Highlights of the Science of Human Development

As evident throughout this textbook, much more research and appreciation of the brain, social context, and the non-Western world has expanded our understanding of human development in the 21st century. This timeline lists a few highlights of the past.

200,000–50,000 BCE With their large brains, long period of child development, and extensive social and family support, early humans were able to sustain life and raise children more effectively than other primates.

c. 400 BCE In ancient Greece, ideas about children from philosophers like Plato (c. 428-348 BCE) and Aristotle (384-322 BCE) influenced further thoughts about children. Plato believed children were born with knowledge. Aristotle believed children learn from experience.

©2016 MACMILLAN

1650–1800 European philosophers like John Locke (1632–1704) and Jean Jacques Rousseau (1712–1778) debate whether children are born as "blank slates" and how much control parents should take in raising them.

1797 First European vaccination: Edward Jenner (1749–1823) publicizes smallpox inoculation, building on vaccination against smallpox in Asia, the Middle East, and Africa.

1750–1850 Beginning of Western laws regulating child labor and protecting the rights of children.

©2016 MACMILLAN

1879 First experimental psychology laboratory established in Leipzig, Germany.

1885 Sigmund Freud (1856–1939) publishes *Studies on Hysteria*, one of the first works establishing the importance of the subconscious and marking the beginning of the theories of psychoanalytic theory.

©2016 MACMILLAN

1895 Ivan Pavlov (1849–1936) begins research on dogs salivation response.

AGENCY ANIMAL PICTURE/GETTY IMAGES

1905 Max Weber (1864–1920), the founder of sociology, writes *The Protestant Work Ethic*, about human values and adult work.

1905 Alfred Binet's (1857–1911) intelligence test published.

1907 Maria Montessori (1870–1952) opens her first school in Rome.

HARVEY WATTS PHOTOGRAPHY/GETTY IMAGES

1913 John B. Watson (1878–1958) publishes *Psychology As the Behaviorist Views It*.

| 50,000 BCE | 400 BCE | 0 | 500 | 1000 | 1500 | 1650 | 1700 |

---

140 BCE In China, imperial examinations are one of the first times cognitive testing is used on young people.

500–1500 During the Middle Ages in Europe, many adults believed that children were miniature adults.

SCALA/ART RESOURCE, NY

1100–1200 First universities founded in Europe. Young people pay to be educated together.

NICHOLAS VEASEY/GETTY IMAGES

1837 First kindergarten opens in Germany, part of a movement to teach young children before they entered the primary school system.

RALF HETTLER/GETTY IMAGES

1859 Charles Darwin (1809–1882) publishes *On the Origin of Species*, sparking debates about what is genetic and what is environmental.

1900 Compulsory schooling for children is established for most children in the United States and Europe.

RALF HETTLE/GETTY IMAGES

1903 The term "gerontology," the branch of developmental science devoted to studying aging, first coined.

FUSE/GETTY IMAGES

1920 Lev Vygotsky (1896–1934) develops sociocultural theory in the former Soviet Union.

1923 Jean Piaget (1896–1980) publishes *The Language and Thought of the Child*.

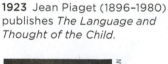
©2016 MACMILLAN

1933 Society for Research on Child Development, the preeminent organization for research on child development, founded.

1939 Mamie (1917–1983) and Kenneth Clark (1914–2005) receive their their research grants to study race in early childhood.

JGI/JAMIE GRILL/GETTY IMAGES

1943 Abraham Maslow (1908–1970) publishes *A Theory of Motivation*, establishing the hierarchy of needs.

1950 Erik Erikson (1902–1994) expands on Freud's theory to include social aspects of personality development with the publication of *Childhood and Society*.

©2016 MACMILLAN

1951 John Bowlby (1907–1990) publishes *Maternal Care and Mental Health*, one of his first works on the importance of parent–child attachment.

MONKEY BUSINESS IMAGES/SHUTTERSTOCK

1953 Publication of the first papers describing DNA, our genetic blueprint.

DIGITAL VISION VECTORS/GETTY IMAGES

1957 Harry Harlow (1905–1981) publishes *Love in Infant Monkeys*, describing his research on attachment in rhesus monkeys.

MARTIN ROGERS/GETTY IMAGES

1961 The morning sickness drug Thalidomide is banned after children are born with serious birth defects, calling attention to the problem of teratogens during pregnancy.

1961 Alfred Bandura (b. 1925) conducts the Bobo Doll experiments, leading to the development of social learning theory.

1979 Urie Bronfenbrenner (1917–2005) publishes his work on ecological systems theory

1986 John Gottman (b. 1942) founded the "Love Lab" at the University of Washington to study what makes relationships work.

1987 Carolyn Rovee-Collier (1942–2014) shows that even young infants can remember in her classic mobile experiments.

FOTOSEARCH/FOTOSEARCH/SUPERSTOCK

1990 The United Nations treaty *Convention on the Rights of the Child* in effect, requiring the best interests of children be considered, and stating that they are not solely the possession of their parents. All UN nations have signed on, except Somalia, South Sudan, and the United States.

TONGRO/GETTY IMAGES

1993 Howard Gardner (b. 1943) publishes *Multiple Intelligences*, a major new understanding of the diversity of human intellectual abilities. Gardner has since revised and expanded his ideas in many ways.

1994 Steven Pinker (b. 1954) publishes *The Language Instinct*, focusing attention on the interaction between neuroscience and behavior, helping developmentalists understand the need for physiological understanding as part of human growth. These themes continue in his later work, such as *How the Mind Works* in 1997.

1800	1900		2000

ANYAIVANOVA/ISTOCK/THINKSTOCK

1953 B.F. Skinner (1904–1990) conducts experiments on rats and establishes operant conditioning.

1955 Emmy Werner (b. 1929) begins her Kauai study, which focuses on the power of resilience.

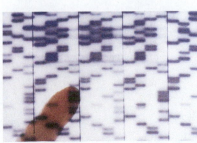
DONNA DAY/EXACTOSTOCK-1598/SUPERSTOCK

1956 K. Warner Schaie's (b. 1928) Seattle Longitudinal Study of Adult Intelligence begins.

1965 Head Start, an early childhood education program, launched in the United States.

1965 Mary Ainsworth (1913–1999) starts using the "Strange Situation" to measure attachment.

©2016 MACMILLAN

1966 Diana Baumrind (b. 1928) publishes her first work on parenting styles.

1972 Beginning of the Dunedin, New Zealand, study—one of the first longitudinal studies to include genetic markers.

TETRA IMAGES/GETTY IMAGES

1990–Present New brain imaging technology allows pinpointing of brain areas involved in everything from executive function to Alzheimer's disease.

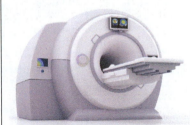
BARIS SIMSEK/GETTY IMAGES

1990 Barbara Rogoff (b. 1950) publishes *Apprenticeship in Thinking*, making developmentalists more aware of the significance of culture and context. Rogoff provided new insights and appreciation of child-rearing in Latin America.

1996 Giacomo Rizzolatti publishes his discovery of mirror neurons.

2000 Jeffrey Arnett conceptualizes emerging adulthood.

2003 Mapping of the human genome is completed.

2013 DSM-5, which emphasizes the role of context in understanding mental health problems, is published.

Present Onward. There are many more discoveries and research chronicled in this book.

BLEND IMAGES/BLEND IMAGES/SUPERSTOCK

The Developing Person
Through the Life Span

TENTH EDITION

The Developing Person

Through the Life Span

Kathleen Stassen Berger

Bronx Community College of the City University of New York

worth publishers
Macmillan Learning
New York

Vice President, Social Sciences and High School: Charles Linsmeier

Executive Editor: Christine Cardone

Developmental Editor: Andrea Musick Page

Editorial Assistant: Melissa Rostek

Executive Marketing Manager: Katherine Nurre

Marketing Assistant: Morgan Ratner

Executive Media Editor: Noel Hohnstine

Senior Media Editor: Laura Burden

Media Editorial Assistant: Nik Toner

Director, Content Management Enhancement: Tracey Kuehn

Managing Editor, Sciences and Social Sciences: Lisa Kinne

Project Manager: Betsy Draper, MPS Limited

Director of Digital Production: Keri deManigold

Media Producer: Elizabeth Dougherty

Production Manager: Stacey B. Alexander

Photo Editor: Sheena Goldstein

Photo Researcher: Rona Tuccillo

Director of Design, Content Management: Diana Blume

Cover and Interior Designer: Blake Logan

Art Manager: Matthew McAdams

Illustrations: Todd Buck Illustrations, MPS Limited, Evelyn Pence, Charles Yuen

Composition: MPS Limited

Printing and Binding: King Printing Co., Inc.

Cover Photograph: Alix Minde/PhotoAlto/Getty Images
Peopleimages/E+/Getty Images, JGI/Jamie Grill/Getty Images,
Peter M. Fisher/Fuse/ Getty Images, Ron Levine/DigitalVision/
Getty Images, Milind Ketkar/Dinodia Photo/age fotostock

Library of Congress Control Number: 2016949294

ISBN-13: 978-1-319-01587-9

ISBN-10: 1-319-01587-5

ISBN-13: 978-1-319-01627-2

ISBN-10: 1-319-0-1627-8

ISBN-13: 978-1-319-01628-9

ISBN-10: 1-319-01628-6

Printed in the United States of America

Third printing

Worth Publishers

One New York Plaza

Suite 4500

New York, NY 10004-1562

www.macmillanlearning.com

Kathleen Stassen Berger received her undergraduate education at Stanford University and Radcliffe College, and then she earned an MAT from Harvard University and an M.S. and Ph.D. from Yeshiva University. Her broad experience as an educator includes directing a preschool, serving as chair of philosophy at the United Nations International School, and teaching child and adolescent development to graduate students at Fordham University in New York and undergraduates at Montclair State University in New Jersey and Quinnipiac University in Connecticut. She also taught social psychology to inmates at Sing Sing Prison who were earning their paralegal degrees.

Currently, Berger is a professor at Bronx Community College of the City University of New York, as she has been for most of her professional career. She began there as an adjunct in English and for the past decades has been a full professor in the social sciences department, which includes sociology, economics, anthropology, political science, human services, and psychology. She has taught introduction to psychology, child and adolescent development, adulthood and aging, social psychology, abnormal psychology, and human motivation. Her students—who come from many ethnic, economic, and educational backgrounds and who have a wide range of ages and interests—consistently honor her with the highest teaching evaluations.

Berger is also the author of *Invitation to the Life Span* and *The Developing Person Through Childhood and Adolescence*. Her developmental texts are currently being used at more than 800 colleges and universities worldwide and are available in Spanish, French, Italian, and Portuguese, as well as English. Her research interests include adolescent identity, immigration, bullying, and grandparents, and she has published articles on developmental topics in the *Wiley Encyclopedia of Psychology* and in publications of the American Association for Higher Education and the National Education Association for Higher Education. She continues teaching and learning from her students as well as from her four daughters and three grandsons.

© 2016 Macmillan

BRIEF CONTENTS

shapecharge/E+/Getty Images

Christopher Hope-Fitch/Moment/Getty Images

Hola Images RF/Getty Images

StarsStudio/iStock/Getty Images

Jupiterimages/DigitalVision/Getty Images

CONTENTS

PART II

The First Two Years

PART IV

Middle Childhood

PART V

Adolescence

PART VII

Adulthood

If human development were simple, universal, and unchanging, there would be no need for a new edition of this textbook. Nor would anyone need to learn anything about human growth. But human development is complex, varied, and never the same.

This is evident to me in small ways as well as large ones. Yesterday, I made the mistake of taking two of my grandsons, aged 6 and 7, to the grocery store, asking them what they wanted for dinner. I immediately rejected their first suggestions—doughnuts or store-made sandwiches. But we lingered over the meat counter. Asa wanted hot dogs and Caleb wanted chicken. Neither would concede.

At least one universal is apparent in this anecdote: Grandmothers seek to nourish grandchildren. But complexity and variability were evident in two stubborn cousins and one confused grandmother.

This small incident is not unlike the headlines in today's newspaper. Indeed, another developmental question seems more urgent now, interweaving what is universally true about humans with what is new and immediate, balancing them in order to move forward with our public and personal lives. I found a compromise for dinner—chicken hot dogs, which both boys ate, with whole wheat buns and lots of ketchup. I do not know the solutions to public dilemmas such as climate change, immigration, gun violence, and systemic racism, but I believe that a deeper and more accurate understanding of human development might help.

That is why I wrote this tenth edition, which presents both the enduring and the current findings from the study of human development. Some of those findings have been recognized for decades, even centuries, and some are new, as thousands of scientists continue to study how humans grow and change with new circumstances. I hope they will help us with the public and private aspects of our lives, moving us all forward from the moment of conception until the last breath.

What's New in the Tenth Edition?

New Material

Every year, scientists discover and explain more concepts and research. The best of these are integrated into the text, with hundreds of new references on many topics, including epigenetics at conception, prenatal protections, infant nutrition, autism spectrum disorder, attachment over the life span, high-stakes testing, drug use and drug addiction, sex education, and diversity of all kinds—ethnic, economic, and cultural. Cognizant of the interdisciplinary nature of human development, I include recent research in biology, sociology, education, anthropology, political science, and more—as well as my home discipline, psychology.

Genetics and social contexts are noted throughout. The interaction of nature and nurture are discussed in many chapters, as neuroscience relates to research on family life. Among the many topics described with new research are the variations, benefits, and hazards of breast-feeding, infant day care, preschool education,

Go with the Flow This boat classroom in Bangladesh picks up students on shore and then uses solar energy to power computers linked to the Internet as part of instruction. The educational context will teach skills and metaphors their peers will not understand.

Forget Baby Henry? Infants left in parked cars on hot days can die from the heat. Henry's father invented a disc to be placed under the baby that buzzes his cell phone if he is more than 20 feet away from the disc. He hopes all absent minded parents will buy one.

single parenthood, exercise, vaccination, same-sex marriage—always noting differences, deficits, and resilience.

No paragraph in this edition is exactly what it was in the ninth edition. To help professors who taught with the earlier texts, or students who have friends who took the course a few years ago, here are some highlights of my updates:

- New figures on the Gini index and neurogenesis (Chapter 1).
- Updated examples of longitudinal research and the ethics of scientific research (Chapter 1).
- Descriptions of newer brain imaging techniques such as fNIRS (functional near infrared spectroscopy) and DTI (diffusion tensor imaging) (Chapter 2).
- *Grandmother hypothesis* added to the discussion of evolutionary theory (Chapter 2).
- New discussion of epigenetics, including examples of type 2 diabetes, drug use, and loneliness (Chapter 3).
- New infographic figure on critical periods in prenatal development (Chapter 4).
- Updated coverage on infant sleep, SIDS, and infant mortality rates (Chapter 5).
- New coverage of bilingualism in babies (Chapter 6).
- New features on emotional expression and adoptive parents' attachment to their children (Chapter 7).
- Updated and reorganized coverage of infant day care (Chapter 7).
- Updated research on childhood obesity and nutrition (Chapter 8).
- Expanded discussion and new research on STEM learning and bilingualism in early childhood (Chapter 9).
- New coverage and data on screen time (Chapter 10).
- New research on gender development and gender differences (Chapter 10).
- Updated coverage of childhood psychopathology, including ADHD, autism spectrum disorder, and specific learning disorders, and special education (Chapter 11).
- New discussion of the U.S. Common Core standards and of Finland's recent education reform (Chapter 12).
- New research on various family structures, both within the United States and internationally (Chapter 13).
- New research on eating disorders and sexual activity during adolescence (Chapter 14).
- Updated coverage of media use among adolescents (Chapter 15).
- Updated coverage of ethnic and gender development, as well as sexual orientation (Chapter 16).
- Updated coverage of teenage drug use, including e-cigarettes (Chapter 16).
- New feature on whether or not emerging adulthood is a worldwide phenomenon (Chapter 17).
- More coverage on exercise and new data on family-planning trends worldwide (Chapter 17).
- Updated new material on college completion and debt (Chapter 18).
- Extensively updated material on dating, cohabitation, and romance in emerging adults (Chapter 19).
- New research on exercise, obesity, and opioid and heroin addiction during adulthood (Chapter 20).
- Updated coverage of the development of expertise in a new, technologically connected era (Chapter 21).
- More coverage of same-sex relationships and marriage (Chapter 22).

- New material on the challenges of balancing work and family (Chapter 22).
- Updated coverage of ageism (Chapter 23).
- New research on the rate and importance of exercise for older adults (Chapter 23).
- Fully updated section and Visualizing Development infographic on neurocognitive disorders (Chapter 24).
- Updated material on caregiving for fragile elders (Chapter 25).
- Updated coverage and data for the "death with dignity" movement (Epilogue).

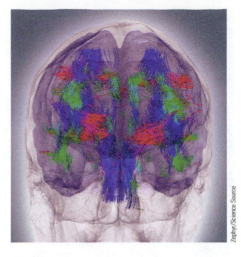

FIGURE 8.1

Mental Coordination? This brain scan of a 38-year-old depicts areas of myelination (the various colors) within the brain. As you see, the two hemispheres are quite similar, but not identical. For most important skills and concepts, both halves of the brain are activated.

New *Inside the Brain* Feature

Since new discoveries abound almost daily in the field of neuroscience, I have added *Inside the Brain* features to several chapters, exploring topics such as the intricacies of prenatal and infant brain development, brain specialization and speech development, brain maturation and emotional development, neuronal growth in adulthood, and brain plasticity in late adulthood.

New and Updated Coverage of Neuroscience

Inclusion of neuroscience is a familiar feature of this book. In addition to the new *Inside the Brain* features, I include the latest, cutting-edge research on the brain in virtually every chapter, often enhancing it with charts, figures, and photos to help students understand the brain's inner workings. A list highlighting this material is available at macmillanlearning.com.

New Online *Data Connections* Activities

Understanding how scientists use data helps students realize that the study of human development is not just a matter of personal experience and common sense. It goes far beyond that—sometimes contradicting old myths and pat conclusions. This edition includes interactive activities, *Data Connections* that allow students to interpret data on topics ranging from breast-feeding to risk taking.

For example, students discover how rates of smoking differ by gender or age during adolescence, which probably is not what they think. These interactive activities will make students more engaged and active learners, while deepening their understanding of the importance of quantitative data. Instructors can assign these activities in the online LaunchPad that accompanies this book.

Renewed Emphasis on Critical Thinking and Application in the Pedagogical Program

As a professor myself, I continue to seek ways to deepen knowledge. Cognitive psychology and research on pedagogy finds that vocabulary, specific knowledge, attention to experience, and critical thinking are all part of learning. This book and many features are designed to foster all four.

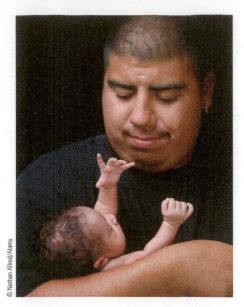

Mutual Joy Ignore this dad's tattoo and earring, and the newborn's head wet with amniotic fluid. Instead recognize that, for thousands of years, hormones and instincts propel fathers and babies to reach out to each other, developing lifelong connections.

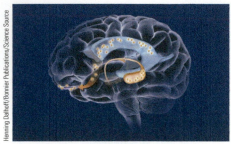

Video Activity: Brain Development: Adolescence features animations and illustrations of the changes that occur in the teenage brain.

We all need to be critical thinkers. Virtually every page of this book presents not only facts but also questions. A new marginal feature, *Think Critically,* encourages student reflection and analysis. There are no pat answers to these questions: They could be used to start a class discussion or begin a long essay.

Every chapter begins with a few *What Will You Know?* questions, one for each major heading. Of course, much of what readers learn will be reflected in new attitudes and perspectives—hard to quantify. But these *What Will You Know?* questions are intended to be provocative and to pose issues that students will remember for decades.

In addition, after every major section, *What Have You Learned?* questions appear. They are designed to help students review what they have just read, a pedagogical technique proven to help retention. Ideally, students will answer the learning objective questions in sentences, with specifics that demonstrate knowledge. Some answers are straightforward, requiring only close attention to the chapter content. Others require comparisons, implications, or evaluations.

Key terms are indicated with bold print and are defined in the margins as well as in the glossary, because expanded vocabulary aids expanded understanding.

To help students become better observers, occasional *Observation Quizzes* accompany a photo or figure. And, since many students reading this book are preparing to be teachers, health care professionals, police officers, or parents, every chapter contains *Especially For* questions that encourage students to apply important developmental concepts just as experts in the field do.

New Integration with LaunchPad

Throughout the book, the margins include LaunchPad call-outs to online videos about either people in a particular context or key scientists who might become role models. For example, Susan Beal, the Australian scientist who revolutionized our understanding of SIDS (sudden infant death syndrome) and infant sleep position, saving millions of babies, is shown to be a person with whom many students can identify. Relevant *Data Connections* activities (described on p. xix) are also highlighted for the reader.

Updated Features

Opposing Perspectives, A View from Science, and A Case to Study

Special topics and new research abound in life-span development. This edition of *The Developing Person Through the Life Span* includes boxed features in every chapter.

Opposing Perspectives focuses on controversial topics—from prenatal sex selection to e-cigarettes. Information and opinions on both sides of each issue are presented, so students can weigh evidence, assess arguments, and reach their own conclusions while appreciating that an opposite conclusion also has merit.

A View from Science explains recent scientific research in more detail, illustrating the benefits of the scientific method for a specific issue.

A Case to Study focuses on particular individuals, helping students to identify the personal implications of what they learn.

Infographics

Information is sometimes better understood visually and graphically. Carefully chosen, updated photos and figures appear on almost every page to accomplish this, with, as always, captions that explain and increase knowledge.

In addition, every chapter of this new edition includes *Visualizing Development*, a full-page illustration of a topic in development. These infographics explain key concepts, from brain development to marriage rates, often with data that encourage students to think of other nations, other cultures, other times. My two awesome editors and I have worked closely with noted designer Charles Yuen to create these infographics, hoping they reinforce key ideas.

Child Development and Nursing Career Correlation Guides

Many students taking this course hope to become nurses or early-childhood educators. This book and accompanying testing material are fully correlated to the NAEYC (National Association for the Education of Young Children) career preparation goals and the NCLEX (nursing) licensure exam. These two supplements are available in LaunchPad.

Ongoing Features

Writing That Communicates the Excitement and Challenge of the Field

Writing about the science of human development should be lively, just as real people are. Each sentence conveys attitude as well as content. Chapter-opening vignettes describe real-life situations. Examples and clear explanations abound, helping students connect theory, research, and experiences.

Coverage of Diversity

Cross-cultural, international, multiethnic, sexual orientation, poverty, age, gender—all of these words and ideas are vital to appreciating how people develop. This is particularly apparent to me, as I have lived in several regions of the United States as well as abroad.

I have learned from my students at the United Nations school, Fordham, Quinnipiac, Sing Sing, and Bronx Community College—all places where people of many backgrounds learn. Research uncovers surprising similarities and notable differences: We have much in common, yet each human is unique. From the discussion of social contexts in Chapter 1 to the coverage of cultural differences in death and dying in the Epilogue, each chapter highlights possibilities and variations.

New research on family structures, immigrants, bilingualism, and gender and ethnic differences in health are among the many topics that illustrate human diversity. Respect for human differences is evident throughout. You will note that examples and research findings from many parts of the world are included, not as add-on highlights but as integral parts of the description of each age. A list of these examples and research is available at macmillanlearning.com.

Current Research from the Field

My mentors welcomed curiosity, creativity, and skepticism; as a result, I am eager to read and analyze thousands of articles and books on everything from the genes that predispose children to autism spectrum disorder to the complications of zygosity.

The recent explosion of research in neuroscience and genetics has challenged me once again, first to understand and then to explain many complex findings and

Imitation is Lifelong As this photo illustrates, at every age, people copy what others do—often to their mutual joy. The new ability at stage six is "deferred imitation"—this boy may have seen another child lie on a tire a few days earlier.

More Dad . . . and Mom Worldwide, fathers are spending more time playing with their children—daughters as well as sons, as this photo shows. Does that mean that mothers spend less time with their children? No—the data show that mothers are spending more time as well.

Political Division At a Trump rally, a group circled to protect the person with a Black Lives Matter sign. Ahead of a presidential election, it is not unusual for protesters to disrupt the opposition's rally. What is unusual is the age and gender divisions. Contrast the protesters in the forefront of this photo and the Trump supporters at the back.

speculative leaps. My students continue to ask questions and share their experiences, always providing new perspectives and concerns.

Topical Organization Within a Chronological Framework

The book's basic organization remains unchanged. Four chapters begin the book with coverage of definitions, theories, genetics, and prenatal development. These chapters function not only as a developmental foundation but also as the structure for explaining the life-span perspective, plasticity, nature and nurture, multicultural awareness, risk analysis, gains and losses, family bonding, and many other concepts that yield insights for all of human development.

The other seven parts correspond to the major periods of development. Each age is discussed in three chapters, one for the biological, one for the cognitive, and one for the social world. The topical organization within a chronological framework is a useful scaffold for students' understanding of the interplay between age and domain.

Photographs, Tables, and Graphs That Are Integral to the Text

Students learn a great deal from this book's illustrations because Worth Publishers encourages authors to choose the photographs, tables, and graphs and to write captions that extend the content. *Observation Quizzes* that accompany many of them inspire readers to look more closely at certain photographs, tables, and figures. The online *Data Connections* further this process by presenting numerous charts and tables that contain detailed data for further study.

Supplements

After teaching every semester for many years, I know well that supplements can make or break a class. Students are now media savvy and instructors use tools that did not exist when they themselves were in college. Many supplements are available for both students and professors. I encourage adopters of my textbook to ask their publisher's representative for guidance as to how these might be used. As an instructor who has used books from many publishers, I think you will find that Worth representatives are a cut above the rest, and you will be happy you asked for help.

LaunchPad with LearningCurve Quizzing and Data Connections Activities

Built to solve key challenges in the course, LaunchPad gives students everything they need to prepare for class and exams, while giving instructors everything they need to quickly set up a course, shape the content to their syllabus, craft presentations and lectures, assign and assess homework, and guide the progress of individual students and the class as a whole.

Our LaunchPad, which can be previewed at www.launchpadworks.com, includes the following:

- An **interactive e-Book** integrates the text and all student media, including the new Data Connections activities, videos, and much more.
- **LearningCurve adaptive quizzing** gives individualized question sets and feedback based on each student's correct and incorrect responses. All of

the questions are tied back to the e-Book to encourage students to read the book in preparation for class time and exams. And, state-of-the-art question-analysis reports allow instructors to track the progress of individual students as well as their class as a whole. A team of dedicated instructors has worked closely to develop more than 5,000 quizzing questions specifically for this book.

- **Video Collection for Human Development** Worth's extensive archive of video clips covers the full range of the course, from classic experiments (like the Strange Situation and Piaget's conservation tasks) to investigations of children's play to adolescent risk taking. Instructors can assign these videos to students through LaunchPad or choose one of 50 popular video activities that combine videos with short-answer and multiple-choice questions. (For presentation purposes, our videos are also available on flash drive.)

- **Instructor's Resources** Now fully integrated with LaunchPad, this collection of resources has been hailed as the richest collection of instructor's resources in developmental psychology. The resources include learning objectives, springboard topics for discussion and debate, handouts for student projects, course-planning suggestions, ideas for term projects, and a guide to audiovisual and online materials.

- **Lecture Slides** We offer two sets of prebuilt slides: one comprised of chapter art and illustrations, and another consisting of comprehensive, book-specific lectures. These slides can be used as is, or they can be customized to fit individual needs.

- **Test Bank and Computerized Test Bank** The test bank includes at least 100 multiple-choice and 70 fill-in-the-blank, true-false, and essay questions per chapter. Good test questions are critical to every course, and we have gone through each and every one of these test questions with care. We have added more challenging questions, and questions are keyed to the textbook by topic, page number, and level of difficulty. Questions are also organized by NCLEX, NAEYC, and APA goals and Bloom's taxonomy. We have also written rubrics for grading all of the short-answer and essay questions in the test bank.

The Diploma computerized test bank guides instructors step by step through the process of creating a test. It also allows them to quickly add an unlimited number of questions; edit, scramble, or re-sequence items; format

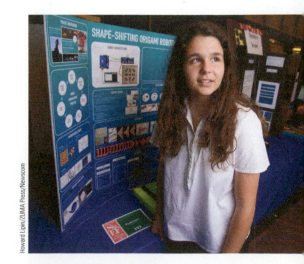

Howard Lipin/ZUMA Press/Newscom

Typical or Extraordinary? Francisca Vasconcelos, a San Diego high school senior, demonstrates formal operational thought. She used origami principles to create a 3D printed robot. She calls herself an "aspiring researcher," and her project won second place in the INTEL 2016 Science Fair. Is she typical of older adolescents, or extraordinarily advanced?

a test; and include pictures, equations, and media links. The accompanying Gradebook enables instructors to record students' grades throughout the course and includes the capacity to sort student records, view detailed analyses of test items, curve tests, generate reports, and add weights to grades. The password-protected test bank is available online to instructors.

Thanks

I would like to thank the academic reviewers who have read this book in every edition and who have provided suggestions, criticisms, references, and encouragement. They have all made this a better book.

I want to mention especially those who have reviewed this edition:

Chris Alas, Houston Community College

Adrienne Armstrong, Lone Star College

William Robert Aronson, Florida International University

T. M. Barratt, Arizona State University

Melissa A. Bright, University of Florida

Alda Cekrezi, Lone Star College

Kristi Cordell-McNulty, Angelo State University

Faith T. Edwards, University of Wisconsin–Oshkosh

Naomi Ekas, Texas Christian University

Michael A. Erickson, Hawaii Pacific University

Diane Klieger Feibel, University of Cincinnati—
     Blue Ash College

Lori Neal Fernald, The Citadel Military
     College of South Carolina

Valerie C. Flores, Loyola University Chicago

Stacie Foster, Arizona State University

Kathryn Frazier, Northeastern University

Christopher Gade, Berkeley City College

Dan Grangaard, Austin Community College

Jiansheng Guo, California State University–East Bay

Pinar Gurkas, Clayton State University

E. Allison Hagood, Arapahoe Community College

Toni Stepter Harris, Virginia State University

Raquel Henry, Lone Star College–Kingwood

Kristina Herndon, George Mason University

Carmon Weaver Hicks, Ivy Tech Community College

Danelle Hodge, California State University–San Bernadino

Richard Marmer, American River College

Jerry Marshall, Green River College

T. Darin Matthews, The Citadel Military
     College of South Carolina

Elizabeth McCarroll, Texas Woman's University

Lisa Montero-Blyer, Broward College

Abigail M. Nehrkorn, West Virginia University

Elif Angel Raynor, Palm Beach State College

Nicole Stalnaker, Lone Star College–University Park

The editorial, production, and marketing people at Worth Publishers are dedicated to meeting the highest standards of excellence. Their devotion of time, effort, and talent to every aspect of publishing is a model for the industry. I particularly would like to thank Andrea Musick Page, Chris Cardone, Stacey Alexander, Diana Blume, Ellie Bruckner, Laura Burden, Matthew Christensen, Tom Churchill, Betsy Draper, Sheena Goldstein, Noel Hohnstine, Lisa Kinne, Tracey Kuehn, Charles Linsmeier, Blake Logan, Jennifer MacMillan, Matthew McAdams, Hilary Newman, Katherine Nurre, Morgan Ratner, Chelsea Roden, Melissa Rostek, Joe Tomasso, Nik Toner, Rona Tuccillo, and Charles Yuen.

Kathleen Stassen Berger

New York
October 2016

the beginnings

The science of human development includes many beginnings. Each of the first four chapters of this text forms one corner of a solid foundation for our study.

Chapter 1 introduces definitions and dimensions, explaining research strategies and methods that help us understand how people develop. The need for science, the power of culture, and the necessity of an ecological approach are all explained.

Without ideas, our study would be only a jumble of observations. Chapter 2 provides organizing guideposts: Five major theories, each leading to many other theories and hypotheses, are described.

Chapter 3 explains heredity. Genes never act alone, yet no development—whether in body or brain, at any time, in anyone—is unaffected by DNA.

Chapter 4 details the prenatal growth of each developing person from a single cell to a breathing, grasping, crying newborn. Many circumstances—from the mother's diet to the father's care to the culture's values—affect development during every day of embryonic and fetal growth.

As you see, the science and the wonder of human life begin long before the first breath. Understanding the beginnings described in each of these chapters prepares us to understand each developing child, and each of us.

Left: Peopleimages/E+/Getty Images
Right: shapecharge/E+/Getty Images

The Science of Human Development

What Will You Know?*

1. Why is science crucial for understanding how people develop?
2. Are people the same, always and everywhere, or is each person unique, changing from day to day and place to place?
3. How are the methods of science used to study development?
4. What must scientists do to make their conclusions valid and ethical?

Insomnia is a serious problem. Many developmentalists study its effects: Inadequate sleep troubles people at night and impairs their health and thinking by day. But I do not know this personally. Instead, I now arrange my life so that I sleep deeply and naturally whenever I wish. My mother said that, as a baby, I never cried at bedtime or naptime, and I always woke up happy. When I lost my temper as a child, my mother suggested I nap. My daughters do that now.

Early every morning I plan my day. My computer automatically inserts time on my sent e-mails: 4 A.M., 5 A.M., 3 A.M. When friends comment on my early productivity, I tell them about my naps.

Sleep is a fitting beginning for this chapter, because it explains that each of us is unique, a product of genes and childhood (nature and nurture) and an architect of our adult lives. Developmentalists notice human diversity: Some people have insomnia and others sleep easily, and scientists search for the causes and consequences of differences. Age is always a factor in diverse pathways, including for sleep: Infants are up at dawn; teenagers sleep late; older adults wake often. Lifelong continuity is also evident: I have always been a morning person.

Why? Did I follow my grandparents' example? (They needed to milk the cows.) Am I a product of this culture (which says "the early bird gets the worm")? Did I want to please my mother? Is it genetic? Genes affect sleep patterns. Do I have morning genes?

My brother lived far away all my adult life, but one August, he stayed with me. When I woke before dawn to write, I was taken aback to see him already up and writing. Then I read that sleep in birds is genetic; that's why we speak of morning larks and night owls. Aha—my brother and I must share a lark gene.

This illustrates the theme of this chapter. Developmentalists notice something curious about human behavior, their own or that of someone else, and then they try to understand its origin and outcome in order to accept it (as I do for naps) or change it (as many do with insomnia). You will learn about the process of scientific discovery, which reveals the many forces that make each of us who we are.

*What Will You Know? questions are a preview *before* each chapter, one for each major heading. They are big ideas that you will still know a decade from now, unlike "What Have You Learned?" questions that are more specific, *after* each major heading.

Left: Sam Diephuis/Getty Images
Top: shapecharge/E+/Getty Images

● Understanding How and Why

The **science of human development** *seeks to understand how and why people—all kinds of people, everywhere, of every age—change over time.* The goal of this science is for the more than 7 billion people on Earth to fulfill their potential. Growth is *multidirectional, multicontextual, multicultural, multidisciplinary,* and *plastic,* five terms that will be explained soon.

First, however, we need to emphasize that developmental study is a *science.* It depends on theories, data, analysis, critical thinking, and sound methodology, just like every other science. All scientists ask questions and seek answers in order to ascertain "how and why."

Science is especially useful when we study people: Lives depend on it. What should pregnant women eat? How much should babies cry? When should children be punished, and how, and for what? Under what circumstances should adults marry, or divorce, or retire, or die? People disagree about all this and more, sometimes vehemently.

The Scientific Method

Facts are often misinterpreted and applications sometimes spring from assumptions, not from data. To avoid unexamined opinions and to rein in personal biases, researchers follow the five steps of the **scientific method** (see Figure 1.1):

1. *Begin with curiosity.* On the basis of theory, prior research, or a personal observation, pose a question.
2. *Develop a hypothesis.* Shape the question into a **hypothesis,** a specific prediction to be examined.
3. *Test the hypothesis.* Design and conduct research to gather **empirical evidence** (data).
4. *Analyze the evidence gathered in the research.* Conclude whether the hypothesis is supported or not.
5. *Report the results.* Share the data, conclusions, and alternative explanations.

As you see, developmental scientists begin with curiosity and then seek the facts, drawing conclusions after careful research.

Replication—repeating the procedures and methods of a study with different participants—is often a sixth and crucial step. Scientists study the reports of other scientists and build on what has gone before. Sometimes they try to duplicate a study exactly; often they follow up with related research (Stroebe & Strack, 2014). Conclusions are revised, refined, rejected, or confirmed after replication.

Obviously, the scientific method is not foolproof. Scientists may draw conclusions too hastily, misinterpret data, or ignore alternative perspectives. Sometimes scientists discover outright fraud (Bouter, 2015). Ideally, before any conclusion

---

science of human development The science that seeks to understand how and why people of all ages and circumstances change or remain the same over time.

scientific method A way to answer questions using empirical research and data-based conclusions.

hypothesis A specific prediction that can be tested.

empirical evidence Evidence that is based on observation, experience, or experiment; not theoretical.

replication Repeating a study, usually using different participants, perhaps of another age, SES, or culture.

FIGURE 1.1
Process, Not Proof Built into the scientific method—in questions, hypotheses, tests, and replication—is a passion for possibilities, especially unexpected ones.

1. Curiosity

2. Hypothesis

3. Test

4. Analyze data and draw conclusions

5. Report the results

is accepted, results are replicated, not only by performing the same research again but also by designing other ways to verify and extend the same hypothesis (Larzelere et al., 2015).

An effort to replicate 100 published studies in psychology found that about one-third failed and another one-third were less conclusive than the original (Bohannon, 2015). The problems usually arose from the research design (Step 3) of the original studies and the pressure to publish. The conclusion: "there is still more work to do to verify whether we know what we think we know" (Open Science Collaboration, 2015, p. 943). That conclusion itself calls for replication—an effort that found a failure rate of only 15 percent (Gilbert et al., 2016).

That is why scientists examine the procedures and results of other scientists. They read publications, attend conferences, send e-mails, and collaborate with colleagues from many nations. Reading widely, thinking critically, and testing hypotheses are the foundation of our study, as the following illustrates.

A VIEW FROM SCIENCE

Are Children Too Overweight?*

Obesity is a serious problem. Over the life span, from infancy to age 60, rates of obesity increase, and with it, rates of diabetes, heart disease, and stroke. The connection between overweight and disease was not always known. Since before written history, mothers realized that underweight children were more likely to die. That led to a logical, but false, assumption: Heavier children were assumed to be healthier (Laraway et al., 2010).

Another untested assumption as recently as 1945 was that heart attacks could not be prevented, or even predicted. Death was fate; doctors were "baffled" by heart failure. Scientists decided to study thousands of adults in Framingham, Massachusetts, to see what they could learn (Levy & Brink, 2005, p. 4).

The Framingham Heart Study began in 1948. By 1990, conclusions from that study had revolutionized adult behavior—a historic example of the scientific method at work. Because of Framingham, cigarette smoking is down, exercise is up, and doctors routinely monitor blood pressure, weight, and cholesterol, advising and prescribing accordingly.

Worldwide, almost a billion premature deaths have been averted. (Heart problems are still the most common cause of death, but now that rarely occurs before age 60.)

That led to a new question: Was childhood obesity a health risk when the children grew up? That thought (Step 1) led to a hypothesis (Step 2) that overweight in childhood impairs health in adulthood.

This hypothesis is now widely assumed to be true. For instance, a poll found that most Californians consider childhood obesity "very serious," with one-third of them rating poor eating

What Will Become of Her? This happy, beautiful girl in Sweden may become an overweight woman . . . or she may not. Research finds that if she slims down by adulthood, she is likely to be healthier than the average woman who was never overweight.

habits as a worse risk to child health than drug use or violence (Hennessy-Fiske, 2011). But is that assumption valid?

The best way to test that hypothesis (Step 3) is to examine adult health in people who had been weighed and measured in childhood. Several researchers did exactly that. Indeed, four studies had data on children's height and weight as well as measurements of the same people as adults. Most (83 percent) of the people in these studies maintained their relative weight (see Figure 1.2a). That means that most overweight children became overweight adults.

From that research, a strong conclusion was reached (Step 4) and published (Step 5): Overweight children are likely to become obese adults, who then are at high risk for cardiovascular disease, diabetes, and early death. For instance, in those four studies, 29 percent of the adults who were overweight all their

---

*Many chapters of this text feature A View from Science, which explains surprising insights from recent scientific research.

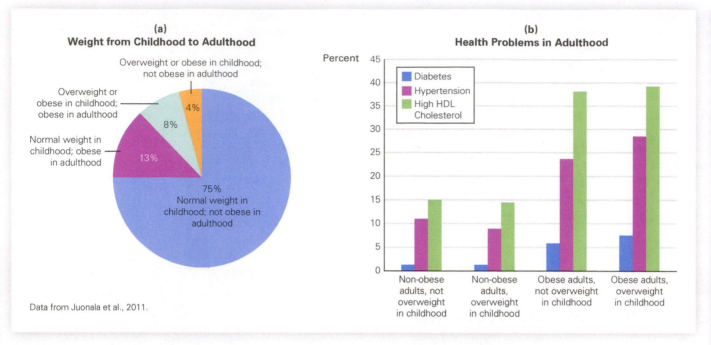

(a)
Weight from Childhood to Adulthood

Overweight or obese in childhood; not obese in adulthood — 4%

Overweight or obese in childhood; obese in adulthood — 8%

Normal weight in childhood; obese in adulthood — 13%

75% Normal weight in childhood; not obese in adulthood

Data from Juonala et al., 2011.

(b)
Health Problems in Adulthood

Percent

- Diabetes
- Hypertension
- High HDL Cholesterol

Non-obese adults, not overweight in childhood
Non-obese adults, overweight in childhood
Obese adults, not overweight in childhood
Obese adults, overweight in childhood

FIGURE 1.2

Not Yet Obese You probably know that more than half of all adults in the United States are overweight, so this chart—with only 21 percent of adults obese—may seem inaccurate. However, three facts explain why the data are accurate: (1) "Obese" is much heavier than overweight; (2) the average adult in this study was 34 years old (middle-aged and older adults are more often obese); and (3) one of the studies that provided much of the longitudinal data was in Finland, where rates of obesity are lower than in the United States.

lives had high blood pressure, compared to 11 percent of those who were never overweight (Juonala et al., 2011).

A new question arose (Step 1), building on those earlier findings. What about overweight children who become normal-weight adults? Have they already harmed their health? That led to a new hypothesis (Step 2): Overweight children will have a higher rate of heart attacks, strokes, diabetes, and death in adulthood, even if they slim down before adulthood. The research design (Step 3) was to measure indications of health in adults who had been overweight as children but who now were normal weight.

The data (Step 4) (see Figure 1.2b) *disproved* the hypothesis: As normal-weight adults, those who had been overweight were *not* at high risk of disease, a conclusion replicated by several studies with quite different populations (Juonala et al., 2011). Scientists were happy with that conclusion—disproving a hypothesis is no less welcome than proving it.

Many other issues, complications, and conclusions regarding weight are discussed later in this book. For now, all you need to remember are the steps of the scientific method and that developmentalists are right: Significant "change over time" is possible.

The Nature–Nurture Controversy

An easy example of the need for science concerns a great puzzle of life, the *nature–nurture debate*. **Nature** refers to the influence of the genes that people inherit. **Nurture** refers to environmental influences, beginning with the health and diet of the embryo's mother and continuing lifelong, including experiences in the family, school, community, and nation.

The nature–nurture debate has many manifestations, among them *heredity–environment, maturation–learning, and sex–gender*. Under whatever name, the basic question is, "How much of any characteristic, behavior, or emotion is the result of genes, and how much is the result of experience?"

Some people believe that most traits are inborn, that children are innately good ("an innocent child") or bad ("beat the devil out of them"). Others stress nurture,

nature In development, nature refers to the traits, capacities, and limitations that each individual inherits genetically from his or her parents at the moment of conception.

nurture In development, nurture includes all of the environmental influences that affect the individual after conception. This includes everything from the mother's nutrition while pregnant to the cultural influences in the nation.

crediting or blaming parents, or neighborhood, or drugs, or even food, when someone is good or bad, a hero or a scoundrel.

Neither belief is accurate. The question is "how much," not "which," because *both* genes and the environment affect every characteristic: Nature always affects nurture, and then nurture affects nature. Even "how much" is misleading, if it implies that nature and nurture each contribute a fixed amount (Eagly & Wood, 2013; Lock, 2013).

A further complication is that the impact of any good or bad experience—a beating, or a beer, or a blessing—might be magnified or inconsequential because of a particular set of genes or events in infancy. Each aspect of nature and nurture depends on other aspects of nature and nurture in ways that vary for each person.

Epigenetics

The science of this interaction is explored in a new discipline called **epigenetics,** which studies the many ways the environment alters genetic expression, beginning with methylation at conception and continuing lifelong. For example, brain formation is directed by genes inherited at conception, but those genes are not alone. Soon, nutrients and toxins affect the prenatal brain, nurture affecting nature. This interaction continues. Even adult social experiences, such as chronic loneliness, change brain structures (Cacioppo et al., 2014).

Sometimes protective factors, in either nature or nurture, outweigh liabilities. As one review explains, "there are, indeed, individuals whose genetics indicate exceptionally high risk of disease, yet they never show any signs of the disorder" (Friend & Schadt, 2014, p. 970). Why? Epigenetics. **[Life-Span Link:** The major discussion of epigenetics is in Chapter 3.]

Dandelions and Orchids

There is increasing evidence of **differential susceptibility**—that sensitivity to any particular experience differs from one person to another because of the particular genes each person has inherited, or what happened to that person years earlier.

Some people are like *dandelions*—hardy, growing and thriving in good soil or bad, with or without ample sun and rain. Other people are like *orchids*—quite wonderful, but only when ideal growing conditions are met (Ellis & Boyce, 2008; Laurent, 2014).

For example, in one study, depression in pregnant women was assessed and then the emotional maturity of their children was measured. Those children who had a particular version of the serotonin transporter gene (5-HTTLPR) were likely to be emotionally immature if their mothers were depressed, but *more* mature than average if their mothers were not depressed (Babineau et al., 2015).

The nature–nurture debate is not merely academic. In a tragic case, an infant's penis was mistakenly destroyed in 1966. His parents had his testicles removed and renamed him Brenda. They raised him as a girl because, at that time, sex differences were thought to originate from the genitals and child rearing (Money & Ehrhardt, 1972). Since he had no male organs, he could be a girl.

But we now know that some male–female differences are genetic and hormonal; they are in the brain, not the body, in nature, not nurture. After a troubled childhood, Brenda chose at age 15 to become David, a man. That may have been too late; he killed himself in 2004 (Diamond & Sigmundson, 1997; The Associated Press, 2004).

Do not make the mistake of concluding that all male–female differences are due to nature. It was once thought that biology made females inferior in math, and thus girls who wanted to be physicists or engineers were advised to choose another

Chopin's First Concert Frederick Chopin, at age 8, played his first public concert in 1818, before photographs. But this photo shows Piotr Pawlak, a contemporary prodigy playing Chopin's music in the same Polish Palace where that famous composer played as a boy. How much of talent is genetic and how much is cultural—a nature–nurture question that applies to both boys, 200 years apart.

JANEK SKARZYNSKI/AFP/Getty Images

epigenetics The study of how environmental factors affect genes and genetic expression—enhancing, halting, shaping, or altering the expression of genes.

differential susceptibility The idea that people vary in how sensitive they are to particular experiences. Often such differences are genetic, which makes some people affected "for better or for worse" by life events. (Also called *differential sensitivity*.)

THINK CRITICALLY: Why not assign a percent to nature and a percent to nurture so that they add up to 100 percent?*

*Think Critically questions occur several times in each chapter. They are intended to provoke thought, not simple responses, and hence have no obvious answers.

career. But in the 1960s millions of women insisted that nurture, not nature, kept women from excelling in math.

Consequently, more girls were allowed to study calculus. Recent international tests find that math scores of the two sexes have become quite similar: In some nations (Russia, Singapore, Algeria, Iran) girls are ahead of boys! The practical implications of that research are that college women are encouraged to become engineers, physicists, or chemists (Brown & Lent, 2016). The scientific implications are, again, that nature and nurture always interact.

WHAT HAVE YOU LEARNED?

1. What are the five steps of the scientific method?

2. What is the difference between asking a question (Step 1) and developing a hypothesis (Step 2)?

3. Why is replication important for scientific progress?

4. What basic question is at the heart of the nature–nurture controversy?

5. When in development does nature begin to influence nurture?

6. What is the difference between genetics and epigenetics?

7. How might differential susceptibility apply to responses to a low exam grade?

The Life-Span Perspective

The **life-span perspective** (Fingerman et al., 2011; Lerner et al., 2010) takes into account all phases of life. This has led to a new understanding of human development as multidirectional, multicontextual, multicultural, multidisciplinary, and plastic (Baltes et al., 2006; Barrett & Montepare, 2015; Raz & Lindenberger, 2013).

Age periods (see Table 1.1) are only a rough guide to life stages, a truism particularly apparent after age 18, when knowing that a particular adult is 25, or 35, or even 65 does not necessarily mean that the person does or does not have a job, a spouse, a young child. Birthdays are significant markers for children; they are imperfect and misleading measures of aging. The dilemma was captured by the social scientist Ashly Montagu, who said, "The idea is to die young, as late as possible."

However, a developmental perspective requires consideration of time. Consequently, even though chronology is imperfect, imprecise, and sometimes flat-out wrong, approximate ages for each period are given in Table 1.1.

Development Is Multidirectional

Multiple changes, in every direction, characterize the life span. Traits appear and disappear, with increases, decreases, and zigzags (see Figure 1.3). An earlier idea—that all development advances until about age 18, steadies, and then declines—has been soundly disproven by life-span research.

Sometimes *discontinuity* is evident: Change can occur rapidly and dramatically, as when caterpillars become butterflies. Sometimes *continuity* is found: Growth can be gradual, as when redwoods add rings over hundreds of years.

Some characteristics do not seem to change at all: The person I am now is an older version of the person I was as an infant. The same is true of you.

---

life-span perspective An approach to the study of human development that takes into account all phases of life, not just childhood or adulthood.

TABLE 1.1	Age Ranges for Different Stages of Development
Infancy	0 to 2 years
Early childhood	2 to 6 years
Middle childhood	6 to 11 years
Adolescence	11 to 18 years
Emerging adulthood	18 to 25 years
Adulthood	25 to 65 years
Late adulthood	65 years and older

As you will learn, developmentalists are reluctant to specify chronological ages for any period of development, because time is only one of many variables that affect each person. However, age is a crucial variable, and development can be segmented into periods of study. Approximate ages for each period are given here.

Humans experience simple growth, radical transformation, improvement, and decline as well as stability, stages, and continuity—day to day, year to year, and generation to generation. Not only do the pace and direction of change vary, but each characteristic follows its own trajectory.

Losses in some abilities occur simultaneously with gains in others. For example, babies lose some ability to distinguish sounds from other languages when they begin talking in whatever language they hear; adults who quit their paid job may become more creative.

The timing of losses and gains, impairments or improvements, varies as well. Some changes are sudden and profound because of a **critical period**, which is either when something *must* occur to ensure normal development or the only time when an abnormality might occur. For instance, the human embryo grows arms and legs, hands and feet, fingers and toes, each over a critical period between 28 and 54 days after conception. After that, it is too late: Unlike some insects, humans never grow replacement limbs.

We know this fact because of a tragic episode. Between 1957 and 1961, thousands of newly pregnant women in 30 nations took *thalidomide,* an antinausea drug. This change in nurture (via the mother's bloodstream) disrupted nature (the embryo's genetic program).

If an expectant woman ingested thalidomide during the critical period for limb formation, her newborn's arms or legs were malformed or absent (Moore et al., 2015, p. 480). Whether all four limbs, or just arms, hands, or fingers were missing depended on exactly when the drug was taken. If thalidomide was ingested only after day 54, no harm occurred.

Life has few such dramatic critical periods. Often, however, a particular development occurs more easily—but not exclusively—at a certain time. That is called a **sensitive period.**

An example is learning language. If children do not communicate in their first language between ages 1 and 3, they might do so later (hence, these years are not critical), but their grammar is impaired (hence, these years are sensitive).

Similarly, childhood is a sensitive period for learning to pronounce a second or third language with a native accent. Many adults master new languages, but strangers ask, "Where are you from?" They detect accents that the speaker does not.

Development Is Multicontextual

The second insight from the life-span perspective is that "human development is fundamentally contextual" (Pluess, 2015, p. 138). Among those many contexts are physical contexts (climate, noise, population density, etc.), family contexts (marital status, family size, members' age and sex), and community contexts (urban, suburban, or rural; multiethnic or not; etc.).

For example, a student might decide on a whim to stop by a social gathering instead of heading straight to the library. The social context of the party (perhaps free drinks and food, lively music, friends) is influential, affecting class the next day. Each of us experiences several contexts each day, some by choice and some involuntarily, and each affects our later thoughts and actions.

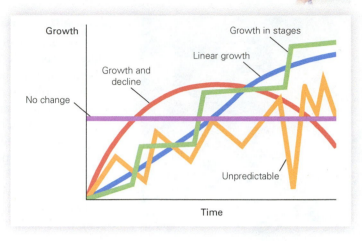

FIGURE 1.3

Patterns of Developmental Growth Many patterns of developmental growth have been discovered by careful research. Although linear (or nonlinear) progress seems most common, scientists now find that almost no aspect of human change follows the linear pattern exactly.

critical period A crucial time when a particular type of developmental growth (in body or behavior) must happen for normal development to occur, or when harm (such as a toxic substance or destructive event) can occur.

sensitive period A time when a certain type of development is most likely, although it may still happen later with more difficulty. For example, early childhood is considered a sensitive period for language learning.

I Love You, Mommy We do not know what words, in what language, her son is using, but we do know that Sobia Akbar speaks English well, a requirement for naturalized U.S. citizens. Here she obtains citizenship for her two children born in Pakistan. Chances are they will speak unaccented American English, unlike Sobia, whose accent might indicate that she learned British English as a second language.

© ZUMA Press, Inc./Alamy

Breathe, Don't Sink Ben Schwenker is learning "drown-proofing," which is important for a skinny 8-year-old because his low body fat (a physiological system) makes floating harder. Ecological systems also make this skill vital, since Ben is in Marietta, a city with thousands of pools, in Georgia, a state bordered by the Atlantic Ocean. Another system is relevant: Ben was diagnosed with autism at age 1; for him, a sense of body strength and autonomy is particularly important.

ecological-systems approach A perspective on human development that considers all of the influences from the various contexts of development. (Later renamed *bioecological theory*.)

FIGURE 1.4

The Ecological Model According to developmental researcher Urie Bronfenbrenner, each person is significantly affected by interactions among a number of overlapping systems, which provide the context of development. *Microsystems*—family, peer group, classroom, neighborhood, house of worship—intimately and immediately shape human development. Surrounding and supporting the microsystems are the *exosystems,* which include all the external networks, such as community structures and local educational, medical, employment, and communications systems, that affect the microsystems. Influencing both of these systems is the *macrosystem,* which includes cultural patterns, political philosophies, economic policies, and social conditions. *Mesosystems* refer to interactions among systems, as when parents and teachers coordinate to educate a child. Bronfenbrenner eventually added a fifth system, the *chronosystem,* to emphasize the importance of historical time.

Ecological Systems

A leading developmentalist, Urie Bronfenbrenner (1917–2005), led the way to considering contexts. Just as a naturalist studying an organism examines the ecology (the relationship between the organism and its environment) of a tiger, or tree, or trout, Bronfenbrenner recommended that developmentalists take an **ecological-systems approach** (Bronfenbrenner & Morris, 2006) regarding humans.

This approach recognizes three nested levels (see Figure 1.4). Most obvious are *microsystems*—each person's immediate social contexts, such as family and peer group. Also important are *exosystems* (local institutions such as school and church) and *macrosystems* (the larger social setting, including cultural values, economic policies, and political processes).

Two more systems affect these three. One is the *chronosystem* (literally, "time system"), which is the historical context. The other is the *mesosystem,* consisting of the connections among the other systems.

Toward the end of his life, Bronfenbrenner renamed his approach *bioecological theory* to highlight the role of biology, recognizing that systems within the body (e.g., the sexual-reproductive system, the cardiovascular system) affect the external systems (Bronfenbrenner & Morris, 2006).

Bronfenbrenner's perspective remains useful. For example, children who have been sexually abused are likely to be abused again, in childhood and adulthood. Why? Is the child to blame, or is the fault in the culture?

Bronfenbrenner would say that this *either/or* is the wrong approach. Psychologists who use Bronfenbrenner's systems approach to analyze repeated sexual victimization conclude that the micro-, macro-, and exosystems all have an impact (Pittenger et al., 2016).

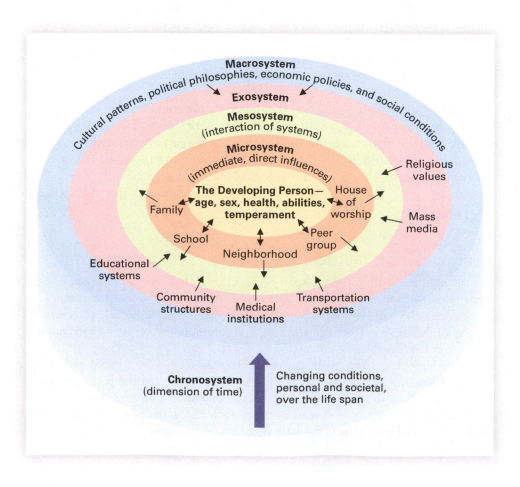

History and Social Class

Two contexts—the historical and the socioeconomic—are basic to understanding people at every period of the entire life span. Consequently, we explain them now.

All persons born within a few years of one another are called a **cohort,** a group defined by its members' shared age. Cohorts travel through life together, affected by the values, events, technologies, and culture of the historical period as it interacts with their age at the time. From the moment of birth, when parents name their baby, historical context affects what may seem like a private and personal choice (see Table 1.2).

If you know someone named Emma, she is probably young: Emma is the most common name for girls born in 2014 but was not in the top 100 until 1996, and not in the top 1,000 in 1990. If you know someone named Mary, she is probably old: About 10 percent of all girls born from 1900 to 1965 were named Mary, but now Mary is unusual.

Two of my daughters, Rachel and Sarah, have names that were common when they were born. One wishes she had a more unusual name, the other is glad she does not. Your own name is influenced by history; your reaction is yours.

In another cohort example, the years 18 to 25 constitute a sensitive period for consolidation of political values. The historical events when a person was a young adult—recently "Occupy Wall Street" or "Black Lives Matter," or, for former cohorts, September 11, 2001, or the assassination of John F. Kennedy—affect later attitudes throughout life.

Indeed, even whether a person is likely to vote for a Democrat or a Republican is affected by which party was in the White House when that person was age 20. Thus, not only do historical events have an impact, but age matters—differential susceptibility again.

Consider attitudes and data about marijuana. In the United States in the 1930s, marijuana was declared illegal, but enforcement was erratic. And some cultures encouraged everyone to smoke "weed." Virtually all of the popular musicians of the 1960s—including the Beatles, Bob Dylan, James Brown, and Bob Marley—not only smoked publicly but also sang about it.

This had a notable effect on high school students, as found in an annual *Monitoring the Future* report (Johnston et al., 1978–2014, continued by Miech et al., 2015). In 1978, only 12 percent thought experimental use of marijuana was harmful, and more than half had tried the drug.

Then in the 1980s, marijuana was labeled a "gateway drug," likely to lead to drug abuse and addiction (Kandel, 2002). People were arrested and jailed for possession of even a few grams. By 1991, when the gateway drug message became widespread, 80 percent of high school seniors thought there was "great risk" in regular use of marijuana, and only 21 percent of high school seniors ever smoked it.

Attitudes gradually shifted again (Johnston et al., 2014 and previous years). By 2014, marijuana use became legal in two states, and medical use was permitted in several others (see Figure 1.5). According to a Gallup poll, more than half (54 percent) of Americans approve of making marijuana use legal, as long as it is used by adults and not in public (Motel, 2014). In 2013, about one-third of high school seniors had themselves used marijuana.

Consequences can be profound. As one of the states that allows both medical and recreational marijuana use, Colorado has had difficulty keeping marijuana from those under age 21, as the law intended (Ghosh et al., 2016). In March 2014, a 19-year-old jumped to his death after

cohort People born within the same historical period who therefore move through life together, experiencing the same events, new technologies, and cultural shifts at the same ages. For example, the effect of the Internet varies depending on what cohort a person belongs to.

TABLE 1.2	Popular First Names
Girls:	
2014: Emma, Olivia, Sophia, Isabella, Ava	
1994: Jessica, Ashley, Emily, Samantha, Sarah	
1974: Jennifer, Amy, Michelle, Heather, Angela	
1954: Mary, Linda, Deborah, Patricia, Susan	
1934: Mary, Betty, Barbara, Shirley, Dorothy	
Boys:	
2014: Noah, Liam, Mason, Jacob, William	
1994: Michael, Christopher, Matthew, Joshua, Tyler	
1974: Michael, Jason, Christopher, David, James	
1954: Michael, James, Robert, John, David	
1934: Robert, James, John, William, Richard	

Information from U.S. Social Security Administration.

Not Generation Some people praise (or criticize) young adults for their attitudes or behavior, but perhaps people should credit (or blame) history instead. Note that even when they were young, the oldest generations did not think that marijuana should be legal, nor were they likely to endorse same-sex marriage or even mothers of young children working outside the home. On many issues, personal experience matters more than age.

Observation Quiz Why is the line for the 1981–1997 cohort much shorter than the line for the older cohorts? (see answer, page 14)* ↑

*Observation Quizzes are designed to help students practice a crucial skill, specifically to notice small details that indicate something about human development. Answers appear on the next page or two.

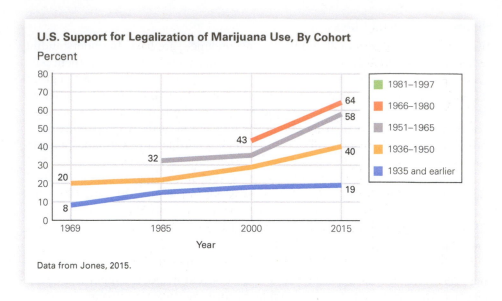

U.S. Support for Legalization of Marijuana Use, By Cohort

Percent

Legend:
- 1981–1997
- 1966–1980
- 1951–1965
- 1936–1950
- 1935 and earlier

Data from Jones, 2015.

socioeconomic status (SES) A person's position in society as determined by income, occupation, education, and place of residence. (Sometimes called *social class*.)

consuming marijuana that was legally purchased in Colorado. As we know from the ecological-systems perspective, suicide has many causes—but no 19-year-old should have been able to buy the drug. (Chapter 13 discusses the developmental consequences of marijuana use; the point here is that cohort effects can be profound.)

The second pervasive context is economic, reflected in a person's **socioeconomic status,** abbreviated **SES.** (Sometimes SES is called *social class*, as in *middle class* or *working class*.) SES reflects education, occupation, and neighborhood, as well as income.

Suppose a U.S. family is comprised of an infant, an unemployed mother, and a father who earns less than $17,000 a year. Their SES would be low if the wage earner is a high school dropout working 45 hours a week at the 2015 federal minimum wage ($7.25 × 45 × 52 = $16,965) and living in a drug-infested neighborhood, but it would be much higher if the wage earner is a postdoctoral student living on campus and teaching part time. Both of these families are officially below the federal poverty line for a family of three ($19,790), but only one is low-SES.

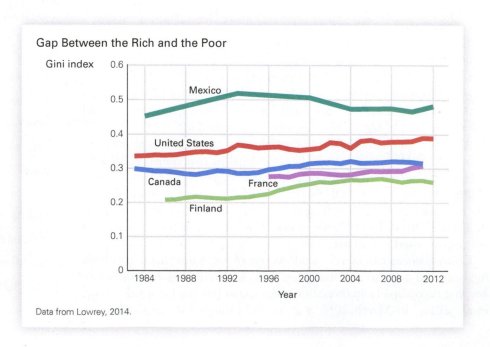

Gap Between the Rich and the Poor

Gini index

Mexico
United States
Canada
France
Finland

Data from Lowrey, 2014.

The Rich Get Richer The Gini index is a measure of income equality, ranging from 0 (everyone equal) to 1 (one person has all the money). Values here are after taxes, which shows that the gap between rich and poor is widening in the United States and Finland but not in other countries. Worldwide, the gap between the rich and the poor is estimated at about 0.63 on the Gini index.

Same Situation, Far Apart: Shelter Rules The homeless shelter in Paris, France *(left)* allows dogs, Christmas trees, and flat-screen televisions for couples in private rooms. The one in Cranston, Rhode Island *(right)* is only for men (no women, children, or dogs), who must leave each morning and wait in line each night for one of the 88 beds. Both places share one characteristic: Some of the homeless are turned away, as there is not room for everyone.

Measuring SES is complex, especially internationally. The United Nations rates the United States and Canada as rich nations, but most people in those nations do not consider themselves rich. (See Figure 1.6.)

SES brings advantages and disadvantages, opportunities and limitations—all affecting housing, health, nutrition, knowledge, and habits. Although low income obviously limits a person, other factors are pivotal, especially education and national policy. Voters choose leaders who decide policies that differentially affect people of various ages and incomes.

For example, Northern European nations eliminate SES disparities as much as possible. By contrast, the largest gaps between rich and poor tend to be in developing nations, especially in Latin America (Ravallion, 2014). Among advanced nations, the United States has "recently earned the distinction of being the most unequal of all developed countries" (Aizer & Currie, 2014, p. 856).

Income differences are not only found by ethnic group but also by age—children and young adults are more often poor compared to middle-aged and older adults. Young children with young parents suffer most: Poverty in early childhood reduces academic achievement even more than poverty during adolescence (Wagmiller et al., 2015).

Historical context matters for SES as well. Worldwide, abject poverty is less common than it was a few decades ago, but the rich are even richer than before. As one economist says, "the rising tide has indeed raised all boats . . . But the big yachts have done better, so overall income inequality is increasing" (Vanneman, quoted in Hvistendahl, 2014, p. 832).

Development Is Multicultural

In order to learn about "all kinds of people, everywhere, at every age," it is necessary to study people of many cultures. For social scientists, **culture** is "the system of shared beliefs, conventions, norms, behaviors, expectations and symbolic representations that persist over time and prescribe social rules of conduct" (Bornstein et al., 2011, p. 30).

culture A system of shared beliefs, norms, behaviors, and expectations that persist over time and prescribe social behavior and assumptions.

🔵🟢 **Observation Quiz** How many children are sleeping here in this photograph? (see answer, page 14) ⬇

Hard Floor, Hard Life These are among the thousands of unaccompanied minors who fled Latin America and arrived in Arizona and Texas in 2014. Developmentalists predict that the effects of their hazardous journey will stay with them, unless sources of resilience—such as caring family and supportive community—are quickly found. Culture and context affect every one lifelong.

social construction An idea that is built on shared perceptions, not on objective reality. Many age-related terms (such as *childhood, adolescence, yuppie,* and *senior citizen*) are social constructions, connected to biological traits but strongly influenced by social assumptions.

Watch **Video: Interview with Barbara Rogoff** to learn more about the role of culture in the development of Mayan children in Guatemala*.

*Throughout the book, the margins contain descriptions of relevant online videos and activities available in LaunchPad. Some contain QR codes, allowing immediate viewing on a smartphone.

difference-equals-deficit error The mistaken belief that a deviation from some norm is necessarily inferior to behavior or characteristics that meet the standard.

Video: Research of Geoffrey Saxe
http://qrs.ly/9c4eoxh

Social Constructions

Thus, culture is far more than food or clothes; it is a set of ideas, beliefs, and patterns. Culture is a powerful **social construction,** that is, a concept created, or *constructed,* by a society. Social constructions affect how people think and act—what they value, ignore, and punish.

Although most adults consider themselves tolerant and value a multicultural perspective, be careful. It is easy to overgeneralize when referring to cultures that are not one's own.

For example, when people speak of Asian culture or Hispanic culture, they may be stereotyping, ignoring cultural differences between people from Korea and Japan, for instance, or those from Mexico and Guatemala. An additional complication is that individuals within every group sometimes rebel against their culture's expected "beliefs, conventions, norms, behaviors."

Thus, the words *culture* and *multicultural* need to be used carefully, especially when they are applied to individuals, including oneself. Each of us is multicultural; our ethnic, national, school, and family cultures sometimes clash. One of my students wrote:

> My mom was outside on the porch talking to my aunt. I decided to go outside; I guess I was being nosey. While they were talking I jumped into their conversation which was very rude. When I realized what I did it was too late. My mother slapped me in my face so hard that it took a couple of seconds to feel my face again.

> *[C., personal communication]*

Notice how my student reflects her culture; she labels her own behavior "nosey" and "very rude." She later wrote that she expects children to be seen but not heard and that her own son makes her "very angry" when he interrupts.

However, her "rude" behavior reflects the influence of U.S. culture, where a curious, talkative child is often encouraged. Many teachers want children to "participate," and many North American parents welcome their children's questions. Do you think my student was nosey or, on the contrary, that her mother should not have slapped her? Your answer reflects your culture.

Deficit or Just Difference?

As with my student's mother, everyone tends to believe that their nation and culture are better than others. This way of thinking has benefits: Generally, people who like themselves are happier, prouder, and more willing to help strangers. However, that belief becomes destructive if it reduces respect, understanding, and appreciation for people from other groups. Too quickly and without thought, differences are assumed to be problems (Akhtar & Jaswal, 2013).

Developmentalists recognize the **difference-equals-deficit error,** which is the assumption that people unlike us (different) are inferior (deficit). Sadly, when humans realize that their ways of thinking and acting are not universal, they tend to believe that people who think or act differently are to be pitied, feared, or encouraged to change.

The difference-equals-deficit error is one reason that a careful multicultural approach is necessary. Never assume that another culture is wrong and inferior—or the opposite, right and superior. Assumptions can be harmful.

For example, one Japanese child, on her first day in a U.S. school, was teased for the food she brought for lunch. The next day, she dumped the contents of her lunchbox in the garbage before lunch—she would rather go hungry than be considered deficient. This example illustrates the problem with judging another

Diverse Complexities

It is often repeated that "the United States is becoming more diverse," a phrase that usually refers only to ethnic diversity and not to economic and religious diversity (which are also increasing and merit attention). From a developmental perspective, two other diversities are also important—age and region, as shown below. What are the implications for schools, colleges, employment, health care, and nursing homes in the notable differences in the ages of people of various groups? And are attitudes about immigration, or segregation, or multiracial identity affected by the ethnicity of one's neighbors?

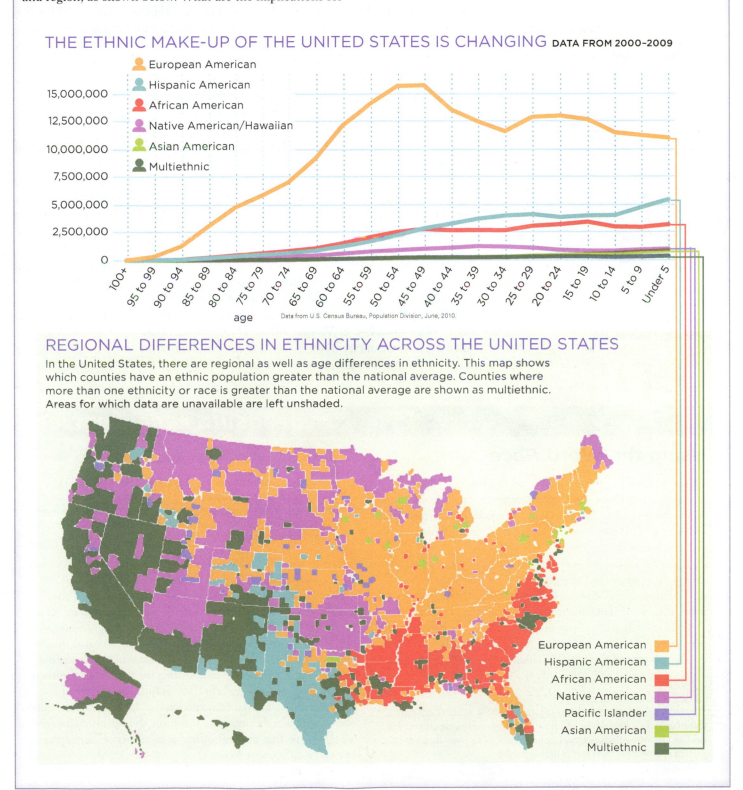

THE ETHNIC MAKE-UP OF THE UNITED STATES IS CHANGING DATA FROM 2000–2009

- European American
- Hispanic American
- African American
- Native American/Hawaiian
- Asian American
- Multiethnic

Data from U.S. Census Bureau, Population Division, June, 2010.

REGIONAL DIFFERENCES IN ETHNICITY ACROSS THE UNITED STATES

In the United States, there are regional as well as age differences in ethnicity. This map shows which counties have an ethnic population greater than the national average. Counties where more than one ethnicity or race is greater than the national average are shown as multiethnic. Areas for which data are unavailable are left unshaded.

- European American
- Hispanic American
- African American
- Native American
- Pacific Islander
- Asian American
- Multiethnic

THINK CRITICALLY: Is harmony within a nation worth the harm of punishing rebels?

culture: A Japanese lunch might, or might not, be more nutritious for children than a typical American one. The children did not know or care; the mothers thought the lunch they packed was best; the student wanted to be accepted.

Ethnic and Racial Groups

ethnic group People whose ancestors were born in the same region and who often share a language, culture, and religion.

Cultural clashes can fuel wars and violence when they are not understood. To prevent that, we need to understand the terms *culture, ethnicity,* and *race.* Members of an **ethnic group** almost always share ancestral heritage and often have the same national origin, religion, and language.

Consequently, ethnic groups often share a culture, but not necessarily (see Figure 1.7). There are "multiple intersecting and interacting dimensions" to ethnic identity (Sanchez & Vargas, 2016, p. 161). People may share ethnicity but differ culturally (e.g., people of Irish descent in Ireland, Australia, and North America), and people of one culture may come from several ethnic groups (consider British culture). [**Life-Span Link:** The major discussion of ethnic identity is in Chapter 19.]

Ethnicity is another social construction, a product of the social context, not biology. It is nurture not nature, and specifics depend on the surroundings. For example, African-born people in North America typically consider themselves African, but African-born people in Africa identify with a more specific ethnic group.

Many Americans are puzzled by civil wars (e.g., in Syria, or Sri Lanka, or Kenya) because people of the same ethnicity seem to be bitter enemies. However, within each of those nations, those opposing sides recognize many ethnic differences between them. Social construction may be potent.

Ethnic identity flourishes when co-ethnics are nearby and outsiders emphasize differences (Sanchez & Vargas, 2016). This is particularly obvious when appearance signifies ethnicity. Race is also a social construction—and a misleading one. There are reasons to abandon, and to keep, the term, as the following explains.

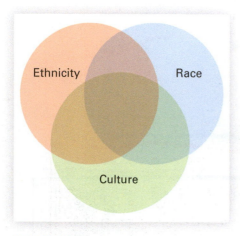

FIGURE 1.7
Overlap—But How Much? Ethnicity, culture, and race are three distinct concepts, but they often—though not always—overlap.

OPPOSING PERSPECTIVES*

Using the Word *Race*

The term **race** categorizes people on the basis of physical differences, particularly outward appearance. Historically, most North Americans believed that race was an inborn biological characteristic. Races were categorized by color: white, black, red, and yellow (Coon, 1962).

It is obvious now, but was not a few decades ago, that no one's skin is really white (like this page) or black (like these letters) or red or yellow. Social scientists are convinced that race is a social construction and that color terms exaggerate minor differences.

Skin color is particularly misleading because dark-skinned people with African ancestors have "high levels of within-population genetic diversity" (Tishkoff et al., 2009, p. 1035) and

race A group of people who are regarded by themselves or by others as distinct from other groups on the basis of physical appearance, typically skin color. Social scientists think race is a misleading concept, as biological differences are not signified by outward appearance.

because many dark-skinned people whose ancestors were not African share neither culture nor ethnicity with Africans.

Race is more than a flawed concept; it is a destructive one. It is used to justify racism, which over the years has been expressed in myriad laws and customs, with slavery, lynching, and segregation directly connected to the idea that race was real. Racism continues today in less obvious ways (some of which are highlighted later in this book), undercutting the goal of our science of human development—to help all of us fulfill our potential.

Since race is a social construction that leads to racism, some social scientists believe that the term should be abandoned. They believe that cultural differences influence development, but racial differences do not.

---

*Every page of this text includes information that requires critical thinking and evaluation. In addition, in almost every chapter you will find an Opposing Perspectives feature in which an issue that has compelling opposite perspectives is highlighted.

A study of census categories used by 141 nations found that only 15 percent use the word *race* on their census forms (Morning, 2008). The United States is the only census that separates race and ethnicity, stating that Hispanics "may be of any race." Cognitively, that may encourage stereotyping (Kelly et al., 2010). One scholar explains:

> The United States' unique conceptual distinction between race and ethnicity may unwittingly support the longstanding belief that race reflects biological difference and ethnicity stems from cultural difference. In this scheme, ethnicity is socially produced but race is an immutable fact of nature. Consequently, walling off race from ethnicity on the census may reinforce essentialist interpretations of race and preclude understanding of the ways in which racial categories are also socially constructed.
>
> *[Morning, 2008, p. 255]*

Concern about the word *race* is relevant for biologists as well as social scientists. As one team writes:

> We believe the use of biological concepts of race in human genetic research—so disputed and so mired in confusion—is problematic at best and harmful at worst. It is time for biologists to find a better way.
>
> *[Yudell et al., 2016, p. 564]*

To avoid racism, should we abandon the word *race*? Is the phrase "Black Lives Matter" a throwback?

Maybe not. There is a powerful opposite perspective (Bliss, 2012). In a nation with a history of racial discrimination, reversing that history may require allowing some people to be proud of their race and other people to recognize the harm of their racism.

The fact that race is a social construction does not make it meaningless. Adolescents who are proud of their racial identity are likely to achieve academically, resist drug addiction, and feel better about themselves (Zimmerman, 2013). Racial pride, but not personal experiences with discrimination, also predicts more positive attitudes about other racial groups. This was found for 15- to 25-year-old Black and Hispanic youth, but not for Whites—who tend not to consider themselves as belonging to a racial group (Sullivan & Ghara, 2015).

It may be that to combat racism, race itself must be acknowledged. Many medical, educational, and economic conditions—from low birthweight to college graduation, from family income to health insurance—reflect racial disparities.

In 2013 in the United States, 13 percent of Black newborns were of low birthweight, but only 7 percent of newborns from other groups were (Martin et al., 2015). That statistic requires that newborns be categorized by race. Does that lead to improvements in the care of pregnant Black women, or to blame?

Some social scientists find that to be color-blind is to be subtly racist (e.g., sociologists Marvasti & McKinney, 2011; anthropologist McCabe, 2011). Two political scientists studying the criminal justice system found that people who claim to be color-blind display "an extraordinary level of naiveté" (Peffley & Hurwitz, 2010, p. 113). Some observers believe that some of the criticism of President Obama springs from racial prejudice and that uninformed anti-racism is actually a new form of racism (Bonilla-Silva, 2015; Sullivan, 2014; Hughey & Parks, 2014).

As you see, strong arguments support both sides. This book sometimes refers to race or color when the original data are reported that way, as in the low birthweight data above. Racial categories may crumble someday, but apparently not yet.

Young Laughter Friendship across ethnic lines is common at every age, when schools, workplaces, and neighborhoods are not segregated. However, past history has an impact: These two girls share so much that they spontaneously laugh together, unaware that this scene in a restaurant could not have happened 50 years ago. Many of the youngest cohorts have trouble understanding lynching, poll taxes, separate swimming pools, or even the historic March on Washington in 1963.

THINK CRITICALLY: To fight racism, must race be named and recognized?

Development Is Multidisciplinary

In order to examine each aspect of human growth, development is often considered in three domains—*biosocial, cognitive,* and *psychosocial.* (Figure 1.8 describes each domain.) Each domain is the focus of several academic disciplines: Biosocial includes biology, neuroscience, and medicine; cognitive includes psychology, linguistics, and education; and psychosocial includes economics, sociology, and

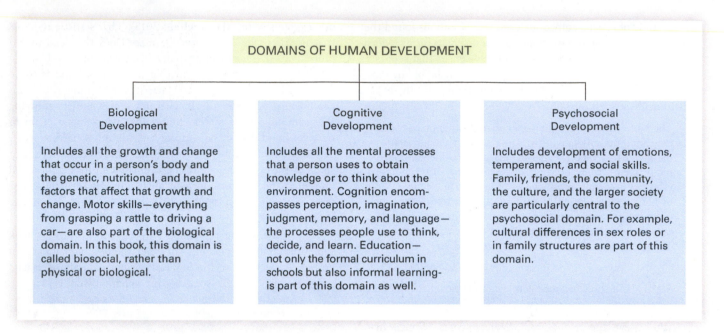

Biological Development

Includes all the growth and change that occur in a person's body and the genetic, nutritional, and health factors that affect that growth and change. Motor skills—everything from grasping a rattle to driving a car—are also part of the biological domain. In this book, this domain is called biosocial, rather than physical or biological.

Cognitive Development

Includes all the mental processes that a person uses to obtain knowledge or to think about the environment. Cognition encompasses perception, imagination, judgment, memory, and language— the processes people use to think, decide, and learn. Education— not only the formal curriculum in schools but also informal learning- is part of this domain as well.

Psychosocial Development

Includes development of emotions, temperament, and social skills. Family, friends, the community, the culture, and the larger society are particularly central to the psychosocial domain. For example, cultural differences in sex roles or in family structures are part of this domain.

FIGURE 1.8

The Three Domains The division of human development into three domains makes it easier to study, but remember that very few factors belong exclusively to one domain or another. Development is not piecemeal but holistic: Each aspect of development is related to all three domains.

history. Typically, each scholar follows a particular thread within one discipline and one domain, using clues and conclusions from other scientists who have concentrated on that same thread.

Accordingly, human development requires insights and information from many scientists, past and present, in many disciplines. Our understanding of every topic benefits from multidisciplinary research; scientists hesitate to apply general conclusions about human life until they are substantiated by several disciplines, each with specialization.

Genetics and Epigenetics

The need for multidisciplinary research is obvious when considering genetic analysis. When the human genome was first mapped in 2003, some people assumed that humans became whatever their genes destined them to be—heroes, killers, or ordinary people. However, multidisciplinary research quickly showed otherwise.

Yes, genes affect every aspect of behavior. But even identical twins, with identical genes, differ biologically, cognitively, and socially. The reasons are many, including how they are positioned in the womb and non-DNA influences in utero, both of which affect birthweight and birth order, and dozens of other epigenetic influences throughout life (Carey, 2012). [**Life-Span Link:** Mapping of the human genome is discussed in Chapter 3.]

Every academic discipline risks becoming a *silo,* that is a storage tank for research in that discipline, isolated from other disciplines. Breaking out of silos can illuminate topics that mystified scientists who were stuck in their own discipline.

One recent example is in economics, which has developed a new specialty called behavioral economics to combine conclusions from psychology, methods from sociology, and analysis from economics (Thaler, 2015; Kahneman, 2011). This specialty might have averted the recession of 2008 if it had been better understood a decade ago.

Overall, multidisciplinary research broadens and deepens our knowledge of human development. People are complex, and to properly grasp all the systems— from the workings of the microbiome in the gut to the effects of climate change in the entire world—requires scientific insights from many disciplines. Adding to this complexity, people change over time. That leads to the final theme of the life-span perspective, plasticity.

Development Is Plastic

The term **plasticity** denotes two complementary aspects of development: Human traits can be molded (as plastic can be), yet people maintain a certain durability of identity (as plastic does). The concept of plasticity in development provides both hope and realism—hope because change is possible, and realism because development builds on what has come before.

Dynamic Systems

Plasticity is basic to our contemporary understanding of human development. This is evident in the **dynamic-systems approach** to development. The idea is that human development is an ongoing, ever-changing interaction between the body and mind and between the individual and every aspect of the environment, including all of the systems described in the ecological-systems approach.

Note the word *dynamic*: Physical contexts, emotional influences, the passage of time, each person, and every aspect of the ecosystem are always interacting, always in flux, always in motion. For instance, a new approach to developing the motor skills of children with autism spectrum disorder stresses the dynamic systems that undergird movement—the changing aspects of the physical and social contexts (Lee & Porretta, 2013). [**Life-Span Link:** Autism spectrum disorder is discussed in Chapter 11.]

Similarly, a dynamic-systems approach to understanding the role of fathers in child development takes into account the sex and age of the child, the role of the mother, and the cultural norms of fatherhood. The result is a complex mix of complementary effects—and, dynamically, this affects the child in diverse ways as plasticity of family systems would predict (Cabrera, 2015).

The dynamic-systems approach builds on the multidirectional, multicontextual, multicultural, and multidisciplinary nature of development. With any developmental topic, stage, or problem, the dynamic-systems approach urges consideration of all the interrelated aspects, every social and cultural factor, over days and years. Plasticity and the need for a dynamic-systems approach are most evident when considering the actual lived experience of each individual. My nephew David is one example.

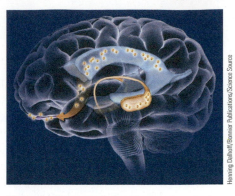

Birth of a Neuron A decade ago, neuroscientists thought that adult brains lost neurons, with age or alcohol, but never gained them. Now we know that precursors of neurons arise in the lateral ventricles (bright blue, center) to become functioning neurons in the olfactory bulb (for smell, far left) and the hippocampus (for memory, the brown structure just above the brain stem). Adult neurogenesis is much less prolific than earlier in life, but the fact that it occurs at all is astounding.

plasticity The idea that abilities, personality, and other human characteristics can change over time. Plasticity is particularly evident during childhood, but even older adults are not always "set in their ways."

dynamic-systems approach A view of human development as an ongoing, ever-changing interaction between the physical, cognitive, and psychosocial influences. The crucial understanding is that development is never static but is always affected by, and affects, many systems of development.

Dynamic Interaction A dynamic-systems approach highlights the ever-changing impact that each part of a system has on all the other parts. This classroom scene reflects the eagerness for education felt by many immigrants, the reticence of some boys in an academic context, and a global perspective (as demonstrated by the world map). These facets emerge from various systems—family, gender, and culture—and they have interacted to produce this moment.

David

My sister-in-law contracted rubella (also called German measles) early in her third pregnancy; it was not diagnosed until David was born, blind and dying. Immediate heart surgery saved his life, but surgery to remove a cataract destroyed one eye.

The doctor was horrified at the unexpected results of surgery, and he decided the cataract on the other eye should not be removed until the virus was finally gone. But one dead eye and one thick cataract meant that David's visual system was severely impaired for the first five years of his life. That affected all of his other systems. For instance, he interacted with other children by pulling their hair. Fortunately, the virus that had damaged the embryo occurred after the critical period for hearing. As dynamic systems might predict, David developed extraordinary listening ability in response to his diminished sight.

The virus harmed many aspects of fetal development—thumbs, ankles, teeth, toes, spine, and brain. David attended three special preschools—for the blind, for children with cerebral palsy, for children who were intellectually disabled. At age 6, when some sight was restored, he entered regular public school, learning academics but not social skills—partly because he was excluded from physical education and recess.

By age 10, David had blossomed intellectually: He had skipped a year of school and was in fifth grade, reading at the eleventh-grade level. Before age 20, he learned to speak a second and a third language. In young adulthood, he enrolled in college.

_____

*Many chapters include the feature A Case to Study. Each person is unique, which means that generalities cannot be validly drawn from one case, but sometimes one example makes a general concept clear.

My Brother's Children Michael, Bill, and David (left to right) are adults now, with quite different personalities, abilities, numbers of offspring (4, 2, and none), and contexts (in Massachusetts, Pennsylvania, and California). Yet despite genes, prenatal life, and contexts, I see the shared influence of Glen and Dot, my brother and sister-in-law—evident here in their similar, friendly smiles.

As development unfolded, the interplay of systems was evident. David's family context allowed him to become a productive and happy adult. He told me, "I try to stay in a positive mood." This was especially important when David's father died in 2014. David accepted the death (he said, "Dad is in a better place") and comforted his mother.

Remember, plasticity cannot erase a person's genes, childhood, or permanent damage. The brain destruction and compensation from that critical period of prenatal development remain. David is now 50. His widowed mother has applied to

TABLE 1.3	Five Characteristics of Development
Characteristic	**Application in David's Story**
Multidirectional. Change occurs in every direction, not always in a straight line. Gains and losses, predictable growth, and unexpected transformations are evident.	David's development seemed static (or even regressive, as when early surgery destroyed one eye), but then it accelerated each time he entered a new school or college.
Multidisciplinary. Numerous academic fields—especially psychology, biology, education, and sociology, but also neuroscience, economics, religion, anthropology, history, medicine, genetics, and many more—contribute insights.	Two disciplines were particularly critical: medicine (David would have died without advances in surgery on newborns) and education (special educators guided him and his parents many times).
Multicontextual. Human lives are embedded in many contexts, including historical conditions, economic constraints, and family patterns.	The high SES of David's family made it possible for him to receive daily medical and educational care. His two older brothers protected him.
Multicultural. Many cultures—not just between nations but also within them—affect how people develop.	Appalachia, where David lived, is more accepting of people with disabilities.
Plasticity. Every individual, and every trait within each individual, can be altered at any point in the life span. Change is ongoing, although it is neither random nor easy.	David's measured IQ changed from about 40 (severely intellectually disabled) to about 130 (far above average), and his physical disabilities became less crippling as he matured.

enter a senior citizen residence: Permission depends on approval to have an adult child living with her. She laughingly said that David gives her a reason for living: If she lives another 12 years, he will be able to stay in senior housing on his own.

Despite David's lifelong dependence on his parents, his listening skills continue to be impressive. He once told me:

> I am generally quite happy, but secretly a little happier lately, especially since November, because I have been consistently getting a pretty good vibrato when I am singing, not only by myself but also in congregational hymns in church. [*He explained vibrato:*] When a note bounces up and down within a quartertone either way of concert pitch, optimally between 5.5 and 8.2 times per second.

David works as a translator of German texts, which he enjoys because, as he says, "I like providing a service to scholars, giving them access to something they would otherwise not have." As his aunt, I have seen him repeatedly overcome disabilities. Plasticity is dramatically evident. This case illustrates all five aspects of the life-span perspective (see Table 1.3).

Differential Susceptibility

Plasticity emphasizes that people can and do change, that predictions are not always accurate. One insight regarding plasticity is *differential susceptibility,* a term mentioned earlier that needs elaboration. The genes and experiences of each person prime him or her to respond in a particular way, and responses are plastic.

Differential susceptibility and plasticity are apparent at every point in the life span, from prenatal development throughout old age. The early months may be especially vulnerable, "for better or for worse" (Hartman & Belsky, 2015), but old people also may change depending on the circumstances.

An experiment involved stressing pregnant rhesus monkeys and then observing how responsive those monkeys were to their newborns. Those stressed mothers who were already nurturing became more nurturing than usual, but those stressed mothers who were less nurturing became worse.

Researchers compared the monkeys born to the stressed mothers with other monkeys born earlier to the same mothers when they were not stressed. The babies of the stressed nurturing mothers were superior to their older siblings, unlike the babies born to the stressed cold mothers. Stress affected them all; differential susceptibility was evident in the specifics (Shirtcliff et al., 2013).

Development is plastic; each life is molded by contexts and events. Genes and earlier events make people vulnerable to later experiences, for better or for worse.

WHAT HAVE YOU LEARNED?

1. What aspects of development show continuity?
2. What is the difference between a critical period and a sensitive period?
3. Why is it useful to know when sensitive periods occur?
4. What did Bronfenbrenner emphasize in his ecological-systems approach?
5. What are some of the social contexts of life?
6. How does cohort differ from age group?
7. How might male–female differences be examples of the difference-equals-deficit error?
8. What is the difference between race and ethnicity?
9. What factors comprise a person's SES?
10. What is the problem with each discipline having its own silo?
11. How is human development plastic?

Video Activity: What's Wrong with This Study? explores some of the major pitfalls of the process of designing a research study.

scientific observation A method of testing a hypothesis by unobtrusively watching and recording participants' behavior in a systematic and objective manner—in a natural setting, in a laboratory, or in searches of archival data.

Using the Scientific Method

To verify or refute a hypothesis (Step 2), researchers seek the best of hundreds of research designs, choosing exactly who and what to study, how and when (Step 3), in order to gather results that will lead to valid conclusions (Step 4) that are worth publishing (Step 5). Often they use statistics to discover relationships between various aspects of the data. (See Table 1.4.)

Every research design, method, and statistic has strengths as well as weaknesses, of which students need to know to assess the conclusions. Consequently, we describe three basic research strategies and then three ways in which developmentalists study change over time.

Observation

Scientific observation requires researchers to record behavior systematically and objectively. Observations often occur in a naturalistic setting such as a home, where people behave normally. Scientific observation can also occur in a laboratory, where scientists record human reactions in various situations, often with wall-mounted video cameras and the scientist in another room.

Observation is crucial to develop hypotheses. However, observation provides issues to explore, not proof.

For example, one study of children arriving at a preschool, several weeks after the start of the year, observed how long parents stayed to hug and kiss their children before saying goodbye. When parents lingered three minutes or more, their "children spent less time involved in the preschool peer social environment," measured

Paul Rodriguez/The Orange County Register/ZUMAPRESS.com/Newscom

Friendly Dogs? Dr. Sabrina Schuck is observing children with ADHD (attention-deficit/hyperactivity disorder), who are singing as part of a 12-week therapy program. She notes specific disruptions (can you see that child's flailing arm?). Half the children in her study have sessions with therapy dogs that are trained not to bark when the children get too lively. Those children were most likely to calm down.

TABLE 1.4	Statistical Measures Often Used to Analyze Research Results
Measure	**Use**
Effect size	Indicates how much one variable affects another. Effect size ranges from 0 to 1: An effect size of 0.2 is called small, 0.5 moderate, and 0.8 large.
Significance	Indicates whether the results might have occurred by chance. If chance would produce the results only 5 times in 100, that is significant at the 0.05 level, once in 100 times is 0.01; once in 1,000 is 0.001.
Cost-benefit analysis	Calculates how much a particular independent variable costs versus how much it saves. This is useful for analyzing public spending, finding that preschool education, or preventative health majors, save money.
Odds ratio	Indicates how a particular variable compares to a standard, set at 1. For example, one study found that, although less than 1 percent of all child homicides occurred at school, the odds were similar for public and private schools. The odds of it in high schools, however, were 18.47 times that of elementary or middle schools (set at 1.0) (MMWR, January 18, 2008).
Factor analysis	Hundreds of variables could affect any given behavior. In addition, many variables (such as family income and parental education) overlap. To take this into account, analysis reveals variables that can be clustered together to form a factor, which is a composite of many variables. For example, SES might become one factor, child personality another.
Meta-analysis	A "study of studies." Researchers use statistical tools to synthesize the results of previous, separate studies. Then they analyze the accumulated results, using criteria that weigh each study fairly. This approach improves data analysis by combining studies that were too small, or too narrow, to lead to solid conclusions.

by whether the child looked at or played with other children (Grady et al., 2012, p. 1690). The authors suggest that this "has implications for not only children's later peer interactions and peer status, but also for children's engagement with school and, ultimately, academic achievement" (Grady et al., 2012, p. 1690).

But those implications are not proven. Perhaps parents of shy children stayed to help the children become more comfortable with school, and those children might become academically strong later on. Thus, the intriguing observations from this study led to two alternative hypotheses: (1) Parental anxiety impairs child social engagement, or (2) shy children benefit from parental support. More research is needed.

The Experiment

The **experiment** establishes what causes what. In the social sciences, experimenters typically impose a particular treatment on a group of volunteer participants or expose them to a specific condition and then note whether their behavior changes.

In technical terms, the experimenters manipulate an **independent variable,** which is the imposed treatment or special condition (also called the *experimental variable*; a *variable* is anything that can vary). They note whether this independent variable affects whatever they are studying, called the **dependent variable** (which *depends* on the independent variable).

Thus, the independent variable is the new, special treatment; any change in the dependent variable is the result. The purpose of an experiment is to find out whether an independent variable affects the dependent variable.

In a typical experiment (as diagrammed in Figure 1.9), two groups of participants are studied. One group, the *experimental group*, is subjected to the particular treatment or condition (the independent variable); the other group, the *comparison group* (also called the *control group*), is not.

experiment A research method in which the researcher tries to determine the cause-and-effect relationship between two variables by manipulating one (called the *independent variable*) and then observing and recording the ensuing changes in the other (called the *dependent variable*).

independent variable In an experiment, the variable that is introduced to see what effect it has on the dependent variable. (Also called *experimental variable*.)

dependent variable In an experiment, the variable that may change as a result of whatever new condition or situation the experimenter adds. In other words, the dependent variable *depends* on the independent variable.

> **THINK CRITICALLY:** If you want to predict who will win the next U.S. presidential race, what survey question would you ask, and who would you ask?

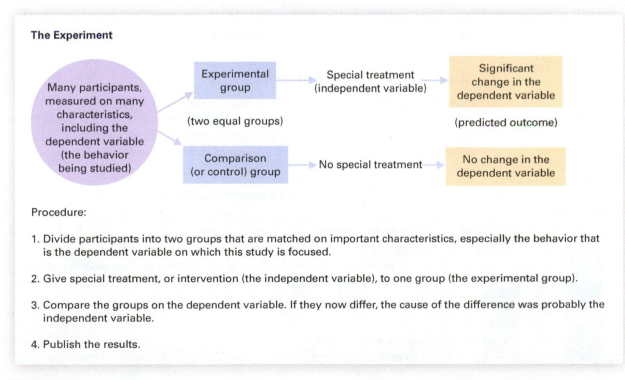

The Experiment

Many participants, measured on many characteristics, including the dependent variable (the behavior being studied)

→ Experimental group → Special treatment (independent variable) → Significant change in the dependent variable

(two equal groups)   (predicted outcome)

→ Comparison (or control) group → No special treatment → No change in the dependent variable

Procedure:

1. Divide participants into two groups that are matched on important characteristics, especially the behavior that is the dependent variable on which this study is focused.

2. Give special treatment, or intervention (the independent variable), to one group (the experimental group).

3. Compare the groups on the dependent variable. If they now differ, the cause of the difference was probably the independent variable.

4. Publish the results.

FIGURE 1.9

How to Conduct an Experiment The basic sequence diagrammed here applies to all experiments. Many additional features, especially the statistical measures listed in Table 1.4 and various ways of reducing experimenter bias, affect whether publication occurs. (Scientific journals reject reports of experiments that were not rigorous in method and analysis.)

© Rick Friedman/Corbis

What Can You Learn? Scientists first establish what is, and then try to change it. In one recent experiment, Deb Kelemen (shown here) established that few children under age 12 understand a central concept of evolution (natural selection). Then she showed an experimental group a picture book illustrating the idea. Success! The independent variable (the book) affected the dependent variable (the children's ideas), which confirmed Kelemen's hypothesis: Children can understand natural selection if instruction is tailored to their ability.

survey A research method in which information is collected from a large number of people by interviews, written questionnaires, or some other means.

🔵🔵 **Especially for Nurses** In the field of medicine, why are experiments conducted to test new drugs and treatments? (see response, page 26)*

cross-sectional research A research design that compares groups of people who differ in age but are similar in other important characteristics.

To follow up on the observation study above, researchers could design an experiment. For example, they could assess the social skills (dependent variable) of hundreds of children in the first week of school and then require parents in half of the classes to linger at drop-off (independent variable, experimental group), and in the other classes, ask the parents to leave immediately (comparison group) or let the parents do whatever they thought best (control group).

In order to draw conclusions, the social skills (dependent variable) of the children could be measured again in several months. A few years later, their school achievement (another dependent variable) could be measured.

The Survey

A third research method is the **survey,** in which information is collected from a large number of people by interview, questionnaire, or some other means. This is a quick, direct way to obtain data. It avoids assuming that the people we know best reflect the opinions of people we do not know.

For example, perhaps you know a 16-year-old who is pregnant, or an adult who hates his job, or an older person who watches television all day. If you surveyed several hundred teenagers, or adults, or older people, you would realize that teenage pregnancy is no longer common, that most people like their jobs, and that older people watch less television than children do.

Unfortunately, although surveys are quick and direct, they are not always accurate. People sometimes lie to please the researcher, and answers are influenced by the wording and the sequence of the questions.

Survey respondents may even lie to themselves. For instance, every two years since 1991, high school students in the United States have been surveyed confidentially. The most recent survey included 13,633 students from all 50 states and from schools large and small, public and private (MMWR, June 13, 2014).

Students are asked whether they had sexual intercourse *before* age 13. Every year, more ninth-grade boys than eleventh-grade boys say they had sex before age 13, yet those eleventh-graders were ninth-graders a few years before (see Figure 1.10). Why? The survey cannot tell us.

Studying Development over the Life Span

In addition to conducting observations, experiments, and surveys, developmentalists must measure how people *change or remain the same over time,* as our definition stresses. Remember that systems are dynamic, ever-changing. To capture that dynamism, developmental researchers use one of three basic research designs: cross-sectional, longitudinal, and cross-sequential.

Cross-Sectional Versus Longitudinal Research

The quickest and least expensive way to study development over time is with **cross-sectional research,** in which groups of people of one age are compared with people of another age. You saw that at the beginning of the chapter: With every decade of age, the proportion of obese people increases.

Cross-sectional design seems simple. However, the people being compared may not be similar in every way except age.

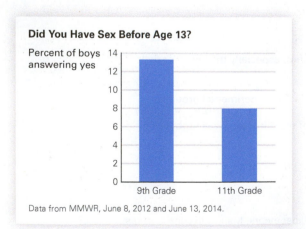

Did You Have Sex Before Age 13?

Percent of boys answering yes

Data from MMWR, June 8, 2012 and June 13, 2014.

FIGURE 1.10

I Forgot? If these were the only data available, you might conclude that ninth-graders have suddenly become more sexually active than eleventh-graders. But we have 20 years of data—those who are ninth-graders now will answer differently by eleventh grade.

---

*Since many students reading this book are preparing to be teachers, health care professionals, police officers, or parents, every chapter contains Especially For questions, which encourage you to apply important developmental concepts just as experts in the field do.

For example, because most women now in their 50s gained an average of a pound every year throughout their adulthood, does this mean that women now age 20 who weigh 140 pounds will, on average, weigh 170 pounds at age 50? Not necessarily.

To help discover whether age itself rather than cohort causes a developmental change, scientists undertake **longitudinal research.** This requires collecting data repeatedly on the same individuals as they age.

For insight about the life span, the best longitudinal research follows the same individuals from infancy to old age. Long-term research requires patience and dedication from a team of scientists, but it can pay off. It is only through longitudinal research that scientists learned that one-third of overweight children become normal-weight adults.

A longitudinal study of 790 children born in Baltimore to low-income parents found that only 4 percent of them graduated from college by age 28 (Alexander et al., 2014). Because this was a longitudinal study, it was able to pinpoint when those children were pushed away from college. Early education and friendly neighbors turned out to be more important than high school policies!

The biggest problem with longitudinal research comes from the historical context. Science, popular culture, and politics alter life experiences. Data collected on people born decades ago may not be relevant for today.

All Smiling, All Multiethnic, All the Same? Cross-sectional research comparing these people would find age differences, but there might be cohort differences as well. Only longitudinal research could find them.

longitudinal research A research design in which the same individuals are followed over time, as their development is repeatedly assessed.

Seven Times of Life These photos show Sarah-Maria, born in 1980 in Switzerland, at seven periods of her life: infancy (age 1), early childhood (age 3), middle childhood (age 8), adolescence (age 15), emerging adulthood (age 19), and adulthood (ages 30 and 36).

Observation Quiz Longitudinal research best illustrates continuity and discontinuity. For Sarah-Maria, what changed over 30 years and what didn't? (see answer, page 26)

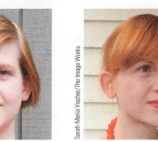

For example, many recent substances might be harmful but are advocated as beneficial, among them *phthalates* and *bisphenol A* (BPA) (chemicals used in manufacturing) in plastic baby bottles, *hydrofracking* (a process used to get gas for fuel from rocks), *e-waste* (from old computers and cell phones), and more. Some nations and states ban or regulate each of these; others do not. Verified, longitudinal data are not yet possible.

A critical example is *e-cigarettes*. They are less toxic (how much less?) to adult organs than combustible cigarettes. Some (how many?) smokers reduce their risk of cancer and heart disease by switching to e-cigs (Bhatnagar et al., 2014). But some teenagers (how many?) are more likely to smoke cigarettes if they start by vaping.

The best research shows that non-smoking teenagers who use e-cigarettes are almost four times as likely to say they "will try a cigarette soon," an ominous result but not longitudinal proof (Parker et al., 2016).

Until rates of addiction and death for e-cig smokers are known, 10 or 20 years from now, no one can be certain if the harm outweighs the benefits (Ramo et al., 2015; Hajek et al., 2014; Dutra & Glantz, 2014). [**Life-Span Link:** The major discussion of e-cigarette use is in Chapter 16.]

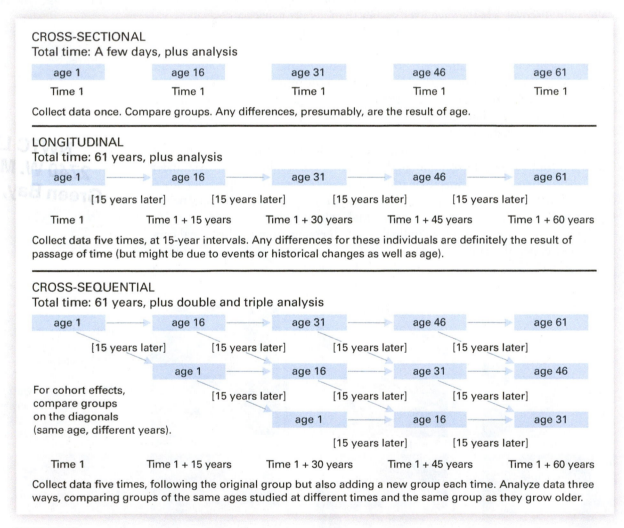

CROSS-SECTIONAL
Total time: A few days, plus analysis

| age 1 | age 16 | age 31 | age 46 | age 61 |
| Time 1 | Time 1 | Time 1 | Time 1 | Time 1 |

Collect data once. Compare groups. Any differences, presumably, are the result of age.

LONGITUDINAL
Total time: 61 years, plus analysis

age 1	→	age 16	→	age 31	→	age 46	→	age 61
[15 years later]	[15 years later]	[15 years later]	[15 years later]
Time 1	Time 1 + 15 years	Time 1 + 30 years	Time 1 + 45 years	Time 1 + 60 years

Collect data five times, at 15-year intervals. Any differences for these individuals are definitely the result of passage of time (but might be due to events or historical changes as well as age).

CROSS-SEQUENTIAL
Total time: 61 years, plus double and triple analysis

age 1 → age 16 → age 31 → age 46 → age 61
[15 years later]   [15 years later]   [15 years later]   [15 years later]
age 1 → age 16 → age 31 → age 46
[15 years later]   [15 years later]   [15 years later]
For cohort effects, compare groups on the diagonals (same age, different years).
age 1 → age 16 → age 31
[15 years later]   [15 years later]

| Time 1 | Time 1 + 15 years | Time 1 + 30 years | Time 1 + 45 years | Time 1 + 60 years |

Collect data five times, following the original group but also adding a new group each time. Analyze data three ways, comparing groups of the same ages studied at different times and the same group as they grow older.

FIGURE 1.11

Which Approach Is Best? Cross-sequential research is the most time-consuming and complex, but it yields the best information. One reason that hundreds of scientists conduct research on the same topics, replicating one another's work, is to gain some advantages of cohort-sequential research without waiting for decades.

Cross-Sequential Research

Scientists have discovered a third strategy, combining cross-sectional and longitudinal research. This combination is called **cross-sequential research** (also referred to as *cohort-sequential* or *time-sequential research*). With this design, researchers study several groups of people of different ages (a cross-sectional approach), follow them over the years (a longitudinal approach), and then combine the results.

A cross-sequential design lets researchers compare findings for, say, 16-year-olds with findings for the same individuals at age 1, as well as with data for people who were 16 long ago, who are now ages 31, 46, and 61 (see Figure 1.11). Cross-sequential research is complicated, in recruitment and analysis, but it lets scientists disentangle age from history.

The first well-known cross-sequential study (the *Seattle Longitudinal Study*) found that some intellectual abilities (vocabulary) increase even after age 60, whereas others (speed) start to decline at age 30 (Schaie, 2005/2013), confirming that development is multidirectional. This study also discovered that declines in adult math ability are more closely related to education than to age, something neither cross-sectional nor longitudinal research could reveal.

Cross-sequential research is useful for young adults as well. For example, drug addiction (called *substance use disorder,* or *SUD*) is most common in the early 20s and decreases by the late 20s. But one cross-sequential study found that the origins of SUD are much earlier, in adolescent behaviors and in genetic predispositions (McGue et al., 2014). Other research finds that heroin deaths are more common after age 30, but the best time to intervene seems to be in emerging adulthood (Carlson et al., 2016). [**Life-Span Link:** The major discussions of substance use disorder are in Chapters 17 and 20.]

cross-sequential research A hybrid research design in which researchers first study several groups of people of different ages (a cross-sectional approach) and then follow those groups over the years (a longitudinal approach). (Also called *cohort-sequential research* or *time-sequential research*.)

WHAT HAVE YOU LEARNED?

1. Why do careful observations not prove "what causes what"?

2. Why do experimenters use a control (or comparison) group as well as an experimental group?

3. What are the strengths and weaknesses of the survey method?

4. Why would a scientist conduct a cross-sectional study?

5. What are the advantages and disadvantages of longitudinal research?

6. What current innovations await longitudinal research?

7. Why do developmentalists use cross-sequential research?

Cautions and Challenges from Science

The scientific method illuminates and illustrates human development as nothing else does. Facts, consequences, and possibilities have emerged that would not be known without science—and people of all ages are healthier, happier, and more capable because of it.

For example, infectious diseases in children, illiteracy in adults, depression in late adulthood, and racism and sexism at every age are much less prevalent today than a century ago. Science deserves credit. Even violent death is less likely, with scientific discoveries and education as likely reasons (Pinker, 2011).

Developmental scientists have also discovered unexpected sources of harm. Video games, cigarettes, television, shift work, asbestos, and even artificial respiration are all less benign than people first thought.

TABLE 1.5   Quiz on Correlation

Two Variables	Positive, Negative, or Zero Correlation?	Why? (Third Variable)
1. Ice cream sales and murder rate	_____	_____
2. Reading ability and number of baby teeth	_____	_____
3. Sex of adult and his or her average number of offspring	_____	_____

For each of these three pairs of variables, indicate whether the correlation between them is positive, negative, or nonexistent. Then try to think of a third variable that might determine the direction of the correlation. The correct answers are printed upside down below.

3. Zero; each child must have a parent of each sex; no third variable

2. Negative; third variable: age

1. Positive; third variable: heat

Answers:

A Pesky Third Variable Correlation is often misleading. In this case, a third variable (the supply of fossil fuels) may be relevant.

As these examples attest, the benefits of science are many. However, there are also serious pitfalls. We now discuss three potential hazards: misinterpreting correlation, depending too heavily on numbers, and ignoring ethics.

Correlation and Causation

Probably the most common mistake in interpreting research is confusing correlation with causation. A **correlation** exists between two variables if one variable is more (or less) likely to occur when the other does. A correlation is *positive* if both variables tend to increase together or decrease together, *negative* if one variable tends to increase while the other decreases, and *zero* if no connection is evident. (Try the quiz in Table 1.5.)

Expressed in numerical terms, correlations vary from +1.0 (the most positive) to −1.0 (the most negative). Correlations are almost never that extreme; a correlation of +0.3 or −0.3 is noteworthy; a correlation of +0.8 or −0.8 is astonishing.

Many correlations are unexpected. For instance: First-born children are more likely to develop asthma than are later-born children; teenage girls have higher rates of mental health problems than do teenage boys; and counties in the United States with more dentists have fewer obese residents. That last study controlled for the number of medical doctors and the poverty of the community. The authors suggest that dentists provide information about nutrition that improves health (Holzer et al., 2014).

At this point, remember that *correlation is not causation*. Just because two variables are correlated does not mean that one causes the other—even if it seems logical that it does. It proves only that the variables are connected somehow. Many mistaken and even dangerous conclusions are drawn because people misunderstand correlation.

Quantity and Quality

A second caution concerns how heavily scientists should rely on data produced by **quantitative research** (from the word *quantity*). Quantitative research data can be categorized, ranked, or numbered and thus can be easily translated across cultures and for diverse populations. One example of quantitative research is the use of children's school achievement scores to compare the effectiveness of education within a school or a nation.

Since quantities can be easily summarized, compared, charted, and replicated, many scientists prefer quantitative research. Statistics require numbers. Quantitative data are easier to replicate and less open to bias, although researchers who choose this method have some implicit beliefs about evidence (Creswell, 2009).

However, when data are presented in categories and numbers, some nuances and individual distinctions are lost. Many developmental researchers thus turn to **qualitative research** (from the word *quality*)—asking open-ended questions, reporting answers in narrative (not numerical) form.

correlation A number between +1.0 and −1.0 that indicates the degree of relationship between two variables, expressed in terms of the likelihood that one variable will (or will not) occur when the other variable does (or does not). A correlation indicates only that two variables are somehow related, not that one variable causes the other to occur.

quantitative research Research that provides data that can be expressed with numbers, such as ranks or scales.

qualitative research Research that considers qualities instead of quantities. Descriptions of particular conditions and participants' expressed ideas are often part of qualitative studies.

Qualitative researchers are "interested in understanding how people interpret their experiences, how they construct their worlds . . ." (Merriam, 2009, p. 5). Qualitative research reflects cultural and contextual diversity, but it is also more vulnerable to bias and harder to replicate. Both types of research are needed.

Ethics

The most important caution for all scientists, especially for those studying humans, is to uphold ethical standards. Each academic discipline and professional society involved in the study of human development has a *code of ethics* (a set of moral principles).

Ethical standards and codes are increasingly stringent. Most educational and medical institutions have an *Institutional Review Board* (IRB), a group that permits only research that follows certain guidelines.

Although IRBs often slow down scientific study, some research conducted before they were established was clearly unethical, especially when the participants were children, members of minority groups, prisoners, or animals. Some argue that serious ethical dilemmas remain (Leiter & Herman, 2015).

Many ethical dilemmas arose in the Ebola epidemic (Rothstein, 2015; Gillon, 2015). Among them: Is it fair to use vaccines whose safety is unproven when such proof would take months? What kind of informed consent is needed to avoid both false hope and false fears? Is it justified to keep relatives away from sick people who might have Ebola, even though social isolation might increase the death rate?

More broadly, is justice served by a health care system that is inadequate in some countries and high-tech in others? Medicine has tended to focus on individuals, ignoring the customs and systems that make some people more vulnerable. One observer noted:

> When people from the United States and Europe working in West Africa have developed Ebola, time and again the first thing they wanted to take was not an experimental drug. It was an airplane that would cart them home.

> [Cohen, 2014, p. 911]

Sadly, some of the benefits (promotion, acclaim) of publishing remarkable, unreplicated findings encourage unethical research. Pressures from politicians and corporations are part of the problem, but nonprofit research groups and academic institutions are also to blame.

As stressed early in this chapter, researchers, like all other humans, have strong opinions, which they expect research to confirm. They might try (sometimes without noticing it) to achieve the results they want. As one team explains:

> Our job as scientists is to discover truths about the world. We generate hypotheses, collect data, and examine whether or not the data are consistent with those hypotheses . . . . [but we] often lose sight of this goal, yielding to pressure to do whatever is justifiable to compile a set of studies we can publish. This is not driven by a willingness to deceive but by the self-serving interpretation of ambiguity . . .

> [Simmons et al., 2011, pp. 1359, 1365]

Obviously, collaboration, replication, and transparency are essential ethical safeguards. Hundreds of questions regarding human development need answers, and researchers have yet to find them. That is the most important ethical mandate of all. For instance:

- Do we know enough about prenatal drugs to protect every fetus?
- Do we know enough about poverty to enable everyone to be healthy?

Video Activity: Eugenics and the Feebleminded: A Shameful History illustrates what can happen when scientists fail to follow a code of ethics.

Especially for Future Researchers and Science Writers Do any ethical guidelines apply when an author writes about the experiences of family members, friends, or research participants? (see response, page 30)

Response for Future Researchers (from page 26) There is no best method for collecting data. The method used depends on many factors, such as the age of participants (infants can't complete questionnaires), the question being researched, and the time frame.

Science and Ebola Ebola was halted as much because of social science as medicine, which has not yet found an effective vaccine. Fortunately, social workers taught practices that were contrary to West African culture—no more hugging, touching, or visiting from one neighborhood to another. Psychologists advised health workers, like this one from Doctors Without Borders, to hold, reassure, and comfort children as much as possible. This girl was *not* among the 5,000 Liberians who died.

John Moore/Getty Images

🔴🔵 **Response for Future Researchers and Science Writers** (from page 29) Yes. Anyone you write about must give consent and be fully informed about your intentions. They can be identified by name only if they give permission. For example, family members gave permission before anecdotes about them were included in this text. My nephew David read the first draft of his story (see pages 20–21) and is proud to have his experiences used to teach others.

THINK CRITICALLY: Can you think of an additional question that researchers should answer?

- Do we know enough about transgender children, or single parenthood, or divorce, or same-sex marriages to ensure optimal development?
- Do we know enough about dying to enable everyone to die with dignity?

The answer to all of these questions is a resounding *NO*.

Scientists and funders tend to avoid questions that might produce unwanted answers. People have strong opinions about drugs, income, sex, families, and death that may conflict with scientific findings and conclusions. Religion, politics, and ethics shape scientific research, sometimes stopping investigation before it begins.

For instance, in 1996, the United States Congress, in allocating funds for the Centers for Disease Control, passed a law stating that "None of the funds made available for injury prevention and control at the Centers for Disease Control and Prevention may be used to advocate or promote gun control." This has stopped some research on the most common means of suicide in the United States, because it might—or might not—be used to advocate gun control (Gostin, 2016).

An even greater question is about the "unknown unknowns," the topics that we assume we understand but do not, hypotheses that have not yet occurred to anyone because our thinking is limited by our cultures and contexts. This probably applies to both sides of the gun debate.

The next cohort of developmental scientists will build on what is known, mindful of what needs to be explored, and will raise questions that no one has thought of before. Remember that the goal is to help everyone fulfill their potential. Much more needs to be learned. The next 24 chapters are only a beginning.

WHAT HAVE YOU LEARNED?

1. Why does correlation not prove causation?
2. What are the advantages and disadvantages of quantitative research?
3. What are the advantages and disadvantages of qualitative research?
4. What is the role of the IRB?
5. Why might a political leader avoid funding developmental research?
6. What questions about human development remain to be answered?

SUMMARY

Understanding How and Why

1. The study of human development is a science that seeks to understand how people change or remain the same over time. As a science, it begins with questions and hypotheses and then gathers empirical data.

2. Replication confirms, modifies, or refutes conclusions, which are not considered solid until they are confirmed by several studies.

3. The universality of human development and the uniqueness of each individual's development are evident in both nature (the genes) and nurture (the environment); no person is quite like another. Nature and nurture always interact, and each human characteristic is affected by that interaction.

4. Crucial to the study of nature and nurture is the concept of differential susceptibility—that genes or experiences affect the likelihood that a person will be affected by the environment.

The Life-Span Perspective

5. The assumption that growth is linear and that progress is inevitable has been replaced by the idea that both continuity (sameness) and discontinuity (sudden shifts) are part of every life and that gains and losses are apparent at every age.

6. Time is a crucial variable in studying human development. A critical period is a time when something *must* occur or when an abnormality might occur. Often a particular development can occur more easily at a particular time, called a sensitive period.

7. Urie Bronfenbrenner's ecological-systems approach notes that each of us is situated within larger systems of family, school, community, and culture, as well as part of a historical cohort. Changes in the context affect all other aspects of the system.

8. Certain experiences or innovations shape people of each cohort because they share the experience of significant historical events. Socioeconomic status (SES) affects each person's opportunities, health, and even abilities at every stage of development.

9. *Culture, ethnicity,* and *race* are social constructions, concepts created by society. Culture includes beliefs and patterns; ethnicity refers to ancestral heritage. Race is also a social construction, sometimes mistakenly thought to be biological.

10. Developmentalists try to avoid the difference-equals-deficit error. Differences are alternate ways to think or act. They are not necessarily harmful.

11. Within each person, every aspect of development interacts with the others, but development can be divided into three domains—biosocial, cognitive, and psychosocial. A multidisciplinary, dynamic-systems approach is needed.

12. Throughout life, human development is plastic. Brains and behaviors to change over time. Plasticity means that change is possible, not that everything can change.

Using the Scientific Method

13. Commonly used research methods are scientific observation, the experiment, and the survey. Each can provide insight and discoveries, yet each is limited. Replication, or using other methods to examine the same topic, is needed.

14. Developmentalists study change over time, often with cross-sectional and longitudinal research. A newer method is cross-sequential, which combines the other two methods.

Cautions and Challenges from Science

15. A correlation shows that two variables are related not that one *causes* the other: Both may be caused by a third variable.

16. Quantitative research provides numerical data. This makes it best for comparing contexts and cultures via verified statistics. By contrast, more nuanced data come from qualitative research, which reports on individual lives. Both are useful.

17. Ethical behavior is crucial in all of the sciences. Results must be fairly gathered, reported, and interpreted.

18. The most important ethical question is whether scientists are designing, conducting, analyzing, publishing, and applying the research that is most critically needed.

KEY TERMS

science of human
  development (p. 4)
scientific method (p. 4)
hypothesis (p. 4)
empirical evidence (p. 4)
replication (p. 4)
nature (p. 6)
nurture (p. 6)
epigenetics (p. 7)
differential susceptibility
  (p. 7)

life-span perspective (p. 8)
critical period (p. 9)
sensitive period (p. 9)
ecological-systems
  approach (p. 10)
cohort (p. 11)
socioeconomic status
  (SES) (p. 12)
culture (p. 13)
social construction (p. 14)

difference-equals-deficit error
  (p. 14)
ethnic group (p. 16)
race (p. 16)
plasticity (p. 19)
dynamic-systems
  approach (p. 19)
scientific observation (p. 22)
experiment (p. 23)
independent variable (p. 23)

dependent variable (p. 23)
survey (p. 24)
cross-sectional research (p. 24)
longitudinal research (p. 25)
cross-sequential research
  (p. 27)
correlation (p. 28)
quantitative research (p. 28)
qualitative research (p. 28)

APPLICATIONS

1. It is said that culture is pervasive but that people are unaware of it. List 30 things you did *today* that you might have done differently in another culture. Begin with how and where you woke up.

2. How would your life be different if your parents were much higher or lower in SES than they are? Consider all three domains.

3. A longitudinal case study can be insightful but is also limited in generality. Interview one of your older relatives, explain what aspects of his or her childhood are unique and what might be relevant for everyone.

Theories

What Will You Know?

1. What is practical about a theory?
2. Do childhood experiences affect adults?
3. Would you be a different person if you grew up in another place or century?
4. Why do we need so many theories?

Larry DePrimo, a 25-year-old police officer on duty in Times Square, saw a barefoot man on a frigid November night, asked his shoe size (12), and bought him all-weather boots and thermal socks. As DePrimo bent down to help the man don his gift, a tourist from Arizona snapped his photo. Days later, the tourist wrote to the New York Police Department, who put the image on their Web site. It went viral.

Then came theories, in half a million comments on Facebook.

Commentators asked: Was this real or a hoax? Was DePrimo's act typical ("most cops are honorable, decent people"), atypical ("truly exceptional"), or in between ("not all NYC cops are short-tempered, profiling, or xenophobic")? Is the officer young and naive? Are his parents proud and wonderful? Was his assignment (anti-terrorism patrol) neglected or boring?

These questions reflect not science but "folk theories," which arise from pre-conceptions and everyday experience (Bazinger & Kühberger, 2012). We all have dozens of folk theories, without realizing that they lead us to opinions that are not shared by people with other folk theories. Nonetheless, this anecdote illustrates three aspects shared by every theory, scientific as well as folk: (1) Behavior can be surprising, (2) humans develop theories to explain everything, and (3) experience and culture matter.

Past experience is particularly powerful. This was apparent with the boots: An advocate for the homeless suspected that the photo was staged; the photographing tourist thought of her father (also a police officer); many commentators criticized someone, among them the mayor (for not helping the poor), the police (for harassing the homeless), journalists (for focusing "on murder and mayhem"), and the barefoot man himself (for choosing his plight).

A year later, DePrimo was promoted. His father, wanting people to understand the totality of his son, said that his service record was the reason, not the boots (Antenucci, 2013). DePrimo himself was pleasantly surprised, commenting on the new detective badge on his shirt: "I look down and it's still unreal to me" (DePrimo, quoted in Antenucci, 2013). The badge is a symbol, infused with decades of theories.

In this chapter, we explain five of the most insightful theories of human development. Three of them—psychoanalytic, behaviorism, and cognitive—have been touchstones for developmentalists for decades and are thus called "grand theories."

Badge and Boots This is Larry DePrimo, a New York City police officer in Manhattan, who astonished many people when he bought boots for a barefoot man on a cold afternoon.

developmental theory A group of ideas, assumptions, and generalizations that interpret and illuminate the thousands of observations that have been made about human growth. A developmental theory provides a framework for explaining the patterns and problems of development.

As you will read, each of these has evolved over the years, with newer versions of the originals set out by Freud, Pavlov, and Piaget.

Two more theories—sociocultural and evolutionary—are newer for developmentalists. Both have arisen from recent research, which has discovered important cultural differences and surprising archeological evidence. Some of the implications and applications of these two are still in flux and undergoing debate, but both merit exploration here.

Simple pronouncements regarding one incident are relatively easy to prove or disprove. DePrimo is from my local precinct. I know his commanding officer; this was not a hoax. Understanding why he did as he did requires more depth: Each of the theories in this chapter has a different perspective.

What Theories Do

Kurt Lewin (1945) once quipped, "Nothing is as practical as a good theory." Like many other scientists, he knew that theories help analysis. Of course, theories differ; some are less adequate than others, and some reflect one culture but not another.

Every theory is an explanation of facts and observations, a set of concepts and ideas that organize the confusing mass of sensations that each of us encounters every moment. Some theories are idiosyncratic, narrow, and useless to anyone except the people who thought of them. Others are much more elaborate and insightful, such as the major theories described in this chapter.

Because they are comprehensive and complex, the grand theories and the newer theories propel science forward, inspiring thousands of scientists to experiment and explain. Scientific theories are similar to folk theories in some ways. However, unlike most folk theories, they lead to new insights and elicit alternate interpretations.

A **developmental theory** is a systematic statement of general principles that provides a framework for understanding how and why people change as they grow older. Facts and observations are connected to patterns of change and explanations, weaving the details into a meaningful whole. A developmental theory is more than a hunch or a hypothesis; it is far more comprehensive than a folk theory. Developmental theories provide insights that are both broad and deep.

Questions and Answers

As you remember from Chapter 1, the first step in the science of human development is to pose a question, which often springs from theory. Among the thousands of important questions are the following, each central to one of the five theories in this chapter:

1. Does the impact of early experience—of breast-feeding or attachment or abuse—linger into adulthood, even if the experience seems to be forgotten?
2. Does learning depend on encouragement, punishment, and/or role models?
3. Do people develop morals, even if no one taught them right from wrong?
4. Does culture determine parents' behavior, such as how to respond to a child's cry?
5. Is survival an inborn instinct, underlying all personal and social decisions?

Each of these five questions is answered "yes" by, in order, the following theories: psychoanalytic, behaviorism, cognitive, sociocultural, and evolutionary. Each question is answered "no" or "not necessarily" by several others. For every answer, more questions arise: Why or why not? When and how? So what? This last question is crucial; the implications and applications of the answers affect everyone's daily life.

To be more specific about what theories do:

- Theories produce *hypotheses.*
- Theories generate *discoveries.*
- Theories offer *practical guidance.*

Facts and Norms

A **norm** is an average or usual event or experience. It is related to the word *normal,* although it has a somewhat different meaning. Something can be outside the norm, but that does not make it abnormal.

To be *abnormal* implies that something is wrong, but norms are neither right nor wrong. A norm is an average—not an arithmetical mean or median, but those mode, a common standard. Thus, norms can be calculated, such as the norm for when infants put two words together (18 months) or when workers retire (62 years). As you learned in Chapter 1, differences from the norm are not necessarily deficits, and cultures vary.

Retirement age is an easy example. Age 62 was the norm in the United States at about 2010. Retirement occured on average at age 60 in most European nations, never in most African nations.

Practice and policy often conflict. In many Asian nations, older people assumed that their families would support them, and thus employers could fire older workers. Now governments provide some pensions and other services, and the laws are changing.

Singapore is an example. Until 2012, employers could require employees to quit at age 62 and reduce a worker's salary after age 60. Then, as the population aged (more elders, fewer young workers), Singapore revised the law. Currently, employers *must* offer healthy 62-year-olds another job (not necessarily at the same salary) until age 65, when retirement can be required.

That is changing again in Singapore. The age at which employers can require retirement is slated to increase to age 67 in 2017, partly because many older workers want to work and there are fewer young workers to support them (Chuan, 2015).

In the United States, the norm for retirement was age 62, but in the past five years it has been inching up for the same reasons. Obviously, a norm is simply a statistic; it is not necessarily good or bad.

Sometimes a norm is an expected behavior, even if it is not the usual practice. For instance, *filial responsibility*—the idea that adults should care for their aged parents—is a norm in most cultures. However, many adult children currently do not follow that norm because their elders were divorced, distant, or destructive (Coleman & Ganong, 2014).

To return to the opening anecdote, it is not the norm for police officers to spend their own money to buy boots for strangers, which is why DePrimo's act generated headlines. But his act should not be called abnormal.

Do not confuse theories with norms or facts. Theories raise questions and suggest hypotheses, and they lead to research to gather empirical data. Those data are facts that suggest conclusions, which may reveal a norm or verify some aspect of a theory. Other interpretations of the data and new research to confirm or refute the theory are possible.

Maremagnum/Getty Images

Give My Regards to Broadway Those lyrics written by George Cohan (1878–1942) are inscribed on his bronze statue overlooking thousands of twenty-first century tourists from every state and nation in Times Square, New York City. Like all five theories in this chapter, this scene depicts the dynamic interaction of old insights and new realities.

norm An average, or typical, standard of behavior or accomplishment, such as the norm for age of walking or the norm for greeting a stranger.

Obviously, the scientific method is needed because "each theory of developmental psychology always has a view of humans that reflects philosophical, economic, and political beliefs" (Miller, 2011, p. 17). A theory begins the process, but then scientists develop hypotheses, design studies, and collect and analyze data that lead to conclusions that undercut some theories and modify others. [**Life-Span Link:** These five steps are explained in Chapter 1.]

Past and Future

Humans spontaneously develop theories about everything they observe. Scientists have realized this for centuries. Charles Darwin wrote, "As soon as the important faculties of the imagination, wonder, and curiosity, together with some power of reasoning, had become partially developed, man would naturally crave to understand what was passing around him, and would have vaguely speculated on his own existence" (Darwin, 1871, quoted in Thomson, 2015, p. 104; Culotta, 2009, and many others).

Quoting Darwin (a controversial figure) evokes theories about creation and evolution, including the theory that science and religion are opposing worldviews, a theory not held by most scientists. Theories are meant to be useful, moving us forward, not stopping thought.

That is why we need developmental theories. Without them we would be reactive and bewildered, blindly following our culture and our prejudices, not helpful to anyone who wonders about their children, their elders, themselves. Hundreds of theories about the life span have been published, some pertaining only to one behavior or age.

Many influential theories focus only on adulthood. One example is **humanism,** which is explained in Chapter 22. Others focus particularly on late adulthood. Disengagement, activity, and stratification theories are discussed in Chapter 25. The five clusters in this chapter are comprehensive, covering the entire life span, each attempting to explain all of human development.

Not surprisingly, given the power of history and experience to shape perspectives, each theory became ascendant in a particular decade during the past 100 years. Of course, all five shed light on current issues—otherwise they would not still be useful. And all echo ideas written by ancient sages, in Greece, China, India, and elsewhere, since humans always "naturally crave to understand." Consider these a touchstone, useful for understanding the rest of this book.

humanism A theory that stresses the potential of all humans for good and the belief that all people have the same basic needs, regardless of culture, gender, or background.

Backpacks or Bouquets? Children worldwide are nervous on their first day of school, but their coping reflects implicit cultural theories. Kindergartner Madelyn Ricker in Georgia shows her new backpack to her teacher, and elementary school students in Russia bring flowers to their teachers.

WHAT HAVE YOU LEARNED?

1. What are the similarities and differences between folk theories and scientific theories?

2. What three things do theories do?

3. How is a norm different from a theory?

4. What is the relationship between theories and facts?

5. Who develops theories—everyone or just scientists?

Grand Theories

In the first half of the twentieth century, two opposing theories—psychoanalytic and behaviorism—dominated the discipline of psychology, each with extensive applications to human development. In about 1960, a third theory—cognitive—arose, and it too was widely applied to development.

These three are called "grand theories" because they are comprehensive, enduring, and far-reaching. In developmental studies, these three theories continue to be useful, which is why they are considered grand and are explained here. But be forewarned: None of them is now considered as grand as developmentalists once believed.

Psychoanalytic Theory: Freud and Erikson

Inner drives, deep motives, and unconscious needs rooted in childhood—especially the first six years—are the focus of **psychoanalytic theory**. These unconscious forces are thought to influence every aspect of thinking and behavior, from the smallest details of daily life to the crucial choices of a lifetime.

psychoanalytic theory A grand theory of human development that holds that irrational, unconscious drives and motives, often originating in childhood, underlie human behavior.

Freud's Ideas

Psychoanalytic theory originated with Sigmund Freud (1856–1939), an Austrian physician who treated patients suffering from mental illness. He listened to his patients' remembered dreams and to their uncensored streams of thought. From that, he constructed an elaborate, multifaceted theory.

According to Freud, development in the first six years of life occurs in three stages, each characterized by sexual interest and pleasure arising from a particular part of the body. In infancy, the erotic body part is the mouth (the *oral stage*); in early childhood, it is the anus (the *anal stage*); in the preschool years, it is the penis (the *phallic stage*), a source of pride and fear among boys and a reason for sadness and envy among girls. Then, after a quiet period (*latency*), the *genital stage* arrives at puberty, lasting throughout adulthood. (Table 2.1 describes stages in Freud's theory.)

Freud maintained that sensual satisfaction (from stimulation of the mouth, anus, or penis) is linked to major developmental stages, needs, and challenges. During the oral stage, for example, sucking provides not only nourishment but also erotic joy and attachment to the mother. Kissing between lovers is a vestige of the oral stage. Next, during the anal stage, pleasures arise from self-control, initially with toileting.

One of Freud's most influential ideas was that each stage includes its own struggles. Conflict occurs, for instance,

Freud at Work In addition to being the world's first psychoanalyst, Sigmund Freud was a prolific writer. His many papers and case histories, primarily descriptions of his patients' symptoms and sexual urges, helped make the psychoanalytic perspective a dominant force for much of the twentieth century.

AKG/Photo Researchers

TABLE 2.1	Comparison of Freud's Psychosexual and Erikson's Psychosocial Stages	
Approximate Age	Freud (Psychosexual)	Erikson (Psychosocial)
Birth to 1 year	*Oral Stage* The lips, tongue, and gums are the focus of pleasurable sensations in the baby's body, and sucking and feeding are the most stimulating activities.	*Trust vs. Mistrust* Babies either trust that others will satisfy their basic needs, including nourishment, warmth, cleanliness, and physical contact, **or** develop mistrust about the care of others.
1–3 years	*Anal Stage* The anus is the focus of pleasurable sensations in the baby's body, and toilet training is the most important activity.	*Autonomy vs. Shame and Doubt* Children either become self-sufficient in many activities, including toileting, feeding, walking, exploring, and talking, **or** doubt their own abilities.
3–6 years	*Phallic Stage* The phallus, or penis, is the most important body part, and pleasure is derived from genital stimulation. Boys are proud of their penises; girls wonder why they don't have them.	*Initiative vs. Guilt* Children either try to undertake many adultlike activities **or** internalize the limits and prohibitions set by parents. They feel either adventurous **or** guilty.
6–11 years	*Latency* Not really a stage, latency is an interlude. Sexual needs are quiet; psychic energy flows into sports, schoolwork, and friendship.	*Industry vs. Inferiority* Children busily practice and then master new skills **or** feel inferior, unable to do anything well.
Adolescence	*Genital Stage* The genitals are the focus of pleasurable sensations, and the young person seeks sexual stimulation and satisfaction in heterosexual relationships.	*Identity vs. Role Confusion* Adolescents ask themselves "Who am I?" They establish sexual, political, religious, and vocational identities **or** are confused about their roles.
Adulthood	Freud believed that the genital stage lasts throughout adulthood. He also said that the goal of a healthy life is "to love and to work."	*Intimacy vs. Isolation* Young adults seek companionship and love **or** become isolated from others, fearing rejection. *Generativity vs. Stagnation* Middle-aged adults contribute to future generations through work, creative activities, and parenthood **or** they stagnate. *Integrity vs. Despair* Older adults try to make sense of their lives, either seeing life as a meaningful whole **or** despairing at goals never reached.

No Choking During the oral stage, children put everything in their mouths, as Freud recognized and as 12-month-old Harper Vasquez does here. Toy manufacturers and lawyers know this, too, which is why many toy packages read "Choking hazard: small parts, not appropriate for children under age 3."

© 2016 Macmillan

when parents wean their babies (oral stage), toilet train their toddlers (anal stage), deflect the sexual curiosity and fantasies of their 5-year-olds (phallic stage), and limit the sexual interests of adolescents (genital stage). According to Freud, the experience and resolution of these conflicts determines personality lifelong.

Freud did not believe that new stages occurred after puberty; rather, he believed that adult personalities and habits were influenced by whatever happened in childhood. Unconscious conflicts rooted in early life are evident in adult behavior—for instance, smoking cigarettes (oral) or keeping a clean and orderly house (anal) or falling in love with a much older partner (phallic).

Erikson's Ideas

Many of Freud's followers became famous theorists themselves—Carl Jung, Alfred Adler, and Karen Horney among them. They acknowledged the importance of the unconscious and of early-childhood experience, but each of them expanded and modified Freud's ideas. For scholars in human development, one neo-Freudian, Erik Erikson (1902–1994), is particularly insightful. He proposed a comprehensive developmental theory that included the entire life span.

Erikson described eight developmental stages, each characterized by a particular challenge, or *developmental crisis* (summarized in Table 2.1). Although Erikson named two polarities at each crisis, he recognized a wide range of outcomes between those opposites. Typically, development at each stage leads to neither extreme but to something in between.

In the stage of *initiative versus guilt,* for example, 3- to 6-year-olds undertake activities that exceed the limits set by their parents and their culture. They leap into swimming pools, pull their pants on backward, make cakes according to their own recipes, and wander off alone.

Erikson thought that such preschool initiatives produce feelings of pride or failure. The result can be lifelong guilt if adults are too critical or if social norms are too strict. Most adults fall somewhere between unbridled initiative and crushing guilt, depending on their early childhood experiences.

As you can see from Table 2.1, Erikson's first five stages are closely related to Freud's stages. Erikson, like Freud, believed that problems of adult life echo unresolved childhood conflicts. He thought the first stage, *trust versus mistrust,* was particularly crucial. For example, an adult who has difficulty establishing a secure, mutual relationship with a life partner may never have resolved that first crisis of early infancy.

Every stage echoes throughout life. For example, in late adulthood, one person may be outspoken while another avoids expressing opinions because each resolved the initiative-versus-guilt stage in opposite ways.

In two crucial aspects, Erikson's stages differ significantly from Freud's:

1. Erikson's stages emphasized family and culture, not sexual urges.
2. Erikson recognized adult development, with three stages after adolescence.

Behaviorism: Conditioning and Learning

The comprehensive theory that dominated psychology in the United States for most of the twentieth century was **behaviorism.** The roots of this theory were in Russia, with Ivan Pavlov, who first described the process of conditioning.

Classical Conditioning

A century ago, Pavlov (1849–1936) did many experiments to examine the link between stimulus and response. While studying salivation in his laboratory, Pavlov noted that his research dogs drooled not only at the smell of food but also, eventually, at the sound of the footsteps of the people bringing food. This observation led Pavlov to perform a famous experiment: He conditioned dogs to salivate when hearing a particular noise.

The Photo Works

Pavlov began by sounding a tone just before presenting food. After a number of repetitions of the tone-then-food sequence, dogs began salivating at the sound even when there was no food. This simple experiment demonstrated **classical conditioning** (also called *respondent conditioning*).

In classical conditioning, a person or animal learns to associate a neutral stimulus with a meaningful stimulus, gradually responding to the neutral stimulus in the same way as to the meaningful

Ted Streshinsky/The LIFE Images Collection/Getty Images

A Legendary Couple In his first 30 years, Erikson never fit into a particular local community, since he frequently changed nations, schools, and professions. Then he met Joan. In their first five decades of marriage, they raised a family and wrote several books. If Erikson had published his theory at age 73 (when this photograph was taken) instead of in his 40s, would he still have described life as a series of crises?

Especially for Teachers Your kindergartners are talkative and always moving. They almost never sit quietly and listen to you. What would Erik Erikson recommend? (see response, p. 41)

behaviorism A grand theory of human development that studies observable behavior. Behaviorism is also called *learning theory* because it describes the laws and processes by which behavior is learned.

classical conditioning The learning process in which a meaningful stimulus (such as the smell of food to a hungry animal) is connected with a neutral stimulus (such as the sound of a tone) that had no special meaning before conditioning. (Also called *respondent conditioning.*)

A Conventional Couple The identity crisis looks like a rejection of social norms, from her multicolored hair to his two-color pants. But Erikson noted that underlying the crisis is the wish to find another teenager who shares the same identity—as these two have done.

A Contemporary of Freud Ivan Pavlov was a physiologist who received the Nobel Prize in 1904 for his research on digestive processes. It was this line of study that led to his discovery of classical conditioning, when his research on dog saliva led to insight about learning.

 Observation Quiz How is Pavlov similar to Freud in appearance, and how do both look different from the other theorists pictured? (see answer, page 42) ↑

one. In Pavlov's original experiment, the dog associated the tone (the neutral stimulus) with food (the meaningful stimulus) and eventually responded to the tone as if it were the food itself. The conditioned response to the tone, no longer neutral but now a conditioned stimulus, was evidence that learning had occurred.

Behaviorists see dozens of examples of classical conditioning. Infants learn to smile at their parents because they associate them with food and play; toddlers become afraid of busy streets if the noise of traffic repeatedly frightens them; students enjoy—or fear—school, depending on what happened in kindergarten.

One example of classical conditioning is *white coat syndrome,* when past experiences with medical professionals (who wore white coats) conditioned a person to be anxious. For that reason, when a doctor or nurse dressed in white takes a patient's blood pressure, anxiety causes the pressure to rise, producing an artificially high number.

White coat syndrome is apparent in about half of the U.S. population over age 80 (Bulpitt et al., 2013), probably because of their childhood experiences. Today, many nurses wear colorful blouses and many doctors wear street clothes: They hope that will prevent conditioned anxiety in newer cohorts.

Behaviorism in the United States

Pavlov's ideas seemed to bypass most European developmentalists but were welcomed in the United States, where they arose in opposition to the psychoanalytic emphasis on the unconscious. The first of three famous Americans who championed behaviorism was John B. Watson (1878–1958), who argued that if psychology was to be a true science, psychologists should examine only what they could see and measure. In his words:

> Why don't we make what we can *observe* the real field of psychology? Let us limit ourselves to things that can be observed, and formulate laws concerning only those things. . . . We can observe *behavior—what the organism does or says.*
>
> *[Watson, 1924/1998, p. 6]*

According to Watson, if psychologists focus on behavior, they will realize that everything can be learned. He wrote:

> Give me a dozen healthy infants, well-formed, and my own specified world to bring them up in and I'll guarantee to take any one at random and train him to become any type of specialist I might select—doctor, lawyer, artist, merchant-chief, and yes, even beggar-man and thief, regardless of his talents, penchants, tendencies, abilities, vocations, and race of his ancestors.
>
> *[Watson, 1924/1998, p. 82]*

Other American psychologists agreed. They developed behaviorism to study observable behavior, objectively and scientifically. For everyone at every age, behaviorists believe there are natural laws of human behavior. Those laws allow simple actions to become complex competencies, as various forces in the environment affect each action.

Learning in behaviorism is far more comprehensive than the narrow definition of learning, which focuses on academic knowledge, such as learning to read or multiply. Instead, for behaviorists, everything that people do and feel is learned.

For example, newborns need to *learn* to suck on a nipple; infants *learn* to smile at a caregiver; preschoolers *learn* to hold hands when crossing the street. Learning continues lifelong: Adults *learn* to budget time and money, to relate to strangers, to favor liberal or conservative candidates for public office, and more.

Behaviorists believe that development occurs not in stages but bit by bit. A person learns to talk, read, and everything else one tiny step at a time.

Operant Conditioning

The most influential North American proponent of behaviorism was B. F. Skinner (1904–1990). Skinner agreed with Watson that psychology should focus on the science of observable behavior. He did not dispute Pavlov's classical conditioning, but, as a good scientist, he built on Pavlov's conclusions with his own experiments. His most famous contribution was to recognize another type of conditioning— **operant conditioning** (also called *instrumental conditioning*)—in which animals (including people) act and then something follows that action.

In other words, Skinner went beyond learning by association, in which one stimulus is paired with another stimulus (in Pavlov's experiment, the tone with the food). He focused instead on what happens after a behavior elicits a particular response. If the consequence that follows is enjoyable, the animal tends to repeat the behavior; if the consequence is unpleasant, the animal does not do that action again.

Consequences that increase the frequency or strength of a particular action are called reinforcers, in a process called **reinforcement** (Skinner, 1953). According to behaviorism, almost all of our daily behavior, from saying "Good morning" to earning a paycheck, can be understood as the result of past reinforcement.

Pleasant consequences are sometimes called *rewards,* but behaviorists do not call them that because what some people consider a reward may actually be a punishment, an unpleasant consequence. For instance, some teachers think they are rewarding children by giving them more recess time, but some children hate recess.

The opposite is true as well: Something thought to be a punishment may actually be reinforcing. For example, parents "punish" their children by withholding dessert. But a particular child might dislike the dessert, so being deprived of it is no punishment.

Sometimes teachers send misbehaving children out of the classroom and principals suspend them from school. However, if a child hates the teacher, leaving class is rewarding, and if a child hates school, suspension is a reinforcement. Indeed, research on school discipline finds that some measures, including school suspension, *increase* later misbehavior (Osher et al., 2010). In order to stop misbehavior, it is more effective to encourage good behavior, to "catch them being good."

In the United States, the rate of suspension is three times higher for African American children than for European American children, and it is higher for children designated as needing special education than for children in regular classrooms. Statistics on school discipline raise a troubling question: Is suspension a punishment for the child, or is it a reward for the teacher? Or an example of prejudice? (Tajalli & Garba, 2014; Shah, 2011).

The true test is the *effect* a consequence has on the individual's future actions, not whether it is intended to be a reward or a punishment. A child, or an adult, who repeats an offense may have been reinforced, not punished, for the first infraction.

Social Learning

At first, behaviorists thought all behavior arose from a chain of learned responses, the result of either the association between one stimulus and another (classical conditioning) or of past reinforcement (operant conditioning). Thousands of experiments inspired by learning theory have demonstrated that both classical conditioning and operant conditioning occur in everyday life. We are all conditioned to react as we do.

operant conditioning The learning process by which a particular action is followed by something desired (which makes the person or animal more likely to repeat the action) or by something unwanted (which makes the action less likely to be repeated). (Also called *instrumental conditioning*.)

reinforcement When a behavior is followed by something desired, such as food for a hungry animal or a welcoming smile for a lonely person.

AP Photo

Rats, Pigeons, and People B. F. Skinner is best known for his experiments with rats and pigeons, but he also applied his knowledge to human behavior. For his daughter, he designed a glass-enclosed crib in which temperature, humidity, and perceptual stimulation could be controlled to make her time in the crib enjoyable and educational. He encouraged her first attempts to talk by smiling and responding with words, affection, or other positive reinforcement.

● **Response for Teachers** (from page 39) Erikson would note that the behavior of 5-year-olds is affected by their developmental stage and by their culture. Therefore, you might design your curriculum to accommodate active, noisy children.

Answer to Observation Quiz (from page 40) Both are balding, with white beards. Note also that none of the other theorists in this chapter have beards—a cohort difference, not an ideological one.

TABLE 2.2	**Three Types of Learning**	

Behaviorism is also called *learning theory* because it emphasizes the learning process, as shown here.

Type of Learning	Learning Process	Result
Classical Conditioning	Learning occurs through association.	Neutral stimulus becomes conditioned stimulus.
Operant Conditioning	Learning occurs through reinforcement and punishment.	Weak or rare responses become strong and frequent—or, with punishment, unwanted responses become extinct.
Social Learning	Learning occurs through modeling what others do.	Observed behaviors become copied behaviors.

social learning theory An extension of behaviorism that emphasizes the influence that other people have over a person's behavior. Even without specific reinforcement, every individual learns many things through observation and imitation of other people. (Also called *observational learning*.)

modeling The central process of social learning, by which a person observes the actions of others and then copies them.

Video Activity: Modeling: Learning by Observation features the original footage of Albert Bandura's famous experiment.

However, research finds that people at every age are social and active, not just reactive. Instead of responding merely to their own direct experiences, "people act on the environment. They create it, preserve it, transform it, and even destroy it . . . in a socially embedded interplay" (Bandura, 2006, p. 167).

That social interplay is the foundation of **social learning theory** (see Table 2.2), which holds that humans sometimes learn without personal reinforcement. As the primary proponent of this theory, Albert Bandura, explains, this learning often occurs through **modeling,** when people copy what they see others do (also called *observational learning*) (Bandura, 1986, 1997).

Modeling is not simple imitation: Some people are more likely to follow or be role models than others. Indeed, people model only some actions, of some individuals, in some contexts. Sometimes people do the opposite of what they have seen. Generally, modeling is most likely when the observer is uncertain or inexperienced (which explains why modeling is especially powerful in childhood) and when the model is admired, powerful, nurturing, or similar to the observer.

Social learning is particularly noticeable in early adolescence, when children want to be similar to their peers despite their parents' wishes. That impulse may continue into adulthood, especially when adults are in an unfamiliar place—perhaps a first-year student in college, or a new immigrant to the United States, or a patient in a hospital.

Learning to Be a Dad Note how the 2-year-old angles the bottle and the doll's body, just as his father does. Even his left hand, gentle on the head, shows that he is learning how to be a good father from watching his dad.

Cognitive Theory: Piaget and Information Processing

According to **cognitive theory,** thoughts and expectations profoundly affect attitudes, values, emotions, and actions. This may seem obvious to you now, but it was not always so clear. Indeed, social scientists describe a "cognitive revolution," which occurred around 1980. Suddenly *how* and *what* people think became important. This added to psychoanalysis (which emphasized hidden impulses) and behaviorism (which emphasized observed actions). A person's thoughts came between those impulses and actions, and they were critically important.

The cognitive revolution began decades ago, but it is not over: Contemporary researchers use new tools to study cognition, with neuroscience, large data, and body-mind connections (e.g., Glenberg et al., 2013; Griffiths, 2015). To understand the impact of cognitive theory on development, we begin with Piaget.

Piaget's Stages of Development

Jean Piaget (1896–1980) transformed our understanding of cognition, leading some people to consider him "the greatest developmental psychologist of all time" (Haidt, 2013, p. 6). His academic training was in biology, with a focus on shellfish—a background that taught him to look closely at small details.

Before Piaget, most scientists believed that babies could not yet think. But Piaget used scientific observation with his own three infants, finding them curious and thoughtful, developing new concepts month by month.

Later he studied hundreds of schoolchildren. From this work, Piaget formed the central thesis of cognitive theory: *How* children think changes with time and experience, and their thought processes affect their behavior. According to cognitive theory, to understand humans of any age, one must understand thinking.

Piaget maintained that cognitive development occurs in four age-related periods, or stages: *sensorimotor, preoperational, concrete operational,* and *formal operational* (see Table 2.3). Each period fosters certain cognitive processes: Infants

cognitive theory A grand theory of human development that focuses on changes in how people think over time. According to this theory, our thoughts shape our attitudes, beliefs, and behaviors.

THINK CRITICALLY: Is your speech, hairstyle, or choice of shoes similar to those of your peers, or of an entertainer, or a sports hero? Why?

TABLE 2.3	Piaget's Periods of Cognitive Development		
	Name of Period	Characteristics of the Period	Major Gains During the Period
Birth to 2 years	Sensorimotor	Infants use senses and motor abilities to understand the world. Learning is active, without reflection.	Infants learn that objects still exist when out of sight (*object permanence*) and begin to think through mental actions. (The sensorimotor period is discussed further in Chapter 6.)
2–6 years	Preoperational	Children think symbolically, with language, yet children are *egocentric,* perceiving from their own perspective.	The imagination flourishes, and language becomes a significant means of self-expression and social influence. (The preoperational period is discussed further in Chapter 9.)
6–11 years	Concrete operational	Children understand and apply logic. Thinking is limited by direct experience.	By applying logic, children grasp concepts of conservation, number, classification, and many other scientific ideas. (The concrete-operational period is discussed further in Chapter 12.)
12 years through adulthood	Formal operational	Adolescents and adults use abstract and hypothetical concepts. They can use analysis, not only emotion.	Ethics, politics, and social and moral issues become fascinating as adolescents and adults use abstract, theoretical reasoning. (The formal-operational period is discussed further in Chapter 15.)

Would You Talk to This Man? Children loved talking to Jean Piaget, and he learned by listening carefully—especially to their incorrect explanations, which no one had paid much attention to before. All his life, Piaget was absorbed with studying the way children think. He called himself a "genetic epistemologist"—one who studies how children gain knowledge about the world as they grow.

cognitive equilibrium In cognitive theory, a state of mental balance in which people are not confused because they can use their existing thought processes to understand current experiences and ideas.

think via their senses; preschoolers have language but not logic; school-age children have simple logic; adolescents and adults can use formal, abstract logic (Inhelder & Piaget, 1958/2013b; Piaget, 1952/2011).

Piaget found that intellectual advancement occurs because humans at every age seek **cognitive equilibrium**—a state of mental balance. The easiest way to achieve this balance is to interpret new experiences through the lens of preexisting ideas. For example, infants grab new objects in the same way that they grasp familiar objects, a child's concept of God is as a loving—or punishing—parent.

At every age, people interpret other people's behavior by assuming that everyone thinks as they themselves do. Adults believe that other people seek sex, or wealth, or admiration because of their own perceptions and priorities.

Like children, people of all ages tend to stick to their old ideas; cognition is easier that way. That is cognitive equilibrium. For instance, once people grasp the concept of "dog," they can see unfamiliar dogs on the street, from Great Danes to Chihuahuas, and expect them to sniff, bark, wag tails, and so on. Some people want to pet all dogs; some people fear them all—but in either case, comfortable generalities of "dogness" are evident.

Achieving equilibrium is not always easy, however. Sometimes a new experience or question is jarring or incomprehensible—such as learning that some dogs (Basenjis) do not bark. Then the individual experiences *cognitive disequilibrium*, an imbalance that creates confusion. As Figure 2.1 illustrates, disequilibrium can

(b)

(a)

How to Think About Flowers A person's stage of cognitive growth influences how he or she thinks about everything, including flowers. *(a)* To an infant in the sensorimotor stage, flowers are "known" through pulling, smelling, and even biting. *(b)* At the concrete operational stage, children become more logical. This boy can understand that flowers need sunlight, water, and time to grow. *(c)* At the adult's formal operational stage, flowers can be part of a larger, logical scheme— for instance, to earn money while cultivating beauty. As illustrated by all three photos, thinking is an active process from the beginning of life until the end.

(c)

cause cognitive growth if people adapt their thinking. Piaget describes two types of cognitive adaptation:

- **Assimilation:** New experiences are reinterpreted to fit, or *assimilate,* into old ideas. [A Basenji could bark if it wanted to.]
- **Accommodation:** Old ideas are restructured to include, or *accommodate,* new experiences. [Some dogs do not bark.]

Accommodation is more difficult than assimilation, but it advances thought. Children—and everyone else—actively develop new concepts when the old ones fail. In Piagetian terms, they *construct* ideas based on their experiences.

Ideally, when two people disagree, adaptation is mutual. Think of a lovers' quarrel: Both parties listen to the other, and the relationship reaches a new equilibrium. They accommodate, and the quarrel strengthens their relationship.

Information Processing

Piaget is credited with discovering that mental constructs affect behavior, an idea now accepted by most social scientists. However, many think Piaget's theories were limited. Neuroscience, cross-cultural studies, and step-by-step understanding of cognition have revealed problems in Piaget's theory.

A newer version of cognitive theory is called **information-processing theory,** inspired by the input, programming, memory, and output of the computer. When conceptualized in that way, thinking is affected by the synapses and neurons of the brain.

Information processing is "a framework characterizing a large number of research programs" (Miller, 2011, p. 266). Instead of interpreting *responses* by infants and children, as Piaget did, this cognitive theory focuses on the *processes* of thought—that is, when, why, and how neurons fire before a response.

Brain activity is traced back to what activated those neurons. Information-processing theorists examine stimuli and responses from the senses, body movements, hormones, and organs, all of which affect thinking (Glenberg et al., 2013). These scientists believe that details of the cognitive process shed light on the outcome.

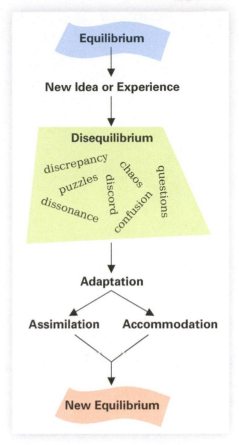

FIGURE 2.1

Challenge Me Most of us, most of the time, prefer the comfort of our conventional conclusions. According to Piaget, however, when new ideas disturb our thinking, we have an opportunity to expand our cognition with a broader and deeper understanding.

assimilation The reinterpretation of new experiences to fit into old ideas.

accommodation The restructuring of old ideas to include new experiences.

information-processing theory A perspective that compares human thinking processes, by analogy, to computer analysis of data, including sensory input, connections, stored memories, and output.

Healthy Control Adults

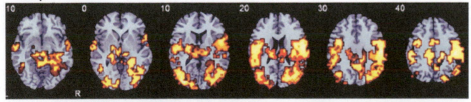

Adults with Childhood ADHD

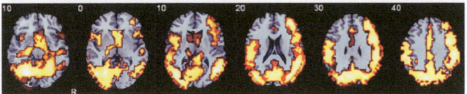

They Try Harder Details of brain scans require interpretation from neurologists, but even the novice can see that adults who have been diagnosed with ADHD (second line of images) reacted differently in this experiment when they were required to push a button only if certain letters appeared on a screen. Sustained attention to this task required more brain power (the lit areas) for those with ADHD. Notice also that certain parts of the brain were activated by the healthy adults and not by those with ADHD. Apparently adults who had problems paying attention when they were children have learned to focus when they need to, but they do it in their own way and with more effort.

Cubillo, Ana; Halari, Rozmin; Smith, Anna; Taylor, Eric & Rubia, Katya. (2012). A review of fronto-striatal and fronto-cortical brain abnormalities in children and adults with Attention deficit hyperactivity disorder (ADHD) and new evidence for dysfunction in adults with ADHD during motivation and attention. *Cortex 48*(2), 194–215. doi: 10.1016/J.cortex.2011.04.007 With Permission From Elsevier

Thus, cognition begins when input is picked up by one of the senses. It proceeds to brain reactions, connections, and stored memories, and it concludes with some form of output. For infants, output consists of moving a hand, making a sound, or staring a split second longer at one stimulus than at another. As a person matures, these scientists study not only words but also hesitations, neuronal activity, and bodily reactions (heartbeat, blood pressure, and the like).

The latest techniques to study the brain have produced insights from neuroscience on the sequence and strength of neuronal communication and have discovered patterns beyond those traced by early information-processing theory. With the aid of sensitive technology, information-processing research has also overturned some of Piaget's findings.

However, the basic tenet of cognitive theory is equally true for Piaget, neuroscience, and information processing: *Ideas matter*. Thus, how children interpret a hypothetical social situation, such as whether they anticipate welcome or rejection, affects the quality of their actual friendships, and how adults think about heaven and hell influences their sexual activity. In every case, ideas frame situations and affect actions.

INSIDE THE BRAIN

Measuring Mental Activity

A hundred years ago, people thought that emotions came from the heart. That's why we still send hearts on Valentine's Day, why we speak of broken hearts or people who are soft- or hard-hearted.

But now we know that everything begins inside the brain. It is foolish to dismiss a sensation with "It's all in your head." Of course it is in your head; everything is.

Until quite recently, the only way scientists could estimate brain activity was to measure heads. Of course, measuring produced some obvious discoveries—babies with shrunken brains (microcephaly) suffered severe intellectual disability, and brains grew bigger as children matured.

Measuring also led to some obvious errors, now discredited. In the nineteenth and early twentieth centuries, many scientists believed the theory that bumps on the head reflected intelligence and character, a theory known as *phrenology*. Psychiatrists would run their hands over a person's skull to measure 27 traits, including spirituality, loyalty, and aggression. Another example was that some scientists said that women could never be professors because their brains were too small (Swaab & Hofman, 1984).

Within the past half-century, neuroscientists developed ways to use electrodes, magnets, light, and computers to measure brain activity, not just brain size (see Table 2.4).

TABLE 2.4	**Some Techniques Used by Neuroscientists to Understand Brain Function**

EEG (electroencephalogram)

The EEG measures electrical activity in the cortex. This can differentiate active brains (beta brain waves—very rapid, 12 to 30 per second) from sleeping brains (delta waves—1 to 3 per second) and brain states that are half-awake, or dreaming. Complete lack of brain waves, called flat-line, indicates brain death.

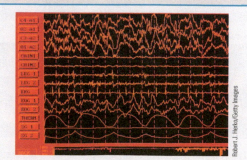

Robert J. Herko/Getty Images

EEG of a participant in a sleep disorder study

*Inside the Brain boxes are new to this edition. The brain is crucial for all of development, so many findings from the study of the brain appear as regular text. Sometimes, however, more details from neurology add to our understanding. This feature presents these details.

ERP (event-related potential)

The amplitude and frequency of brain electrical activity changes when a particular stimulus (called an event) occurs. First the ERP establishes the usual patterns, and then researchers present a stimulus (such as a sound, an image, a word) that causes a blip in electrical activity. ERP indicates how quickly and extensively people react—although this method requires many repetitions to distinguish the response from the usual brain activity.

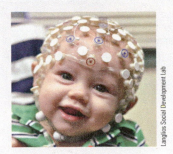

ERP when listening

MRI (magnetic resonance imaging)

The water molecules in various parts of the brain each have a magnetic current, and measuring that current allows measurement of myelin, neurons, and fluid in the brain.

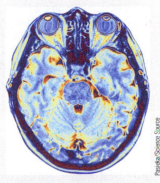

MRI scan of a healthy brain

fMRI (functional magnetic resonance imaging)

In advanced MRI, function is measured as more oxygen is added to the blood flow when specific neurons are activated. The presumption is that increased blood flow means that the person is using that part of the brain. fMRI has revealed that several parts of the brain are active at once—seeing something activates parts of the visual cortex, but it also may activate other parts of the brain far from the visual areas.

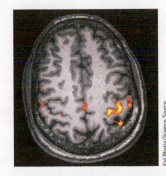

fMRI showing the visual cortex light up while viewing an object

PET (positron emission tomography)

When a specific part of the brain is active, the blood flows more rapidly in that part. If radioactive dye is injected into the bloodstream and a person lies very still within a scanner while seeing pictures or other stimuli, changes in blood flow indicate thought. PET can reveal the volume of neurotransmitters; the rise or fall of brain oxygen, glucose, amino acids; and more. PET is almost impossible to use with children (who cannot stay still) and is very expensive with adults.

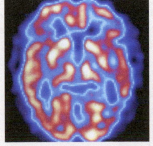

PET scan of normal brain metabolic activity

fNIRS (functional near infrared spectroscopy)

This method also measures changes in blood flow. But, it depends on light rather than magnetic charge and can be done with children, who merely wear a special cap connected to electrodes and do not need to lie still in a noisy machine (as PET or the in the fMRI). By measuring how each area of the brain absorbs light, neuroscientists infer activity of the brain (Ferrari & Quaresima, 2012).

fNIRS of a college student

DTI (diffusion tensor imaging)

DTI is another technique that builds on the MRI. It measures the flow (diffusion) of water molecules within the brain, which shows connections between one area and another. This is particularly interesting to developmentalists because life experiences affect which brain areas connect with which other ones. Thus, DTI is increasingly used by clinicians who want to individualize treatment and monitor progress (Van Hecke et al., 2016).

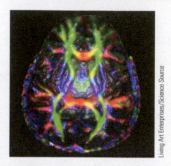

Digitally enhanced DTI scan of normal brain

For both practical and ethical reasons, it is difficult to use these techniques on large, representative samples. One of the challenges of neuroscience is to develop methods that are harmless, quick, acceptable to parents and babies, and comprehensive. A more immediate challenge is to depict the data in ways that are easy to interpret and understand.

Bumps on the head and head size (within limits) were proven irrelevant to intellectual processes. Researchers now study cognitive processes between input and output. Some results are cited later. In this feature we describe methods.

As you see, measurement and interpretation of brain activity is still difficult, but newer techniques are developing. Neuroscientists and developmentalists often disagree about the specific meaning of various results.

Nonetheless, brain imagery has revealed many surprises. For example, fNIRS finds that the brains of newborns are more active when they hear the language that their mother spoke when they were in the womb than when they hear another language (May et al., 2011). fMRI on adolescents has found that a fully grown brain does not mean a fully functioning brain: The prefrontal cortex is not completely connected to the rest of the brain until about age 25. Brain scans of new mothers reveal that babies change their mothers' brains (Kim et al., 2016).

All the tools indicated on the previous pages have discovered brain plasticity and variations not imagined in earlier decades. However, sensitive machines and advanced computer analysis are required for accurate readings. Even then, all we know is whether parts of the brain are functioning and active—or not. Changes in light absorption, or magnetism, or oxygenated blood flow in the brain are miniscule from one moment to the next. Interpreting what that means is more complex.

For example, it would be good to replace the conventional lie detector, which is unreliable, with brain imaging. But current technology is not ready (Rose, 2016).

Variations within and between people make it difficult to know what someone is thinking via brain scans. Once again, this confirms the need for theory: Without an idea of what to look for, or what it might mean, the millions of data points from all brain images might lead to the same trap as earlier measurements of the skull—human bias.

Newer Theories

You have surely noticed that the seminal grand theorists—Freud, Pavlov, Piaget—were all men, scientists who were born in the late nineteenth century and who lived and died in Europe. These background variables are limiting. (Of course, female, non-European, and contemporary theorists are limited by their background as well, but their limitations are not the same.)

A new wave of research and understanding from scientists with more varied experiences who have more extensive global and historical data has led to the two newer theories explored now. The multidisciplinary nature of our study is apparent: Sociocultural theorists benefit from anthropologists who report on cultures in every nation, and evolutionary psychologists use data from archeologists who examine the bones of humans who died 100,000 years ago.

Sociocultural Theory: Vygotsky and Beyond

One hallmark of newer theories is that they are decidedly multicultural, influenced by the growing awareness that cultures shape experiences and attitudes. Whereas once "culture" referred primarily to oddities outside the normative Western experience, it is now apparent that many cultural differences occur within each nation.

Some cultural differences within the United States arise from ethnic and national origins—people whose grandparents lived in Pakistan versus those whose grandparents were in Poland, for instance. Some arise from SES, such as college graduates contrasted with those who dropped out of high school. And some are related to region, age, and gender: An 80-year-old woman in Montana might have a different sociocultural perspective than a 15-year-old boy in Mississippi, even if both are similar in ethnic and economic background. Sociocultural theory considers all of those differences significant.

The central thesis of **sociocultural theory** is that human development results from the dynamic interaction between developing persons and their surrounding society. Culture is not something external that impinges on developing persons but is internalized, integral to everyday attitudes and actions. This idea is so central to our current understanding of human development that it was already stressed in Chapter 1. Here the terms and implications of sociocultural theory are explained in more detail.

sociocultural theory A newer theory which holds that development results from the dynamic interaction of each person with the surrounding social and cultural forces.

Teaching and Guidance

The pioneer of the sociocultural perspective was Lev Vygotsky (1896–1934), a psychologist from the former Soviet Union. Like the other theorists, he was born

Affection for Children Vygotsky lived in Russia from 1896 to 1934, when war, starvation, and revolution led to the deaths of millions. Throughout this turmoil, Vygotsky focused on learning. His love of children is suggested by this portrait: He and his daughter have their arms around each other.

at the end of the nineteenth century, but unlike them, he traveled extensively within his native Russia, studying Asian and European groups of many faiths, languages, and social contexts.

Vygotsky noted that people everywhere were taught the beliefs and habits valued within their culture. He noted many specific cultural variations. For example, his research included how farmers used tools, how illiterate people thought of abstract ideas, and how children learned in school.

In Vygotsky's view, each person, schooled or not, develops with the guidance of more skilled members of his or her society. Those people become tutors or mentors in an **apprenticeship in thinking** (Vygotsky, 2012).

apprenticeship in thinking Vygotsky's term for how cognition is stimulated and developed in people by more skilled members of society.

In earlier centuries, a young person wanting to repair shoes might become an apprentice to an experienced cobbler, learning the trade while assisting the teacher.

Vygotsky believed that children become apprentices to adults, who teach them how to think by explaining ideas, asking questions, and repeating values.

To describe this process, Vygotsky developed the concept of **guided participation,** the method used by parents, teachers, and entire societies to teach novices the skills and habits expected within their culture. Tutors engage learners (*apprentices*) in joint activities, offering "mutual involvement in several widespread cultural practices with great importance for learning: narratives, routines, and play" (Rogoff, 2003, p. 285).

guided participation The process by which people learn from others who guide their experiences and explorations.

Active apprenticeship and sensitive guidance are central to sociocultural theory because each person depends on others to learn. All cultural beliefs are social constructions, not natural laws, according to sociocultural theorists. Customs powerfully protect and unify a community, yet some cultural assumptions need to change. For example, Vygotsky stressed that children with disabilities should be educated (Vygotsky, 1994b). This belief has been enshrined in U.S. law since about 1970, but it is not yet part of every culture.

The Zone of Proximal Development

According to sociocultural theory, all learning is social, whether people are learning a manual skill, a social custom, or a language. As part of the apprenticeship of thinking, a mentor (parent, peer, or professional) finds the learner's **zone of proximal development,** an imaginary area surrounding the learner that contains the skills, knowledge, and concepts that are close (proximal) to being grasped but not yet reached.

zone of proximal development In sociocultural theory, a metaphorical area, or "zone," surrounding a learner that includes all of the skills, knowledge, and concepts that the person is close ("proximal") to acquiring but cannot yet master without help.

Through sensitive assessment of each learner, mentors engage mentees within their zone. Together, in a "process of joint construction," new knowledge is attained (Valsiner, 2006). The mentor must avoid two opposite dangers: boredom and failure. Some frustration is permitted, but the learner must be actively engaged, never passive or overwhelmed (see Figure 2.2).

FIGURE 2.2

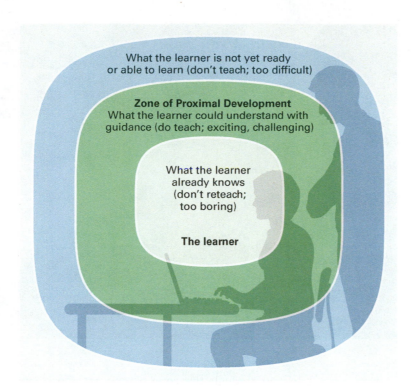

The Magic Middle Somewhere between the boring and the impossible is the zone of proximal development, where interaction between teacher and learner results in knowledge never before grasped or skills not already mastered. The intellectual excitement of that zone is the origin of the joy that both instruction and study can bring.

Consider an example: a father teaching his daughter to ride a bicycle. He begins by rolling her along, supporting her weight while telling her to keep her hands on the handlebars, to push the right and left pedals in rhythm, and to look straight ahead. As she becomes more comfortable and confident, he begins to roll her along more quickly, praising her for steadily pumping.

Within a few lessons over several days or weeks, he jogs beside her, holding only the handlebars. When he senses that she can maintain her balance, he urges her to pedal faster while he loosens his grip. Perhaps without realizing it, she rides on her own. Soon she waves goodbye to her father and she bikes around the block.

Note that this is not instruction by preset rules. Sociocultural learning is active: No one learns to ride a bike by reading and memorizing written instructions, and no good teacher merely repeats a prepared lesson.

Examples from other people and equipment provided by the culture also teach children, according to sociocultural theory. The bicycle-riding child wants to learn because she has seen other children biking, and stores sell tricycles, training wheels, and small bikes without peddles. Those cultural artifacts guide participation.

In another culture, everything might be different. Perhaps no children ride bicycles, or no fathers teach their daughters—or even allow them outside the house unsupervised. Recognizing such cultural differences is crucial for understanding development, according to this theory.

Moreover, within each culture, learners have personal traits, experiences, and aspirations. Consequently, education must be individualized. Some people need more assurance; some seek independence. Some learn best by looking, others by hearing, although no one is exclusively one kind of learner.

A mentor must sense whether support or freedom is needed and how peers can help (they may be the best mentors). Skilled teachers know when the zone of proximal development expands and shifts.

Zone of Excitement Vygotsky believed that other people, especially slightly older peers, and all the artifacts of the culture, teach everyone within their zone of proximal development. What lessons are these children learning about emotions, via frightening yet thrilling experiences? Much depends on the design of the amusement park rides, on the adults who paid, and, here, on the big sister, who encourages the hesitant younger child.

Bruno De Hogues/The Image Bank/Getty Images.

Excursions into and through the zone of proximal development are everywhere. At the thousand or so science museums in the United States, children ask numerous questions, and adults guide their scientific knowledge (Haden, 2010).

In another example, every Western child must learn to sit at the table and eat with a knife and fork. This is a long process. Parents neither spoon-feed their 3-year-olds nor expect them to cut their own meat. Instead they find the proper zone of proximal development, and they provide appropriate tools and guidance.

In general, mentors, attuned to ever-shifting abilities and motivation, continually urge a new competence—the next level, not the moon. For their part, learners ask questions, show interest, and demonstrate progress, all of which informs and inspires the mentors. When education goes well, both mentor and learner are fully engaged and productive within the zone. Particular skills and processes vary enormously, but the overall process is the same.

Remember that all theories are designed to be useful, yet each is distinct. The following is one illustration of the way psychoanalytic, behaviorist, cognitive, and sociocultural theory might apply to common parental concerns.

OPPOSING PERSPECTIVES

Toilet Training—How and When?

Parents hear opposite advice about almost everything regarding infant care, including feeding, responding to cries, bathing, and exercise. Often a particular parental response springs from one of the theories explained in this chapter—no wonder advice is sometimes contradictory.

One practical example is toilet training. In the nineteenth century, many parents believed that bodily functions should be controlled as soon as possible in order to distinguish humans from lower animals. Consequently, they began toilet training in the first months of life (Accardo, 2006). Then, psychoanalytic theory pegged the first year as the oral stage (Freud) or the time when trust was crucial (Erikson), before the toddler's anal stage (Freud) began or autonomy needs (Erikson) emerged.

Consequently, psychoanalytic theory led to postponing toilet training to avoid serious personality problems later on. This was soon part of many manuals on child rearing. For example, a leading pediatrician, Barry Brazelton, wrote a popular book for parents advising that toilet training should not begin until the child is cognitively, emotionally, and biologically ready—around age 2 for daytime training and age 3 for nighttime dryness.

> As a society, we are far too concerned about pushing children to be toilet trained early. I don't even like the phrase "toilet training." It really should be toilet learning.
>
> *[Brazelton & Sparrow, 2006, p. 193]*

By the middle of the twentieth century, many U.S. psychologists had rejected psychoanalytic theory and become behaviorists. Since they believed that learning depends primarily on conditioning, some suggested that toilet training occur whenever the parent wished, not at a particular age.

In one application of behaviorism, children drank quantities of their favorite juice, sat on the potty with a parent nearby to keep them entertained, and then, when the inevitable occurred, the parent praised and rewarded them—a powerful reinforcement. Children were conditioned (in one day, according to some behaviorists) to head for the potty whenever the need arose (Azrin & Foxx, 1974). Cognitive theory would consider such a concerted effort unnecessary, suggesting that parents wait until the child can understand reasons to urinate and defecate in the toilet.

Rejecting all of these theories, some African communities let children toilet train themselves by following slightly older children to the surrounding trees and bushes. This is easier, of course, if toddlers wear no diapers—a practice that makes sense in some climates. Sociocultural practices differ because of the ecological context, and infants adjust.

Meanwhile, some Western parents prefer to start potty training very early. One U.S. mother began training her baby just 33 days after birth. She noticed when her son was about to defecate, held him above the toilet, and had trained him by 6 months (Sun & Rugolotto, 2004).

Such early training is criticized by all of the theories, each in their own way:

- Psychoanalysts would wonder what made her such an anal person, valuing cleanliness and order without considering the child's needs.
- Behaviorists would say that the mother was trained, not the son. She taught herself to be sensitive to his body; she was reinforced when she read his clues correctly.
- Cognitive theory would question the mother's thinking. For instance, did she have an odd fear of normal body functions?
- Sociocultural theory would be aghast that the U.S. drive for personal control took such a bizarre turn.

What is best? Some parents are reluctant to train, and the result, according to one book, is that many children are still in diapers at age 5 (Barone, 2015). Dueling theories and diverse

What to Do? Books on infant care give contradictory advice. Even in this photo one can see that these modern mothers follow divergent parenting practices. One is breast-feeding a 1-year-old; another has toilet-trained her toddler; one sits cross-legged so that her baby can be on her lap, which would be impossible for another—and so on.

parental practices have led the authors of an article for pediatricians to conclude that "despite families and physicians having addressed this issue for generations, there still is no consensus regarding the best method or even a standard definition of toilet training" (Howell et al., 2010, p. 262).

One comparison study of toilet-training methods found that the behaviorist approach was best for older children with serious disabilities but that almost every method succeeded with the average young child. Many sources explain that because each child is different, there is no "right" way: "the best strategy for implementing training is still unknown" (Colaco et al., 2013, p. 49).

That may suggest sociocultural theory, which notes vast differences from one community to another. A study of parents' opinions in Belgium found that mothers without a partner and without much education were more likely to wait too long, age 3 or so (van Nunen et al., 2015). Of course, both too soon and too late are matters of opinion.

What values are embedded in each practice? Psychoanalytic theory focuses on later personality, behaviorism stresses conditioning of body impulses, cognitive theory considers variation in the child's intellectual capacity, and sociocultural theory allows vast diversity.

There is no easy answer, but many parents firmly believe in one approach or another. That confirms the statement at the beginning of this chapter: We all have theories, sometimes strongly held, whether we know it or not.

Evolutionary Theory

You are familiar with Charles Darwin and his ideas, first published 150 years ago, regarding the evolution of plants, insects, and birds over billions of years (Darwin, 1859). But you may not realize that serious research on human development inspired by this theory is quite recent (Simpson & Kenrick, 2013). As a leader in this theory recently wrote:

> Evolutionary psychology . . . is a revolutionary new science, a true synthesis of modern principles of psychology and evolutionary biology.
>
> *[Buss, 2015, p. xv]*

This perspective is not universally accepted by social scientists, but nonetheless this theory has led to new hypotheses and provocative ideas relevant to human development. A leading psycholinguist wrote, "there are major spheres of human experience—beauty, motherhood, kinship, morality, cooperation, sexuality, violence—in which evolutionary psychology provides the only coherent theory" (Pinker, 2003, p. 135).

The basic idea of evolutionary theory in development is that in order to understand the emotions, impulses, and habits of humans over the life span, it is important to understand how those same emotions, impulses, and habits developed within *Homo sapiens* over the past 100,000 years.

Why We Fear Snakes More Than Cars

Evolutionary theory has intriguing explanations for many issues in human development, including a pregnant woman's nausea, 1-year-olds' attachment to their parents, the obesity epidemic, and the diseases of late adulthood. According to this theory, all of these evolved to help people survive many millennia ago.

For example, many people are terrified of snakes; they scream and sweat upon seeing one. Yet snakes cause less than one death in a million, while cars cause more than a thousand times that (OECD, 2014). Why is virtually no one terrified of automobiles? The explanation is that human fears have evolved since ancient times, when snakes were common killers. Thus,

> ancient dangers such as snakes, spiders, heights, and strangers appear on lists of common phobias far more often than do evolutionarily modern dangers such as cars and guns, even though cars and guns are more dangerous to survival in the modern environment.
>
> *[Confer et al., 2010, p. 111]*

Since our fears have not caught up to automobiles, we must use our minds to pass laws regarding infant seats, child-safety restraints, seat belts, red lights, and speed limits. Humanity is succeeding in such measures: The U.S. motor-vehicle death rate has been cut in half over the past 20 years.

Other modern killers—climate change, drug addiction, obesity, pollution—also require social management because instincts are contrary to what we now know about the dangers of each of these. Evolutionary theory contends that recognizing the ancient origins of destructive urges—such as the deadly desire to eat calorie-dense chocolate cake—is the first step in controlling them (King, 2013).

Why We Protect Babies

According to evolutionary theory, every species has two long-standing, biologically based drives: survival and reproduction. Understanding these two drives provides insight into protective parenthood, the death of newborns, infant dependency, child immaturity, the onset of puberty, the formation of families, and much more (Konner, 2010).

Here is one example. Adults consider babies to be cute—despite the reality that babies have little hair, no chins, stubby legs, and round stomachs—all of which are considered unattractive in adults. The reason, evolutionary theory contends, is that adults are instinctually attuned to protect and cherish the young, which was essential 100,000 years ago.

But humans do not always protect every baby. Indeed, another instinct embedded in the genes is that all creatures seek to perpetuate their own genes. That might lead to infanticide of infants who are not one's own, again explained by evolutionary theory. Chimpanzee males who take over a troop kill babies of the deposed male. This occurred among ancient humans as well. The Bible chronicles at least three examples, two for the story of Moses and one for the birth of Jesus. Modern humans, of course, have created laws against such practices—a necessity because evolutional instincts might be murderous (Hrdy, 2009).

It is apparent that humans are much less concerned about deaths of unknown babies than of their own kin, while parents typically sacrifice sleep, money, and even life itself for their offspring. The reason: instincts that developed via evolution from the days when one's own tribe needed protection.

An application of evolutionary theory is found in research on grandmothers. Recently, grandmothers have been studied extensively by women—evidence of the wider perspective of current scientists. Historic data from Africa, Japan, India, and elsewhere led to the *grandmother hypothesis,* that menopause and female longevity were evolutionary adaptations arising from children's survival needs (Hawkes & Coxworth, 2013).

Genetic Links

This inborn urge to protect is explained by a basic concept from evolutionary theory: **selective adaptation.** The idea is that humans today react in ways that promoted survival and reproduction long ago. According to one version of selective adaptation, genes for traits that aid survival and reproduction have been selected over time to allow the species to thrive (see Figure 2.3). Some of the best qualities of people—cooperation, spirituality, and self-sacrifice—may have originated thousands of years ago when groups of people survived because they took care of one another (Rand & Nowak, 2016).

Especially for Teachers and Counselors of Teenagers Teen pregnancy is destructive of adolescent education, family life, and sometimes even health. According to evolutionary theory, what can be done about this? (see response, page 56)

selective adaptation The process by which living creatures (including people) adjust to their environment. Genes that enhance survival and reproductive ability are selected, over the generations, to become more prevalent.

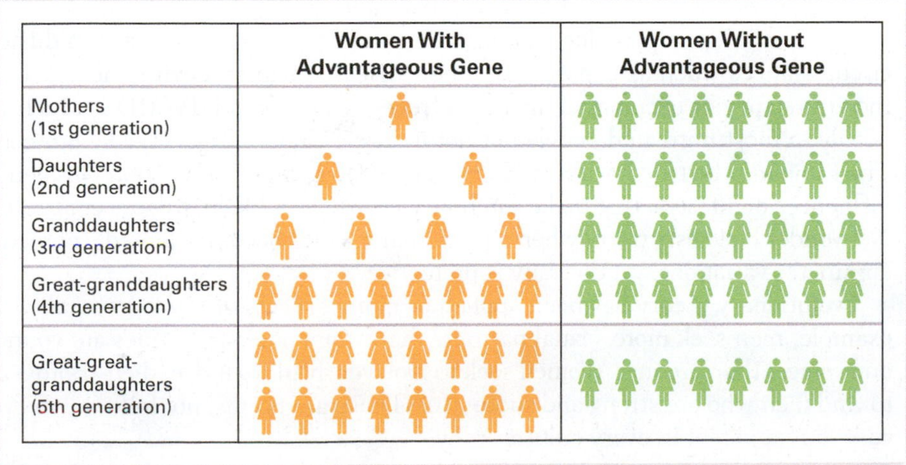

	Women With Advantageous Gene	Women Without Advantageous Gene
Mothers (1st generation)		
Daughters (2nd generation)		
Granddaughters (3rd generation)		
Great-granddaughters (4th generation)		
Great-great-granddaughters (5th generation)		

FIGURE 2.3

Selective Adaptation Illustrated Suppose only one of nine mothers happened to have a gene that improved survival. The average woman had only one surviving daughter, but this gene mutation might mean more births and more surviving children such that each woman who had the gene bore two girls who survived to womanhood instead of one. As you see, in 100 years, the "odd" gene becomes more common, making it a new normal.

Got Milk! Many people in Sweden (like this barefoot preschooler at her summer cottage) drink cow's milk and eat many kinds of cheese. That may be because selective adaptation allowed individuals who could digest lactose to survive in the long northern winters when no crops grew.

Response for Teachers and Counselors of Teenagers (from page 55) Evolutionary theory stresses the basic human drive for reproduction, which gives teenagers a powerful sex drive. Thus, merely informing teenagers of the difficulty of caring for a newborn (some high school sex-education programs simply give teenagers a chicken egg to nurture) is not likely to work. A better method would be to structure teenagers' lives so that pregnancy is impossible—for instance, with careful supervision or readily available contraception.

The process of selective adaptation works as follows: If one person happens to have a trait that makes survival more likely, the gene (or combination of genes) responsible for that trait is passed on to the next generation if that person lives long enough to reproduce. Anyone with such a fortunate genetic inheritance has a better chance than those without that gene to survive, mate, and bear many children—half of whom would inherit genes for that desirable trait.

For example, originally almost all human babies lost the ability to digest lactose at about age 2, when they were weaned from breast milk. Older children and adults were *lactose intolerant,* unable to digest milk (Suchy et al., 2010). In a few regions thousands of years ago, cattle were domesticated and raised for their meat. In those places, "killing the fatted calf" provided a rare feast for the entire community.

In those cattle-raising regions, occasionally a young woman would chance to have an aberrant but beneficial gene for the enzyme that allows digestion of cow's milk. If she drank milk intended for a calf, she would gain weight, experience early puberty, sustain many pregnancies, and have ample breast milk for her thriving offspring.

For all of those reasons, her genes would spread to many children. Thus, the next generation would include more people who inherited that aberrant gene, becoming lactose-tolerant unlike most people. With each generation, their numbers would increase. Eventually, that gene would become the new norm.

Interestingly, there are several distinct versions of lactose tolerance: Apparently different aberrant genes appeared in several cattle-raising regions, and in each area selective adaptation increased the prevalence of that odd gene (Ranciaro et al., 2014).

This process of selective adaptation continues over many generations. The fact that many people now can digest milk, enhancing survival in cattle-raising communities, explains why few Scandinavians are lactose-intolerant but many Africans are—but not where cattle were common in Kenya and Tanzania (Ranciaro et al., 2014).

Once it was understood that milk might make some children sick, better ways to relieve hunger were found. Although malnutrition is still a global problem, fewer children are malnourished today than a few decades ago, partly because nutritionists now know which foods are digestible, nourishing, and tasty for whom. Evolutionary psychology has helped with that.

For groups as well as individuals, evolutionary theory notices how the interaction of genes and environment affects survival and reproduction. Genetic variations are particularly beneficial when the environment changes, which is one reason genetic diversity benefits humanity as a whole.

If a species' gene pool does not include variants that allow survival in difficult circumstances (such as exposure to a new disease or to an environmental toxin), the entire species becomes extinct. One recent example is HIV/AIDS, which was deadly in most untreated people but not in a few who were genetically protected. The same may be true for Ebola. Some people have inborn protection plus genetic influences on lifestyle that make catching the virus less likely (Kilgore et al., 2015). No wonder biologists worry when a particular species becomes inbred. Inbreeding eliminates variations, yet diversity is protective.

Evolutionary theory has been applied to many aspects of human sexuality. For example, men seek more sexual partners than women do, and brides are younger, on average, than grooms. Women seek to look youthful (hair dye, diets, Botox) and to find men who are strong and successful. These are norms, not followed in every case, but apparent in every culture. Why?

Breast-Feeding Diversity

Breast-feeding is an interesting example of cultural variations in child development practices around the world. In some parts of the world, and in some cohorts in each country, mothers breast-feed for years—in other places and in other cultural groups, mothers see formula-feeding as safer and more modern. Rates of breast-feeding seem to vary by cohort and culture. Virtually every scientist and pediatrician is convinced that the benefits of breast milk outweigh any dangers, with numerous advantages evident years after infancy. However, the experiences of each cohort differ from earlier cohorts.

U.S. HISTORICAL BREAST-FEEDING STATISTICS

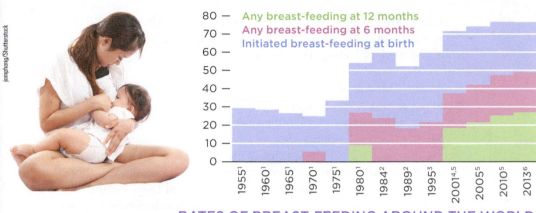

Any breast-feeding at 12 months
Any breast-feeding at 6 months
Initiated breast-feeding at birth

1955[1] 1960[1] 1965[1] 1970[1] 1975[1] 1980[1] 1984[2] 1989[2] 1995[3] 2001[4,5] 2005[5] 2010[5] 2013[6]

Data from (1) Martinez, Gilbert A.; Dodd, David, A. & Samartgedes, Jo Ann. (1981). Milk feeding patterns in the United States during the first 12 months of life. *Pediatrics, 68*(6), 863–868.
(2) Ryan, Alan S.; Rush, David; Krieger, Fritz W. & Lewandowski, Gregory E. (1991). Recent declines in breast-feeding in the United States, 1984 through 1989. *Pediatrics, 88*(4), 719–727.
(3) Ryan, Alan S. (1997). The resurgence of breastfeeding in the United States. *Pediatrics, 99*(4), E12.
(4) Ryan, Alan S.; Zhou, Wenjun & Acosta, Andrew. (2002). Breastfeeding continues to increase into the new millennium. *Pediatrics, 110*(6), 1103–1109. doi: 10.1542/peds.110.6.1103
(5) Centers for Disease Control and Prevention. (2014). Breastfeeding among U.S. children born 2001–2011, CDC National Immunization Survey. Atlanta, GA: National Center for Chronic Disease Prevention and Health Promotion, Centers for Disease Control and Prevention.
(6) Centers for Disease Control and Prevention. (2013, July). Breastfeeding report card—United States, 2013. Atlanta, GA: National Center for Chronic Disease Prevention and Health Promotion, Centers for Disease Control and Prevention.

RATES OF BREAST-FEEDING AROUND THE WORLD

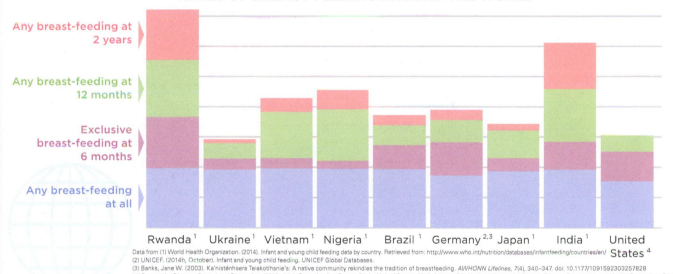

Any breast-feeding at 2 years
Any breast-feeding at 12 months
Exclusive breast-feeding at 6 months
Any breast-feeding at all

Rwanda[1] Ukraine[1] Vietnam[1] Nigeria[1] Brazil[1] Germany[2,3] Japan[1] India[1] United States[4]

Data from (1) World Health Organization. (2014). Infant and young child feeding data by country. Retrieved from: http://www.who.int/nutrition/databases/infantfeeding/countries/en/
(2) UNICEF. (2014b, October). Infant and young child feeding. UNICEF Global Databases.
(3) Banks, Jane W. (2003). Ka'nisténhsera Teiakotíhsnie's: A native community rekindles the tradition of breastfeeding. *AWHONN Lifelines, 7*(4), 340–347. doi: 10.1177/1091592303257828
(4) Centers for Disease Control and Prevention. (2013, July). *Breastfeeding Report Card—United States, 2013*. Atlanta, GA: National Center for Chronic Disease Prevention and Health Promotion, Centers for Disease Control and Prevention.

WHAT AN OBSERVER INFLUENCED BY EACH OF THE FIVE PERSPECTIVES MIGHT SAY ABOUT THESE STATISTICS

① **Psychoanalytic.** The close mother–infant bond is crucial for the child's psychological development. Nations with lower rates of breast-feeding are likely to have higher rates of anxiety and depression among adults.

② **Behaviorist.** Breast-feeding becomes habitual and reinforcing to both mother and child. That is why, among mothers who are breast-feeding at 6 months, many continue—even when nutritionally it is no longer needed.

③ **Cognitive.** Whether or not a woman breast-feeds depends on what she believes. That is why rates of breast-feeding have increased in Western nations over the past few decades.

④ **Sociocultural.** Cultural variations are apparent. All infants need to be fed, but the wide differences from place to place show that how babies are fed depends more on culture than on other factors.

⑤ **Evolutionary (a universal perspective).** Evolutionary needs have always required breast-feeding, but women who wanted to be more "modern" moved away from it. As evolutionary factors have become better understood in the United States, breast-feeding is increasing.

**Many hypotheses spring from each theory. These are possible interpretations—not accepted by everyone or guided by any of these theories.

The evolutionary explanation begins with biology. Since females, not males, become pregnant and breast-feed, in most of human history mothers needed mature, strong men to keep predators away. That helped women fulfill their evolutionary destiny, to bear children who would live long enough to reproduce. Consequently, women chose men who were powerful and then kept them nearby with home cooking and sex. Those choices linger in human instincts: Men seek sexy, fertile partners—more than one, if possible. Women seek faithful, good providers.

Many women reject this evolutionary explanation. They contend that hypothetical scenarios do not reflect actual experience and that patriarchy and sexism, not genes and ancient history, produce mating patterns (Vandermassen, 2005; Varga et al., 2011).

Similar controversies arise with other applications of evolutionary theory. People do not always act as evolutionary theory predicts: Parents sometimes abandon newborns, adults sometimes handle snakes, and so on.

Nonetheless, evolutionary theorists believe that humans need to understand ancient impulses within our species in order to control destructive reactions. The better we know those basic reactions, the better we can overcome them if need be. We can promote diplomacy instead of tribalism and manufacture safer cars and fewer guns. But if we do not know and respect our evolutionary impulses, we cannot modify them.

THINK CRITICALLY: What would happen if lust were the only reason one person would mate with another?

WHAT HAVE YOU LEARNED?

1. Why is the sociocultural perspective particularly relevant within the United States?

2. How do mentors and mentees interact within the zone of proximal development?

3. Why would behaviors and emotions that benefited ancient humans be apparent today?

4. What is the evolutionary explanation for mating patterns and promiscuity?

What Theories Contribute

Each major theory discussed in this chapter has contributed to our understanding of human development (see Table 2.5):

- *Psychoanalytic theories* make us aware of the impact of early-childhood experiences, remembered or not, on subsequent development.
- *Behaviorism* shows the effect that immediate responses, associations, and examples have on learning, moment by moment and over time.
- *Cognitive theories* bring an understanding of intellectual processes, including the fact that thoughts and beliefs affect every aspect of our development.
- *Sociocultural theories* remind us that development is embedded in a rich and multifaceted cultural context, evident in every social interaction.
- *Evolutionary theories* suggest that human impulses need to be recognized before they can be guided.

No comprehensive view of development can ignore any of these theories, yet each has encountered severe criticism: *psychoanalytic theory* for being too

TABLE 2.5	Five Perspectives on Human Development		
Theory	Area of Focus	Fundamental Depiction of What People Do	Relative Emphasis on Nature or Nurture?
Psychoanalytic theory	Psychosexual (Freud) or psychosocial (Erikson) stages	Battle unconscious impulses and overcome major crises.	More nature (biological, sexual impulses, and parent–child bonds)
Behaviorism	Conditioning through stimulus and response	Respond to stimuli, reinforcement, and models.	More nurture (direct environment produces various behaviors)
Cognitive theory	Thinking, remembering, analyzing	Seek to understand experiences while forming concepts.	More nature (mental activity and motivation are key)
Sociocultural theory	Social control, expressed through people, language, customs	Learn the tools, skills, and values of society through apprenticeships.	More nurture (interaction of mentor and learner, within cultures)
Evolutionary	Needs and impulses that originated thousands of years ago	Develop impulses, interests, and patterns to survive and reproduce.	More nature (needs and impulses apply to all humans)

subjective; *behaviorism* for being too mechanistic; *cognitive theory* for undervaluing emotions; *sociocultural theory* for neglecting individual choice; *evolutionary theory* for ignoring the power of modern religion, law, and social norms.

Most developmentalists prefer an **eclectic perspective,** choosing what they consider to be the best aspects of each theory. Rather than adopt any one of these theories exclusively, they make selective use of all of them.

Obviously, all theories reflect the personal background of the theorist, as do all criticisms of theories. Being eclectic, not tied to any one theory, is beneficial because everyone, scientist as well as layperson, is biased. But even being eclectic may be criticized for being too picky or the opposite, too tolerant.

For developmentalists, all of these theories merit study and respect. It is easy to dismiss any one of them, but using several perspectives opens our eyes and minds to aspects of development that we might otherwise ignore. As one overview of seven developmental theories (including those explained here) concludes, "Because no one theory satisfactorily explains development, it is critical that developmentalists be able to draw on the content, methods, and theoretical concepts of many theories" (Miller, 2011, p. 437).

As you will see in many later chapters, theories provide a fresh look at behavior. Imagine a parent and a teacher discussing the learning or behavioral problems of a particular child. Each suggests a possible explanation that makes the other say, "I never thought of that." If they listen to each other with an open mind, together they might understand the child better and agree on a beneficial strategy.

Using five theories is like having five perceptive observers. All five are not always on target, but it is better to use theory to expand perception than to stay in

eclectic perspective The approach taken by most developmentalists, in which they apply aspects of each of the various theories of development rather than adhering exclusively to one theory.

Featuring an interactive time line, the Data Connections activity **Historical Highlights of the Science of Human Development** explores the events and individuals that helped establish the field of developmental psychology.

one narrow groove. A hand functions best with five fingers, although each finger is different and some fingers are more useful than others.

WHAT HAVE YOU LEARNED?

1. What are the criticisms of each of the five theories?

2. Why are most developmentalists eclectic in regard to theories?

3. Why is it useful to know more than one theory to explain human behavior?

SUMMARY

What Theories Do

1. A theory provides a framework of general principles to guide research and to explain observations. Each of the five major developmental theories—psychoanalytic, behaviorist, cognitive, sociocultural, and evolutionary—interprets human development from a distinct perspective, providing a framework for understanding human emotions, experiences, and actions.

2. Theories are neither true nor false. They are not facts; they suggest hypotheses to be tested and interpretations of the myriad human behaviors. Good theories are practical: They aid inquiry, interpretation, and daily life.

3. A norm is a usual standard, either something commonly done or a general ideal. Norms are not theories, although theories may suggest or endorse certain norms. Norms are not necessarily good or bad.

Grand Theories

4. Psychoanalytic theory emphasizes that adult actions and thoughts originate from unconscious impulses and childhood conflicts. Freud theorized that sexual urges arise during three stages of childhood—oral, anal, and phallic—and continue, after latency, in the genital stage.

5. Erikson described eight successive stages of development, each involving a crisis to be resolved as people mature within their context. Societies, cultures, and family members shape each person's development.

6. All psychoanalytic theories stress the legacy of childhood. Conflicts associated with children's erotic impulses have a lasting impact on adult personality, according to Freud. Erikson thought that the resolution of each crisis may linger to affect adult development.

7. Behaviorists, or learning theorists, believe that scientists should study observable and measurable behavior. Behaviorism emphasizes conditioning—a lifelong learning process in which an association between one stimulus and another (classical conditioning) or the consequences of reinforcement and punishment (operant conditioning) guide behavior.

8. Social learning theory recognizes that people learn by observing others, even if they themselves have not been reinforced or punished. Children are particularly susceptible to social learning, but all humans are affected by what they notice in other people.

9. Cognitive theorists believe that thoughts and beliefs powerfully affect attitudes, actions, and perceptions. Piaget proposed four age-related periods of cognition, each propelled by an active search for cognitive equilibrium.

10. Information processing focuses on each aspect of cognition—input, processing, and output. This perspective has benefited from technology, first from understanding computer functioning and more recently by the many ways scientists monitor the brain.

Newer Theories

11. Sociocultural theory explains human development in terms of the guidance, support, and structure provided by knowledgeable members of the society through culture and mentoring. Vygotsky described how learning occurs through social interactions in which mentors guide learners through their zone of proximal development.

12. Evolutionary theory contends that contemporary humans inherit genetic tendencies that have fostered survival and reproduction of the human species for tens of thousands of years. Through selective adaptation, the fears, impulses, and reactions that were useful 100,000 years ago for *Homo sapiens* continue to this day.

13. Evolutionary theory provides explanations for many human traits, from lactose intolerance to the love of babies. Many hypotheses arising from this theory are intriguing but controversial, especially those regarding family life and sexuality.

What Theories Contribute

14. Psychoanalytic, behavioral, cognitive, sociocultural, and evolutionary theories have aided our understanding of human development, yet no single theory describes the full complexity and diversity of human experience. Most developmentalists are eclectic, drawing on many theories.

KEY TERMS

developmental theory (p. 34)
norm (p. 35)
humanism (p. 36)
psychoanalytic theory (p. 37)
behaviorism (p. 39)
classical conditioning (p. 39)

operant conditioning (p. 41)
reinforcement (p. 41)
social learning theory (p. 42)
modeling (p. 42)
cognitive theory (p. 43)
cognitive equilibrium (p. 44)

assimilation (p. 45)
accommodation (p. 45)
information-processing theory
  (p. 45)
sociocultural theory (p. 49)
apprenticeship in thinking (p. 50)

guided participation (p. 50)
zone of proximal development
  (p. 50)
selective adaptation (p. 55)
eclectic perspective (p. 59)

APPLICATIONS

1. Developmentalists sometimes talk about "folk theories," which are theories developed by ordinary people, who may not know that they are theorizing. Choose three sayings that are commonly used in your culture, such as (from the dominant U.S. culture) "A penny saved is a penny earned" or "As the twig is bent, so grows the tree." Explain the underlying assumptions, or theory, that each saying reflects.

2. Cognitive theory suggests the power of thoughts, and sociocultural theory emphasizes the power of context. Find someone who disagrees with you about some basic issue (e.g., abortion, immigration, socialism) and listen carefully to their ideas and reasons. Then analyze how cognition and experience shaped their ideas **and** your own.

3. Ask three people to tell you their theories about male–female differences in mating and sexual behaviors. Which of the theories described in this chapter is closest to each explanation, and which theory is not mentioned?

The New Genetics

What Will You Know?

1. Genetically, how is each zygote unique?
2. How are twins different from other siblings?
3. Who is likely to carry genes that they do not know they have?
4. Why are far more abnormal zygotes created than abnormal babies born?

"She needs a special school. She cannot come back next year," Elissa's middle school principal told us.

We were stunned. Apparently her teachers thought that our wonderful daughter, bright and bubbly (Martin called her "frothy"), was learning-disabled. They had a label for it, "severely spatially disorganized."

Perhaps we should not have been surprised. We knew she misplaced homework, got lost, left books at school, forgot where each class met on which day. But we focused on her strengths in reading, analyzing, and friendship.

I knew the first lesson from genetics: Genes affect everything, not just physical appearance, intellect, and diseases. It dawned on me that Elissa had inherited our behavior. Our desks were covered with papers; our home was cluttered. If we needed masking tape, or working scissors, or silver candlesticks, we had to search in several places. Elissa seemed quite normal to us, but were we spatially disorganized, too?

The second lesson from genetics is that nurture always matters. We had learned to compensate. Since he often got lost, Martin readily asked for directions; since I mislaid documents, I kept my students' papers in clearly marked folders at my office.

There is a third lesson. Whether or not a gene is *expressed,* that is, whether or not it actively affects a person, depends partly on the social context as that person develops. We did not want our genes and habits to impair Elissa. Now that we were aware of her problems, we got help. I consulted a friend who is a professor of special education; Martin found a tutor who knew about disorganized 12-year-olds. Elissa learned to list her homework assignments, check them off when done, put papers carefully in her backpack (not crumpled in the bottom).

We all did our part. We double-checked the list and made sure Elissa had everything when she left for school; Martin attached her bus pass to her backpack; I wrote an impassioned letter telling the principal it would be unethical to expel her; we bought more textbooks so that she could leave one set at school and one at home. The three of us toured other schools, exploring options. Elissa studied diligently, hoping she would stay with her friends.

Success! Elissa aced her final exams, and the principal reluctantly allowed her to return. She became a stellar student and is now a gifted strategist, master organizer, and accomplished professional.

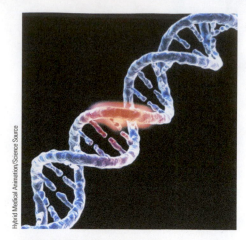

Hybrid Medical Animation/Science Source

Twelve of 3 Billion Pairs This is a computer illustration of a small segment of one gene. Even a small difference in one gene can cause major changes in a person's phenotype.

deoxyribonucleic acid (DNA) The chemical composition of the molecules that contain the genes, which are the chemical instructions for cells to manufacture various proteins.

chromosome One of the 46 molecules of DNA (in 23 pairs) that virtually every cell of the human body contains and that, together, contain all the genes. Other species have more or fewer chromosomes.

gene A small section of a chromosome; the basic unit for the transmission of heredity. A gene consists of a string of chemicals that provide instructions for the cell to manufacture certain proteins.

genome The full set of genes that are the instructions to make an individual member of a certain species.

This chapter explains these three lessons. New discoveries about genes are published every day, leading to many surprises, dilemmas, and choices. I hope your understanding of human genetics will mean that you will never be stunned by what a professional says about your child.

The Genetic Code

First, we review some biology. All living things are composed of cells. The work of cells is done by *proteins*. Each cell manufactures certain proteins according to a code of instructions stored by molecules of **deoxyribonucleic acid (DNA)** at the heart of the cell. These coding DNA molecules are on a **chromosome.**

46 to 20,000 to 3 Billion

Humans have 23 pairs of chromosomes (46 in all), which contain the instructions to make the proteins needed for life and growth (see Figure 3.1). The instructions in the 46 chromosomes are organized into genes, with each **gene** usually at a precise location on a particular chromosome.

Individuals have about 20,000 genes, each directing the formation of specific proteins made from a string of 20 amino acids. The genes themselves are a collection of about 3 billion *base pairs,* which are pairs of four chemicals (adenine paired with thymine, and guanine paired with cytosine).

The entire packet of instructions to make a living organism is called the **genome.** There is a genome for every species and variety of plant and animal—even for every bacterium and virus.

Members of the same species are quite similar genetically—it is estimated that more than 99 percent of any person's base pairs are identical to those of any other person. Knowing the usual genome of *Homo sapiens*, which was decoded in 2001,

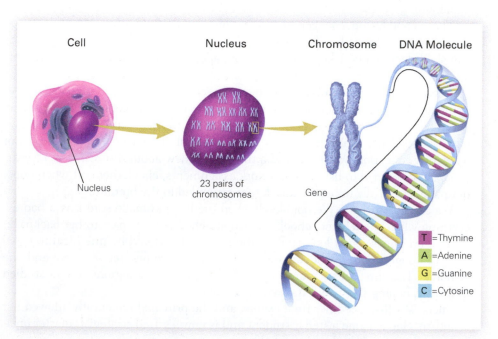

Cell   Nucleus   Chromosome   DNA Molecule

Nucleus

23 pairs of chromosomes

Gene

T = Thymine
A = Adenine
G = Guanine
C = Cytosine

FIGURE 3.1

How Proteins Are Made The genes on the chromosomes in the nucleus of each cell instruct the cell to manufacture the proteins needed to sustain life and development. The code for a protein is the particular combination of four bases, T-A-G-C (thymine, adenine, guanine, and cytosine).

is only the start of understanding human genetics because everyone has a slightly different set of genetic instructions.

Same and Different

It is human nature for people to notice differences more than commonalities. For that reason, before focusing on genetic differences, remember that all people share many crucial similarities, not only with two eyes, hands, and feet but also with the ability to communicate in language, with the capacity to love and hate, with the hope for a meaningful life.

Now consider our many differences. Any gene that varies in the precise sequence of those 3 billion base pairs—sometimes with a seemingly minor transposition, deletion, or repetition—is called an **allele.** Most alleles cause small differences (such as the shape of an eyebrow), but some are crucial. Another way to state this is to say that some genes are *polymorphic* (literally, "many forms"). They may have *single-nucleotide polymorphisms* (abbreviated SNPs, pronounced "snips"), which is a variation in only one part of the code.

Because each person's variations differ from every other person's variations, each of us is unique. You can recognize at a glance that two people are not identical, even if both are the same age, sex, and ethnicity. When you search for a familiar friend among a crowd of thousands, you do not mistakenly greet someone who is quite similar in appearance. Tiny variations in SNPs distinguish not only each face but also each body—inside and out.

allele A variation that makes a gene different in some way from other genes for the same characteristics. Many genes never vary; others have several possible alleles.

Beyond the Genes

RNA (ribonucleic acid, another molecule) and additional DNA surround each gene. In a process called *methylation,* this additional material enhances, transcribes, connects, empowers, silences, and alters genetic instructions. This noncoding material used to be called *junk*—but no longer. The influences of this surrounding material "alter not the gene itself, but rather, the regulatory elements that control the process of gene expression" (Furey & Sethupathy, 2013, p. 705). Methylation continues throughout life, from conception until death.

Obviously, genes are crucial, but even more crucial is whether or not a gene is expressed. The RNA regulates and transcribes genetic instructions, turning some genes and alleles on or off. In other words, a person can have the genetic tendency for a particular trait, disease, or behavior, but that tendency might never appear because it was never turned on. Think of a light switch: A lamp might have a new bulb and an electricity source, but the room stays dark unless the switch is flipped.

Some genetic activation occurs because of prenatal RNA, and some occurs later because of biological factors (such as pollution) and psychological ones (as with social rejection). As already mentioned in Chapter 1, the study of exactly how, why, and when genes change in form and expression is called **epigenetics,** with the Greek root *epi-,* meaning "around, above, below." Epigenetic changes are crucial: Events and circumstances surrounding (around, above, below) the genes determine whether genes are expressed or silenced (Ayyanathan, 2014).

Especially for Scientists A hundred years ago, it was believed that humans had 48 chromosomes, not 46; 20 years ago, it was thought that humans had 100,000 genes, not 20,000 or so. Why? (see response, page 66)

epigenetics The study of how environmental factors affect genes and genetic expression—enhancing, halting, shaping, or altering the expression of genes.

The Microbiome

One aspect of both nature and nurture that profoundly affects each person is the **microbiome,** which refers to all of the microbes (bacteria, viruses, fungi, archaea, yeasts) that live within every part of the body. Some are called "germs" and people try to kill them with germicides and antibiotics, but most microbes are more helpful than harmful. Microbes have their own DNA, reproducing throughout life.

microbiome All of the microbes (bacteria, viruses, and so on) with all of their genes in a community; here, the millions of microbes of the human body.

● ● **Response for Scientists** (from page 65): There was some scientific evidence for the wrong numbers (e.g., chimpanzees have 48 chromosomes), but the reality is that humans tend to overestimate many things, from the number of genes to their grade on the next test. Scientists are very human: They tend to overestimate until the data prove them wrong.

zygote The single cell formed from the union of two gametes, a sperm and an ovum.

copy number variations Genes with various repeats or deletions of base pairs.

The Moment of Conception This ovum is about to become a zygote. It has been penetrated by a single sperm, whose nucleus now lies next to the nucleus of the ovum. Soon, the two nuclei will fuse, bringing together about 20,000 genes to guide development.

● ● **Especially for Medical Doctors** Can you look at a person and then write a prescription that will personalize medicine to their particular genetic susceptibility? (see response, page 69)

There are thousands of varieties of these microbes. Together they have an estimated 3 million different genes—influencing immunity, weight, diseases, moods, and much else that affects us every day (Dugas et al., 2016; Koch, 2015). Particularly intriguing is the relationship between the microbiome and nutrition, since bacteria in the gut break down food for nourishment (Devaraj et al., 2013).

For instance, a careful study in Malawi found that sometimes one twin suffers from malnutrition and the other does not, even when both are fed the same foods in the same quantity (Pennisi, 2016). The microbiome, not the parents, may be to blame, as each twin has different microbes. Mice that are obese or thin change body shape when the microbiome from another mouse with the opposite problem is implanted. This may be true for humans, too (Dugas et al., 2016).

Siblings Not Alike

The differences between siblings are not only in the microbiome but also in the genes themselves. Each reproductive cell (sperm or ovum, called *gametes*) has only one of the two chromosomes that a man or a woman has at each of the 23 locations. This means that each man or woman can produce 2^{23} different gametes—more than 8 million versions of their chromosomes (actually 8,388,608).

When a sperm and an ovum combine, they create a new single cell called a **zygote.** The genes on one of those 8 million possible sperm from the father interacts with the genes on one of the 8 million possible ova from the mother. Your parents could have given you an astronomical number of siblings, each unique.

Even more than that, each zygote carries genes that "are themselves transmitted to individual cells with large apparent mistakes—somatically acquired deletions, duplications, and other mutations" (Macosko & McCarroll, 2013, p. 564). Small variations, mutations, or repetitions in the 3 billion base pairs could make a notable difference in the proteins and thus, eventually, in the person.

Attention has focused on **copy number variations,** which are genes with repeats (from one to hundreds) or deletions of base pairs. Copy number variations are widespread—everyone has them—and they correlate with almost every disease and condition, including heart disease, intellectual disability, mental illness, and many cancers.

Each parent contributes 23 chromosomes, or half the genetic material. When the man's chromosomes pair with the woman's (chromosome 1 from the sperm with chromosome 1 from the ovum, chromosome 2 with chromosome 2, and so on), each gene from each parent connects with its counterpart from the other parent, and the interaction between the two determines the inherited traits of the future person. Since some alleles from the father differ from the alleles from the mother, their combination produces a zygote unlike either parent. Thus, each new person is a product of two parents but is unlike either one.

Genetic diversity helps the species, because creativity, prosperity, and survival is enhanced when one person is unlike another. There is an optimal balance of diversity and similarity for each species: Human societies are close to that optimal level (Ashraf & Galor, 2013).

Male—Female Variations

To further complicate matters, sometimes one-half of a gene pair switches off completely, which may cause a problem if that remaining gene is destructive. For girls, one X of the 23rd pair is deactivated early in prenatal life. The implications of that shutoff are not well understood, but it is known that sometimes that X is from the ovum, sometimes it is from the sperm. Boys, of course, have only one X, so it is always activated.

The fact that X deactivation occurs in girls but not in boys is only one example of the significance of the embryo's sex. Sometimes the same allele affects male and female embryos differently. For instance, women develop multiple sclerosis more often than men, and they usually inherit it from their mothers, not their fathers, probably for genetic as well as epigenetic reasons (Huynh & Casaccia, 2013).

It sometimes matters whether a gene came from the mother or the father, a phenomenon called *parental imprinting*. The best-known example occurs with a small deletion on chromosome 15. If that deletion came from the father's chromosome 15, the child may develop Prader-Willi syndrome and be obese, slow-moving, and stubborn. If that deletion came from the mother's chromosome 15, the child will have Angelman syndrome and be thin, hyperactive, and happy—sometimes too happy, laughing when no one else does.

She Laughs Too Much No, not the smiling sister, but the 10-year-old on the right, who has Angelman syndrome. She inherited it from her mother's chromosome 15. Fortunately, her two siblings inherited the mother's other chromosome 15. If the 10-year-old had inherited the identical deletion on her father's chromosome 15, she would have Prader-Willi syndrome, which would cause her to be overweight, always hungry, and often angry. With Angelman syndrome, however, laughing, even at someone's pain, is a symptom.

Matching Genes and Chromosomes

The genes on the chromosomes constitute the organism's genetic inheritance, or **genotype,** which endures throughout life. Growth requires duplication of the code of the original cell again and again.

Autosomes

In 22 of the 23 pairs of chromosomes, both members of the pair (one from each parent) are closely matched. As already explained, some of the specific genes have alternate alleles, but each chromosome finds its comparable chromosome, making a pair. Those 44 chromosomes are called *autosomes,* which means that they are independent (*auto* means "self") of the sex chromosomes (the 23rd pair).

Each autosome, from number 1 to number 22, contains hundreds of genes in the same positions and sequence. If the code of a gene from one parent is exactly like the code on the same gene from the other parent, the gene pair is **homozygous** (literally, "same-zygote").

However, the match is not always letter-perfect because the mother might have a different allele of a particular gene than the father has. If a gene's code differs from that of its counterpart, the two genes still pair up, but the zygote (and, later, the person) is **heterozygous.** This can occur with any of the gene pairs on any of the autosomes.

Given that only half of a man's genes are on each sperm and only half of a woman's genes are on each ovum, the combination creates siblings who will be, genetically, similar and different. Thus, which particular homozygous or heterozygous genes my brother and I inherited from our parents is a matter of chance, and it has no connection to the fact that I am a younger sister, not an older brother.

Sex Chromosomes

However, for the **23rd pair** of chromosomes, a marked difference is apparent between my brother and me. My 23rd pair matched, but his did not. In that, he is like all males: When gametes combine to form the zygote, half of the time a dramatic mismatch occurs, because some sperm carry an X and some a Y.

genotype An organism's entire genetic inheritance, or genetic potential.

homozygous Referring to two genes of one pair that are exactly the same in every letter of their code. Most gene pairs are homozygous.

heterozygous Referring to two genes of one pair that differ in some way. Typically one allele has only a few base pairs that differ from the other member of the pair.

23rd pair The chromosome pair that, in humans, determines sex. The other 22 pairs are autosomes, inherited equally by males and females.

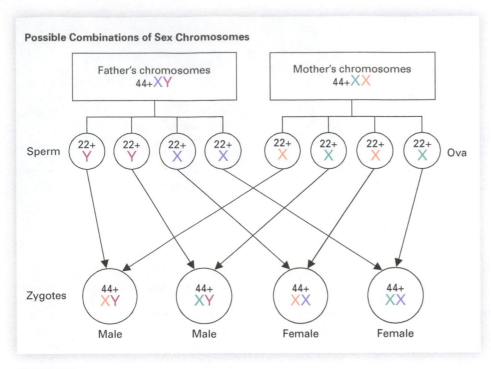

Possible Combinations of Sex Chromosomes

FIGURE 3.2

Determining a Zygote's Sex Any given couple can produce four possible combinations of sex chromosomes; two lead to female children and two lead to male children. In terms of the future person's sex, it does not matter which of the mother's Xs the zygote inherited. All that matters is whether the father's Y sperm or X sperm fertilized the ovum. However, for X-linked conditions it matters a great deal because typically one, but not both, of the mother's Xs carries the trait.

XY A 23rd chromosome pair that consists of an X-shaped chromosome from the mother and a Y-shaped chromosome from the father. XY zygotes become males.

XX A 23rd chromosome pair that consists of two X-shaped chromosomes, one each from the mother and the father. XX zygotes become females.

This is how it happens. In males, the 23rd pair has one X-shaped chromosome and one Y-shaped chromosome. It is called **XY**. In females, the 23rd pair is composed of two X-shaped chromosomes. Accordingly, it is called **XX**.

Because a female's 23rd pair is XX, when her 46 chromosomes split to make ova, each ovum contains either one X or the other—but always an X. And because a male's 23rd pair is XY, half of a father's sperm carry an X chromosome and half a Y.

The X chromosome is bigger and has more genes, but the Y chromosome has a crucial gene, called *SRY*, that directs the embryo to make male hormones and organs. Thus, sex depends on which sperm penetrates the ovum—a Y sperm with the SRY gene, creating a boy (XY), or an X sperm, creating a girl (XX) (see Figure 3.2).

Although sex is determined at conception, for most of history no one knew it until a baby was born and someone shouted "It's a ------!" In former times, millions of pregnant women ate special foods, slept on one side, or repeated certain prayers, all to control the sex of the fetus—which was already male or female.

More Than Sex Organs

That SRY gene directs the embryo to grow a penis, and much more. The Y chromosome causes male hormone production that affects the brain, skeleton, body fat, and muscles, beginning in the first weeks of prenatal development and continuing to the last breath in old age. At conception, there are about 120 males for every 100 females, perhaps because Y sperm swim faster and reach the ovum first (remember, they carry fewer genes, so they are lighter than the X sperm).

Uncertain Sex Every now and then, a baby is born with "ambiguous genitals," meaning that the child's sex is not abundantly clear. When this happens, a quick analysis of the chromosomes is needed to make sure that there are exactly 46 and to see whether the 23rd pair is XY or XX. The karyotypes shown here indicate a normal baby boy *(left)* and girl *(right)*.

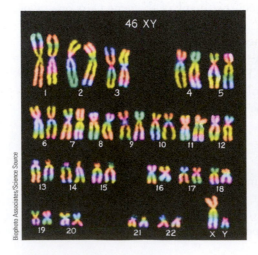

46 XY

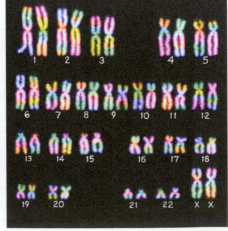

However, male embryos are more vulnerable than female ones (because of fewer genes, again?), so they are less likely to survive. The United Nations reports that, at birth, the natural male/female ratio worldwide is about 104:100; in developed nations it is 105:100, but it is only 103:100 in the poorest nations. Maternal nutrition and prenatal care are the probable reasons.

Biological sex differences become cultural differences as soon as a newborn is named and wrapped in blue or pink. Thousands of gender differences throughout the life span—from toy trucks given to 1-day-old boys to the survival rates of old women—begin with one gene.

Obviously, the impact of that SRY gene goes far beyond the fact that it is only one of about 20,000 genes. It influences thousands of other genetic and cultural forces. Consider sex selection.

Response for Medical Doctors (from page 66): No. Personalized medicine is the hope of many physicians, but appearance (the phenotype) does not indicate alleles, recessive genes, copy number variations, and other genetic factors that affect drug reactions. Many medical researchers seek to personalize chemotherapy for cancer, but although this is urgently needed, success is still experimental, even when the genotype is known.

OPPOSING PERSPECTIVES

Too Many Boys?

In past centuries, millions of newborns were killed because they were the wrong sex, a practice that would be considered murder today. Now the same goal is achieved long before birth in three ways: (1) inactivating X or Y sperm before conception, (2) inserting only male or female zygotes after in vitro conception, or (3) aborting XX or XY fetuses.

Recently, millions of couples have used these methods to choose their newborn's sex. Should this be illegal? It is in at least 36 nations. It is legal in the United States (Murray, 2014).

To some prospective parents, those 36 nations are unfair. Those 36 nations allow similar measures to avoid severely disabled newborns. Why is that legal but sex selection is not? There are moral reasons. But should governments legislate morals? People disagree (Wilkinson, 2015).

One nation that forbids prenatal sex selection is China. This was not always so. In about 1979, China began a "one-child" policy, urging and sometimes forcing couples to have only one child. That achieved the intended goal: fewer children to feed . . . or starve. Severe poverty was almost eliminated.

But advances in prenatal testing combined with the Chinese tradition that sons, not daughters, care for aging parents, led many couples to want their only child to be male. Among the unanticipated results of the one-child policy:

- Since 1980, an estimated 9 million abortions of female fetuses
- Adoption of thousands of newborn Chinese girls by Western families
- By 2010, far more unmarried young men than women

In 1993, the Chinese government forbade prenatal testing for sex selection. In 2013, China rescinded the one-child policy. Yet from 2005 to 2010, the ratio of preschool boys to girls was 117:100, an imbalance that continues (United Nations, Department of Economic and Social Affairs, Population Division, 2015). Despite government policies, many Chinese couples still prefer to have only one child, a boy.

The argument in favor of sex selection is freedom from government interference. Some fertility doctors and many individuals believe that each couple should be able to decide how many children to have and what sex they should be (Murray, 2014).

Why would anyone object to such a private choice? There is a reason: It might harm society. For instance, 30 years after the one-child policy began, many more young Chinese men than women die. The developmental explanation is that unmarried young men take risks to attract women. They become depressed if they remain alone. Thus, the skewed sex ratio among young adults in China increases early death, from accidents and suicide, from drug overdoses and poor health practices, in young men.

That is a warning to every nation. Males are more likely to suffer intellectual disability and substance use disorder; they commit crimes, kill each other, die of heart attacks, and start

My Strength, My Daughter That's the slogan these girls in New Delhi are shouting at a demonstration against abortion of female fetuses in India. The current sex ratio of children in India suggests that this campaign has not convinced every couple.

Manish Swarup/AP Photo

wars more than females do. For instance, the United States Department of Justice reports that, since 1980, 85 percent of

Mama Is 60 Wu Jingzhou holds his newborn twin daughters, born to his 60-year-old wife after in vitro fertilization. Ordinarily, it is illegal in China, as in most other nations, for women to have children after menopause. But an exception was made for this couple because the death of their only child, a young woman named Tingling, was partly the government's fault.

the prison population are men, and primarily because of heart disease and violence, men are about twice as likely as women to die before age 50 (Centers for Disease Control and Prevention, 2014). A nation with more men than women may suffer.

But wait: Chromosomes and genes do not *determine* behavior. Every sex difference is influenced by culture. Even traits that originate with biology, such as the propensity to heart attacks, are affected more by environment (in this case, diet and cigarettes) than by XX or XY chromosomes. Perhaps nurture would change if nature produced more males than females, and then societies would adapt.

Already, medical measures and smoking declines have reduced heart attacks in men. In 1950, four times as many middle-aged men as women died of heart disease; by 2010, the rate was lower for both sexes, but especially for men, 2:1 not 4:1. Lifelong, rates of cardiovascular deaths in the United States are currently close to sex-neutral (Centers for Disease Control and Prevention, 2015). Indeed, every sex difference is strongly influenced by culture and policy.

> **THINK CRITICALLY:** Might laws against prenatal sex selection be unnecessary if culture shifted?

WHAT HAVE YOU LEARNED?

1. How many chromosomes and genes do people have?
2. What is an allele?
3. What effect does the microbiome have?
4. Why is each zygote unique, genetically?
5. What determines whether a baby is a boy or a girl?

New Cells, New People

Within hours after conception, the zygote begins *duplication* and *division*. First, the 23 pairs of chromosomes (carrying all the genes) duplicate to form two complete sets of the genome. These two sets move toward opposite sides of the zygote, and the single cell splits neatly down the middle into two cells, each containing the original genetic code.

These first two cells duplicate and divide, becoming four, which duplicate and divide, becoming eight, and so on. The name of the developing mass of cells changes as it multiplies—from *morula* to *blastocyst,* from *embryo* to *fetus*—and finally, at birth, *baby.* [**Life-Span Link:** Prenatal growth is detailed in Chapter 4.]

Cells and Identity

Nine months after conception, a newborn has about 26 billion cells, all influenced by whatever nutrients, drugs, hormones, viruses, microbes, and so on came from the pregnant woman. Almost every human cell carries a complete copy of the genetic instructions of the one-celled zygote. About half of those genetic instructions came from each parent, but every zygote also has a few spontaneous mutations—about 40 base pair variations that were not inherited.

Adults have about 37 trillion cells, each with the same 46 chromosomes and the same thousands of genes of the original zygote (Bianconi et al., 2013). This explains why DNA testing of any body cell, even from a drop of blood or a snip of hair, can identify "the real father," "the guilty criminal," "the long-lost brother." DNA lingers long after death. Several living African Americans claimed Thomas Jefferson as an ancestor: DNA proved some right and some wrong (Foster et al., 1998).

Indeed, because the Y chromosome is passed down to every male descendant, and because the Y changes very little from one generation to the next, men today have the Y of their male ancestors who died thousands of years ago. Female ancestors also live on. Each zygote has *mitochondria,* biological material that provides energy for the cell. The mitochondria come from the mother, and her mother, and her mother, and thus each person carries evidence of maternal lineage.

Stem Cells

The cells that result from the early duplication and division are called **stem cells;** these cells are able to produce any other cell and thus to become a complete person. After about the eight-cell stage, although duplication and division continue, a third process, *differentiation,* begins. In differentiation, cells specialize, taking different forms and reproducing at various rates depending on where they are located. For instance, some cells become part of an eye, others part of a finger, still others part of the brain. They are no longer stem cells.

Scientists have discovered ways to add genes to certain differentiated cells in a laboratory process that reprograms those cells, making them like stem cells again. Another new method, called CRISPR, has been developed to edit genes (Lander, 2016).

However, scientists do not yet know how to reprogram stem cells to cure genetic conditions without harming other cells. As for CRISPR, it may be used to control the mosquitos who spread malaria, Zika virus, and other diseases. Although human genes could theoretically be edited with CRISPR, the prospect of "designer babies" raises serious ethical questions. At least at the moment, CRISPR is forbidden for human organisms (Lander, 2016; Green, 2015).

In Vitro Fertilization

The ethical implications of CRISPR raise the issue of **in vitro fertilization (IVF),** which was pronounced "sacrilegious," and against God, when attempted in 1960 and when successful in 1978. Over the past half-century, IVF has become "a relatively routine way to have children, with an estimated 5 million babies born to date" (C. Thompson, 2014, p. 361).

IVF is quite different from the typical conception. The woman must take hormones to increase the number of fully developed ova, and the man must ejaculate into a receptacle. Then surgeons remove several ova from the ovaries and technicians combine ova and sperm in a laboratory dish (*in vitro* means "in glass"), often inserting one active sperm into each normal ovum. [**Life-Span Link:** Artificial reproductive technology (ART) is further discussed in Chapter 20.]

Zygotes that fail to duplicate, or blastocysts that test positive for serious genetic diseases, are rejected, but those that seem viable can be inserted into the uterus. Even with careful preparation, fewer than half of the inserted blastocysts successfully implant and grow to become newborns. For both natural and alternative conception, fertility decreases with age, so some young women freeze their ova for IVF years later (Mac Dougall et al., 2013). A slightly higher risk of congenital malformations may occur (Qin et al., 2015).

(a)

(b)

(c)

Anatomical Travelogue/Science Source

First Stages of the Germinal Period The original zygote as it divides into *(a)* two cells, *(b)* four cells, and *(c)* eight cells. Occasionally at this early stage, the cells separate completely, forming the beginning of monozygotic twins, quadruplets, or octuplets.

stem cells Cells from which any other specialized type of cell can form.

in vitro fertilization (IVF) Fertilization that takes place outside a woman's body (as in a glass laboratory dish). The procedure involves mixing sperm with ova that have been surgically removed from the woman's ovary. If a zygote is produced, it is inserted into a woman's uterus, where it may implant and develop into a baby.

Perfectly Legal Nadya Suleman was a medical miracle when her eight newborns all survived, thanks to expert care in a Los Angeles hospital. Soon thereafter, however, considerable controversy began: She was dubbed "Octomom" because—even though already a single mother of six children, including twins—she still opted to undergo in vitro fertilization, which resulted in implantation of her octuplets.

macmillan learning

Video Activity: Identical Twins: Growing Up Apart gives a real-life example of how genes play a significant role in people's physical, social, and cognitive development.

monozygotic (MZ) twins Twins who originate from one zygote that splits apart very early in development. (Also called *identical twins*.) Other monozygotic multiple births (such as triplets and quadruplets) can occur as well.

If IVF children are of normal birthweight, they do as well or better than other babies, not only in childhood health, intelligence, and school achievement but also in self-reported emotional development as teenagers (Wagenaar et al., 2011). The reason might be that their parents are more responsive, at least according to a study in Jamaica (Pottinger & Palmer, 2013).

Thanks to IVF, millions of couples who would have been infertile now have children. Indeed, some parents have children who are not genetically or biologically theirs if others donated the sperm, the ova, and/or the womb. The word *donate* may be misleading, since most donors—often college students—are paid for their sperm, ova, or pregnancy. Since up to three strangers could create a baby for someone else, the "real" parents are considered those who raise a child, not those who conceive it (Franklin, 2013).

Some nations forbid IVF unless a couple provides proof of heterosexual marriage and even proof of financial and emotional health. Several European nations limit the numbers of blastocysts inserted into the uterus at one time, partly because national health care pays for both IVF and newborn care.

The United States has no legal restrictions, although there are SES impediments—the cost is about $20,000 for all the drugs, the monitoring, and the procedure itself. Medical societies provide some oversight. For example, the California Medical Board removed the medical license from the physician who inserted 12 blastocysts in Nadya Suleman. She gave birth to eight surviving babies in 2009, a medical miracle but a developmental disaster.

Twins and More

Thus far we have described natural conception as if one sperm and one ovum resulted in one baby. That is the usual process for primates, but there are many exceptions. To understand multiple conceptions, you first need to understand the difference between monozygotic and dizygotic twins (see Visualizing Development, p. 73).

Monozygotic Twins

Remember that each stem cell contains the entire genetic code. If parents who carry destructive genes use IVF, one cell can be removed at the very early stage of duplication and that cell can be analyzed. If it does not contain the destructive gene, the blastocyst can be implanted. Removing one stem cell at this early stage does not harm development: A healthy baby may be born.

With lower animals, scientists have separated stem cells and allowed two identical animals to develop. This is illegal for humans—each IVF zygote becomes one embryo. However, in one pregnancy in about 250, nature within the woman's body does what scientists are forbidden to do—it splits those early cells and allows each to develop independently. If each of those separated cells then duplicates, divides, differentiates, implants, grows, and survives, multiple births occur.

One separation results in **monozygotic (MZ) twins,** from one (*mono*) zygote (also called *identical twins*). Separations at the four- or eight-cell stage create monozygotic quadruplets or octuplets. Because monozygotic multiples originate from the same zygote, they have identical genetic instructions for appearance, psychological traits, disease vulnerability, and everything else genetic.

Remember, however, that epigenetic influences begin as soon as conception occurs: Monozygotic twins look and act very much alike, but their environment can distinguish one from the other. Epigenetic factors affect genes within hours of conception, and thus the developing blastocysts may differ. Then, the particular spot in the uterus where each twin implants may make one fetus heavier than the other.

Monozygotic twins are fortunate in some ways. They can donate a kidney or other organ to their twin with no organ rejection. They can also befuddle

One Baby or More

Humans usually have one baby at a time, but sometimes twins are born. Most often they are from two ova fertilized by two sperm (*lower left*), resulting in dizygotic twins.

Sometimes, however, one zygote splits in two (*lower right*), resulting in monozygotic twins; if each of these zygotes splits again, the result is monozygotic quadruplets.

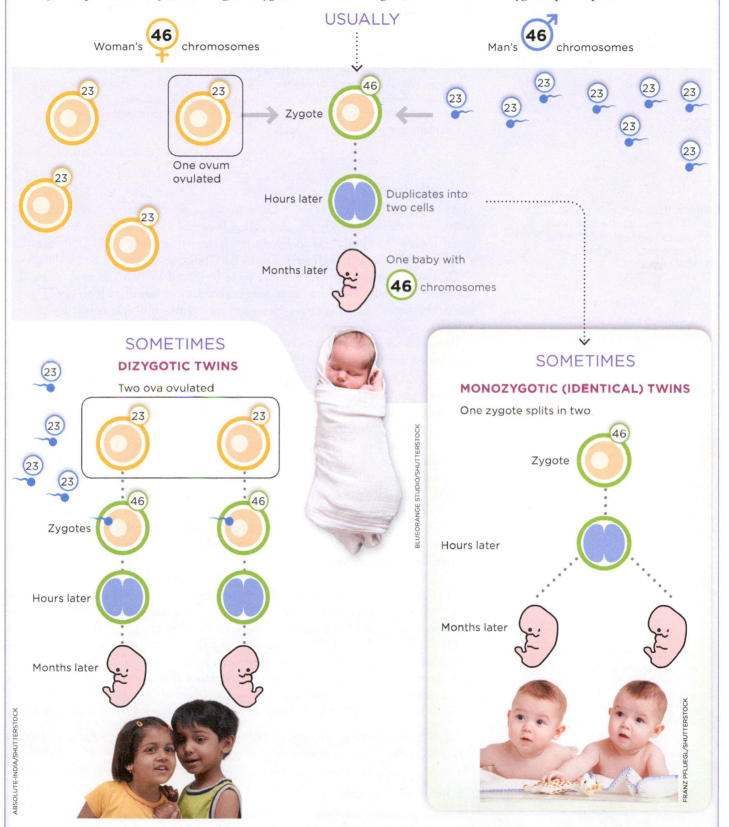

USUALLY

Woman's ♀ **46** chromosomes

Man's ♂ **46** chromosomes

One ovum ovulated

Zygote 46

Hours later — Duplicates into two cells

Months later — One baby with **46** chromosomes

SOMETIMES
DIZYGOTIC TWINS

Two ova ovulated

Zygotes — 46 / 46

Hours later

Months later

SOMETIMES
MONOZYGOTIC (IDENTICAL) TWINS

One zygote splits in two

Zygote 46

Hours later

Months later

BLUEORANGE STUDIO/SHUTTERSTOCK

ABSOLUTE-INDIA/SHUTTERSTOCK

FRANZ PFLUEGL/SHUTTERSTOCK

their parents and teachers, who may need ways (such as different earrings) to tell them apart.

Usually, the twins themselves establish their own identities. For instance, both might inherit equal athletic ability, but one decides to join the basketball team while the other plays soccer.

As one monozygotic twin writes:

> Twins put into high relief *the* central challenge for all of us: self-definition. How do we each plant our stake in the ground, decide how sensitive, callous, ambitious, conciliatory, or cautious we want to be every day? . . . Twins come with a built-in constant comparison, but defining oneself against one's twin is just an amped-up version of every person's life-long challenge: to individuate—to create a distinctive persona in the world.
>
> *[Pogrebin, 2010, p. 9]*

Dizygotic Twins

dizygotic (DZ) twins Twins who are formed when two separate ova are fertilized by two separate sperm at roughly the same time. (Also called *fraternal twins.*)

Most twins are <u>not</u> monozygotic. Once in about 60 conceptions, **dizygotic (DZ) twins** are conceived. They are also called *fraternal twins,* although because *fraternal* means "brotherly" (as in *fraternity*), fraternal is inaccurate. Odds are that a third of DZ twins are both girls, a third both boys, and a third a boy and a girl.

DZ twins began life when two ova were fertilized by two sperm at about the same time. Usually, women release only one ovum per month, which is why most human newborns are singletons. However, sometimes multiple ovulation occurs, a tendency affected by genes.

People sometimes say that twinning "skips a generation," but that is not completely accurate. What it skips is fathers—but not exactly. Since dizygotic twinning requires multiple ovulation, the likelihood of a woman bearing twins depends on her genes, not her husband's. However, a man has half his genes from his mother. If multiple ovulation is in his family, he will not produce twins; but if the X he inherited from his mother encouraged multiple ovulation, his daughters (who always get his X) might.

When dizygotic twinning occurs naturally, the incidence varies by ethnicity. For example, about 1 in 11 Yorubas in Nigeria is a twin, as are about 1 in 45 European Americans, 1 in 75 Japanese and Koreans, and 1 in 150 Chinese. Age matters, too: Older women more often double-ovulate and thus have more twins.

IVF often produces twins, because prospective parents are so eager to have babies that they ignore medical advice to implant only one zygote: The result is more underweight, preterm babies. [**Life-Span Link:** The problems of low birthweight are detailed in Chapter 4.]

After twins are conceived, their chance of survival until birth depends on prenatal circumstances: Sometimes an early sonogram reveals two developing organisms, but only one embryo continues to grow. This *vanishing twin* phenomenon may occur in about 12 percent of pregnancies (Giuffrè et al., 2012).

Like all full siblings, DZ twins have about half of their genes in common. They can differ markedly in appearance, or they can look so much alike that only genetic tests determine their zygosity. In the rare incidence that a woman releases two ova at once and has sex with two men over a short period, it is possible for fraternal twins to have different fathers. Then they share only one-fourth of their genes.

WHAT HAVE YOU LEARNED?

1. What makes a cell a "stem cell"?

2. How does DNA establish identity?

3. What is similar and different in an IVF and a traditional pregnancy?

4. Why is CRISPR illegal for humans?

5. What is the difference between monozygotic and dizygotic twins?

6. Are some pregnancies more likely to be twins than others?

From Genotype to Phenotype

As already explained, when a sperm and an ovum create a zygote, they establish the *genotype*: all the genes of the developing person. That begins several complex processes that combine to form the **phenotype**—the person's appearance, behavior, and brain and body functions.

Nothing is totally genetic, not even such obviously inherited traits as height or hair color, but nothing is untouched by genes. That includes such social traits as working overtime, wanting a divorce, or becoming a devoted parent (Plomin et al., 2013).

Many Factors

The genotype instigates body and brain formation, but the phenotype depends on a combination of genes and the environment, from the moment of conception until the moment of death. Some of those influences change the genes directly, in epigenesis, and some are less direct, via culture and context.

Almost every trait is **polygenic** (affected by many genes) and **multifactorial** (influenced by many factors). A zygote might have the alleles for becoming, say, a musical genius, but that potential may never be expressed. Completely accurate prediction of the phenotype is impossible, even if the genotype is entirely known (Lehner, 2013). One reason is *differential susceptibility*, as explained in Chapter 1. Because of a seemingly minor allele, or a transient environmental influence, a particular person may be profoundly changed—or not affected at all—by experiences.

Remember that all important human characteristics are epigenetic. This is easiest to see with conditions that are known to be inherited, such as cancer, schizophrenia, and autism spectrum disorder (Kundu, 2013; Plomin et al., 2013). It is also apparent with cognitive abilities and personality traits.

Diabetes is a notable example. People who inherit genes that put them at risk do not always become diabetic. Lifestyle factors activate that genetic risk. Then, epigenetic changes make diabetes irreversible. Once a person is diabetic, diet and insulin may control the disease, but the pre-diabetic state never returns (Reddy & Natarajan, 2013).

One dramatic intervention—bariatric surgery—puts diabetes into remission in most (72 percent) patients, but over the years full diabetes returns for more than half of them. Crucial is conscientious diet and exercise (Sjöström et al., 2014).

The same may be true for other developmental changes over the life span. Drug abuse—cocaine, cigarettes, alcohol, and so on—may produce epigenetic changes. A person may still be addicted, even if they have not used the drug for years (Bannon et al., 2014). Treatment and other factors help, of course, but the addict can never use the drug again as an unaffected person could.

In general, some bio-psycho-social influences (such as injury, temperature extremes, drug abuse, and crowding) can impede healthy development, whereas others (nourishing food, loving care, play) can facilitate it, all because of differential susceptibility and epigenetic change. For example, if a person feels lonely and rejected, that feeling affects the RNA, which allows genetic potential for heart disease or social anxiety to be expressed (Slavich & Cole, 2013).

phenotype The observable characteristics of a person, including appearance, personality, intelligence, and all other traits.

polygenic Referring to a trait that is influenced by many genes.

multifactorial Referring to a trait that is affected by many factors, both genetic and environmental, that enhance, halt, shape, or alter the expression of genes, resulting in a phenotype that may differ markedly from the genotype.

Courtesy Kate Nurre

Sisters, But Not Twins, in Iowa From their phenotype, it is obvious that these two girls share many of the same genes, as their blond hair and facial features are strikingly similar. And you can see that they are not twins; Lucy is 7 years old and Ellie is only 4. It may not be obvious that they have the same parents, but they do—and they are both very bright and happy because of it. This photo also shows that their genotypes differ in one crucial way: One of them has a dominant gene for a serious condition.

● **Observation Quiz** Who has that genetic condition? (see answer, page 77) ↑

Human Genome Project An international effort to map the complete human genetic code. This effort was essentially completed in 2001, though analysis is ongoing.

Gene–Gene Interactions

Many discoveries have followed the completion of the **Human Genome Project** in 2001. One of the first surprises was that humans have far fewer than 100,000 genes, the number often cited in the twentieth century.

The total number of genes in a person is about 20,000. The precise number is elusive because—another surprise—it is not always easy to figure out where one gene starts and another ends, or even if a particular stretch of DNA is actually a gene (Rouchka & Cha, 2009). Nor is it always easy to predict exactly how the genes from one parent will interact with the genes from the other. We do, however, know some basics of genetic interaction, as described now.

Additive Heredity

Especially for Future Parents Suppose you wanted your daughters to be short and your sons to be tall. Could you achieve that? (see response, page 79)

Some genes and alleles are *additive* because their effects *add up* to influence the phenotype. When genes interact additively, the phenotype usually reflects the contributions of every gene that is involved. Height, hair curliness, and skin color, for instance, are usually the result of additive genes. Indeed, height is probably influenced by 180 genes, each contributing a very small amount (Enserink, 2011).

Most people have ancestors of varied height, hair curliness, skin color, and so on, so their children's phenotype does not mirror the parents' phenotypes (although the phenotype always reflects the genotype). I see this in my family: Our daughter Rachel is of average height, shorter than her father and me, but taller than either of our mothers. She apparently inherited some of her grandmothers' height genes via our gametes. And none of my children have exactly my skin color—apparent when we borrow clothes from each other and are distressed that a particular shade is attractive on one but ugly on another.

How any additive trait turns out depends partly on all the genes a child happens to inherit (half from each parent, which means one-fourth from each grandparent). Some genes amplify or dampen the effects of other genes, aided by all the other DNA and RNA (not junk!) in the zygote.

© 2016 Macmillan

Genetic Mix Dizygotic twins Olivia and Harrison have half their genes in common, as do all siblings from the same parents. If the parents are close relatives who themselves share most alleles, the nonshared half is likely to include many similar genes. That is not the case here, as their mother (Nicola) is from Wales and their father (Gleb) is from the nation of Georgia, which includes many people of Asian ancestry. Their phenotypes, and the family photos on the wall, show many additive genetic influences.

Dominant–Recessive Heredity

Not all genes are additive. In one nonadditive form, alleles interact in a **dominant–recessive pattern,** when one allele, the *dominant gene,* is more influential than the other, the *recessive gene.* The dominant gene controls the expression of a characteristic even when a recessive gene is the other half of a pair.

dominant–recessive pattern The interaction of a heterozygous pair of alleles in such a way that the phenotype reflects one allele (the dominant gene) more than the other (the recessive gene).

carrier A person whose genotype includes a gene that is not expressed in the phenotype. The carried gene occurs in half of the carrier's gametes and thus is passed on to half of the carrier's children. If such a gene is inherited from both parents, the characteristic appears in the phenotype.

Everyone is a **carrier** of recessive genes, which are *carried* on the genotype but not apparent in their phenotype. For instance, no one would guess, simply by looking at me, that my mother had to stretch to reach 5 feet, 4 inches tall. But Rachel has half of her genes from me, and one of my height genes may be recessive.

Most recessive genes are harmless. For example, blue eyes are determined by a recessive allele and brown eyes by a dominant one, so a child conceived by a blue-eyed parent (who always has two recessive blue-eye genes) and a brown-eyed parent will usually have brown eyes.

"Usually," but not always. Sometimes a brown-eyed person is a carrier of the blue-eye gene. In that case, in a blue-eye/brown-eye couple, every child has at least one blue-eye gene (from the blue-eyed parent) and half of them will have

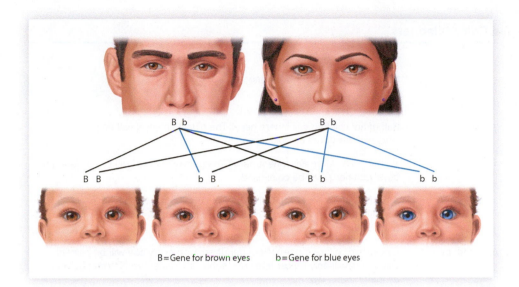

B = Gene for brown eyes   b = Gene for blue eyes

FIGURE 3.3
Changeling? No. If two brown-eyed parents both carry the blue-eye gene, they have one chance in four of having a blue-eyed child. Other recessive genes include the genes for red hair, Rh-negative blood, and many genetic diseases.

🔵🟢 **Observation Quiz** Why do these four offspring look identical except for eye color? (see answer, page 79) ←

a blue-eye recessive gene (from the brown-eyed parent). That half will have blue eyes because they have no dominant brown-eye gene. The other half will have a brown-eye dominant gene and thus have brown eyes but carry the blue-eye gene, like their brown-eyed parent.

This gets tricky if both parents are carriers. If two brown-eyed parents both have the blue-eye recessive gene, the chances are one in four that their child will have blue eyes (see Figure 3.3). This example is simple because it assumes that only one pair of genes is the main determinant of eye color. However, as with almost every trait, eye color is polygenic, with other genes having some influence. Eyes are various shades of blue and brown.

Recessive genes are often carried on the genotype but hidden on the phenotype. A recessive trait appears on the phenotype only when a person inherits the same recessive gene from both parents. Understanding the double recessive might prevent parents from blaming each other if their child has a recessive disease, and it might prevent fathers from suspecting infidelity if a child is unexpectedly blue-eyed.

Mother to Son

A special case of the dominant–recessive pattern occurs with genes that are **X-linked** (located on the X chromosome). If an X-linked gene is recessive—as are the genes for red–green color blindness (by far the most common type of color blindness), several allergies, a few diseases, and some learning disorders—the fact that it is on the X chromosome is critical (see Table 3.1). Boys might have the phenotype; girls are usually only carriers.

To understand this, remember that the Y chromosome is much smaller than the X, containing far fewer genes. For that reason, genes on the X almost never have a match on the Y. Therefore, recessive traits carried on the X usually have no dominant gene on the Y. A boy, XY, with a recessive gene on his X has no corresponding dominant gene on his Y to counteract it, so his phenotype will be affected. A girl will be affected only if she has the recessive trait on both of her X chromosomes.

This explains why males inherit X-linked disorders from their mothers, not their fathers. A study of children from six ethnic groups in Northern India found about nine red–green color-blind boys for every one such girl, but it also found marked variation in overall rates (3 to 7 percent) from one group to another (Fareed et al., 2015).

🔵🟢 **Answer to Observation Quiz** (from page 75): Ellie has a gene for achondroplasia, the most common form of dwarfism, which affects her limb growth, making her a little person. Because of her parents and her sister, she is likely to have a long and accomplished life: Problems are less likely to come from her genotype than from how other people perceive her phenotype.

X-linked A gene carried on the X chromosome. If a male inherits an X-linked recessive trait from his mother, he expresses that trait because the Y from his father has no counteracting gene. Females are more likely to be carriers of X-linked traits but are less likely to express them.

THINK CRITICALLY: If a woman has a color-blind brother, will her sons be color-blind?

TABLE 3.1	The 23rd Pair and X-Linked Color Blindness		
23rd Pair	Phenotype	Genotype	Next Generation
1. XX	Normal woman	Not a carrier	No color blindness from mother
2. XY	Normal man	Normal X from mother	No color blindness from father
3. ⊗X	Normal woman	Carrier from father	Half of her children will inherit her ⊗. The girls with her ⊗ will be carriers; the boys with her ⊗ will be color-blind.
4. X⊗	Normal woman	Carrier from mother	Half of her children will inherit her ⊗. The girls with her ⊗ will be carriers; the boys with her ⊗ will be color-blind.
5. ⊗Y	Color-blind man	Inherited from mother	All of his daughters will have his ⊗. None of his sons will have his X. All of his children will have normal vision unless their mother also had an ⊗ for color blindness.
6. ⊗⊗	Color-blind woman (rare)	Inherited from both parents	Every child will have one ⊗ from her. Therefore, every son will be color-blind. Daughters will only be carriers unless they also inherit an ⊗ from the father, as their mother did.

⊗ = X that carries recessive gene for color-blindness

Nature and Nurture

One goal of this chapter is to help every reader grasp the complex interaction between genotype and phenotype. This is not easy. For decades, in many nations, millions of scientists have struggled to understand this complexity. Each year brings advances in statistics and molecular analysis, new data to uncover various patterns, all resulting in hypotheses to be explored.

Now we examine two complex traits: addiction and visual acuity, in two specific manifestations, alcohol use disorder and nearsightedness. As you will see, understanding the progression from genotype to phenotype has many practical implications.

Alcohol Use Disorder

At various times throughout history, people have considered the abuse of alcohol and other drugs to be a moral weakness, a social scourge, or a personality defect. Historically and internationally, the main focus has been on alcohol, since people everywhere discovered fermentation thousands of years ago. Alcohol has been declared illegal (as in the United States from 1919 to 1933) or considered sacred (as in many Judeo-Christian rituals), and those with the disorder have been jailed, jeered, or burned at the stake.

We now know that inherited biochemistry affects alcohol metabolism. Punishing those with the genes does not stop addiction. There is no single "alcoholic gene," but alleles that make alcoholism more likely have been identified on every chromosome except the Y (Epps & Holt, 2011).

To be more specific, alleles create an addictive pull that can be overpowering, extremely weak, or somewhere in between. Each person's biochemistry reacts to alcohol by causing sleep, nausea, aggression, joy, relaxation, forgetfulness, sex urges, or tears. If metabolism allows people to "hold their liquor," they might drink too much; others (including many East Asians) might sweat and become red-faced after just a few sips. That embarrassing response may lead to abstinence. This inherited "flushing" tendency not only makes alcohol addiction rare, but it also improves metabolism (Kuwahara et al., 2014).

Although genes for biological addiction were the focus of early research, we now know that inherited personality traits (including a quick temper, sensation seeking, and high anxiety) may be pivotal (Macgregor et al., 2009). Social contexts

Welcome Home For many women in the United States, white wine is part of the celebration and joy of a house party, as shown here. Most people can drink alcohol harmlessly; there is no sign that these women are problem drinkers. However, danger lurks. Women get drunk on less alcohol than men, and females with alcohol use disorder tend to drink more privately and secretly, often at home, feeling more shame than bravado. All that makes their addiction more difficult to recognize.

Hero Images Inc./Alamy

matter as well. Some (such as fraternity parties) make it hard to avoid alcohol; others (such as a church social in a "dry" county) make it difficult to swallow anything stronger than lemonade.

Sex (biological—either XX or XY) and gender (cultural) have an impact. For biological reasons (body size, fat composition, metabolism), women become drunk on less alcohol than men. Heavy-drinking females double their risk of mortality compared to heavy-drinking males (Wang et al., 2014). Gender matters also. Many cultures encourage men to drink but not women (Chartier et al., 2014).

Nearsightedness

Age, genes, and culture affect vision as well. The effects of age are easy to notice. Newborns focus only on things within 1 to 3 feet of their eyes; vision improves steadily until about age 10. The eyeball changes shape at puberty, increasing myopia (nearsightedness), and again in middle age, decreasing myopia. The effects of genes and culture on eyesight are more complex.

A study of British twins found that the *Pax6* gene, which governs eye formation, has many alleles that make people somewhat nearsighted (Hammond et al., 2004). That study found almost 90 percent heritability of myopia, so if one monozygotic twin was nearsighted, the other twin was almost always nearsighted, too.

However, **heritability** indicates only how much of the variation in a particular trait, *within a particular population, in a particular context and era* can be traced to genes. For example, the heritability of height is very high (about 95 percent) when children receive good medical care and nutrition, but it is low (about 20 percent) when children are severely malnourished. Children who are chronically underfed are quite short, no matter what their genes. Thus, the British finding of 90 percent heritability of nearsightedness may not be universal.

Indeed, it is not. In some African and Asian communities, vision heritability is close to 0 because some children are severely deprived of vitamin A. For them, eyesight depends less on nature (genes) than nurture: "Because of vitamin A deficiency, more than 250,000 children become blind every year, and half of them die within a year of losing their sight" (Ehrenberg, 2016, p. 25).

Scientists have engineered new strains of the local staples (maize or rice) that are high in vitamin A, and in some nations (Zambia and Cameroon), vitamin A is added to cooking oil and sugar. Added vitamins must be carefully done—excessive, nonfood vitamin A may cause problems, but the consequences are far less serious than the blindness that is prevented (Tanumihardjo et al., 2016).

What about children who are well nourished? Is their vision entirely inherited? Cross-cultural research suggests that it is not (Seppa, 2013a).

One report claimed that "myopia is increasing at an 'epidemic' rate, particularly in East Asia" (Park & Congdon, 2004, p. 21). The first published research on this phenomenon appeared in 1992, when scholars noticed that in army-mandated medical exams of all 17-year-old males in Singapore in 1980, 26 percent were nearsighted but 43 percent were nearsighted in 1990 (Tay et al., 1992).

An article in the leading British medical journal (*The Lancet*) suggests that although genes are to blame for most cases of severe myopia, "any genetic differences may be small" for the common nearsightedness of Asian schoolchildren (I. Morgan et al., 2012, p. 1739). Nurture must somehow be involved. But how?

One possible culprit is homework. As Chapter 12 describes, contemporary East Asian children are amazingly proficient in math and science. Fifty years ago, most Asian children were working; now almost all are diligent students. As their developing eyes focus on their books, those with a genetic vulnerability to myopia may lose acuity for objects far away—which is exactly what nearsightedness means.

Especially for Drug Counselors Is the wish for excitement likely to lead to addiction? (see response, page 81)

Answer to Observation Quiz (from page 77): This is a figure drawn to illustrate the recessive inheritance of blue eyes, and thus eyes are the only difference shown. If this were a real family, each child would have a distinct appearance.

heritability A statistic that indicates what percentage of the variation in a particular trait within a particular population, in a particular context and era, can be traced to genes.

Response for Future Parents (from page 76: Possibly, but you wouldn't want to. You would have to choose one mate for your sons and another for your daughters, and you would have to use sex-selection methods. Even so, it might not work, given all the genes on your genotype. More important, the effort would be unethical, unnatural, and possibly illegal.

Applauding Success These eager young men are freshmen at the opening convocation of Shanghai Jiao Tong University. They have studied hard in high school, scoring high on the national college entrance exam. Now their education is heavily subsidized by the government. Although China has more college students than the United States, the proportions are far lower, since the population of China is more than four times that of the United States.

Observation Quiz Name three visible attributes of these young men that differ from a typical group of freshmen in North America. (see answer, page 83) ↑

A study of Singaporean 10- to 12-year-olds found a positive correlation between nearsightedness (measured by optometric exams) and high achievement, especially in language proficiency (presumably reflecting more reading). Correlation is not proof, but the odds ratio was 2:5 and the significance was 0.001, which makes these data impossible to ignore (Saw et al., 2007). Data from the United States on children playing sports have led some ophthalmologists to suggest that the underlying cause is not time spent studying but inadequate time spent in daylight (I. Morgan et al., 2012). Perhaps if children spent more time outside playing, walking, or relaxing, fewer would need glasses.

Between the early 1970s and the early 2000s, nearsightedness in the U.S. population increased from 25 to 42 percent (Vitale et al., 2009). Urbanization, television, and fear of strangers have kept many U.S. children indoors most of the time, unlike children of earlier generations who played outside for hours each day. One ophthalmologist comments that "we're kind of a dim indoors people nowadays" (Mutti, quoted in Holden, 2010, p. 17). Formerly, genetically vulnerable children did not necessarily become nearsighted; now they do.

Practical Applications

Since genes affect every disorder, no one should be blamed or punished for inherited problems. However, knowing that genes never act in isolation allows prevention after birth. For instance, if alcohol use disorder is in the genes, parents can keep alcohol out of their home, hoping their children become cognitively and socially mature before imbibing. If nearsightedness runs in the family, parents can play outdoors with their children every day.

Of course, playing outdoors and avoiding alcohol are recommended for all children, as are dozens of other behaviors, such as flossing twice a day, saying "please," sleeping 10 hours each night, eating five servings of vegetables a day, and promptly writing thank-you notes. No parent can enforce every recommendation, but awareness of genetic risks can guide priorities.

A CASE TO STUDY

Mickey Mantle

Ignoring the nature–nurture interaction can be lethal. Consider baseball superstar Mickey Mantle, who hit more home runs (18) in World Series baseball than any other player before or since. Most of his male relatives were addicted to alcohol and died before middle age, including his father, who died of Hodgkin's disease (a form of cancer) at age 39.

Mantle became "a notorious alcoholic [because he] believed a family history of early mortality meant he too would die young" (Jaffe, 2004, p. 37). He ignored his genetic predisposition to alcohol use disorder.

At age 46 Mantle said, "If I knew I was going to live this long, I would have taken better care of myself." He never devel-

oped Hodgkin's disease, and if he had, chemotherapy that had been discovered since his father's death would likely have saved him—an example of environment prevailing over genes.

However, drinking destroyed Mantle's liver. He understood too late what he had done. When he was dying, he told his fans at Yankee Stadium: "Please don't do drugs and alcohol. God gave us only one body, and keep it healthy. If you want to do something great, be an organ donor" (quoted in Begos, 2010). Despite a last-minute liver transplant, he died at age 63—15 years younger than most men of his time.

WHAT HAVE YOU LEARNED?

1. Why do humans vary so much in skin color and height?

2. What is the difference between additive and dominant–recessive inheritance?

3. Why don't children always look like their parents?

4. Why are sons more likely to inherit recessive conditions from their mothers instead of their fathers?

5. What genes increase the risk of alcohol use disorder?

6. What suggests that nearsightedness is affected by nurture?

7. What does *heritability* mean?

● Response for Drug Counselors
(from page 79): Maybe. Some people who love risk become addicts; others develop a healthy lifestyle that includes adventure, new people, and exotic places. Any trait can lead in various directions. You need to be aware of the connections so that you can steer your clients toward healthy adventures.

Chromosomal and Genetic Problems

We now focus on conditions caused by an extra chromosome or a single destructive gene. Each person has about 40 alleles that *could* cause serious disease—including some very common ones such as strokes, heart disease, and cancer—but most of those require at least two SNPs, plus particular environmental conditions, before they appear.

If all notable anomalies and disorders are included, 92 percent of people do <u>not</u> develop a serious genetic condition by early adulthood—but that means 8 percent have a serious condition in their phenotype as well as their genotype (Chong et al., 2015). Study of such problems is relevant because:

1. They provide insight into the complexities of nature and nurture.
2. Knowing their origins helps avoid or limit their effects.
3. Information combats prejudice: Difference is not always deficit.

Not Exactly 46

As you know, each sperm or ovum usually has 23 chromosomes, creating a zygote with 46 chromosomes and eventually a person. However, sperm and ova do not always split exactly in half to make gametes. The parents' ages correlate with chromosomal abnormalities, particularly the age of the mother, whose ova began development before she was born. Sperm also are diminished in quantity and normality as men age, although, since men typically release more than 100 million sperm in sex, usually the sperm with 23 chromosomes reach the ova first.

Miscounts are not rare, however. About half of all zygotes have more than or fewer than 46 chromosomes (Milunsky & Milunsky 2016). Almost all of them fail to duplicate, divide, differentiate, and implant, or they are spontaneously aborted before anyone knows that conception occurred.

If implantation does occur, many embryos with chromosomal miscounts are aborted, either by nature (miscarried) or by choice. Ninety-nine percent of fetuses that survive until birth have the usual 46 chromosomes, but for the remaining 1 percent, birth is hazardous. Only 1 newborn in 166 births survives with 45, 47, or, rarely, 48 or 49 chromosomes (Benn, 2016).

Survival is more common if some cells have 46 chromosomes and some 47, (a condition called *mosaicism*), or if only a piece of a chromosome is missing or extra. Advanced analysis suggests that mosaicism of some sort "may represent the rule rather than the exception" (Lupski, 2013, p. 358). Usually this has no detectable effect on development, although cancer is more likely with extra or missing genetic material.

Down Syndrome

If an entire chromosome is missing or added, that leads to a recognizable *syndrome*, a cluster of distinct characteristics that tend to occur together. Usually the cause is three chromosomes at a particular location instead of the usual two

LaunchPad
macmillan learning

Video: Genetic Disorders
http://qrs.ly/pg4eoxw

Monkey Business Images/Shutterstock

Down syndrome A condition in which a person has 47 chromosomes instead of the usual 46, with 3 rather than 2 chromosomes at the 21st site. People with Down syndrome typically have distinctive characteristics, including unusual facial features, heart abnormalities, and language difficulties. (Also called *trisomy-21*.)

REUTERS/Claudia Daut

Universal Happiness All young children delight in painting brightly colored pictures on a big canvas, but this scene is unusual for two reasons: Daniel has trisomy-21, and this photograph was taken at the only school in Chile where typical children and those with special needs share classrooms.

◉ Observation Quiz How many characteristics can you see that indicate Daniel has Down syndrome? (see answer, page 84) ↑

(a condition called a *trisomy*). The most common extra-chromosome condition that results in a surviving child is **Down syndrome,** also called *trisomy-21* because the person has three copies of chromosome 21.

Some 300 distinct characteristics can result from three chromosomes at site 21. No individual with Down syndrome is identical to another, but trisomy usually produces specific physical characteristics—a thick tongue, round face, and slanted eyes, as well as distinctive hands, feet, and fingerprints.

Many people with Down syndrome also have hearing problems, heart abnormalities, muscle weakness, and short stature. They are usually slower to develop intellectually, especially in language, with a notable deficit in hearing sounds that rhyme (Næss, 2016). That extra chromosome affects the person lifelong, but family context, education, and possibly medication can decrease the harm (Kuehn, 2011).

Problems of the 23rd Pair

Every human has at least 44 autosomes and one X chromosome; an embryo cannot develop without those 45. However, about 1 in every 300 infants is born with only one sex chromosome (no Y) or with three or more (not just two) (Benn, 2016); each particular combination of sex chromosomes results in specific syndromes (see Table 3.2).

Having an odd number of sex chromosomes impairs cognition and sexual maturation, with varied specifics depending on epigenetics (Hong & Reiss, 2014). It is not unusual for an affected person to seem to be developing typically until they find that they are infertile, a problem more common in men than women. Then diagnosis reveals the undetected problem.

Gene Disorders

Everyone carries alleles that *could* produce serious diseases or disabilities in the next generation. Most such genes have no serious consequences because they are recessive. The phenotype is affected only when the inherited gene is dominant or when a zygote is homozygous for a particular recessive condition, that is, when the zygote has received the same recessive gene from both parents.

Dominant Disorders

Most of the 7,000 *known* single-gene disorders are dominant (always expressed) (Milunsky & Milunsky, 2016). Severe dominant disorders are infrequent because

TABLE 3.2	Common Abnormalities Involving the Sex Chromosomes		
Chromosomal Pattern	Physical Appearance	Psychological Characteristics	Incidence*
XXY (Klinefelter Syndrome)	Males. Usual male characteristics at puberty do not develop—penis does not grow, voice does not deepen. Usually sterile. Breasts may develop.	Can have some learning disabilities, especially in language skills.	1 in 700 males
XYY (Jacob's Syndrome)	Males. Typically tall.	Risk of intellectual impairment, especially in language skills.	1 in 1,000 males
XXX (Triple X Syndrome)	Females. Normal appearance.	Impaired in most intellectual skills.	1 in 1,000 females
XO (only one sex chromosome) (Turner Syndrome)	Females. Short, often "webbed" neck. Secondary sex characteristics (breasts, menstruation) do not develop.	Some learning disabilities, especially related to math and spatial understanding; difficulty recognizing facial expressions of emotion.	1 in 6,000 females

*Incidence is approximate at birth.
Information from Hamerton & Evans, 2005; Aksglaede et al., 2013; Powell, 2013; Benn, 2016.

people with such disorders usually die in childhood and thus the gene is not passed on to the next generation.

Dominant disorders become common only when they are latent in childhood. That is the usual case with *Huntington's disease,* a fatal central nervous system disorder caused by a copy number variation—more than 35 repetitions of a particular set of three base pairs. Although children with the dominant gene sometimes are affected (Milunsky & Milunsky, 2016), symptoms usually first appear in midlife, when a person could have had several children, as did the original Mr. Huntington. Half of his children inherited his dominant gene, which is why the disease is named after him.

Another exception to the general rule that serious dominant diseases are not inherited is a rare but severe form of Alzheimer's disease. It causes major neurocognitive disorder (formerly called *dementia*) before age 60. (Most forms of Alzheimer's begin after age 70 and are not dominant.) [**Life-Span Link:** Alzheimer's disease and other neurocognitive disorders are discussed in Chapter 24.]

Recessive Disorders

Recessive diseases are more numerous because they are passed down from one generation to the next by carriers who are unaware of their genotype. Most recessive disorders are on the autosomes and thus are not X-linked (Milunsky & Milunsky, 2016). Carrier detection is possible for about 500, and diagnosis of the actual disorder is possible for many more, creating an ethical dilemma. Should someone be told about a genetic disorder if no treatment is available and if the knowledge will not change anything?

Some recessive conditions are X-linked, including hemophilia, Duchenne muscular dystrophy, and **fragile X syndrome,** the last of which is caused by more than 200 repetitions on one gene (Plomin et al., 2013). (Some repetitions are normal, but not this many.) The cognitive deficits caused by fragile X syndrome are the most common form of *inherited* intellectual disability. (Many other forms, such as trisomy-21, are not usually inherited.) Boys are much more often impaired by fragile X than are girls, again because they have only one X.

The Most Common Recessive Disorders

About 1 in 12 North American men and women carries an allele for cystic fibrosis, thalassemia, or sickle-cell disease, all devastating in children of both sexes. These conditions are common because carriers have benefited from the gene.

Consider the most studied example: sickle-cell disease. Carriers of the sickle-cell gene die less often from malaria, which is prevalent and lethal in parts of Africa. Indeed, four distinct alleles cause sickle-cell disease, each originating in a malaria-prone region.

Selective adaptation allowed the gene to become widespread because it protected more people (the carriers) than it killed (those who inherited the recessive gene from both parents). Odds were that if a couple were both carriers and had four children, one would die of sickle-cell disease, one would not be a carrier and thus might die of malaria, but two would be carriers. They would be protected against a common, fatal disease. Consequently, they would likely become parents themselves. In that way, the recessive trait became widespread.

Almost every disease and risk of death is more common in one group than in another (Weiss & Koepsell, 2014). About 11 percent of Americans with African ancestors are carriers of sickle-cell disease; cystic fibrosis is more common among Americans with ancestors from northern Europe because carriers may have been protected from cholera. Dark skin is protective against skin cancer,

Especially for Teachers Suppose you know that one of your students has a sibling who has Down syndrome. What special actions should you take? (see response, page 84)

Especially for Future Doctors Might a patient who is worried about his or her sexuality have an undiagnosed abnormality of the sex chromosome? (see response, page 84)

LaunchPad
macmillan learning

Visit the Data Connections activity **Common Genetic Diseases and Conditions** to learn more about several different types of gene disorders.

fragile X syndrome A genetic disorder in which part of the X chromosome seems to be attached to the rest of it by a very thin string of molecules. The cause is a single gene that has more than 200 repetitions of one triplet.

Answer to Observation Quiz (from page 80): Glasses, not nearsightedness! Rates of corrective lenses (estimated at 85 percent) are as high among university students in the United States, but Americans are more likely to wear contacts. Two other visible differences: uniforms and gender. Except for the military, no U.S. university issues uniforms and the majority of North American students are women. A fourth difference may be inferred from their attentiveness: The graduation rate of incoming college students in China is about 90 percent, compared to about 50 percent in the United States.

and light skin allows more vitamin D to be absorbed from the sun—a benefit if a baby lives where sunlight is scarce.

Genetic Counseling and Testing

Until recently, after the birth of a child with a severe disorder, couples blamed witches or fate, not genes or chromosomes. That has changed, with many young adults concerned about their genes long before parenthood. Virtually everyone has a relative with a serious condition and wonders what their children will inherit.

Knowing the entire genome of a particular individual takes extensive analysis, but the cost has plummeted in recent years from more than a million dollars to less than a thousand. The results sometimes help find the best treatment for a disease, but experts hesitate to recommend full genome screening because most SNPs are "variants of unknown significance" (Couzin-Frankel, 2016, p. 442). In other words, it is not hard for a technician to find something unusual, but no one knows what all the oddities signify.

Some people pay for commercial genetic testing, which often provides misleading information. From the perspective of genetic counselors, a worse problem with commercial testing is that the emotional needs of the person are not addressed. For instance, some people who *might* be carriers of Huntington's disease commit suicide—before symptoms appear, and without treatment that might reduce symptoms and allow years of normal life (Dayalu & Albin, 2015).

Psychological Disorders

Misinformation and mistaken fears are particularly destructive for psychological disorders, such as depression, schizophrenia, and autism spectrum disorder. No doubt genes are a factor in all of these conditions (Plomin et al., 2013). Yet, as with addiction and vision, the environment is crucial—not only what the parents do but also what communities and governments do.

This was confirmed by a study of the entire population of Denmark, where good medical records and decades of free public health make research accurate. If both Danish parents developed schizophrenia, 27 percent of their children developed it; if one parent had it, 7 percent of their children developed it. These same statistics can be presented in another way: Even if both parents developed the disease, almost three-fourths (73 percent) of their children never did (Gottesman et al., 2010). (Some of them developed other psychological disorders, again providing evidence for epigenetics.)

Even more persuasive is evidence for monozygotic twins. If one identical twin develops schizophrenia, often—but not always—the other twin also develops a psychological disorder. Two conclusions are obvious: (1) genes are powerful and (2) schizophrenia is not entirely genetic.

Numerous studies have identified environmental influences on schizophrenia, including fetal malnutrition, birth in the summer, adolescent use of psychoactive drugs, emigration in young adulthood, and family emotionality during adulthood.

Because environment is crucial, few scientists advocate genetic testing for schizophrenia or any psychological condition. They fear that a positive test would lead to depression and stress, factors that might cause a disorder that would not have occurred otherwise. Further, a positive genetic diagnosis might add to discrimination against the mentally ill (Mitchell et al., 2010).

The Need for Counseling

The problems with testing for genes that cause mental disorders are only one of several complications that might emerge. Scientists—and the general public—have

LaunchPad
macmillan learning

Video: Genetic Testing examines the pros and cons of knowing what diseases may eventually harm us or our offspring.

wavebreakmedia/Shutterstock

● ● **Answer to Observation Quiz** (from page 82): Individuals with Down syndrome vary in many traits, but visible here are five common ones. Compared to most children his age, including his classmate beside him, Daniel has a rounder face, narrower eyes, shorter stature, larger teeth and tongue, and—best of all—a happier temperament.

● ● **Response for Teachers** (from page 83): As the text says, "information combats prejudice." Your first step would be to make sure you know about Down syndrome, reading material about it. You would learn, among other things, that it is not usually inherited (your student need not worry about his or her progeny) and that some children with Down syndrome need extra medical and educational attention. This might mean that you need to pay special attention to your student, whose parents might focus on the sibling.

● ● **Response for Future Doctors** (from page 83): That is highly unlikely. Chromosomal abnormalities are evident long before adulthood. It is quite normal for adults to be worried about sexuality for social, not biological, reasons. You could test the karyotype, but that may be needlessly alarmist.

many opinions about genetic testing, and nations have varying policies (Plows, 2011). The problem is that science has revealed much more about genes than anyone imagined a decade ago. Laws and ethics have not kept up with the possibilities, and very few prospective parents can interpret their own genetic history or laboratory results without help.

Some prospective parents seek abortion or sterilization to avoid a disease that is rare; others blithely give birth to one impaired child after another. Legally and ethically in the United States, genetic counselors believe that everyone has "a right to know," but counselors also realize that, in the emotional stress of hearing about their genes, clients misunderstand and misinterpret.

Professionals who have been trained to provide **genetic counseling** help prospective parents understand their genetic risk so that they can make informed decisions. The genetic counselor's task is complicated for many reasons. One is that every week reveals not only new genetic disorders but also new treatments for the disorders that are recognized. A second is that testing is now possible for hundreds of conditions, but accuracy varies. Sometimes a particular gene increases the risk of a problem by only a tiny amount, perhaps 0.1 percent.

Even doctors do not always understand genetics. Consider the experience of one of my students. A month before she became pregnant, Jeannette was required to have a rubella vaccination for her job. Hearing that Jeannette had had the shot, her prenatal care doctor gave her the following prognosis:

> My baby would be born with many defects, his ears would not be normal, he would be intellectually disabled. . . . I went home and cried for hours and hours. . . . I finally went to see a genetic counselor. Everything was fine, thank the Lord, thank you, my beautiful baby is okay.

[Jeannette, personal communication]

It is possible that Jeannette misunderstood what she was told, but that is exactly why the doctor should not have spoken. Genetic counselors are trained to make information clear. If sensitive counseling is available, then preconception, prenatal, or even prenuptial (before marriage) testing is especially useful for:

- individuals who have a parent, sibling, or child with a serious genetic condition
- couples who have had several spontaneous abortions or stillbirths
- couples who are infertile
- couples from the same ethnic group, particularly if they are relatives
- women over age 35 and men over age 40

Genetic counselors follow two ethical rules: (1) Tests are confidential, beyond the reach of insurance companies and public records, and (2) decisions are made by the clients, not by the counselors.

However, these guidelines are not always easy to follow (A. Parker, 2012). One quandary arises when parents already have a child with a recessive disease but tests reveal that the husband does not carry that gene. Should the counselor tell the couple that their next child will not have this disease because the husband is not the biological father of the first?

Another quandary arises when DNA is collected for one purpose—say, to assess the risk of sickle-cell disease—and analysis reveals another quite different problem, such as an extra sex chromosome or a high risk of breast cancer. This problem is new: Even a few years ago, testing was so expensive that it focused on only the feared and named condition. Now counselors learn about thousands of conditions that were not suspected. If no treatment is available, must the person be told?

genetic counseling Consultation and testing by trained experts that enables individuals to learn about their genetic heritage, including harmful conditions that they might pass along to any children they may conceive.

Who Has the Fatal Dominant Disease? The mother, but not the children. Unless a cure is found, Amanda Kalinsky will grow weak and experience significant cognitive decline, dying before age 60. She and her husband, Bradley, wanted children without Amanda's dominant gene for a rare disorder, Gerstmann-Straussler-Scheinker disease. Accordingly, they used IVF and pre-implantation testing. Only zygotes without the dominant gene were implanted. This photo shows the happy result.

Nathan Morgan/The New York Times/Redux

Reach for the Sky Gavin and Jake Barker both have cystic fibrosis, which would have meant early death had they been born 50 years ago. Now their parents pound on their chests twice a day to loosen phlegm— and they can enjoy jumping on the trampoline while wearing special pneumatic vests under their shirts.

THINK CRITICALLY: Instead of genetic counseling, should we advocate health counseling?

The current consensus is that information should be shared if:

1. the person wants to hear it
2. the risk is severe and verified
3. an experienced counselor explains the data
4. treatment is available

That is not as straightforward as it appears. Scientists and physicians disagree about severity, certainty, and treatment. A group of experts recently advocated informing patients of any serious genetic disorder, even when the person does not want to know and when the information might be harmful (Couzin-Frankel, 2013a).

An added complication is that individuals differ in their willingness to hear bad news. What if one person wants to know but other family members—perhaps a parent or a monozygotic twin who has the same condition—do not? We all are carriers. Do we all want specifics?

Sometimes couples make a decision (such as to begin or to abort a pregnancy) that reflects a mistaken calculation of the risk, at least as the professional interprets it (A. Parker, 2012). Even with careful counseling, people with identical genetic conditions often make opposite choices.

For instance, 108 women who already had one child with fragile X syndrome were told that they had a 50 percent chance of having another such child. Most (77 percent) decided to avoid pregnancy with sterilization or excellent contraception, but some (20 percent) deliberately had another child (Raspberry & Skinner, 2011). Always the professional explains probabilities; always the clients decide.

Many developmentalists stress that changes in the environment, not in the genes, are more likely to improve health. In fact, some believe that the twenty-first-century emphasis on genes is a way to avoid focusing on poverty, pollution, pesticides, and so on, even though such factors cause more health problems than genes do (Plows, 2011). A wise genetic counselor notes the many factors in nature and nurture that are relevant, writes a letter explaining the genetic facts and future possibilities, and follows up months and years later to find out what needs more explanation.

As you have read many times in this chapter, genes are part of the human story, influencing every page, but they do not determine the plot or the final paragraph. The remaining chapters describe the rest of the story.

WHAT HAVE YOU LEARNED?

1. What chromosomal miscounts might result in a surviving child?
2. What is the cause and consequence of Down syndrome?
3. How common are recessive conditions?
4. Why is sickle-cell disease very common in some parts of Africa?
5. What is the role of the genetic counselor?
6. What ethical mandates are required of genetic counselors?

SUMMARY

The Genetic Code

1. Genes are the foundation for all development, first instructing the developing creature to form the body and brain, and then affecting thought, behavior, and health lifelong. Human conception occurs when two gametes (a sperm with 23 chromosomes and an ovum with 23 chromosomes) combine to form a single cell called a zygote.

2. A zygote usually has 46 chromosomes (half from each parent), which carry a total of about 20,000 genes. Genes and chromosomes from each parent match up to make the zygote, but the match is not always letter-perfect because of genetic variations called alleles, or polymorphisms.

3. Genetic variations occur in many ways, from the chromosomes of the parent to the epigenetic material surrounding the zygote and the microbiome of every body part. Spontaneous mutations, changing the number or sequences of base pairs, also make each person unique.

4. The most notable mismatch is in the 23rd pair of chromosomes, which is XX in females and XY in males. The sex of the embryo depends on the sperm, since only men have a Y chromosome and thus can make Y gametes.

New Cells, New People

5. The first duplications of the one-celled zygote create stem cells, each of which could become a person if it developed. Monozygotic twins occur if those first stem cells split completely, which rarely occurs. Usually the cluster of cells continues dividing and duplicating throughout development, creating a baby with 26 billion cells and eventually an adult with 37 trillion cells.

6. Dizygotic twins occur if two ova are fertilized by two sperm at about the same time. Genetically, they have half their genes in common, as do all full siblings.

7. In vitro fertilization (IVF) has led to millions of much-wanted babies and also to an increase in multiple births, who often are preterm and of low birthweight. Ethical concerns regarding IVF have quieted, but new dilemmas appear with stem cells and CRISPR.

From Genotype to Phenotype

8. Genes interact in many ways, sometimes additively with each gene contributing to development and sometimes in a dominant–recessive pattern. The environment interacts with the genetic instructions for every trait, making every characteristic polygenic and multifactorial.

9. Genetic makeup can make a person susceptible to many conditions. Examples include substance use disorder (especially alcohol use disorder) and poor vision (especially nearsightedness). Culture and family affect both of these conditions dramatically.

10. Knowing the impact of genes and the environment can help in several ways, including guiding parents to protect their children from potentially harmful genes.

Chromosomal and Genetic Problems

11. Often a gamete has fewer or more than 23 chromosomes, which may create a zygote with 45, 47, or 48 chromosomes. Usually such zygotes do not duplicate, implant, or grow.

12. Infants may survive if they have three chromosomes at the 21st site (Down syndrome) or extra sex chromosomes. They may have intellectual and sexual problems, but they may have a fulfilling life.

13. Everyone is a carrier for genetic abnormalities. Usually these conditions are recessive, not apparent unless the mother and the father both carry the gene. Serious dominant disorders usually do not appear until midlife. Serious recessive diseases can become common if carriers have a health advantage.

14. Genetic testing and counseling can help many couples. Testing provides information about possibilities, but the final decision rests with the couple.

KEY TERMS

deoxyribonucleic acid (DNA) (p. 64)
chromosome (p. 64)
gene (p. 64)
genome (p. 64)
allele (p. 65)
epigenetics (p. 65)
microbiome (p. 65)
zygote (p. 66)

copy number variations (p. 66)
genotype (p. 67)
homozygous (p. 67)
heterozygous (p. 67)
23rd pair (p. 67)
XY (p. 78)
XX (p. 78)
stem cells (p. 71)
in vitro fertilization (IVF) (p. 71)

monozygotic (MZ) twins (p. 72)
dizygotic (DZ) twins (p. 74)
phenotype (p. 75)
polygenic (p. 75)
multifactorial (p. 75)
Human Genome Project (p. 76)
dominant–recessive pattern (p. 76)

carrier (p. 76)
X-linked (p. 77)
heritability (p. 79)
Down syndrome (p. 82)
fragile X syndrome (p. 83)
genetic counseling (p. 85)

APPLICATIONS

1. Pick one of your traits, and explain the influences that both nature *and* nurture have on it. For example, if you have a short temper, explain its origins in your genetics, your culture, and your childhood experiences.

2. Many adults have a preference for having a son or a daughter. Interview adults of several ages and backgrounds about their preferences. If they give the socially preferable answer ("It does not matter"), ask how they think the two sexes differ. Listen and take notes—don't debate. Analyze the implications of the responses you get.

3. Draw a genetic chart of your biological relatives, going back as many generations as you can, listing all serious illnesses and causes of death. Include ancestors who died in infancy. Do you see any genetic susceptibility? If so, how can you overcome it?

4. Given what is known about the genetics of substance use disorders, ask several people how addiction can be prevented. Discuss why answers differ.

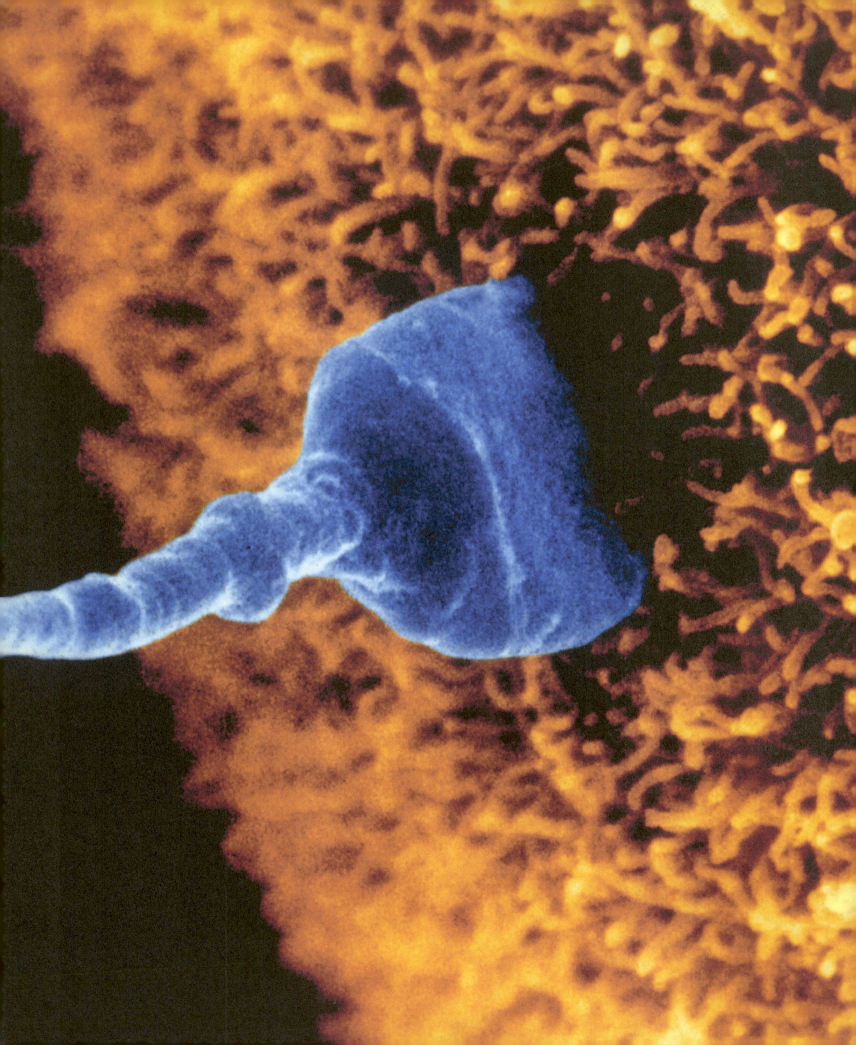

Prenatal Development and Birth

What Will You Know?

1. Why do most zygotes never become babies?
2. Ideally, should all births occur in hospitals?
3. What can a pregnant woman do to ensure a healthy newborn?
4. Why do new mothers and fathers sometimes become severely depressed?

My daughter Elissa had a second child. At 6 A.M. she and her husband were in the labor room of the birthing center; I was with Asa, age 5, in the family waiting room. Several times Asa walked down the hall to see his parents. Usually the midwife opened the labor room door to let us in; Elissa smiled and asked Asa how he was doing. Sometimes we waited until a contraction was over. Then parents and son greeted each other again.

When the baby was born, a nurse came to say, "There's a new person who wants to meet you."

"Let me put this last Lego piece in," Asa said. He then brought his new creation to show his parents, who introduced him to his brother, Isaac, sucking on his mother's breast.

The scientific study of human development is not only about how individuals change over time, it is about historical change—Bronfenbrenner's chronosystem. We will explore many aspects of historical and cultural variations in pregnancy and birth in this chapter, the thought of which struck me forcefully when I remembered the births of my children and witnessed those of my grandchildren.

To be specific, the contrast between Isaac's birth in 2014 and Elissa's own arrival is stark. Back then, midwives were banned and fathers were relegated to waiting rooms, as my husband, Martin, had been for our first two babies. Newly inspired by feminism, I convinced my obstetrician to let Martin stay with me. He wept when he held Elissa, wet and wide-eyed, moments old. Then she was wiped, weighed, wrapped, and wheeled away.

The nurses did not let me touch my daughter until she was 24 hours old. They said that I had no milk, that I needed rest, that she was tired too. By contrast, six hours after Isaac was born, the entire family was home again. Elissa's sister, Sarah, came over; we ordered take-out dinner and I left the new family by 6 P.M. I know that my experience is limited—Elissa and Isaac were born in the same city within a few decades of each other. Millions of other newborns arrive in homes—as did my own mother—often with no trained attendant.

This chapter describes what we now know about prenatal growth and birth, and some of the vast differences from one era, one culture, even one family to another. Possible harm is noted: causes and consequences of diseases,

Left: David M. Phillips/Science Source
Top: shapecharge/E+/Getty Images

malnutrition, drugs, pollution, stress. Fathers, particularly, have become more active partners, and all of us—medical professionals, governments, and family members—affect the early life of each developing person. You will understand many recent changes in prenatal development and birth—not always improvements.

Prenatal Development

The most dramatic and extensive transformation of the life span occurs before birth. To make it easier to study, prenatal development is often divided into three main periods. The first two weeks are called the **germinal period;** the third week through the eighth week is the **embryonic period;** from then until birth is the **fetal period.** (Alternative terms are presented in Table 4.1.)

Germinal: The First 14 Days

You learned in Chapter 3 that the one-celled zygote duplicates, divides, and multiplies. Soon after the 16-cell stage, differentiation begins: The early cells take on distinct characteristics. About a week after conception, the mass of about 100 cells, called a *blastocyst,* forms two distinct parts—a shell that will become the *placenta* and a nucleus that will become the embryo.

The placenta, an understudied "throwaway organ" (Kaiser, 2014a, p. 1073), must achieve **implantation**—that is, it must embed into the nurturing lining of the uterus (see Figure 4.1). This process is far from automatic; more than half of natural conceptions and an even larger proportion of in vitro conceptions never implant, usually because of a chromosomal abnormality (Niakan et al., 2012). Most new life ends before an embryo begins (see Table 4.2).

germinal period The first two weeks of prenatal development after conception, characterized by rapid cell division and the beginning of cell differentiation.

embryonic period The stage of prenatal development from approximately the third week through the eighth week after conception, during which the basic forms of all body structures, including internal organs, develop.

fetal period The stage of prenatal development from the ninth week after conception until birth, during which the fetus gains about 7 pounds (more than 3,000 grams) and organs become more mature, gradually able to function on their own.

implantation The process, beginning about 10 days after conception, in which the developing organism burrows into the uterus, where it can be nourished and protected as it continues to develop.

TABLE 4.1	**Timing and Terminology**

Popular and professional books use various phrases to segment the stages of pregnancy. The following comments may help to clarify the phrases used.

- *Beginning of pregnancy:* Pregnancy begins at conception, which is also the starting point of *gestational age*. However, the organism does not become an *embryo* until about two weeks later, and pregnancy does not affect the woman (and is not confirmed by blood or urine testing) until implantation. Perhaps because the exact date of conception is usually unknown, some obstetricians and publications count from the woman's last menstrual period (LMP), usually about 14 days *before* conception.

- *Length of pregnancy:* Full-term pregnancies last 266 days, or 38 weeks, or 9 months. If the LMP is used as the starting time, pregnancy lasts 40 weeks, sometimes expressed as 10 lunar months. (A lunar month is 28 days long.)

- *Trimesters:* Instead of *germinal period, embryonic period*, and *fetal period*, as used in this text, some writers divide pregnancy into three-month periods called *trimesters*. Months 1, 2, and 3 are called the *first trimester;* months 4, 5, and 6, the *second trimester;* and months 7, 8, and 9, the *third trimester*.

- *Due date:* Although a specific due date based on the LMP is calculated, only 5 percent of babies are born on that exact day. Babies born between two weeks before and one week after that date are considered *full term*. [This is recent; until 2012, three weeks before and two weeks after were considered full term.] Because of increased risks for postmature babies, labor is often induced if the baby has not arrived within 7 days after the due date, although many midwives and doctors prefer to wait to see whether labor begins spontaneously.

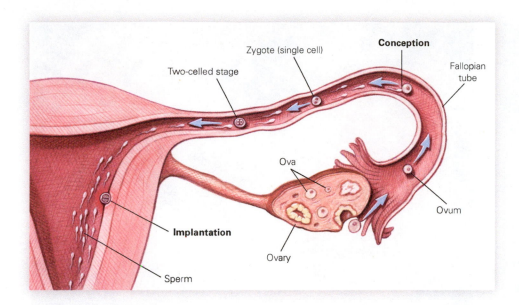

FIGURE 4.1

The Most Dangerous Journey In the first 10 days after conception, the organism does not increase in size because it is not yet nourished by the mother. However, the number of cells increases rapidly as the organism prepares for implantation, which occurs successfully not quite half of the time.

TABLE 4.2	Vulnerability During Prenatal Development

The Germinal Period

An estimated 60 percent of all zygotes do not grow or implant properly and thus do not survive the germinal period. Many of these organisms are abnormal; few women realize they were pregnant.

The Embryonic Period

About 20 percent of all embryos are aborted spontaneously. This is usually called an early *miscarriage,* a term that implies something wrong with the woman when in fact the most common reason for a spontaneous abortion is a chromosomal abnormality.

The Fetal Period

About 5 percent of all fetuses are aborted spontaneously before viability at 22 weeks or are *stillborn,* defined as born dead after 22 weeks. This is much more common in poor nations.

Birth

Because of all these factors, only about 31 percent of all zygotes grow and survive to become living newborn babies. Age of the mother is crucial, with survival of the newborn most likely if the pregnancy lasted at least 36 weeks and the mother was in her early 20s.

Information from Bentley & Mascie-Taylor, 2000; Laurino et al., 2005; Cunningham et al., 2014.

Embryo: From the Third Week Through the Eighth Week

The start of the third week after conception initiates the *embryonic period,* during which the mass of cells takes shape—not yet recognizably human but worthy of a new name, **embryo.** (The word *embryo* is often used loosely, but each early stage has a particular name; here, embryo refers day 14 to day 56.)

First, a thin line (called the *primitive streak*) appears down the middle of the inner mass of cells; it will become the *neural tube* between 20 and 27 days after conception and develop into the central nervous system (the brain and spinal column). The head appears in the fourth week, as eyes, ears, nose, and mouth start to form, and a minuscule blood vessel that will become the heart begins to pulsate.

By the fifth week, buds that will become arms and legs emerge. The upper arms and then forearms, palms, and webbed fingers grow. Legs, knees, feet, and

embryo The name for a developing human organism from about the third week through the eighth week after conception.

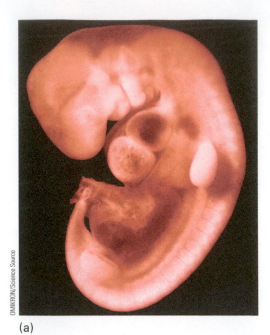

(a)

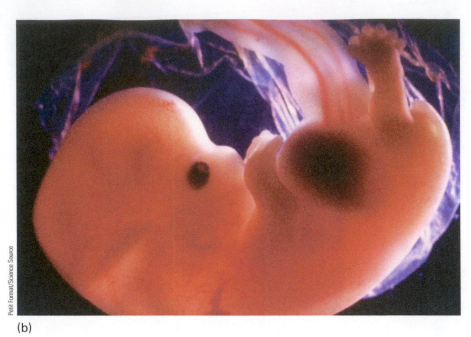

(b)

The Embryonic Period (*a*) At 4 weeks past conception, the embryo is only about 1/8 inch (3 millimeters) long, but already the head has taken shape. (*b*) By 7 weeks, the organism is somewhat less than an inch (2 centimeters) long. Eyes, nose, the digestive system, and even the first stage of toe formation can be seen.

fetus The name for a developing human organism from the start of the ninth week after conception until birth.

ultrasound An image of a fetus (or an internal organ) produced by using high-frequency sound waves. (Also called *sonogram*.)

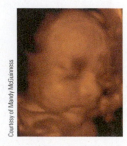

Meet Your Baby The photo at the right is Elisa Clare McGuinness at 22 weeks postconception. She continued to develop well for the next four months, becoming a healthy, 3,572-gram newborn, finally able to meet her family—two parents and an older brother.

webbed toes, in that order, emerge a few days later, each having the beginning of a skeletal structure. Then, 52 and 54 days after conception, respectively, the fingers and toes separate.

As you can see, growth occurs in a *cephalocaudal* (head down literally, "head-to-tail") pattern, and in a *proximodistal* (literally, "near-to-far") pattern, with the extremities forming last. This directional pattern continues until puberty, when it reverses. The feet of a young teenager grow first—the brain last!

At the end of the eighth week after conception (56 days), the embryo weighs just one-thirtieth of an ounce (1 gram) and is about 1 inch (2½ centimeters) long. It has all the basic organs and body parts (except sex organs) of a human being, including elbows and knees. It moves frequently, about 150 times per hour, but this movement is imperceptible and random; it will be many months before deliberate movement occurs.

Fetus: From the Ninth Week Until Birth

The organism is called a **fetus** from the beginning of the ninth week after conception until birth. The fetal period encompasses dramatic change, from a tiny, sexless creature smaller than the final joint of your thumb to a boy or girl about 20 inches (51 centimeters) long.

The Third Month

If the 23rd pair of chromosomes are XY, the SRY gene on the Y triggers the development of male sex organs. Otherwise, female organs develop. The male fetus experiences a rush of the hormone testosterone, affecting many structures and connections in the brain (Filová et al., 2013).

By the end of the third month, the sex organs may be visible via **ultrasound** (in a *sonogram*), which is similar to an X-ray but uses sound waves instead of radiation. The 3-month-old fetus weighs about 3 ounces (87 grams) and is about 3 inches (7.5 centimeters) long. Early prenatal growth is very rapid, with considerable variation, especially in body weight. The numbers just given—3 months, 3 ounces, 3 inches—are rounded off for easy recollection. (Metric measures—100 days, 100 grams, 100 millimeters—are similarly imprecise yet useful.)

Neuronal Birth and Death

In earlier decades, a newborn's chance of survival was pegged to how much the baby weighed. Today we know that weight is a crude predictor—some 1-pound babies live and some 3-pound ones die. The crucial factor is maturation of the brain.

The central nervous system is the first body system to begin development. The embryonic stage starts with the primitive streak, which becomes the neural tube even before the facial features are formed and the first pulsating blood vessel appears.

Already in the third week after conception, some cells specialize to become *neural progenitor cells,* which duplicate and multiply many times until some of them create brain cells (neurons). Neurons do not duplicate; some endure lifelong. Those early neurons migrate to a particular part of the brain (brain stem, cerebellum, hypothalamus, visual cortex, and so on) and specialize, such as some neurons dedicated to seeing faces, others to seeing red and green, others to blue and yellow, and so on.

By mid-pregnancy, the brain has billions of neurons (*neurogenesis*). Earlier, the cortex (the outer part, described in Chapter 5) had been smooth, but now folds and wrinkles (ridges and depressions, called gyri and sulci) allow the human brain to be larger and more complex than the brains of other animals (Stiles & Jernigan, 2010).

Following the proximodistal sequence, the six layers of the cortex are produced, with the bottom (sixth) layer first and then each new layer on top of the previous one so that the top and outer layer is the last to form. Similarly, first the brain stem above the back of the neck, then the midbrain, and finally the forebrain develop and connect.

Detailed study of one crucial brain region, the hippocampus (the major site for memory formation), reveals an explosion of new cells in that area during the fourth month of gestation and then a gradual slowdown of new cell formation (Ge et al., 2015). Although a mid-gestation burst of new neurons and later slowing is characteristic of the entire brain, each part follows its own timetable, as required by the function of each area.

By full term, human brain growth is so extensive that the cortex has many gyri and sulci (see Figure 4.2). Although some huge mammals (whales, for instance) have bigger brains than humans, no other creature needs as many folds because, relative to body size, the human brain is much larger.

Beyond brain growth, with an estimated 86 billion neurons at birth, another process occurs in the final three months of a normal pregnancy—cell death. Programmed cell death, called *apoptosis,* occurs in two prenatal waves. The first wave is easy to understand: Abnormal and immature neurons, such as those with missing or extra chromosomes, are lost. Later in development, however, seemingly normal neurons die such that almost half of all newly formed brain cells are gone before birth (Underwood, 2013).

It is possible that the final three months are the best time for this normal cell death, part of enabling the remaining neurons to establish connections for thinking, remembering, and responding. It is known that surviving preterm babies often have subtle intellectual and emotional deficits. There are many plausible hypotheses for this correlation. Could lack of normal prenatal apoptosis be one of them?

In the final months of pregnancy, the various lobes and areas of the brain are established, and pathways between one area and another are forged. For instance, sound and sight become coordinated: Newborns connect voices heard during pregnancy with faces, recognizing their mothers, for instance. That phenomenal accomplishment occurs within a day or two after birth. Indeed, the fetal brain is attuned to the voices heard much more than to other noises, evidence of neurological plasticity as early as the sixth month after conception (Webb et al., 2015).

Although many connections form in the brain before birth, this process continues for years—the human brain is not fully connected until early adulthood. One of the distinguishing differences between the brains of humans and that of other primates is the extensive prenatal and postnatal growth of axons and dendrites, the connecting fibers between one neuron and another (Gash & Dean, 2015; Collins et al., 2016).

Also in the final months of pregnancy, the membranes and bones covering the brain thicken, which helps prevent "brain bleeds," a hazard of preterm birth if paper-thin blood vessels in the cortex collapse. Newborns have two areas on the top of their heads (*fontanels*) where the bones of the skull have not yet fused. This enables the fetal head to become narrower at

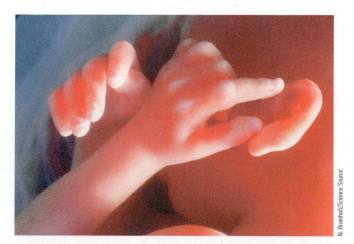

Can He Hear? A fetus, just about at the age of viability, is shown fingering his ear. Such gestures are probably random; but yes, he can hear.

birth, in order to move through the vagina. Fontanels are larger in preterm babies, making them more vulnerable to brain damage. Fontanels gradually close during infancy.

Curiously, some areas of chimpanzee brains are packed with more neurons than human brains, allowing less room for dendrites and axons. Furthermore, myelination, which speeds transmission from one neuron to another, is already about 20 percent complete for the newborn chimp but virtually zero for the human at birth (Gash & Dean, 2015). Thus, brains of the human fetus are designed to be molded by experience after birth.

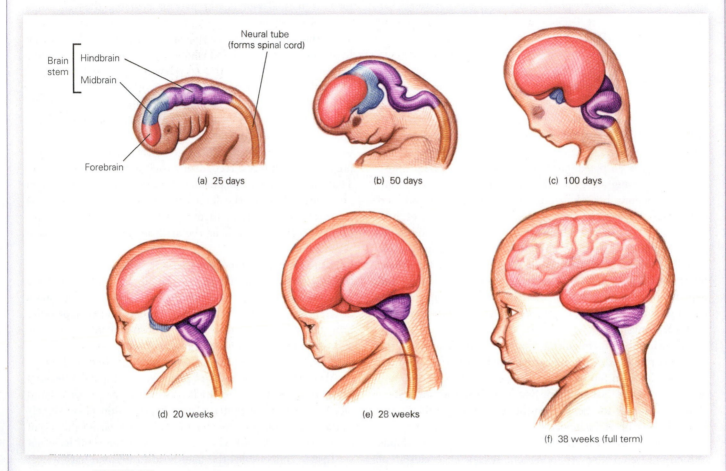

FIGURE 4.2

Prenatal Growth of the Brain Just 25 days after conception *(a)*, the central nervous system is already evident. The brain looks distinctly human by day 100 *(c)*. By the 28th week of gestation *(e)*, at the very time brain activity begins, the various sections of the brain are recognizable. When the fetus is full term *(f)*, all parts of the brain, including the cortex (the outer layers), are formed, folding over one another and becoming more convoluted, or wrinkled, as the number of brain cells increases.

The Middle Three Months

Although movement begins earlier, in the fourth month all of the body parts move, "including stretching, yawning, hand to face contact, swallowing and tongue protrusion." Many future mothers can feel *quickening,* as the first palpable movement is called (DiPietro et al., 2015, p. 33). The heartbeat becomes stronger and more varied—speeding up or slowing down with activity. Digestive and excretory systems develop. Fingernails, toenails, and buds for teeth form, and hair grows (including eyelashes).

The crucial mid-pregnancy development is that the entire central nervous system becomes active, regulating heart rate, breathing, and sucking. Advances in neurological functioning allow the fetus to reach the **age of viability** at the end of this trimester, when a fetus born far too early can survive.

age of viability The age (about 22 weeks after conception) at which a fetus might survive outside the mother's uterus if specialized medical care is available.

Survival is far from automatic. A century ago, if a fetus was born before 30 weeks of gestation, it soon died. Currently, if birth occurs in an advanced neonatal unit, some very immature babies survive.

In Japan, which has excellent neonatal care, 20 percent of 22-week-old newborns survive without major neurological impairment (Ishii et al., 2013). However, the age of viability is stuck at 22 weeks because even the most advanced technology cannot maintain life without some brain response. (Reports of survivors born before 22 weeks are suspect because the date of conception is unknown.)

The Final Three Months

Reaching viability simply means that life outside the womb is *possible*. Many babies born between 22 and 24 weeks die, and survivors born before 27 weeks often develop slowly because they have missed some essential brain development in the uterus (Månsson & Stjernqvist, 2014).

Each day of the final three months improves the odds not only of survival but also of healthy life and normal cognition. (More on preterm birth appears later in this chapter.) Many aspects of prenatal life are awe-inspiring; the fact that an ordinary woman provides a far better home for a fetus than the most advanced medical technology is one of them.

The critical difference between life and death, or between a fragile preterm newborn and a robust one, is maturation of the neurological, respiratory, and cardiovascular systems. In the final three months of prenatal life, the lungs expand and contract, and breathing muscles are exercised as the fetus swallows and spits out amniotic fluid. The valves of the heart go through a final maturation, as do the arteries and veins throughout the body; the testicles of the male fetus descend; brain pathways become stronger.

The fetus usually gains at least 4½ pounds (2.1 kilograms) in the third trimester, increasing to an average of about 7½ pounds (about 3.4 kilograms) at birth. After 36 weeks or more, most newborns are ready to thrive at home on mother's milk—no expert help, oxygenated air, or special feeding required. For thousands of years, that is how humans survived: We would not be alive if any of our ancestors had required intensive newborn care.

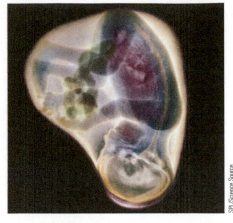

Ready for Birth? We hope not, but this fetus at 27 weeks postconception is viable, although very small. At full term (38 weeks), weight gain would mean that the limbs are folded close to the body, and the uterus is almost completely full.

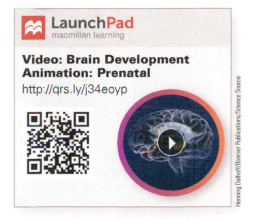

LaunchPad
macmillan learning

Video: Brain Development Animation: Prenatal
http://qrs.ly/j34eoyp

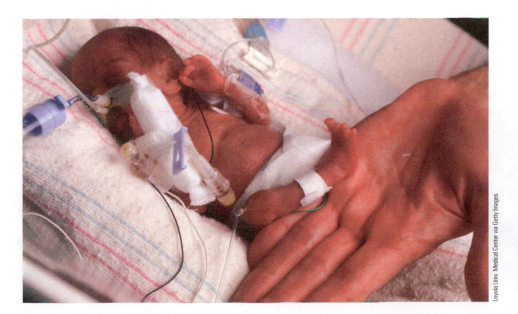

One of the Tiniest Rumaisa Rahman was born after 26 weeks and 6 days, weighing only 8.6 ounces (244 grams). Nevertheless, she has a good chance of living a full, normal life. Rumaisa gained 5 pounds (2,270 grams) in the hospital and then, 6 months after her birth, went home. Her twin sister, Hiba, who weighed 1.3 pounds (590 grams) at birth, had gone home two months earlier. At their one-year birthday, the twins seemed normal, with Rumaisa weighing 15 pounds (6,800 grams) and Hiba 17 pounds (7,711 grams) (Nanji, 2005).

WHAT HAVE YOU LEARNED?

1. What are the three stages of prenatal development?

2. What parts of the embryo form first?

3. When do sex organs appear?

4. What distinguishes a fetus from a baby?

5. What is the prognosis of a baby born after 22 weeks of gestation?

6. What occurs in the final three months of pregnancy?

Birth

About 266 days (38 weeks, although 36–39 weeks is still considered full term) after conception, the fetal brain signals the release of hormones, specifically *oxytocin,* which prepares the fetus for delivery and starts labor. Oxytocin also increases the mother's urge to nurture her baby, continuing in the next months and years in both parents. (Figure 4.3 shows the universal stages of birth.)

The average baby is born after 14 hours of active labor for first births and 7 hours for subsequent births, although often birth takes twice or half as long, with biological, psychological, and social circumstances all significant. The definition of "active" labor varies, which is one reason some women believe they are in active labor for days and others say 10 minutes. Doctors consider active labor as beginning with regular contractions and ending when the fetal head passes through the cervix (Cunningham et al., 2014).

Birthing positions and place vary. Some cultures expect women to be sitting or squatting upright, supported by family members; some doctors insist that women be lying down on their backs; some women give birth in a warm "birthing tub" of water. Most U.S. births now take place in hospital labor rooms with high-tech operating rooms nearby. Another 1 to 6 percent of U.S. births occur in *birthing centers* (not in a hospital), with the rate varying by state. Less than 1 percent occur at home (MacDorman et al., 2014). (Home births are illegal in some U.S. states.)

Choice, Culture, or Cohort? Why do it that way? Both of these women (in Peru, on the *left,* in England, on the *right*) chose methods of labor that are unusual in the United States, where birth stools and birthing pools are uncommon. However, in all three nations, most births occur in hospitals—a rare choice a century ago.

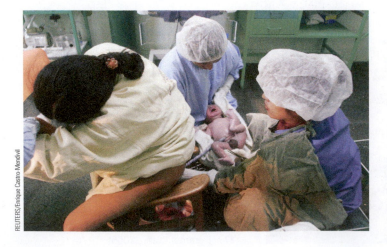

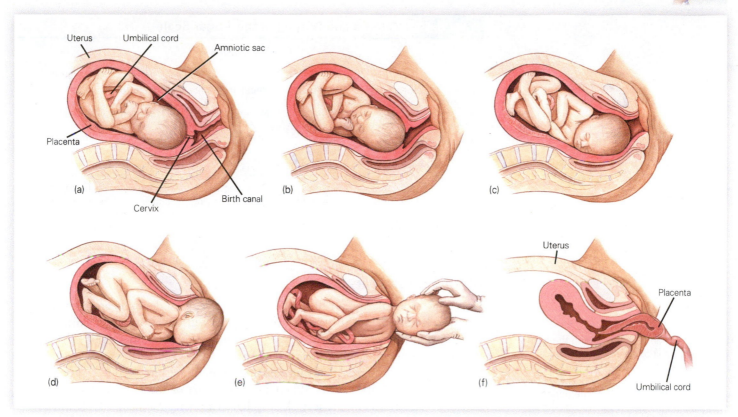

A Normal, Uncomplicated Birth *(a)* The baby's position as the birth process begins. *(b)* The first stage of labor: The cervix dilates to allow passage of the baby's head. *(c)* Transition: The baby's head moves into the "birth canal," the vagina. *(d)* The second stage of labor: The baby's head moves through the opening of the vagina (the baby's head "crowns") and *(e)* emerges completely. *(f)* The third stage of labor is the expulsion of the placenta. This usually occurs naturally, but the entire placenta must be expelled; so birth attendants check carefully. In some cultures, the placenta is ceremonially buried to commemorate its life-giving role.

The Newborn's First Minutes

Newborns usually breathe and cry on their own. Between spontaneous cries, the first breaths of air bring oxygen to the lungs and blood, and the infant's color changes from bluish to pinkish. ("Pinkish" refers to blood color, visible beneath the skin, and applies to newborns of all hues.) Eyes open wide; tiny fingers grab; even tinier toes stretch and retract. The newborn is instantly, zestfully, ready for life.

Nevertheless, there is much to be done. Mucus in the baby's throat is removed, especially if the first breaths seem shallow or strained. The umbilical cord is cut. The baby may be weighed, measured, and examined, and then given to the mother to preserve its body heat and to breast-feed a first meal of *colostrum*, a thick substance that helps the newborn's digestive and immune systems.

One widely used assessment of infant health is the **Apgar scale** (see Table 4.3) (1953/2015). In 1933, when Virginia Apgar earned her M.D., she wanted to work in a hospital but was told that only men did surgery. Consequently, she became an anesthesiologist. She saw that "delivery room doctors focused on mothers and paid little attention to babies. Those who were small and struggling were often left to die" (Beck, 2009, p. D1).

To save those young lives, Apgar developed a simple rating scale of five vital signs—color, heart rate, cry, muscle tone, and breathing—to alert doctors to newborn health. Birth attendants worldwide use the Apgar (using the acronym, Appearance, Pulse, Grimace, Activity, and Respiration) at one minute and again at five minutes after birth, assigning each vital sign a score of 0, 1, or 2. (See Visualizing Development, p. 99.)

Apgar scale A quick assessment of a newborn's health, from 0-10. Below 5 is an emergency—a neonatal pediatrician is summoned immediately. Most babies are at 7, 8, or 9—almost never a perfect 10.

TABLE 4.3	Criteria and Scoring of the Apgar Scale				
Five Vital Signs					
Score	Color	Heartbeat	Reflex Irritability	Muscle Tone	Respiratory Effort
0	Blue, pale	Absent	No response	Flaccid, limp	Absent
1	Body pink, extremities blue	Slow (below 100)	Grimace	Weak, inactive	Irregular, slow
2	Entirely pink	Rapid (over 100)	Coughing, sneezing, crying	Strong, active	Good; baby is crying

Source: Apgar, 1953/2015.

Medical Assistance

How closely any particular birth matches the foregoing depends on many factors. One is whether or not the woman has support and encouragement during labor, provided by the father, other relatives, or a **doula,** who is trained and dedicated to helping mothers in the entire birth process.

Especially if a woman feels intimidated by medical professionals, a doula can be very helpful (Kang, 2014). When a doula is part of the medical team, women use less medication and are less likely to have extensive medical intervention.

Surgery

One-third of U.S. births occur via **cesarean section** (**c-section,** or simply *section*), whereby the fetus is removed through incisions in the mother's abdomen. Midwives are as skilled at delivering babies as physicians, but in most nations only medical doctors can perform surgery of any kind, including at birth. The World Health Organization suggested that c-sections are medically indicated in about 15 percent of births (such as when the pelvis is too small and the fetal head too big for a vaginal birth).

In some nations, cesareans are rare—less than 5 percent. In those nations, birth is often hazardous for both mother and child. Public health workers find that training midwives to perform cesareans and implementing good newborn care saves many lives (Pucher et al., 2013).

doula A woman who helps with the birth process. Traditionally in Latin America, a doula was the only professional who attended childbirth. Now doulas are likely to arrive at the woman's home during early labor and later work alongside a hospital's staff.

cesarean section (c-section) A surgical birth, in which incisions through the mother's abdomen and uterus allow the fetus to be removed quickly, instead of being delivered through the vagina. (Also called simply *section*.)

Mother Laboring, Doula Working In many nations, doulas work to help the birth process, providing massage, timing contractions, and preparing for birth. In the United States, doulas typically help couples decide when to leave home, avoiding long waits between hospital admittance and birth. Here, in Budapest, this expectant mother will have her baby with a licensed midwife at home. Nora Schimcsig is her doula; the two women will be together from this moment in early labor to the first breast-feeding of the newborn.

BEA KALLOS/EPA/Newscom

A Healthy Newborn

Just moments after birth, babies are administered their very first test. The APGAR score is an assessement tool used by doctors and nurses to determine whether a newborn requires any medical intervention. It tests five specific criteria of health, and the medical professional assigns a score of 0, 1, or 2 for each category. A perfect score of 10 is rare—most babies will show some minor deficits at the 1-minute mark, and many will still lose points at the 5-minute mark.

GRIMACE RESPONSE/REFLEXES

(2) A healthy baby will indicate his displeasure when his airways are suctioned—he'll grimace, pull away, cough, or sneeze.

(1) Baby will grimace during suctioning.

(0) Baby shows no response to being suctioned and requires immediate medical attention.

RESPIRATION

(2) A good strong cry indicates a normal breathing rate.

(1) Baby has a weak cry or whimper, or slow/irregular breathing.

(0) Baby is not breathing and requires immediate medical intervention.

PULSE

(2) A pulse of 100 or more beats per minute is healthy for a newborn.

(1) Baby's pulse is less than 100 beats per minute.

(0) A baby with no heartbeat requires immediate medical attention.

APPEARANCE/COLOR

(2) Body and extremities should show good color, with pink undertones indicating good circulation.

(1) Baby has some blueness in the palms and soles of the feet. Many babies exhibit some blueness at both the 1- and 5-minute marks; most warm up soon after.

(0) A baby whose entire body is blue, grey, or very pale requires immediate medical intervention.

ACTIVITY AND MUSCLE TONE

(2) Baby exhibits active motion of arms, legs, body.

(1) Baby shows some movement of arms and legs.

(0) A baby who is limp and motionless requires immediate medical attention.

REFLEXES IN INFANTS

Never underestimate the power of a reflex. For developmentalists, newborn reflexes are mechanisms for survival, indicators of brain maturation, and vestiges of evolutionary history. For parents, they are mostly delightful and sometimes amazing.

THE SUCKING REFLEX A newborn, just a few minutes old, demonstrates that he is ready to nurse by sucking on a doctor's finger.

Astier/BSIP/Science Source/Photo Researchers, Inc.

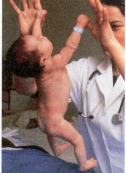

Petit Format/Photo Researchers

THE GRASPING REFLEX When the doctor places a finger on the palm of a healthy infant, he or she will grasp so tightly that the baby's legs can dangle in space.

THE STEP REFLEX A 1-day-old girl steps eagerly forward on legs too tiny to support her body.

Jennie Woodcock; Reflections Photolibrary/Corbis

Pick Up Your Baby! Probably she can't. In this maternity ward in Beijing, China, most patients are recovering from cesarean sections, making it difficult to cradle, breast-feed, or carry a newborn until the incision heals.

Other nations have far more cesareans than the recommended 15 percent. Dramatic increases have occurred in China, where the rate was 5 percent in 1991, 20 percent by 2001, and about 50 percent in 2014 (Hellerstein et al., 2015).

In the United States, the c-section rate rose between 1996 and 2008 (from 21 percent to 34 percent) and now is steady, but variation is dramatic from one hospital to another—from 7 to 70 percent (Kozhimannil et al., 2013). That variation raises questions, since hospitals and doctors might prefer cesareans for reasons other than medical ones—they are easier to schedule, quicker, and require surgeons, anesthesiologists, and several hospital days.

With current technology, cesareans are safe and quick, and welcomed by many women as well as doctors. The disadvantages appear later: more medical complications after birth and less breast-feeding of the newborn (Malloy, 2009).

By age 3, children born by cesarean are twice as likely to be obese: 16 percent compared to 8 percent (Huh et al., 2012). The reason may be that babies delivered vaginally have beneficial bacteria in their microbiome that those delivered surgically do not (Wallis, 2014).

Drugs

In the United States, drugs are usually part of the birth process. The goal is to balance the needs of the mother, the fetus, and the hospital—and people disagree about how best to do that. In about half of U.S. hospital births, doctors use an *epidural,* an injection in the spine that stops feeling in the lower half of the body while keeping the mother awake. One woman, named Resch, had an epidural and a cesarean because her fetus was in a breech position (buttocks first, not head first).

> Resch felt "a lot of rough pushing and pulling" and "a painless suction sensation" as if her body were "a tar pit the baby was wrestled from". She heard the doctor say to the resident: "Hold her up by the hips", and Resch peered down. She saw her daughter for the first time, wet and squirming . . . Resch's husband held the baby next to Resch's cheek. Resch felt "overwhelmed by emotions"—"joy, awe, anxiety, relief, surprise." She gave thanks for her healthy baby, and for modern obstetrical care.
>
> *[Lake, 2012, p. 21]*

Resch was grateful, but critics would be troubled. Sometimes headaches or other side effects are caused by an epidural, but the most common problem is that labor slows down. On average, an epidural adds more than two hours to the time required for a vaginal birth (Cheng et al., 2014). In addition, any anesthetic that enters the woman's bloodstream slows down the baby's reflexes, including sucking and breathing.

Another drug-based medical intervention is *induced labor,* in which labor is started, speeded up, or strengthened with a drug. The rate of induced labor in the United States tripled between 1990 and 2010 and is close to 20 percent. Starting labor before it begins spontaneously increases the likelihood of an epidural and makes cesarean birth more common (Jonsson et al., 2013).

Newborn Survival

The benefits of modern medical measures at birth are evident. A century ago, at least 5 of every 100 newborns in the United States died (De Lee, 1938), as did more than half of those born in developing nations. Birth was hazardous for women as well: It was the most common reason a healthy woman in her 20s might die.

In poor nations even today, complications at birth are often serious. Indeed, one estimate is that worldwide almost 2 million newborns (1 in 70) die each year (Rajaratnam et al., 2010) and almost 300,000 women die in pregnancy or birth. In the poorest nations, the rates may be higher, in that some births are not recorded and some maternal deaths—from an illegal abortion for instance—are not attributed to pregnancy.

Currently in the United States, neonatal mortality is rare: Less than 1 newborn in 250 dies, and most of them were born far too soon. About 40 other nations have even better rates of newborn survival. In developed nations, a woman almost never dies from complications of pregnancy, abortion, or birth—the rate is less than 1 in 10,000.

As you can see from Figure 4.4, U.S. rates have risen while rates have fallen in other nations, but that may be attributed to a change in data collection. A death during pregnancy or within 42 days after birth is now tallied as maternal mortality (Maron, 2015).

Critics point out, however, that survival is not the only measure of success. A particular issue in medically advanced nations is the attention lavished on "miracle babies" who require high-tech medical support, microsurgery, and weeks in the hospital before they go home (Longo, 2013).

Miracle babies often need special care all their lives. The unusual and happy outcomes are published; the public expense of keeping these babies alive and the

Everyone Healthy and Happy A few decades ago in the developing world and a century ago in advanced nations, hospital births were only for birthing women who were near death, and only half of the fetuses survived. That has changed, particularly in Asia, where women prefer to give birth in hospitals. Hospital births themselves are not what they once were. Most new mothers participate in the process: Here Le Thi Nga is about to greet her newborn after pulling with all her strength on the belt that helped her push out the head.

Observation Quiz What evidence shows that, even in Hanoi, technology is part of this birth? (see answer, page 103)

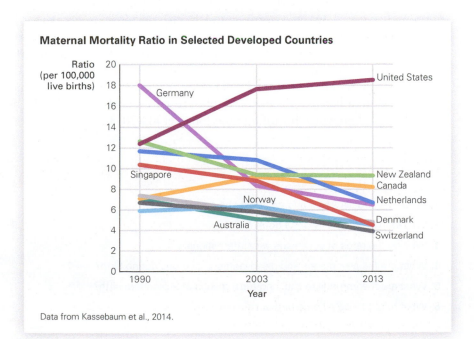

Maternal Mortality Ratio in Selected Developed Countries

Ratio (per 100,000 live births). Germany, Singapore, United States, New Zealand, Canada, Norway, Netherlands, Australia, Denmark, Switzerland. Years 1990, 2003, 2013.

Data from Kassebaum et al., 2014.

FIGURE 4.4

Could It Be? Some argue that U.S. statistics tally increases in childbirth deaths because the definition has become more accurate—including not only deaths immediately after birth but also deaths within the first six weeks. But there is no doubt that maternal mortality in many other nations is lower than the U.S. rates.

private burden borne lifelong by the parents are not publicized. Better prenatal care would prevent many fragile newborns and would save public dollars—but it would not achieve headlines.

Alternatives to Hospital Technology

Questions of costs—emotional as well as financial—abound. For instance, c-section and epidural rates vary more by doctor, hospital, day of the week, and region than by medical complications—even in Sweden, where obstetric care is paid for by the government (Schytt & Waldenström, 2010).

Many hospitals routinely schedule cesareans for breech births and for twins, yet a careful study found that half of the time twins can be safely delivered vaginally (Barrett et al., 2013). Some women who have had a cesarean and then have another pregnancy experience a rare complication (uterine rupture) if they give birth vaginally. As a result, many doctors follow the mantra "once a cesarean, always a cesarean." This may be overly cautious, but juries blame doctors for inaction more than for action. To avoid lawsuits, doctors intervene (Schifrin & Cohen, 2013).

Some women prefer to avoid the medicalization of birth by having their babies at a birthing center or at home. About half of the home births are planned and half not, because of unexpectedly rapid labor. The unplanned ones are hazardous if no one can rescue a newborn in distress.

A study of 13 million U.S. births in homes and hospitals found a slightly higher mortality rate (1.2 babies per thousand) in home births (Grünebaum et al., 2014). However, that correlation does not convince every doctor that hospital births are always best.

A crucial question is the training of the birth attendant. An official group of doctors decided that planned home births are acceptable because women have "a right to make a medically informed decision about delivery," but they also stressed that a trained midwife or doctor be present, that the birth not be high-risk (e.g., no previous cesarean, not carrying twins), and that speedy transportation to a hospital be possible (American College of Obstetricians and Gynecologists Committee on Obstetric Practice, 2011).

Planned home births are more common outside the United States, including 2 percent in England and 30 percent in the Netherlands, where midwives are trained and paid by the government. A British obstetrician notes that home births in the United States are more often chosen by older women and that birth more often occurs a week or more after the due date—risk factors that affect outcomes (Seppa, 2013b).

In the Netherlands, special ambulances called *flying storks* speed mother and newborn to a hospital if needed. Dutch research finds home births better for mothers and no worse for infants (de Jonge et al., 2013).

Especially for Conservatives and Liberals Do people's attitudes about medical intervention at birth reflect their attitudes about medicine at other points in their life span, in such areas as assisted reproductive technology (ART), immunization, and life support? (see response, page 104)

WHAT HAVE YOU LEARNED?

1. Who was Virginia Apgar and what did she do?

2. Why would a woman want a doula?

3. Why do the rates of cesareans vary internationally?

4. What are the advantages and disadvantages of drugs during birth?

5. What are the immediate and long-term results of a cesarean birth?

6. What might make a home birth a safe one?

Problems and Solutions

The early days of life place the future person on the path toward health and success—or not. The troubling consequences of poor nutrition during pregnancy—"a higher risk of type 2 diabetes, obesity, heart disease, insulin resistance, and high blood pressure" (Couzin-Frankel, 2013b, p. 1160)—are not apparent until decades later. Fortunately, healthy newborns are the norm, not the exception. However, if something is amiss, it is often part of a sequence that may become overwhelming (Rossignol et al., 2014).

You just read a small example of such a cascade: Induced labor increases the need for an epidural, which increases the likelihood of a cesarean, which reduces the likelihood of breast-feeding. None of this is necessarily harmful if the fetus is full term and healthy. But if other problems occur during prenatal life, then the baby begins life with handicaps—often not apparent at birth—that other babies do not have.

Harmful Substances

A cascade may begin before a woman realizes she is pregnant. Every week, scientists discover an unexpected **teratogen,** which is anything—drugs, viruses, pollutants, malnutrition, stress, and more—that increases the risk of prenatal abnormalities and birth complications.

But do not be alarmed, like one of my students who said that now that she knew all the things that can go wrong, she never wanted to have a baby. As I explained to her, many problems can be avoided, many potential teratogens do no harm, and much damage can be remedied. Thus, prenatal life is not a dangerous period to be feared; it is a natural process to be protected, resulting in a birth that becomes a joyful memory.

Behavioral Teratogens

Some teratogens cause no physical defects but affect the brain, making a child hyperactive, antisocial, or intellectually disabled. These are **behavioral teratogens.**

Behavioral teratogens can be subtle, yet their effects last a lifetime. That is one conclusion from research on the babies born to pregnant women exposed to the influenza pandemic in 1918, which killed more Americans than World War I. By middle age, although some of these babies became wealthy, happy, and brilliant, on average those born in flu-ravaged regions had less education, more unemployment, and lower income than those born a year earlier (Almond, 2006). They died a few years sooner than those born in 1917 or 1919.

About 20 percent of all children have difficulties that *could* be connected to behavioral teratogens, although the link is not straightforward: The cascade is murky. One of my students wrote:

> I was nine years old when my mother announced she was pregnant. I was the one who was most excited. . . . My mother was a heavy smoker, Colt 45 beer drinker and a strong caffeine coffee drinker.
> One day my mother was sitting at the dining room table smoking cigarettes one after the other. I asked "Isn't smoking bad for the baby?" She made a face and said "Yes, so what?"
> I said "So why are you doing it?"
> She said, "I don't know.". . .
> During this time I was in the fifth grade and we saw a film about birth defects. My biggest fear was that my mother was going to give birth to a fetal alcohol syndrome (FAS) infant. . . . My baby brother was born right on schedule. The doctors claimed a healthy newborn. . . . Once I heard healthy,

teratogen An agent or condition, including viruses, drugs, and chemicals, that can impair prenatal development and result in birth defects or even death.

behavioral teratogens Agents and conditions that can harm the prenatal brain, impairing the future child's intellectual and emotional functioning.

Swing High and Low Adopted by loving parents but born with fetal alcohol syndrome, Philip, shown here at age 11, sometimes threatened to kill his family members. His parents sent him to this residential ranch in Eureka, Montana (nonprofit, tuition $3,500 a month) for children like him. This moment during recess is a happy one; it is not known whether he learned to control his fury.

● **Response for Conservatives and Liberals** (from page 102): Yes, some people are much more likely to want nature to take its course. However, personal experience often trumps political attitudes about birth and death; several of those who advocate hospital births are also in favor of spending one's final days at home.

● **Especially for Judges and Juries** How much protection, if any, should the legal system provide for fetuses? Should women with alcohol use disorder who are pregnant be jailed to prevent them from drinking? What about people who enable them to drink, such as their partners, their parents, bar owners, and bartenders? (see response, page 106)

teratology The scientific study of birth abnormalities, especially on causes of biological disabilities and impairments.

Smoke-free Babies Posters such as this one have had an impact. Smoking among adults is only half of what it was 30 years ago. One-third of women smokers quit when they know they are pregnant, while the other two-thirds cut their smoking in half. Unfortunately, the heaviest smokers are least likely to quit—they need more than posters to motivate them to break the habit.

I thought everything was going to be fine. I was wrong, then again I was just a child. . . .

My baby brother never showed any interest in toys . . . he just cannot get the right words out of his mouth . . . he has no common sense . . .

Why hurt those who cannot defend themselves?

[J., personal communication]

As you remember from Chapter 1, one case proves nothing. J. blames her mother; that may be unfair. Genes, postnatal experiences, and lack of preventive information and services are part of her brother's sorry cascade.

Risk Analysis

Life requires risks: We routinely decide which chances to take and how to minimize harm. To pick an easy example: Crossing the street is risky, yet avoiding street-crossing would harm development. Knowing the danger, we look both ways.

Risk analysis is crucial lifelong (Sheeran et al., 2014). You read in Chapter 3 that pregnancy after age 35 increases the chance of many disorders, but you will read later that mature parents are more likely to have happy marriages, intended pregnancies, and a cooperative parental alliance. Pregnancy at any age entails risks and benefits, joys and concerns. Always, risk analysis is needed; many problems can be prevented or overcome.

Sixty years ago, risk analysis was not applied to prenatal development. It was assumed that the placenta screened out all harmful substances. If a baby had a birth defect, that was fate—unavoidable.

Then two tragic episodes showed otherwise. (1) On an Australian army base, a sudden increase in babies born blind mystified the military doctors. Then they figured it out: The same base experienced a rubella (German measles) epidemic seven months earlier (Gregg, 1941/1991). (2) A tragic rise in British newborns with deformed limbs was traced to maternal use of thalidomide, a new drug for nausea that was widely prescribed in Europe in the late 1950s (Schardein, 1976).

Thus began **teratology,** a science of risk analysis. Although all teratogens increase the *risk* of harm, none *always* cause damage; analysis assesses probabilities, not certainties (Aven, 2011). The impact of teratogens depends on the interplay of many factors, both destructive and constructive—an example of the dynamic-systems perspective described in Chapter 1.

The Critical Time

Timing is crucial. Some teratogens cause damage only during a *critical period* (see Figure 4.5). [**Life-Span Link:** Critical and sensitive periods are described in Chapter 1.] Obstetricians recommend that *before* pregnancy occurs, women should avoid drugs (including cigarettes and alcohol), supplement a balanced diet with extra folic acid and iron, update their immunizations, and gain or lose weight if needed. Indeed, preconception health is at least as important as postconception health (see Table 4.4).

The first days and weeks after conception (the germinal and embryonic periods) are critical for body formation, but health during the entire fetal period affects the brain, and thus behavioral teratogens affect the fetus at any time. Some teratogens that cause preterm birth or low birthweight are particularly harmful in the second half of pregnancy.

In fact, one study found that although smoking cigarettes is always harmful, smokers who quit early in pregnancy had no higher risks of birth complications than did women who never smoked (McCowan et al., 2009). A longitudinal study of 7-year-olds found that, although alcohol is a teratogen throughout pregnancy,

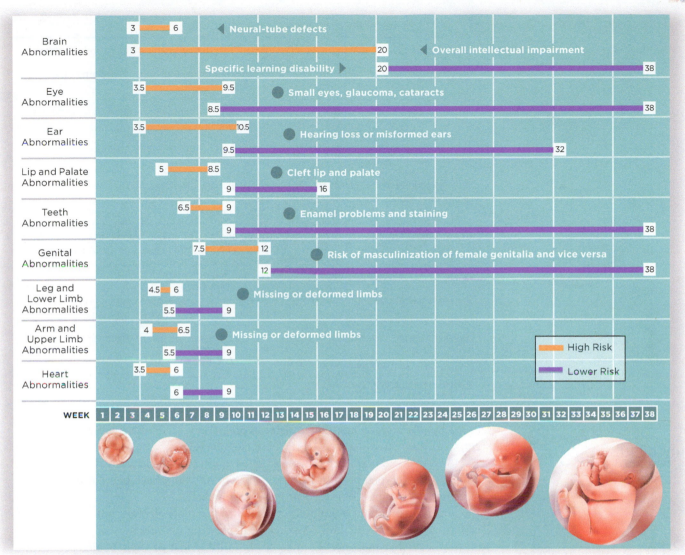

WEEK | 1 | 2 | 3 | 4 | 5 | 6 | 7 | 8 | 9 | 10 | 11 | 12 | 13 | 14 | 15 | 16 | 17 | 18 | 19 | 20 | 21 | 22 | 23 | 24 | 25 | 26 | 27 | 28 | 29 | 30 | 31 | 32 | 33 | 34 | 35 | 36 | 37 | 38

binge drinking is more harmful to the brain in the second half of pregnancy than the first (Niclasen et al., 2014).

Timing may be important in another way. When pregnancy occurs soon after a previous pregnancy, risk increases. For example, one study found that second-born children are twice as likely to have autism spectrum disorder if they are born within a year of the first-born child (Cheslack-Postava et al., 2011).

How Much Is Too Much?

A second factor that affects the harm from teratogens is the dose and/or frequency of exposure. Some teratogens have a **threshold effect;** they are virtually harmless until exposure reaches a certain level, at which point they "cross the threshold" and become damaging. This threshold is not a fixed boundary: Dose, timing, frequency, and other teratogens affect when the threshold is crossed (O'Leary et al., 2010).

Consequently, experts rarely specify thresholds for any particular drug. For example, alcohol, tobacco, and marijuana are more teratogenic, with a lower threshold for each, when all three are combined.

Is there a safe dose for psychoactive drugs? Consider alcohol. During the period of the embryo, a mother's heavy drinking can cause **fetal alcohol syndrome (FAS),** which distorts the facial features of a child (especially the eyes, ears, and

FIGURE 4.5

One More Reason to Plan a Pregnancy
The embryonic period, before a woman knows she is pregnant, is the most sensitive time for causing structural birth defects. However, at no time during pregnancy is the fetus completely safe from harm. Individual differences in susceptibility to teratogens may be caused by a fetus's genetic makeup or peculiarities of the mother, including the effectiveness of her placenta or her overall health. The dose and timing of the exposure are also important.

threshold effect In prenatal development, when a teratogen is relatively harmless in small doses but becomes harmful once exposure reaches a certain level (the threshold).

fetal alcohol syndrome (FAS) A cluster of birth defects, including abnormal facial characteristics, slow physical growth, and reduced intellectual ability, that may occur in the fetus of a woman who drinks alcohol while pregnant.

TABLE 4.4	Before Pregnancy
What Prospective Mothers Should Do	**What Prospective Mothers Really Do (U.S. Data)**
Plan the pregnancy.	At least one-third of all pregnancies are not intended.
Take a daily multivitamin with folic acid.	About 60 percent of women aged 18 to 45 do not take multivitamins.
Avoid binge drinking (defined as four or more drinks in a row).	One in seven women in their childbearing years binge-drink.
Update immunizations against all teratogenic viruses, especially rubella.	Unlike in many developing nations, relatively few pregnant women in the United States lack basic immunizations.
Gain or lose weight, as appropriate.	About one-third of all U.S. women of childbearing age are obese, and about 5 percent are underweight. Both extremes increase complications.
Reassess use of prescription drugs.	Ninety percent of pregnant women take prescription drugs (not counting vitamins).
Develop daily exercise habits.	More than half of women of childbearing age do not exercise.

Data from Bombard et al., 2013; MMWR, July 20, 2012; Brody, 2012; Mosher et al., 2012; U.S. Department of Health and Human Services, 2016; Herd et al., 2016.

Video Activity: Teratogens explores the factors that enable or prevent teratogens from harming a developing fetus.

Especially for Nutritionists Is it beneficial that most breakfast cereals are fortified with vitamins and minerals? (see response, page 109)

Response for Judges and Juries (from page 104): Some laws punish women who jeopardize the health of their fetuses, but a developmental view would consider the micro-, exo-, and macrosystems.

upper lip). As already mentioned, later in pregnancy, alcohol is a behavioral teratogen, with *fetal alcohol effects (FAE)* possible, not FAS.

However, alcohol during pregnancy does not always result in evident harm. If it did, almost everyone born in Europe before 1980 would have been affected, since wine or beer was part of most Europeans' daily diet.

Currently, pregnant women are advised to avoid all alcohol, but many women in France (between 12 and 63 percent, depending on specifics of the research) do not heed that message (Dumas et al., 2014). Most of their babies seem fine. Should all women who might become pregnant refuse a legal substance that most men use routinely? Wise? Probably. Necessary? Maybe not.

Innate Vulnerability

Genes are a third factor that influences the effects of teratogens. When a woman carrying dizygotic twins drinks alcohol, for example, the twins' blood alcohol levels are equal, yet one twin may be more severely affected than the other because of different alleles for the enzyme that metabolizes alcohol. Similar differential susceptibility probably occurs for many teratogens (McCarthy & Eberhart, 2014).

The Y chromosome may be critical. Male fetuses are more likely to be spontaneously aborted, stillborn, or harmed by teratogens than are female fetuses. That is generally true, but the male–female hazard rate differs from one teratogen to another (Lewis & Kestler, 2012).

Genes are important not only at conception but also during pregnancy. One maternal allele results in low levels of folic acid in a woman's bloodstream and hence in the embryo, which can produce *neural-tube defects*—either *spina bifida*, in which the tail of the spine is not enclosed properly (enclosure normally occurs at about week 7), or *anencephaly*, when part of the brain is missing. Neural-tube defects are more common in certain ethnic groups (Irish, English, and Egyptian).

Applying the Research

Remember that no substance is always teratogenic, and no protective measure always succeeds. This is evident in a study of neural-tube disorder (Smithells et al., 2011). In an application of the research, about half of a group of 550 women who had already given birth to a child with the disorder (and hence were genetically at risk) and who wanted another baby and then became pregnant took supplements of folic acid. The other half simply ate normally.

The rate of newborns with neural-tube defects was 1 in 250 among the supplemented mothers and 13 in 300 in the nonsupplemented ones, proof that folic acid helps. But note that almost 96 percent of the women who were at genetic risk but did not take supplements had healthy babies. Also note that one supplemented woman did not. Risk analysis can improve the odds, as it did here, but it does not guarantee.

Results of teratogenic exposure cannot be predicted precisely for each person. Instead, much is known about destructive and damaging teratogens, including what can be done to improve the odds. Optimal weight gain—a protective factor in pregnancy—varies depending on preconception weight: Underweight women need to gain more than average and obese women need to gain less. (See Figure 4.6.)

General health during pregnancy is at least half the battle. Women who maintain good nutrition and avoid drugs and teratogenic chemicals (often found in pesticides, cleaning fluids, and cosmetics) usually have healthy babies. Some medications are necessary (e.g., for women with epilepsy, diabetes, and severe depression), but consultation should begin *before* conception.

Many women assume that herbal medicines or over-the-counter drugs are safe. Not so. As pediatrics professor Allen Mitchell explains, "Many over-the-counter drugs were grandfathered in with no studies of their possible effects during pregnancy" (quoted in Brody, 2013, p. D5). ("Grandfathered" means that if they were legal in days past, they remain legal—no modern testing needed.)

Sadly, a cascade of teratogens is most likely to begin with women who are already vulnerable. For example, cigarette smokers are more often drinkers (as was J.'s mother), and those whose jobs require exposure to chemicals and pesticides (such as migrant workers) are more often malnourished (either too thin or too heavy) and lack access to medical care (Ahmed & Jaakkola, 2007; Hougaard & Hansen, 2007).

Advice from Experts

Although prenatal care is helpful in protecting the developing fetus, even doctors are not always careful. One concern is pain medication. Opioids (narcotics) may damage the fetus. Yet a recent study found that 23 percent of pregnant women on Medicaid are given a prescription for a narcotic (Desai et al., 2014). Hopefully, the doctor didn't realize the patient was pregnant, and the women didn't take the drug.

Worse still is that some obstetricians do not ask about harmful life patterns. For example, one Maryland study found that almost one-third of pregnant women were not asked about alcohol (Cheng et al., 2011). Those who were over age 35 and who were college educated were least likely to be queried. Did their doctors assume they already avoided that teratogen? If so, they were wrong. Older, educated women are the most likely to drink during pregnancy. The rate for pregnant woman overall is 10 percent, but the rate for older pregnant women is 19 percent and for college-educated women, 13 percent (Tan et al., 2015).

Data Connections Activity: Teratogens examines both the effects of various teratogens and the preventive measures that mitigate their risk to a developing fetus.

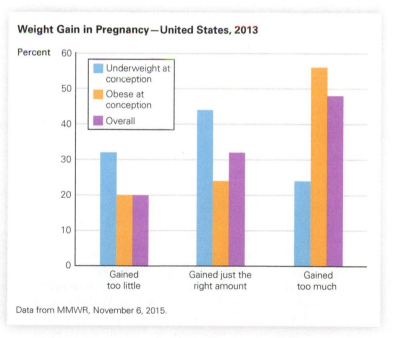

Data from MMWR, November 6, 2015.

FIGURE 4.6

Eating for Two? How much weight women should gain during pregnancy depends on their BMI. When that is taken into account, only about one-third of all women gain the right amount. Fetal health is jeopardized when women gain too little or too much. The ideal is 25–35 pounds for women who are not overweight.

Not the Fetus, the Mother! Alicia Beltran, age 28, shown here pregnant with her first child, confided at her initial prenatal visit that she had been addicted to a painkiller but was now clean (later confirmed by a lab test). She refused a prescription to keep her away from illegal drugs. But that led, when she was 14 weeks pregnant, to the police taking her in handcuffs and shackles to court. She was not represented nor allowed to defend herself, but a state-appointed lawyer for the fetus argued that she should be detained. After more than two months in involuntary confinement, a non-profit lawyer got her released. More than a year later, a judge finally considered her petition that that her constitutional rights had been violated but dismissed the case because the state had dropped the charges.

DARREN HAUCK/The New York Times/Redux

● **Especially for Social Workers**
When is it most important to convince women to be tested for HIV: before pregnancy, after conception, or immediately after birth? (see response, page 111)

To learn what medications are safe in pregnancy, women often consult the Internet. However, a study of 25 Web sites that, together, listed 235 medications as safe found that TERSIS (a group of expert teratologists who analyze drug safety) had declared only 60 (25%) safe. The rest were not *proven* harmful, but TERSIS found insufficient evidence to confirm safety (Peters et al., 2013). The Internet sites sometimes used unreliable data: Some drugs were on the safe list of one site and the danger list of another.

Laws that criminalize substance abuse during pregnancy may keep more women away from prenatal care and hospital births than get them clean. A particular problem is that using drugs (including alcohol) during pregnancy is a crime for which women are arrested and jailed in five states (Minnesota, North Dakota, Oklahoma, South Dakota, and Wisconsin). Is it significant that those states have sizable Native American populations? Other states wait until birth: Several new Alabama mothers have been jailed because their babies had illegal substances in their bloodstream (Eckholm, 2013).

What Is Safe?

As explained in Chapter 1, the scientific method is designed to be cautious. It takes years—for replication, data from alternate designs, and exploration of various hypotheses—to reach sound conclusions. On almost any issue, scientists disagree until the weight of evidence is unmistakable. For example, it took decades before all researchers agreed on such (now obvious) teratogens as rubella, lead, and cigarettes.

One current dispute is whether pesticides should be allowed on the large farms that produce most of the fruits and vegetables for American consumption. No biologist doubts that pesticides harm frogs, fish, and bees, but the pesticide industry insists that careful use (e.g., spraying plants, not workers) does not harm people. Developmentalists, however, worry that pregnant women who breathe these toxins will have children with brain damage. As one scientist said, "Pesticides were designed to be neurotoxic. Why should we be surprised if they cause neurotoxicity?" (Lanphear, quote in Mascarelli, 2013, p. 741).

The United States now bans one pesticide, chlorpyrifos, from household use (it once was commonly used to kill roaches and ants), but chlorpyrifos is still widely used in U.S. agriculture and in homes in other nations. Analysis of umbilical cord blood confirms that fetuses exposed to chlorpyrifos have lower IQs and more behavior problems than other children (Horton et al., 2012). However, Dow Chemical Company, which sells the pesticide, argues that the research does not take into account all the confounding factors (Mascarelli, 2013).

As with every correlation, many causes of those behavior problems are possible. For instance, pregnant women who use roach spray tend to be stressed, living in polluted and violent neighborhoods. Parents who pick sprayed crops tend to move from place to place, which disrupts their children's schooling. Could those factors cause the correlation between babies exposed to pesticides and children who have trouble in school? Is the possibility that this chemical is a teratogen worth the certain cost for agribusiness and grocery shoppers of banning chlorpyrifos?

In this dispute, developmentalists choose to protect the fetal brain, which is why this chapter advises pregnant women to avoid pesticides. However, on many other teratogens, developmentalists themselves are conflicted. Fish consumption is an example.

Pregnant women in the United States are told to eat less fish, but those in the United Kingdom are told to eat more. The reason for these opposite messages is that fish contains mercury (a teratogen) but also DHA (an omega-3 fatty acid that promotes brain development). When scientists weigh the benefits and risks of fish consumption, they wonder whether women can judge each kind of fish and where it swam, choosing benefits while avoiding risks (Lando & Lo, 2014).

To make all of this more difficult, pregnant women are, ideally, happy and calm: Stress and anxiety affect the fetus. Pregnancy often increases fear and anxiety (Rubertsson et al., 2014); scientists do not want to add to the worry. Prospective parents want clear, immediate answers about their daily diet, habits, and circumstances, yet scientists cannot always provide them.

Prenatal Diagnosis

Early prenatal care has many benefits: Women learn what to eat, what to do, and what to avoid. Some serious conditions, syphilis and HIV among them, can be diagnosed and treated in the first prenatal months before they harm the fetus. Tests of blood, urine, fetal heart rate, and ultrasound reassure parents, facilitating the crucial parent–child bond.

In general, early care protects fetal growth, connects women to their particular fetus, makes birth easier, and renders parents better able to cope. When complications (such as twins, gestational diabetes, and infections) arise, early recognition increases the chance of a healthy birth.

Unfortunately, however, about 20 percent of early pregnancy tests *raise* anxiety instead of reducing it. For instance, the level of alpha-fetoprotein (AFP) may be too high or too low, or ultrasound may indicate multiple fetuses, abnormal growth, Down syndrome, or a mother's narrow pelvis. Many such warnings are **false positives;** that is, they falsely suggest a problem that does not exist. Any warning, whether false or true, requires further testing but also leads to worry and soul-searching. Some choose to abort; some do not. Neither decision is easy. Consider the following.

Response for Nutritionists
(from page 106): Useful, yes; optimal, no. Some essential vitamins are missing (too expensive), and individual nutritional needs differ, depending on age, sex, health, genes, and eating habits. The reduction in neural-tube defects is good, but many women don't eat cereal or take vitamin supplements before becoming pregnant.

false positive The result of a laboratory test that reports something as true when in fact it is not true. This can occur for pregnancy tests, when a woman might not be pregnant even though the test says she is, or during pregnancy, when a problem is reported that actually does not exist.

OPPOSING PERSPECTIVES

"What Do People Live to Do?"

John and Martha, both under age 35, were expecting their second child. Martha's initial prenatal screening revealed low alpha-fetoprotein, which could indicate Down syndrome.

Another blood test was scheduled. . . . John asked:

"What exactly is the problem?" . . .

"We've got a one in eight hundred and ninety-five shot at a retarded baby."

John smiled, "I can live with those odds."

"I'm still a little scared."

He reached across the table for my hand. "Sure," he said, "that's understandable. But even if there is a problem, we've caught it in time. . . . The worst-case scenario is that you might have to have an abortion, and that's a long shot. Everything's going to be fine." . . .

"I might *have to have* an abortion?" The chill inside me was gone. Instead I could feel my face flushing hot with anger. "Since when do you decide what I *have* to do with my body?"

John looked surprised. "I never said I was going to decide anything," he protested. "It's just that if the tests show something wrong with the baby, of course we'll abort. We've talked about this."

"What we've talked about," I told John in a low, dangerous voice, "is that I am pro-choice. That means I decide whether or not I'd abort a baby with a birth defect. . . . I'm not so sure of this."

"You used to be," said John.

"I know I used to be." I rubbed my eyes. I felt terribly confused. "But now . . . look, John, it's not as though we're deciding whether or not to have a baby. We're deciding what *kind* of baby we're willing to accept. If it's perfect in every way, we keep it. If it doesn't fit the right specifications, whoosh! Out it goes." . . .

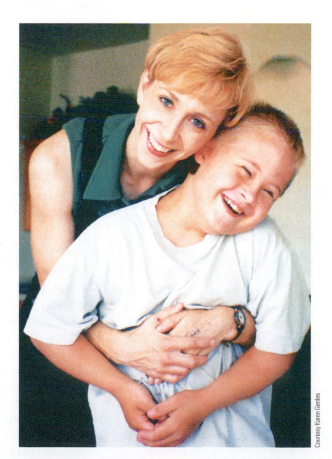

Happy Boy Martha Beck not only loves her son Adam (shown here), but she also writes about the special experiences he has brought into the whole family's life—hers, John's, and their other children's. She is "pro-choice"; he is a chosen child.

Courtesy Karen Gerdes

John was looking more and more confused. "Martha, why are you on this soapbox? What's your point?"

"My point is," I said, "that I'm trying to get you to tell me what you think constitutes a 'defective' baby. What about . . . oh, I don't know, a hyperactive baby? Or an ugly one?"

"They can't test for those things and—"

"Well, what if they could?" I said. "Medicine can do all kinds of magical tricks these days. Pretty soon we're going to be aborting babies because they have the gene for alcoholism, or homosexuality, or manic depression. . . . Did you know that in China they abort a lot of fetuses just because they're female?" I growled. "Is being a girl 'defective' enough for you?"

"Look," he said, "I know I can't always see things from your perspective. And I'm sorry about that. But the way I see it, if a baby is going to be deformed or something, abortion is a way to keep everyone from suffering—*especially* the baby. It's like shooting a horse that's broken its leg. . . . A lame horse dies slowly, you know? . . . It dies in terrible pain. And it can't run anymore.

So it can't enjoy life even if it doesn't die. Horses live to run; that's what they do. If a baby is born not being able to do what other people do, I think it's better not to prolong its suffering."

". . . And what is it," I said softly, more to myself than to John, "what is it that people do? What do we live to do, the way a horse lives to run?"

[Beck, 1999, pp. 132–133, 135]

The second AFP test was in the normal range, "meaning there was no reason to fear . . . Down syndrome" (Beck, 1999, p. 137).

As you read in Chapter 3, genetic counselors help couples weigh options *before* becoming pregnant. John and Martha had had no counseling because the pregnancy was unplanned and their risk for Down syndrome was low. The opposite of a false positive is a false negative, a mistaken assurance that all is well. Amniocentesis later revealed that the second AFP was a false negative. Their fetus had Down syndrome after all. Martha decided against abortion.

Low Birthweight: Causes and Consequences

Some newborns are small and immature. With modern hospital care, tiny infants usually survive, but it would be better for everyone—mother, father, baby, and society—if all newborns were in the womb for at least 36 weeks and weighed more than 2,500 grams (5½ pounds). (Usually, this text gives pounds before grams. But hospitals worldwide report birthweight using the metric system, so grams precede pounds and ounces here.)

The World Health Organization defines **low birthweight (LBW)** as under 2,500 grams. LBW babies are further grouped into **very low birthweight (VLBW),** under 1,500 grams (3 pounds, 5 ounces), and **extremely low birthweight (ELBW),** under 1,000 grams (2 pounds, 3 ounces). Some newborns weigh as little as 500 grams, and they are the most vulnerable—about half of them die even with excellent care (Lau et al., 2013).

Maternal Behavior and Low Birthweight

The causes of low birthweight are many. Twins and other multiples gain weight more slowly than singletons, which is why some nations do not allow multiple zygotes to be implanted in IVF. Remember that fetal weight normally doubles in the last trimester of pregnancy, with 900 grams (about 2 pounds) of that gain occurring in the final three weeks.

Thus, a baby born **preterm** (two or more weeks early; no longer called *premature*) is usually, but not always, LBW. Preterm birth correlates with many of the teratogens already mentioned, part of the cascade.

Not every low-birthweight baby is preterm. Some fetuses gain weight slowly throughout pregnancy and are *small-for-dates,* or **small for gestational age (SGA).** A full-term baby weighing only 2,600 grams and a 30-week-old fetus weighing only 1,000 grams are both SGA, even though the first is not technically low birthweight. Maternal or fetal illness might cause SGA, but maternal drug use is a more common cause. Every psychoactive drug slows fetal growth, with tobacco implicated in 25 percent of all low-birthweight births worldwide.

low birthweight (LBW) A body weight at birth of less than 2,500 grams (5½ pounds).

very low birthweight (VLBW) A body weight at birth of less than 1,500 grams (3 pounds, 5 ounces).

extremely low birthweight (ELBW) A body weight at birth of less than 1,000 grams (2 pounds, 3 ounces).

preterm A birth that occurs two or more weeks before the full 38 weeks of the typical pregnancy—that is, at 36 or fewer weeks after conception.

small for gestational age (SGA) A term for a baby whose birthweight is significantly lower than expected, given the time since conception. For example, a 5-pound (2,265-gram) newborn is considered SGA if born on time but not SGA if born two months early. (Also called *small-for-dates.*)

Another common reason for slow fetal growth is malnutrition. Women who begin pregnancy underweight, who eat poorly during pregnancy, or who gain less than 3 pounds (1.3 kilograms) per month in the last six months more often have underweight infants.

Unfortunately, many risk factors—underweight, undereating, underage, and smoking—tend to occur together. To make it worse, many such mothers live in poor neighborhoods where pollution is high—another risk factor for low birthweight (Stieb et al., 2012).

What About the Father?

The causes of low birthweight just mentioned rightly focus on the pregnant woman. However, fathers—and grandmothers, neighbors, and communities—are often crucial. An editorial in a journal for obstetricians explains: "Fathers' attitudes regarding the pregnancy, fathers' behaviors during the prenatal period, and the relationship between fathers and mothers . . . may indirectly influence risk for adverse birth outcomes" (Misra et al., 2010, p. 99).

As already explained in Chapter 1, each person is embedded in a social network. Since the future mother's behavior impacts the fetus, everyone who affects her also affects the fetus. Her mother, her boss, her mother-in-law, and especially her partner can add to her stress, or mitigate it. Thus, it is not surprising that unintended pregnancies increase the incidence of low birthweight (Shah et al., 2011). Obviously, intentions are in the mother's mind, not her body, and they are affected by the father. Thus, the father's intentions affect her diet, drug use, prenatal care, and so on.

Not only fathers but also the entire social network and culture are crucial (Lewallen, 2011). This is most apparent in what is called the **immigrant paradox.** Many immigrants have difficulty getting education and well-paid jobs; their socioeconomic status is low. Low SES correlates with low birthweight, especially in the United States (Martinson & Reichman, 2016). Thus, newborns born to immigrants are expected to be underweight. But, paradoxically, they are generally healthier in every way, including birthweight, than newborns of U.S.-born women of the same gene pool (García Coll & Marks, 2012).

This paradox was first called the *Hispanic paradox,* because, although U.S. residents born in Mexico or Central or South America average lower SES than Hispanics born in the United States, their newborns have fewer problems. The same paradox is now apparent for immigrants from the Caribbean, from Africa, from Eastern Europe, and from Asia compared to U.S.-born women of those ethnicities. Why? The crucial factor may be fathers, who keep pregnant immigrant women drug-free and healthy, buffering the stress that poverty brings (Luecken et al., 2013).

Consequences of Low Birthweight

You have already read that life itself is uncertain for the smallest newborns. Ranking worse than most developed nations—and just behind Cuba and Croatia—the United States' infant mortality rate (death in the first year) is 34th in the world, about 6 deaths per 1,000 live births, according to the United Nations. The main reason is that the United States has more ELBW newborns.

Worldwide, fewer slightly older newborns die—which is why U.S. infant mortality rates are not decreasing as fast as they are in other nations—but the U.S. death rate of the tiniest babies seems to be rising, not falling (Lau et al., 2013). For survivors born VLBW, every developmental milestone—smiling, holding a bottle, walking, talking—is delayed, even when they are compared to normal weight babies born on the basis of age since conception, not birth age.

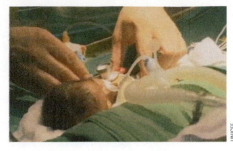

LaunchPad
macmillan learning

Watch **Video: Low Birthweight in India,** which discusses the causes of LBW among babies in India.

immigrant paradox The surprising, paradoxical fact that low-SES immigrant women tend to have fewer birth complications than native-born peers with higher incomes.

Response for Social Workers (from page 108): Testing and then treatment are useful at any time because women who know they are HIV-positive are more likely to get treatment, reduce the risk of transmission, or avoid pregnancy. If pregnancy does occur, early diagnosis is best. Getting tested after birth is too late for the baby.

Low-birthweight babies experience cognitive difficulties as well as visual and hearing impairments. High-risk newborns become infants and children who cry more, pay attention less, disobey, and experience language delays (Aarnoudse-Moens et al., 2009; Stolt et al., 2014).

Research from many nations finds that children who were at the extremes of SGA or preterm have many neurological problems in middle childhood, including smaller brain volume, lower IQs, and behavioral difficulties (Clark et al., 2013; Hutchinson et al., 2013; Howe et al., 2016). Even in adulthood, risks persist: Adults who were LBW are more likely to develop diabetes and heart disease. They also are more likely to experience psychological problems, such as depression and bipolar disorder (Lyall et al., 2016).

Longitudinal data provide both hope and caution. Remember that risk analysis gives probabilities, not certainties—averages are not true in every case. By age 4, some ELBW infants are normal in brain development and overall, especially if they had no medical complications and their mother was well educated. In adulthood, their early arrival may no longer be relevant.

Comparing Nations

In some northern European nations, only 4 percent of newborns weigh under 2,500 grams; in several South Asian nations, including India, Pakistan, and the Philippines, more than 20 percent do. Worldwide, far fewer low-birthweight babies are born than two decades ago; as a result, neonatal deaths have been reduced by one-third (Rajaratnam et al., 2010).

Some nations, China and Chile among them, have improved markedly. In 1970, about half of Chinese newborns were LBW; recent estimates put that number at 2 percent (UNICEF, 2014). In some nations, community health programs aid the growth of the fetus. That has an effect, according to a study provocatively titled *Low birth weight outcomes: Why better in Cuba than Alabama?* (Neggers & Crowe, 2013).

In other nations, notably in sub-Saharan Africa, the LBW rate is rising because global warming, HIV, food shortages, wars, and other problems affect pregnancy. One nation with a troubling rate of LBW is the United States, where the rate fell throughout most of the twentieth century, reaching a low of 7.0 percent in 1990. But then it rose again, with the 2012 rate at 7.99 percent, ranging from less than 6 percent in Alaska to more than 12 percent in Mississippi. The U.S. rate is higher than that of virtually every other developed nation (see Figure 4.7 for a sampling).

Many scientists have suggested hypotheses to explain the troubling U.S. rates. One logical possibility is assisted reproduction, which produces more twins in the United States than in other nations. However, LBW rates rose for naturally conceived babies as well.

Added to the puzzle is that several changes in maternal ethnicity, age, and health since 1990 have decreased LBW averages, not increased them. For instance, although the rate of LBW among African Americans is much higher than the

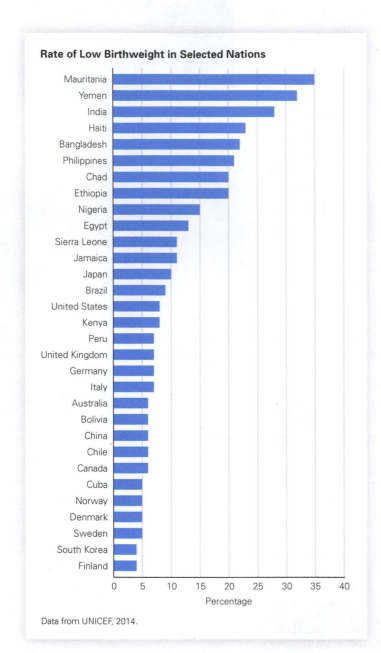

Rate of Low Birthweight in Selected Nations

Data from UNICEF, 2014.

FIGURE 4.7

Getting Better Some public health experts consider the rate of low birthweight to be indicative of national health, since both are affected by the same causes. If that is true, the world is getting healthier, since the LBW world average was 28 percent in 2009 but 16 percent in 2012. When all nations are included, 47 report LBW at 6 per 100 or lower. (The United States and the United Kingdom are not among them.)

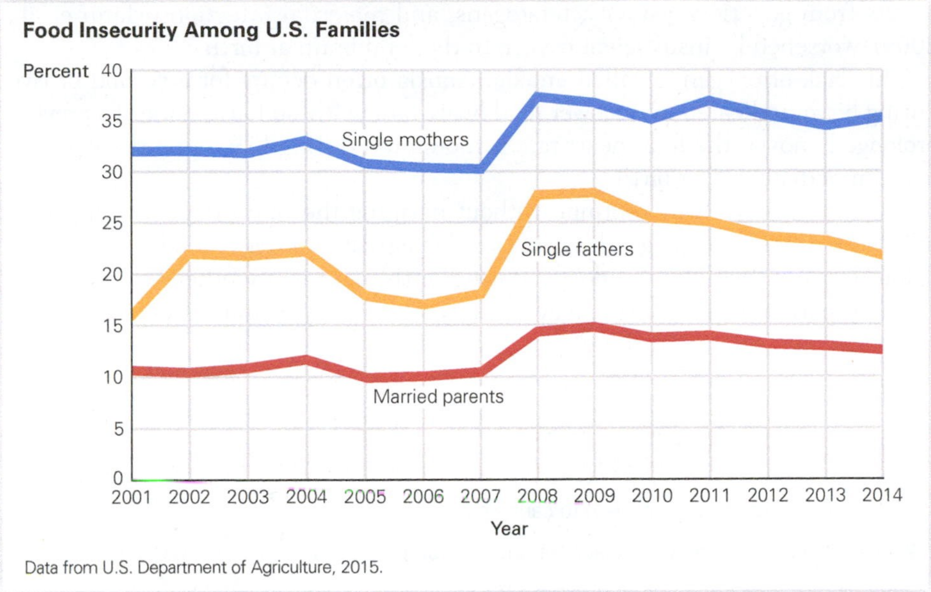

FIGURE 4.8

And Recovery? As you can see, all families were affected by the Great Recession—especially single fathers, who were most likely to lose their jobs and not know how to get food stamps. But why are children of single mothers now hungry almost three times more often than children of married parents? Why did rates for single-mother families stay high after the recession, unlike for other families? The data show correlation; researchers do not agree about causes.

national average (almost 13.2 percent compared with 8 percent), and although younger teenagers have smaller babies than do women in their 20s, the birth rate among both groups was much lower in 2012 than it was in 1990. That should have reduced the LBW average.

Furthermore, maternal obesity and diabetes have increased since 1990; both lead to heavier babies. Yet more underweight babies are born. What could the explanation be?

One possibility is nutrition. In the United States, the U.S. Department of Agriculture (Coleman-Jenson et al., 2015) reported an increase in the rate of *food insecurity* (measured by skipped meals, use of food stamps, and outright hunger) between the first seven years of the twenty-first century and the next seven, from about 11 percent to about 15 percent. Hungry mothers have smaller babies. Food insecurity also increases chronic illness, another correlate of LBW (Seligman & Schillinger, 2010). Food worries are highest in single mothers, a group that has increased since 2000 (see Figure 4.8).

Another possibility is drug use. As you will see in Chapter 16, the rate of smoking and drinking among high school girls reached a low in 1992; it then increased, and then decreased. Most U.S. women giving birth in the first decade of the twenty-first century are in the cohort that experienced rising drug use when they were younger; they may still suffer the effects. If that is the reason, the recent decrease in drug use among teenagers will soon result in fewer LBW babies.

Sadly, in some nations, cigarette smoking trends are ominous. In Asia, more young women are smoking and drinking than did two decades ago. Are LBW rates about to rise in China? Two nations where low birthweight is increasing are Korea and Japan; both have more young women smokers (UNICEF, 2014).

Complications During Birth

Birth complications rarely have a single cause. A fetus may be low-birthweight, preterm, genetically vulnerable, or exposed to teratogens *and* its mother is unusually young, old, small, stressed, or ill. As an example, **cerebral palsy** (a disease marked by difficulties with movement) was once thought to be caused solely by birth procedures (excessive medication, slow breech birth, or use of forceps to pull the fetal head through the birth canal). However, we now know that cerebral palsy

cerebral palsy A disorder that results from damage to the brain's motor centers. People with cerebral palsy have difficulty with muscle control, so their speech and/or body movements are impaired.

results from genetic sensitivity, teratogens, and maternal infection (Mann et al., 2009), worsened by insufficient oxygen to the fetal brain at birth.

This lack of oxygen is called **anoxia.** Anoxia often occurs for a second or two during birth, indicated by a slower fetal heart rate, with no harm done. To prevent prolonged anoxia, the fetal heart rate is monitored during labor, and the Apgar is used immediately after birth.

How long anoxia can continue without harming the brain depends on genes, birthweight, gestational age, drugs in the bloodstream (either taken by the mother before birth or given by the doctor during birth), and many other factors. Thus, anoxia is part of a cascade that may cause cerebral palsy. Almost every other birth complication is also the result of many factors.

anoxia A lack of oxygen that, if prolonged, can cause brain damage or death.

> **THINK CRITICALLY:** Food scarcity, drug use, and unmarried parenthood have all been suggested as reasons for the LBW rate in the United States. Which is it—or are there other factors?

> ### WHAT HAVE YOU LEARNED?
>
> **1.** Why are no teratogens *certain* to cause harm?
>
> **2.** How do we know that the placenta does not screen out all harmful substances?
>
> **3.** What evidence suggests that teratogens are affected by genes and chromosomes?
>
> **4.** Why is it difficult to determine whether behavioral teratogens affected a child?
>
> **5.** What are the causes and consequences of low birthweight?

The New Family

Humans are social creatures, seeking interaction with their families and their societies. We have already seen how crucial social support is during pregnancy. Social interaction may become even more important when a child is born.

The Newborn

Before birth, humans already affect their families through fetal movements and hormones that trigger maternal nurturance (food aversions, increased sleep, and more). At birth, a newborn's appearance (big hairless head, tiny feet, and so on) stirs the human heart, evident in adults' brain activity and heart rate. Fathers are often enraptured by their scraggly newborn and protective of the exhausted mothers, who may appreciate their partners more than before, for hormonal as well as practical reasons.

Newborns are responsive social creatures in the first hours of life (Zeifman, 2013). They listen, stare, cry, stop crying, and cuddle. In the first day or two, a professional might administer the **Brazelton Neonatal Behavioral Assessment Scale (NBAS),** which records 46 behaviors, including 20 reflexes. (See Visualizing Development, p. 99.) Parents watching this assessment are amazed at the newborn's responses—and this fosters early parent–child connection (Hawthorne, 2009).

Technically, a **reflex** is an involuntary response to a particular stimulus. Although many reflexes seem meaningless now, historically reflexes were beneficial, and some are still protective (the eye blink is an example). Their strength varies from one newborn to the next depending on genes, drugs in the bloodstream, and overall health. Newborns have three sets of reflexes that aid survival.

Brazelton Neonatal Behavioral Assessment Scale (NBAS) A test that is often administered to newborns which measures responsiveness and records 46 behaviors, including 20 reflexes.

reflex An unlearned, involuntary action or movement in response to a stimulus. A reflex occurs without conscious thought.

- *Reflexes that maintain oxygen supply.* The *breathing reflex* begins even before the umbilical cord, with its supply of oxygen, is cut. Additional reflexes that maintain oxygen are reflexive *hiccups* and *sneezes,* as well as *thrashing* (moving the arms and legs about) to escape something that covers the face.

- *Reflexes that maintain constant body temperature.* When infants are cold, they *cry, shiver,* and *tuck their legs* close to their bodies. When they are hot, they try to *push away* blankets and then stay still.
- *Reflexes that manage feeding.* The *sucking reflex* causes newborns to suck anything that touches their lips—fingers, toes, blankets, and rattles, as well as natural and artificial nipples of various textures and shapes. In the *rooting reflex,* babies turn their mouths toward anything that brushes against their cheeks—a reflexive search for a nipple—and start to suck. *Swallowing* also aids feeding, as does *crying* when the stomach is empty and *spitting up* when too much is swallowed quickly.

Other reflexes signify brain and body functions. Among them are the:

- *Babinski reflex.* When a newborn's feet are stroked, the toes fan upward.
- *Stepping reflex.* When newborns are held upright, feet touching a flat surface, they move their legs as if to walk.
- *Swimming reflex.* When held horizontally on their stomachs, newborns stretch out their arms and legs.
- *Palmar grasping reflex.* When something touches newborns' palms, they grip it tightly.
- *Moro reflex.* When someone bangs on the table they are lying on, newborns fling their arms outward and then bring them together on their chests, crying with wide-open eyes.

These 18 reflexes and more are evident in normal newborns. The senses are also responsive. New babies listen more to voices than to traffic, for instance. Thus, in many ways newborns connect with the people of their world, who are predisposed to respond (Zeifman, 2013). If the baby performing these actions on the Brazelton NBAS were your own, you would be proud and amazed; that is part of being human.

New Mothers

When birth hormones decrease, between 8 and 15 percent of women experience **postpartum depression,** a sense of inadequacy and sadness (called *baby blues* in the mild version and *postpartum psychosis* in the most severe form).

With postpartum depression, baby care (feeding, diapering, bathing) feels very burdensome. The newborn's cry may not compel the mother to carry and nurse her infant. Instead, the mother may have thoughts of neglect or abuse, thoughts so terrifying that she is afraid of herself. She may be overprotective, insisting that no one else care for the baby. This signifies a fearful mother, not a healthy one.

The first sign that something is amiss may be euphoria after birth. A new mother may be unable to sleep, or to stop talking, or to dismiss irrational worries. After the initial high, severe depression may set in, with a long-term impact on the child. Postpartum depression may not be evident right away; anxiety and depression symptoms may be stronger two months after birth than right away (Kozhimannil & Kim, 2014).

But postpartum depression is not due to hormonal changes alone. From a developmental perspective, some causes of postpartum depression (such as financial stress) predate the pregnancy. Others (such as marital problems) occur during pregnancy; others correlate with birth (especially if the mother is alone and imagined a different birth than actually occurred).

Finally, the characteristics of the baby may be disappointing, (such as health, feeding, or sleeping problems). Successful breast-feeding mitigates maternal depression, one of the many reasons a lactation consultant is an important part of the new mother's support team.

Video: Newborn Reflexes shows several infants displaying the reflexes discussed in this section.

postpartum depression A new mother's feelings of inadequacy and sadness in the days and weeks after giving birth.

Especially for Scientists Research with animals can benefit people, but it is sometimes wrongly used to support conclusions about people. When does that happen? (see response, page 116)

Expecting a Girl She is obviously thrilled and ready, and they bought a crib, but he seems somewhat nervous. Perhaps someone should tell him that his newborn will become a happy and accomplished child and adult, a source of paternal pride and joy for the next 40 years or more.

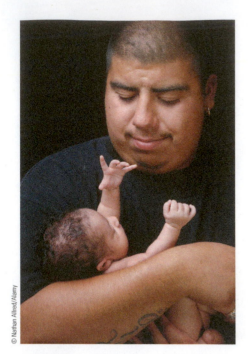

© Nathan Allred/Alamy

Mutual Joy Ignore this dad's tattoo and earring, and the newborn's head wet with amniotic fluid. Instead recognize that, for thousands of years, hormones and instincts propel fathers and babies to reach out to each other, developing lifelong connections.

⬤⬤ Especially for Nurses in Obstetrics
Can the father be of any practical help in the birth process? (see response, page 118)

couvade Symptoms of pregnancy and birth experienced by fathers.

⬤⬤ Response for Scientists (from page 115): Animal research should not, by itself, confirm an assertion that has popular appeal but no scientific evidence. This occurred in the social construction that physical contact was crucial for parent–infant bonding.

New Fathers

As we have seen, fathers-to-be help mothers-to-be stay healthy, nourished, and drug-free. Fathers may be crucial in birth. I observed this when Elissa delivered Asa (now 5, as noted in the opening of this chapter). Asa's birth took much longer than his younger brother's; Elissa's anxiety rose when the doctor and midwife discussed a possible cesarean for "failure to progress" without asking her opinion. Her husband told her, "All you need to do is relax between contractions and push when a contraction comes. I will do the rest." She listened. He did. No cesarean.

Whether or not he is present at birth, the father's legal acceptance of the baby has an impact. A study of all live single births in Milwaukee from 1993 to 2006 (151,869 babies!) found that complications correlated with several expected variables (e.g., maternal cigarette smoking) and one unexpected one—no father listed on the birth record. This connection was especially apparent for European American births: When the mother did not list the father, she was more likely to have long labor, a cesarean section, and so on (Ngui et al., 2009).

Currently, about half of all U.S. women are not married when their baby is born (U.S. Census Bureau, 2014), but fathers may still be on the birth certificate. When fathers acknowledge their role, birth is better for mother and child.

Fathers may experience pregnancy and birth biologically, not just psychologically. Many fathers have symptoms of pregnancy and birth, including weight gain and indigestion during pregnancy and pain during labor (Leavitt, 2009). Among the Papua in New Guinea and the Basques in Spain, husbands used to build a hut when birth was imminent and then lie down to writhe in mock labor (Klein, 1991).

Paternal experiences of pregnancy and birth are called **couvade,** expected in some cultures, a normal variation in many, and considered pathological in others (M. Sloan, 2009). A recent study in India found that most new fathers experienced couvade (Ganapathy, 2014). In the United States, couvade is unnoticed and unstudied, but many fathers are intensely involved with the early development of their future child (Brennan et al., 2007; Raeburn, 2014).

Fathers are usually the first responders when the mother experiences postpartum depression; they may be instrumental in getting the support that the mother and baby need (Cuijpers et al., 2010; Goodman & Gotlib, 2002). But fathers are vulnerable to depression, too, with the same stresses that mothers feel (Gutierrez-Galve et al., 2015). Indeed, sometimes the father experiences more emotional problems than the mother (Bradley & Slade, 2011). Friends and relatives need to help both parents in the first weeks after birth.

Parental Alliance

Remember John and Martha, the young couple whose AFP was a false negative but amniocentesis revealed that their fetus had trisomy-21 (Down syndrome)? One night at 3:00 A.M., after about seven months of pregnancy, Martha was crying uncontrollably. She told John she was scared.

> "Scared of what?" he said. "Of a little baby who's not as perfect as you think he ought to be?"
> "I didn't say I wanted him to be perfect," I said. "I just want him to be normal. That's all I want. Just normal."
> "That is total bullshit. . . . You don't want this baby to be normal. You'd throw him in a dumpster if he just turned out to be normal. What you really want is for him to be superhuman."

"For your information," I said in my most acid tone, "I was the one who decided to keep this baby, even though he's got Down's. You were the one who wanted to throw him in a dumpster."

"How would you know?" John's voice was still gaining volume. "You never asked me what I wanted, did you? No. You never even asked me."

[Beck, 1999, p. 255]

This episode ended well, with a long, warm, and honest conversation between the two prospective parents. Each learned what their fetus meant to the other, a taboo topic until that night.

Their lack of communication up to this point, and the sudden eruption of sorrow and anger, is not unusual, because pregnancy itself raises memories from childhood and fears about the future. Yet honest and intimate communication is crucial throughout pregnancy, birth, and child rearing. Such early communication between new parents helps to form a **parental alliance,** a commitment by both parents to cooperate in raising their child.

The parental alliance is especially beneficial, yet depression in both parents especially likely, when the infant is physically vulnerable, such as having a low birthweight (Helle et al., 2016). Family conflict when a newborn needs extra care increases the risk of child maladjustment and parental divorce (Whiteside-Mansell et al., 2009).

Family Bonding

To what extent are the first hours after birth crucial for the **parent–infant bond,** the strong, loving connection that forms as parents hold, examine, and feed their newborn? It has been claimed that this bond develops in the first hours after birth when a mother touches her naked baby, just as sheep and goats must immediately smell and nuzzle their newborns if they are to nurture them (Klaus & Kennell, 1976).

However, the hypothesis that early skin-to-skin contact is *essential* for human nurturance is false (Eyer, 1992; Lamb, 1982). Substantial research on monkeys begins with *cross-fostering,* a strategy in which newborns are removed from their biological mothers in the first days of life and raised by another female or even a male monkey. A strong and beneficial relationship sometimes develops (Suomi, 2002). Parents may begin to bond with their children before birth, and/or they may bond in the months after birth.

This finding does not contradict the generalization that prospective parents' active involvement in pregnancy, birth, and care of the newborn benefits all three. Factors that encourage parents (biological or adoptive) to nurture their newborns have lifelong benefits, proven with mice, monkeys, and humans (Champagne & Curley, 2010). Beneficial, but not essential.

The benefits of early contact are evident with **kangaroo care,** in which the newborn lies between the mother's breasts, skin-to-skin, listening to her heartbeat and feeling her body heat. A review of 124 studies confirms that kangaroo-care newborns sleep more deeply, gain weight more quickly, and spend more time alert than do infants with standard care, as well as being healthier overall (Boundy et al., 2016). Father involvement may also be important, including father–infant kangaroo care (Feeley et al., 2013).

Kangaroo care benefits babies, not only in the hospital but months later, either because of improved infant adjustment to life outside the womb or because of increased parental sensitivity and effectiveness. Which of these two is the explanation? Probably both.

"Of course I know what he wants when he cries. He wants you."

parental alliance Cooperation between a mother and a father based on their mutual commitment to their children. In a parental alliance, the parents support each other in their shared parental roles.

parent–infant bond The strong, loving connection that forms as parents hold, examine, and feed their newborn.

kangaroo care A form of newborn care in which mothers (and sometimes fathers) rest their babies on their naked chests, like kangaroo mothers that carry their immature newborns in a pouch on their abdomen.

Better Care Kangaroo care benefits mothers, babies, and hospitals, saving space and medical costs in this ward in Manila. Kangaroo care is one reason Filipino infant mortality in 2010 is only one-fifth of what it was in 1950.

As we will see in later chapters, the relationship between parent and child develops over months, not merely hours. Birth is one step of a lifelong journey.

WHAT HAVE YOU LEARNED?

1. How can a newborn be socially interactive?
2. What causes postpartum depression?
3. How are fathers affected by birth?
4. Why is kangaroo care beneficial?
5. When does the parent–infant bond form?

SUMMARY

Prenatal Development

1. The first two weeks of prenatal growth are called the germinal period. Soon the single-celled zygote multiplies into many cells, becoming a *blastocyst,* with more than 100 cells that will eventually form both the placenta and the embryo. The growing organism travels down the fallopian tube and implants in the uterus. More than half the time, implantation fails.

2. The embryonic period, from the third week through the eighth week after conception, begins with the first signs of the future central nervous system. The future heart begins to beat, and the eyes, ears, nose, mouth, and brain form. By the eighth week, the embryo has all of the basic organs and features, except for sex organs.

3. The fetal period extends from the ninth week until birth. In the ninth week, the sex organs develop. By the end of the third month, all of the organs and body structures have formed, although the tiny fetus could not survive outside the womb. At 22 weeks, when the brain can regulate basic body functions, viability is possible but unlikely. Babies born before the 26th week are at high risk of death or disability.

4. The average fetus gains approximately 4½ pounds (2,040 grams) from the sixth month to the ninth month, weighing 7½ pounds (3,400 grams) at birth. Maturation of brain, lungs, and heart ensures survival of more than 99 percent of all full-term babies.

Birth

5. Birth typically begins with contractions that push the fetus out of the uterus and then through the vagina. The Apgar scale, which rates the newborn at one minute and again at five minutes after birth, provides a quick evaluation of the infant's health.

6. Medical assistance speeds contractions, dulls pain, and saves lives. However, many aspects of medicalized birth have been criticized as impersonal and unnecessary, including about half of the cesareans performed in the United States. Contemporary birthing practices are aimed at balancing the needs of baby, parents, and medical personnel.

Problems and Solutions

7. Some teratogens cause physical impairment. Others, called behavioral teratogens, harm the brain and therefore impair cognitive abilities and affect personality.

8. Whether a teratogen harms an embryo or fetus depends on timing, dose, and genes. Public and personal health practices can protect against prenatal complications, with some specifics debatable. Always, however, family members affect the pregnant woman's health.

9. Low birthweight (under 5½ pounds, or 2,500 grams) may arise from early or multiple births, placental problems, maternal illness, malnutrition, smoking, drinking, illicit drug use, and age. Underweight babies experience more medical difficulties and psychological problems for many years. Babies that are small for gestational age (SGA) are especially vulnerable.

10. Every birth complication, such as unusually long and stressful labor that includes anoxia (a lack of oxygen to the fetus), has a combination of causes. Long-term handicaps are not inevitable, but careful nurturing from parents and society may be essential.

The New Family

11. Newborns are primed for social interaction. The Brazelton Neonatal Behavioral Assessment Scale measures 46 newborn behaviors, 20 of which are reflexes.

12. Fathers can be supportive during pregnancy as well as helpful in birth. Paternal support correlates with shorter labor and fewer complications. Some fathers become very involved with the pregnancy and birth, experiencing couvade.

13. Many women feel unhappy, incompetent, or unwell after giving birth. Postpartum depression gradually disappears with appropriate help; fathers can be crucial in baby care, or they can experience depression themselves. Ideally, a parental alliance forms to help the child develop well.

14. Kangaroo care benefits all babies, but especially those who are vulnerable. Mother–newborn interaction should be encouraged, although the parent–infant bond depends on many factors in addition to birth practices.

KEY TERMS

germinal period (p. 90)
embryonic period (p. 90)
fetal period (p. 90)
implantation (p. 90)
embryo (p. 91)
fetus (p. 92)
ultrasound (p. 92)
age of viability (p. 94)
Apgar scale (p. 97)
doula (p. 98)

cesarean section (c-section)
    (p. 98)
teratogen (p. 103)
behavioral teratogens (p. 103)
teratology (p. 104)
threshold effect (p. 105)
fetal alcohol syndrome (FAS)
    (p. 105)
false positive (p. 109)
low birthweight (LBW) (p. 110)

very low birthweight (VLBW)
    (p. 110)
extremely low birthweight
    (ELBW) (p. 110)
preterm (p. 110)
small for gestational age (SGA)
    (p. 110)
immigrant paradox (p. 111)
cerebral palsy (p. 113)
anoxia (p. 114)

Brazelton Neonatal Behavioral
    Assessment Scale (NBAS)
    (p. 114)
reflex (p. 114)
postpartum depression (p. 115)
couvade (p. 116)
parental alliance (p. 117)
parent–infant bond (p. 117)
kangaroo care (p. 117)

APPLICATIONS

1. Go to a nearby greeting-card store and analyze the cards about pregnancy and birth. Do you see any cultural attitudes (e.g., variations depending on the sex of the newborn or of the parent)? If possible, compare those cards with cards from a store that caters to another economic or ethnic group.

2. Interview three mothers of varied backgrounds about their birth experiences. Make your interviews open-ended—let the mothers choose what to tell you, as long as they give at least a 10-minute description. Then compare and contrast the three accounts, noting especially any influences of culture, personality, circumstances, and cohort.

3. People sometimes wonder how any pregnant woman could jeopardize the health of her fetus. Consider your own health-related behavior in the past month—exercise, sleep, nutrition, drug use, medical and dental care, disease avoidance, and so on. Would you change your behavior if you were pregnant? Would it make a difference if you, your family, and your partner did not want a baby?

the first two years

A dults don't change much in a year or two. They might have longer, grayer, or thinner hair; they might gain or lose weight; they might learn something new. But if you saw friends you hadn't seen for two years, you'd recognize them immediately.

Imagine caring for a newborn 24 hours a day for a month and then leaving for two years. On your return, you might not recognize him or her. The baby would have quadrupled in weight, grown a foot taller, and sprouted a new head of hair. Behavior and emotions change, too—less crying, but new laughter and fear—including fear of you.

A year or two is not much compared with the 80 or so years of the average life. However, in their first two years humans reach half their adult height, learn to talk in sentences, and express almost every emotion—not just joy and fear but also love, jealousy, and shame. Invisible changes in the brain are even more crucial, setting the pattern for the life span. The next three chapters describe these radical and awesome changes.●●

The First Two Years:
Biosocial Development

What Will You Know?

1. What part of an infant grows most in the first two years?
2. Are babies essentially blind and deaf at birth?
3. What happens if a baby does not get his or her vaccinations?

Our first child, Bethany, was born when I was in graduate school. At 14 months, she was growing well and talking but had not yet taken her first step. I told my husband that genes were more influential than anything we did. I had read that babies in Paris are among the latest walkers in the world, and my grandmother was French.

To my relief, Bethany soon began walking, and by age 5 she was the fastest runner in her kindergarten class. My genetic explanation was bolstered when our next two children, Rachel and Elissa, were also slow to walk. My students with Guatemalan and Ghanaian ancestors bragged about their infants who walked before a year; those from China and France had later walkers. Genetic, I thought.

Fourteen years after Bethany, Sarah was born. I could finally afford a full-time caregiver, Mrs. Todd. She thought Sarah was the most advanced baby she had ever known, except for her own daughter, Gillian.

"She'll be walking by a year," Mrs. Todd told me. "Gillian walked at 10 months."

"We'll see," I graciously replied.

I underestimated Mrs. Todd. She bounced my delighted baby on her lap, day after day, and spent hours giving her "walking practice." Sarah took her first step at 12 months—late for a Todd, early for a Berger, and a humbling lesson for me.

As a scientist, I know that a single case proves nothing. My genetic explanation might be valid, especially since Sarah shares only half her genes with Bethany and since my daughters are only one-eighth French, a fraction I had conveniently ignored.

Nonetheless, I now recognize that caretakers influence every aspect of biosocial growth. This chapter is filled with examples of caregiving that enables babies to grow, move, and learn. Development is not as genetically determined as it once seemed. Genes provide the outline, but every moment of life after birth shapes and guides the young person to become a distinct, and special, human being.

Body Changes

In infancy, growth is so rapid and the consequences of neglect so severe that gains are closely monitored. Medical checkups, including measurement of height, weight, and head circumference, provide the first clues as to whether an infant is progressing as expected—or not.

© 2016 Macmillan

Video: Physical Development in Infancy and Toddlerhood offers a quick review of the physical changes that occur during a child's first two years.

percentile A point on a ranking scale of 0 to 100. The 50th percentile is the midpoint; half the people in the population being studied rank higher and half rank lower.

Body Size

Newborns lose several ounces in the first three days and then gain an ounce a day for months. Birthweight typically doubles by 4 months and triples by a year. On average, a 7-pound newborn will be 21 pounds at 12 months (9,525 grams, up from 3,175 grams at birth). Height increases, too: A typical baby grows 10 inches (25 centimeters) in a year, measuring about 30 inches (76 centimeters).

Physical growth then slows, but not by much. Most 24-month-old children weigh almost 28 pounds (13 kilograms) and have added another 4 inches (10 centimeters) or so. Typically, 2-year-olds are half their adult height and about one-fifth their adult weight (see Figure 5.1).

Growth is often expressed in a **percentile,** indicating how one person compares to another. Thus, a 3-month-old's weight at the 30th percentile means that 29 percent of 3-month-old babies weigh less and 69 percent weigh more. Healthy babies vary in size, so any percentile between 10 and 90 is okay, as long as the percentile is close to the previous one for that baby.

When an infant's percentile moves markedly up or down, that could signify trouble. A drop suggests poor nutrition; an increase—unless height increases, too—signifies overfeeding.

Parents were once blamed. For babies whose percentile dropped, it was thought that parents made feeding stressful, leading to *failure to thrive.* Now pediatricians consider it "outmoded" to blame parents, because failure to thrive may be caused by allergies, the microbiome, or other medical conditions (Jaffe, 2011, p. 100). Similarly, obesity is now thought to be cultural and genetic, as well as familial.

Sleep

Throughout childhood, regular and ample sleep correlates with normal brain maturation, learning, emotional regulation, academic success, and psychological

FIGURE 5.1

Averages and Individuals Norms and percentiles are useful—most 1-month-old girls who weigh 10 pounds should be at least 25 pounds by age 2. But although females weigh less than males on average lifelong, it is obvious that individuals do not always follow the norms. Do you know a 200-pound woman married to a 150-pound man?

Same Boy, Much Changed All three photos show Conor: first at 3 months, then at 12 months, and finally at 24 months. Note the rapid growth in the first two years, especially apparent in the changing proportions of the head compared to the body and use of the legs.

adjustment (Maski & Kothare, 2013). Sleep deprivation can cause poor health, and vice versa. As with many health habits, sleep patterns begin in the first year.

Patterns of Infant Sleep

Newborns spend most of their time sleeping, about 15 to 17 hours a day. Hours of sleep decrease rapidly with maturity: The norm per day for the first two months is 14¼ hours; for the next three months, 13¼ hours; for 6 to 17 months, 12¾ hours. Remember that norms are simply averages. Among every 20 young infants, their parents report, one baby sleeps nine hours or fewer per day and another one sleeps 19 hours or more (Sadeh et al., 2009).

Over the first few months, the time spent in each stage of sleep changes. Babies born preterm may always seem to be dozing. Full-term newborns dream a lot, as about half their sleep is **REM (rapid eye movement) sleep.** REM sleep declines over the early weeks, as does "transitional sleep," the dozing, half-awake stage. At 3 or 4 months, quiet sleep (also called *slow-wave sleep*) increases markedly.

Sleep varies not only because of biology (maturation and genes) but also because of caregivers. Infants who drink cow's milk and cereal may sleep more soundly—easier for parents but bad for the baby. Social environment matters: If parents respond to predawn cries with food and play, babies wake up early and often, night after night (Sadeh et al., 2009).

Insufficient sleep becomes a problem for parents as well as for infants, because "[p]arents are rarely well-prepared for the degree of sleep disruption a newborn infant engenders, and many have unrealistic expectations about the first few postnatal months." As a result, many parents become "desperate" and institute patterns they may later regret (C. Russell et al., 2013, p. 68).

Where Should Babies Sleep?

Traditionally, most middle-class North American infants slept in cribs in their own rooms; it was feared that they would be traumatized if their parents had sex in the same room. By contrast, most infants in Asia, Africa, and Latin America slept near their parents, a practice called **co-sleeping,** and sometimes in their parents' bed, called **bed-sharing.** In those cultures, nighttime parent–child separation was considered cruel.

REM (rapid eye movement) sleep A stage of sleep characterized by flickering eyes behind closed lids, dreaming, and rapid brain waves.

Especially for New Parents You are aware of cultural differences in sleeping practices, which raises a very practical issue: Should your newborn sleep in bed with you? (see response, page 126)

co-sleeping A custom in which parents and their children (usually infants) sleep together in the same room.

bed-sharing When two or more people sleep in the same bed.

FIGURE 5.2
Awake at Night Why the disparity between Asian and non-Asian rates of co-sleeping? It may be that Western parents use a variety of gadgets and objects—monitors, night-lights, pacifiers, cuddle cloths, sound machines—to accomplish some of what Asian parents do by having their infant next to them.

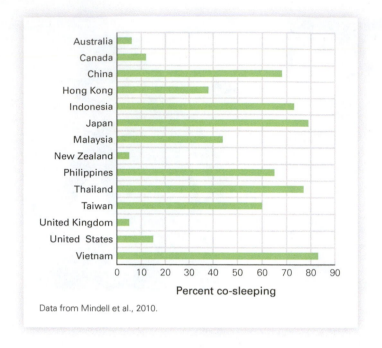

Percent co-sleeping

Data from Mindell et al., 2010.

Infant at Risk? Sleeping in the parents' bed is a risk factor for SIDS in the United States, but don't worry about this Japanese girl. In Japan, 97 percent of infants sleep next to their parents, yet infant mortality is only 3 per 1,000—compared with 7 per 1,000 in the United States. Is this bed, or this mother, or this sleeping position protective?

● ● ▶ Response for New Parents
(from page 125): From the psychological and cultural perspectives, babies can sleep anywhere as long as the parents can hear them if they cry. The main consideration is safety: Infants should not sleep on a mattress that is too soft, nor beside an adult who is drunk or on drugs. Otherwise, families should decide for themselves.

Today, Asian and African mothers still worry more about separation, whereas European and North American mothers worry more about privacy. A 19-nation survey found that parents act on these fears: The extremes were 82 percent of Vietnamese babies co-sleeping compared with 6 percent in New Zealand (Mindell et al., 2010) (see Figure 5.2). Cohort is also significant. In the United States, bed-sharing doubled from 1993 to 2010, from 6.5 percent to 13.5 percent (Colson et al., 2013).

This difference in practice may seem to be related to income, since low-SES families are less likely to have an extra room and more likely to sleep beside their baby (Colson et al., 2013).

But even wealthy Japanese families often sleep together. By contrast, many poor North American families find a separate room for their children. Co-sleeping results primarily from culture and custom, not income. This makes it difficult to change (Ball & Volpe, 2013).

The argument for co-sleeping is that the parents can quickly respond to a hungry or frightened baby. A popular book on infant care advocates "attachment parenting," advising keeping the infant nearby day and night (Sears & Sears, 2001). Babies seem to get as much sleep beside their parents as in their own cribs, although mothers wake up more often (Volkovich et al., 2015).

Co-sleeping does not always mean in the same bed. The argument against bed-sharing rests on a chilling statistic: Sudden infant death syndrome (SIDS), when a baby dies unexpectedly while asleep, is twice as likely when babies sleep beside their parents (Vennemann et al., 2012). Consequently, many experts seek ways to safeguard the practice (Ball & Volpe, 2013). Their advice includes *never* sleeping beside a baby if the parent has been drinking, and *never* using a soft comforter, pillow, or mattress near a sleeping infant.

Babies learn from experience. If they become accustomed to bed-sharing, they may crawl into their parents' bed long past infancy. Parents might lose sleep for years because they wanted more sleep when their babies were small. Developmentalists hesitate to declare either co-sleeping or separate bedrooms best because the issue is "tricky and complex" (Gettler & McKenna, 2010, p. 77). Sleeping alone may encourage independence—a trait appreciated in some cultures, abhorred in others.

Brain Development

From two weeks after conception to two years after birth, the brain grows more rapidly than any other organ, from about 25 percent of adult weight at birth to 75 percent at age 2 (see Figure 5.3). Prenatal and postnatal brain growth (measured by head circumference) affects later cognition (Gilles & Nelson, 2012). If teething or a stuffed-up nose temporarily slows eating, body weight is affected before brain weight, a phenomenon called **head-sparing.** That term expresses well what nature does—protect the brain.

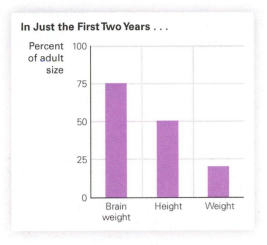

In Just the First Two Years . . .

FIGURE 5.3
Growing Up Two-year-olds are totally dependent on adults, but they have already reached half their adult height and three-fourths of their adult brain size.

head-sparing A biological mechanism that protects the brain when malnutrition disrupts body growth. The brain is the last part of the body to be damaged by malnutrition.

Many other terms in neuroscience are not as self-explanatory, but they are useful to understand the brain. Accordingly, they are explained in the following.

INSIDE THE BRAIN

Neuroscience Vocabulary

To understand the impressive brain growth that occurs throughout childhood, it is helpful to know some of the basic terms of neurological development (see Visualizing Development, p. 131).

Communication within the *central nervous system (CNS)*—the brain and spinal cord—begins with nerve cells, called **neurons.** At birth, the human brain has about 86 billion neurons.

Within and between areas of the central nervous system, neurons are connected to other neurons by intricate networks of nerve fibers called **axons** and **dendrites** (see Figure 5.4). Each neuron has a single axon and numerous dendrites, which spread out like the branches of a tree. The axon of one neuron meets the dendrites of other neurons at intersections called **synapses,** which are critical communication links within the brain.

neuron One of billions of nerve cells in the central nervous system, especially in the brain.

axon A fiber that extends from a neuron and transmits electrochemical impulses from that neuron to the dendrites of other neurons.

dendrite A fiber that extends from a neuron and receives electrochemical impulses transmitted from other neurons via their axons.

synapse The intersection between the axon of one neuron and the dendrites of other neurons.

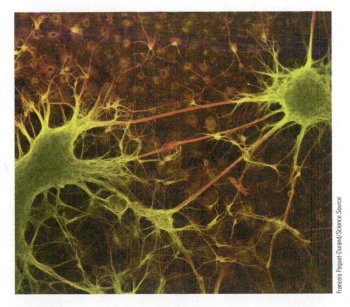

Francois Paquet-Durand/Science Source

FIGURE 5.4
Connecting The color staining on this photo makes it obvious that the two cell bodies of neurons (stained chartreuse) grow axons and dendrites to each other's neurons. This tangle is repeated thousands of times in every human brain. Throughout life, those fragile dendrites will grow or disappear as the person continues thinking.

Neurons communicate by *firing*, or sending electrochemical impulses through their axons to synapses to be picked up by the dendrites of other neurons. The dendrites bring the message to the cell bodies of their neurons, which, in turn, may fire, conveying messages via their axons to the dendrites of other neurons. Some firing is involuntary—such as the reflexes cited in Chapter 4. Most infant brain development requires new connections between one neuron and another, as dendrites grow (Gao et al., 2016).

Axons and dendrites do not touch at synapses. Instead, the electrical impulses in axons typically cause the release of **neurotransmitters,** which stimulate other neurons. There are about 100 neurotransmitters, including dopamine, serotonin, and acetylcholine—all crucial for human development, all mentioned later in this book.

Neurotransmitters carry information from the axon of the sending neuron, across a pathway called the *synaptic gap,* to the dendrites of the receiving neuron, a process speeded up by **myelin,** a coating on the outside of the axon. Myelin increases over childhood—lack of it is one reason infants are slow to react to something pleasurable or painful. [**Life-Span Link:** Myelination is discussed in Chapter 8.]

Some neurons are deep inside the brain in a region called the *hindbrain,* which controls automatic responses such as heartbeat, breathing, temperature, and arousal. Others are in the *midbrain,* in areas that affect emotions and memory. And in humans most neurons (about 70 percent) are in the *forebrain,* especially the **cortex,** the brain's six outer layers (sometimes called the *neocortex*). Most thinking, feeling, and sensing occur in the cortex (Johnson & de Haan, 2015; Kolb & Wishaw, 2015).

The forebrain has two halves and four lobes, which are general regions, each containing many parts. No important human activity is exclusively left- or right-brain, or in one lobe or another. Although each lobe and hemisphere has specialized functions, thousands of connections transmit information among the parts, and much of the specialization is the result of various constraints and experiences, not foreordained by genes (Johnson & de Haan, 2015).

The back of the forebrain is the *occipital lobe,* where vision is located; the sides of the brain are the *temporal lobes,* for hearing; the top is the *parietal lobe,* which includes smell, touch, and spatial understanding, and the front is the *frontal lobe,* which enables people to plan, imagine, coordinate, decide, and create. Humans have a much larger frontal cortex relative to body size than any other animal.

The very front of the frontal lobe is called the **prefrontal cortex.** It is not, as once thought, "functionally silent during most of infancy" (Grossmann, 2013, p. 303), although the prefrontal cortex is very immature at birth. [**Life-Span Link:** Major discussion of adolescent growth of the prefrontal cortex is in Chapter 14.]

Pleasure and pain may arise from the **limbic system,** a cluster of brain areas deep in the forebrain that is heavily involved in emotions and motivation. Two crucial parts of the limbic system are the amygdala and the hippocampus.

The **amygdala** is a tiny structure, about the same shape and size as an almond. It registers strong emotions, both positive and negative, especially fear. The amygdala is present in infancy, but growth depends partly on early experience. Increased amygdala activity may cause terrifying nightmares or sudden terrors.

Another structure in the emotional network is the **hippocampus,** located next to the amygdala. A central processor of memory, especially memory for locations, the hippocampus responds to the amygdala by summoning memory. Some places feel comforting (perhaps a childhood room) and others evoke fear (perhaps a doctor's office), even when the experiences that originated those emotions are long gone.

Sometimes considered part of the limbic system is the **hypothalamus,** which responds to signals from the amygdala and to memories from the hippocampus by producing hormones, especially **cortisol,** a hormone that increases with stress (see Figure 5.5). Another nearby brain structure, the **pituitary,**

---

neurotransmitter A brain chemical that carries information from the axon of a sending neuron to the dendrites of a receiving neuron.

myelin The coating on axons that speeds transmission of signals from one neuron to another.

cortex The outer layers of the brain in humans and other mammals. Most thinking, feeling, and sensing involves the cortex.

prefrontal cortex The area of the cortex at the very front of the brain that specializes in anticipation, planning, and impulse control.

limbic system The parts of the brain that interact to produce emotions, including the amygdala, the hypothalamus, and the hippocampus. Many other parts of the brain also are involved with emotions.

amygdala A tiny brain structure that registers emotions, particularly fear and anxiety.

hippocampus A brain structure that is a central processor of memory, especially memory for locations.

hypothalamus A brain area that responds to the amygdala and the hippocampus to produce hormones that activate other parts of the brain and body.

cortisol The primary stress hormone; fluctuations in the body's cortisol level affect human emotions.

pituitary A gland in the brain that responds to a signal from the hypothalamus by producing many hormones, including those that regulate growth and that control other glands, among them the adrenal and sex glands.

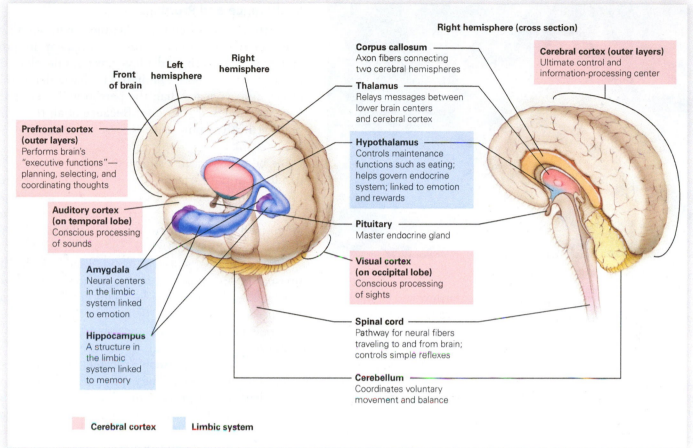

Right hemisphere (cross section)

Corpus callosum
Axon fibers connecting
two cerebral hemispheres

Cerebral cortex (outer layers)
Ultimate control and
information-processing center

Thalamus
Relays messages between
lower brain centers
and cerebral cortex

Front
of brain

Left
hemisphere

Right
hemisphere

**Prefrontal cortex
(outer layers)**
Performs brain's
"executive functions"—
planning, selecting, and
coordinating thoughts

Hypothalamus
Controls maintenance
functions such as eating;
helps govern endocrine
system; linked to emotion
and rewards

**Auditory cortex
(on temporal lobe)**
Conscious processing
of sounds

Pituitary
Master endocrine gland

Amygdala
Neural centers
in the limbic
system linked
to emotion

**Visual cortex
(on occipital lobe)**
Conscious processing
of sights

Hippocampus
A structure in
the limbic
system linked
to memory

Spinal cord
Pathway for neural fibers
traveling to and from brain;
controls simple reflexes

Cerebellum
Coordinates voluntary
movement and balance

■ **Cerebral cortex**   ■ **Limbic system**

FIGURE 5.5

Connections A few of the hundreds of named parts of the brain are shown here. Although each area has particular functions, the entire brain is interconnected. The processing of emotions, for example, occurs primarily in the limbic system, where many brain areas are involved, including the amygdala, hippocampus, and hypothalamus.

responds to the hypothalamus by sending out hormones to various body parts.

Brain research is one area of extensive international collaboration. For example, a 5-billion-dollar, 12-year project in the United States called BRAIN (Brain Research Through Advancing Innovative Neurotechnologies) began in 2014 and is developing new tools (Huang & Luo, 2015). Given new methods and thousands of neuroscientists worldwide, the names and functions of various parts of the brain may be described differently from one source to another.

Thus, the descriptions here are only a beginning. From a developmental perspective, what is crucial to know is that all human thoughts and actions originate in the complexity of the brain, and that understanding the brain adds insight to our effort to understand how humans live their lives. Extensive neurological plasticity is evident as all these parts of the infant brain adapt to experience (Gao et al., 2016).

Aaron McCoy/Photolibrary/Getty Images

Face Lit Up, Brain Too Thanks to scientists at the University of Washington, this young boy enjoys the EEG of his brain activity. Such research has found that babies respond to language long before they speak. Experiences of all sorts connect neurons and grow dendrites.

transient exuberance The great but temporary increase in the number of dendrites that develop in an infant's brain during the first two years of life.

pruning When applied to brain development, the process by which unused connections in the brain atrophy and die.

Exuberance and Pruning

At birth, the brain contains far more neurons than a person needs. Some neurons disappear in programmed cell death, and a few new ones develop. By contrast, the newborn's brain has far fewer dendrites, axons, and synapses than the person will eventually have, and much less myelin. Because of all that, the brain at birth is only half as large as at age 1 (Gao et al., 2016).

To be specific, an estimated fivefold increase in dendrites in the cortex occurs in the 24 months after birth, with about 100 trillion synapses present at age 2. According to one expert, "40,000 new synapses are formed every second in the infant's brain" (Schore & McIntosh, 2011, p. 502).

This extensive *postnatal* brain growth is highly unusual for mammals. It occurs in humans because birth would be impossible if the fetal head grew large enough to contain the extensive networks needed to sustain human development. Because of the need for extensive brain growth after birth, humans must nurture and protect their offspring for a decade or more (Konner, 2010).

Early dendrite growth is called **transient exuberance:** *exuberant* because it is so rapid and *transient* because some of it is temporary. The expansive brain growth is followed by **pruning.** Just as a gardener might prune a rose bush by cutting away some growth to enable more, or more beautiful, roses to bloom, unused brain connections atrophy and die.

As one expert explains it, there is an "exuberant overproduction of cells and connections followed by a several year long sculpting of pathways by massive elimination" (Insel, 2014, p. 1727). Notice the word *sculpting,* as if a gifted artist created an intricate sculpture from raw marble or wood. Human infants are gifted artists, developing their brains as needed for whatever family, culture, or society they happen to be born into.

Thinking and learning require connections among many parts of the brain. This process is made more efficient because some potential connections are pruned (Gao et al., 2016).

For example, to understand any sentence in this text, you need to know the letters, the words, the surrounding text, the ideas they convey, and how they relate to your other thoughts and experiences. Those connections are essential for your comprehension, which differs from other people whose infant brains developed in homes unlike yours. Thus, your brain automatically interprets these roman letters, and, for most of you, is befuddled when viewing Arabic, Cyrillic, or Chinese.

Further evidence of the benefit of cell death comes from a sad symptom of fragile X syndrome (described in Chapter 3), "a persistent failure of normal synapse pruning" (Irwin et al., 2002, p. 194). Without pruning, the dendrites of children with fragile X are too dense and long, making thinking difficult. Similar problems occur for children with autism spectrum disorder: Their brains are unusually large and full, making communication between neurons less efficient and some sounds and sights overwhelming (Lewis et al., 2013).

Thus, pruning is essential. Normally, as brains mature, the process of extending and eliminating dendrites is exquisitely attuned to experience, as the appropriate links in the brain are established, protected, and strengthened

Nature, Nurture, and the Brain

The mechanics of neurological functioning are varied and complex; neuroscientists hypothesize, experiment, and discover more each day. Brain development begins with genes and other biological elements, but hundreds of epigenetic factors affect brain development from the first to the final minutes of life. Particularly important in human development are experiences: Plasticity means that dendrites form or atrophy is response to nutrients and events. The effects of early nurturing experiences are lifelong, as proven many times in mice; research on humans suggests similar effects.

NATURE

Human brains are three times as large per body weight and take years longer to mature than the brains of any other creature, but the basics of brains are the same from mouse to elephant. New dendrites form and unused ones die—especially in infancy and adolescence. Brain plasticity is lifelong.

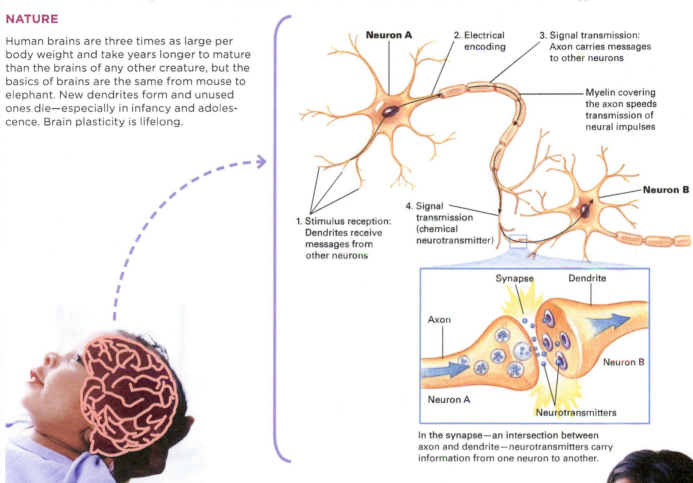

Neuron A

2. Electrical encoding

3. Signal transmission: Axon carries messages to other neurons

Myelin covering the axon speeds transmission of neural impulses

Neuron B

1. Stimulus reception: Dendrites receive messages from other neurons

4. Signal transmission (chemical neurotransmitter)

Synapse   Dendrite

Axon

Neuron B

Neuron A

Neurotransmitters

In the synapse—an intersection between axon and dendrite—neurotransmitters carry information from one neuron to another.

PHOTO: STOCKBYTE/GETTY IMAGES

NURTURE

In the developing brain, connections from axon to dendrite reflect how a baby is treated. In studies of mice, scientists learned that when a mother mouse licks her newborn its methylation of a gene (called Nr3c1) is reduced, allowing increased serotonin to be released by the hypothalamus and reducing stress hormones. Baby mice who were frequently licked and nuzzled by their mothers developed bigger and better brains!

Researchers believe that, just as in rodents, the human mothers who cuddle, cradle, and caress their babies shape their brains for decades.

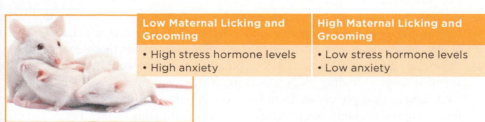

Low Maternal Licking and Grooming	High Maternal Licking and Grooming
• High stress hormone levels • High anxiety	• Low stress hormone levels • Low anxiety

PHOTO: ANYAIVANOVA/ISTOCK/THINKSTOCK

© RUBBERBALL/NICOLE HILL/ALAMY

(Gao et al., 2016). As with the rose bush, pruning needs to be done carefully, allowing further growth.

Without certain experiences, some pruning may occur that limits later thought rather than aids it. One group of scientists speculates that "lack of normative experience may lead to overpruning of neurons or synapses, both of which would lead to reductions of brain activity" (Moulson et al., 2009, p. 1051).

Necessary and Possible Experiences

What are those needed "normative experiences"? A scientist named William Greenough identified two experience-related aspects of brain development (Greenough et al., 1987):

experience-expectant Brain functions that require certain basic common experiences (which an infant can be expected to have) in order to develop normally.

experience-dependent Brain functions that depend on particular, variable experiences and therefore may or may not develop in a particular infant.

- **Experience-expectant growth.** Certain functions require basic experiences in order to develop, just as a tree requires water. Those experiences are part of almost every infant's life, and thus, almost all human brains grow as their genes direct. Brains need and expect such experiences; development would suffer without them.
- **Experience-dependent growth.** Some brain functions depend on particular experiences. These experiences are not essential: They happen in some families and cultures but not in others. Because of experience-dependent experiences, humans can be quite different from one another, yet all fully human.

● **Especially for Parents of Grown Children** Suppose you realize that you seldom talked to your children until they talked to you and that you often put them in cribs and playpens. Did you limit their brain growth and their sensory capacity? (see response, page 134)

The basic, expected experiences *must* happen for normal brain maturation to occur, and they almost always do. For example, in deserts and in the Arctic, on isolated farms and in crowded cities, almost all babies have things to see, objects to manipulate, and people to love them. Babies everywhere welcome such experiences: They look around, they grab for objects, they smile at people. As a result, babies' brains develop. Without such expected experiences, brains wither.

In contrast, dependent experiences *might* happen; because of them, one brain differs from another, even though both brains are developing normally. Experiences vary, such as which language babies hear, what faces they see, whether curiosity is encouraged, or how their mother reacts to frustration. *Depending* on those particulars, infant brains are structured and connected one way or another; some dendrites grow and some neurons thrive while others die (Stiles & Jernigan, 2010).

Consequently, experience-expectant events make all people similar, yet everyone is unique because each undergoes particular experience-dependent events.

The distinction between essential and variable input to the brain's networks can be made for all mammals. But some of the most persuasive research has been done with songbirds. All male songbirds have a brain region dedicated to listening and reproducing sounds (experience-expectant), but birds of the same species produce slightly different songs (experience-dependent) depending on where they live (Konner, 2010).

Birds inherit genes that produce the neurons they need, perhaps dedicated to learning new songs (canaries) or to finding hidden seeds (chickadees). That is experience-expectant: Songs and seeds are essential for those species. Then, depending on their ecological niche, birds *depend* on specific experiences with learning songs or finding seeds (Barinaga, 2003).

A human example comes from face recognition: All infants need to see faces (experience-expectant), but which particular face differences they notice depends on who they see (experience-dependent), as the following explains.

Face Recognition

Unless you have prosopagnosia (face blindness), the *fusiform face area* of your brain is astonishingly adept. Newborns are even quicker to recognize a face that they have seen just once than are older children and adults (Zeifman, 2013). They have no idea which faces are important, so they are primed to stare intently at all of them—unlike adults, who know they can glance at hundreds in a crowd without paying much attention, unless they happen to recognize someone.

Because of experience-expectancies, every face is fascinating early in life: Babies stare at pictures of monkey faces and photos of human ones, at drawings and toys with faces, as well as at live faces. Soon, experience-dependent learning begins (de Heering et al., 2010). By 3 months, babies smile readily at familiar people, differentiate men and women, and distinguish among faces from their own ethnic group (called the *own-race effect*). The own-race effect results from limited multiethnic experience. Indeed, children of one ethnicity, adopted and raised exclusively among people of another ethnicity, recognize differences among people of their adopted group more readily than differences among people of their biological group.

The importance of experience is confirmed by two studies. In the first study, from 6 to 9 months of age infants were repeatedly shown a book with pictures of six monkey faces, each with a name written on the page. One-third of the infants' parents read the names while showing the pictures; another one-third said only "monkey" as they turned each page; the final one-third simply turned the pages with no labeling.

At 9 months, infants in all three groups viewed pictures of six *unfamiliar* monkeys. The infants who had heard names of monkeys were better at distinguishing one new monkey from another than were the infants who saw the same picture book but did not hear each monkey's name (Scott & Monesson, 2010).

Now consider the second study. Most people do not notice the individuality of newborns. However, 3-year-olds with younger siblings were found to be much better at recognizing differences in unfamiliar newborns than were 3-year-olds with no younger brothers or sisters (Cassia et al., 2009). This finding shows, again, that experience matters, contributing to development of dendrites in the fusiform face area.

Distinguishing individual faces is best learned via early exposure, but it is never too late. Adults can learn multiethnic individuality if they try. Infancy is a sensitive period, but plasticity is lifelong.

Dario   Boris   Anice   Iona   Flora   Louis

Iona Is Not Flora If you heard that Dario was not Louis or Boris, would you stare at unfamiliar monkey faces more closely in the future? For 6-month-olds, the answer is yes.

Harming the Infant Body and Brain

Thus far, we have focused on the many normal variations that families offer babies; most infants develop well within their culture. Feeding and health care vary, but every family hopes that their children will survive in good health, and they try to have that happen.

For brain development, it does not matter whether a person learns French or Farsi, or expresses emotions dramatically or subtly (e.g., throwing themselves to the floor or merely pursing their lips, a cultural difference). However, infant brains do not develop well if they do not have the basic experiences that all humans expect and need.

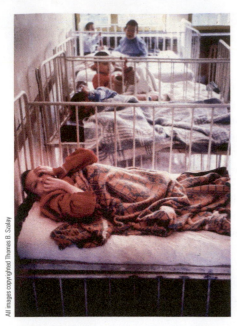

All images copyrighted Thomas B. Szalay

Hands on Head These children in Romania, here older than age 2, probably spent most of their infancy in their cribs, never with the varied stimulation that infant brains need. The sad results are evident here—that boy is fingering his own face, because the feel of his own touch is most likely one of the few sensations he knows. The girl sitting up in the back is a teenager. This photo was taken in 1982; Romania no longer destroys children so dramatically.

shaken baby syndrome A life-threatening injury that occurs when an infant is forcefully shaken back and forth, a motion that ruptures blood vessels in the brain and breaks neural connections.

🔴🔵 **Response for Parents of Grown Children** (from page 132): Probably not. Brain development is programmed to occur for all infants, requiring only the stimulation that virtually all families provide—warmth, reassuring touch, overheard conversation, facial expressions, movement. Extras such as baby talk, music, exercise, mobiles, and massage may be beneficial but are not essential.

Lack of Stimulation

To begin with, infants need stimulation. Some parents put babies in a quiet place, imagining that is needed. Not at all—playing with a young baby, allowing varied sights and sounds, and encouraging movement (arm waving, then crawling, grabbing, and walking) all foster growth. Severe lack of stimulation stunts the brain. As one review explains, "enrichment and deprivation studies provide powerful evidence of . . . widespread effects of experience on the complexity and function of the developing system" (Stiles & Jernigan, 2010, p. 345).

Proof of this came first from research on rodents! In an experiment, some "deprived" rats (raised alone in small, barren cages) were compared with "enriched" rats (raised in large cages with toys and other rats). At autopsy, the brains of the enriched rats were larger and heavier, with more dendrites (Diamond, 1988; Greenough & Volkmar, 1973). Subsequent research with other mammals confirms that isolation and sensory deprivation stunt development, which is sadly evident in longitudinal studies of orphans from Romania, described in Chapter 7.

Stress and the Brain

Some infants experience the opposite problem, too much of the wrong kind of stimulation. If the brain produces an overabundance of cortisol (the stress hormone) early in life (as when an infant is frequently terrified), that makes the brain react oddly to stress lifelong. As a result, years later that child or adult may be hypervigilant (always on the alert) or emotionally flat (never happy, sad, or angry).

Note that this is an emotional response to fear or yelling, not directly caused by physical pain. As just explained, infants should not be protected from every experience. Some stress—not getting an attractive object, being bathed or diapered when the baby does not want it—is part of normal infant life. But a flood of stress hormones is harmful (Propper & Holochwost, 2013).

Worse is the damage that can be done when the adult's stress at a crying baby leads to **shaken baby syndrome.** Because the prefrontal cortex has not yet developed, telling infants to stop crying is pointless because they cannot *decide* to stop crying. Such decisions require brain maturity not yet present. Shaking may stop the crying, because blood vessels in the brain rupture and neural connections break. Pediatricians consider shaken baby syndrome an example of *abusive head trauma* (Christian & Block, 2009). Death is the worst consequence; lifelong intellectual impairment is the more likely one.

Not every infant who has neurological symptoms of head trauma is the victim of abuse: Legal experts worry about false accusations (Byard, 2014). Nonetheless, infants are vulnerable, so the response to a screaming, frustrating baby should be to comfort or walk away, never to shake, yell, or hit.

Lest you cannot imagine the frustration that some parents feel when their baby cries, consider what one mother in Sweden said about her colicky baby, now age 4 and much beloved.

> There were moments when, both me and my husband . . . when she was apoplectic and howling so much that I almost got this thought, 'now I'll take a pillow and put over her face just until she quietens down, until the screaming stops.'
>
> *[Landgren et al., 2012]*

Developmental discoveries about early development have many implications. First, since early growth is so rapid, well-baby checkups are needed often, in order to spot, and treat, any problems. Sight and hearing are springboards for growth, so sensory impairments should be remedied.

Fortunately, one characteristic of infants is called **self-righting,** an inborn drive to compensate and overcome problems. Infants with few toys develop their brains by using sticks, or empty boxes, or whatever is available. Malnourished newborns have *catch-up growth,* so a 5-pound newborn may gain weight faster than an 8-pound one. Plasticity is apparent from the beginning of life (Tomalski & Johnson, 2010).

self-righting The inborn drive to remedy a developmental deficit; literally, to return to sitting or standing upright after being tipped over. People of all ages have self-righting impulses, for emotional as well as physical imbalance.

WHAT HAVE YOU LEARNED?

1. What facts indicate that infants grow rapidly in the first year?

2. Why are pediatricians not troubled when an infant is consistently small, say at the 20th percentile in height and weight?

3. How do sleep patterns change from birth to 18 months?

4. What are the arguments for and against bed-sharing?

5. How can pruning increase brain potential?

6. What is the difference between experience-expectant and experience-dependent growth?

7. What is the effect of stress or social deprivation on early development?

8. What should caregivers remember about brain development when an infant cries?

Perceiving and Moving

Young human infants combine motor ineptness and sensory acuteness (Konner, 2010). What a contrast to kittens, for instance, who are born deaf, with eyes sealed shut, and who stay beside their mother although they can walk. For humans, senses are crucial from birth on; movement skill is not.

Thus, newborns listen and look from day 1, eager to practice every skill as soon as possible. The interaction between the senses and movement is continuous in the early months, with every sensation propelling the infant to attempt new motor skills. Here are the specifics.

sensation The response of a sensory organ (eyes, ears, skin, tongue, nose) when it detects a stimulus.

The Senses

All the senses function at birth. Newborns have open eyes, sensitive ears, and responsive noses, tongues, and skin. Indeed, very young babies use all their senses to attend to everything. For instance, in the first months of life, they smile at everyone and suck almost anything in their mouths.

Sensation occurs when a sensory system detects a stimulus, as when the inner ear reverberates with sound, or the eye's retina and pupil intercept light. Thus, sensations begin when an outer organ (eye, ear, nose, tongue, or skin) meets anything that can be seen, heard, smelled, tasted, or touched.

Genetic selection over more than 100,000 years affects all the senses. Humans cannot hear what mice hear, or see what bats see, or smell what puppies smell; humans do not need those sensory abilities. However, survival requires babies to respond to people, and newborns innately do so with every sense they have (Konner, 2010; Zeifman, 2013).

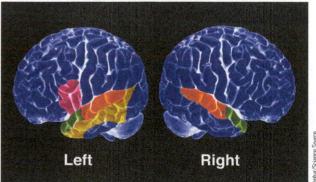

From Sound to Language Hearing occurs in the temporal lobe, in both hemispheres, the green and some of the red parts of the brain. Language comprehension, however, is mostly in the left hemisphere, here shown in the brown region that responds to known words, and Broca's area, the red bulb that produces speech. A person could hear but not understand (a baby) or understand but not speak (if Broca's area is damaged).

Hearing

The sense of hearing develops during the last trimester of pregnancy. At birth, certain sounds trigger reflexes, even without conscious perception. Sudden noises startle newborns, making them cry.

Familiar, rhythmic sounds such as a heartbeat are soothing: That is one reason kangaroo care reduces newborn stress, as the infant's ear rests on the mother's chest. [**Life-Span Link:** Kangaroo care is explained in Chapter 4.] Soon, infants can pinpoint the source of the noise—an ability that requires instant calculation of the difference between when the sound reaches the left and right ears.

Newborn hearing is routinely checked at most hospitals in North America and Europe, since early remediation benefits deaf infants. If they have cochlear implants early in life, their ability to understand and produce language is not delayed—unlike for those whose deafness is remedied later (Tobey et al., 2013). Screening is needed later as well because losses may occur in infancy (Harlor & Bower, 2009).

Seeing

By contrast, vision is immature at birth. Although in mid-pregnancy the eyes open and are sensitive to bright light (if the pregnant woman is sunbathing in a bikini, for instance), the fetus has nothing much to see. Consequently, newborns are legally blind; they focus only on things between 4 and 30 inches (10 and 75 centimeters) away (Bornstein et al., 2005).

Almost immediately, experience combines with maturation of the visual cortex to improve the ability to see shapes and notice details. Vision improves so rapidly that researchers are hard-pressed to describe the day-by-day improvements (Dobson et al., 2009). By 2 months, infants not only stare at faces but also, with perception and cognition, smile. (Smiling can occur earlier but not because of perception.)

Perception requires paying attention to a sensation—most of the things we see and sounds we hear are not perceived because they are meaningless to us. However, with experience, perception builds and visual scanning improves. Thus, 3-month-olds look closely at the eyes and mouth, smiling more at smiling faces than at angry or expressionless ones. They pay attention to patterns, colors, and motion (Kellman & Arterberry, 2006).

Because **binocular vision** (coordinating both eyes to see one image) is impossible in the womb (nothing is far enough away), many newborns seem to use their two eyes independently, momentarily appearing wall-eyed or cross-eyed. Typically, experience leads to rapid focus and binocular vision. Usually between 2 and 4 months, both eyes can focus on a single thing (Wang & Candy, 2010).

This ability aids in the development of depth perception, which has been demonstrated in 3-month-olds, although it was once thought to develop much later. Toddlers who are experienced crawlers and walkers are very adept at deciding whether a given path is safe to cross upright or is best traversed sitting or crawling. This illustrates early coordination of the senses and motor skills (Kretch & Adolph, 2013). (This does *not* mean that toddlers can be trusted not to fall off tables or out of windows.)

Tasting and Smelling

As with vision and hearing, smell and taste rapidly adapt to the social context. Babies appreciate what their mothers eat, prenatally through amniotic fluid, then through breast milk, and finally through smells and spoonfuls of the family dinner.

The foods of a particular culture may aid survival because some natural substances are medicinal. For example, bitter foods provide some defense against malaria; hot spices help preserve food and thus work against food poisoning (Krebs, 2009). Thus, for 1-year-olds, a taste for their family cuisine may save their lives.

Families who eat foods that protected their community in past generations pass on those preferences to their children. Taste preferences endure despite

---

◉◉ Especially for Nurses and Pediatricians The parents of a 6-month-old have just been told that their child is deaf. They don't believe it because, as they tell you, the baby babbles as much as their other children did. What do you tell them? (see response, page 139)

binocular vision The ability to focus the two eyes in a coordinated manner in order to see one image.

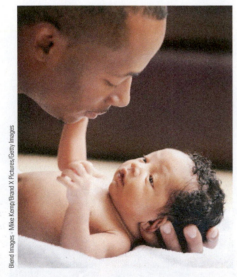

Blend Images - Mike Kemp/Brand X Pictures/Getty Images

Who's This? Newborns don't know much, but they look intensely at faces. Repeated sensations become perceptions, so in about six weeks this baby will smile at Dad, Mom, a stranger, the dog, and every other face. If this father in Utah responds like typical fathers everywhere, by 6 months cognition will be apparent: The baby will chortle with joy at seeing him but become wary of unfamiliar faces.

THINK CRITICALLY: Which is most important in the first year of life, accurate hearing or seeing?

Learning About a Lime As with every other normal infant, Jacqueline's curiosity leads to taste and then to a slow reaction, from puzzlement to tongue-out disgust. Jacqueline's responses demonstrate that the sense of taste is acute in infancy and that quick brain perceptions are still to come.

immigration or when historical circumstances change. Thus, a feeding pattern that was protective may no longer be so. Indeed, when starvation was a threat, families sought high-fat foods; now their descendants enjoy French fries, whipped cream, and bacon, jeopardizing their health.

Adaptation also occurs for the sense of smell. When breast-feeding mothers used a chamomile balm to ease cracked nipples during the first days of their babies' lives, those babies preferred that smell almost two years later, compared with babies whose mothers used an odorless ointment (Delaunay-El Allam et al., 2010).

As babies learn to recognize each person's scent, they prefer to sleep next to their caregivers, and they nuzzle into their caregivers' chests—especially when the adults are shirtless. One way to help infants who are frightened of the bath (some love bathing, some hate it) is for the parent to join the baby in the tub. The smells of the adult's body mixed with the smell of soap, and the pleasant touch, sight, and voice of the caregiver make the entire experience comforting.

Touch and Pain

The sense of touch is acute in infants. Wrapping, rubbing, massaging, and cradling are each soothing to many new babies. Even when their eyes are closed, some infants stop crying and visibly relax when held securely by their caregivers. The newborn's ability to be comforted by touch is tested in the Brazelton NBAS, described in Chapter 4. In the first year of life, infants' heart rates slow and they relax when stroked gently and rhythmically on the arm (Fairhurst et al., 2014).

Pain and temperature are not among the traditional five senses, but they are often connected to touch. Some babies cry when being changed, distressed at the sudden coldness on their skin. Some touches are unpleasant—a poke, pinch, or pat—although this varies from one baby to another.

Scientists are not certain about infant pain (Fitzgerald, 2015). Some experiences that are painful to adults (circumcision, setting of a broken bone) are much less so to newborns, although that does not mean that newborns never feel pain (Reavey et al., 2014). For many newborn medical procedures, from a pin-prick to minor surgery, a taste of sugar right before the event is an anesthetic. Doctors hesitate to use drugs, because that may slow down breathing.

Babies born very early experience many medical procedures that would be painful for adults. The more procedures they undergo, the more impaired their development at age 1, but that outcome could be related to the reasons for those procedures rather than the pain of them (Valeri et al., 2015).

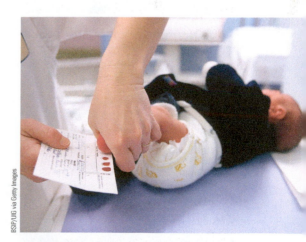

The First Blood Test This baby will cry, but most experts believe the heel prick shown here is well worth it. The drops of blood will reveal the presence of any of several genetic diseases, including sickle-cell disease, cystic fibrosis, and phenylketonuria. Early diagnosis allows early treatment, and the cries subside quickly with a drop of sugar water or a suck of breast milk.

Some people imagine that even the fetus feels pain; others say that the sense of pain does not mature until months later. Digestive difficulty (colic) and teething are said to be painful. However, this is unproven: Crying or lack of crying is an imperfect measure of pain at every stage of life.

Physiological measures, including hormones, heartbeat, and rapid brain waves, are studied to assess infant pain, but the conclusions are mixed. Infant brains are immature: They have some similar responses to pain and some dissimilar ones when compared to adults (Moultrie et al., 2016).

THINK CRITICALLY: What political controversy makes objective research on newborn pain difficult?

Motor Skills

motor skill The learned abilities to move some part of the body, in actions ranging from a large leap to a flicker of the eyelid. (The word *motor* here refers to movement of muscles.)

The most dramatic **motor skill** (any movement ability) is independent walking, which explains why I worried when my 14-month-old daughter had not yet taken a step (as described in the introduction to this chapter). All the basic motor skills, from the newborn's head-lifting to the toddler's stair-climbing, develop in infancy.

Motor skills begin with reflexes, explained in Chapter 4. Reflexes become skills if they are practiced and encouraged. As you saw in the chapter's beginning, Mrs. Todd set the foundation for my fourth child's walking when Sarah was only a few months old. Similarly, some very young babies can swim—if adults build on the swimming reflex by floating with them in calm, warm water.

Gross Motor Skills

gross motor skills Physical abilities involving large body movements, such as walking and jumping. (The word *gross* here means "big.")

Deliberate actions that coordinate many parts of the body, producing large movements, are called **gross motor skills.** These skills emerge directly from reflexes and proceed in a *cephalocaudal* (head-down) and *proximodistal* (center-out) direction. Infants first control their heads, lifting them up to look around. Then they control their upper bodies, their arms, and finally their legs and feet. (See At About This Time, which shows age norms for gross motor skills.)

◐ **Observation Quiz** Which of these skills has the greatest variation in age of acquisition? Why? (see answer, page 140) ↓

Sitting requires muscles to steady the torso. By 3 months, most babies can sit propped up in a lap. By 6 months, they can usually sit unsupported. Babies never propped up (as in some institutions for orphaned children) sit much later.

Crawling is another example of the head-down and center-out direction of skill mastery. As they

AT ABOUT THIS TIME

Age Norms (in Months) for Gross Motor Skills

	When 50% of All Babies Master the Skill	When 90% of All Babies Master the Skill
Sit unsupported	6	7.5
Stands holding on	7.4	9.4
Crawls (creeps)	8	10
Stands not holding	10.8	13.4
Walking well	12.0	14.4
Walk backward	15	17
Run	18	20
Jump up	26	29

Note: As the text explains, age norms are affected by culture and cohort. The first five norms are based on babies from five continents [Brazil, Ghana, Norway, USA, Oman, and India] (World Health Organization, 2006). The next three are from a USA-only source [Coovadia & Wittenberg, 2004; based on Denver II (Frankenburg et al., 1992)]. Mastering skills a few weeks earlier or later does not indicate health or intelligence. Being very late, however, is a cause for concern.

Advancing and Advanced At 8 months, she is already an adept crawler, alternating hands and knees, intent on progress. She will probably be walking before a year.

gain muscle strength, infants wiggle, attempting to move forward by pushing their arms, shoulders, and upper bodies against whatever surface they are lying on.

Usually by 5 months, infants add their legs to this effort, inching forward (or backward) on their bellies. Exactly when this occurs depends partly on how much "tummy time" the infant has had to develop the muscles, and that, of course, is affected by the caregiver's culture (Zachry & Kitzmann, 2011).

Between 8 and 10 months after birth, most infants can lift their midsections and move forward—or sometimes backward first. Some babies never crawl, but they all find some way to move before they can walk (inching, bear-walking, scooting, creeping, or crawling). As soon as they are able, babies walk (falling frequently but getting up undaunted and trying again), since walking is quicker than crawling, and has another advantage—free hands (Adolph et al., 2012). That illustrates the drive that underlies every motor skill: Babies are powerfully motivated to do whatever they can as soon as they can.

Beyond motivations, the dynamic-systems perspective highlights the interaction of strength, maturation, and practice. We illustrate these three with walking.

1. *Muscle strength.* Newborns with skinny legs and 3-month-olds buoyed by water make stepping movements, but 6-month-olds on dry land do not; their legs are too chubby for their underdeveloped muscles. As they gain strength, they stand and then walk—easier for thin babies than heavy ones (Slining et al., 2010).
2. *Brain maturation.* The first leg movements—kicking (alternating legs at birth and then both legs together or one leg repeatedly at about 3 months)—occur without much thought. As the brain matures, deliberate and coordinated leg action becomes possible.
3. *Practice.* Unbalanced, wide-legged, short strides become a steady, smooth gait.

Once toddlers are able to walk by themselves, they practice obsessively, barefoot or not, at home or in stores, on sidewalks or streets, on lawns or in mud. They fall often, but that does not stop them: "they average between 500 and 1,500 walking steps per hour so that by the end of each day, they have may taken 9,000 walking steps and traveled the length of 29 football fields" (Adolph et al., 2003, p. 494).

Fine Motor Skills

Small body movements are called **fine motor skills.** The most valued fine motor skills are finger movements, enabling humans to write, draw, type, tie, and so on. Movements of the tongue, jaw, lips, and toes are fine movements, too.

Regarding hand skills, newborns have a strong reflexive grasp but lack control. During their first 2 months, babies excitedly stare and wave their arms at objects dangling within reach. By 3 months, they can usually touch such objects, but because of limited eye–hand coordination, they cannot yet grab and hold on unless an object is placed in their hands.

By 4 months, infants sometimes grab, but their timing is off: They close their hands too early or too late. Finally, by 6 months, with a concentrated, deliberate stare, most babies can reach, grab, and grasp almost any object that is the right size. Some can even transfer an object from one hand to the other. Toward the end of the first year and throughout the second, finger skills improve as babies master the pincer movement (using thumb and forefinger to pick up tiny objects) and self-feeding (first with hands, then fingers, then utensils) (Ho, 2010). (See At About This Time.)

Bossa Nova Baby? This girl in Brazil demonstrates her joy at acquiring the gross motor skill of walking, which quickly becomes dancing whenever music plays.

● Response for Nurses and Pediatricians (from page 136): Urge the parents to begin learning sign language and investigating the possibility of cochlear implants. Babbling has a biological basis and begins at a specified time in deaf as well as hearing babies. If their infant can hear, sign language does no harm. If the child is deaf, however, lack of communication may be destructive.

fine motor skills Physical abilities involving small body movements, especially of the hands and fingers, such as drawing and picking up a coin. (The word *fine* here means "small.")

LaunchPad
macmillan learning

Video: Fine Motor Skills in Infancy and Toddlerhood
http://qrs.ly/1h4eozr

Success At 6 months, this baby is finally able to grab her toes. From a developmental perspective, this achievement is as significant as walking, as it requires coordination of feet and fingers. Note her expression of determination and concentration.

AT ABOUT THIS TIME

Age Norms (in Months) for Fine Motor Skills

	When 50% of All Babies Master the Skill	When 90% of All Babies Master the Skill
Grasps rattle when placed in hand	3	4
Reaches to hold an object	4.5	6
Thumb and finger grasp	8	10
Stacks two blocks	15	21
Imitates vertical line (drawing)	30	39

Data from World Health Organization, 2006.

🔵 **Answer to Observation Quiz**
(from page 138): Jumping up, with a three-month age range for acquisition. The reason is that the older an infant is, the more impact both nature and nurture have.

As with gross motor skills, fine motor skills are shaped by culture and opportunity. For example, when given "sticky mittens" (with Velcro) that allow grabbing, infants master hand skills sooner than usual. Their perception advances as well (Libertus & Needham, 2010; Soska et al., 2010). More generally, all senses and motor skills expand the baby's cognitive awareness, with practice advancing both skill and cognition (Leonard & Hill, 2014).

Cultural Variations

Caregivers influence every infant move, and every caregiver reflects their culture. All healthy infants develop skills in the same sequence, but the age of acquisition varies because each culture encourages certain kinds of practice.

The importance of context is illustrated by follow-up studies on the "sticky mittens" experiments. Some researchers have given 2-month-olds practice in reaching for toys without sticky mittens. The infants advanced as much as those with special mittens (Williams et al., 2015). It seems that practice of every motor skill advances development, not only of the skill but overall (Leonard & Hill, 2014).

When U.S. infants are grouped by ethnicity, generally African American babies are ahead of Latino babies when it comes to walking. In turn, Latino babies are ahead of those of European descent. Internationally, the earliest walkers are in Africa, where many well-nourished and healthy babies walk at 10 months.

In some African communities, babies are massaged and stretched from birth onward and are encouraged to walk as soon as possible. The latest walkers may be in rural China (15 months), where infants are bundled up against the cold (Adolph & Robinson, 2013).

Cultural patterns affect acquisition of every sensory and motor skill, with the importance of practice evident in hundreds of studies on infant walking (Adolph & Robinson, 2013). In some cultures, babies are discouraged from walking, especially if hazards (poisonous snakes, open fires) are nearby.

Slow development relative to local norms may indicate a problem that should be attended to, as it is much easier to remedy any lag during infancy than later on. Remember the dynamic systems of senses and motor skills: If one aspect of the system lags behind, the other parts may be affected as well.

Surviving in Good Health

Public health measures have dramatically reduced infant death. In 1950, world-wide, one infant in six died before age 1; in 2015, the rate was about 1 in 28 (United Nations, 2015). About 2 million people in the world are alive today who would have died if they had been born 70 years ago. As you can see from Figure 5.6, improvements are everywhere. Infant mortality has been reduced by 900 percent in Poland, Japan, Chile, China, and Finland.

Better Days Ahead

Most child deaths occur in the first month. In the twenty-first century in developed nations, 99.9 percent of 1-month-olds live to adulthood. Public health measures (clean water, nourishing food, immunization) deserve most of the credit.

Not only survival but life itself is better for children, because parents have fewer births and thus attend more to each one. Maternal education is pivotal here. Especially in low-income nations, educated women have far fewer, but much healthier, children than women who never went to school (de la Croix, 2013).

Well Protected Disease and early death are common in Ethiopia, where this photo was taken, but neither is likely for 2-year-old Salem. He is protected not only by the nutrition and antibodies in his mother's milk but also by the large blue net that surrounds them. Treated bed nets, like this one provided by the Carter Center and the Ethiopian Health Ministry, are often large enough for families to eat, read, as well as sleep in together, without fear of malaria-infected mosquitoes.

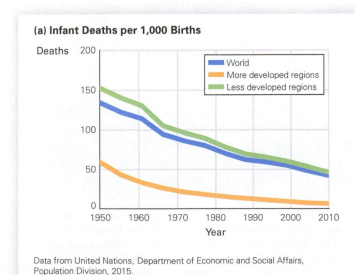

(a) Infant Deaths per 1,000 Births

Data from United Nations, Department of Economic and Social Affairs, Population Division, 2015.

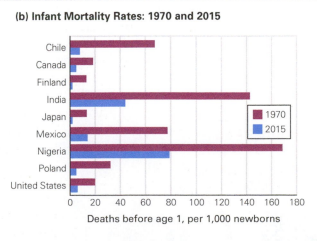

(b) Infant Mortality Rates: 1970 and 2015

Data from World Bank, 2016.

FIGURE 5.6

More Babies Are Surviving Improvements in public health—better nutrition, cleaner water, more widespread immunization—over the past three decades have meant millions of survivors.

Considering Culture

Many cultural variations are simply alternate ways to raise a healthy child. Sometimes, however, one mode of infant care is much better than another. International comparisons then become especially useful. Consider the dramatic worldwide reduction in **sudden infant death syndrome (SIDS).**

Every year until the mid-1990s, tens of thousands of infants died of SIDS, called *crib death* in North America and *cot death* in England. Tiny infants smiled at their caregivers, waved their arms at rattles that their small fingers could not yet grasp, went to sleep, and never woke up. Scientists tested hypotheses (the cat? the quilt? natural honey? homicide? spoiled milk?) to no avail. Sudden infant death was a mystery. Finally, one major risk factor—sleeping on the stomach—was discovered, thanks to the work of one scientist, described below.

sudden infant death syndrome (SIDS)
A situation in which a seemingly healthy infant, usually between 2 and 6 months old, suddenly stops breathing and dies unexpectedly while asleep.

A CASE TO STUDY

Scientist at Work

Susan Beal, a 35-year-old scientist with five young children, began to study SIDS deaths in South Australia. She responded to phone calls, often at 5 or 6 A.M. that another baby had died. Her husband supported her work, often becoming the sole child care provider so she could leave home at a moment's notice.

At first she felt embarrassed to question the parents, sometimes arriving before the police or the coroner. But parents were grateful to talk. Beal realized that parents tended to blame themselves and each other; she reassured them that scientists shared their bewilderment. (Scan the QR code below with your smartphone to watch a short interview with Susan Beal.)

As a scientist, she took detailed, careful notes on dozens of circumstances at each of more than 500 deaths. She found that some things did not matter (such as birth order), and some increased the risk (maternal smoking and lambskin blankets).

A breakthrough came when Beal noticed an ethnic variation: Australian babies of Chinese descent died of SIDS far less often than did those of European descent. Genetic? Most experts thought so. But Beal's notes revealed that almost all SIDS babies died while sleeping on their stomachs, contrary to the Chinese custom of placing infants on their backs to sleep. She developed a new hypothesis: Sleeping position mattered.

To test her hypothesis, Beal convinced a large group of non-Chinese parents to put their newborns to sleep on their backs. Almost none of them died suddenly.

After several years of gathering data, she drew a surprising conclusion: Back-sleeping protected against SIDS. Her published report (Beal, 1988) caught the attention of doctors in the Netherlands, where pediatricians had told parents to put

Public Service Victory Sometimes data and discoveries produce widespread improvements—as in the thousands of lives saved by the "Back to Sleep" mantra. The private grief of mystified parents in Australia is separated by merely 30 years from this subway poster viewed by hundreds of thousands of commuters. Despite many developmental problems—some described in this chapter—the average human life is longer and healthier than it was a few decades ago.

LaunchPad
macmillan learning

http://www.youtube.com/
watch?v=ZIPt5q2QJ91

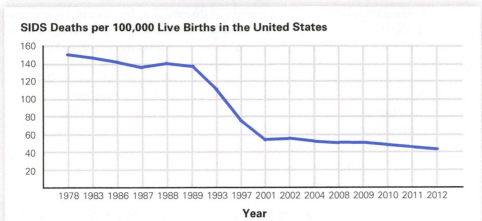

SIDS Deaths per 100,000 Live Births in the United States

Year

Data from National Vital Statistics Reports, Forthcoming; Hoyert & Xu, 2012; Murphy et al., 2012; Kochanek et al., 2011; Miniño et al., 2007; Hoyert et al., 2005; Mathews et al., 2003; Hoyert et al., 1999; Gardner & Hudson, 1996; Macdorman & Rosenberg, 1993; Monthly Vital Statistics Report, 1980.

FIGURE 5.7

Alive Today As more parents learn that a baby should be on his or her "back to sleep," the SIDS rate continues to decrease. Other factors are also responsible for the decline—fewer parents smoke cigarettes in the baby's room.

their babies to sleep on their stomachs. Two Dutch scientists (Engelberts & de Jonge, 1990) recommended back-sleeping; thousands of parents took heed. SIDS was reduced in Holland by 40 percent in one year—a stunning replication.

Replication and application spread. By 1994, a "Back to Sleep" campaign in nation after nation cut the SIDS rate dramatically (Kinney & Thach, 2009; Mitchell, 2009). In the United States in 1984 SIDS killed 5,245 babies; in 1996, that number was down to 3,050; in 2010, it was about 1,700 (see Figure 5.7). In the United States alone, 100,000 children and young adults are alive today who would be dead if they had been born before 1990.

Stomach-sleeping is a proven, replicated risk, but it is not the only one. Other risks include low birthweight, winter, being male, exposure to cigarettes, soft blankets or pillows, bedsharing, and physical abnormalities (in the brainstem, heart, mitochondria, the microbiome (Neary & Breckenridge, 2013; Ostfeld et al., 2010). Most SIDS victims experience several risks, a cascade of biological and social circumstances.

That does not surprise Susan Beal. She sifted through all the evidence and found the main risk—stomach-sleeping—but she continues to study other factors. She praises the courage of the hundreds of parents who talked with her hours after their baby died; the entire world praises her.

Immunization

Diseases that could be deadly (including measles, chicken pox, polio, mumps, rotavirus, and whooping cough) are now rare because of **immunization,** which primes the body's immune system to resist a particular disease. Immunization (often via *vaccination*) is said to have had "a greater impact on human mortality reduction and population growth than any other public health intervention besides clean water" (Baker, 2000, p. 199).

In the first half of the twentieth century, almost every child had one or more of these diseases. Usually they recovered, and then they were immune. Indeed, some parents took their young children to visit a child who had an active case of chicken pox, for instance, hoping the child would catch the disease and then become immune. That protected that child later in life and any infants, who were more likely to die of the disease.

immunization A process that stimulates the body's immune system by causing production of antibodies to defend against attack by a particular contagious disease. Creation of antibodies may be accomplished either naturally (by having the disease), by injection, by drops that are swallowed, or by a nasal spray.

Success and Survival

Beginning with smallpox in the nineteenth century, doctors discovered that giving a small dose of a virus to healthy people stimulates antibodies and provides protection. Stunning successes in immunization include the following:

- Smallpox, the most lethal disease for children in the past, was eradicated worldwide as of 1980. Vaccination against smallpox is no longer needed.

True Dedication This young Buddhist monk lives in a remote region of Nepal, where until recently measles was a common, fatal disease. Fortunately, a UNICEF porter carried the vaccine over mountain trails for two days so that this boy—and his whole community—could be immunized.

Especially for Nurses and Pediatricians A mother refuses to have her baby immunized because she wants to prevent side effects. She wants your signature for a religious exemption, which in some jurisdictions allows the mother to refuse vaccination. What should you do? (see response, page 147)

- Polio, a crippling and sometimes fatal disease, has been virtually eliminated in the Americas. Only 784 cases were reported anywhere in the world in 2003. However, false rumors halted immunization in northern Nigeria. Polio reappeared, sickening 1,948 people in 2005, almost all of them in West Africa. Public health workers and community leaders rallied and Nigeria's polio rate fell again, to 6 cases in 2014. However, poverty and wars in South Asia prevented immunization there: Worldwide, 359 cases were reported in 2014, almost all in Pakistan and Afghanistan (Hagan et al., 2015) (see Figure 5.8).

- Measles (rubeola, not rubella) is disappearing, thanks to a vaccine developed in 1963. Prior to that time, 3 to 4 million cases occurred each year in the United States alone (Centers for Disease Control and Prevention, May 15, 2015). In 2012 in the United States, only 55 people had measles, although globally about 20 million measles cases occurred that year. If a traveler brings measles back to the United States, unimmunized children and adults may catch the disease. That happened in 2014, when 667 people in the United States had measles—the highest rate since 1994 (MMWR, January 8, 2016).

Immunization protects not only from temporary sickness but also from complications, including deafness, blindness, sterility, and meningitis. Sometimes such damage from illness is not apparent until decades later. Having mumps in childhood, for instance, can cause sterility and doubles the risk of schizophrenia in adulthood (Dalman et al., 2008).

Immunization also protects those who cannot be safely vaccinated, such as infants under 3 months and people with impaired immune systems (HIV-positive, aged, or undergoing chemotherapy). Fortunately, each vaccinated child stops transmission of the disease, a phenomenon called *herd immunity*. Usually, if 90 percent of the people in a community (a herd) are immunized, no one dies of that disease.

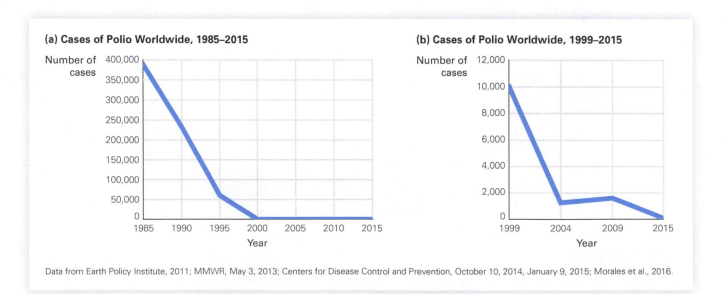

Data from Earth Policy Institute, 2011; MMWR, May 3, 2013; Centers for Disease Control and Prevention, October 10, 2014, January 9, 2015; Morales et al., 2016.

FIGURE 5.8

Not Yet Zero Many public health advocates hope polio will be the next infectious disease to be eliminated worldwide, as is the case in almost all of North America. The number of cases has fallen dramatically worldwide (a). However, there was a discouraging increase in polio rates from 2003 to 2005 (b).

Everywhere, some children are not vaccinated for valid medical reasons, but in 20 of the U.S. states parents are able to refuse vaccination because of "personal belief" (Blad, 2014). One such state is Colorado, where about 81 percent of 1- to 3-year-olds were fully immunized in 2013, a rate far below herd immunity. This horrifies public health workers, who know that the risks of the diseases—especially to babies—are far greater than the risks from immunization of children.

Children may react to immunization by being irritable or even feverish for a day, to the distress of their parents. However, parents do not notice if their child does *not* get polio, measles, or so on. Before the varicella (chicken pox) vaccine, more than 100 people in the United States died each year from that disease, and 1 million were itchy and feverish for a week. Now, far fewer people get chicken pox, and almost no one dies of varicella.

Many parents are concerned about the potential side effects of vaccines, in part because the rare event of one person sickened by vaccination is broadcast widely. Psychologists find that a common source of irrational thinking is overestimating the frequency of a memorable case (Ariely, 2010). As a result, the rate of missed vaccinations in the United States has been rising over the past decade, and epidemics of childhood diseases, such as one that occurred at Disneyland in Anaheim, California, in 2014, are feared.

An example of the benefits of immunization comes from Connecticut, where in 2012 flu vaccination was required for all 6- to 59-month-olds in licensed day-care centers. That winter far fewer young children in Connecticut were hospitalized for flu than previously, although rates rose everywhere else. Meanwhile, Colorado had the highest rate of flu hospitalizations, an increase from previous years (MMWR, March 7, 2014).

Nutrition

As already explained, infant mortality worldwide has plummeted in recent years for several reasons: fewer sudden infant deaths, advances in prenatal and newborn care, and, as you just read, immunization. One more measure is making a huge difference: better nutrition.

Breast Is Best

Ideally, nutrition starts with *colostrum,* a thick, high-calorie fluid secreted by the mother's breasts at birth. This benefit was not understood in some cultures: Again, worldwide research confirmed that colostrum saves infant lives, especially if the infant is preterm (Moles et al., 2015; Andreas et al., 2015). After about three days, the breasts begin to produce milk.

Compared with formula using cow's milk, human milk is sterile, more digestible, and rich in nutrients (Wambach & Riordan, 2014). Allergies and asthma are less common in children who were breast-fed, and in adulthood, their obesity, diabetes, and heart disease rates are lower.

The composition of breast milk adjusts to the age of the baby, with milk for premature babies distinct from that for older infants. Quantity increases to meet the demand: Twins and even triplets can be exclusively breast-fed for months.

Formula is preferable only in unusual cases, such as when the mother uses toxic drugs or is HIV-positive. Even with HIV, however, breast milk without supplementation is advised by the World Health Organization. In some nations, the infants' risk of catching HIV from their mothers is lower than the risk of dying from infections, diarrhea, or malnutrition as a result of bottle-feeding (Williams et al., 2016).

Video: Nutritional Needs of Infants and Children: Breast-Feeding Promotion shows UNICEF's efforts to educate women on the benefits of breast-feeding.

Same Situation, Far Apart: Breast-Feeding
Breast-feeding is universal. None of us would exist if our fore-mothers had not successfully breast-fed their babies for millennia. Currently, breast-feeding is practiced worldwide, but it is no longer the only way to feed infants, and each culture has particular practices.

protein-calorie malnutrition
A condition in which a person does not consume sufficient food of any kind. This deprivation can result in several illnesses, severe weight loss, and even death.

stunting The failure of children to grow to a normal height for their age due to severe and chronic malnutrition.

wasting The tendency for children to be severely underweight for their age as a result of malnutrition.

TABLE 5.1	The Benefits of Breast-Feeding
For the Baby	**For the Mother**
Balance of nutrition (fat, protein, etc.) adjusts to age of baby	Easier bonding with baby
Breast milk has micronutrients not found in formula	Reduced risk of breast cancer and osteoporosis
Less infant illness, including allergies, ear infections, stomach upsets	Natural contraception (with exclusive breast-feeding, for several months)
Less childhood asthma	Pleasure of breast stimulation
Better childhood vision	Satisfaction of meeting infant's basic need
Less adult illness, including diabetes, cancer, heart disease	No formula to prepare; no sterilization
Protection against many childhood diseases, since breast milk contains antibodies from the mother	Easier travel with the baby
Stronger jaws, fewer cavities, advanced breathing reflexes (less SIDS)	**For the Family**
Higher IQ, less likely to drop out of school, more likely to attend college	Increased survival of other children (because of spacing of births)
Later puberty, fewer teenage pregnancies	Increased family income (because formula and medical care are expensive)
Less likely to become obese or hypertensive by age 12	Less stress on father, especially at night

Information from Beilin & Huang, 2008; Riordan & Wambach, 2009; Schanler, 2011; U.S. Department of Health and Human Services, 2011.

Doctors worldwide recommend breast-feeding with no other foods—not even juice—for the first months of life. (Table 5.1 lists some of the benefits of breast-feeding.) Some pediatricians suggest adding foods (rice cereal and bananas) at 4 months; others want mothers to wait until 6 months (Fewtrell et al., 2011).

Breast-feeding was once universal, but by the mid-twentieth century many mothers thought formula was better. Fortunately, that has changed again. In the United States, 79 percent of infants are breast-fed at birth, 49 percent at 6 months (most with other food as well), and 27 percent at a year (virtually all with other food and drink) (Centers for Disease Control and Prevention, 2014). Worldwide, about half of all 2-year-olds are still nursing, usually at night.

Encouragement of breast-feeding from family members, especially new fathers, is crucial. Ideally, nurses visit new mothers weekly at home; such visits (routine in some nations, rare in others) increase the likelihood that breast-feeding will continue.

Malnutrition

Protein-calorie malnutrition occurs when a person does not consume enough food to sustain normal growth. A child may suffer from **stunting,** being short for their age because chronic malnutrition kept them from growing. or **wasting,** being severely underweight for their age and height (2 or more standard deviations below average). Many nations, especially in East Asia, Latin America, and central Europe, have seen improvement in child nutrition in the past decades, with an accompanying decrease in wasting and stunting (see Figure 5.9).

In some other nations, however, primarily in Africa, wasting has increased. And in several nations in South Asia, about one-third of young children are stunted

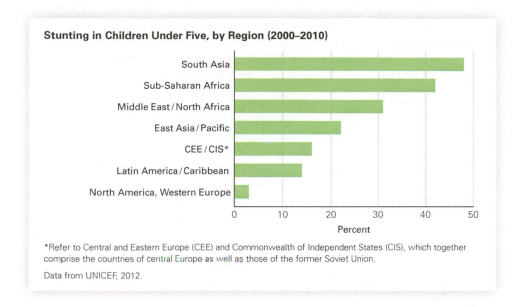

Stunting in Children Under Five, by Region (2000–2010)

South Asia

Sub-Saharan Africa

Middle East / North Africa

East Asia / Pacific

CEE / CIS*

Latin America / Caribbean

North America, Western Europe

0   10   20   30   40   50

Percent

*Refer to Central and Eastern Europe (CEE) and Commonwealth of Independent States (CIS), which together comprise the countries of central Europe as well as those of the former Soviet Union.

Data from UNICEF, 2012.

FIGURE 5.9

Genetic? The data show that basic nutrition is still unavailable to many children in the developing world. Some critics contend that Asian children are genetically small and therefore that Western norms make it appear as if India and Africa have more stunted children than they really do. However, children of Asian and African descent born and nurtured in North America are as tall as those of European descent. Thus, malnutrition, not genes, accounts for most stunting worldwide.

(World Health Organization, 2014). In some nations, the traditional diet for young children or their mothers does not provide sufficient vitamins, fat, and protein for robust health (Martorell & Young, 2012).

Chronically malnourished infants and children suffer in three ways:

1. Their brains may not develop normally. If malnutrition has continued long enough to affect height, it may also have affected the brain. If hunger reduces energy and curiosity, learning suffers.

2. Malnourished children have no body reserves to protect them against common diseases. About half of all childhood deaths occur because malnutrition makes a childhood disease lethal. Precise estimates are unavailable, but there is no doubt that malnutrition increases the death rate from the leading causes—diarrhea and pneumonia—and from milder diseases such as measles (Walker et al., 2013; Imdad et al., 2011).

THINK CRITICALLY: For new mothers in your community, why do some use formula and others breast-feed exclusively for six months?

● Response for Nurses and Pediatricians (from page 144): It is difficult to convince people that their method of child rearing is wrong, although you should try. In this case, listen respectfully and then describe specific instances of serious illness or death from a childhood disease. Suggest that the mother ask her grandparents whether they knew anyone who had polio, tuberculosis, or tetanus (they probably did). If you cannot convince this mother, do not despair: Vaccination of 95 percent of toddlers helps protect the other 5 percent. If the mother has genuine religious reasons, talk to her clergy adviser.

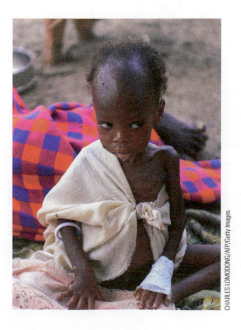

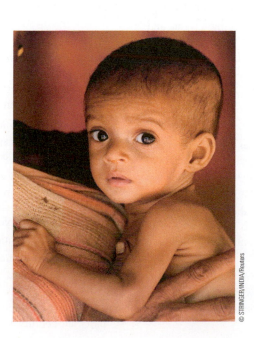

Same Situation, Far Apart: Children Still Malnourished Infant malnutrition is still common in some nations. The 16-month-old at the left is from South Sudan, a nation suffering from civil war for decades, and the 7-month-old boy in India on the right is a twin—a risk for malnutrition. Fortunately, they are getting medical help, and their brains are somewhat protected because of head-sparing.

Courtesy of UNICEF

Video: Malnutrition and Children in Nepal
shows the plight of Nepalese children who
suffer from protein-energy malnutrition (PEM).

3. Some diseases result directly from malnutrition—including both *marasmus* during the first year, when body tissues waste away, and *kwashiorkor* after age 1, when growth slows down, hair becomes thin, skin becomes splotchy, and the face, legs, and abdomen swell with fluid (edema).

Prevention, more than treatment, is needed. Sadly, some children hospitalized for marasmus or kwashiorkor die even after being fed because their digestive systems were already failing (M. Smith et al., 2013). Ideally, prenatal nutrition, then breast-feeding, and then supplemental iron and vitamin A stop malnutrition before it starts. Once malnutrition is apparent, highly nutritious formula (usually fortified peanut butter) often restores weight—but not always.

A combination of factors—genetic susceptibility, poor nutrition, infection, and abnormal bacteria in the digestive system (the microbiome)—may be fatal (M. Smith et al., 2013). Giving severely ill children an antibiotic to stop infection saves lives—but always, prevention is best (Gough et al., 2014).

WHAT HAVE YOU LEARNED?

1. Why is polio still a problem in some nations?

2. Why do doctors worry about immunization rates in the United States?

3. What are the reasons for and against breast-feeding until a child is at least 1 year old?

4. When is it advisable that a woman not breast-feed?

5. What is the relationship between malnutrition and disease?

6. Which is worse, stunting or wasting? Why?

SUMMARY

Body Changes

1. In the first two years of life, infants grow taller, gain weight, and increase in head circumference—all indicative of development. Birthweight doubles by 4 months, triples by 1 year, and quadruples by 2 years, when toddlers weigh about 28 pounds (12.7 kilograms). Two-year-olds are about half their adult height.

2. Medical checkups in the first months of a child's life focus especially on weight, height, and head circumference because early detection of slow growth can halt later problems. Percentile changes can signify difficulties.

3. The amount of time a child sleeps decreases over the first two years. Variations in sleep patterns are normal, caused by both nature and nurture. Bed-sharing is the norm in many developing nations, and co-sleeping is increasingly common in developed ones.

4. Brain size increases dramatically, from about 25 to about 75 percent of adult brain weight in the first two years. Complexity increases as well, with cell growth, development of dendrites, and formation of synapses.

5. Some stimulation is experience-expectant, needed for normal brain development. Both exuberant growth and pruning aid cognition, as the connections that are experience-dependent are strengthened.

6. Experience is vital for brain development. An infant who is socially isolated, overstressed, or deprived of stimulation may be impaired lifelong.

Perceiving and Moving

7. At birth, the senses already respond to stimuli. Prenatal experience makes hearing the most mature sense. Vision is the least mature sense at birth, but it improves quickly. Infants use all their senses to strengthen their early social interactions.

8. The senses of smell, taste, and touch are present at birth, and they help infants respond to their social world. Pain may be experienced, but infant pain is not identical to adult pain.

9. Infants gradually improve their motor skills as they begin to grow and brain maturation continues. Gross motor skills are soon evident, from rolling over to sitting up (at about 6 months), from standing to walking (at about 1 year), from climbing to running (before age 2).

10. Fine motor skills also improve, as infants learn to grab, aim, and manipulate almost anything within reach.

Surviving in Good Health

11. About 2 billion infant deaths have been prevented in the past half-century because of improved health care. One major

innovation is immunization, which has eradicated smallpox and virtually eliminated polio and measles.

12. Public health workers are concerned that some regions of the world, and some states of the United States, have immunization rates that are below herd immunity. Young infants may be most vulnerable to viruses.

13. Breast-feeding is best for infants, partly because breast milk helps them resist disease and promotes growth of every kind.

Most babies are breast-fed at birth, but in North America only half are breast-fed at 6 months, and few of those are exclusively breast-fed, as doctors worldwide recommend.

14. Severe malnutrition stunts growth and can cause death, both directly through marasmus or kwashiorkor and indirectly through vulnerability if a child catches measles, an intestinal virus, or some other illness. Stunting and wasting are both signs of malnutrition.

KEY TERMS

percentile (p. 124)
REM (rapid eye movement) sleep (p. 125)
co-sleeping (p. 125)
bed-sharing (p. 125)
head-sparing (p. 127)
neuron (p. 127)
axon (p. 127)
dendrite (p. 127)
synapse (p. 127)

neurotransmitter (p. 128)
myelin (p. 128)
cortex (p. 128)
prefrontal cortex (p. 128)
limbic system (p. 128)
amygdala (p. 128)
hippocampus (p. 128)
hypothalamus (p. 128)
cortisol (p. 128)
pituitary (p. 128)

transient exuberance (p. 130)
pruning (p. 130)
experience-expectant (p. 132)
experience-dependent (p. 132)
shaken baby syndrome (p. 134)
self-righting (p. 135)
sensation (p. 135)
binocular vision (p. 136)
motor skill (p. 138)
gross motor skills (p. 138)

fine motor skills (p. 139)
sudden infant death syndrome (SIDS) (p. 142)
immunization (p. 143)
protein-calorie malnutrition (p. 146)
stunting (p. 146)
wasting (p. 146)

APPLICATIONS

1. Immunization regulations and practices vary, partly for social and political reasons. Ask at least two faculty or administrative staff members what immunizations the students at your college must have and why. If you hear "It's a law," ask why.

2. Observe three infants (whom you do not know) in public places such as a store, playground, or bus. Look closely at body size and motor skills, especially how much control each baby has over his or her legs and hands. From that, estimate the baby's age in months, and then ask the caregiver how old the infant is.

3. *This project can be done alone, but it is more informative if several students pool responses.* Ask 3 to 10 adults whether they were bottle-fed or breast-fed and, if breast-fed, for how long. If anyone does not know, or if anyone expresses embarrassment about how long they were breast-fed, that itself is worth noting. Do you see any correlation between adult body size and infant feeding?

The First Two Years:
Cognitive Development

What Will You Know?

1. Why did Piaget compare 1-year-olds to scientists?
2. What factors influence whether infants remember what happens to them before they can talk?
3. When and how do infants learn to talk?

"Y ou've been flossing more," my dental hygienist told me approvingly. I am proud. I never flossed as a child (did flossing exist then?), but lately I have flossed every morning. This change was the result of cognition: I read that heart disease and flossing were negatively correlated, and I applied what I know about behavior modification—keeping daily track, with check marks, of when I flossed. But my hygienist was not satisfied.

"You need to brush three minutes each time, and floss twice a day."

"Why?"

"You will have less tartar."

"What is wrong with tartar?"

"It causes gingivitis."

"What is wrong with gingivitis?"

"It causes periodontitis."

"What is wrong with periodontitis?"

She looked at me as if I were incredibly stupid, and replied, "It is terrible, it is expensive, it is time-consuming. You could lose a tooth."

I thought of asking "What's wrong with losing a tooth?" I did not.

How does this apply to infant cognitive development? The negative cascade of daily events, from another minute of brushing to a lost tooth, is not unlike the positive cascade that transforms a newborn into a talking, goal-directed 2-year-old. As you will see, infants learn rapidly, from their first attempt to suck and swallow to their comprehension of some laws of physics, from recognition of their mother's voice to their memory for action sequences that they have witnessed, from a reflexive cry to spoken sentences with several words.

Each day of looking and learning seems insignificant, yet caregiver actions accumulate to turn a newborn into a toddler who thinks, understands, pretends, and explains. This chapter describes in detail those early days and months, which build the intellectual foundation for the later thinking and talking. Everyday actions of infants' caregivers lead to these accomplishments.

The conversation with my dental hygienist is relevant in another way as well. My repeated questioning is similar to infants' drive for new understanding, evident in the six stages of intellectual progression that Piaget describes, and the gradual improvement of infant memory detailed by information-processing theorists. Babies, too, are curious, questioning explorers.

The final topic of this chapter may be most important. How do infants learn so much? What is the best way to nurture early cognition?

Sensorimotor Intelligence

Jean Piaget earned his doctorate in biology in 1918, when most scientists thought infants only ate, cried, and slept. When Piaget became a father, he used his scientific observation skills with his own babies, and, contrary to conventional wisdom, he detailed active learning in infancy. [**Life-Span Link:** Piaget's theory of cognitive development is introduced in Chapter 2.]

Piaget called cognition in the first two years **sensorimotor intelligence.** Early reflexes, senses, and body movements are the raw materials for infant cognition, as now described (see Table 6.1).

sensorimotor intelligence Piaget's term for the way infants think—by using their senses and motor skills—during the first period of cognitive development.

LaunchPad
macmillan learning

Video: Sensorimotor Intelligence in Infancy and Toddlerhood
http://qrs.ly/lj4ep00

© 2016 Macmillan

TABLE 6.1	The Six Stages of Sensorimotor Intelligence

For an overview of the stages of sensorimotor thought, it helps to group the six stages into pairs.

Primary Circular Reactions

The first two stages involve the infant's responses to its own body.

Stage One (birth to 1 month)	*Reflexes:* sucking, grasping, staring, listening
	Example: sucking anything that touches the lips or cheek
Stage Two (1–4 months)	*The first acquired adaptations:* accommodation and coordination of reflexes
	Examples: sucking a pacifier differently from a nipple; attempting to hold a bottle to suck it

Secondary Circular Reactions

The next two stages involve the infant's responses to objects and people.

Stage Three (4–8 months)	*Making interesting sights last:* responding to people and objects
	Example: clapping hands when mother says "patty-cake"
Stage Four (8–12 months)	*New adaptation and anticipation:* becoming more deliberate and purposeful in responding to people and objects
	Example: putting mother's hands together in order to make her start playing patty-cake

Tertiary Circular Reactions

The last two stages are the most creative, first with action and then with ideas.

Stage Five (12–18 months)	*New means through active experimentation:* experimentation and creativity in the actions of the "little scientist"
	Example: putting a teddy bear in the toilet and flushing it
Stage Six (18–24 months)	*New means through mental combinations:* thinking before doing, new ways of achieving a goal without resorting to trial and error
	Example: before flushing the teddy bear again, hesitating because of the memory of the toilet overflowing and mother's anger

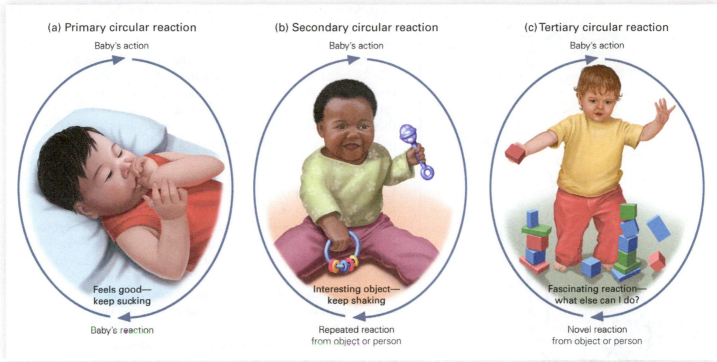

(a) Primary circular reaction

Baby's action

Feels good—
keep sucking

Baby's reaction

(b) Secondary circular reaction

Baby's action

Interesting object—
keep shaking

Repeated reaction
from object or person

(c) Tertiary circular reaction

Baby's action

Fascinating reaction—
what else can I do?

Novel reaction
from object or person

FIGURE 6.1
Never Ending Circular reactions keep going because each action produces pleasure that encourages more action.

Stages One and Two: Primary Circular Reactions

Piaget described the interplay of sensation, perception, action, and cognition as *circular reactions,* emphasizing that, as in a circle, there is no beginning and no end. Each experience leads to the next, which loops back (see Figure 6.1). In **primary circular reactions,** the circle is within the infant's body. Stage one, called the *stage of reflexes,* lasts only a month, as reflexes become deliberate actions; sensation leads to perception, perception leads to cognition, and then cognition leads back to sensation.

Stage two, *first acquired adaptations* (also called *stage of first habits*), begins because reflexes adjust to whatever responses they elicit. Adaptation is cognitive; it includes repeating old patterns (assimilation) and developing new ones (accommodation). [**Life-Span Link:** Assimilation and accommodation are explained in Chapter 2.]

primary circular reactions The first of three types of feedback loops in sensorimotor intelligence, this one involving the infant's own body. The infant senses motion, sucking, noise, and other stimuli and tries to understand them.

Vladimir Godnik/FStop/Punchstock/Getty Images

Time for Adaptation Sucking is a reflex at first, but adaptation begins as soon as an infant differentiates a pacifier from her mother's breast or realizes that her hand has grown too big to fit into her mouth. This infant's expression of concentration suggests that she is about to make that adaptation and suck just her thumb from now on.

"Is **this** the way you plan to spend your peak learning years?"

Still Wrong Parents used to ignore infant cognition. Now some make the opposite mistake, assuming infants learn via active study.

secondary circular reactions The second of three types of feedback loops in sensorimotor intelligence, this one involving people and objects. Infants respond to other people, to toys, and to any other object that they can touch or move.

Here is one example. In a powerful reflex, full-term newborns suck anything that touches their lips (stage one). They must learn to suck, swallow, and suck again without spitting up too much—a major circular reaction that often takes a few days to learn. Then, infants *adapt* their sucking reflex to bottles or breasts, pacifiers or fingers, each requiring specific types of tongue pushing. This adaptation signifies that infants have begun to interpret sensations; as they accommodate, they are thinking—ready for stage two.

During stage two, which Piaget pegged from about 1 to 4 months of age, additional adaptation of the sucking reflex begins. Infant cognition leads babies to suck in some ways for hunger, in other ways for comfort—and not to suck fuzzy blankets or hard plastic. Once adaptation occurs, it sticks.

Adaptation is specific. For instance, 4-month-old breast-fed babies may reject milk from the nipple of a bottle if they have never experienced it. Or, suppose 4-month-olds have discovered how to suck their thumbs and have practiced thumb-sucking to their joy and satisfaction. Then suppose the parents decide that a pacifier is better—perhaps healthier for teeth. That may be too late. The baby may refuse to readapt, spitting out the pacifier and finding the thumb instead. People of all ages tend to stick to their customary ways; early adaptation is one example.

Stages Three and Four: Secondary Circular Reactions

In stages three and four, development advances from primary to **secondary circular reactions.** These reactions extend beyond the infant's body; this circular reaction is between the baby and something else.

During stage three (4 to 8 months), infants attempt to produce exciting experiences, *making interesting sights last*. Realizing that rattles make noise, for example, they wave their arms and laugh whenever someone puts a rattle in their hand. The sight of something delightful—a favorite squeaky toy, a smiling parent—can trigger active efforts for interaction.

Next comes stage four (8 months to 1 year), *new adaptation and anticipation* (also called the *means to the end*). Babies may ask for help (fussing, pointing, gesturing) to accomplish what they want. Thinking is more innovative because adaptation is more complex. For instance, instead of always smiling at Grandpa, an infant might first assess his mood. Stage-three babies continue an experience; stage-four babies initiate and anticipate.

Pursuing a Goal

An impressive attribute of stage four is that babies work hard to achieve their goals. Suppose a 10-month-old girl might crawl over to her mother, bringing a bar of soap as a signal she loves baths, and then start to remove her clothes to make her wishes crystal clear—finally squealing with delight when the bath water is turned on. Similarly, if a 10-month-old boy sees his father putting on a coat to leave, he might drag over his own jacket to signal that he wants to go along.

In both cases, the infant has learned from repeated experience—Daddy may have often brought the baby along when he went out. With a combination of experience and brain maturation, babies become attuned to the goals of others, an ability that is more evident at 10 months than 8 months (Brandone et al., 2014).

Especially for Parents When should parents decide whether to feed their baby only by breast, only by bottle, or using some combination of the two? When should they decide whether or not to let their baby use a pacifier? (see response, page 157)

Object Permanence

Piaget discovered that, until about 8 months, babies do not search for an object that is momentarily out of sight. He thought they did not understand **object permanence**—the concept that objects or people continue to exist when they are not visible. At about 8 months—not before—infants look for toys that have fallen from the crib, rolled under a couch, or disappeared under a blanket.

As another scholar explains:

Many parents in our typical American middle-class households have tried out Piaget's experiment in situ: Take an adorable, drooling 7-month-old baby, show her a toy she loves to play with, then cover it with a piece of cloth right in front of her eyes. What do you observe next? The baby does not know what to do to get the toy! She looks around, oblivious to the object's continuing existence under the cloth cover, and turns her attention to something else interesting in her environment. A few months later, the same baby will readily reach out and yank away the cloth cover to retrieve the highly desirable toy. This experiment has been done thousands of times and the phenomenon remains one of the most compelling in all of developmental psychology.

[Xu, 2013, p. 167]

Piaget studied the development of this concept. He found:

- Infants younger than 8 months do not search for an attractive object momentarily covered by a cloth.
- At about 8 months, infants remove the cloth immediately after the object is covered but not if they have to wait a few seconds.
- At 18 months, they search after a wait but not if they have seen the object put first in one place and then moved to another. They search in the first place, not the second, a mistake Piaget's followers called *A-not-B*. They search where they remember seeing it put (A), not where they saw it moved (to B).
- By 2 years, children fully understand object permanence, progressing through several stages of ever-advanced cognition (Piaget, 1954/2013a).

This research provides many practical suggestions. If young infants fuss because they see something they cannot have (keys, a cell phone, candy), caregivers are advised to put that coveted object out of sight. Fussing stops if object permanence has not yet appeared.

object permanence The realization that objects (including people) still exist when they can no longer be seen, touched, or heard.

By contrast, for toddlers, hiding an object is not enough. It must be securely locked up, lest the child later retrieve it, climbing onto the kitchen counter or under the bathroom sink to do so.

Piaget believed that failure to search before 8 months meant that infants had no concept of object permanence—that "out of sight" literally means "out of mind." However, a series of clever experiments in which objects seemed to disappear while researchers traced babies' eye movements and brain activity revealed that long before 8 months infants are surprised if an object vanishes (Baillargeon & DeVos, 1991; Spelke, 1993).

Further research on object permanence continues to question some of Piaget's conclusions. Many other creatures (cats, monkeys, dogs, birds) develop object permanence faster than human infants. The animal ability seems to be innate, not learned, as wolves can develop it as well as dogs—but neither is adept at A-not-B displacement, as when an object is moved by a hand underneath a cloth that covers it (Fiset & Plourde, 2013). By age 2, children figure this out, but dogs do not.

Family Fun Peek-a-boo makes all three happy, each for cognitive reasons. The 9-month-old is discovering object permanence, his sister (at the concrete operational stage) enjoys making Brother laugh, and their mother understands more abstract ideas—such as family bonding.

Stages Five and Six: Tertiary Circular Reactions

In their second year, infants start experimenting in thought and deed—or, rather, in the opposite sequence, deed and thought. They act first (stage five) and think later (stage six).

Tertiary circular reactions begin when 1-year-olds take independent actions to discover the properties of other people, animals, and things. Infants no longer respond only to their own bodies (primary reactions) or to other people or objects

tertiary circular reactions The third of three types of feedback loops in sensorimotor intelligence, this one involving active exploration and experimentation. Infants explore a range of new activities, varying their responses as a way of learning about the world.

BruesWu/Moment Open/Getty Images

Imitation is Lifelong As this photo illustrates, at every age, people copy what others do–often to their mutual joy. The new ability at stage six is "deferred imitation"—this boy may have seen another child lie on a tire a few days earlier.

(secondary reactions). Their cognition is more like a spiral than a closed circle, increasingly creative with each discovery.

Piaget's stage five (12 to 18 months), *new means through active experimentation,* builds on the accomplishments of stage four. Now goal-directed and purposeful activities become more expansive.

Toddlers delight in squeezing all the toothpaste out of the tube, drawing on the wall, or uncovering an anthill—activities they have never observed. Piaget referred to the stage-five toddler as a **"little scientist"** who "experiments in order to see."

Toddlers' research method is trial and error. Their devotion to discovery is familiar to every adult scientist—and to every parent. Protection is needed.

Finally, in the sixth stage (18 to 24 months), toddlers use *mental combinations,* intellectual experimentation via imagination that can supersede the active experimentation of stage five. Because they combine ideas, stage-six toddlers think about consequences, hesitating a moment before yanking the cat's tail or dropping a raw egg on the floor. They store what they have seen in memory and do it later, an ability Piaget called *deferred imitation.*

The ability to combine ideas allows stage-six toddlers to pretend. For instance, they know that a doll is not a real baby, but they can belt it into a stroller and take it for a walk. Newer research finds that some accomplishments that Piaget pegged for stage six—including pretending and imitation—begin much earlier.

Piaget was right to describe babies as avid and active learners who "learn so fast and so well" (Xu & Kushnir, 2013, p. 28). His main mistake was underestimating how rapidly their learning occurs.

⬤⬤ Especially for Parents One parent wants to put all the breakable or dangerous objects away because the toddler is able to move around independently. The other parent says that the baby should learn not to touch certain things. Who is right? (see response, page 158)

"little scientist" The stage-five toddler (age 12 to 18 months) who experiments without anticipating the results, using trial and error in active and creative exploration.

LaunchPad
macmillan learning

Professor Debra L. Mills, Bangor University, United Kingdom

Video: Event-Related Potential (ERP) Research shows a procedure in which the electrical activity of an infant's brain is recorded to see whether the brain responds differently to familiar versus unfamiliar words.

WHAT HAVE YOU LEARNED?

1. What is a circular reaction?

2. Why did Piaget call his first stage of cognition *sensorimotor* intelligence?

3. How do the first two sensorimotor stages illustrate primary circular reactions?

4. How does a stage-three infant make interesting events last?

5. How is object permanence an example of stage four of sensorimotor intelligence?

6. In sensorimotor intelligence, what is the difference between stages five and six?

7. What implications for caregivers come from Piaget's description of sensorimotor intelligence?

8. What evidence suggests that infants are thinking, not just reacting, before age 1?

Information Processing

To understand cognition, many researchers use their understanding of the workings of a computer, including input, memory, programs, analysis, and output. This emphasis on how the human brain uses experience to advance cognition is basic to an *information-processing approach* to cognition, as described in Chapter 2. This approach has been particularly insightful in understanding infant cognition, since babies are unable to demonstrate what they know with words.

For infants, output might be uncovering a hidden toy, uttering a sound, or simply staring at one photo longer than another. Some recent studies examine changes in brain waves when infants see a picture (Kouider et al., 2013).

To understand information processing in infancy, consider a baby's reaction to an empty stomach. A newborn simply cries as a reflex—no cognition needed. Soon, however, when an infant begins to fuss with hunger, the sound of a mother's voice might lead to looking for her, reaching to be picked up, and nuzzling at her breast—all without crying. By age 1, hunger might make the infant gesture or verbalize. Each step requires information to have been processed.

The information-processing perspective, aided by modern technology, has uncovered many aspects of infant cognition. As one researcher summarizes, "Rather than bumbling babies, they are individuals who . . . can learn surprisingly fast about the patterns of nature" (Keil, 2011, p. 1023). Concepts and categories seem to develop in infants' brains by 6 months or earlier (Mandler & DeLoach, 2012).

The information-processing perspective helps tie together many aspects of infant cognition. In earlier decades, infant intelligence was measured via age of sitting up, grasping, and so on, but we now know that the age at which infants achieve motor skills does not predict later intellectual achievement.

Instead, information-processing research has found that signs of attention correlate with later cognitive ability. Babies who focus intently on new stimuli and then turn away are likely more intelligent than babies who stare aimlessly (Bornstein & Colombo, 2012). Smart babies like novelty.

Now let us look at two specific aspects of infant cognition that illustrate the information-processing approach: affordances and memory. Affordances concern perception or, by analogy, input. Memory concerns brain organization and output—that is, storage and retrieval.

Affordances

Perception, remember, is the processing of information that arrives at the brain from the sense organs. Decades of thought and research led Eleanor and James Gibson to conclude that perception is far from automatic (E. Gibson, 1969; J. Gibson, 1979). Perception—for infants, as for the rest of us—is a cognitive accomplishment that requires selectivity: "Perceiving is active, a process of *obtaining* information about the world. . . . We don't simply see, we look" (E. Gibson, 1988, p. 5).

The environment (people, places, and objects) *affords,* or offers, many opportunities to interact with whatever is perceived (E. Gibson, 1997). Each of these opportunities is called an **affordance.** Which particular affordance is perceived and acted on depends on four factors: (1) the senses, (2) motivation, (3) maturation, and (4) experience.

For example, imagine that you realize you are lost in an unfamiliar city (factor 1). Motivation is high: You need directions (factor 2). Now, you decide

GILKIS-Emielke van Wyk/Gallo Images/Getty Images

What Next? Information-processing research asks what these babies are thinking as they both pull on the same block. Will those thoughts lead to hitting, crying, or sharing?

Especially for Computer Experts In what way is the human mind *not* like a computer? (see response, page 159)

Response for Parents (from page 154): It is easier and safer to babyproof the house because toddlers, being "little scientists," want to explore. However, it is important for both parents to encourage and guide the baby. If having untouchable items prevents a major conflict between the adults, that might be the best choice.

affordance An opportunity for perception and interaction that is offered by a person, place, or object in the environment.

Depth Perception This toddler in a laboratory in Berkeley, California, is crawling on the experimental apparatus called a visual cliff. She stops at the edge of what she perceives as a drop-off.

visual cliff An experimental apparatus that gives the illusion of a sudden drop-off between one horizontal surface and another.

⬤ Response for Parents (from page 156): Both decisions should be made within the first month, during the stage of reflexes. If parents wait until the infant is 4 months or older, they may discover that they are too late. It is difficult to introduce a bottle to a 4-month-old who has never sucked on an artificial nipple or a pacifier to a baby who has already adapted the sucking reflex to a thumb.

⬤ Especially for Parents of Infants When should you be particularly worried that your baby will fall off the bed or down the stairs? (see response, page 161)

whom to ask. You would not ask the first person you see because factors 3 and 4 suggest that the affordance of finding good directions depends on choosing well. You seek someone knowledgeable and approachable, so you evaluate facial expressions, body language, gender, dress, and so on of passersby (Miles, 2009).

Developmentalists studying children emphasize that age, motivation, and experience affect what affordances a child perceives. For example, since toddlers enjoy running as soon as their legs allow it, every open space affords running: a meadow, a building's long hall, a city street. To adults, affordance of running is more limited because of experience: They worry about a bull grazing in the meadow, neighbors behind the hallway doors, or traffic on the street. Because motivation and experience are pivotal in affordances, toddlers move when most adults prefer to stay put.

Variation in affordance is also apparent between and within cultures. City-dwellers complain that visitors from rural areas walk too slowly, yet visitors complain that urbanites are always in a hurry. Sidewalks afford either fast travel or views of architecture, depending on the perceiver.

Research on Early Affordances

Experience always affects which affordances are perceived. This is obvious in studies of depth perception. Research demonstrating this began with an apparatus called the **visual cliff,** designed to provide the illusion of a sudden drop-off between one horizontal surface and another. In a classic research study, 6-month-olds, urged forward by their mothers, wiggled toward Mom over the supposed edge of the cliff, but 10-month-olds, even with their mothers' encouragement, fearfully refused to budge (E. Gibson & Walk, 1960).

Scientists once thought that a visual deficit—specifically, inadequate depth perception—prevented 6-month-olds from seeing the drop, which was why they moved forward. According to this hypothesis, as the visual cortex matured, 10-month-olds perceived that crawling over a cliff afforded falling.

Later research, benefiting from advanced technology and an information-processing approach, found that some 3-month-olds noticed the drop: Their heart rate slowed, and their eyes opened wide when they were placed over the cliff.

Thus, depth perception was not the problem, but until they can crawl, infants do not realize that crawling over an edge affords falling. The difference is in processing affordances, not visual input. Those conclusions were drawn by Eleanor Gibson herself, the scientist who did the early visual cliff research and who explained the concept of affordances (Adolph & Kretch, 2012).

A similar sequence happens with fear. Infants at 9 months pay close attention to snakes and spiders, but they do not yet fear them. A few months later, perhaps because they have learned from others, they are afraid of the creatures (LoBue, 2013).

Very young babies are particularly attuned to emotional affordances, using their limited perceptual abilities and intellectual understanding to respond to smiles, shouts, and so on. Indeed, in one study, babies watched a 3-second video demonstration by an actor whose face was covered (so no visual expression could be seen) as he acted out happiness, anger, or indifference. The results: 6-month-olds can distinguish whether a person is happy or angry by body movements alone (Zieber et al., 2014). Hundreds of information-processing experiments find that infants are able to connect movements, facial expressions, and tone of voice.

Memory

Information-processing research, with detailed behavioral and neurological measures, trace memory in very young babies. Within the first weeks after birth, infants recognize their caregivers by face, voice, and smell.

Selective Amnesia As we grow older, we forget about spitting up, nursing, crying, and almost everything else from our early years. However, strong emotions (love, fear, mistrust) may leave lifelong traces.

Memory improves month by month. In one study, after 6-month-olds had had only two half-hour sessions with a novel puppet, they remembered the experience a month later—an amazing feat of memory for babies who could not talk or even stand up (Giles & Rovee-Collier, 2011).

Instead of noting the many "faults and shortcomings relative to an adult standard," it may be more appropriate to realize that children of all ages remember what they need to remember (Bjorklund & Sellers, 2014, p. 142). Sensory and caregiver memories are apparent in the first month, motor memories by 3 months, and then, at about 9 months, more complex memories (Mullally & Maguire, 2014).

Forget About Infant Amnesia

Before information-processing research, many scientists hypothesized *infant amnesia,* that infants remember nothing. Their evidence was that adults rarely remember events that occurred before they were 3. But the fact that memories fade with time, and that even children cannot verbalize what happened when they were babies, does not mean that memory is absent.

For example, you may not remember your third-grade teacher's name, but that does not mean you had no memory of it when you were in fifth grade; it just means that you do not now remember what you could once easily remember. If you saw a photo of your third-grade teacher, your brain would register that you knew that person, although you might not know his or her name. Then, if presented with four possible names, you probably could choose correctly.

Indeed, if you saw a photo of a grandmother who cared for you every day when you were an infant and who died when you were 2, your brain would still react. Information-processing research finds evidence of very early memories, with visual memories particularly strong (Leung et al., 2016; Gao et al., 2016).

No doubt memory is fragile in the first months of life and improves with age. A certain amount of experience and brain maturation are required to process and recall what happens (Bauer et al., 2010). But some of that experience happens on day 1—or even in the womb, and some memories may begin long before a baby can say them.

Response for Computer Experts (from page 157): Computers differ from humans in dozens of ways, including speed of calculation, ability to network across the world, and vulnerability to viruses. However, in at least one crucial way, the human mind is better: Computers become obsolete or fail within a few years, while human minds keep advancing for decades.

Video: Contingency Learning in Young Infants shows Carolyn Rovee-Collier's procedure for studying instrumental learning during infancy.

He Remembers! Infants are fascinated by moving objects within a few feet of their eyes—that's why parents buy mobiles for cribs and why Rovee-Collier tied a string to a mobile and a baby's leg to test memory. Babies not in her experiment, like this one, sometimes flail their limbs to make their cribs shake and thus make their mobiles move. Piaget's stage of "making interesting sights last" is evident to every careful observer.

reminder session A perceptual experience that helps a person recollect an idea, a thing, or an experience.

Especially for Teachers People of every age remember best when they are active learners. If you had to teach fractions to a class of 8-year-olds, how would you do it? (see response, page 162)

Conditions of Memory

Many studies seek to understand what infants *can* remember, even if they cannot later put memories into words. Memories are particularly evident if:

- Motivation and emotion is high.
- Retrieval is strengthened by reminders and repetition.

The most dramatic proof of infant memory comes from innovative experiments in which 3-month-old infants learned to move a mobile by kicking their legs (Rovee-Collier, 1987, 1990). Babies were laid on their backs and connected to a mobile by means of a ribbon tied to one foot. Virtually every baby began making occasional kicks (as well as random arm movements and noises) and realized that kicking made the mobile move. They then kicked more vigorously and frequently, sometimes laughing at their accomplishment. So far, this is no surprise—observing self-activated movement is highly reinforcing to infants.

When some 3-month-olds had the mobile-and-ribbon apparatus reinstalled and reconnected *one week later,* most started to kick immediately. They remembered their previous experience. But when other 3-month-old infants were retested *two weeks later,* they began with only random kicks. Apparently they had forgotten—evidence that memory is fragile early in life.

Reminders and Repetition

The lead researcher, Carolyn Rovee-Collier, then developed another experiment demonstrating that 3-month-old infants *could* remember after two weeks *if* they had a brief **reminder session** before being retested (Rovee-Collier & Hayne, 1987). In the reminder session, *two weeks* after the initial training, the infants watched the mobile move but were *not* tied to it and were positioned so that they could *not* kick. The next day, when they were again connected to the mobile and positioned so that they could move their legs, they kicked as they had learned to do two weeks earlier.

Apparently, watching the mobile move on the previous day had revived their faded memory. The information about making the mobile move was stored in their brains, but they needed processing time to retrieve it. Other research similarly finds that repeated reminders are more powerful than single reminders and that context is crucial, especially for infants younger than 9 months: Being tested in the same room as the initial experience aids memory (Rovee-Collier & Cuevas, 2009).

A Little Older, a Little More Memory

Older infants retain information for a longer time than younger babies do, with less training or reminding. Many researchers find that by 9 months, memory improves markedly (Mullally & Maguire, 2014). At that age, babies who watch someone else play with a new toy will, the next day, play with it in the same way as he or she had observed. Infants younger than 9 months do not usually do this.

One-year-olds can transfer learning from one object or experience to another, can learn from strangers, and can copy what they see in books and videos. The

Who Is Thinking? They all are. Julie is stretching her sensorimotor intelligence as she rotates a piece to make it fit, while her mother decides whether her 2-year-old is ready for a puzzle with 20 cardboard pieces. But the champion thinker may be baby Samara, as her brain is processing what her eyes see.

dendrites and neurons of several areas of the brain change to reflect remembered experiences. Overall, infants remember not only specific events but also patterns (Keil, 2011). Babies know what to expect from a parent or a babysitter, which foods are delicious, or what details indicate bedtime. Every day of their young lives, infants are processing information and storing conclusions.

● **Response for Parents of Infants**
(from page 158): Constant vigilance is necessary for the first few years of a child's life, but the most dangerous age is from about 4 to 8 months, when infants can move but do not yet fear falling over an edge.

WHAT HAVE YOU LEARNED?

1. How do affordances differ for infants and adults?

2. Why do 10-month-olds refuse to crawl over visual cliffs?

3. What suggests that very young infants have some memory?

4. What conditions help 3-month-olds remember something?

5. How does memory improve between 6 months and 2 years?

Language: What Develops in the First Two Years?

The human linguistic ability at age 2 far surpasses that of full-grown adults from every other species. Very young infants listen intensely, figuring out speech. One scholar explains, "infants are acquiring much of their native language before they utter their first word" (Aslin, 2012, p. 191). How do babies do it?

The Universal Sequence

The sequence of language development is the same worldwide (see At About This Time). Some children learn several languages, some only one; some learn rapidly and others slowly; but they all follow the same path. Even deaf infants who become able to hear (thanks to cochlear implants) follow the sequence, catching up to their age-mates unless they have other disabilities (Fazzi et al., 2011). Those who learn sign language also begin with one word at a time, and then they sign sentences of increasing length and complexity.

Listening and Responding

Newborns prefer to listen to the language their mother spoke when they were in the womb, not because they understand the words, of course, but because they are familiar with the rhythm, the sounds, and the cadence.

Surprisingly, newborns of bilingual mothers differentiate between the languages (Byers-Heinlein et al., 2010). Data were collected on 94 newborns (age 0 to 5 days) in a large hospital in Vancouver, Canada. Half were born to mothers who spoke both English and Tagalog (a language native to the Philippines), one-third to mothers who spoke only English, and one-sixth to mothers who spoke English and Chinese. The bilingual mothers used English in more formal contexts and Chinese or Tagalog with family.

The infants in all three groups sucked on a pacifier connected to a recording of 10 minutes of English or Tagalog matched for pitch, duration, and number of syllables. As evident in the frequency and strength of their sucking, most of the infants with bilingual mothers preferred Tagalog. For the Filipino babies, this was probably because their mothers spoke English in formal settings but not when with family and friends, and thus Tagalog was associated with more interesting talk. Those babies with monolingual mothers preferred English, as both formal and informal English sounds were familiar (Byers-Heinlein et al., 2010).

Ariel Skelley/Getty Images

Who Is Babbling? Probably both the 6-month-old and the 27-year-old. During every day of infancy, mothers and babies communicate with noises, movements and expressions.

child-directed speech The high-pitched, simplified, and repetitive way adults speak to infants and children. (Also called *baby talk* or *motherese*.)

🔴🟣 **Response for Teachers**
(from page 160): Remember the three principles of infant memory: real life, motivation, and repetition. Find something children already enjoy that involves fractions—even if they don't realize it. Perhaps get a pizza and ask them to divide it in half, quarters, eighths, sixteenths, and so on.

Curiously, the Chinese bilingual babies (who had never heard Tagalog) nonetheless preferred it to English. The researchers believe that they liked Tagalog because the rhythm of that language is similar to Chinese (Byers-Heinlein et al., 2010).

Similar results, that babies like to hear familiar language, come from everyday life. Young infants attend to voices more than to mechanical sounds (a clock ticking) and look closely at the facial expressions of someone who is talking to them (Minagawa-Kawai et al., 2011). By 1 year, they are more likely to imitate the actions of a stranger who is speaking their native language than those of a person who speaks another language (Buttelmann et al., 2013).

Infants' ability to distinguish sounds in the language they hear improves, whereas the ability to hear sounds never spoken in their native language (such as a foreign way to pronounce "r" or "l") deteriorates (Narayan et al., 2010). If parents want a child to speak two languages, they should speak both of them to their baby from birth on.

In every language, adults use higher pitch, simple words, repetition, varied speed, and exaggerated emotional tone when talking to infants. This is sometimes called *baby talk,* since it is directed to babies, and sometimes called *motherese,* since mothers universally speak it. But motherese seems wrong, since nonmothers speak it as well. Scientists prefer a more formal term, **child-directed speech.**

AT ABOUT THIS TIME

The Development of Spoken Language in the First Two Years

Age*	Means of Communication
Newborn	Reflexive communication—cries, movements, facial expressions.
2 months	A range of meaningful noises—cooing, fussing, crying, laughing.
3–6 months	New sounds, including squeals, growls, croons, trills, vowel sounds.
6–10 months	Babbling, including both consonant and vowel sounds repeated in syllables.
10–12 months	Comprehension of simple words; speechlike intonations; specific vocalizations that have meaning to those who know the infant well. Deaf babies express their first signs; hearing babies also use specific gestures (e.g., pointing) to communicate.
12 months	First spoken words that are recognizably part of the native language.
13–18 months	Slow growth of vocabulary, up to about 50 words.
18 months	Naming explosion—three or more words learned per day. Much variation: Some toddlers do not yet speak.
21 months	First two-word sentence.
24 months	Multiword sentences. Half the toddler's utterances are two or more words long.

*The ages in this table reflect norms. Many healthy, intelligent children attain each linguistic accomplishment earlier or later than indicated here.

No matter what term is used, child-directed speech fosters learning, and babies communicate as best they can. By 4 months, babies squeal, growl, gurgle, grunt, croon, and yell, telling everyone what is on their minds in response to both their own internal state and their caregivers' words. At 7 months, infants begin to recognize words that are highly distinctive (Singh, 2008): *Bottle, doggie,* and *mama,* for instance, might be differentiated, but not *baby, Bobbie,* and *Barbie.*

Infants also like alliteration, rhymes, repetition, melody, rhythm, and varied pitch (Hayes & Slater, 2008; Schön et al., 2008). Think of your favorite lullaby (itself an alliterative word); obviously, babies prefer sounds over content. Early listening abilities and preferences are the result of early brain function, as the following explains.

INSIDE THE BRAIN

Understanding Speech

One particular research strategy has been a boon to scientists, confirming the powerful curiosity of very young babies. That research method is called **habituation** (from the word *habit*).

Habituation refers to getting accustomed to an experience after repeated exposure, as when the school cafeteria serves macaroni day after day or when infants repeatedly encounter the same sound, sight, toy, or so on. Evidence of habituation is loss of interest (or, for macaroni, loss of appetite).

Using habituation with infants involves repeating one stimulus until the babies lose interest and then presenting another slightly different stimulus (a new sound, sight, or other sensation). Babies indicate that they detect a difference between the two stimuli with a longer or more focused gaze; a faster or slower heart rate; more or less muscle tension around the lips; a change in the rate, rhythm, or pressure of suction on a nipple; or—the newest and most exciting way—a change in brain activation as reflected by the fMRI or DTI. [**Life-Span Link:** DTI, fMRI, ERP, and other types of neuroimaging techniques are described in Chapter 2.]

For example, decades ago scientists used habituation to discover that 1-month-olds can detect the difference between certain sounds, such as "*pah*" and "*bah*" (Eimas et al., 1971). More recently, methods of measuring brain activity reveal that infants respond to some aspects of speech before observable evidence is found (Johnson & de Haan, 2015). For instance, newborns—even if born before full term—can discriminate one syllable from another, evident by activity in their frontal lobes (Mahmoudzadeh et al., 2013).

Other research finds that not only do infants hear differences between sounds, but they also begin the process of learning language very early. For instance, one study found that when infants hear speech, their brains begin to react more notably (registered on ERP, or event-related potential) at the same time that their gaze tends to focus on the mouth more than the eyes (Kushnerenko et al., 2013).

habituation The process of becoming accustomed to an object or event through repeated exposure to it, and thus becoming less interested in it.

Evidence from DTI (diffusion tensor imaging) has found that one of the most complex aspects of learning to talk, specifically activating axons that become pathways within the brain to connect the lobes in order for speech to occur, are bundled over infancy. The specific connected axons are the temporal lobe to hear, the parietal lobe for moving the mouth, the occipital lobe for seeing, and the frontal lobe for thinking (Dubois et al., 2015).

Those "crucial circuits that are required to develop a language system in humans" are similar in structure for infants and adults (Dubois et al., 2015, p. 13). Although the early brain pathways are immature, with scant myelination, advances are evident between 6 and 22 weeks after birth.

Because of maturation of the language areas of the cortex, even 4-month-old infants attend to voices, developing expectations of the rhythm, segmentation, and cadence of spoken words long before comprehension (Minagawa-Kawai et al., 2011).

Soon, infants use their brains to deduce the rules of their native language, such as which syllable is stressed, whether changing inflection matters (as in Chinese), whether certain sound combinations are repeated, and so on. All of this is based on very careful listening to human speech, including speech not directed toward them with words they do not yet understand (Buttelmann et al., 2013).

As you read, Piaget was innovative because he realized that babies can think. Over the past century, and increasingly with brain imagery, it is now apparent that the human brain, even in the first year of life, does more than think. It works hard to enable people to communicate, interact, and create—supporting all the functions that we consider the pinnacle of human intellectual achievement.

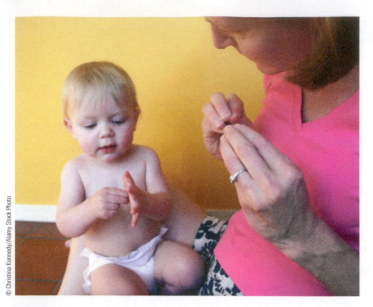

Are You Hungry? Pronunciation is far more difficult than hand skills, but parents want to know when their baby wants more to eat. One solution is evident here. This mother is teaching her 12-month-old daughter the sign for "more," a word most toddlers say several months later.

babbling An infant's repetition of certain syllables, such as *ba-ba-ba*, that begins when babies are between 6 and 9 months old.

Babbling and Gesturing

Between 6 and 9 months, babies repeat certain syllables (*ma-ma-ma, da-da-da, ba-ba-ba*), a vocalization called **babbling** because of the way it sounds. Babbling is experience-expectant; all babies babble, even deaf ones.

Before infants start talking, they become aware of the patterns of speech, such as which sounds are commonly spoken together. A baby who often hears that something is "pretty" expects the sound of *prit* to be followed by *tee* (MacWhinney, 2015) and is startled if someone says "prit-if."

Infants notice the relationship between mouth movements and sound. In one study, 8-month-olds watched a film of someone speaking, with the audio a fraction of second ahead of the video. Even when the actor spoke an unknown language, babies noticed the mistiming (Pons & Lewkowicz, 2014).

Toward the end of the first year, babbling begins to imitate the native language; infants imitate accents, cadence, consonants, and so on of the language they hear. Some caregivers, recognizing the power of gestures, teach "baby signs" to their 6- to 12-month-olds, who communicate with hand signs months before they move their tongues, lips, and jaws to make words. There is no evidence that baby signing accelerates talking (as had been claimed), but it may make parents more responsive, which itself is an advantage (Kirk et al., 2013).

Gestures become a powerful means of communication (Goldin-Meadow, 2015). One early gesture is pointing, a social gesture that requires understanding another person's perspective.

Most animals cannot interpret pointing; most 10-month-old humans look toward wherever someone else points and can already use a tiny index finger (not just a full hand) to point. Pointing is well developed by 12 months, especially when the person who is pointing also speaks (e.g., "look at that") (Daum et al., 2013).

First Words

Finally, at about a year, the average baby utters a few words, understood by caregivers if not by strangers. In the first months of the second year, spoken vocabulary increases gradually (perhaps one new word a week). Meanings are learned rapidly; babies understand about 10 times more words than they can say. Initially, the first words are merely labels for familiar things (*mama* and *dada* are common), but early words are soon accompanied by gestures, facial expressions, and nuances of tone, loudness, and cadence (Saxton, 2010). Imagine meaningful communication in "Dada," "Dada?" and "Dada!" Each is a **holophrase,** a single word that expresses an entire thought.

Show Me Where Pointing is one of the earliest forms of communication, emerging at about 10 months. As you see here, pointing is useful lifelong for humans.

holophrase A single word that is used to express a complete, meaningful thought.

Of course, the thought in the baby's mind may not be what the adult understands. I know this personally. "Mama, mama," my 16-month-old grandson, Isaac, said while I was caring for him when his parents were at work. He looked directly at me when he said it, and he didn't seem wistful. He said, "mama, mama" again, which sounded more like a command than a complaint.

Isaac speaks only a few words that I recognize, and he has his own meanings for many sounds. I remembered that babies understand much more than they say, so I tried, "Mommy's not here." That didn't interest him; he repeated "mama, mama," looking expectantly at me. I know that "mama" means milk in Japanese baby talk (*miruku* is Japanese for milk), so I tried that, offering Isaac milk in his sippy cup. He said, "No, no."

When his father, Oscar, appeared, Isaac grinned broadly, said "mama," and went to cuddle in his arms. I asked Oscar what "mama" means. His answer: "Pick me up."

The Naming Explosion

Spoken vocabulary builds rapidly once the first 50 words are mastered, with 21-month-olds typically saying twice as many words as 18-month-olds (Adamson & Bakeman, 2006). This language spurt is called the **naming explosion** because many early words are nouns, that is, names of persons, places, or things.

Between 12 and 18 months, almost every infant learns the name of each significant caregiver (often *dada, mama, nana, papa, baba, tata*) and sibling (and sometimes each pet). (See Visualizing Development, p. 167) Other frequently uttered words refer to the child's favorite foods (*nana* can mean "banana" as well as "grandma") and to elimination (*pee-pee, wee-wee, poo-poo, ka-ka, doo-doo*).

Notice that all of these words have two identical syllables, each a consonant followed by a vowel. Many words follow that pattern—not just *baba* but also *bobo, bebe, bubu, bibi.* Other early words are only slightly more complicated—*ma-me, ama,* and so on. The meaning of these words varies by language, but every baby says such words, and every culture assigns meaning to them.

Cultural Differences

Cultures and families vary in how much child-directed speech children hear. Some parents read to their infants, teach them signs, and respond to every burp or fart as if it were an attempt to talk. Other parents are much less verbal. They use gestures and touch; they say "hush" and "no" instead of expanding vocabulary.

> **naming explosion** A sudden increase in an infant's vocabulary, especially in the number of nouns, that begins at about 18 months of age.

> ● ● **Especially for Caregivers** A toddler calls two people "Mama." Is this a sign of confusion? (see response, page 166)

Universal or Culture-Specific? Both. All children enjoy music and like to bang on everything from furniture to people. Making noise is fun, but even infants prefer the noises of their community and do their best to repeat them. This boy has learned to play the bongo drums (notice the skilled angle of his hands) thanks to his grandfather.

Jupiterimages/Getty Images

● ● **Response for Caregivers**
(from page 165): Not at all. Toddlers hear several people called "Mama" (their own mother, their grandmothers, their cousins' and friends' mothers) and experience mothering from several people, so it is not surprising if they use "Mama" too broadly. They will eventually narrow the label down to one person, unless both of their parents are women. Usually such parents differentiate, such as one called Mama and the other Mom, or both by their first names.

grammar All of the methods—word order, verb forms, and so on—that languages use to communicate meaning, apart from the words themselves.

mean length of utterance (MLU) The average number of words in a typical sentence (called utterance because children may not talk in complete sentences). MLU is often used to measure language development.

Differences are readily apparent in which sounds capture attention. Infants soon favor the words, accents, and linguistic patterns of their home language. For instance, a study of preverbal Japanese and French infants found that words with the first consonant at the front of the mouth and the second consonant at the back (as in "bat") were preferred by infants in France, but the opposite (as in "tap") was true in Japan. This reflected the language (French or Japanese) that the babies had heard (Gonzalez-Gomez et al., 2014).

The traditional idea that children should be "seen but not heard" is contrary to what developmentalists recommend: Everywhere, infants listen to whatever speech they hear and appreciate the sounds of their culture. Even musical tempo is culture-specific: 4- to 8-month-olds seem to like their own native music best (Soley & Hannon, 2010).

Putting Words Together

Grammar includes all of the methods that languages use to communicate meaning. Word order, prefixes, suffixes, intonation, verb forms, pronouns and negations, prepositions and articles—all of these are aspects of grammar. Grammar can be discerned in holophrases, as one word can be spoken differently depending on meaning. However, grammar becomes essential when babies combine words (Bremner & Wachs, 2010). That typically happens between 18 and 24 months.

For example, "Baby cry" and "More juice" follow grammatical word order. Children do not usually ask "Juice more," and even toddlers know that "cry baby" is not the same as "baby cry." By age 2, children combine three words. English grammar uses subject–verb–object order. Toddlers say "Mommy read book" rather than any of the five other possible sequences of those three words.

Children's proficiency in grammar correlates with sentence length, which is why **mean length of utterance (MLU)** is used to measure a child's language progress (e.g., Miyata et al., 2013). The child who says "Baby is crying" is more advanced than the child who says "Baby crying" or simply the holophrase "Baby."

Theories of Language Learning

Worldwide, people who are not yet 2 years old express hopes, fears, and memories—sometimes in more than one language. By adolescence, people communicate with nuanced words and gestures, some writing poems and lyrics that move thousands of their co-linguists. How is language learned so easily and so well?

Answers come from at least three schools of thought, each connected to a theory introduced in Chapter 2: behaviorism, sociocultural theory, and evolutionary psychology. The first theory says that infants are directly taught, the second that social impulses propel infants to communicate, and the third that infants understand language because of brain advances that began several millennia ago.

Theory One: Infants Need to Be Taught

The seeds of the first perspective were planted in the middle of the twentieth century, when behaviorism was the dominant theory in North American psychology. The essential idea was that learning is acquired, step by step, through association and reinforcement.

B.F. Skinner (1957) noticed that spontaneous babbling is usually reinforced. Typically, when a baby says "ma-ma-ma-ma," a grinning mother appears, repeating the sound and showering the baby with attention, praise, and perhaps food. The baby learns affordances and repeats "ma-ma-ma-ma" when lonely or hungry; through operant conditioning, talking begins.

Early Communication and Language Development

A COMMUNICATION MILESTONES: THE FIRST TWO YEARS

These are norms. Many intelligent and healthy babies vary in the age at which they reach these milestones.

Months	Communication Milestone
0	Reflexive communication—cries, movements, facial expressions
1	Recognizes some sounds
	Makes several different cries and sounds
	Turns toward familiar sounds
3	A range of meaningful noises—cooing, fussing, crying, laughing
	Social smile well established
	Laughter begins
	Imitates movements
	Enjoys interaction with others
6	New sounds, including squeals, growls, croons, trills, vowel sounds
	Meaningful gestures including showing excitement (waving arms and legs)
	Deaf babies express their first signs
	Expresses negative feelings (with face and arms)
	Capable of distinguishing emotion by tone of voice
	Responds to noises by making sounds
	Uses noise to express joy and unhappiness
	Babbles, including both consonant and vowel sounds repeated in syllables
10	Makes simple gestures, like raising arms for "pick me up"
	Recognizes pointing
	Makes a sound (not in recognizable language) to indicate a particular thing
	Responds to simple requests
12	More gestures, such as shaking head for "no"
	Babbles with inflection, intonation
	Names familiar people (like "mama," "dada," "nana")
	Uses exclamations, such as "uh-oh!"
	Tries to imitate words
	Points and responds to pointing
	First spoken words
18	Combines two words (like "Daddy bye-bye")
	Slow growth of vocabulary, up to about 50 words
	Language use focuses on 10–30 holophrases
	Uses nouns and verbs
	Uses movement, including running and throwing, to indicate emotion
	Naming explosion may begin, three or more words learned per day
	Much variation: Some toddlers do not yet speak
24	Combines three or four words together; half the toddler's utterances are two or more words long
	Uses adjectives and adverbs ("blue," "big," "gentle")
	Sings simple songs

SOURCE: AMERICAN ACADEMY OF PEDIATRICS

B UNIVERSAL FIRST WORDS

Across cultures, babies' first words are remarkably similar. The words for mother and father are recognizable in almost any language. Most children will learn to name their immediate family and caregivers between the ages of 12 and 18 months.

Language	Mother	Father
English	mama, mommy	dada. daddy
Spanish	mama	papa
French	maman, mama	papa
Italian	mamma	bebbo, papa
Latvian	mama	te-te
Syrian Arabic	mama	babe
Bantu	be-mama	taata
Swahili	mama	baba
Sanskrit	nana	tata
Hebrew	ema	abba
Korean	oma	apa

R. EKO BINTORO/THINKSTOCK

C MASTERING LANGUAGE (MLU)

Children's use of language becomes more complex as they acquire more words and begin to master grammar and usage. A child's spoken words or sounds (utterances) are broken down into the smallest units of language to determine their length and complexity:

SAMPLES OF UTTERANCES

"Doggie!" = **1**

"Doggie + Sleep" = **2**

"Doggie + Sleep + ing" = **3**

"Shh! + Doggie + Sleep + ing" = **4**

"Shh! + Doggie + is + Sleep + ing" = **5**

"Shh! + The + Doggie + is + Sleep + ing" = **6**

SOURCE: COURTESY OF MONICA KALFUR, SLP

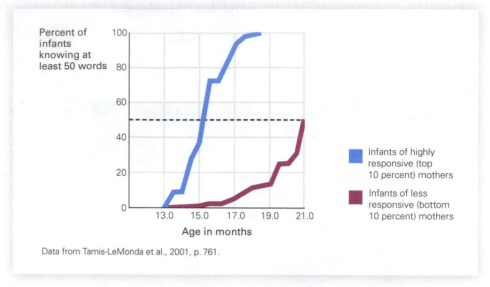

Data from Tamis-LeMonda et al., 2001, p. 761.

FIGURE 6.2

Maternal Responsiveness and Infants' Language Acquisition Learning the first 50 words is a milestone in early language acquisition, as it predicts the arrival of the naming explosion and the multiword sentence a few weeks later. Researchers found that half of the infants of highly responsive mothers (top 10 percent) reached this milestone at 15 months. The infants of non-responsive mothers (bottom 10 percent) lagged significantly behind, with half of them at the 50-word level at 21 months.

Skinner believed that most parents are excellent instructors, responding to their infants' gestures and sounds, thus reinforcing speech. That is what parents usually do (Saxton, 2010). Even in preliterate societies, parents use child-directed speech, responding quickly with high pitch, short sentences, stressed nouns, and simple grammar—exactly the techniques that behaviorists would recommend.

In every culture infants who learn language faster have parents who speak to them more often. Few parents know the theory of behaviorism, but many use behaviorist techniques that Skinner would recommend, because these methods succeed (Tamis-LeMonda et al., 2014).

The core ideas of this theory are the following:

- Parents are expert teachers.
- Repetition strengthens associations, especially when linked to daily life.
- Well-taught infants become articulate, highly verbal children.

Behaviorists note that some 3-year-olds converse in elaborate sentences; others just barely put one simple word with another. Such variations correlate with the amount of language each child has heard. Parents of the most verbal children teach language throughout infancy—singing, explaining, listening, responding, and reading to their children every day, long before the first spoken word (Forget-Dubois et al., 2009) (see Figure 6.2).

According to behaviorists, if adults want children who speak, understand, and (later) read well, they must talk to their infants. A recent application of this theory comes from commercial videos designed to advance toddlers' vocabulary. Typically, such videos use repetition and attention-grabbing measures (sound, tone, color) to encourage babies to learn new words (Vaala et al., 2010). Such videos, and Skinner's theories, have come under attack from many developmentalists, as explained in the following.

● **Especially for Educators** An infant day-care center has a new child whose parents speak a language other than the one the teachers speak. Should the teachers learn basic words in the new language, or should they expect the baby to learn the teachers' language? (see response, page 170)

Language and Video

Toddlers can learn to swim in the ocean, throw a ball into a basket, walk on a narrow path beside a precipice, call on a smartphone, cut with a sharp knife, play a guitar, say a word on a flashcard, recite a poem, utter a curse, and much else—if provided appropriate opportunity, encouragement, and practice. Indeed, toddlers in some parts of the world do each of these things—sometimes to the dismay, disapproval, and even shock of adults from elsewhere.

Infants do what others do, a trait that fosters rapid learning. That same trait challenges caregivers, who try to keep "little scientists" safe. Since language is crucial, many North American parents hope to accelerate talking and understanding, and they covet some free time when they do not need to interact with their toddlers.

Commercial companies cater to parents' wishes. They realize that infants are fascinated by movement, sound, and people. This explains the popularity of child-directed videos—"it's crack for babies," as one mother said (quoted in DeLoache et al., 2010, p. 1572).

Many products are named to appeal to parents, such as *Baby Einstein, Brainy Baby,* and *Mozart for Mommies and Daddies—Jumpstart your Newborn's I.Q.,* and are advertised with testimonials. Scientists consider such advertisements deceptive, since one case proves nothing and only controlled experiments prove cause and effect.

Commercial apps for tablets and smartphones have joined the market, with *Shapes Game HD, VocabuLarry,* and a series called *Laugh and Learn.* Most toddler apps offer free trials that babies enjoy, which prompts parents to pay for more content. This is not surprising: Babies enjoy doing something—like touching a screen—to make interesting sights last, and commercial products seek a profit. Does any video, television program, or app actually teach?

No, according to many scientists, some of whom believe that the truth is the opposite of the commercial claims. A famous study found that infants watching *Baby Einstein* were delayed in language compared to other infants (Zimmerman et al., 2007). The American Association of Pediatricians suggests no screen time (including television, tablets, smartphones, and commercial videos) for children under age 2.

These conclusions are not "robust," the word scientists use to mean that all the evidence agrees. Some interpretations of the evidence endorse absolute prohibition, but others do not.

However, those who sell such products try to convince parents that babies learn from screen time, a conclusion that developmentalists dispute. An author of the original study defends his anti-video conclusions, arguing that "a reanalysis rooted in dissatisfaction with previous results will necessarily be biased

and can only obscure scientific discoveries" (Zimmerman, 2014, p. 138).

Overall, most developmentalists find that, although some educational videos and apps may help older children, screen time during infancy cannot "substitute for *responsive,* loving face-to-face relationships" (Lemish & Kolucki, 2013, p. 335). The crucial factor for intellectual growth seems to be caregiver responsiveness to the individual child, face to face (Richert et al., 2011).

More specifically, infants are less likely to understand and apply what they have learned from books, videos, and apps than what they learn directly from another person (Barr, 2013). One product, *My Baby Can Read,* was pulled off the market in 2012 because experts repeatedly attacked its claims, and the cost of defending lawsuits was too high (Ryan, 2012). But many similar products are still sold, and new ones appear continually.

"Keep in mind, this all counts as screen time."

Caught in the Middle Parents try to limit screen time, but children are beguiled and bombarded from many sides.

The owners of *Baby Einstein* lost a lawsuit in 2009, promised not to claim it was educational, and offered a refund, yet, as one critic notes:

> The bottom line is that this industry exists to capitalize on the national preoccupation with creating intelligent children as early as possible, and it has become a multi-million dollar enterprise. Even after . . . the Baby Einstein Company itself admitted its products are not educational, Baby Einstein products continue to fly off of the shelves.
>
> [Ryan, 2012, p. 784]

One study focused particularly on teaching "baby signs," 18 hand gestures that refer to particular objects (Dayanim & Namy, 2015). The babies in this study were 15 months old, an age when all babies use gestures and are poised to learn object names. The 18 signs referred to common early words, such as *baby, ball, banana, bird, cat,* and *dog.*

In this study, the toddlers were divided into four groups: video only, video with parent watching and reinforcing, book instruction with parent reading and reinforcing, and no instruction. Not surprisingly, the no-instruction group learned words but not signs, and the other three groups learned some signs. The two groups with parent instruction learned most, with the book-reading group remembering signs better than either video group.

● ● **Response for Educators**

(from page 168): Probably both. Infants love to communicate, and they seek every possible way to do so. Therefore, the teachers should try to understand the baby and the baby's parents, but they should also start teaching the baby the majority language of the school.

Theory Two: Social Impulses Foster Infant Language

The second theory is called *social-pragmatic*. It arises from the sociocultural reason for language: communication. According to this perspective, infants communicate because humans are social beings, dependent on one another for survival and joy. All human infants (and no chimpanzees) seek to master words and grammar in order to join the social world in which they find themselves (Tomasello & Herrmann, 2010).

According to this perspective, it is the emotional messages of speech, not the words, that propel communication. Evidence for social learning comes from educational programs for children. Many 1-year-olds enjoy watching television and videos, as the Opposing Perspectives feature explains, but they learn best when adults are actively involved in teaching. In a controlled experiment, 1-year-olds learned vocabulary much better when someone taught them directly than when the same person gave the same lesson on video (Roseberry et al., 2009).

Theory Three: Infants Teach Themselves

A third theory holds that language learning is genetically programmed to begin at a certain age; adults need not teach it (theory one), nor is it a by-product of social interaction (theory two). Instead, it arises from the universal genetic impulse to imitate. That impulse has been characteristic of the human species for 100,000 years. For example, English articles (*the, an, a*) signal that the next word will be the name of an object, and since babies have "an innate base" that primes them to learn, articles facilitate learning nouns (Shi, 2014, p. 9).

Infants and toddlers have always imitated what they hear—not slavishly but according to their own concepts and intentions. Theory three proposes that this is exactly how they learn language (Saxton, 2010). This theory is buttressed by research which finds that variations in children's language ability correlate with differences in brain activity and perceptual ability, evident months before the first words are spoken and apart from the particulars of parental input (Cristia et al., 2014). Some 5-year-olds are far more verbal than others because they were born to be so.

● **Especially for Nurses and Pediatricians** Eric and Jennifer have been reading about language development in children. They are convinced that because language develops naturally, they need not talk to their 6-month-old son. How do you respond? (see response, page 172)

This perspective began soon after Skinner proposed his theory of verbal learning. Noam Chomsky (1968, 1980) and his followers felt that language is too complex to be mastered merely through step-by-step conditioning. Although behaviorists focus on variations among children in vocabulary size, Chomsky focused on similarities in language acquisition—the evolutionary universals, not the differences.

Noting that all young children master basic grammar according to a schedule, Chomsky cited *universal grammar* as evidence that humans are born with a mental structure that prepares them to seek some elements of human language. For example, everywhere, a raised tone indicates a question, and infants prefer questions to declarative statements (Soderstrom et al., 2011). This suggests that infants are

Same Situation, Far Apart: Before Words The Polish babies learning sign language *(left)* and the New York infant interpreting a smile *(right)* are all doing what babies do: trying to understand communication long before they are able to talk.

wired to have conversations, and caregivers universally ask them questions long before they can answer back.

Chomsky labeled this hypothesized mental structure the **language acquisition device (LAD).** The LAD enables children, as their brains develop, to derive the rules of grammar quickly and effectively from the speech they hear every day, regardless of whether their native language is English, Thai, or Urdu.

According to theory three, language is experience-expectant, as the developing brain quickly and efficiently connects neurons to support whichever language the infant hears. Because of this experience expectancy, the various languages of the world are all logical, coherent, and systematic. Then some experience-dependent learning occurs as each brain adjusts to a particular language.

Research supports this perspective as well. As you remember, newborns are primed to listen to speech, and all infants babble *ma-ma* and *da-da* sounds (not yet referring to mother or father). No reinforcement or teaching is required; all a baby needs is time for dendrites to grow, mouth muscles to strengthen, neurons to connect, and speech to be heard. This theory might explain why poets put together phrases that they have never heard to produce novel understanding, and why people hear words in their dreams that make no sense. Thus, the language impulse may arise from the brain, not from other people.

Nature even provides for deaf infants. All 6-month-olds, hearing or not, prefer to look at sign language over nonlinguistic pantomime. For hearing infants, this preference disappears by 10 months, but deaf infants begin signing at that time, which is their particular expression of the universal LAD.

A Hybrid Theory

Which of these three perspectives is correct? Perhaps all of them are true to some extent. In one monograph that included details and results of 12 experiments, the authors presented a hybrid (which literally means "a new creature, formed by combining other living things") of previous theories (Hollich et al., 2000). Since infants learn language to do numerous things—to indicate intention, call objects by name, put words together, talk to family members, sing to themselves, express wishes, remember the past, and much more—some aspects of language learning are best explained by one theory at one age and other aspects by another theory at another age.

Since every human must learn language, nature allows variations so that the goal is attained. Ideally, parents talk often to their infants (theory one), encourage social interaction (theory two), and appreciate innate *impulses* (theory three). Contemporary advocates of a hybrid view conclude that there is no single critical

language acquisition device (LAD) Chomsky's term for a hypothesized mental structure that enables humans to learn language, including the basic aspects of grammar, vocabulary, and intonation.

Steven J. Kazlowski/Alamy

Family Values Every family encourages the values and abilities that their children need to be successful adults. For this family in Ecuador, that means strong legs and lungs to climb the Andes, respecting their parents, and keeping quiet unless spoken to. A "man of few words" is admired. By contrast, many North American parents babble in response to infant babble, celebrate the first spoken word, and stop their conversation to listen to an interrupting child. If a student never talks in class, or another student blurts out irrelevant questions, perhaps the professor should consider cultural influences.

◐● Response for Nurses and Pediatricians (from page 170): Although humans may be naturally inclined to communicate with words, exposure to language is necessary. You may not convince Eric and Jennifer, but at least convince them that their baby will be happier if they talk to him.

period for language acquisition, but rather that the many aspects of language are mastered at various times and in various ways (Balari & Lorenzo, 2015).

A master linguist has concurred that the "the human mind is a hybrid system" which learns some aspects of language in one way and other aspects in another, perhaps using different parts of the brain for each kind of learning (Pinker, 1999, p. 279). Another expert agrees:

> our best hope for unraveling some of the mysteries of language acquisition rests with approaches that incorporate multiple factors, that is, with approaches that incorporate not only some explicit linguistic model, but also the full range of biological, cultural, and psycholinguistic processes involved.

[Tomasello, 2006, pp. 292–293]

The idea that every theory is correct may seem idealistic. However, many scientists who are working on extending and interpreting research on language acquisition arrived at a similar conclusion. They contend that language learning is neither the direct product of repeated input (behaviorism) nor the result of a specific human neurological capacity (LAD). Rather, from an evolutionary perspective, "different elements of the language apparatus may have evolved in different ways," and thus, a "piecemeal and empirical" approach is needed (Marcus & Rabagliati, 2009, p. 281).

What conclusion can we draw from all the research on infant cognition? It is clear that infants are active learners of language and concepts and that they seek to experiment with objects and find ways to achieve their goals. This is the cognitive version of the biosocial developments noted in Chapter 5—that babies strive to roll over, crawl, walk, and so on as soon as they can. One scholar summarizes this as a bio-psycho-social approach to cognition—every aspect and impulse of infant life leads to cognitive development (Nelson, 2015).

WHAT HAVE YOU LEARNED?

1. What communication abilities do infants have before they talk?

2. What aspects of early language development are universal, apparent in every culture?

3. What is typical of the first words that infants speak and the rate at which they acquire them?

4. What are the early signs of grammar in infant speech?

5. According to behaviorism, how do adults teach infants to talk?

6. According to sociocultural theory, why do infants try to communicate?

7. What does the idea that child speech results from brain maturation imply for caregivers?

SUMMARY

Sensorimotor Intelligence

1. Piaget realized that very young infants are active learners who seek to understand their complex observations and experiences. The six stages of sensorimotor intelligence involve early adaptation to experience.

2. Sensorimotor intelligence begins with reflexes and ends with mental combinations. The six stages occur in pairs, with each pair characterized by a circular reaction; infants first react to their

own bodies (primary), then respond to other people and things (secondary), and finally, in the stage of tertiary circular reactions, infants become more goal-oriented, creative, and experimental as "little scientists."

3. Infants gradually develop an understanding of objects. According to Piaget's classic experiments, infants understand object permanence and begin to search for hidden objects at about 8 months. Newer research, using brain scans and other new

methods, finds that Piaget underestimated infant cognition, including his conclusions about when infants understand object permanence and when they defer imitation.

Information Processing

4. Another approach to understanding infant cognition involves information-processing theory, which looks at each step of the thinking process, from input to output. The perceptions of a young infant are attuned to the particular affordances, or opportunities for action, that are present in the infant's world.

5. From a baby's perspective, the world is filled with exciting affordances, and babies are eager to experience all of the opportunities for learning available to them. Adults are more cautious.

6. Infant memory is fragile but not completely absent. Reminder sessions help trigger memories, and young brains learn motor sequences and respond to repeated emotions (their own and those of other people) long before they can remember with words.

7. Memory is multifaceted; infant amnesia is a myth. At about 9 months, infant memories improve, and toddlers can apply what they have learned to new situations.

Language: What Develops in the First Two Years?

8. Language learning, which distinguishes the human species from other animals, is an amazing accomplishment. By age 2, babies are talking to express wishes and memory, as well as what they experience at the moment.

9. Attempts to communicate are apparent in the first weeks and months, beginning with noises, facial expressions, and avid listening. Infants babble at about 6 months, understand words and gestures by 10 months, and speak their first words at about 1 year. Deaf infants make their first signs before 1 year.

10. Vocabulary builds slowly until the infant knows approximately 50 words. Then the naming explosion begins. The tone of holophrases is evidence of grammar, but putting two or three words together in proper sequence is proof.

11. Toward the end of the second year, toddlers put words together in short sentences. Much variation is evident, in part because of context, but all babies should be talking by age 2.

12. Various theories explain how infants learn language as quickly as they do. The three main theories emphasize different aspects of early language learning: that infants must be taught, that their social impulses foster language learning, and that their brains are genetically attuned to language as soon as the requisite maturation has occurred.

13. Each theory of language learning is confirmed by some research. The challenge for developmental scientists has been to formulate a hybrid theory that uses all of the insights and research on early language learning. The challenge for caregivers is to respond to the infant's early attempts to communicate, expecting neither too much nor too little.

KEY TERMS

sensorimotor intelligence (p. 152)
primary circular reactions (p. 153)
secondary circular reactions (p. 154)

object permanence (p. 155)
tertiary circular reactions (p. 155)
"little scientist" (p. 156)
affordance (p. 157)
visual cliff (p. 158)

reminder session (p. 160)
child-directed speech (p. 162)
habituation (p. 163)
babbling (p. 164)
holophrase (p. 164)
naming explosion (p. 165)

grammar (p. 166)
mean length of utterance (MLU) (p. 166)
language acquisition device (LAD) (p. 171)

APPLICATIONS

1. Elicit vocalizations from an infant—babbling if the baby is under age 1, using words if the baby is older. Write down all of the baby's communication for 10 minutes. Then ask the primary caregiver to elicit vocalizations for 10 minutes, and write these down. What differences are apparent between the baby's two attempts at communication? Compare your findings with the norms described in the chapter.

2. Many educators recommend that parents read to babies every day, even before 1 year of age. What theory of language develop-

ment does this reflect and why? Ask several parents if they did so, and why or why not.

3. Test a toddler's ability to pretend and to imitate. Use a doll or a toy car and pretend with it, such as feeding the doll or making the car travel. Then see if the child will do it. This experiment can be more elaborate if the child succeeds.

The First Two Years:
Psychosocial Development

What Will You Know?

1. Does a difficult newborn become a difficult child?
2. What do babies do to indicate how responsive their parents are?
3. Do infants benefit or suffer when cared for by someone other than their mother?

My daughter Bethany came to visit her newest nephew, Isaac, 7 months old. She had visited him many times before, always expressing joy and excitement with her voice, face, and hands. By 2 months, he always responded in kind, with big smiles and waving arms, to her delight. But this time he was more hesitant, and looked away, nuzzling on his mother. Later Bethany tried again, and this time he kept looking and smiling.

"You like me now," she said.

"He always liked you; he was just tired," said Elissa, his mother.

"I know," Bethany told her. "I didn't take it personally."

I appreciated both daughters. Elissa sought to reassure Bethany, and Bethany knew that Isaac's reaction was not really to her, although she wished that he had not turned away. But the person I appreciated most was Isaac, responsive to people as well-loved babies should be, but wary and seeking maternal comfort as he grew closer to a year. Emotions change month by month in the first two years; ideally caregivers change with them.

This chapter opens by tracing infants' emotions as their brains mature and their experiences accumulate. Next we explore caregiver–infant interaction, particularly *synchrony, attachment,* and *social referencing,* and some theories that explain those developments

Finally, we explore a controversy: Who should be infant caregivers and how should they respond? Families and cultures answer this question in many ways. Fortunately, as this chapter explains, despite diversity of temperament and caregiving, most people thrive, as long as their basic physical and emotional needs are met. Isaac, Elissa, and Bethany are all thriving.

Emotional Development

In their first two years, infants progress from reactive pain and pleasure to complex patterns of social awareness (see At About This Time), a movement from basic instinctual emotions to learned emotions and then thoughtful ones (Panksepp & Watt, 2011).

AT ABOUT THIS TIME

Developing Emotions

Birth	Distress; contentment
6 weeks	Social smile
3 months	Laughter; curiosity
4 months	Full, responsive smiles
4–8 months	Anger
9–14 months	Fear of social events (strangers, separation from caregiver)
12 months	Fear of unexpected sights and sounds
18 months	Self-awareness; pride; shame; embarrassment

As always, culture and experience influence the norms of development. This is especially true for emotional development after the first eight months.

Grandpa Knows Best Does her tongue sticking out signify something wrong with her mouth or mind? Some parents might worry, but one advantage of grandparents is that they have been through it before: All babies do something with their fingers, toes, or, as here, tongue (sometimes all three together!) that seems odd but is only a temporary exploration of how their body works.

social smile A smile evoked by a human face, normally first evident in infants about 6 weeks after birth.

separation anxiety An infant's distress when a familiar caregiver leaves; most obvious between 9 and 14 months.

stranger wariness An infant's expression of concern—a quiet stare while clinging to a familiar person, or a look of fear—when a stranger appears.

Early Emotions

At first there is comfort and pain. Newborns are happy and relaxed when fed and drifting off to sleep. They cry when they are hurt or hungry, tired or frightened (as by a loud noise or a sudden loss of support).

Some infants have bouts of uncontrollable crying, called *colic,* probably the result of immature digestion; some have *reflux,* probably the result of immature swallowing. About 20 percent of babies cry "excessively," defined as more than three hours a day, for more than three days a week, for more than three weeks (J. Kim, 2011).

Smiling and Laughing

Soon, crying decreases and additional emotions become recognizable. Curiosity is evident: Infants respond to objects and experiences that are new but not too novel. Happiness is expressed by the **social smile,** evoked by a human face at about 6 weeks. (Preterm babies smile later because the social smile is affected by age since conception, not age since birth.)

Laughter builds as curiosity does; a typical 6-month-old laughs loudly upon discovering new things, particularly social experiences that balance familiarity and surprise, such as Daddy making a funny face. They prefer looking at happy faces over sad ones, even if the happy faces are not looking at them (Kim & Johnson, 2013).

Anger and Sadness

Reactive crying and the positive emotions of joy and contentment are soon joined by negative emotions. Anger is notable at 6 months, usually triggered by frustration, such as when infants are prevented from moving or grabbing.

To investigate infants' response to frustration, researchers "crouched behind the child and gently restrained his or her arms for 2 min[utes] or until 20 s[econds] of hard crying ensued" (Mills-Koonce et al., 2011, p. 390). "Hard crying" is not rare: Infants hate to be strapped in, caged in, closed in, or even just held in place when they want to explore.

In infancy, anger is a healthy response to frustration, unlike sadness, which also appears in the first months. Sadness indicates withdrawal and is accompanied by a greater increase in the body's production of cortisol. Since sadness produces physiological stress (measured by cortisol levels), sorrow negatively impacts the infant. All social emotions, particularly sadness and fear, affect the brain. Caregiving matters. Sad and angry infants whose mothers are depressed become fearful toddlers and depressed children (Dix & Yan, 2014). Abuse and unpredictable responses are likely among the "early adverse influences [that] have lasting effects on developing neurobiological systems in the brain" (van Goozen, 2015, p. 208).

Fear

Fear in response to some person, thing, or situation (not just being startled) soon becomes more frequent and obvious. Two kinds of social fear are typical:

- **Separation anxiety**—clinging and crying when a familiar caregiver is about to leave. Separation anxiety is normal at age 1, intensifies by age 2, and usually subsides after that.
- **Stranger wariness**—fear of unfamiliar people, especially when they move too close, too quickly. Wariness indicates memory, so it is a positive sign.

If separation anxiety remains intense after age 3, impairing a child's ability to leave home, to go to school, or to play with other children, it is considered an emotional disorder. Separation anxiety as a disorder can be diagnosed up to age 18 (American Psychiatric Association, 2013); some clinicians diagnose it in adults as well (Bögels et al., 2013).

Many typical 1-year-olds fear anything unexpected, from a flushing toilet to a popping jack-in-the-box, from closing elevator doors to the tail-wagging approach of a dog. With repeated experience and reassurance, older infants might enjoy flushing the toilet (again and again) or calling the dog (mad if the dog does *not* come). Note the transition from instinct to learning to expectation (Panksepp & Watt, 2011).

Toddlers' Emotions

Emotions take on new strength during toddlerhood, as both memory and mobility advance. For example, throughout the second year and beyond, anger and fear become less frequent but more focused, targeted toward infuriating or terrifying experiences. Similarly, laughing and crying are louder and more discriminating.

The new strength of emotions is apparent in temper tantrums. Toddlers are famous for fury. When something angers them, they might yell, scream, cry, hit, and throw themselves on the floor. Logic is beyond them; if adults respond with anger or teasing, that makes it worse.

One child said, "I don't want my feet. Take my feet off. I don't want my feet." Her mother tried logic, which didn't work, and then said she could get a pair of scissors and cut off the offending feet. A new wail of tantrum erupted, with a loud shriek "Nooooo!" (Katrina, quoted in Vedantam, 2011).

With temper tantrums, soon sadness comes to the fore, at which time comfort—rather than acquiescence or punishment—is helpful (Green et al., 2011).

Social Awareness

Temper can be seen as an expression of selfhood. So can other common toddler emotions: pride, shame, jealousy, embarrassment, disgust, and guilt. These emotions require social awareness.

Such awareness typically emerges from family interactions. For instance, in a study of infant jealousy, when mothers deliberately paid attention to another infant, babies moved closer to their mothers, bidding for attention. Their brain activity also registered social emotions (Mize et al., 2014).

Culture is crucial here, with independence considered a value in some families but not in others. Many North American parents encourage toddler pride (saying, "You did it yourself"—even when that is untrue), but Asian families typically cultivate modesty and shame. Such differences may still be apparent in adult personality and judgment.

Disgust is also strongly influenced by other people as well as by maturation. According to a study that involved children of various ages, many 18-month-olds (but not younger infants) expressed disgust at touching a dead animal. None, however, were yet disgusted when a teenager cursed at an elderly person—something that parents and older children often find disgusting (Stevenson et al., 2010).

Positive emotions also show social awareness in toddlerhood. For instance, toddlers spontaneously try to help a stranger who dropped something or who is searching for a hidden object. This empathy and generosity emerges quite apart from any selfish motives (Warneken, 2015).

© SUZANNE PLUNKETT/Reuters/Corbis

Developmentally Correct Both Santa's smile and Olivia's grimace are appropriate reactions for people of their age. Adults playing Santa must smile no matter what, and if Olivia smiled, that would be troubling to anyone who knows about 7-month-olds. Yet every Christmas, thousands of parents wait in line to put their infants on the laps of oddly dressed, bearded strangers.

Especially for Nurses and Pediatricians Parents come to you concerned that their 1-year-old hides her face and holds onto them tightly whenever a stranger appears. What do you tell them? (see response, page 178)

THINK CRITICALLY: Which is more annoying, people who brag or people who put themselves down?

self-awareness A person's realization that he or she is a distinct individual whose body, mind, and actions are separate from those of other people.

⬤⬤ **Response for Nurses and Pediatricians** (from page 177): Stranger wariness is normal up to about 14 months. This baby's behavior actually might indicate secure attachment!

My Finger, My Body, and Me Mirror self-recognition is particularly important in her case, as this 2-year-old has a twin sister. Parents may enjoy dressing twins alike and giving them rhyming names, but each baby needs to know they are an individual, not just a twin.

© 2016 Macmillan

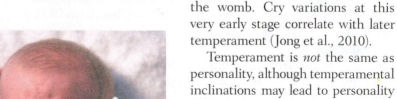

LaunchPad
macmillan learning

Video Activity: Self-Awareness and the Rouge Test shows the famous assessment of how and when self-awareness appears in infancy.

temperament Inborn differences between one person and another in emotions, activity, and self-regulation. It is measured by the person's typical responses to the environment.

No Tears Needed In the first weeks of life, babies produce no tears. However, sadness is obvious—unlike adults who smile when tears betray them. Given what is known about the infant brain, we hope photography did not postpone baby-comforting.

© Peter Casolino/Alamy

Self-Awareness

In addition to social awareness, another foundation for emotional growth is **self-awareness,** the realization that one's body, mind, and activities are distinct from those of other people (Kopp, 2011). Closely following the new mobility that results from walking is an emerging sense of "me" and "mine" that leads the infant to develop a new consciousness of others at about age 1.

In a classic experiment (Lewis & Brooks, 1978), 9- to 24-month-olds looked into a mirror after a dot of rouge had been surreptitiously put on their noses. If they reacted by touching the red dot on their noses, that meant they knew the mirror showed their own faces. None of the babies younger than 12 months did that, although they sometimes smiled and touched the dot on the "other" baby in the mirror.

Between 15 and 24 months, babies become self-aware, touching their own red noses with curiosity and puzzlement. Self-recognition in the mirror/rouge test (and in photographs) usually emerges with two other advances: pretending and using first-person pronouns (*I, me, mine, myself, my*) (Lewis, 2010). Thus, "an explicit and hence reflective conception of the self is apparent at the early stage of language acquisition at around the same age that infants begin to recognize themselves in mirrors" (Rochat, 2013, p. 388).

This is another example of the interplay of all the infant abilities—walking, talking, and emotional self-understanding all work together to make the 18-month-old quite unlike the 8-month-old.

Temperament

Temperament is defined as the "biologically based core of individual differences in style of approach and response to the environment that is stable across time and situations" (van den Akker et al., 2010, p. 485). "Biologically based" means that these traits originate with nature, not nurture. Confirmation that temperament arises from the inborn brain comes from an analysis of the tone, duration, and intensity of infant cries after the first inoculation, before much experience outside the womb. Cry variations at this very early stage correlate with later temperament (Jong et al., 2010).

Temperament is *not* the same as personality, although temperamental inclinations may lead to personality differences. Generally, personality traits (e.g., honesty and humility) are learned, whereas temperamental traits (e.g., shyness and aggression) are genetic. Of course, for every trait, nature and nurture interact as the following makes clear.

Expressing Emotions

Brain maturation is crucial for emotional development, particularly for emotions that are in response to other people. Experience connects the amygdala and the prefrontal cortex (van Goozen, 2015), and it helps infants connect their feelings with those of other people (Missana et al., 2014).

Maturation of the cortex is crucial for the social smile and laughter in the first months of life (Konner, 2010). Jealously may arise before 6 months, when the brain expects maternal attention and the infant sees mother paying heed to another baby (Legerstee, 2013). Similar expectations and reactions occur for fear, self-awareness, and anger. Infant experience may form an adult who cries, laughs, or angers quickly.

An example of the connection between brain development and caregiving came from a study of "highly reactive" infants (i.e., those whose brains naturally reacted with intense fear, anger, and other emotions). Highly reactive 15-month-olds with responsive caregivers (not hostile or neglectful) became less fearful, less angry, and so on. By age 4, they were able to regulate their emotions, presumably because they had developed neurological links between brain excitement and emotional response. However, highly reactive toddlers whose caregivers were less responsive were often overwhelmed by later emotions (Ursache et al., 2013).

Differential susceptibility is apparent here: Innate reactions and caregiver actions together sculpt the brain. Both are affected by ethnicity and culture, with some parents fearful of spoiling and others sympathetic to every sign of distress.

The social smile, for instance, is tentative for almost every face at 2 months, but it soon becomes a quicker and fuller smile at the sight of a familiar, loving caregiver. This occurs because, with repeated experience, the neurons that fire together become more closely and quickly connected to each other (via dendrites).

Every experience activates and prunes neurons. Remember this with baby mice in Chapter 5: Some were licked and nuzzled by their mothers almost constantly, and some were neglected. A mother mouse's licking of her newborn babies allowed more serotonin (a neurotransmitter) to be released by the hypothalamus. That not only increased momentary pleasure (mice love being licked) but also started a chain of epigenetic responses to reduce cortisol from many parts of the brain and body, including the adrenal glands. The effects on both brain and behavior are lifelong.

For optimal development of the brain, parents need to be comforting (as with the nuzzled baby mice) but not overprotective. Fearful mothers tend to raise fearful children, but fathers who offer their infants exciting but not dangerous challenges (such as a game of chase, crawling on the floor) reduce later anxiety (Majdandžić et al., 2013).

By contrast, excessive fear and stress harms the hypothalamus, which grows more slowly if an infant is often frightened.

Brain scans of children who were maltreated in infancy show abnormal responses to stress, anger, and other emotions later on, including to photographs. Some children seem resilient, but many areas of the brain (the hypothalamus, the amygdala, the HPA axis, the hippocampus, and the prefrontal cortex) are affected by abuse that begins in infancy (Bernard et al., 2014; Cicchetti, 2013a).

Thus, all of the infant emotions begin in the brain and are affected by early experiences. Links between the amygdala—the center for fear and other emotions—and the prefrontal cortex are particularly plastic during infancy, which means that experience has a decided impact (Callaghan & Tottenham, 2016).

Although infant brains are particularly moldable, adult brains are also affected by experience. Consequently, caregiver–infant relationships occur in adult brains, not just in actions. Infant crying increases caregivers' cortisol: Some respond with rage, others with tenderness. That brain reaction in the adult affects the baby's brain. Both suffer from their early experiences.

Joseph Farris/CartoonStock

Empathy Wins Crying babies whose caregivers sympathize often become confident, accomplished, and caring children. Sleep deprivation makes anyone unhappy, but this man's response is much better for both of them than anger or neglect.

LaunchPad
macmillan learning

Video: Temperament in Infancy and Toddlerhood

http://qrs.ly/j44ep09

Especially for Nurses Parents come to you with their fussy 3-month-old. They say they have read that temperament is "fixed" before birth, and they are worried that their child will always be difficult. What do you tell them? (see response, page 182)

Denis Doyle/Getty Images

Feliz Navidad Not only is every language and culture distinct, but also each individual has their own temperament. Here children watch the Cortylandia Christmas show in Madrid, Spain, where the Christmas holiday begins on the 24th of December and lasts through January 6th, Three Kings Day. As you see from the three fathers and children, each person has their own reaction to the same event.

Observation Quiz What indicates that each father has his own child on his shoulders? (see answer, page 182) ↑

Temperament Over the Years

In laboratory studies of temperament, infants are exposed to events that are frightening or attractive. Four-month-olds might see spinning mobiles or hear unusual sounds. Older babies might confront a noisy, moving robot or a clown who approaches quickly. During such experiences, some children laugh, some cry, others are quiet, and still others exhibit some combination of these reactions that might be signs of one of four types of babies: easy (40 percent), difficult (10 percent), slow-to-warm-up (15 percent), and hard-to-classify (35 percent).

These four categories originate from the *New York Longitudinal Study* (NYLS). Begun in the 1960s, the NYLS was the first large study to recognize that each newborn has distinct inborn traits (Thomas & Chess, 1977). According to the NYLS, by 3 months infants manifest nine traits that cluster into the four categories just listed.

Although the NYLS began a rich research endeavor, its nine dimensions have not held up in later studies. Generally, only three (not nine) dimensions of temperament are found (Hirvonen et al., 2013; van den Akker et al., 2010; Degnan et al., 2011), each of which affects later personality and school performance. The following three dimensions of temperament are apparent:

> Effortful control (able to regulate attention and emotion, to self-soothe)
> Negative mood (fearful, angry, unhappy)
> Exuberant (active, social, not shy)

Each of these dimensions is associated with distinctive brain patterns as well as behavior. The last of these (exuberance versus shyness) is most strongly traced to genes (Wolfe et al., 2014).

Since these temperamental traits are apparent at birth, some developmentalists seek to discover which alleles affect specific emotions (Johnson & Fearon, 2011). For example, researchers have found that the 7-repeat allele of the DRD4 VNTR gene, when combined with the 5-HTTLPR genotype, results in 6-month-olds who are difficult—they cry often, are hard to distract, and are slow to laugh (Holmboe et al., 2011). Infants with a particular allele of the MOA gene are quick to anger. You need not remember the letters of these alleles, but remember that infant emotions vary, partly for genetic reasons.

Another longitudinal study analyzed temperament in children as they grew, at 4, 9, 14, 24, and 48 months and in middle childhood, adolescence, and adulthood. The scientists designed laboratory experiments with specifics appropriate for the age of the children, collected detailed reports from the mothers and later from the participants themselves, and gathered observational data and physiological evidence, including brain scans.

Past data on each person were reevaluated each time, and cross-sectional and international studies were considered (Fox et al., 2001, 2005, 2013; Hane et al., 2008; Williams et al., 2010; Jarcho et al., 2013).

Half of the participants did not change much over time, reacting the same way and having similar brain-wave patterns when confronted with frightening experiences. Curiously, the participants most likely to change from infancy to age 4 were the inhibited, fearful ones. Least likely to change were the exuberant babies (see Figure 7.1). Apparently, adults coax frightened infants to be brave but let exuberant children stay happy.

The researchers found unexpected gender differences. As teenagers, the formerly inhibited boys were more likely than the average adolescent to use drugs, but the inhibited girls were less likely to do so (L. R. Williams et al., 2010). The most likely explanation is cultural: Shy boys seek to become less anxious by using drugs, but shy girls may be more accepted as they are, or more likely to obey their parents.

Examination of these children in adulthood found, again, intriguing differences between brain and behavior. Those who were inhibited in childhood still showed, in brain scans, evidence of their infant temperament. That confirms that genes affected their traits.

However, learning (specifically cognitive control) was evident: Their behavior was similar to those with a more outgoing temperament, unless other factors caused serious emotional problems. Apparently, most of them had learned to override their initial temperamental reactions—not to erase their innate impulses, but to keep them from impairing adult action (Jarcho et al., 2013).

Continuity and change were also found in another study, which found that angry infants were likely to make their mothers hostile toward them, and, if that happened, such infants became antisocial children. However, if the mothers were loving and patient despite the difficult temperament of the children, hostile traits were not evident later on (Pickles et al., 2013).

Other studies confirm that difficult infants often become easier—*if* their parents provide excellent, patient care (Belsky & Pluess, 2009). How could this be? Some scientists suggest that because fussy and scared children often come to the parents for comfort or reassurance, they are particularly likely to flourish with responsive parenting, but they wither if their parents are rejecting (Stupica et al., 2011). This is differential susceptibility again. If the home is chaotic and the parenting erratic, inborn temperament traits are evident; but if the family is responsive, temperament is less heritable (Saudino & Micalizzi, 2015).

All the research finds that traces of childhood temperament endure, blossoming into adult personality, but it also confirms that innate tendencies are only part of the story. Context always shapes behavior.

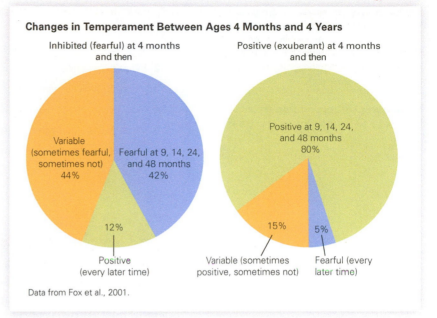

Changes in Temperament Between Ages 4 Months and 4 Years

Inhibited (fearful) at 4 months and then

- Fearful at 9, 14, 24, and 48 months 42%
- Variable (sometimes fearful, sometimes not) 44%
- Positive (every later time) 12%

Positive (exuberant) at 4 months and then

- Positive at 9, 14, 24, and 48 months 80%
- Variable (sometimes positive, sometimes not) 15%
- Fearful (every later time) 5%

Data from Fox et al., 2001.

FIGURE 7.1

Do Babies' Temperaments Change? Sometimes it is possible—especially if they were fearful babies. Adults who are reassuring help children overcome fearfulness. If fearful children do not change, it is not known whether that's because their parents are not sufficiently reassuring (nurture) or because the babies themselves are temperamentally more fearful (nature).

Getty Images/iStockphoto/Getty Images

Faith, Not Fear It is natural for infants to be frightened when swung upside down, but it is also common for fathers to teach their offspring the joy of safe adventures. This boy is unlikely to be a shy, timid toddler, thanks to his active, loving father.

Response for Nurses (from page 180): It's too soon to tell. Temperament is not truly "fixed" but variable, especially in the first few months. Many "difficult" infants become happy, successful adolescents and adults, if their parents are responsive.

Answer to Observation Quiz (from page 180): Watch the facial expressions.

WHAT HAVE YOU LEARNED?

1. What are the first emotions to appear in infants?
2. What experiences trigger anger and sadness in infants?
3. What do typical 1-year-olds fear?
4. How do emotions differ between the first and second year of life?
5. What is the significance of the toddler's reaction to seeing him- or herself in a mirror?
6. Do traits of temperament endure or change as development continues?
7. How does context affect temperament?

The Development of Social Bonds

Humans are, by nature, social creatures, and thus nurture (other people) is crucial. The specifics during infancy depend on the age of the baby, with three kinds of social interactions—synchrony, attachment, and social referencing—each evident in the first two years of life (see Visualizing Development, p. 188).

Synchrony

synchrony A coordinated, rapid, and smooth exchange of responses between a caregiver and an infant.

Early parent–child interactions are described as **synchrony,** a mutual exchange that requires split-second timing. Metaphors for synchrony are often musical—a waltz, a jazz duet—to emphasize that each partner must be attuned to the other, with moment-by-moment responses. Synchrony becomes more frequent and elaborate as the infant matures (Feldman, 2007).

Both Partners Active

Detailed research reveals the symbiosis of adult–infant partnerships. Adults rarely smile at young infants until the infants smile at them, several weeks after birth. That tentative baby smile is like a switch that turns on the adult, who usually grins broadly and talks animatedly (Lavelli & Fogel, 2005).

Open Wide Synchrony is evident worldwide. Everywhere babies watch their parents carefully, hoping for exactly what these two parents—each from quite different cultures—express, and responding with such delight that adults relish these moments.

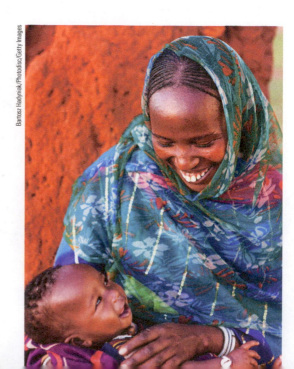

Direct observation reveals synchrony; anyone can see it when watching a caregiver play with an infant who is too young to talk. It is also evident in computer measurement of the millisecond timing of smiles, arched eyebrows, and so on (Messinger et al., 2010). Synchrony is a powerful learning experience for the new human. In every interaction, infants read others' emotions and develop social skills, such as taking turns and watching expressions.

Synchrony usually begins with adults imitating infants (not vice versa), with tone and rhythm (Van Puyvelde et al., 2010). Adults respond to barely perceptible infant facial expressions and body motions. This helps infants connect their internal state with behaviors that are understood within their family and culture.

This relationship is crucial when the infant is at medical risk. The necessity of time-consuming physical care might overwhelm concern about psychosocial needs, yet those needs are as important for long-term health as are the biological ones (Newnham et al., 2009). Responsiveness to the individual, not simply to the impaired human, leads to a strong, mutual love between parents and child (Solomon, 2012).

Hold Me Tight Synchrony is evident not only in facial expressions and noises but also in body positions. Note the mother's strong hands and extended arms, and her daughter's tucked in legs and arms. This is a caregiving dance that both have executed many times.

Neglected Synchrony

Experiments involving the **still-face technique** suggest that synchrony is experience-expectant (needed for normal growth) (Tronick, 1989; Tronick & Weinberg, 1997). [**Life-Span Link:** Experience-expectant and experience-dependent brain function are described in Chapter 5.]

In still-face studies, an infant faces an adult who responds while two video cameras simultaneously record their interpersonal reactions. Frame-by-frame analysis reveals that parents instinctively synchronize their responses to the infants' movements, with exaggerated tone and expression. Babies reciprocate with smiles and flailing limbs.

To be specific, long before they can reach out and grab, infants respond excitedly to caregiver attention by waving their arms. They are delighted if the adult moves closer so that a waving arm can touch the face or, even better, a hand can grab hair. This is the eagerness to "make interesting events last" that was described in Chapter 6. For their part, adults open their eyes wide, raise their eyebrows, smack their lips, and emit nonsense sounds. Hair-grabbing might make adults bob their head back and forth, in a playful attempt to shake off the grab, to the infants' joy, as Isaac did to Bethany in the chapter opening.

In still-face experiments, the adult stops all expression on cue, staring quietly with a "still face" for a minute or two. Sometimes by 2 months, and clearly by 6 months, infants are upset when their parents are unresponsive. Babies frown, fuss, drool, look away, kick, cry, or suck their fingers. By 5 months, they also vocalize, as if to say, "React to me" (Goldstein et al., 2009).

Many studies reach the same conclusion: Synchrony is experience-expectant, not simply experience-dependent. Responsiveness aids psychosocial and biological development, evident in heart rate, weight gain, and brain maturation. Particularly in the first year, mothers who are depressed and anxious are less likely to synchronize their responses, and then babies become less able to respond to social cues (Atzil et al., 2014).

For example, one study looked in detail at 4-month-old infants during and immediately after the still-face episode (Montirosso et al., 2015). The researchers found three clusters, which they called "socially engaged" (33 percent), "disengaged" (60 percent), and "negatively engaged" (7 percent).

When the mothers were still-faced, the socially engaged babies remained active, looking around at other things. When the still face was over, they quickly

still-face technique An experimental practice in which an adult keeps his or her face unmoving and expressionless in face-to-face interaction with an infant.

THINK CRITICALLY: What will happen if no one plays with an infant?

reengaged. The disengaged group became passive, taking longer to return to normal. The negatively engaged were angry and crying, even after the still face ended.

The mothers of each type differed, with the engaged mothers matching the infants' actions (bobbing heads, opening mouth, and so on) and the negative mothers almost never matching and sometimes expressing anger that their baby cried (Montirosso et al., 2015). A lack of synchrony is a troubling sign.

Attachment

Responsive and mutual relationships are important throughout childhood and beyond. However, once infants can walk, the moment-by-moment, face-to-face synchrony is less common.

Instead, **attachment** becomes evident. Actually, attachment is also lifelong, beginning before birth and influencing relationships throughout life (see At About This Time), but thousands of researchers on every continent have focused on

attachment According to Ainsworth, "an affectional tie" that an infant forms with a caregiver—a tie that binds them together in space and endures over time.

AT ABOUT THIS TIME

Stages of Attachment

Birth to 6 weeks	*Preattachment.* Newborns signal, via crying and body movements, that they need others. When people respond positively, the newborn is comforted and learns to seek more interaction. Newborns are also primed by brain patterns to recognize familiar voices and faces.
6 weeks to 8 months	*Attachment in the making.* Infants respond preferentially to familiar people by smiling, laughing, babbling. Their caregivers' voices, touch, expressions, and gestures are comforting, often overriding the infant's impulse to cry. Trust (Erikson) develops.
8 months to 2 years	*Classic secure attachment.* Infants greet the primary caregiver, play happily when he or she is present, show separation anxiety when the caregiver leaves. Both infant and caregiver seek to be close to each other (proximity) and frequently look at each other (contact). In many caregiver–infant pairs, physical touch (patting, holding, caressing) is frequent.
2 to 6 years	*Attachment as launching pad.* Young children seek their caregiver's praise and reassurance as their social world expands. Interactive conversations and games (hide-and-seek, object play, reading, pretending) are common. Children expect caregivers to comfort and entertain.
6 to 12 years	*Mutual attachment.* Children seek to make their caregivers proud by learning whatever adults want them to learn, and adults reciprocate. In concrete operational thought (Piaget), specific accomplishments are valued by adults and children.
12 to 18 years	*New attachment figures.* Teenagers explore and make friendships independent from parents, using their working models of earlier attachments as a base. With formal operational thinking (Piaget), shared ideals and goals become influential.
18 years on	*Attachment revisited.* Adults develop relationships with others, especially relationships with romantic partners and their own children, influenced by earlier attachment patterns. Past insecure attachments from childhood can be repaired rather than repeated, although this does not always happen.

Source: Adapted from Grobman, 2008.

infant attachment. They were inspired by the theories of John Bowlby (1983) and the research of Mary Ainsworth, who described mother–infant relationships in central Africa 60 years ago (Ainsworth, 1967). Attachment studies have led to an application called *attachment parenting,* which prioritizes the mother–infant relationship far more than Ainsworth or Bowlby did.

Mother–infant attachment has been studied in virtually every nation and researched extensively on atypical populations (e.g., infants with Down syndrome, autism spectrum disorder, and so on) as well as typical ones. Attachment has been measured during early and late childhood, adolescence, and adulthood (e.g., Simpson & Rholes, 2015; Grossmann et al., 2014; Tan et al., 2016; Hunter & Maunder, 2016).

Signs of Attachment

Infants show their attachment through *proximity-seeking* (such as approaching and following their caregivers) and through *contact-maintaining* (such as touching, snuggling, and holding). Those attachment expressions are evident when a baby cries if the caregiver closes the door when going to the bathroom, or fusses if a back-facing car seat prevents the baby from seeing the parent.

To maintain contact when driving in a car and to reassure the baby, some caregivers in the front seat reach back to give a hand, or they install a mirror angled so that driver and baby can see each other. Some caregivers take the baby into the bathroom: One mother complained that she hadn't been alone in the bathroom for two years (Senior, 2014). Contact need not be physical: Visual or verbal connections are often sufficient.

Attachment is mutual. Caregivers often keep a watchful eye on their baby, initiating contact with expressions, gestures, and sounds. Before going to sleep at midnight they might tiptoe to the crib to gaze at their sleeping infant, or, in daytime, absentmindedly smooth their toddler's hair.

Attachment is universal, part of the inborn social nature of the human species, with specific manifestations dependent on the culture and age. For instance, Ugandan mothers never kiss their infants, but they often massage them, contrary to Westerners. Adults may phone their mothers every day—even when the mothers are a thousand miles away. Or attached adults may sit in the same room of a large house, each reading quietly.

In some cultures, adults hold hands, hug, touch each others' faces, shoulders, buttocks. Some scholars believe that attachment to infants, from fathers, grandparents, and nonrelatives as well as mothers, is the reason that *Homo sapiens* thrived when other species became extinct (Hrdy, 2009).

Secure and Insecure Attachment

Attachment is classified into four types: A, B, C, and D (see Table 7.1). Infants with **secure attachment** (type B) feel comfortable and confident. The caregiver is a *base for exploration,* providing assurance and enabling discovery. A toddler might, for example, scramble down from the caregiver's lap to play with an intriguing toy but periodically look back and vocalize (contact-maintaining) or bring the toy to the caregiver for inspection (proximity-seeking).

Their mother's presence gives them courage to explore; her departure causes distress; her return elicits positive social contact (such as smiling or hugging) and then more playing. This balanced reaction—being concerned but not overwhelmed by comings and goings—indicates security. Early research was only on mothers. Later, fathers and other caregivers were included since they also could have secure or insecure attachments to an infant.

Video Activity: Mother Love and the Work of Harry Harlow features classic footage of Harlow's research, showing the setup and results of his famous experiment.

secure attachment A relationship in which an infant obtains both comfort and confidence from the presence of his or her caregiver.

Stay In Touch In early infancy, physical contact is often part of secure attachment. No wonder many happy babies travel next to their caregivers in slings, wraps, and snugglies. Note that attachment is mutual—she holds on to the thumb that her father provides.

TABLE 7.1	Patterns of Infant Attachment				
Type	Name of Pattern	In Playroom	Mother Leaves	Mother Returns	Toddlers in Category (%)
A	Insecure-avoidant	Child plays happily.	Child continues playing.	Child ignores her.	10–20
B	Secure	Child plays happily.	Child pauses, is not as happy.	Child welcomes her, returns to play.	50–70
C	Insecure-resistant/ ambivalent	Child clings, is preoccupied with mother.	Child is unhappy, may stop playing.	Child is angry; may cry, hit mother, cling.	10–20
D	Disorganized	Child is cautious.	Child may stare or yell; looks scared, confused.	Child acts oddly—may scream, hit self, throw things.	5–10

insecure-avoidant attachment A pattern of attachment in which an infant avoids connection with the caregiver, as when the infant seems not to care about the caregiver's presence, departure, or return.

insecure-resistant/ambivalent attachment A pattern of attachment in which an infant's anxiety and uncertainty are evident, as when the infant becomes very upset at separation from the caregiver and both resists and seeks contact on reunion.

disorganized attachment A type of attachment that is marked by an infant's inconsistent reactions to the caregiver's departure and return.

Strange Situation A laboratory procedure for measuring attachment by evoking infants' reactions to the stress of various adults' comings and goings in an unfamiliar playroom.

By contrast, insecure attachment (types A and C) is characterized by fear, anxiety, anger, or indifference. Some insecure children play independently without maintaining contact; this is **insecure-avoidant attachment** (type A). The opposite reaction is **insecure-resistant/ambivalent attachment** (type C). Children with this type of attachment cling to their caregivers and are angry at being left.

Ainsworth's original schema differentiated only types A, B, and C. Later researchers discovered a fourth category (type D), **disorganized attachment.** Type D infants may shift suddenly from hitting to kissing their mothers, from staring blankly to crying hysterically, from pinching themselves to freezing in place.

Among the general population, almost two-thirds of infants are secure (type B). About one-third of infants are insecure, either indifferent (type A) or unduly anxious (type C). About 5 to 10 percent of infants fit into none of these categories; they are disorganized (type D), with no consistent strategy for social interaction, even avoidance or resistance. Sometimes they become hostile and aggressive, difficult for anyone to relate to (Lyons-Ruth et al., 1999).

Unlike the first three types, disorganized infants have elevated levels of cortisol in reaction to stress (Bernard & Dozier, 2010). A meta-analysis of 42 studies of more than 4,000 infants found that insecure attachment and especially disorganized attachment predict emotional problems, both externalizing (such as aggression) and internalizing (such as depression) (Groh et al., 2012).

Measuring Attachment

Ainsworth (1973) developed a now-classic laboratory procedure called the **Strange Situation** to measure attachment. In a well-equipped playroom, an infant is observed for eight episodes, each lasting no more than three minutes. First, the child and mother are together. Next, according to a set sequence, the mother and then a stranger come and go. Infants' responses to their mother indicate which type of attachment they have formed.

Researchers are trained to distinguish types A, B, C, and D. They focus on the following:

Exploration of the toys. A secure toddler plays happily.
Reaction to the caregiver's departure. A secure toddler notices when the caregiver leaves and shows some sign of missing him or her.
Reaction to the caregiver's return. A secure toddler welcomes the caregiver's reappearance, usually seeking contact, and then plays again.

© 2016 Macmillan

Excited, Troubled, Comforted This sequence is repeated daily for 1-year-olds, which is why the same sequence is replicated to measure attachment. As you see, toys are no substitute for mother's comfort if the infant or toddler is secure, as this one seems to be. Some, however, cry inconsolably or throw toys angrily when left alone.

Research measuring attachment has revealed that some behaviors that might seem normal are, in fact, a sign of insecurity. For instance, an infant who clings to the caregiver and refuses to explore the toys might be type C. Likewise, adults who say their childhood was happy and their mother was a saint, especially if they provide few specific memories, might be insecure. And young children who are immediately friendly to strangers may never have formed a secure attachment (Tarullo et al., 2011).

Insecure Attachment and the Social Setting

At first, developmentalists expected secure attachment to "predict all the outcomes reasonably expected from a well-functioning personality" (Thompson & Raikes, 2003, p. 708). But this expectation turned out to be naive.

Securely attached infants *are* more likely to become secure toddlers, socially competent preschoolers, high-achieving schoolchildren, and capable parents. Attachment affects early brain development, one reason these outcomes occur (Diamond & Fagundes, 2010). But insecure attachment does not always lead to later problems (Keller, 2014).

Attachment forms in infancy (see Table 7.2), but it may change when the family context changes, such as a new caregiver who is unusually responsive or abusive. The underlying premise—that responsive early parenting leads to secure attachment, which buffers stress and encourages exploration—seems valid. However, attachment behaviors in the Strange Situation provide only one indication of the quality of the parent–child relationship.

Insights from Romania

No scholar doubts that close human relationships should develop in the first year of life and that the lack of such

THINK CRITICALLY: Is the Strange Situation a valid way to measure attachment in every culture, or is it biased toward the Western idea of the ideal mother–child relationship?

TABLE 7.2	Predictors of Attachment Type

Secure attachment (type B) is more likely if:

- The parent is usually sensitive and responsive to the infant's needs.
- The infant–parent relationship is high in synchrony.
- The infant's temperament is "easy."
- The parents are not stressed about income, other children, or their marriage.
- The parents have a working model of secure attachment to their own parents.

Insecure attachment is more likely if:

- The parent mistreats the child. (Neglect increases type A; abuse increases types C and D.)
- The mother is mentally ill. (Paranoia increases type D; depression increases type C.)
- The parents are highly stressed about income, other children, or their marriage. (Parental stress increases types A and D.)
- The parents are intrusive and controlling. (Parental domination increases type A.)
- The parents are active alcoholics. (Alcoholic father increases type A; alcoholic mother increases type D.)
- The child's temperament is "difficult." (Difficult children tend to be type C.)
- The child's temperament is "slow to warm up." (This correlates with type A.)

Developing Attachment

Attachment begins at birth and continues lifelong. Much depends not only on the ways in which parents and babies bond, but also on the quality and consistency of caregiving, the safety and security of the home environment, and individual and family experience. While the patterns set in infancy may echo in later life, they are not determinative.

HOW MANY CHILDREN ARE SECURELY ATTACHED?

The specific percentages of children who are secure and insecure vary by culture, parent responsiveness, context, and specific temperament and needs of both the child and the caregiver. Generally, about a third of all 1-year-olds seem insecure.

50–70%	10–20%	10–20%	5–10%
Securely Attached (Type B)	Avoidant Attachment (Type A)	Ambivalent Attachment (Type C)	Disorganized Attachment (Type D)

ATTACHMENT IN THE STRANGE SITUATION MAY INFLUENCE RELATIONSHIPS THROUGH THE LIFE SPAN

Attachment patterns formed early affect people lifelong, but later experiences of love and rejection may change early patterns. Researchers measure attachment by examining children's behaviors in the Strange Situation where they are separated from their parent and play in a room with an unfamiliar caregiver. These early patterns can influence later adult relationships. As life goes on, people become more or less secure, avoidant, or disorganized.

Securely Attached [Type B]

In the Strange Situation, children are able to separate from caregiver but prefer caregiver to strangers.

Later in life, they tend to have supportive relationships and positive self-concept.

Avoidant [Type A]

In the Strange Situation, children avoid caregiver.

Later in life, they tend to be aloof in personal relationships, loners who are lonely.

Resistant/Ambivalent [Type C]

In the Strange Situation, children appear upset and worried when separated from caregiver; they may hit or cling.

Later in life, their relationships may be angry, stormy, unpredictable. They have few long-term friendships.

Disorganized [Type D]

In the Strange Situation, children appear angry, confused, erratic, or fearful.

Later in life, they can demonstrate odd behavior—including sudden emotions. They are at risk for serious psychological disorders.

THE CONTINUUM OF ATTACHMENT

Avoidance and anxiety occur along a continuum. Neither genes nor cultural variations were understood when the Strange Situation was first developed (in 1965). Some contemporary researchers believe the link between childhood attachment and adult personality is less straightforward than this table suggests.

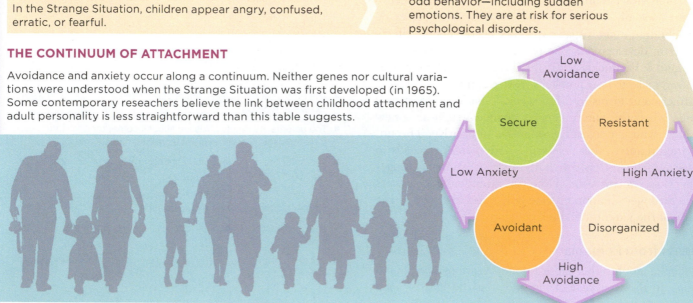

Low Avoidance

Low Anxiety — High Anxiety

High Avoidance

Secure | Resistant | Avoidant | Disorganized

relationships risks dire consequences. Unfortunately, thousands of children born in Romania are proof.

When Romanian dictator Nicolae Ceauşescu forbade birth control and abortions in the 1980s, illegal abortions became the leading cause of death for Romanian women aged 15 to 45 (Verona, 2003), and 170,000 children were abandoned and sent to crowded, impersonal, state-run orphanages (Marshall, 2014). The children were severely deprived of social contact, experiencing virtually no synchrony, play, or conversation.

In the two years after Ceauşescu was ousted and killed in 1989, thousands of those children were adopted by North American, western European, and Australian families. Those who were adopted before 6 months of age fared best; the adoptive parents established synchrony via play and caregiving. Most of these children developed well. Many of those adopted between 6 and 18 months also fared well.

For those adopted later, early signs were encouraging: Skinny infants gained weight and grew faster than other children, developing motor skills they had lacked (H. Park et al., 2011). However, if social deprivation had lasted a year or more, their emotions and intellect suffered.

Many were overly friendly to strangers, a sign of insecure attachment as previously mentioned. At age 11, their average IQ was only 85, which is 15 points lower than the statistical norm. The older they had been at adoption, the worse their cognition was (Rutter et al., 2010). Some became impulsive, angry teenagers. Apparently, the stresses of adolescence and emerging adulthood exacerbated the cognitive and social strains of growing up (Merz & McCall, 2011).

These children are now adults, many with serious emotional or conduct problems. Other research on children adopted nationally and internationally finds that many develop quite well, but every stress—from rejection in infancy to early institutionalization to the circumstances of the adoption process—makes it more difficult for the infant to become a happy, well-functioning adult (Grotevant & McDermott, 2014).

Romanian infants are no longer available for international adoption, even though some are institutionalized. Research confirms that early emotional deprivation, not genes or nutrition, is their greatest problem. Romanian infants develop best in their own families, second best in foster families, and worst in institutions (Nelson et al., 2007). As best we know, this applies to infants everywhere: Families usually nurture their babies better than strangers who care for many infants at once, and the more years children spend in an impersonal institution, the more likely it is they will become socially and intellectually impaired (Julian, 2013).

Fortunately, many institutions have improved or been shuttered, although worldwide, an estimated 8 million children are in orphanages (Marshal, 2014). More-recent adoptees are not as impaired as those Romanian orphans (Grotevant & McDermott, 2014), and many families with adopted children are as strongly attached as any biological family, which the following demonstrates.

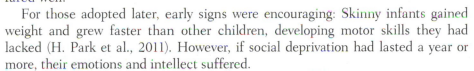

Danger Ongoing Look closely and you can see danger. That bent crib bar could strangle an infant, and that chipped paint could contain lead. (Lead tastes sweet; is that why two of the children are biting it?) Fortunately, these three Romanian infants (photographed in 1990) escaped those dangers to be raised in loving adoptive homes. Unfortunately, the damage of social isolation (note the sheet around the crib) could not be completely overcome: Some young adults who spent their first year in an institution like this still carry emotional scars.

Observation Quiz What three possible dangers do you see? (see answer, page 190) ↑

Can We Bear This Commitment?

Parents and children capture my attention, wherever they are. Today I saw one mother ignoring her stroller-bound toddler on a crowded subway (I wanted to tell her to talk to her child) and another mother breast-feed a happy 7-month-old in a public park (which was illegal three decades ago). I look for signs of secure or insecure attachment—the contact-maintaining and proximity-seeking moves that parents do, seemingly unaware that they are responding to primordial depths of human love.

I particularly observe families I know. I am struck by the powerful bond between parent and child, as strong (or stronger) in adoptive families as in genetic ones.

One adoptive couple is Macky and Nick. I see them echoing my own experiences. Two examples: When Alice was a few days old, I overheard Nick phone another parent, asking which detergent is best for washing baby clothes; when Macky was engrossed in conversation, Nick interrupted to insist that it was time to get the girls home for their nap.

My appreciation of their attachment was cemented by a third incident. In Macky's words:

I'll never forget the Fourth of July at the spacious home of my mother-in-law's best friend. It was a perfect celebration on a perfect day. Kids frolicked in the pool. Parents socialized nearby, on the sun-drenched lawn or inside the cool house. Many guests had published books on parenting; we imagined they admired our happy, thriving family.

My husband and I have two daughters, Alice who was then 7 and Penelope who was 4. They learned to swim early and are always the first to jump in the pool and the last to leave. Great children, and doesn't that mean great parents?

After hours of swimming, the four of us scrambled up to dry land. I went inside to the library to talk with my father, while most people enjoyed hot dogs, relish, mustard, and juicy watermelon.

Suddenly we heard a heart-chilling wail. Panicked, I raced to the pool's edge to see the motionless body of a small child who had gone unnoticed underwater for too long. His blue-face was still. Someone was giving CPR. His mother kept wailing, panicked, pleading, destroyed. I had a shameful thought—thank God that is not my child.

He lived. He regained his breath and was whisked away by ambulance. The party came to a quick close. We four, skin tingling from the summer sun, hearts beating from the near-death of a child who was my kids' playmate an hour before, drove away.

Turning to Nick, I asked, "Can we bear this commitment we have made? Can we raise our children in the face of all hazards—some we try to prevent, others beyond our control?"

That was five years ago. Our children are flourishing. Our confidence is strong and so are our emotions. But it takes only a moment to recognize just how entwined our well-being is with our children and how fragile life is. We are deeply grateful.

A Grateful Family This family photo shows, from left to right, Nick, Penelope, Macky, and Alice with their dog Cooper. When they adopted Alice as a newborn, the parents said, "This is a miracle we feared would never happen."

Answer to Observation Quiz
(from page 189) Social isolation (the sheet around the crib), lead poisoning (note that two babies are biting the painted bars), and injured limbs and even strangulation (note the bent crib slats, farther apart than U.S. law allows).

social referencing Seeking information about how to react to an unfamiliar or ambiguous object or event by observing someone else's expressions and reactions. That other person becomes a social reference.

Many nations now restrict international adoptions, in part because some children were literally snatched from their biological parents to be sent abroad. The number of international adoptees in the United States was 8,668 in 2012, down from 22,884 in 2004.

However, some infants in every nation are deprived of healthy interaction, sometimes within their own families. Ideally, no infant is institutionalized, but if that ideal is not reached, institutions need to change so that psychological health is as important as physical health (McCall, 2013).

Children need responsive caregivers, who could be their biological relatives or could be unrelated. When international adoptions become a pawn in international disputes, as in 2014 between the United States and Russia, children suffer.

Social Referencing

Social referencing refers to seeking emotional responses or information from other people, much as a student might consult a dictionary or other reference work.

Someone's reassuring glance, cautionary words, or a facial expression of alarm, pleasure, or dismay—those are social references.

Even at 8 months, infants notice where other people are looking and use that information to look in the same direction themselves (Tummeltshammer et al., 2014). After age 1, when infants can walk and are "little scientists," their need to consult others becomes urgent as well as more accurate.

Toddlers search for clues in gazes, faces, and body position, paying close attention to emotions and intentions. They focus on their familiar caregivers, but they also use relatives, other children, and even strangers to help them assess objects and events. They are remarkably selective, noticing that some strangers are reliable references and others are not (Fusaro & Harris, 2013).

Social referencing has many practical applications for the infant. Consider mealtime. Caregivers the world over smack their lips, pretend to taste, and say "yum-yum," encouraging toddlers to eat beets, liver, or spinach. Toddlers read expressions, insisting on the foods that the adults *really* like. If mother likes it, and presents it on the spoon, then they eat it—otherwise not (Shutts et al., 2013).

Through this process, some children develop a taste for raw fish or curried goat or smelly cheese—foods that children in other cultures refuse. Similarly, toddlers use social cues to understand the difference between real and pretend eating, as well as to learn which objects, emotions, and activities are forbidden.

Rotini Pasta? Look again. Every family teaches their children to relish delicacies that other people avoid. Examples are bacon (not in Arab nations), hamburgers (not in India), and, as shown here, a witchetty grub. This Australian aboriginal boy is about to swallow an insect larva.

Fathers as Social Partners

Synchrony, attachment, and social referencing are sometimes more apparent with fathers than with mothers. Indeed, fathers often elicit more smiles and laughter from their infants than mothers do. They tend to play more exciting games, swinging and chasing, while mothers do more caregiving and comforting (Fletcher et al., 2013).

Although these generalities hold, and although women do more child care than men in every nation, both parents often work together to raise their children (Shwalb et al., 2013). One researcher who studied many families reports "fathers and mothers showed patterns of striking similarity: they touched, looked, vocalized, rocked, and kissed their newborns equally" (Parke, 2013, p. 121). Differences were apparent from one couple to another, but not from one gender to another—except for smiling (women did it more). Another study, this one of U.S. parents having a second child,

Not Manly? Where did that idea come from? Fathers worldwide provide excellent care for their toddlers and enjoy it, evident in the United States *(left)* and India *(right)*, and in every other nation.

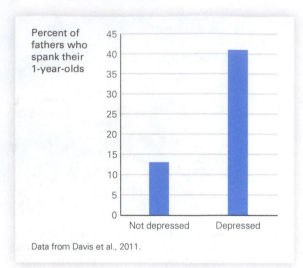

Data from Davis et al., 2011.

FIGURE 7.2

Shame on Who? Not on the toddlers, who are naturally curious and careless, but maybe not on the fathers either. Both depression and spanking are affected by financial stress, marital conflict, and cultural norms; who is responsible for those?

found that mothers used slightly more techniques to soothe their crying infants than fathers did (7.7 versus 5.9), but the study also found that mothers were less distressed by infant crying if their partners were active soothers (Dayton et al., 2015).

It is a stereotype that African American, Latin American, and Asian American fathers are less nurturing and stricter than other men (Parke, 2013). The opposite may be more accurate. Within the United States, contemporary fathers in all ethnic groups are, typically, more involved with their children than their own fathers were.

As with humans of all ages, social contexts are influential: Fathers are influenced by other fathers (Roopnarine & Hossain, 2013; Qin & Chang, 2013). Thus, fathers of every ethnic group may be aware of what other men are doing, and that affects their own behavior.

Stress decreases parent involvement for both sexes. Particularly if income is low, fathers sometimes choose to be uninvolved, a choice less open to mothers (Roopnarine & Hossain, 2013; Qin & Chang, 2013).

Close father–infant relationships teach infants (especially boys) appropriate expressions of emotion, particularly anger. The results may endure: Teenagers are less likely to lash out at friends and authorities if, as infants, they experienced a warm, responsive relationship with their father (Hoeve et al., 2011).

Usually, mothers are caregivers and fathers are playmates, but not always. Each couple, given their circumstances (perhaps immigrant or same-sex), finds some way to help their infant thrive (Lamb, 2010). Traditional mother–father roles may be switched, with no harm to the baby (Parke, 2013).

A constructive parental alliance can take many forms, but it cannot be taken for granted, no matter what the family configuration. Single-parent families, same-sex families, grandparent families, and nuclear families all function best when caregivers cooperate. No form is always constructive. [**Life-Span Link:** Family forms are discussed in Chapter 13.]

Family members affect each other. Paternal depression correlates with maternal depression and with sad, angry, disobedient toddlers (see Figure 7.2). Cause and consequence are intertwined. When anyone is depressed or hostile, everyone (mother, father, baby, sibling) needs help.

WHAT HAVE YOU LEARNED?

1. Why does synchrony affect early emotional development?
2. How is proximity-seeking and contact-maintaining attachment expressed by infants and caregivers?
3. What is the difference in behavior of infants in each of the four types of attachment?
4. How might each of the four types of attachment be expressed in adulthood?
5. What has been learned from the research on Romanian orphans?
6. How is social referencing important in toddlerhood?
7. What distinctive contributions do fathers make to infant development?

LaunchPad
macmillan learning

Video: Theories of Emotional Development in Infancy and Toddlerhood summarizes the theories of personality development described in this section.

Theories of Infant Psychosocial Development

The fact that infants are emotional, social creatures is recognized by everyone who studies babies. However, each of the theories discussed in Chapter 2 has a distinct perspective on this universal reality, as you will now see.

Psychoanalytic Theory

Psychoanalytic theory connects biosocial and psychosocial development. Sigmund Freud and Erik Erikson each described two distinct stages of early development, one in the first year and one beginning in the second year.

Freud: Oral and Anal Stages

According to Freud (1935/1989, 2001), the first year of life is the *oral stage,* so named because the mouth is the young infant's primary source of gratification. In the second year, with the *anal stage,* pleasure comes from the anus—particularly from the sensual satisfaction of bowel movements and, eventually, the psychological pleasure of controlling them.

Freud believed that the oral and anal stages are fraught with potential conflicts. If a mother frustrates her infant's urge to suck—weaning too early or too late, for example, or preventing the baby from sucking a thumb or a pacifier—that may later lead to an *oral fixation.* A person with an oral fixation is stuck (fixated) at the oral stage, and therefore, as an adult, he or she eats, drinks, chews, bites, or talks excessively, still seeking the mouth-related pleasures of infancy.

Similarly, if toilet training is overly strict or if it begins before the infant is mature enough, then the toddler's refusal—or inability—to comply will clash with the wishes of the adult, who denies the infant normal anal pleasures. That may lead to an *anal personality*—an adult who seeks self-control, with an unusually strong need for regularity and cleanliness in all aspects of life. [**Life-Span Link:** Theory of toilet training is discussed in Chapter 2.]

Erikson: Trust and Autonomy

According to Erikson, the first crisis of life is **trust versus mistrust,** when infants learn whether or not the world can be trusted to satisfy basic needs. Babies feel secure when food and comfort are provided with "consistency, continuity, and sameness of experience" (Erikson, 1993a, p. 247). If social interaction inspires trust, the child (later the adult) confidently explores the social world.

The second crisis is **autonomy versus shame and doubt,** beginning at about 18 months, when self-awareness emerges. Toddlers want autonomy (self-rule) over their own actions and bodies. Without it, they feel ashamed and doubtful. Like Freud, Erikson believed that problems in early infancy could last a lifetime, creating adults who are suspicious and pessimistic (mistrusting) or easily shamed (lacking autonomy).

Behaviorism

From the perspective of behaviorism, emotions and personality are molded as parents reinforce or punish a child. Behaviorists believe that parents who respond joyously to every glimmer of a grin will have children with a sunny disposition. The opposite is also true:

> Failure to bring up a happy child, a well-adjusted child—assuming bodily health—falls squarely upon the parents' shoulders. [By the time the child is 3] parents have already determined . . . [whether the child] is to grow into a happy person, wholesome and good-natured, whether he is to be a whining, complaining neurotic, an anger-driven, vindictive, over-bearing slave driver, or one whose every move in life is definitely controlled by fear.
>
> [Watson, 1928/1972, pp. 7, 45]

Later behaviorists recognized that infants' behavior also reflects social learning, as infants learn from other people. You already saw an example, social referencing.

● **Especially for Nursing Mothers** You have heard that if you wean your child too early he or she will overeat or develop alcohol use disorder. Is it true? (see response, page 195)

All Together Now Toddlers in an employees' day-care program at a flower farm in Colombia learn to use the potty on a schedule. Will this experience lead to later personality problems? Probably not.

trust versus mistrust Erikson's first crisis of psychosocial development. Infants learn basic trust if the world is a secure place where their basic needs (for food, comfort, attention, and so on) are met.

autonomy versus shame and doubt Erikson's second crisis of psychosocial development. Toddlers either succeed or fail in gaining a sense of self-rule over their actions and their bodies.

Only in America Toddlers in every nation of the world sometimes cry when emotions overwhelm them, but in the United States young children are encouraged to express emotions, and Halloween is a national custom, unlike in other nations. Candy, dress-up, ghosts, witches, and ringing doorbells after sunset—no wonder many young children are overwhelmed.

proximal parenting Caregiving practices that involve being physically close to the baby, with frequent holding and touching.

distal parenting Caregiving practices that involve remaining distant from the baby, providing toys, food, and face-to-face communication with minimal holding and touching.

working model In cognitive theory, a set of assumptions that the individual uses to organize perceptions and experiences. For example, a person might assume that other people are trustworthy and be surprised by an incident in which this working model of human behavior is erroneous.

Amusing or Neglectful? Depends on the culture. In proximal cultures this father would be criticized for not interacting with his daughter, and the mother would be blamed for letting him do so. But in distal cultures Dad might be admired for multitasking: simultaneously reading the paper, waiting for the bus, and taking the baby to day care.

🔵 **Especially for Pediatricians** A mother complains that her toddler refuses to stay in the car seat, spits out disliked foods, and almost never does what she says. How should you respond? (see response, page 196)

Social learning occurs throughout life (Morris et al., 2007; Rendell et al., 2011). Toddlers express emotions in various ways—from giggling to cursing—just as their parents or older siblings do.

For example, a boy might develop a hot temper if his father's outbursts seem to win his mother's respect; a girl might be coy, or passive-aggressive, if that is what she has seen at home. These examples are deliberately sexist: Gender roles, in particular, are learned, according to social learning. [**Life-Span Link:** Social learning theory is discussed in Chapter 2.]

Parents often unwittingly encourage certain traits in their children. Should babies have many toys, or will that make them too greedy? Should you pick up your crying baby or give her a pacifier? Should you breast-feed until age 2 or longer or switch to bottle-feeding before 6 months?

These questions highlight the distinction between **proximal parenting** (being physically close to a baby, often holding and touching) and **distal parenting** (keeping some distance—providing toys, encouraging self-feeding, talking face-to-face instead of communicating by touch). Caregivers tend to behave in proximal or distal ways very early, when infants are only 2 months old (Kärtner et al., 2010).

Variations in proximal and distal parenting lead to variations in toddler behavior. For instance, toddlers who, as infants, were often held, patted, and hushed (proximal) became toddlers who are more obedient to their parents but less likely to recognize themselves in a mirror (Keller et al., 2010; Keller et al., 2004).

The long-term impact of responses to the behavior of infants is evident when researchers compare child-rearing practices of the Nso people of Cameroon (very proximal) with those of the Greeks in Athens (very distal). In Greece, Cameroon, and many other places, how much adults value individual rather than collective action is related to how much distal or proximal child care they experienced (Borke et al., 2007; Kärtner et al., 2011).

Cognitive Theory

Cognitive theory holds that thoughts determine a person's perspective. Early experiences are important because beliefs, perceptions, and memories make them so, not because they are buried in the unconscious (psychoanalytic theory) or burned into the brain's patterns (behaviorism).

According to many cognitive theorists, early experiences help infants develop a **working model,** which is a set of assumptions that becomes a frame of reference for later life (S. Johnson et al., 2010). It is a "model" because early relationships form a prototype, or blueprint; it is "working" because it is a work in progress, not fixed or final.

Ideally, infants develop "a working model of the self as lovable and competent" because the parents are "emotionally available, loving, and supportive of their mastery efforts" (Harter, 2012, p. 12). However, reality does not always conform to this ideal. A 1-year-old girl might develop a model, based on her parents' inconsistent responses to her, that people are unpredictable. She will continue to apply that model to everyone: Her childhood friendships will be insecure, and her adult relationships will be guarded.

The crucial idea, according to cognitive theory, is that an infant's early experiences themselves are not necessarily pivotal, but the interpretation of those experiences is (Olson & Dweck, 2009). Children may misinterpret their experiences, or parents may offer inaccurate explanations, and these form ideas that affect later thinking and behavior.

In this way, working models formed in childhood echo lifelong. A hopeful message from cognitive theory is that people can rethink and reorganize their thoughts, developing new models. Our mistrustful girl might marry someone who is faithful and loving, so she may gradually develop a new working model. The form of psychotherapy that seems most successful at the moment is called cognitive-behavioral, in which new thoughts about how to behave are developed. In other words, a new working model is developed.

Evolutionary Theory

Remember that evolutionary theory stresses two needs: survival and reproduction. Human brains are extraordinarily adept at those tasks. However, not until after about two decades of maturation is the human brain fully functioning. A child must be nourished, protected, and taught much longer than offspring of any other species. Infant and parent emotions ensure this lengthy protection (Hrdy, 2009).

Emotions for Survival

Infant emotions are part of this evolutionary mandate. All of the reactions described in the first part of this chapter—from the hunger cry to the temper tantrum—can be seen from this perspective (Konner, 2010).

For example, newborns are extraordinarily dependent, unable to walk or talk or even sit up and feed themselves for months after birth. They must attract adult devotion—and they do. That first smile, the sound of infant laughter, and their role in synchrony are all powerfully attractive to adults—especially to parents.

Adults call their hairless, chinless, round-faced, big-stomached, small-limbed offspring "cute," "handsome," "beautiful," "adorable," yet all these characteristics are often considered ugly in adults. Parents willingly devote hours to carrying, feeding, changing, and cleaning their infants, who never say "thank you."

Adaptation is evident. Adults have the genetic potential to be caregivers, and grandparents have done it before, but, according to evolutionary psychology, whether or not that potential is expressed, turning busy adults into devoted caregivers and dependent infants into emotional engines, is ruled by basic survival needs of the species. If humans were motivated solely by money or power, no one would have children. Yet evolution has created adults who find parenting worth every sacrifice.

Same Situation, Far Apart: Safekeeping
Historically, grandmothers were sometimes crucial for child survival. Now, even though medical care has reduced child mortality, grandmothers still do their part to keep children safe, as shown by these two—in the eastern United States *(top)* and Vietnam *(bottom)*.

The Cost of Childrearing

The costs of parenting are substantial: Food, diapers, clothes, furniture, medical bills, toys, and child care (whether paid or unpaid) are just a start. Before a child becomes independent, many parents buy a bigger residence and pay for education—including such luxuries as violin lessons or basketball camp. The emotional costs are greater—worry, self-doubt, fear. A book about parenting is titled *All Joy and No Fun*, highlighting the paradox: People choose to sacrifice time, money, and fun because they find parenting deeply satisfying (Senior, 2014).

Evolutionary theory holds that the emotions of attachment—love, jealousy, even clinginess and anger—keep toddlers near caregivers who remain vigilant. Infants fuss at still faces, fear separation, and laugh when adults play with them—all to sustain caregiving. Emotions are our genetic legacy; we would die without them.

Evolutionary social scientists note that if mothers were the exclusive caregivers of each child until children were adults, a given woman could rear only one or two offspring—not enough for the species to survive. Instead, before the introduction of reliable birth control, the average interval between births for humans was two to four years. Humans birth children at relatively short intervals because of **allocare**—the care of children by people other than the biological parents (Hrdy, 2009).

Allocare is essential for *Homo sapiens'* survival. Compared with many other species (mother chimpanzees space births by four or five years and never let another

Response for Nursing Mothers
(from page 193): Freud thought so, but there is no experimental evidence that weaning, even when ill-timed, has such dire long-term effects.

allocare Literally, "other-care"; the care of children by people other than the biological parents.

● **Response for Pediatricians**
(from page 194): Consider the origins of the misbehavior—probably a combination of the child's inborn temperament and the mother's distal parenting. Acceptance and consistent responses (e.g., avoiding disliked foods but always using the car seat) is more warranted than anger. Perhaps this mother is expressing hostility toward the child—a sign that intervention may be needed. Find out.

chimp hold their babies), human mothers have evolved to let other people help with child care (Kachel et al., 2011). That may be true, and it may be universal for our species—but to understand the varieties of allocare, the next theory is needed.

Sociocultural Theory

Cultural variations are vast in every aspect of infant care. You have read many examples: breast-feeding, co-sleeping, and language development among them.

Each theory just described can be used to justify or criticize certain variations. For example, Westerners expect toddlers to go through the stubborn and defiant "terrible twos"; that is a sign of autonomy, as Erikson described it and as distal parenting encourages. By contrast, parents in some other places expect toddlers to be obedient.

The result is that North American parents are urged to be patient, to lock up valuables, and to have the number for Poison Control ready. Other cultures use shame, guilt, or severe physical punishment (which we consider abuse) to enforce compliance. A study of children in three nations found that the Japanese were highest in shame, the Koreans highest in guilt, and the U.S. children highest in pride (Furukawa et al., 2012).

Infant Day Care

The best way to illustrate the vast cultural differences in infant care is to look closely at one example, infant day care. People have opposite ideas about this topic, depending largely on their cultural background.

About 134 million babies will be born each year from 2010 to 2021 (United Nations, Department of Economic and Social Affairs, Population Division, 2015). Universally, most newborns are cared for primarily by their mothers, but sociocultural differences in allocare soon are evident. Fathers and grandmothers typically provide care from the first days of life, although that is not true in every culture.

In Western cultures, infant care provided by a nonrelative has increased since 1980, although recent trends suggest that stay-at-home mothers are more common than they were a decade ago, at 29 percent in the United States in 2012 (Cohn et al., 2014). Nonetheless, most mothers of infants are in the labor force, especially in the United States where paid maternal leave is uncommon. One expert wrote "the overwhelming majority of mothers (80%) work in the 1st year of their child's life" (Brooks-Gunn et al., 2010, p. 96).

● **Observation Quiz** What three things do you see that suggest good care? (see answer, page 198) →

Contrast This with That Three infants again, but this infant day-care center provides excellent care, as can be seen by comparing this scene with what is depicted in the photo on page 193.

Ted Richardson/Raleigh News & Observer/MCT via Getty Images

FIGURE 7.3

A Changing World No one was offered maternity leave a century ago because the only jobs that mothers had were unregulated ones. Now, virtually every nation has a maternity leave policy, revised every decade or so. (The data on this chart are from 2011—already outdated.) As of 2014, only Australia, Sweden, Iceland, France, and Canada offered policies reflecting gender equality. That may be the next innovation in many nations.

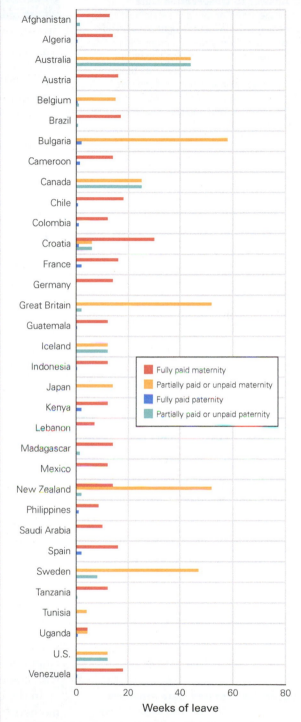

Data from ILO Database on Conditions of Work and Employment Laws, 2011.

Note: In some cases, leave can be shared between parents or other family members. Many nations have increased leave in the past four years.

Cultural variations in early care are evident. Virtually no infant in some of the poorest nations receives regular nonmaternal care unless the mother is incapable, and then a close relative takes over. By contrast, by age 1, 90 percent of infants of the wealthiest families within developed nations are cared for regularly by a nanny or babysitter at home, or by a family day-care provider in her (almost never his) home, or by a trained professional in a day-care center.

Almost every developmentalist agrees with three conclusions.

1. Attachment to someone is beneficial. That someone could be a mother or someone else, or more than one person—and can develop with a variety of care arrangements.
2. Frequent changes and instability are problematic. If an infant is cared for by a neighbor, a grandmother, a day-care center, and then another grandmother, each for only a month or two, or if an infant is with the biological mother, then a foster mother, then back with the biological mother, that is harmful. By age 3, children with unstable care histories are likely to be more aggressive than those with stable care, such as being at the same center with the same caregiver for years (Pilarz & Hill, 2014).
3. Babies benefit from a strong relationship with their parents. Accordingly, most nations provide some paid leave for mothers who are in the workforce; but an increasing trend is to provide paid leave for fathers or to allow family leave to be taken by either parent. The length of paid leave varies from a few days to about 15 months (see Figure 7.3). Laws in many nations guarantee that a mother's job will be open to her when her leave is over. Some cultures expect fathers to stay away from infant care, and others favor equality (Shwalb et al., 2013).

Beyond those three there is no agreed-upon best practice. As one review explained: "This evidence now indicates that early nonparental care environments sometimes pose risks to young children and sometimes confer benefits" (Phillips et al., 2011). The same is true for parental care: Some mothers and fathers are wonderful, some not.

People tend to believe that the practices of their own family or culture are best and that other patterns harm the infant and the parent. Because of the difference-equals-deficit error, assumptions flourish.

International Variations

For ideological as well as economic reasons, center-based infant care is common in France, Israel, China, Chile, Norway, and Sweden, where it is heavily subsidized by the governments. Many families in those nations believe that subsidized infant care is a public right, in much the same way they assume that a public fire department is available if needed. By contrast, center care is scarce in South

TABLE 7.3	**High-Quality Day Care**

High-quality day care during infancy has five essential characteristics:

1. *Adequate attention to each infant.*
   A small group of infants (no more than five) needs two reliable, familiar, loving caregivers. Continuity of care is crucial.

2. *Encouragement of language and sensorimotor development.*
   Infants need language—songs, conversations, and positive talk—and easily manipulated toys.

3. *Attention to health and safety.*
   Cleanliness routines (e.g., handwashing), accident prevention (e.g., no small objects), and safe areas to explore are essential.

4. *Professional caregivers.*
   Caregivers should have experience and degrees/certificates in early-childhood education. Turnover should be low, morale high, and enthusiasm evident.

5. *Warm and responsive caregivers.*
   Providers should engage the children in active play and guide them in problem solving. Quiet, obedient children may indicate unresponsive care.

Asia, Africa, and Latin America, where many parents believe it is harmful. (Table 7.3 lists five essential characteristics of high-quality infant day care, wherever it is located.)

Most nations are between those two extremes. Germany recently began offering paid infant care as a successful strategy to increase the birth rate. In the United States, infant care is paid for almost exclusively by parents, which makes quality infant care unaffordable for many families. One detailed example comes from Australia, where the government attempted to increase the birth rate. Parents were given $5,000 for each newborn, parental leave was paid, and public subsidies provided child-care centers. Yet many Australians still believed that babies need exclusive maternal care (Harrison et al., 2014).

Parents are caught in the middle. For example, one Australian mother of a 12-month-old boy used center care, but said:

> I spend a lot of time talking with them about his day and what he's been doing and how he's feeling and they just seem to have time to do that, to make the effort to communicate. Yeah they've really bonded with him and he's got close to them. But I still don't like leaving him there.
>
> [quoted in Boyd et al., 2013]

Underlying every policy and practice are theories about what is best. In the United States, marked variations are apparent by state and by employer, with some employers being quite generous. Almost no U.S. company pays for paternal leave, with one exception: The U.S. military allows 10 days of paid leave for fathers.

In the United States, only 20 percent of infants are cared for *exclusively* by their mothers (i.e., no other relatives or babysitters) throughout their first year. This is in contrast to Canada, with far more generous maternal leave and lower rates of maternal employment. In the first year of life, most Canadians are cared for only by their mothers (Babchishin et al., 2013). Obviously, these differences are affected by culture, economics, and politics more than by any universal needs of babies.

● **Especially for Day-Care Providers**

A mother who brings her child to you for day care says that she knows she is harming her baby, but economic necessity compels her to work. What do you say? (see response, page 200)

Recent Past and Present

Research two decades ago, led primarily by Jay Belsky, raised questions about the long-term consequences of infant day care (Belsky & Rovine, 1988; Belsky, 2001). Other studies were more positive. For instance, a large study in Canada found that infant girls seemed to develop equally well in various care arrangements. However, Canadian boys from high-income families whose mothers were not exclusive care-givers fared less well than similar boys whose mothers provided all of their care. By age 4, those who had been in day care were slightly more assertive or aggressive, with more emotional problems (e.g., a teacher might note that a kindergarten boy "seems unhappy").

The opposite was true for Canadian boys from low-income families: On average, they benefited from nonmaternal care, again according to teacher reports. The researchers insist that no policy implications can be derived from this study, partly because care varied so much in quality, location, and provider (Côté et al., 2008).

Research in the United States has also found that center care benefits children of low-income families (Peng & Robins, 2010). For less impoverished children, some questions arise. An ongoing longitudinal study by the Early Child Care Network of the National Institute of Child Health and Human Development (NICHD) has followed the development of more than 1,300 children from birth to age 11. Early day care correlated with many cognitive advances, especially in language.

The social consequences were less clear, however. Most analyses find that secure attachment to the mother was as common among infants in center care as among infants cared for at home. Like other, smaller studies, the NICHD research confirms that the mother–child relationship is pivotal.

However, infant day care seemed detrimental if the mother was insensitive *and* the infant spent more than 20 hours a week in a poor-quality program with too many children per group (McCartney et al., 2010). Again, boys in such circumstances had more conflicts with their teachers than did the girls or other boys with a different mix of maternal traits and day-care experiences.

More recent work finds that high-quality care in infancy benefits the cognitive skills of children of both sexes and all income groups, with no evidences of emotional harm, especially when it is followed by good preschool care (Li et al., 2013; Huston et al., 2015). Maybe earlier studies reflect cohort, not infant needs.

Nonetheless, the link between infant day care and later psychosocial problems, although not found in every study, raises concern. For that reason, a large study in Norway is particularly interesting.

Observation Quiz How do the two photographs reflect that the United States values individuality and Bangladesh values the group? (see answer, page 200) ↓

Same Situation, Far Apart: Instead of Mothers Casper, Wyoming *(left)*, is on the opposite side of the Earth from Dhaka, Bangladesh *(right)*, but day care is needed in both places, as shown here.

Response for Day-Care Providers
(from page 198): Reassure the mother that you will keep her baby safe and will help to develop the baby's mind and social skills by fostering synchrony and attachment. Also tell her that the quality of mother–infant interaction at home is more important than anything else for psychosocial development; mothers who are employed full time usually have wonderful, secure relationships with their infants. If the mother wishes, you can discuss ways to be a responsive mother.

Answer to Observation Quiz
(from page 199): In Bangladesh, unlike the U.S. children, all seven are close in age, with close-cropped hair and standard, cotton uniforms. All focus on the same collection of balls, while the Wyoming teacher seems to appreciate the girl who does not want to look at the book.

Norway

In Norway, new mothers are paid at full salary to stay home with their babies for 47 weeks, and high-quality, free center day care is available from age 1 on. Most (62 percent) Norwegian 1-year-olds are in center care, as are 84 percent of the 2-year-olds and 93 percent of the 3-year-olds. By contrast, in the United States maternal leave is unpaid, and if the mother does not return to work after three months, she may lose her job. Infant care is usually privately financed, which may reduce quality for all but the wealthy.

In the United States, reliable statistics are not kept on center care for infants, but only 42 percent of all U.S. 3-year-olds were in educational programs in 2012, according to the National Center for Education Statistics (Kena et al., 2014). Rates increase slightly as maternal education rises, as mothers with more education are more likely to appreciate and be able to afford early education.

Longitudinal results in Norway find no detrimental results of infant center care that begins at age 1. Too few children were in center care before their first birthday to find significant longitudinal results. By kindergarten, Norwegian day-care children had slightly more conflicts with caregivers, but the authors suggest that may be the result of shy children becoming bolder as a result of day care (Solheim et al., 2013).

Quality Care

The issue of the quality of care has become crucial. A professional organization in the United States, the National Association for the Education of Young Children, recently revised its standards for care of babies from birth to 15 months, based on current research (NAEYC, 2014). Breast-feeding is encouraged (via bottles of breast milk that mothers have expressed earlier), babies are always put to sleep on their backs, group size is small (no more than eight infants), and the ratio of adults to babies is 1:4 or fewer.

Many specific practices are recommended to keep infant minds growing and bodies healthy. For instance, "before walking on surfaces that infants use specifically for play, adults and children remove, replace, or cover with clean foot coverings any shoes they have worn outside that play area. If children or staff are barefoot in such areas, their feet are visibly clean" (NAEYC, 2014, p. 59). Another recommendation is to "engage infants in frequent face-to-face social interactions"—including talking, singing, smiling, and touching (NAEYC, 2014, p. 4).

All the research on infant day care confirms that sociocultural differences not only are many but also that they are significant. What seems best for one infant, in one culture, may be quite different from what is best for another infant elsewhere. It is a mistake to judge too broadly—infant day care, or almost any other practice or policy regarding babies, depends on specifics, not generalities.

Conclusion

No matter what form of care is chosen or what theory is endorsed, individualized care with stable caregivers seems best (Morrissey, 2009). Caregiver change is especially problematic for infants because each simple gesture or sound that a baby makes not only merits an encouraging response but also requires interpretation by someone who knows that particular baby well.

For example, "baba" could mean bottle, baby, blanket, banana, or some other word that does not even begin with *b*. This example is an easy one, but similar communication efforts—requiring individualized emotional responses, preferably from a familiar caregiver—are evident even in the first smiles and cries.

A related issue is the growing diversity of baby care providers. Especially when the home language is not the majority language, parents hesitate to let people of another background care for their infants. That is one reason that immigrant parents in the United States often prefer care by relatives instead of by professionals (P. Miller et al., 2014). Relationships are crucial, not only between caregiver and infant but also between caregiver and parent (Elicker et al., 2014).

As is true of many topics in child development, questions remain. But one fact is without question: Each infant needs personal responsiveness. Someone should serve as a partner in the synchrony duet, a base for secure attachment, and a social reference who encourages exploration. Then, infant emotions and experiences—cries and laughter, fears and joys—will ensure that development goes well.

WHAT HAVE YOU LEARNED?

1. According to Freud, what might happen if a baby's oral needs are not met?

2. How might Erikson's crisis of "trust versus mistrust" affect later life?

3. How do behaviorists explain the development of emotions and personality?

4. What does a "working model" mean within cognitive theory?

5. What is the difference between proximal and distal parenting?

6. How does evolution explain the parent–child bond?

7. Why is allocare necessary for survival of the human species?

8. Why do cultures differ on the benefits of infant nonmaternal care?

9. What aspects of infant care are agreed on by everyone?

SUMMARY

Emotional Development

1. Two emotions, contentment and distress, appear as soon as an infant is born. Smiles and laughter are evident in the early months. Between 4 and 8 months of age, anger emerges in reaction to restriction and frustration, and it becomes stronger by age 1.

2. Reflexive fear is apparent in very young infants. Fear of something specific, including fear of strangers and of separation, is typically strong toward the end of the first year.

3. In the second year, social awareness produces more selective fear, anger, and joy. As infants become increasingly self-aware, emotions emerge that encourage an interface between the self and others—specifically, pride, shame, and affection. Self-recognition (measured by the mirror/rouge test) emerges at about 18 months.

4. Temperament is inborn, but the expression of temperament is influenced by the context, with evident plasticity. At least in the United States, parents tend to encourage exuberance and discourage fear.

The Development of Social Bonds

5. Often by 2 months, and clearly by 6 months, infants become more responsive and social, and synchrony is evident. Caregivers and infants engage in reciprocal interactions, with split-second timing.

6. Infants are disturbed by a still face because they expect and need social interaction. Babies of depressed or rejecting parents become depressed or disturbed themselves.

7. Attachment is the relationship between two people who try to be close to each other (proximity-seeking and contact-maintaining). It is measured in infancy by a baby's reaction to the caregiver's presence, departure, and return in the Strange Situation.

8. Secure attachment provides encouragement for infant exploration, and it may influence the person lifelong. Some infants seem indifferent (type A attachment—insecure-avoidant) or overly dependent (type C—insecure-resistant/ambivalent), instead of secure (type B). Disorganized attachment (type D) is the most worrisome.

9. As they become more mobile and engage with their environment, toddlers use social referencing (looking to other people's facial expressions and body language) to detect what is safe, frightening, or fun. Fathers help toddlers become more adventuresome.

10. Infants frequently use fathers as partners in synchrony, as attachment figures, and as social references, developing emotions and exploring their world. Contemporary fathers often play with their infants.

Theories of Infant Psychosocial Development

11. According to all major theories, caregivers are especially influential in the first two years. Freud stressed the mother's impact on oral and anal pleasure; Erikson emphasized trust and autonomy. Both believed that the impact of these is lifelong.

12. Behaviorists focus on learning. They note that parents teach their babies many things, including when to be fearful or joyful, and how much physical and social distance (proximal or distal parenting) is best.

13. Cognitive theory holds that infants develop working models based on their experiences. Interpretation is crucial, and that can change with maturation.

14. Evolutionary theorists recognize that both infants and caregivers have impulses and emotions that have developed over millennia to foster the survival of each new member of the human species. Attachment is one example.

15. Sociocultural theory notes that infant care varies tremendously from one culture or era to another. The impact of nonmaternal care depends on many factors that change from one nation, one family, and even one child to another. For example, attitudes about infant day care vary a great deal, with the impact dependent on the quality of care (responsive, individualized, stable).

16. All theories find and all of the research shows that the relationship between the infant and caregivers is crucial. All aspects of early development are affected by policy and practice.

KEY TERMS

social smile (p. 176)
separation anxiety (p. 176)
stranger wariness (p. 176)
self-awareness (p. 178)
temperament (p. 178)
synchrony (p. 182)
still-face technique (p. 183)

attachment (p. 184)
secure attachment (p. 185)
insecure-avoidant attachment (p. 186)
insecure-resistant/ambivalent attachment (p. 186)

disorganized attachment (p. 186)
Strange Situation (p. 186)
social referencing (p. 190)
trust versus mistrust (p. 193)

autonomy versus shame and doubt (p. 193)
proximal parenting (p. 194)
distal parenting (p. 194)
working model (p. 194)
allocare (p. 195)

APPLICATIONS

1. One cultural factor that influences infant development is how infants are carried from place to place. Ask four mothers whose infants were born in each of the past four decades how they transported them—front or back carriers, facing out or in, strollers or carriages, in car seats or on mother's laps, and so on. Why did they choose the mode(s) they chose? What are their opinions and yours on how such cultural practices might affect infants' development?

2. Video synchrony for three minutes. Ideally, ask the parent of an infant under 8 months of age to play with the infant. If no

infant is available, observe a pair of lovers as they converse. Note the sequence and timing of every facial expression, sound, and gesture of both partners.

3. Contact several day-care centers to try to assess the quality of care they provide. Ask about factors such as adult/child ratio, group size, and training for caregivers of children of various ages. Is there a minimum age? Why or why not? Analyze the answers, using Table 7.3 as a guide.

The Developing Person So Far:
The First Two Years

BIOSOCIAL

Body Changes Over the first two years, body weight quadruples and brain weight triples. Connections between brain cells grow dense, with complex networks of dendrites and axons. Experiences that are universal (experience-expectant) and culture-bound (experience-dependent) aid brain growth, partly by pruning unused connections between neurons.

Perceiving and Moving Brain maturation as well as culture underlies the development of all the senses. Seeing, hearing, and mobility progress from reflexes to coordinated voluntary actions, including focusing, grasping, and walking.

Surviving in Good Health Infant health depends on immunization, parental practices (including "back to sleep"), and nutrition. Breast milk protects health. Survival rates are much higher today than even a few decades ago.

COGNITIVE

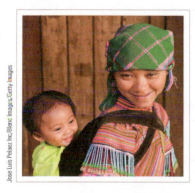

Sensorimotor Intelligence As Piaget describes it, in the first two years, infants progress from knowing their world through immediate sensory experiences to "experimenting" on that world through actions and mental images.

Information Processing Information-processing theory stresses the links between sensory experiences and perception. Infants develop their own ideas regarding the possibilities offered by the objects and events of the world.

Language: What Develops in the First Two Years? Interaction with responsive adults exposes infants to the structures of communication and language. By age 1, infants usually speak a word or two; by age 2, language has exploded—toddlers talk in short sentences and add vocabulary each day.

PSYCHOSOCIAL

Emotional Development Babies soon progress to smiling and laughing at pleasurable objects and events, and experience anger, sadness, and fear. Toddlers develop self-awareness and social awareness, and experience new emotions: pride, shame, embarrassment, disgust, and guilt. Temperament varies, as do the links between emotions and the brain.

The Development of Social Bonds Parents and infants respond to each other by synchronizing their behavior. Toward the end of the first year, secure attachment to the parent sets the stage for the child's increasingly independent exploration of the world. Insecure attachment—avoidant, resistant, or disorganized—signifies a parent–child relationship that hinders learning. Infants' self-awareness and independence are shaped by parents.

Theories of Infant Psychosocial Development All the theories of psychosocial development find that the infant–caregiver relationship is crucial. Infant day care is considered a fundamental right in some places, a luxury in others, and harmful in still others. All aspects of early development are affected by policy and practice.

PART III

early childhood

From ages 2 to 6, children spend most of their waking hours discovering, creating, laughing, and imagining—all the while acquiring the skills they need. They chase each other and attempt new challenges (developing their bodies); they play with sounds, words, and ideas (developing their minds); they invent games and dramatize fantasies (learning social skills and morals). These were once called the *preschool years* because school started in first grade. But first grade is no longer first; most children begin school long before age 6. Therefore, we call these years *early childhood*. By whatever name, the years from 2 to 6 are a time for extraordinary growth, impressive learning, and spontaneous play, joyful not only for young children but also for anyone who knows them.

Left: © 2016 Macmillan
Right: Christopher Hope-Fitch/Moment/Getty Images

Early Childhood:
Biosocial Development

What Will You Know?

1. Do young children eat too much, too little, or the right amount?
2. If children never climb trees or splash in water, do they suffer?
3. Why is injury control more needed than accident prevention?
4. Which is worse, neglect or abuse?

I often took 5-year-old Asa and his female friend, Ada, by subway from their kindergarten in Manhattan to their homes in Brooklyn. Their bodies were quite similar (no visible sex differences yet) but were a marked contrast to the hundreds of fellow subway riders. Of course they were shorter, thinner, with rounder heads and smaller hands, and their feet did not touch the floor when they sat, but that was not the most distinctive difference. Movement was.

I tried to keep their swinging feet from kicking other riders; I kept telling them to hold on to the pole; I explained that they should sit beside me instead of careening up and down the subway car, oblivious to the strangers they bumped into or squeezed by. Enforcing proper subway behavior with 5-year-olds is difficult; I often failed.

That is how nature makes young children: full of energy and action. Adults must guide them and keep them safe while enjoying their exuberance. Most tired subway riders did just that; they smiled, admired, and seemed to sympathize with me. This chapter describes growth during early childhood—in body, brain, and motor skills—and what adults can do to protect it.

Body Changes

In early childhood, as in infancy, the body and brain grow according to powerful epigenetic forces—biologically driven and socially guided, experience-expectant and experience-dependent. [**Life-Span Link:** Experience-expectant and experience-dependent brain development are explained in Chapter 5.] During this period, bodies and brains mature in size and function.

Growth Patterns

Compare an unsteady 24-month-old with a cartwheeling 6-year-old. Body differences are obvious. Height and weight increase in those four years (by about a foot and 16 pounds, or almost 30 centimeters and 8 kilograms), but that is not the most remarkable change. During early childhood, proportions shift radically: Children slim down as the lower body lengthens and fat turns to muscle.

Marc Romanelli/Getty Images

Short and Chubby Limbs No Longer
Siblings in New Mexico, ages 7 and almost 1, illustrate the transformation of body shape and skills during early childhood. Head size is almost the same, but arms are twice as long, evidence of proximo-distal growth.

In fact, the average body mass index (BMI, a ratio of weight to height) is lower at ages 5 and 6 than at any other time of life. [**Life-Span Link:** Body mass index is defined in Chapter 11.] Gone are the infant's protruding belly, round face, short limbs, and large head. The center of gravity moves from the breast to the belly, enabling cartwheels, somersaults, and many other motor skills. The joys of dancing, gymnastics, and pumping legs on a swing become possible; changing proportions enable new achievements.

During each year of early childhood, well-nourished children grow about 3 inches (about 7½ centimeters) and gain almost 4½ pounds (2 kilograms). By age 6, the average child in a developed nation:

- is at least 3½ feet tall (more than 110 centimeters).
- weighs between 40 and 50 pounds (between 18 and 23 kilograms).
- looks lean, not chubby.
- has adultlike body proportions (legs constitute about half the total height).

Nutrition

Although they rarely starve, preschool children sometimes are malnourished, even in nations with abundant food. The main reason is that small appetites are often satiated by unhealthy snacks, crowding out needed vitamins.

Obesity Among Young Children

Adults often encourage children to eat, instinctively protecting them against famine that was common a century ago. Unfortunately, that encouragement may be destructive.

As family income decreases, both malnutrition and obesity increase. Indeed, obesity is a sign of poor nutrition, likely to reduce immunity and later increase disease (Rook et al., 2014).

There are many explanations for the connection between obesity and low SES. Many family habits—less exercise, more television, fewer vegetables, more fast food—are more common in low-SES families than in those with wealthier, more educated parents (Cespedes et al., 2013). In addition, many low-income children live with grandmothers who know firsthand the dangers of inadequate body fat, so they promote eating patterns that, in other times and places, protected against starvation.

Those elders do not realize that traditional diets in low-income nations are healthier than foods advertised in developed nations (de Hoog et al., 2014). Sadly, many of those regions are adopting Western diets and, as a result, "childhood obesity is one of the most serious public health challenges of the twenty-first century. The problem is global and is steadily affecting many low and middle income countries, particularly in urban settings" (Sahoo et al., 2015, p. 188).

A life-span explanation links childhood stress to adult obesity. Children who lived in low-SES families became less attuned to hunger and satiety signals in their bodies, and, when they grow up, eat when they are not hungry (Hill et al., 2016).

For all children, appetite decreases between ages 2 and 6, and obesity increases every year from birth through adolescence. In former times, when most children lived in rural areas and played outside all day, the growth slowdown in early childhood was not noticed. Children did not come inside and had no snacks until their parents called them in for dinner, and then they ate whatever was put before them. Now, many adults fret, threaten, and cajole children to overeat ("Eat all your dinner and you can have ice cream").

One reason parents urge children to eat is that they underestimate their children's weight. A review of 69 studies found that half the parents of overweight children believe their children are thinner than they actually are. This problem was particularly likely for children ages 2 to 5 (Lundahl et al., 2014).

There is some good news in the United States, however. Young children are eating more fruit and are obese less often, from 12.1 percent of 2- to 5-year-olds in 2010 to 8.4 percent in 2012 (Ogden et al., 2014). Both public education and parental action are credited with improvement (MMWR, January 18, 2013; MMWR, August 9, 2013). Many day-care centers have successfully prevented obesity increasing from ages 2 to 5 by increasing exercise and improving snacks (Sisson et al., 2016).

Nutritional Deficiencies

Although many young children consume more than enough calories, they do not always obtain adequate iron, zinc, and calcium. For example, North American children now drink less milk than formerly, which means they ingest less calcium and have weaker bones later on.

Eating a wide variety of fresh foods may be essential for optimal health. Compared with the average child, those preschoolers who eat more dark-green and orange vegetables and less fried food benefit in many ways. They gain bone mass but not fat, according to a study that controlled for other factors that might correlate with body fat, such as gender (girls have more), ethnicity (people of some ethnic groups are genetically thinner), and income (poor children have worse diets) (Wosje et al., 2010).

Sugar is a major problem. Many customs entice children to eat sweets—in birthday cake, holiday candy, desserts, sweetened juice, soda, and so on. Sweetened cereals and drinks (advertised as containing 100 percent of daily vitamins) are a poor substitute for a balanced, varied diet, partly because some nutrients have not yet been identified, much less listed on food labels.

One result: Many children have cavities and decaying teeth before age 6. All children should see a dentist and brush their teeth regularly during early childhood—both practices that were unnecessary before widespread sugar consumption (Gibbons, 2012).

Allergies

An estimated 3 to 8 percent of children are allergic to a specific food, almost always a common, healthy one: Cow's milk, eggs, peanuts, tree nuts (such as almonds and walnuts), soy, wheat, fish, and shellfish are the usual culprits. Diagnostic standards

Catching Up, Slimming Down China has transformed its economy and family life since 1950, with far fewer poor families and malnourished children. Instead, problems and practices of the West are becoming evident, as in these two boys. They are attending a weight-loss camp in Zhengzhou, where the average 8- to 14-year-old child loses 14 pounds in a month.

🔵 **Especially for Nutritionists** A parent complains that she prepares a variety of vegetables and fruits, but her 4-year-old wants only French fries and cake. What should you advise? (see response, page 210)

🔵 **Especially for Early-Childhood Teachers** You know that young children are upset if forced to eat a food they hate, but you have eight 3-year-olds with eight different preferences. What do you do? (see response, page 210)

Apples or Oranges? During early childhood, boys and girls love having a choice, so it is the adults' task to offer good options. Which book before bed? Which colored shirt before school? Which healthy snack before going out to play?

Response for Nutritionists
(from page 209): The nutritionally wise advice would be to offer only fruits, vegetables, and other nourishing, low-fat foods, counting on the child's eventual hunger to drive him or her to eat them. However, centuries of cultural custom make such wisdom difficult. A physical checkup, with a blood test, may be warranted to make sure the child is healthy.

Response for Early-Childhood Teachers (from page 209): Remember to keep food simple and familiar. Offer every child the same food, allowing refusal but no substitutes—unless for all eight. Children do not expect school and home routines to be identical; they eventually taste whatever other children enjoy.

Especially for Early-Childhood Teachers You know you should be patient, but frustration rises when your young charges dawdle on the walk to the playground a block away. What should you do? (see response, page 216)

myelination The process by which axons become coated with myelin, a fatty substance that speeds the transmission of nerve impulses from neuron to neuron.

for allergies vary (which explains the range of estimates), and treatment varies even more (Chafen et al., 2010).

Some experts advocate total avoidance of the offending food—there are peanut-free schools, where no one is allowed to bring a peanut-butter sandwich for lunch—but other experts suggest that tolerance should be gradually increased (Reche et al., 2011). In some cases, giving infants a tiny bit of peanut butter under close medical supervision is beneficial (Gruchalla & Sampson, 2015).

Indeed, exposure to peanuts can begin before birth: A study of pregnant women who ingested peanuts found that their children were less likely to be allergic (Frazier et al., 2014). Fortunately, many childhood food allergies are outgrown, but allergies make a balanced diet even harder.

Brain Growth

By age 2, most neurons have connected to other neurons and substantial pruning has occurred. The 2-year-old's brain already weighs 75 percent of what it will weigh in adulthood; the 6-year-old's brain is 90 percent of adult weight.

Since most of the brain is already present and functioning those of by age 2, what remains to develop? The most important parts! Most important for people, that is.

Although the brains and bodies of other primates are better than humans in some ways (they climb trees earlier and faster, for instance), and although many animals have abilities that humans lack (smell in dogs, for instance), humans have intellectual capacities far beyond any other animal. Although sometime evolution is thought to mean survival of the fittest, the human species developed "a mode of living built on social cohesion, cooperation and efficient planning. It was a question of survival of the smartest" (Corballis, 2011, p. 194).

As the prefrontal cortex matures, social understanding develops. For example, a careful series of tests given to 106 chimpanzees, 32 orangutans, and 105 human 2½-year-olds found that young children were "equivalent . . . to chimpanzees on tasks of physical cognition but far outstripped both chimpanzees and orangutans on tasks of social cognition" such as pointing or following someone's gaze (Herrmann et al., 2007, p. 1365).

Children gradually become better at controlling their emotions when they are with other people. This is directly connected to brain development as time passes and family experiences continue, although how much of such control is due to brain maturation directly and how much is due to learning is disputed (DeLisi, 2014; Kochanska et al., 2009). Nonetheless, gradual self-control and development of the prefrontal cortex is apparent.

After infancy, most of the increase in brain weight occurs because of **myelination.** *Myelin* (sometimes called the *white matter* of the brain; the *gray matter* is the neurons themselves) is a fatty coating on the axons that protects and speeds signals between neurons (see Figure 8.1).

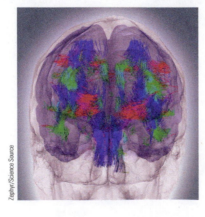

Myelin helps every part of the brain, especially the connections between neurons that are far from each other. It is far more than mere insulation around the axons: "Myelin organizes the very structure of network connectivity . . . and regulates the timing of information flow through individual circuits" (Fields, 2014, p. 266). This is evident in the major link between the left and the right halves of the brain, the corpus callosum, as the following explains.

FIGURE 8.1
Mental Coordination? This brain scan of a 38-year-old depicts areas of myelination (the various colors) within the brain. As you see, the two hemispheres are quite similar, but not identical. For most important skills and concepts, both halves of the brain are activated.

Zaphyr/Science Source

INSIDE THE BRAIN

Connected Hemispheres

The brain is divided into two halves, connected by the **corpus callosum,** a long, thick band of nerve fibers that grows particularly rapidly in early childhood (Ansado et al., 2015). For that reason, compared to toddlers, young children become much better at coordinating the two sides of their brains and, hence, both sides of their bodies. They can hop, skip, and gallop at age 5, unlike at age 2.

Serious disorders result when the corpus callosum fails to develop, almost always including intellectual disability (Cavalari & Donovick, 2014). Abnormal growth of the corpus callosum is one symptom of autism spectrum disorder, as well as dozens of other disorders (Travers et al., 2015; Wolff et al., 2015; Al-Hashim et al., 2016).

To appreciate the corpus callosum, note that each side of the body and brain specializes and is therefore dominant for certain functions. This is **lateralization,** literally, "sidedness."

The entire human body is lateralized, apparent not only in right- or left-handedness but also in the feet, the eyes, the ears, and the brain itself. People prefer to kick a ball, wink an eye, or listen on the phone with their preferred foot, eye, or ear, respectively. Genes, prenatal hormones, and early experiences all affect which side does what.

Astonishing studies of humans whose corpus callosa were severed to relieve severe epilepsy, as well as research on humans and other vertebrates with intact corpus callosa, reveal how the brain's hemispheres specialize. Typically, the left half controls the body's right side as well as areas dedicated to logical reasoning, detailed analysis, and the basics of language. The brain's right half controls the body's left side and areas dedicated to emotional and creative impulses, including appreciation of music, art, and poetry. Thus, the left side notices details and the right side grasps the big picture.

This left–right distinction has been exaggerated, especially when broadly applied to people (Hugdahl & Westerhausen, 2010). No one is exclusively left-brained or right-brained (except individuals with severe brain injury in childhood, who may use half of their brain to do all of the necessary thinking).

Both sides of the brain are usually involved in every skill. That is why the corpus callosum is crucial. As myelination progresses, signals between the two hemispheres become quicker and clearer, enabling children to become better thinkers and to be less clumsy. For example, no 2-year-old can hop on one foot, but most 6-year-olds can—an example of brain balancing. Many songs, dances, and games that young children love involve moving their bodies in some coordinated way—challenging, but fun because of that. Logic (left brain) without emotion (right brain) is a severe impairment, as is the opposite (Damasio, 2012).

Left-handed people tend to have thicker corpus callosa than right-handed people do, perhaps because they need to readjust the interaction between the two sides of their bodies, depending

corpus callosum A long, thick band of nerve fibers that connects the left and right hemispheres of the brain and allows communication between them.

lateralization Literally, sidedness, referring to the specialization in certain functions by each side of the brain, with one side dominant for each activity. The left side of the brain controls the right side of the body, and vice versa.

on the task. For example, most left-handed people brush their teeth with their left hand because using their dominant hand is more natural, but they shake hands with their right hand because that is what social convention requires.

Acceptance of left-handedness is more widespread now than a century ago. More adults in Great Britain and the United States claim to be left-handed today (about 10 percent) than in 1900 (about 3 percent) (McManus et al., 2010). Developmentalists advise against trying to force a left-handed child to become right-handed, since the brain is the origin of handedness.

Left lateralization is an advantage in some professions, especially those involving creativity and split-second actions. A disproportionate number of artists, musicians, and sports stars were/are left-handed, including Pele, Babe Ruth, Monica Seles, Bill Gates, Oprah Winfrey, Jimi Hendrix, Lady Gaga, and Justin Bieber. Five of the past seven presidents of the United States were/are lefties: Gerald Ford, Ronald Reagan, George H.W. Bush, Bill Clinton, and Barack Obama.

Dexterity in Evidence She already holds the pen at the proper angle with her thumb, index finger, and middle finger—an impressive example of dexterity for a 3-year-old. However, *dexter* is Latin for "right"—evidence of an old prejudice no longer apparent here.

Response for Early-Childhood Teachers (from page 214): One solution is to remind yourself that the children's brains are not yet myelinated enough to enable them to quickly walk, talk, or even button their jackets. Maturation has a major effect, as you will observe if you can schedule excursions in September and again in November. Progress, while still slow, will be a few seconds faster.

Maturation of the Prefrontal Cortex

The entire frontal lobe continues to develop for many years after early childhood; dendrite density and myelination are still increasing in emerging adulthood. Nonetheless, neurological control advances significantly between ages 2 and 6, evident in several ways:

- Sleep becomes more regular.
- Emotions become more nuanced and responsive.
- Temper tantrums subside.
- Uncontrollable laughter and tears are less common.

One example of the maturing brain is evident in the game Simon Says. Players are supposed to follow the leader *only* when orders are preceded by the words "Simon says." Thus, if leaders touch their noses and say, "Simon says touch your nose," players are supposed to touch their noses; but when leaders touch their noses and say, "Touch your nose," no one is supposed to follow the example. Young children lose at this game because they impulsively do what they see and hear.

Impulsiveness and Perseveration

Neurons have only two kinds of impulses: on–off or, in neuroscience terms, activate–inhibit. Each is signaled by biochemical messages from dendrites to axons to neurons. The consequences are evident in *executive function* and *emotional regulation,* both discussed in the next two chapters (Barrasso-Catanzaro & Eslinger, 2016; Holmes et al., 2016). Activation and inhibition are necessary for thoughtful adults, who neither leap too quickly nor hesitate too long. A balanced brain is best throughout life: One sign of cognitive loss in late adulthood is when an elderly person becomes too cautious or too impulsive.

Many young children are notably unbalanced neurologically. They are impulsive, flitting from one activity to another. That explains why many 3-year-olds cannot stay quietly on one task, even in "circle time" in preschool, where each child is supposed to sit in place, not talking or touching anyone.

impulse control The ability to postpone or deny the immediate response to an idea or behavior.

perseveration The tendency to persevere in, or stick to, one thought or action for a long time.

Ready to Learn? He is 5 years old, able to sit at a desk with impressive control of fine motor muscles in his upper lip, but probably not able to read the text on the board behind him. Should he be praised or punished? Perhaps neither; in another year or two, he will no longer be admired by his classmates for this trick.

Jessie Jean/Getty Images

Poor **impulse control** signifies a personality disorder in adulthood but not in early childhood. Few 3-year-olds are capable of sustained attention to tasks that adults organize. However, some preschoolers pay too much attention to things that capture their interest. They might show **perseveration,** which is to stick to, or persevere in, one thought or action, such as playing with one toy or holding one fantasy for hours.

Young children may repeat one phrase or question again and again, or cannot stop giggling once they start. That is perseveration. Crying may become uncontrollable because the child is stuck in whatever triggered the tantrum.

No young child is perfect at regulating attention, because immaturity of the prefrontal cortex makes it impossible to moderate the limbic system.

"I would share, but I'm not there developmentally."

Good Excuse It is true that emotional control of selfish instincts is difficult for young children because the prefrontal cortex is not yet mature enough to regulate some emotions. However, family practices can advance social understanding.

Impulsiveness and perseveration are evident. Because the amygdala is not well connected to more reflective parts of the brain, many children become suddenly terrified—even of something that exists only in imagination. Gradually preschoolers are less likely to perseverate, especially if they are taught to do so (Zelazo, 2015).

A study of children from ages 3 to 6 found that the ability to attend to what adults requested gradually increased. That correlated with academic learning and behavioral control (fewer outbursts or tears) (Metcalfe et al., 2013). Development continues as brain maturation (innate) and emotional regulation (learned) allow most children to pay attention and switch activities as needed. By adolescence, most teenagers change tasks at the sound of the school bell.

Especially for Neurologists Why do many experts think the limbic system is an oversimplified explanation of brain function? (see response, page 214)

Stress and the Brain

The relationship between stress and brain activity depends partly on the age of the person and partly on the degree of stress. Both too much and too little impair learning.

In an experiment, brain scans and hormone measurements were taken of 4- to 6-year-olds immediately after a fire alarm (Teoh & Lamb, 2013). As measured by their cortisol levels, some children were upset and some were not. Two weeks later, they were questioned about the event. Those with higher cortisol reactions to the alarm remembered more details than did those with less stress. That conclusion is found in other research as well—some stress, but not too much, aids cognition (Keller et al., 2012).

However, especially with children, when an adult demands answers in a stern, yes-or-no, stressful manner, memories are less accurate. There are good evolutionary reasons for that: People need to remember experiences that arouse their emotions so that they can avoid, or adjust to, similar experiences in the future. On the other hand, the brain protects itself from too much stress by shutting down.

Generally, a balance between arousal and reassurance is needed, again requiring speedy coordination among many parts of the brain. For instance, if children

LaunchPad macmillan learning

Video Activity: The Childhood Stress-Cortisol Connection examines how high cortisol levels can negatively impact a child's overall health.

are witnesses to a crime (a stressful experience) or experience abuse, memory is more accurate when an interviewer is warm and attentive, listening carefully but not suggesting answers (Johnson et al., 2016).

Studies of maltreated children suggest that excessive stress-hormone levels in early childhood permanently damage brain pathways, blunting or accelerating emotional responses lifelong (Evans & Kim, 2013; Wilson et al., 2011). Sadly, this topic leads again to the Romanian children mentioned in Chapter 7.

When some adopted Romanian children saw pictures of happy, sad, frightened, or angry faces, their limbic systems were less reactive than were those of Romanian children who were never institutionalized. Their brains were also less lateralized, suggesting less efficient thinking (C. Nelson et al., 2014). Thus, institutional life, without the stress reduction of loving caretakers, impaired their brains.

WHAT HAVE YOU LEARNED?

1. About how much does a well-nourished child grow in height and weight from ages 2 to 6?

2. Why do many adults overfeed children?

3. How do childhood allergies affect nutrition?

4. Why are today's children more at risk of obesity than children 50 years ago?

5. How much does the brain grow from ages 2 to 6?

6. Why is myelination important for thinking and motor skills?

7. How does brain maturation affect impulsivity and perseveration?

Advancing Motor Skills

Maturation and myelination allow children to move with greater speed, agility, and grace as they age (see Visualizing Development, p. 216). Brain growth, motivation, and guided practice undergird all motor skills.

Gross Motor Skills

Gross motor skills improve dramatically during early childhood. When playing, many 2-year-olds fall down and bump clumsily into each other. By contrast, some 5-year-olds perform coordinated dance steps, tumbling tricks, or sports moves.

There remains much for them to learn, especially in the ability to adjust to other people and new circumstances. Thus, a 5-year-old can sometimes kick a ball with precision, but it is much harder for that child to be a good team player on a soccer team.

Specific Skills

Many North American 5-year-olds can ride a tricycle, climb a ladder, and pump a swing, as well as throw, catch, and kick a ball. A few can do these things by age 3, and some 5-year-olds can already skate, ski, dive, and ride a bike—activities that demand balanced coordination and both brain hemispheres. Elsewhere, some 5-year-olds swim in oceans or climb cliffs.

Adults need to make sure children have a safe space to play, with time, appropriate equipment, and playmates. Children learn best from peers who demonstrate

Practice with the Big Kids Ava is unable to stand as Carlyann can *(left)*, but she is thrilled to be wearing her tutu in New York City's Central Park, with 230 other dancers in a highly organized attempt to break a record for the most ballerinas on pointe at the same moment. Motor skills are developing in exactly the same way on the other side of the world *(right)* as children in Beijing perform in ballet class.

whatever the child is ready to try, from catching a ball to climbing a tree. Of course, culture and locale influence particulars: Some small children learn to skateboard, others to sail.

Recent urbanization concerns many developmentalists. A century ago, children with varied skill levels played together in empty lots or fields without adult supervision, but now more than half the world's children live in cities.

Busy or violent streets not only impede development of gross motor skills but also add to the natural fears of the immature amygdala, compounded by the learned fears of adults. Gone are the days when parents told their children to go out and play, only to return when hunger, rain, or nightfall brought them home. Now many parents fear strangers and traffic, keeping their 3- to 5-year-olds inside (R. Taylor et al., 2009).

That worries many childhood educators who believe that children need space and freedom to play in order to develop well. Indeed, many agree that environment is the third teacher, "because the environment is viewed as another teacher having the power to enhance children's sense of wonder and capacity for learning" (Stremmel, 2012, p. 136). Balancing on branches and jumping over fences, squeezing mud and throwing pebbles, chasing birds and catching bugs—each forbidden now by some adults—educated millions of children in former cohorts.

Environmental Hazards

Observable dangers and restricted exploration are not the only reasons some children are slow to develop motor skills. In addition, children who breathe heavily polluted air exercise less. Often they live in crowded neighborhoods and attend poor schools. Can we be certain that dirty air harms their learning?

Scientists have grappled with this question and answered yes: Environmental substances directly impair brain development in young children, especially those in low-SES families. Of course, many factors impact learning, but the conclusion that pollution harms the brain seems valid. Consider asthma, which keeps some children from playing and reduces oxygen to the brain.

Developing Motor Skills

Every child can do more with each passing year. These examples detail what one child might be expected to accomplish from ages 2 to 6. Of course, each child is unique, and much depends on culture, practice, and maturity.

SKILLS

AVERAGE HEIGHT IN INCHES
BOYS 45.5   GIRLS 45.0

Draw and paint recognizable images
Write simple words
Read a page of print   **6 years**
Tie shoes
Catch a small ball

BOYS 43.0   GIRLS 42.5

Skip and gallop in rhythm
Clap, bang, sing in rhythm
Copy difficult shapes and letters
Climb trees, jump over things   **5 years**
Use a knife to cut
Wash face, comb hair

BOYS 40.5   GIRLS 40.0

Catch a beach ball
Use scissors
Hop on either foot
Feed self with fork
Dress self   **4 years**
Copy most letters
Pour juice without spilling
Brush teeth

Kick and throw a ball
Jump with both feet
Pedal a tricycle
Copy simple shapes   **3 years**
Walk down stairs
Climb ladders

BOYS 37.5   GIRLS 37.0

Run without falling
Climb out of crib
Walk up stairs
Feed self with spoon   **2 years**
Draw spirals

BOYS 34.1   GIRLS 33.5

In the United States, asthma is more prevalent among children who live in poverty than among those who do not. Worldwide, children who live in high-pollution cities have far higher rates of asthma than their peers elsewhere in their nation. Unfortunately, the World Health Organization reports that increasing numbers of children suffer from asthma and half of the world's children live in cities, often in megacities where air pollution is getting worse (World Health Organization, May 7, 2014). [**Life-Span Link:** Asthma is discussed in Chapter 11.]

A recent study conducted in British Columbia, where universal public health care and detailed birth records allow solid longitudinal research, confirmed the connection. Pollution from traffic and industry during early childhood was a cause, not just a correlate, of asthma (N. Clark et al., 2010).

This study began with all 37,401 births in 1999 and 2000 in southwest British Columbia (which includes a major city, Vancouver). By age 3, almost 10 percent (3,482) of these children were asthmatic. Each of those 3,482 was matched on SES, gender, and so on with five other children from the same birth group. Exposure to air pollution (including carbon monoxide, nitric oxide, nitrogen dioxide, particulate matter, ozone, sulfur dioxide, black carbon, wood smoke, car exhausts, and smoke from parents' cigarettes) was carefully measured.

Parents did not always protect their children, partly because they did not know which substances caused poor health. For example, because wood smoke is easy to see and smell, some parents tried to avoid it, but burning wood did not increase asthma.

However, although carbon monoxide emissions are not visible, when compared to their five matched peers, those children who were diagnosed with asthma were more likely to live near major highways, where carbon monoxide is prevalent. Other research finds that cigarette smoke affects a child's brain as well as their breath—a problem not recognized a decade ago (Swan & Lessov-Schlaggar, 2015).

From this and other research, we now know that hundreds of substances in air, food, and water affect the brain and thus impede balance, motor skills, and motivation. Many substances have not been tested, but some—including lead in the water and air, pesticides in the soil or on clothing, bisphenol A (BPA) in plastic, and secondhand cigarette smoke—are known to be harmful.

One new concern is *e-waste,* which refers to discarded computers, cell phones, and other outmoded electronic devices. E-waste may spew pollutants that affect the brains of infants and children, although the data are not yet definitive. As one group of researchers explains: "Although data suggest that exposure to e-waste is harmful to health, more well designed epidemiological investigations in vulnerable populations, especially pregnant women and children, are needed to confirm these associations" (Grant et al., 2013, p. e350).

The administrator of environmental public health in Oregon said, "We simply do not know—as scientists, as regulators, as health professionals—the health impacts of the soup of chemicals to which we expose human beings" (Shibley, quoted in T. Johnson, 2011). Whether you think Shibley is needlessly alarmist or is simply stating the obvious depends on your own perspective—and maybe on your amygdala.

Lead, however, has been thoroughly researched, and there is no doubt that lead is severely toxic. The history of lead exposure in the following illustrates the tortuous path from science to practice.

Eliminating Lead

Lead was recognized as a poison a century ago (Hamilton, 1914). The symptoms of *plumbism,* as lead poisoning is called, were obvious—intellectual disability, hyperactivity, and even death if the level reached 70 micrograms per deciliter of blood.

The lead industry defended the heavy metal. Manufacturers argued that low levels were harmless, and they blamed parents for letting their children eat flaking chips of lead paint (which tastes sweet). Further, since children with high levels of lead in their blood were often from low-SES families, some argued that malnutrition, inadequate schools, family conditions, or a host of other causes were the reasons for their reduced IQ (Scarr, 1985).

I am chagrined to confess that this argument made sense to me when I wrote the first edition of this textbook (Berger, 1980).

Lead remained a major ingredient in paint (it speeds drying) and in gasoline (it raises octane) for most of the twentieth century. Finally, chemical analyses of blood and teeth, with careful longitudinal and replicated research, proved that lead was indeed a poison for all children (Needleman et al., 1990; Needleman & Gatsonis, 1990).

The United States banned lead in paint (in 1978) and automobile fuel (in 1996). The blood level that caused plumbism was set at 40 micrograms per deciliter, then 20, and then 10. Danger is now thought to begin at 5 micrograms, but no level has been proven to be risk-free (MMWR, April 5, 2013). Part of the problem is that the fetus and infant absorb lead at a much higher rate than adults do, so lead's neurotoxicity is especially destructive of developing brains (Hanna-Attisha et al., 2016).

Regulation has made a difference: The percentage of U.S. 1- to 5-year-olds with more than 5 micrograms of lead per deciliter of blood was 8.6 percent in 1999–2001, 4.1 percent in 2003–2006, and 2.6 percent in 2007–2010 (see Figure 8.2).

Cecil, Kim M.; Brubaker, Christopher J.; Adler, Caleb M.; Dietrich, Kim N.; Altaye, Mekibib; Egelhoff, John C., . . . Lanphear, Bruce P. (2008). Decreased brain volume in adults with childhood lead exposure. *PloS Medicine,* 5(5), 741–750. doi: 10.1371/journal.pmed.0050112

Toxic Shrinkage A composite of 157 brains of adults—who, as children, had high lead levels in their blood—shows reduced volume. The red and yellow hot spots are all areas that are smaller than areas in a normal brain. No wonder lead-exposed children have multiple intellectual and behavioral problems.

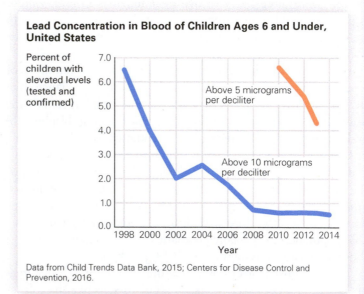

Lead Concentration in Blood of Children Ages 6 and Under, United States

Data from Child Trends Data Bank, 2015; Centers for Disease Control and Prevention, 2016.

FIGURE 8.2

Dramatic Improvement in a Decade When legislators finally accepted the research establishing the damage from lead in paint, gasoline, and water, they passed laws making it exceedingly rare for any child to die or suffer intellectual disability because of plumbism. A decade ago, 10 micrograms in the blood was thought to be completely safe; now less than 1 child in 200 tests at that level, and even 5 micrograms alerts pediatricians and parents to find the source. These national data make the tragedy in Flint, Michigan especially shocking.

Children who are young, low-SES, and/or living in old housing tend to have higher levels (MMWR, April 5, 2013).

Many parents now know to increase their children's calcium intake, wipe window ledges clean, avoid child exposure to construction dust, test drinking water, discard lead-based medicines and crockery (available in some other nations), and make sure children never eat chips of lead-based paint. However, as evident many times in the study of development, private actions alone are not sufficient to protect health. Parents are blamed for obesity, injury, abuse, and neglect, but often the larger community is also to blame.

A stark recent example occurred in Flint, Michigan, where in April 2014 cost-saving officials (appointed by the state to take over the city when the tax base shrunk as the auto industry left) changed the municipal drinking water from Lake Huron to the Flint River. That river contained chemicals that increased lead leaching from old pipes, contaminating the water supply—often used for drinking and mixing infant formula.

The percent of young children in Flint with blood lead levels above 5 micrograms per deciliter doubled in two years, from 2.4 to 4.9 percent, and more than tripled in one neighborhood from 4.6 to 15.7 (Hanna-Attisha et al., 2016). Apparently, the state-appointed emergency manager focused on saving money, ignoring possible brain damage to children who, unlike him, are mostly low-income and African American. This oversight is considered an "abject failure to protect public health" (Bellinger, 2016, p. 1101).

The consequences may harm the community for decades. Remember from Chapter 1 that scientists sometimes use data collected for other reasons to draw new conclusions. This is the case with lead. About 15 years after the sharp decline in blood lead levels in preschool children, the rate of violent crime committed by teenagers and young adults fell sharply. This seems more than coincidence, since some nations reduced lead before others, and those nations saw a reduction in teenage crime earlier than others.

A scientist comparing these trends concluded that some teenagers commit impulsive, violent crimes because their brains were poisoned by lead years ago. The correlation is found not only in the United States but also in every nation that has reliable data on lead and crime—Canada, Germany, Italy, Australia, New Zealand, France, and Finland (Nevin, 2007). Moreover, recent research finds that blood lead levels in early childhood predict later attention deficits and school suspensions (Amato et al., 2013; Goodlad et al., 2013).

There is no doubt that lead, even at low levels in the blood of a young child, harms the brain. That raises questions about the long-term effects of hundreds, perhaps thousands, of new chemicals in the air, water, or soil. It also makes the Flint tragedy more troubling. Developmentalists have known about the dangers of lead for decades. Why didn't the Michigan administrator know better?

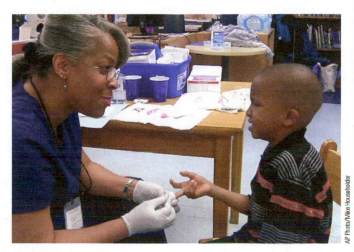

Too Late? Veronica Robinson is a University of Michigan nursing professor who volunteered to provide free lead testing for the children of Flint, Michigan. If 7-year-old Zyontae's level is high, brain damage in early life will trouble him lifelong.

Fine Motor Skills

Fine motor skills are harder to master than gross motor skills. Whistling, winking, and especially writing are difficult. Pouring juice into a glass, cutting food with a knife, and achieving anything more artful than a scribble with a pencil all require a level of muscular control, patience, and judgment that is beyond most 2-year-olds.

Many fine motor skills involve two hands and thus both sides of the brain: The fork stabs the meat while the knife cuts it; one hand steadies the paper while the other writes; tying shoes, buttoning shirts, cutting paper, and zipping zippers require both hands. Brain lateralization is needed. Short, stubby fingers add to the problem. As a result, shoelaces get knotted, paper gets ripped, and zippers get stuck. Parents and teachers need to provide good learning tools (puzzles, art supplies, etc.) with much patience.

Same Situation, Far Apart: Finger Skills
Children learn whatever motor skills their culture teaches. Some master chopsticks, with fingers to spare; others cut sausage with a knife and fork. Unlike these children in Japan *(above left)* and Germany *(above right)*, some never master either, because about one-third of adults worldwide eat directly with their hands.

🟢 **Especially for Immigrant Parents**
You and your family eat with chopsticks at home, but you want your children to feel comfortable in Western culture. Should you change your family's eating customs? (see response, page 222)

What Is It? Wrong question! Better to say "tell me about it" and then perhaps this 4-year-old will explain the fringe she carefully added to the . . .

Academics Before Age 6

Traditional school necessitates fine motor skills and body control. Writing requires finger control, reading print requires eye control, classroom schedules require bladder control, and so on. These are beyond most young children, so even the brightest 3-year-old is not ready for first grade.

Slow maturation is one reason many 6-year-olds are frustrated if their teachers demand that they write neatly and cut straight. Some educators suggest waiting until a child is "ready" for school; some suggest that preschools should focus on readiness; still others suggest that schools should adjust to children, not vice versa.

Fine motor skills—like many other biological characteristics, such as bones, brains, and teeth—mature about six months earlier in girls than in boys. By contrast, boys often are ahead of girls in gross motor skills. These gender differences may be biological, or they may result from practice: Young girls more often dress up and play with dolls (fine motor skills), while boys more often climb and kick (gross motor skills) (Saraiva et al., 2013).

In grade school, girls are, on average, ahead of boys in behavior and reading because of fine motor maturation. Boys, of course, catch up, and they should not be blamed if they are not as accomplished as their female classmates.

Artistic Expression

Young children are imaginative, creative, and not yet self-critical. They love to express themselves, especially if their parents applaud their performances, display their artwork, and otherwise communicate approval. The fact that their fine motor skills are immature, and thus their drawings lack precision, is irrelevant. Perhaps the immaturity of the prefrontal cortex is a blessing, allowing creativity without self-criticism.

All forms of artistic expression blossom during early childhood; 2- to 6-year-olds love to dance around the room, build an elaborate tower of blocks, make music by pounding in rhythm, and put bright marks on shiny paper. In every artistic domain, skill takes both practice and maturation.

For example, when drawing a person, 2- to 3-year-olds usually draw a "tadpole"—a circle head, dots for eyes, sometimes a smiling mouth, and then a line or two beneath to indicate the rest of the body.

Gradually, tadpoles get bodies, limbs, hair, and so on. Children's artwork is not intended to be realistic: It communicates thoughts and self-expression (Papandreou, 2014). It is a mistake for adults to say "that looks like a . . ." or worse, "you forgot the feet."

Cultural and cohort differences are apparent in all artistic skills. Some parents enroll their preschool children in music lessons, hoping they will learn to play. As a result, those preschoolers become better at listening to sounds, evident in listening to speech as well as music. Neurological evidence finds that their brains reflect their new auditory abilities, a remarkable testimony to the role of family and culture (Strait et al., 2013).

WHAT HAVE YOU LEARNED?

1. What three factors help children develop their motor skills?

2. How have cohort changes affected the development of gross motor skills?

3. What is known and unknown about the effects on young children of chemicals in food, air, and water?

4. What are conflicting interpretations of gender differences in motor skills?

5. How does brain maturation affect children's artistic expression?

Injuries and Abuse

In almost all families of every income, ethnicity, and nation, parents want to protect their children while fostering their growth. Yet far more children die from violence—either accidental or deliberate—than from any specific disease.

The contrast between disease and violent (usually accidental) death is most obvious in developed nations, where medical prevention, diagnosis, and treatment make fatal illness rare until late adulthood. In the United States, four times as many 1- to 4-year-olds die of accidents than of cancer, which is the leading cause of disease death during these years (National Center for Health Statistics, 2015). Indeed, in 2013, more 1- to 4-year-old U.S. children were murdered (337) than died of cancer (328). This was not always true, but cancer deaths have decreased during the past half-century, while child homicide has increased.

Avoidable Injury

Worldwide, injuries cause millions of premature deaths among adults as well as children: Not until age 40 does any specific disease overtake accidents as a cause of mortality.

In some nations, malnutrition, malaria, and other infectious diseases *combined* cause more infant and child deaths than injuries do, but those nations also have high rates of child injury. Southern Asia and sub-Saharan Africa have the highest rates of motor-vehicle deaths, even though the number of cars is relatively low (World Health Organization, 2015). Most children who die in such accidents are pedestrians, or are riding—without a helmet—on motorcycles.

Age-Related Dangers

In accidents overall, 2- to 6-year-olds are more often seriously hurt than 6- to 10-year-olds. Why are young children so vulnerable?

Same Situation, Far Apart: Keeping Everyone Safe Preventing child accidents requires action by both adults and children. In the United States *(above left)*, adults passed laws and taught children to use seat belts—including this boy who buckles his stuffed companion. In France *(above right)*, teachers stop cars while children hold hands to cross the street—each child keeping his or her partner moving ahead.

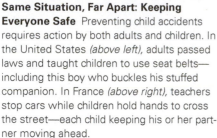

Response for Immigrant Parents (from page 220): Children develop the motor skills that they see and practice. They will soon learn to use forks, spoons, and knives. Do not abandon chopsticks completely, because young children can learn several ways of doing things, and the ability to eat with chopsticks is a social asset.

injury control/harm reduction
Practices that are aimed at anticipating, controlling, and preventing dangerous activities; these practices reflect the beliefs that accidents are not random and that injuries can be made less harmful if proper controls are in place.

Immaturity of the prefrontal cortex makes young children impulsive; they plunge into danger. Unlike infants, their motor skills allow them to run, leap, scramble, and grab in a flash, before a caregiver can stop them. Their curiosity is boundless; their impulses are uninhibited. Then, if they do something that becomes dangerous, such as lighting a fire while playing with matches, fear and stress might make them slow to get help.

Age-related trends are apparent in particulars. Falls are more often fatal for the youngest (under 24 months) and oldest (over 80 years); preschoolers have high rates of poisoning and drowning; motor-vehicle deaths peak during ages 15 to 25.

Generally, as income falls, accident rates rise, but this is not always true. Not only are 1- to 4-year-olds more likely to die of drowning than any other age group, they drown in swimming pools six times more often than older children and adults (MMWR, May 16, 2014). Usually the deadly pool is in their own backyard, a luxury less likely for low-income families.

Injury Control

Instead of using the term *accident prevention,* public health experts prefer **injury control** (or **harm reduction**). Consider the implications. *Accident* implies that an injury is random, unpredictable; if anyone is at fault, it's a careless parent or an accident-prone child. Instead, *injury control* suggests that the impact of an injury can be limited if appropriate controls are in place, and *harm reduction* implies that harm can be minimized.

If young children are allowed to play as necessary to develop their skills, minor mishaps (scratches and bruises) are bound to occur. However, serious injury is unlikely if a child falls on a safety surface instead of on concrete, if a car seat protects the body in a crash, if a bicycle helmet cracks instead of a skull, or if swallowed pills come from a tiny bottle. Reducing harm requires a combined effort from professionals and parents, as I know too well from my own experience described in the following.

"My Baby Swallowed Poison"

Many people think that the way to prevent injury to young children is to educate parents. However, public health research finds that laws that apply to everyone are more effective than education, especially if parents are overwhelmed by the daily demands of child care and money management. Injury rates rise when parents have more than one small child, and not enough money.

For example, thousands of lives have been saved by infant car seats. However, many parents do not voluntarily install car seats. Research has found that parents are more likely to use car seats if given them to take their newborn home from the hospital, and if an expert installs the seat and shows the parents how to use it—not simply tells them or makes them watch a video (Tessier, 2010). New laws mandating car seats and new programs at hospitals have had an effect. In 2013 in the entire United States, only 60 infant passengers died in car accidents, about one-eighth the number in 2003.

The research concludes that motivation and education help, but laws mandating primary prevention are more effective. I know this firsthand. Our daughter Bethany, at age 2, climbed onto the kitchen counter to find, open, and swallow most of a bottle of baby aspirin. Where was I? In the next room, nursing our second child and watching television. I did not notice what Bethany was doing until I checked on her during a commercial.

Bethany is alive and well today, protected by all three levels of prevention defined on the next page. Primary prevention included laws limiting the number of baby aspirin per container; secondary prevention included my pediatrician's written directions when Bethany was a week old to buy syrup of ipecac; tertiary prevention was my phone call to Poison Control.

I told the helpful stranger who answered the phone, "My baby swallowed poison." He calmly asked me a few questions and then advised me to give Bethany ipecac to make her throw up. I did, and she did.

I had bought that ipecac two years before, when I was a brand-new mother and ready to follow every bit of my pediatrician's advice. I might not have done so if the doctor had waited until Bethany was able to climb before he recommended it, because by then I might have had more confidence in my own ability to prevent harm.

I still blame myself, but I am grateful for all three levels of prevention that protected my child. In some ways, my own education helped avert a tragedy. I had chosen a wise pediatrician; I knew the number for Poison Control (FYI: 1-800-222-1222).

As I remember all the mistakes I made in parenting (only a few mentioned in this book), I am grateful for every level of prevention. Without protective laws and a national network to help parents, the results might have been tragic.

Less than half as many 1- to 5-year-olds in the United States were fatally injured in 2014 as in 1984, thanks to laws that limit poisons, prevent fires, and regulate cars. Control has not yet caught up with newer hazards, however. For instance, many new homes in California, Florida, Texas, and Arizona have swimming pools: In those states drowning is a leading cause of child death. According to the American Association of Poison Control Centers' National Poison Data System, children under age 5 are now less often poisoned from pills and more often poisoned because of cosmetics or personal care products (deodorant, hair colorant, etc.) (Mowry et al., 2015, p. 968).

Prevention

Prevention begins long before any particular child, parent, or legislator does something foolish. Unfortunately, no one notices injuries and deaths that did not happen.

Finding the Cause

For developmentalists, two types of analysis are useful to predict and prevent danger. The first is to use a dynamic-systems or ecological approach. Every level must be considered: Causes can be found in the child, the microsystem, the exosystem, and the macrosystem.

For example, when a child is hit by a car, the child might have been impulsive, the parents neglectful (microsystem), the community not child-friendly (no parks,

Solent News/Splash News/Newscom

Forget Baby Henry? Infants left in parked cars on hot days can die from the heat. Henry's father invented a disc to be placed under the baby that buzzes his cell phone if he is more than 20 feet away from the disc. He hopes all absent-minded parents will buy one.

traffic lights, sidewalks, or curbs—all exosystem), and/or the culture may have prioritized fast cars over slow pedestrians (macrosystem). Once all of those factors are recognized, preventive measures on every level become clear, from holding the hand of a young child when crossing the street up to enforcing national speed limits.

The second type of analysis involves understanding statistics. For example, the rate of childhood poisoning decreased markedly when pill manufacturers adopted bottles with safety caps that are difficult for children to open; such a statistic goes a long way in countering individual complaints about inconvenience.

New statistics show a rise in the number of children being poisoned by taking adult recreational drugs, such as cocaine, alcohol, or marijuana, and adult prescription drugs, such as opioids, and being shot by household guns not locked away. Those data can lead to new strategies for prevention (Fine et al., 2012).

Levels of Prevention

Three levels of prevention apply to every health and safety issue.

primary prevention Actions that change overall background conditions to prevent some unwanted event or circumstance, such as injury, disease, or abuse.

secondary prevention Actions that avert harm in a high-risk situation, such as stopping a car before it hits a pedestrian.

tertiary prevention Actions, such as immediate and effective medical treatment, that are taken after an adverse event (such as illness or injury) and that are aimed at reducing harm or preventing disability.

- In **primary prevention,** the overall conditions are structured to make harm less likely. Primary prevention reduces everyone's chance of injury.
- **Secondary prevention** is more targeted, averting harm in high-risk situations or for vulnerable individuals.
- **Tertiary prevention** begins after an injury has already occurred, limiting damage.

In general, tertiary prevention is the most visible of the three levels, but primary prevention is the most effective (L. Cohen et al., 2010). An example comes from data on pedestrian deaths. As compared with 20 years ago, fewer children in the United States today die after being hit by a motor vehicle (see Figure 8.3). How does each level of prevention contribute?

Primary prevention includes sidewalks, pedestrian overpasses, streetlights, and traffic circles. Cars have been redesigned (e.g., better headlights, windows, and

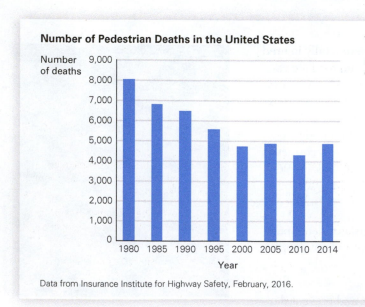

Number of Pedestrian Deaths in the United States

Data from Insurance Institute for Highway Safety, February, 2016.

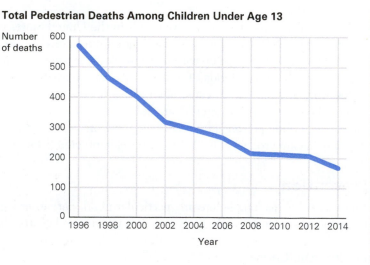

Total Pedestrian Deaths Among Children Under Age 13

FIGURE 8.3

No Matter What Statistic Motor vehicle fatalities of pedestrians, passengers and drivers, from cars, trucks and motorcycles, for people of all ages, are all markedly lower in 2015 than 1995, an especially dramatic difference since the population has increased by a third and the number of cars increased as well. Proof could be shown in a dozen charts, but here is one of the most telling: deaths of child pedestrians. All three levels of prevention, in roads, cars, drivers, police, caregivers, and the children themselves—contributed to this shift.

brakes), and drivers' competence has improved (e.g., stronger penalties for drunk driving). Reduction of traffic via improved mass transit provides additional primary prevention.

Secondary prevention reduces danger in high-risk situations. School crossing guards and flashing lights on stopped schoolbuses are secondary prevention, as are salt on icy roads, warning signs before blind curves, speed bumps, and walk/don't walk signals at busy intersections.

Finally, *tertiary prevention* reduces damage after an accident. Examples include speedy ambulances, efficient emergency room procedures, effective follow-up care, and laws against hit-and-run drivers, all of which have been improved from decades ago. Medical personnel speak of the *golden hour,* the hour following an accident, when a victim should be treated. Of course, there is nothing magical about 60 minutes in contrast to 61 minutes, but the faster an injury victim reaches a trauma center, the better the chance of recovery (Dinh et al., 2013).

Especially for Urban Planners Describe a neighborhood park that would benefit 2- to 5-year-olds. (see response, page 226)

WHAT HAVE YOU LEARNED?

1. What can be concluded from the data on rates of childhood injury?

2. How do injury deaths compare in developed and developing nations?

3. What are some examples of primary prevention?

4. What are some examples of secondary prevention?

Child Maltreatment

Until about 1960, people thought child maltreatment was rare and consisted of a sudden attack by a disturbed stranger, usually a man. Today we know better, thanks to a pioneering study based on careful observation in one Boston hospital (Kempe & Kempe, 1978).

Maltreatment is neither rare nor sudden, and 92 percent of the time the perpetrators are one or both of the child's parents—more often the mother than the father (U.S. Department of Health and Human Services, January 25, 2016). That makes it much worse: Ongoing home maltreatment, with no protector, is much more damaging than a single outside incident, however injurious.

Definitions and Statistics

Child maltreatment now refers to all intentional harm to, or avoidable endangerment of, anyone under 18 years of age. Thus, child maltreatment includes both **child abuse,** which is deliberate action that is harmful to a child's physical, emotional, or sexual well-being, and **child neglect,** which is failure to meet essential needs.

Neglect is worse than abuse. It also is "the most common and most frequently fatal form of child maltreatment" (Proctor & Dubowitz, 2014, p. 27). About three times as many neglect cases occur in the United States as abuse cases, a ratio probably found in many other nations.

To be specific, data on cases of *substantiated* maltreatment in the United States in 2014 indicate that 77 percent were neglect, 17 percent physical abuse, 6 percent emotional abuse, and 8 percent sexual abuse. (A few were tallied in two categories [U.S. Department of Health and Human Services, January 25, 2016].) Ironically, neglect is too often ignored by the public, who are "stuck in an overwhelming and debilitating" concept of maltreatment as something that causes immediate bodily harm (Kendall-Taylor et al., 2014, p. 810).

child maltreatment Intentional harm to or avoidable endangerment of anyone under 18 years of age.

child abuse Deliberate action that is harmful to a child's physical, emotional, or sexual well-being.

child neglect Failure to meet a child's basic physical, educational, or emotional needs.

FIGURE 8.4

Getting Better? As you can see, the number of victims of child maltreatment in the United States has declined in the past decades, an especially good result because the total number of children has increased. One possible explanation is that the legal, social work, and community responses have improved, so fewer children are mistreated. Other less sanguine explanations are possible, however.

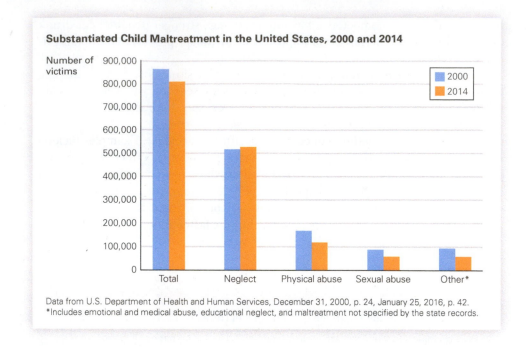

Substantiated Child Maltreatment in the United States, 2000 and 2014

Data from U.S. Department of Health and Human Services, December 31, 2000, p. 24, January 25, 2016, p. 42.
*Includes emotional and medical abuse, educational neglect, and maltreatment not specified by the state records.

substantiated maltreatment Harm or endangerment that has been reported, investigated, and verified.

reported maltreatment Harm or endangerment about which someone has notified the authorities.

Substantiated maltreatment means that a case has been reported, investigated, and verified (see Figure 8.4). In 2014, about 800,000 children suffered substantiated abuse in the United States. Substantiated maltreatment harms about 1 in every 90 children aged 2 to 5 annually.

Reported maltreatment (technically a referral) means simply that the authorities have been informed. Since 1993, the number of children referred to authorities in the United States has ranged from about 2.7 million to 3.6 million per year, with 3.6 million in 2014 (U.S. Department of Health and Human Services, January 25, 2016).

The 5-to-1 ratio of reported versus substantiated cases occurs because:

1. Each child is counted only once, so five verified reports about a single child result in one substantiated case.
2. Substantiation requires proof. Most investigations do not find unmistakable harm or a witness.
3. Many professionals are *mandated reporters,* required to report any signs of *possible* maltreatment. In 2014, two-thirds of all reports came from professionals. Usually an investigation finds no harm (Pietrantonio et al., 2013).
4. Some reports are "screened out" as belonging to another jurisdiction, such as the military or a Native American tribe, who have their own systems. In 2014, many (about 39 percent) referrals were screened out.
5. A report may be false or deliberately misleading (though few are) (Sedlak & Ellis, 2014).

Frequency of Maltreatment

How often does maltreatment actually occur? No one knows. Not all instances are noticed, not all that are noticed are reported, and not all reports are substantiated. Part of the problem is in drawing the line between harsh discipline and abuse, and between momentary and ongoing neglect. If the standard were perfect parenting all day and all night from birth to age 18, as judged by neighbors, professionals, as well as the parent, then every child has been mistreated. Only the most severe cases are tallied.

● **Response for Urban Planners**
(from page 225): The adult idea of a park— a large, grassy open place—is not best for young children. For them, you would design an enclosed area, small enough and with adequate seating to allow caregivers to socialize while watching their children. The playground surface would have to be protective (since young children are clumsy), with equipment that encourages motor skills. Teenagers and dogs should have their own designated area, far from the youngest children.

If we rely on official U.S. statistics, positive trends are apparent. Substantiated child maltreatment increased from about 1960 to 1990 but decreased thereafter (see Figure 8.5). Other sources also report declines, particularly in sexual abuse, over the past two decades. Perhaps national awareness has led to better reporting and then more effective prevention.

Unfortunately, official reports raise doubt. For example, Pennsylvania reports fewer victims than Maine (3,262 compared to 3,823 in 2014), but the child population of Pennsylvania is more than 10 times that of Maine. Why the discrepancy? One hypothesis might be lack of sufficient personnel, but that hypothesis has been proven false: Pennsylvania has 20 times more employees screening and investigating than Maine (2,803 to 145). There is another oddity in the data: Only 3 percent of the Pennsylvania victims are classified as neglected, but 62 percent suffered sexual abuse. (National rates are 75 percent neglect and 8 percent sexual abuse.)

Pennsylvania has the lowest child maltreatment rate of any of the 50 states, but Maine is not highest—Massachusetts is. Does Pennsylvania ignore thousands of maltreated children who would be substantiated victims if they lived in Massachusetts?

How maltreatment is defined is powerfully influenced by culture (one of my students asked, "When is a child too old to be beaten?"). Willingness to report also varies. The United States has become more culturally diverse, and people have become more suspicious of government. Does that reduce reporting but not abuse?

From a developmental perspective, beyond the difficulty in getting accurate data, another problem is that most maltreatment occurs early in life, before children are required to attend school, where a teacher would notice a problem. One infant in 45 is substantiated as maltreated, as is 1 preschooler in 90 (U.S. Department of Health and Human Services, January 25, 2016). Those are substantiated cases; some of the youngest victims never reach outsiders' attention.

Warning Signs

Instead of relying on official statistics and mandated reporters, every reader of this book can recognize developmental problems and prevent harm. Often the first sign of maltreatment is delayed development, such as slow growth, immature communication, lack of curiosity, or unusual social interactions, all evident early in life, before a child comes to the notice of a professional.

In early childhood, maltreated children may seem fearful, startled by noise, defensive and quick to attack, and confused between fantasy and reality. These are symptoms of **post-traumatic stress disorder (PTSD),** first identified in combat veterans, then in adults who had experienced some emotional injury or shock (after a serious accident, natural disaster, or violent crime), and more recently in some maltreated children, who suffer neurologically, emotionally, and behaviorally (Neigh et al., 2009; Weiss et al., 2013).

Table 8.1 lists signs of child maltreatment, both neglect and abuse. None of these signs prove that a child has been abused, but whenever any of them occurs, further investigation is needed. Further, some adults might be troubled by things

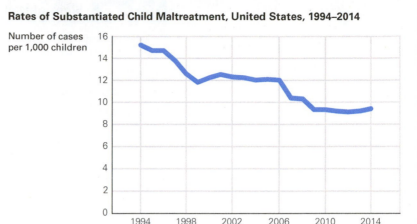

Rates of Substantiated Child Maltreatment, United States, 1994–2014

Data from U.S. Department of Health and Human Services, December 31, 1999, p. 12, December 31, 2000, p. 24, December 31, 2005, p. 26, January, 2010, p. 34, and January 25, 2016, p. 21.

FIGURE 8.5

Still Far Too Many The number of substantiated cases of maltreatment of children under age 18 in the United States is too high, but there is some good news: The rate has declined significantly from its peak (15.3) in 1993.

THINK CRITICALLY: Why might Pennsylvania have so few cases of neglect?

Especially for Nurses While weighing a 4-year-old, you notice several bruises on the child's legs. When you ask about them, the child says nothing and the parent says that the child bumps into things. What should you do? (see response, page 228)

post-traumatic stress disorder (PTSD)
An anxiety disorder that develops as a delayed reaction to having experienced or witnessed a profoundly shocking or frightening event, such as rape, severe beating, war, or natural disaster. Its symptoms may include flashbacks to the event, hyperactivity and hypervigilance, displaced anger, sleeplessness, nightmares, sudden terror or anxiety, and confusion between fantasy and reality.

TABLE 8.1	**Signs of Maltreatment in Children Aged 2 to 10**

Injuries that are unlikely to be accidents, such as bruises on both sides of the face or body; burns with a clear line between burned and unburned skin

Repeated injuries, especially broken bones not properly tended (visible on X-ray)

Fantasy play with dominant themes of violence or sex

Slow physical growth

Unusual appetite or lack of appetite

Ongoing physical complaints, such as stomachaches, headaches, genital pain, sleepiness

Reluctance to talk, to play, or to move, especially if development is slow

No close friendships; hostility toward others; bullying of smaller children

Hypervigilance, with quick, impulsive reactions, such as cringing, startling, or hitting

Frequent absence from school

Frequent change of address

Frequent change in caregivers

Child seems fearful, not joyful, on seeing caregiver

Response for Nurses (from page 227): Any suspicion of child maltreatment must be reported, and these bruises are suspicious. Someone in authority must find out what is happening so that the parent as well as the child can be helped.

that readers of this book know are quite normal, such as preschoolers who do not eat all of their dinner, or who cry when they must stop doing something they enjoy, or who have vivid imaginations.

Consequences of Maltreatment

The consequences of maltreatment involve not only the child but also the entire community. Regarding specifics, much depends on the culture as well as resilience—not only in the child but also in the social context.

Certain customs (such as circumcision, pierced ears, and spanking) are considered abusive among some groups but not in others; their effects vary accordingly. Children suffer if their parents seem to care less than most parents in their neighborhood. If a parent forbids something other children have or punishes more severely or not at all, children might feel unloved.

The long-term effects of maltreatment depend partly on the child's interpretation at the time (punishment considered unfair is especially harmful) and, in adulthood, on the current relationship between the adult and the punishing parent. If the adults have a good relationship (more common if abuse was not chronic), then the adult may recover from past maltreatment (Schafer et al., 2014). It has been said that abused children become abusive parents, but this is not necessarily true (Widom et al., 2015a). Many people avoid repeating the mistakes of their parents, especially if they have friends and partners who show them a better way.

Nonetheless, the consequences of maltreatment may last for decades. The immediate impairment may be obvious, as when a child is bruised, broken, afraid to talk, or failing in school. However, when researchers follow maltreated children over the years, deficits in social skills and self-esteem seem more crippling than physical or intellectual damage.

Maltreated children tend to hate themselves and then hate everyone else. Even if the child was mistreated in the early years and then not after age 5, emotional problems (externalizing for the boys and internalizing for the girls) linger (Godinet et al., 2014). Adult drug abuse, social isolation, and poor health may result from maltreatment decades earlier (Sperry & Widom, 2013; Mersky et al., 2013).

Hate is corrosive. A warm and enduring friendship can repair some damage, but maltreatment makes such friendships less likely. Many studies find that mistreated children typically regard other people as hostile and exploitative; hence, they are less friendly, more aggressive, and more isolated than other children.

The earlier abuse starts and the longer it continues, the worse their relationships are, with physically and sexually abused children likely to be irrationally angry and neglected children often withdrawn (Petrenko et al., 2012). That makes healthy romances and friendships difficult.

Further, finding and keeping a job is a critical aspect of adult well-being, yet adults who were maltreated suffer in this way as well. One study carefully matched 807 children who had experienced substantiated abuse with other children who were of the same sex, ethnicity, and family SES. About 35 years later, long after maltreatment had stopped, those who had been mistreated were 14 percent less likely to be employed than those who had not been abused. The researchers concluded: "abused and neglected children experience large and enduring economic consequences" (Currie & Widom, 2010, p. 111).

In this study, women had more difficulty finding and keeping a job than men. It may be that self-esteem, emotional stability, and social skills are even more important for female employees than for male ones. This study is just one of hundreds of longitudinal studies, all of which find that maltreatment affects people decades after broken bones, or skinny bodies, or medical neglect.

Preventing Maltreatment

Just as with injury control, the ultimate goal with regard to child maltreatment is *primary prevention,* a social network of customs and supports that help parents, neighbors, and professionals protect every child. Neighborhood stability, parental education, income support, and fewer unwanted children all reduce maltreatment.

All of these are examples of primary prevention. Such measures are more effective in the long run, but governments and private foundations are more likely to fund projects that focus on high-risk families (Nelson & Caplan, 2014). The media's focus on shocking examples of parental abuse or social worker neglect ignores the many ways families, communities, and professionals stop maltreatment before it begins.

Secondary prevention involves spotting warning signs and intervening to keep a risky situation from getting worse. For example, insecure attachment, especially of the disorganized type, is a sign of a disrupted parent–child relationship. Thus, insecure attachment should be repaired before it becomes harmful. [**Life-Span Link:** Attachment types are explained in detail in Chapter 7.]

An important aspect of secondary prevention is reporting the first signs of maltreatment. Unfortunately, relatively few reports come from neighbors (5 percent) or relatives (7 percent), who are usually the first to notice when a young child is mistreated. One reason is that they may not know what is normal and what is not. Another reason is that many abusers hide from outsiders, deliberately changing residences and isolating from relatives. Social isolation itself is a worrisome sign.

Tertiary prevention limits harm after maltreatment has occurred. Reporting is the first step; investigating and substantiating is second. The crucial step, however, is helping the caregiver provide better care (specifics may include treating addiction, assigning a housekeeper, locating family helpers, securing better living quarters).

The priority must be child protection. That may mean finding a better caregiver. In every case, **permanency planning** is needed: planning how to nurture the child until adulthood (Scott et al., 2013). Uncertainty, moving, a string of temporary placements, and frequent changes in schools are all destructive.

When children are taken from their parents and entrusted to another adult, that is **foster care.** The other adult might be a stranger or might be a relative, in which case it is called **kinship care.** Foster parents are paid for the child's expenses and trained to provide good care, although specifics vary from state to state. Every year

Family Protection Relatives are a safety net. Ideally, they feed and play with the young members of the family (as these grandfathers do). This is secondary prevention, allowing parents to provide good care. Rarely is tertiary prevention needed. About 1 percent of all U.S. grandparents are foster or adoptive parents of their grandchildren. This does not benefit the adults, but it may be the best solution for mistreated children.

permanency planning An effort by child-welfare authorities to find a long-term living situation that will provide stability and support for a maltreated child. A goal is to avoid repeated changes of caregiver or school, which can be particularly harmful to the child.

foster care A legal, publicly supported system in which a maltreated child is removed from the parents' custody and entrusted to another adult or family, who is reimbursed for expenses incurred in meeting the child's needs.

kinship care A form of foster care in which a relative of a maltreated child, usually a grandparent, becomes the approved caregiver.

Mother–Daughter Love, Finally After a difficult childhood, 7-year-old Alexia is now safe and happy in her mother's arms. Maria Luz Martinez was her foster parent and has now become her adoptive mother.

for the past decade in the United States, almost half a million children have been officially in foster care. At least another million are unofficially in kinship care, because relatives realize that the parents are unable or unwilling to provide good care.

In every nation, most foster children are from low-income, ethnic-minority families—a statistic that reveals problems in the macrosystem as well as the microsystem. In the United States, most foster children have physical, intellectual, and emotional problems that arose in their original families—evidence of their abuse and neglect (Jones & Morris, 2012). Obviously, foster parents need much more than financial subsidies to become good caregivers, a topic further discussed in Chapter 22.

In many cases, the best permanency plan for children is to be adopted by another family, who will care for them lifelong. However, adoption is difficult, for many reasons:

- Judges and biological parents are reluctant to release children for adoption.
- Most adoptive parents prefer infants, but few maltreating adults realize at birth that they cannot be good parents and thus decide that someone else should care for their newborn.
- Some agencies screen out families not headed by heterosexual couples.
- Some professionals insist that adoptive parents be of the same ethnicity and/or religion as the child.

As detailed many times in this chapter, caring for young children is not easy. Parents shoulder most of the burden, and their love and protection usually result in strong and happy children. However, when parents are inadequate and the community is not supportive, complications abound. We all benefit from well-nurtured people; how to achieve that goal is a question we all must answer.

WHAT HAVE YOU LEARNED?

1. Why did few people recognize childhood maltreatment 50 years ago?

2. Why is childhood neglect considered more harmful than abuse?

3. Why is it difficult to know exactly how often child maltreatment occurs?

4. What are the long-term consequences of childhood maltreatment?

5. What are the trends in child maltreatment in the United States?

6. When is foster care a good strategy?

7. Why does permanency planning rarely result in adoption?

SUMMARY

Body Changes

1. Well-nourished children gain weight and height during early childhood at a lower rate than infants do. Proportions change, allowing better body control.

2. Culture, income, and family customs all affect children's growth. Worldwide, an increasing number of children are eating too much unhealthy food, which puts them at risk for many health problems.

3. Although obesity has increased in every nation, in the United States fewer young children are overweight than a decade ago. However, many young children consume too much sugar, which harms their teeth.

4. The brain continues to grow in early childhood, reaching about 75 percent of its adult weight at age 2 and 90 percent by age 6. Much of the increase is in myelination, which speeds transmission of messages from one part of the brain to another.

5. Maturation of the prefrontal cortex allows more reflective, coordinated thought and memory, better planning, and quicker responses. Many young children gradually become less impulsive and less likely to perseverate, although that process continues for many years.

6. The expression and regulation of emotions are fostered by better connections within the limbic system and between that system and other parts of the brain. Childhood trauma may create a flood of stress hormones (especially cortisol) that damage the brain and interfere with learning.

Advancing Motor Skills

7. Gross motor skills continue to develop; clumsy 2-year-olds become 6-year-olds who move their bodies well, guided by their peers, practice, motivation, and opportunity—all of which vary by culture. Playing with other children in safe places helps develop skills that benefit children's physical, intellectual, and social development.

8. Urbanization and chemical pollutants are two factors that hamper development. More research is needed for many elements, but lead is now a proven neurotoxin, and many chemicals increase asthma, decrease oxygen, and impair the brain.

9. Fine motor skills are difficult to master during early childhood. Young children enjoy expressing themselves artistically, which helps them develop their body and finger control. Fortunately, self-criticism is not yet strong.

Injuries and Abuse

10. Accidents cause more child deaths than diseases, with young children more likely to suffer a serious injury or premature death than older children. Close supervision and public safeguards can protect young children from their own eager, impulsive curiosity.

11. In the United States, various preventive measures have reduced the rate of serious injury, but medical measures have reduced disease deaths even faster. Four times as many young children die of injuries than of cancer, the leading cause of disease death in childhood.

12. Injury control occurs on many levels, including long before and immediately after each harmful incident. Primary prevention protects everyone, secondary prevention focuses on high-risk conditions and people, and tertiary prevention occurs after an injury. All three are needed.

Child Maltreatment

13. Child maltreatment includes ongoing abuse and neglect, usually by a child's own parents. Each year, about 3 million cases of child maltreatment are reported in the United States; fewer than 1 million are substantiated, and rates of substantiated abuse have decreased in the past decade.

14. Physical abuse is the most obvious form of maltreatment, but neglect is more common and more harmful. Health, learning, and social skills are all impeded by abuse and neglect, not only during childhood but also decades later.

15. Tertiary prevention may include placement of a child in foster care, including kinship care. Permanency planning is required because frequent changes are harmful to children.

KEY TERMS

myelination (p. 210)
corpus callosum (p. 211)
lateralization (p. 211)
impulse control (p. 212)
perseveration (p. 212)

injury control/harm reduction (p. 222)
primary prevention (p. 224)
secondary prevention (p. 224)
tertiary prevention (p. 224)
child maltreatment (p. 225)

child abuse (p. 225)
child neglect (p. 225)
substantiated maltreatment (p. 226)
reported maltreatment (p. 226)

post-traumatic stress disorder (PTSD) (p. 227)
permanency planning (p. 229)
foster care (p. 229)
kinship care (p. 229)

APPLICATIONS

1. Keep a food diary for 24 hours, writing down what you eat, how much, when, how, and why. Then think about nutrition and eating habits in early childhood. Do you see any evidence in yourself of imbalance (e.g., not enough fruits and vegetables, too much sugar or fat, eating when you are not really hungry)? Did your food habits originate in early childhood, in adolescence, or at some other time?

2. Go to a playground or another place where young children play. Note the motor skills that the children demonstrate, including abilities and inabilities, and keep track of age and sex. What differences do you see among the children?

3. Ask several parents to describe each accidental injury of each of their children, particularly how it happened and what the consequences were. What primary, secondary, or tertiary prevention measures would have made a difference?

4. Think back to your childhood and the friends you had at that time. Was there any maltreatment? Considering what you have learned in this chapter, why or why not?

Early Childhood:
Cognitive Development

What Will You Know?

1. Are young children selfish or just self-centered?
2. Do children get confused if they hear two languages?
3. Is preschool for play or learning?

Asa, not yet 3 feet tall, held a large rubber ball. He wanted me to play basketball with him.

    "We can't play basketball; we don't have a hoop," I told him.

"We can imagine a hoop," he answered, throwing up the ball.

"I got it in," he said happily. "You try."

I did.

"You got it in, too," he announced, and did a little dance.

Soon I was tired, and sat down.

"I want to sit and think my thoughts," I told him.

"Get up," he urged. "You can play basketball and think your thoughts."

Asa is typical. Imagination comes easily to him, and he aspires to the skills of older, taller people in his culture. He thinks by doing, and his vocabulary is impressive; but he does not yet understand that my feelings differ from his, that I would rather sit than throw a ball at an imaginary basket. He does know, however, that I usually respond to his requests.

This chapter describes these characteristics of the young child—imagination, active learning, vocabulary, but also their difficulty in understanding another person's perspective. I hope it also conveys the joy that adults gain when they understand how young children think. When that happens, you might do what I did—get up and play.

Thinking During Early Childhood

You have just learned in Chapter 8 that every year of early childhood advances motor skills, brain development, and impulse control. In Chapter 6, you learned about the impressive development of memory and language in the first two years of life. Each of these developmental advances affects cognition. Thinking during early childhood is multifaceted, creative, and remarkable.

Piaget: Preoperational Thought

Early childhood is the time of **preoperational intelligence,** the second of Piaget's four periods of cognitive development (described in Table 2.3 on p. 45). Piaget called early-childhood thinking *pre*operational because children do not yet use logical operations (reasoning processes) (Inhelder & Piaget, 1964/2013a).

preoperational intelligence
Piaget's term for cognitive development between the ages of about 2 and 6; it includes language and imagination (which involve symbolic thought), but logical, operational thinking is not yet possible at this stage.

Left: Peathegee Inc/Blend Images/Getty Images
Top: Christopher Hope-Fitch/Moment/Getty Images

Red Hot Anger Emotions are difficult for young children to understand, since they are not visible. The Disney-Pixar movie *Inside Out* uses symbolic thought to remedy that—here with green Disgust, red Anger, and purple Fear. What colors are Joy and Sadness?

symbolic thought A major accomplishment of preoperational intelligence that allows a child to think symbolically, including understanding that words can refer to things not seen and that an item, such as a flag, can symbolize something else (in this case, a country).

animism The belief that natural objects and phenomena are alive, moving around, and having sensations and abilities that are human-like.

centration A characteristic of preoperational thought in which a young child focuses (centers) on one idea, excluding all others.

egocentrism Piaget's term for children's tendency to think about the world entirely from their own personal perspective.

focus on appearance A characteristic of preoperational thought in which a young child ignores all attributes that are not apparent.

static reasoning A characteristic of preoperational thought in which a young child thinks that nothing changes. Whatever is now has always been and always will be.

Preoperational children are no longer in the stage of sensorimotor intelligence because they can think in symbols, not just via senses and motor skills. In **symbolic thought,** an object or word can stand for something else, including something out of sight or imagined. Language is the most apparent example of symbolic thought. Words make it possible to think about many things at once.

However, although vocabulary and imagination soar in early childhood, logical connections between ideas are not yet *operational,* which means that young children cannot yet apply their impressive new linguistic ability to comprehend reality.

The word *dog,* for instance, is at first only the family dog sniffing at the child, not yet a symbol (Callaghan, 2013). By age 2, the word becomes a symbol: It can refer to a remembered dog, or a plastic dog, or an imagined dog. Symbolic thought allows for the language explosion (detailed later in this chapter), which enables children to talk about thoughts and memories. Nonetheless, if asked to define the differences between dogs and cats, preschoolers have difficulty contrasting the essential qualities of "dogness" from those of "catness."

Symbolic thought helps explain **animism,** the belief of many young children that natural objects (such as a tree or a cloud) are alive and that nonhuman animals have the same characteristics as the child. Many children's stories include animals or objects that talk and listen (Aesop's fables, *Winnie-the-Pooh, Goodnight Moon, The Day the Crayons Quit*). Preoperational thought is symbolic and magical, not logical and realistic. Childish animism gradually disappears as the mind becomes more mature (Kesselring & Müller, 2011).

Obstacles to Logic

Piaget described symbolic thought as characteristic of preoperational thought. He noted four limitations that make logic difficult until about age 6: centration, focus on appearance, static reasoning, and irreversibility.

Centration is the tendency to focus on one aspect of a situation to the exclusion of all others. Young children may, for example, insist that Daddy is a father, not a brother, because they center on the role that he fills for them. This illustrates a particular type of centration that Piaget called **egocentrism**—literally, "self-centeredness." Egocentric children contemplate the world exclusively from their personal perspective.

Egocentrism is *not* selfishness. One 3-year-old chose to buy a model car as a birthday present for his mother: His "behavior was not selfish or greedy; he carefully wrapped the present and gave it to his mother with an expression that clearly showed that he expected her to love it" (Crain, 2011, p. 133).

A second characteristic of preoperational thought is a **focus on appearance** to the exclusion of other attributes. For instance, a girl given a short haircut might worry that she has turned into a boy. In preoperational thought, a thing is whatever it appears to be—evident in the joy young children have in wearing the hats or shoes of a grown-up, clomping noisily and unsteadily around the living room.

Third, preoperational children use **static reasoning.** They believe that the world is stable, unchanging, always in the state in which they currently encounter it. Many children cannot imagine that their own parents were ever children. If they are told that Grandma is their mother's mother, they still do not understand how people change with maturation. One preschooler wanted his grandmother to tell his mother to never spank him because "she has to do what her mother says."

The fourth characteristic of preoperational thought is **irreversibility.** Preoperational thinkers fail to recognize that reversing a process sometimes restores whatever existed before. A young girl might cry because her mother put lettuce on her sandwich. She might reject the food even after the lettuce is removed because she believes that what is done cannot be undone.

irreversibility A characteristic of preoperational thought in which a young child thinks that nothing can be undone. A thing cannot be restored to the way it was before a change occurred.

Conservation and Logic

Piaget highlighted several ways in which preoperational intelligence disregards logic. A famous set of experiments involved **conservation,** the notion that the amount of something remains the same (is conserved) despite changes in its appearance.

Suppose two identical glasses contain the same amount of pink lemonade, and the liquid from one of these glasses is poured into a taller, narrower glass. When young children are asked whether one glass contains more or, alternatively, if both glasses contain the same amount, those younger than 6 answer that the narrower glass (with the higher level) has more. (See Figure 9.1 for other examples.)

All four characteristics of preoperational thought are evident in this mistake. Young children fail to understand conservation because they focus (*center*) on what they see (*appearance*), noticing only the immediate (*static*) condition. It does not occur to them that they could reverse the process and re-create the level of a moment earlier (*irreversibility*).

Piaget's original tests of conservation required children to respond verbally to an adult's questions. Later research has found that when the tests of logic are simplified or made playful, young children may succeed. They may indicate via eye

conservation The principle that the amount of a substance remains the same (i.e., is conserved) even when its appearance changes.

LaunchPad
macmillan learning

Video Activity: Achieving Conservation focuses on the cognitive changes that enable older children to pass Piaget's conservation-of-liquid task.

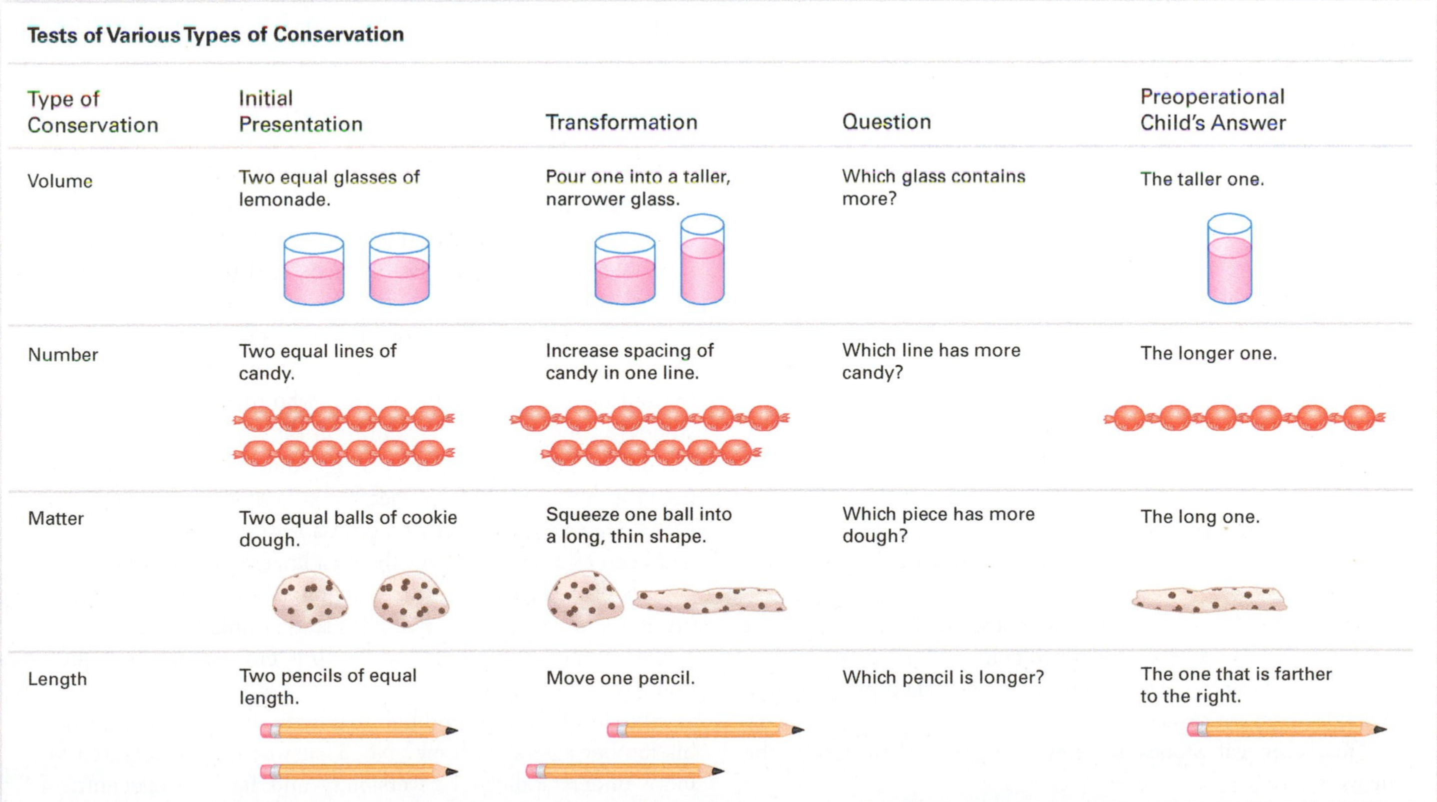

Tests of Various Types of Conservation

Type of Conservation	Initial Presentation	Transformation	Question	Preoperational Child's Answer
Volume	Two equal glasses of lemonade.	Pour one into a taller, narrower glass.	Which glass contains more?	The taller one.
Number	Two equal lines of candy.	Increase spacing of candy in one line.	Which line has more candy?	The longer one.
Matter	Two equal balls of cookie dough.	Squeeze one ball into a long, thin shape.	Which piece has more dough?	The long one.
Length	Two pencils of equal length.	Move one pencil.	Which pencil is longer?	The one that is farther to the right.

FIGURE 9.1

Conservation, Please According to Piaget, until children grasp the concept of conservation at (he believed) about age 6 or 7, they cannot understand that the transformations shown here do not change the total amount of liquid, candies, cookie dough, and pencils.

Easy Question; Obvious Answer *(above left)* Sadie, age 5, carefully makes sure both glasses contain the same amount. *(above right)* When one glass of pink lemonade is poured into a wide jar, she triumphantly points to the tall glass as having more. Sadie is like all 5-year-olds; only a developmental psychologist or a 7-year-old child knows better.

movements or gestures that they know something before they can say it in words (Goldin-Meadow & Alibali, 2013). Further, conservation and many more logical ideas are understood bit by bit, with active, guided experience. Glimmers of understanding may be apparent as young as age 4 (Sophian, 2013).

As with sensorimotor intelligence in infancy, Piaget underestimated what preoperational children could understand. Piaget was right about his basic idea, however: Young children are not very logical (Lane & Harris, 2014). Their cognitive limits make smart 3-year-olds sometimes foolish, as Caleb is.

A CASE TO STUDY

Stones in the Belly

As we were reading a book about dinosaurs, my 3-year-old grandson, Caleb, told me that some dinosaurs (*sauropods*) have stones in their bellies. It helps them digest their food and then poop and pee.

I was amazed, never having known this before.

"I didn't know that dinosaurs ate stones," I said.

"They don't eat them."

"Then how do they get the stones in their bellies? They must swallow them."

"They don't eat them."

"Then how do they get in their bellies?"

"They are just there."

"How did they get there?"

"They don't eat them," said Caleb. "Stones are dirty. We don't eat them."

I dropped it, as I knew that his mother had warned him not to eat pebbles, and I didn't want to confuse him. However, my question apparently puzzled him. Later he asked my daughter, "Do dinosaurs eat stones?"

"Yes, they eat stones so they can grind their food," she answered.

At that, Caleb was quiet.

In all of this, preoperational cognition is evident. Caleb is bright; he can name several kinds of dinosaurs, as can many young children.

But logic eludes Caleb. He is preoperational, not operational.

It seemed obvious to me that dinosaurs must have swallowed the stones. However, in his static thinking, Caleb said the stones "are just there." He rejected the thought that dinosaurs ate stones because he has been told that stones are too dirty to eat.

Caleb is egocentric, reasoning from his own experience, and animistic, in that he thinks other creatures think and act as he himself does. He trusts his mother, who told him never to eat stones, or, for that matter, sand from the sandbox, or food that fell on the floor. My authority as grandmother was clearly less than the authority of his mother, but at least he considered what I said. He was skeptical that a dinosaur would do something he had been told not to do, but the idea lingered rather than being completely rejected. Of course, the implications of my status as his mothers' mother are beyond his static thinking.

Like many young children, Caleb is curious, and my question raised his curiosity.

Should I have expected him to tell me that I was right, when his mother agreed with me? No. That would have required far more understanding of reversibility and far less egocentrism than most young children can muster.

Vygotsky: Social Learning

For decades, the magical, illogical, and self-centered aspects of cognition dominated our conception of early-childhood thought. Scientists were understandably awed by Piaget.

Vygotsky emphasized another side of early cognition—that each person's thinking is shaped by other people's wishes and goals. His focus on the sociocultural aspects of development contrasted with Piaget's emphasis on the individual.

Mentors

Vygotsky believed that cognitive development is embedded in the social context at every age (Vygotsky, 1987). He stressed that children are curious and observant of everything in their world. They ask questions—about how machines work, why weather changes, where the sky ends—and seek answers from more knowledgeable mentors, who might be their parents, teachers, older siblings, or just a stranger. The answers they get are affected by the mentors' perceptions and assumptions—that is, their culture—which shapes their thought.

As you remember from Chapter 2, children learn through *guided participation,* as mentors teach them. Parents are their first guides, although children are guided by many others, too.

According to Vygotsky, children learn because their mentors do the following:

- Present challenges.
- Offer assistance (without taking over).
- Add crucial information.
- Encourage motivation.

Learning from mentors indicates intelligence; according to Vygotsky, "What children can do with the assistance of others might be in some sense even more indicative of their mental development than what they can do alone" (1980, p. 85).

Scaffolding

Vygotsky believed that all individuals learn within their **zone of proximal development (ZPD),** an intellectual arena in which new ideas and skills can be mastered. *Proximal* means "near," so the ZPD includes the ideas and skills children are close to mastering but cannot yet demonstrate independently. Learning depends, in part, on the wisdom and willingness of mentors to provide **scaffolding,** or temporary sensitive support, to help children within their developmental zone.

Good mentors provide plenty of scaffolding, encouraging children to look both ways before crossing the street (pointing out speeding trucks, cars, and buses while holding the child's hand) or letting them stir the cake batter (perhaps covering the

● **Especially for Nutritionists** How can Piaget's theory help you encourage children to eat healthy foods? (see response, page 239)

zone of proximal development (ZPD) Vygotsky's term for the skills—cognitive as well as physical—that a person can exercise only with assistance, not yet independently.

scaffolding Temporary support that is tailored to a learner's needs and abilities and aimed at helping the learner master the next task in a given learning process.

Learning to Button Most shirts for 4-year-olds are wide-necked without buttons, so preschoolers can put them on themselves. But the skill of buttoning is best learned from a mentor, who knows how to increase motivation.

Count by Tens A large, attractive abacus could be a scaffold. However, in this toy store the position of the balls suggests that no mentor is nearby. Children are unlikely to grasp the number system without a motivating guide.

Observation Quiz Is the girl above right-handed or left-handed? (see answer, page 240) ↑

overimitation When a person imitates an action that is not a relevant part of the behavior to be learned. Overimitation is common among 2- to 6-year-olds when they imitate adult actions that are irrelevant and inefficient.

Especially for Driving Instructors Sometimes your students cry, curse, or quit. How would Vygotsky advise you to proceed? (see response, page 240)

child's hand on the spoon handle, in guided participation). Crucial in every activity is joint engagement, when both learner and mentor are actively involved together in the ZPD (Adamson et al., 2014).

Culture matters. In some families and cultures, book-reading is a time for conversation and questions; in others, it is a time for telling the child to be quiet and listen. Parents scaffold whatever they deem important. One study of parents in the United States found that many book-reading parents of Chinese descent pointed out problems that misbehavior caused for the book's characters, while many Mexican Americans highlighted the emotions of the characters (Luo et al., 2014).

Overimitation

Sometimes scaffolding is inadvertent, as when children copy something that adults would rather the child not do. Young children curse, kick, and worse because someone else showed them how.

More benignly, children imitate meaningless habits and customs, a trait called **overimitation.** Children are eager to learn from mentors, allowing "rapid, high-fidelity intergenerational transmission of tool-use skills and for the perpetuation and generation of cultural forms" (Nielsen & Tomaselli, 2010, p. 735).

Overimitation was demonstrated in a series of experiments with 3- to 6-year-olds, 64 of them from San communities (pejoratively called Bushmen) in South Africa and Botswana, and, for comparison, 64 from cities in Australia and 19 from aboriginal communities within Australia. Australian middle-class adults often scaffold for children with words and actions, but San adults rarely do. The researchers expected the urban Australian children but not the San children to follow adult demonstrations (Nielsen et al., 2014). The researchers were wrong.

In part of the study, one by one some children in each group observed an adult perform irrelevant actions such as waving a red stick above a box three times and then using that stick to push down a knob to open the box, which could be easily and more efficiently opened by merely pulling down the same knob by hand. Then children were given the stick and the box. No matter what their culture, they followed the adult example, waving the stick three times and not using their hands directly.

Same or Different? Which do you see? Most people focus on differences, such as ethnicity or sex. But a developmental perspective appreciates similarities: book-reading to a preliterate child cradled on a parent's lap.

Other children did not see the demonstration. When they were given the stick and asked to open the box, they simply pulled the knob. Then they observed an adult do the stick-waving opening—and they copied those inefficient actions, even though they already knew the easy way to open the box. Apparently, children everywhere learn from others through observation as well as from explicit guidance. Across cultures, overimitation is striking and generalizes to other similar situations.

Overimitation is part of a universal trait of young children to follow what adults do. They are "socially motivated" by nature, and that impulse makes them ready to learn as long as the adults structure and guide that learning. Adults do exactly that, using eye contact and facial expressions to facilitate learning (Heyes, 2016).

The process is exquisitely designed in that adults enjoy transmitting knowledge and, for their part, children are automatic imitators—especially when copying is not too difficult: They imitate adults who seem to know what they are doing, even if the adults are not deliberately teaching (Tomasello, 2016; Keupp et al., 2016).

That is exactly what Vygotsky expected and explained: Children are attuned to culture.

Language as a Tool

Although all of the objects of a culture guide children, Vygotsky thought language is pivotal.

First, internal dialogue, called **private speech,** is evident when young children talk aloud to review, decide, and explain events to themselves (and, incidentally, to anyone else within earshot) (Al-Namlah et al., 2012). Older preschoolers are more circumspect, sometimes whispering. Audible or not, private speech aids cognition and self-reflection; adults should encourage it (Perels et al., 2009; Benigno et al., 2011). Many adults use private speech as they talk to themselves when alone or write down ideas.

Second, language advances thinking by facilitating the social interaction that is vital to learning (Vygotsky, 2012). This **social mediation** function of speech occurs as mentors guide mentees in their zone of proximal development, learning numbers, recalling memories, and following routines.

STEM Learning

A practical use of Vygotsky's theory concerns STEM (science, technology, engineering, math) education. Many adults are currently concerned that too few college students choose a STEM career.

Developmentalists find that a person's interest in such vocations begins with learning about numbers and science (counting, shapes, fractions, molecular struc-

private speech The internal dialogue that occurs when people talk to themselves (either silently or out loud).

social mediation Human interaction that expands and advances understanding, often through words that one person uses to explain something to another.

I Want a Pet Young children are more fascinated than afraid of snakes, spiders, and—as shown here at the London Pet Show—scorpions. Although some children are temporarily cautious, phobias are learned, not innate. Many children want a pet; science education may begin here.

ture, the laws of motion) in early childhood. An understanding of math develops month by month, before age 6, as children learn to:

- Count objects, with one number per item (called *one-to-one correspondence*).
- Remember times and ages (bedtime at 8 P.M., a child is 4 years old, and so on).
- Understand sequence (first child wins, last child loses).
- Know which numbers are greater than others (e.g., that 7 is greater than 4).
- Understand how to make things move, from toy cars to soccer balls.
- Appreciate temperature effects, from ice to steam.

Especially in math, computers can promote learning. Educational software becomes "a conduit for collaborative learning" (Cicconi, 2014, p. 58), as Web 2.0 (interactive) programs respond to the particular abilities and needs of each child. In preschool classrooms, several children can work together, each mentoring the others, talking aloud as the computer prompts them. Educators disapprove when a screen undercuts human interaction, but they recognize that computers might be learning tools, just as books might be (Alper, 2013).

By age 3 or 4, children's brains are mature enough to comprehend numbers, store memories, and recognize routines. Whether or not children actually demonstrate such understanding depends on what they hear and how they participate in various activities within their families, schools, and cultures.

Some 2-year-olds hear sentences such as "One, two, three, takeoff," "Here are two cookies," "Dinner in five minutes" several times a day. They are encouraged to touch an interesting bit of moss, or are alerted to the phases of the moon outside their window, or learn about the relationship between pace and steepness of a hill they are climbing.

Other children never hear such comments—and they have a harder time with math in first grade, with science in the third grade, and with STEM curricula when they are older. If words mediate between brain potential and comprehension, this process begins long before formal education.

One manifestation of children's impressive learning ability is in the development of **executive function,** the ability to use the mind to plan, remember, inhibit some impulses, and execute others. This is an ability that develops throughout life, allowing students of all ages to learn from experience, but it first is evident and measured during early childhood (Eisenberg & Zhou, 2016).

executive function The cognitive ability to organize and prioritize the many thoughts that arise from the various parts of the brain, allowing the person to anticipate, strategize, and plan behavior.

Usually these three components comprise executive function: working memory, cognitive flexibility, and inhibitory control—which is the ability to focus on a task and ignore distractions. For instance, one test of executive function during the preschool years is to ask a child to say "night" when seeing a picture of the sun and to say "day" when seeing a picture of the moon. Children who are able to do this are flexible, able to stop their initial impulse. During the preschool years, various programs inspired by Vygotsky (e.g., Tools of the Mind) promote executive function (Liew, 2012).

Children's Theories

Piaget and Vygotsky both recognized that children work to understand their world. No contemporary developmental scientist doubts that. They recognize that young children do more than gain words and concepts; they develop theories to help them understand and remember—theories that arise from both brain maturation and personal experience (Baron-Cohen et al., 2013).

Theory-Theory

theory-theory The idea that children attempt to explain everything they see and hear by constructing theories.

Humans of all ages want explanations, as Chapter 2 emphasizes. **Theory-theory** refers to the idea that children naturally construct theories to explain whatever they see and hear. In other words, the theory about how children think is that they construct a theory.

According to theory-theory, the best explanation for cognition is that humans seek reasons, causes, and underlying principles to make sense of their experience. That requires curiosity and thought, connecting bits of knowledge and observations, which is what young children do. Humans always want theories (even false ones sometimes suffice) to help them understand the world. Especially in childhood, theories are subject to change as new evidence accumulates (Meltzoff & Gopnik, 2013; Bridgers et al., 2016).

Exactly how do children seek explanations? They ask questions, and, if they are not satisfied with the answers, they develop their own theories. For example, one child thought his grandpa died because God was lonely; another thought thunder occurred because God was rearranging the furniture.

Children follow the same processes that scientists do: asking questions, developing hypotheses, gathering data, and drawing conclusions. Of course, their methods lack the rigor of scientific experiments, but questions of physics, biology, and the social sciences are explored: "infants and young children not only detect statistical patterns, they use those patterns to test hypotheses about people and things" (Gopnik, 2012, p. 1625). Their conclusions are not always correct: Like all good scientists, they allow new data to promote revision, although, like all humans, they sometimes stick to their old theories instead of newer versions.

One common theory-theory is that everyone intends to do things correctly. For that reason, when asked to repeat something ungrammatical that an adult says, children often correct the grammar. They theorize that the adult intended to speak grammatically but failed to do so (Over & Gattis, 2010).

This is an example of a general principle: Children theorize about intentions before they imitate what they see. As you have read, when children saw an adult wave a stick before opening a box, the children theorized that, since the adult did it deliberately, stick-waving must somehow be important.

Theory of Mind

Mental processes—thoughts, emotions, beliefs, motives, and intentions—are among the most complicated and puzzling phenomena that humans encounter every day. Adults wonder why people fall in love with the particular persons they do, why they vote for the candidates they do, or why they make foolish choices—from signing for a huge mortgage to buying an overripe cucumber. Children are likewise puzzled about a playmate's unexpected anger, a sibling's generosity, or an aunt's too-wet kiss.

To know what goes on in another's mind, people develop a *folk psychology,* which includes ideas about other people's thinking, called **theory of mind.** Theory of mind is an emergent ability, slow to develop but typically beginning in most children at about age 4 (Carlson et al., 2013).

Some aspects of theory of mind develop sooner, and some later. Longitudinal research finds that the preschool years typically begin with 2-year-olds not knowing that other people think differently than they do but end with 6-year-olds having a well developed theory of mind (Wellman et al., 2011).

Part of theory of mind is understanding that someone else might have a mistaken belief. For example, a child watches a puppet named Max put a toy dog into

theory of mind A person's theory of what other people might be thinking. In order to have a theory of mind, children must realize that other people are not necessarily thinking the same thoughts that they themselves are. That realization seldom occurs before age 4.

Especially for Social Scientists Can you think of any connection between Piaget's theory of preoperational thought and 3-year-olds' errors in this theory-of-mind task? (see response, page 242)

Candies in the Crayon Box Anyone would expect crayons in a crayon box, but once a child sees that candy is inside, he expects that everyone else will also know that candies are inside!

Macmillan Publishers

Response for Social Scientists
(from page 241): According to Piaget, preschool children focus on appearance and on static conditions (so they cannot mentally reverse a process). Furthermore, they are egocentric, believing that everyone shares their point of view. No wonder they believe that they had always known the puppy was in the blue box and that Max would know that, too.

Video: Theory of Mind: False-Belief Tasks

http://qrs.ly/ba4ep0i

© 2016 Macmillan

a red box. Then Max leaves and the child sees the dog taken out of the red box and put in a blue box.

When Max returns, the child is asked, "Where will Max look for the dog?" Without a theory of mind, most 3-year-olds confidently say, "In the blue box"; most 6-year-olds correctly say, "In the red box."

Theory of mind actually develops gradually, progressing from knowing that someone else might have different desires (at about age 3) to knowing that someone might hide their true feelings (about age 6). Culture matters. Even within one nation, regional differences appear, not in the universal progression but in specific examples (Duh et al., 2016). The most notable variations, however, are neurological, not cultural: Children who are deaf or have autism are remarkably slow to develop theory of mind (Carlson et al., 2013).

The development of theory of mind can be seen when young children try to escape punishment by lying. Their faces often betray them: worried or shifting eyes, pursed lips, and so on.

Parents sometimes say, "I know when you are lying," and, to the consternation of most 3-year-olds, parents are usually right.

In one experiment, 247 children, aged 3 to 5, were left alone at a table that had an upside-down cup covering dozens of candies (Evans et al., 2011). The children were told *not* to peek, and the experimenter left the room.

For 142 children (57 percent), curiosity overcame obedience. They peeked, spilling so many candies onto the table that they could not put them back under the cup. The examiner returned, asking how the candies got on the table. Only one-fourth of the participants (more often the younger ones) told the truth.

The rest lied, and their skill increased with their age. The 3-year-olds typically told hopeless lies (e.g., "The candies got out by themselves"); the 4-year-olds told unlikely lies (e.g., "Other children came in and knocked over the cup"). Some of the 5-year-olds, however, told plausible lies (e.g., "My elbow knocked over the cup accidentally").

Brain and Context

This particular study was done in Beijing, China, but the results seem universal: Older children are better liars (see Figure 9.2). Beyond the age differences, the experimenters found that the more logical liars were also more advanced in theory of mind and executive functioning (Evans et al., 2011). That finding occurs in many studies: Both theory of mind and executive function advance as memory improves, experience builds, and the prefrontal cortex matures (Devine & Hughes, 2014).

Children who are slow in language development are also slow in theory of mind, a finding that makes developmentalists suggest that underlying deficits—genetic or neurological—may be crucial for both. Developmentalists suggest that, in addition to specific efforts to improve language skills, therapists need to consider ways to advance executive function (Nilsson & de López, 2016).

Social interactions with other children advance theory of mind and executive function. This is especially evident when the other children are siblings of about the same age (McAlister & Peterson, 2013). As one expert in theory of mind quipped, "Two older siblings are worth about a year of chronological age" (Perner, 2000, p. 383).

Indeed, many studies have found that a child's ability to develop theories correlates with neurological maturation, which also correlates with advances in executive processing—the reflective,

FIGURE 9.2

Better with Age? Could an obedient and honest 3-year-old become a disobedient and lying 5-year-old? Apparently yes, as the proportion of peekers and liars in this study more than doubled over those two years. Does maturation make children more able to think for themselves or less trustworthy?

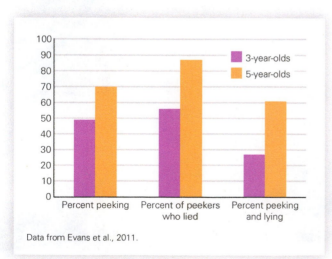

Data from Evans et al., 2011.

anticipatory capacity of the mind (Mar, 2011; Baron-Cohen et al., 2013). Detailed studies find that theory of mind activates several brain regions (Koster-Hale & Saxe, 2013). This makes sense, as theory of mind is a complex ability that humans develop in social contexts, so it is not likely to reside in just one neurological region.

Evidence for crucial brain maturation comes from the other research on the same 3- to 5-year-olds whose lying was studied. The children were asked to say "day" when they saw a picture of the moon and "night" when they saw a picture of the sun. They needed to inhibit their automatic reaction. Their success indicated advanced executive function, which correlated with maturation of the prefrontal cortex.

Even when compared to other children who were the same age, those who failed the day–night tests typically told impossible lies. Their age-mates who were high in executive function told more plausible lies (Evans et al., 2011).

Does the crucial role of neurological maturation make culture and context irrelevant? Not at all: Nurture is always important. The reason that formal education traditionally began at about age 6 is that at that point maturation of the prefrontal cortex naturally allows sustained attention, but many experiences before age 6 can advance brain development and thus ready a child for learning (Blair & Raver, 2015).

Those experiences before age 6 occur naturally as children develop theory of mind in talking with adults or in playing with other children. As brothers and sisters argue, agree, compete, and cooperate, and as older siblings fool younger ones, it dawns on 3-year-olds that not everyone thinks as they do.

By age 5, siblings have learned how to persuade their younger brothers and sisters to give them a toy. Meanwhile, younger siblings figure out how to gain sympathy by complaining that their older brothers and sisters have victimized them. Parents, beware: Asking, "Who started it?" may be irrelevant.

Still Angry Was Mom tired of telling the older sister to play gently? From her expression, it looks as if the younger one doesn't understand why her sister is mad. Do you?

Jamie Grill/Iconica/Getty Images

WHAT HAVE YOU LEARNED?

1. What is not logical about preoperational thought?

2. What is the difference between egocentrism in a child and selfishness in an adult?

3. How does guided participation increase a child's zone of proximal development?

4. Why did Vygotsky think that talking to oneself is an aid to cognition?

5. Why does theory-theory develop?

6. What factors advance theory of mind?

Language Learning

Learning language is the premier cognitive accomplishment of early childhood. Two-year-olds use short, telegraphic sentences ("Want cookie," "Where Daddy go?"), omitting adjectives, adverbs, and articles. By contrast, 5-year-olds seem to be able to say almost anything (see At About This Time) using every part of speech.

A Sensitive Time

Brain maturation, myelination, scaffolding, and social interaction make early childhood ideal for learning language. As you remember from Chapter 1, scientists

AT ABOUT THIS TIME

Language in Early Childhood

Approximate Age	Characteristic or Achievement in First Language
2 years	*Vocabulary:* 100–2,000 words *Sentence length:* 2–6 words *Grammar:* Plurals; pronouns; many nouns, verbs, adjectives *Questions:* Many "What's that?" questions
3 years	*Vocabulary:* 1,000–5,000 words *Sentence length:* 3–8 words *Grammar:* Conjunctions, adverbs, articles *Questions:* Many "Why?" questions
4 years	*Vocabulary:* 3,000–10,000 words *Sentence length:* 5–20 words *Grammar:* Dependent clauses, tags at sentence end ("...didn't I?" "...won't you?") *Questions:* Peak of "Why?" questions; many "How?" and "When?" questions
6 years and up	*Vocabulary:* 5,000–30,000 words *Sentence length:* Some seem unending ("...and...who...and...that...and...") *Grammar:* Complex, depending on what the child has heard, with some children correctly using the passive voice ("Man bitten by dog") and subjunctive ("If I were...") *Questions:* Some about social differences (male–female, old–young, rich–poor) and many other issues

Video Activity: Language Acquisition in Young Children features video clips of a new sign language created by deaf Nicaraguan children and provides insights into how language evolves.

once thought that early childhood was a *critical period* for language learning—the *only* time when a first language could be mastered and the best time to learn a second or third one.

It is easy to understand why they thought so. Young children have powerful motivation and ability to sort words and sounds into meaning (theory-theory). That makes them impressive language learners. However, the critical-period hypothesis is false: Many people learn a new language after age 6.

Instead, early childhood is a *sensitive period* for language learning—for rapidly and easily mastering vocabulary, grammar, and pronunciation. Young children are language sponges; they soak up every verbal drop they encounter.

One of the valuable (and sometimes frustrating) traits of young children is that they talk about many things to adults, to each other, to themselves, to their toys—unfazed by misuse, mispronunciation, ignorance, stuttering, and so on (Marazita & Merriman, 2010). Language comes easily partly because preoperational children are not self-critical about what they say. Egocentrism has advantages; this is one of them.

The Vocabulary Explosion

The average child knows about 500 words at age 2 and more than 10,000 at age 6 (Herschensohn, 2007). That's more than six new words a day. These are averages: Estimates of vocabulary size at age 6 vary from 5,000 to 30,000.

Comprehension is always greater than production, but language proficiency is difficult to measure. Tests vary (Hoffman et al., 2014). For example, after children listened to a book about a raccoon that saw its reflection in the water, they were asked what *reflection* means. Here are five answers:

1. "It means that your reflection is yourself. It means that there is another person that looks just like you."
2. "Means if you see yourself in stuff and you see your reflection."
3. "Is like when you look in something, like water, you can see yourself."
4. "It mean your face go in the water."
5. "That means if you the same skin as him, you blend in." (Hoffman et al., 2014, pp. 471–472)

In another example, when a story included "a chill ran down his spine," children were asked what *chill* meant. One child answered, "When you want to lay down and watch TV—and eat nachos" (Hoffman et al., 2014, p. 473).

Who knows the vocabulary word? None? All? Some number in between?

Fast-Mapping

Children develop interconnected categories for words, a kind of grid or mental map that makes speedy vocabulary acquisition possible. Learning a word after one exposure is called **fast-mapping** (Woodward & Markman, 1998) because, rather than figuring out the exact definition after hearing a word used in several contexts, children hear a word once and quickly stick it into a category in their mental language grid. *Mother* can mean any caregiving woman, for instance.

Picture books offer many opportunities to advance vocabulary through scaffolding and fast-mapping. A mentor might encourage the next steps in the child's zone of proximal development, such as that tigers have stripes and leopards spots, or, for an older child, that calico cats are almost always female and that lions with manes are always male.

This process explains children's learning of colors. Generally, 2-year-olds fast-map color names (K. Wagner et al., 2013). For instance, "blue" is used for some greens or grays. It is not that children cannot see the hues. Instead, they apply words they know to broad categories and have not yet learned the boundaries that adults use, or specifics such as chartreuse, turquoise, olive, navy. As one team of scientists explains, adults' color words are the result of slow-mapping (K. Wagner et al., 2013), which is not what young children do.

Words and the Limits of Logic

Closely related to fast-mapping is a phenomenon called *logical extension:* After learning a word, children use it to describe other objects in the same category. One child told her father she had seen some "Dalmatian cows" on a school trip to a farm. Instead of criticizing her foolishness, he remembered the Dalmatian dog she had petted the weekend before. He realized that she saw Holstein cows, not Jersey ones.

Bilingual children who don't know a word in the language they are speaking often insert a word from the other language, code-switching in the middle of a sentence. That mid-sentence switch may be considered wrong, but actually that is evidence of the child's drive to communicate. Soon, children realize who understands which language, and they avoid substitutions when speaking to a monolingual person. That illustrates theory of mind.

Some words are particularly difficult for every child, such as, in English, *who/whom, have been/had been, here/there, yesterday/tomorrow.* More than one child has awakened on Christmas morning and asked, "Is it tomorrow yet?" A child told

fast-mapping The speedy and sometimes imprecise way in which children learn new words by tentatively placing them in mental categories according to their perceived meaning.

to "stay there" or "come here" may not follow instructions because the terms are confusing. It might be better to say, "Stay there on that bench" or "Come here to hold my hand." Every language has difficult concepts that are expressed in words; children everywhere learn them eventually.

Abstractions are particularly difficult; actions are easier to understand. A hole is to dig; love is hugging; hearts beat.

Acquiring Grammar

Remember from Chapter 6 that *grammar* includes structures, techniques, and rules that communicate meaning. Knowledge of grammar is essential for learning to speak, read, and write. A large vocabulary is useless unless a person knows how to put words together. Each language has its own grammar rules; that's one reason children speak in one-word sentences first.

Children apply rules of grammar as soon as they figure them out, using their own theories about how language works and their experience regarding when and how often various rules apply (Meltzoff & Gopnik, 2013). For example, English-speaking children quickly learn to add an *s* to form the plural: Toddlers follow that rule when they ask for two cookies or more blocks.

Soon they add an *s* to make the plural of words they have never heard before, even nonsense words. If preschoolers are shown a drawing of an abstract shape, told it is called a *wug,* and are then shown two of these shapes, they say there are two *wugs.* Children realize that words have a singular and a plural before they use that grammar form themselves (Zapf & Smith, 2007).

Sometimes children apply the rules of grammar when they should not. This error is called **overregularization**. By age 4, many children overregularize that final *s,* talking about *foots, tooths,* and *mouses.* This signifies knowledge, not lack of it: Many children first say words correctly (*feet, teeth, mice*), repeating what they have heard. Later, they are smart enough to apply the rules of grammar, and overregularize, assuming that all constructions follow the rules (Ramscar & Dye, 2011). The child who says, "I goed to the store" needs to hear, "Oh, you went to the store?" rather than criticism.

More difficult to learn is an aspect of language called **pragmatics**—knowing which words, tones, and grammatical forms to use with whom (Siegal & Surian, 2012). In some languages, it is essential to know which set of words to use when a person is older, or when someone is not a close friend, or when grandparents are on the mother's side or the father's.

overregularization The application of rules of grammar even when exceptions occur, making the language seem more "regular" than it actually is.

pragmatics The practical use of language that includes the ability to adjust language communication according to audience and context.

Camels Protected, People Confused Why the contrasting signs? Does everyone read English at the international airport in Chicago (O'Hare) but not on the main road in Tunisia?

English does not make those distinctions, but pragmatics is important for early-childhood learning nonetheless. Children learn variations in vocabulary and tone depending on the context, and once theory of mind is established, on the audience.

Knowledge of pragmatics is evident when a 4-year-old pretends to be a doctor, a teacher, or a parent. Each role requires different speech. On the other hand, children often blurt out questions that embarrass their parents ("Why is that lady so fat?" or "I don't want to kiss Grandpa because his breath smells."): The pragmatics of polite speech require more social understanding than many young children possess.

Learning Two Languages

Language-minority people (those who speak a language that is not their nation's dominant one) suffer if they do not also speak the majority language (Rosselli et al., 2016). In the United States, those who are not proficient in English have lower school achievement, diminished self-esteem, and inadequate employment, as well as many other problems. Fluency in English erases these liabilities; fluency in another language then becomes an asset.

Early childhood is the best time to learn languages. Neuroscience finds that if adults mastered two languages when they were young, both languages are located in the same areas of the brain with no detriment to the cortex structure (Klein et al., 2014). Being bilingual seems to benefit the brain lifelong, further evidence for plasticity. Indeed, the bilingual brain may provide some resistance to neuro-cognitive disorder due to Alzheimer's disease (formerly called Alzheimer's dementia) in old age (Costa & Sebastián-Gallés, 2014).

Adults can also master the grammar and vocabulary of an unfamiliar language, but pronunciation, idioms, and exceptions to the rules are rarely mastered after puberty. Do not equate pronunciation and spoken fluency with comprehension and reading ability. Many adults who speak the majority language with an accent are nonetheless proficient in the language and culture (difference is not deficit).

From infancy on, hearing is more acute than vocalization. Almost all young children mispronounce whatever language they speak, blithely unaware of their mistakes. They comprehend more than they say, they hear better than they speak, and they learn rapidly as long as people speak to them.

Language Loss and Gains

Language-minority parents fear that their children will make a *language shift,* becoming more fluent in the school language than in their home language. Language shift occurs everywhere when theory-theory leads children to conclude that their first language is inferior to another one (Bhatia & Ritchie, 2013).

Some language-minority children in Mexico shift to Spanish; some children of Canada's First Nations (as native peoples are called there) shift to French; some children in the United States shift to English. In China, all speak some form of Chinese, but some shift occurs from Mandarin, Cantonese, and so on to another.

Remember that young children are preoperational: They center on the immediate status of their language (not on future usefulness or past glory), on appearance more than substance. No wonder many shift toward the language of the dominant culture. Since language is integral to culture, if a child is to become fluently

Bilingual Learners These are Chinese children learning a second language. Could this be in the United States? No, this is a class in the first Chinese-Hungarian school in Budapest. There are three clues: the spacious classroom, the letters on the book, and the trees outside.

ATTILA KISBENEDEK/AFP/Getty Images

● **Especially for Immigrant Parents**
You want your children to be fluent in the language of your family's new country, even though you do not speak that language well. Should you speak to your children in your native tongue or in the new language? (see response, page 250)

bilingual, everyone who speaks with the child should show appreciation of both cultures, and children need to hear twice as much talk as usual (Hoff et al., 2012). Learning one language well makes it easier to learn another (Hoff et al., 2014).

The same practices can make a child fluently trilingual, as some 5-year-olds are. If young children are immersed in three languages, they may speak all three without an accent—except whatever accent their mother, father, and friends have. [**Life-Span Link:** Bilingual education and differences in language learning are discussed further in Chapter 12.]

Listening, Talking, and Reading

Because understanding the printed word is crucial, a meta-analysis of about 300 studies analyzed which activities in early childhood aided reading later on. Both vocabulary and phonics (precise awareness of the sounds of words) predicted literacy (Shanahan & Lonigan, 2010). Five specific strategies and experiences were particularly effective for children of all income levels, languages, and ethnicities.

1. *Code-focused teaching.* In order for children to read, they must "break the code" from spoken to written words. It helps if they learn the letters and sounds of the alphabet (e.g., "A, alligators all around" or, conventionally, "B is for baby").
2. *Book-reading.* Vocabulary as well as familiarity with pages and print will increase when adults read to children, allowing questions and conversation.
3. *Parent education.* When parents know how to stimulate cognition (as in book-reading), children become better readers. Adults need to use words to expand vocabulary.
4. *Language enhancement.* Within each child's zone of proximal development, mentors can expand vocabulary and grammar, based on the child's knowledge and experience.
5. *Preschool programs.* Children learn from teachers, songs, excursions, and other children. (We discuss variations of early education next, but every study finds that preschools advance language acquisition.)

WHAT HAVE YOU LEARNED?

1. What is the evidence that early childhood is a sensitive time for learning language?
2. How does fast-mapping aid the language explosion?
3. How is overregularization a cognitive advance?
4. What in language learning shows the limitations of logic in early childhood?
5. What are the advantages of teaching a child two languages?
6. How can the language shift be avoided in children?

Early-Childhood Schooling

Today, virtually every nation provides some early-childhood education, sometimes financed by the government, sometimes privately, sometimes only for a privileged few, and sometimes for almost every child (Georgeson & Payler, 2013).

In France, Denmark, Norway, and Sweden, more than 95 percent of all 3- to 5-year-olds are enrolled in government-sponsored schools. Norway also pays for education for 1- and 2-year-olds, and 80 percent of them attend (Ellingsaeter, 2014). The reasons for the international variations are historical, economic, and

"We teach them that the world can be an unpredictable, dangerous, and sometimes frightening place, while being careful not to spoil their lovely innocence. It's tricky."

Tricky Indeed Young children are omnivorous learners, picking up habits, curses, and attitudes that adults would rather not transmit. Deciding what to teach—by actions more than words—is essential.

political, but one message from child development research has reached almost every parent and politician worldwide—young children are amazingly capable and eager to learn.

Homes and Schools

Developmental research does not translate directly into specific practices in early education, so no program can legitimately claim to follow Piaget or Vygotsky exactly (Hatch, 2012). This general finding should reassure parents: Young children learn in a variety of settings, and a close relationship to their mothers is maintained whether or not they are in day care full-time. However, developmental theories and understanding of children can inspire educators, suggest hypotheses, and advance ideas.

Beyond the amazing potential of young children to learn, another robust conclusion from research on children's learning seems not yet universally understood: Quality matters (Gambaro et al., 2014). If the home learning environment is poor, a good preschool program aids health, cognition, and social skills. If, instead, a family provides excellent learning, children still benefit from attending a high-quality preschool, but they do not benefit as much as less fortunate children.

Indeed, it is better for children to be in excellent home care than in a low-quality, overcrowded day-care center. One expert criticizes inadequate subsidies that result in low-quality care: "Parents can find cheap babysitting that's bad for their kids on their own. They don't need government help with that" (Barnett, quoted in Samuels & Klein, 2013, p. 21).

Quality is difficult to judge, and competition does not necessarily improve it: "[B]ecause quality is hard for parents to observe, competition seems to be

Response for Immigrant Parents (from page 248): Children learn by listening, so it is important to speak with them often. Depending on how comfortable you are with the new language, you might prefer to read to your children, sing to them, and converse with them primarily in your native language and find a good preschool where they will learn the new language. The worst thing you could do is to restrict speech in either tongue.

Especially for Teachers In trying to find a preschool program, what should parents look for? (see response, page 252)

Especially for Unemployed Early-Childhood Teachers You are offered a job in a program that has ten 3-year-olds for every adult. You know that is too many, but you want a job. What should you do? (see response, page 252)

dominated by price" (Gambaro et al., 2014, p. 22). To save money and make a profit, programs hire fewer teachers—so saving money may reduce quality.

Quality cannot be judged by the name of a program or by its sponsorship. Educational institutions for 3- to 5-year-olds are called preschools, nursery schools, day-care centers, pre-primary programs, pre-K classes, and kindergartens. Sponsors can be public (federal, state, or city), private, religious, or corporate. Further, children, parents, and cultures differ, so an excellent program for one child might be less effective for another.

Professional assessment of quality also seems inadequate, if the goal of preschool is to further math, reading, and social skills (Sabol et al., 2013). However, one aspect—child–teacher interaction—does correlate with more learning. A bad sign is a teacher who sits and watches; look for teachers who talk, laugh, guide, and play with the children.

In order to sort through this variety, we review some distinctions among types of programs. One broad distinction concerns the program goals. Is the goal to encourage each child's creative individuality (*child-centered*) or to prepare the child for formal education (*teacher-directed*), or is it to prepare low-SES children for school (*intervention*, such as *Head Start*)?

Child-Centered Programs

Many programs are called *child-centered*, or *developmental*, because they stress each child's development and growth. Teachers in such programs believe children need to follow their own interests rather than adult directions. For example, they agree that "children should be allowed to select many of their own activities from a variety of learning areas that the teacher has prepared" (Lara-Cinisomo et al., 2011). The physical space and the materials (such as dress-up clothes, art supplies, puzzles, blocks, and other toys) are arranged to allow exploration.

Most child-centered programs encourage artistic expression. Some educators argue that young children are gifted in seeing the world more imaginatively than

Tibet, China, India, and . . . Italy? Over the past half-century, as China increased its control of Tibet, thousands of refugees fled to northern India. Tibet traditionally had no preschools, but young children adapt quickly, as in this preschool program in Ladakh, India. This Tibetan boy is working a classic Montessori board.

© infocusphotos.com/Alamy

older people do. According to advocates of child-centered programs, this peak of creative vision should be encouraged; children need many opportunities to tell stories, draw pictures, dance, and make music for their own delight.

That does not mean that academics are ignored. Advocates of math learning, for instance, believe that children have a natural interest in numbers and that child-centered schools can guide those interests as children grow (Stipek, 2013).

Child-centered programs are often influenced by Piaget, who emphasized that each child will discover new ideas if given a chance, or by Vygotsky, who thought that children learn from playing, especially with other children, with adult guidance.

Montessori Schools

One type of child-centered school began in the slums of Rome in 1907, when Maria Montessori opened a nursery school (Standing, 1998). She believed that children needed structured, individualized projects to give them a sense of accomplishment. Her students completed puzzles, used sponges and water to clean tables, traced shapes, and so on.

Contemporary **Montessori schools** still emphasize individual pride and achievement, presenting many literacy-related tasks (e.g., outlining letters and looking at books) to young children. Specific materials differ from those that Montessori developed, but the underlying philosophy is the same. Children seek out learning tasks; they do not sit quietly in groups while a teacher instructs them. That makes Montessori programs child-centered (Lillard, 2013).

> **Montessori schools** Schools that offer early-childhood education based on the philosophy of Maria Montessori, which emphasizes careful work and tasks that each young child can do.

Reggio Emilia

Another form of early-childhood education is **Reggio Emilia,** named after the town in Italy where it began. In Reggio Emilia, children are encouraged to master skills that are not usually taught in North American schools until age 7 or so, such as writing and using tools. Although many educators worldwide admire the Reggio philosophy and practice, it is expensive to duplicate in other nations—there are few dedicated Reggio Emilia schools in the United States.

Reggio schools do not provide large-group instruction, with lessons in, say, forming letters or cutting paper. Instead, hands-on activities chosen by individual children, such as drawing, cooking, and gardening, are stressed. Measurement of achievement, such as standardized testing to see whether children recognize the 26 letters of the alphabet, is antithetical to the conviction that each child should explore and learn in his or her own way. Each child's learning is documented via scrapbooks, photos, and daily notes—not to measure progress but to help the child and the parent take pride in accomplishments (Caruso, 2013).

> **Reggio Emilia** A program of early-childhood education that originated in the town of Reggio Emilia, Italy, and that encourages each child's creativity in a carefully designed setting.

> **Child-Centered Pride** How could Rachel Koepke, a 3-year-old from a Wisconsin town called Pleasant Prairie, seem so pleased that her hands (and cuffs) are blue? The answer arises from northern Italy—Rachel attended a Reggio Emilia preschool that encourages creative expression.

Appreciation of the arts is evident. Every Reggio Emilia school originally had a studio, an artist, and space to encourage creativity (Forbes, 2012). Children's art is displayed on white walls and hung from high ceilings, and floor-to-ceiling windows open to a spacious, plant-filled playground. Big mirrors are part of the schools' décor—again, with the idea of fostering individuality and self-expression. However, individuality does not mean that children do not work together. On the contrary, group projects are encouraged.

Often those group projects include exploring some aspect of the natural world. One analysis of Reggio Emilia in the United States found "a science-rich context that

ELIZABETH FLORES KRT/Newscom

Response for Teachers
(from page 250): Tell parents to look at the
people more than the program. Parents
should see the children in action and note
whether the teachers show warmth and
respect for each child.

**Response for Unemployed Early-
Childhood Teachers** (from page 250):
It would be best for you to wait for a job
in a program in which children learn well,
organized along the lines explained in this
chapter. You would be happier, as well as
learn more, in a workplace that is good for
children. Realistically, though, you might feel
compelled to take the job. If you do, change
the child/adult ratio—find a helper, perhaps
a college intern or a volunteer grandmother.
But choose carefully—some adults are
not helpful at all. Before you take the job,
remember that children need continuity:
You can't leave simply because you find
something better.

triggered and supported preschoolers' inquiries and effectively engaged preschoolers' hands, heads, and hearts with science" (Inan et al., 2010, p. 1186).

Teacher-Directed Programs

Teacher-directed preschools stress academics, often taught by one adult to the entire group. The curriculum includes learning the names of letters, numbers, shapes, and colors according to a set timetable; every child naps, snacks, and goes to the bathroom on schedule as well. Children learn to sit quietly and listen to the teacher. Praise and other reinforcements are given for good behavior, and time-outs (brief separation from activities) are imposed to punish misbehavior.

The goal of teacher-directed programs is to make all children "ready to learn" when they enter elementary school. For that reason, basic skills are stressed, including precursors to reading, writing, and arithmetic, perhaps through teachers asking questions that children answer together in unison. Behavior is also taught, as children learn to respect adults, to follow schedules, to hold hands when they go on outings, and so on.

Children practice forming letters, sounding out words, counting objects, and writing their names. If a 4-year-old learns to read, that is success. (In a child-centered program, that might arouse suspicion that there was too little time to play or socialize.)

Many teacher-directed programs were inspired by behaviorism, which emphasizes step-by-step learning and repetition, with reinforcement (praise, gold stars, prizes) for accomplishment. Another inspiration for teacher-directed programs comes from information-processing research indicating that children who have not learned basic vocabulary and listening skills by kindergarten often fall behind in primary school. Many state legislatures mandate that preschoolers master specific concepts, an outcome best achieved by teacher-directed learning (Bracken & Crawford, 2010).

Comparing Child-Centered and Teacher-Directed Learning

Most developmentalists advocate child-centered programs. They fear that the child's joy and creativity will be squashed if there are specific goals set for all

Learning from One Another Every nation creates its own version of early education. In this scene in Kuala Lumpur, Malaysia, note the head coverings, uniforms, and distance between the sexes. None of these elements would be found in most early-childhood-education classrooms in North America or Europe, but none of them enhances or inhibits learning for these children.

MOHD RASFAN/AFP/Getty Images

children. On the other hand, many parents and legislators want proof that children are learning things that will help them read, add, and so on.

As Penelope Leach wrote, "Goals come from the outside. . . . It is important that people see early learning as coming from inside children because that's what makes clear its interconnectedness with play, and therefore the inappropriateness of many 'learning goals'" (Leach, 2011, p. 17). More specifically, one developmentalist writes, "why should we settle for unimaginative goals . . . like being able to identify triangles and squares, or recalling the names of colors and seasons" (Christakis, 2016).

Many developmentalists resist legislative standards and academic tests for young children, arguing that social skills and creative play are essential for healthy development but difficult to measure. A truly brilliant child is characterized by all the complex skills of executive function, not the easy-to-measure skills of letter recognition (Golinkoff & Hirsch-Pasek, 2016). [**Life-Span Link:** Children's play is discussed in Chapter 10.]

Finding the right balance between formal and informal assessment, and between child-centered and teacher-directed learning, is a goal of many educators who hope each child has the education that works best for him or her (Fuligni et al., 2012).

Intervention Programs

Several programs designed for children from low-SES families were established in the United States decades ago. Some solid research on the results of these programs is now available.

Head Start

In the early 1960s, millions of young children in the United States were thought to need a "head start" on their formal education to foster better health and cognition before first grade. Consequently, since 1965, the federal government has funded a massive program for 4-year-olds called **Head Start**.

The goals for Head Start have changed over the decades, from lifting families out of poverty to promoting literacy, from providing dental care and immunizations

Head Start A federally funded early-childhood intervention program for low-income children of preschool age.

If You're Happy and You Know It Gabby Osborne (pink shirt) has her own way of showing happiness, not the hand-clapping that Lizalia Garcia tries to teach. The curriculum of this Head Start class in Florida includes learning about emotions, contrary to the wishes of some legislators, who want proof of academics.

to teaching Standard English, from focusing on 4-year-olds to including 2- and 3-year-olds. Although initially most Head Start programs were child-centered, they have become increasingly teacher-directed as waves of legislators have approved and shaped them. Children learn whatever their particular teachers emphasize. Not surprisingly, specific results vary by program and cohort.

For example, many low-income 3- and 4-year-olds in the United States are not typically exposed to math. After one Head Start program engaged children in a board game with numbers, their mathematical understanding advanced significantly (Siegler, 2009).

A 2007 congressional reauthorization of funding for Head Start included a requirement for extensive evaluation to answer three questions:

1. What difference does Head Start make to key outcomes of development and learning (in particular, school readiness) for low-income children?
2. How does Head Start affect what parents do with their children?
3. Under what circumstances and for whom does Head Start achieve the greatest impact?

The answers were not as dramatic as either advocates or detractors had hoped (U.S. Department of Health and Human Services, 2010). Head Start improved literacy and math skills, oral health, and parental responsiveness during early childhood. However, many academic benefits faded by first grade. One explanation is that, unlike when Head Start began, many children in the comparison group were enrolled in other early-childhood programs—sometimes excellent ones, sometimes not. Another explanation is that the elementary schools for low-SES children were of low quality, so the Head Start children sank back to the norm.

The research found that benefits were strongest for children in poverty, or in rural areas, or with disabilities (U.S. Department of Health and Human Services, 2010). They are least likely to find other sources of early education, largely because of their parents' income, location, and stress (Crosnoe et al., 2016).

The data show that most Head Start children of every background advanced in many areas of language and social skills, but by elementary school the comparison children often caught up. However, there was one area in which the Head Start children maintained their superiority—vocabulary.

That finding also supports what you just learned about language development. Any good preschool will introduce children to words they would not learn at home. Children will fast-map those words, gaining a linguistic knowledge base that facilitates expanded vocabulary throughout life.

A recent study of children born in 2001 found that those who went to Head Start were advanced in math and language, but, compared to similar children who had only their mother's care, they had more behavior problems, according to their teachers (R. Lee et al., 2014). Of course, one interpretation of that result is that the teachers reacted negatively to the self-assertion of the Head Start children, rating the children's attitude a problem when really it was the teachers who needed attitude adjustment.

Long-Term Gains from Intensive Programs

This discussion of philosophies, practices, and programs may give the impression that the research on early-childhood cognition is contradictory. That is not true. Specifics are debatable, but empirical evidence and longitudinal evaluation find that preschool education advances learning. Ideally, each program has a curriculum that guides practice, all the adults collaborate, and experienced teachers respond to each child.

The best longitudinal evidence comes from three intensive programs that enrolled children for years—sometimes beginning with home visits in infancy, sometimes continuing in after-school programs through first grade. One program, called *Perry* (or *High/Scope*), was spearheaded in Michigan (Schweinhart & Weikart, 1997); another, called *Abecedarian,* got its start in North Carolina (Campbell et al., 2001); a third, called *Child–Parent Centers,* began in Chicago (Reynolds, 2000). All focused on children from low-SES families.

All three programs compared experimental groups of children with matched control groups, and all reached the same conclusion: Early education has substantial long-term benefits that become most apparent when children are in the third grade or later. By age 10, children who had been enrolled in any one of these three programs scored higher on math and reading achievement tests than did other children from the same backgrounds, schools, and neighborhoods. They were less likely to be placed in classes for children with special needs, or to repeat a year of school, or to drop out of high school before graduation.

An advantage of decades of longitudinal research is that teenagers and adults who received early education can be compared with those who did not. For all three programs, early investment paid off. In adolescence, the children who had undergone intensive preschool education had higher aspirations, possessed a greater sense of achievement, and were less likely to have been abused. As young adults, they were more likely to attend college and less likely to go to jail. As middle-aged adults, they were more often employed, paying taxes, healthy, and not needing government subsidies (Reynolds & Ou, 2011; Schweinhart et al., 2005; Campbell et al., 2014).

All three research projects found that providing direct cognitive training, with specific instruction in various school-readiness skills, was useful. Each child's needs and talents were considered—a circumstance made possible because the

Frank Porter Graham Child Development Institute

Lifetime Achievement The baby in the framed photograph escaped the grip of poverty. The woman holding it proved that early early education can transform children. She is Frances Campbell, who spearheaded the Abecedarian Project. The baby's accomplishments may be the more impressive of the two.

child/adult ratio was low. This combined child-centered and teacher-directed programs, with all the teachers working together on the same goals, so children were not confused. The parents reinforced what the children learned. In all three, teachers deliberately involved parents, and each program included strategies to enhance the home–school connection.

These programs were expensive (ranging from $6,000 to $18,000 annually per young child in 2014 dollars). From a developmental perspective, the decreased need for special education and other social services later on made early education a "wise investment" (Duncan & Magnuson, 2013, p. 128). Additional benefits to society over the child's lifetime, including increased employment and tax revenues, as well as reduced crime, are worth much more than the cost of the programs.

Among developed nations, the United States is an outlier, least likely to support new mothers or young children. However, in the past decade, some states (e.g., Oklahoma, Georgia, Florida, New Jersey, and Illinois) and some cities (e.g., New York, Boston, Cleveland, San Antonio, and Los Angeles) have offered preschool to every 4-year-old. Although this investment generally results in fewer children needing special education later on, implementation and results are controversial—a topic for further research.

As of 2014, 40 states sponsored some public education for young children—usually only for 4-year-olds. More than a million children (1,347,072) attended state-sponsored preschools. Although these numbers include some 3-year-olds, it is estimated that 29 percent of all 4-year olds were in state-sponsored preschool, twice as many as a decade earlier (Barnett et al., 2015). About another 10 percent attended the federal program, Head Start, and an estimated 3 percent were in special publicly-funded programs for children with disabilities (U.S. Department of Education, 2015).

Most state programs pay only for children living in poverty, but some wealthy families pay tuition for preschool education. Private schools may be very expensive—as much as $30,000 a year. Not surprisingly, in the United States, families in the highest income quartile are more likely to have their 3- and 4-year-olds in an educational program than the national average (see Visualizing Development, p. 257).

The increases in government-sponsored preschool for 4-year-olds is good news, but developmentalists note that in the United States, unlike in Europe, almost half of all 4-year-olds and most 3-year-olds are not in any educational program. The children least likely to be in such programs are Spanish-speaking, or if the family income is slightly above poverty-level, or if the mother is not employed. In all three situations, a good early-education program would be especially helpful.

The other problem is that states save money in ways that do not promote learning. Spending per child has been decreasing. In inflation-adjusted dollars, per-pupil spending by states was $5,129 per child in 2002 and $4,121 in 2014 (Barnett et al., 2015). That means less child-centered learning (which is more expensive) and more teacher-directed education.

Compared to a decade ago, much more is known about early cognition: 2- to 4-year-olds are capable of learning languages, concepts, math, theory of mind, and much more. What a child learns before age 6 is pivotal for later schooling and adult life. The amazing potential of young children is also a theme of the next chapter, where we discuss other kinds of learning—in emotional regulation, social skills, and more.

Early-Childhood Schooling

Preschool can be an academic and social benefit. Around the world, increasing numbers of children are enrolled in early-childhood education.

Programs are described as "teacher-directed" or "child-centered," but in reality, most teachers' styles reflect a combination of both approaches. Some students benefit more from the order and structure of a teacher-directed classroom, while others work better in a more collaborative and creative environment.

TEACHER-DIRECTED APPROACH
Focused on Getting Preschoolers Ready to Learn

Direct instruction
Teacher as formal authority
Students learn by listening
Classroom is orderly and quiet
Teacher fully manages lessons
Fosters autonomy of each individual
Encourages academics
Students learn from teacher

CHILD-CENTERED APPROACH
Focused on Individual Development and Growth

Teacher as facilitator
Teacher as delegator
Students learn actively
Classroom is designed for collaborative work
Students influence content
Fosters collaboration among students
Encourages artistic expression
Students learn from each other

WORTH PUBLISHERS

DIFFERENT STUDENTS, DIFFERENT TEACHERS

There is no "one right way" to teach children. Each approach has potential benefits and pitfalls. A classroom full of creative, self-motivated students can thrive when a gifted teacher acts as a competent facilitator. But students who are distracted or annoyed by noise, or who are shy or intimidated by other children, can blossom under an engaging and encouraging teacher in a more traditional environment.

Done Well

Teacher-Directed	Child-Centered
• engaging teacher	• emphasizes social skills and emotion regulation
• clear, consistent assessment	• encourages critical thinking
• reading and math skills emphasized	• builds communication skills
• quiet, orderly classroom	• fosters individual achievement
• all students treated equally	• encourages creativity and curiosity

Teacher-Directed ←→ **Child-Centered**

Teacher-Directed	Child-Centered
• bored students	• chaotic/noisy classrooms
• passive learning	• students may miss/avoid important knowledge and skills
• less independent, critical thinking	• inconclusive assessment of student progress
• teacher may dominate	• some students may dominate classroom

Done Poorly

SUMMARY

Thinking During Early Childhood

1. Piaget stressed the egocentric and illogical aspects of thought during early childhood. He called this stage of thinking preoperational intelligence because young children do not yet use logical operations to think about their observations and experiences.

2. Young children, according to Piaget, sometimes focus on only one thing (centration) and see things only from their own viewpoint (egocentrism), remaining stuck on appearances and current reality. They may believe that living spirits reside in inanimate objects and that nonhuman animals have the same characteristics they themselves have, a belief called animism.

3. Vygotsky stressed the social aspects of childhood cognition, noting that children learn by participating in various experiences, guided by more knowledgeable adults or peers. Such guidance assists learning within the zone of proximal development, which encompasses the knowledge children are close to understanding and the skills they can almost master.

4. According to Vygotsky, the best teachers use various hints, guidelines, and other tools to provide a child with a scaffold for new learning. Language is a bridge that provides social mediation between the knowledge that the child already has and the learning that the society hopes to impart. For Vygotsky, words are tools for learning.

5. Children develop theories, especially to explain the purpose of life and their role in it. One theory about children's thinking is called "theory-theory"—the hypothesis that children develop theories because all humans innately seek explanations for everything they observe.

6. An example of the developing cognition of young children is theory of mind—an understanding of what others may be thinking. Theory of mind begins at around age 4, partly as a result of maturation of the brain. Culture and experiences also influence its development.

Language Learning

7. Language develops rapidly during early childhood, a sensitive period but not a critical one for language learning. Vocabulary increases dramatically, with thousands of words added between ages 2 and 6. In addition, basic grammar is mastered.

8. Many children learn to speak more than one language, gaining cognitive as well as social advantages. Early childhood is the best time to learn two languages. The benefits of bilingualism are lifelong. Pronunciation lags behind production, which lags behind comprehension.

Early-Childhood Schooling

9. Organized educational programs during early childhood advance cognitive and social skills, although specifics vary a great deal. The quality of a program cannot be judged by the name or by appearance.

10. Montessori and Reggio Emilia are two child-centered programs that began in Italy and are now offered in many nations. They stress individual interests of each child, including creative play, inspired by Piaget and Vygotsky.

11. Behaviorist principles led to many specific practices of teacher-directed programs. Children learn to listen to teachers and become ready for kindergarten.

12. Head Start is a U.S. federal government program primarily for low-income children. Longitudinal research finds that early-childhood education reduces the risk of later problems, such as needing special education. High-quality programs increase the likelihood that a child will become a law-abiding, gainfully employed adult.

13. Many types of preschool programs are successful. It is the quality of early education that matters. The training, warmth, and continuity of early-childhood teachers benefit children in many ways.

14. Some nations provide early education for all 3- and 4-year-olds. The United States is slower on this metric, with only about half of all 4-year-olds in preschool, and far fewer 3-year-olds.

KEY TERMS

preoperational intelligence
   (p. 233)
symbolic thought (p. 234)
animism (p. 234)
centration (p. 234)
egocentrism (p. 234)
focus on appearance (p. 234)

static reasoning (p. 234)
irreversibility (p. 235)
conservation (p. 235)
zone of proximal development
   (ZPD) (p. 237)
scaffolding (p. 237)

overimitation (p. 238)
private speech (p. 239)
social mediation (p. 239)
executive function (p. 240)
theory-theory (p. 240)
theory of mind (p. 241)

fast-mapping (p. 245)
overregularization (p. 246)
pragmatics (p. 246)
Montessori schools (p. 251)
Reggio Emilia (p. 251)
Head Start (p. 253)

APPLICATIONS

The best way to understand thinking in early childhood is to listen to a child, as Applications 1 and 2 require. If some students have no access to children, they should do Application 3 or 4.

1. Replicate one of Piaget's conservation experiments. The easiest one is conservation of liquids (Figure 9.1). Work with a child under age 5 who tells you that two identically shaped glasses contain the same amount of liquid. Then carefully pour one glass of liquid into a narrower, taller glass. Ask the child if one glass now contains more or if the glasses contain the same amount.

2. To demonstrate how rapidly language is learned, show a preschool child several objects and label one with a nonsense word that the child has never heard. (*Toma* is often used; so is *wug*.) Or choose a word the child does not know, such as *wrench, spatula,* or the name of a coin from another nation. Test the child's fast-mapping.

3. Theory of mind emerges at about age 4, but many adults still have trouble understanding other people's thoughts and motives. Ask several people why someone in the news did whatever he or she did (e.g., a scandal, a crime, a heroic act). Then ask your informants how sure they are of their explanation. Compare and analyze the reasons as well as the degrees of certainty. (One person may be sure of an explanation that someone else thinks is impossible.)

4. Think about an experience in which you learned something that was initially difficult. To what extent do Vygotsky's concepts (guided participation, zone of proximal development) explain the experience? Write a detailed, step-by-step account of your learning process as Vygotsky would have described it.

Early Childhood:
Psychosocial Development

What Will You Know?

1. Why do 2-year-olds have more sudden tempers, tears, and terrors than 6-year-olds?
2. What do children learn from playing with each other?
3. What happens if parents let their children do whatever they want?

I was early to pick up my grandson, so I waited while the after-school teacher tried to encourage imagination in a circle of 4-year-olds.

"What would you like to be?" she asked, expecting them to say some sort of animal, perhaps a bear or a lion, or some sort of professional, perhaps a teacher or a police officer.

One girl said "princess"; another said "ballerina." All of the girls smiled approvingly. One boy said "Superman"; my grandson said "Spider-Man." Smiles from the boys. The teacher kept trying. She asked another boy.

"Spider-Man," he said.

"Think of something else," she said.

"I can't," he answered, and his best friend laughed.

That was not what the teacher expected. She switched activities; she had them all sing a song they knew.

I was surprised, too. This was 2014, in Brooklyn, New York. The parents of these children resist gender stereotypes. I once asked my son-in-law to use his "man hands" to open a stubborn jar of tomato sauce, and my daughter, scowling, said "that's sexist, Mom."

If I had remembered this chapter, I might not have been surprised. Preschoolers have definite ideas of male–female roles, often more rigid than their parents. They insist on their own opinions even when adults ask them to think of something else. Their self-confidence and the importance of peer approval are part of growing up, as is the fact that these children sat in a circle and listened to each other. The social world of the young child expands, sometimes in ways that adults do not expect.

Emotional Development

Controlling the expression of feelings, called **emotional regulation,** is the preeminent psychosocial task between ages 2 and 6. Emotional regulation is a lifelong endeavor, but it develops most rapidly in early childhood (Gross, 2014; Lewis, 2013).

By age 6, most children can be angry, frightened, sad, anxious, or proud without the explosive outbursts of temper, or terror, or tears of 2-year-olds. Depending on training and temperament, some emotions are easier for a child to control than others, but even temperamentally angry or fearful children learn to regulate their emotions (Moran et al., 2013; Tan et al., 2013; Suurland et al., 2016).

emotional regulation The ability to control when and how emotions are expressed.

self-concept A person's understanding of who he or she is, in relation to self-esteem, appearance, personality, and various traits.

In the process of emotional regulation, children develop their **self-concept,** which is their idea of who they are. Remember that 1-year-olds begin to recognize themselves in the mirror, the start of self-awareness. In early childhood they begin to understand some of their characteristics, which include what emotions they feel and how they express them. That is probably true for all children everywhere, although specifics of parental guidance and encouragement make a difference (LeCuyer & Swanson, 2016).

Indeed, for all aspects of self-concept and emotional regulation, culture and family matter. Children may be encouraged to laugh/cry/yell, or the opposite, to hide their emotions. Some adults guffaw, slap their knees, and stomp their feet for joy; others cover their mouths if a smile spontaneously appears. Anger is regulated in almost every culture, but the expression of it—when, how, and to whom—varies a great deal. No matter what the specifics, parents teach emotional regulation (Kim & Sasaki, 2014).

effortful control The ability to regulate one's emotions and actions through effort, not simply through natural inclination.

Emotional regulation is also called **effortful control** (Eisenberg et al., 2014), a term which emphasizes that controlling outbursts is not easy. Effortful control is more difficult when people—of any age—are in pain, or tired, or hungry. Effortful control, executive function, and emotional regulation are similar constructs, with much overlap. Executive function emphasizes cognition; effortful control emphasizes temperament; both are aspects of emotional regulation.

initiative versus guilt Erikson's third psychosocial crisis, in which children undertake new skills and activities and feel guilty when they do not succeed at them.

Initiative Versus Guilt

Emotional regulation is part of Erikson's third developmental stage, **initiative versus guilt.** *Initiative* includes saying something new, expanding an ability, beginning a project, expressing an emotion. Depending on what happens when they try a new action, children feel proud or guilty.

Usually, North American adults encourage enthusiasm, effort, and pride in their 2- to 6-year-olds. If a project fails—the block tower falls down, the playmate turns away—adults usually suggest trying again and blaming the block or the playmate, thus helping the child avoid feeling guilty.

If, instead, parents ignore rather than guide joy and pride, or worse, blame the child for being ignorant, clumsy, or so on, the child may not learn emotional regulation. For both genetic and behavioral reasons, parents who blame their children and who have poor emotional regulation themselves are likely to have children who do not learn how to regulate their own emotions (Bridgett et al., 2015).

Guidance, yes; brutal honesty, no. Preschool children are usually proud of themselves, overestimating their skills. As one team expressed it:

> Compared to older children and adults, young children are the optimists of the world, believing they have greater physical abilities, better memories, are more skilled at imitating models, are smarter, know more about how things work, and rate themselves as stronger, tougher, and of higher social standing than is actually the case.
>
> *[Bjorklund & Ellis, 2014, p. 244]*

That protective optimism helps young children try new things, and initiative advances learning of all kinds. As Erikson predicted, their optimistic self-concept protects them from guilt and shame.

If young children knew the true limits of their ability, they would not imagine becoming an NBA forward, a Grammy winner, a billionaire inventor. That might discourage them from trying to learn new things (Bjorklund & Ellis, 2014). Initiative is a driving force for young children, and that is as it should be.

Agnieszka Kirinicjanow/Getty Images

Genuinely Helpful Children of all ages can be helpful to their families, but their actions depend on family and cohort. Thirty years ago more children gathered freshly laid eggs than recycled plastic milk bottles. Indeed, no blue recycling bins existed until tens of thousands of environmentalists advocated reducing our carbon footprint.

● **Observation Quiz** Does this mother deserve praise? (see answer, page 265) ↑

Pride and Prejudice

In the United States, pride quickly includes gender, size, and heritage. Except for a very few who want to be the other sex, girls are happy to be girls; boys to be boys; both are glad they aren't babies. "Crybaby" is an insult; praise for being "a big kid" is welcomed; pride in doing something better than a younger child is expressed. Bragging is common.

Many young children believe that whatever they are is good. They feel superior to children of the other sex, or of another nationality or religion. This arises because of maturation: Cognition enables them to understand group categories, not only of ethnicity, gender, and nationality, but even categories that are irrelevant. They remember more about cartoon characters whose names begin with the same letter as theirs (Ross et al., 2011).

One amusing example occurred when preschoolers were asked to explain why one person would steal from another, as occurred in a story about two fictional tribes, the Zaz and the Flurps. As you would expect from theory-theory, the preschoolers readily found reasons. Their first explanation illustrated their belief that group loyalty was more important than any personal characteristic.

> "Why did a Zaz steal a toy from a Flurp?"
> "Because he's a Zaz, but he's a Flurp . . . They're not the same kind . . ."

Then they were asked to explain a more difficult case, when group loyalty was insufficient.

> "Why did a Zaz steal a toy from a Zaz?"
> "Because he's a very mean boy."

> [Rhodes, 2013, p. 259]

Proud Peruvian In rural Peru, a program of early education (Pronoei) encourages community involvement and traditional culture. Preschoolers, like this girl in a holiday parade, are proud to be themselves, and that helps them become healthy and strong.

Brain Maturation

The new initiative that Erikson describes results from myelination of the limbic system, growth of the prefrontal cortex, and a longer attention span—all the result of neurological maturation. Emotional regulation and cognitive maturation develop together, each enabling the other to advance (Bell & Calkins, 2011; Lewis, 2013; Bridgett et al., 2015).

Normally, neurological advances in the prefrontal cortex at about age 4 or 5 make children less likely to throw tantrums, pick fights, or giggle during prayer. Throughout early childhood, violent outbursts, uncontrolled crying, and terrifying *phobias* (irrational, crippling fears) diminish.

The capacity for self-control, such as not opening a present immediately if asked to wait and not expressing disappointment at an undesirable gift, becomes more evident. Consider the most recent time you gave someone a gift. If the receiver was a young child, you probably could tell whether the child liked the present. If the receiver was an adult, you might not have known.

In one study, researchers asked children to wait eight minutes while their mothers did some paperwork before opening a wrapped present in front of them (Cole et al., 2010). The children used strategies to help them wait, including distractions and private speech.

Keisha was one of the study participants:

> "Are you done, Mom?" . . . "I wonder what's in it" . . . "Can I open it now?"
> Each time her mother reminds Keisha to wait, eventually adding, "If you keep interrupting me, I can't finish and if I don't finish . . ." Keisha plops in her chair, frustrated. "I really want it," she laments, aloud but to herself. "I want to talk to Mommy so I won't open it. If I talk, Mommy won't finish. If she doesn't finish, I can't have it." She sighs deeply, folds her arms, and scans the room. . . . The

THINK CRITICALLY: At what age, if ever, do people understand when pride becomes prejudice?

Video Activity: Can Young Children Delay Gratification? illustrates how most young children are unable to overcome temptation even when promised an award.

Learning Emotional Regulation Like this girl in Hong Kong, all 2-year-olds burst into tears when something upsets them—a toy breaks, a pet refuses to play, or it's time to go home. A mother who comforts them and helps them calm down is teaching them to regulate their emotions.

intrinsic motivation A drive, or reason to pursue a goal, that comes from inside a person, such as the desire to feel smart or competent.

extrinsic motivation A drive, or reason to pursue a goal, that arises from the need to have one's achievements rewarded from outside, perhaps by receiving material possessions or another person's esteem.

● ● Especially for College Students
Is extrinsic or intrinsic motivation more influential in your study efforts? (see response, page 266)

imaginary friends Make-believe friends who exist only in a child's imagination; increasingly common from ages 3 through 7. They combat loneliness and aid emotional regulation.

research assistant returns. Keisha looks at her mother with excited anticipation. Her mother says, "OK, now." Keisha tears open the gift.

[Cole et al., 2010, p. 59]

This is a recent example of the famous marshmallow test, which now has longitudinal results (Mischel et al., 1972). Children could eat one marshmallow immediately or get two marshmallows if they waited—sometimes as long as 15 minutes. Young children who delayed gobbling up a marshmallow became more successful as teenagers, young adults, and even middle-aged adults—doing well in college, for instance, and having happy marriages (Mischel, 2014).

Of course, this is correlation, not causation: Some preschoolers who did not wait became successful in later life. But emotional regulation in preschool predicts academic achievement and later success. Many factors are crucial.

- **Maturation matters.** Three-year-olds are notably poor at impulse control. By age 6 they are better, and effortful control continues to improve throughout childhood.
- **Learning matters.** In the zone of proximal development, children learn from mentors, who offer tactics for delaying gratification.
- **Culture matters.** In the United States many parents tell their children not to be afraid; in Japan they tell them not to be too proud; in the Netherlands, not to be too moody. Children try to do whatever their culture asks.

Motivation

Motivation is the impulse that propels someone to act. It comes either from a person's own desires or from the social context.

Intrinsic motivation arises from within, when people do something for the joy of doing it: A musician might enjoy making music even if no one else hears it. Intrinsic motivation is thought to advance creativity, innovation, and emotional well-being (Weinstein & DeHaan, 2014). Erikson's psychosocial needs are intrinsic: The young child feels compelled to initiate things, from walking along a ledge to exploring an anthill.

Extrinsic motivation comes from outside the person, when people do something to gain praise or some other reinforcement. A musician might play for applause or money. Social rewards are powerful lifelong: Four-year-olds hold an adult hand crossing the street because they are praised for doing so—and punished if they forget. If an extrinsic reward stops, the behavior may stop unless it has become a habit. Then it is continued because it feels right (intrinsic).

Intrinsic motivation is crucial for children. They play, question, exercise, create, and explore for the sheer joy of it. That serves them well. For example, a longitudinal study found that 3-year-olds who were strong in intrinsic motivation were, two years later, advanced in early math and literacy (Mokrova et al., 2013).

Child-centered preschools, as described in Chapter 9, depend on children's intrinsic motivation to talk, play, learn, and move. That is effective: Children enjoy activity for its own pleasures. When playing a game, few young children keep score; intrinsic joy is appreciated more than winning. In fact, young children often think they won when objective scores would say they lost; in this case, the children may really be winners.

Intrinsic motivation is apparent when children invent dialogues for their toys, concentrate on creating a work of art or architecture, or converse with **imaginary friends.** Such conversations with invisible companions are rarely encouraged by adults (thus no extrinsic motivation), but from about age 2 to 7, imaginary friends are increasingly common. Children know that their imaginary friends are invisible and pretend, but conjuring them up meets various intrinsic psychosocial needs (M. Taylor et al., 2009).

The distinction between extrinsic and intrinsic motivation may be crucial in understanding how and when to praise something the child has done. Praise may be effective when it is connected to the particular production, not to a general trait. For example, the adult might say, "You worked hard and created a good drawing," not "You are a great artist." The goal is to help the child feel happy that effort paid off, which is what children are inclined to think. That motivates future action (Zentall & Morris, 2010).

In a set of experiments which suggest that specific praise for effort is better than generalized statements, some 4- to 7-year-old boys were told that boys are good at a particular game. Knowing this *decreased* their scores on the game. The same thing happened when girls were told that girls were good at the game. The children apparently feared that they would not be as good as most children of their sex. They "felt less happy and less competent, liked the game less, [and] were less persistent" (Cimpian, 2013, p. 272).

By contrast, other children were told that one particular child was good at the game. That led them to believe that personal effort mattered. That belief was motivating; their scores were higher than those told that boys or girls in general were good.

WHAT HAVE YOU LEARNED?

1. How might protective optimism lead to a child's acquisition of new skills and competencies?

2. What did Erikson think was crucial for young children?

3. What is an example (not in the text) of intrinsic motivation?

4. What is an example (not in the text) of extrinsic motivation?

5. Why do child-centered preschools need children to be intrinsically motivated?

Play

Play is timeless and universal—apparent in every part of the world over thousands of years. Many developmentalists believe that play is the most productive as well as the most enjoyable activity that children undertake (Elkind, 2007; Bateson & Martin, 2013; P. Smith, 2010). Not everyone agrees. Whether play is essential for normal growth or is merely fun is "a controversial topic of study" (Pellegrini, 2011, p. 3).

This controversy underlies many of the disputes regarding preschool education, which increasingly stresses academic skills. One consequence is that "play in school has become an endangered species" (Trawick-Smith, 2012, p. 259). Among the leading theorists of human development, Vygotsky is well known for his respect for child's play, which makes a playing child "a head taller" than his or her actual height (Vygotsky, 1980).

Especially for Professors One of your students tells you about a child who plays, sleeps, and talks with an imaginary friend. Does this mean that child is emotionally disturbed? (see response, page 266)

Especially for Teachers of Young Children Should you put gold stars on children's work? (see response, page 266)

Answer to Observation Quiz (from page 262): Yes—even if you don't consider recycling important. Notice her face and body: She is smiling and kneeling, and her hands are on her legs, all suggesting that she knows how to encourage without interfering. Even more commendable is her boys' behavior: Many brothers would be grabbing, shoving, and throwing, but, at least at this moment, shared cooperation is evident. Kudos to Mom.

JGI/Jamie Grill/Blend Images/Getty Images

Real or Fake? This photo may be staged, but the children show the power of imagination—each responding to his or her cape in their own way. Sociodramatic play is universal; children do it if given half a chance.

Some educators want children to play less in order to focus on reading and math; others predict emotional and academic problems for children who rarely play (Golinkoff & Hirsh-Pasek, 2016). Children want to be active. If children are kept quiet for a long time, they tend to play more vigorously when they finally have the chance (Pellegrini, 2013).

Playmates

Young children play best with *peers,* that is, people of about the same age and social status. Although infants are intrigued by other children, most infant play is either solitary or with a parent. Some maturation is required for play with peers (Bateson & Martin, 2013).

The Historical Context

Children everywhere have always played, but specifics vary with culture and cohort (Roopnarine et al., 2015). Some developmentalists fear that play is subverted currently by three factors: (1) the current push toward early mastery of academic skills, (2) the "swift and pervasive rise of electronic media," and (3) adults who lean "more toward control than freedom" (Chudacoff, 2011, p. 108).

As you remember, one dispute in preschool education is the proper balance between unstructured, creative play and teacher-directed learning. Before the electronic age, most families had several children, and few mothers worked outside the home. The children played outside with all of their neighbors, boys and girls, of several ages. A century ago, American sociologist Mildred Parten described five stages of play, each more advanced than the previous one:

1. *Solitary:* A child plays alone, unaware of other children playing nearby.
2. *Onlooker:* A child watches other children play.
3. *Parallel:* Children play in similar ways but not together.
4. *Associative:* Children interact, sharing toys, but not taking turns.
5. *Cooperative:* Children play together, creating dramas or taking turns.

Parten (1932) described play as intrinsic, with children gradually advancing, from age 1 to 6, from solitary to cooperative play.

Research on contemporary children finds much more age variation than Parten did, perhaps because family size is smaller and parents invest heavily in each child. Many Asian parents successfully teach 3-year-olds to take turns, share, and otherwise cooperate (stage 5). Many North American children, encouraged to be individuals, still engage in parallel play at age 6 (stage 3).

Social Play

Play can be divided into two kinds: *pretend play* when a child is alone and *social play* that occurs with playmates. One meta-analysis of the research on pretend play and social play (Lillard et al., 2013) reports that evidence is weak or mixed regarding pretend play but that social play has much to commend it. If social play is prevented, children are less happy and less able to learn, which suggests that social play is one way that children develop their minds and social skills.

Such an advance can be seen over the years of early childhood. Toddlers are too self-absorbed to be good playmates, but they learn quickly. By age 6, most children are quite skilled: Some know how to join a peer group, manage conflict, take turns, find friends, and keep the action going (Şendil & Erden, 2014; Göncü & Gaskins, 2011). Parents need to find playmates, because even the most playful parent is

Response for College Students (from page 264): Both are important. Extrinsic motivation includes parental pressure and the need to get a good job after graduation. Intrinsic motivation includes the joy of learning, especially if you can express that learning in ways others recognize. Have you ever taken a course that was not required and was said to be difficult? That was intrinsic motivation.

Response for Professors (from page 265): No, unless the child is over age 10. In fact, imaginary friends are quite common, especially among creative children. The child may be somewhat lonely, though; you could help him or her find a friend.

Response for Teachers of Young Children (from page 265): Perhaps, but only after the work is completed and if the child has put genuine effort into it. You do not want to undercut intrinsic motivation, as happens with older students who know a particular course will be an "easy A."

Less Play, Less Safe?

Play is universal—all young children do it when they are with each other, if they can. For children, play takes up more time than anything else, whether their family is rich or poor.

WHAT 3-YEAR-OLDS DO WITH THEIR TIME

	Working Class	Middle Class
United States European Americans		
African Americans		
Kenya		
Brazil		

Legend:
- 😐 Play
- 📝 School and homework
- 🔨 Work
- Conversation
- ❓ Other

[These represent the percentages of time spent in each type of activity, out of 20 hours observed.]

DATA FROM TUDGE ET AL., 2006

However, many developmentalists worry that active play has decreased as screen time has increased, especially in the United States (on average screen time is 2.1 hours per day for 2- to 4-year-olds).

Parents worry that children will be injured if they play outside, but the data suggest the opposite. Only 166 out of every thousand children need to go to the emergency room per year, and almost all of those were injured in the home, or in a car.

PERCENT OF KIDS WHOSE PARENTS PLAY OUTDOORS WITH THEM

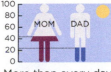
More than every day

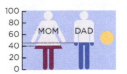
A few times a week

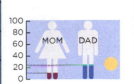
A few times a month

Rarely or never

No serious injury

HOSPITAL

166

From what kind of injuries do young children suffer?
Compare 1- to 4-year-olds and 5- to 14-year-olds

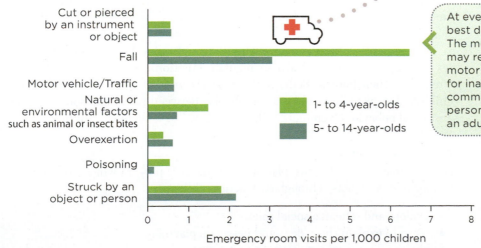

- Cut or pierced by an instrument or object
- Fall
- Motor vehicle/Traffic
- Natural or environmental factors such as animal or insect bites
- Overexertion
- Poisoning
- Struck by an object or person

■ 1- to 4-year-olds
■ 5- to 14-year-olds

Emergency room visits per 1,000 children
0 1 2 3 4 5 6 7 8

At every age, physical fitness is the best defense against accidental injury. The most common injury, falls—which may result from poor balance and motor control—is more problematic for inactive children. The next most common injury is being struck by a person—almost always that person is an adult at home.

DATA FROM EMERGENCY ROOM VISITS, 2009–2010, CHILDSTATS.GOV.

iStockphoto/Giulio Fornasar/Getty Images

Finally Cooperating The goal of social play—cooperation—is shown by these two boys who, at ages 8 and 11, are long past the associative, self-absorbed play of younger children. Note the wide-open mouths of laughter over a shared video game—a major accomplishment.

rough-and-tumble play Play that mimics aggression through wrestling, chasing, or hitting, but in which there is no intent to harm.

> **THINK CRITICALLY:** Is "play" an entirely different experience for adults than for children?

sociodramatic play Pretend play in which children act out various roles and themes in stories that they create.

outmatched by another child at negotiating the rules of tag, at play-fighting, at pretending to be sick, at killing dragons, and so on.

As they become better playmates, children learn emotional regulation, empathy, and cultural understanding. Specifics vary, but "play with peers is one of the most important areas in which children develop positive social skills" (Xu, 2010, p. 496).

Active Play

Children need physical activity to develop muscle strength and control. Peers provide an audience, role models, and sometimes competition. For instance, running skills develop best when children chase or race each other, not when a child runs alone.

Active social play—not solitary play—correlates with peer acceptance and a healthy self-concept and may help regulate emotions (Becker et al., 2014; Sutton-Smith, 2011). Adults need to remember this when they want children to sit still and be quiet.

Among nonhuman primates, deprivation of social play warps later life, rendering some monkeys unable to mate, to make friends, or even to survive alongside other monkeys (Herman et al., 2011; Palagi, 2011). Might the same be true for human primates?

Rough and Tumble

The most common form of active play is called **rough-and-tumble play** because it looks quite rough and because the children seem to tumble over one another. The term was coined by British scientists who studied animals in East Africa (Blurton-Jones, 1976). They noticed that young monkeys often chased, attacked, rolled over in the dirt, and wrestled quite roughly without injuring one another, all while seeming to smile (showing a *play face*).

When these scientists returned to London, they saw that puppies, kittens, and even their own children engaged in rough-and-tumble play, like baby monkeys. Children chase, wrestle, and grab each other, developing games like tag and cops-and-robbers, with various conventions, facial expressions, and gestures to signify "just pretend."

Rough-and-tumble play happens everywhere (although cops-and-robbers can be "robots-and-humans" or many other iterations) and has probably been common among children for thousands of years (Fry, 2014). It is much more common among boys than girls and flourishes best in ample space with minimal supervision (Pellegrini, 2013).

Many scientists think that rough-and-tumble play helps the prefrontal cortex develop, as children learn to regulate emotions, practice social skills, and strengthen their bodies (Pellis & Pellis, 2011). Indeed, some believe that play in childhood, especially rough-and-tumble play between father and son, may prevent antisocial behavior (even murder) later on (Fry, 2014; Wenner, 2009).

Sociodramatic Play

Another major type of active play is **sociodramatic play,** in which children act out various roles and plots. Through such acting, children:

- explore and rehearse social roles.
- learn to explain their ideas and persuade playmates.
- practice emotional regulation by pretending to be afraid, angry, brave, and so on.
- develop self-concept in a nonthreatening context.

Sociodramatic play builds on pretending, which emerges in toddlerhood. But remember that solitary pretending may not advance various skills; dramatic pretending with peers does. As children combine their imagination with that of their friends, they advance in theory of mind (Kavanaugh, 2011).

Everywhere, as they age from 2 to 6, children increasingly prefer to play with children of their own sex. For example, a day-care center in Finland allowed extensive free play. The boys often enacted dramas of good guys versus bad guys. In this episode, four boys did so, with Joni as the bad guy. Tuomas directed the drama and acted in it.

Joy Supreme Pretend play in early childhood is thrilling and powerful. For this dancing 7-year-old from Park Slope, Brooklyn, pretend play overwhelms mundane realities, such as an odd scarf or awkward arm.

Tuomas: . . . and now he [Joni] would take me and would hang me. . . . this would be the end of all of me.

Joni: Hands behind!

Tuomas: I can't help it . . . I have to.
[The two other boys follow his example.]

Joni: I would put fire all around them.
[All three brave boys lie on the floor with hands tied behind their backs. Joni piles mattresses on them, and pretends to light a fire, which crackles closer and closer.]

Tuomas: Everything is lost!
[One boy starts to laugh.]

Petterl: Better not to laugh, soon we will all be dead. . . . I am saying my last words.

Tuomas: Now you can say your last wish. . . . And now I say I wish we can be terribly strong.
[At that point, the three boys suddenly gain extraordinary strength, pushing off the mattresses and extinguishing the fire. Good triumphs over evil, but not until the last moment, because, as one boy explains, "Otherwise this playing is not exciting at all."]

[adapted from Kalliala, 2006, p. 83]

LaunchPad
macmillan learning

Video: The Impact of Media in Early Childhood

http://qrs.ly/on4ep0n

Good Over Evil or Evil Over Good? Boys everywhere enjoy "strong man" fantasy play, as the continued popularity of Spider-Man and Superman attests. These boys follow that script. Both are Afghan refugees now in Pakistan.

As with this example, boys' sociodramatic play often includes danger and then victory over evil. By contrast, girls typically act out domestic scenes, with themselves as the adults. In the same day-care center where Joni piled mattresses on his playmates, preparing to burn them, the girls say their play is "more beautiful and peaceful . . . [but] boys play all kinds of violent games" (Kalliala, 2006, p. 110).

The prevalence of sociodramatic play varies by culture, with parents often following cultural norms. Some cultures find make-believe frivolous and discourage it; in other cultures, parents teach toddlers to be lions, or robots, or ladies drinking tea. Then children elaborate on those themes (Kavanaugh, 2011). Many children are avid television watchers, and they act out superhero themes.

That children copy superheroes and villains from TV and tablet screens is troubling to many developmentalists, who prefer dramas from a child's imagination. This is not to say that screen time is necessarily bad: By the preschool years, unlike in infancy, children can learn from videos, especially if adults watch with them. However, children rarely select educational programs over fast-paced cartoons with characters who hit, shoot, and kick. They act out what they have seen.

Stopped in Her Tracks The birthday balloon or the tiny horse on the floor is no match for the bright images on the screen, designed to capture every child's attention. Are you critical of the parents who bought, placed, and turned on that large television for their 2-year-old or the culture that allows such programming? Would you report this as child neglect?

empathy The ability to understand the emotions and concerns of another person, especially when they differ from one's own.

prosocial behavior Actions that are helpful and kind but are of no obvious benefit to oneself.

antisocial behavior Actions that are deliberately hurtful or destructive to another person.

In North America, most children have more than an hour of screen time every day (Carson et al., 2013; Fletcher et al., 2014). That troubles developmentalists for many reasons. One is simply time—the more children are glued to screens, especially when the screen is their own hand-held device, the less they spend in active, social play (see Figure 10.1). Further, much of the most attractive media teaches aggression and reinforces gender and ethnic stereotypes.

Learning Emotional Regulation

The development of emotional regulation benefits playful interactions not from watching a screen. Young children enjoy playing with each other, and they gradually learn what actions and reactions make a good playmate.

Empathy and Antipathy

As theory of mind develops and children have experience with other children, they develop **empathy,** an understanding of other people's feelings and concerns. Empathy leads to compassion and **prosocial behavior**—helpfulness and kindness without any obvious personal benefit. Prosocial actions and preferences increase from ages 1 to 6. Empathetic preschoolers become first graders who are likely to share, help, and play with other children (Z. Taylor et al., 2013).

The opposite can also happen. Children might dislike other children, especially those who are mean in rough-and-tumble play, or who insist on their own way in sociodramatic play. Antipathy may lead to **antisocial behavior,** which includes verbal insults, social exclusion, and physical assaults.

Both prosocial and antisocial behavior are innate and universal (Séguin & Tremblay, 2013). Two-year-olds find it hard to share, even to let another child use a crayon that they have already used. Preschool children have a sense of ownership: A teacher's crayon should be shared, but if a child owns it, the other children believe that he or she is allowed to be selfish (Neary & Friedman, 2014).

FIGURE 10.1

Learning by Playing Fifty years ago, the average child spent three hours a day in outdoor play. Video games and television have largely replaced that playtime, especially in cities. Children seem safer if parents can keep an eye on them, but what are the long-term effects on brain and body?

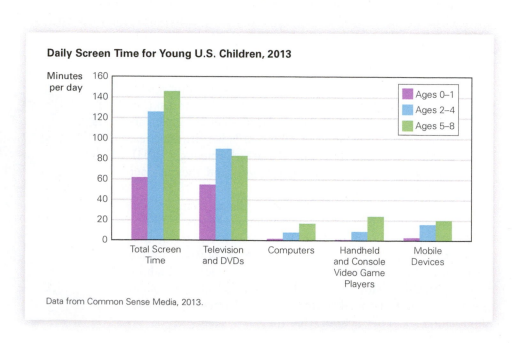

Data from Common Sense Media, 2013.

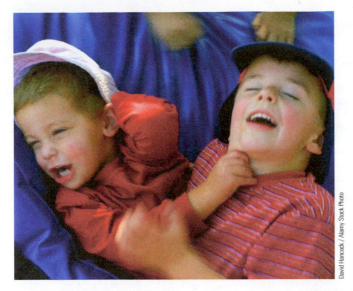

Pinch, Poke, or Pat Antisocial and prosocial responses are actually a sign of maturation: Babies do not recognize the impact of their actions. These children have much more to learn, but they already are quite social.

Generally, antisocial behavior diminishes over the preschool years, especially as social understanding increases. Parents and teachers help children learn how to take turns and share, increasing emotional maturity, or slowing it down if they neither discuss nor respond to emotions (Z. Taylor et al., 2013; Richards et al., 2014). Neighborhood and school stress also decrease empathy and increase antipathy, as well as fueling the emotional problems that some children develop (Flouri & Sarmadi, 2016). In other words, context is crucial.

The most troubling problems are the externalizing ones, when children's anger leads them to hit, kick, and hurt other people. For aggression, emotional regulation is essential.

Aggression

Researchers recognize four general types of aggression, each of which is evident in early childhood (see Table 10.1). Two forms decrease over the years, one increases, and one can either increase or decrease—with destructive consequences.

Instrumental aggression is common among 2-year-olds, who often want something and try to get it. This is called *instrumental* because the aggression is a tool, or instrument, to get something that is desired. The harm in grabbing a toy, and hitting, if someone resists, is not understood.

Because instrumental aggression naturally occurs, **reactive aggression** is also common among young children. Almost every child reacts when hurt, whether or not the hurt was deliberate. The reaction may not be controlled—a child might punch in response to an unwelcome remark—but as the prefrontal cortex matures, the impulse to strike back becomes modified. Both instrumental aggression and reactive aggression are less often physical when children develop emotional regulation and theory of mind (Olson et al., 2011).

Relational aggression (usually verbal) destroys self-esteem and disrupts social networks, becoming more common as well as more hurtful as children mature. A child might spread rumors or tell others not to play with so-and-so. In early childhood, relational aggression is usually quite direct: A young child might tell another, "You can't be my friend" or "You are fat," hurting the other child's

Video: Interview with Lawrence Walker discusses what parents can do to encourage their children's moral development.

instrumental aggression Behavior that hurts someone else because the aggressor wants to get or keep a possession or a privilege.

reactive aggression An impulsive retaliation for another person's intentional or accidental action, verbal or physical.

relational aggression Nonphysical acts, such as insults or social rejection, aimed at harming the social connection between the victim and other people.

TABLE 10.1	The Four Forms of Aggression	
Type of Aggression	Definition	Comments
Instrumental aggression	Hurtful behavior that is aimed at gaining something (such as a toy, a place in line, or a turn on the swing) that someone else has	Often increases from age 2 to 6; involves objects more than people; quite normal; more egocentric than antisocial.
Reactive aggression	An impulsive retaliation for a hurt (intentional or accidental) that can be verbal or physical	Indicates a lack of emotional regulation, characteristic of 2-year-olds. A 5-year-old can usually stop and think before reacting.
Relational aggression	Nonphysical acts, such as insults or social rejection, aimed at harming the social connections between the victim and others	Involves a personal attack and thus is directly antisocial; can be very hurtful; more common as children become socially aware.
Bullying aggression	Unprovoked, repeated physical or verbal attack, especially on victims who are unlikely to defend themselves	In both bullies and victims, a sign of poor emotional regulation; adults should intervene before the school years. (Bullying is discussed in Chapter 8.)

bullying aggression Unprovoked, repeated physical or verbal attacks, especially on victims who are unlikely to defend themselves.

feelings. However, the sting of relational aggression is far less painful at age 3 than age 8.

The fourth and most ominous type is **bullying aggression,** done to dominate. Bullying aggression occurs among young children but should be stopped by kindergarten, before it becomes more harmful. Not only does it destroy self-esteem and thus learning, it eventually harms the bullies, who learn destructive habits. A 4-year-old bully may be friendless; a 10-year-old bully may be feared and admired; a 50-year-old bully may be hated and lonely. [**Life-Span Link:** An in-depth discussion of bullying appears in Chapter 13.]

Between ages 2 and 6, as the brain matures and empathy increases, children learn to use aggression selectively, and that decreases both internalizing and externalizing problems (Ostrov et al., 2014). Parents, peers, and preschool teachers are pivotal mentors in this learning process.

A longitudinal study found that close teacher–student relationships in preschool predicted less aggression and less victimization in elementary school. The probable reason—close relationships led children to want to please the teachers, who guided them toward prosocial, not antisocial, behavior (Runions & Shaw, 2013).

WHAT HAVE YOU LEARNED?

1. Why might playing with peers help children build muscles and develop self-control?

2. What do children learn from rough-and-tumble play?

3. What do children learn from sociodramatic play?

4. Why do many experts want to limit children's screen time?

5. How might children develop empathy and antipathy as they play with one another?

6. What is the connection between empathy and prosocial behavior?

7. What are the similarities and differences of the four kinds of aggression?

8. What are the developmental changes in each form of aggression over the years of early childhood?

Challenges for Caregivers

Every developmentalist realizes that caring for a young child is challenging. At this age, children are energetic and curious. That helps them learn and grow but also tests the emotions and skills of any adult.

Styles of Caregiving

The more developmentalists study parents, the more styles of parenting they see. International variations are stark—from those who are so strict that they seem abusive to those who are so lenient that they seem neglectful. Variations are also apparent within each nation, within each ethnic group, and even within each neighborhood. Appreciation of culture makes developmentalists hesitate to say one style is best, but appreciation of the needs of children makes it hard not to judge.

Baumrind's Categories

Although thousands of researchers have traced the effects of parenting on child development, the work of one person, 50 years ago, is especially influential. In her original research, Diana Baumrind (1967, 1971) studied 100 preschool children, all from California, almost all middle-class European Americans.

She found that parents differed on four important dimensions:

1. *Expressions of warmth.* Some parents are warm and affectionate; others are cold and critical.
2. *Strategies for discipline.* Parents vary in how they explain, criticize, persuade, and punish.
3. *Expectations for maturity.* Parents vary in expectations for responsibility and self-control.
4. *Communication.* Some parents listen patiently; others demand silence.

On the basis of these dimensions, Baumrind identified three parenting styles (summarized in Table 10.2). A fourth style, not described by Baumrind, was suggested by other researchers.

Authoritarian parenting. The authoritarian parent's word is law, not to be questioned. Misconduct brings strict punishment, usually physical. Authoritarian parents set down clear rules and hold high standards. They do not expect children to offer opinions; discussion about emotions and expressions of affection are rare. One adult from authoritarian parents said that "How do you feel?" had only two possible answers: "Fine" and "Tired."

Permissive parenting. Permissive parents (also called *indulgent*) make few demands, hiding any impatience they feel. Discipline is lax, partly because they have low expectations for maturity. Permissive parents are nurturing and accepting, listening to whatever their offspring say, including cursing at the parent.

Authoritative parenting. Authoritative parents set limits, but they are flexible. They encourage maturity, but they usually listen and forgive (not punish) if the child falls short. They consider themselves guides, not authorities (unlike authoritarian parents) and not friends (unlike permissive parents).

Neglectful/uninvolved parenting Neglectful parents are oblivious to their children's behavior; they seem not to care. Their children do whatever they want. This is quite different from permissive parents, who care very much about their children.

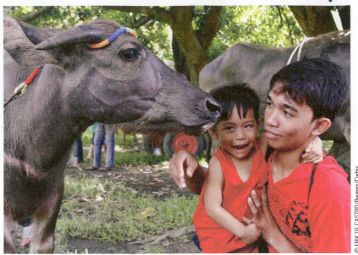

Protect Me from the Water Buffalo These two are at the Carabao Kneeling Festival. In rural Philippines, hundreds of these large but docile animals kneel on the steps of the church, part of a day of gratitude for the harvest.

Observation Quiz Is the father above authoritarian, authoritative, or permissive? (see answer, page 274)

Especially for Political Scientists Many observers contend that children learn their political attitudes at home, from the way their parents teach them. Is this true? (see response, page 274)

authoritarian parenting An approach to child rearing that is characterized by high behavioral standards, strict punishment for misconduct, and little communication from child to parent.

permissive parenting An approach to child rearing that is characterized by high nurturance and communication but little discipline, guidance, or control. (Also called *indulgent parenting*.)

authoritative parenting An approach to child rearing in which the parents set limits but listen to the child and are flexible.

neglectful/uninvolved parenting An approach to child rearing in which the parents are indifferent toward their children and unaware of what is going on in their children's lives.

TABLE 10.2	Characteristics of Parenting Styles Identified by Baumrind					
					Communication	
Style	Warmth	Discipline	Expectations of Maturity	Parent to Child	Child to Parent
Authoritarian	Low	Strict, often physical	High	High	Low
Permissive	High	Rare	Low	Low	High
Authoritative	High	Moderate, with much discussion	Moderate	High	High

Answer to Observation Quiz (from page 273): It is impossible to be certain based on one moment, but the best guess is authoritative. He seems patient and protective, providing comfort and guidance, neither forcing (authoritarian) nor letting the child do whatever he wants (permissive).

The following long-term effects of parenting styles have been reported, not only in the United States but in many other nations as well (Baumrind, 2005; Baumrind et al., 2010; Chan & Koo, 2011; Huver et al., 2010; Rothrauff et al., 2009; Deater-Deckard, 2013).

- *Authoritarian* parents raise children who become conscientious, obedient, and quiet but not especially happy. Such children may feel guilty or depressed, internalizing their frustrations and blaming themselves when things don't go well. As adolescents, they sometimes rebel, leaving home before age 20.
- *Permissive* parents raise children who lack self-control, especially in the give-and-take of peer relationships. Inadequate emotional regulation makes them immature and impedes friendships, so they are unhappy. They tend to continue to live at home, still dependent on their parents in adulthood.
- *Authoritative* parents raise children who are successful, articulate, happy with themselves, and generous with others. These children are usually liked by teachers and peers, especially in cultures that value individual initiative (e.g., the United States).
- *Neglectful/uninvolved* parents raise children who are immature, sad, lonely, and at risk of injury and abuse, not only in early childhood but also lifelong.

Problems with the Research

Baumrind's classification schema has been soundly criticized. You can probably already see some of the ways her research was flawed:

- She did not consider socioeconomic differences.
- She was unaware of cultural differences.
- She focused more on parent attitudes than on parent actions.
- She overlooked children's temperamental differences.
- She did not recognize that some "authoritarian" parents are also affectionate.
- She did not realize that some "permissive" parents provide extensive verbal guidance.

Response for Political Scientists (from page 273): There are many parenting styles, and it is difficult to determine each one's impact on children's personalities. At this point, attempts to connect early child rearing with later political outlook are speculative.

More recent research finds that a child's temperament powerfully affects caregivers. Good caregivers treat each child as an individual who needs personalized care. For example, fearful children require reassurance, while impulsive ones need strong guidelines. Parents of such children may, to outsiders, seem permissive or authoritarian.

Overprotection may be a consequence, not a cause, of childhood anxiety (McShane & Hastings, 2009; Deater-Deckard, 2013). Every child needs some protection and guidance; some more than others. The right balance depends on the particular child, as differential susceptibility makes clear.

A study of parenting at age 2 and children's competence in kindergarten (including emotional regulation and friendships) found "multiple developmental pathways," with the best outcomes dependent on both the child and the adult (Blandon et al., 2010). Such studies suggest that simplistic advice—from a book, a professional, or a neighbor who does not know the child—may be misguided. Longitudinal, careful observation of parent–child interactions is needed before judging that a caregiver is too lax or too rigid.

As the following suggests, given a multicultural and multicontextual perspective, developmentalists realize that many parenting practices are sometimes effective. But that does not mean that all families function equally well—far from it. Signs of emotional distress, including a child's anxiety, aggression, and inability to play with others, indicate that the family may not be the safe haven of support and guidance that it should be.

"He's just doing that to get attention."

Pay Attention Children develop best with lots of love and attention. They shouldn't have to ask for it!

Harry Bliss The New Yorker Collection/The Cartoon Bank

A VIEW FROM SCIENCE

Culture and Parenting Style

Culture powerfully affects caregiving style. This is obvious internationally. In some nations, parents are expected to beat their children; in other nations, parents are arrested if they lay a hand on their children. Some parents think they should never praise their children; elsewhere parents think they should tell their children they are wonderful, even when they are not.

Differences are evident in multiethnic nations including the United States, where parents of Chinese, Caribbean, or African heritage are often stricter than those of European backgrounds. However, children of some ethnic minority families seem to thrive with strict parents, *if* the parents also express love and appreciation (Parke & Buriel, 2006; F. Ng et al., 2014).

A detailed study of Mexican American mothers of 4-year-olds noted 1,477 instances when the mothers tried to change their children's behavior. Most of the time the mothers simply uttered a command and the children complied (Livas-Dlott et al., 2010).

This simple strategy, with the mother asserting authority and the children obeying without question, might be considered authoritarian. Almost never, however, did the mothers use physical punishment or even harsh threats when the children did not immediately do as they were told—which happened 14 percent of the time. For example:

Hailey [the 4-year-old] decided to look for another doll and started digging through her toys, throwing them behind her as she dug. Maricruz [the mother] told Hailey

she should not throw her toys. Hailey continued to throw toys, and Maricruz said her name to remind her to stop. Hailey continued her misbehavior, and her mother repeated "Hailey" once more. When Hailey continued, Maricruz raised her voice but calmly directed, "Hailey, look at me." Hailey continued but then looked at Maricruz as she explained, "You don't throw toys; you could hurt someone." Finally, Hailey complied and stopped.

[Livas-Dlott et al., 2010, p. 572]

Note that the mother's first three efforts failed, and then a "look" accompanied by an explanation (albeit inaccurate in that setting, as no one could be hurt) succeeded. The Mexican American families did not fit any of Baumrind's categories; respect (*respeto*) for adult authority did not mean an authoritarian relationship. Instead, the relationship shows evident caring (*cariño*) (Livas-Dlott et al., 2010).

As with *respeto* and *cariño* (values evident in Latino parents), parenting in every culture includes strategies that need to be recognized and appreciated (Butler & Titus, 2015). However, the research finds that harsh or cold parenting is always harmful (Dyer et al., 2014). (The consequences of harsh punishment are discussed at the end of this chapter.) Parental affection allows children to develop self-respect and to become compassionate adults, no matter what the parenting styles or culture (Deater-Deckard, 2013; Eisenberg et al., 2013).

Discipline

Children misbehave. They do not always do what adults think they should do. Sometimes they do not know better, but sometimes they deliberately ignore a request, perhaps doing exactly what they have been told not to do. Since misbehavior is part of growing up, and since children need guidance to keep them safe and strong, parents must respond.

Physical Punishment

In the United States, young children are slapped, spanked, or beaten more often than are infants or older children, and more often than children in Canada or western Europe. Spanking is more frequent:

- in the southern United States than in New England.
- by mothers than by fathers.
- among conservative Christians than among nonreligious families.
- among African Americans than among European Americans.
- among European Americans than among Asian Americans.
- among U.S.-born Hispanics than among immigrant Hispanics.
- in low-SES families than in high-SES families.

(MacKenzie et al., 2011; S. Lee et al., 2015; Lee & Altschul, 2015).

These are general trends: Contrary to their generalization, many African American mothers living in the South never spank their children, and many secular, European American, high-SES fathers in New England routinely spank their children. Local norms matter, but parents make their own decisions.

Most adults believe that their upbringing helped them become the person they are, and consequently they think that their own past was proper. Moreover, physical punishment (called **corporal punishment** because it hurts the body) usually succeeds momentarily because immediately afterward children are quiet.

However, longitudinal research finds that children who are physically punished are more likely to be disobedient and to become bullies, delinquents, and then abusive adults (Gershoff et al., 2012). They are also less likely to learn quickly in school or to enroll in college (Straus & Paschall, 2009).

In fact, longitudinal research finds that children who are *not* spanked are more likely to develop self-control. As spanking increases, so does misbehavior (Gershoff, 2013). The correlation between spanking and later aggression holds for children of all ethnic groups.

In 43 nations (mostly in Europe), corporal punishment is illegal; in many nations on other continents, it is the norm. A massive study of low- and moderate-income nations found that 63 percent of 2- to 5-year-olds had been physically punished (slapped, spanked, hit with an object) in the past month (Deater-Deckard & Lansford, 2016).

In more than 100 nations, physical punishment is illegal in schools, but each state of the United States sets laws, and teachers may legally paddle children in 19 of them. Overall, in the United States in one recent year, 218,466 children were corporally punished at school. Sixteen percent of those children had intellectual disabilities, and a disproportionate number were African American boys (Morones, 2013; Gershoff et al., 2015). Worldwide, boys are punished slightly more often than girls.

Although some adults believe that physical punishment will "teach a lesson" of doing the right thing, others argue that the lesson that children learn is that "might makes right." It is true that children who were physically disciplined tend to use corporal punishment on others—first on their classmates, and later on their wives or husbands, and then their children. However, many people believe that children sometimes need spanking—a controversial idea, as the following explains.

corporal punishment Punishment that physically hurts the body, such as slapping, spanking, etc.

Is Spanking OK?

Opinions about spanking are influenced by past experience and cultural norms. That makes it hard for opposing perspectives to be understood by people on the other side (Ferguson, 2013). Try to suspend your own assumptions as you read this.

What might be right with spanking? Over the centuries many parents have done it, so it has stood the test of time. Indeed, in the United States, parents who never spank are unusual. Spanking seems less common in the twenty-first century than in the twentieth (Taillieu et al., 2014), but 85 percent of U.S. adolescents who were children at the end of the twentieth century remember being slapped or spanked by their mothers (Bender et al., 2007). More than one-third of the mothers in low- and middle-income nations believe that to raise a child well, physical punishment is essential (Deater-Deckard & Lansford, 2016).

One pro-spanking argument is that the correlations reported by developmentalists (between spanking and later depression, low achievement, aggression, crime, and so on) may be caused by a third variable, not spanking itself. A suggested third variable is child misbehavior: Perhaps disobedient children cause spanking, not vice versa. Such children may become delinquent, depressed, and so on not because they were spanked but in spite of being spanked.

Noting problems with correlational research, one team explains, "Quite simply, parents do not need to use corrective actions when there are no problems to correct" (Larzelere & Cox, 2013, p. 284). These authors point out that every disciplinary technique, if used frequently, correlates with misbehavior, but the punishment may be the result, not the cause. Further, since parents who spank their children tend to have less education and less money than other parents, SES may be the underlying reason spanked children average lower academic achievement.

If that is true, the solution is to reduce poverty, not to forbid spanking. When researchers try to eliminate the effect of every third variable, especially SES, they find a smaller correlation between spanking and future problems than most other studies do (Ferguson, 2013).

What might be wrong with spanking? One problem is adults' emotions: Angry spankers may become abusive. Children are sometimes seriously injured and even killed by parents who use corporal punishment. One pediatrician who hesitates to argue against all spanking, everywhere, nonetheless has observed that physical injury is common when parents discipline children. He says that parents should never spank in anger, cause bruises that last more than 24 hours, use an object, or spank a child under age 2 (Zolotor, 2014).

Another problem is the child's immature cognition. Many children do not understand why they are spanked. Parents assume the transgression is obvious, but children may think the parents' anger, not the child's actions, caused spanking (Harkness et al., 2011). Most parents tell their children why they are being spanked, but children are less likely to listen or understand when they are being hit.

Almost all of the research finds that children who are spanked suffer in many ways. They are more depressed, more antisocial, more likely to hate school, and less likely to have close friends. Many continue to suffer in adulthood.

Yet there are exceptions, spanked children who become happy and successful adults. For example, one U.S. study found that conservative Protestant parents spanked their children more often than other parents, but if that spanking occurred only in early (not middle) childhood, the children did not develop low self-esteem and increased aggression (Ellison et al., 2011).

The authors of the study suggest that, since spanking was the norm in that group, the children did not think they were unloved. Moreover, religious leaders tell parents never to spank in anger. As a result, their children may "view mild–to–moderate corporal punishment as legitimate, appropriate, and even an indicator of parental involvement, commitment, and concern" (Ellison et al., 2011, p. 957).

As I write these words, I realize which perspective is mine. I am one of many developmentalists who believe that alternatives to spanking are better for the child and a safeguard against abuse. Indeed, the same study that found spanking common in developing nations also reported that 17 percent of the children experienced severe violence (Bornstein et al., 2016).

Yet a dynamic-systems, multicultural perspective reminds us all that everyone is influenced by background and context. I know that I am; so is every scientist, and so are you.

Smack Will the doll learn never to disobey her mother again?

● **Especially for Parents** Suppose you agree that spanking is destructive, but you sometimes get so angry at your child's behavior that you hit him or her. Is your reaction appropriate? (see response, page 280)

psychological control A disciplinary technique that involves threatening to withdraw love and support and that relies on a child's feelings of guilt and gratitude to the parents.

Bad Boy or Bad Parent? For some children in some cultures, standing in the corner may be an effective punishment. Much depends on whether this boy knows if his parents' anger or his own behavior put him there.

time-out A disciplinary technique in which a child is separated from other people for a specified time.

induction A disciplinary technique in which the parent tries to get the child to understand why a certain behavior was wrong. Listening, not lecturing, is crucial.

Many studies of children from all family constellations and backgrounds find that physical punishment of young children correlates with delayed theory of mind and increased aggression (Olson et al., 2011). To prove cause without a doubt would require many parents of monozygotic twins to raise them identically, except that one twin would be spanked often and the other never. Of course, that is unethical as well as impossible.

Nonetheless, most developmentalists wonder why parents would take the chance. The best argument in favor of spanking is that alternative punishments may be worse (Larzelere et al., 2010; Larzelere & Cox, 2013). Let us consider alternatives.

Alternatives to Spanking

Another common method of discipline is called **psychological control,** in which children's shame, guilt, and gratitude are used to control their behavior (Barber, 2002). Psychological control may reduce academic achievement and emotional understanding, just as spanking is thought to do (Alegre, 2011).

Consider Finland, one of the nations where corporal punishment is now forbidden. Parents were asked about psychological control (Aunola et al., 2013). If parents strongly agreed with the following questions, they were considered to use psychological control:

1. "My child should be aware of how much I have done for him/her."
2. "I let my child see how disappointed and shamed I am if he/she misbehaves."
3. "My child should be aware of how much I sacrifice for him/her."
4. "I expect my child to be grateful and appreciate all the advantages he/she has."

The higher the parents scored on these four measures of psychological control, the lower the children's math scores were—and this connection grew stronger over time. Moreover, the children tended to have negative emotions (depression, anger, and so on). Thus, psychological control may have some of the same consequences as corporal punishment.

Another disciplinary technique often used with young children in North America is the **time-out,** in which a misbehaving child is required to sit quietly, without toys or playmates, for a short time. Time-out is not to be done in anger, or for too long; it is recommended that parents use a calm voice and that the time-out last only one to five minutes (Morawska & Sanders, 2011). Time-out works as a punishment if the child really enjoys "time-in," when the child is happily engaged with the parents or with peers.

Time-out is favored by many experts. For example, in the large, longitudinal evaluation of the Head Start program highlighted in Chapter 9, an increase in time-outs and a decrease in spankings were considered signs of improved parental discipline (U.S. Department of Health and Human Services, 2010).

However, the same team who criticized the correlation between spanking and misbehavior also criticized the research favoring time-out. They added, "misbehavior is motivated by wanting to escape from the situation . . . time-out reinforces the misbehavior" (Larzelere & Cox, 2013, p. 289).

Often combined with the time-out is another alternative to physical punishment and psychological control—**induction,** in which the parents talk extensively with the offender, helping the child understand why his or her behavior was wrong.

Ideally, time-out allows children to calm down. Then a strong and affectionate parent–child relationship means that children explain their emotions and parents listen carefully. Children can explain what they *might have* done instead of what *was* done, although such hypothetical reasoning is difficult—maybe impossible—for young children.

Induction takes time and patience. Since 3-year-olds confuse causes with consequences, they cannot answer "Why did you do that?" or appreciate a long explanation. Simple induction ("Why did he cry?") may be more appropriate, but even that is hard before a child develops theory of mind. Nonetheless, induction seems to pay off over time. Children whose parents used induction when they were 3-year-olds became children with fewer externalizing problems in elementary school (Choe et al., 2013b).

Becoming Boys or Girls: Sex and Gender

Another challenge for caregivers is raising a child with a healthy understanding of sex and gender (Wilcox & Kline, 2013). In early childhood, some children identify as transgender, wanting to be a gender that is not their biological sex. This presents their parents with a challenge that almost no parent anticipated a decade ago (Rahilly, 2015).

Biology determines whether an embryo is male or female (except in rare cases): Those XX or XY chromosomes normally shape organs and produce hormones. But genes create **sex differences,** which are biological, not **gender differences,** which are culturally prescribed. Theoretically, the distinction between sex and gender seems straightforward, but complexity is evident in practice. Scientists need to "treat culture and biology not as separate influences but as interacting components of nature and nurture" (Eagly & Wood, 2013, p. 349).

Although the 23rd pair of chromosomes are crucial, the entire culture creates gender differences, beginning with the blue or pink caps put on newborns' heads. Before age 2, children use gender labels (*Mrs., Mr., lady, man*) consistently. By age 4, children believe that certain toys (such as dolls or trucks) and roles (Daddy, Mommy, nurse, teacher, police officer, soldier) are reserved for one sex or the other.

She Understands? Children who are spanked remember the pain and anger but not the reason for the punishment. It is better for parents to explain what the misbehavior was. However, sometimes explanations are not understood.

sex differences Biological differences between males and females, in organs, hormones, and body type.

gender differences Differences in the roles and behaviors of males and females that are prescribed by the culture.

Same Situation, Far Apart: Culture Clash? He wears the orange robes of a Buddhist monk, and she wears the hijab of a Muslim girl. Although he is at a week-long spiritual retreat led by the Dalai Lama and she is in an alley in Pakistan, both carry universal toys—a pop gun and a bride doll, identical to those found almost everywhere.

● ● **Response for Parents** (from page 278): No. The worst time to spank a child is when you are angry. You might seriously hurt the child, and the child will associate anger with violence. You would do better to learn to control your anger and develop other strategies for discipline and for prevention of misbehavior.

There is much that young children do not yet understand. One little girl said she would grow a penis when she got older, and one little boy offered to buy his mother one. A 3-year-old went with his father to see a neighbor's newborn kittens. Returning home, he told his mother that there were three girl kittens and two boy kittens. "How do you know?" she asked. "Daddy picked them up and read what was written on their tummies," he replied.

In one preschool, the children themselves decided that one wash-up basin was for boys and the other for girls. A girl started to use the boys' basin.

> **Boy:** This is for the boys.
> **Girl:** Stop it. I'm not a girl and a boy, so I'm here.
> **Boy:** What?
> **Girl:** I'm a boy and also a girl.
> **Boy:** You, now, are you today a boy?
> **Girl:** Yes.
> **Boy:** And tomorrow what will you be?
> **Girl:** A girl. Tomorrow I'll be a girl. Today I'll be a boy.
> **Boy:** And after tomorrow?
> **Girl:** I'll be a girl.
>
> *[Ehrlich & Blum-Kulka, 2014, p. 31]*

Although they do not understand that sex is inborn, many preschoolers are quite rigid about male–female roles. Despite their parents' and teachers' wishes, children say, "No girls [or boys] allowed." Most children consider ethnic discrimination immoral, but they accept some sex discrimination (Møller & Tenenbaum, 2011). Transgender children, likewise, are insistent that they are not the sex that their parents thought (Rahilly, 2015).

Why are male and female distinctions important to 5-year-olds and considered valid by 10-year-olds? All of the major theories "devote considerable attention to gender differences. . . . the primary difference among the theories resides in the causal mechanism responsible" (Bornstein et al., 2016, pp. 10, 11). Each of the five comprehensive theories in Chapter 2 has an explanation of causes.

phallic stage Freud's third stage of development, when the penis becomes the focus of concern and pleasure.

Psychoanalytic Theory

Freud (1938/1995) called the period from about ages 3 to 6 the **phallic stage,** named after the *phallus,* the Greek word for penis. At age 3 or 4, said Freud, boys become aware of their male sexual organ. They masturbate, fear castration, and develop sexual feelings toward their mother.

Test Your Imagination Preschool children have impressive imaginations and strong social impulses. When two friends are together, they launch into amazing fun, drinking tea, crossing swords, wearing special masks and bracelets, or whatever. Adults may be more limited—can you picture these two scenes with genders switched, the boys in the tea party and the girls in the sword fight?

These feelings make every young boy jealous of his father—so jealous, according to Freud, that he wants to replace his dad. Freud called this the **Oedipus complex,** after Oedipus, son of a king in Greek mythology. Abandoned as an infant and raised in a distant kingdom, Oedipus returned to his birthplace and, without realizing it, killed his father and married his mother. When he discovered the horror, he blinded himself.

Freud believed that this ancient story (immortalized in *Oedipus Rex,* a play written by Sophocles and first presented in Athens in 429 B.C., still presented in Freud's day as well as in the twenty-first century) dramatizes the overwhelming emotions that all 5-year-old boys feel about their parents—both love and hate. Every boy feels guilty about his incestuous and murderous impulses. In self-defense, he develops a powerful conscience called the **superego,** which is quick to judge and punish.

That marks the beginning of morality, according to psychoanalytic theory. This theory contends that a boy's fascination with superheroes, guns, kung fu, and the like arises from his unconscious impulse to kill his father. Further, an adult man's homosexuality, homophobia, or obsession with guns, prostitutes, or hell arises from problems at the phallic stage.

Freud offered several descriptions of the moral development of girls. One, called the *Electra complex,* is again named after an ancient Greek drama. Freud thought girls also want to eliminate their same-sex parent (mother) and become intimate with the opposite-sex parent (father). That explains why many 5-year-old girls dress in frills and lace, and are happy to be "daddy's girl."

According to this theory, children cope with their guilt about their strong impulses toward their parents through **identification;** that is, they try to become like the same-sex parent. Consequently, young boys copy their fathers' mannerisms, opinions, and actions, and girls copy their mothers'. That is why they exaggerate the male or female role. The next stage, *latency,* is devoted to repressing sexual urges.

Many psychologists criticize psychoanalytic theory as being unscientific. That was my opinion in graduate school, so I dismissed Freud's ideas and I deliberately dressed my baby girls in blue, not pink, so that they would not follow stereotypes. However, scientists seek to reconcile experience with theory. My daughters made me reconsider. (See next page.)

Behaviorism

Behaviorists believe that virtually all roles, values, and morals are learned. To behaviorists, gender distinctions are the product of ongoing reinforcement and punishment, as well as social learning. Such learning is evident in early childhood.

For example, a boy who asks for a train and a doll for his birthday is more likely to get the train. Boys are rewarded for boyish requests, not for girlish ones. Indeed, the push toward traditional gender behavior in play and chores (washing dishes versus fixing cars) is among the most robust findings of decades of research on this topic (Eagly & Wood, 2013).

Gender differentiation may be subtle, with adults unaware that they are reinforcing traditional masculine or feminine behavior. For example, a study of parents talking to young children found that numbers were mentioned more often with the

Oedipus complex The unconscious desire of young boys to replace their father and win their mother's romantic love.

superego In psychoanalytic theory, the judgmental part of the personality that internalizes the moral standards of the parents.

identification An attempt to defend one's self-concept by taking on the behaviors and attitudes of someone else.

© SWNS/Splash News/Corbis

Banned from Children's Church Club
This 5-year-old loves pink, wears princess dresses, and plays with Barbie dolls. Such girlish behavior is not unusual in 5-year-olds, but this child is not welcome because Romeo Clark is a boy.

The Berger Daughters

It began when my eldest daughter, Bethany, was about 4 years old:

Bethany: When I grow up, I'm going to marry Daddy.
   Me: But Daddy's married to me.
Bethany: That's all right. When I grow up, you'll probably be dead.
   Me: [*Determined to stick up for myself*] Daddy's older than me, so when I'm dead, he'll probably be dead, too.
Bethany: That's OK. I'll marry him when he gets born again.

I was dumbfounded, without a good reply. Bethany saw my face fall, and she took pity on me:

Bethany: Don't worry, Mommy. After you get born again, you can be our baby.

The second episode was a conversation I had with Rachel when she was about 5:

Rachel: When I get married, I'm going to marry Daddy.
   Me: Daddy's already married to me.
Rachel: [*With the joy of having discovered a wonderful solution*] Then we can have a double wedding!

The third episode was considerably more graphic. It took the form of a "Valentine" left on my husband's pillow on February 14th by my daughter Elissa.

Finally, when Sarah turned 5, she also said she would marry her father. I told her she couldn't, because he was married to me. Her response revealed one more hazard of watching TV: "Oh, yes, a man can have two wives. I saw it on television."

As you remember from Chapter 1, a single example (or four daughters from one family) does not prove that Freud was correct. I still think he was wrong on many counts. But his description of the phallic stage seems less bizarre than I once thought.

Pillow Talk Elissa placed this artwork on my husband's pillow. My pillow, beside it, had a less colorful, less elaborate note—an afterthought. It read, "Dear Mom, I love you too."

boys (Chang et al., 2011). This may be a precursor to the boys becoming more interested in math and science later on.

According to social learning theory, people model themselves after people they perceive to be nurturing, powerful, and yet similar to themselves. For young children, those people are usually their parents.

Ironically, adults are the most gender-typed of their entire lives when they are raising young children. If an employed woman is ever to leave her job to become a housewife, it is when she has a baby. Fathers tend to work longer hours and mothers work fewer when children arrive. Since children learn gender roles from their parents, it is no surprise that they are quite sexist (Hallers-Haalboom et al., 2014). They follow the examples they see, unaware that their very existence changed adult behavior.

Reinforcement for distinct male and female behaviors is widespread. As the President of the Society for Research in Child Development observes, "parents, teachers, and peers . . . continue to encourage, model, and enforce traditional gender messages" (Liben, 2016, p. 24). The 3-year-old boy who brings his carefully dressed Barbie doll to preschool will be punished—not physically, but with words and social exclusion—by his male classmates.

Cognitive Theory

Cognitive theory offers an alternative explanation for the strong gender identity that becomes apparent at about age 5 (Kohlberg et al., 1983). Remember that cognitive theorists focus on how children understand various ideas. One idea that children develop regards the sexes. They construct a **gender schema,** an understanding of male–female differences (Bem, 1981; Martin et al., 2011).

As cognitive theorists point out, young children tend to perceive the world in simple, egocentric terms, as explained in Chapter 5. Therefore, they categorize male and female as opposites. Nuances, complexities, exceptions, and gradations about gender (and about everything else) are beyond them.

During the preoperational stage, appearance trumps logic. One group of researchers who endorse the cognitive interpretation note that "young children pass through a stage of gender appearance rigidity; girls insist on wearing dresses, often pink and frilly, whereas boys refuse to wear anything with a hint of femininity" (Halim et al., 2014, p. 1091).

In research reported by this group, parents discouraged stereotypes, but that did not necessarily sway a preschool girl who wanted a bright pink tutu and a sparkly tiara. The child's gender schema overcame the words of parents who disparaged gender stereotypes. In effect, children develop a theory-theory to explain what they experience.

Cognitive theory recognizes that not all parents think sexual distinctions are wrong. "Sometimes gender-traditional messages are conveyed deliberately . . . Many fathers and mothers dream of raising their sons and daughters to join them in traditional masculine and feminine pastimes" (Liben, 2016, p. 24). Gender schema are everwhere (Starr & Zurbriggen, 2016). Deliberate messages added to children's simplistic thinking can explain all gender stereotypes, according to cognitive theory.

Sociocultural Theory

In many ways, all societies promote gender distinction. Although national policies impact gender roles and although many fathers are active caregivers, women do much more child care, house cleaning, and meal preparation than do men. This is true even when women are the primary wage-earners for their families (as are about 40 percent of mothers in the United States) as well as worldwide (Bornstein & Putnick, 2016).

Furthermore, cultures socialize young girls and boys differently. For example, two 4-year-old girls might hug each other and hear "how sweet," but a boy who hugs a boy might be pushed away. Already by age 6, rough-and-tumble play is the only accepted way that boys touch each other. It is no surprise that such play is much more common in boys than girls.

Parents encourage gender differences sometimes without realizing it. For instance, a massive study of 41 low- and middle-income nations found that fathers took their young boys outside more often than their girls. They also were more likely to read to, tell stories to, and count with their sons. The mothers tended to be more unisex in their activities (Bornstein & Putnick, 2016).

gender schema A cognitive concept or general belief based on one's experiences—in this case, a child's understanding of sex differences.

By age 6, children are astute "gender detectives," seeking out ways that males and females differ in their culture and then trying to follow the lead of others of their sex. Mia is one example:

> On her first day of school, Mia sits at the lunch table eating a peanut butter and jelly sandwich. She notices that a few boys are eating peanut butter and jelly, but not one girl is. When her father picks her up from school, Mia runs up to him and exclaims, "Peanut butter and jelly is for boys! I want a turkey sandwich tomorrow."
>
> [*Quoted in Miller et al., 2013, p. 307*]

Evolutionary Theory

Evolutionary theory holds that sexual passion is one of humankind's basic drives, because all creatures have a powerful impulse to reproduce. Since biology requires an ovum and a sperm to make a baby, males and females follow their evolutionary mandate by trying to look attractive to the other sex—walking, talking, and laughing in gendered ways. If girls see their mothers wearing makeup and high heels, they want to do likewise.

This evolutionary drive may explain why, already in early childhood, boys have a powerful urge to become like the men, and girls like the women. This will prepare them, later on, to mate and conceive a new generation.

Thus, according to this theory, over millennia of human history, genes, chromosomes, and hormones have evolved to allow survival. Genes dictate that young boys are more active (rough-and-tumble play) and girls more domestic (playing house) because that prepares them for adulthood, when fathers defend against predators and mothers care for the home and children. To deny that is to deny nature. This means that transgender children, who identify as the other sex, have a difficult childhood. The entire culture pushes them to be whatever sex was on their birth certificate.

What Is Best?

Each major developmental theory strives to explain the ideas that young children express and the roles they follow. No consensus has been reached. That challenges caregivers because they know they should not blindly follow the norms of their culture, yet they also know that they need to provide guidance regarding male–female differences and everything else.

Regarding sex or gender, those who contend that nature (sex) is more important than nurture tend to design, cite, and believe studies that endorse their perspective. That has been equally true for those who believe that nurture (gender) is more important than nature. Only recently has a true interactionist perspective, emphasizing how nature affects nurture and vice versa, been endorsed (Eagly & Wood, 2013).

Some of the latest research suggests that our culture's emphasis on sex differences blinds us to the reality, a *gender similarities hypothesis,* that the two sexes have far more in common than traditional theories recognize. Perhaps instead of looking for sex differences, we should notice sex similarities. In early childhood, boys and girls are alike in many ways.

Indeed, this seems to be true for all aspects of development in early childhood. No matter which sex or ethnic group or culture, these three chapters emphasize that all children need good nutrition, intellectual stimulation, and other children to play with, always protected and encouraged by adults. The results are evident: By age 6, children everywhere are eager to grow and learn beyond the familiar comfort of their homes, as the next three chapters explain.

THINK CRITICALLY: Should children be encouraged to combine both male and female characteristics (called *androgyny*), or is learning male and female roles crucial for becoming a happy man or woman?

LaunchPad
macmillan learning

Video Activity: The Boy Who Was a Girl presents the case of David/Brenda Reimer as an exploration of what it means to be a boy or a girl.

SUMMARY

Emotional Development

1. Emotional regulation is crucial during early childhood. It occurs in Erikson's third developmental stage, initiative versus guilt. Children normally feel pride when they demonstrate initiative, but sometimes they feel guilt or even shame at an unsatisfactory outcome.

2. Emotional regulation is made possible by maturation of the brain, particularly of the prefrontal cortex, as well as by experiences with parents and peers.

3. Intrinsic motivation is apparent in a preschooler's concentration on a drawing or a conversation with an imaginary friend. It may endure when extrinsic motivation stops.

Play

4. All young children enjoy playing—preferably with other children of the same sex, who teach them lessons in social interaction that their parents do not.

5. Active play takes many forms, with rough-and-tumble play fostering social skills and sociodramatic play developing emotional regulation.

6. Prosocial emotions lead to caring for others; antisocial behavior includes instrumental, reactive, relational, and bullying aggression.

Challenges for Caregivers

7. Three classic styles of parenting have been identified: authoritarian, permissive, and authoritative. Generally, children are more

successful and happy when their parents express warmth and set guidelines.

8. A fourth style of parenting, neglectful/uninvolved, is always harmful. The particulars of parenting reflect the culture as well as the temperament of the child.

9. Parental punishment can have long-term consequences, with both corporal punishment and psychological control teaching lessons that few parents want their children to learn.

10. Even 2-year-olds correctly use sex-specific labels. Young children become aware of gender differences in clothes, toys, playmates, and future careers.

11. Freud emphasized that children are attracted to the opposite-sex parent and eventually seek to identify, or align themselves, with the same-sex parent. Behaviorists hold that gender-related behaviors are learned through reinforcement and punishment (especially for males) and social modeling.

12. Cognitive theorists note that simplistic preoperational thinking leads to gender schemas and therefore stereotypes. Sociocultural theory notes that every society and culture organizes life in gendered ways. Thus children express those social norms. Evolutionary theory contends that biological differences are crucial for the survival and reproduction of the species.

13. All five theories of gender-role development are plausible, which poses a challenge for caregivers who must determine which set of values they choose to teach.

KEY TERMS

emotional regulation (p. 261)
self-concept (p. 262)
effortful control (p. 262)
initiative versus guilt (p. 262)
intrinsic motivation (p. 264)
extrinsic motivation (p. 264)
imaginary friends (p. 264)
rough-and-tumble play (p. 268)
sociodramatic play (p. 268)

empathy (p. 270)
prosocial behavior (p. 270)
antisocial behavior (p. 270)
instrumental aggression
   (p. 271)
reactive aggression (p. 271)
relational aggression (p. 271)
bullying aggression (p. 272)
authoritarian parenting (p. 273)

permissive parenting (p. 273)
authoritative parenting (p. 273)
neglectful/uninvolved parenting
   (p. 273)
corporal punishment (p. 276)
psychological control (p. 278)
time-out (p. 278)
induction (p. 278)
sex differences (p. 279)

gender differences (p. 279)
phallic stage (p. 280)
Oedipus complex (p. 281)
superego (p. 281)
identification (p. 281)
gender schema (p. 283)

APPLICATIONS

1. Adults tend to believe that the way their parents raised them helped them become the people they are. Ask three people how their parents encouraged and disciplined them, and assess whether that indeed had an impact on adult personality.

2. Gender indicators often go unnoticed. Go to a public place (park, restaurant, busy street) and spend at least 10 minutes recording examples of gender differentiation, such as articles of clothing, mannerisms, interaction patterns, and activities.

Quantify what you see, such as baseball hats on eight males and two females. Or (better, but more difficult) describe four male–female conversations, indicating gender differences in length and frequency of talking, interruptions, vocabulary, and so on.

3. Analyze the intrinsic and extrinsic motivation for attending college. Do you think that one type or the other is more influential in your achievement? Explain.

The Developing Person So Far:
Early Childhood

BIOSOCIAL

Body Changes Children continue to grow from ages 2 to 6, but at a slower rate. Normally, the BMI (body mass index) is lower at about ages 5 and 6 than at any other time of life. Children often eat too much unhealthy food, putting themselves at risk for obesity and other problems. The proliferation of neural pathways and myelination continues. Parts of the brain connect, allowing better lateralization of the brain's left and right hemispheres and better coordination of the left and right sides of the body. This also leads to a decline in impulsivity and perseveration and better emotional expression and regulation.

Advancing Motor Skills Play is important for development; increasingly children are getting too little. Urbanization and pollution are also problematic, causing asthma, lead poisoning, and other impairments. Young children are still developing fine motor skills, and artistic expression helps them improve body and finger control.

Injuries and Abuse Far more children worldwide die of avoidable accidents than of diseases. Child abuse and neglect require primary, secondary, and tertiary prevention.

Child Maltreatment Maltreated children suffer ongoing abuse (most obvious) and neglect (most common), usually by their own parents. Both tertiary prevention and permanency planning are needed to mitigate the ill effects of maltreatment.

COGNITIVE

Thinking During Early Childhood Piaget stressed the young child's egocentric, illogical perspective, which prevents the child from grasping concepts such as conservation. Vygotsky stressed the cultural context, noting that children learn from mentors—which include parents, teachers, peers—and from the social context. Children develop their own theories, including a theory of mind, as they realize that not everyone thinks as they do.

Language Learning Language develops rapidly. By age 6, the average child knows 10,000 words and demonstrates extensive grammatical knowledge. Young children can become balanced bilinguals during these years if their social context is encouraging.

Early-Childhood Education Young children are avid learners. Child-centered, teacher-directed, and intervention programs, such as Head Start, can all nurture learning.

PSYCHOSOCIAL

Emotional Development Self-esteem is usually high during early childhood. Self-concept emerges in Erikson's stage of initiative versus guilt, as does the ability to regulate emotions. Externalizing problems may be the result of too little emotional regulation; internalizing problems may result from too much control.

Play All young children play, and they play best with peers. Play helps children develop physically and teaches emotional regulation, empathy, and cultural understanding.

Challenges for Caregivers A caregiving style that is warm and encouraging, with good communication as well as high expectations (called authoritative), is most effective in promoting the child's self-esteem, autonomy, and self-control. The authoritarian and permissive styles are less beneficial, although cultural variations are apparent.

middle childhood

Every age has joys and sorrows, gains and losses. But if you were pushed to choose one best period, you might select middle childhood. From ages 6 to 11, children grow steadily as they master new athletic skills, learn thousands of words, and enter a wider social world. Life is safe and healthy; the dangers of adolescence (drugs, early sex, violence) are still distant.

But not always. For some children, these years are the worst, not the best. They hate school or fear home; they may suffer with asthma or learning disorders, or they may be bullied or isolated. Adults don't always see these years as simple ones. Instead, they argue about diet and schooling, about treatment for children with special needs, about the effects on children of single parenthood or divorce or poverty. The next three chapters describe the joys and complications of middle childhood. ●●

Left: © 2016 Macmillan
Right: PhotoAlto/Jerome Gorin/Getty Images

Middle Childhood:
Biosocial Development

What Will You Know?

1. Does physical activity affect psychological health?
2. Why are IQ tests not used as often as they were a few decades ago?
3. Should children who are special—with unusual gifts or disabilities—be in special classes?

My daughter seemed lonely in the early weeks of first grade. Her teacher told me that she was admired, not rejected, and that she might become friends with Alison, who was also shy and bright. I spoke to Alison's mother, a friendly woman named Sharon, and we arranged a play date. Soon Bethany and Alison became best friends, as the teacher had predicted.

Unpredicted, however, is that Sharon became my friend. She and her husband, Rick (an editor of a fashion magazine), had one other child, a pudgy boy two years older than Alison. When my daughter and Alison were in fifth grade, I mentioned to Rick my interest in longitudinal research. He recalled a friend, a professional photographer, who took pictures of Alison and her brother every year. The friend wanted the pictures for his portfolio; Rick was happy to oblige. Rick then retrieved an old album with stunning portrayals of brother–sister relationships and personality development from infancy on. Alison was smiling and coy, even as an infant, and her brother was gaunt and serious until Alison was born, when he seemed to relax.

Rick welcomed my interest; Sharon did not.

"I hate that album," she said, slamming it shut. She explained that she told the pediatrician that she thought her baby boy was hungry, but the doctor insisted she stick to a four-hour breast-feeding schedule and told her to never give him formula. That's why she hated that album; it was evidence of an inexperienced mother heeding a doctor while starving her son.

Decades later, I am still friends with Sharon. Her genes and early life made her a large woman, but she carries her large frame well—she is neither too heavy nor too thin. Her adult son, however, is not only big—he is obese. His photo as a thin, serious infant haunts me now as well.

Did Sharon cause his obesity by underfeeding him when he was little, or by overfeeding him later on? Or did genes and culture interact in a destructive way? Or was he rebelling against his father, whose profession glorifies appearance?

Middle childhood is usually a happy time. But this chapter describes some problems of this period, including obesity, asthma, and a host of intellectual disabilities, all caused by the interaction of genes and environment, nature and nurture. Consequences and solutions are complex: Sharon and Rick are among the many parents who wonder what they could have done differently and whether it is too late to help their grown children. I wonder, too.

Left: knape/E+/Getty Images
Top: PhotoAlto/Jerome Gorin/Getty Images

middle childhood The period between early childhood and early adolescence, approximately from ages 6 to 11.

A Healthy Time

Genes and environment safeguard **middle childhood,** as the years from about 6 to 11 are called (Konner, 2010). Fatal diseases and accidents are rare; both nature and nurture make these years the healthiest of the entire life span. In the United States in 2013, the death rate for 5- to 14-year-olds was half of the rate for 1- to 4-year-olds and one-sixth the rate for 15- to 24-year-olds. From then on, disease fatalities increase steadily every year (National Center for Health Statistics, 2015).

Relatively good health has always been true everywhere in middle childhood, but this is even more apparent today. Worldwide, the current death rate in middle childhood is about one-fourth what it was in 1950 (United Nations, Department of Economic and Social Affairs, Population Division, 2015). In the United States in 1950, the death rate per 100,000 children aged 5 to 14 was 60; in 2013, it was 13. Likewise, minor illnesses, such as ear infections, infected tonsils, measles, and flu, are much less common than a few decades ago (National Center for Health Statistics, 2015).

Expert Eye-Hand Coordination The specifics of motor-skill development in middle childhood depend on the culture. These flute players are carrying on the European Baroque musical tradition that thrives among the poor, remote Guarayo people of Bolivia.

Slower Growth, Greater Strength

Unlike infants or adolescents, school-age children grow slowly and steadily, in body and brain. That makes self-care easy—from dressing to bathing, from making lunch to getting to school. Brain maturation allows children to sit in class without breaking pencils, tearing papers, or elbowing classmates. In these middle years, children are much more self-sufficient than younger children and not yet troubled by adolescent body changes.

Teeth

Important to the individual child is the loss of baby teeth. Some children are eager for the Tooth Fairy to replace their lost tooth with money—and some are told to

Global Decay Thousands of children in Bangalore, India gathered to brush their teeth together, part of an oral health campaign. Music, fast food, candy bars, and technology have been exported from the United States, and many developing nations have their own versions (Bollywood replaces Hollywood). Western diseases have also reached many nations; preventive health now follows.

Observation Quiz Beyond toothbrushes, what other health tools do most children here have that their parents did not? (see answer, page 294) →

brush carefully because the Tooth Fairy likes clean teeth. Each permanent tooth arrives on schedule, from about ages 6 to 12, with girls a few months ahead of boys.

In earlier times, many children neither brushed their teeth nor saw a dentist, and fluoride was never added to water. That's why many of the oldest-old have missing teeth, replaced with implants or dentures—no longer common among younger cohorts.

Currently, most school-age children brush their teeth, and many communities—including all of the larger U.S. cities—add fluoride to drinking water. According to a national survey, about 75 percent of U.S. children saw a dentist for preventive care in the past year. For most (70 percent), their teeth were in good shape (Ida & Rozier, 2013). In 2011, one city in Canada (Calgary) stopped adding fluoride to the water. The teeth of second-grade children suffered compared to children in a similar city (Edmonton) (McLaren et al., 2016).

Children's Health Habits

The health that most school-age children naturally enjoy depends on daily habits, including diet, exercise, and sleep. Unfortunately, children who have poor health for economic or social reasons (such as no regular medical care) are vulnerable lifelong, even if their socioeconomic status improves, because genes are affected by childhood lifelong (Miller & Chen, 2010; Blair & Raver, 2012).

Peers and parents are crucial. If children see that others routinely care for their own health, social learning pushes them to do the same. Camps for children with asthma, cancer, diabetes, sickle-cell disease, and other chronic illnesses are beneficial because the example of other children and the guidance of knowledgeable adults help children learn self-care. That needs to become a habit in childhood—not a matter of parental insistence—lest teenage rebellion lead to ignoring special diets, pills, warning signs, and doctors (Dean et al., 2010; Naughton et al., 2014).

Physical Activity

Beyond the sheer fun of playing, the benefits of physical activity—especially games with rules, which children are now able to follow—can last a lifetime. Exercise not only improves physical health and reduces depression but may also improve academic achievement (Ridgers et al., 2012).

Are They Having Fun? Helmets, uniforms, and competition—more appropriate for adults? Children everywhere want to do what the adults do, so probably these ones are proud of their ice hockey team.

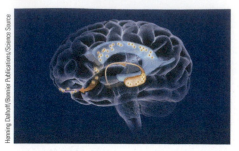

Video Activity: Brain Development: Middle Childhood depicts the changes that occur in a child's brain from age 6 to age 11.

selective attention The ability to concentrate on some stimuli while ignoring others.

Pay Attention Some adults think that computers make children lazy, because they can look up whatever they don't know. But imagine the facial expressions of these children if they were sitting at their desks with 30 classmates, listening to a lecture.

reaction time The time it takes to respond to a stimulus, either physically (with a reflexive movement such as an eyeblink) or cognitively (with a thought).

Answer to Observation Quiz
(from page 292): Water bottles, sun visors, and I.D. badges—although the latter might not be considered a healthy innovation.

Brain Development

How could body movement improve intellectual functioning? A review of the research suggests several possible mechanisms, including direct benefits of better cerebral blood flow and increased neurotransmitters, as well as indirect results from better moods (Singh et al., 2012). A new concept in psychology is *embodied cognition,* the idea that human thoughts are affected by body health, comfort, position, and so on (L. Smith, 2005). Many recent studies have found that cognition and action are closely aligned in children. A well-functioning body helps a child to learn.

Underlying body functioning is brain functioning. Remember *executive control,* the ability to inhibit some impulses to focus on others. Neurological advances allow children to pay special heed to the most important elements of their environment. **Selective attention,** the ability to concentrate on some stimuli while ignoring others, improves markedly at about age 7.

Selective attention is partly the result of maturation, but it is also greatly affected by experience, particularly the experience of playing with others. School-age children not only notice various stimuli (which is one form of attention) but also select appropriate responses when several possibilities conflict (Wendelken et al., 2011).

For example, in kickball, soccer, basketball, and baseball, it is crucial to attend to the ball, not to dozens of other stimuli. Thus, in baseball, young batters learn to ignore the other team's attempts to distract them, fielders start moving into position as soon as the bat connects, and pitchers adjust to the height, handedness, and past performance of the players. Another physical activity that seems to foster *executive function* is karate, which requires inhibition of some reactions in order to execute others (Alesi et al., 2014).

Similar advances occur in **reaction time,** which is how long it takes to respond to a stimulus. Preschoolers are sometimes frustratingly slow in putting on their pants, eating their cereal, throwing a ball. Reaction time is shorter every year of childhood, thanks to increasing myelination. Skill at games is an obvious example, from scoring on a video game, to swinging at a pitch, to kicking a soccer ball toward a teammate—all of which improve every year from 6 to 11, depending partly on practice.

Neighborhood Play

In addition to brain development, playing games teaches cooperation, problem solving, and respect for teammates and opponents of many backgrounds. Where can children reap these benefits?

Neighborhood play is an ideal way to develop many skills. Rules and boundaries are adapted to the context (out of bounds is "past the tree" or "behind the truck"). Dozens of running and catching games go on forever—or at least until dark. Neighborhood play is active, interactive, and inclusive—any child can play. One scholar notes:

> Children play tag, hide and seek, or pickup basketball. They compete with one another but always according to rules, and rules that they enforce themselves without recourse to an impartial judge. The penalty for not playing by the rules is not playing, that is, social exclusion.

[Gillespie, 2010, p. 298]

For school-age children, "social exclusion" is a steep price. Most learn to cooperate, playing for hours every day.

Unfortunately, modern life has undercut informal neighborhood play. Vacant lots and empty fields have largely disappeared, and parents fear "stranger danger"—thinking that a stranger might hurt their child (which is exceedingly rare) and ignoring the many benefits of outside play, which are universal. As one advocate of more unsupervised, creative childhood play sadly notes:

> Actions that would have been considered paranoid in the '70s—walking third-graders to school, forbidding your kid to play ball in the street, going down the slide with your child in your lap—are now routine.
>
> [Rosin, 2014]

Many parents enroll their children in organizations that offer—depending on the culture—tennis, karate, cricket, rugby, baseball, or soccer. Unfortunately, in every nation, childhood sports leagues are less likely to include children with special needs or low SES. Neighborhood leagues—Little League and so on—are scarce in inner-city neighborhoods. As a result, the children most likely to benefit are least likely to participate. The reasons are many, the consequences sad (Dearing et al., 2009). Another group with low participation is older girls, again a group particularly likely to benefit from athletic activity (Kremer et al., 2014).

Idyllic Two 8-year-olds, each with a 6-year-old sister, all four daydreaming or exploring in a very old tree beside a lake in Denmark—what could be better? Ideally, all of the world's children would be so fortunate, but most are not.

Exercise in School

When opportunities for neighborhood play are scarce, physical education in school is a logical alternative. However, in the United States schools are pressured to focus on test scores, so time for physical education and recess has declined. According to a nationwide survey of 10,000 third graders, about one-third of all U.S. schoolchildren have less than 15 minutes of recess each day. Some have no recess at all, a deprivation more likely in low-SES, urban, public schools.

The researchers write: "many children from disadvantaged backgrounds are not free to roam their neighborhoods or even their own yards unless they are accompanied by adults. . . . recess periods may be the only opportunity for them to practice their social skills with other children" (Barros et al., 2009, p. 434). In 2013, the American Academy of Pediatricians released a policy statement that "recess is a crucial and necessary component of a child's development," imploring educators never to punish children by reducing recess.

The same schools that eliminate recess often cut physical education to allow more time for reading and math. Even when gym class is required, schools find reasons to cancel it. For instance, although Alabama law requires at least 30 minutes of physical education each day, a study of all primary schools in one low-income district found that cancellations resulted in an average of only 22 minutes of gym a day. No school in this district had after-school sports (Robinson et al., 2014).

Paradoxically, eliminating recess may reduce children's mastery of reading and math, contrary to what many in the United States believe. Other nations make different choices.

Health Problems in Middle Childhood

Although health generally improves in middle childhood, some chronic conditions, including Tourette syndrome, stuttering, and allergies, often worsen. Even

⬤⬤ Especially for Physical Education Teachers A group of parents of fourth- and fifth-graders have asked for your help in persuading the school administration to sponsor a competitive sports team. How should you advise the group to proceed? (see response, page 296)

● ● **Response for Physical Education Teachers** (from page 295): Discuss with the parents their reasons for wanting the team. Children need physical activity, but some aspects of competitive sports are better suited to adults than to children.

childhood obesity In a child, having a BMI above the 95th percentile, according to the U.S. Centers for Disease Control's 1980 standards for children of a given age.

childhood overweight In a child, having a BMI above the 85th percentile, according to the U.S. Centers for Disease Control's 1980 standards for children of a given age.

● ● **Especially for Medical Professionals** You notice that a child is overweight, but you are hesitant to say anything to the parents, who are also overweight, because you do not want to offend them. What should you do? (see response, page 299)

● ● **Especially for Parents** Suppose that you always serve dinner with the television on, tuned to a news broadcast. Your hope is that your children will learn about the world as they eat. Can this practice be harmful? (see response, page 300)

Same Situation, Far Apart Children have high energy but small stomachs, so they enjoy frequent snacks more than big meals. Yet snacks are typically poor sources of nutrition. Who is healthier: the American boy crunching buttered popcorn as he watches a 3-D movie, or the Japanese children eating *takoyaki* (an octopus dumpling) as part of a traditional celebration near Tokyo?

minor problems—glasses, coughing, nose blowing, a visible birthmark—can make children self-conscious, interfering with friendship formation.

Not always, of course. Researchers increasingly recognize "that the expression and outcome for any problem will depend on the configuration and timing of a host of surrounding circumstances" (Hayden & Mash, 2014, p. 49). Parents and children are not merely reactive: In a dynamic-systems manner, individuals and contexts influence each other. Consider two examples: obesity and asthma.

Childhood Obesity

Childhood overweight is usually defined as a BMI above the 85th percentile, and **childhood obesity** is defined as a BMI above the 95th percentile for children of a particular age. In 2012, 18 percent of 6- to 11-year-olds in the United States were obese (Ogden et al., 2014).

Childhood obesity is increasing worldwide, having more than doubled since 1980 in all three nations of North America (Mexico, the United States, and Canada) (Ogden et al., 2011). Since 2000, rates seem to have leveled off in the United States, but they continue to increase in most other nations, including the most populous two, China and India (Gupta et al., 2012; Ji et al., 2013) (see Visualizing Development, p. 298).

Childhood overweight correlates with asthma, high blood pressure, and elevated cholesterol (especially LDL, the "lousy" cholesterol). If a child is critically ill (rare in middle childhood), obesity adds to the risk, making death more likely (P. Ross et al., 2016). But for the vast majority of children, obesity is not a medical problem as much as a social one. As excessive weight builds, school achievement decreases, self-esteem falls, and loneliness rises (Harrist et al., 2012).

Loneliness may be the worst of these for school-age children, since during these years friends are particularly important. A reciprocal relationship is apparent: Children with poor social skills and few friends are more likely to become obese and vice versa (Jackson & Cunningham, 2015; Vandewater et al., 2015).

What Causes Childhood Obesity?

There are "hundreds if not thousands of contributing factors" for childhood obesity, from the cells of the body to the norms of the society (Harrison et al., 2011, p. 51). Dozens of genes affect weight by influencing activity level, hunger, food preferences, body type, and metabolism. New genes and alleles that affect obesity—and that never act alone—are discovered virtually every month (Dunmore, 2013).

Knowing that genes are involved may slow down the impulse to blame people for being overweight. However, genes cannot explain why obesity rates have increased dramatically, since genes change little from one generation to the next (Harrison et al., 2011). Instead, cultural and cohort changes must be responsible, evident not only in North America but worldwide. For example, a review in India acknowledges genes but focuses on sugary drinks, portion sizes, chips, baked goods, and candy (Sahoo et al., 2015).

Look at the figure on obesity among 6- to 11-year-olds in the United States (see Figure 11.1).

At first glance, one might think that the large ethnic gaps (such as only 9 percent of Asian Americans but 26 percent of Hispanic Americans) might be genetic. But look at gender: Non-Hispanic white *girls* are twice as likely to be obese as boys, but in the other groups *boys* are more often obese than girls. Something cultural, not biological, must be the reason. Further evidence that social context, not genes, affects obesity was found in a study that controlled for family income and early parenting: Ethnic differences in childhood obesity almost disappeared (Taveras et al., 2013).

What are those parenting practices that make children too heavy? Obesity rates rise if: infants are not breast-fed and begin eating solid foods before 4 months; preschoolers have televisions in their bedrooms and drink large quantities of soda; school-age children sleep too little but have several hours each day of "screen time" (TV, videos, games), rarely playing outside (Hart et al., 2011; Taveras et al., 2013).

Although family habits in infancy and early childhood can set a child on the path to obesity, during middle childhood children themselves have *pester power*—the ability to get adults to do what they want (Powell et al., 2011). Often they pester their parents to buy calorie-dense foods that are advertised on television.

On average, all these family practices changed for the worse toward the end of the twentieth century in North America and are spreading worldwide. For instance, family size has decreased, and as a result, pester power has increased, and more food is available for each child. That makes childhood obesity collateral damage of a reduction in birth rate—a worldwide trend in the early twenty-first century.

Attempts to limit sugar and fat clash with the goals of many corporations, since snacks and processed foods are very profitable. On the plus side, many schools now have policies that foster good nutrition. A national survey in the United States found that schools are reducing all types of commercial food advertising. However, vending machines are still prevalent in high schools, and free food coupons are often used as incentives in elementary schools (Terry-McElrath et al., 2014).

Overall, simply offering healthy food is not enough to convince children to change their diet; context and culture are crucial (Hanks et al., 2013). Communities can build parks, bike paths, and sidewalks, and nations can decrease subsidies for sugar and corn oil and syrup.

Rather than trying to zero in on any single factor, a dynamic-systems approach is needed: Many factors, over time, make a child overweight (Harrison et al., 2011). Changing just one factor is not enough.

FIGURE 11.1

Heavier and Heavier The incidence of obesity (defined here as the 95th percentile or above, per the Centers for Disease Control and Prevention 2000 growth charts) increases with age. Infants and preschoolers have lower rates than schoolchildren, which suggests that nurture is more influential than nature.

Observation Quiz Are boys more likely to be overweight than girls? (see answer, page 300) ➔

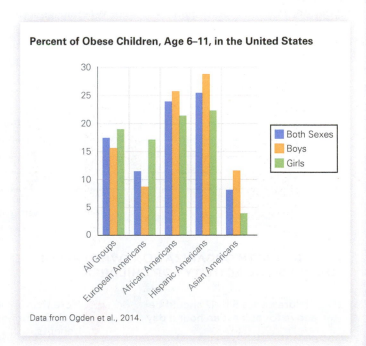

Percent of Obese Children, Age 6–11, in the United States

Data from Ogden et al., 2014.

Childhood Obesity Around the Globe

Obesity now causes more deaths worldwide than malnutrition. Reductions are possible. A multi-faceted prevention effort—including mothers, preschools, pediatricians, grocery stores, and even the White House—has reduced obesity in the United States for 2- to 5-year-olds. It was 13.9 percent in 2002 and was 8.4 percent in 2012. However, obesity rates from age 6 to 60 remain high everywhere.

DATA FROM M. NG ET AL., 2014.

Percentage of
Overweight
2- to 19-Year-Olds

- No data
- Less than 10%
- 10–15%
- 15–20%
- 20–25%
- 25–30%
- Over 30%

ADS AND OBESITY

Nations differ in children's exposure to televised ads for unhealthy food. The amount of this advertising continues to correlate with childhood obesity (e.g., Hewer, 2014). Parents can reduce overweight by limiting screen time and playing outside with their children. The community matters as well: When neighborhoods have no safe places to play, rates of obesity soar.

DATA FROM LOBSTEIN AND DIBB, 2005.

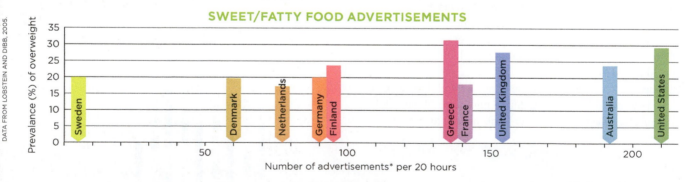

SWEET/FATTY FOOD ADVERTISEMENTS

Prevalence (%) of overweight

Sweden, Denmark, Netherlands, Germany, Finland, Greece, France, United Kingdom, Australia, United States

Number of advertisements* per 20 hours

INFORMATION FROM WORLD HEALTH ORGANIZATION, 2011.

WORLD HEALTH ORGANIZATION (WHO) RECOMMENDATIONS FOR PHYSICAL ACTIVITY FOR CHILDREN

1 Children ages 5 to 17 should be active for at least an hour a day.

2 More than an hour of exercise each day brings additional benefits.

3 Most physical activity should be aerobic. Vigorous activities should occur 3 times per week or more.

WHO also recommends daily exercise for adults of every age—including centenarians.

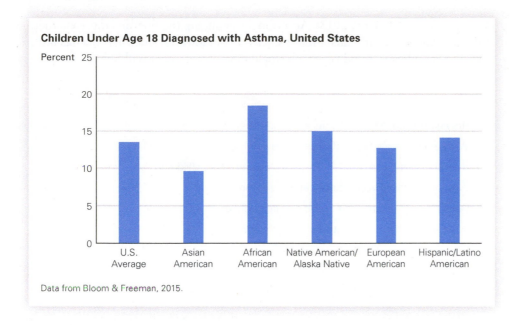

Children Under Age 18 Diagnosed with Asthma, United States

Data from Bloom & Freeman, 2015.

FIGURE 11.2

Not Breathing Easy Of all U.S. children younger than 18, almost 14 percent have been diagnosed at least once with asthma. Why are African American children more likely to have asthma? Puerto Rican children have even higher rates (not shown). Is that nature or nurture, genetics or pollution?

🔴 **Response for Medical Professionals** (from page 296): You need to speak to the parents, not accusingly (because you know that genes and culture have a major influence on body weight) but helpfully. Alert them to the potential social and health problems their child's weight poses. Most parents are very concerned about their child's well-being and will work with you to improve the child's snacks and exercise levels.

Asthma

Asthma is a chronic inflammatory disorder of the airways that makes breathing difficult. Sufferers have periodic attacks, sometimes requiring a rush to the hospital emergency room, a frightening experience for children who know that asthma might kill them (although it almost never does in childhood). Childhood asthma continues in adulthood about half the time, when it can be fatal (Banks & Andrews, 2015). But the most serious problem related to asthma in middle childhood is social, not medical. Childhood friendships thrive between children who are almost never absent, yet asthma is the most common reason children miss school.

In the United States, childhood asthma rates have tripled since 1980, with 14 percent of U.S. 5- to 11-year-olds diagnosed with asthma at some time. About two-thirds of those ever diagnosed still have asthma (National Center for Health Statistics, 2014). (See Figure 11.2.)

Researchers have found many causes of asthma. Some alleles have been identified, as have many aspects of modern life—carpets, pollution, house pets, airtight windows, parental smoking, cockroaches, dust mites, less outdoor play. None acts in isolation. A combination of genetic sensitivity to allergies, early respiratory infections, and compromised lung functioning increases wheezing and shortness of breath (Mackenzie et al., 2014).

Some experts suggest a *hygiene hypothesis*: that "the immune system needs to tangle with microbes when we are young" (Leslie, 2012, p. 1428). Children may be overprotected from viruses and bacteria. In their concern about hygiene, parents prevent exposure to minor infections, diseases, and family pets that would strengthen their child's immunity. This hypothesis is supported by data showing that (1) first-born children develop asthma more often than later-born ones; (2) asthma and allergies are less common among farm-dwelling children; and (3) children born by cesarean delivery (very sterile) have a greater incidence of asthma. Overall, it may be "that despite what our mothers told us, cleanliness sometimes leads to sickness" (Leslie, 2012, p. 1428).

Remember the microbiome—those many bacteria that are within our bodies. Some are in the lungs and act to increase or

asthma A chronic disease of the respiratory system in which inflammation narrows the airways from the nose and mouth to the lungs, causing difficulty in breathing. Signs and symptoms include wheezing, shortness of breath, chest tightness, and coughing.

Pride and Prejudice In some city schools, asthma is so common that using an inhaler is a sign of pride, as suggested by the facial expressions of these two boys. The "prejudice" is beyond the walls of this school nurse's room, in a society that allows high rates of childhood asthma.

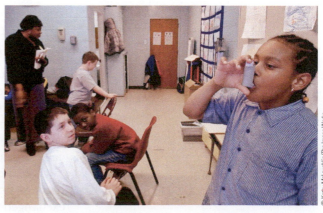

Response for Parents
(from page 296): Habitual TV watching correlates with obesity, so you may be damaging your children's health rather than improving their intellect. Your children would probably benefit more if you were to make dinner a time for family conversation about world events.

Answer to Observation Quiz (from page 297): Overall, no. But in some groups, yes. Rates of obesity among Asian American boys are almost three times higher than among Asian American girls.

developmental psychopathology
The field that uses insights into typical development to understand and remediate developmental disorders.

comorbid Refers to the presence of two or more unrelated disease conditions at the same time in the same person.

decrease asthma (Huang, 2013). Accordingly, changing the microbiome—via diet, drugs, or exposure to animals—may treat asthma. However, since asthma has multiple and varied causes and types, no single kind of treatment will help everyone.

WHAT HAVE YOU LEARNED?

1. How do childhood health habits affect adult health?
2. What are the advantages of physical play during middle childhood?
3. How could the brain be affected by playing with other children?
4. Why does a thin 6-year-old not need to eat more?
5. What roles do nature and nurture play in childhood asthma?
6. What are the hazards of asthma in childhood?

Children with Special Brains and Bodies

Developmental psychopathology links usual with unusual development, especially when the unusual results in special needs (Cicchetti, 2013b; Hayden & Mash, 2014). Every topic already described, including "genetics, neuroscience, developmental psychology, . . . must be combined to understand how psychopathology develops and can be prevented" (Dodge, 2009, p. 413).

This topic is relevant lifelong because "[e]ach period of life, from the prenatal period through senescence, ushers in new biological and psychological challenges, strengths, and vulnerabilities" (Cicchetti, 2013b, p. 458). Turning points, opportunities, and past influences are always apparent.

At the outset, four general principles should be emphasized.

1. *Abnormality is normal,* meaning that everyone typically has some aspects of behavior that are quite unusual. Thus, most people sometimes act oddly. The opposite is also true: Everyone with a serious disorder is, in many respects, like everyone else. This is particularly apparent with children.
2. *Disability changes year by year.* Most disorders are **comorbid,** which means that more than one problem is evident in the same person. The disorder that seems most severe may become much milder, but another problem may appear.
3. *Life may get better or worse.* Prognosis is uncertain. Many children with severe disabilities (e.g., blindness) become productive adults. Conversely, some conditions (e.g., conduct disorder) become more disabling.
4. *Diagnosis and treatment reflect the social context.* Each individual interacts with the surrounding setting—including family, school, community, and culture—to modify, worsen, or even create psychopathology.

Measuring the Mind

The importance of this last item is evident in a basic question—does a particular person have a disorder or not? In ancient times, if adults were strong and hardworking, that made them solid members of the community, not disordered. No one was singled out if they could not think quickly, read well, or sit still. If someone had an obvious disability, such as being blind or deaf, he or she received special care; no need for diagnosis.

Over the centuries, however, humans have placed more value on brain functioning. Books were printed so that everyone might read them; money was exchanged for daily food and housing; voters chose leaders instead of kings inheriting kingdoms. This meant that learning ability became crucial.

Currently, only about 1 percent of all children are diagnosed with obvious physical impairments. But in many nations another 10 to 20 percent are thought to need special education because of something amiss in their thinking. For that, the social context matters.

Aptitude, Achievement, and IQ

The potential to master a specific skill or aptitude to learn a certain body of knowledge is called **aptitude.** A child's brain has the potential to read and write (true for most people), or an adult has the aptitude for becoming a talented soccer player, seamstress, chef, artist, or whatever (potentials that only some people have).

People assumed that, for **intelligence,** one general aptitude (often referred to as *g*, for general intelligence) could be assessed by answers to a series of questions testing vocabulary, memory, puzzle completion, and so on. The number of correct answers was compared to the average for children of a particular age, and an IQ score was found. The advantage of intelligence tests is that scores correlated with school achievement and often predicted which children would have difficulty mastering the regular curriculum.

Originally, IQ tests produced a score that was literally a quotient: Mental age (the average chronological age of children who answer a certain number of questions correctly) was divided by the chronological age of a child taking the test. The answer from that division (the quotient) was multiplied by 100.

Thus, if the average 9-year-old answered, say, exactly 60 questions correctly, then everyone who got 60 questions correct—no matter what their chronological age—would have a mental age of 9. Obviously, for children whose mental age was the same as their chronological age (such as a 9-year-old who got 60 questions right), the IQ would be 100 ($9 \div 9 = 1 \times 100 = 100$), exactly average.

If a 6-year-old answered the questions as well as a typical 9-year-old, the score would be $9 \div 6 \times 100$, or 133. If a 12-year-old answered only 60 questions correctly, the IQ would be 75 ($9 \div 12 \times 100$). The current method of calculating IQ is more complex, but the basic idea is the same: *g* is calculated based on the average mental age of people of a particular chronological age. (See Figure 11.3.)

What is actually learned, not one's learning potential (aptitude), is called **achievement.** School achievement tests compare scores to norms established for each grade. For example, children of any age who read as well as the average third-grader would be at the third-grade level in reading achievement.

It was once assumed that aptitude was a fixed characteristic, present at birth. Longitudinal data show otherwise. Young children with a low IQ can become

Typical 7-Year-Old? In many ways this boy is typical. He likes video games and school, he usually appreciates his parents, and he gets himself dressed every morning. This photo shows him using blocks to construct a design to match a picture, one of the 10 kinds of challenges that comprise the WISC, a widely used IQ test. His attention to the task is not unusual for children his age, but his actual performance is more like that of an older child. That makes his IQ score significantly above 100.

aptitude The potential to master a specific skill or to learn a certain body of knowledge.

intelligence The ability to learn and understand various aspects of life, traditionally focused on reading and math, and more recently on the arts, movement, and social interactions.

achievement test A measure of mastery or proficiency in reading, mathematics, writing, science, or some other subject.

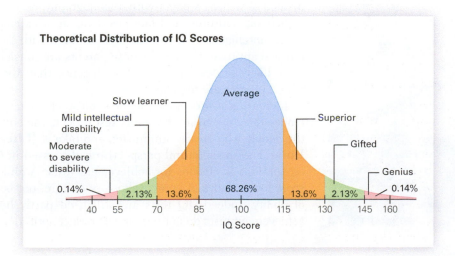

Theoretical Distribution of IQ Scores

Moderate to severe disability — 0.14%
Mild intellectual disability — 2.13%
Slow learner — 13.6%
Average — 68.26%
Superior — 13.6%
Gifted — 2.13%
Genius — 0.14%

40   55   70   85   100   115   130   145   160

IQ Score

FIGURE 11.3

In Theory, Most People Are Average
Almost 70 percent of IQ scores fall within the "normal" range. Note, however, that this is a norm-referenced test. In fact, actual IQ scores have risen in many nations; 100 is no longer exactly the midpoint. Furthermore, in practice, scores below 50 are slightly more frequent than indicated by the normal curve (shown here) because severe disability is the result not of normal distribution but of genetic and prenatal factors.

Observation Quiz If a person's IQ is 110, what category is he or she in? (see answer, page 302)

Flynn effect The rise in average IQ scores that has occurred over the decades in many nations.

Answer to Observation Quiz (from page 301): He or she is average. Anyone with a score between 85 and 115 has an average IQ.

multiple intelligences The idea that human intelligence is composed of a varied set of abilities rather than a single, all-encompassing one.

Especially for Teachers What are the advantages and disadvantages of using Gardner's nine intelligences to guide your classroom curriculum? (see response, page 304)

A Gifted Child Georgie Pocheptsov is an artist, and his family and culture recognized his talent by buying art supplies, giving him time and a place to paint, and selling his creations. Did he lose anything because of his talent, as Picasso did?

© Brownie Harris/CORBIS

above average or even gifted adults, like my nephew David (discussed in Chapter 1). Indeed, the average IQ scores of entire nations have risen substantially every decade for the past century—a phenomenon called the **Flynn effect,** named after the researcher who first described it (Flynn, 1999, 2012).

Most psychologists now agree that the brain is like a muscle, affected by mental exercise—which often is encouraged or discouraged by the social setting. This is proven in language and music (brains literally grow with childhood music training) and is probably true in other domains (Moreno et al., 2015; Zatorre, 2013). Both speed and memory are crucial for *g*, and they are affected by experience, evident in the Flynn effect.

Many Intelligences

Since scores change over time, IQ tests are much less definitive than they were once thought to be. Some scientists doubt whether any single test can measure the complexities of the human brain, especially if the test is designed to measure *g*, one general aptitude. According to some experts, children inherit and develop many abilities, some high and some low, rather than any *g* (e.g., Q. Zhu et al., 2010).

Two leading developmentalists (Robert Sternberg and Howard Gardner) are among those who believe that humans have **multiple intelligences,** not just one. Sternberg originally described three kinds of intelligence: analytic, creative, and practical (2008; 2011). His ideas are discussed when we explore adult intelligence in Chapter 21.

Gardner originally described seven intelligences: linguistic, logical-mathematical, musical, spatial, bodily-kinesthetic (movement), interpersonal (social understanding), and intrapersonal (self-understanding), each associated with a particular brain region (Gardner, 1983). He subsequently added an eighth (naturalistic: understanding nature, as in biology, zoology, or farming) and a ninth (spiritual/existential: thinking about life and death) (Gardner, 1999, 2006; Gardner & Moran, 2006).

Although everyone has some of all nine intelligences, Gardner believes each individual excels in particular ones. For example, someone might be gifted spatially but not linguistically (a visual artist who cannot describe her work) or might have interpersonal but not naturalistic intelligence (an astute clinical psychologist whose houseplants die). Gardner's concepts influence teachers in many primary schools, where children might demonstrate their understanding of a historical event via a poster with drawings instead of writing a paper with a bibliography.

Schools, cultures, and families dampen or expand particular intelligences. If two children are born with creative, musical aptitude, the child whose parents are musicians is more likely to develop musical intelligence than the child whose parents are tone deaf.

Increasing awareness of the sociocultural perspective has made educators aware that every test reflects the culture of the people who create, administer, and take it. [**Life-Span Link:** The sociocultural perspective is discussed in Chapter 2.] This is obvious for achievement tests: A child may score low because of home, school, or culture, not because of ability. Indeed, IQ tests are still used partly because achievement tests do not necessarily reflect aptitude.

Brain Scans

Another way to indicate aptitude is to measure the brain directly, avoiding cultural biases. In childhood, brain scans do not correlate with scores on IQ tests, but they do later on (Brouwer et al., 2014). Brain scans can measure speed of reaction, which may underlie adult IQ. However, the variation in brain scans and IQ scores in children suggests flaws in one or the other (or both) of these measures (Goddings & Giedd, 2014).

Neurological measures may be no more accurate than paper-and-pencil tests. For example, although it seems logical that less brain activity means less intelligence, that is not always the case. In fact, heightened brain activity may be a sign of a disorder, not of intelligence (e.g., Xiang et al., 2016). Treatment effectiveness may be indicated by reduced brain activity (Thomas & Viljoen, 2016).

Another example of interpretation problems is in measuring the cortex. A thicker cortex sometimes correlates with high IQ, which makes sense because that is where most thinking occurs. However, in 9- to 11-year-olds, a thinner cortex predicts greater vocabulary (Menary et al., 2013; Karama et al., 2009). (Extensive vocabulary is pivotal for many aspects of intelligence and school achievement.)

Brain patterns in creative children differ from those who score high on IQ tests, again a result that is difficult to interpret (Jung & Ryman, 2013). Thus, there are many reasons psychologists do not rely on children's brain scans to indicate intelligence or diagnose psychopathology.

Neuroscientists and psychologists agree, however, on three generalities:

1. *Brain development depends on experiences.* Thus, a brain scan is accurate only for when it is done, not for the future.
2. *Dendrites form and myelination changes throughout life.* Middle childhood is crucial, but developments before and after these years are also significant.
3. *Children with disorders often have unusual brain patterns, and training may change those patterns.* However, brain complexity and normal variation mean that diagnosis and remediation are far from perfect.

Special Needs in Middle Childhood

Problems with testing are not the only reason diagnosis of psychopathology is complex (Hayden & Mash, 2014; Cicchetti, 2013b). One cause can have many (multiple) final manifestations, a phenomenon called **multifinality** (many final forms). The opposite is also apparent: Many causes can result in one symptom, a phenomenon called **equifinality** (equal in final form).

For example, an infant who has been flooded with stress hormones may become hypervigilant or irrationally placid, may be easily angered or quick to cry, or may not be affected (multifinality). Or a nonverbal child may have autism spectrum disorder or be hard of hearing, electively mute, or pathologically shy (equifinality).

The complexity of diagnosis is evident in the *Diagnostic and Statistical Manual of Mental Disorders*, 5th edition (American Psychiatric Association, 2013), referred to as DSM-5. A major problem is differentiating typical childish behavior and pathology. Some suggest that childhood psychopathology was underdiagnosed in early editions of the DSM and now is overdiagnosed (Hayden & Mash, 2014).

To illustrate the many complexities, we discuss three particularly common and troubling disorders, attention-deficit/hyperactivity disorder (ADHD), specific learning disorder, and autism spectrum disorder (ASD). The online DSM-5 Appendix lists the criteria for these three; professionals need to study dozens of disorders in much more detail.

multifinality A basic principle of developmental psychopathology which holds that one cause can have many (multiple) final manifestations.

equifinality A basic principle of developmental psychopathology which holds that one symptom can have many causes.

Download the **DSM-5 Appendix** to learn more about the terminology and classification of childhood psychopathology.

Almost Impossible The concentration needed to do homework is almost beyond Clint, age 11, who takes medication for ADHD. Note his furrowed brow, resting head, and sad face.

Observation Quiz Can Clint do his homework by himself? (see answer, p. 308) ↑

attention-deficit/hyperactivity disorder (ADHD) A condition characterized by a persistent pattern of inattention and/or by hyperactive or impulsive behaviors; ADHD interferes with a person's functioning or development.

Response for Teachers (from page 302): The advantages are that all of the children learn more aspects of human knowledge and that many children can develop their talents. Art, music, and sports should be an integral part of education, not just a break from academics. The disadvantage is that they take time and attention away from reading and math, which might lead to less proficiency in those subjects on standard tests and thus to criticism from parents and supervisors.

Attention-Deficit/Hyperactivity Disorder

Someone with **attention-deficit/hyperactivity disorder (ADHD)** is often inattentive and unusually active and impulsive, interfering with his or her ability to learn. The diagnosis in DSM-5 says that symptoms must start before age 12 (in DSM-IV it was age 7) and must impact daily life. (DSM-IV said *impaired*, not just *impacted*.) Thus, more children are considered ADHD than was the case 10 years ago.

Some impulsive, active, and creative behaviors are normal for children and healthy. However, children with ADHD "are so active and impulsive that they cannot sit still, are constantly fidgeting, talk when they should be listening, interrupt people all the time, can't stay on task, . . . accidentally injure themselves." All this makes them "difficult to parent or teach" (Nigg & Barkley, 2014, p. 75).

There is no biological marker for ADHD. Although some brain patterns are distinct, they are not proof of the disorder. Nor is there any definitive written test. Instead, diagnosis depends on parent and teacher reporting actual behavior, confirmed by careful observation by a professional who has seen many children that age. The origin is thought to be neurological, with problems in brain regulation either because of genes, complications of pregnancy, or toxins (such as lead) (Nigg & Barkley, 2014).

ADHD is often comorbid with other intellectual disabilities and depression, again, definitive biological markers are not usually found with any common disorder.

One surprising comorbidity is deafness: Children with severe hearing loss are affected in balance and activity, and that may make them develop ADHD (Antoine et al., 2013). The path may be direct or indirect: Whatever caused their hearing loss may also affect their activity level. When one brain insult causes many symptoms, that is multifinality; when many causes (deafness, toxins, illnesses) produce one disorder (ADHD), that is equifinality.

Although in 1980 about 5 percent of all U.S. 4- to 17-year-olds were diagnosed with ADHD, more recent rates are 7 percent of 4- to 9-year-olds, 13 percent of 10- to 13-year-olds, and 15 percent of 14- to 17-year-olds (Schwarz & Cohen, 2013). These numbers are called "astronomical" by one pediatric neurologist (Graf, quoted in Schwarz & Cohen, 2013) and "preposterous . . . a concoction to justify the giving out of medicine at unprecedented and unjustifiable levels" (Conners, quoted in Schwarz, 2013, p. A1).

Rates of ADHD in most other nations are lower than in the United States, but they are rising everywhere (e.g., Al-Yagon et al., 2013; Hsia & Maclennan, 2009; van den Ban et al., 2010). Most research finds the highest rates in North America and the lowest rates in East Asia (Erskine et al., 2013), but since diagnosis depends on judgment, international comparisons may be invalid. Increases anywhere raise three concerns:

- *Misdiagnosis.* If ADHD is diagnosed when another disorder is the problem, treatment might make the problem worse (Miklowitz & Cicchetti, 2010). Many psychoactive drugs alter moods, so a child with disruptive mood dysregulation (formerly called bipolar disorder) might be harmed by ADHD medication.

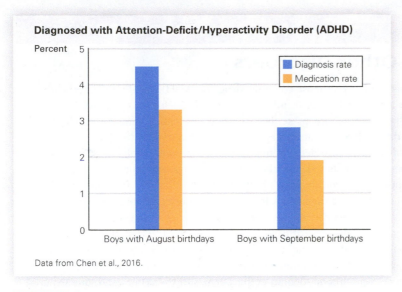

Data from Chen et al., 2016.

FIGURE 11.4

One Month Is One Year In the Taiwanese school system, the cutoff for kindergarten is September 1, so some boys enter school a year later because they were born a few days later. Those who are relatively young among their classmates are less able to sit still and listen. They are twice as likely to be given drugs to quiet them down.

- *Drug abuse.* Although drugs sometimes are therapeutic for true ADHD cases, some adolescents seek a diagnosis of ADHD in order to obtain legal amphetamines.
- *Normal behavior considered pathological.* In young children, high activity, impulsiveness, and curiosity are typical. When children are diagnosed as abnormal, that may affect their self-concept and adult expectations.

"Normal considered pathological" is one interpretation of data on 378,000 children in Taiwan, a Chinese nation whose rates of ADHD are increasing (Chen et al., 2016). Boys who were born in August, and hence entered kindergarten when they just turned 5, were diagnosed with ADHD at the rate of 4.5 percent, whereas boys born in September, starting kindergarten when they were almost 6, were diagnosed at the rate of 2.8 percent. Diagnosis typically occurred years after kindergarten, but August birthday boys were at risk throughout their school years. (See Figure 11.4.)

This suggests that neurological immaturity, not neurological deficit, is sometimes the problem. Changes in the school curriculum or expectations may be a better solution than medication.

A related issue regards the sex ratio: Boys are far more often diagnosed as having ADHD than girls, usually because their mothers and female teachers find them impossible to control. One review states "boys outnumber girls 3-to-1 in community samples and 9-to-1 in clinical samples" (Hasson & Fine, 2012, p. 190). Could typical male activity be one reason?

Treatment for ADHD involves (1) training for the family and the child, (2) special education for teachers, and (3) medication. But, as equifinality suggests, most disorders vary in causes, so treatment that helps one child does not necessarily work for another (Mulligan et al., 2013).

Drugs may help, but they are not a cure. Adults disagree about treatment, especially with drugs, as the following explains.

Especially for Health Workers
Parents ask that some medication be prescribed for their kindergarten child, who they say is much too active for them to handle. How do you respond? (see response, page 308)

Drug Treatment for ADHD and Other Disorders

Because many adults are upset by children's moods and actions, and because any physician can write a prescription to quiet a child, thousands of U.S. children may be overmedicated. *But because many parents do not recognize that their child needs help, or they are suspicious of drugs and psychologists (Moldavsky & Sayal, 2013; Rose, 2008), thousands of children may suffer needlessly. Many child psychologists believe that the public discounts the devastation and lost learning that occur when a child's serious disorder is not recognized or treated. On the other hand, many parents are suspicious of drugs and psychotherapy and avoid recommended treatment (Gordon-Hollingsworth et al., 2015).

In the United States, more than 2 million people younger than 18 take prescription drugs to regulate their emotions and behavior. The rates are about 14 percent for teenagers (Merikangas et al., 2013), about 10 percent for 6- to 11-year-olds, and less than 1 percent for 2- to 5-year-olds (Olfson et al., 2010). In China, parents rarely use psychoactive medication for children: A Chinese child with ADHD symptoms is thought to need correction rather than medication (Yang et al., 2013). An African child who does not pay attention may be beaten. Wise or cruel?

The most common drug for ADHD is Ritalin (methylphenidate), but in middle childhood at least 20 other psychoactive drugs are prescribed to treat depression, anxiety, intellectual disability, autism spectrum disorder, disruptive mood dysregulation disorder, and many other conditions (see Figure 11.5). Some parents welcome the relief that drugs may provide; others refuse to medicate their children because they fear the consequences, among them later drug abuse or shorter height. Neither of those consequences has been proven. Indeed, long-term benefits including less drug abuse sometimes occur (Craig et al., 2015).

Worrisome is that some research finds that medicating ADHD children increases the risk of severe mental illness in adulthood (Moran et al., 2015). On the other hand, one expert argues that teachers and doctors underdiagnose and undertreat African American children, and that increases another outcome—prison. If disruptive African American boys are punished, not treated, for ADHD symptoms that should be recognized and altered in childhood, they may join the "school-to-prison pipeline" (Moody, 2016).

All professionals agree that finding the best drug at the right strength is difficult, in part because each child's genes and personality are unique, and in part because children's weight and metabolism change every year. Given all that, it is troubling that only half of all children who take psychoactive drugs are evalu-

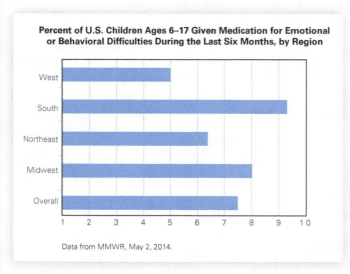

Percent of U.S. Children Ages 6–17 Given Medication for Emotional or Behavioral Difficulties During the Last Six Months, by Region

Data from MMWR, May 2, 2014.

FIGURE 11.5

One Child in Every Classroom Or maybe two, if the class has more than 20 students or is in Alabama. This figure shows the percent of 6- to 17-year-olds prescribed psychoactive drugs in the previous six months. About half of these children have been diagnosed with ADHD, and the rest have anxiety, mood, and other disorders. These data are averages, gathered from many communities. In fact, some schools, even in the South, have very few medicated children, and others, even in the West, have several in every class. The regional variations evident here are notable, but much more dramatic are rates by school, community, and doctor—some of whom are much quicker to medicate children than others.

A Family Learning When Anthony Suppers was diagnosed with ADHD, his mother Michelle (shown here) realized she had it, too. That helps Anthony, because his mother knows how important it is to have him do his homework at his own desk as soon as he comes home from school.

ated and monitored by a mental health professional (Olfson et al., 2010) and that pharmaceutical companies advertise ADHD drugs as beneficial for children (Schwarz, 2013). Most professionals believe that contextual interventions (instructing caregivers and schools on child management) should be tried before drugs (Daley et al., 2009; Leventhal, 2013; Pelham & Fabiano, 2008), many parents wonder whether professionals really understand.

Ethnic differences are found in parent responses, teacher responses, and treatment for children with ADHD symptoms. In the United States, when African American and Hispanic children are diagnosed with ADHD or other psychological disorders, parents are less likely to give them medication or engage in other forms of professional therapy compared to European American parents (Morgan et al., 2013; Gordon-Hollingsworth et al., 2015). Income differences are evident as well: In the United States, children on Medicaid (the health program for low-SES families) are more likely to be prescribed ADHD medication than middle-class children (Schwarz, 2013).

Genes, culture, health care, education, religion, and stereotypes all affect ethnic and economic differences. As two experts explain, "disentangling these will be extremely valuable to improving culturally competent assessment in an increasingly diverse society" (Nigg & Barkley, 2014, p. 98). Given the emotional and practical implications of that tangle, opposing perspectives are not surprising.

Specific Learning Disorders

The DSM-5 diagnosis of **specific learning disorder** now includes problems in both perception and processing of information causing low achievement in reading, math, or writing (including spelling) (Lewandowski & Lovett, 2014). Disabilities in these areas undercut academic achievement, destroy self-esteem, and qualify a child for special education (according to U.S. law) or formal diagnosis (according to DSM-5). Hopefully, such children find (or are taught) ways to compensate, and other abilities shine.

The most commonly diagnosed learning disorder is **dyslexia**—unusual difficulty with reading. No single test accurately diagnoses dyslexia (or any learning disorder) because every academic achievement involves many distinct factors. One child with a reading disability might have trouble sounding out words but excel in comprehension and memory of printed text; another child might have the opposite problem. Dozens of types and causes of dyslexia have been identified: No specific strategy helps every child (O'Brien et al., 2012). Historically, some children with dyslexia figured out themselves how to cope—as did Hans Christian Andersen and Winston Churchill.

Early theories hypothesized that visual difficulties—for example, reversals of letters (reading *god* instead of *dog*) and mirror writing (*b* instead of *d*)—were the cause of dyslexia, but we now know that dyslexia more often originates with speech and hearing difficulties (Gabrieli, 2009; Swanson, 2013). An early warning occurs if a 3-year-old does not talk clearly or has not had a naming explosion. [**Life-Span Link:** Language development in early childhood is explained in Chapter 6.]

Another common learning disorder is **dyscalculia,** unusual difficulty with math. For example, when asked to estimate the height of a normal room, second-graders with dyscalculia might answer "200 feet," or, when shown two cards, say the 5 and 8 of hearts, and asked which is higher, a child might correctly answer 8—but only after using their fingers to count the number of hearts on each card (Butterworth et al., 2011).

Although learning disorders can appear in any skill, such as in music or movement (as Gardner's theory of multiple intelligences predicts), only one more disorder is recognized by DSM-5: *dysgraphia,* difficulty in writing. Neat writing is rare at age 6, but fine motor skills improve every year, so a child should be able to write easily and legibly by age 10. Penmanship was once a major subject in school: Now reading and math are more emphasized, and current learning goals in the United States (the Common Core) include keyboarding, not writing (Zubrzycki, 2012). One result is that dysgraphia is common, but less often diagnosed and treated.

specific learning disorder A marked deficit in a particular area of learning that is not caused by an apparent physical disability, by an intellectual disability, or by an unusually stressful home environment.

dyslexia Unusual difficulty with reading; thought to be the result of some neurological underdevelopment.

dyscalculia Unusual difficulty with math, probably originating from a distinct part of the brain.

LaunchPad
macmillan learning

Video: Dyslexia: Expert and Children
http://qrs.ly/cg4ep0v

© 2016 Macmillan

Happy Reading Those large prism glasses keep the letters from jumping around on the page, a boon for this 8-year-old French boy. Unfortunately, each child with dyslexia needs individualized treatment: These glasses help some, but not most, children who find reading difficult.

BSIP/IIG Via Getty Images

autism spectrum disorder (ASD)
A developmental disorder marked by difficulty with social communication and interaction—including difficulty seeing things from another person's point of view—and restricted, repetitive patterns of behavior, interests, or activities.

LaunchPad
macmillan learning

Video: Current Research into Autism Spectrum Disorder explores why the causes of ASD are still largely unknown.

Response for Health Workers
(from page 305): Medication helps some hyperactive children but not all. It might be useful for this child, but other forms of intervention should be tried first. Compliment the parents on their concern about their child, but refer them to an expert in early childhood for an evaluation and recommendations. Behavior-management techniques geared to the particular situation, not medication, should be the first strategy.

Answer to Observation Quiz
(from p. 304) Maybe, but he often needs help. Clint is not writing the answers here.

Autism Spectrum Disorder

Of all the children with special needs, those with **autism spectrum disorder (ASD)** are probably the most puzzling. Their problems are sometimes severe, but both the causes and treatments are hotly disputed. Thomas Insel, director of the National Institute of Mental Health, describes the parents and other advocates of children with autism as "the most polarized, fragmented community I know" (quoted in Solomon, 2012, p. 280).

A century ago, autism was considered a rare disorder affecting fewer than 1 in 1,000 children with "an extreme aloneness that, whenever possible, disregards, ignores, shuts out anything . . . from the outside" (Kanner, 1943). In the middle of the twentieth century, very few children were thought to have autism, and those few were usually completely nonverbal and severely impaired. Most children who developed such symptoms were diagnosed as "mentally retarded" or, by the end of the twentieth century, as having a "pervasive developmental disorder." (The term "mental retardation," in DSM-IV, has been replaced with "intellectual disability" in DSM-5.)

The DSM-5 expanded the term *autism* to *autism spectrum disorder,* which now includes mild, moderate, or severe categories. Children who were said to have Asperger syndrome now have "autism spectrum disorder without language or intellectual impairment" (American Psychiatric Association, 2013, p. 32).

All children with ASD find it difficult to understand the emotions of others, which makes them feel alien, like "an anthropologist on Mars," as Temple Grandin, an educator and writer with ASD, expressed it (quoted in Sacks, 1995). Consequently, they are less likely to talk or play with other children, and they are delayed in developing theory of mind.

Children with severe ASD may never speak, rarely smile, and typically play for hours with one object (such as a spinning top or a toy train). Mildly impaired children may not seem unusual at first, and they may be talented in some specialized area, such as drawing or geometry, although social skills are delayed. Many (46 percent) score average or above on IQ tests (MMWR, March 28, 2014).

Most children with ASD show signs in early infancy (no social smile, for example, or less gazing at faces and eyes than most toddlers). Some improve by age 3; others deteriorate (Klinger et al., 2014). Late onset occurs with several brain disorders, including *Rett syndrome,* in which a newborn girl (boys with the Rett gene never survive) has "normal psychomotor development through the first 5 months after birth," but then her brain develops very slowly, severely limiting movement and language (Bienvenu, 2005).

Many children with ASD have an opposite problem—too much neurological activity, not too little. Their head grows too fast, and by age 2 it is larger than average. Their sensory cortex may be hypersensitive, making them unusually upset by noise, light, and other sensations. Literally hundreds of genes and dozens of brain abnormalities are more common in people diagnosed with autism than in the general population.

Over the past two decades, far more children are diagnosed with ASD, and far fewer with intellectual disability. In the United States, among 8-year-olds, 1 child in every 68 (1 boy in 42; 1 girl in 189) is said to have ASD (MMWR, March 28, 2014). That's more than four times as many boys as girls. The other disparity is ethnic: About one-third more European American than Hispanic, Asian, or African American children are diagnosed with ASD.

The reasons for that increase are disputed. It could be caused by the environment—chemicals in the food, pollution in the air and water—or it could be that more professionals are aware of ASD and that more parents realize that education is finally available (Klinger et al., 2014). No definitive measure diagnoses ASD, making comparisons difficult.

As more children are diagnosed, some people wonder whether ASD is a disorder needing a cure or whether contemporary culture expects everyone to be fluent talkers, gregarious, and flexible—the opposite of people with ASD. Instead of those expectations, some advocate **neurodiversity,** the idea that human brains make us each diverse in our abilities and needs. Instead of trying to make all children alike, we might welcome the neurological variation of human beings (Kapp et al., 2013; Silberman, 2015).

Neurodiversity is a logical extension of the criticism of IQ tests. If there are multiple intelligences, then it is restrictive and prejudicial to expect everyone to be the same. Some people are impaired in interpersonal intelligence (one of Gardner's nine), and they may suffer from ASD. But those same people might have other strengths to be appreciated, even celebrated.

The neurodiversity perspective leads to new criticisms of the many treatments for ASD. When a child is diagnosed with ASD, parental responses vary from irrational hope to deep despair, from blaming doctors and chemical additives to feeling guilty for their genes, for their behavior during pregnancy, or for the circumstances they allowed at their child's birth. Many parents sue schools, or doctors, or the government; many spend all of their money and change their lives; many subject their children to treatments that are, at best, harmless, and at worst, painful and even fatal.

A sympathetic observer describes one child who was medicated with

> Abilify, Topamax, Seroquel, Prozac, Ativan, Depakote, trazodone, Risperdal, Anafranil, Lamictal, Benadryl, melatonin, and the homeopathic remedy, Calms Forté. Every time I saw her, the meds were being adjusted again . . . [he also describes] physical interventions—putting children in hyperbaric oxygen chambers, putting them in tanks with dolphins, giving them blue-green algae, or megadosing them on vitamins . . . usually neither helpful nor harmful, though they can have dangers, are certainly disorienting, and cost a lot.

> [Solomon, 2012, pp. 229, 270]

Diagnosis and treatment are difficult; an intervention that seems to help one child proves worthless for another. It is known, however, that biology is crucial (genes, copy number abnormalities, birth complications, prenatal injury, perhaps chemicals during fetal or infant development) family nurture is not the cause.

Not a Cartoon At age 3, Owen Suskind was diagnosed with autism. He stopped talking and spent hour after hour watching Disney movies. His father said his little boy "vanished," as chronicled in the documentary *Life Animated*. Now, at age 23 (shown here), Owen still loves cartoons, and he still has many symptoms of autism spectrum disorder. However, he also has learned to speak and has written a movie that reveals his understanding of himself, *The Land of the Lost Sidekicks*.

THINK CRITICALLY: Many adults are socially inept, insensitive to other people's emotions, and poor at communication—might they have been diagnosed as on the spectrum if they had been born more recently?

neurodiversity The idea that people with special needs have diverse brain structures, with each person having neurological strengths and weaknesses that should be appreciated, in much the same way diverse cultures and ethnicities are welcomed.

WHAT HAVE YOU LEARNED?

1. When would an educator give an aptitude test instead of an achievement test?

2. Should traditional IQ tests be discarded? Why or why not?

3. What might be the explanation for the Flynn effect?

4. Should brain scans replace traditional intelligence tests? Why or why not?

5. What is the difference between multifinality and equifinality?

6. Why is medication used for some children with ADHD?

7. What is the difference between ADHD and normal child behavior?

8. What are dyslexia, dyscalculia, and dysgraphia?

9. How might an adult have a learning disorder that has never been diagnosed?

10. What are the symptoms of autism spectrum disorder?

11. Who is likely to welcome the concept of neurodiversity?

• Special Education

The overlap of the biosocial, cognitive, and psychosocial domains is evident to developmentalists, as is the need for parents, teachers, therapists, and researchers to work together to help each child. However, deciding whether or not a child should be designated as needing special education is not straightforward, nor is it closely related to individual needs. Parents, schools, and therapists often disagree about how to help children, or even whether help is needed, as the following case illustrates.

A CASE TO STUDY

Lynda Is Getting Worse

Researchers asked 158 child psychologists—half of them from England and half from the United States—to diagnose an 11-year-old girl with the following symptoms.

> Parents say Lynda has been hyperactive, with poor boundaries and disinhibited behavior since she was a toddler. . . . Lynda has taken several stimulants since age 8. She is behind in her school work, but IQ normal. . . . At school she is oppositional and "lazy" but not disruptive in class. Psychological testing, age 8, described frequent impulsivity, tendencies to discuss topics unrelated to tasks she was completing, intermittent expression of anger and anxiety, significantly elevated levels of physical activity, difficulties sitting still, and touching everything. Over the past year Lynda has become very angry, irritable, destructive and capricious. She is provocative and can be cruel to pets and small children. She has been sexually inappropriate with peers and families, including expressing interest in lewd material on the Internet, Play Girl magazine, hugging and kissing peers. She appears to be grandiose, telling her family that she will be attending medical school, or will become a record producer, a professional wrestler, or an acrobat. Throughout this period there have been substantial marital difficulties between the parents.

> *[Dubicka et al., 2008, appendix p. 3]*

Most (81 percent) of the clinicians diagnosing Lynda thought she had ADHD, and most thought she had another disorder as well. Almost all of the Americans suggested a second and often a third disorder, with 75 percent of them specifying bipolar disorder (now called disruptive mood dysregulation disorder). Only 33 percent of the British psychologists agreed (Dubicka et al., 2008).

Clinicians did not finger the family context or teachers' attitudes, but a developmental approach would consider the entire context. The school, for instance, focused only on academics, and since Lynda did not have a learning disorder and was not disruptive, the teachers' only complaint was that she was lazy. "Lazy" is a word that signifies serious problems in the school or the child—yet the teachers did not realize it.

More troubling is that the parents did not get the treatment Lynda or they themselves needed. They thought she was hyperactive at age 2, but not until age 8 did they have her tested. At that point they put her on medication, but they did not find an appropriate educational setting for her or revamp their own parenting. Ideally, they themselves should have been tested to discover any genetic or familial effects, and they should have sought counseling for their marriage. Children whose parents are hostile to each other often act out in the ways that Lynda did, with unexpected anger, depression, and sexual interest. Many studies find that school and home environments can be crucial for a young child with ADHD (Nigg & Barkley, 2014).

Puberty is the time for increased sexual interest and defiance of parental authority. Thus, it is not surprising that 11-year-old Lynda is getting worse. Family interaction, especially a parental alliance, might have forestalled the problem, and special education, beginning in preschool, might have avoided difficulties with Lynda and with their relationship, both of which became more troubling when she reached puberty—a result that developmentalists could have predicted years earlier.

Of course, this is speculation. It is impossible to know what would have happened if intensive intervention had taken place for the entire family, and if good education had been found when Lynda was a toddler. In any case, the four principles of developmental psychopathology suggest that developmental patterns and social contexts needed to be considered. Life may become better or worse (principle three). Without treatment Lynda got worse, and will continue to do so. Special education, ideally, begins early and includes the entire family. That might have led to improvement, as apparently testing and three years of medication did not.

Labels, Laws, and Learning

In the United States, recognition that the distinction between typical and atypical is not clear-cut (the first principle of developmental psychopathology) led to a series of reforms in the treatment and education of children with special needs. According to the 1975 Education of All Handicapped Children Act, all children can learn, and all must be educated in the **least restrictive environment (LRE).**

That law has been revised several times, but the goal remains the same. No child should be segregated from other children unless efforts to remediate problems within the regular classroom have been tried and failed. Further, every child merits schooling: None should be considered uneducable.

Consequently, LRE usually means educating most children with special needs within a regular class (a practice once called *mainstreaming*) rather than in a special classroom or school. Sometimes a child is sent for a few hours a week to a *resource room,* with a teacher who provides targeted tutoring. Sometimes a class is an *inclusion class,* which means that children with special needs are "included" in the general classroom, with "appropriate aids and services" (ideally from a trained teacher who works with the regular teacher).

A more recent educational strategy is called **response to intervention (RTI)** (Al Otaiba et al., 2015; Jimerson et al., 2016; Ikeda, 2012). First, all children are taught specific skills; for instance, learning the sounds that various letters make. Then the children are tested, and those who did not master the skill receive special "intervention"—practice and individualized teaching, usually within the regular class. Then they are tested again, and, if need be, intervention occurs again. Only when a child does not respond adequately to repeated, focused intervention is he or she referred for special education.

If the child is found to need special education, the school proposes an **individual education plan (IEP).** Parents are consulted, and they must agree with the IEP. The idea is that schools need to "design learning pathways for each individual sufferer." The label, or specific diagnosis, is supposed to lead to effective remediation. Yet this rarely occurs in practice, educators do not always know the best way to remediate learning difficulties (Butterworth & Kovas, 2013).

least restrictive environment (LRE)
A legal requirement that children with special needs be assigned to the most general educational context in which they can be expected to learn.

response to intervention (RTI)
An educational strategy intended to help children who demonstrate below-average achievement in early grades, using special intervention.

individual education plan (IEP) A document that specifies educational goals and plans for a child with special needs.

The Tuscaloosa News, Dusty Compton/AP Photo

All Together Now Kiemel Lamb *(top center)* leads children with ASD in song, a major accomplishment. For many of these children, music is soothing, words are difficult, and handholding in a group is almost impossible.

● **Observation Quiz** What is the adult: child ratio here? (see answer, p. 312) ←

FIGURE 11.6

Nature or Nurture Communities have always had some children with special needs, with physical, emotional, and neurological disorders of many kinds. In some eras, and even today in some nations, the education of such children was neglected. Indeed, many children were excluded from normal life. Now in the United States every child is entitled to school. As you see, the specific label for such children has changed over the past decades, because of nurture, not nature. Thus teratogens before and after birth, coupled with changing parental and community practice, probably caused the rise in autism spectrum disorder and developmental delay, the decrease in intellectual disability, and the fluctuation in learning disorders apparent here.

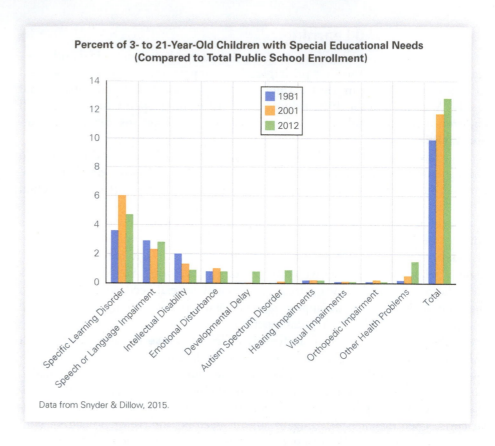

Percent of 3- to 21-Year-Old Children with Special Educational Needs (Compared to Total Public School Enrollment)

Data from Snyder & Dillow, 2015.

Why don't educators know what to do? A major problem is that most research on remediation focuses on the less common problems. For example, in the United States, "research funding in 2008–2009 for autistic spectrum disorder was 31 times greater than for dyslexia and 540 times greater than for dyscalculia" (Butterworth & Kovas, 2013, p. 304). Nor do educational categories necessarily reflect actual needs.

As Figure 11.6 shows, the proportion of children designated with special needs in the United States rose from 10 percent in 1980 to 13 percent in 2011, primarily because more children are called "learning disabled" or "speech impaired" (National Center for Education Statistics, 2013b). Most educators do not believe that the actual number of children with these problems has increased: Instead, teachers are more likely to think that the children they have trouble teaching must have some sort of disorder and parents are more likely to agree. An alternative explanation for the rise in numbers is that there are more teratogens in the air, water, and food.

Internationally, the connection between special needs and education varies, again for cultural and historical reasons more than for child-related ones (Rotatori et al., 2014). In many African and Latin American nations, almost no child with special needs receives targeted public education; in many Asian nations, diagnosis depends primarily on physical disability. The U.S. school system designates more children as having special needs than does any other nation: Whether this is a reason for national pride or shame depends on one's perspective.

Early Intervention

One conclusion from all the research on special education is that diagnosis and intervention often occur too late, or not at all. The numbers of children in public schools who are designated as needing special education increase as children grow

◗◗ Answer to Observation Quiz
(from p. 311) About 1:1. The advantage of segregated classes for children with special needs is a low adult/child ratio.

older, which is the opposite of what would occur if early intervention were successful. This is apparent in each of the disorders we have discussed.

There is no separate education category for ADHD, though that disorder is most troubling to parents and teachers. To receive special services, teachers designate children with ADHD as having a specific learning disorder. Since most disorders are comorbid, the particular special needs category chosen by a school psychologist may not be the diagnosis given by a private psychologist. One result is that teachers, therapists, and parents may work at cross-purposes to educate a child.

Even at age 4, children with ADHD symptoms tend to have difficulties making and keeping friends. Longitudinal research finds that poor early peer relationships worsens their ADHD more than ADHD characteristics worsens peer relationships (Stenseng et al., 2016). That suggests a target for early schooling: Help young children make friends.

Traditionally, specific learning disorders were diagnosed *only* if a child had difficulty with a particular school subject that made his or her achievement scores at least two years below IQ (as a 9-year-old with an average IQ who read at the first-grade level). In addition, the child must have adequate hearing and vision, and there could be no other explanation for the delay in reading, such as that the family was abusive or the home language was not English.

All this meant a "wait to fail" approach, that learning disorders were not diagnosed until third grade or later, even though signs were apparent long before. This meant that bad learning strategies, low self-esteem, and hatred of school might already be established in first and second grade. As one expert says, "We need early identification, and. . . . early intervention. If you wait until third grade, kids give up" (Shaywitz, cited in Stern, 2015).

A similar problem occurs with autism spectrum disorder. You read that signs of autism appear in infancy, but children are not usually diagnosed until age 4, on average (MMWR, March 28, 2014). This is long after many parents have noticed something amiss in their child, and years after the most effective intervention can begin.

Experts now recognize that parents are crucial in the early treatment of autism, long before first grade (Wainer et al., 2016). Generally, parents of children with special needs are eager to help them. However, few parents know exactly what educational supports their children need or the difference between normal toddler activity and worrisome signs that may explain why parents postpone seeking a diagnosis. Taking action, not postponing it, mitigates problems. Especially for young children with ASD, parents who spend hours each day teaching language and social interaction in the ways that research finds helpful can make a major difference.

In fact, some children diagnosed with ASD before age 4 no longer have it later on—an outcome that seems to be related to intense social intervention in the early years (Kroncke et al., 2016). Such children may still have other problems, and even with early intervention most children with ASD remain symptomatic in adulthood, but the fact that any child can overcome the social and cognitive symptoms of the disorder is another argument for early intervention.

Gifted and Talented

Children who are unusually gifted are often thought to have special educational needs as well. But they are not covered by federal laws in the United States. Instead, each U.S. state selects and educates gifted and talented children in a particular way. That leads to controversy.

Some children score very high on IQ tests, and some are *divergent thinkers,* who find many solutions and even more questions for every problem. These two characteristics do not always overlap: A high-IQ child might be a *convergent thinker,* quickly aware of the correct answer for every problem and impatient with the child who is more creative.

This raises a controversial question for educators: Should children who are unusually intelligent, talented, or creative be skipped, segregated, enriched, or home-schooled? Each of these solutions has been tried and found lacking.

Historically, most children did not attend school, and, if a family recognized their gifted or talented child, they might teach the child themselves or hire a special coach or tutor if they could afford it. For example, Mozart composed music at age 3 and Picasso created works of art at age 4. Both boys had fathers who recognized their talent. Mozart's father transcribed his earliest pieces and toured Europe with his gifted son; Picasso's father removed him from school in second grade so he could create all day.

Although intense early education at home nourished their talent, neither Mozart nor Picasso had happy adult lives. Mozart had a poor understanding of math and money. He had six children, only two of whom survived infancy, and he died in debt at age 35. Picasso regretted never learning to read or write, and he had four children by three women—one child with the wife he married at age 17.

When school attendance became universal, another solution for gifted children was found—they could skip early grades and join other children of the same mental age, not their chronological age. This practice was called **acceleration.** Today it is rarely done, because many accelerated children never learned how to get along with others. As one woman remembers:

> Nine-year-old little girls are so cruel to younger girls. I was much smaller than them, of course, and would have done anything to have a friend. Although I could cope with the academic work very easily, emotionally I wasn't up to it. Maybe it was my fault and I was asking to be picked on. I was a weed at the edge of the playground.

> *[Rachel, quoted in Freeman, 2010, p. 27]*

Calling herself a weed suggests that she never overcame her conviction that she was less cherished than the other children. Her intellectual needs may have been met by skipping two grades, but her emotional and social needs were severely neglected.

My own father skipped three grades, graduating from high school at age 14. Because he attended a one-room school, and because he was the middle child of five, his emotional and social needs were met until he began college—almost failing because of his immaturity. He recovered, but some other children do not. A chilling example comes from:

> Sufiah Yusof [who] started her maths degree at Oxford [the leading University in England] in 2000, at the age of 13. She too had been dominated and taught by her father. But she ran away the day after her final exam. She was found by police but refused to go home, demanding of her father in an email: "Has it ever crossed your mind that the reason I left home was because I've finally had enough of 15 years of physical and emotional abuse?" Her father claimed she'd been abducted and brainwashed. She refuses to communicate with him. She is now a very happy, high-class, high-earning prostitute.

> *[Freeman, 2010, p. 286]*

The fate of the creative child may be worse than the intellectually gifted child. They joke in class, resist drudgery, ignore homework, and bedevil their teachers.

acceleration Educating gifted children alongside other children of the same mental, not chronological, age.

Gifted. Then What? Mercan Türkoğlu won a Bambi, the German equivalent of an Oscar, awarded for her star performance in the film *Three Quarter Moon.* She is German of Turkish ancestry, Muslim, and a talented actress. What education will best prepare her for adulthood?

They may become innovators, inventors, and creative forces in the future, but they also may take psychoactive drugs, drop out of high school, or leave college before graduating because they feel more stifled than challenged. Among the well-known creative geniuses who were poor students were Albert Einstein, Sigmund Freud, Isaac Newton, Oliver Sachs, Steve Jobs, and hundreds of thousands of others, probably some of whom you know personally.

One such person was Charles Darwin, whose "school reports complained unendingly that he wasn't interested in studying, only shooting, riding, and beetle-collecting" (Freeman, 2010, p. 283). At the behest of his physician father, Darwin entered college to study medicine, but he found the instruction dull and dropped out. Without a degree, he began his famous five-year trip around South America at age 22, collecting the specimens and developing the theory of evolution—which disputed conventional religious dogma as only a highly creative person could do.

Since both acceleration and intense parental tutoring have led to later social problems, a third education strategy has become popular, at least in the United States. Children who are bright, talented, and/or creative—all the same age but each with special abilities—are taught as a group in their own exclusive classroom. Ideally, such children are neither bored nor lonely; each is challenged and appreciated by their classmates.

There is research that supports that strategy. Neuroscience has recently discovered that children who develop their musical talents with extensive practice in early childhood grow specialized brain structures, as do child athletes and mathematicians (Moreno et al., 2015). Since plasticity means that children learn whatever their context teaches, talents may be enhanced with special education. This becomes an argument for gifted and talented classes in elementary school.

Classes for gifted students require unusual teachers, bright and creative, able to appreciate divergent thinking and to challenge the very intelligent. They must be flexible, giving a 7-year-old artist freedom, guidance, and inspiration for magnificent art and simultaneously providing patient, step-by-step reading instruction if that same child is a typical new reader. Similarly, a 7-year-old classmate who reads at the twelfth-grade level might have immature social skills, needing a teacher who finds another child to befriend him or her and who then helps both of them share, compromise, and take turns.

However, the argument against such special classes is that every child needs such teachers, no matter what the child's abilities or disabilities. Many educators complain that the U.S. system of education, in which each school district and sometimes each school hires and assigns teachers, results in the best teachers having the most able students. Should it be the opposite?

The trend for gifted students to have gifted teachers is furthered by *tracking,* putting children with special needs together, and allowing private or charter schools to select certain students and leave the rest behind. The problem is worse if the gifted and non-gifted students are in the same school—the regular students try less, and the gifted students think they know more than they do (Herrmann et al., 2016; Van Houtte, 2015).

Mainstreaming, IEPs, and so on were developed when parents and educators saw that segregation of children with special needs led to less learning and impaired adult lives. The same may happen if gifted and talented children are separated from the rest. This is controversial, and it is discussed in the next chapter.

Some nations (China, Finland, Scotland, and many others) educate all children together, assuming that every child could be a high achiever if he or she worked hard, guided by effective teachers. Every special and ordinary form of education can benefit by applying what we know about children's minds (De Corte, 2013). That is the topic of the next chapter.

WHAT HAVE YOU LEARNED?

1. What do mainstreaming and inclusion have in common?

2. Why is response to intervention considered an alternative to special education?

3. Why is it easier to help a child with special needs at age 6 than at age 10?

4. Why might children who have high IQs no longer be likely to skip grades?

5. What are the arguments for and against special classes for gifted children?

SUMMARY

A Healthy Time

1. Middle childhood is a time of steady growth and few serious illnesses. During these years, health habits, including daily oral care, protect children from later health problems.

2. Physical activity aids health and joy in many ways. However, current social and environmental conditions make informal neighborhood play uncommon and school exercise less prevalent than formerly. Children who most need physical activity may be least likely to have it.

3. Childhood obesity is a worldwide epidemic. Although genes are part of the problem, too little exercise and the greater availability of unhealthy foods are the main reasons today's youth are heavier than their counterparts of 50 years ago. Parents and policies share the blame.

4. The incidence of asthma is increasing overall. The causes include genes and the microbiome; the triggers include specific allergens.

5. Brains continue to develop during middle childhood. Experience enhances coordination of brain impulses, and selective attention develops as children play.

Children with Special Brains and Bodies

6. Developmental psychopathology uses an understanding of typical development to inform the study of unusual development. Four general lessons have emerged: Abnormality is normal; disability changes over time; a condition may get better or worse in adolescence and adulthood; diagnosis depends on context.

7. IQ tests quantify intellectual aptitude. Mental age rises as chronological age does, with children whose mental age is more than, or less than, their chronological age having high or low IQ scores, respectively. Most IQ tests emphasize language and logic, and they predict school achievement. Scores change over time, as culture and experience enhance particular abilities.

8. Achievement tests measure accomplishment, often in specific academic areas. Aptitude and achievement are correlated, both

for individuals and for nations, and have risen in the past decades as Flynn documented.

9. Critics of IQ testing contend that intelligence is manifested in multiple ways, which makes *g* (general intelligence) too narrow and limited. Some psychologists stress that people have multiple intelligences, include creative and practical abilities. Gardner describes nine distinct intelligences.

10. Children with attention-deficit/hyperactivity disorder (ADHD) have potential problems in three areas: inattention, impulsiveness, and activity. Stimulant medication helps many children with ADHD to concentrate and learn, but any drug use by children is controversial.

11. DSM-5 recognizes learning disorders that impair learning in school, specifically dyslexia (unusual difficulty with reading), dyscalculia (unusual difficulty with math), and dysgraphia (unusual difficulty with writing).

12. Children on the autism spectrum typically have problems with social interaction and language. They often exhibit restricted, repetitive patterns of behavior, interests, and activities. Many causes are hypothesized. ASD originates in the brain. No expert now believes that the cause is inadequate parenting or early vaccinations. Treatments are diverse and controversial.

Special Education

13. About 13 percent of all school-age children in the United States receive special education services. These begin with an IEP (individual education plan) and assignment to the least restrictive environment (LRE), usually within the regular classroom.

14. Diagnosis and special education typically occur much later than seems best. Parents, teachers, and professionals need to come together to help children with special needs.

15. Some children are unusually intelligent, talented, or creative, and some states and nations provide special education for them. The traditional strategy—skipping a grade—no longer seems beneficial, but special classes for gifted and talented children are controversial. They may harm those left behind.

KEY TERMS

middle childhood (p. 292)
selective attention (p. 294)
reaction time (p. 294)
childhood obesity (p. 296)
childhood overweight (p. 296)
asthma (p. 299)
developmental psychopathology
  (p. 300)

comorbid (p. 300)
aptitude (p. 301)
intelligence (p. 301)
achievement test (p. 301)
Flynn effect (p. 302)
multiple intelligences (p. 302)
multifinality (p. 303)
equifinality (p. 303)

attention-deficit/hyperactivity
  disorder (ADHD) (p. 304)
specific learning disorder
  (p. 307)
dyslexia (p. 307)
dyscalculia (p. 307)
autism spectrum disorder
  (ASD) (p. 308)

neurodiversity (p. 309)
least restrictive environment
  (LRE) (p. 311)
response to intervention (RTI)
  (p. 311)
individual education plan (IEP)
  (p. 311)
acceleration (p. 314)

APPLICATIONS

1. Compare play spaces for children in different neighbor-hoods—ideally, urban, suburban, and rural areas. Note size, safety, and use. How might children's weight and motor skills be affected by the differences you observe?

2. Should every teacher be skilled at teaching children with a wide variety of needs, or should some teachers specialize in particular kinds of learning difficulties? Ask professors in your education department? What does the curriculum of your college promote?

3. Parents of children with special needs often consult Internet sources. Pick one disorder and find 10 sites that describe causes and educational solutions. How valid, how accurate, and how objective is the information? What disagreements do you find? How might parents react to the information provided?

4. How inclusive are the elementary schools (public, charter and private) in your community? Get data on ethnic, economic, and ability grouping. Then analyze whether this is best.

Middle Childhood: Cognitive Development

CHAPTER 12

What Will You Know?

1. Does cognition improve naturally with age, or is teaching crucial to its development?
2. Why do children use slang, curse words, and bad grammar?
3. What type of school is best during middle childhood?

At age 9, I wanted a puppy. My parents said no; we already had Dusty, our family dog. I dashed off a poem, promising "to brush his hair as smooth as silk" and "to feed him milk." Twice wrong. Not only poor cadence, but also, puppies get sick on cow's milk. But my father praised my poem; I got Taffy, a blonde cocker spaniel.

At age 10, my daughter Sarah wanted her ears pierced. I said no, it would be unfair to her three older sisters, who had had to wait for ear-piercing until they were teenagers. Sarah wrote an affidavit and persuaded all three to sign "No objection." She got gold posts.

Children's wishes differ by cohort and their strategies by context. I knew that my father loved my childish poems, but Sarah knew that my lawyer husband and I wouldn't budge for doggerel but that signed documents might work. We were both typical children, wanting something that we did not need and figuring out how to get it. Depending on their circumstances, children learn to divide fractions, text friends, memorize baseball stats, load rifles, and persuade parents.

This chapter describes the cognitive accomplishments that make all that possible. We begin with Piaget, Vygotsky, and information processing. Then we discuss applications of those theories to language and formal education, nationally and internationally. Everyone agrees that extensive learning occurs; adults disagree sharply about what and how to teach.

Building on Theory

Learning is rapid. By age 11, some children beat their elders at chess, play music that adults pay to hear, publish poems, and win trophies for spelling or sports or some other learned skill. Others survive on the streets or kill in wars, mastering lessons that no child should know. How do they learn so quickly?

Piaget and Concrete Thought

Piaget called middle childhood the time for **concrete operational thought,** characterized by new logical abilities. *Operational* comes from the Latin word *operare,* meaning "to work; to produce." By calling this period operational, Piaget emphasized

concrete operational thought
Piaget's term for the ability to reason logically about direct experiences and perceptions.

How the Mind Works The official dictionary used for the Scripps National Spelling Bee has 472,000 words, which makes rote memorization impossible. Instead, winners recognize patterns, roots, and exceptions—all possible in middle childhood.

productive thinking. Piaget's theory is considered a classic stage theory, in that concrete operational thinking is a more advanced kind of thinking than preoperational but less advanced than the next stage (formal operational).

However, Piaget also recognized that children do not leap wholesale to a new conceptual level but advance step by step within each stage. He called this *horizontal décalage*—the idea that at each level (like a horizon, seeming flat) concepts appear in sequence over months or even years. One example is with conservation (explained in Chapter 9). Preoperational children do not understand the concept of conservation, but concrete operational children do.

However, some types of conservation are understood before other types—7-year-olds typically know that two balls of clay have the same matter no matter what shape they are, but not until a year or two later does the child understand that weight is also conserved no matter what shape. That is horizontal décalage.

The main characteristic of this stage is that children can apply their new cognitive skills to *concrete* situations, which are situations grounded in actual experience, like the concrete of a cement sidewalk. Concrete thinking arises from what is visible, tangible, and real, not abstract and theoretical (as at the next stage, formal operational thought). Children become more systematic, objective, scientific—and educable.

A Hierarchy of Categories

classification The logical principle that things can be organized into groups (or categories or classes) according to some characteristic that they have in common.

One logical operation is **classification,** the organization of things into groups (or *categories* or *classes*) according to some characteristic that they share. For example, *family* includes parents, siblings, and cousins. Other common classes are animals, toys, and food. Each class includes some elements and excludes others; each is part of a hierarchy.

Food, for instance, is an overarching category, with the next-lower level of the hierarchy being meat, grains, fruits, and so on. Most subclasses can be further divided: Meat includes poultry, beef, and pork, each of which can be divided again. Adults realize that items at the bottom of a classification hierarchy belong to every higher level: Bacon is always pork, meat, and food, but most food, meat, and pork are not bacon. This mental operation of moving up and down the hierarchy is beyond preoperational children.

Piaget devised many classification experiments. In one, he showed a child a bunch of nine flowers—seven yellow daisies and two white roses. Then the child is asked, "Are there more daisies or more flowers?" Until about age 7, most children answer, "More daisies." The youngest children offer no justification, but some 6-year-olds explain that "there are more yellow ones than white ones" or "because daisies are daisies, they aren't flowers" (Piaget et al., 2001). By age 8, most children can classify: "More flowers than daisies," they say.

Other Logical Concepts

Several logical concepts were already discussed in Chapter 9, including the most famous accomplishment of concrete operational children, *conservation.*

seriation The concept that things can be arranged in a logical series, such as the number sequence or the alphabet.

Another example of concrete logic is **seriation,** the knowledge that things can be arranged in a logical *series*. Seriation is crucial for using (not merely memorizing) the alphabet or the number sequence. By age 5, most children can count up to 100, but because they do not yet grasp seriation, they cannot correctly estimate where any particular two-digit number would be placed on a line that starts at 0 and ends at 100 (Meadows, 2006).

Logic allows children to understand math. Children at the stage of concrete operational thought eventually understand that 15 is always 15 (conservation), that numbers from 20 to 29 are all in the 20s (classification), that 134 is less than 143 (seriation), and that if $5 \times 3 = 15$, then $15 \div 5 = 3$ (reversibility). [**Life-Span Link:** These concepts are explained in Chapter 9 and detailed in a recently reissued classic, Inhelder & Piaget, 2013a.] By age 11, children use mental categories and subcategories more flexibly, inductively, and simultaneously than they did at age 6.

Vygotsky and Culture

Like Piaget, Vygotsky felt that educators should consider children's thought processes, not just the outcomes. He appreciated the fact that children are curious, creative learners. For that reason, Vygotsky believed that an educational system based on rote memorization rendered the child "helpless in the face of any sensible attempt to apply any of this acquired knowledge" (Vygotsky, 1994a, pp. 356–357).

The Role of Instruction

Unlike Piaget, who thought children would discover most concepts themselves, Vygotsky stressed direct instruction from teachers and other mentors who provided the needed scaffold between potential and knowledge by engaging each child in his or her zone of proximal development. [**Life-Span Link:** Vygotsky's theory is discussed in Chapters 2 and 9.]

Internationally as well as nationally, children who begin education at age 4 or 5, not 6 or 7, tend to be ahead in academic achievement compared to those who enter later, an effect noted even at age 15, although not in every nation (Sprietsma, 2010). Vygotsky would explain the variation in impact by noting that early education is far more interactive, and hence better, in some places than in others.

Play with peers, screen time, dinner with families, neighborhood scenes . . . every experience, from birth on, teaches a child, according to Vygotsky. The particular lessons vary by culture.

Cultural Variations

Culture and context affect more than academic learning. A stunning example comes from Varanasi, a city in northeast India. Many Varanasi children have an extraordinary sense of spatial orientation: They know whether they are facing north or south, even when they are inside a room with no windows. In one experiment, children were blindfolded, spun around, and led to a second room, yet some still knew which way they were then facing (Mishra et al., 2009).

Further research in Varanasi found that some religious traditions emphasize north/south/east/west orientations instead of left–right ones (Dasen & Mishra, 2013). This is evident in language: Instead of "the dog is sleeping by the door," someone might say, "the dog is sleeping southeast." Children who learn north/south/east/west in order to communicate have an internal sense of direction by middle childhood.

Culture affects *how* children learn, not just what they learn. Whereas many traditional Western schools expect children to learn directly, by listening to a teacher and demonstrating what they have learned with individually written homework and tests, some other cultures consider learning to occur mostly indirectly, by observation and joint activity (Rogoff, 2016).

For example, one study found that children born and raised in the United States from Native American cultures were accustomed to learning by observation. They

Math and Money Third-grader Perry Akootchook understands basic math, so he might beat his mother at "spinning for money," shown here. Compare his concrete operational skills with those of a typical preoperational child, who would not be able to play this game and might give a dime for a nickel.

Especially for Teachers How might Piaget's and Vygotsky's ideas help in teaching geography to a class of third-graders? (see response, page 324)

Girls Can't Do It As Vygotsky recognized, children learn whatever their culture teaches. Fifty years ago, girls were in cooking and sewing classes. No longer. This 2012 photo shows 10-year-olds Kamrin and Caitlin in a Kentucky school, preparing for a future quite different from that of their grandmothers.

Never Lost These children of Varanasi sleep beside the Ganges River in the daytime. At night they use their excellent sense of direction to guide devotees from elsewhere.

A Boy In Memphis Moziah Bridges (known as Mo Morris) created colorful bowties, which he first traded for rocks in elementary school. He then created his own company (Mo's Bows) at age 9, selling $300,000 worth of ties to major retailers by age 14. He is shown here with his mother, who encouraged his entrepreneurship.

were better at remembering an overheard folktale than other U.S. children (Tsethlikai & Rogoff, 2013).

Information Processing

Contemporary educators and psychologists find both Piaget and Vygotsky insightful. International research confirms the merits of their theories (Griffin, 2011; Mercer & Howe, 2012). Piaget described universal changes; Vygotsky noted cultural impact. However, both grand theories of child cognition are limited, especially regarding specifics of school curriculum. Each domain of achievement may follow a particular path (Siegler, 2016). Developmentalists now recognize the merits and pitfalls of a third approach to understanding cognition.

The *information-processing perspective* benefits from technology that allows much more detailed data and analysis than was possible for Piaget or Vygotsky. [**Life-Span Link:** Information processing is introduced in Chapter 2.] Accordingly, as in information processing in computers, people can access large amounts of information. They then (1) seek relevant information (as a search engine does), (2) analyze (as software programs do), and (3) express conclusions (as a printout might do). By tracing the paths and links of each of these functions, scientists better understand the learning process.

The brain's gradual growth, now seen in neurological scans, confirms the usefulness of the information-processing perspective. So do data on children's school achievement: Absences, vacations, new schools, and even new teachers may set back a child's learning because learning each day builds on the learning of the previous day. Brain connections and pathways are forged from repeated experiences, allowing advances in processing. Without careful building and repetition of various skills, fragile connections between neurons break.

One of the leaders of the information-processing perspective is Robert Siegler. He has studied the day-by-day details of children's cognition in math (Siegler & Chen, 2008). Apparently, children do not suddenly grasp the logic of the number system, as Piaget expected at the concrete operational stage. Instead, number understanding accrues gradually, with new and better strategies for calculation tried, ignored, half-used, abandoned, and finally adopted (Siegler, 2016). Siegler compared the acquisition of knowledge to waves on an ocean beach when the tide is rising. There is substantial ebb and flow; eventually a new level is reached.

One example is the ability to estimate where a number might fall on a line, such as where the number 53 would be placed on a line from 0 to 100. This skill predicts later math achievement (Libertus et al., 2013). U.S. kindergartners are usually lost when asked to do this task; Chinese kindergartners are somewhat better (Siegler & Mu, 2008). Everywhere, proficiency gradually builds from the first grade on, predicting later math skills (Feigenson et al., 2013). Many information-processing experts. Now advocate giving children practice with number lines in order to develop later math skills, such as the ability to do multiplication and division.

Curiously, knowing how to count to high numbers seems less important for math mastery than being able to estimate magnitude (Thompson & Siegler, 2010). For example, understanding the size of fractions (e.g., that 3/16 is smaller than 1/4) is connected to a thorough grasp of the relationship between one number and another, a skill that predicts later math achievement internationally, according to a study of schoolchildren in China, Belgium, and the United States (Torbeyns et al., 2015).

Overall, information processing guides teachers who want to know exactly which concepts and skills are crucial foundations for mastery, not only for math but for reading, writing, and science as well. For example, in the beginning of middle childhood, children are typically stumped when a scientific experiment leads to surprising results. By age 10, they are able to generate hypotheses to explain it (Piekny & Maehler, 2013). This suggests that science may be interesting to young children at every stage, but expecting them to think like scientists, developing hypotheses and testing them, might be premature.

From brain research, information processing, and longitudinal studies of children's learning, we now know that children learn step by step, gradually advancing as neurological connections spread from one domain to another. However, the major pitfall of information processing is in application.

Children advance one day and regress the next (Siegler, 2016). Patience, allowing knowledge from various domains to come together, is a good strategy for middle-childhood educators, but specifics for any individual, child are unknown. As explained in detail in the following, information from various parts of the brain is combined in regions called *hubs* to achieve the learning that occurs in middle childhood; how to strengthen those hubs is the next question.

LaunchPad
macmillan learning

Arithmetic Strategies: The Research of Robert Siegler
http://qrs.ly/o84ep10

Video provided by Geetha Ramani and Robert Siegler, Carnegie Mellon University.

INSIDE THE BRAIN

Coordination and Capacity Development

Recall that emotional regulation, theory of mind, and left–right coordination emerge in early childhood. The maturing corpus callosum connects the hemispheres of the brain, enabling balance and two-handed coordination, while myelination adds speed. Maturation of the prefrontal cortex—the executive part of the brain—allows the child to plan, monitor, and evaluate.

In middle childhood, increasing maturation results in connections between the various lobes and regions of the brain. Such connections are crucial for the complex tasks that children must master, which require "smooth coordination of large numbers of neurons" (Stern, 2013, p. 577). Certain areas of the brain, called *hubs*, are locations where massive numbers of axons meet. Hubs tend to be near the corpus callosum, and damage to them correlates with notable brain dysfunction (as in neurocognitive and other mental disorders) (Crossley et al., 2014).

Because of hubs, brain connections formed in middle childhood are crucial. Consider learning to read. Reading is not instinctual: Our ancestors never did it, and until recent centuries, only a few scribes and scholars could interpret letters written on papyrus, carved in wood, or chiseled into stone. Consequently, the brain has no areas dedicated to reading in the way it does for talking or gesturing (Sousa, 2014).

Instead, reading uses many parts of the brain—one for sounds, another for recognizing letters, another for sequencing, another for comprehension and more. By working together, these parts first foster listening, talking, and thinking, and then they put it all together (Lewandowski & Lovett, 2014).

Quick reaction time and selective attention (both explained in Chapter 11) aid every social and academic skill. For instance, being able to calculate when to utter a witty remark and when to stay quiet is something few 6-year-olds can do. By age 10, some children can (1) realize that a comment could be made and (2) decide what it could be, (3) think about the other person's possible response, and in the same split second (4) know when something should NOT be said.

Children with reading difficulties are variable as well as slow in reaction time. That makes their reading erratic (Tamm et al., 2014). Fluent reading—possible at age 8 or so—requires (1) seeing a long sequence of letters, (2) segmenting them as words, (3) differentiating words spelled alike (such as *read* and *read*, *bark* and *bark*), (4) considering context to grasp unfamiliar words, (5) recognizing oddities and ironies, and (6) understanding meaning related to the previous sentences. For fluency, reactions must be quick and automatic.

Automatization, the process by which a sequence of thoughts and actions is repeated until no conscious thought is required, aids quick reaction time. At first, almost all voluntary behaviors require careful thought. After many repetitions, neurons fire in sequence, and less thinking is needed because the firing of one neuron sets off a chain reaction.

Consider again learning to read. At first, eyes (sometimes aided by a guiding finger) focus intensely, painstakingly making out letters and sounding out each one. This leads to the perception of syllables and then words. Eventually, the process becomes so routine that as people drive along on a highway, they read billboards that they have no interest in reading.

Automatization aids all academic skills. One longitudinal study of second-graders—from the beginning to the end of the school year—found that each type of academic proficiency aided each other type. Thus, learning became more automatic as automatization fostered more learning (Lai et al., 2014).

Learning a second language, reciting the multiplication tables, and writing one's name are all slow at first, but automatization makes each effortless by adulthood. Not just academic knowledge but also habits and routines that are learned in childhood echo lifelong—and are hard to break. That's automatization.

automatization A process in which repetition of a sequence of thoughts and actions makes the sequence routine so that it no longer requires conscious thought.

Memory

Many scientists who study memory take an information-processing approach. They have learned that various methods of input, storage, and retrieval affect the increasing cognitive ability of the schoolchild. Each of the three major steps in the memory process—sensory memory, working memory, and long-term memory—is affected by both maturation and experience.

Three Steps of Memory

sensory memory The component of the information-processing system in which incoming stimulus information is stored for a split second to allow it to be processed. (Also called the *sensory register*.)

Sensory memory (also called the *sensory register*) is the first component of the human information-processing system. It stores incoming stimuli for a split second, with sounds retained slightly longer than sights. To use terms explained in Chapter 5, *sensations* are retained for a moment, and then some become *perceptions*. This first step of sensory awareness is already quite good in early childhood. Sensory memory improves slightly until about age 10 and remains adequate until late adulthood.

working memory The component of the information-processing system in which current conscious mental activity occurs. (Formerly called *short-term memory*.)

Once some sensations become perceptions, the brain selects the meaningful ones and transfers them to working memory for further analysis. It is in **working memory** that current, conscious mental activity occurs. Processing, not mere exposure, is essential for getting information into working memory; for this reason, working memory improves markedly in middle childhood (Cowan & Alloway, 2009). That enables children to become much better learners, as they can organize material into chunks that help them understand and remember bits of knowledge.

Working memory is particularly important for reading in that each letter, word, and sentence needs to be connected with the other letters, words, and sentences—all held in the memory for long enough for better processing of what has been read. Children do some of this on their own as their brains mature, but good teachers help children connect ideas, allowing working memory to become a powerful tool (Cowan, 2014) (see Table 12.1).

Response for Teachers

(from page 321): Here are two of the most obvious ways. (1) Use logic. Once children can grasp classification and class inclusion, they can understand cities within states, states within nations, and nations within continents. Organize your instruction to make logical categorization easier. (2) Make use of children's need for concrete and personal involvement. You might have the children learn first about their own location, then about the places where relatives and friends live, and finally about places beyond their personal experience (via books, photographs, videos, and guest speakers).

Cultural differences are evident. For example, many Muslim children are taught to memorize all 80,000 words of the Quran, so they learn strategies to remember long passages. These strategies are unknown to non-Muslim children, and they help the Muslim children with other cognitive tasks (Hein et al., 2014). A very different example is the ability to draw a face, an ability admired by U.S. children. They learn strategies to improve their drawing, such as knowing where

TABLE 12.1	Advances in Memory from Infancy to Age 11
Child's Age	**Memory Capabilities**
Under 2 years	Infants remember actions and routines that involve them. Memory is implicit, triggered by sights and sounds (an interactive toy, a caregiver's voice).
2–5 years	Words are now used to encode and retrieve memories. Explicit memory begins, although children do not yet use memory strategies. Children remember things by rote (their phone number, nursery rhymes).
5–7 years	Children realize that they need to remember some things, and they try to do so, usually via rehearsal (repeating an item again and again). This is not the most efficient strategy, but repetition can lead to automatization.
7–9 years	Children can learn new strategies, including visual clues (remembering how a particular spelling word looks) and auditory hints (rhymes, letters), evidence of brain functions called the visual-spatial sketchpad and phonological loop. Children benefit from organizing things to be remembered.
9–11 years	Memory becomes more adaptive and strategic as children become able to learn various memory techniques from teachers and other children. They can organize material themselves, developing their own memory aids.

Information from Meadows, 2006.

to put the eyes, mouth, and chin when drawing a face. (Few spontaneously draw the eyes mid-face rather than at the top, but most learn to do so.)

Finally, information from working memory may be transferred to **long-term memory,** to be stored for minutes, hours, days, months, or years. The capacity of long-term memory—how much can be crammed into one brain—is huge by the end of middle childhood. Together with sensory memory and working memory, long-term memory organizes ideas and reactions, fostering more effective learning over the years (Wendelken et al., 2011).

Crucial to long-term memory is not merely *storage* (how much material has been deposited) but also *retrieval* (how readily past learning can be brought into working memory). For everyone at every age, retrieval is easier for some memories (especially of vivid, emotional experiences) than for others. And for everyone, long-term memory is imperfect: We all forget and distort memories and need strategies for accurate recall. Some schools teach this more than others—just as some Islamic children memorize the Quran and some children memorize Shakespeare, or the books of the Bible, or the Gettysburg Address.

Knowledge and Memory

The more people already know, the better they can learn. Having an extensive **knowledge base,** or a broad body of knowledge in a particular subject, makes it easier to remember and understand related new information. As children gain knowledge during the school years, they become better able to judge what is true or false, what is worth remembering, and what is insignificant (Woolley & Ghossainy, 2013).

Three factors facilitate increases in the knowledge base: past experience, current opportunity, and personal motivation. The last item in this list explains why children's knowledge bases are not what their parents or teachers might prefer. Some schoolchildren memorize words and rhythms of hit songs, know plots and characters of television programs, or can recite the names and histories of basketball players. Yet they do not know whether World War I was in the nineteenth or twentieth century or whether Pakistan is in Asia or Africa.

Motivation provides a clue for teachers: New concepts are learned best if they are connected to personal and emotional experiences. For example, children who are from South Asia, or who have classmates from there, learn the boundaries of Pakistan if their teachers acknowledge and appreciate their student's background.

Control Processes

The neurological mechanisms that put memory, processing speed, and the knowledge base together are **control processes;** they regulate the analysis and flow of information within the brain. Emotional regulation and executive function are control processes (and are explained in Chapters 10 and 11). Two other terms are often used to refer to cognitive control—*metacognition* (sometimes called "thinking about thinking") and *metamemory* (knowing about memory).

Control processes require the brain to organize, prioritize, and direct mental operations, much as the CEO (chief executive officer) of a business organizes, prioritizes, and directs business operations. For that reason, control processes are also called *executive processes,* and the ability to use them is called *executive function* (already mentioned in Chapter 9); these processes allow a person to step back from the specifics of learning and thinking and consider more general goals and strategies.

long-term memory The component of the information-processing system in which virtually limitless amounts of information can be stored indefinitely.

knowledge base A body of knowledge in a particular area that makes it easier to master new information in that area.

Especially for Teachers How might your understanding of memory help you teach a 2,000-word vocabulary list to a class of fourth-graders? (see response, page 326)

What Does She See? It depends on her knowledge base and personal experiences. Perhaps this trip to an aquarium in North Carolina is no more than a break from the school routine, with the teachers merely shepherding the children to keep them safe. Or, perhaps she has learned about sharks and dorsal fins, about scales and gills, about warm-blooded mammals and cold-blooded fish, so she is fascinated by the swimming creatures she watches. Or, if her personal emotions shape her perceptions, she feels sad about the fish in their watery cage or finds joy in their serenity and beauty.

control processes Mechanisms (including selective attention, metacognition, and emotional regulation) that combine memory, processing speed, and knowledge to regulate the analysis and flow of information within the information-processing system. (Also called *executive processes.*)

Fortunate Child or Too Fortunate?
Mothers everywhere help children with homework, as this mother does. Is it ever true that parents should let their children struggle, and fail?

Executive function becomes more evident and significant among 10-year-olds than among 4- or 6-year-olds, although some older children still act impulsively (Masten, 2014; Bjorklund et al., 2009). Generally, however, students learn to listen to their teacher, ignoring classmates who are chewing gum or passing notes. That deliberate selectivity is an example of a control process at work. Children can decide to do their homework before watching television or to review their spelling words before breakfast, creating mnemonics to remember the tricky ones. All of these signify executive function.

Control processes improve with age and experience. For instance, in one study, children took a fill-in-the-blanks test and indicated how confident they were about each answer. Then they were allowed to delete some questions, with the remaining ones counting more. Already by age 9, they were able to estimate correctness; by age 11, they were skilled at knowing what to delete (Roebers et al., 2009).

Sometimes, experience that is not directly related has an impact. This seems to be true for fluently bilingual children, who must learn to inhibit one language while using another. They are advanced in control processes, obviously in language but also in more abstract measures of control (Bialystok, 2010).

Such processes develop spontaneously as the prefrontal cortex matures, but they can also be taught. Teaching can be explicit, more so in some nations (e.g., Germany) than in others (e.g., the United States) (Bjorklund et al., 2009). Examples that may be familiar include spelling rules ("*i* before *e* except after *c*") and ways to remember how to turn a lightbulb ("lefty-loosey, righty-tighty"). Preschoolers ignore such rules or use them only on command; 7-year-olds begin to use them; 9-year-olds can create and master more complicated rules. Efforts to teach executive control succeed if the particular neurological maturation of the child is considered, as information processing would predict (Karbach & Unger, 2014).

> ### WHAT HAVE YOU LEARNED?
>
> 1. What did Piaget mean when he called cognition in middle childhood *concrete operational thought*?
>
> 2. What items would be in a class other than food or family, such as transportation or plants?
>
> 3. How do Vygotsky and Piaget differ in their explanation of cognitive advances in middle childhood?
>
> 4. How are the children of Varanasi an example of Vygotsky's theory?
>
> 5. How does information-processing theory differ from traditional theories of cognitive development?
>
> 6. According to Siegler, what is the pattern of learning math concepts?
>
> 7. What aspects of memory improve markedly during middle childhood?
>
> 8. How and why does the knowledge base increase in middle childhood?
>
> 9. How might control processes help a student learn?

Response for Teachers
(from page 325): Children this age can be taught strategies for remembering by forming links between working memory and long-term memory. You might break down the vocabulary list into word clusters, grouped according to root words, connections to the children's existing knowledge, applications, or (as a last resort) first letters or rhymes. Active, social learning is useful; perhaps in groups the students could write a story each day that incorporates 15 new words. Each group could read its story aloud to the class.

Language

As you will remember, many aspects of language advance during early childhood. By age 6, children have mastered the basic vocabulary and grammar of their first language.

Many also speak a second language fluently. That increases their knowledge base, enabling more advanced learning and thinking in every subject and in every aspect of language—vocabulary, comprehension, speaking ability, and grammar (Language and Reading Research Consortium, 2015). Here are some specifics.

Vocabulary

By age 6, children use every part of speech—adjectives, adverbs, interjections, and conjunctions, as well as thousands of nouns and verbs—to form sentences that sometimes go on and on. Vocabulary builds during middle childhood because concrete operational children are more logical; they can understand prefixes, suffixes, compound words, phrases, and metaphors, even if they have not heard them before. For example, 2-year-olds know *egg*, but 10-year-olds also know *egg salad*, *egg-drop soup, egghead, a good egg*, and *last one in is a rotten egg*.

In middle childhood, some words become pivotal for understanding what is taught in middle school, such as *negotiate, evolve, allegation, deficit, molecules*. Consequently, vocabulary expansion is part of the curriculum in every elementary school classroom.

Understanding Metaphors

Metaphors, jokes, and puns are comprehended. Some jokes ("What is black and white and read all over?" and "Why did the chicken cross the road?") are funny only during middle childhood. Younger children don't understand why they provoke laughter, and teenagers find them lame and stale.

But the new cognitive flexibility of 6- to 11-year-olds allows them to enjoy puns, unexpected answers to normal questions, as well as metaphors and similes. A lack of metaphorical understanding, or an inability to see the humor in a pun, indicates a cognitive problem (Thomas et al., 2010).

Metaphors are context specific, building on the knowledge base. An American who lives in China notes phrases that U.S. children understand but that children in cultures without baseball do not, including "dropped the ball," "on the ball," "play ball," "throw a curve," "strike out" (Davis, 1999). If a teacher says "keep your eyes on the ball," some immigrant children might not pay attention because they are looking for that ball.

Adjusting Language to the Context

Another aspect of language that advances markedly in middle childhood is pragmatics, defined in Chapter 9. Pragmatics is evident when a child knows which words to use with teachers (never calling them a *rotten egg*) and informally with friends (who can be called rotten eggs or worse). As children master pragmatics, they become more adept at making friends. Shy 6-year-olds cope far better with the social pressures of school if they use pragmatics well (Coplan & Weeks, 2009). By contrast, children with autism spectrum disorder are usually very poor at pragmatics (Klinger et al., 2014).

Pragmatics are important lifelong, as an elderly, white, former college president realized when he was unexpectedly arrested, convicted, and imprisoned with hundreds of young, minority men. He said that he benefited from his knowledge as a linguist, knowing "the impact that delivering an expletive with just the right tone had on his fellow inmates" (Mangan, 2016).

Mastery of pragmatics allows children to change styles of speech, or "linguistic codes," depending on their audience. Each code includes many aspects of language—not just vocabulary, but also tone, pronunciation, gestures, sentence

Go With the Flow This boat classroom in Bangladesh picks up students on shore and then uses solar energy to power computers linked to the Internet as part of instruction. The educational context will teach skills and metaphors their peers will not understand.

Jonas Gratzer/LightRocket via Getty Images

Especially for Parents You've had an exhausting day but are setting out to buy groceries. Your 7-year-old son wants to go with you. Should you explain that you are so tired that you want to make a quick solo trip to the supermarket this time? (see response, page 331)

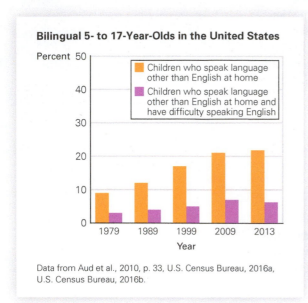

Bilingual 5- to 17-Year-Olds in the United States

Data from Aud et al., 2010, p. 33, U.S. Census Bureau, 2016a, U.S. Census Bureau, 2016b.

FIGURE 12.1

Hurray for Teachers More children in the United States are now bilingual and more of them speak English well, from about 40 percent of the bilingual children in 1980 to 82 percent in 2011.

English Language Learners (ELLs)
Children in the United States whose proficiency in English is low—usually below a cutoff score on an oral or written test. Many children who speak a non-English language at home are also capable in English; they are *not* ELLs.

immersion A strategy in which instruction in all school subjects occurs in the second (usually the majority) language that a child is learning.

bilingual schooling A strategy in which school subjects are taught in both the learner's original language and the second (majority) language.

ESL (English as a Second Language)
A U.S. approach to teaching English that gathers all of the non-English speakers together and provides intense instruction in English. Students' first languages are never used; the goal is to prepare them for regular classes in English.

length, idioms, and grammar. Sometimes the switch is between *formal code* (used in academic contexts) and *informal code* (used with friends); sometimes it is between standard (or proper) speech and dialect or vernacular (used on the street). Code is used in texting—numbers (411), abbreviations (LOL), emoticons (:-D), and spelling (r u ok?), which children now do a dozen or more times a day.

Some children may not realize that informal expressions are wrong in formal language, or what is gained by elegant use of precise vocabulary. All children need instruction in the formal code because the logic of grammar (whether *who* or *whom* is correct or how to spell *you*) is almost impossible to deduce, as is the spelling of many words. The peer group teaches the informal code, and each local community transmits dialect, metaphors, and pronunciation; schools must convey the formal code.

Speaking Two Languages

Code changes are obvious when children speak one language at home and another at school. Every nation includes many such children; most of the world's 6,000 languages are not school languages. For instance, English is the language of instruction in Australia, but 17 percent of the children speak 1 of 246 other languages at home (Centre for Community Child Health & Telethon Institute for Child Health Research, 2009). In the United States, about one school-age child in four has a home language that is not English (see Figure 12.1).

In addition, many other children speak a dialect of English (the United States is said to have more than two dozen dialects) with distinct word use, pronunciation, and grammar. The ability to switch codes correlates with school achievement and benefits from teachers who appreciate and respect the home language while speaking and teaching the school language (Terry et al., 2016). Many children learn two or more codes—easiest in early childhood, possible in middle childhood, and increasingly difficult after puberty.

If children learn two languages in the first three years of life, no brain differences are detectable between monolingual and bilingual children. However, from about age 4 through adolescence, the older children are when they learn a second language, the more likely their brains will change to accommodate the second language, with greater cortical thickness on the left side (the language side) and thinness on the right (Klein et al., 2014). This reflects what we know about language learning: In infancy and early childhood, language is learned effortlessly; in middle childhood, some work (indicated by brain growth) is required.

Educators and political leaders in the United States argue about how to teach English to **English Language Learners (ELLs),** who are people whose first language is not standard English. One strategy is called **immersion,** in which instruction occurs entirely in the new language. The opposite strategy begins by teaching children in their first language until the second language is taught as a "foreign" tongue (a strategy rare in the United States but common elsewhere).

Between these extremes lies **bilingual schooling,** with instruction in two languages, and **ESL (English as a Second Language),** with all non-English speakers taught English in one multilingual group, who will soon join English-only classes. Every method for teaching a second language sometimes succeeds and sometimes fails. A major problem is that children's language-learning abilities change with age: In middle school, the youngest children learn a new language much more quickly than the older children (Stevens, 2015; Palacios & Kibler, 2016). Language learning depends not only on the child but also on the literacy of the home environment (frequent reading, writing, and listening in any language helps); the warmth, training, and skill of the teacher; and the national context. If parents might be deported, that adds to stress and impairs language learning, especially in middle childhood (Brabeck & Sibley, 2016; Dearing et al., 2016).

Specifics differ for each state, grade, family, and child, but the general trends are discouraging. Unless a child is already bilingual at age 5, ELLs fall further behind their peers with each passing year, leaving school at higher rates than other students their age (Han, 2012). For instance, in Pennsylvania in 2009, the percentage of fourth-graders proficient in reading was 74 percent for the non-ELLs but only 30 percent for the ELLs. The gap in math scores was not quite as wide, but in every subject and every grade, the gap widened as children grew older (O'Conner et al., 2012).

Months or Years? ESL classes, like this one in Canada, often use pictures and gestures to foster word learning. How soon will these children be ready for instruction?

Differences in Language Learning

Learning to speak, read, and write the school language is pivotal for primary school education. Some differences in ability may be innate: A child with an intellectual disability will have trouble with both the school and home languages. It is a mistake to assume that a child who does not speak English well has a disability (difference is not deficit), but it is also is a mistake to assume that such a child's only problem is lack of English knowledge (deficits do occur among all children, no matter what their background).

To discover whether a child has difficulty learning language, testing in the home language is best—even when the child has been speaking the second language from kindergarten on (Erdos et al., 2014). Often the language gap between one child and another is caused neither by brain abnormality nor by the home language. Two social factors have a major impact: SES and expectations.

Socioeconomic Status

Decades of research throughout the world have found a strong correlation between academic achievement and socioeconomic status. Language is a major reason. Not only do children from low-SES families usually have smaller vocabularies than those from higher-SES families, but their grammar is also simpler (fewer compound sentences, dependent clauses, and conditional verbs) and their sentences are shorter (Hart & Risley, 1995; Hoff, 2013). That slows down school learning in every subject.

Brain scans confirm that development of the hippocampus is particularly affected by SES, as is language learning (Jednoróg et al., 2012). That is correlation, not causation. Consequently, many researchers have asked why low SES affects language learning. Possibilities include inadequate prenatal care, blood lead levels, no breakfast, crowded households, few books at home, teenage parents, authoritarian child rearing, inexperienced teachers, poor neighborhood role

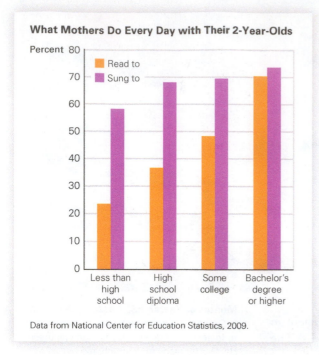

What Mothers Do Every Day with Their 2-Year-Olds

Data from National Center for Education Statistics, 2009.

FIGURE 12.2

Red Fish, Blue Fish As you can see, most mothers sing to their little children, but the college-educated mothers are much more likely to know that book-reading is important. Simply knowing how to turn a page or hearing new word combinations (hop on pop?) correlates with reading ability later on.

models . . . the list could go on and on (Van Agt et al., 2015; Kolb & Gibb, 2015; Rowe et al., 2016). All of these conditions correlate with low SES and less learning, but it is difficult to isolate the impact of any specific one.

However, one factor seems to be a cause, not just a correlate: language heard early on. For this, the mother's education seems crucial. Most less-educated parents use simpler vocabulary and talk much less to their infants and young children than more-educated parents do. For instance, among mothers of 2-year-olds, 24 percent of those with less than a high school education read books daily to their children, but 70 percent of the mothers with at least a B.A. did (National Center for Education Statistics, 2009) (see Figure 12.2).

Although education often correlates with book-reading, not every educated mother reads to her child. Adult habits reflect this. Children who grow up in homes with many books accumulate, on average, three more years of education than children who live in homes with no books (Evans et al., 2010).

It is also important to engage children in conversation about the interesting sights around them. Another way to surround children with language is to sing to a child, not just a few simple songs but dozens of songs with varied vocabulary in many stanzas. Then discussions about the meaning of words come naturally. Ideally, several adults read to, sing to, and converse with each child daily.

Interestingly, a study found that vocabulary is learned better if the same words are heard from several people, so a child needs more than just the mother talking to him or her. Of course, this can be challenging to adults. Taking my grandson on the subway, he asked me what a "zombie apocalypse" was. It was part of an ad for buying food, so I had to explain not only the words but also why a grocer would tell people to prepare for such a thing.

Crucial is that adults expect children to learn, and continually expand vocabulary and the knowledge base, as I tried to do. Although substantial research has found that children are influenced by adults' positive expectations, the relationship between expectation and achievement becomes complicated as children grow older. One crucial factor seems to be whether parents and teachers have shared expectations, rather than working at cross-purposes. It is also true that children may rebel against expectations if they feel the expectations are unrealistic (Froiland & Davison, 2014). This is particularly likely with authoritarian parenting—high standards, without much warmth.

Expectations do not necessarily follow income lines, especially among immigrant families. Many first generation children are very good students: They try to validate their parents' decision to leave their native land (Ceballo et al., 2014; Fuller & García Coll, 2010). Their parents expect them to study hard, and they do.

Priorities This family in London is low-income, evident in the stained walls, peeling paint, and old toilet, but that does not necessarily limit the girl's future. More important is what she learns about values and behavior. If this scene is typical, this mother is teaching her daughter about appearance and obedience. What would happen if the child had to care for her own grooming? Tangles? Short hair? Independence? Linguistic advances?

Observation Quiz What in the daughter's behavior suggests that maternal grooming is a common event in her life? (see answer, page 332) →

WHAT HAVE YOU LEARNED?

1. How does learning language progress between the ages of 6 and 10?
2. How does a child's age affect the understanding of metaphors and jokes?
3. Why would a child's linguistic code be criticized by teachers but admired by friends?
4. What factors in a child's home and school affect language-learning ability?
5. What does the research find about children whose home language is not the school language?
6. How and why does low SES affect language learning?

Response for Parents (from page 328): Your son would understand your explanation, but you should take him along if you can do so without losing patience. You wouldn't ignore his need for food or medicine, so don't ignore his need for learning. While shopping, you can teach vocabulary (does he know pimientos, pepperoni, polenta?), categories (root vegetables, freshwater fish), and math (which size box of cereal is cheaper?). Explain in advance that you need him to help you find items and carry them and that he can choose only one item that you wouldn't normally buy. Seven-year-olds can understand rules, and they enjoy being helpful.

Teaching and Learning

As we have just described, school-age children are great learners, using logic, developing strategies, accumulating knowledge, and expanding language. In every nation, new responsibilities and formal instruction begin at about age 6 because that is when the human body and brain are ready for them. Traditionally, this learning occurred at home, but now United Nations data find that more than 95 percent of the world's 7-year-olds are in school; that is where their parents and political leaders want them to be. (See Visualizing Development on p. 343 for U.S. and international statistics on education in middle childhood.)

Indeed, in many developing nations, the number of students in elementary school exceeds the number of school-age children, because many older children are enrolled in primary education, trying to master the basics. In 2014, Ghana, El Salvador, and China were among the nations with significantly more students in primary school than the total population of children in middle childhood (UNESCO, 2014).

hidden curriculum The unofficial, unstated, or implicit patterns within a school that influence what children learn. For instance, teacher background, organization of the play space, and tracking are all part of the hidden curriculum—not formally prescribed, but instructive to the children.

International Schooling

Everywhere, children are taught to read, write, and do arithmetic, as the brain matures. Some of the sequences recognized universally are listed in the accompanying At About This Time tables.

Differences by Nation

Beyond literacy and math, nations vary in what they expect. All want their children to be good citizens. However, there is no consensus as to what good citizenship means or what developmental paths should be followed for children to learn it (Cohen & Malin, 2010). Accordingly, many children simply follow their parents' example regarding everything from picking up trash to supporting a candidate for president.

Differences between one nation and another, and, in the United States, between one school and another, are stark in the **hidden curriculum**—all of the implicit values and assumptions that underlie the course offerings, schedules, tracking, teacher characteristics, discipline, teaching methods, sports competitions, student government, extracurricular activities, and so on.

Whether and how students should talk in class is part of the hidden curriculum, taught from kindergarten on. In the

AT ABOUT THIS TIME

Math

Age	Norms and Expectations
4–5 years	■ Count to 20. ■ Understand one-to-one correspondence of objects and numbers. ■ Understand *more* and *less*. ■ Recognize and name shapes.
6 years	■ Count to 100. ■ Understand *bigger* and *smaller*. ■ Add and subtract one-digit numbers.
8 years	■ Add and subtract two-digit numbers. ■ Understand simple multiplication and division. ■ Understand word problems with two variables.
10 years	■ Add, subtract, multiply, and divide multidigit numbers. ■ Understand simple fractions, percentages, area, and perimeter of shapes. ■ Understand word problems with three variables.
12 years	■ Begin to use abstract concepts, such as formulas and algebra.

Math learning depends heavily on direct instruction and repeated practice, which means that some children advance more quickly than others. This list is only a rough guide, meant to illustrate the importance of sequence.

AT ABOUT THIS TIME

Reading

Age	Norms and Expectations
4–5 years	■ Understand basic book concepts. For instance, children learning English and many other languages understand that books are written from front to back, with print from left to right, and that letters make words that describe pictures. ■ Recognize letters—name the letters on sight. ■ Recognize and spell own name.
6–7 years	■ Know the sounds of the consonants and vowels, including those that have two sounds (e.g., *c, g, o*). ■ Use sounds to figure out words. ■ Read simple words, such as *cat, sit, ball, jump*.
8 years	■ Read simple sentences out loud, 50 words per minute, including words of two syllables. ■ Understand basic punctuation, consonant–vowel blends. ■ Comprehend what is read.
9–10 years	■ Read and understand paragraphs and chapters, including advanced punctuation (e.g., the colon). ■ Answer comprehension questions about concepts as well as facts. ■ Read polysyllabic words (e.g., *vegetarian, population, multiplication*).
11–12 years	■ Demonstrate rapid and fluent oral reading (more than 100 words per minute). ■ Vocabulary includes words that have specialized meaning in various fields. For example, in civics, *liberties, federal, parliament,* and *environment* all have special meanings. ■ Comprehend paragraphs about unfamiliar topics. ■ Sound out new words, figuring out meaning using cognates and context. ■ Read for pleasure.
13+ years	■ Continue to build vocabulary, with greater emphasis on comprehension than on speech. Understand textbooks.

Reading is a complex mix of skills, dependent on brain maturation, education, and culture. The sequence given here is approximate; it should not be taken as a standard to measure any particular child.

Teacher Technique Some children are riveted by TV but distracted at school. Has this teacher found a solution, or is she making the problem worse?

United States, children are encouraged to express opinions—perhaps by raising their hands, but always verbal, active, and engaged.

When I taught at United Nations International School, one student, newly arrived from India, was very quiet, so I called on him. He immediately stood up to answer—to the surprise of his classmates. Soon he learned to stay seated, but at least in the first year after his arrival, he spoke only when required directly.

In general, North American students are taught to speak their minds, even when they are irrational. This correlates with later active citizenship (Lin, 2014). Some of my students at the United Nations school, encouraged to speak out, returned to their homelands to lead protests. I now wonder if their fellow countrymen thought them disrespectful, foolish, or perhaps ruined by their education abroad.

The hidden curriculum may also be the underlying reason for a disheartening difference in whether elementary school students ask their teachers for help. In one study, middle-class children requested special assistance more often than low-SES students did. The researchers found that the low-SES students wanted

Same Situation, Far Apart: Spot the Hidden Curriculum Literacy is central to the curriculum for schoolchildren everywhere, no matter how far apart they live. However, in the U.S. classroom at the left, boys and girls learn together, clothes are casual, history books are paperback and illustrated, and children of every background read the same stories with the same patriotic—but not religious—themes. The hidden curriculum is quite different for the boy memorizing his holy book on the right.

to avoid special attention, fearing it would lead to criticism (Calarco, 2014). For that reason, the hidden curriculum meant that middle-class students benefited from having middle-class teachers, an advantage contrary to what the teachers hoped or intended.

Indeed, if teachers' gender, ethnicity, or economic background is unlike their students, children may conclude that education is irrelevant for them. If the school has gifted classes, the hidden message may be that the rest of the students are not capable. This is not the school's intention, but it is internalized by the students.

The physical setting of the school also sends a hidden message. Some schools have spacious classrooms, wide hallways, and large, grassy playgrounds; others have cramped, poorly equipped classrooms and cement play yards. In some nations, school is held outdoors, with no chairs, desks, or books; classes are canceled when it rains. What does that tell the students?

Room to Learn? In the elementary school classroom in Florida (left), the teacher is guiding two students who are working to discover concepts in physics—a stark contrast to the Filipino classroom on the right, in a former storeroom. Sometimes the hidden curriculum determines the overt curriculum, as shown here.

International Testing

Over the past two decades, more than 50 nations have participated in at least one massive international test of educational achievement. Longitudinal data reveal that when achievement rises, the national economy advances with it; this sequence seems causal, not merely correlational (Hanushek & Woessmann, 2009). Apparently, better-educated adults become more productive workers.

Science and math achievement are tested in the **Trends in Math and Science Study (TIMSS)**. The main test of reading is the **Progress in International Reading Literacy Study (PIRLS)**. These tests are given every few years, with East Asian nations usually ranking at the top. The rank of the United States has risen over the past two decades, but it is still below several other nations in eastern and western Europe as well as in Asia (see Tables 12.2 and 12.3). Most developing nations in Africa or South America do not give these tests, but when they do, their scores are low. Improvement is possible, however, as illustrated on the following page.

Trends in Math and Science Study (TIMSS) An international assessment of the math and science skills of fourth- and eighth-graders. Although the TIMSS is very useful, different countries' scores are not always comparable because sample selection, test administration, and content validity are hard to keep uniform.

Progress in International Reading Literacy Study (PIRLS) Inaugurated in 2001, a planned five-year cycle of international trend studies in the reading ability of fourth-graders.

TABLE 12.2 TIMSS Ranking and Average Scores of Math Achievement for Fourth-Graders, 2007 and 2011

Rank*	Country	Score 2007	Score 2011
1.	Singapore	599	606
2.	Korea	597	605
3.	Hong Kong	667	602
4.	Chinese Taipei	576	591
5.	Japan	568	585
6.	N. Ireland	**	562
7.	Belgium	**	549
8.	Finland	**	545
9.	England	541	542
10.	Russia	544	542
11.	United States	531	541
12.	Netherlands	535	540
	Canada (Quebec)	519	533
	Germany	525	528
	Canada (Ontario)	512	518
	Australia	516	516
	Italy	507	508
	Sweden	491	504
	New Zealand	492	486
	Iran	402	431
	Yemen	224	248

*The top 12 groups in 2011 are listed in order, but after that, not all the jurisdictions that took the test are listed. Some nations have improved over the past 15 years (notably, Hong Kong, England) and some have declined (Austria, Netherlands), but most continue about where they have always been.

**Northern Ireland, Belgium, and Finland did not participate in the 2007 TIMSS assessment.

Information from Provasnik et al., 2012; Mullis et al., 2012a.

TABLE 12.3 PIRLS Distribution of Reading Achievement for Fourth-Graders, 2006 and 2011

Country	Score 2006	Score 2011
Hong Kong	564	571
Russian Federation	565	568
Finland	**	568
Singapore	558	567
N. Ireland	**	558
United States	540	556
Denmark	546	554
Chinese Taipei	535	553
Ireland	**	552
England	539	552
Canada	549	548
Italy	551	541
Germany	548	541
Israel	512	541
New Zealand	532	531
Australia	**	527
Poland	519	526
France	522	520
Spain	513	513
Iran	421	457
Colombia	**	448
Indonesia	405	428
Morocco	323	310

Information from from Mullis et al., 2007; Mullis et al., 2012b.

Finland

Finland's scores on international tests increased dramatically after a wholesale reform of their public education system (see Figure 12.3). Reforms occurred in several waves (Sahlberg 2011, 2015). Finland abolished ability grouping in 1985; curriculum reform to encourage collaboration and active learning began in 1994. Now, during middle childhood, all children learn together—no tracking—and teachers are mandated to work with each child to make sure he or she masters the curriculum. Learning difficulties are remediated in the early grades, within the regular classroom.

Over the past two decades, strict requirements for becoming a teacher have been put in place. Only the top 3 percent of Finland's high school graduates are admitted to teachers' colleges. They study five years at the university at no charge, earning a master's degree in the theory and practice of education.

Finnish teachers are granted more autonomy within their classrooms than is typical in other nations. Since the 1990s, they have had more time and encouragement to work with colleagues (Sahlberg, 2011, 2015). They are encouraged to respond to each child's temperament as well as skills. A study of first-graders found that this strategy led to achievement, particularly in math (Viljaranta, et al., 2015).

Buildings are designed to foster collaboration, with comfortable teacher's lounges (Sparks, 2012). This reflects a hidden curriculum that teachers are professionals, a valued resource trusted to work together to teach the children well.

Unlike the United States, where teachers can be fired if their students' test scores do not improve, Finland has no system-wide tests until high school. Instead, teachers devise their own ways to measure what their students have learned. The teachers also belong to a union, which encourages them all to work for their collective welfare. All children attend public school—there are no schools funded by private tuition.

A major emphasis is on the future lives of the citizens. Since those who are poorly educated and who drop out of high school become a burden on the society, counseling for later life is a priority. Children of all ages are challenged and advised "to become engaged learners, fulfilled individuals, and compassionate, productive citizens" (Robinson, 2015, p. 205). High-quality, individualized teaching with long-term goals rather than short-term test scores might be the reason for Finland's success.

Critics contend, instead, that success occurs because of Finland's small population (5.5 million—less than the average state of the United States), or culture, or location (between the former Soviet Union and the Scandinavian nations, making political thought over the decades a volatile compromise between ideals and practice).

Advocates reply that no other nation or state has instituted these reforms, not because they cannot but because they do not have high expectations for all of their children. In Finland, every child is assumed to have strengths and weaknesses, so teachers seek the right approach to foster learning. Almost no child is designated for special education because *all* are given individualized attention; they strive to meet expectations. One bit of evidence: Teenagers can choose vocational education, leaving school, or academic high school. Most (94 percent) choose academics. (Sahlberg, 2011, 2015).

The Finnish minister of education believes that expectations are crucial, not only for individual children but also for entire nations. He said:

> "When President Kennedy was making his appeal for advancing American science and technology by putting a man on the moon by the end of the 1960's, many said it couldn't be done. . . . But he had a dream. Just like Martin Luther King a few years later had a dream. Those dreams came true. Finland's dream was that we want to have a good public education for every child regardless of where they go to school or what kind of families they come from, and many even in Finland said it couldn't be done" (Sahlberg, quoted in Partanen, 2011).

According to international assessment, they did it!

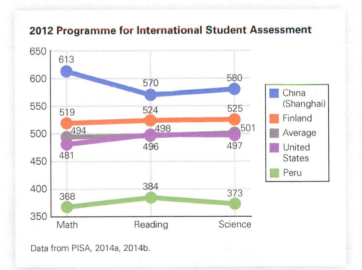

2012 Programme for International Student Assessment

China (Shanghai): Math 613, Reading 570, Science 580
Finland: Math 519, Reading 524, Science 525
Average: Math 494, Reading 498, Science 501
United States: Math 481, Reading 496, Science 497
Peru: Math 368, Reading 384, Science 373

Data from PISA, 2014a, 2014b.

FIGURE 12.3

Lifelong Learning Finnish elementary school students do not score much better or worse than their United States peers on the TIMSS or PIRLS, but educators in Finland do not believe that tests in childhood are the best measure of learning. Instead they prefer to focus on using knowledge later on, as measured by a test further described in Chapter 15, the PISA. Shown here are PISA scores for 15-year-olds. Finland is among the highest nations, and the United States is middling (just slightly below the overall average). Thirty nations are below the United States and thirty nations are higher. For comparison, this graph also shows the highest (Shanghai) and lowest (Peru) nations.

Sharing Answers After individually subtracting 269 from 573, these two third-graders check their answers in two ways—first by adding and then by showing their work to each other. As you can see, he is not embarrassed at his mistake because students in this class enjoy learning from each other.

International tests reflect educational approaches in various nations, as well as cultural values. TIMSS experts videotaped 231 math classes in Japan, Germany, and the United States (Stigler & Hiebert, 2009). The U.S. teachers taught math at a lower level than did their German and Japanese counterparts, presenting more definitions disconnected to prior learning. Few U.S. students seemed engaged in math because they felt the teachers "seem to believe that learning terms and practicing skills is not very exciting" (Stigler & Hiebert, 2009, p. 89).

By contrast, the Japanese teachers were excited about math instruction, working collaboratively and structuring lessons so that the children developed proofs and alternative solutions, both alone and in groups. Teachers used social interaction and followed an orderly sequence (building lessons on previous knowledge). Japanese teaching reflected all three theories of cognition: children's creative discovery from Piaget, collaborative learning from Vygotsky, and sequencing from information processing. Since Japanese students excel on the TIMSS, the teachers' use of strategies from all three theories may lead to student success.

Problems with International Benchmarks

Elaborate and extensive measures are in place to make the PIRLS and the TIMSS valid. For instance, test items are designed to be fair and culture-free, and participating children represent the diversity (economic, ethnic, etc.) of each nation's child population. Consequently, most social scientists respect the data gathered from these tests.

The tests are far from perfect, however. Designing test items that are equally challenging to every student in every nation is impossible. Should fourth-graders be expected to understand fractions, graphs, and simple geometry, or should the test examine only basic operations with whole numbers? Once such general issues are decided to give every child an equal chance, specific items need to be written, again equally fair in every culture. The following item was used to test fourth-grade math:

> Al wanted to find out how much his cat weighed. He weighed himself and noted that the scale read 57 kg. He then stepped on the scale holding his cat and found that it read 62 kg. What was the weight of the cat in kilograms?

This requires simple subtraction, yet 40 percent of U.S. fourth-graders got it wrong. Were they unable to subtract 57 from 62, or did they not understand the example, or did the abbreviation for kilograms confuse them because—unlike children in most nations—they are more familiar with pounds? On this item, children from Yemen were at the bottom, with 95 percent of them failing. Is that because few of them have cats for pets or weigh themselves on a scale? As you see, national and cultural contexts may affect test scores.

Gender Differences in School Performance

In addition to marked national, ethnic, and economic differences, gender differences in achievement scores are reported. The PIRLS finds girls ahead of boys in verbal skills in every nation by an average of 16 points. The female advantage is not that high in the United States, with the 2011 PIRLS finding girls 10 points ahead. This meant that they were ahead of the average boy by about 2 percent—an advantage similar to Canada, Germany, and the Netherlands, which may mean that those nations are more gender-equitable than other nations.

Historically, boys were ahead of girls in math and science. However, TIMSS reported that those gender differences among fourth-graders in math narrowed or disappeared in 2011. In most nations, boys are still slightly ahead, with the United States showing the greatest male advantage (9 points—about 2 percent). However,

"Big deal, an A in math. That would be a D in any other country."

in many nations, girls were ahead, sometimes by a great deal, such as 14 points in Thailand and 35 points in Kuwait. Such results support the *gender-similarities hypothesis* (see Chapter 10) that males and females are similar academically in middle childhood, with "trivial" exceptions later on (Hyde et al., 2008, p. 494).

Unlike test results, classroom performance during elementary school does show gender differences. Girls have higher report card grades overall, including in math and science, with reasons having to do with brain maturation (girls are better able to sit still, manipulate a pencil) and culture (girls are more rewarded for "good" behavior, which includes listening to the teacher). At puberty, girls' grades dip, especially in science, a topic explored in Chapter 15.

Many reasons for adult gender differences have been suggested, with the social context of childhood classrooms being crucial (Legewie & DiPrete, 2012).

The hidden curriculum may favor young girls. Since most elementary school teachers are women, girls in the early grades may feel (or be) more encouraged than boys.

The popularity of alternate explanations has shifted. Analysts once attributed the female advantage in elementary school to the faster maturation of the female body. Now explanations more often consider socio cultural factors. (The same switch in explanations, from biology to culture, appears for male advantages later on.)

Future Engineers After-school clubs now encourage boys to learn cooking and girls to play chess, and both sexes are active in every sport. The most recent push is for STEM (Science, Technology, Engineering and Math) education—as in this after-school robotics club.

Schooling in the United States

Although most national tests indicate improvements in U.S. children's academic performance over the past decade, when they are compared with children in other nations, they are far from the top. A particular concern is that achievement is affected by income and ethnicity in the United States more than in other nations (McNeil & Blad, 2014). Some high-scoring nations have more ethnic groups, economic diversity, and immigrants than the United States, so diversity itself is not the reason.

As of 2014 in the United States, the nation's public schools are said to have become "majority minority," which means that most students are from groups that once were called minorities—such as African American, Latino, or Asian American (Krogstad & Fry, 2014). From a developmental perspective, the terms *majority* and *minority* are misleading, since the majority category includes many children whose ancestors came from distinct parts of Europe, and the minority category likewise includes many groups.

This ethnic diversity could be beneficial. Given the values as well as the reality of U.S. society, most parents want children to learn about other groups during elementary school. This is best done with personal contact between equals (e.g., students in the same classroom) with a teacher who guides the students toward mutual respect. In fact, however, this does not usually happen, since schools are more segregated than they were 40 years ago (Rosiek & Kinslow, 2016).

Even when students from different backgrounds are in the same schools, they are not necessarily seen as equals. In the United States, although many educators and political leaders try to eradicate performance disparities linked to a child's background, the gap between fourth-grade European Americans and their Latino

Video Activity: Educating the Girls of the World examines the situation of girls' education around the world while stressing the importance of education for all children.

and African American peers is as wide as it was 15 years ago (Snyder & Dillow, 2013). Furthermore, the gap between low- and high-income U.S. students is widening, as is the gap between Native Americans and other groups (Maxwell, 2012).

Financial support may be the reason for the U.S. variations by race and income, since notable disparities are apparent from one community to another, and those follow residential segregation. This is true from state to state as well: Massachusetts and Minnesota are consistently at the top of state achievement, and West Virginia, Mississippi, and New Mexico are at the bottom—in part because of the investment in education within those states and the proportion of students of high or low SES (which itself affects state spending) (Pryor, 2014).

National Standards

National Assessment of Educational Progress (NAEP) An ongoing and nationally representative measure of U.S. children's achievement in reading, mathematics, and other subjects over time; nicknamed "the Nation's Report Card."

For decades, the United States government has sponsored tests called the **National Assessment of Educational Progress (NAEP)** to measure achievement in reading, mathematics, and other subjects. The NAEP has high standards, rating fewer children proficient than do state tests. For example, New York's tests reported 62 percent proficient in math, but the NAEP found only 32 percent; 51 percent were proficient in reading on New York's state tests but only 35 percent according to NAEP (Martin, 2014).

Since states tend to vary in what they expect children to learn and then design tests that favor their students, the governors of all 50 states designated a group of experts to develop high national standards, the *Common Core,* finalized in 2010. The standards are explicit, with half a dozen or more specific expectations for achievement in each subject for each grade. (Table 12.4 provides a sample of the specific standards.) Various testing companies have attempted to measure student accomplishments.

Choices and Complications

Most states and teachers initially favored of the Common Core, because high standards and accountability are aspirational goals shared by many. However, as testing increased, and implementation of the Common Core began in classrooms, many

TABLE 12.4	The Common Core: Sample Items for Each Grade	
Grade	Reading and Writing	Math
Kindergarten	Pronounce the primary sound for each consonant	Know number names and the count sequence
First	Decode regularly spelled one-syllable words	Relate counting to addition and subtraction (e.g., by counting 2 more to add 2)
Second	Decode words with common prefixes and suffixes	Measure the length of an object twice, using different units of length for the two measurements; describe how the two measurements relate to the size of the unit chosen
Third	Decode multisyllabic words	Understand division as an unknown-factor problem; for example, find 32 ÷ 8 by finding the number that makes 32 when multiplied by 8
Fourth	Use combined knowledge of all letter–sound correspondences, syllable patterns, and morphology (e.g., roots and affixes) to read accurately unfamiliar multisyllabic words in context and out of context	Apply and extend previous understandings of multiplication to multiply a fraction by a whole number
Fifth	With guidance and support from peers and adults, develop and strengthen writing as needed by planning, revising, editing, and rewriting, or trying a new approach	Graph points on the coordinate plane to solve real-world and mathematical problems

Information from National Governors Association, 2010.

turned against it. A poll by Education Next found only 12 percent of teachers were opposed to the Common Core in 2013; a year later, 40 percent were opposed (Gewertz, 2014). Likewise, many state legislators as well as the general public are critical of the Common Core. This illustrates a general finding: Issues regarding how best to teach children, and what they need to learn, are controversial among teachers, parents, and political leaders. Ten other controversial issues are listed here.

Ten Questions

1. Should public education be a priority for public funds, or should wealthy parents be able to pay for smaller class size, special curricula, and expensive facilities (e.g., a stage, a pool, a garden) in private education? All told, about 11 percent of students in the United States attend *private schools* (see Figure 12.4). Other nations have higher and lower rates. Economic factors are a major concern: Because they are funded primarily by tuition, private schools usually have few poor children.

2. Should parents be given **vouchers** to pay for some tuition at whatever private school they wish? That might make private school more affordable, but in Wisconsin only 20 percent of the parents who used vouchers for private schools had had their children in public schools. Most were already paying private school tuition. If Wisconsin rates are true more generally, vouchers further increase inequality in schooling. In addition, vouchers may pay for religious schools, which some believe is contrary to the U.S. principle of separation of church and state.

3. Should more **charter schools** open or close? Charters are public schools funded and licensed by states or local districts, exempt from some regulations, especially those negotiated by teacher unions (hours, class size, etc.). Some admit students by lottery, but most have some control over admissions and expulsions, which makes them more ethnically segregated, enrolling fewer children with special needs (Stern et al., 2015). Some charter schools are remarkably successful; others are not (Peyser, 2011). Overall, more children (especially African American boys) and teachers leave or are expelled from charter schools than from other schools, a disturbing statistic. However, for some charters, children who stay learn more and are more likely to go to college than their peers in regular schools (Prothero, 2016).

4. **Home schooling** occurs when parents avoid both public and private schools by educating their children at home. In most states, authorities set standards for what a child must learn, but home-schooling families decide specifics of curriculum, schedules, and discipline. About 2 percent of all children were home-schooled in 2003, about 3 percent in 2007, and perhaps 4 percent in 2012 (Snyder & Dillow, 2013; Ray, 2013). Home schooling requires an adult at home, usually the mother in a two-parent family.

   The major criticism of home schooling is not academic (some mothers are conscientious teachers, especially in the early grades) but social: Children have no interaction with classmates. To compensate, many home-schooling parents plan activities with other home-schooling families, or they enroll their children in various classes (Sparks, 2012).

5. Should public education be free of *religion* to avoid bias toward one religion or another? In the United States, thousands of parochial schools were founded

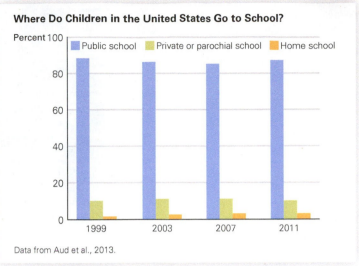

Where Do Children in the United States Go to School?

Data from Aud et al., 2013.

FIGURE 12.4

Where'd You Go to School? Note that although home schooling is still the least-chosen option, the number of home-schooled children is increasing. Not shown is the percentage of children attending the nearest public school, which is decreasing slightly because of charter and magnet schools. More detailed data indicate that the average home-schooled child is a 7-year-old European American girl living in a rural area of the South with an employed father and a stay-at-home mother.

voucher Public subsidy for tuition payment at a nonpublic school. Vouchers vary a great deal from place to place, not only in amount and availability but also in restrictions as to who gets them and what schools accept them.

charter school A public school with its own set of standards that is funded and licensed by the state or local district in which it is located.

home schooling Education in which children are taught at home, usually by their parents.

William Widmer/Redux

Plagiarism, Piracy, and Public School Charter schools often have special support and unusual curricula, as shown here. These four children are learning about copyright law in a special summer school class at the ReNEW Cultural Arts Academy in New Orleans.

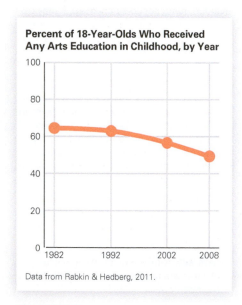

Percent of 18-Year-Olds Who Received Any Arts Education in Childhood, by Year

Data from Rabkin & Hedberg, 2011.

FIGURE 12.5

Focus on Facts As achievement test scores become the measure of learning, education in art, music, and movement has been squeezed out. Artists worry that creativity and imagination may be lost as well.

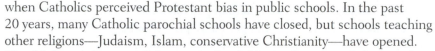 **Especially for School Administrators** Children who wear uniforms in school tend to score higher on reading tests. Why? (see response, page 342)

when Catholics perceived Protestant bias in public schools. In the past 20 years, many Catholic parochial schools have closed, but schools teaching other religions—Judaism, Islam, conservative Christianity—have opened.

6. Should *the arts* be part of the curriculum? Music, drama, and the visual arts are essential in some places, not in others. Half of all U.S. 18- to 24-year-olds say they had no arts education in childhood, either in school or anywhere else (Rabkin & Hedberg, 2011) (see Figure 12.5). By contrast, schools in Finland consider arts education essential, with a positive impact on learning (Nevanen et al., 2014).

7. Should children learn a *second language* in primary school? In Canada and in most European nations, almost every child studies two languages by age 10. Many African children know three languages before high school—their home language plus two other school languages. In the United States, less than 5 percent of children under age 11 study a language other than English in school (Robelen, 2011). The developmental fact that young children learn languages better than older children is lost in fears about immigration and globalization.

8. Can *computers* advance education? Some enthusiasts hope that connecting schools to the Internet or, even better, giving every child a laptop will advance learning. For example, both the state of Maine and the city of Los Angeles tried to have a computer for every child. The results are not dramatic, however. Sometimes computers improve achievement, but not always. Widespread, sustainable advances are elusive (Lim et al., 2013). Technology may be only a tool—a twenty-first-century equivalent of chalk—that depends on a creative, trained teacher to use well.

9. Are *class sizes* too big? Parents typically think that a smaller class size encourages more individualized education. That is a belief that motivates many parents to choose private schools or home schooling. However, mixed evidence comes from nations where children score high on international tests. Sometimes they have large student/teacher ratios (Korea's average is 28-to-1) and sometimes small (Finland's is 14-to-1).

10. Should teachers nurture *soft skills* such as empathy, cooperation, and integrity as part of the school curriculum, even though these skills cannot be tested by multiple-choice questions? Many scholars argue that soft skills are crucial not only for academic success but also for employment (Reardon, 2013). This idea is becoming increasingly popular, as noted in the following.

True Grit or Test Achievement?

Thousands of social scientists—psychologists, educators, sociologists, economists—have realized that, for cognitive development from middle childhood through late adulthood, characteristics beyond IQ scores, test grades, and family SES are sometimes pivotal.

One leading proponent of this idea is Paul Tough, who wrote: "We have been focusing on the wrong skills and abilities in our children, and we have been using the wrong strategies to help nurture and teach those skills" (Tough, 2012, p. xv). Instead of focusing on test scores, Tough believes we should focus on characteristics, particularly *grit* (persistence and effort).

Many scientists agree that executive control processes with many names (grit, emotional regulation, conscientiousness, resilience, executive function, effortful control) develop over the years of middle childhood. Over the long term, these aspects of character predict achievement in high school, college, and adulthood. Developmentalists disagree about exactly which qualities are crucial for achievement, with grit considered crucial by some and not others (Ivcevic & Brackett, 2014; Duckworth & Kern, 2011). However, no one denies that success depends on personal traits.

This concept appears in almost every previous chapter of this textbook, from the discussion of plasticity in Chapter 1 to the evidence in Chapter 11 regarding children who overcome notable intellectual disabilities. One of the best longitudinal studies we have (the Dunedin study of an entire cohort of children from New Zealand) found that measures of self-control before age 10 predicted health, happiness, education, and accomplishment many years later, even when IQ and SES were already taken into account (Moffitt et al., 2011).

Among the many influences on children, a pivotal one is having at least one adult who encourages accomplishment. For many children that adult is their mother, although, especially when parents are neglectful or abusive, a teacher, a religious leader, a coach, or someone else can be the mentor and advocate who helps a child overcome adversity (Masten, 2014).

Remember that school-age children are ready for intellectual growth (Piaget) and are responsive to mentors (Vygotsky). These universals were evident in one study that occurred in two places, 12,000 miles apart: the northeastern United States and Taiwan. More than 200 mothers were asked to recall and then discuss with their 6- to 10-year-olds two learning-related incidents that they knew their child experienced. In one incident, the child had a "good attitude or behavior in learning"; in the other, "not perfect" (J. Li et al., 2014).

All of the mothers were married and middle-class, and all tried to encourage their children, stressing the value of education and the importance of doing well in school. The researchers noted that the mothers differed in the attitudes they were trying to encourage in their children. The Taiwanese mothers were about 50 percent more likely to mention what the researchers called "learning virtues," such as practice, persistence, and concentration—all of which are part of grit. The American mothers were 25 percent more likely to mention "positive affect," such as happiness and pride.

This distinction is evident in the following two excepts:

First, Tim and his American mother discussed a "not perfect" incident.

Mother: I wanted to talk to you about . . . that time when you had that one math paper that . . . mostly everything was wrong and you never bring home papers like that. . . .

Tim: I just had a clumsy day.

Mother: You had a clumsy day. You sure did, but there was, when we finally figured out what it was that you were doing wrong, you were pretty happy about it . . . and then you were happy to practice it, right? . . . Why do you think that was?

Tim: I don't know, because I was frustrated, and then you sat down and went over it with me, and I figured it out right with no distraction and then I got it right.

Mother: So it made you feel good to do well?

Tim: Uh-huh.

Mother: And it's okay to get some wrong sometimes.

Tim: And I, I never got that again, didn't I?

The next excerpt occurred when Ren and his Taiwanese mother discuss a "good attitude or behavior."

Mother: Oh, why does your teacher think that you behave well?

Ren: It's that I concentrate well in class.

Mother: Is your good concentration the concentration to talk to your peer at the next desk?

Ren: I listen to teachers.

Mother: Oh, is it so only for Mr. Chang's class or is it for all classes?

Ren: Almost all classes like that. . . .

Mother: So you want to behave well because you want to get an . . . honor award. Is that so?

Ren: Yes.

Mother: Or is it also that you yourself want to behave better?

Ren: Yes. I also want to behave better myself.

[J. Li et al., 2014, p. 1218]

Both Tim and Ren are likely to be good students in their respective schools. When parents support and encourage their child's learning, almost always the child masters the basic skills required of elementary school students, and almost never does the child become crushed by life experiences. Instead, the child has sufficient strengths to overcome most challenges (Masten, 2014).

The specifics of parental encouragement affect the child's achievement. Some research has found that parents in Asia emphasize that education requires hard work, whereas parents in North America stress the joy of learning. Could it be, as one group of researchers contend, that U.S. children are happier but less accomplished than Asian ones (F. Ng et al., 2014)?

Laura Embry/ZUMA Press/Newscom

Loved and Rewarded Marissa Ochoa, a third-grade public school teacher near San Diego, California, is shown moments after she learned that she won $5,000 as a star educator. Which do you think is more rewarding to her, the money or the joy of her students?

Who Decides?

An underlying issue for almost any national or international school is the proper role of parents. In most nations, matters regarding public education—curriculum, funding, teacher training, and so on—are set by the central government. Almost all children attend the local school, whose resources and standards are similar to those of the other schools in that nation. The parents' job is to support the child's learning by checking homework and so on.

In the United States, however, local districts provide most of the funds and guidelines, and parents, as voters and volunteers, are often active in their child's school. Although most U.S. parents send their children to the nearest public school, almost one-third send their children to private schools or charter schools, or educate them at home. Parental choices may vary for each child, depending on the child's characteristics, the parents' current economic status, and the political rhetoric at the time. Every option has strengths and weaknesses, both for the child and for society.

It is difficult for parents to decide the best school for their child, partly because neither the test scores of students in any of these schools nor the moral values a particular school may espouse correlate with the cognitive skills that developmentalists seek to foster (Finn et al., 2014). Thus, parents may choose a school that advertises what the parents value, but the school may not actually be the best educational experience for their child.

Statistical analysis raises questions about home schooling and about charter schools (Lubienski et al., 2013; Finn et al., 2014), but as our discussion of NAEP, Common Core, TIMSS, and so on makes clear, the evidence allows many interpretations. As one review notes, "the modern day, parent-led home-based education movement . . . stirs up many a curious query, negative critique, and firm praise" (Ray, 2013, p. 261).

Schoolchildren's ability to be logical and teachable, now that they are no longer preoperational and egocentric, makes this a good time to teach them—they will learn whatever adults deem important. Parents, politicians, and developmental experts all agree that school is vital for development, but disagreements about teachers and curriculum—hidden or overt—abound.

Response for School Administrators (from page 340): The relationship reflects correlation, not causation. Wearing uniforms is more common when the culture of the school emphasizes achievement and study, with strict discipline in class and a policy of expelling disruptive students.

WHAT HAVE YOU LEARNED?

1. What do all nations have in common regarding education in middle childhood?

2. How does the hidden curriculum differ from the stated school curriculum?

3. What are the TIMSS and the PIRLS?

4. What are the national and international differences in school achievement of girls and boys?

5. What are the strengths and liabilities of national and international tests?

6. What are the differences among charter schools, private schools, and home schools?

7. Which of the ten controversies are most contentious in your community, and why?

Education in Middle Childhood Around the World

Only a decade ago, gender differences in education around the world were stark, with far fewer girls in school than boys. Now girls have almost caught up. However, many of today's children suffer from past educational inequality: Recent data find that the best predictor of childhood health and learning is an educated mother.

WORLDWIDE PRIMARY SCHOOL ENROLLMENT, 2011

Enrollments in elementary school are increasing around the world, but poor countries still lag behind more wealthy ones, and in all countries, more boys attend school than girls. These data are for almost all 6- to 11-year-olds. About 15 percent leave school by age 10.

BARBARA DELGADO/SHUTTERSTOCK

Countries	All	Poor	All	Poor	All	Poor
			BOYS		**GIRLS**	

DATA FROM THE WORLD BANK, 2014.

WORLDWIDE, BASIC ELEMENTARY EDUCATION LEADS TO:

LESS −
- Child and maternal mortality
- Transmission of HIV
- Early marriage and childbirth
- War

MORE +
- Better-paying jobs
- Agricultural productivity
- Use of medical care
- Voting

INFORMATION FROM HANUSHEK & WOESSMANN, 2007.

HOW ARE U.S. FOURTH-GRADERS DOING?

Primary school enrollment is high in the United States, but not every student is learning. While numbers are improving, less than half of fourth-graders are proficient in math and reading.

PROFICIENCY LEVELS FOR U.S. FOURTH-GRADERS

MATHEMATICS
- Proficient 34%
- Advanced 8%
- Below Basic Level 17%
- Basic Understanding 41%

READING
- Proficient 27%
- Advanced 8%
- Below Basic Level 32%
- Basic Understanding 33%

DATA FROM NATIONAL CENTER FOR EDUCATION STATISTICS, 2013A, FIGURES 4 AND 5.

CHANGE IN AVERAGE SCORES FOR U.S. FOURTH-GRADERS

NAEP (NATIONAL ASSESSMENT OF ACADEMIC PROGRESS)

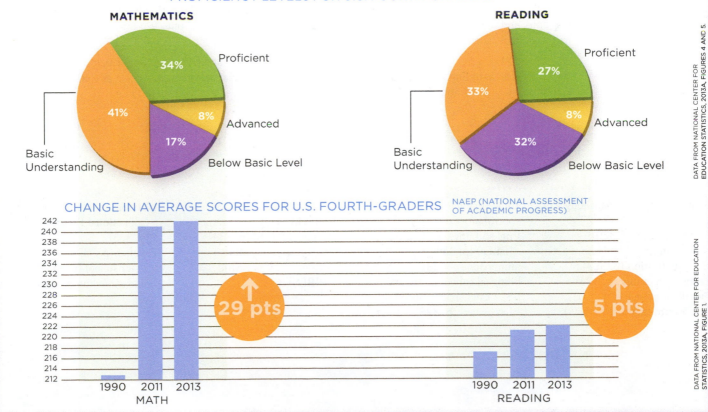

29 pts (MATH: 1990, 2011, 2013)

5 pts (READING: 1990, 2011, 2013)

DATA FROM NATIONAL CENTER FOR EDUCATION STATISTICS, 2013A, FIGURE 1.

SUMMARY

Building on Theory

1. According to Piaget, middle childhood is the time of concrete operational thought, when egocentrism diminishes and logical thinking begins. School-age children can understand classification, conservation, and seriation.

2. Vygotsky stressed the social context of learning, including the specific lessons of school and learning from peers and adults. Culture affects not only what children learn but also how they learn.

3. An information-processing approach examines each step of the thinking process, from input to output, using the computer as a model. This approach is useful for understanding memory, perception, and expression.

4. Memory begins with information that reaches the brain from the sense organs. Then selection processes, benefiting from past experience, allow some information to reach working memory. Finally, long-term memory indefinitely stores images and ideas that can be retrieved when needed.

5. A broader knowledge base, logical strategies for retrieval, and faster processing advance every aspect of memory and cognition. Control processes are crucial. Children become better at controlling and directing their thinking as the prefrontal cortex matures.

Language

6. Language learning advances in many practical ways, including expanded vocabulary, as words are logically linked together and as an understanding of metaphors begins.

7. Children excel at pragmatics during middle childhood, often using one code with their friends and another in school. Many children become fluent in the school language while speaking their first language at home.

8. Children of low SES are usually lower in linguistic skills, primarily because they hear less language at home and because adult expectations for their learning are low. This is not inevitable for low-SES families, however.

Teaching and Learning

9. Nations and experts agree that education is critical during middle childhood. Almost all of the world's children now attend primary school and learn to read, write, and calculate. Many other aspects of curriculum vary from nation to nation and, within the United States, from school to school.

10. The hidden curriculum may be more influential on children's learning than the formal curriculum. Some believe elementary schools favor girls, although internationally, gender similarities seem to outweigh gender differences.

11. International assessments are useful as comparisons, partly because few objective measures of learning are available. Reading is assessed with the PIRLS, math and science with the TIMSS. On both measures, children in East Asia excel, and children in the United States are in the middle ranks.

12. In the United States, the National Assessment of Educational Progress (NAEP) is a test that may raise the standard of education. The Common Core, developed with the sponsorship of the governors of the 50 states, was an effort to raise national standards and improve accountability, but it is now controversial.

13. Nations differ in how much overall control the central government has on education and how much choice and influence parents have. Unlike almost all other countries, in the United States, each state, each district, and sometimes each school retains significant control. Education is a political issue as much or more than a developmental one.

14. Disagreements about curriculum and sponsorship of school for young children are frequent. Some parents choose charter schools, others prefer private schools, and still others opt for home schooling. More research is needed to discover what is best.

KEY TERMS

concrete operational thought (p. 319)
classification (p. 320)
seriation (p. 320)
automatization (p. 323)
sensory memory (p. 324)
working memory (p. 324)
long-term memory (p. 325)

knowledge base (p. 325)
control processes (p. 325)
English Language Learners (ELLs) (p. 328)
immersion (p. 328)
bilingual schooling (p. 328)
ESL (English as a Second Language) (p. 328)

hidden curriculum (p. 331)
Trends in Math and Science Study (TIMSS) (p. 334)
Progress in International Reading Literacy Study (PIRLS) (p. 334)

National Assessment of Educational Progress (NAEP) (p. 338)
voucher (p. 339)
charter school (p. 339)
home schooling (p. 339)

APPLICATIONS

1. Visit a local elementary school and look for the hidden curriculum. For example, do the children line up? Why or why not, when, and how? Does gender, age, ability, or talent affect the grouping of children or the selection of staff? What is on the walls? Are parents involved? If so, how? For everything you observe, speculate about the underlying assumptions.

2. Interview a 6- to 11-year-old child to find out what he or she knows *and understands* about mathematics. Relate both correct and incorrect responses to the logic of concrete operational thought.

3. What do you remember about how you learned to read? Compare your memories with those of two other people, one at least 10 years older and the other at least 5 years younger than you are. Can you draw any conclusions about effective reading instruction? If so, what are they? If not, why not?

4. Talk to two parents of primary school children. What do they think are the best and worst parts of their children's education? Ask specific questions and analyze the results.

Middle Childhood:
Psychosocial Development

What Will You Know?

1. What helps some children thrive in a difficult family, school, or neighborhood?
2. Should parents marry, risking divorce, or not marry, and thus avoid divorce?
3. What can be done to stop a bully?
4. Why would children lie to adults to protect a friend?

> "But Dad, that's not fair! Why does Keaton get to kill zombies and I can't?"
>
> "Well, because you are too young to kill zombies. Your cousin Keaton is older than you, so that's why he can do it. You'll get nightmares."
>
> "That's soooo not fair."
>
> "Next year, after your birthday, I'll let you kill zombies."
>
> *[adapted from Asma, 2013]*

This conversation between a professor and his 8-year-old illustrates social development in middle childhood, explained in this chapter. All children want to do what the bigger children do, and all parents seek to protect their children, sometimes ineffectively. Throughout middle childhood, issues of parents and peers, fairness and justice, inclusion and exclusion are pervasive. Age takes on new importance, as concrete operational thinking makes chronology more salient. Age cutoffs are frequent in schools, camps, and athletic leagues.

In the excerpt above, the professor hoped his son would no longer want to kill zombies when he was 9, but if Keaton is still killing zombies in a year, the father's promise will be remembered.

The Nature of the Child

As explained in the previous chapter, steady growth, brain maturation, and intellectual advances make middle childhood a time for more independence (see At About This Time). One practical result is that between ages 6 and 11, children learn to care for themselves. They not only hold their own spoon but also make their own lunch, not only zip their own pants but also pack their own suitcases, not only walk to school but also organize games with friends.

Over the same years, parent–child interactions shift from primarily physical care (bathing, dressing, and so on) to include more conversation about choices and values, a trend particularly apparent with boys and their fathers (Keown & Palmer, 2014). Children listen to adults but express their own ideas as well.

The drive for independence expands the social world. School-age children venture outdoors alone to play with friends, if their parents let them. Some experts think that parents should do just that (Rosin, 2014).

Learning from Each Other: Middle childhood is prime time for social comparison. Swinging is done standing, or on the belly, or twisted, or head down (as shown here) if someone else does it.

social comparison The tendency to assess one's abilities, achievements, social status, and other attributes by measuring them against those of other people, especially one's peers.

industry versus inferiority The fourth of Erikson's eight psychosocial crises, during which children attempt to master many skills, developing a sense of themselves as either industrious or inferior, competent or incompetent.

Self-Concept

Throughout the centuries and in every culture, school-age children develop a much more realistic understanding of who they are and what they can do. They busily master whatever skills their culture values.

Social Comparison

In middle childhood, the self-concept becomes more complex and logical, as cognitive development and social awareness increase. Children realize they are not the fastest, smartest, prettiest, best. At some point between ages 6 and 11, when they win a race with their mother, it dawns on them that she could have run faster if she had tried.

Crucial during middle childhood is **social comparison**— comparing one's self to others (Davis-Kean et al., 2009; Dweck, 2013). Ideally, social comparison helps school-age children value themselves and abandon the imaginary, rosy self-evaluation of preschoolers. The self-concept becomes more realistic, incorporating comparison to peers and judgments from the overall society (Davis-Kean et al., 2009).

Over the years of middle childhood, children develop pride in their gender and background (Corenblum, 2014). Parents and teachers help by noting heroes who were female, African American, Latino, Muslim, Jewish, and so on. Of course, European American boys need heroes, too.

Affirming pride is an important counterbalance, because, for all children, increasing self-understanding and social awareness come at a price. Self-criticism and self-consciousness rise from ages 6 to 11, and "by middle childhood . . . this [earlier] overestimate of their ability or judgments decreases" (Davis-Kean et al., 2009, p. 184) while global self-esteem falls. Children's self-concept becomes influenced by the opinions of others, even by other children whom they do not know (Thomaes et al., 2010).

Erikson's Insights

With regard to his fourth psychosocial crisis, **industry versus inferiority,** Erikson noted that the child "must forget past hopes and wishes, while his exuberant imagination is tamed and harnessed to the laws of impersonal things," becoming "ready to apply himself to given skills and tasks" (Erikson, 1993a, pp. 258, 259).

Think of learning to read and to add, both of which are painstaking and boring. Slowly sounding out "Jane has a dog" or writing "3 + 4 = 7" for the 100th time is not exciting. Yet school-age children busily practice reading and math: They are intrinsically motivated to read a page, finish a worksheet, memorize a spelling word, color a map, and so on. Adults can encourage this.

This was apparent in the mother–son dialogue in Chapter 12, page 341. When Tim's mother wrote out many new math problems of the kind that had him "clumsy" in class, he did "the whole thing lickety split . . . [which made him] very happy" (Li et al.,

---

AT ABOUT THIS TIME

Signs of Psychosocial Maturation over the Years of Middle Childhood*

Children responsibly perform specific chores.
Children make decisions about a weekly allowance.
Children can tell time and have set times for various activities.
Children have homework, including some assignments over several days.
Children are punished less often than when they were younger.
Children try to conform to peers in clothes, language, and so on.
Children voice preferences about their after-school care, lessons, and activities.
Children are responsible for younger children, pets, and, in some places, work.
Children strive for independence from parents.

*Of course, culture is crucial. For example, giving a child an allowance is typical for middle-class children in developed nations since about 1960. It was rare, or completely absent, in earlier times and other places.

Same Situation, Far Apart: Helping at Home Sichuan, in China, and Virginia, in the United States, provide vastly different contexts for child development. Children everywhere help their families with household chores, as these two do, but gender expectations vary a great deal.

2014, p. 1218). Similarly, children enjoy collecting, categorizing, and counting whatever they gather—perhaps stamps, stickers, stones, or seashells. That is industry.

Overall, children judge themselves as either *industrious* or *inferior*—deciding whether they are competent or incompetent, productive or useless, winners or losers. Self-pride depends not necessarily on actual accomplishments but on how others view one's accomplishments. As Erikson said:

> In this, children cannot be fooled by empty praise and condescending encouragement. They may have to accept artificial bolstering of their self-esteem in lieu of something better, but [they gain] . . . strength only from wholehearted and consistent recognition of real accomplishment, [that is] of achievement that has meaning in the culture.
>
> [Erikson, 1993a, pp. 235–236]

Social rejection is both a cause and a consequence of feeling inferior (Rubin et al., 2013). The culture that is most salient in middle childhood is the culture of children, especially from peers of the same sex. Indeed, boys who write "Girls stay out!" and girls who insist that "Boys stink!" are typical. From a developmental perspective, this temporary antipathy (which Freud called *latency*) is a dynamic and useful stage. Children strive to be recognized for "real accomplishment" by their peers, shifting away from sexual interests until the hormones of puberty rise (Knight, 2014).

One component of self-concept has received considerable research attention (Dweck, 2013). As children become more self-aware, they benefit from praise for their process, for *how* they learn and *how* they relate to others, not for static qualities such as intelligence and popularity. This encourages a *growth mindset*. Instead of being told that "failure is not an option," they are encouraged to "fail again, fail better" (Smith & Henriksen, 2016, p. 6). [**Life-Span Link:** Dweck's research on whether intelligence is inborn or learned is further discussed in Chapter 15.]

For example, children who fail a test may be devastated *if* failure means they are not smart. However, process-oriented children consider failure a "learning opportunity," a time to advance metacognition by planning a better way to study.

Self-conscious emotions (pride, shame, guilt) develop during middle childhood, guiding social interaction. During these years, if those same emotions are

Watch **Video: Interview with Carol Dweck** to learn about how children's mindsets affect their intellectual development.

THINK CRITICALLY: When would a realistic, honest self-assessment be harmful?

uncontrolled, they can overwhelm a healthy self-concept, leading to psychopathology (Muris & Meesters, 2014).

Thus, as with most developmental advances, the potential for psychological growth is evident. However, advance is not automatic—family and social context affect whether a more realistic, socially attuned self-concept will be a burden or a blessing, and cultures vary.

Protect or Puncture Self-Esteem?

Unrealistically high self-esteem seems to reduce effortful control (described in Chapter 10), which leads to lower achievement and increased aggression. The same problems appear if self-esteem is unrealistically low. Children may be too self-critical or not self-critical enough (Robins et al., 2012; Baumeister, 2012).

Many cultures teach children to be modest, not prideful. For example, Australians say, "tall poppies are cut down"; the Chinese say, "the nail that sticks up is hammered"; and the Japanese discourage social comparison aimed at making oneself feel superior. That perspective is not held by everyone, even in those cultures.

A trio of researchers, acknowledging that "Whether high or low self-esteem is associated with increased aggression remains a topic of debate" (Teng et al., 2015, p. 45), surveyed 52 studies of self-esteem in Chinese children. They found that low self-esteem correlated with aggression, and thus they recommended that Chinese families and schools should not criticize children so much.

On the other hand, a study of fourth-grade students in the Netherlands found that "inflated self-esteem" (indicated by agreeing with items such as "I am a great example for other kids to follow") predicted bullying aggression among boys (not girls) (Reijntjes et al., 2015). These researchers were particularly concerned about child narcissism, an exaggerated pride that may be pathological.

Self-esteem is often encouraged in the United States. If 8-year-olds say that they want to be president when they grow up, adults usually smile and say, "That would be wonderful." Children's successes and ambitions are praised—even unlikely ones.

Teachers hesitate to criticize, especially in middle childhood. Some report card categories use phrases such as "on grade level" and "needs improvement" instead of letter grades. No child fails. This may lead to "social promotion," a much-criticized practice of passing children to the next grade whether or not they have mastered the work.

A backlash against age-based promotion is implicit when schools are closed because the children score low on achievement tests. A recent wave of educational reform in the United States tests children from the third grade on, promoting them only if they have achieved proficiency. The wave has already produced an opposing counterwave, with parents opting out of testing and politicians criticizing Common Core standards. Obviously culture, cohort, and age all influence attitudes about achievement, standards, and self-esteem. Should children be praised less or criticized less?

Resilience and Stress

Although early experiences are powerful, some children seem unscathed by early stress. They have been called "resilient" or even "invincible." Current thinking about resilience, with insights from dynamic-systems theory, emphasizes that no one is impervious to past history or current context (see Table 13.1). Many suffer lifelong harm from early maltreatment, some weather early storms, and a few become stronger (Masten, 2014).

Differential susceptibility is apparent, because of genes and early child rearing, preschool education, and culture. As Chapter 1 explains, some children are hardy, more like dandelions than orchids, but all are influenced by their situation (Ellis & Boyce, 2008).

Two leading researchers have defined **resilience** as "a dynamic process encompassing positive adaptation within the context of significant adversity" (Luthar et al., 2000, p. 543) and "the capacity of a dynamic system to adapt successfully to

resilience The capacity to adapt well to significant adversity and to overcome serious stress.

disturbances that threaten system function, viability, or development" (Masten, 2014, p. 10). Note that both definitions emphasize:

- Resilience is *dynamic*, not a stable trait. A given person may be resilient at some periods but not at others. The effects from one period reverberate as time goes on.
- Resilience is a *positive adaptation*. For example, if parental rejection leads a child to a closer relationship with another adult, that is positive adaptation.
- Adversity must be *significant*, a threat to the processes of development or even to life itself, not merely a minor stress.

Same Situation, Far Apart: Play Ball In the war in the Ukraine *(left)*, volunteers guard the House of Parliament against a Russian takeover, and in Liberia *(right)*, thousands have died from the Ebola epidemic. Nonetheless, one boy practices his soccer kick and four boys celebrate a soccer goal in 2015. Children can ignore national disasters as long as they have familiar caregivers nearby and a chance to play.

Observation Quiz How can you tell that the Liberian boys are celebrating a soccer victory instead of the end of an epidemic? (see answer, page 352) ↑

TABLE 13.1	Dominant Ideas About Resilience, 1965 to Present
1965	All children have the same needs for healthy development.
1970	Some conditions or circumstances—such as "absent father," "teenage mother," "working mom," and "day care"—are harmful for every child.
1975	All children are *not* the same. Some children are resilient, coping easily with stressors that cause harm in other children.
1980	Nothing inevitably causes harm. Both maternal employment and preschool education, once thought to be risks, are often helpful.
1985	Factors beyond the family, both in the child (low birthweight, prenatal alcohol exposure, aggressive temperament) and in the community (poverty, violence), can be very risky for children.
1990	Risk–benefit analysis finds that some children are "invulnerable" to, or even benefit from, circumstances that destroy others.
1995	No child is invincible. Risks are always harmful—if not in education, then in emotions; if not immediately, then long term.
2000	Risk–benefit analysis involves the interplay among many biological, cognitive, and social factors, some within the child (genes, disability, temperament), the family (function as well as structure), and the community (including neighborhood, school, church, and culture).
2008	Focus on strengths, not risks. Assets in child (intelligence, personality), family (secure attachment, warmth), community (schools, after-school programs), and nation (income support, health care) must be nurtured.
2010	Strengths vary by culture and national values. Both universal ideals and local variations must be recognized and respected.
2012	Genes as well as cultural practices can be either strengths or weaknesses; differential susceptibility means identical stressors can benefit one child and harm another.
2015	Communities are responsible for child resilience. Not every child needs help, but every community needs to encourage healthy child development.

Answer to Observation Quiz
(from page 351) They are hugging the ball.

Cumulative Stress

One important discovery is that stress accumulates over time, with many minor disturbances (called "daily hassles") building to a major impact. A long string of daily hassles is more devastating than an isolated major stress.

Almost every child can withstand one trauma. Repeated stresses, daily hassles, and multiple traumatic experiences make resilience difficult (Masten, 2014; Catani et al., 2010). The social context—especially supportive adults who do not blame the child—is crucial.

A chilling example comes from the "child soldiers" in the 1991–2002 civil war in Sierra Leone (Betancourt et al., 2013). Children witnessed and often participated in murder and rape. When the war was over, 529 war-affected youth, then aged 10 to 17, were interviewed. Many were pathologically depressed or anxious.

These war-damaged children were interviewed again two and six years later. Surprisingly, many had overcome their trauma and were functioning like typical children. Recovery was more likely if they were in middle childhood, not adolescence, when the war occurred. Furthermore, if at least one caregiver survived, if their communities did not reject them, and if their daily routines were restored, the children usually regained emotional normality.

An example from the United States comes from children living in a shelter for homeless families (Cutuli et al., 2013; Obradović, 2012). Compared to other children from the same kinds of families (typically high-poverty, single-parent), they were "significantly behind their low-income, but residentially more stable peers" in every way (Obradović et al., 2009, p. 513).

The probable reasons: Residential disruption, added to other stresses, was too much. They suffered physiologically, as measured by cortisol levels, blood pressure, and weight, and psychologically, as indicated by lower school achievement and fewer friends. Again, however, protective factors buffered the impact: Having a parent with them who provided affection, hope, and stable routines enabled some homeless children to be resilient.

Similar results were found in a longitudinal study of children exposed to a sudden, wide-ranging, terrifying wildfire in Australia. Almost all of the children suffered stress reactions at the time, but 20 years later the crucial factor for recovery

Same Situation, Far Apart: Praying Hands Differences are obvious between the Northern Indian girls entering their Hindu school and the West African boy in a Christian church, even in their clothes and hand positions. But underlying similarities are more important. In every culture, many 8-year-olds are more devout than their elders. That is especially true if their community is under stress. Faith aids resilience.

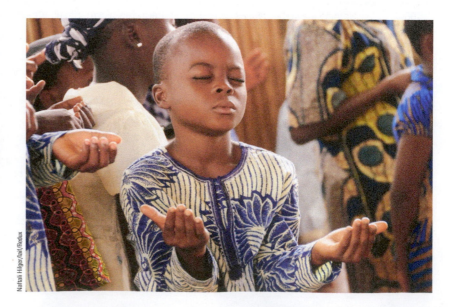

was not their proximity to the blaze but whether they had been separated from their mothers (McFarlane & Van Hooff, 2009).

Cognitive Coping

These examples are extreme, but the general finding appears in other research as well. Disasters take a toll, but factors in the child (especially problem-solving ability), in the family (consistency and care), and in the community (good schools and welcoming religious institutions) all increase resilience (Masten, 2014).

A pivotal factor is the child's interpretation of events (Lagattuta, 2014). Cortisol increases in low-income children *if* they interpret circumstances connected to their family's poverty as a personal threat and *if* the family lacks order and routines (thus increasing daily hassles) (E. Chen et al., 2010). When low-SES children do not take things personally and their family is not chaotic, resilience is more likely.

Do you know adults who grew up in low-SES families but seem strengthened, not destroyed, by that experience? If so, they probably did not consider themselves poor, perhaps because all of the children they knew had similar circumstances. They may have shared a bed with a sibling, eaten macaroni day after day, worn used clothes, and walked to school. However, if their family was loving and neither chaotic nor hostile, poverty did not harm them lifelong.

Overall, children's interpretation of circumstances (poverty, divorce, war, and so on) is crucial. Some consider their situation a temporary hardship; they look forward to leaving childhood behind. If they also have personal strengths, such as creativity and intelligence, they may shine in adulthood—evident in thousands of success stories, from Abraham Lincoln to Oprah Winfrey.

The opposite reaction is **parentification,** when children feel responsible for the entire family. They become caretakers, including of their actual parents. Here again, interpretation is crucial. Children suffer if they feel burdened and unable to escape, but if they feel helpful and adults respect their contribution, they may be resilient. The difference depends partly on community values (Khafi et al., 2014).

Video Activity: Child Soldiers and Child Peacemakers examines the state of child soldiers in the world and then explores how adolescent cognition impacts the decisions of five teenage peace activists.

> **THINK CRITICALLY:** Is there any harm in having the oldest child take care of the younger ones? Why or why not?

parentification When a child acts more like a parent than a child. Parentification may occur if the actual parents do not act as caregivers, making a child feel responsible for the family.

WHAT HAVE YOU LEARNED?

1. How do Erikson's stages of cognition for preschool- and school-age children differ?

2. Why is social comparison particularly powerful during middle childhood?

3. Why do cultures differ in how they value pride or modesty?

4. What factors help a child become resilient?

5. Why and when might minor stresses be more harmful than major stresses?

6. How might a child's interpretation affect the ability to cope with repeated stress?

Families and Children

No one doubts that genes affect personality as well as ability, that peers are vital, and that schools and cultures influence what, and how much, children learn. Some experts have gone further, suggesting that genes, peers, and communities are so influential that parenting has little impact—unless it is grossly abusive (Harris, 1998, 2002; McLeod et al., 2007). This suggestion arose from studies about the impact of the environment on child development.

Family Unity Thinking about any family—even a happy, wealthy family like this one—makes it apparent that each child's family experiences differ. For instance, would you expect this 5-year-old boy to be treated the same way as his two older sisters? And how about each child's feelings toward the parents? Even though the 12-year-olds are twins, one may favor her mother while the other favors her father.

Observation Quiz The 12-year-olds are twins. Can you see any differences in their shared environment? (see answer, page 357) ↑

Shared and Nonshared Environments

Many studies find that children are much less affected by *shared environment* (influences that arise from being in the same environment, such as two siblings living in one home, raised by their parents) than by *nonshared environment* (e.g., the experiences in the school or neighborhood that differ between one child and another).

Almost all personality traits and intellectual characteristics can be traced to the combined influence of genes and nonshared environments, with little left over for shared influences. Traits that some people believe arise from family circumstances, such as psychopathology, happiness, and sexual orientation (Burt, 2009; Långström et al., 2010; Bartels et al., 2013) also can be traced primarily to genes and nonshared environment, not families.

Could it be that parents are merely caretakers, providing only the basics (food, shelter)? Might normal household restrictions, routines, values, and responses be irrelevant? If a child becomes a murderer or a hero, maybe that is genetic and nonshared, so the parents deserve neither blame nor credit!

Recent findings, however, reassert parent power. The analysis that nonshared influences are powerful was correct, but it is not true that siblings raised together share the same environment.

For example, if relocation, divorce, unemployment, or a new job occurs in a family, the impact on each child depends on age, genes, and gender. Moving to another town upsets school-age children more than infants; divorce harms boys more than girls; poverty hurts preschoolers the most; and differential susceptibility is always relevant. If siblings share the same dysfunctional family, one child may become antisocial, another pathologically anxious, and a third resilient, capable, and strong (Beauchaine et al., 2009).

Further, parents do not treat each of their children the same. Even identical twins might not share family experiences, as the following makes clear.

A VIEW FROM SCIENCE

"I Always Dressed One in Blue Stuff . . ."

To separate the effects of genes and environment, many researchers have studied twins. As you remember from Chapter 3, some twins are dizygotic (DZ), with only half of their genes in common, and some are monozygotic (MZ), genetically identical (some MZ twins differ because of epigenetic factors after conception, but genetically, MZ twins come from one ovum and one sperm producing one zygote). Typically MZ and DZ twins are raised together, so researchers assumed a shared environment.

In prior research, if MZ twins had the same trait but DZ twins did not, scientists assumed that the trait was genetic. However, if MZ and DZ twins were similar in any intellectual or personality characteristic, their shared environment was considered the reason. Studies of thousands of twins led to the conclusion that genes and nonshared environment were far more significant for intelligence and personality than shared environment—i.e., their parents' values and practices.

Comparing MZ and DZ twins is a useful research strategy. However, conclusions are now tempered by another finding:

Siblings raised in the same households do not necessarily share the same home environment.

Researchers compared 1,000 sets of MZ twins reared by their biological parents. Their mothers' descriptions ranged from very positive ("my ray of sunshine") to very negative ("I wish I never had her. . . . She's a cow, I hate her") (quoted in Caspi et al., 2004, p. 153). Many mothers saw personality differences between their twins. For example, one mother said:

> Susan can be very sweet. She loves babies . . . she can be insecure . . . she flutters and dances around. . . . There's not much between her ears. . . . She's exceptionally vain, more so than Ann. Ann loves any game involving a ball, very sporty, climbs trees, very much a tomboy. One is a serious tomboy and one's a serious girlie girl. Even when they were babies I always dressed one in blue stuff and one in pink stuff.

> [quoted in Caspi et al., 2004, p. 156]

Some mothers rejected one twin and favored the other:

He was in the hospital and everyone was all "poor Jeff, poor Jeff" and I started thinking, "Well, what about me? I'm the one's just had twins. I'm the one's going through this, he's a seven-week-old baby and doesn't know a thing about it . . ." I sort of detached and plowed my emotions into Mike. [Jeff's twin brother.]

[quoted in Caspi et al., 2004, p. 156].

This same mother later blamed Jeff for favoring his father: "Jeff would do anything for Don but he wouldn't for me, and no matter what I did for either of them [Don or Jeff] it wouldn't be right" (p. 157). She said Mike was much more lovable.

The researchers measured each twin's personality at age 5 (assessing, among other things, antisocial behavior reported by teachers) and again two years later. They found that if a mother was more negative toward one of her twins, that twin *became* more antisocial, more likely to fight, steal, and hurt others at age 7 than at age 5, unlike the favored twin.

These researchers do not deny that many other nonshared factors—peers, teachers, and so on—have an impact. But parents matter. This will surprise no one who has a brother or a sister. Children from the same home do not always share the same experiences.

Family Structure and Family Function

Family structure refers to the legal and genetic connections among related people. Legal connections may be via marriage, years of cohabitation, or adoption. Genetic connections may be from parent to child, or between siblings, cousins, grandparents and grandchildren, and so on.

Family function refers to how the people in a family work together to care for the family members. Some families function well; others are dysfunctional. Some family functions are needed by everyone at every age, such as love and encouragement. Beyond that, what people need from their families differs depending on how old they are: Infants need responsive caregiving; teenagers need guidance; young adults need freedom; the aged need respect.

Always, function is more influential on human development than structure.

The Needs of Children in Middle Childhood

What do school-age children need from their families? Ideally, five things:

1. *Physical necessities.* Although 6- to 11-year-olds eat, dress, and go to bed without help, families provide basic needs, such as food, clothing, and shelter.
2. *Learning.* The prime learning years are in middle childhood: Families can support, encourage, and guide education.
3. *Self-respect.* Because children from age 6 to 11 become self-critical and socially aware, families can provide opportunities for success (in academics, sports, the arts, and so on) or shame.
4. *Peer relationships.* Families can choose schools and neighborhoods with friendly children and then arrange play dates, group activities, overnight trips, and so on.
5. *Harmony and stability.* Families can provide protective, predictable routines within a home that is a safe, peaceful haven.

The final item on the list above is especially crucial in middle childhood: Children cherish harmony and stability; they do not like conflict and change (Turner et al., 2012). Ironically, many parents move from one neighborhood or school to another during these years, not realizing that frequent moves may harm children academically and psychologically (Cutuli et al., 2013).

The need for continuity is evident for U.S. children in military families. Enlisted parents have higher incomes, better health care, and more education than do civilians from the same backgrounds. But they move. As a scientist reports, "military parents are continually leaving, returning, leaving again. . . . School work suffers, more for boys than for girls, . . . reports of depression and behavioral problems go up when a parent is deployed" (Hall, 2008, p. 52).

family structure The legal and genetic relationships among relatives living in the same home. Possible structures include nuclear family, extended family, stepfamily, single-parent family, and many others.

family function The way a family works to meet the needs of its members. Children need families to provide basic material necessities, to encourage learning, to help them develop self-respect, to nurture friendships, and to foster harmony and stability.

Especially for Scientists How would you determine whether or not parents treat all of their children the same? (see response, page 357)

Stay Home, Dad The rate of battle deaths for U.S. soldiers is lower for those deployed in Iraq and Afghanistan than for any previous conflict, thanks to modern medicine and armor. However, psychological harm from repeated returns and absences is increasing, especially for children.

About half of the military personnel on active duty have children, who usually learn to cope with the stresses they experience (Russo & Fallon, 2014). To help them, the U.S. military has instituted special programs, such as after-school sports that encourage positive friendships and abilities. Caregivers are encouraged to avoid changes in the child's life: no new homes, new rules, or new schools (Lester et al., 2011).

Diverse Structures

nuclear family A family that consists of a father, a mother, and their biological children under age 18.

Children flourish, or suffer, in many family structures. The most common structure during middle childhood is the **nuclear family,** which is made up of two parents and their biological children (see Table 13.2). Other two-parent structures include adoptive, foster, grandparents without parents, stepfamilies, and same-sex couples. Probably the most complex structure is the *blended family,* with children from each of two remarried parents, who often then have a baby of their own. Blended families are idealized in the media, but relatively few children live within them.

single-parent family A family that consists of only one parent and his or her children.

A third of U.S. children live in a **single-parent family.** Rates change depending on the age of the child: Infants and adolescents are more often in single-parent households than are 6- to 11-year-olds.

extended family A family of relatives in addition to the nuclear family, usually three or more generations living in one household.

Extended families consist of relatives residing with parents and children. Usually the additional persons are grandparents; sometimes they are uncles, aunts, or cousins. Shared households are common in some nations but less so in the United States. Rates vary depending on family culture: Extended families in the United States are more frequent in low-income, African American, and immigrant families. When they do not live in the same household, families in all of those groups tend to have more frequent interaction (R. Taylor et al., 2013).

polygamous family A family consisting of one man, several wives, and their children.

In many nations, a **polygamous family** (one husband with two or more wives) is an acceptable family structure, although polygamous families are atypical everywhere. In the United States, polygamy is illegal, and rare.

Same Situation, Far Apart: Happy Families The boys in both photos are about 4 years old. Roberto lives with his single mother in Chicago *(left)*. She pays $360 a month for her two children to attend a day-care center. The youngest child in the Balmedina family *(right)* lives with his nuclear family—no day care needed—in the Philippines. Which boy has the better life? The answer is not known; family function is more crucial than family structure.

AP Photo/Charles Rex Arbogast

Greg Elms/Getty Images

Divorce

Scientists try to provide analysis and insight based on empirical data (of course), but the task goes far beyond reporting facts. Regarding divorce, thousands of studies and several opposing perspectives need to be considered, analyzed, and combined—no easy task. One scholar who has attempted to do so is Andrew Cherlin, who has written 13 books and over 200 articles since 1988.

Among the puzzling facts that need interpretation are:

1. The United States leads the world in the rates of marriage, divorce, and remarriage, with almost half of all marriages ending in divorce.
2. Single parents, cohabiting parents, and stepparents sometimes provide good care for their estimated 40 million U.S. children, but children usually do best living with both of their married, biological parents.
3. Divorce is a process, not a decree: It affects academic achievement and psychosocial development for years, even decades.
4. Custody disputes and outcomes often harm children. Noncustodial parents, especially fathers, often become less connected to their children.

Answer to Observation Quiz
(from page 354) Their appearance and clothes are very similar. However, their relationship with their mother may differ.

Response for Scientists
(from page 355): Proof is very difficult when human interaction is the subject of investigation, since random assignment is impossible. Ideally, researchers would find identical twins being raised together and would then observe the parents' behavior over the years.

TABLE 13.2   Family Structures (percent of U.S. 6- to 11-year-olds in each type)*

Two-Parent Families (69%)

1. **Nuclear family** (56%). Named after the nucleus (the tightly connected core particles of an atom), the nuclear family consists of a man and a woman and their biological offspring under 18 years of age. In middle childhood, about half of all children live in nuclear families. About 10 percent of such families also include a grandparent, and often an aunt or uncle, living under the same roof. Those are *extended* families.

2. **Stepparent family** (9%). Divorced fathers usually remarry; divorced mothers remarry about half the time. If the stepparent family includes children born to two or more couples (such as children from the spouses' previous marriages and/or children of the new couple), that is a *blended family.*

3. **Adoptive family** (2%). Although as many as one-third of infertile couples adopt children, they usually adopt only one or two. Thus, only 2 percent of children are adopted, although the overall percentage of adoptive families is higher than that.

4. **Grandparents alone** (1%). Grandparents take on parenting for some children when biological parents are absent (dead, imprisoned, sick, addicted, etc.). That is a *skipped generation* family.

5. **Two same-sex parents** (1%). Some two-parent families are headed by a same-sex couple, whose legal status (married, step-, adoptive) varies.

Single-Parent Families (31%)

One-parent families are increasing, but they average fewer children than two-parent families. So in middle childhood, only 31 percent of children have a lone parent.

1. **Single mother—never married** (14%). In 2010, 41 percent of all U.S. births were to unmarried mothers; but when children are school age, many such mothers have married or have entrusted their children to their parents' care. Thus, only about 14 percent of 6- to 11-year-olds, at any given moment, are in single-mother, never-married homes.

2. **Single mother—divorced, separated, or widowed** (12%). Although many marriages end in divorce (almost half in the United States, fewer in other nations), many divorcing couples have no children. Others remarry. Thus, only 12 percent of school-age children currently live with single, formerly married mothers.

3. **Single father** (4%). About 1 father in 25 has physical custody of his children and raises them without their mother or a new wife. This category increased at the start of the twenty-first century but has decreased since 2005.

4. **Grandparent alone** (1%). Sometimes a single grandparent (usually the grandmother) becomes the sole caregiving adult for a child.

More Than Two Adults (15%) [Also listed as two-parent or single-parent family]

1. **Extended family** (15%). Some children live with a grandparent or other relatives, as well as with one (5 percent) or both (10 percent) of their parents This pattern is most common with infants (20 percent) but occurs in middle childhood as well.

2. **Polygamous family** (0%). In some nations (not the United States), men can legally have several wives. This family structure is more favored by adults than children. Everywhere, polyandry (one woman, several husbands) is rare.

---

*Less than 1 percent of children under age 12 live without any caregiving adult; they are not included in this table.

The percentages in this table are estimates, based on data in U.S. Bureau of the Census, Current Population Reports (2015), and *America's Families and Living Arrangements,* 2011. The category "extended family" in this table is higher than most published statistics, since some families do not tell official authorities about relatives living with them.

Each of these is troubling. The problem, Cherlin (2009) contends, is that the entire culture is conflicted: Marriage is idolized, but so is personal freedom. As a result, many North Americans assert their independence by marrying without consulting their parents or community. If they have a baby, child care becomes overwhelming and family support is lacking. That strains the marriage, precipitating divorce.

However, because marriage is the ideal, divorcing adults blame their former mate or their own poor choice, not the institution or the culture, according to Cherlin. Consequently, they seek another marriage, which may lead to another divorce. (Divorced adults marry more often than single adults their age, and the risk of divorce rises if a person has already been divorced.) Divorces allow freedom for the adults but may harm the children.

This leads to a related insight. Cherlin suggests that the main reason children are harmed by divorce—as well as by cohabitation, single parenthood, and stepparenthood—is not the legal status of their parents but the instability in residence, in school, in family members, and—this may be crucial—in the relationship between child and parent. Divorced parents often become stricter or more lenient, imposing premature responsibility or freedom, keeping family secrets or telling the child things that relieve the adult's anger or loneliness but that confuse and distress the child.

To make this more complex, sometimes divorce is better for children than an ongoing, destructive family. As one scientist who has also studied divorced families for decades wrote:

> Although divorce leads to an increase in stressful life events, such as poverty, psychological and health problems in parents, and inept parenting, it also may be associated with escape from conflict, the building of new more harmonious fulfilling relationships, and the opportunity for personal growth and individuation.

> [Hetherington, 2006, p. 204]

Connecting Structure and Function

The fact that family function is more influential than family structure does not make structure irrelevant. Structure affects function. Some structures make it easier for parents to provide the five family functions mentioned earlier (physical necessities, learning, self-respect, friendship, and harmony/stability).

Two-Parent Families

On average, adults are better parents when they live with their own children, day after day, and when they form a strong and cooperative alliance. One scholar summarizes the conclusions of dozens of studies: "Children living with two biological married parents experience better educational, social, cognitive, and behavioral outcomes" (Brown, 2010, p. 1062).

Some of those benefits are correlates, not direct causes. For instance, education, earning potential, and emotional maturity all correlate with marriage, birth, and staying married. One data point is illustrative: Most highly educated women having their first baby are married (78 percent) at conception; most less educated women are not (only 11 percent) (Gibson-Davis & Rackin, 2014).

Thus, brides and grooms tend to have personal assets *before* marriage and parenthood, and they bring those assets to their new family. That means that the correlation between child success and married parents occurs partly because of *who* marries, not because of the wedding. Indeed, for some very low-SES women, marrying a

Didn't Want to Marry This couple was happily cohabiting and strongly committed to each other but didn't wed until they learned that her health insurance would not cover them unless they were legally married. Twenty months after marriage, their son was born.

man who is also a high-school dropout with no steady job would actually undercut their ability to give their baby attention. They may be better mothers not married!

Income also correlates with family structure. Usually, married couples live apart from their parents if everyone can afford it. This means that, at least in the United States, an extended family suggests that someone is financially dependent, not that a child has many loving adults at home.

These two factors—mate selection and income—explain some of the correlation between nuclear families and child well-being, but not all of it (Brown, 2010). The fact that the nuclear family is "not as strong as it appears" does not make marriage irrelevant. Ideally, marriage produces mutual affection and support, and then both partners become wealthier and healthier than either would alone. Further, when both parents live with their children day and night, a *parental alliance* is likely to form and benefit the child.

Shared parenting decreases the risk of abuse and neglect. Having two parents in the house makes it more likely that someone will read to the children, check their homework, invite their friends over, buy them new clothes, and save for their college education. Of course, having two married parents does not guarantee an alliance. One of my students wrote:

> My mother externalized her feelings with outbursts of rage, lashing out and breaking things, while my father internalized his feelings by withdrawing, being silent and looking the other way. One could say I was being raised by bipolar parents. Growing up, I would describe my mom as the Tasmanian devil and my father as the ostrich, with his head in the sand. . . . My mother disciplined with corporal punishment as well as with psychological control, while my father was permissive. What a pair.
>
> [C, 2013]

This student never experienced a well-functioning parental alliance. That may help explain why she is now a single parent, having twice married, given birth, and divorced. For everyone, childhood family experiences echo in adulthood.

Adoptive and same-sex parents usually function well for children, not only in middle childhood but lifelong. Stepfamilies *can* also function well, if the biological parent has chosen a partner who will be a good parent. Especially when children are under age 2 and the stepparent and the biological parent develop a strong, healthy relationship, the children who live with them may thrive (Ganong et al., 2011).

No structure is guaranteed to function well, but particular circumstances for all three family types—same-sex, adoptive, and step—can nudge in one direction or the other. Unfortunately, instability occurs more often in non-nuclear families. They move from one place to another more often, and the family composition changes—new babies arrive, older children join or depart. Stepchildren create "complex" structures, affecting all of the children (including those who are the biological offspring of both parents) in school and in life (Brown et al., 2015).

Middle American Family This photo seems to show a typical breakfast in Brunswick, Ohio—Cheerios for 1-year-old Carson, pancakes that 7-year-old Carter does not finish eating, and family photos crowded on the far table.

Observation Quiz What is unusual about this family? (see answer, page 360) ↑

Don't Judge We know this is a mother and her child, but structure and function could be wonderful or terrible. These two could be half of a nuclear family, or a single mother with one adoptive child, or part of four other family structures. That does not matter as much as family function: If this scene is typical, with both enjoying physical closeness in the great outdoors, this family functions well.

 **Answer to Observation Quiz** (from page 359) Both parents are women. The evidence shows that families with same-sex parents are similar in many ways to families with opposite-sex parents, and children in such families develop well.

Especially for Single Parents You have heard that children raised in one-parent families will have difficulty in establishing intimate relationships as adolescents and adults. What can you do about this possibility? (see response, page 363)

LaunchPad
macmillan learning

Check out the Data Connections activity **Family Structure in the United States and Around the World.**

FIGURE 13.1

Possible Problems As the text makes clear, structure does not determine function, but raising children is more difficult as a single parent, in part because income is lower. African American families have at least one asset, however. They are more likely to have grandparents who are actively helping with child care.

Harmony is also more difficult in stepfamilies (Martin-Uzzi & Duval-Tsioles, 2013). Children may be expected to share a home and even a bedroom with other children raised with other values who are now called their brothers and sisters. Further, loyalty to both biological parents is challenged by ongoing disputes between them. A solid parental alliance is difficult for the three adults, two of whom had such profound disagreements that they divorced and one who is a stranger to the child.

Indeed, some observers suggest that, for children, polygamy is preferable to divorce, remarriage, and stepparenthood. The reason for this suggestion is that most fathers who have divorced their first wife and married another are less involved with children from their first marriage than if they had been polygamous, living with both wives (Calder & Beaman, 2014).

Finally, the grandparent family is often idealized, but reality is much more complex. If a household has grandparents and parents, the grandparents may be care-receivers more than caregivers. Further, the two adult generations often disagree about discipline, diet, and much else.

Sometimes grandparents provide full-time care with no parents present. The hope is that their experience and maturity will benefit the grandchildren. But that may not happen. Grandchildren whose parents have left them often have health or behavioral problems that are difficult for the grandparents to handle (Hayslip et al., 2014).

Single-Parent Families

On average, single parents have less income, time, and stability than do two adults together. Most single parents fill many roles—including wage earner, daughter, or son—making it hard to provide steady emotional and academic support for their children. About half have a live-in partner, who adds to the complexity of the parenting role.

Rates of single parenthood and single grandparenthood are far higher among African Americans than other ethnic groups (see Figure 13.1). This makes children from single-parent, African American families feel less stigmatized, but it does not lighten the burden on the parents. If a single parent is depressed (and many are), that compounds the problem. The following case is an example.

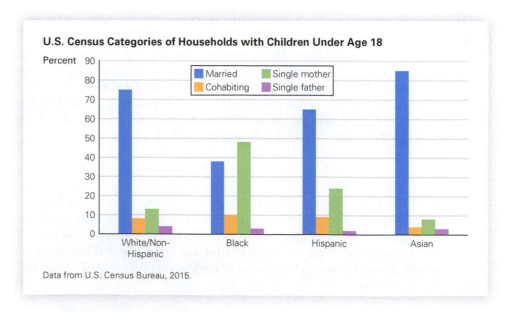

U.S. Census Categories of Households with Children Under Age 18

Data from U.S. Census Bureau, 2015.

How Hard Is It to Be a Kid?

Neesha's fourth-grade teacher referred her to the school guidance team because Neesha often fell asleep in class, was late 51 days, and was absent 15 days. Although she was only 10 years old and had missed much of the fourth grade, testing found Neesha's achievements above average. She scored at the seventh-grade level in reading and writing, and at the fifth-grade level in math. Since ability was not Neesha's problem, something psychosocial must be amiss.

The counselor spoke to Neesha's mother, Tanya, a depressed single parent who was worried about paying rent on the tiny apartment where she had moved when Neesha's father left three years earlier. He lived with his girlfriend, now with a new baby. Tanya said she had no problems with Neesha, who was "more like a little mother than a kid," unlike her 15-year-old son, Tyrone, who suffered from fetal alcohol effects and whose behavior worsened when his father left.

Tyrone was recently beaten up badly as part of a gang initiation, a group he considered "like a family." He was currently in juvenile detention after being arrested for stealing bicycle parts. Note the nonshared environment here: Although the siblings grew up together, 12-year-old Tyrone became rebellious when their father left, whereas 7-year-old Neesha became parentified, "a little mother."

The school counselor spoke with Neesha.

Neesha volunteered that she worried a lot about things and that sometimes when she worries she has a hard time falling asleep . . . it was hard to wake up. Her mom was sleeping late because she was working more nights cleaning offices. . . . Neesha said she got so far behind that she just gave up. She was also having problems with the other girls in the class, who were starting to tease her about sleeping in class and not doing her work. She

said they called her names like "Sleepy" and "Dummy." . . . at first it made her very sad, and then it made her very mad. That's when she started to hit them to make them stop.

[Wilmshurst, 2011, pp. 152–153]

Neesha is coping with poverty, a depressed mother, an absent father, a delinquent brother, and classmate bullying. She seems resilient—her achievement scores are impressive. But shortly after the counselor spoke with her,

The school principal received a call from Neesha's mother, who asked that her daughter not be sent home from school because she was going to kill herself. She was holding a loaded gun in her hand and she had to do it, because she was not going to make this month's rent. . . . While the guidance counselor continued to keep the mother talking, the school contacted the police, who apprehended mom . . . The loaded gun was on her lap. . . . The mother was taken to the local psychiatric facility.

[Wilmshurst, 2011, pp. 154–155]

Whether Neesha will be able to cope with her problems depends on whether she can find support beyond her family. Perhaps the school counselor will help:

When asked if she would like to meet with the school psychologist once in a while, just to talk about her worries, Neesha said she would like that very much. After she left the office, she turned and thanked the psychologist for working with her, and added, "You know, sometimes it's hard being a kid."

[Wilmshurst, 2011, p. 154]

Although family structure encourages or undercuts healthy function, contrary to the averages, thousands of stepparents provide excellent care, thousands of single-parent families are wonderful, and thousands of nuclear families are dysfunctional. Culture and national policy are always influential—providing support or shame (Abela & Walker, 2014).

For example, a study of children in the slums of Mumbai, India, found that children in nuclear families had *more* psychological disorders than children in extended families, presumably because grandparents, aunts, and uncles provided extra care and stability (Patil et al., 2013). However, another study in India found that college students who injured themselves (e.g., *cutting*) were more often from extended families than nuclear ones (Kharsati & Bhola, 2014). One explanation is that these two studies had different populations: College students tend to be from wealthier families, unlike the children in Mumbai.

A Wedding, or Not? Family Structures Around the World

Children fare best when both parents actively care for them every day. This is most likely to occur if the parents are married, although there are many exceptions. Many developmentalists now focus on the rate of single parent-hood, shown on this map. Some single parents raise children well, but the risk of neglect, poverty, and instability in single-parent households increases the chances of child problems.

RATES OF SINGLE PARENTHOOD

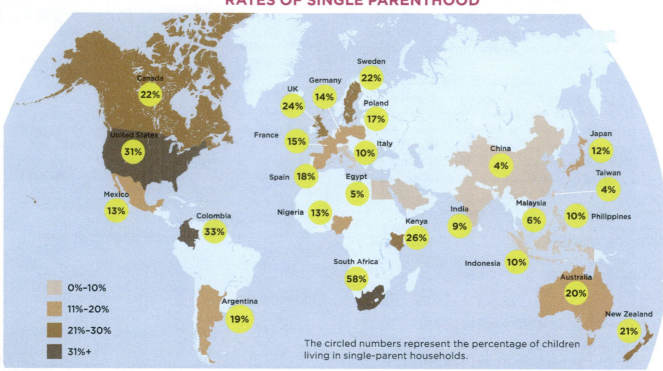

Canada 22%
Sweden 22%
Germany 14%
UK 24%
Poland 17%
France 15%
Italy 10%
Japan 12%
United States 31%
China 4%
Taiwan 4%
Spain 18%
Egypt 5%
Mexico 13%
Nigeria 13%
India 9%
Malaysia 6%
10% Philippines
Colombia 33%
Kenya 26%
Indonesia 10%
South Africa 58%
Australia 20%
Argentina 19%
New Zealand 21%

Legend:
0%–10%
11%–20%
21%–30%
31%+

The circled numbers represent the percentage of children living in single-parent households.

DATA FROM WILCOX, 2011.

A young couple in love and committed to each other—

what next?

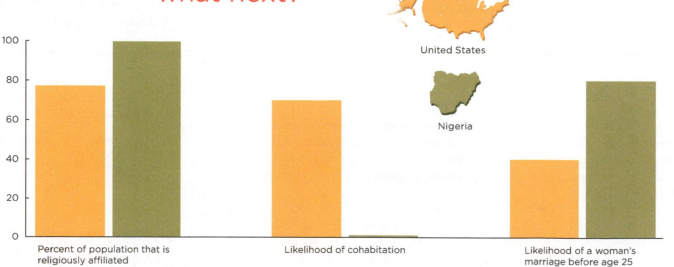

United States

Nigeria

Percent of population that is religiously affiliated

Likelihood of cohabitation

Likelihood of a woman's marriage before age 25

DATA FROM COPEN ET AL., 2013 AND U.S. CENSUS BUREAU, 2012.

Cohabitation and marriage rates change from year to year and from culture to culture. These two examples are illustrative and approximate. Family-structure statistics like these often focus on marital status and may make it seem as if Nigerian children are more fortunate than American children. However, actual household functioning is more complex than that, and involves many other factors.

Family Trouble

Two factors impair family function in every structure, ethnic group, and nation: low income and high conflict. Many families experience both: Financial stress increases conflict and vice versa.

Wealth and Poverty

Family income correlates with both function and structure. Marriage rates fall in times of recession. Divorce itself becomes less common, probably because it is costly to divorce, but home foreclosure increases the rate of family dissolution (Cohen, 2014; Schaller, 2013). Low SES correlates with many problems because "risk factors pile up in the lives of some children, particularly among the most disadvantaged" (Masten, 2014, p. 95).

Several scholars have developed the *family-stress model,* which holds that any risk (such as low income, divorce, single parenthood, or unemployment) damages a family *only if* it increases stress on the parents, who then become less patient and responsive to their children.

If economic hardship is ongoing, if uncertainty about the future is high, if education is low—all of these may increase adult hostility and stress (Valdez et al., 2013; Evans & Kim, 2013; D. Lee et al., 2013). Reaction to wealth may also cause difficulty. If wealthy parents pressure their children to maintain high achievement, the stress can lead the children to use drugs, commit crimes, and fail in school—all of which are more common in children of very wealthy parents compared to parents with average income (Luthar & Barkin, 2012). Again, it is not the money itself; it is the money's effect on the parents.

Conflict

Every researcher agrees that family conflict harms children, especially when adults fight about child rearing. Such fights are more common in stepfamilies, divorced families, and extended families, but nuclear families are not immune. Children suffer if they witness fights between the parents or among siblings (Turner et al., 2012).

Some researchers wonder whether children are emotionally troubled in families with feuding parents because of their inherited genes, not because of what they see. Perhaps the parents' genes lead to marital problems and then their children have those same genes. If that is the case, then family conflict is not the source of the child's problems.

That hypothesis is plausible but was proven false. Researchers studied conflict in married adult twins (388 monozygotic pairs and 479 dizygotic pairs) who had an adolescent child. The researchers analyzed genes and family life for all of the pairs and all of the teenagers. Thus, they compared the problems of each child with those of his or her cousin, who had half (MZ parent) or a quarter (DZ parent) of the same genes (Schermerhorn et al., 2011).

Via complex statistical calculation, the researchers found that, although genes had some influence, witnessing family conflict and experiencing divorce had a more powerful effect. It correlated with externalizing problems in boys and internalizing problems in girls (Schermerhorn et al., 2011).

THINK CRITICALLY: Can you describe a situation in which having a single parent would be better for a child than having two parents?

● **Response for Single Parents** (from page 360): Do not get married mainly to provide a second parent for your child. If you were to do so, things would probably get worse rather than better. Do make an effort to have friends of both sexes with whom your child can interact.

You Idiot! Ideally, parents never argue in front of the children, as these two do here. However, *how* they argue is crucial. Every couple disagrees about specifics of family life; dysfunctional families call each other names. Hopefully, he said, "I know how to fit this bike into the car" and she answered, "I was just trying to help," rather than either one escalating the fight by saying, "It was your stupid idea to take this trip!"

© PhotoAlto/Alamy

The Peer Group

Peers become increasingly important in middle childhood. With their new awareness of reality (concrete operations), children are painfully aware of their classmates' opinions, judgments, and accomplishments.

The Culture of Children

child culture The idea that each group of children has games, sayings, clothing styles, and superstitions that are not common among adults, just as every culture has distinct values, behaviors, and beliefs.

Child culture includes customs, rules, and rituals that are passed down to younger children from slightly older ones. Jump-rope rhymes, insults, and superstitions are part of peer society. So are clothes: Many children reject clothes that parents buy as too loose, too tight, too long, too short, or wrong in color, style, brand, or decoration.

Language is another manifestation of child culture, because communication with peers is vital. Parents may proudly note how well their children speak a second language, but they may be distressed when their children spout their peers' curses, accents, and slang.

Independence from adults is acclaimed. Peers pity those (especially boys) whose parents kiss them ("mama's boy"), tease those who please the teachers ("teacher's pet," "suck-up"), and despise those who betray children to adults ("tattletale," "grasser," "snitch," "rat"). Keeping secrets from parents and teachers is a moral mandate.

Because they value independence, children find friends who defy authority, sometimes harmlessly (passing a note in class), sometimes not (shoplifting, smoking). If a bully teases or isolates a child, it is hard for the other children to defend the one who is shunned.

Friendships

Teachers often try to separate friends, but developmentalists find that friends teach each other academic and social skills (Bagwell & Schmidt, 2011). Moreover, children learn faster and feel happier when they have friends. If they had to choose between being friendless but popular (looked up to by many peers) or having close friends but being unpopular (ignored by peers), most would choose to have friends (Bagwell & Schmidt, 2011). A wise choice.

Friendships become more intense and intimate over the years of middle childhood, as social cognition and effortful control advance. Six-year-olds may befriend anyone of the same sex and age who is willing to play with them. By age 10, children demand more of their friends. They share secrets and expect loyalty.

No Toys Boys in middle childhood are happiest playing outside with equipment designed for work. This wheelbarrow is perfect, especially because at any moment the pusher might tip it.

E.Harazaki Photography/Flickr RF/Getty Images

Compared to younger children, older children change friends less often, become more upset when a friendship breaks up, and find it harder to make new friends.

Older children tend to choose friends whose interests, values, and backgrounds are similar to their own. By the end of middle childhood, close friendships are almost always between children of the same sex, age, ethnicity, and socioeconomic status (Rubin et al., 2013). This occurs not because children naturally become more prejudiced in middle childhood (they do not) but because they seek friends who understand and agree with them.

Gender differences persist in activities (girls converse more whereas boys play more active games), but both boys and girls want best friends. Having no close friends at age 11 predicts depression at age 13 (Brendgen et al., 2010).

If parents focus only on academic accomplishment, they may seriously harm their children's friendship networks. For example, one mother worked as a school aide and saw that her daughter was not being academically challenged in a bilingual class. Accordingly, she got the child transferred to an English-only class, where she had no friends and the teacher resented having an additional student. This student became my student in college and remembers:

> When I was in elementary school from kindergarten to third grade I was in a bilingual class. However, my mother decided she wanted me in an English class, and I was immediately switched. When I was in the bilingual class I was never bullied but in my new class I was bullied every day. A lot of the kids would call me four eyes, ugly, a nerd, and a fly.
>
> I never really had any friends and the only time any of my peers would speak to me was if we had to do a group assignment. I was even bullied by the teacher because my mother worked in the school and she didn't really get along with my mother. One day she put me in the corner because I sneezed. She told me I was "disturbing the class". Another time I raised my hand to go to the bathroom and she told me I could not go. I was trying to obey her and hold it in until lunch time but I couldn't so I asked her again and she said no again. . . . I peed on myself. She then called the janitor to clean it up. I was so embarrassed I went into the closet and cried. The janitor called my mother and she came to the classroom with a change of clothes.
>
> Another day when going to lunch we were all lined up going down the stairs and I stood all the way in the back so I wouldn't get picked on. Huge mistake. Some of the boys pushed me down the stairs. I had a busted lip, broken glasses, a black eye, a huge knot on my forehead. . . . I hated to go to school, I wished to go back to the bilingual class where everyone treated me nice.

[Personal communication, 2016]

Popular and Unpopular Children

The particular qualities that make a child liked or disliked depend on culture, cohort, and sometimes the local region or school. For example, shyness is not valued in North America, especially for boys in middle childhood, but this is not universally the case.

Consider research on shy children in China. A 1990 survey in Shanghai found that shy children were liked and respected (X. Chen et al., 1992). Twelve years later, Chinese culture had shifted and a survey from the same schools found shy children less popular than their shy predecessors had been (X. Chen et al., 2005).

A few years later, a third study in rural China found that shyness was still valued; it predicted adult adjustment (X. Chen et al., 2009). By contrast, a fourth study from a Chinese city found that shyness in middle childhood predicted unhappiness later on—unless the shy child was also academically superior, in which case shyness was not a disability (X. Chen et al., 2013).

"Oh yeah? Well, my vocabulary is bigger than _your_ vocabulary!"

Better Than Children of both sexes, all ethnic groups, and every religion, nation, and family think they are better than children of other groups. They can learn not to blurt out insults, but a deeper understanding of the diversity of human experience and abilities requires maturation.

THINK CRITICALLY: Do adults also choose friends who agree with them, or whose background is similar to their own?

Other traits also vary in how much they are admired. At every age, children who are outgoing, friendly, and cooperative are well liked. In the United States, by the end of middle childhood, a second set of traits also predicts popularity: being dominant and somewhat aggressive (Shi & Xie, 2012).

There are three types of unpopular children. Some are *neglected,* not rejected; they are ignored, but not shunned. The other two types are actively rejected: **aggressive-rejected,** disliked because they are antagonistic and confrontational, and **withdrawn-rejected,** disliked because they are timid and anxious.

aggressive-rejected A type of childhood rejection, when other children do not want to be friends with a child because of his or her antagonistic, confrontational behavior.

Considerable change in social status occurs among children from year to year, as the class composition changes. Teachers can make a difference, if they are warm toward the disliked child (Hughes & Im, 2016). They also can make it worse, as occurred for my student.

withdrawn-rejected A type of childhood rejection, when other children do not want to be friends with a child because of his or her timid, withdrawn, and anxious behavior.

Both aggressive-rejected and withdrawn-rejected children misinterpret social situations, lack emotional regulation, and may be mistreated at home, which increases the risk of rejection at school (Stenseng et al., 2015). Unless they are guided toward friendship with at least one other child, they may become bullies and/or victims.

Bullies and Victims

bullying Repeated, systematic efforts to inflict harm on other people through physical, verbal, or social attack on a weaker person.

Bullying is defined as repeated, systematic attacks intended to harm those who are unable or unlikely to defend themselves. It occurs in every nation, in every community, and in every kind of school (religious or secular, public or private, progressive or traditional, large or small). Victims are chosen because they are powerless, with many possible traits.

As one boy explained:

> You can get bullied because you are weak or annoying or because you are different. Kids with big ears get bullied. Dorks get bullied. You can also get bullied because you think too much of yourself and try to show off. Teacher's pet gets bullied. If you say the right answer too many times in class you can get bullied. There are lots of popular groups who bully each other and other groups, but you can get bullied within your group too. If you do not want to get bullied, you have to stay under the radar, but then you might feel sad because no one pays attention to you.
>
> [*quoted in Guerra et al., 2011, p. 306*]

LaunchPad
macmillan learning

Bullying: Interview with Nikki Crick

http://qrs.ly/nq4ep13

© 2016 Macmillan

Bullying may be any of four types:

- *Physical* (hitting, pinching, shoving, or kicking)
- *Verbal* (teasing, taunting, or name-calling)
- *Relational* (destroying peer acceptance)
- *Cyber* (bullying that uses cell phones, computers, and other electronic devices)

The first three types are common in primary school and begin even earlier, in preschool. (Cyberbullying is more common later on, and it is discussed in Chapter 15.)

A key word in the definition of bullying is *repeated.* Almost every child experiences an isolated attack or is called a derogatory name at some point. Victims of bullying, however, endure shameful experiences again and again—being forced to hand over lunch money, to laugh at insults, to drink milk mixed with detergent, and so on—with no one defending them. Victims tend to be "cautious, sensitive, quiet . . . lonely and abandoned at school. As a rule, they do not have a single good friend in their class" (Olweus, 1999, p. 15).

Although it is often thought that victims are particularly unattractive or odd, this is not usually the case. Victims are chosen because of their emotional

Who Suffers More? Physical bullying is typically the target of antibullying laws and policies, because it is easier to spot than relational bullying. But being rejected from the group, especially with gossip and lies, may be more devastating to the victim and harder to stop. It may be easier for the boy to overcome victimization than for the girl.

vulnerability and social isolation, not their appearance. Children new to a school or a class, or whose background and home culture are unlike that of their peers, are especially vulnerable.

Remember the three types of unpopular children. Neglected children are not victimized; they are ignored, "under the radar." If their family relationships are good, they suffer less even if they are bullied (which they usually are not) (Bowes et al., 2010).

Withdrawn-rejected children are often victims; they are isolated, feel depressed, and are friendless. Aggressive-rejected children are called **bully-victims** (or *provocative victims*), with neither friends nor sympathizers. They suffer the most because they strike back ineffectively, which increases the bullying (Dukes et al., 2009).

Unlike bully-victims, most bullies are *not* rejected. Although some have low self-esteem, others are proud; they are pleased with themselves and have friends who admire them and classmates who fear them (Guerra et al., 2011). As already mentioned, some are quite popular, with bullying seen as a form of social dominance and authority (Pellegrini et al., 2011).

Male bullies usually physically attack smaller, weaker boys. Female bullies usually use words to attack shyer, more soft-spoken girls. Young boys can sometimes bully girls, but by puberty (about age 11), boys who bully girls are not admired (Veenstra et al., 2010), although sexual teasing is. Especially in the final years of middle childhood, boys who are thought to be gay become targets, with suicide attempts being one consequence (Hong et al., 2012).

bully-victim Someone who attacks others and who is attacked as well. (Also called *provocative victims* because they do things that elicit bullying.)

Causes and Consequences of Bullying

Bullying may originate with a genetic predisposition or a brain abnormality, but when a toddler is aggressive, parents, teachers, and peers usually teach emotional regulation and effortful control. However, if home life is stressful, if discipline is ineffectual, if siblings are hostile, or if attachment is insecure, vulnerable young children develop externalizing and internalizing problems, becoming bullies or victims (Turner et al., 2012).

Peers are crucial. Some peer groups approve of relational bullying, and then children entertain their classmates by mocking and insulting each other (Werner & Hill, 2010). On the other hand, when students themselves disapprove, the incidence of bullying plummets (Guerra & Williams, 2010). Television makes it worse. Programs designed for children often include admired characters with sharp tongues and high status—and the screen never shows the effect on the victims (Coyne, 2016).

Age matters. For most of childhood, bullies are disliked; but a switch occurs at about age 11, when bullying becomes a way to gain social status (Caravita & Cillessen, 2012). In addition, some behaviors that adults might consider bullying are accepted by children as part of social interaction, and some social dominance has been part of human development for centuries. It is crucial to understand when aggression is harmful (Bjorklund & Hawley, 2014). If children think teachers are clueless, punishing the wrong person for the wrong thing, that does not help the real victims.

The consequences of bullying can echo for years. Many victims become depressed; many bullies become increasingly cruel (Willoughby et al., 2014). Victims suffer for decades, especially if they blame themselves for their plight (Perren et al., 2013).

Unless bullies are deterred, they and their victims risk impaired social understanding, lower school achievement, and relationship difficulties. Decades later they have higher rates of psychological disorders (Copeland et al., 2013; Ttofi et al., 2014). Compared to other adults the same age, former bullies are more likely to die young, be jailed, or have destructive marriages.

Can Bullying Be Stopped?

Many victims find ways to halt ongoing bullying—by ignoring, retaliating, defusing, or avoiding. Friends defend each other and restore self-esteem (Bagwell & Schmidt, 2011). Friendships help individuals, but what can be done to halt a culture of bullying?

We know what does *not* work: simply increasing students' awareness of bullying, instituting zero tolerance for fighting, or putting bullies together in a therapy group or a classroom (Baldry & Farrington, 2007; Monks & Coyne, 2011). This last measure tends to make daily life easier for some teachers, but it increases aggression. Another strategy is to talk to the parents of the bully, but this may backfire. Since one cause of bullying is poor parent–child interaction, talking to the parents may "create even more problems for the child, for the parents, and for their relationship" (Rubin et al., 2013, p. 267).

The school community as a whole—teachers and bystanders, parents and aides, bullies and victims—needs to change. In fact, the entire school can either increase the rate of bullying or decrease it (Juvonen & Graham, 2014). For example, a Colorado study found that when the overall school climate encouraged learning and cooperation, children with high self-esteem were unlikely to be bullies; when the school climate was hostile, those with high self-esteem were often bullies (Gendron et al., 2011).

Again, peers are crucial: They must do more than simply notice bullying, becoming aware without doing anything to counter it. In fact, some bystanders feel morally disengaged from the victims, which increases bullying. Others are sympathetic but feel powerless (Thornberg & Jungert, 2013). However, if they empathize with victims, feel effective (high in effortful control), and refuse to admire bullies, classroom aggression is reduced (Salmivalli, 2010).

Efforts to change the entire school are credited with recent successful efforts to decrease bullying in 29 schools in England (Cross et al., 2011), throughout Norway, in Finland (Kärnä et al., 2011), and often in the United States (Allen, 2010; Limber, 2011). Among the aspects of successful programs are role-playing and cooperative learning, so bystanders become likely to intervene.

Further, the head of the school needs to encourage all of the teachers to focus on social interactions, not just on academics. Punishing the bullies might backfire, in that they may gain respect among their peers for defying adults. If adults target

THINK CRITICALLY: The text says that both former bullies and former victims suffer in adulthood. Which would you rather be, and why?

Patrick Hardin/CartoonStock

"He followed me home — can I punch him?"

Much to Learn Children do not always know when something is hurtful, and adults do not always know when to intervene.

●● **Especially for Parents of an Accused Bully** Another parent has told you that your child is a bully. Your child denies it and explains that the other child doesn't mind being teased. (see response, page 370)

overt bullying, the result may be more bullying where adults might not see it, such as in bathrooms, the edge of the playground, the social media.

Evaluation is critical: Programs that seem good might be harmful. Longitudinal research on whole-school efforts finds that some programs make a difference and some do not, with variations depending on the age of the children and the indicators (peer report of bullying or victimization, teacher report of incidents reported, and so on). Intervention is more effective in the earlier grades.

Objective follow-up efforts suggest that bullying can be reduced but not eliminated. It is foolhardy to blame only the bully and, of course, wrong to blame the victim: The entire school community—including the culture of the school—needs to change. That leads to the final topic of this chapter, the moral development of children.

Wonderfully Conventional Krysta Caltabiano displays her poster, "Ways to Be a Good Citizen," which won the Good Citizenship Contest sponsored by the Connecticut Secretary of State.

Observation Quiz Why is Krysta's poster a good example of Erikson's industry versus inferiority stage? (see answer, page 371) ↑

WHAT HAVE YOU LEARNED?

1. How does what children wear reflect the culture of children?

2. In what ways do friendships change from the beginning to the end of middle childhood?

3. How is a child's popularity affected by culture and cohort?

4. What are the similarities and differences between boy bullies and girl bullies?

5. How might bullying be reduced?

Children's Moral Values

Middle childhood is prime time for moral development. Many forces drive children's growing interest in moral issues. Three of them are (1) child culture, (2) personal experience, and (3) empathy. The culture of children includes ethical mandates, such as loyalty to friends and keeping secrets. Fairness is seen as equality, not equity. (In the opening anecdote of this chapter, a boy argued that it was "so unfair" that he could not kill zombies.) Personal experiences also matter.

For all children, empathy increases in middle childhood as they become more socially perceptive. This increasing perception can backfire, however. One example was just described: Bullies become adept at picking victims (Veenstra et al., 2010). An increase in social understanding makes noticing and defending rejected children possible, but in some social contexts, bystanders may decide to be self-protective rather than to intervene (Pozzoli & Gini, 2013).

Children who are slow to develop theory of mind—which, as discussed in Chapter 5, is affected by family and culture—are also slow to develop empathy (Caravita et al., 2010). School-age children can think and act morally, but they do not always do so.

The authors of a study of 7-year-olds "conclude that moral *competence* may be a universal human characteristic, but that it takes a situation with specific demand characteristics to translate this competence into actual prosocial performance" (van Ijzendoorn et al., 2010, p. 1).

Moral Reasoning

Piaget wrote extensively about the moral development of children as they developed and enforced their own rules for playing games together (Piaget, 1932/2013b). His emphasis on how children think about moral issues led to a famous description of cognitive stages of morality (Kohlberg, 1963).

Kohlberg's Levels of Moral Thought

Lawrence Kohlberg described three levels of moral reasoning and two stages at each level (see Table 13.3), with parallels to Piaget's stages of cognition.

preconventional moral reasoning
Kohlberg's first level of moral reasoning, emphasizing rewards and punishments.

conventional moral reasoning
Kohlberg's second level of moral reasoning, emphasizing social rules.

postconventional moral reasoning
Kohlberg's third level of moral reasoning, emphasizing moral principles.

- **Preconventional moral reasoning** is similar to preoperational thought in that it is egocentric, with children most interested in their personal pleasure or avoiding punishment.
- **Conventional moral reasoning** parallels concrete operational thought in that it relates to current, observable practices: Children watch what their parents, teachers, and friends do, and they try to follow suit.
- **Postconventional moral reasoning** is similar to formal operational thought because it uses abstractions, going beyond what is concretely observed, willing to question "what is" in order to decide "what should be."

According to Kohlberg, intellectual maturation advances moral thinking. During middle childhood, children's answers shift from being primarily preconventional to being more conventional: Concrete thought and peer experiences help children move past the first two stages (level I) to the next two (level II). Postconventional reasoning is not usually present until adolescence or adulthood, if then.

Kohlberg posed moral dilemmas to school-age boys (and eventually girls, teenagers, and adults). The most famous example of these dilemmas involves a poor man

● ● **Response for Parents of an Accused Bully** (from page 368) The future is ominous if the charges are true. Your child's denial is a sign that there is a problem. (An innocent child would be worried about the misperception instead of categorically denying that any problem exists.) You might ask the teacher what the school is doing about bullying. Family counseling might help. Because bullies often have friends who egg them on, you may need to monitor your child's friendships and perhaps befriend the victim. Talk about the situation with your child. Ignoring the situation might lead to heartache later on.

TABLE 13.3 Kohlberg's Three Levels and Six Stages of Moral Reasoning

Level I: Preconventional Moral Reasoning
The goal is to get rewards and avoid punishments; this is a self-centered level.

- *Stage one: Might makes right* (a punishment-and-obedience orientation). The most important value is to maintain the appearance of obedience to authority, avoiding punishment while still advancing self-interest. Don't get caught!
- *Stage two: Look out for number one* (an instrumental and relativist orientation). Everyone prioritizes his or her own needs. The reason to be nice to other people is so that they will be nice to you.

Level II: Conventional Moral Reasoning
Emphasis is placed on social rules; this is a parent- and community-centered level.

- *Stage three: Good girl and nice boy.* The goal is to please other people. Social approval is more important than any specific reward.
- *Stage four: Law and order.* Everyone must be a dutiful and law-abiding citizen, even when no police are nearby.

Level III: Postconventional Moral Reasoning
Emphasis is placed on moral principles; this level is centered on ideals.

- *Stage five: Social contract.* Obey social rules because they benefit everyone and are established by mutual agreement. If the rules become destructive or if one party doesn't live up to the agreement, the contract is no longer binding. Under some circumstances, disobeying the law is moral.
- *Stage six: Universal ethical principles.* Universal principles, not individual situations (level I) or community practices (level II), determine right and wrong. Ethical values (such as "life is sacred") are established by individual reflection and religious ideas, which may contradict egocentric (level I) or social and community (level II) values.

named Heinz, whose wife was dying. He could not pay for the only drug that could cure his wife, a drug that a local druggist sold for 10 times what it cost to make.

> Heinz went to everyone he knew to borrow the money, but he could only get together about half of what it cost. He told the druggist that his wife was dying and asked him to sell it cheaper or let him pay later. But the druggist said "no." The husband got desperate and broke into the man's store to steal the drug for his wife. Should the husband have done that? Why?

[Kohlberg, 1963, p. 19]

The crucial element in Kohlberg's assessment of moral stages is not what a person answers but the reasons given. For instance, suppose a child says that Heinz should steal the drug. That itself does not indicate the child's level of moral reasoning. The reason could be that Heinz needs his wife to care for him (preconventional), or that people will blame him if he lets his wife die (conventional), or that a human life is more important than obeying a law (postconventional).

Or suppose another child says that Heinz should not steal. The reason could be that he will go to jail (preconventional), or that stealing is against the law (conventional), or that for a community to function, no one should take another person's livelihood (postconventional).

Criticisms of Kohlberg

Kohlberg has been criticized for not appreciating cultural or gender differences. For example, in some cultures, loyalty to family overrides any other value, so moral people might avoid postconventional actions that hurt their family. Also, Kohlberg's original participants were all boys, which may have led him to discount nurturance and relationships, thought to be more valued by females than males (Gilligan, 1982).

Overall, Kohlberg seemed to value abstract principles more than individual needs and to prioritize rational thinking. However, emotions may be more influential than logic in moral development (Haidt, 2013). Thus, according to critics of Kohlberg, emotional regulation, empathy, and social understanding, all of which develop throughout childhood, may be more crucial for morality than intellectual development is.

Later research finds that cultural contexts as well as maturation are important, with politics and religion having a major influence (Haidt, 2013). Considering both age and religion, one study of mainline and evangelical Protestants in the United States found that children of both groups were similar in that fairness was important and individual rights and needs were considered.

For example, when asked if money should be given to a panhandler, a child from an evangelical home said no "because they could go out to the store and buy cigarettes or something that is not good for them" and one from a mainline background also said no because you should give them "food and water . . . they'll be able to live for a longer amount of time" (Jensen & McKenzie, 2016, p. 458). Divergence was somewhat evident even for children, but more apparent with age, as evangelical adults were more likely to assert that God and religion were influential in their moral decisions. One conclusion is that middle childhood is the time for religious education of some sort—with the outcome evident later on.

What Children Value

Many lines of research have shown that children develop their own morality, guided by peers, parents, and culture (Killen & Smetana, 2014). Some prosocial

Answer to Observation Quiz

(from page 369) The industry stage emphasizes being busy and careful. Each square, painstakingly drawn, illustrates a very specific action that a citizen can take.

Kinzie Riehm/Image Source/Getty Images

Heavy Lift Carrying your barefoot little sister across a muddy puddle is not easy, but this 7-year-old has internalized family values. Note her expression: She and many other children her age are proud to do what they consider the right thing.

🔵🔵 **Observation Quiz** What indicates that this sister often carries her younger sibling? (see answer, page 374) ↑

THINK CRITICALLY: If one of your moral values differs from that of your spouse, your parents, or your community, should you still try to teach it to your children? Why or why not?

values are evident in early childhood. Among these values are caring for close family members, cooperating with other children, and not hurting anyone intentionally. Even very young children think stealing is wrong, and even infants seem to appreciate social support and punish mean behavior (Hamlin, 2014).

As children become more aware of themselves and others in middle childhood, they realize that one person's values may conflict with another's. Concrete operational cognition, which gives children the ability to understand and use logic, propels them to think about moral rules and advance their theory of mind (Devine et al., 2016).

Adults Versus Peers

When child culture conflicts with adult morality, children often align themselves with peers. A child might lie to protect a friend, for instance. Friendship itself has a hostile side: Many close friends reject other children who want to join a game, or conversation, with friends (Rubin et al., 2013). They may protect a bully if he or she is a friend. Almost no child will answer a substitute teacher's angry "who threw that spitball?" because no child wants to be called a "tattletale," a term that signifies the value of loyalty to peers over responsiveness to adults.

The conflict between the morality of children and that of adults is evident in the value that children place on education. Adults usually prize school and respect teachers, but children may encourage one another to skip class, cheat on tests, harass a substitute teacher, and so on.

Three common imperatives among 6- to 11-year-olds are the following:

- Protect your friends.
- Don't tell adults what is happening.
- Conform to peer standards of dress, talk, behavior.

These principles can explain both apparent boredom and overt defiance, as well as standards of dress that mystify adults (such as jeans so loose that they fall off or so tight that they impede digestion—both styles worn by my children, who grew up in different cohorts). Clothing choices may seem like mere social conformity, but children may elevate it to a standard of right and wrong, not unlike adults who might consider immoral a woman who does not wear a head covering, or does wear a revealing dress even. Children might call such criticism itself immoral, as one girl accused her mother of "slut-shaming" when the mother told her her skirt was too short.

This conflict between adult values and peer friendship is evident in one boy. Paul said:

> I think right now about going Christian, right? Just going Christian, trying to do good, you know? Stay away from drugs, everything. And every time it seems like I think about that, I think about the homeboys. And it's a trip because a lot of the homeboys are my family, too, you know?

[quoted in Nieto, 2000, p. 249]

Paul chose the friends, and he ended up in jail. Fortunately, peers sometimes may help one another act ethically, so if several children band together to stop a bully, they usually succeed, teaching bullies that their actions are not admired.

All this does not mean that parents, teachers, and religious institutions are irrelevant. During middle childhood, morality can be scaffolded just as cognitive skills are, with mentors—peers or adults—using moral dilemmas to advance moral understanding while also advancing the underlying moral skills of empathy and emotional regulation (Hinnant et al., 2013).

Developing Moral Values

Over the years of middle childhood, moral judgment becomes more comprehensive. Gradually children become better at taking psychological as well as physical harm into account, considering intentions as well as consequences.

For example, in one study 5- to 11-year-olds saw pictures depicting situations in which a child hurt another in order to prevent further harm (such as stopping a friend from climbing on a roof to retrieve a ball) or when one child was simply mean (such as pushing a friend off the swings so that the child could swing). The younger children were more likely to judge based on results—if anyone got hurt that was wrong—but the older children considered intention, so some hurt was acceptable.

When the harm was psychological, not physical (hurting the child's feelings, not hitting), more than half of the older children considered intentions, but only about 5 percent of the younger children did. Compared to the younger children, the older children were more likely to say justifiable harm was OK but unjustifiable harm should be punished (Jambon & Smetana, 2014).

Another detailed examination of morality began with an update of one of Piaget's moral issues: whether punishment should seek *retribution* (hurting the transgressor) or *restitution* (restoring what was lost). Piaget found that children advance from retribution to restitution between ages 8 and 10 (Piaget, 1932/2013b).

To learn how this occurs, researchers asked 133 children who were 9 years old to consider this scenario:

> Late one afternoon there was a boy who was playing with a ball on his own in the garden. His dad saw him playing with it and asked him not to play with it so near the house because it might break a window. The boy didn't really listen to his dad, and carried on playing near the house. Then suddenly, the ball bounced up high and broke the window in the boy's room. His dad heard the noise and came to see what had happened. The father wonders what would be the fairest way to punish the boy. He thinks of two punishments. The first is to say: "Now, you didn't do as I asked. You will have to pay for the window to be mended, and I am going to take the money from your pocket money." The second is to say: "Now, you didn't do as I asked. As a punishment you have to go to your room and stay there for the rest of the evening." Which of these punishments do you think is the fairest?
>
> *[Leman & Björnberg, 2010, p. 962]*

The children were split almost equally, half for paying for the window and half for being sent to the room, in their initial responses. Then, 24 pairs were formed of children who had opposite views. Each pair was asked to discuss the issue and try to reach an agreement. (The other 85 children did not discuss it.) Six pairs were boy–boy, six were boy–girl with the boy favoring restitution, six were boy–girl with the girl favoring restitution, and six were girl–girl.

The conversations typically took only five minutes, and the retribution side was more often chosen. Piaget would consider that a moral backslide, since more restitution advocates than retribution advocates switched sides. However, several

Restore Harm or Hurt the Transgressor? Nine-Year-Olds' Responses

Data from Leman & Björnberg, 2010.

FIGURE 13.2

Benefits of Time and Talking The graph on the left shows that most children, immediately after their initial punitive response, became even more likely to seek punishment rather than to repair damage. However, after some time and reflection, they affirmed the response Piaget would consider more mature. The graph on the right indicates that children who had talked about the broken window example moved toward restorative justice even in examples that they had not heard before, which was not true for those who had not talked about the first story.

⬤⬤ **Answer to Observation Quiz**

(from page 372) The legs and arms of the younger child suggest that she has learned how to hold her body to make carrying possible.

weeks later all of the children were queried again. At that point, many responses changed toward the more advanced restitution response (see Figure 13.2).

The researchers wrote, "conversation on a topic may stimulate a process of individual reflection that triggers developmental advances" (Leman & Björnberg, 2010, p. 969). Parents and teachers take note: Raising moral issues, and letting children discuss them, advances morality—not immediately, but soon.

Think again about the opening anecdote for this chapter (killing zombies). The parent used age as a criterion, and the child rejected that argument. A better argument might raise a higher standard, for instance that killing, even in fantasy, is not justified. The child might disagree, but such conversations might help the child think more deeply about moral values. That deeper thought might protect the child during adolescence, when life-changing moral issues arise, as described in the next three chapters.

WHAT HAVE YOU LEARNED?

1. Using your own example, illustrate Kohlberg's three levels of moral reasoning.

2. What are the main criticisms of Kohlberg's theory?

3. What three values are common among school-age children?

4. What seems to advance moral thought from the beginning to the end of middle childhood?

SUMMARY

The Nature of the Child

1. Children develop their self-concept during middle childhood, basing it on a more realistic assessment of their competence than they had in earlier years. They strive for independence from parents and admiration from peers.

2. Erikson emphasized industry, when children busily strive to master various tasks. If they are unable to do so, they feel inferior. Self-respect is always helpful, but high self-esteem may reduce effortful control and is not valued in every culture. Low self-esteem is also harmful.

3. Both daily hassles and major stresses take a toll on children, with accumulated stresses more likely to impair development than any single event on its own. Resilience is aided by the child's interpretation of the situation and the availability of supportive adults, peers, and institutions.

Families and Children

4. Families influence children in many ways, as do genes and peers. Although most siblings share a childhood home and parents, each sibling experiences different (nonshared) circumstances within the family.

5. The five functions of a supportive family are: meet children's physical needs; encourage learning; nurture friendships; foster self-respect; and provide a safe, stable, and harmonious home. Function is more important than structure, but structure may make it easier to function well.

6. The most common family structure is the nuclear family. Other two-parent families include adoptive, same-sex, grandparent, and stepfamilies, each of which sometimes functions well for children. However, each also has vulnerabilities.

7. On average, children have fewer emotional problems and learn more in school if they live with two parents rather than one, especially if the parents cooperate, forming a strong parental alliance.

8. Single-parent families have higher rates of instability—for example, in where they live and in who is in the household. On average, such families have less income, which may cause stress. Nonetheless, some children fare better than they would if the child's other parent were present.

9. Income affects family function, for two-parent as well as single-parent households. Poor children are at greater risk for emotional and behavioral problems if the stresses that often accompany poverty hinder effective parenting.

10. No matter what the family SES, instability and conflict are harmful. Children suffer even when the conflict does not involve them directly, but their parents or siblings fight.

The Peer Group

11. Peers teach crucial social skills during middle childhood. Each cohort of children has a culture, passed down from slightly older children. Close friends are wanted and needed.

12. Popular children may be cooperative and easy to get along with or may be competitive and aggressive. Much depends on the age and social context.

13. Rejected children may be neglected, aggressive, or withdrawn. Aggressive and withdrawn children have difficulty with social cognition; their interpretation of the normal give-and-take of childhood is impaired.

14. Bullying of all sorts—physical, verbal, relational, and cyber—is common, with long-term consequences for both bullies and victims. Bullies themselves may be admired, which makes their behavior more difficult to stop.

15. Overall, a multifaceted, long-term, whole-school approach, with parents, teachers, and bystanders working together, seems to be the best way to halt bullying. Careful evaluation is needed to discover whether a particular strategy changes the school culture.

Children's Moral Values

16. School-age children seek to differentiate right from wrong. Peer values, cultural standards, and family practices are all part of their personal morality.

17. Children advance in moral thinking as they mature. Kohlberg described three levels of moral reasoning, each related to cognitive maturity. His description has been criticized for ignoring cultural and gender differences and for stressing rationality at the expense of emotions.

18. When values conflict, children often choose loyalty to peers over adult standards of behavior. As children grow older, especially when they discuss moral issues, they develop more thoughtful answers to moral questions, considering intentions as well as consequences.

KEY TERMS

social comparison (p. 348)
industry versus inferiority
  (p. 348)
resilience (p. 350)
parentification (p. 353)
family structure (p. 355)

family function (p. 355)
nuclear family (p. 356)
single-parent family (p. 356)
extended family (p. 356)
polygamous family (p. 356)
child culture (p. 364)

aggressive-rejected (p. 366)
withdrawn-rejected (p. 366)
bullying (p. 366)
bully-victim (p. 367)
preconventional moral
  reasoning (p. 370)

conventional moral reasoning
  (p. 370)
postconventional moral
  reasoning (p. 370)

APPLICATIONS

1. Go someplace where many school-age children congregate (such as a schoolyard, a park, or a community center) and use naturalistic observation for at least half an hour. Describe what popular, average, withdrawn, and rejected children do. Note at least one potential conflict. Describe the sequence and the outcome.

2. Focusing on verbal bullying, describe at least two times when someone said something hurtful to you and two times when you said something that might have been hurtful to someone else. What are the differences between the two types of situations?

3. How would your childhood have been different if your family structure had been different, such as if you had (or had not) lived with your grandparents, if your parents had (or had not) gotten divorced, if you had (or had not) been adopted?

The Developing Person So Far:
Middle Childhood

BIOSOCIAL

A Healthy Time During middle childhood, children grow more slowly than they did earlier or will during adolescence. Physical play is crucial for development. Genes as well as immunization protect against contagious diseases, and medical awareness and care have improved over the past decades. Obesity and asthma have genetic roots and psychosocial consequences. Brain maturation continues, leading to faster reactions and better self-control.

Children with Special Brains and Bodies Children have multiple intellectual abilities, most of which are not reflected in standard IQ tests. Some children have ADHD, a specific learning disorder, or autism spectrum disorder, but diagnosis, treatment, and outcome vary and depend on context.

Special Education Many children have special learning needs. Early recognition, targeted education, and psychological support can help them.

COGNITIVE

Building on Theory Beginning at about age 7, Piaget noted, children attain concrete operational thought, including the ability to understand the logical principles of classification. Vygotsky emphasized that children become more open to learning from mentors, both teachers and peers. Information-processing abilities increase, including greater memory, knowledge, control, and metacognition. Executive function improves

Language Children's increasing ability to understand the structures and possibilities of language enables them to extend the range of their cognitive powers and to become more analytical and expressive in vocabulary. Children have the cognitive capacity to become bilingual and bicultural, although much depends on the teacher.

Teaching and Learning International comparisons reveal marked variations in the overt and hidden curricula, as well as in learning, between one nation and another. In recent years, the Common Core standards have been adapted *and* criticized.

PSYCHOSOCIAL

The Nature of the Child Theorists agree that many school-age children develop competencies, emotional control, and attitudes to defend against stress. Some children are resilient, coping well with problems and finding support in friends, family, school, religion, and community, although no child is invincible.

Families and Children Parents continue to influence children, especially as they exacerbate or buffer problems in school and the community. During these years, families need to meet basic needs, encourage learning, foster self-respect, nurture friendship, and—most important—provide harmony and stability. Nuclear families often provide this, but one-parent, foster, same-sex, or grandparent families can also function well for children. Household income, low conflict, and family stability benefit children of all ages.

The Peer Group Children depend on friends for help, loyalty, and sharing of mutual interests. Rejection and bullying become serious problems.

Children's Moral Values Moral development, influenced by peers, advances during these years. Children develop moral standards that they try to follow, although these differ from the moral standards of adults.

adolescence

A century ago, puberty began at age 15 or so. Soon after that age, most girls married and most boys found work. It is said that *adolescence begins with biology and ends with culture*. If so, then a hundred years ago, adolescence lasted a few months.

Now adolescence lasts much longer. Puberty starts before the teen years, and adult responsibilities are shunned for decades. Indeed, a few observers describe a *Peter Pan Syndrome*—men who "won't grow up," too self-absorbed to love and care for anyone else (Kiley, 1983; Snow, 2015). That is unfair to men and to teenagers, but there is no doubt that few 18-year-olds are ready to shoulder all of the burdens of adulthood.

In the next three chapters (covering ages 11 to 18), we begin with biology (Chapter 14), consider cognition (Chapter 15), and then discuss culture (Chapter 16). Adolescence attracts extremes, arousing the highest hopes and the worst fears of parents, teachers, police officers, social workers, and children themselves. Patterns and events can catapult a teenager to destruction or celebration. Understanding this phase of development is the first step toward ensuring that the teenagers you know, and the millions you have never met, experience a fulfilling, not devastating, adolescence. ●●

Adolescence:
Biosocial Development

What Will You Know?

1. How can you predict when puberty will begin for a particular child?
2. Why do many teenagers ignore their nutritional needs?
3. What makes teenage sex often a problem instead of a joy?

I overheard a conversation among three teenagers, including my daughter Rachel, all of them past their awkward years and now becoming beautiful. They were discussing the imperfections of their bodies. One spoke of her fat stomach (what stomach? I could not see it), another of her long neck (hidden by her silky, shoulder-length hair). Rachel complained about her fingers and her feet!

The reality that children become men and women is no shock to any adult. But for teenagers, heightened self-awareness often triggers surprise or even horror, joy, and despair at the specifics of their growth. Like these three, adolescents pay attention to details. Gender differences become significant. Girls bond as they discuss their flaws; boys more often boast, yet almost all teenagers are simultaneously self-focused and social, needing each other.

This chapter describes the biosocial specifics of growing bodies and emerging sexuality. It all begins with hormones, but other invisible changes may be even more potent—such as the timing of neurological maturation that does not yet allow adolescents like these three to realize that minor imperfections are insignificant.

Puberty Begins

Puberty refers to the years of rapid physical growth and sexual maturation that end childhood, producing a person of adult size, shape, and sexuality. The forces of puberty are unleashed by a cascade of hormones that produce external growth and internal changes, including heightened emotions and sexual desires.

The process normally starts sometime between ages 8 and 14. Most biological growth and maturation ends about four years after the first signs appear, although some individuals (especially boys) add height, weight, and muscle until age 20 or so. Over the past decades, the age of puberty has decreased, perhaps for both sexes, although the evidence is more solid for girls (Biro et al., 2013; Herman-Giddens, 2013).

For girls, the observable changes of puberty usually begin with nipple growth. Soon a few pubic hairs are visible, followed by a peak growth spurt, widening of the hips, the first menstrual period (**menarche**), a full pubic-hair pattern, and breast maturation (Susman et al., 2010). The average age of menarche is about 12 years, 4 months (Biro et al., 2013), with any age from 10 to 15 considered neither precocious nor delayed.

✦ Puberty Begins
Unseen Beginnings
Brain Growth
INSIDE THE BRAIN: Lopsided Growth
When Will Puberty Begin?
A VIEW FROM SCIENCE: Stress and Puberty
Too Early, Too Late

✦ Growth and Nutrition
Growing Bigger and Stronger
Diet Deficiencies
Eating Disorders

✦ Sexual Maturation
Sexual Characteristics
Sexual Activity
Sexual Problems in Adolescence

puberty The time between the first onrush of hormones and full adult physical development. Puberty usually lasts three to five years. Many more years are required to achieve psychosocial maturity.

menarche A girl's first menstrual period, signaling that she has begun ovulation. Pregnancy is biologically possible, but ovulation and menstruation are often irregular for years after menarche.

🔵🟢 **Especially for Parents of Teenagers**
Why would parents blame adolescent moods on hormones? (see response, page 385)

spermarche A boy's first ejaculation of sperm. Erections can occur as early as infancy, but ejaculation signals sperm production. Spermarche may occur during sleep (in a "wet dream") or via direct stimulation.

pituitary A gland in the brain that responds to a signal from the hypothalamus by producing many hormones, including those that regulate growth and sexual maturation.

adrenal glands Two glands, located above the kidneys, that respond to the pituitary, producing hormones.

HPA (hypothalamus–pituitary– adrenal) axis A sequence of hormone production originating in the hypothalamus and moving to the pituitary and then to the adrenal glands.

gonads The paired sex glands (ovaries in females, testicles in males). The gonads produce hormones and mature gametes.

HPG (hypothalamus–pituitary–gonad) axis A sequence of hormone production originating in the hypothalamus and moving to the pituitary and then to the gonads.

estradiol A sex hormone, considered the chief estrogen. Females produce much more estradiol than males do.

testosterone A sex hormone, the best known of the androgens (male hormones); secreted in far greater amounts by males than by females.

For boys, the usual sequence is growth of the testes, initial pubic-hair growth, growth of the penis, first ejaculation of seminal fluid (**spermarche**), appearance of facial hair, a peak growth spurt, deepening of the voice, and final pubic-hair growth (Biro et al., 2001; Herman-Giddens et al., 2012; Susman et al., 2010). The typical age of spermarche is 13 years, almost a year later than menarche. Again age varies markedly. The averages here are for well-nourished adolescents in the United States.

Unseen Beginnings

The changes just listed are visible, but the entire process begins with an invisible event—a marked increase in hormones. *Hormones* are body chemicals that regulate hunger, sleep, moods, stress, sexual desire, immunity, reproduction, and many other bodily functions and processes, including puberty. Throughout adolescence, hormone levels correlate with physiological changes and self-reported developments (Shirtcliff et al., 2009).

Production of many hormones is regulated deep within the brain, where biochemical signals from the hypothalamus signal another brain structure, the **pituitary,** to go into action. The pituitary produces hormones that stimulate the **adrenal glands,** located above the kidneys at either side of the lower back. The adrenal glands produce more hormones. Many hormones that regulate puberty follow this route, known as the **HPA (hypothalamus–pituitary–adrenal) axis** (see Figure 14.1).

Sex Hormones

Late in childhood, the pituitary activates not only the adrenal glands—the HPA axis—but also the **gonads,** or sex glands (ovaries in females; testes, or testicles, in males), following another sequence called the **HPG (hypothalamus–pituitary–gonad) axis.** One hormone in particular, GnRH (gonadotropin-releasing hormone), causes the gonads to enlarge and dramatically increase their production of sex hormones, chiefly **estradiol** in girls and **testosterone** in boys. These hormones affect the body's shape and function and produce additional hormones that regulate stress and immunity (Young et al., 2008).

Estrogens (including estradiol) are female hormones and *androgens* (including testosterone) are male hormones, although both sexes have some of both. The ovaries produce high levels of estrogens, and the testes produce dramatic increases in androgens. This "surge of hormones" affects bodies, brains, and behavior before any visible signs of puberty appear, "well before the teens" (Peper & Dahl, 2013, p. 134).

The activated gonads soon produce mature ova or sperm, released in menarche or spermarche. Conception is possible, although peak fertility occurs four to six years later.

Hormonal increases may also that precipitate psychopathology. In both genders, adolescence is the peak time for the emergence of many disorders (Powers & Casey, 2015). The rush of hormones at puberty puts some vulnerable children over the edge, although hormones are never the sole cause (Tackett et al., 2014; Rudolph 2014; Remington & Seeman, 2015). Probably because of sex differences in hormones, adolescent males are almost twice as likely as females to develop schizophrenia, and females are more than twice as likely to become severely depressed.

For everyone, one psychological effect of estrogen and testosterone is new interest in sexuality. For most teenagers this comes as a sudden shock that the other sex is not necessarily stupid (as many children think); for some teenagers this comes as an attraction to same-sex partners, again an unanticipated surprise.

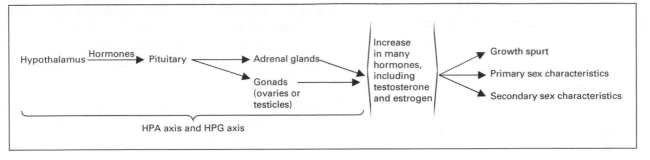

FIGURE 14.1

Biological Sequence of Puberty Puberty begins with a hormonal signal from the hypothalamus to the pituitary gland, both deep within the brain. The pituitary, in turn, sends a hormonal message through the bloodstream to the adrenal glands and the gonads to produce more hormones.

Usually a young adolescent's first sexual objects are safely unattainable—a film star, a popular singer, a teacher—but by mid-adolescence, fantasies may settle on another young person. Hormones also direct adolescents toward typical sexual roles and interactions, perhaps a product of selective fitness for the human species (Sisk, 2016). Of course, sexual identity and gender roles are increasingly complex, because of the combination of puberty, norms, and variations—a topic discussed in Chapter 16.

Although emotional surges, nurturant impulses, and lustful urges arise with hormones, remember that body, brain, and behavior always interact. Sexual thoughts themselves can *cause* physiological and neurological processes, not just result from them. Cortisol levels rise at puberty, and that makes adolescents quicker to become angry or upset (Goddings et al., 2012; Klein & Romeo, 2013). Then those emotions, in turn, increase levels of various hormones. Bodies, brains, and behavior all affect one another.

For example, when people react to emerging breasts or beards, those reactions evoke adolescent thoughts and frustrations, which then raise hormone levels, propel physiological development, and trigger more emotions. Because of hormones,

THINK CRITICALLY: If a child seems to be unusually short or unusually slow in reaching puberty, would you give the child hormones? Why or why not?

Especially for Teenagers Some 14-year-olds have unprotected sex and then are relieved to realize that conception did not occur. Does this mean they do not need to worry about contraception? (see response, page 385)

Do They See Beauty? Both young women—the Mexican 15-year-old preparing for her Quinceañara and the Malaysian teen applying a rice facial mask—look wistful, even worried. They are typical of teenage girls everywhere, who do not realize how lovely they are.

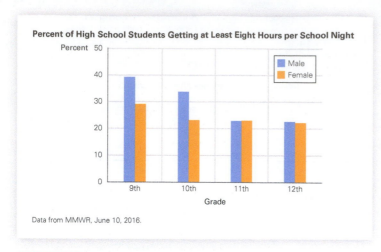

Percent of High School Students Getting at Least Eight Hours per School Night

Data from MMWR, June 10, 2016.

FIGURE 14.2

Sleepyheads Three of every four high school seniors are sleep deprived. Even if they go to sleep at midnight, as many do, they must get up before 8 A.M., as almost all do. Then all day they are tired.

🔵 **Observation Quiz** As you see, the problems are worse for the girls. Why is that? (see answer, page 387) ↑

circadian rhythm A day–night cycle of biological activity that occurs approximately every 24 hours.

emotions are more likely to be expressed during adolescence (with shouts and tears), and that affects everyone's next reactions. Thus, the internal and external changes of puberty are cyclical and reciprocal, each affecting the other.

Body Rhythms

Because of hormones, the brain of every living creature responds to environmental changes over the hours, days, and seasons. For example, time of year affects body weight and height: Children gain weight more rapidly in winter and grow taller more quickly in summer. Another example is seasonal affective disorder (SAD), when people become depressed in winter. Those are seasonal changes, but many *biorhythms* are on a 24-hour cycle, called the **circadian rhythm.** (*Circadian* means "about a day.") Puberty interacts with biorhythms.

For most people, daylight awakens the brain. That's why people experiencing jet lag are urged to take an early-morning walk. But at puberty, night may be more energizing, making some teens wide awake and hungry at midnight but half asleep, with no appetite or energy, all morning.

In addition to circadian changes at puberty, some individuals (especially males) are naturally more alert in the evening than in the morning, a genetic trait called *eveningness.* Puberty plus eveningness increases risk (drugs, sex, delinquency), in part because teenagers are awake when adults are asleep. If they must wake up in the morning, many teenagers are sleep deprived (Roenneberg et al., 2012).

Added to the circadian sleep debt, "the blue spectrum light from TV, computer, and personal-device screens may have particularly strong effects on the human circadian system" (Peper & Dahl, 2013, p. 137). Watching late-night TV, working on a computer, or texting friends at 10 P.M. interferes with sleepiness. As a result, many adolescents find early bedtime and early rising almost impossible.

Sleep deprivation and irregular sleep schedules increase several proven dangers, including insomnia, nightmares, mood disorders (depression, conduct disorder, anxiety), and falling asleep while driving. Adolescents are particularly vulnerable to all of these (see Figure 14.2). In addition, sleepy students do not learn as well as well-rested ones.

Oblivious to adolescent biorhythms, some parents set early curfews or stay awake until their child comes home at night. They might drag their teenager out of bed for school—the same child who, a decade earlier, was commanded to stay in bed until dawn.

Some municipalities also fight adolescent biology. In 2014, Baltimore implemented a law that requires everyone under age 14 to be home by 9 P.M., and 14- to 16-year-olds to be off the streets by 10 P.M. on school nights and 11 P.M. on weekends. This assumes that home is a happy, safe place where teenagers will go to sleep early, and it restricts the teen's ability to socialize or study with friends.

Several enlightened school districts have revised their schedules. Minneapolis high schools changed their start time from 7:15 A.M. to 8:40 A.M.; attendance and graduation rates improved. School boards in South Burlington (Vermont), West Des Moines (Iowa), Tulsa (Oklahoma), Arlington (Virginia), Palo Alto (California), and Milwaukee (Wisconsin) voted to start high school later, from an average of 7:45 A.M. to an average of 8:30 A.M. (Tonn, 2006; Snider, 2012). Unexpected advantages appeared: more efficient energy use, less adolescent depression, fewer visits to the school nurse, and in Tulsa, unprecedented athletic championships.

Most high schools, however, remain stuck in schedules set before the hazards of sleep deprivation were known. Although "the science is there; the will to change is not" (Snider, 2012, p. 25).

One example comes from Fairfax, Virginia, with two opposing groups: SLEEP (Start Later for Excellence in Education Proposal) versus WAKE (Worried About Keeping Extra-Curriculars) argued. A reporter wrote that allowing high school students to sleep longer

> would hinder teams without lighted practice fields. Hinder kids who work after-school jobs to save for college or to help support their families. Hinder teachers who work second jobs or take late-afternoon college classes. Hinder commuters who would get stopped behind more buses during peak traffic times. Hinder kids who might otherwise seek after-school academic help, or club or team affiliation. Hinder families that depend on high school children to watch younger siblings after school. Hinder community groups that use school and park facilities in the late afternoons and evenings.

> [*Williams, 2009*]

He wrote that science was on the side of change but reality was not. To developmentalists, of course, science *is* reality. In 2009, the Fairfax school board voted to keep the high school start time at 7:20 A.M. The SLEEP advocates kept trying. On the eighth try, the Fairfax school board in 2012 finally set a goal: High schools should not start before 8 A.M. They hired a team to figure out how to implement that goal. But as of 2014, the Fairfax school board had not yet agreed on a new start time.

They have new motivation. In August 2014, the American Academy of Pediatrics concluded that high schools should not begin until 8:30 or 9 A.M., because adolescent sleep deprivation causes a cascade of intellectual, behavioral, and health problems. The doctors noted that 43 percent of high schools in the United States start *before* 8 A.M. Most developmentalists, pediatricians, and education researchers wonder why adult traditions are preserved while adolescent learning is ignored.

Brain Growth

A more ominous example of the disconnect between what science tells us and what adolescents do concerns adolescent involvement in cars, guns, sex, and drugs, all of which result in injury and even death. A chilling example comes from teenage driving (legal at age 16 in most U.S. localities). Per mile driven, teenage drivers are three times more likely to die in a motor-vehicle crash than drivers over age 20 (Insurance Institute for Highway Safety, 2013b).

Sequence of Changes

Many aspects of adolescent growth are uneven, with no harm done. However, the usual sequence of brain maturation, propelled by hormones that activate the limbic system at puberty, can lead to danger. The prefrontal cortex matures steadily, advancing gradually year by year. The limbic system, however, is affected more by hormones (the HPG axis) and thus grows dramatically in early adolescence. Consequently, for contemporary teenagers, emotions may overwhelm rational thought for a decade. The limbic system makes powerful sensations—loud music, speeding cars, strong drugs—compelling.

Pubertal hormones target the amygdala directly (Romeo, 2013). The instinctual and emotional areas of the adolescent brain develop ahead of the reflective, analytic areas. Puberty means emotional rushes, unchecked by caution. Immediate impulses thwart long-term planning and reflection. My friend said to his

Response for Parents of Teenagers (from page 382): If something causes adolescents to shout "I hate you," to slam doors, or to cry inconsolably, parents may decide that hormones are the problem. This makes it easy to disclaim personal responsibility for the teenager's anger. However, research on stress and hormones suggests that this comforting attribution is too simplistic.

Response for Teenagers (from page 383): No. Early sex has many hazards, but it is true that pregnancy is less likely (although quite possible) before age 15. However, this may lead to a false sense of security: Conception is more likely in the late teens than at any other period in the life span.

Video Activity: Brain Development: Adolescence features animations and illustrations of the changes that occur in the teenage brain.

THINK CRITICALLY: Given the nature of adolescent brain development, how should society respond to adolescent thoughts and actions?

Fawkes, Not Fake Bonfires, fireworks, burning effigies, and—shown here—sparklers are waved in memory of Guy Fawkes, who tried to burn down the British Parliament and destroy the king in 1605. In theory, Guy Fawkes Night celebrates his capture; in fact it is time for rebellion.

🌐 **Especially for Health Practitioners** How might you encourage adolescents to seek treatment for STIs? (see response, page 388)

neighbor, who had given his son a red convertible for high school graduation, "Why didn't you just give him a loaded gun?" The mother of the 20-year-old who killed 20 first-graders and 7 adults (including the mother) in Newtown, Connecticut, did just that.

It is not that the prefrontal cortex shuts down. Actually, it continues to develop throughout adolescence and beyond. Maturation doesn't stop, but the balance and coordination between the various parts of the brain are off-kilter (Casey et al., 2011).

When stress, arousal, passion, sensory bombardment, drug intoxication, or deprivation is extreme, the adolescent brain is flooded with impulses that overwhelm the cortex and might shame an adult. Teenagers brag about being so drunk that they were "wasted," "bombed," "smashed"—a state most adults try to avoid and would not admit if it occurred.

Indeed, such sensations might be sought. Many teenagers choose to spend a night without sleep, to eat nothing all day, to exercise in pain, to play music at deafening loudness, or to risk a sexually transmitted infection by not using a condom. The parts of the brain dedicated to analysis are immature until long after the first hormonal rushes and sexual urges begin.

A common example comes from reading and sending text messages while driving. Teenagers know that this is illegal, but the "ping" of a text message evokes emotions that compel attention. In one survey, among U.S. high school seniors who have driven a car in the past month, 61 percent texted while driving (MMWR, June 10, 2016). This neurological disconnect is further explained in the following.

INSIDE THE BRAIN

Lopsided Growth

Instead of beginning this box in the usual way, with data from neuroscience, we begin with one teenage boy and his father.

Laurence Steinberg is a noted expert on adolescence (e.g., Steinberg, 2014, 2015). He is also a father.

> When my son, Benjamin, was 14, he and three of his friends decided to sneak out of the house where they were spending the night and visit one of their girlfriends at around two in the morning. When they arrived at the girl's house, they positioned themselves under her bedroom window, threw pebbles against her windowpanes, and tried to scale the side of the house. Modern technology, unfortunately, has made it harder to play Romeo these days. The boys set off the house's burglar alarm, which activated a siren and simultaneously sent a direct notification to the local police station, which dispatched a patrol car. When the siren went off, the boys ran down the street and right smack into the police car, which was heading to the girl's home. Instead of stopping and explaining their activity, Ben and his friends scattered and ran off in different directions through the neighborhood. One of the boys was caught by the police and taken back to his home, where his parents were awakened and the boy questioned.
>
> I found out about this affair the following morning, when the girl's mother called our home to tell us what Ben had done. . . . After his near brush with the local police,

> Ben had returned to the house out of which he had snuck, where he slept soundly until I awakened him with an angry telephone call, telling him to gather his clothes and wait for me in front of his friend's house. On our drive home, after delivering a long lecture about what he had done and about the dangers of running from armed police in the dark when they believe they may have interrupted a burglary, I paused.
>
> "What were you thinking?" I asked.
>
> "That's the problem, Dad," Ben replied, "I wasn't."
>
> *[Steinberg, 2004, pp. 51, 52]*

Steinberg's son was right: When emotions are intense, especially when friends are nearby, cortisol floods the brain, causing the prefrontal cortex to shut down. This shutdown is not reflected in questionnaires that require teenagers to respond to paper-and-pencil questions regarding hypothetical dilemmas. On those tests, most teenagers think carefully and answer correctly. In fact, when strong emotions are not activated, teenagers may be more logical than adults (Casey & Caudle, 2013). They remember facts that they have learned in biology or health class about sex and drugs. They know exactly how HIV is transmitted and how alcohol affects the brain. However,

the prospect of visiting a hypothetical girl from class cannot possibly carry the excitement about the possibility of surprising someone you have a crush on with a visit in the middle of the night. It is easier to put on a hypothetical condom during an act of hypothetical sex than it is to put on a real one when one is in the throes of passion. It is easier to just say no to a hypothetical beer than it is to a cold frosty one on a summer night."

[Steinberg, 2004, p. 53]

Ben reached adulthood safely. Other teenagers, with less cautious police or less diligent parents, do not. Brain immaturity makes teenagers vulnerable to social pressures and stresses, which typically bombard young people today (Casey & Caudle, 2013).

Brain scans confirm that emotional control, revealed by fMRI studies, is not fully developed until adulthood, because the prefrontal cortex is limited in connections and engagement (Luna et al., 2013; Hartley & Somerville, 2015) (see Figure 14.3).

Longitudinal research finds that heightened arousal occurs in the brain's reward centers, specifically the nucleus accumbens, a region of the ventral striatum that is connected to the limbic system, when an adolescent's brain is compared to his or her brain in childhood or adulthood (Braams et al., 2015).

Teens seek excitement and pleasure, especially the social pleasure of a peer's admiration (Galván, 2013). In fact, when other teens are watching, they find it thrilling to take dramatic risks that produce social acclaim, risks they would not dare take alone (Albert et al., 2013). Interestingly, the same reward regions of the brain that are highly activated when peers are watching show decreased activation when the adolescent's mother is nearby (Telzer et al., 2015).

The research on adolescent brain development confirms two insights regarding adolescent growth in general. First, physiological changes triggered by puberty are dramatic, unlike those of either childhood or adulthood. Second, the social context matters—the body and brain of humans respond not only to hormones and physical maturation but also to the friends and family nearby.

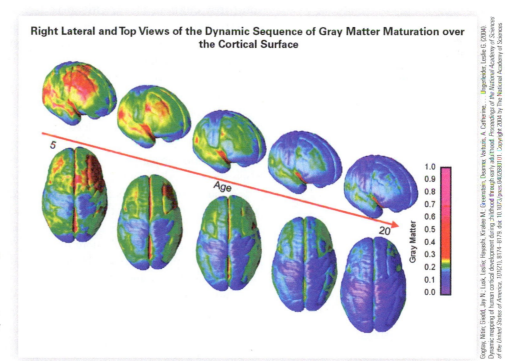

FIGURE 14.3

Same People, But Not the Same Brain These brain scans are part of a longitudinal study that repeatedly compared the proportion of gray matter from childhood through adolescence. (Gray matter refers to the cell bodies of neurons, which are less prominent with age as some neurons are unused.) Gray matter is reduced as white matter increases, in part because pruning during the teen years (the last two pairs of images here) allows intellectual connections to build. As the authors of one study that included this chart explained, teenagers may look "like an adult, but cognitively they are not there yet" (Powell, 2006, p. 865).

Right Lateral and Top Views of the Dynamic Sequence of Gray Matter Maturation over the Cortical Surface

Gogtay, Nitin; Giedd, Jay N.; Lusk, Leslie; Hayashi, Kiralee M.; Greenstein, Deanna; Vaituzis, A. Catherine;... Ungerleider, Leslie G. (2004). Dynamic mapping of human cortical development during childhood through early adulthood. *Proceedings of the National Academy of Sciences of the United States of America, 101*(21), 8174 - 8179. doi: 10.1073/pnas.0402680101. Copyright 2004 by The National Academy of Sciences

When Will Puberty Begin?

Normally, pubertal hormones begin to accelerate sometime between ages 8 and 14, and visible signs of puberty appear a year later. That six-year range is too great for many parents, teachers, and children, who want to know when a given child will begin puberty. Fortunately, if a child's genes, gender, body fat, and stress level are known, prediction within a year or two is possible.

Genes and Gender

Genetic sex differences have a marked effect. In height, the average pubescent girl is about two years ahead of the average boy. Sex affects sequence as well. The

Answer to Observation Quiz

(from page 384): Girls tend to spend more time studying, talking to friends, and getting ready in the morning. Other data show that many girls get less than 7 hours of sleep per night.

Ancient Rivals or New Friends? One of the best qualities of adolescents is that they identify more with their generation than their ethnic group, here Turk and German. Do the expressions of these 13-year-olds convey respect or hostility? Impossible to be sure, but given they are both about mid-puberty (face shape, height, shoulder size), and both in the same school, they may become friends.

🔵🔵 **Especially for Parents Worried About Early Puberty** Suppose your cousin's 9-year-old daughter has just had her first period, and your cousin blames hormones in the food supply for this "precocious" puberty. Should you change your young daughter's diet? (see response, page 390)

secular trend The long-term upward or downward direction of a certain set of statistical measurements, as opposed to a smaller, shorter cyclical variation. As an example, over the last two centuries, because of improved nutrition and medical care, children have tended to reach their adult height earlier and their adult height has increased.

🔴🟠 **Response for Health Practitioners** (from page 386): Many adolescents are intensely concerned about privacy and fearful of adult interference. This means that your first task is to convince the teenagers that you are nonjudgmental and that everything is confidential.

female height spurt occurs *before* menarche; the male increase in height occurs *after* spermarche. Therefore, unlike height, for hormonal and sexual changes, girls are less than a year ahead of boys. This means that a sixth-grade boy with sexual fantasies about the taller girls in his class is neither perverted nor precocious; his hormones are simply ahead of his height.

Overall, about two-thirds of the variation in age of puberty is genetic—not only the genes associated with the XX or XY chromosomes but also in the genes common in families and ethnic groups (Dvornyk & Waqar-ul-Haq, 2012; Biro et al., 2013). If both of a child's parents were early or late to reach puberty, the child will likely be early or late as well.

On average, African Americans reach puberty about seven months before European or Hispanic Americans; Chinese Americans average several months later. The significance of all these changes is more gender than sex, more cultural than genetic.

Body Fat and Chemicals

Another influence on the onset of puberty is body fat, which itself is partly genetic and partly cultural. Heavy girls (over 100 pounds) reach menarche years earlier than thinner ones do, especially if girls are underweight because of malnutrition.

In some nations, inadequate food delays growth of every kind; but in developed nations, poor eating habits can result in overweight and, thus, early puberty. This is suggested by a study which found that girls who regularly drank several sugar-sweetened beverages each day were likely to experience earlier menarche (Carwile et al., 2015). Although extreme underweight always delays puberty, body fat may be less necessary for boys. Indeed, one study found that male obesity may delay puberty (Tackett et al., 2014).

Malnutrition explains why youths reach puberty later in some parts of Africa, while their genetic relatives in North America mature much earlier. For example, girls in northern Ghana reach menarche more than a year later (almost age 14) than African American girls in the United States (just past 12). Ghanaian girls in rural areas—where malnutrition is more common—are behind those in urban areas (Ameade & Garti, 2016). A more dramatic example arises from sixteenth-century Europe, where puberty is thought to have begun several years later than it does today.

All of the data suggest that in recent centuries puberty has begun at younger and younger ages. This is an example of what is called the **secular trend,** which is earlier or greater growth as nutrition and medicine improved. Increased food availability has led to more weight gain in childhood, promoting earlier puberty and taller average height. Over the nineteenth and twentieth centuries, because of the secular trend, every generation reached puberty before the previous one (Floud et al., 2011; Fogel & Grotte, 2011).

One curious bit of evidence of the secular trend is in the height of U.S. presidents. James Madison, the fourth president, was shortest at 5 feet, 4 inches; recent presidents have been much taller. The secular trend has stopped in most nations because childhood nutrition allows everyone to attain their genetic potential. Young men no longer look down at their short fathers, or girls at their mothers, unless their parents were born in nations where hunger was common.

Some scientists suspect that precocious (before age 8) or delayed (after age 14) puberty may be caused by hormones in the food supply, especially in milk. Cattle are fed steroids to increase bulk and milk production, and hundreds of chemicals and hormones are used to produce most of the food that children consume. All of these substances *might* affect appetite, body fat, and sex hormones, with effects at puberty (Clayton et al., 2014; Wiley, 2011; Synovitz & Chopak-Foss, 2013).

Leptin, a hormone that is naturally produced by the human body, definitely affects the onset of puberty. Leptin is essential for appetite, energy, and puberty. However, too much leptin correlates with obesity, early puberty, and then early termination of growth. Thus, the heaviest third-grade girl may become the tallest fifth-grader and then the shortest high school graduate.

Most research on leptin has been done with mice; the effects are more complicated for humans (Bohlen, 2016). In fact, none of the data on the effects on humans of hormones and other chemicals, whether natural or artificial, are easy to interpret. It seems that the female body is especially sensitive not only to leptin but also to other factors in the environment, but the exact effects, at which dose, are controversial. It is known, however, that many hormones and chemicals, both natural and artificial, affect puberty (Wolff et al., 2015).

Stress

Stress hastens puberty, especially if a child's parents are sick, drug-addicted, or divorced, or if the neighborhood is violent and impoverished. One study of sexually abused girls found that they began puberty seven months earlier, on average, than did a matched comparison group (Trickett et al., 2011). Particularly for girls who are genetically sensitive, puberty comes early if their family interaction is stressful but late if their family is supportive (Ellis et al., 2011; James et al., 2012).

This may explain the fact that many internationally adopted children experience early puberty, especially if their first few years of life were in an institution or a chaotic home. An alternative explanation is that their age at adoption was underestimated: Puberty may seem early but really be at the expected time (Hayes, 2013).

Developmentalists have known for decades that puberty is influenced by genes, hormones, and body fat. The effect of stress is a newer discovery, as the following explains.

leptin A hormone that affects appetite and is believed to affect the onset of puberty. Leptin levels increase during childhood and peak at around age 12.

A VIEW FROM SCIENCE

Stress and Puberty

Emotional stress, particularly when it has a sexual component, tends to precipitate puberty. Girls growing up in dysfunctional families or chaotic neighborhoods reach menarche sooner than girls in more isolated, peaceful homes. For example, a large longitudinal study in England found that when a girl's biological father was not in the home (which often meant a stressed mother and other men in the child's life), menarche tended to occur earlier and the incidence of depression rose (Culpin et al., 2015).

This connection has been found in developing nations as well as developed ones. For example, in Peru, if a girl was physically and sexually abused, she was much more likely (odds ratio 1.56) to have her first period before age 11 than if she had not been abused (Barrios et al., 2015).

Hypothetically, the connection between stress and early puberty could be indirect. For example, perhaps children in dysfunctional families eat worse and watch TV more frequently and that makes them overweight, which correlates with menarche before age 11. Or, perhaps they inherit genes for early puberty from their distressed mothers, and those genes led the mothers

to become pregnant too young, creating a stressful family environment. Either obesity or genes could cause early puberty, and then stress would be a by-product, not a cause.

However, several longitudinal studies show a direct link between stress and puberty. For example, one longitudinal study of 756 children found that parents who demanded respect, who often spanked, and who rarely hugged their babies were, a decade later, likely to have daughters who reached puberty earlier than other girls in the same study (Belsky et al., 2007). Perhaps harsh parenting increases cortisol, which precipitates puberty.

A follow-up of the same girls at age 15, controlling for genetic differences, found that harsh treatment in childhood increased sexual problems (more sex partners, pregnancies, sexually transmitted infections) but *not* other risks (drugs, crime) (Belsky et al., 2010). This suggests that stress triggers earlier increases of sex hormones but not generalized rebellion. The direct impact of stress on puberty seems proven.

Why would higher cortisol accelerate puberty? The opposite effect—delayed puberty—makes more sense. In such a scenario, stressed teens would still look and act childlike, which might evoke adult protectiveness rather than lust or anger. Protection is especially needed in conflict-ridden or stressed single-parent homes, yet such homes produce earlier puberty and less parental nurturance. Is this a biological mistake? Not according to evolutionary theory:

> Maturing quickly and breeding promiscuously would enhance reproductive fitness more than would delaying development, mating cautiously, and investing heavily in parenting. The latter strategy, in contrast, would make biological sense, for virtually the same reproductive-fitness-enhancing reasons, under conditions of contextual support and nurturance.
>
> [Belsky et al., 2010, p. 121]

In other words, thousands of years ago, when harsh conditions threatened survival of the species, adolescents needed to reproduce early and often, lest the entire community become extinct. By contrast, in peaceful times with plentiful food, puberty could occur later, allowing children to postpone maturity and instead enjoy extra years of nurturance from their biological parents and grandparents. Genes evolved to respond differently to war and peace.

Of course, this evolutionary benefit no longer applies. Today, early sexual activity and reproduction are more destructive than protective of communities. However, since the genome has been shaped over millennia, a puberty-starting allele that responds to social conditions will respond in the twenty-first century as it did thousands of years ago. This idea complements current behavioral genetic understanding of differential susceptibility (Harkness, 2014). Because of genetic protections, not every distressed girl experiences early puberty, but also for genetic reasons, family stress may speed up age of menarche.

Tom Hopkins/Aurora Creative/Getty Images

Celebrating Bodies The awkwardness of female maturation should not blind us to the other truth: Most girls enjoy friendship and changing bodies, as shown here.

● **Observation Quiz** Which girl is the leader? (See answer, page 392) ↑

⬤⬤ **Response for Parents Worried About Early Puberty** (from page 388): Probably not. If she is overweight, her diet should change, but the hormone hypothesis is speculative. Genes are the main factor; she shares only one-eighth of her genes with her cousin.

Too Early, Too Late

For a society's health, early puberty is problematic: It increases the rate of emotional and behavioral problems (Dimler & Natsuaki, 2015). For most adolescents, these links between puberty, stress, and hormones are irrelevant. Only one aspect of timing matters: their friends' schedules. No one wants to be too early or too late.

Girls

Think about the early-maturing girl. If she has visible breasts at age 10, the boys her age tease her; they are unnerved by the sexual creature in their midst. She must fit her developing body into a school chair designed for smaller children; she might hide her breasts in large T-shirts and bulky sweaters; she might refuse to undress for gym. Early-maturing girls tend to have lower self-esteem, more depression, and poorer body image than do other girls (Galvao et al., 2014; Compian et al., 2009).

Some early-maturing girls have older boyfriends, who are attracted to their womanly shape and girlish innocence. Having an older boyfriend bestows status among young adolescents, but it also increases the rate of drug and alcohol use (Mrug et al., 2014). Early-maturing girls enter abusive relationships more often than other girls do. Is that because their social judgment is immature?

Boys

Early maturation is more harmful than helpful for females no matter when they were born, but cohort matters for males. Early-maturing boys who were born around 1930 often became leaders in high school and earned more money as adults (Jones, 1965; Taga et al., 2006). Since about 1960, however, the risks associated with early male maturation have outweighed the benefits.

In the twenty-first century, early-maturing boys are more aggressive, law-breaking, and alcohol-abusing than the average boy (Mendle et al., 2012). Although most of the research on the connection between the timing of puberty and conduct problems has been on boys in the United States, similar findings come from many parts of the world, including a recent large study in contemporary China (Sun et al., 2016).

This is not surprising. A boy with rapidly increasing testosterone, whose body looks more like a man than a child, whose brain is more affected by emotions than logic, and who seeks approval from peers more than adults, is likely to trouble parents, peers, schools, and the police.

Early puberty is particularly stressful if it happens suddenly: The boys most likely to become depressed are those for whom puberty was both early and quick (Mendle et al., 2010). In adolescence, depression is often masked as anger. That fuming, flailing 12-year-old may be more sad than mad.

Late puberty may also be difficult, especially for boys (Benoit et al., 2013). Slow-developing boys tend to be more anxious, depressed, and afraid of sex. Girls are less attracted to them, coaches less often want them on their teams, peers bully or tease them. If a 14-year-old boy still looks childish, he may react in ways (clowning, fighting, isolating) that are not healthy for him.

Ethnic Differences

Puberty that is late by world norms, at age 14 or so, is not troubling if one's friends are late as well. Well-nourished Africans tend to experience puberty a few months earlier and Asians a few months later than Europeans, but they all function well if their peers are on the same schedule (Al-Sahab et al., 2010). This is also true within nations such as the United States and Canada that are home to many teenagers with roots elsewhere. Peer groups that are multiethnic may reflect ethnic differences, however, and that may create tension among the adolescents.

The specific impact of early puberty varies not only by sex but also by culture. For instance, one study found that, in contrast to European Americans, early-maturing African American girls were not depressed, but early-maturing African American boys were (Hamlat et al., 2014a, 2014b).

European research finds that early-maturing Swedish girls were likely to encounter problems with boys and early drug abuse, but similar Slovak girls were not, presumably because parents and social norms kept Slovak girls under tight control (Skoog & Stattin, 2014). Finally, early-maturing Mexican American boys were likely to experience trouble (with police and with peers) if they lived in neighborhoods with few Mexican Americans, but not if they lived in ethnic enclaves (R. White et al., 2013).

None of this is true for all children from these groups. However, research confirms that contextual factors interact with biological ones. Always, relationships with peers, parents, and community make off-time puberty better or worse (Benoit et al., 2013).

WHAT HAVE YOU LEARNED?

1. What are the first visible signs of puberty?
2. What body parts of a teenage boy or girl are the last to reach full growth?
3. How do hormones affect the physical and psychological aspects of puberty?
4. Why do adolescents experience sudden, intense emotions?
5. How does the circadian rhythm affect adolescents?
6. What are the consequences of sleep deprivation?
7. What are the sex differences in the growth spurt?
8. What are the ethnic and cultural differences in the timing of puberty?
9. How are girls affected by early puberty?
10. How are boys affected by off-time puberty?

Answer to Observation Quiz (from page (390): Impossible to know, but it looks like the one who is most developed is also leading the group.

growth spurt The relatively sudden and rapid physical growth that occurs during puberty. Each body part increases in size on a schedule: Weight usually precedes height, and growth of the limbs precedes growth of the torso.

Growth and Nutrition

Puberty entails transformation of every body part, with each change affecting all of the others. Here we discuss biological growth and the nutrition that fuels that growth. Then we will focus on sexual maturation.

Growing Bigger and Stronger

The first set of changes is called the **growth spurt**—a sudden, uneven jump in size that turns children into adults. Growth proceeds from the extremities to the core (the opposite of the earlier proximodistal growth). Thus, fingers and toes lengthen before hands and feet, hands and feet before arms and legs, arms and legs before the torso. Growth is not always symmetrical: One foot, one breast, or even one ear may grow later than the other.

Because the torso is the last body part to grow, many pubescent children are temporarily big-footed, long-legged, and short-waisted. If young teenagers complain that their jeans don't fit, they are probably correct—even if those same jeans fit when their parents bought them a month earlier. (Advance warning about rapid body growth occurs when parents first have to buy their children's shoes in the adult section.)

Sequence: Weight, Height, Muscles

As the growth spurt begins, children eat more and gain weight. Exactly when, where, and how much weight they gain depends on heredity, hormones, diet, exercise, and sex. By age 17, the average girl has twice the percentage of body fat as her male classmate, whose increased weight is mostly muscle.

A height spurt follows the weight spurt; a year or two later a muscle spurt occurs. Thus, the pudginess and clumsiness of early puberty are usually gone by late adolescence. Keep in mind, however, that puberty may dislodge the usual relationship between height and overweight or underweight. A child may be eating too much or too little, but that may not be apparent in conventional measures of BMI (Golden et al., 2012).

At puberty, all of the muscles grow. Arm muscles develop particularly in boys, doubling in strength from age 8 to 18. Other muscles are gender-neutral. For instance, both sexes run faster with each year of adolescence, with boys not much faster than girls (unless the girls choose to slow down) (see Figure 14.4).

Organ Growth

In both sexes, lungs triple in weight; consequently, adolescents breathe more deeply and slowly. The heart (another muscle) doubles in size as the heartbeat slows, decreasing the pulse rate while increasing blood pressure (Malina et al., 2004). Consequently, endurance improves: Some teenagers can run for miles or dance for hours. Red blood cells increase in both sexes, but dramatically more so in boys, which aids oxygen transport during intense exercise.

Both weight and height increase *before* muscles and internal organs: To protect immature muscles and organs, athletic training and weight lifting should be tailored to an adolescent's size the previous year. Sports injuries are the most common school accidents, and they increase at puberty. One reason is that the height spurt precedes increases in bone mass, making young adolescents particularly vulnerable to fractures (Mathison & Agrawal, 2010).

FIGURE 14.4

Little Difference Both sexes develop longer and stronger legs during puberty.

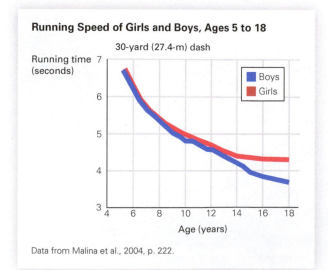

Running Speed of Girls and Boys, Ages 5 to 18

Data from Malina et al., 2004, p. 222.

One organ system, the lymphoid system (which includes the tonsils and adenoids), *decreases* in size, so teenagers are less susceptible to respiratory ailments. Mild asthma, for example, often switches off at puberty—half as many teenagers as children are asthmatic (MMWR, June 8, 2012). In addition, teenagers have fewer colds and allergies than younger children. This reduction in susceptibility is aided by growth of the larynx, which also deepens the voice, dramatically noticeable in boys.

Another organ system, the skin, becomes oilier, sweatier, and more prone to acne. Hair also changes, becoming coarser and darker. New hair grows under arms, on faces, and over sex organs (pubic hair, from the same Latin root as *puberty*).

Diet Deficiencies

All of the changes of puberty depend on adequate nourishment, yet many adolescents do not eat well. Teenagers often skip breakfast, binge at midnight, guzzle down unhealthy energy drinks, and munch on salty, processed snacks. One reason for their eating patterns is that their hormones affect the circadian rhythm of their appetites; another reason is that their drive for independence makes them avoid family dinners, refusing to eat what their mothers say they should. In 2015, only 16 percent of U.S. high school seniors ate the recommended three or more servings of vegetables a day (MMWR, June 10, 2016).

Deficiencies of iron, calcium, zinc, and other minerals are especially common during adolescence. Because menstruation depletes iron, anemia is more common among adolescent girls than among any other age or sex group. This is true everywhere, especially in South Asia and sub-Saharan Africa, where teenage girls rarely eat iron-rich meat and green vegetables.

Reliable laboratory analysis of blood iron on a large sample of young girls in developing nations is not available, but all indications suggest that many are anemic. One study of a select group of 168 girls, ages 13 to 16, from one school in India found that two-thirds were anemic, with school grades lower among those who were iron-deficient (Tarun et al., 2016).

Another study on 18- to 23-year-old college women in Saudi Arabia found that a fourth (24 percent) were clinically anemic and another fourth (28 percent) were iron-deficient, although not technically anemic (Al-Sayes et al., 2011). These numbers are especially troubling since almost all college women in Saudi Arabia are in good health, from wealthy families, and have never been pregnant. They are among the better-nourished young women in that nation; rates of anemia are undoubtedly higher among younger, poorer girls.

Boys everywhere may also be iron-deficient if they engage in physical labor or intensive sports: Muscles need iron for growth and strength. The cutoff for iron-deficiency anemia is higher for boys than for girls because boys require more iron to be healthy (Morón & Viteri, 2009). Yet, in developed as well as developing nations, many adolescents of both sexes spurn iron-rich foods in favor of chips, sweets, and fries.

Similarly, although the daily recommended intake of calcium for teenagers is 1,300 milligrams, the average U.S. teen consumes less than 500 milligrams a day. About half of adult bone mass is acquired from ages 10 to 20, which means that many contemporary teenagers will develop osteoporosis (fragile bones), a major cause of disability, injury, and death in late adulthood, especially for women.

One reason for calcium deficiency is that milk drinking has declined. In 1961, most North American children drank at least 24 ounces (about three-fourths of

For the Audience Teenage eating behavior is influenced by other adolescents. Note the evident approval from the slightly older teenager, not from the younger boys. Would the eater have put his head back and mouth wide open if the only onlookers were his parents?

Diet Worldwide, adolescent obesity is increasing. Parental responses differ, from indifference to major focus. For some U.S. parents the response is to spend thousands of dollars trying to change their children, as is the case for the parents of these girls, eating breakfast at Wellspring, a California boarding school for overweight teenagers that costs $6,250 a month. Every day, these girls exercise more than 10,000 steps (tracked with a pedometer) and eat less than 20 grams of fat (normal is more than 60 grams).

body image A person's idea of how his or her body looks.

a liter) of milk each day, providing almost all (about 900 milligrams) of their daily calcium requirement. Fifty years later, only 10.2 percent of high school students drank that much milk, and 21.5 percent (more girls than boys) drank no milk at all (MMWR, June 10, 2016).

The decline of milk drinking is one reason for the prevalent deficiency in vitamin D. Skipping breakfast and avoiding dairy products are common for adolescents of every group, particularly African Americans, affecting later health (Van Horn et al., 2011). Some find milk difficult to digest, but other products—cheese or yogurt, for instance—could replace milk. Too many adolescents choose soda and chips.

Choices Made

Many economists advocate a "nudge" to encourage people to make better choices, not only in nutrition but also in all other aspects of their lives (Thaler & Sunstein, 2008). Teenagers are often nudged by peers and institutions in the wrong direction. Deficiencies result from the choices that young adolescents are enticed to make.

Fast-food establishments cluster around high schools, often with extra seating that encourages teenagers to eat and socialize. This is especially true for high schools with large Hispanic populations, who are most at risk for obesity (Taber et al., 2011). Forty-five percent of Hispanic girls in U.S. high schools describe themselves as overweight, as do 28 percent of Hispanic boys (MMWR, June 10, 2016). Price further influences food choices, especially for adolescents, and unhealthy fast foods are cheaper than healthy ones.

Nutritional deficiencies increase when schools have vending machines that offer soda and snacks (Rovner et al., 2011). An increasing number of laws require schools to encourage healthy eating, but effects are more apparent in elementary schools than in high schools (Mâsse et al., 2013; Terry-McElrath et al., 2014).

The data show that rates of obesity are falling in childhood but not in adolescence. In 2003, only three U.S. states (Kentucky, Mississippi, Tennessee) had high school obesity rates at 15 percent or more; in 2015, 30 states did (MMWR, June 10, 2016). In Latin America, the nutritional focus is on preventing underweight, not preventing overweight; yet overall, about one teenager in four is overweight or obese (Rivera et al., 2014).

Body Image

One reason for poor nutrition among teenagers is anxiety about **body image**—that is, a person's idea of how his or her body looks. Few teenagers welcome every change in their bodies. Instead, they tend to focus on and exaggerate imperfections (as did the three girls in the anecdote that opens this chapter). Two-thirds of U.S. high school girls are trying to lose weight, one-third think they are overweight, and only one-sixth are actually overweight or obese (MMWR, June 10, 2016).

Few adolescents are happy with their bodies, partly because very few look like the bodies portrayed online and in magazines, movies, and television programs that are marketed to teenagers (Bell & Dittmar, 2011). Unhappiness with appearance—especially with weight for girls—is documented worldwide: in South Korea, China, and Greece (Kim & Kim, 2009; Chen & Jackson, 2009; Argyrides & Kkeli, 2015).

Dissatisfaction with body image is not only depressing but also can be dangerous. Many teenagers eat erratically and take drugs to change their bodies.

Teenagers try new diets, go without food for 24 hours (as did 19 percent of U.S. high school girls in one typical month), or take diet drugs (6.6 percent) (MMWR, June 13, 2014). Many eat oddly (e.g., only rice or only carrots), begin unusual diets, or exercise intensely.

Eating Disorders

Dissatisfaction with body image can be dangerous, even deadly. Many teenagers, mostly girls, eat erratically or ingest drugs (especially diet pills) to lose weight; others, mostly boys, take steroids to increase muscle mass. [**Life-Span Link:** Teenage drug abuse is discussed in Chapter 16.] Eating disorders are rare in childhood but increase dramatically at puberty, accompanied by distorted body image, food obsession, and depression (Le Grange & Lock, 2011). (See Visualizing Development, page 396.)

Adolescents sometimes switch from obsessive dieting to overeating to overexercising and back again. Here, we describe two eating disorders that are particularly likely to begin in adolescence.

Anorexia Nervosa

A body mass index (BMI) of 18 or lower, or loss of more than 10 percent of body weight within a month or two, indicates **anorexia nervosa,** a disorder characterized by voluntary starvation and a destructive and distorted attitude about one's own body fat. The affected person becomes very thin, risking death by organ failure. Staying too thin becomes an obsession.

Although anorexia existed earlier, it was not identified until about 1950, when some high-achieving, upper-class young women became so emaciated that they died. Soon anorexia was evident among teenagers and young adults of every income, nation, and ethnicity; the rate spikes at puberty and again in emerging adulthood. Certain alleles increase the risk of developing anorexia (Young, 2010), with higher risk among girls with close relatives who suffer from eating disorders or severe depression. Although far more common in girls, some boys are also at risk.

Binge Eating

About three times as common as anorexia is **bulimia nervosa.** This disorder is clinically present in 1 to 3 percent of female teenagers and young adults in the United States. They overeat compulsively, consuming thousands of calories within an hour or two, and then purge through vomiting or laxatives. Most are close to normal in weight and therefore unlikely to starve. However, they risk serious health problems, including damage to their gastrointestinal systems and cardiac arrest from electrolyte imbalance.

Bingeing and purging are common among adolescents. For instance, a 2013 survey found that *in the last 30 days*, 6.6 percent of U.S. high school girls and 2.2 percent of boys vomited or took laxatives to lose weight, with marked variation by state, from 3.6 percent in Nebraska to 9 percent in Arizona (MMWR, June 13, 2014).

A disorder that is newly recognized in DSM-5 is *binge eating disorder*. Some adolescents periodically and compulsively overeat, quickly consuming large amounts of ice cream, cake, or any snack food until their stomachs hurt. When bingeing becomes a disorder, overeating is typically done in private, at least weekly for several months. The sufferer does not purge (hence this is not bulimia) but feels out of control, distressed, and depressed.

Can't Wait If he asked his parents or his friends what they thought of his looks, they might wonder why he asked—his features are even and attractive, and boys are not supposed to care very much. However, both sexes are often self-conscious about their looks, especially during puberty when everything changes. Note that he is in early adolescence (the proportions of his hands are bigger than his head, and he does not yet have facial hair), which is when details of appearance are most troubling.

anorexia nervosa An eating disorder characterized by self-starvation. Affected individuals voluntarily undereat and often overexercise, depriving their vital organs of nutrition. Anorexia can be fatal.

bulimia nervosa An eating disorder characterized by binge eating and subsequent purging, usually by induced vomiting and/or use of laxatives.

Not Just Dieting Elize, seen here sitting in a café in France, believes that she developed anorexia after she went on an extreme diet. Success with that diet led her to think that even less food would be better. She is recovering, but, as you can see, she is still too thin.

SATISFIED WITH YOUR BODY?

Probably not, if you are a teenager. At every age, accepting who you are—not just ethnicity and gender, but also body shape, size, and strength—correlates with emotional health. During the adolescent years, when everyone's body changes dramatically, body dissatisfaction rises. As you see, this is particularly true for girls—but if the measure were satisfaction with muscles, more boys would be noted as unhappy.

BODY DISSATISFACTION CORRELATES WITH...

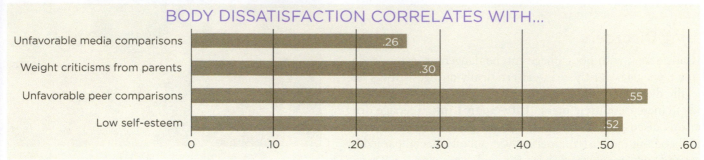

Unfavorable media comparisons	.26
Weight criticisms from parents	.30
Unfavorable peer comparisons	.55
Low self-esteem	.52

Scale: 0 .10 .20 .30 .40 .50 .60

Data from Van Vonderen & Kinnally, 2012.

GENDER DIFFERENCES IN BODY DISSATISFACTION

Females of all ages tend to be dissatisfied with their bodies, but the biggest leap in dissatisfaction occurs when girls transition from early to mid-adolescence (Makinen et al., 2012).

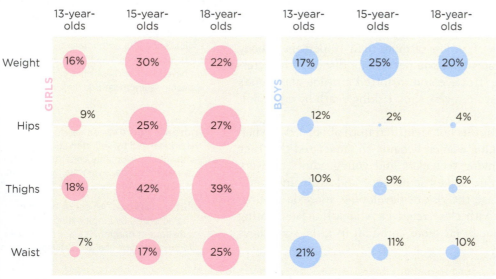

GIRLS

	13-year-olds	15-year-olds	18-year-olds
Weight	16%	30%	22%
Hips	9%	25%	27%
Thighs	18%	42%	39%
Waist	7%	17%	25%

BOYS

	13-year-olds	15-year-olds	18-year-olds
Weight	17%	25%	20%
Hips	12%	2%	4%
Thighs	10%	9%	6%
Waist	21%	11%	10%

Data from Weinshenker, 2014; Rosenblum & Lewis, 1999.

SOCIAL MEDIA AND BODY DISSATISFACTION

- The more time teenage girls spend on social media, the higher their body dissatisfaction.
- 86% of teens say that social network sites hurt their body confidence.

(Proudzme, 2013; Tiggemann & Stater, 2013)

NUTRITION AND EXERCISE

High school students are told, at home and at school, to eat their vegetables and not care about their looks. Is that good advice, when they listen more to their peers and follow social norms? Fortunately, some eventually learn that, no matter what their body type, good nutrition and adequate exercise make a person feel more attractive, energetic, and happy.

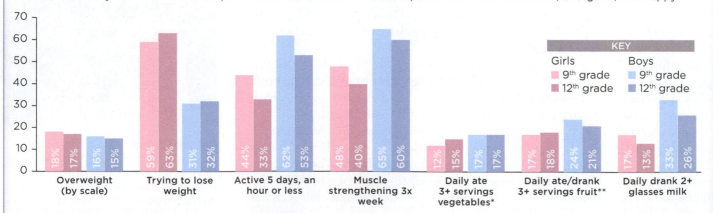

KEY

	Girls	Boys
9th grade	Girls 9th grade	Boys 9th grade
12th grade	Girls 12th grade	Boys 12th grade

	Girls 9th	Girls 12th	Boys 9th	Boys 12th
Overweight (by scale)	18%	17%	16%	15%
Trying to lose weight	59%	63%	31%	32%
Active 5 days, an hour or less	44%	33%	62%	53%
Muscle strengthening 3x week	48%	40%	65%	60%
Daily ate 3+ servings vegetables*	12%	15%	17%	17%
Daily ate/drank 3+ servings fruit**	17%	18%	24%	21%
Daily drank 2+ glasses milk	17%	13%	33%	26%

*Vegetables includes salad greens, and excludes French fries.
**Fruits include a glass of 100% fruit juice.

Data from MMWR, June 10, 2016.

Life-Span Consequences

From a life-span perspective, teenage eating disorders are not limited to adolescence, even though this is the age when first signs typically appear. The origins begin much earlier, in family eating patterns if parents do not help their children eat sensibly—when they are hungry, without food being a punishment or a reward.

For all eating disorders, family function (not structure) is crucial (Tetzlaff & Hilbert, 2014). During the teen years, many parents do not recognize serious eating disorders, and thus they delay getting the help that their children need (Thomson et al., 2014). Much of the problem arises from the social emphasis on appearance. Since pubescent girls normally add body fat and experience a body type that differs from the cultural ideal, eating disorders become a risk (Smolak & Levine, 2015).

Problems continue. Many eating disorders are unrecognized until emerging adulthood. Unless adolescents with disordered eating patterns learn better patterns, they are vulnerable later on. Perhaps 5 percent die of anorexia—death usually coming 10 years or more after initial symptoms. Most survive but experience depression and anxiety or health complications such as heart disease, infertility, or osteoporosis. Chance of recovery is better if diagnosis occurs during early adolescence (not adulthood), and hospitalization is brief (Meczekalski et al., 2013; Errichiello et al., 2016).

WHAT HAVE YOU LEARNED?

1. What is the pattern of growth in adolescent bodies?

2. What complications result from the sequence of growth (weight/height/muscles)?

3. Why are many teenagers deficient in iron and calcium?

4. Why are many adolescents unhappy with their appearance?

Sexual Maturation

Sexuality is multidimensional, complicated, and variable—not unlike human development overall. Here we consider biological changes at puberty and some cohort variations. Other aspects of sexuality are discussed in Chapters 16, 17, 20, and 23.

Sexual Characteristics

The body characteristics that are directly involved in conception and pregnancy are called **primary sex characteristics**. During puberty, every primary sex organ (the ovaries, the uterus, the penis, and the testes) increases dramatically in size and matures in function. Reproduction becomes possible.

At the same time that maturation of the primary sex characteristics occurs, secondary sex characteristics develop. **Secondary sex characteristics** are bodily features that do not directly affect reproduction (hence they are secondary) but that signify masculinity or femininity.

One secondary characteristic is body shape. Young boys and girls have similar shapes, but at puberty males widen at the shoulders and grow about 5 inches taller than females, while girls widen at the hips and develop breasts. Those female curves are often considered signs of womanhood, but neither breasts nor wide hips are required for conception; thus, they are secondary, not primary, sex characteristics.

The pattern of hair growth at the scalp line (widow's peak), the prominence of the larynx (Adam's apple), and several other anatomical features differ for men

primary sex characteristics The parts of the body that are directly involved in reproduction, including the vagina, uterus, ovaries, testicles, and penis.

secondary sex characteristics Physical traits that are not directly involved in reproduction but that indicate sexual maturity, such as a man's beard and a woman's breasts.

and women; all are secondary sex characteristics that few people notice. Facial and body hair increases in both sexes, affected by sex hormones as well as genes.

Visible facial and chest hair is sometimes considered a sign of manliness, although hairiness in either sex depends on genes as well as on hormones. Girls often pluck or wax any facial hair they see and shave their legs, while boys may proudly grow sideburns, soul patches, chinstraps, moustaches, and so on—with specifics dependent on culture and cohort.

Often teenagers cut, style, or grow the hair on their heads in ways their parents do not like, as a sign of independence. To become more attractive, many adolescents spend considerable time, money, and thought on growing, gelling, shaving, curling, straightening, highlighting, brushing, combing, styling, dyeing, wetting, and/or drying. In many ways, visible hair is far more than a growth characteristic; it is a display of sexuality.

Secondary sex characteristics are important psychologically, if not biologically. Breasts are an obvious example. Many adolescent girls buy "minimizer," "maximizer," "training," or "shaping" bras in the hope that their breasts will conform to an idealized body image.

During the same years, many overweight boys are horrified to notice a swelling around their nipples—a temporary result of the erratic hormones of early puberty. If a boy's breast growth is very disturbing, tamoxifen or plastic surgery can reduce the swelling, although many doctors prefer to let time deal with the problem (Morcos & Kizy, 2012).

Sexual Activity

Primary and secondary sex characteristics such as menarche, spermarche, and body shape are not the only evidence of sex hormones. Fantasizing, flirting, hand-holding, staring, standing, sitting, walking, displaying, and touching are all done in particular ways to reflect sexuality. As already explained, hormones trigger sexual thoughts, but the culture shapes thoughts into enjoyable fantasies, shameful obsessions, frightening impulses, or actual contact (see Figure 14.5).

Masturbation is common in both sexes, for instance. One cross-sectional study of 14- to 17-year-olds in the United States reported that 74 percent of the boys

Video: Romantic Relationships in Adolescence explores teens' attitudes and assumptions about romance and sexuality.

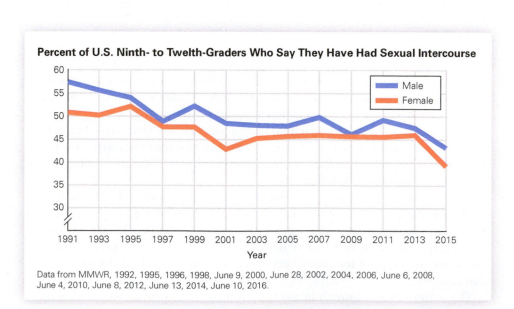

Percent of U.S. Ninth- to Twelth-Graders Who Say They Have Had Sexual Intercourse

Data from MMWR, 1992, 1995, 1996, 1998, June 9, 2000, June 28, 2002, 2004, 2006, June 6, 2008, June 4, 2010, June 8, 2012, June 13, 2014, June 10, 2016.

FIGURE 14.5

Boys and Girls Together Boys tend to be somewhat more sexually experienced than girls during the high school years, but since the Youth Risk Behavior Survey began in 1991, the overall trend has been toward equality in rates of sexual activity.

and 48 percent of the girls said they masturbated (Robbins et al., 2011). However, their attitudes vary, from private sin to mutual pleasure (Driemeyer et al., 2016).

A study on sexual behaviors such as hand-holding and cuddling among young adolescents found that biological maturation was only one factor in whether or not such activities occurred: Especially among young European Americans, those girls with lower self-esteem were more likely to engage in sexual intimacy (Hipwell et al., 2010).

The distinction between early and later sexual experience during adolescence may be significant. A detailed longitudinal study in Finland found that those who were depressed and rebellious were more likely to use drugs and more likely to have sexual intercourse before age 14 (Kaltiala-Heino et al., 2015). That had flipped by age 19, when those who had experienced intercourse were less likely to be depressed (Savioja et al., 2015). Emotions regarding sexual experience, like the rest of puberty, are strongly influenced by social norms.

Indeed, everyone is influenced by hormones and society, biology and culture. All adolescents have sexual interests that they did not previously have (biology), which produce behaviors engaged in by teenagers in some nations that teenagers of other nations would not do (culture).

Social norms regarding male–female differences are quite powerful. Traditionally, males were thought to have stronger sexual urges than females, which is why adolescent boys are supposed to "make the first move," from asking for a date to trying for a kiss. Then, girls were supposed to slow down the boys' advances. This was called the *double standard,* in that behaviors of boys and girls were held to different standards. Many adolescents still expect boys and girls to approach heterosexual interactions differently, with boys more insistent and girls more hesitant. As one teen explained, "that's just how it is" (Tolman et al., 2016).

In many nations including the United States, rates of sexual activity are now almost even. For example, among high school seniors, 57 percent of the girls and 59 percent of the boys have had sexual intercourse, with most of them sexually active in the past three months. The one notable difference among high school students is in the number of partners: 9 percent of the girls and 14 percent of the boys have had four or more (MMWR, June 10, 2016).

In the United States, every gender, ethnic, and age group is less sexually active than the previous cohort. Between 1991 and 2015, intercourse experience among African American high school students decreased 40 percent (to 49 percent); among European Americans, down 120 percent (to 40 percent); and among Latinos, down 19 percent (to 43 percent) (MMWR, June 10, 2016).

These were responses to an anonymous questionnaire. As you know from Chapter 1, some inaccuracies may have occurred, but the trends are solid in that the same questions were asked over the decades. Many reasons for the trends have been suggested: better sex education, fear of HIV/AIDS, new realization of the problems of pregnancy, better understanding of abortion, less male–female intimacy . . . more research is needed.

The trend toward later sexual activity is international, although because marriage occurs later, rates of premarital sex are rising. More teenagers worldwide are virgins than was true a decade ago, a trend documented in China, where, unlike former cohorts, first intercourse does not occur until age 20, on average (Yu et al., 2013). Data from the United States show earlier experience but the same trends.

Steve Coleman/OJO Images RF/Getty Images

Everywhere Glancing, staring, and—when emotions are overwhelming—averting one's eyes are part of the universal language of love. Although the rate of intercourse among teenagers is lower than it was, passion is expressed in simple words, touches, and, as shown here, the eyes on a cold day.

LaunchPad
macmillan learning

Check out the Data Connections activity **Sexual Behaviors of U.S. High School Students,** which examines how sexually active teens really are.

Who Should Teens Talk to About Contraception? This teenage girl is discussing contraception with her gynecologist.

In 2015, half (50 percent) of eleventh-graders said they have had intercourse; in 1991, two-thirds (62 percent) said they did.

All of these examples demonstrate that a universal experience (rising hormones) that produces another universal experience (growth of primary and secondary sex characteristics) is influenced by cohort, gender, and culture. The most important contextual influence for adolescents' sexual activity is their close friends, a more powerful force than more general norms for their sex or ethnic group (van de Bongardt et al., 2015).

Sexual Problems in Adolescence

Sexual interest and interaction are part of adolescence; healthy adult relationships are more likely to develop when adolescent impulses are not haunted by shame and fear (Tolman & Mc-Clelland, 2011). Although guidance is needed, teenagers are neither depraved nor degenerate in experiencing sexual urges. Before focusing on the hazards of adolescent sex, we should note that several "problems" are less troubling now than in earlier decades. Here are three specifics:

- *Teen births have decreased.* In the United States, births to teenage mothers (aged 15 to 19) decreased 25 percent between 2007 and 2011 across race and ethnicity, with the biggest drop among Hispanic teens (J. Martin et al., 2010; Centers for Disease Control and Prevention, June 16, 2014). [The 2011 rate was the lowest in 40 years.] Similar declines are evident in other nations. The most dramatic results are from China, where the teen pregnancy rate was cut in half from 1960 to 2010 (reducing the 2015 projection of the world's population by about 1 billion).
- *The use of "protection" has risen.* Contraception, particularly condom use among adolescent boys, has increased markedly in most nations since 1990 (Santelli & Melnikas, 2010). The U.S. Youth Risk Behavior Survey found that 63 percent of sexually active ninth-grade boys used a condom during their most recent intercourse (MMWR, June 10, 2016) (see Table 14.1).
- *The teen abortion rate is down.* In general, the teen abortion rate in the United States has declined every year since abortion became legal. The rate today is about half that of 20 years earlier (Kost & Henshaw, 2013), even as the rate among older women has increased. The reason is not only that intercourse is less frequent but also that contraception is more prevalent.

These are positive trends, but many aspects of adolescent sexual activity remain problematic.

Sex Too Soon

Sex can, of course, be thrilling and affirming, providing a bonding experience. However, compared to a century ago, adolescent sexual activity—especially if it results in birth—is more hazardous because four circumstances have changed:

1. Earlier puberty and weaker social taboos result in some very young teens having sex. Early sex correlates with depression, drug abuse, and lifelong problems (Kastbom et al., 2015).
2. If early sex leads to pregnancy and birth, most teenage girls have no partners to help. A century ago, teenage mothers were often married; now, in the United States, 86 percent are unwed (Shattuck & Kreider, 2013).

TABLE 14.1	Condom Use Among 15-Year-Olds (Tenth Grade)	
Country	Sexually Active (% of total)	Used Condom at Last Intercourse (% of those sexually active)
France	20	84
England	29	83
Canada	23	78
Russia	33	75
Israel	14	72
United States	41	60

Data from MMWR, June 4, 2010, June 10, 2016; Nic Gabhainn et al., 2009.

quavondo/Getty Images

See the Joy Some young mothers are wonderful, as seems the case here. This mother–infant pair have many advantages, not only their mutual love but also a supportive community. (Note the floor of the playroom—colorful, nontoxic and soft—perfect for toddlers.)

3. Raising a child has become more complex and expensive, and family helpers are scarce. The strategy that most teenage mothers used in former times—having their mother raise the child—is less readily available, as most young grandmothers are employed (Meyer, 2014).

4. Sexually transmitted infections are more common and more dangerous (Satterwhite et al., 2013).

As you read, teen births are declining, as are teen abortions. However, the U.S. rate of adolescent pregnancy is the highest of any developed nation (true among every ethnic group). Such pregnancies are risky. If a pregnant girl is under 16 (most are not), she is more likely than older pregnant teenagers to experience complications—including spontaneous or induced abortion, high blood pressure, stillbirth, preterm birth, and low birthweight. This is true worldwide, as documented in a study of low-income nations (Ganchimeg et al., 2014).

There are many reasons for these hazards besides age. Poverty and lack of education correlate with teen pregnancy and with every problem just listed (Santelli & Melnikas, 2010). Beyond that, younger pregnant teenagers are often malnourished and postpone prenatal care. After birth, adolescents are less often the responsive mothers that newborns need, so insecure attachment is more common. [**Life-Span Link:** Attachment types and the importance of early attachment were discussed in Chapter 7.]

Even if sexually active adolescents avoid pregnancy, early intercourse increases psychosocial problems. A study of 3,923 adult women in the United States found that those who *voluntarily* had sex before age 16 were more likely to divorce later on, whether or not they became pregnant or later married their first sexual partner. The same study found that adolescents of any age whose first sexual experience was unwanted (either "really didn't want it" or "had mixed feelings about it") were also more likely to later experience divorce (Paik, 2011).

Forced sex is much worse, of course, as now explained.

Sexual Abuse

Teenage births are risky, but sometimes mother and baby develop well. However, sexual abuse is always devastating: It harms development lifelong. **Child sexual abuse** is defined as any sexual activity (including fondling and photographing) between a juvenile and an adult, with age 18 the usual demarcation (although

child sexual abuse Any erotic activity that arouses an adult and excites, shames, or confuses a child, whether or not the victim protests and whether or not genital contact is involved.

Especially for Parents Worried About Their Teenager's Risk Taking You remember the risky things you did at the same age, and you are alarmed by the possibility that your child will follow in your footsteps. What should you do? (see response, page 404)

legal age varies by state). Girls are particularly vulnerable, although boys are also at risk.

The rate of sexual abuse increases at puberty, a particularly sensitive time because many young adolescents are confused about their own sexual urges and identity (Graber et al., 2010). Virtually every adolescent problem, including pregnancy, drug abuse, eating disorders, and suicide, is more frequent in adolescents who are sexually abused.

This is true worldwide. Although solid numbers are unknown for obvious reasons, it is apparent that millions of girls in their early teens are forced into marriage or prostitution each year. Adolescent girls are common victims of sex trafficking, not only because their youth makes them more alluring but also because their immaturity makes them more vulnerable (McClain & Garrity, 2011). Some believe they are helping their families by earning money to support them; others are literally sold by their families (Montgomery, 2015).

A United Nations report (2009) on trafficking for sexual exploitation found that most nations have laws against the practice, but almost half of the nations have *never* convicted anyone of the crime. Another global report on child sexual abuse, reported retrospectively by adults, found regional and gender variations—lower levels in East Asia, higher levels for girls in Australia and for boys in Africa—but the authors emphasize that accurate data are hard to find and difficult to compare (Stoltenborgh et al., 2011).

When U.S. children suffer sexual abuse, they are usually not trafficked but instead are abused in their own homes by a family member. Typically, the victim is a young adolescent who is prevented from the usual friendships and romances that teach a child how to develop a healthy and satisfying life. Sometimes the abusing family member is a biological parent, but often it is a stepfather, older sibling, or uncle. Young people who are sexually exploited tend to fear sex and to devalue themselves lifelong, with higher rates of virtually every developmental problem (Pérez-Fuentes et al., 2013).

For example, in one longitudinal study in Washington, D.C., of 84 reported victims of child sexual abuse (all girls), each of them was interviewed six times over 23 years (Trickett et al., 2011). In order to isolate the effects of abuse, the researchers also followed the development of individuals from the same backgrounds (SES, ethnicity, and so on) who were not sexually abused.

Every problem examined was worse in the victims than in their peers who were not victimized. Among the examples: Sex was thought of as dirty, shameful, and dangerous; few were overweight as children, but 42 percent were obese in their 20s; school achievement was lower; rates of self-harm were higher; repeated victimization—both sexual and physical—was more common in adulthood (Trickett et al., 2011).

From a developmental perspective, their ability to care for their children is particularly important. Almost half of the girls who were abused became mothers, having a total of 78 children. Of those children, three died in infancy and nine were permanently removed from their mothers, who had severely maltreated them. These rates were much higher than rates among the mothers from the same income and ethnic groups who were not victimized.

Early in this chapter, we noted that the HPA axis regulates puberty and many other physiological responses. Many of the formerly abused women had abnormal HPA regulation, with alteration of their cortisol responses. That condition produced heightened stress reactions in early adolescence but then abnormally low stress responses in adulthood.

Fortunately, now that child sexual abuse is recognized and reported more often, it has become less common, with "large declines in sexual abuse from 1992 to

2010" in the United States (Finkelhor & Jones, 2012, p. 3). Worldwide, about 13 percent of women say they were sexually abused as children (Stoltenborgh et al., 2011). Of course, even one instance is too many.

Our discussion of sexual abuse focuses on girls because they are the most common victims. However, teenage boys may be sexually abused as well, a direct attack on their fledgling identity as men (Dorais, 2009). Disclosure of past abuse is particularly difficult for men, which makes reliable statistics difficult (Collin-Vézina et al., 2015).

Remember that perpetrators of all kinds of abuse are often people known to the child. After puberty, although sometimes abusers are parents, coaches, or other authorities, often they are other teenagers. In the most recent U.S. Youth Risk Behavior Survey of high school students, 15 percent of the girls and 5 percent of the boys said that they had been kissed, touched, or forced to have sex within a dating relationship when they did not want to (MMWR, June 10, 2016). Sex education is discussed in Chapter 16; obviously teenagers have much to learn.

Sexually Transmitted Infections

Unlike teen pregnancy and sexual abuse, the other major problem of teenage sex shows no signs of abating. A **sexually transmitted infection (STI)** (sometimes called a sexually transmitted disease [STD]) is any infection transmitted through sexual contact. Worldwide, sexually active teenagers have higher rates of the most common STIs—gonorrhea, genital herpes, and chlamydia—than do sexually active people of any other age group.

In the United States, half of all new STIs occur in people ages 15 to 25, even though this age group has less than one-fourth of the sexually active people (Satterwhite et al., 2013). Rates are particularly high among sexually active adolescents, ages 15 to 19 (Gavin et al., 2009). Biology provides one reason: Pubescent girls are particularly likely to catch an STI compared to fully developed women, probably because adult women have more vaginal secretions that reduce infections. Further, if symptoms appear, teens are less likely to alert their partners or seek treatment unless pain requires it.

A survey of adolescents in a U.S. pediatric emergency department found that half of the teenagers (average age 15) were sexually active and 20 percent of those had an STI—although that was not usually the reason they came for medical help (Miller et al., 2015).

There are hundreds of STIs. *Chlamydia* is the most frequently reported one; it often begins without symptoms, yet it can cause permanent infertility.

Worse is *human papillomavirus (HPV)*, which has no immediate consequences but increases the risk of "serious, life-threatening cancer" in both sexes (MMWR, July 25, 2014, p. 622). Immunization before the first intercourse has reduced the rate of HPV, but in 2013 among 13- to 17-year-olds, only 38 percent of the girls and 14 percent of the boys had all three recommended doses (MMWR, July 25, 2014).

National variations in laws and rates of STIs are large. Rates among U.S. teenagers are higher than those in any other medically advanced nation but lower than rates in some developing nations. HIV rates are not declining, despite increased awareness.

Once again, it is apparent that a universal experience (the biology of puberty) varies remarkably depending on national and family context. As we stated earlier, adolescence begins with biology and ends with culture. You will see more examples in the next chapter, as you learn that schools for adolescents vary a great deal in how and what they teach.

LaunchPad
macmillan learning

The Data Connections activity **Major Sexually Transmitted Infections: Some Basics** offers more information about the causes, symptoms, and rates of various STIs.

sexually transmitted infection (STI)
A disease spread by sexual contact, including syphilis, gonorrhea, genital herpes, chlamydia, and HIV.

WHAT HAVE YOU LEARNED?

1. What are examples of the difference between primary and secondary sex characteristics?
2. Why are there fewer problems caused by adolescent sexuality now than a few decades ago?
3. What are the problems with adolescent pregnancy?
4. Among sexually active people, why do adolescents have more STIs than adults?
5. What are the effects of child sexual abuse?

SUMMARY

Puberty Begins

1. Puberty refers to the various changes that transform a child's body into an adult one. Even before the teenage years, biochemical signals from the hypothalamus to the pituitary gland to the adrenal glands (the HPA axis) increase production of testosterone, estrogen, and various other hormones, which cause the body to grow rapidly and become capable of reproduction.

2. Some emotional reactions, such as quick mood shifts, are directly caused by hormones, as are thoughts about sex. The reactions of others to adolescents and the adolescents' own reactions to the physical changes they are undergoing also trigger emotional responses, which, in turn, affect hormones.

3. Hormones regulate all of the body rhythms of life, by day, by season, and by year. Changes in these rhythms in adolescence often result in sleep deprivation, partly because the natural circadian rhythm makes teenagers wide awake at night. Sleep deprivation causes numerous health and learning problems.

4. Various parts of the brain mature during puberty and in the following decade. The regions dedicated to emotional arousal (including the amygdala) mature before those that regulate and rationalize emotional expression (the prefrontal cortex).

5. Puberty normally begins anytime from about age 8 to about age 14. The young person's sex, genetic background, body fat, and level of stress all contribute to this variation in timing.

6. Girls generally begin and end puberty before boys do, although the time gap in sexual maturity is much shorter than the two-year gap in reaching peak height. Girls from divorced families or stressful neighborhoods are likely to reach puberty earlier.

Growth and Nutrition

7. The growth spurt is an acceleration of growth in every part of the body. Peak weight usually precedes peak height, which is then followed by peak muscle growth. This sequence makes adolescents particularly vulnerable to sports injuries. The lungs and the heart also increase in size and capacity.

8. All of the changes of puberty depend on adequate nourishment, yet adolescents do not always make healthy food choices. One reason for poor nutrition is the desire to lose (or, less often, gain) weight because of anxiety about body image. This is a worldwide problem, involving cultural as well as biological factors.

9. The precursors of eating disorders are evident during puberty. Many adolescents eat too much of the wrong foods or too little food overall. Deficiencies of iron, vitamin D, and calcium are common, affecting bone growth and overall development.

10. Because of the sequence of brain development, many adolescents seek intense emotional experiences, unchecked by rational thought. For the same reason, adolescents are quick to react, explore, and learn. As a result, adolescents take risks, bravely or foolishly, with potential for harm as well as for good.

Sexual Maturation

11. Male–female differences in bodies and behavior become apparent at puberty. The maturation of primary sex characteristics means that by age 13 or so, after experiencing menarche or spermarche, teenagers are capable of reproducing, although peak fertility is several years later.

12. Secondary sex characteristics are not directly involved in reproduction but signify that the child is becoming a man or a woman. Body shape, breasts, voice, body hair, and numerous other features differentiate males from females. Sexual activity is influenced more by culture than by physiology.

13. In the twenty-first century, teenage sexual behavior has changed for the better in several ways. Hormones and growth may cause sexual thoughts and behaviors at younger ages, but teen pregnancy is far less common, condom use has increased, and the average age of first intercourse has risen.

14. Among the problems that adolescents still face is the urge to become sexually active before their bodies and minds are ready. Birth before age 16 takes a physical toll on a growing girl; it also puts her baby at risk of physical and psychological problems.

15. Sexual abuse is more likely to occur in early adolescence than at other ages. Girls are more often the victims than boys are. The perpetrators are often family members or close friends of the family. Rates of child sexual abuse are declining in the United States, but globalization has probably increased international sex trafficking.

16. Untreated STIs at any age can lead to infertility and even death. Rates among sexually active teenagers are rising for many reasons, with HIV/AIDS not yet halted. Immunization to prevent HPV is decreasing rates of vaginal cancer in adulthood, but most teenagers are not immunized.

KEY TERMS

puberty (p. 381)
menarche (p. 381)
spermarche (p. 382)
pituitary (p. 382)
adrenal glands (p. 382)
HPA (hypothalamus–pituitary–adrenal) axis (p. 382)

gonads (p. 382)
HPG (hypothalamus–pituitary–gonad) axis (p. 382)
estradiol (p. 382)
testosterone (p. 382)
circadian rhythm (p. 384)
secular trend (p. 388)

leptin (p. 389)
growth spurt (p. 392)
body image (p. 394)
anorexia nervosa (p. 395)
bulimia nervosa (p. 395)
primary sex characteristics (p. 397)

secondary sex characteristics (p. 397)
child sexual abuse (p. 401)
sexually transmitted infection (STI) (p. 403)

APPLICATIONS

1. Visit a fifth-, sixth-, or seventh-grade class. Note variations in the size and maturity of the students. Do you see any patterns related to gender, ethnicity, body fat, or self-confidence?

2. Interview two to four of your friends who are in their late teens or early 20s about their memories of menarche or spermarche, including their memories of others' reactions. Do their comments indicate that these events are or are not emotionally troubling for young people?

3. Talk with someone who became a teenage parent. Were there any problems with the pregnancy, the birth, or the first years of parenthood? Would the person recommend teen parenthood? What would have been different had the baby been born three years earlier or three years later?

4. Adult reactions to puberty can be reassuring or frightening. Interview two or three people about how adults prepared, encouraged, or troubled their development. Compare that with your own experience.

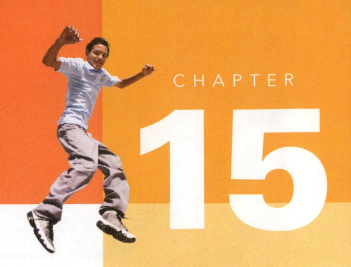

Adolescence:
Cognitive Development

What Will You Know?

1. Why are young adolescents often egocentric?
2. Why does emotion sometimes overwhelm reason?
3. Is cyberbullying worse than direct bullying?
4. What kind of school is best for teenagers?

I have taught at four universities, educating thousands of college students. Most of the curriculum is standard. That allows me to focus on updating, adding current examples, and adjusting to the particular class. Depending on the topic and students, my methods change—lecture, discussion, polls, groups, video clips, pair/share, role-play, written responses, quizzes, and more.

No class is exactly like any other. Groups are dynamic, because of the individuals and interactions. Ideally, I recognize who needs encouragement ("Good question"), who needs prompts ("Do you agree with . . . ?"), who should think before they speak ("What is your evidence?"), whose background needs to be understood by others ("Is that what it was like when you were a child in . . . ?"). Deciding who should learn what, when, and how is my challenge and my joy.

A few years ago, I taught an introductory course for college credit to advanced high school students. They grasped concepts quickly, they studied diligently, they completed papers on time—in all of those ways they were good students. But they presented new pedagogical challenges. One day I introduced psychoanalysis.

Student: I don't agree with Freud.
   Me: You don't have to agree, just learn the terms and ideas.
Student: Why should I do that?
   Me: You need to understand Freud, so you can then disagree.
Student: But I have my own ideas, and I like them better than Freud's.

I was taken aback. None of my students had ever been so egocentric as to claim that their own wonderful ideas meant that they didn't need to bother with Freud. College students do not usually agree with psychoanalytic theory: Some express insightful critiques. But none have resisted learning about Freud, deciding in advance that they liked their ideas better.

Then I remembered: Bright as they were, these students thought like adolescents. I adjusted my teaching.

This chapter describes adolescent cognition, sometimes brilliant, sometimes theoretical, and sometimes egocentric. Then we describe how adolescents are taught—in middle school, in high school, and around the world—and how that aligns or clashes with adolescent cognition.

All Eyes on Me Egocentrism and obsession with appearance are hallmarks of adolescence, as shown by these high school cheerleaders. Given teenage thinking, it is not surprising that many boys and girls seek stardom, sometimes making competition within teams and between schools fierce. Cooperation and moderation are more difficult.

adolescent egocentrism A characteristic of adolescent thinking that leads young people (ages 10 to 13) to focus on themselves to the exclusion of others.

Logic and Self

Brain maturation, additional years of schooling, moral challenges, increased independence, and intense conversations all occur between the ages of 11 and 18. These aspects of adolescents' development propel impressive cognitive growth, as teenagers move from egocentrism to logic.

Egocentrism

During puberty, young people center on themselves, in part because maturation of the brain and body heightens self-consciousness. Young adolescents grapple with conflicting feelings about their parents and friends, examine details of their physical changes, think deeply (but not always realistically) about their future. They *ruminate,* going over problems via phone, text, conversation, social media, and private, quiet self-talk (as when they lie in bed, unable to sleep) about each nuance of everything they have done, are doing, and might do. Others act impulsively, blurting out words that they later regret. And most do both, zigzagging from thoughtfulness to thoughtlessness.

Adolescent egocentrism—that is, adolescents thinking intensely about themselves and about what others think of them—was first described by David Elkind (1967). He found that, egocentrically, adolescents regard themselves as much more unique, special, and admired or hated than anyone else considers them to be. Egocentric adolescents have trouble understanding other points of view.

For example, few girls are attracted to boys with pimples and braces, but one boy's eagerness to be seen as growing up kept him from realizing this, according to his older sister:

> Now in the 8th grade, my brother has this idea that all the girls are looking at him in school. He got his first pimple about three months ago. I told him to wash it with my face soap but he refused, saying, "Not until I go to school to show it off." He called the dentist, begging him to approve his braces now instead of waiting for a year. The perfect gifts for him have changed from action figures to a bottle of cologne, a chain, and a fitted baseball hat like the rappers wear.
>
> *[adapted from E., personal communication]*

Egocentrism leads adolescents to interpret everyone else's behavior as if it were a judgment on them. A stranger's frown or a teacher's critique can make a teenager conclude that "No one likes me" and then deduce that "I am unlovable" or even "I can't leave the house." More positive casual reactions—a smile from a sales clerk or an extra-big hug from a younger brother—could lead to "I am great" or "Everyone loves me."

Acute self-consciousness about physical appearance may be more prevalent between the ages of 10 and 14 than at any other time, in part because every adolescent notices that the changes in his or her particular body during puberty do not exactly conform to norms, ideals, and fantasies (Guzman & Nishina, 2014). Most young adolescents would rather not stand out from their peers, hoping instead to blend in, although they may want to flaunt adult standards.

Piercings, shaved heads, torn jeans—all contrary to adult conventions—signify connection to youth culture. Notice groups of adolescents waiting in line for a midnight show, or clustering near their high school, and you will see that counterculture appearance conforms with a social group.

Because adolescents are focused on their own perspectives, their emotions may not be grounded in reality. A study of 1,310 Dutch and Belgian adolescents found that egocentrism was strong. For many of these teenagers, self-esteem and loneliness were closely tied to their *perception* of how others saw them, not to their actual popularity or acceptance among their peers. Gradually, after about age 15, some gained more perspective and became less depressed (Vanhalst et al., 2013).

The Imaginary Audience

Egocentrism creates an **imaginary audience** in the minds of many adolescents. They believe they are at center stage, with all eyes on them, and they imagine how others might react to their appearance and behavior.

One woman remembers:

> When I was 14 and in the 8th grade, I received an award at the end-of-year school assembly. Walking across the stage, I lost my footing and stumbled in front of the entire student body. To be clear, this was not falling flat on one's face, spraining an ankle, or knocking over the school principal—it was a small misstep noticeable only to those in the audience who were paying close attention. As I rushed off the stage, my heart pounded with embarrassment and self-consciousness, and weeks of speculation about the consequence of this missed step were set into motion. There were tears and loss of sleep. Did my friends notice? Would they stop wanting to hang out with me? Would a reputation for clumsiness follow me to high school?
>
> [Somerville, 2013, p. 121]

This woman became an expert on the adolescent brain. She remembered from personal experience that "adolescents are hyperaware of others' evaluations and feel they are under constant scrutiny by an imaginary audience" (Somerville, 2013, p. 124).

Fables

The **personal fable** is the belief that one is unique, destined to have a heroic, fabled, even legendary life. Some 12-year-olds plan to star in the NBA, or to become billionaires, or to cure cancer. Some believe they are destined to die an early, tragic death. For that reason, statistics about smoking, junk food, vaping, or other destructive habits are of no import. One of my young students said "that's just a statistic," dismissing its relevance.

Adolescents markedly overestimate the chance that they will die soon. One study found that teens estimate 1 chance in 5 that they will die before age 20, when in fact the odds are less than 1 in 1,000. Even those most at risk of early death (urban African American males) survive at least to age 20 more than 99 times in 100. Sadly, if adolescents think that they will die young, they are likely to risk jail, HIV, drug addiction, and so on (Haynie et al., 2014). If someone dies, the response is fatalistic ("his number was up"), unaware that a self-fulfilling prophecy was part of the problem.

The personal fable may coexist with the **invincibility fable,** the idea that death will not occur unless it is destined. This is another reason that some adolescents believe that fast driving, unprotected sex, or addictive drugs will do them no harm. In every nation, most army volunteers—hoping for combat—are under age 20. Young recruits take more risks than older, more experienced soldiers (Killgore et al., 2006).

Similarly, teens post comments on Snapchat, Instagram, Facebook, and so on, and they expect others to understand, laugh, admire, or sympathize. Their

imaginary audience The other people who, in an adolescent's egocentric belief, are watching and taking note of his or her appearance, ideas, and behavior. This belief makes many teenagers very self-conscious.

personal fable An aspect of adolescent egocentrism characterized by an adolescent's belief that his or her thoughts, feelings, and experiences are unique, more wonderful, or more awful than anyone else's.

invincibility fable An adolescent's egocentric conviction that he or she cannot be overcome or even harmed by anything that might defeat a normal mortal, such as unprotected sex, drug abuse, or high-speed driving.

Duck, Duck, Goose Far more teens are injured in bicycle accidents than hunting ones, because almost all young people ride bicycles and relatively few are hunters. However, especially when no adult is present, young hunters are less likely to wear blaze orange, to attend safety classes, and to be licensed to hunt. Most likely these boys will return home safe, without the duck they seek. However, guns and off-road vehicles are leading causes of death for those under age 18, so this scene is not a comforting one.

Typical or Extraordinary? Francisca Vasconcelos, a San Diego high school senior, demonstrates formal operational thought. She used origami principles to create a 3D printed robot. She calls herself an "aspiring researcher," and her project won second place in the INTEL 2016 Science Fair. Is she typical of older adolescents, or extraordinarily advanced?

THINK CRITICALLY: How should you judge the validity of the idea of adolescent egocentrism?

formal operational thought In Piaget's theory, the fourth and final stage of cognitive development, characterized by more systematic logical thinking and by the ability to understand and systematically manipulate abstract concepts.

macmillan learning

Video Activity: The Balance Scale Task shows children of various ages completing the task and gives you an opportunity to try it as well.

imaginary audience is other teenagers, not parents, teachers, college admission officers, or future employers who might have another interpretation (boyd, 2014).

Too much can be made of these fables and adolescent egocentrism overall. Indeed, one team of researchers considers adolescent egocentrism a "largely discredited notion" (Laursen & Hartl, 2013, p. 1266). Nonetheless, they and many others find some truth in it.

Formal Operational Thought

Piaget described a shift in early adolescence to **formal operational thought** as adolescents move past concrete operational thinking and consider abstractions, including "assumptions that have no necessary relation to reality" (Piaget, 1950/2001, p. 163). Is Piaget correct? Many educators think so. They adjust the curriculum between primary and secondary school, reflecting a shift from concrete thought to formal, logical thought. Here are three examples:

- *Math.* Younger children multiply real numbers, such as $4 \times 3 \times 8$; adolescents multiply unreal numbers, such as $(2x)(3y)$ or even $(25xy^2)(-3zy^3)$.
- *Social studies.* Younger children study other cultures by considering daily life—drinking goat's milk or building an igloo, for instance. Adolescents consider the effect of GNP (gross national product) and TFR (total fertility rate) on global politics.
- *Science.* Younger students grow carrots and feed gerbils; adolescents study invisible particles and distant galaxies.

Piaget's Experiments

Piaget and his colleagues devised a number of tasks to assess formal operational thought (Inhelder & Piaget, 1958/2013b). In these tasks, "in contrast to concrete operational children, formal operational adolescents imagine all possible determinants . . . [and] systematically vary the factors one by one, observe the results correctly, keep track of the results, and draw the appropriate conclusions" (P. Miller, 2011, p. 57).

One of their experiments (diagrammed in Figure 15.1) required balancing a scale by hooking weights onto the scale's arms. To master this task, a person must realize the reciprocal interaction between distance from the center and heaviness of the weight.

Balancing was not understood by the 3- to 5-year-olds. By age 7, children balanced the scale by putting the same amount of weight on each arm, but they didn't realize that the distance from the center mattered. By age 10, children experimented with the weights, using trial and error, not logic. Finally, by about age 13 or 14, some children hypothesized about reciprocity, realizing that a heavy weight close to the center can be counterbalanced with a light weight far from the center on the other side (Piaget & Inhelder, 1972).

Hypothetical-Deductive Reasoning

One hallmark of formal operational thought is the capacity to think of possibility, not just reality. "Here and now" is only one of many possibilities, including "there and then," "long, long ago," "not yet," and "never." As Piaget said:

> The adolescent . . . thinks beyond the present and forms theories about everything, delighting especially in considerations of that which is not. . . .

[Piaget, 1950/2001, p. 163]

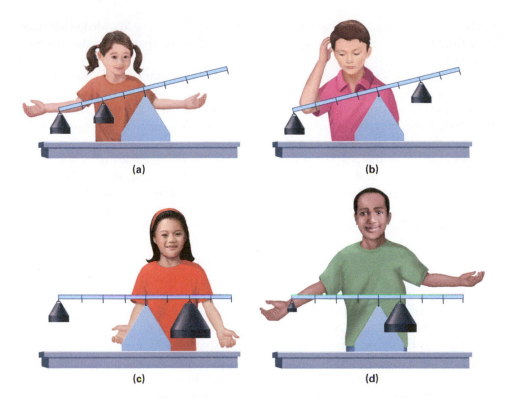

How to Balance a Scale Piaget's balance-scale test of formal reasoning, as it is attempted by *(a)* a 4-year-old, *(b)* a 7-year-old, *(c)* a 10-year-old, and *(d)* a 14-year-old. The key to balancing the scale is to make weight times distance from the center equal on both sides of the center; the realization of that principle requires formal operational thought.

hypothetical thought Reasoning that includes propositions and possibilities that may not reflect reality.

deductive reasoning Reasoning from a general statement, premise, or principle, through logical steps, to figure out (deduce) specifics. (Also called *top-down reasoning*.)

inductive reasoning Reasoning from one or more specific experiences or facts to reach (induce) a general conclusion. (Also called *bottom-up reasoning*.)

Adolescents are therefore primed to engage in **hypothetical thought,** reasoning about *if–then* propositions. Consider the following question, adapted from De Neys & Van Gelder, 2009:

> If all mammals can walk,
> And whales are mammals,
> Can whales walk?

Children answer "No!" They know that whales swim, not walk; the logic escapes them. Some adolescents answer "Yes." They understand the conditional *if,* and therefore the counterfactual phrase "if all mammals."

> *Possibility* no longer appears merely as an extension of an empirical situation or of action actually performed. Instead, it is *reality* that is now secondary to *possibility.*
>
> [*Inhelder & Piaget, 1958/2013b, p. 251; emphasis in original*]

Hypothetical thought transforms perceptions, not necessarily for the better. Adolescents might criticize everything from their mother's spaghetti (it's not *al dente*) to the Gregorian calendar (it's not the Chinese or Jewish one). They criticize what *is* because of their hypothetical thinking about what might be and their growing awareness of other families and cultures (Moshman, 2011).

In developing the capacity to think hypothetically, by age 14 or so adolescents become more capable of **deductive reasoning,** or *top-down reasoning,* which begins with an abstract idea or premise and then uses logic to draw specific conclusions. In the example above, "if all mammals can walk" is a premise. By contrast, **inductive reasoning,** or *bottom-up reasoning,* predominates during the

Triple Winners Sharing the scholarship check of $100,000, these high school students are not only high achievers but also have learned to collaborate within a comprehensive public school (Hewlett). In Long Island, New York. They were taught much more than formal operational logic.

school years, as children accumulate facts and experiences (the knowledge base) to aid their thinking. Since they know whales cannot walk, that knowledge trumps the logic.

In essence, a child's reasoning goes like this: "This creature waddles and quacks. Ducks waddle and quack. Therefore, this must be a duck." This is inductive: It progresses from particulars ("waddles" and "quacks") to a general conclusion ("a duck"). By contrast, deduction progresses from the general to the specific: "If it's a duck, it will waddle and quack."

An example of the progress toward deductive reasoning comes from how children, adolescents, and adults change in their understanding of the causes of racism. Even before adolescence, almost every American is aware that racism exists—and almost everyone opposes it. However, children tend to think the core problem is that some people are prejudiced. Using inductive reasoning, they think that the remedy is to argue against racism when they hear other people express it. By contrast, older adolescents think, deductively, that racism is a society-wide problem that requires policy solutions.

This example arises from a study of adolescent opinions regarding policies to remedy racial discrimination (Hughes & Bigler, 2011). Not surprisingly, most students of all ages in an interracial U.S. high school recognized disparities between African and European Americans and believed that racism was a major cause.

However, the age of the students made a difference. Among those who recognized marked inequalities, older adolescents (ages 16 to 17) more often supported systemic solutions (e.g., affirmative action and desegregation) than did younger adolescents (ages 14 to 15). Hughes and Bigler wrote: "[D]uring adolescence, cognitive development facilitates the understanding that discrimination exists at the social-systemic level . . . [and] racial awareness begins to inform views of race-conscious policies during middle adolescence" (2011, p. 489).

As you know from previous chapters, many researchers have criticized Piaget's description of the stages of cognition. Many also criticize his description of formal operational thinking. Nonetheless, something shifts in cognition after puberty. Piaget was correct in recognizing that many older adolescents think more logically and hypothetically than most children do.

● **Especially for Natural Scientists** Some ideas that were once universally accepted, such as the belief that the sun moved around Earth, have been disproved. Is it a failure of inductive or deductive reasoning that leads to false conclusions? (see response, page 415)

WHAT HAVE YOU LEARNED?

1. How does adolescent egocentrism differ from early-childhood egocentrism?
2. What perceptions arise from belief in the imaginary audience?
3. Why are the personal fable and the invincibility fable called "fables"?
4. What are the practical implications of adolescent cognition?
5. What are the advantages of using inductive rather than deductive reasoning?

Two Modes of Thinking

Advanced logic in adolescence is counterbalanced by the increasing power of intuition. Most cognitive psychologists recognize that thinking occurs in two ways, called **dual processing.** The terms and descriptions of these two modes of thought vary, including intuitive/analytic, implicit/explicit, creative/factual, contextualized/decontextualized, unconscious/conscious, gist/quantitative, emotional/intellectual, experiential/rational, hot/cold, systems 1 and 2. Although they interact and can overlap, each mode is independent (Kuhn, 2013) (see Visualizing Development, page 414).

dual processing The notion that two networks exist within the human brain, one for emotional processing of stimuli and one for analytical reasoning.

The thinking described by the first half of each pair is easier and quicker, preferred in everyday life. Sometimes, however, circumstances necessitate the second mode, when deeper thought is demanded. The discrepancy between the maturation of the limbic system and the prefrontal cortex reflects this duality. [**Life-Span Link:** Timing differences in maturation of various parts of the brain are discussed in Chapter 14.]

Dual Processing During Development

To some extent, both modes of thinking reflect inborn temperament. Most children who are impulsive by nature learn to regulate their reactions in childhood, but a dual-processing perspective suggests that regulation may break down during adolescence (Henderson et al., 2015).

In describing adolescent cognition, we use the terms *intuitive* and *analytic,* defined as follows:

- **Intuitive thought** begins with a belief, assumption, or general rule (called a *heuristic*) rather than logic. Intuition is quick and powerful; it feels "right."
- **Analytic thought** is the formal, logical, hypothetical-deductive thinking described by Piaget. It involves rational analysis of many factors whose interactions must be calculated, as in the scale-balancing problem.

Examples of Dual Processing

When the two modes of thinking conflict, people of all ages sometimes use one and sometimes the other: We are all "predictably irrational" at times (Ariely, 2010), but adolescent brains are increasingly myelinated, which makes thought occur with lightning speed. That may make them "fast and furious" intuitive thinkers, unlike their teachers and parents, who prefer slower, analytic thinking. The result: "people who interact with adolescents often are frustrated by the mercurial quality of their decisions" (Hartley & Somerville, 2015, p. 112).

To test yourself on intuitive and analytic thinking, answer the following:

1. A bat and a ball cost $1.10 in total. The bat costs $1 more than the ball. How much does the ball cost?
2. If it takes 5 minutes for 5 machines to make 5 widgets, how long would it take 100 machines to make 100 widgets?
3. In a lake, there is a patch of lily pads. Every day the patch doubles in size. If it takes 48 days for the patch to cover the entire lake, how long would it take for the patch to cover half the lake?

[From Gervais & Norenzayan, 2012, p. 494]

Answers are on page 416. As you see, the quick, intuitive responses may be wrong.

Paul Klaczynski conducted dozens of studies comparing the thinking of children, young adolescents, and older adolescents (usually 9-, 12-, and 15-year-olds) (Holland & Klaczynski, 2009; Klaczynski, 2001, 2011; Klaczynski et al., 2009). Variation in thinking was evident at every age.

Klaczynski reports that almost every adolescent is analytical and logical on some problems but not on others, with some passing the same questions that others fail. As they grow older, adolescents sometimes gain in logic and sometimes regress, with the social context and training in statistics becoming major influences on cognition (Klaczynski & Felmban, 2014).

intuitive thought Thought that arises from an emotion or a hunch, beyond rational explanation, and is influenced by past experiences and cultural assumptions.

analytic thought Thought that results from analysis, such as a systematic ranking of pros and cons, risks and consequences, possibilities and facts. Analytic thought depends on logic and rationality.

Impressive Connections This robot is about to compete in the Robotics Competition in Atlanta, Georgia, but much more impressive are the brains of the Oregon high school team (including Melissa, shown here) who designed the robot.

● **Observation Quiz** Melissa seems to be working by herself, but what sign do you see that suggests she is part of a team who built this robot? (see answer, page 415) ↑

Thinking in Adolescence

We are able to think both intuitively and analytically, but adolescents tend to rely more on intuitive thinking than do adults.

INDUCTIVE vs. DEDUCTIVE REASONING

INDUCTIVE: Conclusion reached after many of the following. Note that the problem is that the adolescent's nimble mind can rationalize many specifics. Only when the evidence is overwhelming is the conclusion reached.

DEDUCTIVE: The principle is the starting point, not the end point.

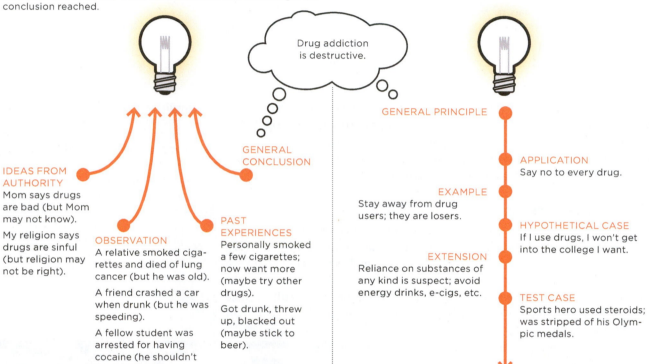

Drug addiction is destructive.

GENERAL CONCLUSION

IDEAS FROM AUTHORITY
Mom says drugs are bad (but Mom may not know).

My religion says drugs are sinful (but religion may not be right).

OBSERVATION
A relative smoked cigarettes and died of lung cancer (but he was old).

A friend crashed a car when drunk (but he was speeding).

A fellow student was arrested for having cocaine (he shouldn't have carried it).

PAST EXPERIENCES
Personally smoked a few cigarettes; now want more (maybe try other drugs).

Got drunk, threw up, blacked out (maybe stick to beer).

GENERAL PRINCIPLE

APPLICATION
Say no to every drug.

EXAMPLE
Stay away from drug users; they are losers.

HYPOTHETICAL CASE
If I use drugs, I won't get into the college I want.

EXTENSION
Reliance on substances of any kind is suspect; avoid energy drinks, e-cigs, etc.

TEST CASE
Sports hero used steroids; was stripped of his Olympic medals.

CHANGES IN AGE

INTUITIVE THINKING

ANALYTICAL THINKING

age

YOUNGER

OLDER

This singer is cute and fun = I'll listen to her

This singer is very popular
+ She sometimes writes her own songs
+ She makes creative videos
+ I agree with her morals = I'll listen to her music

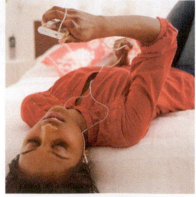

As people age, their thinking tends to move from intuitive processing to more analytic processing. Virtually all cognitive psychologists note these two alternative processes and describe a developmental progression toward more dispassionate logic with maturity. However, the terms used and the boundaries between the two vary. They are roughly analogous to Kahneman's System 1 (which "operates automatically and quickly") and System 2 ("the conscious, reasoning self") (Kahneman, 2011, pp. 20–21), as well as to the traditional distinction between inductive and deductive reasoning, and to Piaget's concrete operational versus formal operational thought. Although experts vary in their descriptions, and individuals vary in when and how they use these two processes, overall adolescents tend to favor intuitive rather than analytic thinking.

In dozens of studies, being smarter as measured by an intelligence test does not advance logic as much as having more experience, in school and in life. Using statistics and respecting experts helps adolescents think rationally—but they do not always do so (Kail, 2013). Even though teenagers *can* use logic, sometimes stereotypes grow stronger, and then "social variables are better predictors of age differences in heuristics and biases than cognitive abilities" (Klaczynski & Felmban, 2014, pp. 103–104). Competence (i.e., intellectual ability) does not always predict performance.

Preferring Emotions

Why not use formal operational thinking? Klaczynski's young adolescents had all learned the scientific method in school, so they knew that scientists use empirical evidence and deductive reasoning. But they did not always think like scientists. Why not?

Dozens of experiments and extensive theorizing have found some answers (Albert & Steinberg, 2011). Essentially, logic is more difficult than intuition, and it requires questioning ideas that are comforting and familiar. Once people of any age reach an emotional conclusion (sometimes called a "gut feeling"), they resist changing their minds. Prejudice is not seen as prejudice; people develop reasons to support their feelings.

As people gain experience in making decisions and thinking things through, they may become better at knowing when analysis is needed (Milkman et al., 2009). For example, in contrast to younger students, when judging whether a rule is legitimate, older adolescents are more suspicious of authority and more likely to consider mitigating circumstances (Klaczynski, 2011). That may be wise—sometimes.

Both suspicion of authority and awareness of context advance reasoning, but both also complicate simple issues or lead to impulsive but destructive actions. Indeed, suspicion of authority may propel adolescents to respond illogically. One of my students quoted a Supreme Court decision to a police officer who was about to arrest her cousin. When the officer grabbed her cousin, she bit his hand—and spent months in jail. [Then I appeared in court on her behalf; the judge released her because he listened to me but not to her, an example of the "social variables" that Klaczynski describes.]

That example may be an outlier, but similar results were found in a longitudinal survey that repeatedly queried more than 7,000 adolescents, beginning at age 12 and ending at age 24, about their ideas, activities, and plans. The results were "consistent with neurobiological research indicating that cortical regions involved in impulse control and planning continue to mature through early adulthood [and that] subcortical regions that respond to emotional novelty and reward are more responsive in middle adolescence than in either children or adults" (Harden & Tucker-Drob, 2011, p. 743).

Specifically, this longitudinal survey traced sensation seeking (e.g., "I enjoy new and exciting experiences") from early adolescence to the mid-20s. Increases were notable from ages 12 to 14 (see Figure 15.2). Sensation seeking leads to intuitive thinking, direct from the gut to the brain. The researchers also studied impulsivity, as indicated by agreement with statements such as "I often get in a jam because I do things without thinking." A decline in impulsive action occurred more gradually as analytic thinking increased.

Response for Natural Scientists (from page 412): Probably both. Our false assumptions are not logically tested because we do not realize that they might need testing.

Answer to Observation Quiz (from page 413): The flag on the robot matches her T-shirt. Often teenagers wear matching shirts to signify their joint identity.

THINK CRITICALLY: When might an emotional response to a problem be better than an analytic one?

FIGURE 15.2

Look Before You Leap As you can see, adolescents become less impulsive as they mature, but they still enjoy the thrill of a new sensation.

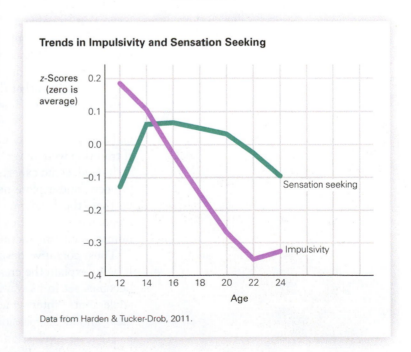

Trends in Impulsivity and Sensation Seeking

Data from Harden & Tucker-Drob, 2011.

Answers	Intuitive	Analytic
1.	10 cents	5 cents
2.	100 minutes	5 minutes
3.	24 days	47 days

On average, sensation seeking accelerated rapidly at puberty, and both sensation seeking and impulsivity slowly declined with maturation. However, trajectories varied individually: Sensation seeking did not necessarily correlate with impulsivity. Thus, biology (the HPA axis) is not necessarily linked to experience (the prefrontal cortex) (Harden & Tucker-Drob, 2011). Both affect behavior: Risky sex correlates with sensation seeking and with impulsivity (Charnigo et al., 2013), but each has an independent impact.

My student was past the age of peak sensation seeking, and as a girl, she had less testosterone (which fuels sensation seeking) than a boy might have. In her education, she had gained a formal understanding of the laws regarding arrest. However, she was still impulsive.

Better Thinking

Sometimes adults conclude that more mature thought processes are wiser. The judge thought that I understood things about the police that my student did not. Many adults conclude that irrational thinking leads impulsive teenagers to risk addiction by using drugs or to risk pregnancy and HIV/AIDS by not using a condom.

But adults may themselves be egocentric in making such judgments if they assume that adolescents share their values. Parents want healthy, long-lived children, so they blame faulty reasoning when adolescents risk their lives. Judges want law-abiding citizens. Adolescents, however, value social warmth and friendship, and their hormones and brains are more attuned to those values than to long-term consequences (Crone & Dahl, 2012).

A 15-year-old who is offered a cigarette, for example, might rationally choose peer acceptance and the possibility of romance over the distant risk of cancer. Think of a teenager who wants to be "cool" or "bad," and then decide whether he or she might say, "No, thank you, my mother told me not to smoke."

Furthermore, weighing alternatives and thinking of future possibilities can be paralyzing. The systematic, analytic thought that Piaget described is slow and costly, not fast and frugal, wasting precious time when a young person wants to act. Some risks are taken impulsively, and that is not always bad.

On average, logic increases from adolescence to adulthood (and then decreases somewhat in old age) (De Neys & Van Gelder, 2009; Kuhn, 2013). Always, however, the specific context, including superstitions and assumptions, makes a difference: We cannot assume that adolescent decisions are better than, or worse than, those of either children or adults (Furlan et al., 2013). It is not that they do not know better; it is that they evaluate differently (Hartley & Somerville, 2015).

Societies need some people who question assumptions, and adolescents are primed to question everything, often raising issues that need to be raised. As social and ecological circumstances change, someone needs to question traditions. If tradition were never questioned, customs would ossify, and societies would die.

Indeed, some experts suggest that the adolescent impulse to take risks, respond to peers, and explore new ideas is adaptive in some contexts (Ernst, 2016). It may be that "the fundamental task of adolescence—to achieve adult levels of social competence—requires a great deal of learning about the social complexities of human social interactions" (Peper & Dahl, 2013, p. 135).

Thus, cognitive development in adolescence "confers benefits as well as risks. It helps explain the creativity of adolescence and early adulthood, before the brain becomes set in its ways" (Monastersky, 2007, p. A17). The emotional intensity of adolescents "intertwines with the highest levels of human endeavor: passion for ideas and ideals, passion for beauty, passion to create music and art" (Dahl, 2004, p. 21). One application: Since adolescents are learning life lessons, adults need to ensure that those lessons are positive ones.

Impulses, Rewards, and Reflection

The brain maturation process described in Chapter 14 is directly related to the dual processes just explained. Because the limbic system is activated by puberty while the prefrontal cortex is "developmentally constrained," maturing more gradually, adolescents are swayed by their intuition instead of by analysis (Hartley & Somerville, 2015, p. 109).

One specific is that the connection between the ventral striatum and the prefrontal cortex changes during puberty, and that increases risk taking. Hormones, especially testosterone (rapidly increasing in boys but also increasing less dramatically in girls), fuel new adolescent emotional impulses (Peper & Dahl, 2013). According to one review, many studies confirm that adolescents show "heightened activity in the striatum, both when anticipating rewards and when receiving rewards" (Crone et al., 2016, p. 360).

In choosing between a small but guaranteed reward and a large, possible reward, adolescent brains show more activity for the larger reward than the brains of children or adults. This means that when teenagers weigh the possible results of a particular risky action, their brains make them more inclined to imagine success than to fear failure. Whether this makes them brave and bold or foolish and careless is a matter of judgment, but the judge should know that neurological circuits tip the balance toward action.

Another crucial aspect of adolescent brains is that social rejection by peers is deeply felt, with activation throughout the limbic system as well as other subcortical areas. Social impulses are crucial for humans lifelong, but the brain is sensitive to particular kinds at particular ages (Nelson et al., 2016). Thus, mother rejection is especially hurtful in infancy, as is a breakup with a romantic partner in emerging adulthood. Adolescents are particularly sensitive to peer rejection

Neurological sensitivity may explain why teens readily follow impulses that promise social approval from friends. In experiments in which adults and adolescents, alone or with peers, play video games in which taking risks might lead to crashes or gaining points, adolescents are much more likely than adults are to risk crashing, especially when they are with peers. There are notable differences in brain activity (specifically in the ventral striatum) between adolescents and adults. When they are with other adults, the adults' brains give more signals of caution (inhibition)—opposite to adolescents' brains when they are with peers (Albert et al., 2013) (see Figure 15.3).

This peer influence is apparent in both sexes but is stronger in boys—particularly when they are with other boys (de Boer et al., 2016). This explains why boys die accidental deaths during adolescence twice as often as girls, and why deaths per motor-vehicle crash are much higher in adolescence than later

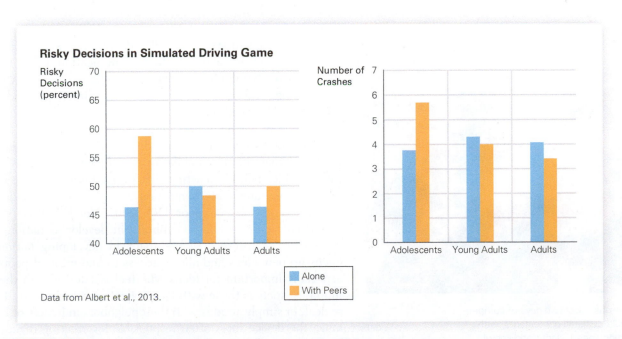

Data from Albert et al., 2013.

FIGURE 15.3

Losing Is Winning In this game, risk taking led to more crashes and fewer points. As you see, adolescents were strongly influenced by the presence of peers, so much so that they lost points they would have kept if they had played alone. In fact, sometimes they laughed when they crashed instead of bemoaning their loss. Note the contrast with emerging adults, who were more likely to take risks when alone.

on. Teenage drivers like to fill (or overfill) their cars with teen passengers who will admire them for speeding, passing trucks, beating trains at railroad crossings, and so on. Of course, that is not true for every young driver, but the number of passengers injured per driver is highest for passengers aged 15 to 17 (Bergen et al., 2014).

This impulse is aided by a third brain change in adolescence. Compared to children, there is a substantial increase in myelination between the emotional and action parts of the brain. This increase in white matter means rapid responses. As a result, adolescents act before slower-thinking adults can stop them (Hartley & Somerville, 2015).

Don't blame teen crashes on inexperience; blame it on the brain. Some states now prohibit teen drivers from transporting other teenagers, reducing deaths and banning one source of adolescent excitement. Teens advocate some laws, such as those that protect the environment; they do not advocate this one.

WHAT HAVE YOU LEARNED?

1. When might intuition and analysis lead to contrasting conclusions?

2. What mode of thinking—intuitive or analytic—do most people prefer, and why?

3. How might intuitive thinking increase risk taking?

4. How does egocentrism account for the clashing priorities of parents and adolescents?

5. When is intuitive thinking better than analytic thinking?

Digital Natives

Adults over age 50 grew up without the Internet, instant messaging, Twitter, blogs, cell phones, smartphones, MP3 players, tablets, 3-D printers, or digital cameras. At first, the Internet was only for the military and then primarily for businesses and the educated elite. Until 2006, only students at a few highly selective colleges could join Facebook.

In contrast, today's teenagers have been called *digital natives*, although if that implies that they know everything about digital communication, it is a misnomer (boyd, 2014). No doubt, however, adolescents have been networking, texting, and clicking for definitions, directions, and data all their lives. Their cell phones are always nearby.

Not All Thumbs After two days of competition among 22 qualified contestants, with tests of texting speed, clarity, and knowledge, 15-year-old Kate Moore of Des Moines, Iowa, was declared champion. She won a trophy and $50,000. She has texted hundreds of friends for years.

Connection to peers has always been important to teenagers, and has always been feared by adults—who in earlier generations predicted that the automobile, or the shopping mall, or rock and roll would lead children astray. A huge gap between those with and without computers was bemoaned a decade ago; it divided boys from girls and rich from poor (Dijk, 2005; Norris, 2001). No longer.

Virtually every school and library in developed nations is connected to the Internet, as are many in developing nations. This opens up new ideas and allows access to like-minded people, both especially important for teens who feel isolated within their communities, such as those with Down syndrome, or who are LGBTQ, or deaf, or simply at odds with their neighbors in beliefs or behavior.

As costs tumble, the device most often responsible for creating digital natives among low-SES adolescents of every ethnic group is the smartphone, used primarily to connect with friends (Madden et al., 2013). African American and Latino American teenagers are more likely than European American teens to say they are online "almost constantly" (34 percent, 32 percent, 19 percent) (Lenhart, 2015, p. 2).

Although discrepancies in number and quality of devices still follow SES lines, the most notable divide is now age: Each older generation is less likely to use the Internet than the next younger one. That may explain why people bemoaning the effects of technology on adolescent minds tend to be over age 50.

Technology and Cognition

In general, educators accept—even welcome—students' facility with technology. In many high schools, teachers use laptops, smartphones, and so on as tools for learning. In some districts, students are required to take at least one class completely online. There are "virtual" schools in which students earn all of their credits via the Internet, never entering a school building, and school districts that give everyone a tablet instead of a textbook.

Some programs and games have been designed for high school classes. For example, 10 teachers were taught how to use a game (Mission Biotech) to teach genetics and molecular biology. Their students—even in advanced classes but especially in general education—scored higher on tests of the standard biology curriculum than students who did not use the game (Sadler et al., 2013). It seems that, when carefully used, computer games enhance learning.

Most secondary students check facts, read explanations, view videos, and thus grasp concepts they would not have understood without technology. Almost every high school student in the United States uses the Internet for research, finding it quicker and its range of information more extensive than books on library shelves. And for some adolescents, the Internet is their only source of information about health and sex.

We already know from research before the technology explosion that instruction, practice, conversation, and experience within the zone of proximal development advance adolescent thought. Technology does not change that, although it may speed up the process. It also may subvert some kinds of learning. It encourages rapid shifts of attention, multitasking without reflection, and visual learning instead of invisible analysis (Greenfield, 2009).

A major concern is that adolescents do not evaluate what they see on the screen as carefully as they should; nor do they pause to consider the implications of a message they send on impulse. Messages endure and can be seen by hundreds, sometimes thousands, of unintended recipients, sometimes with unanticipated harm to others or oneself (boyd, 2014).

Sexual Abuse?

Parents worry about sexual abuse via the Internet. Research is reassuring: Although predators lurk online, most teens never encounter them. Sexual abuse is a serious problem, but if sexual abuse is defined as a perverted older stranger taking technological advantage of an innocent teen, it is "extremely rare" (Mitchell et al., 2013, p. 1226).

Between 2000 and 2010, the number of teenagers online rose dramatically, but the percentage of those who say that someone online tried to get them to talk about sex declined from 10 percent in 2000 to 1 percent in 2010. Those 1 percent were almost always solicited by another young person whom the teenager knew in person—a Facebook friend, for instance (Mitchell et al., 2013). Teenagers are actually more suspicious of strangers than they were before the Internet, and perhaps not suspicious enough of friends, coaches, clergy, and relatives.

Of course, abuse can be devastating. Ten years out of high school, adolescent bullies and victims—online or offline, sexual or otherwise—are less likely to have

Something Worth Sharing But what is it? Is it the same as boys everywhere, or is it something specific to their culture? The four are in England: We do not know if they see a football (soccer) score, a prime minister's proclamation, or a sexy female.

FIGURE 15.4

Access or Addiction? As we know from research on substance use disorder, use is not necessarily addiction. As you see, teenagers have no trouble accessing video games, and most decide to play. When does play become a compulsion, no longer a choice?

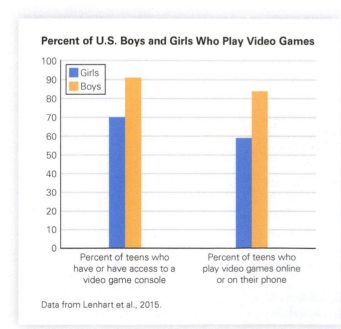

Percent of U.S. Boys and Girls Who Play Video Games

Data from Lenhart et al., 2015.

graduated from high school or college and less likely to have good jobs or any job at all (Sigurdson et al., 2014). Parents and teachers need to worry less about online strangers and more about teens who victimize each other.

Sexual abuse is one of the main reasons that more than half of all parents restrict their 13- to 17-year-olds' technology use. More than 90 percent of parents discuss online behavior and appropriate Web sites with their teenagers, and "nearly half (48%) of parents know the password to their teen's email account, while 43% know the password to their teen's cell phone and 35% know the password to at least one of their teen's social media accounts" (Anderson, 2016, p. 3).

Virtually all teenagers use social media, and those in romantic relationships usually flirt online. But most of their romantic relationships begin in person, with only 6 percent of 13- to 17-year olds ever having had a romantic relationship that began online. If the sexual aspect of a relationship makes them uncomfortable, they block the sender or unfriend them (Lenhart et al., 2015).

Although teenagers enjoy staying in touch with their dating partners via the Internet—and most do it several times a day—when the relationship ends, sometimes it turns ugly. Of those who have broken up with a dating partner, 15 percent report being threatened online and 5 percent report being pressured to engage in sexual activity they did not want (Lenhart et al., 2015).

Addiction

For some adolescents, chat rooms, message boards, video games, and Internet gambling undercut active play, schoolwork, and friendship—a worldwide problem (Tang et al., 2014). A study of almost 2,000 older children and adolescents in the United States found that the *average* person played video games two hours a day. Some played much more, and only 3 percent of the boys and 21 percent of the girls never played (Gentile, 2011) (see Figure 15.4). Almost all (92 percent) 13- to 17-year-olds in the United States go online every day, and 24 percent say they are online "almost constantly" (Lenhart, 2015, p. 16).

When do these tendencies become truly addictive as opposed to normal teen behavior? Many adolescents in the first survey admit that video game playing takes time away from household chores and homework. Worse, one-fourth used video games to escape from problems, and one-fifth had "done poorly on a school assignment or test" because of spending too much time on video games. The heaviest users got lower school grades and had more physical fights than did the average users (Gentile, 2011).

Using criteria for addiction developed by psychiatrists for other addictions (gambling, drugs, and so on), an estimated 3 percent of U.S. adolescents suffer from Internet addiction, almost always with other disorders as well (Jorgenson et al., 2016) (see Table 15.1). Those rates are low according to research in other nations, with rates of 15 percent in Turkey, 12 percent in India, 22 percent in Hong Kong (Şaşmaz et al., 2014; Yadav et al., 2013; Shek & Yu, 2016).

Reviewing research from many nations, one team of researchers reports addiction rates from 0 to 26 percent. The variation was caused more by differing definitions and procedures among researchers than by differences among students in any particular place (Y. Lee et al., 2015).

TABLE 15.1	Signs of Substance Use Disorder
In General	**How It Might Apply to Internet Addiction***
1. Impairs desired activity and accomplishment, notable in failed personal goals and broken promises to oneself.	1. Person denies, or lies about, how much time is spent online, which interferes with study, homework completion, household chores, or job-related concentration.
2. Normal cognitive processes—memory, motivation, logic—are impaired.	2. Person is less able to think deeply and analytically, or to remember things not on line, such as personal phone numbers, appointment times.
3. Social interactions disrupted, either disconnections when in a social group, or isolation from other people.	3. Person spends less time with family, face-to-face communication with friends. Person ignores social interactions to check texts.
4. Basic body maintenance and health disturbed, such as loss of sleep, changed appetite, hygiene.	4. Person does not remember or care to do usual health maintaining activities, internet interferes with sleep, healthy eating, and so on.
5. Withdrawal symptoms: person is agitated, physically or mentally, when unable to attain substance.	5. Person is angry or depressed when internet not available, as when cell phones are banned from class, or parents restrict use, or connections broken.
6. Increasing dependence: Need for substance or activity increases over time, as brain patterns change.	6. Person increases time spent; wants more devices (laptop, watch, tablet).

*This list is speculative. DSM-5 finds insufficient evidence of Internet addiction, and does not use the word "addiction" because of "uncertain definition and potentially negative connotation" (American Psychiatric Association, 2013, p. 485).

Remember that correlation is not causation, so perhaps low school achievement, depression, aggression, and so on lead to video game playing and social media obsession rather than vice versa. Some scholars worry that adults tend to pathologize normal teen behavior, particularly in China, where rehabilitation centers are strict—some would say abusive—in keeping teenagers from Internet use (Bax, 2014).

Most screen time occurs in the child's own bedroom. About half of all parents place no restrictions on technology use, as long as their adolescent is safe at home. Other parents place many restrictions on their children—not only regarding technology but also on contact with peers, either at home or in a public place (such as a movie theater or store). To socialize, their children may log in privately (boyd, 2014).

Whether extensive use of the Internet qualifies as an addiction is controversial. The psychiatrists who wrote the DSM-5, after careful consideration of the evidence, did not include it as an addiction. Instead, they wrote that further study was needed.

Cyber Danger

Now we consider an Internet use that everyone agrees is harmful and seems most real: **cyberbullying,** when electronic devices are used to harass someone, with rumors, lies, embarrassing truths, or threats. Cyberbullies are usually already bullies

cyberbullying Bullying that occurs when one person spreads insults or rumors about another by means of social media posts, e-mails, text messages, or cell phone videos.

Consequences Unknown Few adolescents think about the consequences of their impulsive rage, responses, or retorts on social media or smartphones. This educator at a community center tries to explain that victims can be devastated—rarely suicidal, but often depressed.

or victims or both, with bully-victims especially likely to engage in, and suffer from, cyberbullying. [**Life-Span Link:** Bullying is discussed in Chapter 13.]

Worst in Adolescence

Technology does not create bullies, but it allows another means to act and a larger audience, expanding the hurt (Giumetti & Kowalski, 2015). Texted and posted rumors and insults can reach thousands, day and night, with shame magnified by the imaginary audience. Photos and videos of someone drunk, naked, or crying can be easily sent to dozens of others, who may send it further or post it on public sites for anyone to see. Since young adolescents act quickly without reflection, cyberbullying is particularly prevalent and thoughtlessly cruel between ages 11 and 14.

Cyberbullying is most damaging when the self-concept is fragile, when sexual impulses are new, and when impulsive thoughts precede analytic ones—all of which characterize many young adolescents. The most serious consequence is deep depression, added to the typical rise in depression at puberty. In extreme cases, cyberbullying may trigger suicide (Bonanno & Hymel, 2013; Geoffroy et al., 2016).

The school climate is a powerful antidote for cyberbullying (Guo, 2016). When students consider school a good place to be—with supportive teachers, friendly students, opportunities for growth (clubs, sports, theater, music), and the like—those with high self-esteem are less likely to engage in cyberbullying. They not only disapprove of it, they stop it by blocking bullies and deleting messages. However, when the school climate is negative, those with high self-esteem may become bullies (Gendron et al., 2011).

A complication is that adolescents may be too trusting of technology while many adults are ignorant about possibilities and protection. Few parental actions and school policies successfully prevent it. However, it not only harms individuals but can also poison the school climate. Adolescents need more protection than most adults realize (boyd, 2014).

Sexting

sexting Sending sexual content, particularly photos or videos, via cell phones or social media.

The vulnerability of adolescence was tragically evident in the suicide of a California 15-year-old, Audrie Pott (Sulek, 2013). At a weekend sleepover, Audrie and her friends found alcohol. She got so drunk that she blacked out, or passed out. The next Monday, three boys in her school bragged that they had had sex with her, showing pictures to classmates. The next weekend, Audrie hanged herself. Only then did her parents and teachers learn what had happened.

One aspect of this tragedy will not surprise adolescents: **sexting,** as sending sexual photographs is called. As many as 30 percent of adolescents report having received sexting photos, with marked variation by school, gender, and ethnicity and often in attitude: Many teens send their own sexy "selfies" and are happy to receive sext messages (Temple et al., 2014). Of those in romantic relationships, 63 percent have sent flirtatious messages online, and 23 percent have sent sexual pictures or videos (Lenhart et al., 2015). As with Internet addiction, researchers have yet to agree on how to measure sexting or how harmful it is and for whom.

Two dangers are evident: (1) Pictures may be forwarded without the naked person's knowledge, and (2) senders of erotic self-images risk serious depression if the reaction is not what they wished (Temple et al., 2014). Remember that body image formation is crucial during early adolescence and that many teens have distorted self-concepts and unrealistic fantasies—no wonder sexting is fraught with trouble.

Other Hazards

Internet connections allow troubled adolescents to connect with others who share their prejudices and self-destructive obsessions, such as anorexia or cutting. The people they connect with are those who confirm and inform their twisted cognition. This is another reason that parents and teachers need to continue their close relationships with their adolescents. Note the absence of adults at Audrie's alcohol-fueled sleepover, rape, cyberbullying, and suicide.

The danger of technology lies not in the equipment but in the mind. As is true of many aspects of adolescence (puberty, brain development, egocentric thought, contraception, and so on), context, adults, peers, and the adolescent's own personality and temperament "shape, mediate, and/or modify effects" of technology (Oakes, 2009, p. 1142).

One careful observer claims that, instead of being *native* users of technology, many teenagers are *naive* users—believing they have privacy settings that they do not have, trusting sites that are markedly biased, misunderstanding how to search for and verify information (boyd, 2014). Educators can help with all of this—but only if they themselves understand technology and teens.

Teens are intuitive, impulsive, and egocentric, often unaware of the impact of what they send, overestimating the validity of what they read, choosing immediate attraction over eventual gain. Adults should know better.

> **THINK CRITICALLY:** The older people are, the more likely they are to be critical of social media. Is that wisdom or ignorance? Why?

WHAT HAVE YOU LEARNED?

1. What benefits come from adolescents' use of technology?
2. Why is adult fear of online adult predators exaggerated?
3. How do video games affect student learning?
4. Who is most apt and least apt to be involved in cyberbullying?
5. Why might sexting be a problem?
6. How might the term "digital native" be misleading?

Secondary Education

What does our knowledge of adolescent thought imply about school? Educators, developmentalists, political leaders, and parents wonder exactly which curricula and school structures are best for 11- to 18-year-olds. There are dozens of options: academic/skills, single-sex/co-ed, competitive/cooperative, large/small, public/private, charter/voucher, and more.

To complicate matters, adolescents are far from a homogeneous group. As a result,

> some youth thrive at school—enjoying and benefiting from most of their experiences there; others muddle along and cope as best they can with the stress and demands of the moment; and still others find school an alienating and unpleasant place to be.

[*Eccles & Roeser, 2011, p. 225*]

Given all of these variations, no school structure or pedagogy is best for everyone. Various scientists, nations, schools, and teachers try many strategies, some based on opposite but logical hypotheses. To begin to analyze this complexity, we present definitions, facts, issues, and possibilities.

Definitions and Facts

Each year of school advances human potential, a fact recognized by leaders and scholars in every nation and discipline. As you have read, adolescents are capable of deep and wide-ranging thought, no longer limited by concrete experience, yet they are often egocentric and impulsive. Quality matters: A year can propel thinking forward or can have little impact (Hanushek & Woessmann, 2010).

secondary education Literally, the period after primary education (elementary or grade school) and before tertiary education (college). It usually occurs from about ages 12 to 18, although there is some variation by school and by nation.

Secondary education—traditionally grades 7 through 12—denotes the school years after elementary or grade school (known as *primary education*) and before college or university (known as *tertiary education*). Adults are healthier and wealthier if they complete primary education, learning to read and write, and then continue on through secondary and tertiary education. This is true within nations and between them.

Even cigarette smoking by European American adults—seemingly unrelated to education—is almost three times as common among those with no high school diploma than it is among those with bachelor's degrees (40 percent versus 14 percent, respectively) (National Center for Health Statistics, 2016). This is typical: Data on almost every condition, from every nation and ethnic group, confirm that high school and college graduation correlates with better health, wealth, and family life. Some reasons are indirectly related to education (e.g., income and place of residence), but even when poverty and toxic neighborhoods are equalized, education confers benefits.

Partly because political leaders recognize that educated adults advance national wealth and health, every nation is increasing the number of students in secondary schools. Education is compulsory until at least age 12 almost everywhere, and new high schools and colleges open daily in developing nations. The two most populous countries, China and India, are characterized by massive growth in education.

In many nations, two levels of secondary education are provided. Traditionally, secondary education was divided into junior high (usually grades 7 and 8) and senior

Now Learn This Educators and parents disagree among themselves about how and what middle school children need to learn. Accordingly, some parents send their children to a school where biology is taught via dissecting a squid *(left)*, others where obedience is taught via white shirts and lining up *(right)*.

Observation Quiz Although the philosophy and strategy of these two schools are quite different, both share one aspect of the hidden curriculum, what is it? (see answer, page 426)

high (usually grades 9 through 12). As the average age of puberty declined, **middle schools** were created for grades 5 or 6 through 8.

Middle School

Adjusting to middle school is bound to be stressful, as teachers, classmates, and expectations all change. Regarding learning, "researchers and theorists commonly view early adolescence as an especially sensitive developmental period" (McGill et al., 2012, p. 1003). Yet many developmentalists find middle schools to be "developmentally regressive" (Eccles & Roeser, 2010, p. 13), which means learning goes backward.

Increasing Behavioral Problems

For many middle school students, academic achievement slows down and behavioral problems increase. Puberty itself is part of the problem. At least for other animals studied, especially when they are under stress, learning is reduced at puberty (McCormick et al., 2010).

For people, the biological and psychological stresses of puberty are not the only reason learning suffers in early adolescence. Cognition matters, too: How much new middle school students like their school affects how much they learn (Riglin et al., 2013). This applies to students of every ethnic group, with declines in academics particularly steep for young adolescents of ethnic minorities as they become more aware of low social expectations for them (Dotterer et al., 2009; McGill et al., 2012; Hayes et al., 2015).

Even if there were no discrimination in the larger society, students have reasons to dislike middle school. Bullying is common, particularly in the first year (Baly et al., 2014). Parents are less involved than in primary school, partly because students want more independence. Unlike primary school, when each classroom had one teacher, middle school teachers have hundreds of students. They become impersonal and distant, opposite to the direct, personal engagement that young adolescents need (Meece & Eccles, 2010).

> **middle school** A school for children in the grades between elementary school and high school. Middle school usually begins with grade 6 and ends with grade 8.

> ●● **Especially for Teachers** You are stumped by a question your student asks. What do you do? (see response, page 427)

A CASE TO STUDY

James, the High-Achieving Dropout

A longitudinal study in Massachusetts followed children from preschool through high school. James was one of the most promising. In his early school years, he was an excellent reader whose mother took great pride in him, her only child. Once James entered middle school, however, something changed:

> Although still performing well academically, James began acting out. At first his actions could be described as merely mischievous, but later he engaged in much more serious acts, such as drinking and fighting, which resulted in his being suspended from school.
>
> [Snow et al., 2007, p. 59]

Family problems increased. James and his father blamed each other for their poor relationship, and his mother bragged "about how independent James was for being able to be left alone to fend for himself," while James said that other students were afraid of him but still associated with him. He "described himself as isolated and closed off" (Snow et al., 2007, p. 59).

James's experience is not unusual. Generally, aggressive and drug-using students are admired in middle school more than those who are conscientious and studious—a marked difference from elementary school (Rubin et al., 2013). Academics become less important.

This is true not only for African American boys like James. There is "an abundance of evidence of middle school declines on a number of academic outcomes" (McGill et al., 2012). Beginning at puberty, girls' interest in math and science decreases if they and their peers perceive it as not being feminine (Leaper et al., 2012).

Unfortunately, middle school achievement is a strong predictor of high school achievement, which is a strong predictor of whether or not a young person will earn a college degree. At the end of primary school, James planned to go to college; in middle school, he said he had "a complete lack of motivation"; in tenth grade, he dropped out.

More Like Him Needed In 2014 in the United States, half the public school students were tallied as non-white and non-Hispanic, and half are male. Meanwhile, only 17 percent of teachers are non-white and non-Hispanic, and only 24 percent are male. This Gardena, California high school teacher is a welcome exception in two other ways—he rarely sits behind his desk and he uses gestures as well as his voice to explain.

● **Especially for Middle School Teachers** You think your lectures are interesting and you know you care about your students, yet many of them cut class, come late, or seem to sleep through it. What do you do? (see response, page 428)

● **Answer to Observation Quiz**
(from page 424): Both are single-sex. What does that teach these students?

entity theory of intelligence An approach to understanding intelligence that sees ability as innate, a fixed quantity present at birth; those who hold this view do not believe that effort enhances achievement.

incremental theory of intelligence An approach to understanding intelligence which holds that intelligence can be directly increased by effort; those who subscribe to this view believe they can master whatever they seek to learn if they pay attention, participate in class, study, complete their homework, and so on.

As was true for James, the early signs of a future high school dropout are found in middle school. Those students most at risk are low-SES boys from minority ethnic groups, yet almost no middle school has male guidance counselors or teachers who are African American or Latino American. Given the egocentric and intuitive thinking of many young adolescents, they may stop trying to achieve if they do not see role models of successful, educated men (Morris & Morris, 2013).

Finding Acclaim

To pinpoint the developmental mismatch between students' needs and the middle school context, note that just when egocentrism leads young people to feelings of shame or fantasies of stardom (the imaginary audience), schools typically require them to change rooms, teachers, and classmates every 40 minutes or so. That limits both public acclaim and new friendships.

Recognition for academic excellence is especially elusive because middle school teachers grade more harshly than their primary school counterparts. Effort without accomplishment is not recognized, and achievement that was earlier "outstanding" is now only average. Acclaim for after-school activities is also elusive, because many art, drama, dance, and other programs put adolescents of all ages together, and 11- to 13-year-olds are not as skilled as older adolescents.

Finally, when athletic teams become competitive, those with fragile egos protect themselves by not trying out. If sports require public showers, that is another reason for students in early puberty to avoid them. Special camps for basketball, soccer, and so on are usually expensive—beyond the reach of low-SES families. Ironically, one of the factors that keeps students engaged in secondary school is participation on a sports team: Those who most need engagement may be least likely to get it.

As noted in the discussion of the brain, peer acceptance is more cherished at puberty than at any other time. Physical appearance—from eyebrows to foot size—suddenly becomes significant; status symbols—from gang colors to trendy sunglasses—take on new meaning; expensive clothes are coveted; and sexual conquests are flaunted. All of this adds stress to middle school students, who may have no psychic energy left for homework.

Coping with Middle School

One way middle school students avoid feelings of failure in academics is to quit trying. Then they can blame a low grade on their choice ("I didn't study") rather than on their ability. Pivotal is how they think of their potential.

If they hold to the **entity theory of intelligence** (i.e., that ability is innate, a fixed quantity present at birth), then they conclude that nothing they do can improve their academic skill. If they think they are "born stupid" at math, or language, or whatever, they mask their self-assessment by claiming not to study, try, or care. Thus, entity belief relieves stress, but it also reduces learning.

By contrast, if adolescents adopt the **incremental theory of intelligence** (i.e., that intelligence can increase if they work to master whatever they seek to understand), they will pay attention, participate in class, study, complete their homework, and learn. That is also called *mastery motivation,* an example of intrinsic motivation. [**Life-Span Link:** Intrinsic and extrinsic motivation are discussed in Chapter 10.]

This is not hypothetical. In the first year of middle school, students with entity beliefs do not achieve much, whereas those with mastery motivation improve academically, true in many nations (e.g., Diseth et al., 2014; Zhao & Wang, 2014; Burnette et al., 2013).

This is true between ethnic groups within nations as well. For example, in Australia, indigenous (Maori) youth tend to have much lower achievement scores than Australian youth of British descent, but the difference is more attitudinal than ethnic. Most Maori youth, and most of their teachers, hold the entity theory, but students who subscribe to the incremental theory achieve as much as their nonindigenous peers (Tarbetsky et al., 2016).

Believing that skills can be mastered and that effort pays off is also crucial for learning social skills (Dweck, 2013). Students want good peer relationships, but some are convinced that no one likes them. That self-perception may lead to social avoidance and a downward spiral of feelings of rejection (Zimmer-Gembeck, 2016). Adults must first change these students' attitudes and then help them change their behavior.

Teachers, parents, schools, and cultures allow the hidden curriculum to express the entity theory, encouraging children to compete, not to learn from each other (Eccles & Roeser, 2011). International comparisons reveal that educational systems that track students into higher or lower classes, that expel low-achieving students, and that allow competition between schools for the brightest students (all reflecting entity, not incremental, theory) also show lower average achievement and a larger gap between the scores of students at the highest and lowest score quartiles (OECD, 2011).

High School

Many of the patterns and problems of middle school continue in high school, although once the sudden growth and unfamiliar sex impulses of puberty are less acute, and with maturation and experience, adolescents are better able to cope with school. They become increasingly able to think abstractly, analytically, hypothetically, and logically (all formal operational thought), as well as subjectively, emotionally, intuitively, and experientially. High school curricula and teaching methods often require the formal mode.

THINK CRITICALLY: Would there be less bullying if more schools were multiethnic?

● Response for Teachers

(from page 425): Praise a student by saying, "What a great question!" Egos are fragile, so it's best to always validate the question. Seek student engagement, perhaps asking whether any classmates know the answer or telling the student to discover the answer online or saying you will find out. Whatever you do, don't fake it; if students lose faith in your credibility, you may lose them completely.

● Especially for High School Teachers

You are much more interested in the nuances and controversies than in the basic facts of your subject, but you know that your students will take high-stakes tests on the basics and that their scores will have a major impact on their futures. What should you do? (see response, page 429)

Same Situation, Far Apart: How to Learn
Although developmental psychologists find that adolescents learn best when they are actively engaged with ideas, most teenagers are easier to control when they are taking tests (*left,* Winston-Salem, North Carolina, United States) or reciting scripture (*right,* Kabul, Afghanistan).

● **Response for Middle School Teachers** (from page 426): Students need both challenge and involvement; avoid lessons that are too easy or too passive. Create small groups; assign oral reports, debates, role-plays, and so on. Remember that adolescents like to hear one another's thoughts and their own voices.

high-stakes test An evaluation that is critical in determining success or failure. If a single test determines whether a student will graduate or be promoted, it is a high-stakes test.

The College-Bound

From a developmental perspective, the fact that high schools emphasize formal thinking makes sense, since many older adolescents are capable of abstract logic. In several nations, attempts are underway to raise standards so that all high school graduates will be ready for college, where analysis is required.

A mantra in the United States is "college for all," intended to encourage low achievers to aspire for tertiary education, although some authors believe the effect may be the opposite (Carlson, 2016). One result of the emphasis on college is that more students take classes that are assessed by externally scored exams, either the IB (International Baccalaureate) or the AP (Advanced Placement). Such classes have high standards and satisfy some college requirements if the student scores well. In 2013, such classes were taken by one-third of all high school graduates, compared to less than one-fifth (19 percent) in 2003 (Adams, 2014).

Another indicator of increasing standards are requirements for an academic diploma and restrictions on vocational or general diplomas. Most U.S. schools require two years of math beyond algebra, two years of laboratory science, three years of history, four years of English, and two years of a language other than English.

In addition to mandated courses, 74 percent of U.S. public high school students are required to pass a **high-stakes test** in order to graduate. (Any exam for which the consequences of failing are severe is called "high-stakes.") A decade ago, no state required exit exams. Increased testing is evident in every state, but it is controversial, as the following explains.

Testing

Secondary students in the United States take many more tests than they did even a decade ago. This includes many high-stakes tests—not only tests to earn a high school diploma but also tests to get into college (the SAT and ACT, achievement and aptitude) and tests to earn college credits (the AP and IB) while in high school.

High-stakes tests have become part of the culture, necessary to pass third, fifth, and eighth grades, and even to enter special kindergarten classes. Further, the Common Core, explained in Chapter 12, requires testing in reading and math, and the 2016 federal educational reform, the ESSA (Every Student Succeeds Act) requires standardized testing from the third grade on.

Tests also have high stakes for teachers, who may earn extra pay or lose their job based on how their students score, and for schools, which gain resources or are shuttered because of test scores. Entire school systems are rated on test scores. This is said to be one reason that widespread cheating on high-stakes tests occurred in Atlanta beginning in 2009 (Severson & Blinder, 2014).

Opposing perspectives on testing are voiced in many schools, parent groups, and state legislatures. In 2013, Alabama dropped its high-stakes test for graduation in the same year that Pennsylvania instituted such a test, but opposing voices have postponed implementation of that requirement. A 2007 law in Texas required 15 tests for graduation; in 2013, Texas law reduced that to four tests (Rich, 2013).

Overall, high school graduation rates in the United States have increased every year for the past decade, reaching 82 percent in 2014 after four years in high school. Rates of students who take five years to graduate, or who drop out, are also reduced (see Figure 15.5). Some say that increased tests and higher standards are part of the reason, but others contend that the high-stakes tests discourage some students while making graduation too easy for others who are adept at test-taking (Hyslop, 2014).

Students who fail high-stakes tests are often those with intellectual disabilities, one-third of whom do not graduate (Samuels, 2013), and those who attend schools in low-income neighborhoods. Some argue that the tests punish these students, when the real culprit is the school, the community, or the entire nation. Passing graduation exit exams does not correlate with excellence in college, but failing them increases the risk of harm—including prison later on (Baker & Lang, 2013).

Ironically, in the same decade during which U.S. schools are raising requirements, many East Asian nations, including China, Singapore, and Japan (all with high scores on international tests), have moved in the opposite direction. Particularly in Singapore, national high-stakes tests are being phased out, and local autonomy is increasing (Hargreaves, 2012).

International data support both sides of this controversy. One nation whose children generally score well is South Korea, where high-stakes tests have resulted in extensive studying. Many South Korean parents hire tutors to teach their children after school and on weekends to improve their test scores (Lee & Shouse, 2011). Almost all Korean students graduate from high school, and most attend college—but that accomplishment is not valued by many Korean educators, including Seongho Lee, a professor of education in Korea. He says that "oversupply in college education is a very serious social problem" creating "an army of the unemployed" (quoted in Fischer, 2016, p. A25).

On the opposite side of the globe, students in Finland also score well on international tests but have no national tests until the end of high school. Nor do they spend much time on homework or after-school education. A Finnish expert proudly states that "schoolteachers teach in order to help their students learn, not to pass tests" (Sahlberg, 2011, p. 26).

The most recent international data suggest that U.S. high school students are not doing well, despite more high-stakes tests. As reviewed in Chapter 12, two international tests, the TIMSS (Trends in International Mathematics and Science Study) and the PIRLS (Progress in International Reading Literacy Study), find that the United States is far from the top on student learning. A third test, the PISA (described soon), also shows the United States lagging. That is leading to a reexamination of U.S. education policies and practices, yet opposing perspectives are evident.

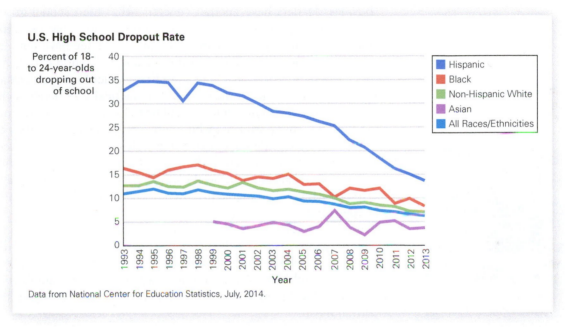

U.S. High School Dropout Rate

Percent of 18- to 24-year-olds dropping out of school

Legend:
- Hispanic
- Black
- Non-Hispanic White
- Asian
- All Races/Ethnicities

Year

Data from National Center for Education Statistics, July, 2014.

FIGURE 15.5

Mostly Good News This depicts wonderful improvements in high school graduation rates, especially among Hispanic youth, who drop out only half as often as they did 20 years ago. However, since high school graduation is increasingly necessary for lifetime success, even the rates shown here may not have kept pace with the changing needs of the economy. Future health, income, and happiness for anyone who drops out may be in jeopardy.

Alternatives to College

In the United States, a sizable minority (about 30 percent) of high school graduates do not enter college. Moreover, of those who enter public community colleges, most (about three-fourths) do not complete their associate's degree within three years, and almost half of those entering public or private four-year schools do not graduate. Some simply take longer or enter the job market first, but even 10 years after the usual age for high school graduation, only 34 percent of U.S. young adults have earned a bachelor's degree (National Center for Education Statistics, 2013c).

Rates are much lower in many of the largest cities. For example, only 18 percent of the approximately 60,000 ninth-grade students entering public schools in the district of Philadelphia managed to graduate on time from high school and then complete at least two years of college (Center for Education Policy, 2013).

● ● Response for High School Teachers (from page 427): It would be nice to follow your instincts, but the appropriate response depends partly on pressures within the school and on the expectations of the parents and administration. A comforting fact is that adolescents can think about and learn almost anything if they feel a personal connection to it. Look for ways to teach the facts your students need for the tests as the foundation for the exciting and innovative topics you want to teach. Everyone will learn more, and the tests will be less intimidating to your students.

The 82 percent who fell off track are often a disappointment to their parents: In Philadelphia and nationwide, almost all parents hope their children will graduate from college. The students may be a disappointment to themselves as well. Many quit high school before their senior year, but among the graduating Philadelphia seniors, 84 percent plan to go to college but only 47 percent enroll the following September. Some will begin college later, but their chance of college completion is low.

These sobering statistics underlie another debate among educators. Should students be encouraged to "dream big" early in high school, aspiring for tertiary learning? This suggestion originates from studies that find a correlation between dreaming big in early adolescence and going to college years later (Domina et al., 2011a, 2011b). Others suggest that college is a "fairy tale dream" that may lead to low self-esteem (Rosenbaum, 2011). If adolescents fail academic classes, will they feel bored, stupid, and disengaged?

Business leaders have another concern—that high school graduates are not ready for the demands of work because their education has been too abstract, or the standards for writing and analyzing too low. They have not learned enough through discussion, emotional maturation, and real-world experience.

Internationally, vocational education that explicitly prepares students for jobs via a combination of academic classes and practical experience seems to succeed better than a general curriculum (Eichhorst et al., 2012). On the other hand, for some students, many students whose test scores suggest that they could succeed at a four-year college do not enroll. Some high schools are more encouraging than others. For example, students who entered high school with high achievement scores in two major cities in neighboring states (Albuquerque, New Mexico and Fort Worth, Texas) had markedly different college enrollment rates (about 83 percent compared to 58 percent) (Center for Education Policy, 2012).

Overall, the data present a dilemma for educators. Suggesting that a student should *not* go to college may be racist, classist, sexist, or worse. On the other hand, many students who begin college do not graduate, so they lose time and gain debt when they could have advanced in a vocation. Everyone agrees that adolescents need to be educated for life as well as for employment, but it is difficult to decide what that means.

Measuring Practical Cognition

Employers usually provide on-the-job training, which is much more specific and current than what high schools can provide. They hope their future employees will have learned in secondary school how to think, explain, write, concentrate, and get along with other people.

As one executive of Boeing (which hired 33,000 new employees in two years) wrote:

> We believe that professional success today and in the future is more likely for those who have practical experience, work well with others, build strong relationships, and are able to think and do, not just look things up on the Internet.

> [Stephens & Richey, 2013, p. 314]

Those skills are hard to measure, especially on national high-stakes tests or on the two international tests explained in Chapter 12, the PIRLS and the TIMSS.

The third in the set of international tests mentioned above, the **PISA (Programme for International Student Assessment),** was designed to measure students' ability to apply what they have learned. The PISA is taken by 15-year-olds, an age chosen because some 15-year-olds are close to the end of their formal

San Diego Union-Tribune/ZUMAPRESS/Newscom

What Do They Need to Learn? Jesse Olascoaga and José Perez here assemble a desk as part of a class in Trade Tech High School in Vista, California. Are they mastering skills that will lead to a good job? Much depends on what else they are learning. It may be collaboration and pride in work well done, in which case this is useful education.

THINK CRITICALLY: Is it more important to prepare high school students for jobs or for college?

PISA (Programme for International Student Assessment) An international test taken by 15-year-olds in 50 nations that is designed to measure problem solving and cognition in daily life.

school career. The questions are supposed to be practical, measuring knowledge that might apply at home or on the job. As a PISA report described it:

> The tests are designed to generate measures of the extent to which students can make effective use of what they have learned in school to deal with various problems and challenges they are likely to experience in everyday life.

> *[PISA, 2009, p. 13]*

For example, among the 2012 math questions is this one:

> Chris has just received her car driving license and wants to buy her first car. The table below shows the details of four cars she finds at a local car dealer.

What car's engine capacity is the smallest?

A. Alpha   B. Bolte   C. Castel   D. Dezal

Model	Alpha	Bolte	Castel	Dezal
Year	2003	2000	2001	1999
Advertised price (zeds)	4800	4450	4250	3990
Distance travelled (kilometers)	105 000	115 000	128 000	109 000
Engine capacity (liters)	1.79	1.796	1.82	1.783

For that and the other questions on the PISA, the calculations are quite simple—most 10-year-olds can do them; no calculus, calculators, or complex formulas required. However, almost half of the 15-year-olds worldwide got that question wrong. (The answer is D.) One problem is decimals: Some students do not remember how to interpret them when a practical question, not an academic one, is asked. Even in Singapore and Hong Kong, one out of five 15-year-olds got this question wrong. Another problem is that distance traveled is irrelevant, yet many students are distracted by it.

Overall the U.S. students score lower on the PISA compared to many other nations, including Canada, the nation most similar to it in ethnicity and location. Compared to peers in other nations, the 2012 results rank the U.S. 15-year-olds 36th in math, 28th in science, and 24th in reading—all lower than in 2009, when the U.S. scores were 31st, 23rd, and 17th.

Some 2012 results were not surprising (China, Japan, Korea, and Singapore were all high), but some were unexpected (high scores for Finland, Poland, and Estonia). The lowest results were Peru, Indonesia, and Qatar. The results reflect the educational systems, not geography, since low-scoring Indonesia is close to Singapore.

International analysis finds that the following items correlate with high achievement of high school students on the PISA (OECD, 2010, p. 6):

- Leaders, parents, and citizens value education overall, with individualized approaches to learning so that all students learn what they need.
- Standards are high and clear, so every student knows what he or she must do, with a "focus on the acquisition of complex, higher-order thinking skills."
- Teachers and administrators are valued, and they are given "considerable discretion . . . in determining content" and sufficient salary as well as time for collaboration.
- Learning is prioritized "across the entire system," with high-quality teachers assigned to the most challenging schools.

The PISA and international comparisons of high school dropout rates suggest that U.S. secondary education can be improved, especially for those who do not go to college. Surprisingly, students who are capable of passing their classes, at least as measured on IQ tests, drop out almost as often as those who are less capable. Persistence, engagement, and motivation seem more crucial than intellectual ability alone (Archambault et al., 2009; Tough, 2012). Again, as in middle school, the incremental (effort-based) theory of education may be crucial.

Variability

An added complication is that adolescents themselves vary: Some are thoughtful, some are impulsive, some are ready for analytic challenges, some are egocentric. All of them, however, need personal encouragement.

A study of student emotional and academic engagement from fifth grade to eighth grade found that, as expected, the overall average was a slow and steady decline of engagement, but a distinctive group (about 18 percent) were highly engaged throughout while another distinctive group (about 5 percent) experienced precipitous disengagement year by year (Li & Lerner, 2011). The 18 percent are likely to do well in high school; the 5 percent are likely to drop out, but some of them are late bloomers who could succeed in college if given time and encouragement. Thus, schools and teachers need many strategies if they hope to reach every adolescent.

Similar complications are evident in one recent strategy for advancing academic achievement—separating the boys and the girls. Some studies find that teenagers, benefit from being with others of their own sex, but other studies find the opposite. The data are complicated by selection effects: Single-sex schools are more often private, not public, and have smaller class size, wealthier families, and more selective admissions. All of those factors improve achievement—so the single-sex characteristic may be irrelevant.

Perhaps the age of the students is a crucial variable. A meta-analysis found some academic advantage to single-sex education in middle school but none in high school (Pahlke et al., 2014). As one review states, "both proponents and critics of single-sex schooling have studies that support their positions, stagnating the policy debate" (Pahlke & Hyde, 2016, p. 83). It also may be that the emphasis on academic achievement is too narrow: If the goal of secondary education is to prepare students for life, then coeducation may be better.

Now let us return to general conclusions for this chapter. The cognitive skills that boost national economic development and personal happiness are creativity, flexibility, relationship building, and analytic ability. Whether or not an adolescent is college-bound, those skills are exactly what the adolescent mind can develop—with proper education and guidance. Every cognitive theorist and researcher believes that adolescents' logical, social, and creative potential is not always realized, but that it can be. Does that belief end this chapter on a hopeful note?

WHAT HAVE YOU LEARNED?

1. Why have most junior high schools disappeared?

2. What characteristics of middle schools make them more difficult for students than elementary schools?

3. Why does puberty affect a person's ability to learn?

4. How do beliefs about intelligence affect motivation and learning?

5. What are the advantages and disadvantages of high-stakes testing?

6. What are the problems with Advanced Placement classes and tests?

7. Should high schools prepare everyone for college? Why or why not?

8. How does the PISA differ from other international tests?

SUMMARY

Logic and Self

1. Cognition in early adolescence may be egocentric, a kind of self-centered thinking. Adolescent egocentrism gives rise to the personal fable, the invincibility fable, and the imaginary audience.

2. Formal operational thought is Piaget's term for the last of his four periods of cognitive development. He tested and demonstrated formal operational thought with various problems that students in a high school science or math class might encounter.

3. Piaget realized that adolescents are no longer earthbound and concrete in their thinking; they imagine the possible, the probable, and even the impossible, instead of focusing only on what is real. They develop hypotheses and explore, using deductive reasoning. However, few developmentalists find that adolescents move suddenly from concrete thinking to formal thinking.

Two Modes of Thinking

4. Many cognitive theories describe two types of thinking during adolescence. One set of names for these two types is intuitive and analytic. Both become more forceful during adolescence, but brain development means that intuitive, emotional thinking matures before analytic, logical thought.

5. Few teenagers always use logic, although they are capable of doing so. Emotional, intuitive thinking is quicker and more satisfying, and sometimes better, than analytic thought.

6. Neurological as well as survey research finds that adolescent thinking is characterized by more rapid development of the limbic system and slower development of the prefrontal cortex. Peers further increase emotional impulses, so adolescents may make choices that their parents believe to be foolish.

Digital Natives

7. Adolescents use technology, particularly the Internet, more than people of any other age. They reap many educational benefits, and many teachers welcome the accessibility of information and the research advances made possible by the Internet. Social connections are encouraged as well.

8. However, technology can be destructive. Some adolescents may be addicted to video games, some use smartphones and instant messages for cyberbullying, some find like-minded peers to support eating disorders and other pathologies, some engage in sexting. Overall, adults may mistakenly attribute normal teen behavior to technology use.

Secondary Education

9. Achievement in secondary education—after primary education (grade school) and before tertiary education (college)—correlates with the health and wealth of individuals and nations.

10. In middle school, many students struggle both socially and academically. One reason may be that middle schools are not structured to accommodate egocentrism or intuitive thinking. Students' beliefs about the nature of intelligence—entity or incremental—may also affect their learning.

11. Education in high school emphasizes formal operational thinking. In the United States, the demand for more accountability has led to an increase in the requirements for graduation and to more Advanced Placement (AP) classes and high-stakes testing.

12. A sizable number of high school students do not graduate or go on to college, and many more leave college without a degree. Current high school education does not seem to meet their needs.

13. The PISA test, taken by many 15-year-olds in 50 nations, measures how well students can apply the knowledge they have been taught. Students in the United States seem to have particular difficulty with such tests.

KEY TERMS

adolescent egocentrism (p. 408)
imaginary audience (p. 409)
personal fable (p. 409)
invincibility fable (p. 409)
formal operational thought (p. 410)

hypothetical thought (p. 411)
deductive reasoning (p. 411)
inductive reasoning (p. 411)
dual processing (p. 412)
intuitive thought (p. 413)
analytic thought (p. 413)

cyberbullying (p. 421)
sexting (p. 422)
secondary education (p. 424)
middle school (p. 425)
entity theory of intelligence (p. 426)

incremental theory of intelligence (p. 426)
high-stakes test (p. 428)
PISA (Programme for International Student Assessment) (p. 430)

APPLICATIONS

1. Describe a time when you overestimated how much other people were thinking about you. How was your mistake similar to and different from adolescent egocentrism?

2. Talk to a teenager about politics, families, school, religion, or any other topic that might reveal the way he or she thinks. Do you hear any adolescent egocentrism? Intuitive thinking? Systematic thought? Flexibility? Cite examples.

3. Think of a life-changing decision you have made. How did logic and emotion interact? What would have changed if you had given the matter more thought—or less?

4. Describe what happened and what you thought in the first year you attended a middle school or a high school. What made it better or worse than later years in that school?

Adolescence:
Psychosocial Development

What Will You Know?

1. Why might a teenager be into sports one year and into books the next?
2. Should parents back off when their teenager disputes every rule, wish, or suggestion they make?
3. Who are the best, and worst, sources of information about sex?
4. Should we worry more about teen suicide or juvenile delinquency?
5. Why are adolescents forbidden to drink and smoke, but adults can do so?

It's not easy being a teenager, as the previous chapters make clear, but neither is it easy being the parent of one. Sometimes I was too lenient. For example, once my daughter came home late. I was worried, angry, and upset, but I did not think about punishing her until she asked, "How long am I grounded?" And sometimes I was too strict. For years I insisted that my daughters and their friends wash the dinner dishes—until all of my children told me that none of their friends had such mean mothers.

At times, parents like me ricochet. When our children were infants, my husband and I had discussed how we would react when they became teenagers: We were ready to be firm, united, and consistent regarding illicit drugs, unsafe sex, and serious lawbreaking. More than a decade later, when our children actually reached that stage, none of those issues appeared. Instead, we reacted inconsistently to unanticipated challenges. My husband said, "I knew they would become adolescents. I didn't expect us to become parents of adolescents."

This chapter is about adolescents' behavior and their relationships with friends, parents, and the larger society. It begins with identity and ends with drugs, both of which might appear to be the result of personal choice but actually are strongly affected by other people. I realize now that my children's actions and my reactions were influenced by personal history (I washed family dishes as a teenager) and by current norms (their friends did not).

Identity

Psychosocial development during adolescence is often understood as a search for a consistent understanding of oneself. Self-expression and self-concept become increasingly important at puberty. Each young person wants to know, "Who am I?"

According to Erik Erikson, life's fifth psychosocial crisis is **identity versus role confusion**: Working through the complexities of finding one's own identity is the primary task of adolescence (Erikson, 1968/1994). He said that this crisis is

identity versus role confusion
Erikson's term for the fifth stage of development, in which the person tries to figure out "Who am I?" but is confused as to which of many possible roles to adopt.

Left: Stuart Hughs/The Image Bank/Getty Images
Top: Hola Images RF/Getty Images

No Role Confusion These are high school students in Junior ROTC training camp. For many youths who cannot afford college, the military offers a temporary identity, complete with haircut, uniform, and comrades.

identity achievement Erikson's term for the attainment of identity, or the point at which a person understands who he or she is as a unique individual, in accord with past experiences and future plans.

role confusion A situation in which an adolescent does not seem to know or care what his or her identity is. (Sometimes called *identity* or *role diffusion*.)

foreclosure Erikson's term for premature identity formation, which occurs when an adolescent adopts his or her parents' or society's roles and values wholesale, without questioning or analysis.

moratorium An adolescent's choice of a socially acceptable way to postpone making identity-achievement decisions. Going to college is a common example.

Video Activity: Adolescence Around the World: Rites of Passage presents a comparison of adolescent initiation customs in industrialized and developing societies.

THINK CRITICALLY: Since identity is formed lifelong, is your identity now different from what it was five years ago?

resolved with **identity achievement,** when adolescents have reconsidered the goals and values of their parents and culture, accepting some and discarding others, forging their own identity.

The result is neither wholesale rejection nor unquestioning acceptance of social norms (Côté, 2009). With their new autonomy, teenagers maintain continuity with the past so that they can move to the future. Each person must achieve his or her own identity. Simply following parental footsteps does not work, because the social context of each generation differs.

Not Yet Achieved

Erikson's insights have inspired thousands of researchers. Notable among those was James Marcia, who described and measured four specific ways in which young people cope with the identity crisis: (1) role confusion, (2) foreclosure, (3) moratorium, and finally (4) identity achievement (Marcia, 1966).

Over the past half-century, major psychosocial shifts have lengthened the duration of adolescence and made identity achievement more complex (Côté & Levine, 2015). However, the above three way stations on the road to identity achievement still seem evident (Kroger & Marcia, 2011).

Role confusion is the opposite of identity achievement. It is characterized by lack of commitment to any goals or values. Erikson originally called this *identity diffusion* to emphasize that some adolescents seem diffuse, unfocused, and unconcerned about their future. Perhaps worse, adolescents in role confusion see no goals or purpose in their life, and thus they flounder, unable to move forward (Hill et al., 2013).

Identity **foreclosure** occurs when, in order to avoid the confusion of not knowing who they are, young people accept traditional roles and values (Marcia, 1966; Marcia et al., 1993). They might follow customs transmitted from their parents or culture, never exploring alternatives. Or they might foreclose on an oppositional, *negative identity*—the direct opposite of whatever their parents want—again without thoughtful questioning. Foreclosure is comfortable. For many, it is a temporary shelter, to be followed by more exploration (Meeus, 2011).

A more mature shelter is **moratorium,** a time-out that includes some exploration, either in breadth (trying many things) or in depth (following one path but with a tentative, temporary commitment). Moratoria are rare before age 18, and hence they are discussed in Chapter 19. We begin the description of the search for identity in adolescence, where Erikson originally placed it, but scholars agree that establishing identity is a lifelong process (Meeus, 2011).

Four Arenas of Identity Formation

Erikson (1968/1994) highlighted four aspects of identity: religious, political, vocational, and sexual. Terminology and timing have changed, yet the crucial question remains: Does the person ponder the possibilities and actively seek an identity (Lillevoll et al., 2013)?

Religious Identity

Most adolescents begin to question some aspects of their faith, but their *religious identity* is similar to that of their parents. Few reject religion if they have grown up following a particular faith, especially if they have a good relationship with their parents (Kim-Spoon et al., 2012).

They may express their religious identity more devoutly. A Muslim girl might start to wear a headscarf, a Catholic boy might study for the priesthood, or a Baptist teenager might join a Pentecostal youth group, each surprising their parents. However, few teenagers have a crisis of faith unless unusual circumstances propel it (King & Roeser, 2009). Almost no young Muslims convert to Judaism, and almost no teenage Baptists become Hindu—although such conversions can occur in adulthood as the search for religious identity continues.

Same Situation, Far Apart: Religious Identity Awesome devotion is characteristic of adolescents, whether devotion is to a sport, a person, a music group, or—as shown here—a religion. This boy *(left)* praying on a Kosovo street is part of a dangerous protest against the town's refusal to allow building another mosque. This girl *(right)* is at a stadium rally for young Christians in Michigan, declaring her faith for all to see. While adults see differences between the two religions, both teens share not only piety but also twenty-first century clothing. Her t-shirt is a recent innovation, and on his jersey is Messi 10, for a soccer star born in Argentina.

Political Identity

Parents also influence their children's *political identity*. In the twenty-first century in the United States, more adults identify as independent than Republican, Democrat, or any other party. Their teenage children reflect their lack of party affiliation. Some adolescents proudly say that they do not care about politics, echoing the parents' generation without realizing it.

Adolescents tend to be more liberal than their parents, especially on social issues (LGBTQ rights, reproduction, the environment), but major political shifts do not usually occur until later (P. Taylor, 2014). For example, Hillary Clinton's parents were Republican and she was a Young Republican at age 17, not becoming a Democrat until age 21.

Related to political identity is *ethnic identity*, a topic not discussed by Erikson. In the United States and Canada, almost half of all current adolescents are of African, Asian, Latino, or Native American (aboriginal in Canada) heritage. Many of them also have ancestors of another ethnic group. Although official government categories are very broad, teenagers forging their personal ethnic identity must become more specific.

Hispanic youth, for instance, must figure out how having grandparents from Mexico, Peru, or Cuba, and/or California, Texas, or New York, affects them. Many Latinos (some identifying as Chicano) also have ancestors from Spain, Africa, and /or indigenous groups such as the Maya or Inca (Mao et al., 2007). Similarly, those who are European American must decide the significance of having grandparents from, say, Italy, Ireland, or Sweden. No teenager adopts, wholesale, their ancestors' identity, but every one reflects, somehow, their family's history.

Vocational Identity

Vocational identity originally meant envisioning oneself as a worker in a particular occupation. Choosing a future career made sense for teenagers a century ago, when most girls became housewives and most boys became farmers, small businessmen, or factory workers. Those few in professions were mostly generalists (doctors did family medicine, lawyers handled all kinds of cases, teachers taught all subjects).

Early vocational identity is no longer appropriate. No teenager can realistically choose among the tens of thousands of careers; most adults change vocations (not just employers) many times. Currently, vocational identity is best seen as a dynamic, flexible path: Adults eventually find a career, or, even better, a calling, that can lead to a variety of specific jobs (Skorikov & Vondracek, 2011).

It is a myth that having a job will keep teenagers out of trouble and establish vocational identity (Staff & Schulenberg, 2010). Research that controlled for SES

A Person, Not a Stereotype In the United States in 2015, the identity crisis became manifest with massive marches like the one shown here in Madison, Wisconsin, after no charges were filed against police officer Matt Kenny, who killed 19-year-old Tony Robinson.

● **Observation Quiz** Do you see any evidence of religious identity? (see answer, page 440) ↑

gender identity A person's acceptance of the roles and behaviors that society associates with the biological categories of male and female.

found that adolescents who are employed more than 20 hours a week during the school year tend to quit school, fight with parents, smoke cigarettes, and hate their jobs—not only when they are teenagers but also later on (although sometimes work that is steady and not too time-consuming may be beneficial) (Osilla et al., 2015; Mortimer, 2010).

Typically, teenagers spend their wages on clothes, cars, drugs, fast food, and music, not on supporting their families or saving for college (Mortimer, 2013). Grades fall: Employment interferes with school work and attendance. This is true not only in the United States; similar results are found in South Korea (Lee et al., 2016).

Gender Identity

The fourth type of identity described by Erikson is *sexual identity*. As you remember from Chapter 10, *sex* and *sexual* refer to biological characteristics, whereas *gender* refers to cultural and social attributes that differentiate males and females. A half-century ago, Erikson and other theorists thought of the two sexes as opposites (Miller & Simon, 1980). They assumed that adolescents who were confused about sexual identity would soon adopt "proper" male or female roles (Erikson, 1968/1994; A. Freud, 1958/2000).

Thus, adolescence was once a time for "gender intensification," when people increasingly identified as male or female. No longer (Priess et al., 2009). Erikson's term *sexual identity* has been replaced by **gender identity** (Denny & Pittman, 2007), which refers primarily to a person's self-definition as male, female, or transgender.

Gender identity often (not always) begins with the person's biological sex and leads to a gender role, but many adolescents (who reach the questioning stage of hypothetical reasoning that Piaget described) question aspects of gender roles. This often troubles their parents and grandparents.

Gender roles once meant that only men were employed; they were *breadwinners* (good providers) and women were *housewives* (married to their houses). As women entered the labor market, gender roles expanded but were still strong (nurse/doctor, secretary/businessman, pink collar/blue collar). Even today, women in every nation do far more child care and elder care than men. There is a "slow but steady pace of change in gender divisions of domestic labor . . . combined with a persistence of gender differences and inequalities" (Doucet, 2015, p. 224).

Now, gender roles are changing everywhere. The speed and specifics of the change vary dramatically by culture and cohort, which makes gender identity complicated for many youth. All adolescents are vulnerable to feelings of depression and anxiety as they try to sort out their identity, but this is particularly true of those who are transgender or nonconforming in other ways (Reisner et al., 2016). Fluidity and uncertainty regarding sexuality and gender is particularly common during early adolescence, which adds to the difficulty of self-acceptance.

Among Western psychiatrists in former decades, people who had "a strong and persistent cross-gender identification" were said to have *gender identity disorder,* a serious diagnosis according to DSM-IV. However, the DSM-5 instead describes *gender dysphoria,* when people are distressed at their biological gender. This is not simply a change in words: A "disorder" means something is amiss with the individual, no matter how he or she feels about it, whereas in dysphoria the problem is in the distress, which can be mitigated by social conditions and/or by perception (Zucker et al., 2013).

What has not changed are sexual drives as hormone levels increase. As Erikson recognized, many adolescents are confused regarding when, how, and with whom to express those drives. Some foreclose by exaggerating male or female roles; others seek a moratorium by avoiding all sexual contact. Some who feel their gender identity is fragile aspire to a gender-stereotypic career (Sinclair & Carlsson, 2013). Choosing a career to establish gender identity, rather than to use skills, follow interests, and affirm values, is another reason why settling on a vocational identity during adolescence may be premature.

WHAT HAVE YOU LEARNED?

1. What is Erikson's fifth psychosocial crisis, and how is it resolved?

2. How does identity foreclosure differ from identity moratorium?

3. What has changed over the past decades regarding political identity in the United States?

4. What role do parents play in the formation of an adolescent's religious and political identity?

5. Why is it premature for today's adolescents to achieve vocational identity?

6. What assumptions about sexual identity did most adults hold 50 years ago?

7. What variations in sexual identity are apparent worldwide?

8. What is the difference between gender identity disorder and gender dysphoria?

Relationships with Adults

Adolescence is often depicted as a period of waning adult influence, when children distance themselves from their elders. This picture is only half true. Adult influence is less immediate but no less important.

Parents

The fact that caregiver–adolescent relationships are pivotal does not mean that they are peaceful (Laursen & Collins, 2009). Disputes are common because the adolescent's drive for independence, arising from biological as well as psychological impulses and social expectations, clashes with the adult's desire for control.

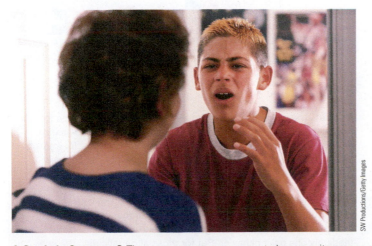

A Study in Contrasts? These two teenagers appear to be opposites: one yelling at his mother and the other conscientiously helping his father. However, adolescent moods can change in a flash, especially with parents. Later in the day, these two might switch roles.

🔵 **Answer to Observation Quiz**
(from page 438): Yes, notice the two marchers in liturgical vestments at the far right.

Normally, conflict peaks in early adolescence, especially between mothers and daughters. The most common conflict is not fighting but instead *bickering*—repeated, petty arguments (more nagging than fighting) about routine, day-to-day concerns such as cleanliness, clothes, chores, and schedules. Each generation tends to misjudge the other, and that adds to the conflict. Parents (usually biological parents, but this includes grandparents and others who are caregivers) think that their offspring resent them more than they actually do, and adolescents imagine that their parents want to dominate them more than they actually do (Sillars et al., 2010).

A VIEW FROM SCIENCE

Parents, Genes, and Risks

Research on human development has many practical applications. This was evident in a longitudinal study of African American families in rural Georgia that involved 611 parents and their 11-year-olds (Brody et al., 2009). Half of them were assigned to the comparison group, with no special intervention. The other half were invited to seven two-hour training sessions. Groups were small, and leaders were well prepared and selected to be likely role models. Parents and their 11-year-olds were taught in two separate groups for an hour and then brought together.

The parents learned the following:

- The importance of being nurturing and involved
- The importance of conveying pride in being African American (called *racial socialization*)
- How monitoring and control benefit adolescents
- Why clear norms and expectations reduce substance use
- Strategies for communication about sex

The 11-year-olds learned the following:

- The importance of having household rules
- Adaptive behaviors when encountering racism
- The need for making plans for the future
- The differences between them and peers who use alcohol

After that first hour, the parents and 11-year-olds were led in games, structured interactions, and modeling designed to improve family communication and cohesion. Three years after the intervention, both the experimental and comparison groups were reassessed regarding sex and alcohol/drug activity. The results were disappointing: The intervention helped, but not very much.

Then, four years after the study began, the researchers read new research that found heightened risks of depression, delinquency, and other problems for people with the short allele of the 5-HTTLPR gene. To see whether this applied to their African American teenagers, they collected and analyzed the DNA of 16-year-olds who had been, at age 11, in either the special training group or the comparison group. As Figure 16.1 shows, the training had virtually no impact on those with the long allele, but it had a major impact on those with the short one.

That 14 hours or fewer of training (some families skipped sessions) had an impact on genetically sensitive boys is amazing, given all of the other influences surrounding these boys over the years. Apparently, since the parent–child relationship is crucial throughout adolescence, those seven sessions provided insights and connections that affected each vulnerable dyad from then on.

Genetic sensitivity was crucial. In a follow-up study when the boys were 19, those boys with the short 5-HTTLPR gene had increased levels of many indicators of poor health—physical and psychological—if their family environment was not supportive (Brody et al., 2013). Again, nature and nurture work together.

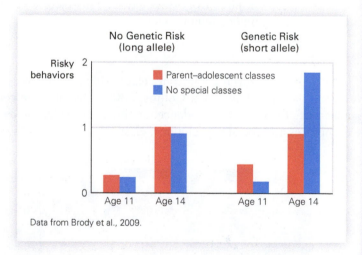

Data from Brody et al., 2009.

FIGURE 16.1

Not Yet The risk score was a simple one point for each of the following: had drunk alcohol, had smoked marijuana, had had sex. As shown, most of the 11-year-olds had done none of these. By age 14, most had done one (usually had drunk beer or wine)—except for those at genetic risk who did not have the seven-session training. Some of them had done all three, and many had done at least two. As you see, for those youths without genetic risk, the usual parenting was no better or worse than the parenting that benefited from the special classes: The average 14-year-old in either group had tried only one risky behavior. But for those at genetic risk, the special program made a decided difference.

Unspoken concerns need to be aired so that both generations better understand each other. Bickering begins with squabbling and nagging, but ideally it leads to each person understanding the needs of the other—something not to be taken for granted as puberty awakens new worries and concerns (McLaren & Sillars, 2014).

Some bickering may indicate a healthy family, since close relationships almost always include conflict. A study of mothers and their adolescents suggested that "although too much anger may be harmful . . . some expression of anger may be adaptive" (Hofer et al., 2013, p. 276). In this study, as well as generally, the parent–child relationship usually improved with time (Tighe et al., 2016; Tsai et al., 2013).

Crucial is that caregivers avoid becoming stricter or more lenient, and they instead adapt to the adolescent's need for increased independence. One review of dozens of studies found that the effects of conflict varied a great deal but that "parent–adolescent conflict might signal the need for families to adapt and change . . . to accommodate adolescents' increasing needs for independence and egalitarianism" (Weymouth et al., 2016, p. 107).

Cultural Differences

Several researchers have compared parent–child relationships in various cultures: Everywhere, parent–child communication and encouragement reduce teenage depression, suicide, and low self-esteem, and increase aspirations and achievements (e.g., Kwok & Shek, 2010; Leung et al., 2010; Qin et al., 2009). However, expectations, interactions, and behavior vary by culture (Brown & Bakken, 2011).

Parent–child conflict is less evident in cultures that stress **familism,** the belief that family members should sacrifice personal freedom and success to care for one another. Most refugee youth (Palestinian, Syrian, Iraqi) in Jordan agreed that parents had a right to decide their children's hairstyles, clothes, and music—contrary to what most U.S. teenagers believe (Smetana et al., 2016). In many traditional cultures, if adolescents do something parents would not approve of, the teens keep it quiet.

By contrast, many U.S. adolescents deliberately provoke an argument by boldly proclaiming what should be allowed, even if it is something they themselves never do (Cumsille et al., 2010). The parents' job is to listen, not punish.

If an impulsive, fearful, adventurous child is raised in a supportive family, he or she is less likely to do drugs than the average adolescent. The opposite is true in a harsh family (Rioux et al., 2016). Thus, when U.S. teenagers say something that upsets their parents (the specifics vary by family—a teenager might defend gun possession, or abortion, or profanity), parents should engage, not explode or ignore.

Closeness Within the Family

Family closeness may be crucial. Specifically:

1. Communication (Do family members talk openly with one another?)
2. Support (Do they rely on one another?)
3. Connectedness (How emotionally close are they?)
4. Control (Do parents encourage or limit adolescent autonomy?)

No social scientist doubts that the first two, communication and support, are helpful, perhaps essential, for healthy development. Patterns set in place during childhood continue, ideally buffering some of the turbulence of adolescence. Regarding the next two, connectedness and control, consequences vary and

THINK CRITICALLY: When do parents forbid an activity they should approve of, or ignore a behavior that should alarm them?

familism The belief that family members should support one another, sacrificing individual freedom and success, if necessary, in order to preserve family unity and protect the family from outside forces.

Video: Parenting in Adolescence examines how family structure can help or hinder parent–teen relationships.

"So I blame you for everything—
whose fault is that?"

parental monitoring Parents' ongoing awareness of what their children are doing, where, and with whom.

observers differ in what they see. How do you react to this example, written by one of my students?

> I got pregnant when I was sixteen years old, and if it weren't for the support of my parents, I would probably not have my son. And if they hadn't taken care of him, I wouldn't have been able to finish high school or attend college. My parents also helped me overcome the shame that I felt when . . . my aunts, uncles, and especially my grandparents found out that I was pregnant.
>
> *[I., personal communication]*

My student is grateful to her parents, but did teenage motherhood give her parents too much control, preventing her from establishing her own identity? Indeed, had they unconsciously encouraged her dependence by neither chaperoning nor explaining contraception? I's parents were immigrants from South America, and culture may be a factor, endorsing less independence that would be the norm for native-born adolescents.

A related issue is **parental monitoring**—that is, parental knowledge about each child's whereabouts, activities, and companions. Many studies have shown that when parental knowledge is the result of a warm, supportive relationship, adolescents are likely to become confident, well-educated adults, avoiding drugs and risky sex. However, if the parents are cold, strict, and punitive, monitoring may lead to rebellion.

Adolescents play an active role in monitoring. A "dynamic interplay between parent and child behaviors" is evident because teenagers choose what to reveal (Abar et al., 2014, p. 2177). Most are selective in what they disclose to their parents (Brown & Bakken, 2011).

Thus, monitoring may signify a mutual, close interaction (Kerr et al., 2010). But if adolescents resist telling their parents much of anything, they may develop problems such as aggression against peers, lawbreaking, and drug abuse (Laird et al., 2013). Lack of communication is a symptom more than the cause.

WHAT HAVE YOU LEARNED?

1. Why do parents and adolescents often bicker?
2. How do parent–adolescent relationships change over time?
3. When is parental monitoring a sign of a healthy parent–adolescent relationship?
4. How might a parent–child relationship be too close?

More Familiar Than Foreign? Even in cultures with strong and traditional family influence, teenagers choose to be with peers whenever they can. These boys play at Cherai Beach in India.

● **Observation Quiz** What evidence do you see that traditional norms remain in this culture? (see answer, page 444) ↑

Peer Power

Adolescents rely on peers to help them navigate the physical changes of puberty, the intellectual challenges of high school, and the social changes of leaving childhood. Friendships are important at every stage, but during early adolescence popularity (not just friendship) is coveted (LaFontana & Cillessen, 2010).

Peers do not negate the need for parental support: Healthy communication and support from parents make constructive peer relationships likely. However, parental support alone is not sufficient.

In one experiment, children and adolescents had to give a speech, with or without their parents' support. For 9-year-olds, the parents' presence relieved stress, as indicated by cortisol reduction as well as visible signs. For 15-year-olds, however, the parents' presence was no help (Hostinar et al., 2015). Especially when parents are harsh or neglectful, peer support can be crucial (Birkeland et al., 2014).

Peer Pressure

Peer pressure is the idea that peers will push a teenager to do something that adults disapprove, such as using drugs or breaking laws. It is true that adolescents are influenced by their friends, but peer pressure can be more helpful than harmful. This is especially true in early adolescence, when adults do not seem to understand biological and social stresses.

Many caregivers fear the power of social media as corruptive of innocent youth, but adolescents use social media to strengthen existing friendships (boyd, 2014). Of course, since most people post successes, not failures, some teens feel that they are less attractive, less social, or less competent than their peers, but that danger does not originate with the computer. Teens who have supportive friends offline are likely to benefit from online social interaction (Khan et al., 2016). Regarding social media and substance (alcohol and drugs) use, some drugs are promoted but abuse is not (Moreno & Whitehill, 2016).

Peers may be particularly important for adolescents of minority and immigrant groups as they strive to achieve ethnic identity (not confused or foreclosed). The larger society provides stereotypes and prejudice; parents seem stuck in past prejudices, although, ideally, they also describe ethnic heroes (Umana-Taylor et al., 2010); and then peers help with self-esteem. For example, a study of Hispanic adolescents found that those who experienced ethnic prejudice were more likely to abuse drugs, but not if their parents and peers made them proud to identify as Hispanic or Latino (Grigsby et al., 2014).

Given the myelination and maturation of parts of the brain, it is not surprising that the most influential peers are those nearby at the moment. This was found in a study in which all the eleventh-graders in several public schools in Los Angeles were offered a free online SAT prep course (worth $200) that they could take if they signed up on a paper that the organizers distributed (Bursztyn & Jensen, 2014).

In this study, students were *not* allowed to talk before deciding whether or not to accept the offer. So they did not know that although all of the papers had identical, detailed descriptions of the SAT program, one word differed in who would learn of their decision—either no other students or only the students in that particular class.

peer pressure Encouragement to conform to one's friends or contemporaries in behavior, dress, and attitude; usually considered a negative force, as when adolescent peers encourage one another to defy adult authority.

Matthew Staver/Bloomberg via Getty Images

Everyday Danger After cousins Alex and Arthur, ages 16 and 20, followed family wishes to shovel snow around their Denver home, they followed their inner risk impulses and jumped from the roof. Not every young man can afford the expense of motocross or hang gliding, but almost everyone leaps into risks that few 40-year-olds would dare.

A CASE TO STUDY

The Naiveté of Your Author

Adults are sometimes unaware of adolescents' desire for respect from their contemporaries. I did not recognize this at the time with my own children:

- Our oldest daughter wore the same pair of jeans in tenth grade, day after day. She washed them each night by hand and asked me to put them in the dryer early each morning. My husband was bewildered. "Is this some weird female ritual?" he asked. Years later, she explained that she was afraid that if she wore different pants each day, her classmates would think she cared about her clothes, which would prompt them to criticize her choices. To avoid imagined criticism, she wore only one pair of jeans.

- Our second daughter, at 16, pierced her ears for the third time. When I asked if this meant she would do drugs, she

laughed at my naiveté. I later saw that many of her friends had multiple holes in their ear lobes.

- At age 15, our third daughter was diagnosed with cancer. My husband and I weighed opinions from four physicians, each explaining treatment that would minimize the risk of death. She had other priorities: "I don't care what you choose, as long as I keep my hair." (Now her health is good; her hair grew back.)

- Our youngest, in sixth grade, refused to wear her jacket (it was new; she had chosen it), even in midwinter. Not until high school did she tell me why—she wanted her classmates to think she was tough.

In retrospect, I am amazed that I was unaware of the power of peers.

● **Answer to Observation Quiz**
(from page 442): The girls are only observers, keeping a respectful distance.

● **Especially for Parents of a Teenager**
Your 13-year-old comes home after a sleepover at a friend's house with a new, weird hairstyle—perhaps cut or colored in a bizarre manner. What do you say and do? (see response, page 448)

deviancy training Destructive peer support in which one person shows another how to rebel against authority or social norms.

Social or Solitary? Adults have criticized the Internet for allowing teenagers to keep friends at a distance. By contrast, sitting around an outdoor fire is romanticized as a bonding experience. Which is more accurate here? Are these two girls about to talk about what they are reading?

THINK CRITICALLY: Why is peer pressure thought to be much more sinister than it actually is?

The two versions were:

> *Your decision to sign up for the course will be kept completely private from everyone, <u>except</u> the other students in the room.*
>
> *Your decision to sign up for the course will be kept completely private from everyone, <u>including</u> the other students in the room.*

A marked difference was found if students thought their classmates would learn of their decision, with the honors students more likely to sign up and the non-honors students less likely if they thought their classmates would know. To make sure this was a peer effect, not just divergent motivation and ability between honors and non-honors students, the researchers compared 107 students who took exactly two honors classes and several non-honors classes. Some happened to be sitting in an honors classroom when they filled out their sign-up sheets; others were not.

When the decisions of the two-honors subgroup were kept totally private, acceptance rates were similar (72 and 79 percent) no matter which class students were in at the moment. But, if they thought their classmates might know their decision, imagined peer pressure affected them. When in an honors class, 97 percent signed up for the SAT program. Of those in a non-honors class, only 54 percent signed up, a 43-percent difference (Bursztyn & Jensen, 2014).

Selecting Friends

Of course, peers *can* lead one another into trouble. Collectively, they may provide **deviancy training,** whereby one person shows another how to resist social norms (Dishion et al., 2001). However, innocent teens are not corrupted by deviants. Adolescents choose their friends and models—not always wisely, but never randomly.

A developmental progression can be traced: The combination of "problem behavior, school marginalization, and low academic performance" at age 11 leads to gang involvement two years later, deviancy training two years after that, and violent behavior at age 18 or 19 (Dishion et al., 2010, p. 603). This cascade is not inevitable; adults need to engage marginalized 11-year-olds instead of blaming their friends years later.

To further understand the impact of peers, examination of two concepts is helpful: *selection* and *facilitation*. Teenagers *select* friends whose values and interests they share, abandoning former friends who follow other paths. Then, friends *facilitate* destructive or constructive behaviors. It is easier to do wrong ("Let's all skip school on Friday") or right ("Let's study together for the chem exam") with friends. Peer facilitation helps adolescents do things they are unlikely to do alone.

Thus, adolescents select and facilitate, choose and are chosen. Happy, energetic, and successful teens have close friends who themselves are high achievers, with no major emotional problems. The opposite also holds: Those who are drug users, sexually active, and alienated from school choose compatible friends.

A study of identical twins from ages 14 to 17 found that selection typically precedes facilitation, rather than the other way around. Those who *later* rebelled chose lawbreaking friends at age 14 more often than their more conventional twin did (Burt et al., 2009).

Research on teenage cigarette smoking also found that selection preceded peer pressure (Kiuru et al., 2010), and yet another study found that young adolescents tend to select peers who drink alcohol and then start drinking themselves (Osgood et al., 2013). Finally, a third study, of teenage sexual activity, again found that selection was the crucial peer influence on behavior (van de Bongardt et al., 2015). In general, peers provide opportunity, companionship, and encouragement for what young adolescents already are inclined to do.

Selection and facilitation are evident lifelong, but the balance between the two shifts. Early adolescence is a time of selection; the facilitation is evident in later adolescence. From ages 20 to 29, selection processes are more influential again, as young adults abandon some of their high school friends and establish new friendships (Samek et al., 2016).

Romance

Video: Romantic Relationships in Adolescence explores teens' attitudes and assumptions about romance and sexuality.

One of the most compelling selection effects occurs with romance. Adolescents choose and are chosen by romantic partners, and then together they affect almost everything—not only sexual interactions but also music preferences, college plans, tattoos, and so on.

First Love

Teens' first romances typically occur in high school, with girls having a steady partner more often than boys. Exclusive commitment is the ideal, but the fluidity and rapidity of the selection process mitigate against permanency. "Cheating," flirting, switching, and disloyalty are rife. Breakups are common, as are unreciprocated crushes. Emotions range from exhilaration to despair, leading to impulsive sex, cruel revenge, and deep depression. Peer support can be vital: Friends help adolescents cope with romantic ups and downs (Mehta & Strough, 2009).

Contrary to adult fears, many teenagers have platonic friends of both sexes (Kreager et al., 2016). They also have romances that do not include intercourse. In the United States in 2016, more than 40 percent of all graduating seniors were virgins. Most of them had dated someone but not had sex with them (see Figure 16.2). Norms vary markedly from group to group, school to school, city to city, and nation to nation.

For instance, twice as many high school students in Philadelphia as in San Francisco say they have had intercourse (52 percent versus 26 percent) (MMWR, June 10, 2016). Obviously, within every city are many subgroups, all with their own norms. For example, girls from religious families with supportive parent–child relationships tend to be romantically involved with boys from similar families, and their shared values slow down sexual activity (Kim-Spoon et al., 2012).

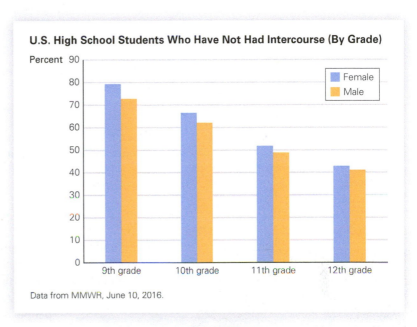

U.S. High School Students Who Have Not Had Intercourse (By Grade)

Data from MMWR, June 10, 2016.

FIGURE 16.2

Many Virgins For 30 years, the Youth Risk Behavior Survey has asked high school students from all over the United States dozens of confidential questions about their behavior. As you can see, about one-fourth of all students have already had sex by the ninth grade, and more than one-third have not yet had sex by their senior year—a group whose ranks have been increasing in recent years. Other research finds that sexual behaviors are influenced by peers, with some groups all sexually experienced by age 14 and others not until age 18 or older.

sexual orientation A term that refers to whether a person is sexually and romantically attracted to others of the same sex, the opposite sex, or both sexes.

Same-Sex Romances

Some adolescents are attracted to peers of the same sex. **Sexual orientation** refers to the direction of a person's erotic desires. One meaning of *orient* is "to turn toward"; thus, sexual orientation refers to whether a person is romantically attracted to (turned on by) people of the other sex, the same sex, or both sexes. Sexual orientation can be strong, weak, overt, secret, or unconscious.

Obviously, culture and cohort are powerful (Bailey et al., 2016). Some cultures accept youth who are gay, lesbian, bisexual, or transgender (the census in India asks people to identify as male, female, or Hijra [transgender]). Other cultures criminalize them (as do 38 of the 53 African nations), even killing them (Uganda). Worldwide, many gay youths date members of the other sex to hide their orientation; deception puts them at risk for binge drinking, suicidal thoughts, and drug

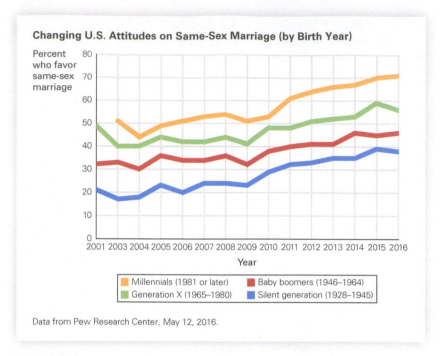

Changing U.S. Attitudes on Same-Sex Marriage (by Birth Year)

Percent who favor same-sex marriage

Legend:
- Millennials (1981 or later)
- Generation X (1965–1980)
- Baby boomers (1946–1964)
- Silent generation (1928–1945)

Data from Pew Research Center, May 12, 2016.

FIGURE 16.3

Young and Old Everyone knows that attitudes about same-sex relationships are changing. Less well known is that cohort differences are greater than the shift over the first decade of the twenty-first century.

use. Those hazards are less common in cultures where same-sex partnerships are accepted, especially when parents affirm their offspring's sexuality (see Figure 16.3).

At least in the United States, adolescents have similar difficulties and strengths whether they are gay or straight (Saewyc, 2011). However, lesbian, gay, bisexual, and transgender youth have a higher risk of depression and anxiety, for reasons from every level of Bronfenbrenner's ecological-systems approach (Mustanski et al., 2014). [**Life-Span Link:** Ecological systems are described in Chapter 1.]

Sexual orientation is surprisingly fluid during the teen years. Girls often recognize their orientation only after their first sexual experiences; many adult lesbians had other-sex relationships in adolescence (Saewyc, 2011).

In one study, 10 percent of sexually active teenagers had had same-sex partners, but many of those 10 percent nonetheless identified as heterosexual (Pathela & Schillinger, 2010). In that study, those most at risk of sexual violence and sexually transmitted infections were those who had partners of both sexes. This specific finding is confirmed by more general studies (e.g., Russell et al., 2014).

Sex Education

Many adolescents have strong sexual urges but minimal logic about pregnancy and disease, as might be expected from the 10-year interval between maturation of the body and of the brain. Millions of teenagers worry that they are oversexed, undersexed, or deviant, unaware that thousands, maybe millions, of people are just like them.

As a result, "students seem to waffle their way through sexually relevant encounters driven both by the allure of reward and the fear of negative consequences" (Wagner, 2011, p. 193). They have much to learn. Where do they learn it?

From the Media

Many adolescents learn about sex from the media. The Internet is a common source. Unfortunately, Web sites are often frightening (featuring pictures of diseased sexual organs) or mesmerizing (containing pornography), and young adolescents are particularly naive.

Girls Together These two girls from Sweden are comfortable lying close to one another. Many boys of this age wouldn't want their photograph taken if they were this close to each other. Around the world, there are cultural and gender norms about what are acceptable expressions of physical affection among friends during adolescence.

Media consumption peaks at puberty. The television shows and videos most watched by teenagers include sexual content almost seven times per hour (Steinberg & Monahan, 2011). That content is alluring: Almost never does a character on the screen develop an STI, deal with an unwanted pregnancy, or mention (much less use) a condom.

Adolescents with intense exposure to sexual content on the screen and in music are more often sexually active, but the direction of this correlation is controversial (R. Collins et al., 2011; Steinberg & Monahan, 2011). The connection is not immediate and direct. Instead, the sexual media may increase an adolescent's focus on external appearance and seeing the body as an object, which may lead to greater sexual activity (Vandenbosch & Eggermont, 2015). One analysis concludes that "the most important influences on adolescents' sexual behavior may be closer to home than to Hollywood" (Steinberg & Monahan, 2011, p. 575).

From Parents and Peers

As that quote implies, sex education begins at home. Every study finds that parental communication influences adolescents' behavior, and many programs of sex education explicitly require parental participation (Silk & Romero, 2014). However, embarrassment and ignorance are common on both sides.

Many parents underestimate their own child's sexual activity, while fearing that the child's social connections are far too sexual (Elliott, 2012).

What should parents tell their children? That is the wrong question, according to a longitudinal study of thousands of adolescents. Teens who were most likely to risk an STI had parents who warned them to stay away from all sex. In contrast, adolescents were more likely to remain virgins if they had a warm relationship with their parents—specific information was less important than open communication (Deptula et al., 2010). Parents should not shy away from discussions about sex, but honest conversation between parent and child provides better protection than detailed sex-related discussion (Hicks et al., 2013).

Especially when parents are silent, forbidding, or vague, adolescent sexual behavior is strongly influenced by peers. Boys learn about sex from other boys (Henry et al., 2012), girls from other girls, with the strongest influence being what peers say they have done, not something abstract (Choukas-Bradley et al., 2014).

Partners also teach each other. However, their lessons are more about pleasure than consequences: Most U.S. adolescent couples do not decide together *before* they have sex how they will prevent pregnancy and disease, and what they will do if their prevention efforts fail. Adolescents were asked whom they discussed sexual issues with. Friends were the most common confidants, then parents, and last of all dating partners. Indeed, only half of them had *ever* discussed anything about sex with their sexual partner (Widman et al., 2014).

From Educators

Sex education from teachers varies dramatically by nation. The curriculum for middle schools in most European nations includes information about masturbation, same-sex romance, oral and anal sex, and specific uses and failures of various methods of contraception—subjects almost never covered in U.S. classes, even in high school. Rates of teenage pregnancy in most European nations are less than half of those in the United States. Perhaps curriculum is the reason, although obviously curriculum is part of the larger culture, and cultural differences regarding sex are vast.

Within the United States, the timing and content of sex education vary by state and community. Some high schools provide comprehensive education, free condoms, and medical treatment; others provide nothing. Some schools begin sex education in the sixth grade; others wait until senior year of high school. Some middle school sex-education programs successfully increase condom use and delay the age when adolescents become sexually active, but other programs have no impact (Hamilton et al., 2013; Kirby & Laris, 2009).

One controversy has been whether sexual abstinence should be taught as the only acceptable strategy. It is true, of course, that abstaining from sex (including oral and anal sex) prevents STIs, and that abstinence precludes pregnancy, but longitudinal data on abstinence-only education, four to six years after adolescents were taught, are disappointing. For instance, about half of the students in both

To Be a Woman Here Miley Cyrus performs for thousands of fans in Brooklyn, New York. Does pop culture make it difficult for teenagers of both sexes to reconcile their own sexual impulses with the images of their culture?

Especially for Sex Educators
Suppose adults in your community never talk to their children about sex or puberty. Is that a mistake? (see response, page 449)

THINK CRITICALLY: Are teenagers drawn to sexy images because they are sexually active, or does the media cause them to be sexually involved?

LaunchPad macmillan learning

Check out the Data Connections activity **Sexual Behaviors of U.S. High School Students,** which examines how sexually active teens really are.

Laugh and Learn Emotions are as crucial as facts in sex education.

⬤⬤ **Response for Parents of a Teenager**
(from page 444): Remember: Communicate, do not control. Let your child talk about the meaning of the hairstyle. Remind yourself that a hairstyle in itself is harmless. Don't say "What will people think?" or "Are you on drugs?" or anything that might give your child reason to stop communicating.

Download the **DSM-5 Appendix** to learn more about the terminology and classification of various disorders.

Blot Out the World Teenagers sometimes despair at their future, as Anthony Ghost-Redfeather did in South Dakota. He tried to kill himself, and, like many boys involved in parasuicide, he is ashamed that he failed.

the experimental group (abstinence-only) and in the control group (more comprehensive sex education) had had sex by age 16 (Trenholm et al., 2007). Students in the abstinence group knew slightly less about preventing disease and pregnancy, but their sexual activity was as frequent as their more knowledgeable peers.

Some social scientists contend that the problem is that U.S. educators and parents present morals and facts to adolescents, but teen behavior is driven by social values and emotions. Sexual behavior does not spring from the prefrontal cortex: Knowing how and why to use a condom does not guarantee a careful, wise choice when passions run high. Consequently, effective sex education must engage emotions more than logic and involves role-playing with other teens and frank discussions with parents (Suleiman & Brindis, 2014).

WHAT HAVE YOU LEARNED?

1. How does the influence of peers and parents differ for adolescents?
2. Why do many adults misunderstand the role of peer pressure?
3. What is the role of parents, peers, and society in helping an adolescent develop an ethnic identity?
4. How do adolescents choose romantic partners, and what do they do together?
5. How does culture affect sexual orientation?
6. From whom do adolescents usually learn about sex?
7. What does the research say about sex education in schools?

Sadness and Anger

Adolescence can be a wonderful time. Nonetheless, troubles plague about 20 percent of youths. For instance, one specific survey of more than 10,000 13- to 17-year-olds in the United States found that 23 percent had a disorder in the past month (Kessler et al., 2012). Most disorders are comorbid, with several problems occurring at once, and some are temporary—not too serious and soon outgrown. However, some are very serious.

We need to distinguish between pathology and normal moodiness, between behavior that is seriously troubled versus merely unsettling. Sometimes negative emotions become intense, chronic, even deadly.

Depression

The general emotional trend from early childhood to early adolescence is toward less confidence and higher rates of depression. Then, gradually, self-esteem increases in late adolescence and early adulthood. A dip in self-esteem at puberty is found for children of every ethnicity and gender (Fredricks & Eccles, 2002; Greene & Way, 2005; Kutob et al., 2010; Zeiders et al., 2013), with notable individual differences.

Universal trends, as well as family effects, are apparent. A report from China also finds a dip in self-esteem at seventh grade (when many Chinese adolescents experience puberty) and then a gradual rise. Recent cohorts of Chinese teenagers have lower self-esteem than earlier cohorts. The authors ascribe this to reduced social connections: Many youth have no siblings or cousins, many parents are employed far from their children, and divorce has become more common (Liu & Xin, 2014).

Self-esteem tends to be higher in boys than girls, African Americans than European Americans, who themselves have higher self-esteem than Asian Americans.

All studies find notable variability among people the same age, yet continuity within each person. Severe depression may lift, but it rarely disappears (Huang, 2010). Context and values matter.

The cultural norm of familism may be protective. For immigrant Latino youth, self-esteem and ethnic pride are higher than for most other groups, and a rise over the years of adolescence is common. When compared to the high rates of depression among European American girls, the Latina rise in self-esteem is particularly notable (Zeiders et al., 2013). Perhaps familism is the reason: Latinas become increasingly helpful at home, which makes their parents appreciative and them proud, unlike other U.S. teenage girls.

On the other hand, some families expect high achievement for every adolescent, and teens are quick to criticize themselves and everyone else when any sign of failure appears (Bleys et al., 2016). The danger is perfectionism, and when a teenager realizes that it is impossible to be perfect, depression may result (Damian et al., 2013). Perfectionism is considered one cause of teenage eating disorders (Wade et al., 2016).

Major Depressive Disorder

Some adolescents sink into **major depression,** a deep sadness and hopelessness that disrupts all normal, regular activities. The causes, including genes and early care, predate adolescence. Then the onset of puberty—with its myriad physical and emotional ups and downs—pushes some vulnerable children, especially girls, into despair. The rate of serious depression more than doubles during this time, to an estimated 15 percent, affecting about 1 in 5 girls and 1 in 10 boys, probably for many reasons, biological (hormonal) and cultural.

Differential susceptibility is apparent. One study found that the short allele of the serotonin transporter promoter gene (5-HTTLPR) increased the rate of depression among girls everywhere but increased depression among boys only if they lived in low-SES communities (Uddin et al., 2010). It is not surprising that vulnerability to depression is partly genetic, but why does neighborhood affect boys more than girls? Perhaps cultural factors depress females everywhere, but boys may be protected unless jobs, successful adult men, and encouragement within their community are scarce.

A cognitive explanation for gender differences in depression focuses on **rumination**—talking about, brooding, and mentally replaying past experiences. Girls ruminate much more than boys, and rumination often leads to depression (Michl et al., 2013). However, when rumination occurs with a close friend after a stressful event, the friend's support may be helpful (Rose et al., 2014). This is thought to be one reason girls are less likely to commit suicide. Differential susceptibility again.

Suicide

Serious, distressing thoughts about killing oneself (called **suicidal ideation**) are most common at about age 15. More than one-third (40 percent) of U.S. high school girls felt so hopeless that they stopped doing some usual activities for two weeks or more in the previous year (an indication of depression), and nearly one-fourth (23 percent) seriously thought about suicide. The corresponding rates for boys were 20 percent and 12 percent (MMWR, June 10, 2016).

Suicidal ideation can lead to **parasuicide,** also called *attempted suicide* or *failed suicide.* Parasuicide includes any deliberate self-harm that could have been lethal. *Parasuicide* is the best word to use because "failed" suicide implies that to die is to succeed (!). Suicide "attempt" is likewise misleading because, especially in adolescence, the difference between attempt and completed suicide may be luck and prompt treatment, not intent.

major depression Feelings of hopelessness, lethargy, and worthlessness that last two weeks or more.

rumination Repeatedly thinking and talking about past experiences; can contribute to depression.

suicidal ideation Thinking about suicide, usually with some serious emotional and intellectual or cognitive overtones.

parasuicide Any potentially lethal action against the self that does not result in death. (Also called *attempted suicide* or *failed suicide.*)

FIGURE 16.4

Sad Thoughts Completed suicide is rare in adolescence, but serious thoughts about killing oneself are frequent. Depression and parasuicide are more common in girls than in boys, but rates are high even in boys. There are three reasons to suspect that the rates for boys are underestimates: Boys tend to be less aware of their emotions than girls are, boys consider it unmanly to try to kill themselves and fail, and completed suicide is also higher in males than in females.

Observation Quiz Does thinking seriously about suicide increase or decrease during high school? (see answer, page 452) ➡

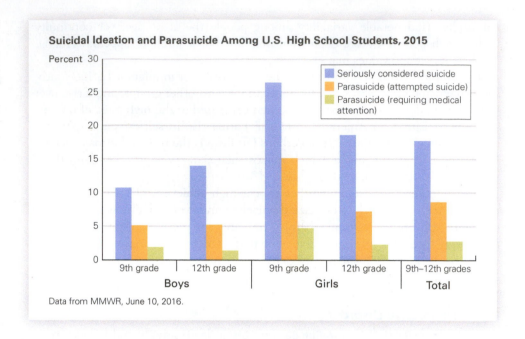

Suicidal Ideation and Parasuicide Among U.S. High School Students, 2015

Data from MMWR, June 10, 2016.

As you see in Figure 16.4, parasuicide can be divided according to instances that require medical attention (surgery, pumped stomach, etc.) and those that do not, but any parasuicide is a warning. If there is a next time, the person may die. Thus, parasuicide must be taken very seriously.

An ominous sign, particularly for adolescent boys from low-SES families, is a Google search for "how to kill yourself" (Ma-Kellams et al., 2016). Among U.S. high school students in 2015, 11.6 percent of the girls and 5.5 percent of the boys attempted suicide in the previous year (MMWR, June 10, 2016).

Although suicidal ideation during adolescence is common, completed suicides are not. The U.S. annual rate of completed suicide for people aged 15 to 19 (in school or not) is less than 8 per 100,000, or 0.008 percent, which is only half the rate for adults aged 20 and older (Parks et al., 2014). This is an important statistic to keep in mind whenever someone claims that adolescent suicide is "epidemic." It is not.

THINK CRITICALLY: Why would suicide rates increase with income?

Because they are more emotional and egocentric than logical and analytical, adolescents are particularly affected when they hear about someone's suicide, either through the media or from peers (Niedzwiedz et al., 2014). That makes them susceptible to **cluster suicides,** which are several suicides within a group over a brief span of time. For that reason, media portrayals of a tragic suicide may inadvertently trigger more deaths.

cluster suicides Several suicides committed by members of a group within a brief period.

Delinquency and Defiance

Like low self-esteem and suicidal ideation, bouts of anger are common in adolescence. In fact, a moody adolescent could be both depressed and delinquent because externalizing and internalizing behavior are closely connected during these years (Loeber & Burke, 2011). This may explain suicide in jail: Teenagers jailed for assault (externalizing) are higher suicide risks (internalizing) than adult prisoners.

Especially for Journalists You just heard that a teenage cheerleader jumped off a tall building and died. How should you report the story? (see response, page 452)

Externalizing actions are obvious. Many adolescents slam doors, curse parents, and tell friends exactly how badly other teenagers (or siblings or teachers) have behaved. Some teenagers—particularly boys—"act out" by breaking laws. They steal, damage property, or injure others.

One issue is whether teenage anger is not only common but also necessary for normal development. That is what Anna Freud (Sigmund's daughter, herself a prominent psychoanalyst) thought. She wrote that adolescent resistance to parental authority was "welcome . . . beneficial . . . inevitable." She explained:

> We all know individual children who, as late as the ages of fourteen, fifteen or sixteen, show no such outer evidence of inner unrest. They remain, as they have been during the latency period, "good" children, wrapped up in their family relationships, considerate sons of their mothers, submissive to their fathers, in accord with the atmosphere, idea and ideal of their childhood background. Convenient as this may be, it signifies a delay of their normal development and is, as such, a sign to be taken seriously.

[A. Freud, 1958/2000, p. 37]

However, most contemporary psychologists, teachers, and parents are quite happy with well-behaved, considerate teenagers, who often grow up to be happy adults. A 30-year longitudinal study found that adults who had never been arrested usually earned degrees, "held high-status jobs, and expressed optimism about their own futures" (Moffitt, 2003, p. 61).

In Every Nation Everywhere, older adolescents are most likely to protest against government authority. *(left)* Younger adolescents in Alabama celebrate the 50-year anniversary of the historic Selma-to-Montgomery march across the Pettus Bridge. In that historic movement, most of those beaten and killed were under age 25. *(right)* In the fall of 2014, thousands of students in Hong Kong led pro-democracy protests, which began peacefully but led, days later, to violent confrontations, shown here as they began.

> **THINK CRITICALLY:** If parents and society became more appreciative of this stage of life, rather than fearful of it, might that lead to healthier and more peaceful teenagers?

Breaking the Law

Both the prevalence (how widespread) and the incidence (how frequent) of criminal actions are higher during adolescence than earlier or later. Arrest statistics in every nation reflect this fact, with 30 percent of African American males and 22 percent of European American males being arrested at least once before age 18 (Brame et al., 2014).

We do not know how many young people have broken the law but not been caught, or caught but not arrested. Confidential self-reports suggest that most adolescents (male or female) break the law at least once before age 20. Boys are three times as likely as girls to be caught, arrested, and convicted. In general, youth of minority ethnic groups, and low-SES families, are more likely to be arrested.

Regarding gender, it is true that boys are more overtly aggressive and rebellious at every age, but this may be nurture, not nature (Loeber et al., 2013). Some studies find that female aggression is typically limited to family and friends, and it is therefore less likely to lead to an arrest.

Determining accurate gender, ethnic, and income differences in actual lawbreaking, not just in arrests, is complex. Both self-reports and police responses may be biased. For instance, research in the Netherlands found that one-third of those interrogated by the police later denied any police contact (van Batenburg-Eddes et al., 2012).

Who Is Happy? At least six people are directly involved here, not only Janelle Evans and her second child (shown here), but also her first child (Jace), her mother, and the two estranged fathers of the two boys. Indirectly, millions more are involved, as Janelle had Jace when she was a high school senior, as featured on *Teen Mom,* an MTV reality show. Her mother won custody of Jace. Janelle has had six boyfriends, numerous arrests, one marriage, and, in 2016, she became pregnant again.

adolescence-limited offender A person whose criminal activity stops by age 21.

life-course-persistent offender A person whose criminal activity typically begins in early adolescence and continues throughout life; a career criminal.

● ● **Answer to Observation Quiz**
(from page 450): Both. It increases for boys but decreases for girls.

● ● **Response for Journalists**
(from page 450): Since teenagers seek admiration from their peers, be careful not to glorify the victim's life or death. Facts are needed, as is, perhaps, inclusion of warning signs that were missed or cautions about alcohol abuse. Avoid prominent headlines or anything that might encourage another teenager to do the same thing.

On the other hand, adolescents sometimes say that they committed a crime when they did not. Overall, in the United States, about 20 percent of confessions are false, and that is more likely before age 20. There are many reasons that a young person might confess falsely: Brain immaturity makes them less likely to consider long-term consequences, and sometimes they prioritize protecting family members, defending friends, and pleasing adults—including the police (Feld, 2013; Steinberg, 2009).

Many researchers distinguish between two kinds of teenage lawbreakers (Monahan et al., 2013), as first proposed by Terri Moffitt (2001, 2003).

1. Most juvenile delinquents are **adolescence-limited offenders,** whose criminal activity stops by age 21. They break the law with their friends, facilitated by their chosen antisocial peers.
2. Some delinquents are **life-course-persistent offenders,** who break the law before and after adolescence as well as during it. Their lawbreaking is more often done alone than as part of a gang, and the cause is neurological impairment (either inborn or caused by early experiences). Symptoms include not only childhood defiance but also early problems with language and learning.

During adolescence, the criminal records of both types may be similar. However, if adolescence-limited delinquents can be protected from various snares (such as quitting school, entering prison, drug addiction), they outgrow their criminal behavior. This is confirmed by other research: Few delinquent youths who are not imprisoned continue to be criminals in early adulthood (Monahan et al., 2009).

Causes of Delinquency

The best way to reduce adolescent crime is to notice earlier behavior that predicts lawbreaking and to change patterns before puberty. Strong and protective social relationships, emotional regulation, and moral values from childhood keep many teenagers from jail. In early adolescence, three signs predict delinquency:

1. *Stubbornness* can lead to defiance, which can lead to running away. Runaways are often victims as well as criminals (e.g., falling in with prostitutes and petty thieves).
2. *Shoplifting* can lead to arson and burglary. Things become more important than people.
3. *Bullying* can lead to assault, rape, and murder.

Each of these pathways demands a different response. Stubbornness responds to social support—the rebel who feels understood, not punished, will gradually become less impulsive and irrational. The second pathway requires strengthening human relationships and moral education. Those who exhibit the third behavior present the most serious problem. Bullying should have been stopped in childhood, as Chapters 10 and 13 explained, and these adolescents need to develop other ways to connect with people.

In all cases, early warning signs are present, and intervention is more effective earlier than later (Loeber & Burke, 2011). Childhood family relationships are crucial, particularly for girls (Rhoades et al., 2015).

Adolescent crime in the United States and many other nations has decreased in the past 20 years. Only half as many juveniles under age 18 are currently arrested for murder than was true in 1990. No explanation for this decline is accepted by all scholars. Among the possibilities:

- fewer high school dropouts (more education means less crime);
- wiser judges (using more community service than prison);
- better policing (arrests for misdemeanors are up, which may warn parents);

- smaller families (parents are more attentive to each of 2 children than each of 12);
- better contraception and legal abortion (wanted children are less likely to become criminals);
- stricter drug laws (binge drinking and crack use increase crime);
- more immigrants (who are more law-abiding);
- less lead in the blood (early lead poisoning reduces brain functioning); and more.

Nonetheless, adolescents remain more likely to break the law than adults. To be specific, the arrest rate for 15- to 17-year-olds is twice that for those over 18. The disproportion is true for almost every crime (fraud, forgery, and embezzlement are exceptions) (FBI, 2015).

WHAT HAVE YOU LEARNED?

1. What is the difference between adolescent sadness and clinical depression?
2. Why do many adults think adolescent suicide is more common than it is?
3. How can rumination contribute to gender differences in depression?
4. Why are cluster suicides more common in adolescence than in later life?
5. What are the similarities between life-course-persistent and adolescence-limited offenders?

LaunchPad
macmillan learning

Video: Risk Taking in Adolescence: Substance Abuse
http://qrs.ly/xf4ep1k

Drug Use and Abuse

Hormonal surges, the brain's reward centers, and cognitive immaturity make adolescents particularly attracted to the sensations produced by psychoactive drugs. But their immature bodies and brains make drug use especially hazardous.

Variations in Drug Use

Most teenagers try *psychoactive drugs,* that is, drugs that activate the brain. Cigarettes, alcohol, and many prescription medicines are as addictive and damaging as illegal drugs such as cocaine and heroin.

Age Trends

For many developmental reasons, adolescence is a sensitive time for experimentation, daily use, and eventual addiction to psychoactive drugs (Schulenberg et al., 2014). Both prevalence and incidence of drug use increase from about ages 10 to 25 and then decrease when adult responsibilities and experiences make drugs less attractive. Most worrisome is drinking alcohol and smoking cigarettes before age 15, because early use escalates. That makes depression, sexual abuse, bullying, and later addiction more likely (Merikangas & McClair, 2012; Mennis & Mason, 2012).

Although drug use increases every year from ages 10 to 21, one drug follows another pattern—*inhalants* (fumes from aerosol containers, glue, cleaning fluid, etc.). Sadly, the youngest adolescents are most likely to try inhalants, because inhalants are easiest to get and the adolescents' cognitive immaturity makes them less likely to understand the risk of one-time use—brain damage and even death.

A Man Now This boy in Tibet is proud to be a smoker—in many Asian nations, smoking is considered manly.

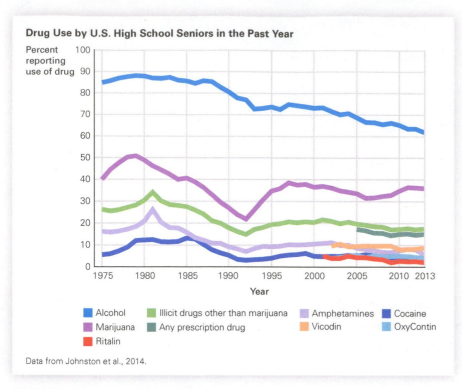

Drug Use by U.S. High School Seniors in the Past Year

Percent reporting use of drug

Legend:
- Alcohol
- Marijuana
- Ritalin
- Illicit drugs other than marijuana
- Any prescription drug
- Amphetamines
- Vicodin
- Cocaine
- OxyContin

Data from Johnston et al., 2014.

FIGURE 16.5

Rise and Fall By asking the same questions year after year, the Monitoring the Future study shows notable historical effects. It is encouraging that something in society, not in the adolescent, makes drug use increase and decrease and that the most recent data show a decline. However, as Chapter 1 emphasized, survey research cannot prove what causes change.

Cohort differences are evident, even over a few years. Use of most drugs has decreased in the United States since 1976 (see Figure 16.5), with the most recent decreases in synthetic narcotics and prescription drugs (Johnston et al., 2014). As mentioned in Chapter 1, vaping (using e-cigarettes) is increasing rapidly during adolescence. Data from the past few years shows that cigarette smoking in down, but vaping is escalating. As you read in Chapter 1, this bodes ill for later cigarette use (Park et al., 2016).

Longitudinal data show that the availability of drugs does not have much impact on use: Most high school students say that they could easily get alcohol, cigarettes, and marijuana if they wish. Most U.S. states prohibit purchase of e-cigarettes by those under age 18, but younger teens can buy them from 116 Internet vendors with no problem (Nikitin et al., 2016). Availability does not affect use, but perception of risks does, and that varies markedly from cohort to cohort (Miech et al., 2016).

Harm from Drugs

Many researchers find that drug use before maturity is particularly likely to harm body and brain growth. However, adolescents typically deny that they ever could become addicted. Few adolescents notice when they or their friends move past *use* (experimenting) to *abuse* (experiencing harm) and then to *addiction* (needing the drug to avoid feeling nervous, anxious, sick, or in pain).

Each drug is harmful in a particular way. An obvious negative effect of *tobacco* is that it impairs digestion and nutrition, slowing down growth. This is true not only for cigarettes but also for bidis, cigars, pipes, chewing tobacco, and probably e-cigarettes. Since internal organs continue to mature after the height spurt, drug-using teenagers who appear to be fully grown may damage their developing hearts, lungs, brains, and reproductive systems.

OPPOSING PERSPECTIVES

E-Cigarettes: Path to Addiction or Healthy Choice?

Controversial is the use of *e-cigarettes,* which are increasingly available and often tried by adolescents. If using e-cigs, or vaping, helps smokers quit, then e-cigarettes literally save lives. Smokers with asthma, heart disease, or lung cancer who find it impossible to stop smoking cigarettes are often able to switch to vaping with notable health benefits (Burstyn, 2014; Franck et al., 2014; Hajek et al., 2014).

However, the fear is that adolescents who try e-cigarettes will become addicted to nicotine as well as being harmed from some other ingredients. Part of the problem is that e-cigarettes are marketed with flavors and appearance that make them

attractive to teenagers. It is known that menthol cigarettes and hookah bars increase the rate of cigarette smoking among young people (Giovino et al., 2012; Sterling & Mermelstein, 2011); e-cigs may do the same (Park et al., 2016).

A victory of North American public health has been a marked reduction in smoking of regular cigarettes. Not only are there only half as many adult smokers as there were in 1950, there are numerous public places where smoking in forbidden, and many people now forbid anyone to smoke in their homes. In the United States in 2010, such homes are the majority (83 percent), an increase from almost zero in 1970 and 43 percent in

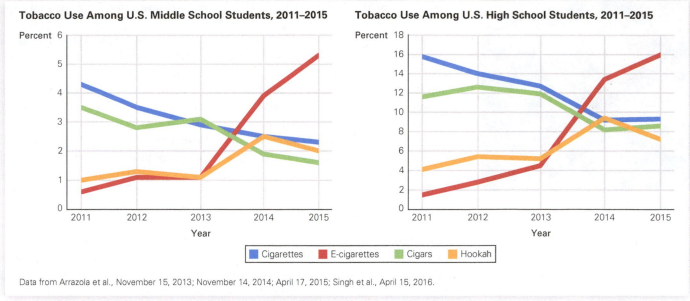

Data from Arrazola et al., November 15, 2013; November 14, 2014; April 17, 2015; Singh et al., April 15, 2016.

FIGURE 16.6

Rise and Fall These data are frightening to public health advocates, who see that the steady decline in cigarette smoking among teens is halted just as e-cigs increase.

1992. Many of those homes have no smoking residents, but cigarettes are banned at 46 percent of the homes where a smoker lives (MMWR, September 5, 2014). Adolescent smoking has markedly declined, primarily because adolescents now consider smoking much more harmful than they did a few decades ago (Miech et al., 2016) (see Figure 16.6).

That is a reason to celebrate, but therein lies the danger. If e-cigarettes make smoking more acceptable, will adolescents pick up the habits that their elders gave up?

E-cigs are illegal for people under age 18, but they are marketed in flavors like bubble gum, can be placed for a fee in Hollywood movies, and are permitted in many public places. If the image of smoking changes from a "cancer stick" to a "glamour accessory," will public health progress stop?

The argument from distributors of e-cigarettes is that they are a healthier alternative to cigarettes, that people should be able to make their own choices, and that the fear of adolescent vaping is exaggerated—part of the irrational fear that everything teenagers do is trouble. As with all opposing perspectives, attitudes depend on who is judging.

Choose Your Flavor Mint- and chocolate-flavored e-cigarettes are particularly popular among adolescents.

Alcohol is the most frequently abused drug in North America. Heavy drinking impairs memory and self-control by damaging the hippocampus and the prefrontal cortex, perhaps distorting the reward circuits of the brain lifelong (Guerri & Pascual, 2010). Adolescence is a particularly sensitive period, because the regions of the brain that are connected to pleasure are more strongly affected by alcohol during adolescence than at later ages. That makes teenagers less

Especially for Police Officers You see some 15-year-olds drinking beer in a local park when they belong in school. What do you do? (see response, page 457)

Relaxing on Marijuana? Synthetic marijuana ("K-2," or "Spice") can be a deadly drug, evident in this young man unconscious on a Harlem sidewalk. Since secret chemicals are mixed and added in manufacturing, neither laws nor hospitals can keep up with new toxic substances.

● **Especially for Parents Who Drink Socially** You have heard that parents should allow their children to drink at home, to teach them to drink responsibly and not get drunk elsewhere. Is that wise? (see response, page 459)

Choose Your Weed No latte or beer offered here, although this looks like the place where previous generations bought drinks. Instead, at A Greener Today in Seattle, Washington, customers ask for 1 of 20 possibilities—all marijuana.

conscious of the "intoxicating, aversive, and sedative effects" of alcohol (Spear, 2013, p. 155).

Marijuana seems harmless to many people (especially teenagers), partly because users seem more relaxed than inebriated. Yet adolescents who regularly smoke marijuana are more likely to drop out of school, become teenage parents, be depressed, and later be unemployed. Some of this may be correlation, not causation, but a longitudinal study that used neurological evidence showed decreasing connections with the brain as well as lower intelligence among adolescents who used marijuana habitually compared to a control group who did not use marijuana (Camchong et al., 2016).

It seems that marijuana affects memory, language proficiency, and motivation—all of which are especially crucial during adolescence (Chassin et al., 2014). Many developmentalists fear that more acceptance of marijuana among adults will lead to less learning, reduced motivation, and poorer health among teenagers.

As noted, some people suggest that the connection between drug use (including cigarettes, alcohol, marijuana, and illegal drugs) and later low achievement and poor health are correlations, not causes. It is true that depressed and abused adolescents are more likely to use drugs, and that whether or not they use drugs, they are more likely to become depressed and abused adults. Might the stress of adolescence lead to drug use, and then might drugs reduce anxiety rather than make problems worse? A plausible hypothesis, but a disproven one.

Longitudinal research suggests that drug use *causes* more problems than it solves, often *preceding* anxiety disorders, depression, and rebellion (Maslowsky et al., 2014). Further, adolescents who use alcohol, cigarettes, and marijuana recreationally as teenagers are more likely to abuse these and other drugs after age 20 (Moss et al., 2014).

Longitudinal studies of twins (which control for genetics and family) find that, many problems predate drug use, with genes and neighborhoods a partial cause of addiction as well as conduct disorder in adolescence. However, while drugs should not be blamed for all problems, they do not help (Lynskey et al., 2012; Korhonen et al., 2012; Verweij et al., 2016).

Most adolescents covet the drugs that slightly older youth use. Many 18-year-olds will buy drugs for younger siblings and classmates, supposedly being kind.

New Zealand lowered the age for legal purchase of alcohol from 20 to 18 in 1999, and the nation experienced an uptick in hospital admission for intoxication, car crashes, and injuries from assault in both 18- to 19-year-olds and 16- to 17-year-olds (Kypri et al., 2006, 2014). Developmentalists rightly fear adolescent drug use but are not sure how best to reduce it.

Preventing Drug Abuse: What Works?

Drug abuse is progressive, beginning with a social occasion and ending alone. The first use usually occurs with friends; occasional use seems to be a common expression of friendship or generational solidarity. An early sign of trouble is lower school achievement, but few notice that as soon as they should (see Visualizing Development, p. 458, for school dropout rates). Overall drug use, legal and illegal, bought on the street and prescribed by doctors, has decreased among adolescents in recent years. (E-cigs are an exception.)

The Monitoring the Future study found that in 2015:

- 17 percent of high school seniors report having had five drinks in a row in the past two weeks.
- 6 percent smoked cigarettes every day for the past month.
- 6 percent smoked marijuana every day.

[Miech et al., 2016]

These figures are ominous, suggesting that addiction is the next step. Drug use is a topic in the next chapter as well, because the variety of drugs, including "club" drugs, and the obvious harm is apparent for 18- to 25-year-olds. The other class of drugs often abused in adolescence is prescription drugs, usually obtained from family and friends but sometimes directly from a physician. These can be addictive as well.

Remember that most adolescents think they are exceptions, sometimes feeling invincible, sometimes extremely fearful of social disapproval, but almost never worried that they themselves will become addicts. They rarely realize that every psychoactive drug excites the limbic system and interferes with the prefrontal cortex.

Because of these neurological reactions, drug users are more emotional (varying from euphoria to terror, from paranoia to rage) than they would otherwise be. They are also less reflective. Moodiness and impulsivity are characteristic of adolescents, and drugs make them worse. Every hazard—including car crashes, unsafe sex, and suicide—is more common among teens who have taken a psychoactive drug.

With harmful drugs, as with many other aspects of life, each generation prefers to learn things for themselves. A common phenomenon is **generational forgetting,** the idea that each new generation forgets what the previous generation learned (Chassin et al., 2014; Johnston et al., 2012). Mistrust of the older generation, added to loyalty to one's peers, leads not only to generational forgetting but also to a backlash. When adults forbid something, that is a reason to try it, especially if the adolescent realizes that some adults exaggerate the dangers. If a friend passes out from drug use, adolescents may hesitate to get medical help.

Some antidrug curricula and advertisements actually make drugs seem exciting. Antismoking announcements produced by cigarette companies (such as a clean-cut young person advising viewers to think before they smoke) actually increase use (Strasburger et al., 2009).

This does not mean that trying to halt early drug use is hopeless. Massive ad campaigns by public health advocates in Florida and California cut adolescent smoking almost in half, in part because the publicity appealed to the young. Public health advocates have learned that teenagers respond to graphic images. In one example:

> A young man walks up to a convenience store counter and asks for a pack of cigarettes. He throws some money on the counter, but the cashier says "that's not enough." So the young man pulls out a pair of pliers, wrenches out one of his teeth, and hands it over. . . . A voiceover asks: "What's a pack of smokes cost? Your teeth."
>
> [Krisberg, 2014]

Parental example and social changes also make a difference. Throughout the United States, higher prices, targeted warnings, and better law enforcement have led to a marked decline in cigarette smoking among younger adolescents. Looking internationally, laws have an effect. In Canada, cigarette advertising is outlawed, and cigarettes packs have graphic pictures of diseased lungs, rotting teeth, and so on; fewer Canadian 15- to 19-year-olds smoke.

In the past three chapters, we see that the universal biological processes do not lead to universal psychosocial problems. Sharply declining rates of teenage

Response for Police Officers (from page 455): Avoid both extremes: Don't let them think this situation is either harmless or serious. You might take them to the police station and call their parents. These adolescents are probably not life-course-persistent offenders; jailing them or grouping them with other lawbreakers might encourage more crime.

THINK CRITICALLY: Might the fear of adolescent drug use be foolish, if most adolescents use drugs whether or not they are forbidden?

generational forgetting The idea that each new generation forgets what the previous generation learned. As used here, the term refers to knowledge about the harm drugs can do.

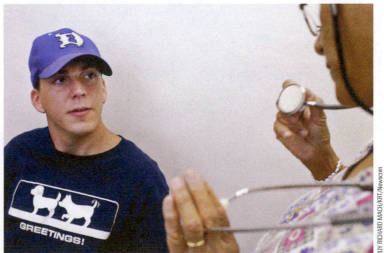

Serious Treatment A nurse checks Steve Duffle's blood pressure after a dose of Naltrexone, a drug with many side effects that combats severe addiction, in this case addiction to heroin. Steve was 24 when this photo was taken.

How Many Adolescents Are in School?

Attendance in secondary school is a psychosocial topic as much as a cognitive one. Whether or not an adolescent is in school reflects every aspect of the social context, including national policies, family support, peer pressures, employment prospects, and other economic concerns. Rates of violence, delinquency, poverty, and births to girls younger than 17 increase as school attendance decreases.

PERCENTAGE OF SECONDARY SCHOOL-AGED CHILDREN NOT IN SCHOOL

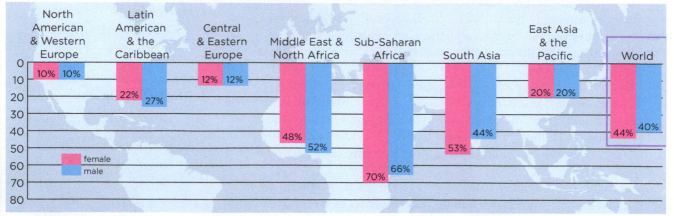

DATA FROM UNESCO, 2011; UNICEF, JULY, 2014.

SELECTED SECONDARY SCHOOL GRADUATION RATES

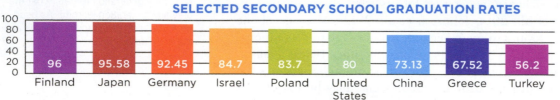

Finland	Japan	Germany	Israel	Poland	United States	China	Greece	Turkey
96	95.58	92.45	84.7	83.7	80	73.13	67.52	56.2

DATA FROM OECD, 2013.

U.S. HIGH SCHOOL GRADUATION RATE, CLASS OF 2012

In the United States, the poorest students are five times more likely to drop out of school than the wealthiest.

(RUMBERGER, 2012)

Almost a third of U.S. girls who drop out of school do so because they are pregnant. This is both a cause and a consequence.

(SHUGER, 2012)

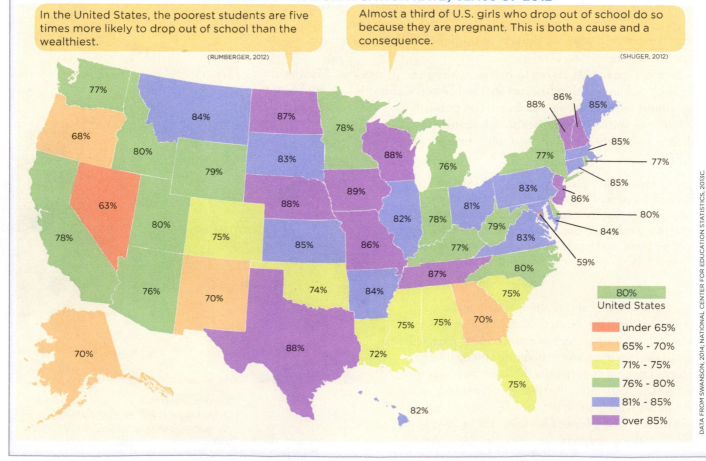

DATA FROM SWANSON, 2014; NATIONAL CENTER FOR EDUCATION STATISTICS, 2013C.

births and abortions (Chapter 14), increasing numbers graduating from high school (Chapter 15), and less misuse of legal drugs and use of illegal drugs are apparent in many nations.

Adolescence starts with puberty; that much is universal. But what happens next depends on parents, peers, schools, communities, and cultures.

Response for Parents Who Drink Socially (from page 456): No. Alcohol is particularly harmful for young brains. It is best to drink only when your children are not around. Children who are encouraged to drink with their parents are more likely to drink when no adults are present. It is true that adolescents are rebellious, and they may drink even if you forbid it. But if you allow alcohol, they might rebel with other drugs.

WHAT HAVE YOU LEARNED?

1. Why are psychoactive drugs particularly attractive in adolescence?

2. Why are psychoactive drugs particularly destructive in adolescence?

3. What specific harm occurs with tobacco products?

4. Why are developmentalists particularly worried about e-cigarettes?

5. What methods to reduce adolescent drug use are successful?

SUMMARY

Identity

1. Adolescence is a time for self-discovery. According to Erikson, adolescents seek their own identity, sorting through the traditions and values of their families and cultures.

2. Many young adolescents foreclose on their options without exploring possibilities, and many experience role confusion. Older adolescents might seek a moratorium. Identity achievement takes longer for contemporary adolescents than it did a half-century ago when Erikson first described it.

3. Identity achievement occurs in many domains, including religion, politics, vocation, and sex. Each of these remains important over the life span, but timing, contexts, and often terminology have changed since Erikson and Marcia first described them. Achieving vocational and gender identity is particularly difficult in adolescence.

Relationships with Adults

4. Parents continue to influence their growing children, despite bickering over minor issues. Ideally, communication and warmth remain high within the family, while parental control decreases and adolescents develop autonomy.

5. There are cultural differences in the timing of conflicts and in the particulars of parental monitoring. Too much parental control is harmful, as is neglect. Parents need to find a balance between granting freedom and providing guidance.

Peer Power

6. Peers and peer pressure can be beneficial or harmful, depending on the particular friends. Adolescents select their friends, including friends of the other sex, who then facilitate constructive and/or destructive behavior. Adolescents seek the approval of their peers, sometimes engaging in risky behavior to gain such approval.

7. Like adults, adolescents experience diverse sexual needs and may be involved in short-term or long-term romances, depending in part on their peer group.

8. Some youths are sexually attracted to people of the same sex. Depending on the culture and cohort, they may have a more difficult adolescence than others, including being bullied or worse.

9. Many adolescents learn about sex from peers and the media—sources that do not provide a balanced picture. Ideally, parents are the best teachers about sex, but many are silent and naive.

10. Age of first intercourse has become later, on average, over the past decades with more than a third of high school seniors still virgins. Young couples rarely discuss contraception and pregnancy.

11. Most parents want schools to teach adolescents about sex. Education varies from nation to nation, with some nations providing comprehensive education beginning in the early grades. In the United States, no curriculum (including abstinence-only programs) markedly changes the age at which adolescents become sexually active, although some help reduce rates of pregnancy and STIs.

Sadness and Anger

12. Almost all adolescents become self-conscious and self-critical. A few become chronically sad and depressed. Many adolescents (especially girls) think about suicide, and some attempt it. Few adolescents actually kill themselves; most who do so are boys.

13. At least in Western societies, almost all adolescents become more independent and angry as part of growing up, although most still respect their parents. Breaking the law as well as bursts of anger are common; boys are more likely to be arrested for violent offenses than are girls.

14. Adolescence-limited delinquents should be prevented from hurting themselves or others; their criminal behavior will disappear with maturation. Life-course-persistent offenders are aggressive in childhood and may continue to be so in adulthood. Early intervention—before the first arrest—is crucial.

Drug Use and Abuse

15. Most adolescents experiment with drugs, especially alcohol and tobacco, although such substances impair growth of the body and the brain. Age, gender, community, and parental factors are influential. Availability is often not an issue—teenagers seem able to get the drugs that they want. Perception of harm makes a difference, and that changes by cohort and affects drug use.

16. Alcohol and marijuana are particularly harmful in adolescence, as they affect the developing brain and threaten the already shaky impulse control. However, adults who exaggerate harm or who abuse drugs themselves are unlikely to prevent teen drug use.

17. Prevention and moderation of adolescent drug use and abuse are possible. Antidrug programs and messages need to be carefully designed to avoid a backlash or generational forgetting. Price, perception, and parents have an effect.

KEY TERMS

identity versus role confusion (p. 435)

identity achievement (p. 436)

role confusion (p. 436)

foreclosure (p. 436)

moratorium (p. 436)

gender identity (p. 438)

familism (p. 441)

parental monitoring (p. 442)

peer pressure (p. 443)

deviancy training (p. 444)

sexual orientation (p. 445)

major depression (p. 449)

rumination (p. 449)

suicidal ideation (p. 449)

parasuicide (p. 449)

cluster suicides (p. 450)

adolescence-limited offender (p. 452)

life-course-persistent offender (p. 452)

generational forgetting (p. 457)

APPLICATIONS

1. Interview people who spent their teenage years in U.S. schools of various sizes, or in another nation, about the peer relationships in their high schools. Describe and discuss any differences you find.

2. Locate a news article about a teenager who committed suicide. Can you find evidence in the article that there were warning signs that were ignored? Does the report inadvertently encourage cluster suicides?

3. Research suggests that most adolescents have broken the law but that few have been arrested or incarcerated. Ask 10 of

your fellow students whether they broke the law when they were under 18 and, if so, how often, in what ways, and with what consequences. (Assure them of confidentiality.) What hypothesis arises about lawbreaking in your cohort?

4. Cultures have different standards for drug use among children, adolescents, and adults. Interview three people from different cultures (not necessarily from different nations; each SES, generation, or religion can be said to have a culture) about their culture's drug-use standards. Ask your respondents to explain the reasons for any differences.

The Developing Person So Far:
Adolescence

BIOSOCIAL

Puberty Begins Puberty begins adolescence, as the child's body becomes much bigger (the growth spurt) and male/female differention occurs, including menarche and spermarche. Hormones of the HPA and HPG axes influence growth and sexual maturation as well as body rhythms, which change so that adolescents are more wakeful at night. The normal range for the beginning of puberty is age 8 to age 14.

Growth and Nutrition Many teens do not get enough iron or calcium because they often consume fast food and soda instead of family meals and milk. Some suffer from serious eating disorders such as anorexia, bulimia, and bingeing. The limbic system typically matures faster than the prefrontal cortex. As a result, adolescents are more likely to act impulsively.

Sexual Maturation Both sexes experience increased hormones, new reproductive potential, and primary as well as secondary sexual characteristics. Every adolescent is more interested in sexual activities, with possible hazards of early pregnancy and sexual abuse.

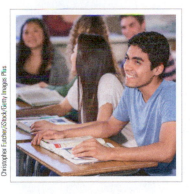

COGNITIVE

Logic and Self Adolescents think differently than younger children do. Piaget stressed the adolescent's new analytical ability—using abstract logic (part of formal operational thought).

Two Modes of Thinking Adolescents use two modes of cognition, intuitive reasoning and analytic thought. Intuitive thinking is experiential, quick, and impulsive, unlike formal operational thought; intuitive processes sometimes crowd out analytical ones.

Digital Natives Technology has both positive and negative aspects, including reduced isolation and cyberbullying.

Secondary Education Secondary education promotes individual and national success. International tests find marked differences in achievement. In the United States, high-stakes tests and more rigorous course requirements before high school graduation are intended to improve standards. Graduation rates are rising.

PSYCHOSOCIAL

Identity Adolescent development includes a search for identity, as Erikson described. Adolescents combine childhood experiences, cultural values, and their unique aspirations in forming an identity. The contexts of identity are religion, politics/ethnicity, vocation, and gender.

Relationships with Adults Families continue to be influential, despite rebellion and bickering. Adolescents seek autonomy but also rely on parental support. Parental guidance and ongoing communication promote adolescents' psychosocial health.

Peer Power The influence of friends and peers of both sexes is increasingly powerful in adolescence. Parents are the best teachers when it comes to sex, but many adolescents get their information primarily from peers and the media.

Sadness and Anger Depression and rebellion may become serious problems. Many adolescents break the law, but delinquency may be limited to adolescent years. Some, however, are life-course-persistent offenders.

Drug Use and Abuse Adolescents are attracted to psychoactive drugs, yet such drugs are particularly harmful during the teen years. Rates of substance use are decreasing, except for a dramatic increase in e-cigarettes (vaping).

emerging adulthood

Until **very recent history,** three roles traditionally signified adulthood: employee, spouse, and parent. Those roles were coveted and expected, soon after puberty. But in the past few decades, millions of young people have spent years on the border between adolescence and adulthood. Their bodies were fully grown by about age 18, but they did not want to cross over into adulthood.

Postponing adult roles was first evident among college students in rich nations. Their stage of life was labeled "youth" or "late adolescence" or "early adulthood." But millions more young people now hover before full adulthood. The world's teen birth rate has plummeted, marriage age has increased, and a billion people hope to attend college or are already there, expecting to work in their preferred occupation someday—but not yet.

Many developmentalists believe that a major shift has occurred in life-span development. A new chronological period has appeared from about age 18 to 25, named **emerging adulthood.** ●●

emerging adulthood The period of life between the ages of 18 and 25. Emerging adulthood is now widely thought of as a distinct developmental stage.

Left: Image Source/Getty Images
Right: StarsStudio/iStock/Getty Images

Emerging Adulthood:
Biosocial Development

What Will You Know?

1. Why are emerging adults quite healthy, even though they may avoid doctors?
2. What has changed in the sexual activity of emerging adults?
3. Why would anyone risk his or her life unnecessarily?

I t's my family's tradition to take a family member to a restaurant on his or her birthday. We adults do not like to notice that the years keep coming, but we value traditions. It was my turn.

"How does it feel to be your age?" Elissa asked me.

"I don't feel old," I said, "but the number makes me think that I am."

"Twenty-five is old, too," Sarah said. (She had turned 25 two weeks earlier.)

We laughed, but we all understood. Although age 18 or 21 was once considered the beginning of adulthood, age 25 has become a new turning point. By about age 18, the biological changes of adolescence are complete: A person is literally "grown up." But many people do not consider themselves adults (which is what Sarah meant by *old*) until age 25 or later.

As this chapter explains, emerging adults are at their prime in biosocial characteristics. Bodies are ready for hard work and reproduction. In former centuries, most 20-year-olds were married and employed.

However, much has changed. New freedoms bring new risks. More young adults die violently than from any disease, and almost none of them wants baby after baby, although their bodies are ready for that. This chapter describes both the possibilities and the vulnerabilities of emerging adulthood.

Growth and Strength

The bodies of emerging adults are ready for hard work and easy birth. However, as you will see, the ability to carry stones, plow fields, or haul water better than older adults is no longer admired, and if a contemporary young couple had a baby every year, their neighbors would be more appalled than approving.

Strong and Active Bodies

Maximum height is usually reached by age 16 for girls and age 18 for boys, except for a few late-maturing boys who gain another inch or two by age 21. Maximum strength soon follows. During emerging adulthood, muscles grow, bones strengthen, and shape changes, with males gaining more arm muscle and females more fat (Whitbourne & Whitbourne, 2014). By age 22, women have

TABLE 17.1	U.S. Deaths from the Top Three Causes (Heart Disease, Cancer, and Chronic Lower Respiratory Disease)
Age Group	Annual Rate per 100,000
15–24	6
25–34	17
35–44	55
45–54	193
55–64	515
65–74	1,123
75–84	2,545
85+	6,224

Data from National Center for Health Statistics, 2014.

developed adult breasts and hips, and men have reached full shoulder width and upper-arm strength.

Every body system—including the digestive, respiratory, circulatory, muscular, and sexual-reproductive systems—functions optimally. Serious diseases are not yet apparent (see Table 17.1), and some childhood ailments are outgrown.

For both sexes, muscles are powerful, if a person regularly uses them to keep them strong. People aged 18 to 25 are best able to race up a flight of stairs, to lift a heavy load, or to grip an object with maximum force. Strength gradually decreases with age, with some muscles weakening more quickly than others. Back and leg muscles shrink faster than the arm muscles, for instance (McCarter, 2006). This is apparent in older baseball players who still hit home runs long after they no longer steal bases.

In a large U.S. survey, 96.4 percent of 18- to 24-year-olds rated their health as good, very good, or excellent. Only 3.6 percent rated it fair or poor, a significant improvement over other adults and over emerging adults from two decades ago (National Center for Health Statistics, 2015). Very few report any limitations on their activities due to chronic health conditions.

However, emerging adults may have precursors of poor health, evident in laboratory analysis of blood, urine, and body fat. A study of biological aging found that some people age three times faster than others, with about half of the difference between fast and slow aging evident by age 26 (Belsky et al., 2015). As a result, by their mid-30s some people have bodies like those in their 20s and some like those in their 40s.

If getting an annual medical checkup were the way to stay healthy, then most emerging adults would be sick: They avoid doctors. The average 18- to 25-year-old in the United States sees a health professional once a year, and that includes those who are pregnant or injured. This compares with about six medical visits per year for typical adults over age 65 (who are less often injured and never pregnant). In fact, one-third of all emerging-adult men never saw a medical professional in 2013 (National Center for Health Statistics, 2015).

Similarly, although the Centers for Disease Control recommends the flu shot each year for everyone over 6 months of age, less than one-third of those aged 18 to 45 comply (National Center for Health Statistics, 2015). Their reasons? It's not guaranteed and it takes time (ignoring the time saved by preventing the flu).

What a Body Can Do Here at age 27, Tobin Heath leaps to celebrate her goal at the soccer World Cup Final in Vancouver, the most recent of seven years of star performances. Every young adult can have moments when their bodies and minds crescendo to new heights.

A New Stage, or Just Weird?

The term *emerging adulthood* was coined by Jeffrey Arnett, a college professor in Missouri who listened to his own students and realized that they were neither adolescents nor adults. As a good researcher, he also queried young adults of many backgrounds in other regions of the United States, he read published research about "youth" or "late adolescence," and he thought about his own life. His research led him to name a new stage, requiring a new label. Many others agreed; the term *emerging adult* caught on.

But some scientists disagree. Instead of a universal stage, they suggest that emerging adulthood is a cultural phenomenon for privileged youth who have had good childhood health and who can afford to postpone work and family commitments (Munson et al., 2013). Some scholars are particularly critical of professors at U.S. universities who study their own students and then draw conclusions about all humankind.

Instead, conclusions based on American college students may apply only to those who are WEIRD—from Western, Educated, Industrialized, and Rich Democracies (Henrich et al., 2010). Most of the world's people are poor (even low-SES Americans are rich by global measures), never reach college, and live in nations without regular elections. WEIRD people are unusual, when compared to the world's 6 billion people.

Arnett himself acknowledged that too much of developmental science focuses on only 5 percent of humanity, and he suggested a broader perspective (Arnett, 2008). He notes that college students in the United States tend to have two additional traits that are not typical, even for emerging adults within the United States—they are more often white, female, and from high-income families (Arnett, 2016).

Indeed, Arnett might agree with Joseph Henrich, the Canadian professor who developed the acronym WEIRD. Henrich wrote, "many psychologists . . . tend to think of cross-cultural research as a nuisance, necessary only to confirm the universality of their findings (which are usually based on WEIRD undergraduates)" (Henrich, 2015, p. 86).

If WEIRD people differ in notable ways from others, perhaps "emerging adulthood"—when young adults become autonomous and independent, forging a future untethered by parents, postponing marriage, parenthood, and work commitments—is a WEIRD anomaly. Another worldview, and expectation for young adults, may be evident in cultures where social interdependence—not dependence—is the ideal (Yeung & Alipio, 2013).

However, one study of personality development among youth in 62 nations found that an emerging adult transition was evident everywhere. They also found that the chronological age when emerging adulthood ended was strongly affected by job responsibility.

When work began at age 20 or earlier (as in Pakistan, Malaysia, and Zimbabwe), personality maturation was rapid. When work began late (as in the Netherlands, Canada, and the United States), emerging adulthood lasted much longer, sometimes past age 25 (Bleidorn et al., 2013).

Data suggesting that emerging adulthood is a trend in every nation, not just the WEIRD ones, come from statistics on average ages of marriage. A century ago, most women married in their teens. Now, in sub-Saharan Africa the average marriage age is 21 for women and 25 for men; in East Asia, 26 and 28; in Western Europe, 31 and 33. North Americans have been marrying later in every recent decade: The current average is 27 for women and 29 for men (American Community Survey, 2014).

Data on childbearing, college attendance, and career commitment show similar worldwide trends. This leads most scholars to believe that although emerging adulthood was first recognized in Missouri, it is now evident worldwide.

Bodies in Balance

Fortunately, bodies are naturally healthy during emerging adulthood. The immune system is strong, fighting off everything from the sniffles to cancer and responding well to vaccines. Usually, blood pressure is normal, teeth have no new cavities, heart rate is steady, the brain functions well, and lung capacity is sufficient (Whitbourne & Whitbourne, 2014).

Rates of illness are so low that many diagnostic tests, such as PSA (for prostate cancer), mammograms (for breast cancer), and colonoscopies (for colon cancer), are not recommended until middle age or later, unless family history or warning signs suggest otherwise.

Three Protective Functions

The young adult body is so strong and healthy that few emerging adults are aware that their organs and cells are aging. Three body functions protect them.

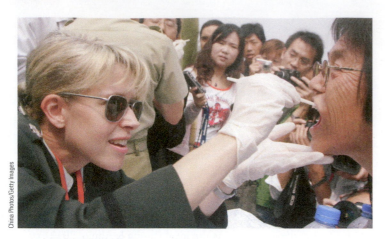

Open Wide China has almost a billion adults who never saw dentists when they were young. They now have "Love Teeth Day," when, as shown here, professionals check their teeth and remedy any serious losses.

organ reserve The capacity of organs to allow the body to cope with stress, via extra, unused functioning ability.

homeostasis The adjustment of all of the body's systems to keep physiological functions in a state of equilibrium. As the body ages, it takes longer for these homeostatic adjustments to occur.

allostasis A dynamic body adjustment, related to homeostasis, that affects overall physiology over time. The main difference is that homeostasis requires an immediate response, whereas allostasis requires longer term adjustment.

allostatic load The stresses of basic body systems that burden overall functioning, eventually causing hypertension, obesity, and diabetes.

First, each organ has extra power, not usually needed, to be tapped when necessary, a phenomenon called **organ reserve.** That reserve shrinks each year of adulthood so that by old age a strain—shoveling snow, catching the flu, minor surgery—can overwhelm the body. At first, however, organ reserve allows speedy recovery from physical demands, such as exercising too long, staying awake all night, or drinking too much alcohol. Emerging adults do all of these, and they usually recover quickly.

Closely related to organ reserve is **homeostasis**—a balance between various body reactions that keeps every physical function in sync with every other one. For example, if the air temperature rises, people sweat, move slowly, and thirst for cold drinks—three aspects of body functioning that cool them. Homeostasis is quickest in early adulthood, partly because all of the organs have power in reserve for sudden demands.

The next time you read about a rash of heat-wave deaths (Australia in 2014 and India and Pakistan in 2016), note the age of the victims. Because homeostasis takes longer, the body dissipates heat less efficiently with age. Sometimes the demands temporarily overwhelm the heart, kidneys, or other organs. Even middle-aged adults are less protected from temperature changes—or any other stress on the body—than emerging adults (Larose et al., 2013).

Related to homeostasis is **allostasis,** a dynamic body adjustment that gradually changes overall physiology. The main difference between homeostasis and allostasis is time: Homeostasis requires an immediate response from body systems, whereas allostasis refers to long-term adjustment.

Allostasis depends on the biological circumstances of every earlier time of life, beginning at conception. The process continues, with early-adulthood conditions affecting later life, as evident in a measure called **allostatic load.** Although organ reserve usually protects emerging adults, the effects accumulate because some of that reserve is spent to maintain health, gradually adding to the overall load.

Because of the protective effects of homeostasis and allostasis, few emerging adults reach the threshold that results in serious illness. The immune system is another factor that keeps the body in balance. However, already by early adulthood, childhood health affects metabolism, weight, lung capacity, and cholesterol. As allostatic load builds, the risk of chronic disease later in life increases.

Examples of Load and Balancing

Consider sleep. One night's poor sleep makes a person tired the next day—that is homeostasis, the body's effort to maintain equilibrium. But if poor sleep quality is typical every day in youth, then appetite, mood, and activity adjust (more, down, less) to achieve homeostasis, while allostatic load rises. By mid- and late adulthood, years of inadequate sleep reduce overall health (McEwen & Karatsoreos, 2015; Carroll et al., 2014) (see Figure 17.1).

Another obvious example is nutrition. If severe malnutrition characterizes fetal or infant development, later on the person might eat too much, becoming obese. Childhood obesity increases the risk of adult obesity—not always, as Chapter 1 explains, but often.

Of course, appetite is affected by much more than fetal development. How much a person eats on a given day is affected by many factors, as the peripheral nervous system sends messages to the brain. An empty stomach triggers hormones, stomach pains, low blood sugar, and so on, all signaling time to eat. If that is occasional, the cascade of homeostatic reactions makes you suddenly realize at 6 P.M. that you haven't eaten since breakfast. Dinner becomes a priority; your body tells you that food is needed.

But if a person begins a severe diet, ignoring hunger messages for days and weeks, rapid weight loss soon triggers new homeostatic reactions, allowing the person to function with reduced daily calories. That makes it harder to lose more weight (Tremblay & Chaput, 2012).

Over the years, allostasis is evident. If a person overeats or starves day after day, the body adjusts: Appetite increases or decreases accordingly. But that day-after-day homeostasis increases allostatic load.

Obesity is one cause of diabetes, heart disease, high blood pressure, and so on—all the result of physiological adjustment (allostasis) to daily overeating (Sterling, 2012). At the opposite extreme, allostasis allows people with anorexia to feel energetic, not hungry, but the burden on their organs may eventually kill them.

Remember that the first signs of eating disorders appear in adolescence, as teenagers try to adjust to the cultural demands for thinness and their body's new need for more food. Teenagers wolf down large quantities, losing control of their consumption; or they drastically undereat, again compulsively, when childhood habits, genes, body image, and the pressures of puberty all combine. Most young people find a more balanced eating pattern by emerging adulthood, although some do not, making "emerging adulthood . . . a critical risk period in the development and prevention of disordered eating" (Goldschmidt et al., 2016, p. 480).

One particularly risky time is when a young person begins college far from home: Many freshmen eat too much or too little. A review of the literature found that these problems are more common in the United States than in Europe, but a large survey in the Netherlands also found that the average student gained weight in the first months of college, while some lost too much. To be specific, 26 percent gained more than 5 pounds in those months, and 6 percent lost more than 5 pounds—both unhealthy amounts (de Vos et al., 2015).

Another example comes from exercise. After a few minutes of exertion, the heart beats faster and breathing becomes heavier—these are homeostatic responses. Because of organ reserve, such temporary stresses on the body in early adulthood are no problem. Over time, homeostasis adjusts and the heart, lungs, and muscles allow longer and more intense exercise. That decreases allostatic load by reducing the health risks of the cardiovascular system.

The opposite is also true, as found in an impressive longitudinal study, CARDIA (Coronary Artery Risk Development in Adulthood), which began with thousands of healthy 18- to 30-year-olds, many (3,154) reexamined 7 and 20 years later. Those who were the least fit at the first assessment (more than 400 of them) were four times more likely to have diabetes and high blood pressure in middle age.

In CARDIA, problems began but were unnoticed (except in blood work) when participants were in their 20s. Organ reserve allowed these participants to function quite well. Nonetheless, each year their allostatic load increased, unless their daily habits changed (Camhi et al., 2013). A disproportionate number of those who were least fit at age 20 had died by age 65.

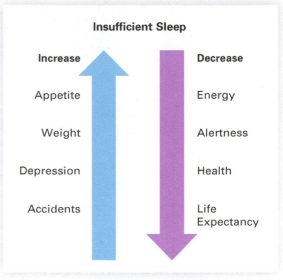

FIGURE 17.1

Don't Set the Alarm? Every emerging adult sometimes sleeps too little and is tired the next day—that is homeostasis. But years of poor sleep habits reduce years of life—a bad bargain. That is allostatic load.

A Moment or a Lifetime These three in New Delhi enjoy free pizza at the opening of the 600th Domino's in India, just one of more than 5,000 outside the United States. Cheese and pepperoni may satisfy homeostatic drive, but they now increase the allostatic load in every nation.

Every day matters. Consider astronauts. They are chosen because they are skilled and in excellent health, with strong immune systems. However, after spaceflight, their immune systems are temporarily devastated, proof that the body is affected by experience, not solely by genes and aging (Crucian et al., 2013).

A more common example comes from data on adults who, as children, suffered from poverty, neglect, and abuse. That affects all of the functions of the body, impairing health in middle age, even if the childhood problems stopped decades ago (Widom et al., 2015b).

Add organ reserve to homeostasis and allostasis and it is clear why health habits in emerging adulthood affect vitality in old age. Because of organ reserve, a heart attack is unlikely before midlife, but years of physical stress affect overall body functioning. Thus, a person may die of a heart attack at age 50 because of cholesterol, hypertension, obesity, and cigarette smoking at age 20.

Even in the smaller changes of aging, such as the wearing down of the teeth or loss of cartilage in the knees, serious reductions are not normally evident until later in life. For example, brushing and flossing reduce mouth bacteria, but if a person never brushes or sees a dentist, all three aspects of body functioning prevent gum disease in emerging adulthood. The consequences appear later, when tooth loss reflects decades of ignoring dental health.

Looking Good

Partly because of their overall health, strength, and activity, most emerging adults look vital and attractive. The oily hair, pimpled faces, and awkward limbs of adolescence are gone, and the wrinkles and hair loss of middle adulthood have not yet appeared. Body shape is often good: Emerging adults are obese about half as often as middle-aged adults.

The organ that protects people from the elements, the skin, is clear and taut—characteristics that change markedly with time (Whitbourne & Whitbourne, 2014). The attractiveness of young skin is one reason that newly prominent fashion models, popular singers, and film stars tend to be in their early 20s, looking fresh and glamorous. Most emerging adults value appearance more than older adults do.

A study of college students (average age 19.5) who viewed a television reality show depicting plastic surgery found that most students—male and female, of many ethnicities—rated the show positively. Comments included "I was amazed at how quickly and easily they turned her into a gorgeous young lady," and "It seemed like the story of an ugly duckling turning into a swan" (Markey and Markey, 2012, p. 212). Students who noted the shallowness of focusing on appearance were in the minority.

Because good looks are so important, it is not surprising that emerging adults spend more money on clothes and shoes than adults of any other age. When they exercise, their main reason is to maintain—or attain—fit, slender, attractive bodies, unlike older adults, whose main exercise motive is health. New students in college, no matter what their ethnicity, usually care a great deal about looking good (Gillen & Lefkowitz, 2012).

Concern about appearance may be connected to sexual drives, since appearance attracts sexual interest, and young adults hope to be attractive. Furthermore, in these years many people are job hunting. Attractiveness (in clothing, body, and face) correlates with better jobs and higher pay (Fletcher, 2009). Women particularly focus on appearance, especially weight, because other people sometimes decide to date, or to employ, them based on superficial appearance (Fikkan & Rothblum, 2012; A. Morgan et al., 2012).

No wonder emerging adults try to look their best. Usually they succeed.

Staying Healthy

Emerging adults experiment and select from many options. We drill down on two vital choices that help emerging adults stay healthy, exercise and nutrition, and then discuss a third domain—sex, which can be a source of health or illness.

Exercise

Exercise protects against serious illness lifelong, even if a person smokes and over-eats. It reduces blood pressure, strengthens the heart and lungs, and makes depression, osteoporosis, diabetes, arthritis, major neurocognitive disorder, and some cancers less likely. Health benefits from exercise are substantial for men and women, old and young, former sports stars and those who never joined an athletic team.

By contrast, sitting for many hours correlates with almost every chronic illness. Every movement—gardening, light housework, walking up the stairs or to the bus—helps. Walking briskly for 30 minutes a day, five days a week, is good; more intense exercise (swimming, jogging, bicycling, and the like) is better; and adding muscle-strengthening exercise is best.

Activity

There is good news here. Most emerging adults are quite active, getting aerobic exercise by climbing stairs, jogging to the store, joining intramural college and company athletic teams, playing sports at local parks, biking, hiking, swimming, and so on. In the United States, emerging adults walk more and drive less than older adults.

Not only are emerging adults the most active age group, but they have improved over the past decades. In 2013, the full standard for aerobic exercise was met by 62 percent, and the standard for muscle-strengthening exercise was met by 33 percent. Indeed, 30 percent met both standards, compared to only 18 percent of middle-aged adults (U.S. Department of Health and Human Services, 2016). Those standards, first issued in 2008 and reissued in May 2016, are:

1. *Aerobic exercise,* several days a week, with the weekly total being a combination of 150 minutes of moderate exercise (walking, swimming, bicycling slowly) or 75 minutes of intense exercise (jogging, racing, bicycling fast), at least 10 minutes at a time.
2. *Muscle-strengthening exercise,* including all of the major muscle groups (legs, hips, back, abdomen, chest, shoulders, and arms) at least twice a week. Resistance training and the like should reach the level that another set would be almost impossible.

In general, more activity is better, with 300 or even 450 minutes (not 150) a weekly goal. The upper limit beyond that, when no more health benefits occur, is not known, and anything is better than zero. It is possible to overuse one particular

See the Sweat This is "hot yoga," a 90-minute class in London with 26 positions, two breathing exercises, in 105-degree heat (40.5 C). Homeostasis allows young adults to stretch their muscles more easily in an over-heated room.

set of muscles, especially if this means neglect of another set, but everyone is advised to incorporate activity into daily life—walking or biking (not driving), climbing stairs (not taking elevators), stretching while cleaning the house, squatting and standing while gardening, and the like. Labor-saving devices may be disability-promoting devices!

Reaching the Goal

The U.S. government's activity guidelines give an example of an emerging adult, a college student named Anita, who initially was not exercising as she should:

> Anita plays league basketball (vigorous-intensity activity) 4 days each week for 90 minutes each day. She wants to reduce her risk of injury from doing too much of one kind of activity (this is called an overuse injury). . . . Anita starts out by cutting back her basketball playing to 3 days each week. She begins to bicycle to and from campus (30 minutes each way) instead of driving her car. She also joins a yoga class that meets twice each week. . . . Eventually, Anita is bicycling 3 days each week to and from campus in addition to playing basketball. Her yoga class helps her to build and maintain strength and flexibility.

> *[U.S. Department of Health and Human Services, 2016]*

Intense basketball 360 minutes a week might seem to be enough, but it was not. At the end of her readjustment, Anita had 450 minutes of aerobic exercise and was using all of her muscle groups in yoga. Finally, she was considered a shining example of a healthy person.

Past generations quit exercising when marriage, parenthood, and career became more demanding. Young adults today, aware of this tendency, can choose friends and communities that support, rather than preclude, staying active. Two factors encourage activity:

1. *Friendship.* People exercise more if their friends do so, too. Because social networks typically shrink with age, adults need to maintain, or begin, friendships that include movement, such as meeting a friend for a jog instead of a beer or playing tennis instead of going to a movie.
2. *Communities.* Some neighborhoods have walking and biking paths, safe fields and parks, and subsidized pools and gyms. Most colleges provide these amenities, which increases student exercise. Health experts cite extensive research showing that community design, safety, and neighbor friendliness promotes walking and biking, reducing obesity, hypertension, and depression (Nehme et al., 2016; Yu & Lippert, 2016).

Eating Well

Nutrition is another lifelong habit embedded in culture. At every life stage, diet affects future development. For example, a program in Guatemala provided adequate nutrition to pregnant women and children under age 3. Benefits appeared 20 years later—the children of these women had more education and better jobs than a comparable group of emerging adults who had not been such fortunate babies (Martorell et al., 2010).

The Ideal Weight

For body weight, there is a homeostatic **set point,** or settling point, that makes people eat when hungry and stop eating when full. Extreme dieting or overeating may alter the set point: Eating disorders such as anorexia, bulimia, and obesity may worsen in early adulthood, although more often the odd eating habits of

Especially for Emerging Adults Seeking a New Place to Live People move more often between the ages of 18 and 25 than at any later time. Currently, real estate agents describe sunlight, parking, and privacy as top priorities for their young clients. What else might emerging adults ask when seeking a new home? (see response, page 474)

set point A particular body weight that an individual's homeostatic processes strive to maintain.

adolescents become more rational (Goldschmidt et al., 2016). [**Life-Span Link:** Eating disorders are discussed in detail in Chapter 14; habits of weight loss are discussed in Chapter 20.]

The **body mass index (BMI)**—the ratio between weight and height—is used to determine whether a person is below, at, or above normal weight. A BMI below 18 is a symptom of anorexia, between 20 and 25 indicates a normal weight, above 25 is considered overweight, and 30 or more is called obese. About half of all emerging U.S. adults are within the normal BMI range, as are less than one-third of adults aged 25 to 65.

Fortunately, once emerging adults become independent, they can change childhood eating patterns. Some do. As a generation, U.S. young adults consume more bottled water, organic foods, and nonmeat diets than do older adults, becoming more fit than their parents were at the same age. Not all is well, however. Emerging adults are also most likely to drink sugar-sweetened soda and juice, with men—especially men living in the South—consuming the largest amounts (Kumar et al., 2014).

Particular nutritional hazards await young adults who are immigrants or children of immigrants. If they decide to "eat American," they might avoid curry, hot peppers, or wasabi—each of which has been discovered to have health benefits. Instead they might indulge in fast food, which tends to be high in fat, sugar, and salt. Although older immigrants overall are healthier than native-born Americans, their young-adult offspring have significantly higher rates of obesity and diabetes than their parents, particularly if their national origin is African or South Asian (Oza-Frank & Narayan, 2010).

No matter what their ancestry, today's emerging adults are heavier than past cohorts, and as they age they gain weight—about a pound a year, according to the CARDIA study. Specifics of diet matter: CARDIA found that fast foods, high-fat diets, and diet soda each had independent effects, with the cumulative allostatic load increasing every marker of poor health (Duffey et al., 2012).

Sex

The sexual-reproductive system is at its most efficient during emerging adulthood. Conception is quicker; miscarriage less common; serious birth complications unusual; orgasms more frequent; and testosterone (the hormone associated with sexual desire) higher for both sexes at age 20 than at age 40. Whether this is a blessing or a curse depends on context.

body mass index (BMI) The ratio of a person's weight in kilograms divided by his or her height in meters squared.

Not Married But . . . Postponing parenthood does not mean postponing contact, although each culture does it differently. Amanda Hawn and Nate Larsen *(left)* have just moved into their California apartment, and two emerging adults in Beijing *(right)* keep their balloon from falling during "Singles Day," a new Chinese custom celebrated on November 11.

🔵 **Observation Quiz** Why is Single's Day on November 11 each year? (see answer, page 474) ⬇

Peter DaSilva/The New York Times/Redux

Li Muyi/ChinaFotoPress/Getty Images

● **Response for Emerging Adults Seeking a New Place to Live**
(from page 472): Since neighborhoods have a powerful impact on health, a person could ask to see the nearest park, to meet a neighbor who walks to work, or to contact a neighborhood sports league.

● **Answer to Observation Quiz**
(from page 473): November 11 is written 11/11. In China, singles are supposed to stay upright but close.

Then and Now

Historically, most babies were born to women under age 25, and peak newborn survival occurred when mothers were aged 18 to 25. Women married before age 20, and couples happily had many children. Hormones, neurotransmitters, and organs were designed, over thousands of years, to propagate the human race, and religious mandates developed so that everyone would "be fruitful and multiply. Fill the earth," as God is quoted as telling the first people in the Book of Genesis.

However, the Earth now seems overfull, making these physiological and genetic impulses liabilities. The religious concern is less about avoiding extinction and more about depleting water and fossil fuels.

Because of the past thousands of years of genetic adaptation, the bodies of emerging adults still want sex, but their minds know they are not ready for parenthood. Nor do they want many children: One or two seems to be enough. A solution, of course, is celibacy, at least until a late marriage, but for many emerging adults, the preferred solution is premarital sex with reliable birth control.

International Standards

Availability and acceptance of contraception and abortion vary widely from nation to nation, as do preferences for one mode or the other. Some nations ban every form; other nations allow many choices.

Public health workers decry the lack of family planning in many areas of the world. One estimate covering 21 developing nations reported that 61 percent of the women of childbearing age had an "unmet need" for contraception, in part because of their nations' laws. Indications of their need were the women's expressed

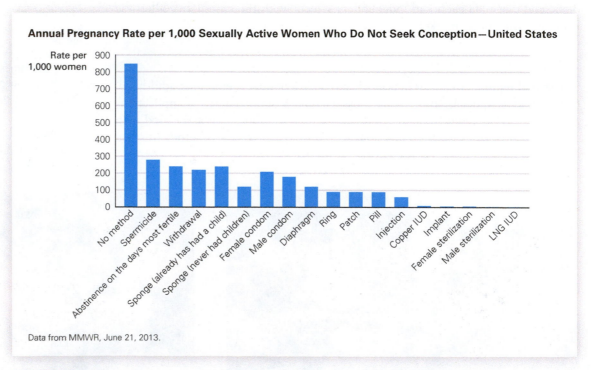

Annual Pregnancy Rate per 1,000 Sexually Active Women Who Do Not Seek Conception—United States

Data from MMWR, June 21, 2013.

FIGURE 17.2

In Real Life These numbers are for typical use, not perfect use. For instance, abstinence on fertile days would produce a pregnancy rate much lower than shown here *if* a woman knew exactly when she was fertile, and *if* she never had sex three days before or three days after that date.

desire and births spaced less than two years, an interval that increases illness and infant death (Moore et al., 2015).

The World Health Organization updated information on family planning. The chance of a sexually active woman becoming pregnant unintentionally within a year ranges from 85 percent if she uses no contraception to less than 1 percent if she uses the most effective methods (MMWR, June 21, 2013) (see Figure 17.2).

Since emerging adults are at peak fertility, if a young man and a young woman have frequent sex with no attempt to limit conception, conception is likely in three months. That would mean four pregnancies per couple per year, but once a woman is pregnant, ovulation almost always ceases until several weeks after the birth—longer with exclusive breast-feeding.

That fertility rate worked well in former centuries; it prevented extinction of the human species. Now early motherhood and large families increase poverty and premature death.

As couples and nations have understood the new demographics, the birth rate has fallen to half of what it was 50 years ago, a reduction worldwide as well as in the United States (United Nations, 2015). Emerging adults are the main reason for this shift. Indeed, women over age 30 are having *more* children than they did 20 years ago, while teenagers and young adults are having far fewer.

Opinions and Problems

Attitudes toward premarital sex are changing, historically and by generation (Twenge et al., 2015). Most adults over age 65 believe that premarital sex is wrong, and almost all emerging adults believe that it is acceptable. Attitudes are affected not only by age but also by culture, with 9 of every 10 people from the Middle East disapproving of premarital sex but only 1 in 9 Europeans disapproving (see Figure 17.3).

Sexually Transmitted Infections

There is no disagreement about another consequence of sexual freedom: sexually transmitted infections (STIs). Half of all new cases worldwide occur in people younger than 26 (Satterwhite et al., 2013, Gewirtzman et al., 2011). The overall incidence of STIs is highest among emerging adults (although the rate among sexually active teenagers is even higher).

The single best way to prevent STIs is lifelong celibacy or monogamy, because most STIs, including HIV/AIDS, are transmitted primarily via sex with more than one partner. STIs would also be limited if sexually active people, after the end of one relationship, were celibate for six months and then tested, treated, and cured for any STI before having a new partner.

However, current practice is far from that ideal. Most emerging adults practice *serial monogamy,* beginning a new relationship soon after one ends. At times a new sexual liaison overlaps an existing one, and sometimes a steady relationship is interspersed with a fling with someone else. Rapid transmission of STIs is one result.

In addition, globalization fuels the spread of every contagious disease (Herring & Swedlund, 2010). With international travel, an STI caught from an infected sex worker in one place quickly arrives in another nation. HIV, for instance, has several

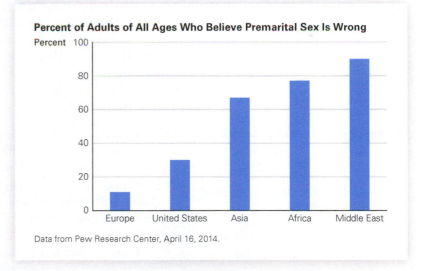

Percent of Adults of All Ages Who Believe Premarital Sex Is Wrong

Data from Pew Research Center, April 16, 2014.

FIGURE 17.3

Everybody Is Doing It Cultural variation regarding sex before marriage, evident in this figure, illustrates a paradox: Sex is essential for community survival, yet attitudes about who, how, when, and why are diametrically opposite from one place, one era, and even one person to another.

Especially for Nurses When should you suspect that a patient has an untreated STI? (see response, page 476)

THINK CRITICALLY: What are the benefits and risks of other innovations, such as the smartphone, bypass surgery, frozen food, or air conditioning?

Response for Nurses (from page 475): Always. In this context, "suspect" refers to a healthy skepticism, not to prejudice or disapproval. Your attitude should be professional rather than judgmental, but be aware that education, gender, self-confidence, and income do not necessarily mean that a given patient is free of an STI.

Especially for Couples Counselors Sex is no longer the main reason for divorce—money is. If you are counseling a cohabiting couple who want to marry, do you still need to ask them about sex? (see response, page 478)

variants, each of which is prevalent in a specific part of the world—but all variants are found in every nation. Emerging adults are prime STI vectors (those who spread disease) as well as the most common victims.

Emotional Stress

Another problem caused by the sexual activity of emerging adults is increased anxiety and depression. New relationships tend to make people anxious and happy, but breakups are depressing. Anxiety and depression are affected directly by increasing and decreasing activity in the brain, as well as by social experience (Fisher, 2016a).

Contemporary emerging adults have more sexual partners than do somewhat older adults. Human physiological responses affect neurological patterns as well as vice versa, which means that sexual relationships trigger the brain systems for attachment (as well as for romantic love), leading to "complex, unanticipated emotional entanglement" (Fisher, 2016b, p. 12).

"Unanticipated emotional entanglement" produces unanticipated stress because people disagree about sex and reproduction. Generally speaking, attitudes about the purpose of sex fall into one of three categories (Laumann & Michael, 2001):

1. *Reproduction.* About one-fourth of all people in the United States (more women than men; more older adults than younger ones) believe that the primary purpose of sex is reproduction. Emerging adults with this perspective are likely to marry young, pressured not only by their parents but also by their values and sexual desires.
2. *Relationship.* Half of the people in the United States (more women than men) believe that the main purpose of sex is to strengthen pair bonding. This is the dominant belief among emerging adults. Their preferred sequence is dating, falling in love, deciding to be faithful, having sex, perhaps living together, and finally (if both are "ready"), marriage and parenthood.
3. *Recreation.* About one-fourth of all adults (more men than women, especially young men) believe that sex is primarily for enjoyment (Katz & Schneider, 2013). Ideally, both partners achieve orgasm, without commitment. [**Life-Span Link:** Hookups are discussed in Chapter 19.]

Assumptions about the purpose of sex are often mutual when partners share religion and culture, with religious beliefs particularly influential (Luquis et al., 2012). In that case, both partners have similar attitudes about fidelity, pregnancy, love, and abortion: no debate needed. Currently, however, many emerging adults leave their childhood community and "have a number of love partners in their late teens and early twenties before settling on someone to marry" (Arnett, 2004, p. 73). Each partner may have attitudes that the other does not.

Partners may feel misused and misled because "choices about sex are not the disassociated, disembodied, hedonistic and sensuous affairs of the fantasy world; they are linked, and rather tightly linked by their social embeddedness, to other domains of our lives" (Laumann & Michael, 2001, p. 22). An unplanned pregnancy may make one partner assume that marriage is the solution and the other partner expect an abortion. Each might be shocked at their lover's reaction.

Even the decision to have sex is fraught with misunderstanding. It is not uncommon for one partner to think past intercourse began with consent but the other partner to disagree.

If a person is ever to experience sexual assault, the first (and sometimes only) episode is more likely to occur during the seven years of emerging adulthood than during adolescence or during the 50 or more remaining years after age 25. This is true for both men and women (Breiding et al., 2014). Of course, sexual violence is more than mistaken communication, but since the most common perpetrators are romantic partners, illusions regarding another's motives and desires are part of the problem.

Added complications are gender identity and sexual orientation (discussed in Chapters 16 and 19). Formerly, almost everyone identified as either male or female, heterosexual or homosexual. Now some emerging adults identify as both, or neither. Many change their expressed orientation during emerging adulthood, a sexual fluidity more common in women than men (Bailey et al., 2016). Obviously, this complicates sexual partnerships.

If partners hold differing assumptions about the purpose of sex, the signs of consent, or their gender or sexual orientation, emotional pain and frustration are likely. One might accuse the other of betrayal, an accusation that the other considers completely unfair. The more partners a person has from ages 18 to 25, the more break-ups occur—each stressful. This may contribute to psychopathology in emerging adulthood, our next topic.

Could It Happen to You? Lady Gaga sang "Til It Happens to You" at the Academy Awards in 2016, holding hands with victims of sexual assault. As explained in the movie *The Hunting Ground*, unwanted sexual comments and actions have been part of the college experience for decades, but now thousands of victims say, "No more."

WHAT HAVE YOU LEARNED?

1. How does the physical activity of emerging adults compare with that of older adults?

2. What are the benefits of physical exercise?

3. What indicates that nutrition in emerging adulthood is sometimes better and sometimes worse than for older adults?

4. What has changed to make premarital sex more common?

5. What are the cohort and cultural differences in attitudes toward premarital sex?

6. How has the birth rate changed in the past 50 years?

7. Why are STIs more common today than they were 50 years ago?

8. What are the three commonly cited reasons to have sexual intercourse?

Psychopathology

Most emerging adults enjoy their freedom from childhood restrictions and adulthood responsibilities. The many stresses and anxieties of adolescence—high school, parental monitoring, erratic hormones, peer pressures, irrational fantasies—are over, or at least less intense. Self-esteem is usually higher in emerging adulthood than earlier, and suicidal thoughts are less common.

This is not true for everyone, however. Many are flourishing, but some are struggling (Piumatti & Rabaglietti, 2015). Although physical health and strength peaks during these years, with almost no new diseases, the same is not true for psychological health. Psychologists increasingly recognize these years as a time of growing happiness and resilience for most people *and* increasing incidence of psychopathology (Madewell & Ponce-Garcia, 2016).

We need to clarify why this topic appears in this chapter on biosocial development in emerging adulthood. Although psychopathology is evident during these years, and although biological causes (especially genes) are implicated, placement here does NOT mean that the causes are all biological nor that this age period causes illness.

Todd Heisler/The New York Times/Redux

diathesis–stress model The view that psychological disorders, such as schizophrenia, are produced by the interaction of a genetic vulnerability (the diathesis) and stressful environmental factors and life events.

Response for Couples Counselors (from page 476): Yes. The specifics of sex—frequency, positions, preferences—are no longer a taboo topic for most couples, but the couple still needs to discuss exactly what sex means to each of them. Issues of contraception, fidelity, and abortion can drive partners apart, each believing that he or she is right and the other is rigid, or loose, or immoral, or hidebound, or irresponsible, or unloving, and so on.

Talk to Her College counselors once focused on transfers and credits. Now psychopathology takes most of their time. This is Judy Esposito, a social worker at Stony Brook University whose job is to help students with mental illness.

As Chapter 1 emphasizes, every age has its own problems, including some psychological disorders. Further, every disorder is caused by a combination of inherited genes, past childhood, and current stress.

Most psychologists and psychiatrists accept the **diathesis–stress model,** which "views psychopathology as the consequence of stress interacting with an underlying predisposition (biological, psychosocial, or sociocultural) to produce a specific disorder" (Hooley, 2004, p. 204). You will recognize that this model is related to the dynamic-systems model described in Chapter 1—that all systems of the body, mind, and social context interact and influence one another as time goes on.

Psychopathology appears here because in the beginning of adulthood, many people find new ways to adapt to life. They may move to another city or nation, enroll in college, begin a new job, make new friends, and recognize and treat whatever psychological problems they have. Psychopathology is multicontextual, multidirectional, and multifaceted; it is hoped that disorders might be recognized and treated before the rest of adulthood takes over.

Multiple Stresses of Emerging Adults

Except for major neurocognitive disorder (dementia), emerging adults experience more of every diagnosed psychological disorder (sometimes called *mental illness*) than any older group. Their rate of newly diagnosed mental illness is almost double that of adults over age 25 (SAMHSA, 2009). Most serious disorders start in adolescence and grow worse in emerging adulthood, and many are comorbid and untreated. That means, for instance, that an overly anxious young adult may also be depressed (comorbid) but get no professional help for either disorder (Wittchen, 2012).

Why the uptick in emerging adulthood? One reason may be the sexual freedom just described, which sometimes causes anxiety, depression, drug abuse, and disease. If that disease is HIV, the first reaction of many is to consider suicide, although with treatment suicidal ideation lessens (Stine et al., 2013).

In addition, parents are less involved in the day-to-day life of their adult offspring than they were earlier, which means that distressed young adults are on a tightrope without the safety net of parental protection.

The effects are reciprocal; problems in any domain are likely to affect other domains. For example, not having a job may lead to psychopathology—perhaps depression, perhaps substance abuse, perhaps anxiety. One study found that depression was three times as common among unemployed emerging adults as among employed ones (McGee & Thompson, 2015). Similar results were found in Australia: A downward trend in well-being in many aspects of life was evident in the cohort that entered the labor market when overall unemployment rates were higher (Parker et al., 2016).

Most people can withstand stress in one domain of their lives, but many emerging adults are hit from several directions. Multiple identity crises are likely to cause depression and anxiety (Crocetti et al., 2012). Vocational, financial, educational, and interpersonal stresses may combine during these years because

> for the first time in their lives, young adults are faced with independence and its inherent rights and responsibilities. Given the novelty of these challenges, young adults may lack the requisite skills to effectively cope and subsequently experience negative mental health outcomes, including depression and anxiety.

[Cronce & Corbin, 2010, p. 92]

College counselors report an increasing number of students with serious psychological problems. This is particularly true for students at small, private, four-year colleges, where about 18 percent of the student body consult college therapists at least once during their four years (Sander, 2013).

Only half as many students go to the counseling center at large public universities as at small private colleges. The reason for this difference is unknown. It could have to do with the counseling center itself, or the college support for counseling, or the attitudes of the students. Or it could be the ecological setting: Many students at small private colleges are far from home, living on campus, unmarried, with large debts and uncertain future employment. That combination may be overwhelming.

Strength in any one domain of an emerging adult's life is protective; the combination of stressors causes breakdown. Family context has an effect, for better or worse. Having a job may be pivotal, according to results from a program to secure employment for people with serious mental disorders. Benefits were particularly apparent for the emerging adults (Burke-Miller et al., 2012).

Research in England has focused particularly on young adults who are **NEET (Not in Education, Employment, or Training).** They are at high risk for psychopathology (Cornaglia et al., 2015).

Thus, the demands of emerging adulthood may cause psychopathology when added to preexisting vulnerability. As a result, many disorders appear: Some (e.g., anorexia and bulimia) we have already discussed, and others (extreme risk taking and substance abuse) are discussed soon. First we note three other common categories of psychopathology: mood disorders, anxiety disorders, and schizophrenia.

NEET (Not in Education, Employment, or Training) Refers to older adolescents and young adults who are not in any future-oriented program and are not employed. This is a new term, because the economic recession that began in about 2007 led to a sizable number of NEET people, with many social problems.

Depressive Disorders

Before they reach age 30, 8 percent of U.S. residents suffer from major depressive disorder, with 18- to 29-year-olds three times as often suffering from this illness as those over age 60 (American Psychiatric Association, 2013). Symptoms appear, disappear, and reappear—which means that the individual, the family, and the society suffer repeatedly.

The social cost of depression is estimated to be higher than that of most physical illnesses, including cancer and heart disease, since mood disorders may begin in early adulthood (or before) and can prevent a person from fully functioning for decades (Wittchen, 2012).

The most common sign of major depressive disorder is loss of interest or lack of pleasure in nearly all activities for two weeks or more. Other difficulties—in sleeping, concentrating, eating, friendships, and feeling hopeful—are also present (American Psychiatric Association, 2013).

Major depressive disorder may be rooted in biochemistry, specifically in neurotransmitters and hormones. However, as the diathesis–stress model explains, problems that are more prevalent in late adolescence and emerging adulthood (e.g., romantic breakups, arrests, drug use) can trigger latent depression that would not emerge if life were less stressful.

At all ages, women are more often depressed than men, but according to research on thousands of young adults in 15 nations, men are particularly vulnerable to depression resulting from loss of a romantic partner. Marriage typically relieves male depression, but divorce may plummet men into despair (Scott et al., 2009; Seedat et al., 2009). Day-to-day relationship interaction is particularly important for women, who can be depressed even within a romantic partnership (Whitton & Kuryluk, 2013).

Depression is particularly debilitating in emerging adulthood because it undercuts accomplishments—higher education, vocational choices, romantic commitment, a steady job—that normally occur in the 20s. Thus, depression at this stage impairs the rest of adulthood (Howard et al., 2010; Zarate, 2010).

Failure to get treatment is common among depressed emerging adults. They distance themselves from anyone who might know them well enough to get professional help. Paradoxically, not only is depression common in emerging adulthood, it also

Don't Worry Isaiah Schaffer was wounded twice as a soldier in Iraq and now suffers from PTSD. Evident in the photo are two ways in which he is learning to readjust to civilian life. He is buying a book for his young daughter, and he has his trusty service dog, Meghan, by his side. Meghan calms him when being in public suddenly triggers a panic attack.

is likely to be relieved with therapy. Social support—which for women means a close friend to talk with and for men means assistance getting in control of their lives—is especially helpful (Martínez-Hernáez et al., 2016).

Anxiety Disorders

Another major set of disorders, evident in one-fourth of all U.S. residents below the age of 25, is anxiety disorders. These include panic attacks, post-traumatic stress disorder (PTSD), and phobia.

Anxiety disorders are even more prevalent than depression. This is true worldwide, according to the World Mental Health surveys of the World Health Organization (Kessler et al., 2009). Incidence statistics vary from study to study, depending partly on definition and cutoff score, but all research finds that many emerging adults are anxious about themselves, their relationships, and their future.

Age and genetic vulnerability shape the symptoms of anxiety disorders. For instance, everyone with PTSD has had a frightening experience—such as a near-death encounter in battle or a rape at gunpoint—yet most people who have had such experiences do not develop PTSD. Young adults, especially if they have no support from close friends or relatives, are more likely to develop this disorder than are people of other ages (Grant & Potenza, 2010).

One reason may be that young adults face a higher rate of trauma (military combat, rape, serious accidents); another reason is that young adults are less protected by parents or spouses (Odlaug et al., 2010). In other words, experience and social support both matter, and that makes emerging adults vulnerable.

Indeed, every anxiety disorder is affected by culture and context. In the United States, social phobia—fear of talking to other people—is common, preventing young adults from enrolling in college, from making friends, from applying for jobs. For all those reasons, a ten-year longitudinal study found that emerging adults with social phobia became 30-year-olds with less income and less success than other adults (Mojtabai et al., 2015).

Recovering A young Japanese man sits alone in his room, which until recently was his self-imposed prison. He is one of thousands of Japanese young people (80 percent of whom are male) who have the anxiety disorder known as *hikikomori*.

In Japan, a severe social phobia, affecting an estimated 100,000 young adults, is *hikikomori,* which means "pull away" (Teo, 2010). The hikikomori sufferer stays in his (or, less often, her) room almost all the time for six months or more, a reaction to extreme anxiety about the social and academic pressures of high school and college. Hikikomori is considered an outgrowth of the stresses experienced by NEET young adults (Uchida & Norasakkunkit, 2015).

The close connection between Japanese mothers and children—and the fact that Japanese parents usually have only one or two children—makes this particular social phobia more common in that nation. The symptoms of hikikomori are also evident among emerging adults in Korea, India, and the United States (Teo et al., 2015). Complications with attachment, coupled with shyness and anxiety, are thought to cause the problem (Krieg & Dickie, 2013).

Every nation has many anxious young adults. Twice as many women as men are affected, and rates are higher in the United States than elsewhere (American Psychiatric Association, 2013). For example, the severe anxiety about food and weight that underlies eating disorders, although evident among emerging adults in every nation, is especially common in the United States. Apparently, anxiety rises every-where when young people are expected to enter the adult world. Symptoms vary.

Schizophrenia

About 1 percent of all adults experience schizophrenia, becoming overwhelmed by disorganized and bizarre thoughts, delusions, hallucinations, and emotions (American Psychiatric Association, 2013). The psychotic episodes that character-ize schizophrenia occur at every age and in every nation, but, again, some cultures, ages, and contexts have much higher rates than others. Half of all sufferers had their first serious episode during adolescence or emerging adulthood (McGrath et al., 2016).

No doubt the cause of schizophrenia is partly genetic, although most people with this disorder have no immediate family members diagnosed with it. Beyond genetics, several other risk factors are known (McGrath & Murray, 2011). One is malnutrition when the brain is developing: Women who are severely malnour-ished in the early months of pregnancy are twice as likely to have a child with schizophrenia.

Another is extensive social pressure. Schizophrenia is higher among immigrants than among their relatives who stayed in the home country, and the rate triples when young immigrant adults have no familial supports (Bourque et al., 2011). Drug use increases the risk, another reason incidence peaks in emerging adulthood.

Diagnosis is most common from ages 18 to 24, with men particularly vulner-able. Men who have had no symptoms by age 35 almost never develop schizophre-nia. Women who develop schizophrenia are also usually young adults, but some older women are diagnosed as well (Anjum et al., 2010).

This raises the question: Does something in the body, mind, or social surround-ings trigger schizophrenia? The diathesis–stress model of mental illness suggests that the answer is yes for all three.

There are dozens of other disorders. The DSM-5 lists 22 major categories, each with many specific disorders. All of them are found in every nation and at every age, although the three just mentioned more often appear in emerging adulthood than later. All of them also have a neurological component, but none of them is solely biological.

Taking Risks

Many emerging adults bravely, or foolishly, risk their lives. Extreme risk taking is not usually considered path-ological, but accidents, homicides, and suicides are the three leading causes of death among people aged 15 to 25—killing more of them than all diseases combined (see Figure 17.4). This is the case even in nations where infectious diseases and malnutrition are rampant. It was also true historically: Young males have always ex-perienced what demographers call an *accident hump* at about age 20 (Goldstein, 2011).

Emerging adult men are the most common killers and victims, murdered at three times the rate of men 20 years older (the U.S. annual rate per 100,000 is 20 compared to 7 for adults aged 45).

Whether extreme risk taking is a sign of mental imbalance is debatable. The data confirm that emerging adults are more likely than older adults to have sex

Especially for Immigrants What can you do in your adopted country to avoid or relieve the psychological stresses of immigration? (see response, page 482)

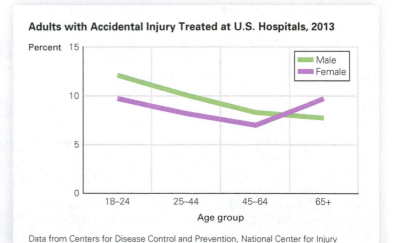

Adults with Accidental Injury Treated at U.S. Hospitals, 2013

Data from Centers for Disease Control and Prevention, National Center for Injury Prevention and Control, Division of Analysis, Research, and Practice Integration, 2013.

FIGURE 17.4

Send Them Home Accidents, homicides, and suicides occur more frequently during emerging adulthood than later. Fewer young adults stay in the hospital, however. They are usually stitched, bandaged, injected, and sent home.

● **Response for Immigrants**
(from page 481): Maintain your social supports. Ideally, emigrate with members of your close family, and join a religious or cultural community where you will find emotional understanding.

without a condom, drive without a seat belt, carry a loaded gun, ride a motorcycle without a helmet, and overdose on drugs. Is that sane?

Risk taking is not only age-related, it is gender-related. Young men find it difficult to walk away from another man's insult, or even an accidental push. Hormones, energy, and neurons once helped young men defend their families against predators and perform strenuous physical work, such as killing tigers and building shelters. Now those same impulses need other outlets, such as contact sports (e.g., football and wrestling) and "extreme sports" (e.g., freestyle motocross—riding a motorcycle off a ramp, catching "big air," doing tricks while falling, and hoping to land upright), described in the following.

A CASE TO STUDY

An Adrenaline Junkie

The fact that extreme sports are age-related is evident in Travis Pastrana, "an extreme sports renaissance man—a pro adrenaline junkie/daredevil/speed demon—whatever you want to call him" (Giblin, 2014). After several almost-fatal accidents, Pastrana won the 2006 X Games freestyle motocross competition at age 22 with a double backflip because, he explained, "The two main things are that I've been healthy and able to train at my fullest, and a lot of guys have had major crashes this year" (quoted in Higgins, 2006, p. D-7).

Four years later, Pastrana set a new record for leaping through big air in an automobile, as he drove over the ocean from a ramp on the California shoreline to a barge more than 250 feet out. He crashed into a barrier on the boat but emerged, seemingly ecstatic and unhurt, to the thunderous cheers of thousands of young adults on the shore (Roberts, 2010).

In 2011, a broken foot and ankle sidelined Pastrana temporarily, but he returned to the acclaim of his cohort, winning races rife with flips and other hazards. In 2013, after some more serious injuries, he said he was "still a couple of surgeries away" from racing on a motorcycle, so he turned to auto racing.

In 2014, at age 30, after becoming a husband and a father (twice), he quit. He says that his most hazardous race days are over. He is an icon for the next generation of daredevil young men.

Many young adults are fans or participants of contact sports and extreme sports; they find golf, bowling, and so on too tame (Breivik, 2010). As the authors of one study of dirt-bikers (off-road motorcyclists) explain, particularly from ages 18 to 24 there is a "developmental lag between impulse control and cognitive evaluation of risk" (Dwane, 2012, p. 62). Thrill overwhelms reason.

The specifics depend on peers, publicity, alcohol, and gender. For instance, no one thought of bungee jumping until a small group of emerging-adult British men formed the Dangerous Sports Club. They told the press they would try bungee jumping on April Fools' Day in 1979. On that day, they all backed out, telling the reporters it was an April Fools' joke. But later, after

drinking, one was filmed bungee jumping. Thousands saw the video, and bungee jumping became a fad (Søreide, 2012).

A similar story holds for other extreme sports—hang gliding, ice climbing, pond swooping, base jumping—that were never imagined until one daredevil young adult inspired thousands of others. Media coverage (especially photos and videos) and social networking create a rush, and young men follow the trend without thinking about dangers.

The conclusion that risk taking is biological, wired into the male of the species, is suggested by research on another primate, the orangutan. As they leap from branch to branch, male orangutans are more likely than females to grab onto flimsy branches that might break—even though males weigh much more, which means the risk of falling is much greater (Myatt & Thorpe, 2011).

Dangerous Pleasure Here, Travis Pastrana prepares to defy death once again as a NASCAR driver. Two days later, his first child was born, and two months later, he declared his race record disappointing. At age 30 he quit, declaring on Facebook that he would devote himself to his wife and family. Is that maturation, fatherhood, or failure?

Drug Abuse

Although risk taking has many benefits, the risk-taking impulse sometimes goes awry, with alcohol and other drugs making it worse. **Substance use disorder (SUD)** is recognized as a psychological disorder in the DSM-5.

SUD occurs whenever a person uses a drug that is harmful to physical, cognitive, or psychosocial well-being. Neither dose nor the specific substance is the determining factor for SUD; the potential for harm is. Thus, even occasional cigarette smoking can be abuse, since that always impairs health, but some other drug use—legal or not—may not be abuse. Some believe that alcohol in moderation is helpful (it correlates with less heart disease in middle age), but excessive alcohol is the most common SUD in the United States.

The problem is that many emerging adults think they are merely users when they are abusers. Denial is common, and harmful. This is obvious in the phenomenon of outdoor music festivals held during warm weather, in or near the major cities of North America. Typically, thousands of emerging adults come to dance, drink, and drug for hours, ignoring the strain on their organs.

In 2013, one such festival in New York City drew 40,000 people each day of the Labor Day weekend, from 11 A.M. on. The temperature was between 85 and 90 degrees, alcohol was sold, and many people used "club drugs," especially MDMA (3,4 methylenedioxymethamphetamine).

Two people died, both college students, one aged 20 and one 23. Hospital emergency care was required for 20 others (Ridpath et al., 2014). Hundreds more came to the medical tent but were not transported to a hospital. It is not known how many of the other 40,000 were affected over the next few days.

That tragedy led to the cancellation of the third day and some new safety measures for this festival the following year. One was denying admission to anyone who was visibly intoxicated; another was having roving scouts whose mission was to take impaired patrons to the medical tent (Ridpath et al., 2014).

That did not stop fatalities, nor did it keep emerging adults away. In 2016, more than 40 festivals took place in North America, from Austin to Vancouver. Over 90 percent of the attendees are emerging adults (the minimum age for the New York City event was 18).

Drug abuse can lead to **drug addiction,** when the absence of a drug causes intense cravings and repeated use. The craving can be physical (e.g., to stop the shakes, to settle the stomach, or to fall asleep) or psychological (e.g., to quiet anxiety or lift depression). Withdrawal symptoms are signs of addiction.

Although cigarettes and alcohol can be as addictive and destructive as illegal drugs, part of the lure of illegal drugs for risk-taking emerging adults is that they are against the law: They like the thrill of buying, carrying, and using, risking arrest and prison. No wonder illegal drug use peaks between ages 18 to 25 and then declines more sharply than use of cigarettes and alcohol (see Figure 17.5).

It may be surprising, however, that drug abuse—particularly of alcohol and marijuana—is more common among college students than among other emerging adults. The overall binge-drinking rate among U.S. college students in 2010 was 37 percent, compared to 28 percent for their age-mates not in college (Johnston et al., 2011). For everyone in or not in college, binge drinking arises from the same drive as extreme sports or other risks—with the same possible consequence (death).

Being with peers, especially for college men, seems to encourage drug abuse. By contrast, those emerging adults least likely to abuse drugs are women living with their parents. As with this distinction, patterns of use, abuse, and addiction vary historically and culturally as well as with age: rising during emerging adulthood and falling with maturity.

substance use disorder (SUD)
The ingestion of a drug to the extent that it impairs the user's biological or psychological well-being.

Video: College Binge Drinking shows college students engaging in (and rationalizing) this risky behavior.

drug addiction A condition of drug dependence in which the absence of the given drug in the individual's system produces a drive—physiological, psychological, or both—to ingest more of the drug.

FIGURE 17.5

Too Old for That As you can see, emerging adults are the biggest substance abusers, but illegal drug use drops much earlier than does cigarette use or binge drinking.

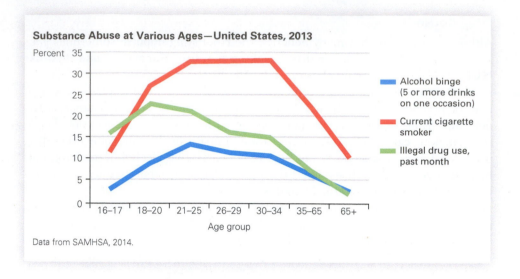

Substance Abuse at Various Ages—United States, 2013

Data from SAMHSA, 2014.

With drugs as with many other risks, the immediate benefits obscure the eventual costs. Many young adults use alcohol to reduce social anxiety—a problem as they enter college, start a new job, speak to strangers, or embark on a romance. Similarly, more than half of all college students and more than half of all U.S. soldiers in Afghanistan use "energy drinks," with high doses of caffeine, to stay awake. Few know that such drinks correlate with dangerous driving and sexual assault (especially when combined with alcohol), and that high doses of caffeine can be lethal (Snipes et al., 2014; Sepkowitz, 2013).

Indeed, no matter what the drug, crossing the line between use and abuse does not always ring alarms in the user. This was apparent in a study of ketamine use among young adults in England, who justified its use—"a bargain"—even after signs of addiction became apparent (Moore & Measham, 2008). (Ketamine has medical uses, but it is often used recreationally.) A complication with ketamine and many other drugs is that they are potent mood changers: Many depressed or anxious emerging adults self-medicate, treating one psychological disorder by creating another (Duman & Aghajanian, 2012).

Although family members and physicians often try to stop drug abuse, intervention is least likely during emerging adulthood. During these years, parents keep their distance, young adults avoid doctors, and drug users are unlikely to marry. Thus, abuse can continue unchecked for years.

Social Norms

One discovery from the study of human development that might improve health among emerging adults is the power of *social norms,* which are customs within a particular society. Social norms exert a particularly strong influence on college students. Since these students want approval from their new peers, social norms matter.

Some social norms benefit emerging adults. This is evident from rates of obesity, since young adults watch their weight in order to be attractive to others, and from rates of exercise, since young adults join sports teams and gyms partly because norms encourage it. However, some norms push emerging adults in destructive directions.

A problem is the *availability error,* the human tendency to remember dramatic events or individuals, not the quiet people or more common events

Brave or Foolish?

Many adults, especially women like me, find risk taking and drug abuse foolish, perhaps pathological. But the fact that I don't want to skydive, or watch men in helmets tackle each other, or use drugs, does not justify criticism of those who do.

Super Bowl Sunday attracts more TV viewers than any other show; advertisers spend 4 million dollars for a 30-second commercial. Some people vote for a president because he is the kind of man they can imagine having a beer with. The specific here is that, in 2004, "57% of undecided voters would rather have a beer with Bush than Kerry" (Benedetto, 2004). Bush won. That should tell me something.

I rationalize my disapproval by noting the serious injuries that many risk-taking young adults sustain. Scientists know that neither enjoyment nor popularity makes something good. (Many things that people enjoy—from eating potato chips to shooting heroin—are harmful.) But whenever I avoid something that millions of others enjoy, I wonder if my perspective is too narrow.

Our society would suffer if young adults were always timid, traditional, and afraid of innovation. They need to befriend strangers, try new foods, explore ideas, travel abroad, and sometimes risk their lives. Enrolling in college, moving to a new state or nation, getting married, having a baby—all are risky. So is starting a business, filming a documentary, entering a sports contest, enlisting in the military, and joining the Peace Corps.

Many occupations are filled with risk takers—police officers, military recruits, financial traders, firefighters, construction workers, and forest rangers among them. Society needs all those workers. If a young man cannot find work that satisfies his need for risk, he might climb mountains, sail oceans, skydive, bungee jump, pond swoop, parkour, cage fight, do potholing (in caves), or kayak over waterfalls. Serious injury is not the goal, but danger adds to the thrill.

Those who choose such sports do not harm anyone but themselves, so why does it trouble me? One study found that facing fear was exhilarating and transformative, improving self-esteem without harming anyone. The researchers suggest that "extreme sports are good for your health" (Brymer & Schweitzer, 2013, p. 477).

But can the same arguments be used for psychoactive drugs? Many Europeans consider drug use a "victimless crime"; they wonder why Americans imprison drug users who hurt no one (Cao & Zhao, 2012). Am I culturally narrow, or limited by my age and gender? Or are extreme risks and psychoactive drug use cultural disorders that are rightly discussed in this section of the book? Opposing perspectives!

Getting High Climbing may be the most sober way to enjoy the thrills of emerging adulthood. The impulse to do so is universal, illustrated with two examples here: a limestone cliff called "the Egg" in Yangshuo, Guangxi Zhuang, China, and an Art of Motion festival in Santorini, Greece.

Andrew Burton/Getty Images

What the F— Happened? That's what 30-year-old Reggie Colby asks. He says he had a happy childhood, tried heroin at age 18, married and dropped out of college, joined the army, and became addicted after an injury in Afghanistan. Since then he has been dishonorably discharged, divorced, and estranged from his daughter. Now he is sheltered by an overpass in Camden, New Jersey, two days after serving time in jail for stealing food. "What happened?" is the right question. Did the stress of emerging adulthood have anything to do with it?

social norms approach A method of reducing risky behavior that uses emerging adults' desire to follow social norms by making them aware, through the use of surveys, of the prevalence of various behaviors within their peer group.

THINK CRITICALLY: Why are wealthier emerging adults more likely to drink too much alcohol than their less wealthy counterparts?

🔵 **Especially for Substance Abuse Counselors** Can you think of three possible explanations for the more precipitous drop in the use of illegal drugs compared to legal ones? (see response, page 487)

(Kahneman, 2011). You probably have noticed the availability error in people who judge everyone of a certain ethnic or national background because of what one member of that group has done. The availability error is evident in college, if one flashy, noisy, classmate announces "I didn't study at all for this test." Some hapless students might then ignore the many classmates who studied hard (they don't announce it) and mistakenly conclude that studying is not common. They might then fail the next test.

The availability error promotes drug use in emerging adults. They are in social settings (colleges, parties, concerts, sports events) where risk takers—especially drug users and drinkers—are noticed and admired.

That may explain why use of alcohol and other drugs escalates during emerging adulthood, particularly among college students. The costs are substantial. Not only are drug-using emerging adults less likely to graduate from college, secure a good job, or become responsible adults, the number of U.S. college students who die each year from alcohol-related injuries is estimated at close to 2,000 (National Institute on Alcohol Abuse and Alcoholism, 2015). That is far more than the number of college suicides (about 1,000 per year).

An understanding of the perceptions and needs of emerging adults, as well as the realization that college students abuse drugs even more than others their age, has led to a promising effort to reduce alcohol abuse on college campuses. This is the **social norms approach,** which begins with the idea that students seek to conform to the norm for drinking and drug use.

About half of the colleges in the United States have surveyed alcohol use on their campuses and reported the results. Almost always, students overestimate how much the average student drinks and underestimate how their peers judge drunk students who are loud, hungover, and disruptive (C. Lee et al., 2010). Ironically, those students whose estimates are farthest from accurate are often those who are isolated and depressed. They then drink to be like everyone else, becoming more depressed.

In general, when survey results are reported and college students realize that most of their classmates study hard, avoid binge drinking, refuse drugs, and are sexually abstinent, faithful, or protected, they are more likely to follow these social norms. This depends partly on the student's own self-image, on his or her past experiences, on parental expectations, and on the influence of friends (Simons-Morton et al., 2016).

Gender is an important factor. If college men think that drinking is part of being a man, then the fact that the overall average (which includes women) is low might make them drink more (Mahalik et al., 2015). Especially for men, the norms of their immediate peers are crucial, evident if they live in a college fraternity. For women, parental alcohol use may be more significant (Mahalik et al., 2015).

When emerging adults are at a party or festival where many people are drinking and using drugs, they tend to perceive the positive effects more than the negative ones (LaBrie et al., 2011). That makes them "join in the fun," which encourages abuse. This helps to explain why people who are trying to stop a habit need to avoid people and contexts that might encourage the habit they want to break. [**Life-Span Link:** The challenges of breaking a habit are discussed in Chapter 20.]

Implications of Risks and Norms

One of my older students, John (about age 30), told the class about his experience as an emerging adult. At first, he spoke with amused pride. But by the end of his narrative, he was troubled, partly because John had become the father of a little boy he adored. He did not want his son to become a reckless young man.

John told us that, during a vacation break in his first year of college, he and two of his male friends were sitting, bored, on a beach. One friend proposed swimming to an island, barely visible on the horizon. The three young men impulsively set out. After swimming for a long time, John realized that he was only about one-third of the way there, that he was tired, that the island was merely an empty spit of sand, and that he would have to swim back.

John turned around and swam back to shore. The friend who made the proposal eventually reached the island. The third friend became exhausted and might have drowned if a passing boat had not rescued him.

What does this episode signify about the biosocial development of emerging adults? It is easy to understand why John started swimming. Male ego, camaraderie, boredom, and the overall context made this an attractive adventure. Many young men like to use their strong arms, legs, and lungs; their impulse is to act, not to think of consequences.

Like John, many adults fondly remember past adventures. They forget the friends who became addicts, who caught STIs, who had abortions or unwanted births, or who died young. Emerging adulthood is a strong and healthy age, but it is not without serious risks. Why swim to a distant island? More thinking is needed, as described in the next chapter.

Before and After These housemates are "pre-gaming," drinking before they go out together to a college party. Camaraderie and alcohol reduce anxiety—temporarily. Picture these six at 8 A.M. the next day.

WHAT HAVE YOU LEARNED?

1. What is the usual pattern of well-being during emerging adulthood?

2. Why do depressed people tend not to seek help?

3. What is one common anxiety disorder in the United States?

4. What evidence suggests that schizophrenia is not based solely on genes?

5. What are the social benefits of risk taking?

6. Which sports are more attractive to emerging adults than to other adults?

7. Why are serious accidents more common during emerging adulthood than later in adulthood?

8. What are the differences among drug use, abuse, and addiction?

9. Why are social norms particularly powerful in emerging adulthood?

Response for Substance Abuse Counselors (from page 486): Legal drugs could be more addictive, or the thrill of illegality may diminish with age, or the fear of arrest may increase. In any case, treatment for young-adult substance abusers may need to differ from that for older ones.

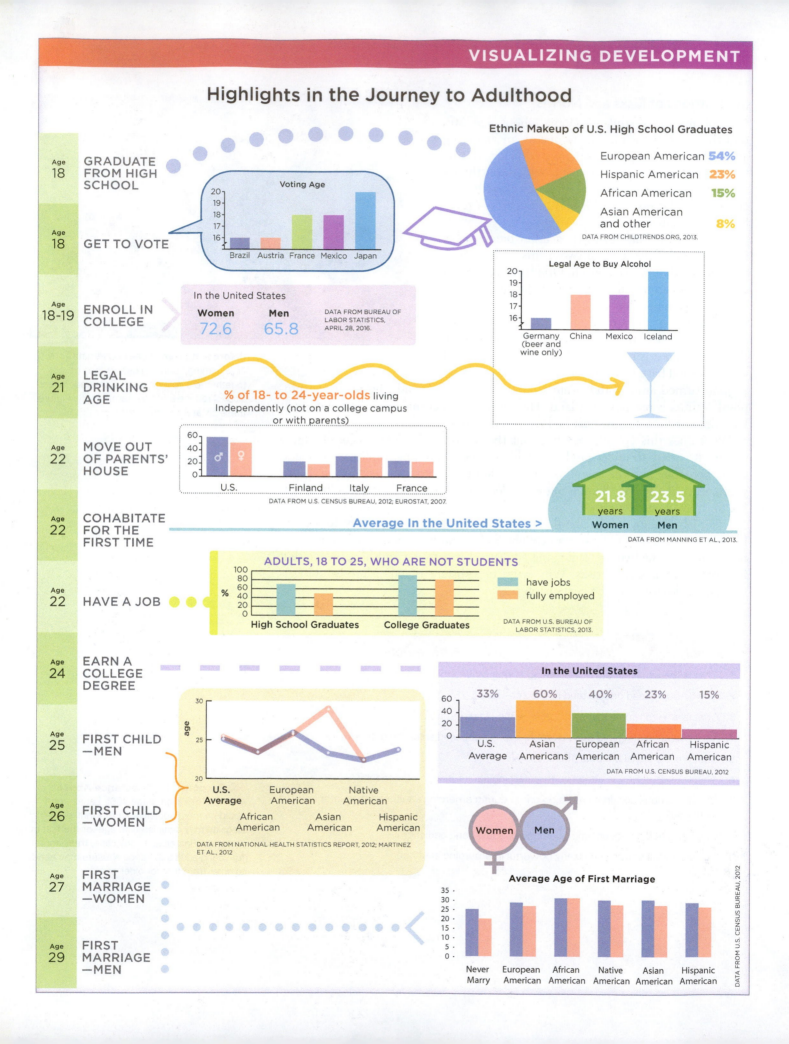

Highlights in the Journey to Adulthood

Age 18 — GRADUATE FROM HIGH SCHOOL

Age 18 — GET TO VOTE

Age 18-19 — ENROLL IN COLLEGE

Age 21 — LEGAL DRINKING AGE

Age 22 — MOVE OUT OF PARENTS' HOUSE

Age 22 — COHABITATE FOR THE FIRST TIME

Age 22 — HAVE A JOB

Age 24 — EARN A COLLEGE DEGREE

Age 25 — FIRST CHILD —MEN

Age 26 — FIRST CHILD —WOMEN

Age 27 — FIRST MARRIAGE —WOMEN

Age 29 — FIRST MARRIAGE —MEN

Voting Age
Brazil, Austria, France, Mexico, Japan

Ethnic Makeup of U.S. High School Graduates

European American	**54%**
Hispanic American	**23%**
African American	**15%**
Asian American and other	**8%**

DATA FROM CHILDTRENDS.ORG, 2013.

In the United States

Women	Men
72.6	65.8

DATA FROM BUREAU OF LABOR STATISTICS, APRIL 28, 2016.

Legal Age to Buy Alcohol
Germany (beer and wine only), China, Mexico, Iceland

% of 18- to 24-year-olds living Independently (not on a college campus or with parents)
U.S., Finland, Italy, France

DATA FROM U.S. CENSUS BUREAU, 2012; EUROSTAT, 2007.

Average In the United States >

21.8 years	23.5 years
Women	Men

DATA FROM MANNING ET AL., 2013.

ADULTS, 18 TO 25, WHO ARE NOT STUDENTS
High School Graduates, College Graduates
- have jobs
- fully employed

DATA FROM U.S. BUREAU OF LABOR STATISTICS, 2013.

age
U.S. Average, European American, Native American, African American, Asian American, Hispanic American

DATA FROM NATIONAL HEALTH STATISTICS REPORT, 2012; MARTINEZ ET AL., 2012

In the United States

U.S. Average	Asian Americans	European American	African American	Hispanic American
33%	60%	40%	23%	15%

DATA FROM U.S. CENSUS BUREAU, 2012

Women / Men

Average Age of First Marriage
Never Marry, European American, African American, Native American, Asian American, Hispanic American

DATA FROM U.S. CENSUS BUREAU, 2012

SUMMARY

Growth and Strength

1. Emerging adulthood, from about age 18 to age 25, is a newly recognized period of development characterized by postponing parenthood, marriage, and career commitment, while attaining additional education.

2. Most emerging adults are strong and healthy. All of the body systems function optimally during these years; immunity is strong; death from disease is rare.

3. Organ reserve and homeostasis help ensure that emerging adults recover quickly from infections and injuries. The allostatic load builds, as some people age much more quickly than others.

4. Emerging adults are usually physically and sexually attractive, more concerned with their appearance than they will be later in life. Such concerns may be related to sexual drives as well as the need for employment, as attractive appearance correlates to better jobs and higher pay.

Staying Healthy

5. Emerging adults tend to exercise more than older adults, as well as to improve their nutrition compared to the habits of adolescents, although some still suffer from inactivity and eating disorders. Habits established in emerging adulthood affect health in the rest of adulthood.

6. Reproduction is most successful during emerging adulthood because both male and female bodies are at their most fertile. However, most emerging adults want to postpone parenthood. Premarital sex with reliable contraception is the most common pattern in the United States.

7. Although pregnancy before age 25 is half as common worldwide as it was 50 years ago, sexually transmitted infections are much more common currently now than in earlier times. Because lifelong monogamy is no longer the norm, STIs are especially prevalent among emerging adults.

8. Most young adults in the United States believe that sexual relationships before marriage are acceptable. However, having several partners arouses unexpected emotions as well as disagreements about the purpose of sex—reproduction, relationship, or recreation.

Psychopathology

9. Generally, well-being increases during emerging adulthood, but so does the incidence of psychological disorders. The diathesis–stress model of mental illness suggests that the roots of such problems begin early and that the stresses of this stage push some people over the edge.

10. Depression, anxiety, and schizophrenia are apparent at every period of life, but some social contexts that are more prevalent during emerging adulthood tend to worsen these problems. Therapy can help, but many young adults do not seek it. Social support may be crucial.

11. Risk taking increases during emerging adulthood, particularly among young men. Some risks are worth taking, but thrills are dangerous. Extreme sports are an example.

12. Context is crucial for risk taking and drug use, with social norms particularly powerful during these years. Substance use disorders are more common in emerging adulthood than at any other time.

KEY TERMS

emerging adulthood (p. 463)
organ reserve (p. 468)
homeostasis (p. 468)
allostasis (p. 468)

allostatic load (p. 468)
set point (p. 472)
body mass index (BMI) (p. 473)

diathesis–stress model (p. 478)
NEET (Not in Education, Employment, or Training) (p. 479)

substance use disorder (SUD) (p. 483)
drug addiction (p. 483)
social norms approach (p. 486)

APPLICATIONS

1. Describe an incident during your emerging adulthood when taking a risk could have led to disaster. What were your feelings at the time? What would you do if you knew that a child of yours was about to do the same thing?

2. Describe the daily patterns of someone you know who has unhealthy habits related to eating, exercise, drug abuse, risk taking, or some other aspect of lifestyle. What would it take for that

person to change his or her habits? Consider the impact of time, experience, medical advice, and fear.

3. Use the library or the Internet to investigate changes over the past 50 years in the lives of young adults in a particular nation or ethnic group. What caused those changes? Are they similar to the changes reported in this text?

Emerging Adulthood: Cognitive Development

CHAPTER 18

What Will You Know?

1. How is adult thinking different from that of adolescents?
2. Are adults more moral or more religious than adolescents?
3. How does college affect a person's thinking processes?

On the bench outside my grandson's class sat a small boy, alone. He told me that another boy made a comment he considered hostile to immigrants. Since his parents were born in another nation, he got into a fight with that other boy. The teacher sent him to the hall. He seemed quite proud of himself.

I could have explained why fighting is bad, or I could have praised him for his loyalty to his parents, or I could have defended his teacher, or I could have supported his ethnic pride by telling him about my friends from the same nation as his parents. Instead, I just nodded.

In this incident, I thought as an adult. Cognition in adulthood considers many perspectives, combining emotions and logic, the personal and the political. Compared to children, who are quick to judge, adults weigh values, interests, and strategies.

Developmentalists themselves use many approaches to analyze adult cognition.

- The *stage approach* describes a new shift in the characteristics of thought.
- The *psychometric approach* analyzes intelligence longitudinally via various tests.
- The *information-processing approach* studies neurological encoding, storage, and retrieval.

Each of these approaches includes adults of every age, and each has merit. None is exclusive, nor confined to any particular chronological period. To make it easier to study, each of the three chapters on adult cognition (Chapters 18, 21, and 24) takes one of these approaches.

This chapter focuses on the idea that adults think at a higher stage than adolescents; Chapter 21 follows the psychometrics of thinking from age 20 to age 100; and Chapter 24 explains changes in information processing over adulthood. In each of these chapters you will read examples of adults at many ages, because the cognitive characteristics of adulthood do not follow chronological cutoffs. For example, college education is discussed in this chapter. But not all college students are emerging adults, nor are all emerging adults in college.

I hope that all adults are, at least, past the preoperational egocentrism of that small boy, who reacted with fisticuffs to a political opinion (which may also have been expressed egocentrically). But not every adult would have responded as dispassionately as I did. And, since I think like an adult, I question myself, wondering if I should have done something other than nod.

Left: Hero Images/Getty Images
Top: StarsStudio/iStock/Getty Images

A New Level of Thinking

Piaget changed our understanding of cognitive development by recognizing that maturation does not simply add knowledge; it allows a leap forward at each stage, first from sensorimotor to preoperational (because of symbolic thought), and then from preoperational to concrete to formal (each with a marked advance in logic).

Although formal operational thought is the final stage of Piaget's theory, many cognitive psychologists find that postadolescent thinking is a cut above earlier thought. Adults are more practical and flexible, combining intuition and analysis. Instead of dual processing, adult thought is dialectical, which means that adults can consider and integrate opposite, and conflicting, ideas.

Postformal Thought

Some developmentalists have labeled this fifth stage of cognitive development **postformal thought,** a "type of logical, adaptive problem-solving that is a step more complex than scientific formal-level Piagetian tasks" (Sinnott, 2014, p. 3). As one group of scholars explained, in postformal thought "one can conceive of multiple logics, choices, or perceptions . . . in order to better understand the complexities and inherent biases in 'truth'" (Griffin et al., 2009, p. 173).

Postformal thinkers do not wait for someone else to present a problem to solve. They take a flexible and comprehensive approach, considering various aspects of a situation beforehand, anticipating problems, and dealing with difficulties rather than denying, avoiding, or procrastinating. As a result, postformal thought is practical as well as creative (Kallio, 2011; Su, 2011).

As you remember from Chapter 15, adolescents use two modes of thought (dual processing) but have difficulty combining them. They use formal analysis to learn science, distill principles, develop arguments, and resolve the world's problems. Alternatively, they think spontaneously and emotionally about personal issues, such as what to wear, whom to befriend, whether to skip class. For personal issues, they prefer quick actions and reactions, only later realizing the consequences.

Postformal thinkers are less impulsive and reactive. They take a more flexible and comprehensive approach, with forethought, noting difficulties and anticipating problems, instead of denying, avoiding, or procrastinating. As a result, postformal thinking is practical, creative, and imaginative (Wu & Chiou, 2008). It is particularly useful in human relationships (Sinnott, 2014).

postformal thought A proposed adult stage of cognitive development, following Piaget's four stages, that goes beyond adolescent thinking by being more practical, more flexible, and more dialectical (i.e., more capable of combining contradictory elements into a comprehensive whole).

Try **Video Activity: Brain Development: Emerging Adulthood** for a quick look at the changes that occur in a person's brain between ages 18 and 25.

Crammed Together Students flock to the Titan Student Union at Cal State Fullerton for the biannual All Night Study before final exams, making cramming a social experience. This is contrary to what scientific evidence has shown is the best way to learn—that is, through distributed practice, which means studying consistently throughout the semester, not bunching it all at the end. Is cramming simply the result of poor time management or is it a rational choice?

An Example: Using Time Well

One way to contrast postformal and formal thinking is to consider a practical problem, time use. Many scholars using varied techniques study how adults spend time, and several nations provide massive data. For example, each year the U.S. Department of Labor asks thousands of adults what they did on the previous day. Since postformal thinking is characterized by strategic flexibility and reconciling conflicting demands, time allocation may signify thought processes.

The best use of time is not simple: International studies find that adult happiness and health are connected to enough, but not too much, sleep, exercise, work, leisure, and so on (Gershuny, 2011). Substantial variation occurs by culture, age, gender, and cohort, although generally people procrastinate less over the years of adulthood. That correlates with more success and happiness (Steel, 2011; Steel & Ferrari, 2013; Beutel et al., 2016).

Contrast adults with adolescents, who tend to be impulsive, reacting quickly and procrastinating irrationally. In adulthood, postformal intellectual skills are harnessed to real educational, occupational, and interpersonal concerns. Conclusions and consequences matter; setting priorities includes postponing some tasks in order to accomplish others.

You can see evidence that time management improves after adolescence by comparing the expectations of high school and college instructors. Most college professors assume that their students can manage time. Therefore, they distribute a syllabus on day one with assignments and due dates for the entire semester.

Adult students planning their work on a term paper that is due in a month think of personal emotions and traits (e.g., anxiety, perfectionism), other obligations (at home and at work), and practical considerations (rewriting, library reserves, computer and printer availability, formatting). Adolescents might ignore all of this until the last

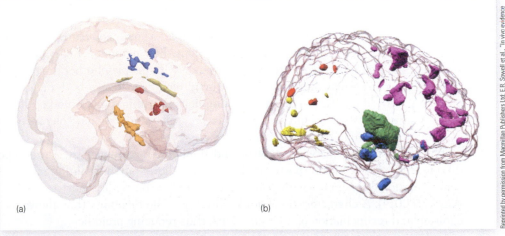

Courtesy Craig Bennett & Abigail Baird. Republished with permission of John Wiley & Sons Inc., from Anatomical Changes in the Emerging Adult Brain, Human Brain Mapping, Abigail Baird and Craig Bennett, 27(9) Sept 2006; permission conveyed through Copyright Clearance Center, Inc.

Reprinted by permission from Macmillan Publishers Ltd: E.R. Sowell et al., "In vivo evidence for post-adolescent brain maturation in frontal and striatal regions," Nature Neuroscience 2, 859-861 (1999)

(a)   (b)

Thinking Away from Home *(a)* Entering a residential college means experiencing new foods, new friends, and new neurons. A longitudinal study of 18-year-old students at the beginning and end of their first year in college (Dartmouth) found increases in the brain areas that integrate emotion and cognition—namely, the cingulate (blue and yellow), caudate (red), and insula (orange). Researchers also studied one-year changes in the brains of students over age 25 at the same college and found no dramatic growth. *(b)* Shown here are the areas of one person's brain changes from age 14 to 25. The frontal cortex (purple) demonstrated many changes in particular parts, as did the areas for processing speech (green and blue)—a crucial aspect of young adult learning. Areas for visual processing (yellow) showed less change.

Researchers now know that brains mature in many ways between adolescence and adulthood; scientists are not yet sure of the cognitive implications.

moment: Teachers of teenagers combat their poor time-management skills by having intermediary due dates (topic chosen, outline, bibliography, first draft, and so on).

Many adult writers consider rewriting again and again a crucial part of the creative process: Few younger students have time for that. Postformal cognition also helps adults to work together, coordinating collaboration, as in a parental alliance, a work team, or a group study session.

To study how young adults work together, and the importance of time management, professors in four nations (United Sates, Germany, Portugal, and Spain) required student teams to produce a major project by the end of the course. Periodically, the researchers assessed the teams' work. When teammates shared expectations for time allocation, and coordinated the scheduling of their individual efforts, everyone's satisfaction increased (Standifer et al., 2015).

Stereotypes

Postformal thought allows adults to question childhood assumptions. Young adults show many signs of such flexibility. The very fact that emerging adults marry later, sometimes crossing ethnic or religious lines to do so, indicates that, couple by couple, thinking is not determined by childhood culture or by traditional norms. Early experiences are influential, but postformal thinkers are not stuck in them.

Consider stereotypes. We all have them, developed in childhood. Remember the prejudices of boys about girls, and vice versa, that develop in almost every child during preoperational egocentric thinking. When my 6-year-old daughter said that she didn't like boys, and I said, "Daddy is a boy and you like him," she said he was an exception.

Some gender prejudices tumble when the hormones of puberty take over—that same daughter told me, at age 11, that she liked boys. But other examples of childhood prejudice—about race, religion, nationality, or even children who live on one city block versus children living a block away—are more durable. Teenage gangs depend on them. Every adult probably holds some childish stereotypes, as well. Fortunately, postformal thinking allows less stereotyped thinking (Chang & Chiou, 2014).

Research on ethnic prejudice is an easy example. Many people are less prejudiced about other ethnic or religious groups than their parents. This is a cohort change, resulting in part from broader experience with people of other groups.

However, people may overestimate their own tolerance. Tests—both on a computer and with brain scans—often reveal implicit discrimination (Amodio, 2014). Thus, many adults have both unconscious prejudice and rational tolerance—a combination that illustrates dual processing.

The wider the gap between explicit and implicit, the stronger the stereotype (Shoda et al., 2014). Ideally, postformal reasoning allows rational thinking to overcome emotional reactions, with responses dependent on reality, not stereotypes (Sinnott, 2014). A characteristic of adult thinking is the flexibility that allows recognition and reconciliation of contradictions, thus reducing prejudice.

Unfortunately, many people do not recognize their own stereotypes, even when false beliefs harm them. One of the most pernicious results is **stereotype threat,** arising in people who worry that other people might judge them as stupid, lazy, oversexed, or worse because of their ethnicity, sex, age, or appearance. Stereotype threat is apparent at every age, when children and adults become aware of what other people might think.

The central concept of stereotype threat is that people have a stereotype that other people think in a stereotypical manner. Then the *possibility* of being stereotyped arouses emotions and hijacks memory, disrupting cognition (Schmader, 2010), as further explained on the next page.

stereotype threat The thought in a person's mind that their appearance or behavior will be misread to confirm another person's oversimplified, prejudiced attitudes.

Stereotype Threat

One statistic has troubled social scientists for decades: African American men have lower grades in high school and earn far fewer college degrees than African American women. Among the women, aged 25 to 36 years, 23 percent hold bachelor's degrees; only 17 percent of the men do (Kena et al., 2015). This cannot be genetic, since the women have the same genes (except for one of the 46 chromosomes) as the men, and it cannot be neighborhood or SES, since families raise their boys and girls together.

Most scientists blame the historical context as well as current discrimination, which falls particularly hard on men. African American women have an easier time finding employment, and African American men are 17 times more often in prison than women. (For every group, more men than women are in prison, but the sex ratio among African Americans is twice the ratio overall.) The unarmed African Americans who are killed are almost always men (recent examples that became nationally known: Martin, Brown, Garner, Gray, Scott).

Another hypothesis focuses on parenting. According to one study, African American mothers grant far more autonomy to their teenage boys and hold higher and stricter standards for their teenage girls (Varner & Mandara, 2014). These researchers suggest that if sons and daughters were treated equally, most gender differences in achievement would disappear.

One African American scholar, Claude Steele, thought of a third possibility. Perhaps the problem originated in the minds of young men, who hypothesized what was in the minds of other people. Steele labeled this *stereotype threat*, a "threat in the air," not in reality (Steele, 1997). The mere *possibility* of being negatively stereotyped may disrupt cognition and emotional regulation.

Steele suspected that African American males, aware of the stereotype that they are poor students, become anxious in educational settings. Their anxiety may increase stress hormones that reduce their ability to respond to intellectual challenges.

Then, if they score low, they protect their pride by denigrating academics. They come to believe that school doesn't matter, that people who are "book smart" are not "street smart." That belief leads them to disengage from high school and college, which results in lower achievement. The greater the threat, the worse they do (Taylor & Walton, 2011).

Stereotype threat is more than a hypothesis. Hundreds of studies show that anxiety reduces achievement. The threat of a stereotype not only reduces achievement in African American men, it causes women to underperform in math, older people to be forgetful, bilingual students to stumble with English, and every member of a stigmatized minority in every nation to handicap themselves because of what they imagine others might think (Inzlicht & Schmader, 2012).

Athletic prowess, health habits, and vocational aspiration may also be impaired if stereotype threat makes people anxious

The Threat of Bias If students fear that others expect them to do poorly because of their ethnicity or gender, they might not identify with academic achievement and therefore do worse on exams than they otherwise would have.

(Aronson et al., 2013). Every sphere of life may be affected. One recent example is that stereotype threat makes blind people underemployed because they hesitate to learn new skills (Silverman & Cohen, 2014).

The harm from anxiety is familiar to those who study sports psychology. When star athletes unexpectedly underperform (called "choking"), stereotype threat arising from past team losses may be the cause (Jordet et al., 2012). Many female players imagine that they are not expected to play as well as men (e.g., someone told them "you throw like a girl"), and that itself impairs performance (Hively & El-Alayli, 2014).

The worst part of stereotype threat is that it is self-imposed. People who are alert to the possibility of prejudice are not only hypersensitive when it occurs, but their minds are hijacked, undercutting potential. Their initial reaction may be to try harder to prove the stereotype wrong, and if that extra effort fails, they stop trying (Mangels et al., 2012; Aronson et al., 2013).

No one, including Steele, believes that stereotype threat is the only reason for unfair disparities in success and achievement. However, many developmentalists seek ways to eliminate, or at least reduce, stereotype threat. Fortunately, many successes have been reported (Inzlicht & Schmader, 2012; Spencer et al., 2016; Pennington et al., 2016), although "clearing the air" is not simple.

Reminding people of their own potential, and the need to pursue their personal goals, is a beginning. Over the years of adulthood, people may confront their internalized self-doubts. Perhaps success in college or on the job, or years of affirmation from a partner, or coping with a health or family crisis, may undercut stereotype threat.

THINK CRITICALLY: What imagined criticisms impair your own achievement, and how can you overcome it?

Limits of Piaget?

As you have read, some developmentalists dispute Piaget's stage theory of childhood cognition. The ranks of dissenters swell regarding this fifth stage. Two scholars writing about emerging adulthood ask, "Who needs stages anyway?" (Hendry & Kloep, 2011).

Piaget himself never used the term *postformal*. If a cognitive *stage* requires a new set of intellectual abilities (such as the symbolic use of language that distinguishes sensorimotor from preoperational thought), then adulthood has no stages. But that definition may be too narrow.

One scholar believes that Piaget would have described a postformal stage if he had turned his attention from children to adults. As this scholar writes:

> we hypothesize that there exists, after the formal thinking stage, a fifth stage of post-formal thinking, as Piaget had already studied its basic forms and would have concluded the same thing, had he the time to do so.
>
> [Lemieux, 2012, p. 404]

Several other scholars criticize Piaget because he did not recognize the limits of formal operational thinking. They contend:

> Piaget assumed that formal operations was the penultimate level of cognitive development, but since about 1980, a number of researchers offered critiques of the implication that cognitive growth abated in adolescence. Instead, a number of proposals appeared that, though independent, converged on an extension of Piaget's theory. These extensions proposed that thinking needs to be integrated with emotional and pragmatic aspects, rather than only dealing with the purely abstract.
>
> [Labouvie-Vief, 2015, p. 89]

The term *fifth stage* may not be completely accurate as Piaget would define it, and *postformal* may imply a depth of intellectual thought that few people attain, but adults can and often do reach a new cognitive level when their brains and life circumstances allow it.

Dialectical Thought

Cross-cultural research suggests that adult thought, at its best, may become **dialectical thought,** which some believe is the most advanced cognitive process (Basseches, 1984, 1989; Riegel, 1975). The word *dialectic* refers to the philosophical concept, developed by Hegel two centuries ago, that every idea or truth bears within itself the opposite idea or truth.

To use the words of philosophers, each idea, or **thesis,** implies an opposing idea, or **antithesis.** Dialectical thought involves considering both of these poles of an idea simultaneously and then forging them into a **synthesis**—that is, a new idea that integrates the original and its opposite. Note that the synthesis is not a compromise; it is a new concept that incorporates both original ones in some transformative way (Lemieux, 2012).

For example, many young children idolize their parents (thesis), many adolescents are highly critical of their parents (antithesis), and many emerging adults appreciate their parents and forgive their shortcomings, which they attribute to their parents' background, historical conditions, and age (synthesis).

Because ideas can engender their opposites, the possibility of change is continuous. Each new synthesis deepens and refines the thesis and antithesis that initiated it, with "cognitive development as the dance of adaptive transformation" (Sinnott, 2009, p. 103). Thus, dialectical thinking involves the constant integration

dialectical thought The most advanced cognitive process, characterized by the ability to consider a thesis and its antithesis simultaneously and thus to arrive at a synthesis. Dialectical thought makes possible an ongoing awareness of pros and cons, advantages and disadvantages, possibilities and limitations.

thesis A proposition or statement of belief; the first stage of the process of dialectical thinking.

antithesis A proposition or statement of belief that opposes the thesis; the second stage of the process of dialectical thinking.

synthesis A new idea that integrates the thesis and its antithesis, thus representing a new and more comprehensive level of truth; the third stage of the process of dialectical thinking.

of beliefs and experiences with all of the contradictions and inconsistencies of daily life. Change throughout the life span is multidirectional, ongoing, and often surprising—a dynamic, dialectical process.

Appreciation that life is a series of thesis/antithesis/synthesis is implicit in the work of every great developmentalist. For instance:

- Educators who agree with Vygotsky that learning is a social interaction within the zone of proximal development (with learners and mentors continually adjusting to each other) take a dialectical approach to education (Vianna & Stetsenko, 2006).
- Piaget could be considered a dialectical thinker, in that he thought conflict between new and old ideas was the fuel that fired a new stage of development (Lemieux, 2012).
- Dialectical processes are readily observable by life-span researchers, who believe that "the occurrence and effective mastery of crises and conflicts represent not only risks but also opportunities for new development" (Baltes et al., 1998, p. 1041).
- Arnett, who coined the term *emerging adulthood,* wrote that brain organization allows the young adult to move past dualism to multiplicity (Tanner & Arnett, 2011), which can be seen as moving past thesis and antithesis, arriving at a synthesis that recognizes the many aspects of truth.
- Erikson described two opposites at each stage (intimacy versus isolation, generativity versus stagnation) causing a psychosocial "crisis" needing a synthesis to allow forward movement.

New demands, roles, responsibilities, and conflicts become learning opportunities for the dialectical thinker. Students might take a class in an unfamiliar subject, employees might apply for an uncertain promotion, young adults might leave their parents' home and move to another town or nation. In such situations, when comfort collides with the desire for growth, dialectical thinkers find a new synthesis, gaining insight. This basic idea underlies all continuing education—that people of all ages keep learning because challenges require it (Su, 2011).

A "Broken" Marriage

Now consider an example of dialectical thought familiar to many: the end of a love affair. A nondialectical thinker might believe that each person has stable, enduring, independent traits. Faced with a troubled romance, then, a nondialectical thinker concludes that one partner (or the other) is at fault, or perhaps the relationship was a mistake from the beginning because the two were a bad match.

By contrast, dialectical thinkers see people and relationships as constantly evolving; partners are changed by time as well as by their interaction. Therefore, a romance becomes troubled not because the partners are fundamentally incompatible, or because one or the other is fatally flawed, but because they have changed without adapting to each other. Marriages do not "break" or "fail"; they either continue to develop over time (dialectically) or they stagnate as the two people move apart.

Everyone is upset when a relationship ends, but neurological immaturity may make adolescents overcome by jealousy or despair, unable to find the synthesis (Fisher, 2006). Older couples may think dialectically and move from former thesis ("I love you because you are perfect") to antithesis ("I hate you—you are selfish and mean") to synthesis ("Neither of us is perfect, but together we can grow").

A dialectic perspective not only encourages adults to work together on their relationships but also helps them cope in a breakup. Many adults feel guilty after divorce, switching from blaming their partner to blaming themselves (Kiiski

MIGUEL ROJO/AFP/Getty Images

Stop the Man-Hating, She Said Emma Watson (most famous for her role as Hermione Granger in the Harry Potter movies) here speaks in Uruguay, following up on her United Nations speech for HeForShe—an organization that calls for men to advocate for women's rights. Using dialectical reasoning, Watson argues that women need to stop blaming men for their plight, and men need to realize that equal rights for women will help them, too. No more man-hating (thesis); no more woman-hating (antithesis). HeForShe: a new synthesis.

objective thought Thinking that is not influenced by the thinker's personal qualities but instead involves facts and numbers that are universally considered true and valid.

subjective thought Thinking that is strongly influenced by personal qualities of the individual thinker, such as past experiences, cultural assumptions, and goals for the future.

● ● Especially for Someone Who Has to Make an Important Decision Which is better, to go with your gut feelings or to consider pros and cons as objectively as you can? (see response, page 500)

et al., 2013). Some manage a dialectical response: seeing their divorce as an opportunity to look at themselves more closely and make necessary changes, thus moving from the thesis (my partner was bad) and antithesis (I am bad) to synthesis (I can learn from this) (Määttä & Uusiautti, 2012).

Combining the Facts and Emotions

A more general example of synthesis is combining objective and subjective thought. **Objective thought** uses abstract, impersonal logic; **subjective thought** arises from personal experiences and perceptions; formal operational thinking values impersonal logic and devalues subjective emotions.

Purely objective, logical thinking may be maladaptive when one is navigating the complexities and commitments of adult life, especially for the social understanding needed for productive families, workplaces, and neighborhoods. Subjective feelings and individual experiences must be taken into account because objective reasoning alone is limited, rigid, and impractical.

Yet subjective thinking is also limited. Truly mature thought involves an interaction between abstract, objective forms of processing and expressive, subjective forms.

Without this new synthesis of intellect and emotion, behavioral extremes (such as those that lead to binge eating, anorexia, obesity, addiction, and violence) and cognitive extremes (such as believing that one is the best or the worst person on Earth) are common. Those are typical of the egocentrism of adolescence—and of some adults as well. By contrast, dialectical thinkers are better able to balance personal experience with knowledge.

As an example of such balance, an emerging adult student of mine wrote:

> Unfortunately, alcoholism runs in my family. . . . I have seen it tear apart not only my uncle but my family also. . . . I have gotten sick from drinking, and it was the most horrifying night of my life. I know that I didn't have alcohol poisoning or anything, but I drank too quickly and was getting sick. All of these images flooded my head about how I didn't want to ever end up the way my uncle was. From that point on, whenever I have touched alcohol, it has been with extreme caution. . . . When I am old and gray, the last thing I want to be thinking about is where my next beer will come from or how I'll need a liver transplant.

[Laura, personal communication]

Laura's thinking about alcohol is postformal in that it combines knowledge (e.g., of alcohol poisoning) with emotions (images flooding her head). Note that she is cautious, not abstinent; she has both objective awareness of her genetic potential and subjective experience of wanting to be part of the crowd. She combines both modes of thought to reach a conclusion that works for her, without needing searing personal experiences (becoming an uncontrollable heavy drinker and reaching despair) and then needing the other extreme (avoiding even one sip).

This development of postformal thought regarding alcohol is seen in most U.S. adults over time. As explained in the previous chapter, those in their early 20s are more likely than people of any other age to abuse alcohol and other drugs. With personal experience and learning from others (social norms), however, cognitive maturity leads most adults to drink occasionally and moderately from then on.

Looking at all of the research makes it apparent that adolescents tend to use either objective *or* subjective reasoning, but adults can combine the two. Of course, adults do not necessarily do so. But learning from experience helps adults combine both kinds of thought. This happens to college teachers as well, as shown by the following example.

College Advancing Thought

One of the leading thinkers in adult cognition is Jan Sinnott, a professor and past editor of the *Journal of Adult Development*. She describes the first course she taught:

> I did not think in a postformal way. . . . Teaching was good for passing information from the informed to the uninformed. . . . I decided to create a course in the psychology of aging . . . with a fellow graduate student. Being compulsive graduate students had paid off in our careers so far, so my colleague and I continued on that path. Articles and books and photocopies began to take over my house. And having found all this information, we seem to have unconsciously sworn to use all of it. . . .
>
> Each class day, my colleague and I would arrive with reams of notes and articles and lecture, lecture, lecture. Rapidly! . . . The discussion of death and dying came close to the end of the term (naturally). As I gave my usual jam-packed lecture, the sound of note taking was intense. But toward the end of the class . . . an extremely capable student burst into tears and said she had to drop the class. . . . Unknown to me, she had been the caretaker of an older relative who had just died in the past few days. She had not said anything about this significant experience when we lectured on caretaking. . . . How could she? . . . We never stopped talking. "I wish I could tell people what it's really like," she said.

> *[Sinnott, 2008, pp. 54–55]*

Sinnott changed her lesson plan. In the next class, she asked that student to share her experiences.

In the end, the students agreed that this was a class when they . . . synthesized material and analyzed research and theory critically.

> *[Sinnott, 2008, p. 56]*

Sinnott writes that she still lectures and gives multiple-choice exams, but she also realizes the impact of the personal story. She combines analysis and emotion; she includes the personal experiences of the students. Her teaching became postformal, dialectical, and responsive.

Culture and Dialectics

Several researchers have compared cognition in East Asian and North American adults, focusing on dialectical thought. It may be that ancient Greek philosophy led Europeans and Americans to use analytic, absolutist logic—to take sides in a battle between right and wrong, good and evil—whereas Confucianism, Buddhism, and Taoism led the Chinese and other Asians to seek compromise, the "Middle Way."

For whatever reason, several researchers find that Asians tend to think holistically, about the whole rather than the parts, seeking the synthesis because "in place of logic, the Chinese developed a dialectic" (Nisbett et al., 2001, p. 294). One example is in judging emotions: Westerners are more likely to pay close attention to facial expressions, and Asians are more likely to consider the context, such as surrounding circumstances (Matsumoto et al., 2012).

This may leave Asians open to more possibilities and make them less likely to conclude that one answer is the only correct one. For example, a study of Canadians, some of them immigrants from China and others native-born, found that the Asian Canadians were more likely to consider many perspectives and thus were less opinionated and more indecisive (L. Li et al., 2014).

Another series of studies compared three groups of students: Koreans in Seoul, South Korea; Korean Americans who had lived most of their lives in the United States; and U.S.-born European Americans. Individuals in all three groups were told the following:

> Suppose that you are the police officer in charge of a case involving a graduate student who murdered a professor. . . . As a police officer, you must establish motive.

> *[Choi et al., 2003, p. 48]*

🔴🟠 **Response for Someone Who Has to Make an Important Decision**
(from page 498): Both are necessary. Mature thinking requires a combination of emotions and logic. To make sure you use both, take your time (don't just act on your first impulse) and talk with people you trust. Ultimately, you will have to live with your decision, so do not ignore either intuitive or logical thought.

Political Division At a Trump rally, a group circled to protect the person with a Black Lives Matter sign. Ahead of a presidential election, it is not unusual for protesters to disrupt the opposition's rally. What is unusual is the age and gender divisions. Contrast the protesters in the forefront of this photo and the Trump supporters at the back.

Participants were given a list of 97 items of information and were asked to identify the ones they would want to know as they looked for the killer's motive. Some of the 97 items were clearly relevant (e.g., whether the professor had publicly ridiculed the graduate student), and virtually everyone in all three groups chose them. Some were clearly irrelevant (e.g., the student's favorite color), and almost everyone left them out.

Other items were questionable (e.g., what the professor was doing that fateful night; how the professor was dressed). Compared with both groups of Americans, the students in Korea asked for 15 more items, on average. The researchers suggest that their culture had taught these students to include the entire context in order to find a holistic synthesis (Choi et al., 2003).

Of course, too much can be made of the distinction between Asian and North American thought. Research on dialectical thinking finds that the Chinese, for instance, are more likely to believe that someone can be good and bad at the same time (Boucher et al., 2009), but certainly some Westerners (including your author) agree.

Most developmentalists believe that flexible thinking is more advanced than simply sticking to one thesis. Piaget defined intelligence as the ability to advance when intellectual disequilibrium occurred.

For example, students who get an F on a test in a subject they thought they knew experience disequilibrium, but the intelligent student does not blame others and become depressed. Instead, he or she talks to others (perhaps including the professor) and develops new strategies for learning. Disequilibrium and then rethinking is more likely to occur as adults share their thoughts and experiences with each other, reaching conclusions that they would not have found on their own.

An Example: Working Together

Seeing advantages and disadvantages in every course of action, weighing personal and political consequences, is characteristic of dialectical thought but is not the "fast and furious" thinking that some people prefer. True dialectical thought allows people to reflect on other viewpoints, considering them with respect even when they seem, at first, ridiculous.

Consider this problem:

> Every card in a pack has a letter on one side and a number on the other. Imagine that you are presented with the following four cards, each of which has something on the back. Turn over only those cards that will confirm or disconfirm this proposition: *If a card has a vowel on one side, then it always has an even number on the other side.*
>
> E 7 K 4
>
> Which cards must be turned over?

The difficulty of this puzzle is "notorious in the literature of human reasoning" (Moshman, 2011, p. 50). Fewer than 10 percent of college students solve it when working independently. Almost everyone wants to turn over the E and the 4—and almost everyone is mistaken.

However, when groups of college students who had guessed wrong on their own then had a chance to discuss the problem together, 75 percent got it right: They avoided the 4 card (even if it has a consonant on the other side, the statement could still be true) and selected the E and the 7 cards (if the 7 has a vowel on the other side, the proposition is proved false).

As in this example, adults can think things through and change their minds after listening (Moshman, 2011). Think about a time when you thought one thing that is opposite to what you now think. Probably a combination of logic and social

TASOS KATOPODIS/AFP/Getty Images

experience caused you to develop your new view. This is cognitive flexibility, duel processing becoming a synthesis.

WHAT HAVE YOU LEARNED?

1. Why did scholars choose the term *postformal* to describe the fifth stage of cognition?

2. How does postformal thinking differ from typical adolescent thought?

3. Why is time management a cognitive issue?

4. How could stereotype threat affect a person's cognition?

5. What is the relationship between thesis, antithesis, and synthesis?

6. How is combining subjective and objective thought an example of dialectical thought?

7. Why does the term *broken home* indicate a lack of dialectical thought?

8. How does listening to opposing opinions demonstrate cognitive flexibility?

THINK CRITICALLY: Can you see dialectical thinking when you remember what you believed as a child?

Morals and Religion

As already explained in earlier chapters, the process of developing morals begins in childhood. Children combine the values of their parents, their culture, and their peers with their own sensibilities as they mature. However, that is only the beginning.

Moral Advances in Adulthood

Many researchers believe that adult responsibilities, experiences, and education are crucial in shaping a person's ethics. They believe that young adults begin a process that continues at least through middle age. Although adolescents may espouse moral principles, some researchers find that they are unlikely to apply those principles when making decisions about daily life. By contrast, with maturation and experience, adults increasingly consider their moral values (Nucci & Turiel, 2009).

James Rest has studied moral development all his life. He says:

> Dramatic and extensive changes occur in young adulthood (the 20s and 30s) in the basic problem-solving strategies used to deal with ethical issues. . . . These changes are linked to fundamental reconceptualizations in how the person understands society and his or her stake in it.
>
> *[Rest, 1993, p. 201]*

Rest found that college education may propel adults to shift their moral reasoning. This is especially likely if coursework includes extensive discussion of moral issues or if the student's future profession (such as law or medicine) requires ethical decisions.

Measuring Moral Growth

What is the best way to assess development of moral thinking? In Kohlberg's scheme, people discuss standard moral dilemmas, responding to various probes. Over decades of longitudinal research, Kohlberg thought that cognitive maturation and moral advances occur together (see Chapter 13).

The **Defining Issues Test (DIT)** is another way to measure moral thinking. The DIT presents a series of questions with specific choices, including the option "can't decide." For example, in one DIT dilemma, a news reporter must decide whether to publish some old personal information that will damage a political candidate. Respondents rank their priorities from personal benefits ("credit for investigative reporting") to higher goals ("serving society").

Defining Issues Test (DIT) A series of questions developed by James Rest and designed to assess respondents' level of moral development by having them rank possible solutions to moral dilemmas.

In the DIT, the ranking of items leads to a number score, which correlates with other aspects of adult cognition, experience, and life satisfaction (Schiller, 1998). These correlations suggest that people who are more caring about other people are also more satisfied with their lives and that moral development advances with age.

However, correlations are not proof. In general, DIT scores rise with age because adults gradually become less doctrinaire and self-serving and more flexible. However, most of the evidence comes from North American young adults—the WEIRD people (Rest et al., 1999; Thoma & Dong, 2014). [**Life-Span Link:** The concept of WEIRD is discussed in Chapter 17.]

Critics complain that the DIT measures only some aspects of moral development, and it is not sensitive to cross-cultural differences (Hannah et al., 2011; Wilhelm & Gunawong, 2016). Not only cognitive maturation but also religious conviction, post-formal thought, moral courage, and social support are crucial in actual moral decisions according to critics of the DIT. It is difficult to measure all of these factors, especially because one person's moral choice may be the opposite of another's.

Teaching Ethics in the Professions

The DIT has often been used on college campuses, in business, nursing, pharmacy, engineering, accounting departments, and so on, to measure advances in moral thought. For instance, one such course for business students in Arkansas exposed students to five major faiths (almost all of the students were Christian and a few were Jewish, so learning about Buddhism, Hinduism, and Islam was new to them).

The instructors asked students to write, and rewrite, a "personal mission statement" as one indication of learning in the course (Herzog et al., 2016). Here are two of the final statements:

> [My mission is] being an authentic, genuine and reliable leader that others can admire, look up to and aspire to be. Establish and create a work environment that is welcoming and accepting of all people who come from different backgrounds, experiences and walks of life. Challenge myself to seek opportunities to try or learn something new as often as possible. Vow to surround myself with individuals different from myself, ask questions and search for answers in order to cultivate growth.

Another wrote:

> I was very interested in the idea of learning more about the world religions and how they hold power over the hearts and minds of so many people. In doing so I had hoped to strengthen my own beliefs as well. I feel as though I have accomplished both of these initiatives. Learning from the many speakers we have had has been incredibly insightful. The Buddhist monk was especially interesting to me. His illustration of Logic and reason as a sort of salvation from the world was incredible. While I disagree with him in this it was an amazing experience to hear from him about his beliefs.

By the end of the course, many students thought in the adult mode, welcoming ideas that they did not know before. Their DIT scores were higher than those of students in the same curriculum who did not take this course. Many reaffirmed their own religious beliefs in the process.

Faith and Practice

The five faith traditions study in Arkansas raises a question. What happens to religious beliefs from ages 18 to 65? There is a paradox here: From adolescence to adulthood, people are *less* likely to attend religious services but *more* likely to see themselves as having religious convictions (Barry et al., 2012). Most young adults consider themselves at least as spiritual as they were when younger (Smith & Snell, 2009).

Spiritual struggles—including "questioning one's religious/spiritual beliefs; feeling unsettled about spiritual and religious matters; struggling to understand evil, suffering, and death; [and] feeling angry at God" (Bryant & Astin, 2008, p. 2)—are not unusual at the beginning of adulthood. Maturation may move adults past the doctrinaire religion of childhood to a more flexible, dialectical, postformal faith.

To describe this process, James Fowler (1981, 1986) developed a now-classic sequence of six stages of faith, building on the work of Piaget and Kohlberg. Before any thought occurs, a person is at "zero," when religion simply reflects children's relationship with their parents. Then thought begins.

- *Stage 1: Intuitive-projective faith.* Faith is magical, illogical, imaginative, and filled with fantasy, especially about the power of God and the mysteries of birth and death. It is typical of children ages 3 to 7.
- *Stage 2: Mythic-literal faith.* Individuals take the myths and stories of religion literally, believing simplistically in the power of symbols. God is seen as rewarding those who follow divine laws and punishing others. Stage 2 is typical from ages 7 to 11, but it also characterizes some adults. Fowler cites a woman who says extra prayers at every opportunity, to put them "in the bank."
- *Stage 3: Synthetic-conventional faith.* This is a conformist stage. Faith is conventional, reflecting concern about other people and favoring "what feels right" over what makes intellectual sense. Fowler quotes a man whose personal rules include "being truthful with my family. Not trying to cheat them out of anything. . . . I'm not saying that God or anybody else set my rules. I really don't know. It's what I feel is right."
- *Stage 4: Individual-reflective faith.* Faith is characterized by intellectual detachment from the values of the culture and from the approval of other people. College may be a springboard to stage 4, as young people learn to question the authority of parents, professors, and other authorities and to rely instead on their own understanding of the world. Faith becomes an active commitment.
- *Stage 5: Conjunctive faith.* Faith incorporates both emotional ideas (such as the power of prayer and the love of God) and rational conscious values (such as the worth of life compared with that of property). People are willing to accept contradictions. That is postformal thinking. Fowler says that this cosmic perspective is seldom achieved before middle age.
- *Stage 6: Universalizing faith.* People at this stage have a powerful vision of universal compassion, justice, and love that compels them to live their lives in a way that others may think is either saintly or foolish. A transforming experience is often the gateway to stage 6, as happened to Moses, Muhammad, the Buddha, and Paul of Tarsus, as well as more recently to Mohandas Gandhi, Martin Luther King, Jr., and Mother Teresa (now Saint Teresa of Calcutta). Stage 6 is rarely achieved.

If Fowler is correct, faith, like other aspects of cognition, progresses from a simple, self-centered, one-sided perspective to a more complex, altruistic (unselfish), and many-sided view. That seems plausible, but quantitative data are limited (Parker, 2010).

Other data indicate that people are more likely to identify with a particular religion, less often claiming to be spiritual but not religious, over the years of adulthood (see Figure 18.1) (Pew Research Center, May 12, 2015).

Praise God? Rituals and ceremonies are remarkably diverse. Some worshipers kiss the ground five times a day, or reach for heaven seven times (as these women do in London, England *[bottom]*). Some worshipers shout "Amen," while others pray quietly (like these students at Zion Bible College in Massachusetts *[top]*). Nonetheless, as people everywhere grow older, they seem to believe in something greater than themselves.

The Data Connections activity **Religious Identity: Young Adults versus Older Cohorts** further explores the religious behaviors and beliefs of U.S. adults.

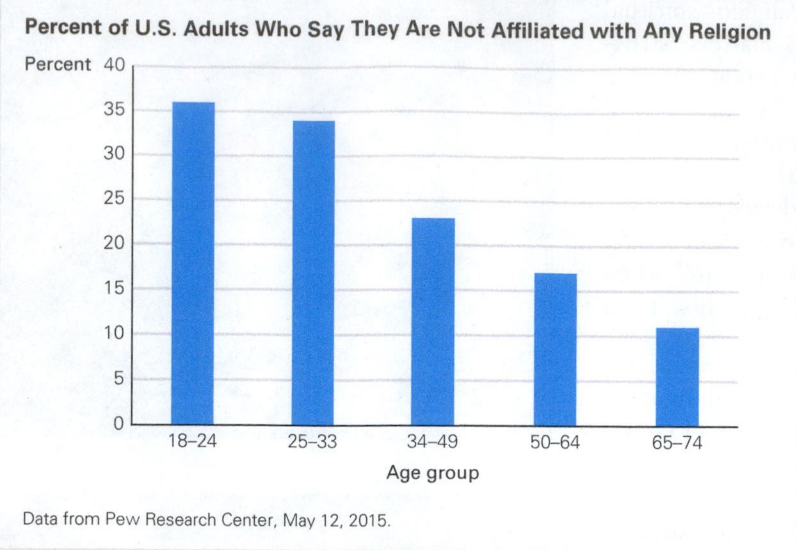

Percent of U.S. Adults Who Say They Are Not Affiliated with Any Religion

Data from Pew Research Center, May 12, 2015.

FIGURE 18.1

Explain This The trends are clear but the reasons are not. Are older adults wiser, or more traditional? Many of the unaffiliated younger adults pray often and believe in God—does that make their lack of religious identity foolish or profound?

morality of care In Gilligan's view, moral principles that reflect the tendency of females to be reluctant to judge right and wrong in absolute terms because they are socialized to be nurturing, compassionate, and nonjudgmental.

morality of justice In Gilligan's view, moral principles that reflect the tendency of males to emphasize justice over compassion, judging right and wrong in absolute terms.

Interpreting this is complicated, however. Of those who say they are unaffiliated, less than 15 percent are atheists, and many pray, believe in God, and consider themselves quite moral. The interpretation of these statistics, in studying adult cognition, depends a great deal on the perspective of the person doing the interpreting. Indeed, that is true for all estimates of moral and religious development.

Gender Differences

In general, more women than men of every age attend religious services and identify with a religion. What this means for morality is debatable, however.

Kohlberg found that males were more likely to reach the highest level of morality, but another Harvard professor, Carol Gilligan, argued that Kohlberg's six stages were insensitive to the morality of women. She contends that women typically must decide about child care and reproduction, about parenthood and abortion. Struggling with those issues may advance moral thinking.

According to Gilligan, girls are raised to develop a **morality of care.** They give human needs and relationships the highest priority. In contrast, boys develop a **morality of justice;** they are taught to distinguish right from wrong (Gilligan, 1981; Gilligan et al., 1990).

However, other researchers have found that education, specific dilemmas (some situations evoke care and some justice), and culture correlate more strongly than gender with whether a person's moral judgments emphasize relationships or absolutes (Juujärvi, 2005; Vikan et al., 2005; Walker, 1984). How a woman or a man responds to a moral question may depend on their culture, not their gender.

Which Era? What Place?

Overall, the power of culture and cohort makes it difficult to prove that morality or religious beliefs advance over the years of adulthood, or the opposite. For example, compared to younger adults in the United States, older people tend to be less supportive of same-sex marriage and more troubled by divorce and single parenthood but more supportive of spending public money for mass transit and health.

Do these age trends suggest that adults become more, or less, moral? Or perhaps asking the question is, itself, an indication of age-related morality. Younger people are less likely to think that various issues, including those just mentioned, are moral ones.

Another prominent theorist of moral development is Jonathan Haidt, who has considered morals in many cultures, as well as many groups within the United States. He contends that five distinct clusters of moral values can be discerned:

(1) Care for others; harm no one.

(2) Promote freedom; avoid oppression.

(3) Be fair; do not cheat.

(4) Seek purity; avoid contamination.

(5) Respect authority; do not break laws.

If one group prioritizes the first two and another group the last two, then each group will interpret the middle one, fairness, differently. This may explain why people of different religious, political, or cultural backgrounds may consider each other immoral; they prioritize differently (Haidt, 2013).

For instance, in 2011 a law was passed in France forbidding covering one's face in public with a veil, burka, or ski mask. The reason was said to be protection of the public (avoiding harm), but the regulation made no exception for devout Muslim women (obeying authority, avoiding contamination) or people who are outside in subzero temperatures (personal freedom). No wonder the law was considered immoral by some but necessary for justice by others.

Contrasting moral standards make it difficult to judge whether morality is stronger among adults than teenagers, or among middle-aged adults than younger ones. Such judgments are bound to raise objections among those deemed less moral.

Nonetheless, an argument can be made that the process (though not necessarily the outcome) of moral thinking improves with age. At least adults may be more dialectical, because increasing experience broadens one's perspective. As one scholar explains it, "The evolved human brain has provided humans with cognitive capacity that is so flexible and creative that every conceivable moral principle generates opposition and counter principles" (Kendler, 2002, p. 503).

Four studies comparing adults of several ages find that, over the years of adulthood, people become less interested in their own financial gain and more interested in the welfare of others (Freund & Blanchard-Fields, 2014). However, as these researchers note, their study was cross-sectional: It could be that something in their past experiences made the older adults more likely to care for others.

Although quantitative research does not allow the firm conclusion that morality increases over adulthood, qualitative research does. Evidence for moral growth abounds in biographical and autobiographical literature. Most readers of this book probably know someone (or might *be* that someone) who had a narrow, shallow outlook on the world at age 18 and then developed a broader, deeper perspective, with more empathy, after adolescence.

WHAT HAVE YOU LEARNED?

1. Why do adults make more decisions involving morality than adolescents do?
2. Why do people disagree as to whether or not something is a moral issue?
3. What is the difference between the DIT and Kohlberg's measures of morality?
4. How are Fowler's stages of faith similar to Kohlberg and Piaget?

Cognitive Growth and Higher Education

Many readers of this textbook have a personal interest in the final topic of this chapter, the relationship between college and cognition. The evidence is encouraging: College graduates are not only healthier and wealthier than other adults, on average, but they are also deeper and more flexible thinkers. However, as you have learned in this chapter, every thesis has an antithesis. That means that every positive result of college has a downside, as you will see.

Health and Wealth

Education improves health and wealth. The data on virtually every physical condition, and every indicator of material success, show that college graduates are ahead of high school graduates, who themselves are ahead of those without a high school diploma. The evidence is so clear that scientists wonder whether selection effects or historical trends, rather than college learning itself, produce such positive correlations (Fletcher & Frisvold, 2011). Let us look at the data.

Evidence of Long-Term Benefits

In the United States, each added level of education correlates with everything from happy marriages to strong teeth, from spacious homes to long lives, from healthy children to working digestive systems (U.S. Department of Health and Human Services, 2015; American Community Survey, 2015). Evidence from many other nations, with and without national health insurance, again finds that education correlates with better health and more wealth (Maskileyson, 2014). In developing nations, one of the most effective ways to improve child health and national economy is to increase education, especially of women (Sperling & Winthrop, 2016; Hagues et al., 2016; Ssozi & Amlani, 2015).

Selection effects *are* powerful here. In the United States and in most other nations, a young person's intelligence and family background compound the benefits of college. According to the U.S. Center for Education Statistics, parental SES is the strongest predictor of whether or not someone will earn a college degree, with 60 percent of those of high SES earning a bachelor's degree compared to 14 percent of those with low family SES (Kena et al., 2015). Many parents who are not wealthy sacrifice to enable their children to attend college.

But, selection effects are not the only reason college graduates have healthier and wealthier lives than their peers. When students of equal ability and family background are compared, education still makes a notable difference in later health and wealth. The average 25- to 34-year-old makes $20,000 a year more with at least a bachelor's degree compared to those with only a high school diploma (Kena et al., 2015) (see Visualizing Development, p. 508). The benefits are especially apparent when those from low-SES families are compared.

Most contemporary students seek the financial benefits of college. Among the "very important" reasons students in the United States enroll in college are "to get a better job" (86 percent) and "to make more money" (73 percent). "Gaining a general education and an appreciation of ideas" is a secondary goal; this is "very important" to 71 percent (Chronicle of Higher Education, 2015).

One of my 18-year-old students wrote:

> A higher education provides me with the ability to make adequate money so I can provide for my future. An education also provides me with the ability to be a mature thinker and to attain a better understanding of myself. . . . An education provides the means for a better job after college, which will support me and allow me to have a stable, comfortable retirement.

> *[E., personal communication]*

Worries about retirement may seem premature for an emerging adult, but E. is not alone in thinking about finances. About two-thirds of first-year students at four-year colleges in the fall of 2014 were concerned about paying for college (Chronicle of Higher Education, 2015).

Overall, about 40 percent of full-time college students are working for pay during the school year (Kena et al., 2015). Many more are working in summer. Even with that, only about 20 percent rely solely on their parents or their own earnings to pay for college. More than half of U.S. students take out loans, and about two-thirds have scholarships or grants, with many colleges providing a deep discount on tuition (Chronicle of Higher Education, 2015).

The longitudinal data make it clear that a college degree is worth the expense, that investing in college education returns the initial expense more than five

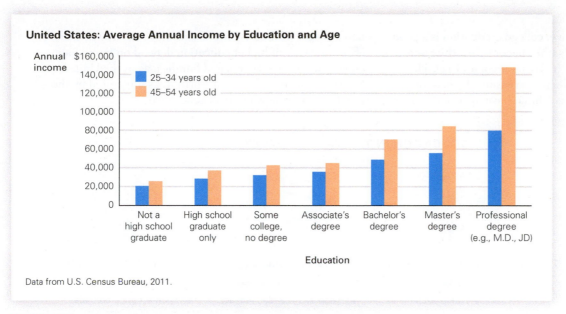

United States: Average Annual Income by Education and Age

Data from U.S. Census Bureau, 2011.

FIGURE 18.2

Older, Wiser, and Richer Adolescents find it easier to think about their immediate experiences (a boring math class) rather than their middle-age income, so some drop out of high school to take a job that will someday pay $500 a week. But over an average of 40 years of employment, someone who completes a master's degree earns half a million dollars more than someone who leaves school in eleventh grade. That translates into about $90,000 for each year of education from twelfth grade to a master's. The earnings gap is even wider than those numbers indicate because this chart compares adults who have jobs, yet finding work is more difficult for those with less education.

times. This means that if a degree-earning student spends a nickel now, he or she will get a quarter back in 20 years, or if a degree costs $200,000, the lifetime return will be a million dollars (see Figure 18.2).

But Without a Degree?

However, there is a major problem with that calculation. Although most freshmen expect to graduate, many leave college before that happens. The financial benefits come primarily from the diploma, yet the costs come from enrolling. Money is a major reason students drop out before completing a degree (McKinney & Burridge, 2015).

To be specific, six years after enrolling full time at a college designed to award a bachelor's degree after four years, less than half of the students have graduated. Rates depend partly on which college the student attends. In 2013, the six-year graduation rate at private, for-profit colleges was only 34 percent; at public institutions, 50 percent; at private, nonprofit colleges, 58 percent (Chronicle of Higher Education, 2014).

One effort to improve graduation rates has been to make college loans easier to obtain. In 2013, 59 percent of students borrowed money to pay for tuition (Chronicle of Higher Education, 2015). The interest on those loans is high, as is the default rate—about 25 percent.

Students at for-profit colleges are more likely to obtain loans and more likely to default on them, perhaps because those colleges have the lowest graduation rates. That is one reason many analysts suggest that federal loans may burden students, taxpayers, and society without increasing learning, graduation, or later employment (Best & Best, 2014; Webber, 2015).

Why Study?

From a life-span perspective, college graduation is a good investment, for individuals (they become healthier and wealthier) and for nations (national income rises). That long-term perspective is the main reason why nations that control enrollment, such as China, have opened dozens of new colleges in the past two decades. However, when the effort and cost of higher education depend on immediate choices made by students and families, as in the United States, many decide it is not worth it, as illustrated by the number of people who earn bachelor's degrees.

EDUCATION IN THE UNITED STATES

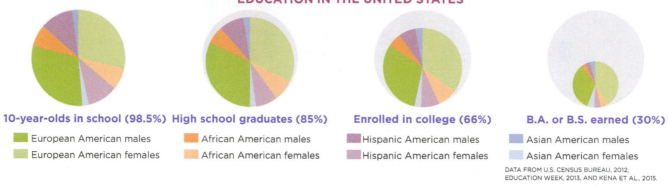

10-year-olds in school (98.5%) **High school graduates (85%)**   **Enrolled in college (66%)**   **B.A. or B.S. earned (30%)**

- 🟩 European American males
- 🟩 European American females
- 🟧 African American males
- 🟧 African American females
- 🟪 Hispanic American males
- 🟪 Hispanic American females
- 🟦 Asian American males
- 🟦 Asian American females

DATA FROM U.S. CENSUS BUREAU, 2012,
EDUCATION WEEK, 2013, AND KENA ET AL., 2015.

AMONG ALL ADULTS

The percentage of U.S. residents with high school and college diplomas is increasing as more of the oldest cohort (often without degrees) dies and the youngest cohorts aim for college. However, many people are insufficiently educated and less likely to find good jobs.

Almost two-thirds of all adults and more than four-fifths of all Hispanics Americans have no college degrees. International data find that many European and East Asian nations have higher rates of degree holders than the United States.

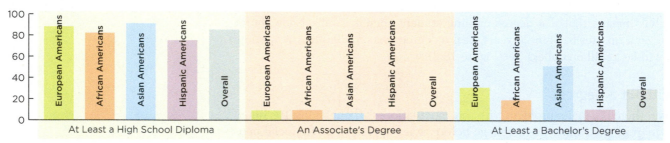

DATA FROM U.S. CENSUS BUREAU, 2013B.

INCOME IMPACT

Over an average of 40 years of employment, someone who completes a master's degree earns $500,000 more than someone who leaves school in eleventh grade. That translates into about $90,000 for each year of education from twelfth grade to a master's. The earnings gap is even wider than those numbers indicate because this chart includes only adults who have jobs, yet finding work is more difficult for those with less education.

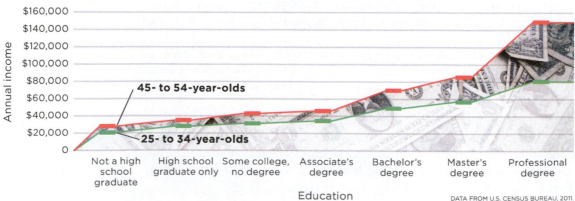

DATA FROM U.S. CENSUS BUREAU, 2011.

JUPITERIMAGES/THINKSTOCK/PHOTOS.COM>>/
GETTY IMAGES PLUS

College and Cognition

Developmentalists are more concerned about lifetime cognition than about lifetime income. College certainly improves verbal and quantitative abilities, adds knowledge of specific subject areas, and teaches skills in various professions. But does that lead to better thinking?

Classic Research

According to one comprehensive review:

> Compared to freshmen, seniors have better oral and written communication skills, are better abstract reasoners or critical thinkers, are more skilled at using reason and evidence to address ill-structured problems for which there are no verifiably correct answers, have greater intellectual flexibility in that they are better able to understand more than one side of a complex issue, and can develop more sophisticated abstract frameworks to deal with complexity.

> *[Pascarella & Terenzini, 1991, p. 155]*

Note that many of these abilities characterize postformal thinking.

Thinking may become more reflective and expansive with *each year* of college. According to one classic study (Perry, 1981, 1998), cognition progresses through nine levels of complexity over the four years that lead to a bachelor's degree, moving from a simplistic either/or dualism (right or wrong, success or failure) to a relativism that recognizes a multiplicity of perspectives.

Perry found that the college experience itself causes this progression: Peers, professors, books, and class discussion all stimulate new questions and thoughts. In general, the more years of higher education and of life experience a person has, the deeper and more dialectical that person's reasoning becomes (Pascarella & Terenzini, 1991).

Especially for Those Considering Studying Abroad Given the effects of college, would it be better for a student to study abroad in the first year or last year of a college education? (see response, page 511)

Current Reality

But wait. You probably noticed that Perry's study was first published decades ago. Hundreds of other studies published toward the end of the twentieth century also conclude that college advances cognition. However, since you know that cohort and culture are influential, you might wonder if Perry's findings are still valid. Good question!

Many recent books say that the college experience has changed for the worse. Notably, a longitudinal study of a cross section of U.S. college students found only half as much growth in critical thinking, analysis, and communication over the four years than had occurred two decades earlier, as measured by widely used national tests. These scholars found that, over the first two years, almost half of the students made no cognitive advances at all (Arum & Roksa, 2011).

They offered many explanations, each confirmed by data. Compared to decades ago, students study less, professors expect less, and students avoid classes that require reading at least 40 pages a week or writing 20 pages a semester. Administrators and faculty still profess hope for intellectual growth, but rigorous classes are optional, canceled, or chosen by few. Most students major in business, fewer in history or literature (which require more writing, reading, and analysis).

Some observers of the current college scene blame the exosystem for forcing colleges to follow a corporate model with students as customers to be satisfied rather than youth who need to be challenged (Deresiewicz, 2014). Customers, apparently, demand dormitories and sports facilities that are costly, and students take out loans to pay for them.

Are students getting what they want and need? There are opposing perspectives on this.

Why College?

Many students attend college primarily for career reasons (see Figure 18.3). They want jobs with good pay; they select majors and institutions accordingly, not for intellectual challenge and advanced communication skills. Business is the most popular major. Students and parents seek to gain skills that will lead to jobs, with many students expecting to enter the health professions or criminal justice (the latest, most popular field and a prime metric for political leaders).

The basic problem may be that students no longer seek to challenge themselves intellectually. For instance, in 1972, when many current professors were in college, 75 percent of undergraduates believed that a "very important" reason to go to college was to "develop a meaningful philosophy of life." In 2013, only 45 percent agreed.

This reveals an underlying mismatch: Many students want to earn a degree as easily as possible, but most professors want every student to think critically and deeply about history, philosophy, and literature. Adults, including parents who have never attended college, believe that "acquiring specific skills and knowledge" is the most important goal of higher education. For them, success is a high-paying job; failure is a college graduate who works as a barista.

In the Arum and Roksa report (2011), students majoring in business and other career fields were less likely to gain in critical thinking compared to those in the liberal arts (courses that demand more reading and writing). Ironically, a follow-up study found that those students who spent most of their college time socializing rather than studying were likely to be unemployed or have low-income jobs. What they had gained from college was a sense that things would get better, but not the critical-thinking skills or the self-discipline that are needed for adult success (Arum & Roksa, 2014).

It may be comforting to know that no nation has reached consensus on the purpose of college. For example, in China, where the number of college students now exceeds the U.S. number (but remember that the Chinese population is much larger), the central government has fostered thousands of new institutions of higher learning.

The main reason is that the Chinese leaders believe that the purpose of higher education is to advance the economy by providing more skilled workers. They are less interested in deeper intellectual understanding and critical thinking. However, even in that centralized government, disagreement about the goals and practices of college is evident (Ross & Wang, 2013).

In 2009, a new Chinese university (called South University of Science and Technology of China, or SUSTC) was founded to encourage analysis and critical thinking. SUSTC did not require prospective students to take the national college entry exam (*Gao Kao*); instead, "creativity and passion for learning" are the admission criteria (Stone, 2011, p. 161).

It is not clear whether SUSTC is successful, again because people disagree about how to measure success. The Chinese government praised SUSTC's accomplishments but has not allowed other universities to alternate admission criteria (Shenzhen Daily, 2014). Some in the first graduating class of 34 were offered postgraduate admission to Yale, Oxford, and Cambridge, which may indicate a successful institution.

In 2015, the government agreed to give credit to students graduating from SUSTC. However, the government also insisted that future students take the Gao Kao, and SUSTC agreed. Is this success or failure (Bing, 2015)?

Especially for High School Teachers One of your brightest students doesn't want to go to college. She would rather keep waitressing in a restaurant, where she makes good money in tips. What do you say? (see response, page 512)

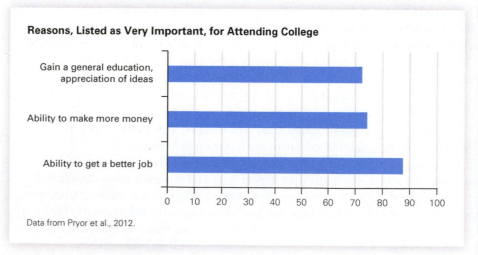

Reasons, Listed as Very Important, for Attending College

Data from Pryor et al., 2012.

FIGURE 18.3

Cohort Shift Decades before these data were collected, students thought new ideas and a philosophy of life were prime reasons to go to college—they were less interested in jobs, careers, and money. If this thinking causes a conflict between student motivation and professors' goals, who should adjust?

Better Instruction

There are many critics of college. However, in several ways colleges may be markedly better than they were a few decades ago. A major improvement is that classroom instruction is changing.

Current instructors seek engaged learners, not passive students. Many professors still lecture, but they include more student involvement. An exposition of how this is done begins with a quote from a Canadian satirist, Stephen Leacock.

> Most people tire of the lecture in ten minutes; clever people can do it in five. Sensible people never go to lectures at all.
>
> *[quoted in Chaudhury, 2011, p. 13]*

College instructors are well aware of the criticism implied by Leacock. Professors used to be "a sage on the stage," that is, an expert who lectures from the front of the room. Instead, more instructors seek to be "a guide on the side." Pedagogy has changed to include more projects, teamwork, and discussion.

One particular version of updated instruction is called the *flipped class,* in which students are required to watch videos and do practice exercises on their computers before class. Then class time is used for discussion, with the professor prodding and encouraging but not lecturing. From a developmental perspective, it seems that flipped classrooms combine insights from two developmental theorists, Piaget and Skinner, an example of a thesis and antithesis leading to a new synthesis. As two professors write:

> The flipped classroom is a new pedagogical method, which employs asynchronous video lectures and practice problems as homework, and active, group-based problem solving activities in the classroom. It represents a unique combination of learning theories once thought to be incompatible—active, problem-based learning activities founded upon a constructivist ideology and instructional lectures derived from direct instruction methods founded upon behaviorist principles.
>
> *[Bishop & Verleger, 2013]*

In general, students prefer flipped classes and learn more in them. One detailed study found that the number of students earning D, F, or W (withdraw without a grade) in an introductory course on networking was 49 percent before the flipped classroom and only 7 percent when the same class was flipped (Nwosisi et al., 2016).

Many instructors use some technology; the flipped classroom requires students to do some work online. In addition, most colleges and universities offer some classes completely online, with students doing all of their homework and reading on their laptops and tablets when they wish, and with tests and final grades delivered over the Internet. Online courses are particularly attractive to students in rural areas far from college, or those unable to leave home because they have young children or mobility problems, or those serving in the armed forces far from their home college.

Indeed, in at least 79 colleges in the United states, more than one-third of students take *all* of their courses online, including 36 (mostly for-profit schools) in which the entire curriculum for every student is online (Chronicle of Higher Education, 2015). Such students need never meet an instructor or a classmate face-to-face in order to earn their degree.

● **Response for Those Considering Studying Abroad** (from page 509):
Since one result of college is that students become more open to other perspectives while developing their commitment to their own values, foreign study might be most beneficial after several years of college. If they study abroad too early, some students might be either too narrowly patriotic (they are not yet open) or too quick to reject everything about their national heritage (they have not yet developed their own commitments).

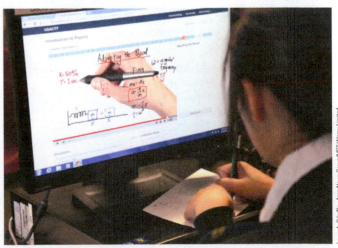

Writing on the Wall In Oakland, California, Selina Wong is learning physics online from a MOOC offered by San Jose University. The most common criticism of online courses is that they are not interactive, but, as you see, this is not always true.

massive open online course (MOOC)
A course that is offered solely online for college credit. Typically, tuition is very low, and thousands of students enroll.

🔴🟣 **Response for High School Teachers**
(from page 510): Even more than ability, motivation is crucial for college success, so don't insist that she attend college immediately. Since your student has money and a steady job (prime goals for today's college-bound youth), she may not realize what she would be missing. Ask her what she hopes for, in work and lifestyle, over the decades ahead.

The possibilities for online courses have led to another phenomenon, the **massive open online course (MOOC),** in which thousands of students enroll. Students in MOOCs often live in places where few rigorous or specialized classes are accessible. The first MOOC offered by Massachusetts Institute of Technology (MIT) and Harvard enrolled 155,000 students from 194 nations, including 13,044 from India (Breslow et al., 2013).

For the most part, data from MOOCs and from completely online colleges have been disappointing. Only 4 percent of the students in that first MOOC completed the course. MOOCs are most successful if students are highly motivated, adept at computer use, and have the needed prerequisites (Reich, 2015). Completion rates have risen in later courses, but almost always the dropout rate is more than 80 percent.

One critical article cites statistics, not only of the MIT course and of another with 37,000 registrants in the University of California at Irvine, but also Duke University:

> Duke opened an astronomy course to 60,000 registered students, but only 16,700 even tried a problem set, and 2,900 contributed to discussion forums . . . in general, the huge registration figures [of many MOOCs] seemed to have more to do with aspiration than with education.

> [Kolowich, 2016, p. A27]

Culture and Cohort Ideally, college brings together people of many backgrounds who learn from each other. This scene from a college library in the United Arab Emirates would not have happened a few decades ago. The dress of these three suggests that culture still matters, but worldwide, education is recognized as benefiting every young person in every nation.

In theory, a MOOC saves instructional costs, because a professor sets up the lessons but provides no individualized attention. However, it seems that college education is not a spectator sport (Kolowich, 2013). Active personalized engagement is needed.

This would not surprise anyone who understands adult cognitive development. Students learn best in MOOCs if they have another classmate, or a local expert, as a personal guide. This is true for all kinds of college learning: Face-to-face interaction seems to improve motivation and learning. As you know regarding cognitive development, books and online information may help, but challenging conversations and new experiences are the most effective ways to advance cognition. This leads to the next topic.

Diversity

One additional aspect of college has changed radically for the better in recent years. A century ago, virtually all college graduates, in the United States and elsewhere, were men of European American descent. Few colleges existed in Africa or Asia. Now most college students are women, and worldwide, most graduates are non-White.

Massification

massification The idea that establishing institutions of higher learning and encouraging college enrollment can benefit everyone (the masses).

As Asian and African nations became independent of colonial rule, and political leaders recognized the power of education, the number of college students has increased dramatically in virtually every nation. The result is called **massification,** the idea that college is not just for the elite but for almost everyone (the masses) (Altbach et al., 2010).

The United States was the first major nation to endorse massification, beginning with federal legislation to establish land-grant colleges in every state. (Iowa was the first, in 1864.) Now every state has publicly supported universities. As a

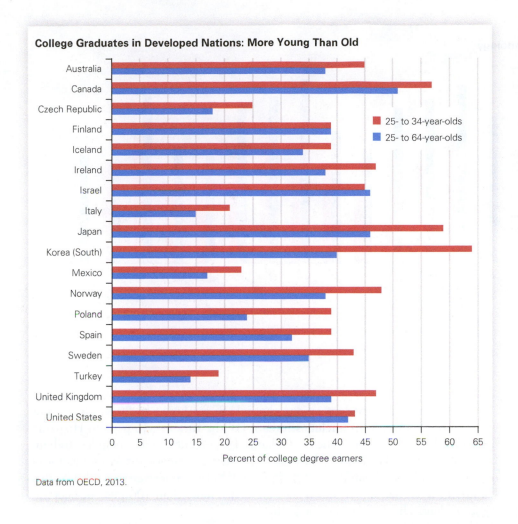

College Graduates in Developed Nations: More Young Than Old

Legend:
- 25- to 34-year-olds
- 25- to 64-year-olds

Percent of college degree earners

Data from OECD, 2013.

FIGURE 18.4

How Things Have Changed This chart reveals two things. First, it shows whether young college graduates have grandparents and parents who did not attend college—dramatically true in Korea and Poland. Second, it reveals whether public support for college has increased in the past twenty years—not true in the United States, Israel, and Finland. In the United States, although more people begin college, fewer graduate, partly because the income gap is wider than it once was while public funding is reduced. Finding four years of tuition money is increasingly difficult for North Americans, and college loans are seen as a boon to banks but not individuals—making young adults wary of signing on the dotted line.

result, throughout the twentieth century, the United States led the world in the percentage of college graduates (see Figure 18.4).

In the twenty-first century, however, most other nations increased public funding for tertiary education while the United States decreased it. As a result, 11 other nations have a higher proportion of 25- to 34-year-olds who are college graduates (OECD, 2013). This is the reason for "declining wages . . . [and] living standards of many Americans" according to one analysis (Greenstone & Looney, 2012, p. 32).

Another consequence is that, although almost every nation has seen improvement in the skills of its citizens, international tests find that young adults in the United States lag behind those in several other nations in reading comprehension, problem solving, and especially math (see Figure 18.5).

A report highlighting those results is particularly critical of the disparity in education between the rich and the poor, stating "to put it bluntly, we no longer share the growth and prosperity of the nation the way we did in the decades between 1940 and 1980" (Goodman et al., 2015, p. 2). That report argues that greater diversity is needed, not only ethnic but also economic.

Many Forms of Diversity

All over the world, people of African, Asian, Arab, and Hispanic heritage whose parents could not attend college are now enrolled. This is also true in the United States, where 20 percent of students beginning college in 2014 are the first generation of their family to attend college.

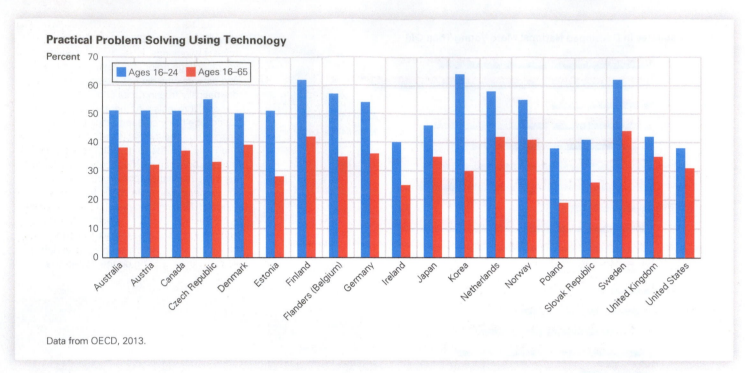

Practical Problem Solving Using Technology

Data from OECD, 2013.

FIGURE 18.5

Blue Is Higher Except... Since blue is for emerging adults and red is for adults of all ages (including emerging ones), it is no surprise that massification has produced higher scores among the young adults than the old ones. Trouble appears when young adults score about the same as older ones.

Observation Quiz In which nation do emerging adults excel the most compared to older adults, and in which nation is the contrast smallest? (see answer, page 516) ↑

Ethnic diversity is evident among those U.S. freshmen of 2014: 68 percent were European American (includes Italian, Polish, Turkish), 16 percent Hispanic (includes Mexican, Puerto Rican, Cuban), 13 percent Asian (includes Indian, Chinese, Korean), 11 percent Black (includes African Americans as well as those of African and Caribbean ethnicity), 4 percent Native American (includes Native Hawaiians and Alaska Natives). Those totals are more than 100 percent because some students checked two ethnic groups.

Almost all (97 percent) of those students are native to the United States, but 3 percent are citizens of other nations, including more than 1 percent from China. India and Korea are the next two sending nations, but the fourth may be a surprise: Saudi Arabia, which sponsored 60,000 students in U.S. colleges in 2015.

The reason for the large number of Saudis is that King Abdullah was troubled by the prejudices of many Americans after September 11, 2001. In 2005, he instituted a program of college scholarships in the United States. The goal was not only that Saudi young people would come to the United States and learn English and important skills but that they would also teach by their presence. U.S. students could see for themselves that almost all Saudis are conscientious, nonviolent, respectful individuals, devoted to their Muslim faith.

In that effort, the King recognized the potential of diversity in colleges. For many students, college is where they meet their first acquaintance from another ethnic group, or their first Jew or Episcopalian or atheist, or their first person whose family is very rich or very poor. Other forms of diversity are students who are parents, or who are older than 30, or who have served in the military, or who have overcome drug addiction.

As laws and policies of the past few decades have made discrimination based on disabilities illegal, many students have classmates who are blind, in wheelchairs, are intellectually disabled, and so on—again making it possible for the college experience to expand the mind.

Beyond ethnic, economic, and experiential diversity is diversity of gender and sexual orientation. In 1970, at least two-thirds of college students were male, often educated in exclusively male institutions. Now, in every developed nation (except

Germany), more than half of college students are female, with women enrolled in virtually every college and every curriculum. That includes fields that once were exclusively male, such as physics and engineering. During the same years, thousands of LGBT college students have made their identities known.

A historic example is Virginia Military Institute (VMI), a state-supported military academy that had never admitted women since its founding in 1839. Administrators at the college said that women could not do the physical tasks required at VMI, and besides, no woman would want to be an army officer. However, in 1997 the U.S. Supreme Court ruled (7–1) that, as a public institution, VMI could not discriminate based on sex alone. In 2015, 11 percent (about 185) of VMI students were female.

A current example is the student protest of the 2016 North Carolina law removing some protections for LGBT students and requiring transgender students to use the bathrooms designated for their natal sex. Almost 1,000 colleges in the United States, including several in North Carolina, have nondiscrimination policies regarding gender identity (Dirks, 2016). This has included admissions, dorm assignments, and bathrooms, now often unisex, with private stalls, a practice accepted by students for decades. North Carolina's law clashes with federal law and college practice, which alerted many students to the diversity among them.

Diversity of every kind *can* advance cognition. Honest conversations among people of varied backgrounds and perspectives lead to intellectual challenge and deeper thought, with benefits lasting for years after graduation (Pascarella et al., 2014). Colleges that make use of their diversity—via curriculum, assignments, discussions, cooperative education, learning communities, residence halls, and so on—stretch student understanding, not only of other people but also of themselves (Harper & Yeung, 2013).

Educating Congress Justin Neisler is a medical student, about to testify before Congress. As an openly gay man, he hopes to serve LGBTQ youth, a group with many unmet medical needs. However, he and all his classmates have a major problem: The clash between their idealism and the money they owe for their education—a median of $170,000 for new M.D.s in 2012.

Not as Diverse as the Numbers Suggest

Of course, the fact that there are LGBT students in every university does not necessarily mean that students understand the needs of those students. Moreover, the numbers overstate diversity: Although one-third of U.S. college students are non-European, it is not true that most colleges are one-third non-European.

Instead, some colleges are almost exclusively African American or Latino or Native American. Many other colleges are 90 percent or more European American. No kind of diversity just mentioned is spread equally, in part because diversity is not equally distributed nationwide.

Students at virtually all community colleges commute from their homes. Since neighborhoods are quite segregated ethnically and economically, community colleges are as well. Furthermore, at residential colleges, most students come from nearby areas (usually within 100 miles of their childhood home), so the student body is quite different in, for instance, Alaska or Alabama.

Students with distinct backgrounds—rich or poor, politically conservative or liberal, disabled or not, and so on—tend to seek colleges with similar students and then befriend those students who are like themselves. People tend to be quiet about atypical experiences—such as having fought in a war, or being transgender, or having a disability. This is a natural human tendency: No one is comfortable as a token, speaking for all people of whatever particular background.

However, opportunities for intellectual growth are missed if diversity is not sought and celebrated. The importance of this has recently been highlighted in two movements on college campus: African American students protesting that

Unlike Their Parents Both photos show large urban colleges in the United States (California and New York), with advantages the older college generations did not have: wireless technology (in use by all three on the top) and classmates from 50 nations (evident in the bottom photo).

macmillan learning

Video: The Effects of Mentoring on Intellectual Development: The University-Community Links Project shows how an after-school study enhancement program has proven beneficial for both its mentors and the at-risk students who attend it.

● **Answer to Observation Quiz**
(from page 514) Most—Korea; least—the United States or the United Kingdom.

colleges do not reflect their needs, and women protesting that their sexual abuse is not responded to with respect and speed.

In both cases, college presidents, deans, and trustees thought they were welcoming African American and female students on their campuses, and in both cases students say much more needs to be done. These two examples had nationwide attention in 2016, and many campuses have fired deans, hired diversity officers, and improved investigations of sexual abuse as a result. As time goes on, we will see whether those changes have an effect, and whether other groups contend that they are not really understood and welcomed either.

Evaluating the Changes

Thus, it is true that college advances thought as well as lifetime income, that technology has changed instruction, and that every institution of higher education is more diverse than it was 50 years ago. It is not true that every institution responds to any of the recent changes, including technology and diversity, in ways that respect the needs of all students. Emerging adults, like people of every age, tend to feel most comfortable with people who agree with them. Critical thinking develops outside the personal comfort zone, when cognitive dissonance requires deeper thought.

The crucial factor for technology seems to be interaction with the professor or with peers; the crucial factor for diversity seems to be honest talk with someone unlike oneself. This can occur spontaneously, or it can be facilitated by a professor. Ideally, the professors themselves are of many backgrounds, and that helps them respect the diversity of their students and teach them to learn from each other. That is cognitive development, that is openness and flexibility, that is postformal thought.

It is time to consider again what today's students get from college. As you see, many signs suggest that college education is as important as it ever was, producing not only better health, and more lifetime earnings, but also better thinking. Technology can be used to improve instruction, massification means that more students attend college, and increasing diversity means that more students of many backgrounds are now in college.

For those in this new stage of development—emerging adulthood—college provides a chance to postpone commitment while exploring new ideas and preparing for adulthood. For those coming to college after time spent in the labor market, college leads to a desirable career shift. However, as we have just described, every aspect of college has mixed consequences. We need to avoid seeing only the positive or the negative.

For many readers of this textbook, none of these findings are surprising. Students learn to think deeply and analytically, as postformal adults do. In many ways, college in the United States can be seen as a thesis and antithesis, as each aspect has a downside. The hope is that you will combine the advantages of college education and the hazards of each innovation, forging a new synthesis. Can you do it?

WHAT HAVE YOU LEARNED?

1. What are the economic benefits of a college education?

2. Why do many students not graduate from college?

3. Why would some people suggest that college loans are not helpful to certain students?

4. What are the educational benefits of college?

5. According to Perry, how does a student's thinking change over his or her college career?

6. What is the clash between students' and professors' goals for college education?

7. What kinds of diversity are found among current college students?

8. How does diversity affect learning in college?

SUMMARY

A New Level of Thinking

1. Many researchers believe that in adulthood the complex and conflicting demands of daily life produce a new cognitive perspective. Postformal thinking is not the automatic result of maturation, so it is not a traditional "stage," but it is a higher level of thought.

2. Choosing how to use time is one of the challenges of adulthood. With postformal thinking, adults are less likely to procrastinate and more likely to coordinate conflicting demands.

3. Stereotypes and stereotype threat interrupt thinking processes and thus can make people seem intellectually less capable. Ideally, adults find ways to overcome such liabilities.

4. Piaget thought the highest level of thinking was formal operational, which began in adolescence and continued through all of adult life. Some scientists believe he was mistaken, in that he did not realize that more advanced cognition was possible.

5. Dialectical thinking synthesizes complexities and contradictions. Instead of seeking absolute, immutable truths, dialectical thought recognizes that people and situations are dynamic and ever-changing.

6. One hallmark of dialectical thought is the ability to combine emotions and rational analysis. This ability is particularly useful in responding to social understanding and actions, because each relationship requires complex and flexible responses.

7. Dialectical thought may be more typical in Asian cultures than in Western ones. However, working together and considering many perspectives is useful for everyone, as adults realize.

Morals and Religion

8. Thinking about questions of morality, faith, and ethics may also progress in adulthood. Specific moral opinions are strongly influenced by culture and context, but adults generally become less self-centered as they mature.

9. As people mature, life confronts them with ethical decisions, including many related to human relationships and the diversity of humankind. According to Fowler, religious faith also moves beyond culture-bound concepts toward universal principles.

10. In many academic fields, coursework is designed to raise ethical issues. Progress can be measured with the Defining Issues Test.

Cognitive Growth and Higher Education

11. Research over the past several decades indicates not only that college graduates are wealthier and healthier than other adults but also that they think at a more advanced level. Over the years of college, students gradually become less inclined to seek absolute truths from authorities and more interested in making their own decisions.

12. College instruction is more likely to focus on engaging students than on lecturing to them. Technology allows flipped classes, online classes, and MOOCs. Personal engagement still seems to be a catalyst for cognitive growth.

13. Contemporary college students are far more diverse than college students were a few decades ago. In every nation, the sheer number of students has multiplied. Ethnically, economically, and experientially, and in many other ways, student diversity can help expand the perspectives of college students.

KEY TERMS

postformal thought (p. 492)
stereotype threat (p. 494)
dialectical thought (p. 496)
thesis (p. 496)

antithesis (p. 496)
synthesis (p. 496)
objective thought (p. 498)
subjective thought (p. 498)

Defining Issues Test (DIT) (p. 501)
morality of care (p. 504)
morality of justice (p. 504)

massive open online course (MOOC) (p. 512)
massification (p. 512)

APPLICATIONS

1. Read a biography or autobiography that includes information about the person's thinking from age 18 to age 60, paying particular attention to practical, flexible, or dialectical thought. How did personal experiences, education, and ideas affect the person's thinking?

2. Some ethical principles are thought to be universal, respected by people of every culture. Think of one such idea and analyze whether it is accepted by each of the world's major religions.

3. Statistics on changes in students and in colleges are fascinating, but only a few are reported here. Compare your nation, state,

or province with another. Analyze the data and discuss causes and implications of differences.

4. One way to assess cognitive development during college is to study yourself or your classmates, comparing thoughts and decisions at the beginning and end of college. Since case studies are provocative but not definitive, identify some hypotheses that you might examine and explain how you would do so.

Emerging Adulthood: Psychosocial Development

What Will You Know?

1. How does the recent economic recession affect emerging adults?
2. How is a family more than a collection of individuals?
3. In spouse abuse, is it better for partners to be counseled or to separate?

W e are all affected by our cohort and culture, although we might not know it at the time. I certainly did not. When I was 20, my two closest friends (Phoebe and Peggy) and I talked about becoming wives and mothers. We were happy, describing our wedding dresses to each other and naming our imagined children. We expected to be dependent on our husbands for financial security and independent from our parents.

The culture shifted. By age 50, none of us had followed the path we anticipated. We were much closer to our parents than we thought we would be, and all six of them—still married to their childhood sweethearts—were surprised at our lives. Now that I think about it, I am surprised, too.

Phoebe never married or had children. She started a business, becoming a millionaire who bought a house near the Pacific Ocean. Peggy married at age 21, earned a Ph.D., divorced in her 30s, and then married a former priest. They had one child, born when she was 40. After several academic jobs, she found work that she loves, as a craniofacial massage therapist.

I married at age 25 to a man different in many ways from the men I was dating when I was 20. I also always was employed full-time except for one year, at age 26, when I was pregnant with our first child and studying full-time for my Ph.D. I once told a stranger that I had four children and was teaching five days a week.

"All from the same husband?" she asked incredulously. Yes, an odd path.

This chapter discusses the ongoing identity exploration of emerging adults. As happened to us, social norms shift and emerging adults make choices they would not have made in earlier times. Young adults still have friendships and romances, and they are probably more connected to their parents than was true in former times, but fewer marry and have children. Personality traits endure (that's why Phoebe and Peggy are still my friends), and happiness may continue as well.

Twelve years ago, I complained to Phoebe that, even though my daughters were all past age 20, none was a wife or mother. She smiled, put her hand on mine, and said, "Please notice. I never married or had children. I am very happy." So is Peggy. So am I.

Continuity and Change

A theme of human development is that continuity and change are evident throughout life. In emerging adulthood, the continuity from childhood is apparent amidst new achievements. As you remember, the identity crisis begins in adolescence, but

Left: Philippe Roy/Cultura/Getty Images
Top: StarsStudio/iStock/Getty Images

JUNG YEON-JE/AFP/Getty Images

Grown Up Now? In Korean tradition, age 19 signifies adulthood, when people can drink alcohol and, in modern times, vote. In 2011, administrators invited 100 19-year-olds to a public Coming of Age ceremony, shown here, that had begun centuries before. Emerging adults are torn between old and new. For example, in many nations, coming of age ceremonies are exclusive to one gender, but here boys and girls participate.

it is not usually resolved until adulthood. Emerging adults ponder all four arenas of identity—religious commitments, gender roles, political loyalties, and career options—trying to reconcile their plans for the future with beliefs acquired in the past.

As explained in Chapter 16, the identity crisis sometimes causes confusion or foreclosure (see Table 19.1). A more mature response is to seek a moratorium, postponing identity achievement and avoiding marriage and parenthood while exploring possibilities. Our current culture offers many moratoria: attending college, joining the military, taking on religious mission work, working as an intern in government, academia, and industry.

Sometimes the moratorium is time-limited (e.g., signing up for a stint in the army or the two-year commitment of Teach for America). All moratoria reduce the pressure to achieve identity, and all may be seen as "floundering" haphazardly or "sagely avoiding foreclosure and premature commitment in a treacherous job market" (Konstam, 2015, p. 95).

Emerging adults do what is required (as students, soldiers, missionaries, or whatever), which explains why a moratorium is considered more mature than role confusion. However, they also postpone settling down. This respite gives them time to achieve identity.

Ethnic Identity

Aspects of identity respond to the historical context, even as the search for self-determination continues. As one expert explains, "identity development . . . from the teenage years to the early 20s, if not through adulthood, . . . has been extended to explain the development of ethnic and racial identity" (Whitbourne et al., 2009, p. 1328). Ethnic identity includes Erikson's political and religious identities, both crucial in our modern, multiethnic world.

Dreamers and Adoptees

Establishing identity is never easy, but it can become especially difficult for two particular groups within the United States.

TABLE 19.1	Erikson's Eight Stages of Development	
Stage	Virtue/Pathology	Possible in Emerging Adulthood If Not Successfully Resolved
Trust vs. mistrust	Hope/withdrawal	Suspicious of others, making close relationships difficult
Autonomy vs. shame and doubt	Will/compulsion	Obsessively driven, single-minded, not socially responsive
Initiative vs. guilt	Purpose/inhibition	Fearful, regretful (e.g., very homesick in college)
Industry vs. inferiority	Competence/inertia	Self-critical of any endeavor, procrastinating, perfectionistic
Identity vs. role diffusion	Fidelity/repudiation	Uncertain and negative about values, lifestyle, friendships
Intimacy vs. isolation	Love/exclusivity	Anxious about close relationships, jealous, lonely
Generativity vs. stagnation	Care/rejection	[In the future] Fear of failure
Integrity vs. despair	Wisdom/disdain	[In the future] No "mindfulness," no life plan

Information from Erikson, 1982/1998.

Members of one large group (estimated at close to 1 million) are called "dreamers." They are unauthorized immigrants to the United States who meet five criteria:

- They are under age 31.
- They entered the United States before age 16.
- They lived continuously in the United States for at least five years.
- They have never been convicted of a felony or a serious misdemeanor.
- They graduated from a U.S. high school or served in the armed forces.

Legally, they could be deported, but their identity is obviously multifaceted. Under current law, they cannot become citizens of the United States, but their ethnic and political identity is quite different from their peers in their original nation.

Members of another large group were adopted internationally and raised in the United States, usually by parents who are from a background quite different from that of their children. An estimated 300,000 children were adopted internationally between 2003 and 2013. As each cohort becomes adult, they must reconcile many identities: racial, ethnic, national, immigrant, and adoptee (Pinderhughes & Rosnati, 2015; Manzi et al., 2014). Their success at that complex task affects their entire lives—enriching them or undermining their later development.

Everyone Else

Dreamers and adoptees obviously have complex identities to establish, but every emerging adult must establish their ethnic and political identity. About half of all emerging adults in the United States have ancestors who were not European, but that simply describes who they are not— they need to figure out the specifics of having ancestors from China, or Colombia, or Cameroon, or wherever.

Many young Americans have a mixed heritage, with forebears from several cultures, each distinct from the current youth culture. Becoming proud of one's heritage—bicultural and biracial as it may be—correlates with healthy psychosocial development (Nguyen & Benet-Martínez, 2013).

As many young adults in the United States with non-European backgrounds struggle to establish their ethnic identity, young adults of European backgrounds also seek to figure out their ethnic identity—as Irish or Italian or whatever. Establishing an ethnic identity was once easier, because neighbors were more likely to be from the same group. As emerging adults enter colleges and workplaces in a global economy, they need to know their own roots so that they can respect the roots of others.

One study found that Hispanic college students who resisted both assimilation and alienation fared best: They were most likely to maintain their ethnic identity, deflect stereotype threat, and become good students (Rivas-Drake & Mooney, 2009). That seems true for every group.

Global Identity Bruno chose Mars as his last name because "I'm out of this world." It represents an inspired combination of his parents' ethnicities: Filipino, Hungarian, Ukrainian, and Puerto Rican. His music is rock, rap, soul, R & B, and hip-hop, a mixture that made him a global superstar.

Christopher Polk/Getty Images for Clear Channel/Getty Images

Political Choices

One example of the reality that today's emerging adults must find their own way is in voting patterns. In former times, growing up in a particular community established political identity. People supported the Democrats or Republicans because that was the party of their parents, their classmates, their church. That is much less true today.

For the first time in 70 years of U.S. history, millions of young adults voted in 2008 for a candidate that their grandparents did not. To be specific, 66 percent of those between 18 and 29 voted for Barack Obama, as did only 45 percent of those over 65—a 21-percent gap.

This was not true for earlier cohorts. As recently as the 2000 presidential contest, when both candidates were quite similar in ethnicity, gender, and age, only a 2-percent difference appeared between older and younger voters.

Of course, there are many plausible explanations, but one is ethnic identity: The fact that President Obama is biracial was easily accepted by the younger generation, who had come to terms with their own ethnicity and thus could accept someone of another background. Many older Americans never thought much about their own ethnic background because they never needed to; they grew up when immigration was at a historic low.

Generally, having a firm identity frees a person to interact with people of other identities. More than other age groups, emerging adults tend to know people of many backgrounds. They become more aware of history, customs, and prejudices.

As emerging adults undergo cognitive development, many of them strive to combine objective and subjective identity: They take courses in history, ethnic studies, and sociology, or that multi-faith course explained in Chapter 18. They may also seek close friends, lovers, and affinity groups whose identity struggles are similar to their own.

Gender Identity

Similar to ethnic identity, gender identity has become more important for every emerging adult in current times. As noted in Chapter 16, the concept of gender identity has broadened for everyone, as a young person no longer simply follows a traditional male or female identity, but is confronted with a range of options.

Establishing a gender identity, and being proud of it, is not easy, in part because many childhood religious and community assumptions pushed people to be traditionally masculine or feminine. For some, clashes with their traditional background leads to depression and even suicide (Gibbs & Goldbach, 2015).

Establishing gender identity is important for all youth, not only sexual minority ones (Maas et al., 2015). Many generational clashes focus on gender norms—in dress, hairstyle, vocation, and so on.

Vocational Identity

Establishing a vocational identity is considered part of growing up, not only by developmental psychologists influenced by Erikson but also by emerging adults themselves—many of whom go to college to prepare for a good job. Emerging adulthood is a "critical stage for the acquisition of resources"—including the education, skills, and experience needed for lifelong family and career success (Tanner et al., 2009, p. 34) (see Table 19.2).

Help from Adults

Achieving vocational identity may be more difficult than ever. Adults are of little help. Parents usually know only their particular job and employer, not labor-market projections in the next decade. High school guidance counselors in the United States have an *average* caseload of 367 students a year, many of whom want to apply to a dozen colleges and some who need time-consuming emotional support to prevent violence, suicide, or drug addiction (The College Board, 2012).

College counselors may also be overwhelmed. One strategy that many emerging adults use is to consider John Holland's description (1997) of

TABLE 19.2	Top Six "Very Important" Objectives in Life*	
Being well off financially		78%
Raising a family		75%
Making more money		71%
Helping others		69%
Becoming an authority in my field		59%
Obtaining recognition in my special field		56%

*Based on a national survey of students entering four-year colleges in the United States in the fall of 2010.

Data from Chronicle of Higher Education, 2010.

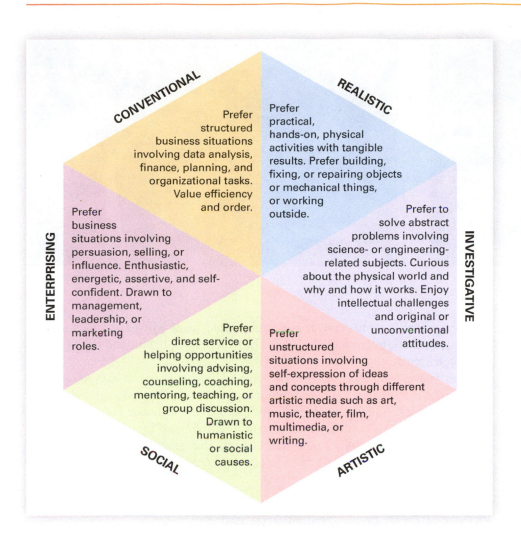

FIGURE 19.1

Happy at Work John Holland's six-part diagram helps job seekers realize that income and benefits are not the only goals of employment. Workers have healthier hearts and minds if their job fits their personal preferences.

six possible interests (see Figure 19.1). However, even if they earn a degree (most don't, as you saw in Chapter 18) and know what they want (again, most don't), they still may be unable to find the work they hope for (Konstam, 2015). This has been particularly true since the economic downturn that began in 2008: Emerging adults are the age group with the highest rate of unemployment (Ruetschlin & Draut, 2013).

One problem is that many young adults consider their job part of their identity, and this makes it difficult for them to accept just any job. As one psychologist wrote:

> career choices faced by individuals inevitably raise the question of the meaning that they intend to give their lives. To choose their work or sector in which they want to evolve, is also to consider the purpose of their existence, the priorities (physical, spiritual, social, aesthetic, etc.) that they want to give, the choices that they wish to operate, the overall style of life that they wish to give themselves.
>
> [Bernaud, 2014, p. 36]

Thus, for many younger adults, vocational identity is not just about finding a job, or finding a job they like, it is about establishing who they want to be and then becoming that person. No wonder achieving vocational identity is difficult.

The Economic Recession

Today's job market has made development of vocational identity even harder. A life-span perspective suggests that young adults may still be affected by their

Ordinary Workers Most children and adolescents want to be sports heroes, star entertainers, billionaires, or world leaders—yet fewer than one in 1 million succeed in doing so.

New Jobs, New Workers This barista in Germany *(left)* and these app developers in India *(right)* work at very different jobs. Yet they may have much in common: If they are like other emerging adults, their current employment is not what they imagined in high school, and not what they will be doing in 10 years.

discouragement, unemployment, and underemployment when the financial picture improves (M. Johnson et al., 2011). The experiences, habits, and fears of early adulthood are not easily forgotten.

Many young people take a series of temporary jobs. Between ages 18 and 25, the average U.S. worker has held seven jobs, with the college-educated changing jobs more than the high school graduate (U.S. Bureau of Labor Statistics, 2015). Part of the reason is that they do not want to climb, rung by rung, a career ladder: They would rather try various kinds of work. But, another part of it is that the recession has meant that more older adults are keeping their jobs, making fewer openings for the young.

Personality in Emerging Adulthood

Continuity and change are evident in personality as well (McAdams & Olson, 2010). Of course, personality is shaped lifelong by genes and early experiences. If self-doubt, anxiety, depression, and so on are present in adolescence, they are typically evident years later. Traits that are present at age 18 rarely disappear by age 25.

Yet personality is not static. After adolescence, new dimensions appear. Indeed, emerging adulthood has been called the "crucible of personality development" (Roberts & Davis, 2016).

As the preceding two chapters emphasize, emerging adults make choices that break with the past. Their freedom from a settled lifestyle allows shifts in attitude and personality. Not only is success in school affected *by* personality but it also *affects* personality (Klimstra et al., 2012). In other words, college success can alter personality traits for the better.

Rising Self-Esteem

The choices that emerging adults make often lead to a rise in self-esteem. Setting one's own goals and making new friends makes people proud to be agents and authors of their own lives (McAdams, 2013).

One study traced the experiences of 3,912 U.S. high school seniors for five years. Generally, chosen transitions, whether entering college, starting a job, leaving home, or getting married, increased well-being. Those who went away from home to college as independent adults showed the largest gains, while those who became single parents or who still lived with their parents showed the least. Even the latter, however, tended to be happier than they had been in high school (see Figure 19.2) (Schulenberg et al., 2005).

Logically, the many stresses and transitions of emerging adulthood might be expected to reduce self-esteem. However, only a minority experience a decline in self-esteem during these years (Nelson & Padilla-Walker, 2013). As detailed in Chapter 17, some develop serious psychological disorders (Twenge et al., 2010), but most do not.

Of course, this depends on the social context as well as on age. Becoming financially independent, which is a marker of adulthood, is more difficult in current times than it once was. That reduces self-esteem.

A recent study in Australia found, as expected, that self-esteem generally rose after adolescence but that the economic downturn had an effect. Those cohorts who were beginning their push toward independence just when the economic recession reduced job openings were less satisfied with their lives, not only their work lives but also their social lives (Parker et al., 2016). The authors fear that the effects may last lifelong because:

> the danger of macroeconomics events, like the [global financial crisis], would be the potential to knock youth off a typical developmental track: delaying transitions, interfering with increasing independence from parents, and extending periods of career and educational uncertainty.
>
> [Parker et al., 2016, p. 641]

These authors note that, because of various federal interventions, the recession was relatively mild for emerging adults in Australia. Unemployment of that age group rose from 9 percent to 14 percent, compared to a change from 10 percent to 18 percent in the United States, and higher in Europe. Research in France, Ireland, and many other places finds a marked negative impact of the recession on youth self-esteem (Lannegrand-Willems et al., 2015; E. Power et al., 2015).

Many observers consider ages 18 to 24 a particularly vulnerable time for personality development, when the social context—economic recession or not—influences the priorities, attitudes, and assumptions of each young person (Schoon, 2006; Steinberg, 2014).

Worrisome Children Grow Up

Shifts toward positive development were found in another longitudinal study that began with 4-year-olds who were at the extremes of either of the two traits known to have strong genetic roots: extreme shyness and marked aggression. Those two traits continued to be evident throughout childhood. But, by emerging adulthood many of these children had changed for the better (Asendorpf et al., 2008).

This is not to say that old patterns disappeared. For example, those who had been aggressive 4-year-olds continued to have conflicts with their parents and friends. They were more likely to quit school and leave jobs before age 25. Half of them had been arrested at least once, another sign of their unusually aggressive personalities.

Yet, unexpectedly, these aggressive young adults had as many friends as their average peers did. They wanted more education than they already had, and their self-rating on conscientiousness was at least equal to the self-ratings of a control group who had been less aggressive as children. Their arrests were usually for minor offenses, typically adolescent-limited, not life-course-persistent. As emerging adults,

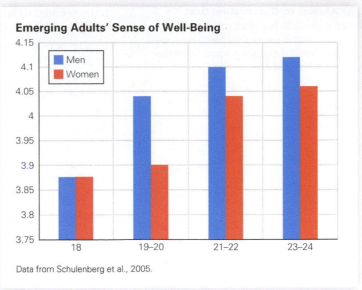

Emerging Adults' Sense of Well-Being

Data from Schulenberg et al., 2005.

FIGURE 19.2

Worthy People This graph shows a steady, although small, rise in young adults' sense of well-being from age 18 to age 24, as measured by respondents' ratings of statements such as "I feel I am a person of worth." The ratings ranged from 1 (complete disagreement) to 5 (complete agreement). The average rating was actually quite high at age 18, and it increased steadily over the years of emerging adulthood.

Observation Quiz It looks as if well-being more than doubled between age 18 and the early 20s. Is that right? (See answer, page 526.) ↑

most seemed to be developing well, controlling their anger and putting their childhood problems behind them. [**Life-Span Link:** Adolescence-limited and life-course-persistent offenders are discussed in Chapter 16.]

As for the emerging adults who had been shy, they were "cautious, reserved adults" (Asendorpf et al., 2008, p. 1007), slower than average to secure a job, choose a career, or find romance (at age 23, two-thirds had no current partner). However, they were no more anxious or depressed than others of their cohort, and their self-esteem was *not* low. They had many friends, whom they saw often. Their delayed employment and later marriage were accepted, even envied, by their outgoing peers. The personality trait (shyness) that was a handicap in childhood had become an asset.

Plasticity

In the research just discussed and in other research as well, plasticity (which, as you remember, refers to the idea that development is both moldable and durable, like plastic) is evident. Personality is not fixed by age 5, or 15, or 20, as it was once thought to be. Emerging adults are open to new experiences (a reflection of their adventuresome spirit), an attitude that allows personality shifts as well as eagerness for more education (McAdams & Olson, 2010; Tanner et al., 2009).

plasticity genes Genes and alleles that make people more susceptible to environmental influences, for better or worse. This is part of differential sensitivity.

Clearly, genes do not determine behavior, but they do make a person more, or less, susceptible to environmental forces. Some genes have been called **plasticity genes** (Simons et al., 2013). A person who inherits them is affected, for better or for worse, by going to college, leaving home, becoming independent, moving to a new city, finding satisfying work and performing it well, making new friends, committing to a partner.

Although total change does not occur, since genes, childhood experiences, and family circumstances affect people lifelong, personality can shift. Plasticity—both neurological and cultural—is evident (Taber-Thomas & Perez-Edgar, 2015).

Remember differential susceptibility. Increased well-being may underlie another shift: Emerging adults may become less self-centered and more caring of others, or they may become focused on their own personal gain (Freund & Blanchard-Fields, 2014; Eisenberg et al., 2005; Padilla-Walker et al., 2008). Because of plasticity, whatever happens can be the foundation of the next psychosocial stage of development, which we now discuss.

WHAT HAVE YOU LEARNED?

1. For whom is ethnic identity difficult and why?

2. Why is gender identity more difficult to establish currently than in former times?

3. How has the recession affected vocational identity?

4. What is the usual path of self-esteem from adolescence through emerging adulthood?

5. What evidence is there that personality can change?

---

intimacy versus isolation The sixth of Erikson's eight stages of development. Adults seek someone with whom to share their lives in an enduring and self-sacrificing commitment. Without such commitment, they risk profound aloneness and isolation.

Close Family and Friends

In Erikson's theory, after achieving identity, people experience the crisis of **intimacy versus isolation.** Social isolation is harmful at every age and in every culture (Holt-Lunstad et al., 2015). Humans have a powerful desire to share their personal lives with someone else. Without intimacy, adults suffer from loneliness. Erikson explains:

> The young adult, emerging from the search for and the insistence on identity, is eager and willing to fuse his identity with others. He is ready for intimacy, that is, the capacity to commit himself to concrete affiliations and partnerships and to develop the ethical strength to abide by such commitments, even though they call for significant sacrifices and compromises.
>
> *[Erikson, 1993a, p. 263]*

Other theorists have different words for the same human need—*affiliation, affection, interdependence, communion, belonging, love*—but all developmentalists note the importance of social connections lifelong. That first social smile in infancy, becoming synchrony and attachment, is the precursor to adult intimacy, especially if the child develops a positive working model of social connections (Chow & Ruhl, 2014; Phillips et al., 2013).

Soon we will explore the usual route that intimacy takes in emerging adulthood, with romantic relationships. First, however, we look at the source of intimacy, the family bond.

Emerging Adults and Their Parents

It is hard to overestimate the importance of the family during any time of the life span. Although it is composed of individuals, a family is much more than the persons who belong to it. In the dynamic synergy of a well-functioning family, children grow, adults find support, and everyone is part of a unit that gives meaning to, and provides models for, aspirations and decisions.

If anything, parents today are more important to emerging adults than ever. Two experts in human development write, "with delays in marriage, more Americans choosing to remain single, and high divorce rates, a tie to a parent may be the most important bond in a young adult's life" (Fingerman & Furstenberg, 2012).

Linked Lives

Emerging adults hope to set out on their own, often leaving their childhood home and parents behind. They strive for independence. But parents continue to be crucial.

All members of each family have **linked lives;** that is, the experiences and needs of family members at one stage of life are affected by those at other stages (Elder, 1998; Macmillan & Copher, 2005; Settersten, 2015). We have seen many examples of this in earlier chapters. If the parents fight, children suffer—even if no one lays a hand on them. Family financial stress and parental alliances shape children's lives. Brothers and sisters can be abusers or protectors, role models for good or for ill.

The same historical conditions that gave rise to the stage now called emerging adulthood have strengthened links between parents and their adult children. Because of demographic changes over the past few decades, most middle-aged parents who have young-adult children do not also have infants or young children who need constant care. Parental habits continue, focused now on adults.

Many emerging adults still live at home, though the percentage varies from nation to nation. Almost all unmarried young adults in Italy and Japan live with their parents. Fewer do so in the United States, but the rates are rising: In 2016, more emerging adults lived with their parents than in any other setting (e.g., with a spouse, with roommates, alone).

The reasons are largely financial: Many parents can no longer afford to underwrite their young-adult children's independent living as they once did (Furstenberg,

linked lives Lives in which the success, health, and well-being of each family member are connected to those of other members. This includes those of another generation, as in the relationship between parents, grandparents, and children.

Brilliant, Unemployed, and Laughing This is not an unusual combination for contemporary college graduates. Melissa, in Missoula, Montana, graduated summa cum laude from George Washington University and is now one of the many college graduates who live with their parents. The arrangement provides many financial and family benefits, but it is not known who cooked dinner and who will wash the dishes.

2010). When they do not live at home, emerging adults see their parents, on average, several times a week and phone or text them even more often (Fingerman et al., 2012b).

Strong links between emerging adults and their parents are evident in attitudes as well. A detailed Dutch study found substantial agreement between parents and their adult children on contentious issues: cohabitation, same-sex partnerships, and divorce. Some generational differences appeared, but when parents were compared with their own children (not young adults in general), "intergenerational congruence" was apparent, especially when the adult children lived with their parents, as did about one-fourth of the sample (Bucx et al., 2010, p. 131).

Nationally and internationally, it is a mistake to put too much emphasis on whether or not a young adult still lives at home. Sharing living quarters is *not* the best indicator of a supportive relationship. Emerging adults who live independently but who previously had close relationships with their parents are likely to stay on the path they have already traveled. For instance, one predictor of adult health and habits is the adult's previous relationship with parents.

Those who are living with their parents, especially the "boomerang" group who once were independent and who now need to save money because they are not employed, are often depressed. However, those who are employed, and have always lived at home but are planning to move out someday, are sometimes quite happy (Copp et al., 2015). Thus, the details of family interaction continue to be more important than who lives where.

Financial Support

At least according to legend, in former years when children reached age 18 or so they left the family home, and parents no longer were responsible for them. The term "empty nest" came from the idea that, like little birds, children left to establish their own lives. That does not seem accurate today.

It certainly is not the case financially. Parents of all income levels in the United States provide substantial help to their adult children, for many reasons (Padilla-Walker et al., 2012). A major one is that the parent generation has more income. On average, households with the highest average income are headed by someone aged 45 to 54.

This harks back to the concept of linked lives, in that the parents use their money to support their adult children. Often parents of emerging adults are employed, with some seniority, and are not yet paying for their own health care or retirement. In nations such as the United States, where neither college nor preschool education is free, parental financial help may be crucial for the emerging adult's later financial and personal success (Furstenberg, 2010).

This observation is not meant to criticize earlier cohorts; parents have always wanted to help their offspring. Now, however, more of them are able to give both money and time. For example, very few young college students can pay all of their tuition and living expenses on their own. Parents provide support that is added to loans, part-time employment, and partial scholarships.

About half of all emerging adults in the United States receive cash from their parents in addition to tuition, medical care, food, and other material support. Most are also given substantial gifts of time, such as help with laundry, moving, household repairs, and, if the young adult becomes a parent, free child care. Earning a college degree or raising small children is especially hard without family help.

"This property comes complete with grown-up children left behind by the vendors."

No Thanks Even living with one's own children is problematic.

It may be that providing too much financial help slows down the process of becoming an adult, since financial self-sufficiency is often considered a mark of adulthood (Padilla-Walker et al., 2012). Of course, taking longer to reach adulthood may be a blessing, with the adult child eventually attaining more education and a better job.

It is not clear whether parents who are able to provide major financial help should do so, but it is clear that some help is almost always needed and provided. Young adults from low-income families are likely to remain low-SES, because their parents cannot afford to lift them up (Fingerman et al., 2012b).

Emotional Support

Financial support is less essential in many European nations, where college tuition is free or less expensive, where early-childhood education is considered a public right, and where housing and health care are less costly. Accordingly, parents in Europe usually spend less on their adult children. However, European parents support their adult children in many other ways—the urge to support grown children is universal; specifics depend on family resources and national policies (Brandt & Deindl, 2013).

Family involvement has many advantages, especially if the young adult becomes a parent and the new grandparents provide free child care. Parenthood before age 25 in the United States is a major impediment to higher education and career success, which may explain why emerging adults postpone it (Furstenberg, 2010).

Some Westerners believe that family dependence is stronger in developing nations. For example, many African young adults marry someone approved by their parents and work to support their many relatives—siblings, parents, cousins, uncles, and so on. Individuals sacrifice personal goals, and "collectivism often takes precedence and overrides individual needs and interests," which makes the family "a source of both collective identity and tension" (Wilson & Ngige, 2006, p. 248).

In cultures with arranged marriages, parents not only provide practical support (such as child care) and emotional encouragement, they may also protect their grown child if the chosen marriage is a disaster. For instance, if the husband beats the wife, if the wife refuses sex, if the husband never works, or the wife never cooks, then the parents intervene. Of course, young spouses and their parents everywhere are influenced by their culture, which advises when the parents should intervene.

Too Little or Too Much?

Sometimes adults provide too much or too little nonfinancial support. One example is children in foster care: At age 18, they are considered adults, able to take their place in society. Given all that is now known, this is far too young (Avery & Freundlich, 2009); most 18-year-olds are not ready to manage life on their own.

Some financial help is available for former foster children (food stamps, college scholarships), but more important may be the adult emotional support and encouragement that emerging adults need. If foster children do not have that, they are at high risk of almost every problem an adult might have.

This was very evident in a study of 65 former foster-care young adults, ages 18 to 26, in Sweden, where financial support is readily available. Emotional support from adults, however, was much needed and often absent (Höjer & Sjöblom, 2014). For instance, many emerging adults are troubled by which bills to pay, which purchases to make, which job interviews to seek, where to live, and so on. They need some wise adult to listen to them and encourage them. Biological children, aged 18 to 25, engage in such conversations with their parents. Foster children may have no one.

Who Needs It? Is Sophia grateful that her mother is making her bed as she moves into her freshman dorm at Saint Joseph's College in Maine? Your answer may be influenced by whether you identify with the mother or the daughter.

helicopter parents The label used for parents who hover (like a helicopter) over their emerging-adult children. The term is pejorative, but parental involvement is sometimes helpful.

● Especially for Family Therapists More emerging-adult children today live with their parents than ever before, yet you have learned that families often function better when young adults live on their own. What would you advise? (see response, page 532)

At the opposite extreme, some parents keep their adult children too dependent. The most dramatic example is the so-called **helicopter parent,** hovering over their emerging-adult child, ready to swoop down if any problem arises (Fingerman et al., 2012a). This occurs not only at college but also in the workplace, with parents sometimes complaining to their adult child's work supervisor about a bad performance review (Karl & Peluchette, 2016).

The rise in the number of college students living at home, or attending college near home, could be ascribed to financial concerns, and that certainly is part of it. But, it also could result from parental reluctance to let go, the so-called "Velcro parent." If the child does manage to leave, parents may do many things for adult college students—washing their laundry, sending them cookies, editing their college papers, paying their phone bills—that keep the child dependent, not learning from their mistakes.

One mother explains that her son doesn't come home from college as often as she would like, but when he does, he brings bags of dirty laundry that she washes, and:

> I always send him back with some food and maybe a little bit of money as well. . . . I just feel that he is my baby, and I feel as though I am still providing for him if I at least know he is eating right and has enough money.

[quoted in Hendry & Kloep, 2011, p. 84]

It is not easy to know when to intervene and support and when to allow an adult child to chart a path unlike the one the parents think best. Parents, adult children, and cultures disagree about this. In mainstream American culture, unsolicited parental advice is not welcome. Yet among many cultures (including some American subcultures) parents advise their grown children about everything from clothing styles to marriage partners—they would consider themselves remiss not to do so (Chentsova-Dutton & Vaughn, 2012). Americanized emerging adults might see such comments as hostile and intrusive, whereas their parents might consider that reaction selfish and rude.

Parental advice and assistance may create another problem. If a family has more than one child, the children may perceive favoritism. Often one sibling seems to receive more encouragement, money, or practical help and another hears more criticism. From the parents' perspective, each child has unique needs, requiring different treatment. But such variations may cause resentment, reduce sibling closeness, increase conflict, and lead to depression, in the favored as well as the less favored child (Jensen et al., 2013).

We need to be careful here. Given the reality that emerging adults are not yet mature, and the lifelong need for family support, it may be that parental involvement of all kinds benefits the children. One scholar argues that criticizing helicopter parents arises from a destructive wish that every child be self-sufficient—which might make everyone isolated and lonely (Kohn, 2016).

Friendship

Parents are one long-standing support that helps emerging adults meet their need for intimacy. Friends are another, a source that is important lifelong but perhaps particularly so in emerging adulthood. Friends strengthen our emotional and physical health (Seyfarth & Cheney, 2012). They probably expand our thinking as well via *self-expansion* (Aron et al., 2013), the idea that other people enlarge our understanding as we absorb their experiences and ideas.

Same Situation, Far Apart: Good Friends Together These smiling emerging adults show that friendship matters everywhere. Culture matters, too. Would the eight Florida college students celebrating a twenty-first birthday at a Tex-Mex restaurant *(left)* be willing to switch places with the two Tibetan workers *(right)*?

Friends in Emerging Adulthood

Friendships "reach their peak of functional significance during emerging adulthood" (Tanner & Arnett, 2011, p. 27). Since fewer emerging adults have the family obligations that come with spouses, children, or frail parents, they have time for friendship. Friends provide needed companionship and critical support. Unlike relatives, friends are chosen. They are selected because they are loyal, trustworthy, supportive, and enjoyable, and the choice is mutual, not obligatory.

Thus, friends understand and comfort each other when romance turns sour, and they share experiences and provide useful information about everything from what college to attend to what shoes to wear. One crucial question for emerging adults is what and how to tell parents news that might upset them: Friends help with that, too. Remember Peggy, my good friend. When she told her parents about her divorce, she and her husband brought me along.

People tend to make more friends during emerging adulthood than at any later period, and they rely on these friends. They often use social media to extend and deepen friendships that begin face-to-face, becoming more aware of the day-to-day tribulations and celebrations of their friends (Burstein, 2013).

Some older adults originally feared that increasing Internet use would diminish the number or quality of friendships. That fear has been proven false. If anything, heavy Internet users tend to have more face-to-face friends than do nonusers. They also form opinions, learn about political events, and learn from others, all examples of self-expansion that might not have occurred without social media (Vallor, 2012; Wang & Wellman, 2010).

A switch occurs with friendship over the years of adulthood. Young adults want many friends, and they gather them, befriending classmates, attending parties, speaking to strangers at concerts, on elevators, in parks, and so on. At about age 30, the quality of friends becomes more important than the quantity (Carmichael et al., 2015). Consequently, some friends made in early adulthood fade away, but other friendships deepen.

There is a paradox here. Not only do young adults, on average, have more friends and acquaintances than adults of other ages, they also have higher rates of loneliness. The only adult age group that is more often lonely are adults over age 80 (Luhmann & Hawkley, 2016).

THINK CRITICALLY: How can a person with many friends also be lonely?

Gender and Friendship

It is a mistake to imagine that men and women have opposite friendship needs. All humans seek intimacy, throughout their lives. Claiming that men are from Mars and women are from Venus ignores reality: People are from Earth (Hyde, 2007).

● **Response for Family Therapists**
(from page 530): Remember that family function is more important than family structure. Sharing a home can work out well if contentious issues—like sexual privacy, money, and household chores—are clarified before resentments arise. You might offer a three-session preparation package to explore assumptions and guidelines.

● **Especially for Young Men** Why would you want at least one close friend who is a woman? (see response, page 534)

Nonetheless, for cultural and biological reasons, some sex differences have been found according to a meta-analysis of 37 studies (Hall, 2011). Men tend to share activities and interests, and they talk about external matters—sports, work, politics, cars. They are less likely to tell other men of their failures, emotional problems, and relationship dilemmas; if they do, they expect practical advice, not sympathy.

Women's friendships are typically more intimate and emotional. They expect to share secrets with their friends and engage in self-disclosing talk, including difficulties with their health, romances, sex life, and relatives. Women reveal their weaknesses and problems and expect an attentive and sympathetic ear, a shoulder to cry on.

Physical touch shows sex differences as well. Men are less likely to touch each other except in aggressive activities, such as competitive athletics or military combat. The butt slapping or body slamming immediately after a sports victory, or the sobbing in a buddy's arms in the aftermath of a battlefield loss, are less likely in everyday life. By contrast, many women routinely hug friends in greeting or farewell; men might fist bump or hand slap.

Lest this discussion seem to imply that female friendships are better because they are closer, research finds that men are more tolerant; they demand less from their friendships than women do, and thus they have more friends (Benenson et al., 2011). One specific detail from college dormitories is revealing: When strangers of the same sex are assigned as roommates (as occurs for first-year students at residential colleges), more women than men request a change (Benenson et al., 2009).

Male–Female Friendships

As already noted, gender differences are cultural, not biological. Norms are changing—are there also changes in other-gender friendships? Yes. For one thing, male–female friendships are no longer rare (Lewis et al., 2011).

It used to be assumed that cross-sex friendships were preludes to romance. No longer. In fact, physical attraction to a friend is more often considered a problem than an asset (Bleske-Rechek et al., 2012). Outsiders should not assume that every male–female relationship is sexual.

Cross-sex friendships sometimes end when couples become romantically committed, because partners want to avoid the possible jealousy that might arise and friends themselves want to avoid any hint of sexual tension (O'Meara, 1989; Williams, 2005). If a "just friendly" relationship becomes sexual, romance with a third person is almost impossible (Bleske-Rechek et al., 2012).

Past research assumed that adults were always heterosexual, but now that fewer adults hide their sexuality, researchers studying many aspects of life include people of all sexual orientations. One such study focused on friendships among 25,185 adults, including 1,361 who were sexual minorities (Gillespie et al., 2015).

Although earlier research had found that people who were sexual minorities had more friends than others, in part because they had fewer close relationships with family members, this research did not find that. The number of friends was quite similar among people of every sexual orientation. The researchers suggest that the culture may have shifted, so younger people particularly can establish similar friendship patterns no matter what their orientation (Gillespie et al., 2015).

One question was how many same-sex and cross-sex friendships the participants had. As earlier research on heterosexual adults had reported, most people had more same-sex friends, a trend particularly apparent for the older cohorts.

Most people had at least three or more friends of the same sex and at least two of the other sex. Gay men under age 30 tended to have the highest number of cross-sex friends, perhaps because such friendships avoid the usual sexual tension between young men and young women.

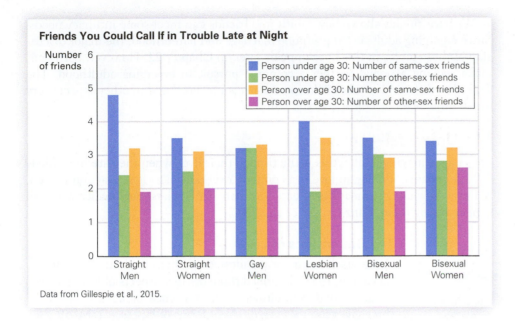

Friends You Could Call If in Trouble Late at Night

Data from Gillespie et al., 2015.

FIGURE 19.3
Same, Yet Different The authors of this study were struck by how similar the friendship patterns of sexual minority and majority people were. As you see, the one noticeable trend is age, not sexuality. People over 30 reported fewer friends overall, and fewer other-sex friends in particular, from an average of 2.6 to an average of 2.1.

In this study, participants were asked how many friends they could discuss sex with, celebrate their birthdays with, or call if in trouble late at night (see Figure 19.3). Not surprisingly, all groups thought of more people to celebrate birthdays with than to talk about sex with. Generally, the number of friends to call when in trouble was between those two.

In this study, having more or fewer friends did not correlate with life satisfaction, but for everyone, satisfaction with friendship strongly predicted overall life satisfaction (Gillespie et al., 2015). As you can see from the figure, all groups tended to have more friends before age 30 than afterward.

WHAT HAVE YOU LEARNED?

1. How does the idea of linked lives apply to emerging adults?

2. What kinds of support do parents provide their grown children?

3. What are the advantages and disadvantages of having a "helicopter parent"?

4. What special difficulties occur for emerging adults who were foster children?

5. How are friendships different for young and older adults?

6. How does sexual orientation affect friendship?

Finding a Partner

All close relationships have much in common—not only in the psychic needs they satisfy but also in the behaviors they require. Each ongoing relationship demands some personal sacrifice, including vulnerability that brings deeper self-understanding and shatters the isolation of too much self-protection. To establish intimacy, the young adult must

> face the fear of ego loss in situations which call for self-abandon: in the solidarity of close affiliations [and] sexual unions, in close friendship and in physical combat, in experiences of inspiration by teachers and of intuition from the recesses of the self. The avoidance of such experiences . . . may lead to a deep sense of isolation and consequent self-absorption.

> *[Erikson, 1993a, pp. 263–264]*

● **Response for Young Men**
(from page 532): Not for sex! Women
friends are particularly responsive to deep
conversations about family relationships,
personal weaknesses, and emotional
confusion. But women friends might be
offended by sexual advances, bragging,
or advice giving. Save these for a future
romance.

We have already shown how family and friends can meet some intimacy needs. Since emerging adults often postpone marriage and parenthood, the major discussion of those topics in this book appears later, in Chapter 22. However, hormones make seeking a sexual partner a common pursuit in emerging adulthood. The form that this seeking takes is in some aspects universal and in other aspects very much influenced by culture, as you will see.

The Universal—Love

For many emerging adults, this is the time in their lives when they are most likely to find romance. Falling in love is a common experience, as is sexual connection, but exactly what that means is affected by many particulars, personality, age, and gender among them (Sanz Cruces et al., 2015).

The Dimensions of Love

"Love" itself has many manifestations. In a classic analysis, Robert Sternberg (1988) described three distinct aspects of love: passion, intimacy, and commitment. The presence or absence of these three gives rise to seven different forms of love (see Table 19.3).

Early in a relationship, *passion* is evident in falling in love, an intense physical, cognitive, and emotional onslaught characterized by excitement, ecstasy, and euphoria. The entire body and mind, hormones and neurons, are activated; the person is obsessed (Sanz Cruces et al., 2015). Passionate love is difficult to measure. In fact, 33 scales attempt to measure it, each one distinct although overlap is also common (Hatfield et al., 2012).

Intimacy is knowing someone well, sharing secrets as well as sex. This aspect of a romance is reciprocal, with each partner gradually revealing more of himself or herself as well as accepting more of the other's revelations. The moonstruck joy of passionate love can become bittersweet as intimacy and commitment increase. As one observer explains, "Falling in love is absolutely no way of getting to know someone" (Sullivan, 1999, p. 225).

The research is not clear about the best schedule for passion and intimacy, whether they should progress slowly or quickly, for instance. According to some research, they are not always connected, as lust arises from a different part of the brain than affection (Langeslag et al., 2013; Fisher, 2016a).

Commitment takes time and effort, at least for those who follow the current Western pattern of love and marriage. It grows through decisions to be together, mutual caregiving, shared possessions, and forgiveness (Schoebi et al., 2012). Social forces strengthen or undermine commitment; that's why in-laws are often the topic of jokes and arguments and why a spouse might be unhappy with their mate's close friends.

Commitment is also affected by the culture. In fact, when cultures endorse arranged marriages, commitment occurs early on, before passion or intimacy. A study of husbands and wives in arranged marriages reports that the commitment by both partners to make the marriage work led to love, not vice versa (Epstein et al., 2013). One husband says:

> Perhaps I could say that love involves commitment or [that] marriage is a commitment to love. From the beginning I was committed to love [my wife]. Sometimes I have been challenged to keep the commitment or just challenged to love her, but I do my best to be a loving husband. Loving her is usually easy but sometimes not.

[quoted in Epstein et al., 2013, pp. 352–353]

TABLE 19.3 Sternberg's Seven Forms of Love

Form of Love	Present in the Relationship?		
	Passion	Intimacy	Commitment
Liking	No	Yes	No
Infatuation	Yes	No	No
Empty love	No	No	Yes
Romantic love	Yes	Yes	No
Fatuous love	Yes	No	Yes
Companionate love	No	Yes	Yes
Consummate love	Yes	Yes	Yes

Information from Sternberg, 1988.

Having friends and acquaintances who do, or do not, endorse the value of a committed relationship affects each couple. An odd correlation was found in Sweden: Couples who lived in detached houses (with yards between them) broke up more often than did couples living in attached dwellings (such as apartments). Perhaps "single-family housing might have deleterious effects on couple stability due to the isolating lack of social support for couples staying together" (Lauster, 2008, p. 901). In other words, suburban couples may be too far from their neighbors to receive encouraging and helpful advice when conflicts arise.

When children are born, passion may fade for both partners, but commitment increases. This may be one reason why most sexually active young adults try to avoid pregnancy unless they believe their partner is a lifelong mate. [**Life-Span Link:** The relationship of parenthood to marital satisfaction is discussed in Chapter 22.]

The Ideal and the Real

In Europe in the Middle Ages, love, passion, and marriage were considered to be distinct phenomena, with "courtly love" disconnected from romance, which was also distinct from lifelong commitment (Singer, 2009). Currently, however, the Western ideal of consummate love includes all three components: passion, intimacy, and commitment.

For developmental reasons, this ideal is difficult to achieve. Passion seems to be sparked by unfamiliarity, uncertainty, and risk, all of which are diminished by the familiarity and security that contribute to intimacy and by the time needed for commitment.

In short, with time, passion may fade, intimacy may grow and stabilize, and commitment may deepen. This pattern occurs for all types of couples—married, unmarried, and remarried; gay, lesbian, and straight; young, middle-aged, and old; in arranged, guided, and self-initiated relationships. In this chapter we focus on the young, many of whom shy away from commitment. The reason may be that they are trying to coordinate their identity with that of a life partner—not an easy task (Shulman & Connolly, 2013).

Emerging adults sometimes refer to *friends with benefits,* implying that sexual passion is an extra benefit, not the core aspect of a friendship. As with other friendships, shared confidences and loyalty are the important parts of the relationship. To use Sternberg's triadic theory, the relationship is intimate but not passionate.

However, such friendships make it emotionally difficult to establish a romantic relationship with someone else (Collibee & Furman, 2016). Perhaps that is part of the goal—friends with benefits are a way to avoid commitment.

Variations by Culture and Cohort

Thus far we have described the universal drives of young adults in partner-finding, drives that have been part of the human species for thousands of years. It seems that love is a universal emotion, and thus passion, intimacy, and commitment have been built into every culture. Those three aspects of love are satisfied in various ways, but every culture, and every human being, seems to strive to accomplish all three.

Now we look at the many differences between one culture and another.

Hookups

A **hookup** is a sexual interaction between partners who do not know each other well, perhaps having met just a few hours before. The phrase, and the experience, arose from emerging adults, first on college campuses in the United States, with scholars describing a new *hookup culture* (Bogle, 2008). When such a relationship

THINK CRITICALLY: Does the success of marriages between people who met online indicate that something is amiss with more traditional marriages?

hookup A sexual encounter between two people who are not in a romantic relationship. Neither intimacy nor commitment is expected.

occurred in prior generations, it was either prostitution or illicit, as in a "fling" or a "dirty secret." No longer.

Hookups are more common among first-year college students than among those about to graduate, perhaps because older students want partners, and, as one put it, "if you hook up with somebody it probably is just a hookup and nothing is going to come of it" (quoted in Bogle, 2008, p. 38). Lonely people are more likely to hook up, which explains the higher rate among first-year students (Owen et al., 2011).

The desire for physical sex without emotional commitment is stronger in young men than in young women, either for hormonal (testosterone) or cultural (women want committed fathers if children are born) reasons. In a U.S. survey of 18- to 24-year-olds who had completed at least one year of college, 56 percent of the men but only 31 percent of the women say they had had a hookup (Monto & Carey, 2014).

One sociologist wrote:

> While women are preparing for adult life, guys are in a holding pattern. They're hooking up rather than forming the kind of intimate romantic relationships that will ready them for a serious commitment; taking their time choosing careers that will enable them to support a family; and postponing marriage, it seems, for as long as they possibly can.
>
> *[Kimmel, 2008, p. 259]*

As contraception, employment, and college education have changed women's lives, this "guy" pattern includes more females. The hookup rates for the women were about twice as high in the twenty-first century as in the end of the twentieth century, although the men's rates did not increase as much (Monto & Carey, 2014). Nonetheless, women are less likely to hook up, and they are less happy when they do.

Indeed, some of the current college awareness of date rape and sexual assault may be fueled by women's reluctance to be involved in casual sex and men's assumption that their dates share their sexual desires. Of course, this topic is complicated by many old myths and falsehoods: about men (they can't control themselves), about women (they want sex even when they don't admit it), and about rape itself (an attack by a stranger, or involving a woman who is drugged, not an aggressive act between acquaintances) (Deming et al., 2013).

The ideal sexual interaction during emerging adulthood is obviously a complex topic, one that cannot be described in a few paragraphs here. However, as has been apparent many times in this text, the body and the psyche function together, so the hope that sex can occur with no psychic consequences is an illusion (Fisher, 2016b). The hookup is not merely a physical activity.

Interestingly, emerging adults of both sexes who want a serious relationship with someone recognize this. They are likely to begin their courtship with covert glances, spoken pleasantries, direct gazing, casual touch, serious talk, all before beginning sexual interaction (Fisher, 2016b). They want to get to know a person, not merely hook up (Regnerus & Uecker, 2011).

Monogamy

Another aspect of sexual interaction that seems to be affected by culture is monogamy and polygamy. Although polygamy is legal in about a third of all nations, 90 percent of the men in those nations marry only one wife.

Polygamy is rare among younger couples, for whom love is the primary reason for marriage. A study of couples in Kenya, where polygamy is legal, found that actual or suspected sexual infidelity was the most common reason for breaking up (S. Clark et al., 2010), and a study in the United States found that emerging adults

LaunchPad
macmillan learning

The Data Connections activity **Technology and Romance: Trends for U.S. Adults** examines how emerging adults find romantic partners.

thought sexual fidelity was crucial for a good, enduring marriage (Meier et al., 2009). Although most U.S. emerging adults find premarital sex acceptable, only about 5 percent consider extramarital sex sometimes okay, an approval rate that is similar in men and women and that is actually slightly lower than 20 years ago (Monto & Carey, 2014).

Humans apparently find it difficult to sustain more than one sexual/romantic relationship at a time. The reasons may arise from deep in the human psyche. The evolution of the human species shows benefits of monogamy, including children growing up with two parents cooperating in their child rearing (Puts, 2016; Kramer & Russell, 2015). This "monogamy hypothesis" is not accepted by everyone.

Although monogamy is the most common pattern, with bigamy being a crime in the United States, the U.S. pattern is actually "serial monogamy," which means one sex partner at a time. Thus, it is acceptable for a couple to marry, be faithful, then divorce, and then remarry, being faithful again to the new partner.

It has been suggested that the natural instinct is to have sex with several people over a lifetime, as most younger adults in the United States do (Barash, 2016). An argument for monogamy in marriage is that children fare better if two parents take care of them.

However, this can be seen as an argument for polygamy. It may be better for children to have a father who remains married to his first wife and then marries a second wife rather than divorcing the first and remarrying. In the latter case, many fathers after divorce become distant from the children of their first wife.

With polygamy, the children's father remains in daily contact, even when his relationship to their mother has changed (Barash, 2016). On the other hand, the evidence suggests that in polygamous households, women and children suffer more often than they benefit (Bennion & Joffe, 2016). [**Life-Span Link:** The importance of father involvement with children is further discussed in Chapter 22.]

> **THINK CRITICALLY:** Which pattern would you personally prefer: lifelong monogamy, serial monogamy, or polygamy, and why?

Finding Each Other and Living Together

One major innovation of the current cohort of emerging adults is the use of social networks, as the online connections between dozens or hundreds of people are called. Almost all (83 percent) U.S. 18- to 29-year-olds use social networking sites to keep in contact (Duggan & Brenner, 2013). Such sites often indicate whether an individual is, or is not, in a committed relationship. There are sites for people seeking someone of particular ethnicity, political values, gender identity, sexual preferences, religious beliefs—all very useful if a young person has definite preferences.

Many young adults seeking romance join one or more matchmaking Web sites that provide dozens of potential partners to meet and evaluate. A problem with such matches is that passion is hard to assess without meeting in person. As one journalist puts it, many people encounter "profound disappointment when the process ends in a face-to-face meeting with an actual, flawed human being who doesn't look like a JPEG or talk like an e-mail message" (Jones, 2006, p. 13).

Emerging adults overcome this problem by filtering their online connections, meeting only those who seem promising, and then arranging a second meeting with very few. Often physical attraction is the gateway to a relationship, but intimacy and then commitment require much more.

How to Find Your Soul Mate Tiago and Mariela met on a dating site for people with tattoos, connected on Skype, moved in together, and soon were engaged to marry.

Observation Quiz Which part of this is unusual for contemporary emerging adults? (See answer, page 538)

choice overload Having so many possibilities that a thoughtful choice becomes difficult. This is particularly apparent when social networking and other technology make many potential romantic partners available.

The large number of possible partners for young adults—the thousands of fellow students at most colleges or the hundreds of suggestions that some matchmaking sites provide—cause a potential problem, **choice overload,** when too many options are available. Choice overload makes some people unable to choose and increases second thoughts after a selection is made (Iyengar & Lepper, 2000; Reutskaja & Hogarth, 2009).

Choice overload has been proven with many consumer goods—jams, chocolates, pens, restaurants—but it may apply to mate selection as well. Having many complex options that require weighing present and future advantages and disadvantages (trade-offs are inevitable in partner selection) may be overwhelming (Scheibehenne et al., 2010). That may impact divorce rates, which are higher for first marriages between young adults (who have more choices) than for those who marry after age 30.

Because Internet dating sites offer a plethora of choices, overload makes people who choose one particular person to meet in person wonder whether they should have chosen someone else (D'Angelo & Toma, 2016). Fortunately, most people overcome this liability. Millions of recent marriages in the United States began with online matches. When online connections lead to face-to-face interactions and then to marriage, the likelihood of happy marriages is as high or higher than when the first contact was made in person (Cacioppo et al., 2013).

Answer to Observation Quiz
(from page 537): Wedding plans.

Changing Historical Patterns

Love, romance, and lasting commitment are all of primary importance for emerging adults. As already mentioned, a defining characteristic of emerging adults is that they marry later: In the United States, the average age at first marriage was 29 for men and 27 for women in 2015. This was three years later than in 2000 and six years later than in 1950.

Marriage is later partly because it is not what it once was. Historically marriage was a legal and religious arrangement that was the exclusive avenue for sexual expression, the only legitimate prelude to childbearing, and a lifelong source of intimacy and support. Now sex almost always begins before marriage, and 40 percent of all babies are born to unmarried women (Martin et al., 2015). In the United States, a majority of emerging adults (52 percent) think being a good parent is one of the most important goals of life; less than one-third (30 percent) say the same about a good marriage (Wang & Taylor, 2011).

Further evidence for this cultural shift is found in U.S. statistics:

- Slightly less than half of all adults are married, living with their spouse.
- Only a third of all emerging adults, ages 18 to 25, are married.
- The divorce rate is about half the marriage rate, not because more people are divorcing but because fewer people are marrying.
- Women having their first baby under age 30 are more often unmarried than married (American Community Survey, 2015).

Such statistics make some people fear that marriage is a dying institution. However, few developmentalists agree with that assessment, partly because emerging adults may be postponing, not abandoning, marriage. In fact, young adults may have higher expectations for marriage than previous cohorts did, and they still see marriage as a marker of maturity and success (Cherlin, 2009). The efforts that gay and lesbian couples made to achieve marriage equality, the backlash in "defense of marriage," and the 400,000 same-sex couples who wed suggest the power of the institution.

What does seem to have occurred, however, is a change in the relationship between love and marriage (Abbott, 2011; Coontz, 2005). Three distinct patterns were evident in the twentieth century.

- In about one-third of the world's families, love did not lead to marriage because parents arranged matches that joined two families together.
- In roughly another one-third of families, adolescents met only a select group (single-sex schools keep them from unsuitable mates). Some then decided to marry, and young men asked the young women's fathers for "her hand in marriage." Parents supervised interactions and then bestowed their blessing. (When parents disapproved, young people separated or eloped—neither of which is typical today.)
- The third type are called *love marriages,* which distinguishes them from the first two. Young people meet thousands of others, sometimes falling in love and having sex, but they are not expected to marry until they are able to be independent, both financially and emotionally.

Love, Not Marriage Andrew and Jessica decided to raise their daughter together but not to marry. They live in White Bear, Minnesota, a relatively conservative area, but cohabiting couples are increasingly common everywhere.

The "one-third" suggested for each of the first two types is a rough approximation. In former times, nearly all marriages were of the first type, and the rest were of the second type. Currently, the practice in developing nations often blends these two types. For example, in modern India most brides believe they have a choice, because they see the photograph and résumé of their future husband. They can veto the choice, but that is rare; two-thirds do not. Most do not meet their husbands until their wedding day (Allendorf & Pandian, 2016).

The final pattern is relatively new, although familiar to most readers of this book, and is becoming the most common one. The choices of the young couple tilt toward personal qualities observable at the moment—appearance, hygiene, sexuality, a sense of humor—and not to qualities that parents value, such as religion, ethnicity, and evidence of long-term stability.

For instance, a person who has been married and divorced is seen much more negatively by parents than by unpartnered adults (Buunk et al., 2008). In parts of India, love marriages have become more popular than arranged marriages, but marrying someone of a higher or lower caste is still much more troubling to the parents than to the emerging adults (Allendorf, 2013).

For Western emerging adults, love is considered a prerequisite for marriage, according to a survey of 14,121 individuals of many ethnic groups and sexual orientations (Meier et al., 2009). They were asked to rate from 1 to 10 the importance of money, same racial background, long-term commitment, love, and faithfulness for a successful marriage or a serious, committed relationship. Faithfulness was the most important of all (rated 10 by 89 percent) and love was almost as high (rated 10 by 86 percent). By contrast, most thought that being the same race was not important (57 percent rated it 1, 2, or 3).

This survey was conducted in North America, but emerging adults worldwide share similar values. Halfway around the world, emerging adults in Kenya also reported that love was the main reason for couples to form and endure; money was less important (S. Clark et al., 2010).

Parents have no say in love marriages, because they cannot know whether or not their child truly is in love with the prospective partner. However, parental support may be crucial in sustaining a marriage. The lack of parental support may explain the statistics on the previous page. Divorce and single parenthood are more common when parents have no say in their adult child's choices.

My Students, My Daughters, and Me

I married late for my cohort (at age 25) to a man my parents never met until we were very much a couple. I had children late for my cohort (two by age 30 and another two by age 40). Of my four children, only one is married—and she and her husband decided to marry so that they could both have health insurance. My other three daughters are older than I was when I married and they are still single. I am proud of all four; they are admirable women working in professions that I respect. But sometimes I wonder why they did not marry.

Few of my young college students have children, and even fewer of them are currently married. I pay close attention to their thoughts about love and marriage. Emerging adult Kerri wrote:

All young girls have their perfect guy in mind, their Prince Charming. For me he will be tall, dark, and handsome. He will be well educated and have a career with a strong future . . . a great personality, and the same sense of humor as I do. I'm not sure I can do much to ensure that I meet my soul mate. I believe that is what is implied by the term *soul mate;* you will meet them no matter what you do. Part of me is hoping this is true, but another part tells me the idea of soul mates is just a fable.

[Personal communication]

Kerri's classmate Chelsea, also an emerging adult, wrote:

I dreamt of being married. The husband didn't matter specifically, as long as he was rich and famous and I had a long, off-the-shoulder wedding dress. Thankfully, my views since then have changed. . . . I have a fantastic boyfriend of almost two years who I could see myself marrying, as we are extremely compatible. Although we are different, we have mastered . . . communication and compromise. . . . I think I will be able to cope with the trials and tribulations life brings.

[Personal communication]

Neither of these students is naive. Kerri uses the words *Prince Charming* and *fable* to express her awareness that her ideas are childish, and Chelsea seems to have moved beyond her "long, off-the-shoulder wedding dress." As a scientist, I read about divorce and the pain of separation; I do not want that for my children or my students. They are wise to be wary of marriage.

But as a mother, I wish everyone would have loving partners, committed to them for life. When my daughters were babies I imagined them in homes with lawns, picket fences, children, a dog, and a cat. Ridiculous. Foolish. Not logical. Bad for the planet.

Even worse, I sometimes blame myself. Did I promote female independence too much, forgetting to highlight my happy marriage? Certainly my daughters are like millions of their peers, and like most of my students, influenced by their context as I was. My postformal mind makes me realize that their attitudes and practices may be better in the twenty-first century than are my own.

Cohabitation

cohabitation An arrangement in which a couple lives together in a committed romantic relationship but are not formally married.

The fact that marriage is often postponed, and that sex sometimes occurs without commitment, does not mean that emerging adults do not hope for a committed romantic partnership. In fact, having a steady partner is still sought (Regnerus & Uecker, 2011). This makes sense for human development: Young adults in romantic relationships tend to be happier and healthier than their single peers.

What has changed is the rise of **cohabitation,** as living with an unmarried partner is called. Cohabitation was relatively unusual 50 years ago: In the United States, less than 1 percent of all households were comprised of a cohabiting man and woman (see Figure 19.4). Now cohabitation is the norm. It is unusual for a couple to marry without ever having lived with a partner.

Cohabitation rates vary from nation to nation. Almost everyone in some nations cohabits at some point—perhaps later marrying someone else, perhaps later living alone, or living with someone who is a friend or family member. Two-thirds of all newly married couples in the United States lived with their partner before marriage (Manning et al., 2014), as did most couples in Canada (especially Quebec), northern Europe, England, and Australia. Many couples in Sweden, France, Jamaica, and Puerto Rico live with a partner for decades, sometimes all their lives, never marrying.

FIGURE 19.4

More Together, Fewer Married As you see, the number of cohabiting male–female households in the United States has increased dramatically over the past decades. These numbers are an underestimate: Couples do not always tell the U.S. Census Bureau that they are living together, nor are cohabitants counted within their parents' households. Same-sex couples (not tallied until 2000) are also not included here.

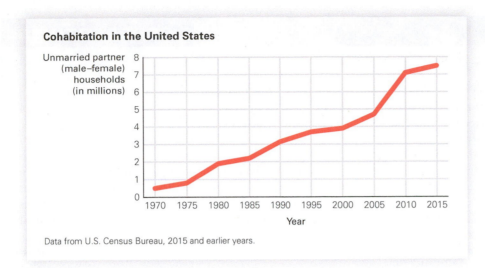

Cohabitation in the United States

Unmarried partner (male–female) households (in millions)

Year

Data from U.S. Census Bureau, 2015 and earlier years.

In the United States, the differences between couples who cohabit for years and those who cohabit for a shorter time and then either split up or marry is affected powerfully by education. Thirty years ago, college graduates were less likely to marry than other adults; now the opposite is true.

Although marriage rates are down and cohabitation up in every demographic group, education increases the chance of marriage and marital childbearing. Cohabiting couples without college degrees have children about five times as often as couples the same age who have graduated from college (Lundberg et al., 2016). The probable reason is not that college graduates know something that others do not; instead they are more likely to have a steady, well-paying job, which often is considered a requirement for marriage. Some young women who cannot find a suitable mate decide that they would rather have a child than an unemployable husband.

In some other nations—including Japan, Ireland, and Italy—cohabitation is not yet the norm, although it is becoming increasingly common. For example, Spain was once a nation where cohabitation was unusual; now one-third of all couples in Spain live together before they marry, a pattern that has become accepted and preferred (Dominguez-Folgueras & Castro-Martin, 2013). Given the popularity of this practice as well as the cultural differences, researchers have opposing opinions about cohabitation, as the following discusses.

Probably Married This couple with two young children could be cohabiting or married, but probably the latter—because this is Germany, where two-thirds of the children are born to married parents. If they were in France, they would probably be cohabiting, since more than half of French newborns have unmarried parents.

Cohabitation

Many emerging adults consider cohabitation to be a wise choice as a prelude to marriage, a way for people to make sure they are compatible before tying the knot and thus reducing the chance of divorce. However, research suggests otherwise.

Contrary to widespread belief, living together before marriage does not prevent problems after a wedding. In a meta-analysis, a team of researchers examined the results of 26 scientific studies of the consequences of cohabitation for the subsequent stability and quality of marriages and found that those who had lived together were more likely to divorce (Jose et al., 2010).

Some emerging adults want to avoid customs and institution and believe that cohabitation allows a couple to have the advantages of marriage without the legal and institutional trappings. But cohabitation is unlike marriage in many ways. Cohabiters are less likely to pool their money, less likely to have close relationships with their parents or their partner's parents, less likely to take care of their partner's health, more likely to be criminals, and more likely to break up (Forrest, 2014; Guzzo, 2014; Hamplová et al., 2014).

Particularly problematic is *churning,* when couples live together, then break up, and then come back together. Churning relationships have high rates of verbal and physical abuse (Halpern-Meekin et al., 2013) (see Figure 19.5). Cohabitation is fertile ground for churning because the partners are less committed to each other than if they were married, but they cannot slow down their relationship as easily as if they were not living together.

Although the research suggests many problems with cohabitation, most emerging adults do it, and most of their grandparents did not. Of course, humans tend to justify whatever they do. In this case, cohabiting adults typically think they have found intimacy without the restrictions of marriage, but they may be fooling themselves.

But might the research, mostly done by middle-aged adults who studied cohabiting couples 10 or 20 years ago, be outdated? In 1990, cohabiting couples were more rebellious and less religious than those who did not cohabit; that

might explain why they were more likely to divorce if they did marry. More recent research finds fewer negative outcomes of cohabitation (Copen et al., 2013).

Marriage still seems the ideal in the United States, according to many people. When same-sex couples were finally allowed to marry, about 400,000 couples did so—many of whom had been cohabiting for decades. They, at least, see advantages to marriage that cohabitation did not offer, primarily advantages related to love and commitment, although there are many legal advantages as well.

Again, however, an opposing perspective is evident. Almost twice that many gay and lesbian couples continue to live together without marrying; they prefer it that way. Two perspectives—could both be right?

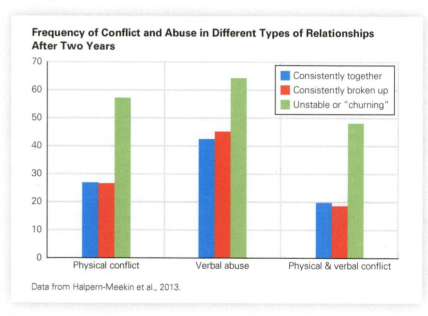

Data from Halpern-Meekin et al., 2013.

FIGURE 19.5

Love You, Love You Not In a longitudinal study of unmarried emerging adults (half men, half from two-parent homes, two-thirds European American, all from Toledo, Ohio) who had had a serious dating or cohabiting relationship in the past two years, some (15 percent) had broken up and not reunited, some (41 percent) had been together without breaking up, and some (44 percent) were churners, defined as having broken up and gotten together again with their partner. As you see, young-adult relationships are often problematic, but churning correlates with the stormiest relationships, with half of churners fighting both physically and verbally.

The meaning and consequences of cohabitation and marriage vary from couple to couple, true no matter what their education level or sexual orientation; it would be oversimplification to pronounce cohabitation always good or bad. However, one definite advantage and one clear disadvantage have been found in study after study.

The advantage is economic: People save money by living together, so cohabitation is better financially than living alone. The disadvantage occurs if children are born: Cohabiting partners have lower incomes than married partners, are less committed to child rearing, and their children are less likely to excel in school, graduate, and go to college (Manning, 2015; Wimer et al., 2016).

In all patterns of sexual and romantic development, community culture matters. Research in 30 nations finds that acceptance of cohabitation within the nation affects the happiness of those who cohabit. Within each of those 30 nations, demographic differences (such as education, income, age, and religion) matter for everyone, (Soons & Kalmijn, 2009), but generally those who are within a community where everyone cohabits are least likely to be harmed by it.

What Makes Relationships Succeed?

As already stated, friendships and romances have much in common. They satisfy the need for intimacy. Friends and mates are selected in similar ways, with mutual commitments gradually increasing until someone becomes a lifelong best friend or a chosen partner. Best friends sometimes part, and long-term marriages may end in divorce. That is not the plan nor the usual sequence.

Changes Over Time

From a developmental perspective, note that relationships evolve over time, sometimes getting better and sometimes worse. Among the factors that lead to improvement are good communication, financial security (more income or new employment), and the end of addiction or illness. Among the factors that stress a marriage are children, with young infants and early adolescents particularly trying for both parents (Cui & Donnellan, 2009).

Another developmental factor is maturity. In general, the younger the partners, the more likely they are to fight and separate, perhaps because, as Erikson recognized, intimacy is elusive before identity is achieved. An emerging adult who finally achieves identity might think, "I finally know who I am, and the person I am does not belong with the person you are."

Similarity tends to solidify commitment, probably because similar people are more likely to understand each other. Anthropologists distinguish between **homogamy,** or marriage within the same tribe or ethnic group, and **heterogamy,** marriage outside the group.

Especially for Social Scientists Suppose your 25-year-old Canadian friend, never married, says, "Look at the statistics. If I marry now, there is a 50/50 chance I will get divorced." What three statistical facts allow you to insist, "Your odds of divorce are much lower"? (see response, page 544)

homogamy Defined by developmentalists as marriage between individuals who tend to be similar with respect to such variables as attitudes, interests, goals, socioeconomic status, religion, ethnic background, and local origin.

heterogamy Defined by developmentalists as marriage between individuals who tend to be dissimilar with respect to such variables as attitudes, interests, goals, socioeconomic status, religion, ethnic background, and local origin.

Same Situation, Far Apart: The Bride and Groom Weddings everywhere involve special gowns and apparel—notice the gloves in Bali *(left)*, and his headpiece in Malaysia *(right)*. They also involve families. In many places, the ceremony includes the new couple promising to care for their parents—a contrast to the U.S. custom of fathers giving away their daughter to the groom.

Traditionally, homogamy meant marriage between people of the same age, religion, SES, and ethnicity. For contemporary partners, homogamy and heterogamy also refer to similarity in interests, attitudes, and goals. Educational and economic similarity are becoming increasingly important, and ethnic similarity is becoming less so (S. Clark et al., 2010; Hamplová, 2009; Schoen & Cheng, 2006).

The data are clear on this issue. One in seven current marriages in the United States is officially counted as interethnic (Wang, 2012). Very broad ethnic categories are used. For example, Black people from Africa, the Caribbean, and America are considered one ethnic group; Asians from more than a dozen nations are another ethnicity; European ancestry is a third category, lumping eastern, western, northern, and southern Europe together.

Thus, a marriage between a Pakistani and a Chinese person would *not* be categorized as interethnic. Nor would a marriage between a person of Greek heritage and one of Norwegian ancestry, even though the couple might be well aware of ethnic differences.

Given the reality of cultural differences in every tiny detail of daily life, few marriages in the United States are truly homogamous. My husband used to be upset with me for not wrapping cheese tightly before putting it in the refrigerator; he forgave me when he saw that my parents did the same thing.

One thorny issue that arises among couples who live together involves the allocation of domestic work, which varies dramatically by culture. In some cultures and in the United States in earlier decades, if the husband had a good job and the wife kept the household running smoothly, each partner was content. This is no longer the case.

Many twenty-first-century U.S. wives work outside the home and want their husbands to do much more housework than the men might prefer. On the other hand, many fathers want to be actively involved in child rearing, something women once assumed was their domain.

Today, partners expect each other to be friends, lovers, and confidants, as well as wage earners and caregivers, with both partners cooking, cleaning, and caring for children—a worldwide trend, with notable cultural differences (Wong & Goodwin, 2009). Happier relationships are those in which both partners are hardworking as well as adept at emotional perception and expression.

As women earn more money and men do more housework, increased shared responsibilities may increase marital satisfaction. Although many aspects of marriage have changed over the decades (some increasing happiness, some not), in general, couples seem as happy with their relationships as they ever were. Unhappy couples divorce, usually early. Of all 25- to 29-year-olds who have ever married, one-fifth have already divorced or separated (American Community Survey, 2015).

Long-term marriage still sometimes ends in divorce, but that is less common. Indeed, because fewer people are marrying before age 25, the U.S. divorce rate for first marriages has decreased since 2000. (The statistic that half of U.S. marriages end in divorce is true, but that includes repeat divorces. If four new brides marry and three of them stay married for life but one divorces, remarries, divorces, remarries, and divorces again, that is a 50 percent divorce rate caused by 25 percent of the women.)

Learning to Listen

No relationship is always smooth; each individual has unique preferences and habits. Again, I know this personally. My husband was much more bothered by disorganization than I was, something we had not realized when we were dating.

But early in our marriage, he bought a plastic container that fit in a drawer in the kitchen and organized all of the silverware, separating salad forks and dinner forks, soup spoons and table spoons, and so on. I was furious. I liked my way, resented his actions, and blurted out half a dozen reasons why what he did, and what was implied, was wrong. Fortunately, we figured out what was beneath my anger, and that fight became a joke in later decades.

If a couple "fights fair," using humor and attending to each other's emotions as they disagree, conflict can contribute to commitment and intimacy (Gottman et al., 2002). According to John Gottman, who has videotaped and studied thousands of couples, conflict is less predictive of separation than disgust because disgust closes down intimacy.

Every social scientist agrees that communication skills are crucial (Wadsworth & Markman, 2012). Much depends on how a conflict ends—with better understanding, with resentment, or, worst of all, with distancing, silence, and perhaps a breakup that neither partner wanted (Halpern-Meekin et al., 2013).

One particularly destructive pattern is called **demand/withdraw interaction**—when one partner insists on talking and the other avoids it (e.g., "We need to talk about this" is met with "No—I'm too busy"). This pattern is part of a downward spiral, as increased demanding leads to slammed doors and angry exits (Merrill & Afifi, 2012).

An international study of young adults in romantic relationships (again, some dating, some cohabiting, some married) in Brazil, Italy, Taiwan, and the United States found that women were more likely to *demand* and men to *withdraw*. When those gender roles were reversed, the pattern was still harmful. The authors explain:

> If couples cannot resolve their differences, then demand/withdraw interaction is likely not only to persist but also to become extreme. We believe that demand and withdraw may potentiate each other so that demanding leads to greater withdrawal and withdrawal leads to greater demanding. This repeated but frustrating and painful interaction can then damage relationship satisfaction.
>
> *[Christensen et al., 2006, p. 1040]*

Traditional gender roles may be part of the problem. Boys may be socialized to be strong and silent and girls to ruminate and cry. Both partners need to learn to listen to each other.

Sometimes the problem is as simple as neither partner recognizing the other's love gestures. A study of how husbands and wives expressed their affection for each other found many similarities (physical touch, sweet words) but also some differences. Men, for instance, thought they were expressing love when they shared household chores with their wives; the women did not always see it that way (Schoenfeld et al., 2012).

Brick By Brick Open communication between partners—with words, body language, gestures, and touch—is crucial. Demand/withdraw patterns build walls.

demand/withdraw interaction
A situation in a romantic relationship wherein one partner wants to address an issue and the other refuses, resulting in opposite reactions—one insistent on talk while the other cuts short the conversation.

Intimate Partner Violence

Emerging adults are more likely to be victims and perpetrators of domestic abuse than people of any other age. A nationwide survey of 14,155 men and women in the United States found that 32 percent of the women and 28 percent of the men had experienced physical violence from an intimate partner (married, cohabiting, or dating) in their lifetime, with abuse most likely to begin between ages 18 and 25 (MMWR, September 5, 2014).

Marital Status in the United States

Adults seek committed partners, but do not always find them—age, cohort, and culture are always influential. Some choose to avoid marriage, more commonly in northern Europe and less commonly in North Africa than in the United States. As you see, in 2010, U.S. emerging adults were unlikely to marry, middle-aged adults had the highest rates of separation or divorce, and widows often chose to stay alone while widowers often remarried.

MARITAL STATUS IN THE UNITED STATES (PERCENT)

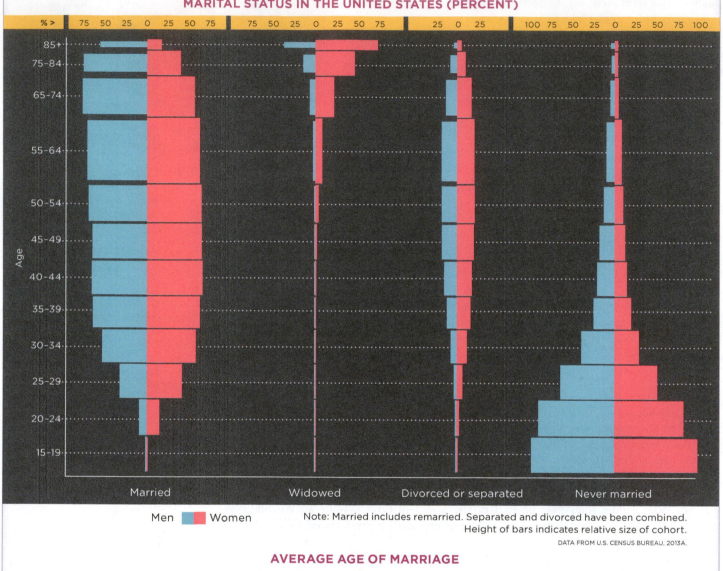

Men ■ Women

Note: Married includes remarried. Separated and divorced have been combined. Height of bars indicates relative size of cohort.

DATA FROM U.S. CENSUS BUREAU, 2013A.

AVERAGE AGE OF MARRIAGE

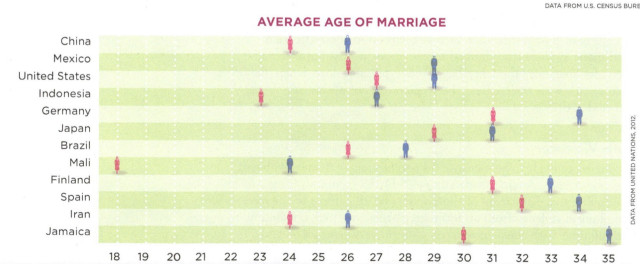

DATA FROM UNITED NATIONS, 2012.

Why this time of life? Inexperience, hormones, and freedom from parental supervision all play a part, but one aspect is directly related to being an emerging adult. Having a job or being in college is somewhat protective, but a sizable proportion of young adults are, at least temporarily, in neither. A correlate of intimate partner violence is that one partner is *NEET* (not in education, employment, or training). For them, abuse is more likely—true for women and for men, for marriages and cohabitants (Alvira-Hammond et al., 2014).

Surveys from other nations report even higher rates of abuse than in the United States. Iranian researchers and social workers are particularly concerned about the rate of domestic abuse in their country, and consequently there are many reports on its prevalence. A meta-analysis estimated that 49 percent of Iranian women had been abused (Kharazmi et al., 2015), and a qualitative study of Iranian men found that abuse was not uncommon among men (Nouri et al., 2016).

Another meta-analysis, this one in India, put the rate of women's abuse at 40 percent. However, that analysis included many studies with widely different reported rates. The scientists note that, from one study to another, one nation to another, and one cohort to another, the definition of abuse (cursing? slapping? beating?) varies so much that prevalence is difficult to compare (Kalokhe et al., 2016). Much depends on the survey questions, how they are asked, and to whom. However, everyone agrees that alcohol and other drugs make violence more severe.

It has been suggested that abuse has become less common in the United States because police are now more likely to take women's complaints seriously. Ethnic differences are often found, but interpreting them is difficult. Some studies of intimate partner violence among Hispanic Americans report higher rates than among European Americans; other studies report lower rates (Cunradi, 2009). Both results are plausible.

Traditionally, women, not men, were asked whether they experienced spousal abuse. It was assumed that women were victims and men were abusers. It is true that more women are seriously injured or killed by male lovers than vice versa, evident in every hospital emergency room or set of police reports.

However, when the definition of abuse includes threats, insults, and slaps, as well as physical battering, some studies find *more* abusive women than men (Archer, 2000; Fergusson et al., 2005; Swan et al., 2008). A meta-analysis found that the triggers for abuse are similar in women and men (Birkley & Eckhardt, 2015).

The original, mistaken assumption that violence was always male abuser/female victim occurred because abusive men are physically stronger and therefore cause more injuries that bring victims to a hospital. Moreover, men are reluctant to admit that they are victims, and outsiders are less likely to believe them. Likewise, same-sex couples hesitate to publicly acknowledge conflict. However, in domestic violence and most other aspects of relationships, they are similar in many ways to heterosexual couples, with some added stress if they have not openly acknowledged their sexual orientation (Edwards et al., 2015).

Social scientists have identified numerous causes of domestic violence, including youth, poverty, personality (such as poor impulse control), mental illness (such as antisocial personality disorder), and substance use disorder. Developmentalists note that many children who are harshly punished, sexually abused, or witness domestic assault grow up to become abusers or victims themselves. Neighborhood chaos is also a factor, as is the cultural acceptance of violence (Olsen et al., 2010).

Context Changes Shirley Hendricks signs documents sealing the deal on her new life. A former drug addict, victim, and perpetrator of couple violence, Shirley is now safe from abuse—much to the joy of her parole officer (in back). She has a new job, and she and her son now have a new home.

Knowing these causes points toward primary prevention. Halting child maltreatment, for instance, averts some later abuse. For tertiary prevention, it is useful to learn more about each abusive relationship. An article for physician assistants, for instance, alerted them to the early signs of intimate partner violence, considered a preventable health problem that all medical professionals should recognize and halt (Collett & Bennett, 2015).

Researchers differentiate two forms of partner abuse, each of which has distinct causes, patterns, and means of prevention (M. P. Johnson, 2011; Johnson & Ferraro, 2000; Swan et al., 2008).

situational couple violence Fighting between romantic partners that is brought on more by the situation than by the deep personality problems of the individuals. Both partners are typically victims and abusers.

Situational couple violence occurs when both partners fight—with words, slaps, and exclusion (leaving home, refusing sex, and so on)—and yet both partners are sometimes caring and affectionate. The *situation* brings out the anger, and then the partners abuse each other. This is the most common form of domestic conflict, with women at least as active in situational violence as men.

Situational couple violence can be reduced with maturation and counseling; both partners need to learn how to interact without violence. Often the roots are in the culture, not primarily in the individuals, which makes it possible for adults who love each other to learn how to overcome the culture of violence (Olsen et al., 2010).

intimate terrorism A violent and demeaning form of abuse in a romantic relationship, in which the victim (usually female) is frightened to fight back, seek help, or withdraw. In this case, the victim is in danger of physical as well as psychological harm.

Intimate terrorism is more violent, more demeaning, and more likely to lead to serious harm (see Figure 19.6). Usually intimate terrorism involves a male abuser and female victim, although the sex roles can be reversed (Dutton, 2012). Terrorism is dangerous to the victim and to anyone who intervenes. It is also difficult to treat because the terrorist gets some satisfaction from abuse, and the victim often submits and apologizes.

Social isolation makes it hard for outsiders to know what is happening, much less to stop it. With intimate terrorism, the victim needs to be immediately separated from the abuser, relocated in a safe place, and given help to restore independence.

The scientist who originally distinguished these two forms of intimate partner abuse says it is a mistake to ask a cross section of people about their current relationship, since those most severely abused will not, or cannot, answer honestly. However, when asking about ex-spouses, many people of both sexes admit to being victims of intimate terrorism (M. P. Johnson et al., 2014).

FIGURE 19.6

Fair Fight? Close relationships include passion and intimacy, which almost always lead to conflict at some point. Ideally, arguments should be dealt with using humor and love, yet if a woman is murdered, most likely her lover/husband is the killer.

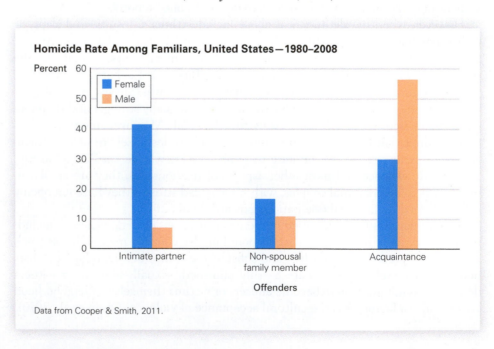

Homicide Rate Among Familiars, United States—1980–2008

Data from Cooper & Smith, 2011.

Concluding Hopes

Asking people about their lives, and encouraging them to talk to each other, seems good advice for every problem noted in these chapters on emerging adults. In Chapter 17, John realized the harm in risk taking when he talked about his own experiences and thought about his son, and young adults generally limit their drug abuse when they know what others are thinking. In Chapter 18, it was shown that listening to the experiences and beliefs of others, particularly in college classes, advances postformal thought. In this chapter, we emphasized the benefits of having friends and lovers who help expand one's mind.

As we think about the experiences of emerging adults overall, it is apparent that this stage of life has many pitfalls as well as benefits. These years may be crucial to long-term well-being, because "decisions made during the transition to adulthood have a particularly long-lasting influence on the remainder of the life course because they set individuals on paths that are sometimes difficult to change" (Thornton et al., 2007, p. 13).

Fortunately, most emerging adults, like humans of all ages, have strengths as well as liabilities. Many survive risks, overcome substance abuse, think more deeply, combat loneliness, and deal with other problems through further education, maturation, friends, and family. If they postpone marriage, prevent parenthood, and avoid a set career until their identity is firmly established and their education is complete, they may be ready and eager for all of the commitments and responsibilities of adulthood (described in the next chapters).

WHAT HAVE YOU LEARNED?

1. What are three aspects of love, according to Sternberg?

2. What is the difference between friends with benefits and hooking up?

3. Why is cohabitation much more common than it once was?

4. What are three cultural differences in the way emerging adults find their marriage partner?

5. Why might it be difficult for romantic partners to listen to each other?

6. What are the implications for prevention in knowing the difference between common couple violence and intimate terrorism?

SUMMARY

Continuity and Change

1. Personality can change in early adulthood. Genes and childhood influences are always factors, but many people improve their personal characteristics once they are able to make their own choices.

2. For today's youth, the identity crisis continues into adulthood. In multiethnic nations, ethnic identity becomes important but difficult to achieve, and it requires complex psychosocial adjustment.

3. Vocational identity requires knowing what career one will have. Few young adults are certain about their career goals. Many

societies offer some moratoria on identity achievement (such as college) that allows postponement of vocational identity.

4. Current economic circumstances make vocational identity particularly difficult. Many adults of all ages switch jobs, with turnover particularly quick in emerging adulthood. Most short-term jobs are not connected to the young person's skills or ambitions.

5. Many emerging adults find an appropriate combination of education, friendship, and achievement that improves their self-esteem. Even unusually aggressive or shy children can become quite happy adults.

Close Family and Friends

6. Family support is needed lifelong. Family members have linked lives, always affected by one another and often helping one another at every age.

7. In most nations, emerging adults and their parents are closely connected. Sometimes this means living in the same household, but even when it does not, alienation of the two generations is unusual.

8. Especially in nations with less public support for young adults, parents often pay college costs, provide free child care, and contribute in other ways to their young-adult children's welfare. Parental financial and emotional support for emerging adult children usually is helpful, but it may also impede independence.

9. Friendships are helpful at every age, particularly in emerging adulthood when people tend to have more friends than at other ages. Close friendships typically include some other-sex as well as same-sex friends, with few differences found for adults of various sexual orientations. Women tend to exchange more confidences and physical affection with their friends than men do.

Finding a Partner

10. Romantic love is complex, involving passion, intimacy, and commitment. In some nations, commitment is crucial and parents arrange marriages with that in mind. Among emerging adults in developed nations, passion is more important but does not necessarily lead to marriage.

11. Many emerging adults use social networking and matchmaking sites on the Internet to expand and deepen their friendship circles and mating options. This has advantages and disadvantages.

12. Cohabitation is increasingly common, with marked national variations. This arrangement does not necessarily improve marital happiness or stability.

13. Marriages work best if couples are able to communicate well. Conflict is part of many intimate relationships. The pattern called demand/withdraw interaction harms a partnership.

14. Spouse abuse is common worldwide. In common couple violence, both partners need to learn how to love each other. In other cases (intimate terrorism), the abused spouse (almost always the woman) needs to leave the man and be protected from him.

KEY TERMS

plasticity genes (p. 526)
intimacy versus isolation (p. 526)
linked lives (p. 527)

helicopter parents (p. 530)
hookup (p. 535)
choice overload (p. 538)
cohabitation (p. 540)

homogamy (p. 543)
heterogamy (p. 543)
demand/withdraw interaction (p. 545)

situational couple violence (p. 548)
intimate terrorism (p. 548)

APPLICATIONS

1. Talk to three people you would expect to have contrasting views on love and marriage (differences in age, gender, upbringing, experience, and religion might affect attitudes). Ask each the same questions and then compare their answers.

2. Analyze 50 marriage announcements (with photographs of the couples) in the newspaper. How much homogamy and heterogamy are evident?

3. Vocational identity is fluid in early adulthood. Talk with several people over age 30 about their work history. Are they doing what they expected they would be doing when they were younger? Are they settled in their vocation and job? Pay attention to their age when they decided on their jobs. Was age 25 a turning point?

The Developing Person So Far:
Emerging Adulthood

BIOSOCIAL

Growth and Strength Bodies are generally strong, healthy, and active. Well-functioning organ systems provide protection through homeostasis, allostasis, and organ reserve. Good health habits include improving nutrition, increasing exercise, and avoiding dangerous risks and addictive drugs. Unfortunately, many emerging adults struggle to maintain good habits.

Sexual Activity Sexual and reproductive potential are at their peak. Emerging adults typically satisfy their strong sexual appetites with a series of relationships that may last months or years. Sexually transmitted infections are a particular risk for this age group.

Psychopathology Although most emerging adults cope well with their new freedom, for some the stresses of this period make psychopathology more common, including major depression, anxiety, and schizophrenia.

Taking Risks Risk taking is common during emerging adulthood, with men more prone to taking risks than women. Some risk taking is involved in developmental tasks such as leaving home or starting a new job. Some risks are beneficial, others are not.

COGNITIVE

Postformal Thought Emerging adults may reach a fifth stage of cognition, called postformal thought, characterized by practical, flexible, and dialectical reasoning.

Morals and Religion Adults learn to balance emotions and logic, and the experiences of adulthood move individuals toward deeper reflection and moral analysis. Religious faith may become more mature.

Cognitive Growth and Higher Education Tertiary education aims to advance critical thinking as well as to develop communication and practical skills. Usually these goals are achieved. More and more emerging adults attend college, a trend particularly apparent among women (who traditionally achieved less education than men), members of minority groups, and in developing nations—especially in Asia and Africa. As a result, emerging adults everywhere are exposed to a wider range of ideas and values.

PSYCHOSOCIAL

Continuity and Change Emerging adults continue on the path toward identity achievement, finding vocational and ethnic identity particularly difficult as economic pressures and ethnic diversity increase. Personality patterns, inherited or developed in childhood, become more stable—although change is possible at every stage.

Emerging Adults and Their Parents Families of origin continue to be supportive of their emerging-adult children, offering financial and emotional help and often providing a home as well. The impact of living with one's parents depends not only on the habits and personality of the emerging adult but also on cultural norms.

Intimacy Friendships become very important as a buffer against the stresses of emerging adulthood and as a way to find romantic partners. Many emerging adults cohabit with a partner, with the intent of getting married someday (but not just yet). Relationship problems, including domestic violence, are more common in emerging adulthood than later on.

adulthood

We now begin the seventh part of this text. These three chapters cover 40 years (ages 25 to 65), when bodies mature, minds master new material, and people work productively.

Adulthood spans such a long period because no particular year is a logical divider. Adults of many ages marry; raise children; care for aging parents; are hired and fired; grow richer or poorer; experience births, deaths, weddings, divorces, illness, and recovery. Thus, adulthood is punctuated by joys and sorrows which can occur at any time. Most days are neither happy nor sad; they are quite similar to the day before or the day after.

Although events are not programmed by age, they are not random: Adults build on their past, creating their own ecological niche, preparing their future. They choose their activities, communities, and habits.

Culture and context are crucial. For instance, marriage and then divorce are chosen by many adults in the United States, but marriage rates vary by nation and generation, and, until recently, divorce was impossible in three nations (Chile, Malta, and the Philippines). Some experiences—midlife crisis, sandwich generation, and empty nest among them—were once assumed to occur to everyone, but they rarely happen. As you will see, adulthood is not what most people think, or thought, or will experience. ●●

Adulthood:
Biosocial Development

What Will You Know?

1. When does a person start to show his or her age?
2. Should a woman bear children before age 30, 40, or 50?
3. How can a person be vitally healthy *and* severely disabled?

Jenny was in her early 30s, a star student in my human development class. She told the class that she was divorced, raising her 7-year-old son, 10-year-old daughter, and two orphaned teenage nephews in a huge public housing tower in a south Bronx neighborhood infamous for guns, gangs, and drugs. She spoke enthusiastically about free activities for her children—public parks, museums, the zoo, Fresh Air camp. We were awed by her creativity, optimism, and energy.

A year later, Jenny came to my office to speak privately. She was about to graduate with honors and had found a job that would enable her family to leave their dangerous neighborhood. She sought my advice because she was four weeks pregnant. The father, Billy, was a married man who told her he would not leave his wife but would pay for an abortion. She loved him and feared he might end their relationship if she did not terminate the pregnancy.

I did not advise her, but I listened intently. I learned that she thought she was too old to have another infant; that she was a carrier for sickle-cell anemia, which had complicated her other pregnancies; that her crowded apartment was no longer "babyproof"; that her son needed special care because he had a speech impediment; that she was not opposed to abortion. She was eager to get on with her adult life, and a baby would stop that.

After a long conversation, Jenny thanked me profusely for helping her reach a decision—although I had only asked questions, provided facts, and nodded. Then she surprised me. "I'll have the baby. Men come and go, but children are always with you."

Despite feeling "too old" to have another baby, Jenny was relatively young. Nonetheless, she was a typical adult in many ways. Wondering about bearing and rearing children is common among 25- to 65-year-olds, as are worries about genes, health, and aging.

This chapter explains some of the choices people make about their bodies and their futures. First you will learn about physiological changes in strength, appearance, and body functions, including changes in vision, hearing, and sexual responses, as well as ways to slow down aging. You will learn who is likely to age quickly and who is likely to have a long, healthy life. Jenny is one of the latter. At the end of this chapter, you will read how her adulthood progressed after she left my office.

senescence The process of aging, whereby the body becomes less strong and efficient.

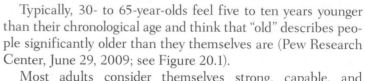

Growing Older

"Aging, we are all doing it," a subway poster proclaims. That poster is designed to make us think. Although we are all aging, few of us realize it because organ reserve and homeostasis (described in Chapter 17) allow declines to be unnoticed until middle adulthood or later.

Typically, 30- to 65-year-olds feel five to ten years younger than their chronological age and think that "old" describes people significantly older than they themselves are (Pew Research Center, June 29, 2009; see Figure 20.1).

Most adults consider themselves strong, capable, and healthy. Economic analysis supports this perception: Adults ages 26 to 60 contribute more to the society than those older or younger, adding a surplus to support those not yet, or no longer, "in their prime" (Zagheni et al., 2015).

As always, genes are crucial. **Senescence,** as the aging process is called, is genetically coded for every species. Our human genes allow us to live 50 to over 100 years—longer than dogs but 100 years shorter than tortoises. A few of us inherit genes that will allow us to live more than a century.

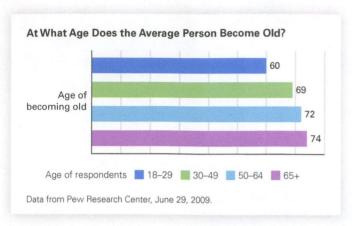

Data from Pew Research Center, June 29, 2009.

FIGURE 20.1

Not Old Yet When people are asked when someone is "old," their answers depend on how old they themselves are. The trend continues—my mother, in her 80s and living in a senior residence, complained that she did not belong there because too many of the people were old.

However, *within* each species, environment (both personal choices and the social context) is more important than genes in allowing one individual to live twice as long and with more vitality than another. Variation in aging among humans, currently and over the centuries, is vast, but this is *not* primarily because of genes (Robert & Labat-Robert, 2015). Now some specifics.

The Experience of Aging

Every organ, every body system, indeed every cell, slows down with age. For that reason, in our culture, aging is often linked to disease and decline, but that link may be broken. Aging—everyone does it; impairment—many avoid it.

Blood Pressure

Avoiding the negative consequences of aging is clearer with an example. With age, blood pressure increases. High blood pressure (*hypertension*) increases the risk of heart disease and stroke. Worldwide, hypertension is the leading risk factor for disease, particularly in Asia, North Africa, the Middle East, and Eastern Europe (Murray et al., 2012).

Just Keep Rolling Along After four years in Iraq and two in Afghanistan with the U.S. Marines, Jared McCallum sought new challenges. He hiked the Appalachian Trail (2,180 miles) and, on September 1, 2014, began rowing the Mississippi River. Here, on October 1, he is at Rock Island, Iowa.

But risk need not be reality. The hearts of most 25- to 65-year-olds beat strong, even as blood pressure rises. In the United States, if pressure gets above 140/90, few adults notice any problems, but a medical checkup alerts them to the risk. Then, exercising, losing weight, avoiding salt, and perhaps medication all lower blood pressure, and thus lower the risk. Control of blood pressure is a major reason that the age-adjusted rate of heart deaths in the United States in 2014 was less than a third of what it was 50 years earlier (National Center for Health Statistics, 2016).

Thus, the link between rising blood pressure and disease is broken. As they grow older, adults are more likely to see a doctor and therefore know when their blood pressure is high. Further, organ reserve usually allows healthy blood circulation throughout the adult years, and homeostasis helps each part of the body adjust to changes in other parts. If a person understands how to keep the body strong, which means reducing dangers (such a hypertension) before they cause disease, then aging is not a problem.

Breathing

Another example is breathing. Because of homeostasis, the body naturally maintains a certain level of oxygen in the blood whether a person is old or young, awake

Observation Quiz Is Jared closer to 30, 40, or 50? (see answer, page 559) ↑

or asleep, exercising or resting (Dominelli & Sheel, 2012). Aging affects this; on average, oxygen dispersal into the bloodstream from the lungs drops about 4 percent per decade after age 20. Thus, older adults may become "winded" after running fast, or they may pause after climbing a long flight of stairs to "catch their breath." That is homeostatic.

Those people who are heavy smokers, especially if they are obese, might reach a point in adulthood when their lungs are seriously impaired. They develop emphysema or chronic obstructive pulmonary disease (COPD), the fourth most common cause of death after age 45 (National Center for Health Statistics, 2016).

But impairment need not occur. Adults can maintain their breathing by exercising regularly and avoiding pollutants, including cigarette smoke. If a smoker quits by age 30, lung functioning gradually improves. As a result, ex-smokers have stronger lungs at age 40 than they did at age 20. Indeed, an estimated 10 years of life is gained by stopping smoking (Jha et al., 2013).

This has practical applications. Suppose a 50-year-old who is winded when climbing several flights of stairs wants to run a marathon. That's possible—if he or she spends a year or more doing practice runs, eating and sleeping well, not smoking, and so on. Like the muscles of the legs, the lungs can be strengthened with judicious exercise.

The word "judicious" refers to judgment. People judge how to protect their bodies. Improved functioning with age is not automatic—quite the opposite. If reduced organ reserve combines with senescence, allostatic load might become too heavy. Then, not only breathing but life itself is threatened.

In the short term, people may combat the anxieties of life by smoking, eating junk food, or sitting rather than exercising, but that momentary homeostasis can lead to compromised body functioning with age. This explains why stress early in life impairs health later on. [**Life-Span Link:** Organ reserve, homeostasis, and allostasis are discussed in Chapter 17.]

The Brain with Age

Like every other body part, the brain slows down. Neurons fire more slowly, and reaction time lengthens because messages from the axon of one neuron are not picked up as quickly by the dendrites of other neurons. New neurons and dendrites appear, but others atrophy: Brain size decreases, with fewer neurons and synapses in adulthood than in adolescence.

As a result, multitasking becomes harder, processing takes longer, and some complex working-memory tasks (e.g., repeating a series of eight numbers, then adding the first four, deleting the fifth one, subtracting the next two, and multiplying the new total by the last one—all in your head) may become impossible (Fabiani & Gratton, 2009).

But remember from Chapter 1 that gains and losses are evident at every point of the life span. This is true for the brain. As one expert describes it:

> The human brain is in a continuous state of flux defined by periods of relative development and periods of relative degeneration that together engender processes of growth, maturation, repair, and deterioration across the life span.
>
> [Sherin & Bartzokis, 2011, p. 333]

Gains? Brain growth? In adulthood? Yes! Myelination continues and dendrites grow, depending on experience. An adult who performs a particular action, time and time again, becomes better and quicker at it because of changes in the brain.

It is true that neurological losses occur, but, as with blood pressure and breathing, brain changes are not usually significant until late in life. On tests of knowledge, people improve every decade until at least age 70. This is explained in Chapter 21. The following explains more about the biological changes in the adult brain.

LaunchPad
macmillan learning

Video: Brain Development Animation: Middle Adulthood

http://qrs.ly/g94sqlu

Henning Dalhoff/Bonnier Publications/Science Source

Especially for Drivers A number of states have passed laws requiring that hands-free technology be used by people who use cell phones while driving. Do those measures cut down on accidents? (see response, page 559)

Neurons Forming in Adulthood

It has long been known that brains slow down with age and that some parts of the brain shrink in size. It also has long been known that neurons are formed rapidly during prenatal development and that most of those neurons are eliminated by pruning, especially in infancy and in early adolescence. It was thought that brain growth and *neurogenesis* (the formation of neurons) stopped long before adulthood.

But in the past two decades, as a review explains, scientists have been surprised to learn that parts of the brain grow and gain neurons during adulthood (Ming & Song, 2011). Not only do dendrites form and pathways strengthen, but new neurons are born. One area that gains brain cells is the hippocampus, the brain structure most prominent in memory (Bergmann et al., 2015). That neurogenesis "appears to contribute significantly to hippocampal plasticity across the life span" (Kempermann et al., 2015).

The specific area of the hippocampus where new neurons settle is the *dentate gyrus,* a region activated in forming new memories and exploring new places. One conclusion of the new research is that the adult human brain is characterized by amazing plasticity (Kemperman et al., 2015).

This means that, for adults between ages 25 and 65, shrinkage of parts of their brains are accompanied by neurological expansion and reorganization (Sherin & Bartzokis, 2011). Those new brain cells facilitate learning and memory (Lepousez et al., 2015).

For most adults, cognitive reserves, homeostasis, and allostasis protect the brain, and neurogenesis allows new learning. Adults may be slower, losing to a teenager at a video game, but their analysis is more comprehensive. This is one reason that judges, bishops, and world leaders are almost always at least 50 years old.

A comprehensive understanding of human biology requires that we temper this encouraging conclusion. For about 1 percent of all adults, brain loss is significant between ages 25 and 65, and compensation is inadequate. However, the cause is pathology, not normal aging (Schaie, 2005/2013). (More specifics of cognitive changes with age are discussed in the next chapter.)

If severe brain loss occurs before age 65, one of the following is the cause:

- *Drug abuse.* All psychoactive drugs can harm the brain, especially alcohol abuse over decades, which can cause Wernicke-Korsakoff syndrome ("wet brain").
- *Poor circulation.* Everything that impairs blood flow—such as hypertension and cigarette smoking—impairs circulation in the brain and thus harms thinking.
- *Viruses.* Various membranes, called the *blood–brain barrier,* protect the brain from most viruses, but a few—including HIV and the prion that causes mad cow disease—cross that barrier and destroy neurons.

- *Genes.* About 1 in 1,000 persons inherits a dominant gene for Alzheimer's disease, and even fewer people inherit genes for other severe neurocognitive disorders.

For 99 percent, experience continues to advance brain development in adulthood. Connections between various parts of the brain are strengthened with age. Adults are better able to understand how one aspect of life impacts another. This can happen on a global scale—adults can understand the connection between famine in South Sudan and electricity use in North Dakota—as well as on a more personal level.

This just happened to me. A houseguest knocked on my door and abashedly apologized for breaking one of my plates. My response: "Do you know I have four children? Plates break all the time."

My intent was to assure her that the broken dish didn't bother me. In my mind, having raised four daughters was evidence that I understood that things are often broken, lost, or damaged, and my experience has taught me that the people are more valuable than the things. But her puzzled expression suggested that my brain's connection of her apology with my motherhood was confusing.

Probably at every age, we need to remember that other people's brains function differently from our own. If someone says something that does not make sense, do not immediately conclude that their brain is scrambled. Ask them to explain.

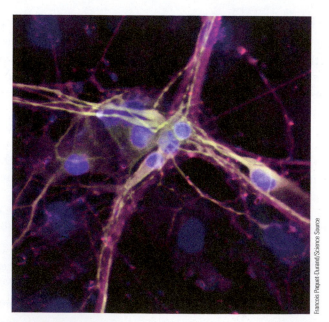

Francois Paquet-Durand/Science Source

Neurons Growing Even in adulthood, dendrites grow (yellow in this picture). Here the cells are in a laboratory and the growth is cancerous, but we now know that healthy neurons develop many new connections in adulthood.

Outward Appearance

Knowing that aging of the vital internal organs is not usually devastating in adulthood is comforting: Bodies can function well at age 30 or age 60, if people take care of themselves. However, visible changes with age are problematic in an age-conscious society. Losing hair or getting wrinkles, moving stiffly or getting shorter, needing glasses or hearing aids—all of these are signs of aging that we now discuss. Few adults want to look old. Eventually everyone does.

Skin and Hair

The first visible signs of age are in the skin, which becomes dryer, rougher, and less even in color. Collagen, the main component of the connective tissue of the body, decreases by about 1 percent per year, starting at age 20. By age 30, the skin is thinner and less flexible, the cells just beneath the surface are more variable, and wrinkles become visible, particularly around the eyes.

Hormones and diet have an effect—fat slows down wrinkling—but aging is apparent in all four layers of the skin, with "looseness, withering, and wrinkling" particularly notable at about age 50 for women, as part of lower estrogen during menopause (Piérard et al., 2015, p. 98).

Wrinkles are not the only sign of skin senescence. Especially on the face (the body part most exposed to sun, rain, heat, cold, and pollution), skin becomes less firm. Age spots, tiny blood vessels, and other imperfections appear. These are visible by age 40 in people who work outside all day, every day (usually farmers, sailors, and construction workers), but they are more troubling to people who associate looking young with sexual attractiveness.

In addition, veins on the legs and wrists become more prominent, and toenails and fingernails become thicker (Whitbourne & Whitbourne, 2014). Changes in appearance are barely noticeable from one year to the next, but if you meet three typical sisters, ages 18, 28, and 38, their skin tells you who is older. By age 60, all faces have aged significantly—some much more than others. The smooth, taut, young face is gone.

Hair usually becomes gray and thinner, first at the temples by age 40 and then over the rest of the scalp. This change does not affect health, but since hair is a visible sign of aging, many adults spend substantial money and time on coloring, thickening, styling, and more.

Both men and women lose hair, but the pattern differs. Women's hair becomes thinner overall, whereas some men lose hair on the top of their heads but not on the sides. That is *male pattern baldness*. I saw a man wearing a T-shirt that read, "This is not a bald spot; it is a solar plate for a sex machine." It is true that male pattern baldness correlates with hormones; it also correlates with increased risk of prostate cancer (Zhou et al., 2016).

Body hair (on the arms, legs, and pubic area) also becomes less dense over the 40 years of adulthood. An occasional thick, unwanted hair may appear on the chin, inside the nose, or in some other place. That has no known correlates with any disease, although many adults are distressed at this and at other signs of aging.

Shape and Agility

The body changes shape between ages 25 and 65. A "middle-age spread" increases waist circumference; all of the muscles weaken; pockets of fat settle on the abdomen, the upper arms, the buttocks, and the chin; people stoop slightly when they stand (Whitbourne & Whitbourne, 2014). This is apparent in everyone by age 50,

Response for Drivers (from page 557): No. Car accidents occur when the mind is distracted, not the hands.

Orange County Register/ZUMAPRESS.com

Look Your Age? Jennifer Roe is used to getting Botox injections—she has been doing this since she was 21. She is among an estimated one million young women who fear any sign of aging and turn to these injections, or even plastic surgery, to prevent the first wrinkle.

THINK CRITICALLY: Is the saying "beauty is only skin deep" accurate?

Answer to Observation Quiz (from page 556): He is closest to 30, 28 to be exact. Clues: He still has the strength, stamina, and risk-taking adventurousness of an emerging adult. Another clue is the contextual and historical: His two years as a marine in Afghanistan must have been recent.

Alex Menendez/Getty Images

Keep Up the Good Work Michael Phelps won a record number of gold medals in the 2008 Olympics in Beijing at age 23, and five in Rio de Janeiro at age 31. Like many athletes, swimmers usually peak in their early 20s, but in many adults, muscles used often stay strong into the 30s. Experience has advantages: Phelps was chosen to be a captain of the 2016 U.S. Olympic team, and became the most decorated Olympian of all time during those games.

presbycusis A significant loss of hearing associated with senescence. Presbycusis usually is not apparent until after age 60.

C Flanigan/FilmMagic/Getty Images

Compensation All the senses decline with age. Too many people accept losses as inevitable, ignoring the many forms of compensation available, becoming socially isolated and depressed. Instead, compensation is possible in two ways. One is to increase use of other senses and abilities. Stevie Wonder illustrates this well—he relies on hearing and touch, which have enabled him to sell over 100 million records and win 25 Grammys. The other way to compensate is more direct: Many technological and medical interventions are available for every sensory loss.

but the beginnings are apparent to the individual much earlier—when the woman who was proud of being a size 4 realizes that she is now a size 6, or the father who easily swung his first child around finds that the same movements are a little harder for the second child.

By late middle age, even if they stretch to their tallest, adults are shorter than they were, because back muscles, connective tissue, and bones lose density, making the vertebrae in the spine shrink. People lose about an inch (2 to 3 centimeters) by age 65, a loss in the trunk because cushioning between spinal disks is reduced. As torsos shrink, waists widen, hence the dreaded middle-age spread.

Muscles weaken; joints lose flexibility; stiffness is more evident; bending is harder; agility is reduced. Rising from sitting on the floor, twisting in a dance, or even walking "with a spring in your step" is more difficult. A strained back, neck, or other muscle may occur.

The Senses

All the senses become less acute with the passage of time, although nurture always plays a role—as first explained with nearsightedness in Chapter 3. Each part of each organ is on a particular timetable.

Vision

Vision seems to be one unified sense, but actually some 30 distinct brain areas as well as at least a dozen aspects of the eye combine to allow sight. Peripheral vision (at the sides) narrows faster than frontal vision; some colors fade more than others; nearsightedness and farsightedness follow different paths.

Nearsightedness is particularly affected by age. It increases gradually in childhood and more rapidly in adolescence; then it stabilizes, reversing in midlife. Because of changes in the shape of the lens, often nearsightedness is reduced in the 50s but farsightedness (difficulty seeing close objects) increases. This explains why 40-year-olds hold the newspaper much farther away than 20-year-olds do: Their near focus is blurry, but far focus is better (Aldwin & Gilmer, 2013).

Other aspects of vision are also affected by age. It takes longer for the eyes to adjust to darkness (as when entering a dark theater after being in daylight) or to adjust to glare (as when headlights of an oncoming car cause temporary blindness) (Aldwin & Gilmer, 2013). Motion perception (how fast is that car approaching?) and contrast sensitivity (is that a bear, a tree, or a person?) slows down (Owsley, 2011). The lens of the eye thickens; brighter lighting is needed.

Hearing

Hearing is most acute at about age 10, again with specific intrapersonal variations. Sounds at high frequencies (a small child's voice) are lost earlier than sounds at low frequencies (a man's voice). Although some middle-aged people hear much better than others, everyone's hearing is less acute with age.

Actually, hearing is always limited: No one hears a conversation a hundred feet away; "shouting distance" is limited. Because deafness is rarely absolute, gradual losses are not noticed. **Presbycusis** (literally, "aging hearing") is rarely diagnosed until about age 60, although whispers become inaudible years earlier.

An alarming study suggests that presbycusis may become apparent long before old age. High school students (1,512 of them) reported whether they experienced any symptoms of hearing loss (ringing, muffled sounds, temporary deafness). Almost one-third said yes, unaware that loud music on their headphones or at concerts might damage the hairs of the inner ear (Vogel et al., 2010). Many nations mandate ear protection for construction workers, but no laws protect against loud music.

The Sexual-Reproductive System

One more set of changes needs to be discussed. Many adults worry about the aging of their sexual and reproductive systems. Definite changes occur, somewhat differently for men and women. Whether they are for the better or worse depends as much on the person's attitude as on the actual details.

Sexual Responsiveness

Sexual arousal occurs more slowly and orgasm takes longer with senescence. However, some say that sexual responses improve with age. Could that be? Might familiarity with one's own body and with that of one's partner make slower response more often a pleasure than a problem?

A U.S. study of women aged 40 and older found that sexual activity decreased each decade but that sexual satisfaction did not (Trompeter et al., 2012). A British study of more than 2,000 adults in their 50s found that almost all of them were sexually active (94 percent of the men and 76 percent of the women) and, again, that most were quite satisfied with their sex lives (D. Lee et al., 2015).

Variability is evident. A study of 38,207 adults in the United States who had been in a committed relationship for more than three years found that about half (55 percent of the women and 43 percent of the men) were highly satisfied with their sex lives but about a third (27 percent of the women and 41 percent of the men) were not (Frederick et al., 2016). Interestingly, age was not a major factor, but variety of sex acts (including oral sex) and quality of sexual communication was.

Long-Lasting Joy In every nation and culture, many couples who have been together for decades continue to delight in their relationship. Talk shows and headline stories tend to focus on bitter divorces, ignoring couples like these who are clearly happy together.

Indeed, for some couples, physiological slowdowns are counterbalanced by reduced anxiety and better communication, as partners become more familiar with their own bodies and those of their mates and are willing to talk about it. Distress at slower responsiveness seems less connected to biology than to troubled interpersonal relationships and unrealistic fears and expectations (Burri & Spector, 2011; DeLamater, 2012).

Overall, the research finds that some adults are sexually satisfied, even thrilled, with their sex lives, and some are unhappy. Although sexual satisfaction tends to be highest in the early months of a relationship, some long-married couples report that their happiness with their sex lives is as strong as it was early on (Frederick et al., 2016).

Variations in Sexuality

Male–female differences could be biological or cultural. Wives sometimes said, "Not tonight, I have a headache," because they did not want to become pregnant with an unwanted baby, for whom they would provide exclusive care. No more.

Some experts say that, without the fear of pregnancy, women are as sexual as men. However, comparisons are difficult. If two people both say they are highly aroused, sexually, does that mean that they are equally aroused, or is one person's "highly aroused" unlike another's?

Pornography

Regarding male–female differences, there is some evidence that sex is more important for men than for women. For instance, men are much more likely to view pornography (Petersen & Hyde, 2011). Reports vary greatly depending on who is surveyed and how, but it is generally agreed that "pornography is both prevalent and normative in many cultures across the world, including United States' culture" (Stewart & Szymanski, 2012, p. 257). Rates of viewing are probably increasing (Price et al., 2016).

High rates of pornography viewing are reported, with disapproval, by groups that promote religious dedication. For instance, Proven Men reports that 79 percent of men and 42 percent of women were frequent viewers (Digital Journal, August 14, 2014). Perhaps because pornography is controversial (some women believe it objectifies women and relationships), objective surveys are more likely outside the United States. Universally, rates are highest among adolescents and gradually decrease (Price et al., 2016). A survey of high school seniors in Italy found that virtually all of the boys and 67 percent of the girls viewed porn (Romito & Beltramini, 2011).

One concern is that viewing pornography correlates with harmful sexual acts (e.g., violence, or with children), for which far more men are arrested than women (Faust et al., 2015).

Sexual Variations

Every large study finds a vast range of sexuality and sexual satisfaction, not only between men and women but between one individual and another. Some people are strongly heterosexual or homosexual, and others less so; some people are pansexual and others bisexual. Beyond that, sexual urges of any kind vary. Some adults are asexual, not interested or aroused by sex. This is apparent more in attitude than in biology (Brotto & Yule, 2011). On the other hand, some people think about sex almost all the time.

Very few people, male or female, ever commit a harmful sexual act (estimates vary widely), so arrest rates do not reflect normal sexuality. Further, correlation is not causation. Both men and women, of varying sexualities, *can* be sexually aroused by viewing sexual images (Spape et al., 2014). Many choose never to look, and some seem unable to stop looking.

THINK CRITICALLY: Is your attitude about pornography influenced more by your body, your mind, or your background?

● **Especially for Young Men** A young man who impregnates a woman is often proud of his manhood. Is this reaction valid? (see response, page 564)

Viewing actions are related to culture and age, in that older men and women view less. This may be a sign of reduced sexual arousal, less computer expertise, or greater wisdom, in that pornography interferes, at least temporarily, with rational thinking, acute hearing, and healthy relationships (Grov et al., 2011; Laier et al., 2014; Oliver et al., 2016).

Biology and age do not seem to be the most important factor. Sexual arousal, orgasm, and, as we will soon see, fertility and menopause are all connected to senescence, but the effects, and even the occurrence, are strongly influenced by the mind (Pfaus et al., 2014). As many say: "The most important human sexual organ is between the . . . ears."

Do You Want a Baby?

One of the mandates of developmental study is to understand historical and cultural influences on human development. Therefore, in explaining adult sexual behavior, we need to consider contraception.

Avoiding Pregnancy

Before about 1960, birth control was erratic: Many women avoided sex because they did not want pregnancy. This may have been the origin of the idea that women are less interested in sex than are men. Now contraception has transformed female sexuality, affecting men as well—in some nations but not in all of them.

As with every aspect of sexuality, local values shape patterns. For example, most couples in India rely on female sterilization to control family size. An estimated half of all women are sterilized by age 30, but virtually no men in India have a vasectomy (Sunita & Rathnamala, 2013). In the United States, young women are rarely sterilized, but the most popular contraception is the birth control pill, which is almost never used for contraception in Japan (Matsumoto et al., 2011). In the United States, sterilization is common after age 35 and involves a fair number of men: 44 percent of sexually active women and 20 percent of the men, with higher rates for both in couples who already have children.

Some form of contraception is used by about 90 percent of sexually active U.S. women of every ethnic group (93 percent European American, 90 percent African American, 91 percent Hispanic American), but ethnic norms are evident in sterilization: Almost twice as many African American and Hispanic American women are sterilized as European American women, but far fewer African American or Hispanic American men are (National Center for Health Statistics, 2016).

Seeking Pregnancy

Rates of **infertility** (failure to conceive after one year of trying) vary from nation to nation, primarily because the rate increases when medical care is scarce (Gurunath et al., 2011). Worldwide, an estimate of primary infertility (never able to conceive naturally) is about 2 percent of all young couples, and secondary infertility (inability to have a second child after five years of trying) is about 10 percent (Mascarenhas et al., 2012).

Age matters. In the United States, about 12 percent of all adult couples do not conceive after one year of trying, partly because many postpone childbearing. Peak fertility is at about age 18.

If couples in their 40s try to conceive, about half fail (a 50-percent infertility rate) and the other half risk various complications. Of course, risk is not reality: In 2014 in the United States, 118,464 babies were born to women age 40 and older. Most of those babies become healthy, well-loved children.

We need to put age and fertility into perspective. By far, most babies born in the United States have mothers aged 23 to 33, and only about 3 percent are born to

infertility The inability to conceive a child after trying for at least a year.

Remembering Younger Days When Chris McNulty was diagnosed with cancer, he and his wife decided to freeze his sperm so they could later have children. He died, but his widow used his sperm five years after his death. Her twin sons, Kyle and Cole, are the result *(left)*. Bala Ram Devi Lohan and his wife Rajo *(right)* wanted a child but tried for 40 years without success. Finally, a donor egg and Bala Ram's sperm produced a zygote, implanted in Rajo's uterus. She gave birth to a 3-pound, 4-ounce girl, shown here with her happy parents, ages 70 and 72.

women over 40. However, the age trends over the past two decades are dramatic: The teenage birth rate is half of what it was, and older women are the only ones whose birth rate is rising (Hamilton et al., 2015).

When couples are infertile, either or both partners may be the problem. A common reason for male infertility is low sperm count. Conception is most likely if a man ejaculates more than 20 million sperm per milliliter of semen, two-thirds of them mobile and viable, because each sperm's journey to the ovum is aided by millions of fellow travelers.

Depending on the man's age, each day about 100 million sperm reach maturity after a developmental process that lasts about 75 days. Anything that impairs body functioning over those 75 days (e.g., fever, radiation, drugs, time in a sauna, stress, environmental toxins, alcohol, cigarettes) reduces sperm number, shape, and motility (activity), making conception less likely. Sedentary behavior, perhaps particularly watching television, also correlates with lower sperm count (Gaskins et al., 2013).

As with men, women's fertility is affected by anything that impairs physical functioning—including disease, smoking, extreme dieting, and obesity. Many infertile women do not realize that they have contracted one specific disease that impairs conception—*pelvic inflammatory disease (PID)*. PID creates scar tissue that may block the fallopian tubes, preventing sperm from reaching an ovum (Brunham et al., 2015).

Fertility Treatments

In the past 50 years, medical advances have solved about half of all fertility problems. Surgery can repair some problems directly, and *assisted reproductive technology (ART)* overcomes obstacles such as a low sperm count and blocked fallopian tubes. Some ART procedures, including in vitro fertilization (IVF), were explained in Chapter 3.

What was not discussed was the impact on the parents, who may be depressed if they are unable to have a baby. Infertility, and fertility measures, affect the psyche, not just the body. People may question their own morality (is parenthood selfish?) and their partner's wishes. Remember that communication is crucial for a satisfying adult sex life; this is especially true when ART is involved.

Some ART is morally acceptable to virtually everyone, especially when couples anticipate disease-related infertility. For example, many cancer patients freeze their ova. When the treatment is over, if they want a baby, their IVF success rate (about one-third of attempts) is similar to those who freeze their ova for reasons not related to cancer (Cardozo et al., 2015).

● ● Response for Young Men
(from page 562): The answer depends on a person's definition of what a man is. No developmentalist would define a man simply as someone who has a high sperm count.

Some healthy young women freeze their ova for IVF years later because the age of the ova is a significant factor in success rates (Mac Dougall et al., 2013). When women over 40 have babies via IVF, most use donor ova (Hamilton et al., 2015).

ART has helped millions who thought they could never have a baby. The most dramatic example is with HIV-positive adults. Three decades ago, doctors recommended sterilization and predicted early death. Now, they can live happily for decades, using condoms for sex and taking antiviral drugs.

If an HIV-positive woman wants a child, drugs and a Cesarean almost always protect the fetus. If an HIV-positive man wants a child, his sperm can be collected, washed, and used in IVF to achieve conception (Sauer et al., 2009). Indeed, conception for HIV-positive men can occur naturally with virus-suppressing drugs, but IVF is safer (Wu & Ho, 2015).

The Sexual-Reproductive System in Middle Age

During adulthood, the level of sex hormones circulating in the bloodstream declines—suddenly in women, gradually in men. Both sexes are affected by those changes, with some taking hormones to replace the hormones lost. That may be ill-advised—as you will see.

Menopause

For women, sometime between ages 42 and 58 (the average age is 51), ovulation and menstruation stop because of a marked drop in production of several hormones. This is **menopause.** The age of natural menopause is affected primarily by genes (17 have been identified) (D. Morris et al., 2011; Stolk et al., 2012) and normal aging but also by smoking (earlier menopause), exercise (later), and moderate alcohol consumption (later) (Taneri et al., 2016).

Menopause is connected to many physical reactions beyond the cessation of menstruation and ovulation. The symptoms include vaginal dryness and body temperature disturbances, including hot flashes (feeling hot), hot flushes (looking hot), and cold sweats (feeling chilled). Those physical responses can be hardly noticeable, or they can be dramatic—interfering with sleep, which can make a woman tired and irritable.

The psychological effects of menopause vary a great deal, with some women sad that they can no longer become pregnant and other women happy for the same reason. Anthropologist Margaret Mead famously said, "There is no more creative force in the world than the menopausal woman with zest." Some menopausal women are depressed, some are moody, and others are more energetic (Judd et al., 2012).

menopause The time in middle age, usually around age 50, when a woman's menstrual periods cease and the production of estrogen, progesterone, and testosterone drops. Strictly speaking, menopause is dated one year after a woman's last menstrual period, although many months before and after that date are menopausal.

Pausing, Not Stopping During the years of menopause, these two women experienced more than physiological changes: Jane Goodall (*left*) was widowed, and Ellen Johnson-Sirleaf (*right*) was imprisoned. Both, however, are proof that post-menopausal women can be productive. After age 50, Goodall (shown visiting a German zoo at age 70) founded and led several organizations that educate children and protect animals, and Johnson-Sirleaf (shown speaking to the International Labor Organization at age 68) became the president of Liberia.

In the United States, about one in four women has a *hysterectomy* (surgical removal of the uterus), which may include removal of her ovaries. If she was pre-menopausal, removal of the ovaries suddenly reduces estrogen and therefore causes menopausal symptoms. Early menopause, surgical or not, correlates with various health problems later on (Hunter, 2012), which suggests that estrogen is protective of health in some ways.

Hormone Replacement

hormone replacement therapy (HRT) Taking hormones (in pills, patches, or injections) to compensate for hormone reduction. HRT is most common in women at menopause or after removal of the ovaries, but it is also used by men as their testosterone decreases. HRT has some medical uses but also carries health risks.

Toward the end of the twentieth century, millions of post-menopausal women used **hormone replacement therapy (HRT).** Some did so to alleviate symptoms of menopause, others to prevent osteoporosis (fragile bones), heart disease, strokes, or cognitive loss. Correlational studies found that these diseases occurred less often among women taking HRT.

However, that correlation was misleading. In a multiyear study of thousands of women, half (the experimental group) took HRT and half (the control group) did not. The results were a shock: Taking estrogen and progesterone *increased* the risk of heart disease, stroke, and some types of cancer (U.S. Preventive Services Task Force, 2002).

The most dramatic difference was an increase in breast cancer, at the rate of 6 per year for 1,000 women taking HRT compared to 4 per 1,000 for women who did not take the hormone (Chlebowski et al., 2013). The women had been randomly assigned to the experimental or control group, which meant that the results were solid. The study was halted before scheduled because the researchers were convinced that the experimental group was at risk.

How could the previous research have been mistaken? In retrospect, scientists realized that, without random assignment, simply comparing women who chose HRT with women who did not resulted in women with higher SES being compared with women of lower SES (who could not afford HRT). Benefits were the result of some women's education and health care, not of HRT.

Scientists agree that HRT has some uses: It reduces hot flashes, decreases osteoporosis, and may improve hearing, but the costs need to be considered (Frisina & Frisina, 2016). Some experts still argue that for younger women the benefits may outweigh the risks (Langer et al., 2012). However, international research confirms a greater risk of breast cancer (Pizot et al., 2016), and, "In most countries, HRT is only recommended for climacteric symptoms, at a dose as small as possible and for a limited period of time" (Kanis et al., 2013, p. 44).

Andropause?

andropause A term coined to signify a drop in testosterone levels in older men, which normally results in reduced sexual desire, erections, and muscle mass. (Also called *male menopause*.)

Do men undergo anything like menopause? Some say yes, suggesting that the term **andropause** (or *male menopause*) should be used to signify age-related lower testosterone levels, which reduces sexual desire, erections, and muscle mass (Samaras et al., 2012). Even with erection-inducing drugs such as Viagra and Levitra, sexual desire and speed of orgasm decline with age, as do many other physiological and cognitive functions.

But most experts think that "andropause" is misleading because it implies a sudden drop in reproductive ability or hormones. That does not occur in men, some of whom produce viable sperm at age 80 and older. Sexual inactivity and anxiety reduce testosterone—superficially similar to menopause but with a psychological, not physiological, cause. In addition, some medical conditions and treatments reduce testosterone.

To combat their hormonal decline, some men take HRT. Of course, their H is the hormone testosterone, not estrogen. The result seems to be less depression, more sexual desire, and leaner bodies. (Some women also take smaller amounts of testosterone to increase their sexual desire.)

Weighing costs and benefits is again needed (Hackett, 2016). One recent study found that men who took testosterone for years had lower rates of cardiovascular disease and fewer deaths, but in the short term more deaths occurred than usual (Wallis et al., 2016). These scientists rightly call for longitudinal randomized studies, a wise suggestion given the results from women's HRT.

WHAT HAVE YOU LEARNED?

1. How does sexual arousal change with age?

2. How does contraception vary from one culture to another?

3. How is male and female sexual behavior similar and not similar?

4. What impairs fertility in men and in women?

5. What are the effects of menopause?

6. How do male changes in sexual behavior differ from female ones?

7. What are the consequences of HRT in women and in men?

Habits: Good and Bad

Surely you have noticed in the previous descriptions of the physical effects of aging that much depends on the habits of the person. Allostatic load, described in Chapter 17, builds quickly or slowly, so some adults seem decrepit by age 50 while others seem youthful. Measured by 18 indicators of health and aging—as well as appearance in photographs—some 26- to 38-year-olds age three years per chronological year, and some age hardly at all (Belsky et al., 2015).

Exercise, nutrition, and drugs influence how long, how strong, and how full each adult life is. We describe the impact of each of these in turn.

Exercise

Many people have sought the secret sauce, the fountain of youth, the magic bullet that will slow, or stop, or even reverse the effects of senescence. Few realize that it has already been found. Thousands of scientists, studying every disease of aging, have found something that helps every condition—exercise.

Regular physical activity protects against serious illness even if a person overeats, smokes, or drinks (all discussed soon). Exercise reduces blood pressure, strengthens the heart and lungs, promotes digestion, and makes depression, diabetes, osteoporosis, strokes, arthritis, and several cancers less likely. Health benefits from exercise are substantial for men and women, old and young, former sports stars and those who never joined a team (Aldwin & Gilmer, 2013).

Moving the body protects both mental health and physical health. Surroundings are key. Neighborhoods high in walkability (paths, sidewalks, etc.) reduce time driving and watching television (Kozo et al., 2012). This relationship between the surroundings, movement, and health is causal, not merely correlational: Exercise strengthens the immune system (Davison et al., 2014). Moreover, active people feel energetic, which increases other good habits.

Exercise maintains flexibility and strength, evident in those who do yoga or swim laps in late adulthood. The same is true for internal muscles—the heart, the lungs, the digestive system. By contrast, sitting for long hours correlates with almost every unhealthy condition, especially heart disease and diabetes, both

Taking Turns Workers such as Josh Baldonado at this insurance company must sign up to use one of the 30 treadmill workstations so that they can exercise as they work. The company moves their phones and computers to their workstations, and the company benefits from fewer absences and lower health care costs.

Playground? Cities that create play space for people of all ages keep the residents active, like these young men in Hong Kong *(left)* and Rio de Janeiro *(right).*

● **Observation Quiz** Young men and women everywhere play ball, but at least five cultural differences are apparent between these two scenes. What are they? (see answer, p. 571) ↑

causing additional health hazards. Even a little movement—gardening, light housework, walking up the stairs or to the bus—helps. Some research suggests that intensity is unnecessary: Regular exercise is (Ross et al., 2015).

How Much and When?

Unfortunately, exercise takes time and effort. It cannot be put in a pill and sold. Perhaps this is one reason that no corporation subsidizes research to understand and promote it. Consequently, scientists do not know exactly which exercise—and for how long—is best, nor how to get every adult to do it.

As one cardiologist said, "It's almost like we have something more powerful than any drug that we have for cardiovascular disease—physical activity—but we don't know how to dose it" (Ashley, cited in Servick, 2015, p. 1307). For example, is it more important to exercise a little every day than to exercise a lot on weekends?

Several studies have found that overweight people are sometimes healthier than trim ones. The crucial difference is body fitness: A heavy person who exercises regularly and well is less at risk for all of the diseases of aging than a normal-weight person who does not move much (Ahima & Lazar, 2013). A recent meta-analysis of breast cancer rates found that physical activity reduced the risk, no matter how heavy the woman was (Pizot et al., 2016).

Exercise is the main reason that some people age more quickly than others and also the reason that some parts of the body are stronger than others. Muscles respond to use—even a few weeks of bed rest weakens the legs substantially. The fibers for Type II muscles (the fast ones needed for forceful actions) are reduced much faster than Type I fibers (for slower, more routine movement) (Nilwik et al., 2013). This means that, as they age, adults become less able to win a 100-meter dash than a marathon, or less able to lift heavy rocks for a few minutes than to pick vegetables for hours.

Particularly for Type II muscles, exercise has been shown to make a dramatic difference (Nilwik et al., 2013). That may be because people use Type I muscles routinely, to walk around the house, to carry the plates to the table, to brush the teeth, to step into the shower, to move the spoon to the mouth. Those basic muscles do not atrophy except in unusual circumstances, unlike the muscles needed to run a mile, lift weights, or do push-ups.

Historical Change

Cohort changes are evident. Adults do not move their legs, arms, or even hands as much as adults did a century ago, thanks to many modern devices, from the automobile to the TV remote. Fortunately, some adults fight the lazy comfort of modern life. More than half (54 percent) meet either the U.S. weekly goal of 150 minutes of moderate exercise *or* 75 minutes of intense exercise. That is much better than 15 years ago, when only 41 percent met either benchmark (National Center for Health Statistics, 2015).

Of course, it is better to meet both goals, and only 21 percent did so—with lower rates as adults grow older. That 21 percent is nonetheless a cohort improvement. In 1998, only 14 percent of adults aged 25 to 65 did (National Center for Health Statistics, 2015).

The aging of the adult body is most evident in sports that require strength, agility, and speed: Gymnasts, boxers, and basketball players are among the athletes whose bodies slow down in their 20s. These are physiological slowdowns: The intellectual and emotional gains of adulthood may compensate for physical changes; some 30-year-olds are more valuable teammates than younger athletes.

Although there is no pill that duplicates exercise, that does not stop people from trying to find one. As you saw, many older adult men take testosterone because it adds lean body mass. Many doctors are skeptical about the benefits, even though many pharmaceutical companies advertise "T" to make a man's body young again.

One doctor wrote that men would be better off learning about "the health benefits of physical activity. . . . Tell them to take the $1,200 they'll spend on testosterone per year and join a health club; buy a Stairmaster—they'll have money left over for their new clothes" (Casey, 2008, p. 48).

"The fresh mountain air is starting to depress me."

Just Give Me the Usual Even bad habits feel comfortable—that's what makes them habits.

Drugs

That doctor's suspicion of T is shared by many who are wary of any medication that interferes with natural body processes. Others—doctors as well as adults of all backgrounds—seek drugs to solve many physical and emotional problems. The data suggest benefits and dangers.

Medication

In the past month in the United States, more than 40 percent of 25- to 44-year-olds and almost 70 percent of 45- to 64-year-olds took at least one prescription drug, according to surveys completed between 2010 and 2012. About 12 percent of adults took three or more prescription drugs in the past month.

About half of those prescriptions were for chronic conditions (such as high blood pressure) and about half were for pain. Prescribed psychoactive drugs were also common: 8 percent of young adults and 14 percent of those aged 45 to 64 took antidepressants (National Center for Health Statistics, 2015).

Over the past 50 years, prescription medication has cut the adult death rate in half and markedly reduced disability. Childhood diabetes (type 1), for instance, was once a death sentence; now diet and insulin allow diabetics to reach the highest levels of success, as Supreme Court Justice Sonia Sotomayor did. She began injecting herself at age 7; now she takes newer medication that is more precisely calibrated to her daily needs (Sotomayor, 2014).

There is no accurate tally of over-the-counter drugs, but almost every adult frequently takes vitamins, analgesics, laxatives, antihistamines, or some other medication. One benefit of growing older might be wisdom regarding drug use: Adults

At Risk in Bangalore A man puffs on a bidi, a flavored cigarette. He is at risk of being among the 1 million Indians who die each year of smoking-related causes.

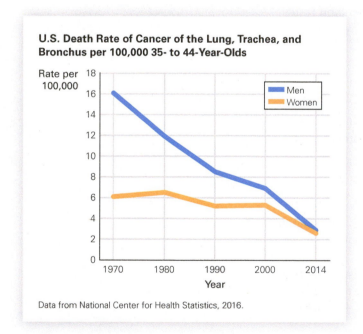

U.S. Death Rate of Cancer of the Lung, Trachea, and Bronchus per 100,000 35- to 44-Year-Olds

Data from National Center for Health Statistics, 2016.

FIGURE 20.2

No More Cancer Sticks The rates of lung cancer deaths dropped dramatically about a decade after smoking rates decreased. Other age groups of adults show similar results, although improvements are not as dramatic for older adults because they learned too late about the damage done to their lungs. In another few decades we will know whether e-cigarettes reverse this trend.

tell each other what works, doctors adjust their prescribing, and each person knows his or her personal reactions to various drugs.

Illegal Drugs and Coffee

Most adults take drugs that affect their mood. Almost everyone uses caffeinated soda and coffee, and a few take illegal drugs. Some improvement over adulthood is evident. As described in Chapter 17, illegal drug abuse decreases markedly over adulthood—often before age 25 and almost always by age 40. Past data show reduced use of marijuana, although recent legal changes may affect adult use, and we need to analyze data for another decade to understand the effect.

New evidence on coffee is good news: We now know that the effect of coffee varies genetically, and adults learn how coffee affects them (Cornelis et al., 2015). For some, coffee does no harm but reduces various problems, including depression and type 2 diabetes (Palatini, 2015). For others, coffee disrupts nighttime sleep and undercuts daytime efficiency. Adults adjust accordingly.

Tobacco

Always, culture and SES matter. This is shown dramatically in use of tobacco, considered the leading risk factor for many diseases. Rates are quite different depending on nation, SES, gender, and cohort.

In the United States, high-SES people are less likely to smoke. However, in poor nations, rates of smoking *increase* with income, because poor people cannot afford cigarettes. Traditionally in Asia, women rarely smoked, but as their income rises, rates of smoking are increasing rapidly (Lortet-Tieulent et al., 2014).

The World Health Organization calls tobacco "the single largest preventable cause of death and chronic disease in the world today," with 1 billion smoking-related deaths projected between 2010 and 2050, most in low-income nations where rates of abject poverty are declining (Blas & Kurup, 2010, p. 199).

Cigarette smoking in the United States illustrates marked cohort and gender effects. During World War II (1941–1945), American soldiers (always men) were given free cigarettes. Then in 1964, the U.S. surgeon general first reported on the health risks of smoking, with many follow-up reports in the next few decades. As a result, many former soldiers quit.

Meanwhile, some women celebrated another historical happening, women's liberation, by smoking—encouraged by cigarette advertisements. (One brand launched in 1968, Virginia Slims, used the slogan "you've come a long way baby.")

In the 1960s, more than half of U.S. adult men and more than a third of women smoked. Over the next decades, as research became clearer on smoking, cancer, heart disease, and secondhand smoke, both sexes had decreased smoking. Recent data show that only 21 percent of adult men (aged 25 to 65) and 17 percent of women are smokers. Rates peak at about age 30 and then decrease, indicating the advantages of maturation among adults (National Center for Health Statistics, 2016). By age 60, more adults are former smokers than current smokers.

The changes over the past decades are reflected in lung cancer deaths. A half-century ago in the United States, five times as many men as women died of lung cancer. More recently, rates are closer to equal, because "women who smoke like men die like men who smoke" (Schroeder, 2013, p. 389). In the past decades, adults of both sexes quit smoking and lung cancer was reduced by 500 percent—not primarily because of better medical care but because of wiser adults (see Figure 20.2).

Not only cohort but also culture has a strong effect on both smoking and gender differences. Almost half of the adults of both sexes in Germany, Denmark, Poland, Holland, Switzerland, and Spain smoke. A joke in Europe is "if you want to stop smoking, go to America."

Alcohol

The harm from cigarettes is dose-related: Each puff, each day, each breath of secondhand smoke makes cancer, heart disease, strokes, and emphysema more likely. No such linear harm results from drinking alcohol.

In fact, some alcohol may be beneficial: Adults who drink wine, beer, or spirits *in moderation*—never more than two drinks a day—live longer than abstainers. Some scientists consider this a misleading correlation because some of those abstainers were formerly heavy drinkers, so their death rate reflects damage done by alcohol (Chikritzhs et al., 2015; Knott et al., 2015). Whether that is true or not is debatable, but everyone agrees that excessive drinking is harmful.

To be specific, alcohol abuse destroys brain cells, is a major cause of liver damage and several cancers, contributes to osteoporosis, decreases fertility, and accompanies many suicides, homicides, and accidents—all while wreaking havoc in families. Even moderate consumption is unhealthy if it leads to smoking, overeating, casual sex, or other destructive habits.

Alcohol abuse also shows age, gender, cohort, and cultural differences. For example, the risk of accidental death while drunk is most common among young men: Law enforcement in the United States has cut their drunk-driving rate in half. However, middle-aged parents who abuse alcohol are more harmful to other people, because of their neglect and irrational rage (Blas & Kurup, 2010).

In the United States, about one in three adults under age 45 have gotten drunk in the past year, as have about one in five adults over age 45. Rates of alcohol abuse are higher among men than women, higher among European Americans than African or Hispanic Americans, and higher among the wealthy than the poor (National Center for Health Statistics, 2015).

In general, low-income nations have more abstainers, more abusers, and fewer moderate drinkers than more affluent nations (Blas & Kurup, 2010). In developing nations, prevention and treatment strategies for alcohol use disorder have not been established, regulation is rare, and laws are lax (Bollyky, 2012). Thus, alcohol is particularly lethal to a community as national income falls.

The Opioid Epidemic

As you see, most of the data on adult use of drugs are positive in the United States. Prescription drugs allow more people to survive and thrive, illegal drug use decreases as adults grow old, cigarette smoking is markedly reduced, and a better understanding of alcohol abuse is leading to fewer people with alcohol use disorder.

However, there is one serious drug problem that increases after age 25. That problem is addiction to opioids, both prescription drugs and street heroin.

Wishful Thinking Would you like to be her, with a thin cigarette in your hand? If this was her usual appearance, she would now be at risk for cancer and heart disease.

● ● **Especially for Doctors and Nurses** If you had to choose between recommending various screening tests and recommending various lifestyle changes to a 35-year-old, which would you do? (see response, page 573)

THINK CRITICALLY: How would you apportion blame for drug addiction?

● ● **Answer to Observation Quiz** (from p. 568) Shoes or bare feet, pants or shorts, skyscrapers or smaller buildings, basketball or soccer, large open space or small fenced area.

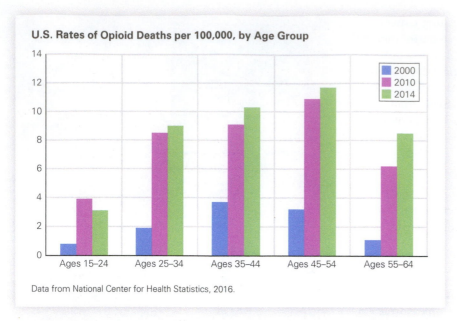

U.S. Rates of Opioid Deaths per 100,000, by Age Group

Data from National Center for Health Statistics, 2016.

FIGURE 20.3

Bad News Which is more troubling: that rates of opioid deaths have more than tripled in a decade, that rates continue to rise, or that rates in middle age are almost four times the rates for emerging adults? The answer depends partly on your age, and whether or not you are a public health worker.

Pain Killer "Never meant to cause you any pain," sang Prince in "Purple Rain." But his own pain led to an addiction to fentanyl (a potent synthetic opioid) and then death, hurting us all.

Abuse of prescribed medication is increasing, as are deaths from all opioids (see Figure 20.3). (Heroin is an opioid, as it comes from opium.) One reason is that such drugs are first given by a doctor to reduce pain, insomnia, or psychological distress. That makes it harder for adults to recognize the early signs of addiction, and thus, some seek more prescriptions rather than trying to quit. Danger ahead.

For example, after the trial of a man (age 33) who killed four people to get pills for himself and his addicted wife (age 30), the local attorney general said, "the genesis of the current prescription pill and heroin epidemic lies squarely at the feet of the medical establishment," (Spota quoted in James, 2012).

Of course, doctors feel unjustly accused for illegal prescription use. Addiction of all kinds raises the question as to who is to blame—and answers range from the addict to the dealer or doctor to the entire society.

Prescription opioids are thought to be one cause of an epidemic of heroin deaths, which have more than tripled from 2010 to 2014 (National Center for Health Statistics, 2016). In 2014, 47,055 drug overdose deaths occurred in the United States, almost all among adults.

One cause is thought to be that adults become addicted to prescription pain medication and then find it hard to get enough from a doctor to feed their addiction. Some switch to heroin, a more available and less expensive drug. Rates of opioid and heroin abuse are higher in men than women, in states east of the Mississippi than west of it (but California is catching up), and among 25- to 44-year-olds than among emerging or older adults (Rudd et al., 2016).

Part of the problem is that, until recently, most adults—doctors, spouses, friends of addicts, and addicts themselves—were unaware of the danger. Greater knowledge of the harm from prescription opioids and of heroin, as well as wider distribution of naloxone (an antidote that saves life if given immediately when someone overdoses) is needed. Given the history of lung cancer and cigarette smoking, we can hope for similar decreases in opioid deaths soon.

Nutrition

At every stage of life, nourishment is essential, affecting life and death. Scientists agree that nutrition is a factor in almost every adult ailment.

Many specific foods—nuts, blueberries, broccoli, tempeh—have been touted as superfoods, and many specific diets—low-carb, low-fat, low-gluten—have been advocated. Here is not the place to analyze specifics, although one diet—the so-called Mediterranean diet, high in fiber, fish, and olive oil—is proven to protect against heart disease and may decrease rates of breast cancer and colon cancer (Estruch et al., 2013; Romagnolo & Selmin, 2016).

Diet is increasingly important as adults grow older, because metabolism decreases by one-third between ages 20 and 60, and digestion become less efficient. This means that, to stay the same weight, adults need to eat less and move more as they grow older. Since overall calories must decline, more fruits and vegetables and fewer sweets and fats must be consumed each year. That is not what typically happens.

Prevalence of Obesity

Healthy eating and good health care are important for all adults, whether or not they are overweight. Indeed, some people may be genetically destined to be outside the boundaries of normal weight. In the United States, Asian American adults have significantly lower rates of obesity (11 percent) and African Americans have higher rates (48 percent).

It is possible that the BMI cutoffs should be altered for these groups. Alternatively, weight might be one reason that African Americans have more premature deaths and Asian Americans fewer than the overall U.S. average.

In the United States, adults gain an average of 1 to 2 pounds each year, much more than prior generations did. Over the 40 years of adulthood, that adds 40 to 80 pounds. As a result, two-thirds of U.S. adults are overweight, defined as a body mass index (BMI) of 25 or more. [**Life-Span Link:** BMI is explained in Chapter 17.]

Overweight is not necessarily a health risk, but too much body fat almost always is. More than one-third of all U.S. men and women age 25 to 65 are obese (with a BMI over 30), and 6 percent are morbidly obese (with a BMI over 40) (National Center for Health Statistics, 2015).

If BMI numbers seem abstract, picture a person who is 5 feet, 8 inches tall. If that person weighs 150 pounds, the BMI is about 23, a normal weight. If he or she weighs 200 pounds, the BMI is 30, which makes that person obese. If he or she weighs more than 260 pounds, the BMI is over 40, making that person morbidly obese.

Worldwide, half a billion people are obese. Rates seem to have reached a plateau in the United States, but many developing nations are reporting rapidly increasing rates (see Visualizing Development, page 574). This is particularly true in North Africa and Asia. Malnutrition once was their most prevalent nutritional problem; now obesity is (M. Ng et al., 2014).

Consequences of Obesity

A meta-analysis found that mortality rates by age for adults who were overweight but not obese were *lower* than the average rates, a conclusion that comforted many larger adults (Flegal et al., 2013). However, be careful. Some of those overweight people have a high BMI because muscle weighs more than fat, so their BMI is high while the fat content of their body is not. Excess body fat (no matter what the BMI) increases the risk of almost every chronic disease.

One example is diabetes, which causes eye, heart, and foot problems as well as early death. Although diabetes is partly genetic, the genetic tendency is exacerbated by excess fat. The United States is the world leader in both obesity and diabetes.

A new hypothesis is that an obese, insulin-resistant mother affects the fetus not only because of her genes but also because of her prenatal health. Pregnant women who are obese and diabetic tend to have children who become overweight and insulin-resistant. The children also have other signs of poor health in adulthood (called *metabolic syndrome*) that predispose them to diabetes and heart disease (Smith & Ryckman, 2015).

The consequences of obesity are psychological as well as physical, since adults who are obese are targets of scorn and prejudice. They are less likely to be chosen as marriage partners, as employees, and even as friends. The stigma leads them to avoid medical checkups, to eat more, and to exercise less—impairing their health far more than their weight alone (Puhl & Heuer, 2010).

Perhaps the goal should be to lose enough pounds to protect health rather than to reach normal weight. The culture's emphasis on an ideal BMI and a svelte shape may encourage unhealthy dieting and then eating disorders, including overeating

● ● **Response for Doctors and Nurses** (from page 571): Obviously, much depends on the specific patient. Overall, however, far more people develop a disease or die because of years of poor health habits than because of various illnesses that are not spotted early. With some exceptions, age 35 is too early to detect incipient cancers or circulatory problems, but it's prime time for stopping cigarette smoking, curbing alcohol abuse, and improving exercise and diet.

Should Adults Know Better? This photo of adults all reaching simultaneously is staged, evident because most adults have learned not to grab. However, doughnuts and other unhealthy foods are routinely offered at business meetings and office parties. After the photo, which of these people took doughnuts, and which made healthier choices?

LaunchPad
macmillan learning

Try the Data Connections activity **Body Mass Index** for a demonstration of how BMI is determined.

Adult Overweight Around the Globe

A century ago, being overweight was a sign of affluence, as the poor were less likely to enjoy a calorie-rich diet and more likely to be engaged in physical labor. Today, that link is less clear. Overweight—defined as having a body mass index (BMI) over 25—is common across socioeconomic groups and across borders, and obesity (a BMI over 30) is a growing health threat worldwide.

OVERWEIGHT AND GDP

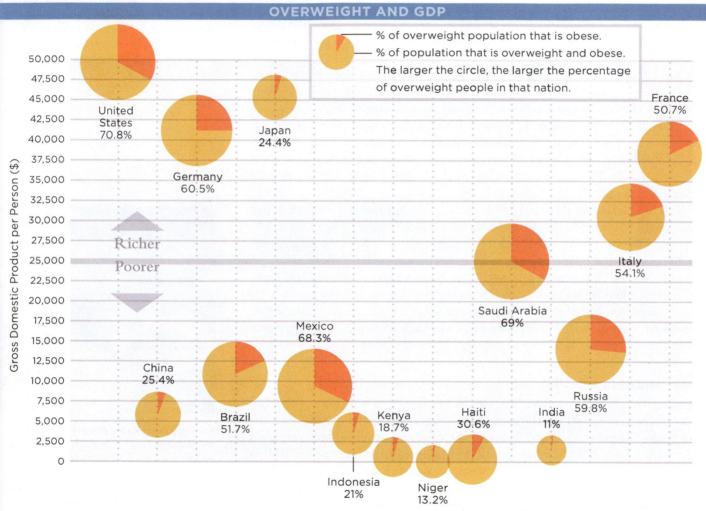

% of overweight population that is obese.

% of population that is overweight and obese. The larger the circle, the larger the percentage of overweight people in that nation.

United States 70.8%
Japan 24.4%
France 50.7%
Germany 60.5%
Italy 54.1%
Richer
Poorer
Saudi Arabia 69%
Mexico 68.3%
China 25.4%
Russia 59.8%
Brazil 51.7%
Kenya 18.7%
Haiti 30.6%
India 11%
Indonesia 21%
Niger 13.2%

Gross Domestic Product per Person ($)

International cutoff weights for overweight and obesity are set at various levels. These numbers show proportions of adults whose BMI is over 25.

DATA FROM WORLD HEALTH ORGANIZATION, 2013; WORLD BANK, 2013.

OBESITY IN THE UNITED STATES

While common wisdom holds that overweight and obesity correlate with income, recent data suggest that culture and gender may play a bigger role. Obesity tends to be less prevalent among wealthy American women; for men, the patterns are less consistent.

Male **Female**

$$$ = Income 350%+ of poverty level
$$ = Income 130% to 349% of poverty level
$ = Income less than 130% of poverty level

OBESITY RATES (U.S.)

% 60

$$$ $$ $ $$$ $$ $ $$$ $$ $ $$$ $$ $

Total   European Americans   African Americans   Mexican Americans

DATA FROM PEW RESEARCH CENTER, 2013.

(Shai & Stampfer, 2008). This may explain why more women than men are of healthy weight (do they care more?) or obese (do they give up if they can't stay thin?).

Losing and Gaining

International politics may decrease weight and increase health. In Cuba from 1991 to 1995, boycotts from the United States led to a national economic crisis. That meant less meat to eat and more walking for transport. The average adult lost 14 pounds, which reduced Cuban rates of diabetes and heart disease. When the crisis was over, people regained weight, and the diabetes rate doubled (Franco et al., 2013). Very human, but not very healthy.

Cultural habits make a difference for everyone. The typical U.S. family consumes more meat and fat and less fiber than people in other parts of the world. For example, the Chinese traditionally ate many vegetables mixed with small bits of meat or fish; few had a weight problem. Some blame the recent weight increase in China on increasing urbanization and industrialization, which has led to a new taste for American food as well as the ability to get it (Chen et al., 2016). In 2016, McDonald's had more than 2,000 restaurants in China (not including several hundred in Taiwan).

One specific culprit in weight gain may be sugar, either sucrose or fructose (added to many packaged foods and beverages through corn syrup). A study that reduced sugar in foods found that people lost weight, and another study in 175 nations found a correlation between national sugar consumption and diabetes (Te Morenga et al., 2013; Basu et al., 2013).

Obviously, we should not rely on genes, or hope for an economic crisis, to protect our health. However, many people do not seem to be able to control eating before it becomes dangerous. Many public health advocates have sought to learn how to help people maintain a healthy weight, as well as quit smoking, exercise more, drink in moderation, use painkillers only when pain is acute, and so on. The answer differs depending on the person's stage, as the following explains.

Exercise Equipment Although expensive full-body machines are bought with good intentions, they often collect dust after a few weeks. More useful equipment is readily available, such as a jump rope, running shoes, or—shown here—a hula hoop.

THINK CRITICALLY: Why did it take an economic crisis for Cubans to lose weight?

OPPOSING PERSPECTIVES

A Habit Is Hard to Break

In this feature, unlike the others, the opposing perspectives are within each person: human emotions opposed to human knowledge. In this tug-of-war, emotions often win, and scientists are trying to figure out how to tilt the balance in favor of knowledge.

Everyone knows that cigarette smoking, alcohol abuse, overeating, and sedentary behavior are harmful, yet almost everyone has at least one of these destructive habits. Why don't we all shape up and live right?

Many social scientists have focused on this disconnect between knowledge and action. One insight, inspired in part by social learning theory, is that changing a habit is a long, multistep process, sometimes conceptualized as five "stages of change" (Norcross et al., 2011; Gökbayrak et al., 2015). Tactics that work at one step fail at another. One list of these steps is (1) denial, (2) awareness, (3) planning, (4) implementation, and (5) maintenance.

1. *Denial* occurs because all bad habits begin and continue for a reason. That makes denial a reasonable act of self-defense, clinging to the reason rather than changing the habit. For example, many adult smokers began as teenagers, using cigarettes to achieve important goals: to be socially accepted, to appear mature, and/or to control weight. Before they realized it, they were addicted.

With many addictions, hearing how bad it is triggers anger, anxiety, defiance. That leads to *more* smoking, drinking, or so on (Maxfield et al., 2014; Ben-Zur & Zeidner, 2009).

Denial may prevent others from criticizing a habit. For instance, one out of eight smokers lies to his or her doctor about smoking. Younger adults are especially likely to lie (Curry et al., 2013). Denial protects against stress; people hide cigarettes, bottles, or other signs, to avoid confrontation.

2. *Awareness* is attained by the person him- or herself, not from someone else. Sometimes awareness comes after a dramatic event—a doctor predicting death from smoking, a

night in jail because of drinking, tipping the scale at 200 pounds (which seems much more than 199).

If someone else tries to encourage awareness by stating facts (e.g., telling a smoker about lung cancer), that can create a backlash. However, *motivational interviewing* may help.

In that interview, the individual is asked about the costs and benefits of the habit. Often people fluctuate between denial and dawning awareness; a good listener tips the balance by affirming what is said about the downside of the habit and stressing the person's power of choice (Magill et al., 2014). However, motivational interviewing must be carefully done, lest denial rather than awareness is encouraged.

Self-efficacy—the belief that people have the power to change—is pivotal (Martin et al., 2010). This self-affirmation does not have to be directly connected to the desired change. For example, when people in a nutrition program had to write about their values and recall one time when they expressed those values, that increased the number of fruits and vegetables they ate during the next 3 months (Harris et al., 2014).

3. *Planning* is best when it is specific, such as setting a date for quitting and putting strategies in place to overcome the obstacles. A series of studies has found that humans tend to underestimate the power of their own impulses, which arise from brain patterns, not logic (Belin et al., 2013). Thus, plans must include strategies to defend against momentary wavering. Overconfidence makes it difficult to break a habit.

In one study, researchers gave students who were entering or leaving a college cafeteria a choice of packaged snacks, promising them about $10 (and the snack) if they did not eat the snack for a week. Students entering the cafeteria, presumably aware of the demands of hunger, planned to avoid temptation by choosing a less desirable snack. Most (61 percent) earned the money. However, many of those who had just eaten chose a more desirable snack. Few (39 percent) earned the money because most ate the food before the week was up (Nordgren et al., 2009).

4. *Implementation* is changing the habit according to the plan. One crucial factor is social support, such as (1) letting others know the date and details of the plan and enlisting their help, (2) finding a buddy, or (3) joining a group (Weight Watchers, Alcoholics Anonymous, or another program). Private efforts often fail.

Implementation must reflect the values, circumstances, and supports of the individual. For instance, prayer was an effective part of implementation to improve diet and exercise of older Mexican American women (Schwingel et al., 2015). That would not help everyone.

Past successes increase self-efficacy. Going without a drug for a day is a reason for celebration, as well as proof that another day is possible. Checking off days on a calendar, rewarding oneself with a gift bought with money saved, listing past accomplishments—all of these make future success more likely.

5. *Maintenance* is the most difficult step. Although quitting any entrenched habit is painful, many addicts have quit several times, recovered, and then relapsed. Dieters go on and off diets so often that this pattern has a name—*yo-yo dieting*. Sadly, once implementation succeeds, people are overconfident. They forget the power of temptation.

Willpower may be like a muscle, slowly gaining strength with activity but subject to muscle fatigue if overused (Baumeister & Tierney, 2012). A man who has stopped abusing alcohol might party with friends who drink, confident that he will stick to soda; a dieter serves dessert to the rest of her family, certain that she will be able to resist a taste herself; someone who joined the gym will skip a day, planning to do twice as much tomorrow.

Such actions are risky. The dieter who skips the dessert uses so much willpower that she is defenseless at midnight, when leftover cake beckons. Maintenance fades when faced with stress. Many people who restart a bad habit explain that they did so because of a divorce, a new job, a rebellious teenager, or so on.

Of course, sooner or later every adult experiences a stressor; that is why maintenance strategies are crucial. When stress combines with opportunity, people mistakenly think that one cigarette, one drink, one slice of cake, one skipped day of exercise, and so on, is inconsequential—which it would be if the person stopped there.

Unfortunately, the human mind is geared toward all or nothing; neurons switch on or off, not halfway. For that reason, one puff of a cigarette makes the next one more likely, one potato chip awakens the urge for another, and so on. With alcohol, the drink itself scrambles the mind; people are less aware of their cognitive lapses under the influence and thus drink more after that first drink (Sayette et al., 2009).

Once a person is aware of a destructive habit (step 2), it is not hard to plan and implement an improvement (steps 3 and 4). But sticking to it (step 5) is difficult if the context includes an unanticipated push in the opposite direction. Think again about the relationship between national culture and cigarette smoking: Almost all adult smokers want to quit, but whether they do depends on much more than their private wishes.

Ideally, young adults take stock of all their habits and make sure that each year is an improvement rather than an added pound or two. For the morbidly obese, surgery may be the best option.

Each year, about 200,000 U.S. residents undergo bariatric surgery to restrict weight gain. The rate of complications is high: About 2 percent die during or soon after the operation, and about 10 percent need additional surgery. Patients have fewer complications if they lose weight in preparation for the surgery (Claes et al., 2015). That could be an aspect of homeostasis—the body is getting ready to adjust to a better diet.

Over time, surgery that reduces obesity saves lives because morbid obesity is a serious risk to survival. The greatest benefits seem to occur for people with diabetes: 70 percent find that their diabetes disappears, usually not to return (Arterburn et al., 2013; Chen et al., 2016).

THINK CRITICALLY: Why might survivors of bariatric surgery live longer than the average person?

Measuring Health

Measuring health is not nearly as simple as it appears. Four measures are often used, each with advantages and disadvantages, as you will now see.

Mortality

Death is the final evidence of loss of health. **Mortality** is usually expressed as the annual number of deaths per hundred thousand in the population. This measure allows valid comparisons between nations and groups.

For example, it is useful to know that, worldwide, women live four years longer than men. In the United States the death rate ranges from 6.5 for Asian American girls aged 5 to 14, to 15,286 for European American, non-Hispanic men over age 85 (National Center for Health Statistics, 2016).

A drawback of this measure is that knowing death rates might not help with prevention. Causes are not necessarily accurate (was that suicide?) or recognized. For instance, when a baby dies of measles, national immunization, breast-feeding, and clean water rates are relevant. But the death certificate does not list that.

mortality Death. As a measure of health, mortality usually refers to the number of deaths each year per hundred thousand members of a given population.

Morbidity

Morbidity (from the Latin word for "disease"), includes illnesses and impairments of all kinds—acute and chronic, physical and psychological. Chronic diseases may be reveal more about the health of a population than death rate. For instance, the sex ratio of morbidity is opposite to mortality: More women than men suffer almost every illness, a recognition that may change what some see as a male bias in medical care.

A focus on morbidity helps prevent years of suffering (a woman with heart disease that impairs her life for years). For instance, not enough research has focused on Alzheimer's because, although it is major cause of morbidity, usually victims die of some other cause.

A disadvantage is that morbidity may be undiagnosed or overdiagnosed. For instance, almost all men eventually have prostate cancer. Diagnosis produces increased morbidity (incontinence, impotence, crippling anxiety) even though prostate cancer is unlikely to cause death for most of them. The American Council of Physicians notes the "limited potential benefits and substantial harm of screening for prostate cancer" (Qaseem et al., 2013). Traditionally, morbidity is higher in nations with lower mortality because of earlier diagnosis.

morbidity Disease. As a measure of health, morbidity usually refers to the rate of diseases in a given population—physical and emotional, acute (sudden) and chronic (ongoing).

Disability

Disability refers to difficulty in performing "activities of daily life" because of a "physical, mental, or emotional condition." Disability does not necessarily equal morbidity: In the United States, of the adults who are disabled, only 29 percent consider their health fair or poor (National Center for Health Statistics, 2016).

This measure has led to a useful indicator, **disability-adjusted life years,** or **DALYs,** which measures how much a person's life is hampered by a disability.

disability Difficulty in performing normal activities of daily life because of some physical, mental, or emotional condition.

disability-adjusted life years (DALYs) A measure of the reduced quality of life caused by disability.

For instance, a person born with a disability that reduces functioning by about 10 percent, who then lives to age 70, would be said to have 63 DALYs because the disability is considered to have cost that person seven healthy, active years (10 percent of 70). Whether or not a disability impairs a person depends as much on the social context as on the specific condition. Thus, making homes and stores accessible might reduce disability.

An analysis of DALYs in 188 nations for 306 diseases since 1990 found that the world disease burden has undergone a major shift. In 1990, the main cause of DALYs was diseases that could be passed from one person to another—diarrhea, HIV/AIDS, tuberculosis, and so on. In the past decades, DALYs have increased for diseases affected by each person's genes and lifestyle. Dramatic increases in DALYs have occurred for major depressive disorder—which does not kill people (unless they kill themselves) but destroys their daily life. Another new problem is "road rage"—now the fifth most common cause of DALYs (C. Murray et al., 2015). That indicates what national and personal measures are needed.

A downside of this measure is that many people with various disabilities object to someone deciding how much their life is impaired because of them. Further, some nations object that the focus on DALYs tilts toward wealthy nations who have the luxury of making daily life better for everyone, whereas poor nations still have high rates of communicable diseases that should be eliminated.

Vitality

vitality A measure of health that refers to how healthy and energetic—physically, intellectually, and socially—an individual actually feels.

Vitality refers to how healthy and energetic—physically, intellectually, and socially—an individual feels. A person can feel terrific despite having a serious disease or disability. A study of adult cancer survivors found that fatigue was a problem for many, but some seemed quite vital despite their history (Deng et al., 2015). Such research can help everyone become more vital, as detailed in this chapter, with habits of exercise, nutrition, and so on.

quality-adjusted life years (QALYs) A measure of how many years of high-quality life a person lives. This is distinct from DALYs, in that a person could have a disability and nonetheless have a high quality of life.

One way to measure vitality is to calculate **quality-adjusted life years (QALYs).** If people are fully vital, their quality of life is 100 percent, which means that a year of their life equals one QALY. A healthy, happy, energetic person who lives 70 years has 70 QALYs. If one year included surgery and a difficult recovery, with an estimated 50 percent reduction in quality of life, then that person's QALY would be 69 and a half.

Considering QALYs is needed to evaluate medical treatment, because simply saving a life (decreasing mortality) or reducing disability may not be a boon if the quality of life is gone. For example, a study at many German hospitals for patients with schizophrenia, randomized to receive traditional or newer antipsychotic drugs, found significant improvement in QALYs as reported by the patients. The study also found slightly more adverse physiological effects from the new drugs (Gründer et al., 2016). Thus, vitality increased even as morbidity did. This information is useful in assessing any medical measure.

People disagree about vitality. As already seen in the sections on exercise and nutrition, specific recommendations vary a great deal, in part because measuring vitality is difficult. Traditional physician training emphasizes morbidity and mortality; psychologists focus more on disability and vitality. Individuals disagree even more.

Overall, doctors are concerned about adverse physiological effects; patients want to be able to do what they want to do, joyfully. Obviously, mortality, morbidity, disability, and vitality are all worthy considerations: Balancing them is difficult. No society spends enough to enable everyone to live life to the fullest. Without some measure of disability and vitality, the best health care goes to whomever has the most money, or whatever morbidity tugs hardest at the public's heart strings.

Correlating Income and Health

As every measure of health indicates, ethnicity, income, and place of residence are all relevant. For example, the overall risk of dying for a U.S. resident at some point between ages 25 and 65 is about 15 percent, but for some it is as high as 50 percent (e.g., Sioux men in South Dakota) or less than 2 percent (Asian women in Connecticut) (Lewis & Burd-Sharps, 2010). The U.S. government recently focused on health disparities among ethnic groups in the United States, and mortality gaps were apparent (National Center for Health Statistics, 2016).

Money and education protect health. Well-educated, financially secure adults live longer and avoid morbidity and disability more than their fellow citizens. Even in nations with good universal health care, the poorest people have shorter lives, on average.

Perhaps education is the pivot here, as educated people learn healthy habits. Obesity and cigarette smoking in the United States are almost twice as common among adults with the least education compared to those with college degrees. Or perhaps higher income allows access to better medical care as well as distance from pollution and street crime.

For whatever reason, the differences can be dramatic. The 10 million U.S. residents with the highest SES (and the best health care) outlive—by about 30 years—the 10 million with the lowest SES who live in rundown areas (Lewis & Burd-Sharps, 2010).

SES protects health between nations as well as within them. Compared to developing nations, rich countries have lower rates of disease, injury, and early death. For example, a baby born in 2015 in a developed nation can expect to live to age 78; but if that baby happens to be born in a least-developed nation, life expectancy is only 62 (see Figure 20.4). The extremes are separated by 33 years: Life expectancy in Hong Kong is 84; in Angola 51—a marked improvement over 1950, when it was only 30 (United Nations, 2015).

Without doubt, low SES harms human development in every way, evident in statistics on mortality, morbidity, disability, and vitality. Unfortunately, more often in the United States than in most nations, babies born poor are unlikely to escape their SES, as their education, health care, job prospects, and so on are all likely to work against them; they therefore enter adulthood already impaired. Is there any hope?

That question returns us to Jenny, whose story began this chapter. When I first met her, she was among the poorest 10 million people in the United States, living in a Bronx neighborhood known as "Gunsmoke Territory" because of its high homicide rate. She is also African American, and people of her ethnicity tend to have higher allostatic load.

Her decision to have another baby—with no promise of marriage or of the father's support—made me fear that she would never escape from poverty. My fear was not prejudice: Lifelong poverty is the usual future for low-income mothers of four who have another child, out of wedlock, with a married man.

But those statistics do not reflect Jenny's intelligence, creativity, and attitude. She made the best of available government help. Her tuition was paid by a Pell

> **THINK CRITICALLY:** Should taxpayers subsidize kidney dialysis for young college students or intensive care for severely disabled 80-year-olds? Would it matter, though, if those damaged kidneys were the result of drug abuse, or if that older person were a former president?

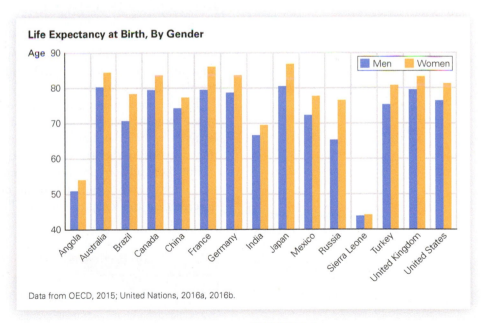

Life Expectancy at Birth, By Gender

Data from OECD, 2015; United Nations, 2016a, 2016b.

FIGURE 20.4

More Widows Than Widowers Women live longer than men, but it matters where they live. The cause is probably both nature and nurture: Biology is that extra X chromosome, more estrogen, or less testosterone; and in most nations, men have fewer social supports, suppress their emotions, and use more harmful drugs.

Grant, she lived in public housing, her children went to public schools, she found parks and museums where her children could play and learn.

She also applied what she learned: I saw her help her children with their homework; find speech therapy for her son; provide love, supervision, and protection for all of them. She convinced Billy to be tested for sickle cell (it was negative). She "babyproofed" her apartment, locking up the poisons, covering electric outlets, getting her landlord to put guards on the windows.

She knew when and how to access social support, evidenced by her seeking me out as well as befriending the teachers of her children. She offered her classmates many examples of how to connect with the other people in their lives.

After giving birth to a healthy, full-term baby girl, she found work tutoring children in her home so that she could earn some money while caring for her newborn. When the baby was a little older, she went back to college, earning her B.A. on a full scholarship. Her professors recognized her intelligence; she was chosen to give the graduation speech. She then found work as a receptionist in a city hospital, a union job that provided medical insurance for her family. That allowed her to move her family to a safer part of the Bronx.

Although Jenny is exceptional, she is not unique: Some low-income people are able to overcome the potential stressors of poverty (Chen & Miller, 2012). One strategy is to choose their friends (I was one of them) and lovers (I later met Billy; I liked him) carefully.

Billy did not abandon Jenny. He sometimes visited her and the daughter he did not want, providing emotional and financial support. His wife became suspicious, hired a private investigator, and then delivered an ultimatum: Stop seeing Jenny or obtain a divorce. He chose Jenny. Soon after that, they married and moved to Florida.

Jenny continues to do well, although, as a developmentalist would predict, Jenny could not completely escape the toll of her early life. For instance, she developed diabetes and must watch her diet carefully. But she bikes, swims, and gardens almost every day. She works full-time in education, having earned a master's degree. She and Billy seem happy together. I met the son who had a speech impediment: He earned a Ph.D. and is an assistant professor. Jenny's daughters are also college graduates.

This example might give the impression that escaping from poverty is easy; all of the longitudinal data show that it is not. Nor do most poor children thrive as Jenny's children did. For her two teenage nephews, Jenny's help came too late—they were lost to the streets of the South Bronx.

But the study of human development is not only about statistics and generalities. Each person is buffeted by all of the habits, conditions, and circumstances described in this chapter, but we all make choices that affect our future. Jenny chose well.

THINK CRITICALLY: How often do people who grow up in poverty stay in poverty?

WHAT HAVE YOU LEARNED?

1. How much should an adult exercise?

2. Why do some experts think exercise is more important than weight?

3. What are the trends in weight in the United States?

4. How does lung cancer reflect trends in smoking cigarettes?

5. Which groups are smoking more and which are smoking less?

6. Who is most likely to suffer from opioid abuse?

7. Why would SES predict health, even in a nation with free, public health care?

SUMMARY

Growing Older

1. Senescence causes a universal slowdown during adulthood, but aging does not necessarily mean impairment. Blood pressure, breathing, and brains usually function well throughout adulthood.

2. A person's appearance undergoes gradual but noticeable changes as middle age progresses, including more wrinkles, less hair, and more fat, particularly around the abdomen. People lose some height because of compression of the spine.

3. Senescence is apparent in the sense organs. Vision becomes less sharp with age. Nearsightedness decreases and farsightedness increases in midlife. Hearing also becomes less acute.

The Sexual-Reproductive System

4. Sexual responsiveness slows down with age, as does speed of recovery after orgasm. This is only a physical decline; many couples find that, overall, sexual relations improve with age, especially if they communicate well. Some evidence (e.g., watching pornography) suggests that sexual activity is more important for men than for women. However, this is not proven.

5. Fertility problems become more common with increased age, for many reasons. The most common one for men is a reduced number of sperm, and for women, ovulation failure or blocked fallopian tubes. For both sexes, not only youth but also health—especially sexual health—correlates with fertility.

6. At menopause, as a woman's menstrual cycle stops, ovulation ceases and levels of estrogen are markedly reduced. This hormonal change produces various symptoms, although most women find menopause to be much less troubling than they had expected. Hormone replacement therapy was once common, but it increases the risk of breast cancer.

7. Hormone production declines in men, too, though not as suddenly as in women. Men produce viable sperm lifelong. Some men take extra testosterone, but hormone replacement therapy in men seems to have health benefits and costs.

Habits: Good and Bad

8. Exercise is the key to good health, both physical and psychological. Adults in the United States are exercising more than they did a decade ago but less than they did a century ago.

9. North Americans are smoking far less than they once did, and rates of lung cancer and other diseases are falling, largely for that reason. Women cut down on smoking later than men did, and in many nations, female smoking is increasing.

10. Moderate drinking of alcohol may be beneficial for heart health, but excessive drinking is a major health problem. This is particularly true in poor nations.

11. Good health habits include not gaining too much weight. Today's adults worldwide are faring worse than did previous generations on this metric. This is especially true in the United States. There is a worldwide "epidemic of obesity," as more people have access to abundant food and overeat as a result. That is one reason the rates of diabetes are rising.

12. There are many ways to measure health. Mortality and morbidity are the most reliable for international comparisons, but disability and vitality are more important to individuals.

13. Aging and health status can be greatly affected by SES. In general, those who have more education and money are more likely to live longer and avoid illness than their poorer counterparts. However, low SES does not inevitably lead to poor health since genes and health habits are protective; avoiding drugs and obesity is possible at any income level.

KEY TERMS

senescence (p. 556)
presbycusis (p. 560)
infertility (p. 563)
menopause (p. 565)

hormone replacement therapy (HRT) (p. 566)
andropause (p. 566)
mortality (p. 577)

morbidity (p. 577)
disability (p. 577)
disability-adjusted life years (DALYs) (p. 577)

vitality (p. 578)
quality-adjusted life years (QALYs) (p. 578)

APPLICATIONS

1. Guess the age of five adults, ideally of different ages. Then ask them how old they are. Analyze the clues you used for your guesses and the reactions to your question.

2. Find a speaker willing to come to your class who is an expert on weight loss, adult health, smoking, or drinking. Write a one-page proposal explaining why you think this speaker would be good and what topics he or she should address. Give this proposal to your instructor, with contact information for your speaker. The instructor will call the potential speakers, thank

them for their willingness, and decide whether or not to actually invite them to speak.

3. Attend a gathering for people who want to stop a bad habit or start a good one, such as an open meeting of Alcoholics Anonymous or another 12-step program, an introductory session of Weight Watchers or Smoke Enders, or a meeting of prospective gym members. Report on who attended, what you learned, and what your reactions were.

Adulthood:
Cognitive Development

What Will You Know?

1. Do people get smarter as they get older?
2. Are people who are high in analytic intelligence also high in practical intelligence?
3. Does stress make a person sick and confused?
4. Is everyone an expert at something?

One of my daughters, herself a professor, was on the committee to select a new college president. She told me that she is happy with the new leader. He came from outside academia and took a huge pay cut to accept the appointment, and now he is improving the institution in many ways.

"You must be glad they selected the one you wanted," I said.

"He's not the one I wanted. I didn't even want to interview him. Others on the committee outvoted me; I am glad they did."

She was unimpressed with his résumé because she is a scholar and he had few publications. But she heard others' opinions, thought again about her criteria, listened with an open mind during his interview, and now is pleased with his leadership.

This illustrates adult cognition at its best. Adults have ideas, quite logical ones, but ideally they also listen to others. Everyone has areas of knowledge in which they are experts, but adults can consider other perspectives, experiences, and emotions.

As you read this chapter, you will realize that cognition is multifaceted. Some abilities improve with age; others do not. Each person becomes an expert at particular skills and knowledge. Ideally, adults become better able to appreciate their own ideas and those of everyone else.

Remember that many research strategies are used to describe cognitive development from emerging adulthood through old age. Chapter 18 described postformal thinking as well as the impact of college. Chapter 24 will take an information-processing perspective, highlighting the aspects of processing that slow down and describing neurocognitive disorders. This chapter follows the psychometric approach (*metric* means "measure"; *psychometric* refers to the measurement of psychological characteristics) and considers various kinds of intelligence, including those that produce experts of one sort or another.

I am proud that my adult daughter realized that the new president is smart and talented, albeit not in the metrics familiar to her (publications, citations). She was thinking as an adult.

Does Intelligence Change with Age?

For most of the twentieth century, everyone—scientists and the general public alike—assumed that there was such a thing as "intelligence," some kind of physical thing, like a lump in the brain that some people had more of than others.

Psychometricians began to see that scores on IQ tests can change markedly from childhood to adulthood, but they thought this was primarily due to imperfect tests, not changing intelligence. They asserted that intelligence was useful to measure because it generally predicted education, income, and longevity (Arden et al., 2016). They knew that the link between childhood intelligence and adult outcomes is erratic, but they considered averages and found that once a person reaches age 20 or so, IQ seems fairly stable, heavily influenced by genetics, and predictive of later life (Plomin & Deary, 2015).

As one scholar begins a book on intelligence:

> Homer and Shakespeare lived in very different times, more than two thousand years apart, but they both captured the same idea: we are not all equally intelligent. I suspect that anyone who has failed to notice this is somewhat out of touch with the species.
>
> *[Hunt, 2011a, p. 1]*

One leading theoretician, Charles Spearman (1927), proposed that there is a single entity, **general intelligence,** which he called *g*. Spearman contended that although *g* cannot be measured directly, it can be inferred from various abilities, such as vocabulary, memory, and reasoning.

IQ tests had already been developed to identify children who needed special instruction, but Spearman promoted the idea that everyone's overall intelligence could be measured by combining test scores on a diverse mix of items. A summary IQ number could reveal whether a person is a superior, typical, or slow learner, or, using labels of 100 years ago that are no longer used, a genius, imbecile, or idiot. [**Life-Span Link:** See Chapter 11 for the theoretical distribution of IQ scores.]

The belief that there is a *g* continues to influence thinking on intelligence (Nisbett et al., 2012). Many neuroscientists search for genetic underpinnings of intellectual capacity. Many other scientists also seek the one common factor that undergirds IQ—perhaps prenatal brain development, experiences in infancy, or physical health. No one has succeeded in finding *g* or any particular intelligence gene. Some contend that no *g* exists. As one scholar who specializes in the study of intelligence states, "Intelligent researchers will likely continue to disagree about *g*" (Gignac, 2016, p. 84).

Some aspects of brain function in the prefrontal cortex hold promise as the source of *g* (Barbey et al., 2013; Roca et al., 2010). Alternatively, the size of a particular part of the adult midbrain (the caudate nuclei) correlates with adult IQ (Grazioplene et al., 2015). However, given the plasticity of the brain, this could be a consequence rather than a cause of intelligence.

Age and Intelligence

Although most psychometricians throughout the twentieth century assumed that intelligence could be measured and quantified via IQ tests, they disagreed about interpreting the data—especially about whether *g* rises or falls after age 20 or so (Hertzog, 2011). Methodology was one reason for that disagreement. Consider the implications of the three methods used for studying human development introduced in Chapter 1: cross-sectional, longitudinal, and cross-sequential.

LaunchPad
macmillan learning

Video Activity: Research Methods and Cognitive Aging explores how various research methods have been employed to study how intelligence changes with age.

general intelligence (*g*) The idea of *g* assumes that intelligence is one basic trait, underlying all cognitive abilities. According to this concept, people have varying levels of this general ability.

Cross-Sectional Declines

For the first half of the twentieth century, psychologists thought that children gained intelligence each year, reaching a peak in late adolescence. They believed that intelligence gradually declines over the adult years so that a very old person has about as much intelligence as a child. Younger adults were considered smarter than older ones.

This belief was based on the best evidence available at that time. For instance, the U.S. Army tested the aptitude of all draftees in World War I. When the scores of men of various ages were compared, it seemed apparent that intellectual ability reached its peak at about age 18, stayed at that level until the mid-20s, and then declined (Yerkes, 1923).

Hundreds of other cross-sectional studies of IQ in many nations confirmed that younger adults outscored older ones. Age-related decline in IQ was considered proven. The two classic IQ tests, the Stanford-Binet and the WISC/WAIS, are still normed to peak in late adolescence. [**Life-Span Link:** Intelligence and IQ tests are introduced in Chapter 11.]

Smart Enough for the Trenches? These young men were drafted to fight in World War I. Younger men (about age 17 or 18) did better on the military's intelligence tests than slightly older ones did.

● **Observation Quiz** In addition to intellectual ability, what two aspects of this test situation might affect older men differently than younger ones? (see answer, page 586) ↑

Longitudinal Improvements

Shortly after the middle of the twentieth century, Nancy Bayley and Melita Oden (1955) analyzed the intelligence of the adults who had been originally selected as child geniuses by Lewis Terman decades earlier. Bayley was an expert in intelligence testing. She knew that "invariable findings had indicated that most intellectual functions decrease after about 21 years of age" (Bayley, 1966, p. 117). Instead, she found that the IQ scores of these gifted individuals *increased* between ages 20 and 50.

Bayley wondered if their high IQ in childhood protected them from age-related declines. To find out, she retested a large group of adults who had been selected and tested in infancy to be typical (not high IQ) of the population. Their childhood intelligence varied, as would be expected in the general population. However, unexpectedly, their IQ scores did not peak in adolescence; the scores continued to rise.

Why did these new data contradict previous conclusions? As you remember from Chapter 1, cross-sectional research can be misleading because each cohort has unique life experiences. The quality and extent of adult education, cultural opportunities (travel, movies), and sources of information (newspapers, radio, and later, television and the Internet) change every decade. No wonder adults studied longitudinally grow in intelligence.

Earlier cross-sectional research did not take into account the fact that most of the older adults had left school before eighth grade. It was unfair to compare their IQ at age 70 to that of 20-year-olds, almost all of whom attended high school. In retrospect, it is not surprising that the older military volunteers scored lower, not because their minds were declining but because their education was inferior. Cross-sectional comparisons would show younger generations scoring better than the older ones, but longitudinal data find that most individuals increase in IQ from age 20 to age 60.

Powerful evidence that younger adults score higher because of education and health, not because of youth, comes from longitudinal research from many nations. Recent cohorts outscore previous ones. As you remember from Chapter 11, this is the *Flynn effect*.

It is now considered unfair—and scientifically invalid—to compare the IQ scores of adults of various ages to learn about age-related changes. Older adults will score lower, but that does not mean that they have lost intellectual power. Longitudinal research finds that they are more likely to gain, not lose ability, as explained above.

Developmentalists agree that longitudinal studies are more accurate than cross-sectional ones in measuring development over the years. However, longitudinal research on IQ has three drawbacks:

- Repeated testing provides practice, and that itself may improve scores.
- Some participants are not available for retesting because they move without forwarding addresses, or refuse to be retested, or die. They often are those whose IQs are declining. Since more of the brighter people remain, that skews the results of longitudinal research.
- Unusual events (e.g., a major war or a breakthrough in public health) affect each cohort. In addition, more gradual changes—such as widespread use of the Internet or less pollution—make it hard to predict the future based on the history of the past.

Will babies born today be smarter adults than babies born in 2000? Probably. But that is not guaranteed: Cohort effects might make a new generation score lower, not higher, than their elders. New data on the Flynn effect find that generational increases have slowed down in developed nations, albeit not in developing ones (Meisenberg & Woodley, 2013). Thus, health and educational benefits may be less dramatic for the next generation than they were 50 years ago.

Cross-Sequential Research

The best method to understand the effects of aging without the complications of historical change is to combine cross-sectional and longitudinal research, a strategy pioneered by a graduate student at the University of Washington in 1956.

For his Ph.D. research, K. Warner Schaie tested a cross section of 500 adults, aged 20 to 50, on five standard primary mental abilities considered to be the foundation of intelligence: (1) verbal meaning (vocabulary), (2) spatial orientation, (3) inductive reasoning, (4) number ability, and (5) word fluency (rapid verbal associations). His cross-sectional results showed age-related decline in all five abilities, as others had found before. This suggested that biological changes of aging (nature) determined intelligence and that every aspect of IQ was affected, as proponents of *g* might expect (Schaie, 1958). But Schaie was not content with that conclusion.

Schaie thought he might study them longitudinally as well, to confirm the results that were now appearing in various publications. He then had a brilliant idea, to combine longitudinal and cross-sectional methods. Seven years later, he retested his initial participants (longitudinal) and also tested a new group of people who were the same age that his earlier sample had been. Consequently, he could compare people not only to their own previous scores but also to people currently as old as his original group had been when first tested.

The Famous Seattle Study

Seattle Longitudinal Study The first cross-sequential study of adult intelligence. This study began in 1956 and is repeated every seven years.

Schaie did so over his entire career, retesting and adding a new group every seven years. Known as the **Seattle Longitudinal Study,** this was the first *cross-sequential* study of adult intelligence. Schaie confirmed and extended what others had found: Cross-sectional research shows declines, but longitudinal research shows improvement in most mental abilities during adulthood (Schaie, 2005/2013). So, *g* varies more than others thought.

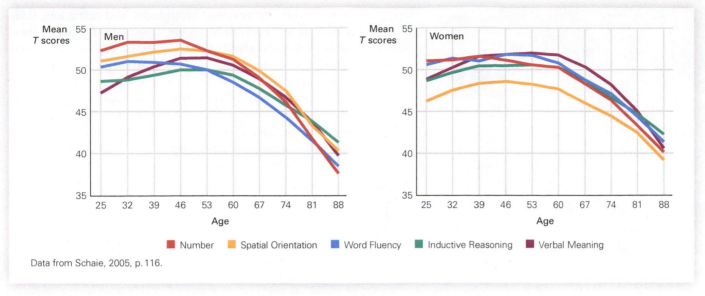

Data from Schaie, 2005, p. 116.

FIGURE 21.1

Age Differences in Intellectual Abilities Cross-sectional data on intellectual abilities at various ages would show much steeper declines. Longitudinal research, in contrast, would show more notable rises. Because Schaie's research is cross-sequential, the trajectories it depicts are more revealing: None of the average scores for the five abilities at any age is above 55 or below 35, which means that the average person of every age still is able to function, intellectually.

As Figure 21.1 shows, Schaie found that each ability at each age has a distinct pattern. Men were initially better at number skills and women at verbal skills, but the two sexes grew closer over time. This reflected trends in the overall culture, which allowed people of both sexes to nurture all of their abilities.

The figure shows that some abilities increase over the years of adulthood. As many other scientists have found, vocabulary is particularly likely to increase. Schaie found that everyone declined by age 60 in at least one of their basic abilities, but not until age 88 did everyone decline from their earlier scores in all five skills.

Other researchers from many nations have found similar trends, although specifics differ (Hunt, 2011a). IQ scores typically increase, or are at least maintained, in adulthood, with timed items showing a decline but verbal items an increase. Individuals and abilities may show marked intellectual ups or downs year by year. Some fade by middle age; others not until decades later (W. Johnson et al., 2014; Kremen et al., 2014).

Cohort Changes

Schaie confirmed the Flynn effect: IQ rises when nations improve childhood nutrition and education, although experts disagree as to what specific factors are most important (Rindermann et al., 2016). As with individuals, the average IQ scores of some nations decrease instead of increase, as happened in France over the past decade (Dutton & Lynn, 2015).

Schaie discovered other cohort changes. Each successive cohort (born at seven-year intervals from 1889 to 1973) scored higher in adulthood than did the previous generations in verbal memory and inductive reasoning. However, number ability (math) peaked for those born in 1924 and then declined slowly in future cohorts until about 1970 (Schaie, 2005/2013).

School curricula influenced these differences: By the mid-twentieth century, reading, writing, and self-expression were more emphasized than they had been

Especially for Older Brothers and Sisters If your younger siblings mock your ignorance of current TV shows and beat you at the latest video games, does that mean your intellect is fading? (see response, page 588)

THINK CRITICALLY: If an adult lived in another nation, would he or she be smarter? And, because of that, would that adult live longer and healthier?

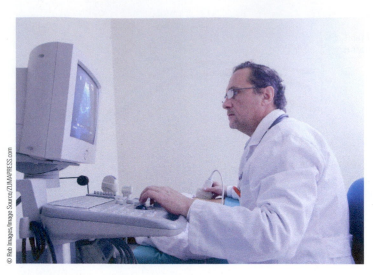

Cohort Changes This expert examining a sonogram illustrates the benefits of recent history. His lifetime experience has made him a better judge of healthy or diseased tissue. Another cohort change is evident here: This photo was taken in Valparaiso, Chile, where the 2015 death rate is only one-third of what it was in 1950.

earlier, while memorizing "math facts" and doing long division were less central. Moreover, fewer adults practice their math skills every day: Scanners at stores, cash registers, and calculators on smartphones make math skills atrophy.

Other cohort effects are that women have increased in IQ since they entered the labor market, and age-related declines appear for everyone about a decade later than they used to (Schaie, 2005/2013), probably because of better communication, education, and health. Nature and nurture interact—and adults are smarter because of it.

Putting It All Together

Many studies using sophisticated designs and statistics have supplanted early cross-sectional, longitudinal, and cross-sequential studies. No study is perfect, because "no design can fully sanitize a study so as to solve the age-cohort-period identification problem" (Hertzog, 2010, p. 5). Cultures, eras, and individuals vary substantially regarding which cognitive abilities are nurtured and tested.

But one conclusion has been verified. From about age 20 to age 70, national values, specific genes, and education are all more influential on IQ scores than is chronological age (W. Johnson et al., 2014).

It is hard to predict intelligence for any particular person, even if genes and age are known. For instance, a study of Swedish twins aged 41 to 84 found differences in verbal ability among the monozygotic twins with equal education. In theory, scores should have been identical, but they were not. As expected, however, age had an effect: Memory and spatial ability declined over time (Finkel et al., 2009).

Considering all of the research, adult intellectual abilities measured on IQ tests sometimes rise, fall, zigzag, or stay the same as age increases. Specific patterns are affected by each person's experiences, with "virtually every possible permutation of individual profiles" (Schaie, 2013, p. 497). This illustrates the life-span perspective: Intelligence is multidirectional, multicultural, multicontextual, and plastic. Although scores on several subtests decline, especially on timed tests, overall ability is usually maintained until late adulthood.

WHAT HAVE YOU LEARNED?

1. Many scientists have searched for the source of *g*; how successful have they been?

2. What does cross-sectional research on IQ throughout adulthood usually find?

3. What does longitudinal research on IQ throughout adulthood usually find?

4. How do historical changes affect the results of longitudinal research?

5. How does cross-sequential research control for cohort effects?

6. Why does IQ vary as much as it does?

Response for Older Brothers and Sisters (from page 587): No. While it is true that each new cohort might be smarter than the previous one in some ways, cross-sequential research suggests that you are smarter than you used to be. Knowing that might help you respond wisely—smiling quietly rather than insisting that you are superior.

Components of Intelligence: Many and Varied

Responding to all of these data, developmentalists are now looking closely at patterns of cognitive gain and loss. They contend that, because virtually every pattern is possible, it is misleading to ask whether intelligence either increases or decreases; it does not move in lockstep with age. There may be "vast domains of cognitive performance . . . that may not follow a common, age-linked trajectory of decline" (Dannefer & Patterson, 2008, p. 116).

Many psychologists describe distinct intellectual abilities, each of which independently rises and falls. Math slowdowns are often apparent by age 40, but verbal ability often keeps rising (Schaie, 2005/2013). Most researchers agree that there are many forms of intelligence (Roberts & Lipnevich, 2012; Goldstein et al., 2015).

We consider here only two proposals, one that posits two distinct abilities and the other, three. [**Life-Span Link:** Gardner's theory of multiple intelligences describes nine abilities, an idea with implications for childhood education, as explained in Chapter 11.]

Two Clusters of Intelligence

In the 1960s, a leading personality researcher, Raymond Cattell, teamed up with a promising graduate student, John Horn, to study intelligence tests. They concluded that adult intelligence is best understood by grouping various measures into two categories, which they called *fluid* and *crystallized*.

Fluid Intelligence

As its name implies, **fluid intelligence** is like water, flowing to its own level no matter where it happens to be. Fluid intelligence is quick and flexible, enabling people to learn anything, even things that are unfamiliar and unconnected to what they already know. Curiosity, learning for the joy of it, solving abstract puzzles, and the thrill at discovering something new are marks of fluid intelligence (Silvia & Sanders, 2010).

People high in fluid abilities can draw inferences, understand relationships between concepts, and readily process new ideas and facts in part because their working memory is large and flexible. Someone high in fluid intelligence is quick and creative with words and numbers and enjoys intellectual puzzles. The kinds of questions that test fluid intelligence among Western adults might be:

What comes next in each of these two series?*

    4 9 1 6 2 5 3
    V X Z B D

Puzzles are often used to measure fluid intelligence, with speedy solutions given bonus points (as on many IQ tests). Immediate recall—of nonsense words, of numbers, of a sentence just read—is one indicator because working memory is crucial for fluid intelligence, especially in timed tests (Chuderski, 2013; Nisbett et al., 2012).

Since fluid intelligence appears to be disconnected from past learning, it may seem impractical. Not so. A study of adults aged 34 to 83 found that stressors did not vary by age but did vary by fluid intelligence. People high in fluid intelligence were more exposed to stress but were less likely to suffer from it: They used their intellect to turn stress into positive experiences (Stawski et al., 2010).

The ability to detoxify stress may be one reason that high fluid intelligence in emerging adulthood leads to longer life and higher IQ later on. Fluid intelligence is associated with openness to new experiences and overall brain health (Ziegler et al., 2012; Silvia & Sanders, 2010). (Ways to cope with stress are discussed later in this chapter, when you will see that adaptive cognition provides the best defense against the problems of life.)

fluid intelligence Those types of basic intelligence that make learning of all sorts quick and thorough. Abilities such as short-term memory, abstract thought, and speed of thinking are all usually considered part of fluid intelligence.

---

* The correct answers are 6 and F. The clue is to think of multiplication (squares) and the alphabet: Some series are much more difficult to complete.

crystallized intelligence Those types of intellectual ability that reflect accumulated learning. Vocabulary and general information are examples. Crystallized intelligence increases with age, while fluid intelligence declines.

Crystallized Intelligence

The accumulation of facts, information, and knowledge as a result of education and experience is called **crystallized intelligence**. The size of a person's vocabulary, the knowledge of chemical formulas, and the long-term memory for dates in history all indicate crystallized intelligence. Tests designed to measure this intelligence might include questions like these:

> What is the meaning of the word *eleemosynary*?
> Who was Descartes?
> Explain the difference between a tangent and a triangle.
> Why does the city of Peking no longer exist?

Although such questions seem to measure achievement more than aptitude, these two are connected, especially in adulthood. Intelligent adults read widely, think deeply, and remember what they learn, so their achievement reflects their aptitude. Thus, crystallized intelligence is an outgrowth of fluid intelligence (Nisbett et al., 2012).

Vocabulary, for example, improves with reading. Using the words *joy, ecstasy, bliss*, and *delight*—each appropriately, with distinct nuances (quite apart from the drugs, perfumes, or yogurts that use these names)—is a sign of intelligence. Remember the knowledge base (Chapter 12): As people know more, they learn more. That explains why education (e.g., high school, college, post-graduate) is considered a rough indicator of adult IQ (Nisbett et al., 2012).

Both Together Now

To reflect the total picture of a person's intellectual aptitude, both fluid and crystallized intelligence must be measured (Hunt, 2011a). Age complicates the IQ calculation because scores on items measuring fluid intelligence decrease with age, whereas scores on items measuring crystallized intelligence increase. Further, there is some overlap between the two kinds of intelligence, such that someone high in fluid intelligence is likely to become high in crystalized intelligence (Ziegler et al., 2012).

Think Before Acting Both of these adults need to combine fluid and crystallized intelligence, insight and intuition, logic and experience. One *(left)* is a surgeon, studying X-rays before picking up her scalpel. The other *(right)* appears to be an architect, using working memory and abstract reasoning.

The combination of these two types of intelligence makes IQ fairly steady from age 30 to age 70. Although slowdown in reaction time and, hence, in some aspects of fluid intelligence begins at age 20 or so, it is rarely apparent until massive declines affect crystallized intelligence. Only then do overall IQ scores fall.

Horn and Cattell wrote that they had:

> shown intelligence to both increase and decrease with age—depending upon the definition of intelligence adopted, fluid or crystallized! Our results illustrate an essential fallacy implicit in the construction of omnibus measures of intelligence.
>
> [Horn & Cattell, 1967, p. 124]

In other words, it may be foolish to try to measure *g,* a single omnibus intelligence, because components need to be measured separately. In testing for *g,* real developmental changes will be masked because fluid and crystallized abilities cancel each other out.

Three Forms of Intelligence

Robert Sternberg (1988, 2003, 2011, 2015) agrees that a single intelligence score is misleading. As first mentioned in Chapter 11, Sternberg proposed three fundamental forms of intelligence: analytic, creative, and practical, each of which can be tested. (See Table 21.1.)

Analytic intelligence includes all of the mental processes that foster academic proficiency by making efficient learning, remembering, and thinking possible. Thus, it draws on abstract planning, strategy selection, focused attention, and information processing, as well as on verbal and logical skills.

Strengths in those areas are valuable in emerging adulthood, particularly in college and in graduate school. Multiple-choice tests and brief essays that call forth remembered information, with only one right answer, indicate analytic intelligence.

analytic intelligence A form of intelligence that involves such mental processes as abstract planning, strategy selection, focused attention, and information processing, as well as verbal and logical skills.

TABLE 21.1	Sternberg's Three Forms of Intelligence		
	Analytic Intelligence	**Creative Intelligence**	**Practical Intelligence**
Mental processes	▪ Abstract planning ▪ Strategizing ▪ Focused attention ▪ Verbal skills	▪ Imagination ▪ Appreciation of the unexpected or unusual ▪ Originality ▪ Vision	▪ Adaptive actions ▪ Understanding and assessing daily problems ▪ Applied skills and knowledge
Valued for	▪ Analyzing ▪ Learning and understanding ▪ Remembering ▪ Thinking	▪ Intellectual flexibility ▪ Sense of humor ▪ Future hopes ▪ Works of art	▪ Adaptability ▪ Concrete knowledge ▪ Real-world experience ▪ Effective action
Indicated by	▪ Multiple-choice tests ▪ Brief essays ▪ Recall of information ▪ Logic	▪ Inventiveness ▪ Innovation ▪ Resourcefulness	▪ Performance in real situations ▪ "Street smarts" ▪ Accomplishments

Based on Sternberg, 1988, 2003, 2011, 2015.

creative intelligence A form of intelligence that involves the capacity to be intellectually flexible and innovative.

practical intelligence The intellectual skills used in everyday problem solving. (Sometimes called *tacit intelligence*.)

Creative intelligence involves the capacity to be intellectually flexible and innovative. Creative thinking is divergent rather than convergent, valuing the unexpected, imaginative, and unusual rather than standard and conventional answers. Sternberg developed tests of creative intelligence that include writing a short story titled "The Octopus's Sneakers" or planning an advertising campaign for a new doorknob. Those with many novel ideas earn high scores.

Practical intelligence involves the capacity to adapt one's behavior to the demands of a given situation. This capacity includes an accurate grasp of the expectations and needs of the people involved and an awareness of the particular skills that are called for, along with the ability to use these insights effectively. Practical intelligence is sometimes called *tacit intelligence* because it is not obvious on tests. Instead, it comes from "the school of hard knocks" and is sometimes called "street smarts," not "book smarts."

The Three Intelligences in Adulthood

The benefits of practical intelligence in adult life are obvious once we recall the cognitive tasks of adulthood. Few adults need to define obscure words or deduce the next element in a number sequence (analytic intelligence); and few need to write a new type of music, restructure local government, or invent a new gadget (creative intelligence). Ideally, those few have already found a niche for themselves and have learned to rely on people with practical intelligence to implement their analytic or creative ideas.

Almost every adult needs practical intelligence. Adults must deal with challenges: maintaining a home; advancing a career; managing money; sifting information from media, mail, and the Internet; addressing the emotional needs of lovers, relatives, neighbors, and colleagues (Blanchard-Fields, 2007). Schaie found that scores on tests of practical intelligence were steadier than scores on other kinds of tests from age 20 to age 70, with no notable decrement, in part because these skills are needed throughout life (Schaie, 2005/2013).

Practical intelligence is the most useful of the three. Without it, a solution found by analytic intelligence might fail because people resist academic brilliance as unrealistic and elite, as the term *ivory tower* implies.

The history of medicine is filled with intelligent ideas that were rejected. For example, the idea that stomach ulcers were caused by bacteria was not believed until an Australian internist deliberately drank infectious broth that made him sick. Similarly, a stunningly creative idea may be rejected as ridiculous rather than sensible—if it is not accompanied by practical intelligence.

The general need for practical intelligence is clear if you imagine a business manager, a school principal, a political leader, or a parent trying to change routine practices—perhaps for a good reason, because the old way was inefficient or destructive, but without practical intelligence. If the new procedures are not compatible with the group and are misunderstood, then the workers, teachers, voters, or family members will misinterpret them, predict failure, and refuse to change.

Flexibility is needed for practical intelligence (K. Sloan, 2009), and, as you remember from Chapter 18, this characterizes postformal thought. Ideally, practical intelligence continues to be refined throughout adulthood as each new experience provides feedback. Failures can be either defeats or learning opportunities. This

© Peter Beck/Corbis

Smart Farmer; Smart Teacher This school field trip is not to a museum or a fire station but to a wheat field, where children study grains that will become bread. Like this creative teacher, modern farmers use every kind of intelligence. To succeed, they need to analyze soil, fertilizer, and pests (analytic intelligence); to anticipate market prices and food fads (creative intelligence); and to know what crops and seed varieties grow in each acre of their land as they manage their workers (practical intelligence).

idea is relevant for students in college (Smith, 2015), but it may be even more crucial in the daily frustrations of adult life.

No abstract test can assess practical intelligence because context is crucial. Instead, to measure this kind of intelligence, adults need to be observed coping with daily life. In hiring a new employee, a hiring committee might describe an actual situation and ask how the applicant would handle it. Such tests might be better predictors of performance than traditional ability tests (Campion et al., 2014).

For instance, in one test of management ability, a prospective employee is asked:

> *You assign a new project to one of your subordinates, who protests, saying it cannot be done without more resources and time. Rank your possible responses, from best to worst. Explain your reasoning.*
>
> *a. You find someone else to do the job.*
> *b. You ask your subordinate to figure out how it can be done with current constraints.*
> *c. You reallocate work, to give your subordinate more time.*
> *d. You fire the subordinate.*
> *e. You ask your supervisor what to do.*
> *f. You postpone the new task until you find more resources.*
>
> *[Salter & Highhouse, 2009]*

Situational tests can be used in many fields. They are often used in the medical professions: Review books have been made for would-be doctors preparing for such tests (e.g., Varian & Cartwright, 2013). Because practical intelligence is crucial on the job, probationary periods, internships, and apprenticeships are common.

Everyone should use the strengths and guard against the limitations of each type. Choosing which intelligence to use takes wisdom, which Sternberg considers a fourth ingredient of successful intelligence. He writes:

> One needs creativity to generate novel ideas, analytical intelligence to ascertain whether they are good ideas, practical intelligence to implement the ideas and persuade others of their value, and wisdom to ensure that the ideas help reach a common good.
>
> *[Sternberg, 2012, p. 21]*

[**Life-Span Link:** Wisdom is discussed in Chapter 24.]

Age and Culture

Which kind of intelligence is most needed and valued depends partly on age and partly on culture. Think about Sternberg's three types. Analytic intelligence is usually valued in high school and college, as students try to remember and analyze various ideas. However, although students who are considered "smart" usually have analytic intelligence, that is not enough in adulthood.

Creative intelligence is prized if life circumstances change and new challenges arise; it is much more valued in some cultures and countries than in others (Kaufman & Sternberg, 2006). In times of social upheaval, or in certain professions (such as the arts), creativity is a better predictor of accomplishment than is IQ. However, creativity can be too innovative, causing creative people to be ignored, scorned, or even killed. Many creative geniuses—Vincent Van Gogh and Igor Stravinsky, for example—were unrecognized until years after they died.

Think about these three intelligences cross-culturally. Creative individuals would be critical of tradition and therefore would be tolerated only in some political environments. Analytic individuals might be seen as absentminded, head-in-the-clouds dreamers. Practical intelligence, though valued less within school settings, might be most useful.

Yet practical intelligence could be used for evil as well as good. Some major corporations and religious movements—Enron and Jonestown come to mind—succeeded

What Kind of Intelligence? Adult intelligence is difficult to assess because context is crucial. What kind of intelligence would you need to successfully herd camels in Saudi Arabia, or to drive a taxi using an app that connects you to customers in Bejing?

because of the practical intelligence of the leaders. Wisdom is essential to consider the long-term, ethical implications of practical ideas, yet wisdom includes the recognition that one person's wisdom might be another's folly.

Difficult as it is to determine who is truly smart, it is even more difficult to judge which nation or ethnic group is smartest, in part because each culture has its own standards to determine the combination of abilities, and sometimes those standards make sense in one place more than in another.

Currently in the United States, of Gardner's nine intelligences, linguistic and mathematical intelligence are prized, and those two abilities are the core of most tests of aptitude and achievement. But in some other cultures, the ability to dance (kinesthetic intelligence), or to grow herbs (naturalistic intelligence), or to pray (existential intelligence) might be more crucial.

In another specific example, there is a test to measure intelligent parenting, called the KIDI (Knowledge of Infant Development). In the United States, high scores on the KIDI often correlate with intelligent baby care (e.g., Howard, 2010; McMillin et al., 2015).

However, sometimes criteria that are well suited in one cultural context might not be useful in another. This was illustrated by a social scientist who did research among the Ache, an ethnic group who live in the jungle in Paraguay. The Ache tribal people were respectful and deferential to the researcher on repeated visits, until she and her husband arrived at their study site with their infant daughter in tow. The Ache greeted her in a whole new way. They took her aside and in friendly and intimate but no-nonsense terms told her all the things she was doing wrong as a mother. . . .

> This older woman sat with me and told me I *must* sleep with my daughter. They were horrified that I had a basket with me for her to sleep in. . . . here was a group of forest hunter-gatherers, people living in what Westerners would call basic conditions, giving instructions to a highly educated woman from a technologically sophisticated culture.
>
> *[Hurtado, quoted in Small, 1998, pp. 213–214]*

The intelligent way to care for an infant in the United States (a basket would allow easy transport and would protect against SIDS) was not intelligent for the Ache, where a baby who didn't sleep with her mother might be poisoned by snakes, bitten by wild dogs, or kidnapped by strangers (that did happen among the Ache).

It is not obvious when a custom is a result of cultural wisdom (as for the Ache), when it is a foolish or even harmful idea that somehow became popular (as was the idea that cigarette smoking is sophisticated), and when it ushers in a social advance. A controversial idea from Earl Hunt, a psychologist who studies intelligence, is that the nations with the most advanced economies and greatest national wealth are those that make best use of **cognitive artifacts**—that is, ways to amplify and extend general cognitive ability (Hunt, 2012).

Historically, written language, the number system, universities, and the scientific method were cognitive artifacts. Each of these artifacts extended human intellectual abilities by allowing people to learn more quickly and extensively than they previously had. Sheer survival (in earlier centuries, more newborns died than lived) and longer life (few people survived to age 50) resulted from cognitive artifacts. The germ theory of disease, for instance, was developed because doctors were able to do research, write, publish, and then learn from each other (Hunt, 2011a).

In more recent times, preventive health care, clean water, electricity, global travel, and the Internet have resulted in advanced societies. According to this idea, smart people are better able to use the cognitive artifacts of their society to advance their own intelligence. Then they develop more cognitive artifacts, and the whole community benefits.

For instance, developed nations provide preschool and kindergarten to all children, unlike in former times when first grade was really first. That increases the average IQ of the new generation, which eventually advances the nation. However, although generally that strategy works, it also is true that implementation is crucial—sometimes early education makes no difference (Muennig, 2015). In other words, a cognitive artifact depends partly on the people who use it.

Education at every level is often considered a cultural artifact, since in earlier times many people had no schooling. The benefits of education as an artifact were shown in a meta-analysis of 167 nations comparing disaster deaths and education, measured by the proportion of women, aged 20 to 39, with at least an eighth-grade education (Lutz et al., 2014). The hypothesis was that educated people are more likely to use various cognitive artifacts, such as safer housing construction, stockpiling supplies, physical and mental health care, understanding warnings. Elaborate statistical testing found that "female education is indeed strongly associated with a reduction in disaster fatalities" but national wealth was not (Lutz et al., 2014, p. 1061).

cognitive artifacts Intellectual tools passed down from generation to generation that may assist in learning within societies.

Everyone Laughing Cognitive artifacts need not be specific inventions, such as the airplane or the printing press, but can be a phrase or joke that captures and crystallizes public thought. Here Jon Stewart works with writers to find the right words that will make millions laugh.

WHAT HAVE YOU LEARNED?

1. Why would a person prefer to have greater crystallized intelligence than fluid intelligence?

2. Why would a person prefer to have greater fluid intelligence than crystallized intelligence?

3. If you want to convince your professors that you are smart, what might you do and what intelligence does that involve?

4. If you want to convince your neighbors to compost their food and yard waste, what might you do and what kind of intelligence does that involve?

5. What kinds of tests could measure creative intelligence?

6. What cognitive artifact has most benefited you and how did that happen?

Selective Gains and Losses

Aging neurons, cultural pressures, historical conditions, and past education all affect adult cognition. None of these can be controlled directly by an individual. Nonetheless, many researchers believe that adults can make crucial choices about intellectual development, deciding whether or not to develop their minds.

Optimization with Compensation

selective optimization with compensation The idea that people compensate for physical and cognitive losses, becoming more proficient in activities or topics that they choose.

Paul and Margret Baltes (1990) developed a theory called **selective optimization with compensation** to describe the "general process of systematic functioning" (Baltes, 2003, p. 25), by which people maintain a balance in their lives as they grow older. They believe that people seek to *optimize* their development, *selecting* the best way to *compensate* for physical and cognitive losses, becoming more proficient at activities they want to perform well.

Selective optimization with compensation applies to every aspect of life, ranging from choosing friends to playing baseball. Each adult seeks to maximize gains and minimize losses, practicing some abilities and ignoring others. Choices are critical, because any ability can be enhanced or diminished, depending on how, when, and why a person uses it. It is possible to "teach an old dog new tricks," but learning requires that adults *want* to learn those new tricks.

When adults are motivated to do well, few age-related deficits are apparent. However, compared with younger adults, older adults are less motivated to put forth their best effort when the task at hand is not particularly engaging (Hess et al., 2009b). That works against them if they take an IQ test.

As Baltes and Baltes (1990) explain, selective optimization means that each adult selects certain aspects of intelligence to optimize and neglects the rest. If the ignored aspects happen to be the ones measured on intelligence tests, then IQ scores will fall, even if the adult's selection improves (optimizes) other aspects of intellect. The brain is plastic over the entire life span, developing new dendrites and activation sequences, adjusting to whatever the person chooses to learn (Karmiloff-Smith, 2010).

An Example: East Timor

For example, suppose someone is highly motivated to learn about a particular area of the world, perhaps East Timor, a tiny nation that has been independent since 2002. That person goes to the library, selecting key articles and the two dozen books in English about East Timor, ignoring other interesting topics (*selection*). Selection might also include getting someone else to do the tasks this person finds less interesting, such as paying bills on time and balancing the checkbook.

Then suppose that person's aging vision makes it hard to read the fine print of some news articles about East Timor. That requires *compensation*—new glasses, a magnifier, increased font size. The person might also notice that memory is sometimes shaky, so note-taking strategies may include color coding, file folders, and underlining. The result: If a local lawmaker or history buff wants to know about genocide, or Indonesia, or the United Nations, then that person who specialized in East Timor can provide knowledge that few others have (*optimization*).

If the expert on East Timor takes an IQ test that includes *tamarind* as a vocabulary word, that person might score high. However, the same person might fail math questions, since someone else managed the finances. Thus, knowledge increases in depth but decreases in breadth as people grow older.

Multitasking

One example of selective optimization is multitasking, which becomes more difficult with every passing decade (Reuter-Lorenz & Sylvester, 2005). Actually, multitasking slows down everyone of every age, but awareness of the slowdown is more acute with age.

This fact is obvious when people drive a car while talking on a cell phone. Such behavior is dangerous for everyone but particularly for older drivers, because as the brain focuses on the conversation, the neurological shift needed to react to a darting pedestrian is slower (Asbridge et al., 2013). Some jurisdictions require drivers to use hands-free phones, as if the distraction originates in the arms. These misguided laws have not reduced traffic accidents resulting from cell phone use because the multitasking brain is the problem, not the arms.

Some say that passenger conversation is as distracting as cell phone talk, but that is not true: Years of practice have taught adult passengers (though not young children) when to stop talking so that the driver can focus on the road (Charlton, 2009). If passengers do not quiet down on their own, experienced drivers stop listening and replying because they know they must concentrate.

This is why statements such as "I can't do everything at once" and "Don't rush me" are more often spoken by older adults than by teenagers. Adults compensate for slower thinking by selecting one task at a time. Resources within the brain are increasingly limited with age, but compensation allows optimal functioning (Freund, 2008).

One father tried to explain this concept to his son as follows:

I told my son: triage
Is the main art of aging.
At midlife, everything
Sings of it. In law
Or healing, learning or play,
Buying or selling—above all
In remembering—the rule is
Cut losses, let profits ring.
Specifics rise and fall
By selection.

[Hamill, 1991]

Accumulating Stressors

Many people prioritize immediate comfort over long-term health and cognition. Those are momentary gains that lead to long-term losses. As we saw in Chapter 20, choices regarding foods, drugs, exercise, and health care affect blood circulation in the brain, reducing intellect. In addition, harmful choices increase stress. Stressors do not merely correlate with illness of all kinds—they *cause* illness, as hundreds of studies on the immune system have found (Prenderville et al., 2015; Reed & Raison, 2016).

Sometimes people are told "it's all in your head" when they complain of physical ailments. That is neither fair nor accurate. A recent comparison between stress-free adults and adults who were caring for a family member with brain cancer found that the caregivers had signaling factors in their brains that increased expression of genes for inflammation. Thus, basic immunity suffers when stress is high (G. Miller et al., 2014). As in this case, caregiving is sometimes necessary as well as commendable. But it takes a toll on the caregiver.

Indeed, many demands of modern life increase stress, and those demands may become **stressors**—experiences, circumstances, or conditions that affect a person. A stress is external. When stresses are internalized, they becoming stressors.

Video Activity: The Effects of Psychological Stress outlines the explanations and causes of stress and then allows students to evaluate the stress in their own lives.

stressor Any situation, event, experience, or other stimulus that causes a person to feel stressed. Many circumstances that seem to be stresses become stressors for some people but not for others.

A Moment or a Lifetime Appearances are deceptive. It looks as if the South Carolina mother *(left)* whose son was just rescued from a flood is more stressed than the father *(right)* from Syria who is walking to Macedonia. However, recovery from stress often depends on the attitudes of other people. The mother is aided by six visible professionals; the father is with other refugees who will be refused entry at the border.

One developmental question is whether adults experience more stress currently than adults did in former times. Modern conditions have reduced some stresses—fewer people are killed and fewer die young.

However, the rate and scope of disasters—caused by human and natural events—is increasing. Floods, earthquakes, raging fires, and landslides are in the news almost every day, and news of terrorism, mass shootings, and civil wars punctuate our lives. Each causes stress not only for everyone who lives through such events but also for people who read about them (Leaning & Guha-Sapir, 2013).

The World Health Organization defines disasters as unexpected events—both from nature (floods, earthquakes, and so on) and from nurture (bombs, epidemics)—that cause at least 10 deaths and 100 serious injuries. The rate between 2000 and 2010 was 10 times that of a century ago and 3 times the rate 20 years earlier (Leaning & Guha-Sapir, 2013).

Globalization and high-speed communication networks can mean that each disaster adds stress to millions far from the event—think of television and Internet footage of 9/11, or the earthquake and tsunami in Japan, or beheadings in Syria. Research finds that watching immediate coverage of disasters increases acute stress reactions to later disasters—even for people far from the trauma and personally unaffected (Garfin et al., 2015).

Modern communication has advantages, of course. But knowing about the rest of the world can be stressful. Think about the Zika virus. Every pregnant person (the United States has about 4 million of them) who sees a mosquito is stressed.

In addition, personal events that are stressful—divorce, intellectual disabilities, relocation, immigration, job loss—are more common than they were, so every adult experiences more stress. Finally, every life has many minor stresses called *hassles*—traffic jams, noise at night, rude strangers, computer malfunction. Hassles, because they are ongoing and chronic, may be more damaging during adulthood than major stresses.

Thus, every adult experiences many stresses, and every adult may have his or her physical and psychological health harmed by them. The question is whether adults learn better coping measures as they mature. It is not clear that they do, but evidence suggests that they might (Aldwin, 2010).

Coping Methods

Adults use many destructive ways to cope with stress: drug abuse, obesity, too much sleep, too little exercise, smoking, drinking, eating sweets, avoiding doctors. Adults choose all of these, and all impair thought while reducing stress—temporarily. Stress affects more than logic; chronic stress increases depression and other psychological illnesses that impair thinking, and it attacks the brain itself (Marin et al., 2011; McEwen & Gianaros, 2011).

Reactions to stress can cause yet more stress, which means that stressors accumulate. For example, a longitudinal study of married couples in their 30s found that if the husband's health deteriorated, the chance of divorce increased. Thus, one reaction to the stress of illness was to do something that increased stress. This effect was apparent with all couples, particularly for well-educated European Americans (Teachman, 2010).

The rate of divorce also increases when parents have children with special needs (Price, 2010). Conversely, for some couples having a child with serious problems brings partners closer together (Solomon, 2012). Apparently, having a child with special needs is always stressful and thus creates a stressor. But how people then cope with that stressor is crucial to their mental health.

Coping involves cognition because people choose what to do.

1. **Avoidant coping,** ignoring a problem, either literally forgetting it or hiding it (one person who owed back taxes threw all official letters under his bed, unopened), is the worst way of coping—it increases depression and the risk of suicide.
2. **Problem-focused coping** is attacking a stressor directly—for instance, by confronting a difficult boss, or by moving out of a dangerous neighborhood.
3. **Emotion-focused coping** is changing emotional reactions—for instance, from anger to acceptance, making the stressor disappear and becoming stronger and more empathic because of it.

Biologically and culturally, the two sexes may respond differently to stress. Men tend to be problem-focused, reacting in a "fight-or-flight" manner. Their sympathetic nervous system (faster heart rate, increased adrenaline) prepares them for attack or escape. Their testosterone level rises when they confront a problem and decreases if they fail. From childhood, boys are encouraged to fight back, and adult men are more likely to rage openly, use force, or disappear.

Females, however, may be emotion-focused, likely to "tend and befriend"—that is, to seek the company of other people when they are under pressure. Their bodies produce oxytocin, a hormone that leads them to seek confidential and caring interactions (Taylor, 2006; Taylor et al., 2000). Their first reaction when something goes wrong might be to call a friend. A woman might be troubled if a man won't talk about his problems; a man might get upset if a woman does not take his advice and solve her problems.

This distinction appeared among 634 mothers and fathers who had lost a baby, either stillborn at birth or dying within the first days and months of life (D. Christiansen et al., 2014). The women were more likely to anxiously seek social support from other people (sometimes overprotecting another child), and the men were more likely to avoid attachment (sometimes spending hours away from home).

Gender differences should not be exaggerated. Both problem- and emotion-focused coping can be effective; everyone should sometimes fight and sometimes

Especially for Doctors and Nurses A patient complains of a headache or stomachache, but laboratory tests and CAT scans find no physical cause. What could it be? (see response, page 600)

avoidant coping A method of responding to a stressor by ignoring, forgetting, or hiding it.

problem-focused coping A strategy to deal with stress by tackling a stressful situation directly.

emotion-focused coping A strategy to deal with stress by changing feelings about the stressor rather than changing the stressor itself.

Win McNamee/Getty Images

Nine Were Killed, and Then... Coping with the 2015 murder of nine people at a prayer meeting in Charleston, South Carolina, led some people to depression, others to revenge, others to forgiveness. Most—black and white—turned their emotions to public mourning (shown here) and then anger at the Confederate flag flying above the State House, where South Carolina government leaders work. The legislators, mostly white, took action, voting 94 to 20 to take the flag down. Both emotion-focused and problem-focused coping were evident.

Response for Doctors and Nurses
(from page 599): Stressors increase allostatic load, so the headache or stomachache could be caused by stress. Be careful, however, because both you and the patient may be engaged in avoidant coping. The patient may deny the stress and blame you for suggesting it, and you yourself may be avoiding responsibility. Emotional and contextual problems impact physical health, so medical experts cannot dismiss them.

religious coping The process of turning to faith as a method of coping with stress.

Marriage in Trouble? Stephanie Brown, a marriage counselor, is helping a couple understand each other. When people have trouble dealing with life—from global problems such as the Syrian civil war to more personal problems like family arguments—counselors can help the individuals. But the root cause is often in the social and political context, not the people. That is the case here: This is Project Sanctuary, a six-day retreat for military couples. Such couples have high rates of divorce.

befriend. In the study of bereaved parents, the researchers noted that both parents sometimes suffered from PTSD (post-traumatic stress disorder) and suggested that they could help each other (D. Christiansen et al., 2014). A review suggests that gender differences, including fight-or-flight versus tend-and-befriend responses, are much smaller in reality than in popular assumptions (Carothers & Reis, 2013).

Choosing Methods

Not only do people need to figure out the best strategy to deal with each particular problem, but they also need to figure out when other people will help and when they will not (Aldwin, 2007). Getting social support is generally a good strategy—other people provide suggestions, lighten a load, and add humor or perspective (Fiori & Denckla, 2012). But sometimes other people criticize, distract, or delay a person's coping. Choose carefully.

Another kind of choice is needed, not just who but how. The best coping strategy depends on the situation. Worse than either problem- or emotion-focused coping is avoidant coping—denying a problem until it escalates or takes a physical toll, such as causing high blood pressure, digestive difficulties, or even a heart attack. Avoidance increases allostatic load.

Age brings an advantage here. Emerging adulthood is "a time of heightened hassles." Once life settles down, some stresses (dating, job hunting, moving) occur less frequently. Adults "are more adept at arranging their lives to minimize the occurrence of stressors" (Aldwin, 2007, p. 298). (See Visualizing Development, p. 601.)

Further, experience may teach adults how to handle stresses. Crucial is the sense of control, which may build during adulthood if various stresses are successfully met (Skinner & Zimmer-Gembeck, 2010).

For example, although Hurricane Katrina occurred years ago, survivors continue to cope with the aftermath, and social scientists continue to study them. Children's success at coping depended on the presence and reactions of their parents. Adults' coping varied a great deal.

One team considered religious beliefs before and after the disaster. Victims who believed in a vengeful and punishing God continued to suffer for years, but those who believed that God is caring and benevolent coped well, experiencing *post-traumatic growth,* the opposite of PTSD (Chan & Rhodes, 2013).

This illustrates a type of emotional coping called **religious coping,** believing that there is divine purpose for problems. Social scientists find that religious coping is particularly likely when people have unexpected illnesses or disasters. As with other forms of coping, religious coping sometimes mitigates a stressor, and other times it makes it worse (Burke et al., 2013; Thuné-Boyle et al., 2013). During adulthood, religious faith and practice tend to increase; past experience overcoming stress may be one reason.

Of course, natural disasters, such as earthquakes, and personal tragedies, such as the death of a loved one, are always stressful at the time. The surprise is that they may be overcome, with many adults reinterpreting events. Instead of dwelling

Stress in Adulthood

Stresses and coping strategies differ from generation to generation. Developmentalists believe that emerging adults today may have more stresses than in the past because education is increasingly important and unemployment is higher. However, adults without jobs or supportive families may be more stressed than emerging adults since they feel more responsible for their problems. Fortunately, the ability to cope may improve with age.

Just as there are many ways to cope with stress, there are many ways to measure it. One common way is to simply ask people what stresses them and another way is experience sampling—beeping people at random times to find out what they are doing and feeling at the moment. As you see from the charts below, the results may differ.

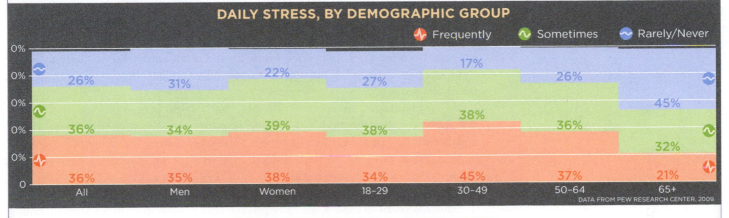

DAILY STRESS, BY DEMOGRAPHIC GROUP

Frequently   Sometimes   Rarely/Never

	All	Men	Women	18–29	30–49	50–64	65+
Rarely/Never	26%	31%	22%	27%	17%	26%	45%
Sometimes	36%	34%	39%	38%	38%	36%	32%
Frequently	36%	35%	38%	34%	45%	37%	21%

DATA FROM PEW RESEARCH CENTER, 2009.

WHAT CAUSES STRESS IN DAILY LIFE

Depending on exactly how the question is phrased, adults identify different triggers for their daily stress. For many, it is work, family, health, and safety concerns that worry them. But, surprisingly, the activity that is most stressful is housework.

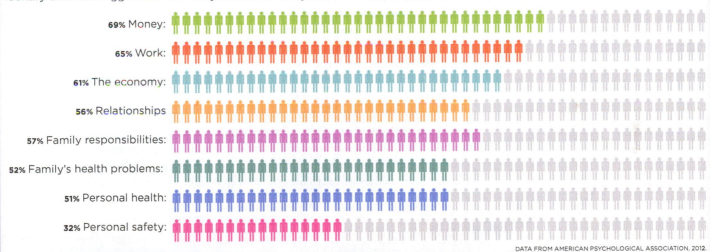

69% Money:

65% Work:

61% The economy:

56% Relationships

57% Family responsibilities:

52% Family's health problems:

51% Personal health:

32% Personal safety:

DATA FROM AMERICAN PSYCHOLOGICAL ASSOCIATION, 2012.

ACTIVITIES THAT ARE LEAST STRESSFUL, RANKED BY WOMEN IN TEXAS, 2004

= most stressful activities   = least stressful activities

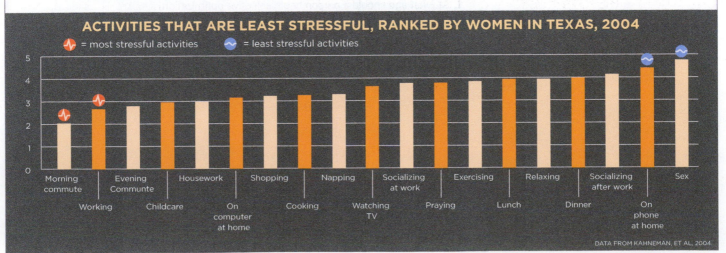

Morning commute · Working · Evening Commute · Childcare · Housework · On computer at home · Shopping · Cooking · Napping · Watching TV · Socializing at work · Praying · Exercising · Lunch · Relaxing · Dinner · Socializing after work · On phone at home · Sex

DATA FROM KAHNEMAN, ET AL, 2004.

on their misfortune, they emphasize their good fortune—not "why me?" but "it could have been worse." Some adults reinterpret stress as challenges, not stressors, even if outsiders would consider them threats (Reich et al., 2010).

In fact, one study of Israeli ex-prisoners of war found that, seventeen years after their release, those who were most likely to reach post-traumatic growth were those who initially experienced post-traumatic stress (Dekel et al., 2012). In other words, the immediate experience of stress does not necessarily harm adult development lifelong; depending on the adults' reaction to it, the stress may have positive effects.

Similar results are found in women who survive breast cancer: They often experience post-traumatic growth, although specifics vary by the age of the woman (Boyle et al., 2016). Since every decade of an adult's life is likely to bring some stresses, if the adult manages to cope well, every decade can also bring post-traumatic growth.

When challenges are successfully met, not only do people feel more effective and powerful, but the body's damaging responses to stressors—increased heart and breathing rates, hormonal changes, immune system breakdowns, cognitive lapses, and so on—are averted. Indeed, effective coping may strengthen the immune system and promote health (Bandura, 1997). For adults, potential stressors can become positive turning points (Reich et al., 2010; Tugade, 2010).

Humans seem to have a recovery reserve that is activated under stress, similar to the organ reserve explained in Chapter 17. According to a related set of studies, it seems that extra effort and alertness are summoned when emergencies arise, even if those affected are overtired and in a noisy environment. This reserve works well in the moments of the emergency, especially if people feel there is something they can do. Thousands stood in long lines to donate blood after 9/11; teachers in New Orleans after Katrina were eager to get back to work; the New York City Pride March was the largest ever after the 2016 killing of 49 Latino LGBT individuals in Orlando, Florida; volunteers stacked sandbags day and night when a flooded river threatened towns in the Midwest; and so on.

This may explain a familiar reaction to final exams in college: Some students study intensely, perform well . . . and then collapse, maybe even getting sick as the immune system shuts down after their last exam. More research is needed, but it seems possible that adults call forth extra energy and gradually develop better coping methods as they adapt to life (Masten & Wright, 2010; Aldwin & Gilmer, 2013).

WHAT HAVE YOU LEARNED?

1. At what age should a person begin selective optimization?
2. What is the connection between stress and health?
3. In what situations is emotion-focused coping the best?
4. In what situations is problem-focused coping the best?
5. Why is religious coping more emotion-focused than problem-focused?

Expert Cognition

Another way to describe selective optimization is to say that everyone develops *expertise*, becoming a selective expert. Adults are not restrained, as most children and adolescents are, by a requirement to learn and do some of everything. Instead, adults are free to specialize in activities that are personally meaningful—anything from car repair to gourmet cooking, from illness diagnosis to fly fishing. As people develop expertise in some areas, they pay less attention to others. Selection is key to the time management described in Chapter 18.

For example, each adult chooses to watch only a few of the dozens of channels on television, many people delete hundreds of unread emails every day, some have no interest in attending certain events for which others wait in line for hours.

Culture and context guide people in this process. Many adults born 60 years ago are much better than more recent cohorts at writing letters with distinctive and legible handwriting because in childhood they practiced penmanship for hours, became experts in it, and maintained that expertise. Today's schools, and therefore today's children, make other choices. Some adults never send hand-written letters, but virtually all can read, unlike a century ago when many adults were illiterate.

An **expert,** as cognitive scientists define it, is not necessarily someone with rare and outstanding proficiency. To researchers it means more—and less—than that. An expert is a specialist in some aspect of life or knowledge. Expertise is not in-nate, although it may begin with inherited abilities that are later developed.

After time and effort, some people have accumulated knowledge, practice, and experience that transform them—they enter a higher league than most people. The quality as well as the quantity of their cognition is advanced. Expert thought is (1) intuitive, (2) automatic, (3) strategic, and (4) flexible, as we now describe.

Intuitive

Novices follow formal procedures and rules. Experts rely more on past experiences and immediate contexts; their actions are therefore more intuitive and less stereo-typical than those of the novice. The role of experience and intuition is evident, for example, during surgery. Outsiders might think medicine is straightforward, but experts understand the reality:

> Hospitals are filled with varieties of knives and poisons. Every time a medication is prescribed, there is potential for an unintended side effect. In surgery, col-lateral damage is inherent. External tissue must be cut to allow internal access so that a diseased organ may be removed, or some other manipulation may be performed to return the patient to better health.
>
> *[Dominguez, 2001, p. 287]*

In one study, many surgeons saw the same video footage of a gallbladder opera-tion and were asked to talk about it. The experienced surgeons anticipated and described problems twice as often as did the residents (who had also removed gallbladders, just not as many) (Dominguez, 2001).

Data on physicians indicate that the single most important question to ask a surgeon is "How often have you performed this operation?" The novice, even with the best, most recent training, is less skilled than the expert.

Another study asked expert chefs to describe how they conceived of their ex-traordinarily sumptuous dishes. They spoke of sudden insight, not step-by-step analysis (Stierand & Dörfler, 2015).

This is true in psychotherapy as well, according to a study that compared nov-ices and experts—all with the requisite academic knowledge. The therapists were asked to talk aloud as they analyzed a hypothetical case. The experts did more "forward thinking," using inferences and developing a possible treatment plan. The novices were less likely to think about the social relationships of the person and more likely to stick to a description of *what is* rather than wonder about what might be (Eells et al., 2011).

In **Video: Expertise in Adulthood: An Expert Discusses His Work,** Kenneth Davis discusses his research on how the neuro-transmitter acetylcholine affects memory.

expert Someone with specialized skills and knowledge developed around a particular activity or area of specific interest.

A classic example of expert intuition is *chicken-sexing*—the ability to tell whether a newborn chicken is male or female. As David Myers tells it:

> Poultry owners once had to wait five to six weeks before the appearance of adult feathers enabled them to separate cockerels (males) from pullets (hens). Egg producers wanted to buy and feed only pullets, so they were intrigued to hear that some Japanese had developed an uncanny ability to sex day-old chicks. . . . Hatcheries elsewhere then gave some of their workers apprenticeships under the Japanese. . . . After months of training and experience, the best Americans and Australians could almost match the Japanese, by sexing 800 to 1,000 chicks per hour with 99 percent accuracy. But don't ask them how they do it. The sex difference, as any chicken-sexer can tell you, is too subtle to explain.
>
> *[Myers, 2002, p. 55]*

The example of chicken-sexing is cited by philosophers because it is not based on certain, verifiable knowledge. Only six weeks later is it obvious that a chick will become an egg-laying hen. Thus, experts cannot articulate reasons and criteria for their intuition, or why they know what they know (Greco, 2014). That is what makes the expert intuitive.

A VIEW FROM SCIENCE

Who Wins in Soccer?

One experiment that studied the relationship between expertise and intuition involved 486 college students who were asked to predict the winners of soccer games not yet played. The students who were avid fans (the experts) made better predictions when they had a few minutes of unconscious thought instead of when they had the same number of minutes to mull over their choice (see Figure 21.2). Those who didn't care much about soccer (the nonexperts) did worse overall, but they did especially poorly when they had time to use unconscious intuition (Dijksterhuis et al., 2009).

The details of this experiment are intriguing. For 20 seconds, all participants were shown a computer screen with four soon-to-be-played soccer matches and were asked to predict the winners. One-third of the predictions were made immediately, one-third were made after two minutes of conscious thought, and one-third were made after two minutes when *only* unconscious thought could occur—because people randomly assigned to that group were required to calculate a series of mind-taxing math questions during those two minutes.

Nonexperts did no better than chance. They did worse after thinking about their answer, especially when the thought was unconscious. Perhaps the stress of doing math interfered with their thinking. By contrast, the predictions of the experts were not much better than those of the nonexperts when they guessed immediately, a little better when they had two minutes to think, and best of all after unconscious thought. Apparently, the experts' knowledge of soccer helped them most when they were consciously thinking of something else.

This experiment has led to many follow-up studies, including in medicine, where intuition sometimes finds a diagnosis that a textbook would not. A recent meta-analysis cautioned against applying this finding too broadly: Medical knowledge,

and thoughtful analysis, may lead to better conclusions than intuition (Vadillo et al., 2015). Hopefully, your doctor is expert enough to realize that.

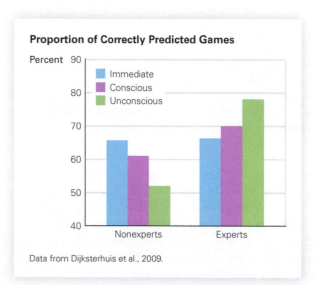

Proportion of Correctly Predicted Games

Data from Dijksterhuis et al., 2009.

FIGURE 21.2

If You Don't Know, Don't Think! Undergraduates at the University of Amsterdam were asked to predict winners of four World Cup soccer matches in one of three conditions: (1) immediate—as soon as they saw the names of the nations that were competing in each of the contests, (2) conscious—after thinking for two minutes about their answers, and (3) unconscious—after two minutes of solving distracting math tasks. As you can see, the experts were better at predicting winners after unconscious processing, but the nonexperts became less accurate when they thought about their answers, either consciously or unconsciously.

Automatic

The experiment with soccer predictions (shown on p. 604) confirms that many elements of expert performance are automatic. That is, the complex action and thought required by most people have become routine for experts, making it appear that most aspects of the task are performed instinctively. Experts process incoming information quickly, analyze it efficiently, and then act in well-rehearsed ways that make their efforts appear unconscious. In fact, some automatic actions are no longer accessible to the conscious mind.

For example, adults are much better at tying their shoelaces than children are (adults can do it in the dark, without thinking about their movements), but they are much worse at describing how they do it. When experts think, they engage in "automatic weighting" of various unverbalized factors. This automatic thinking can be disrupted by the words that nonexperts use, which distort rather than clarify the thinking process (Dijksterhuis et al., 2009, p. 1382).

This is apparent if you are an experienced driver and try to teach someone else to drive. Excellent drivers who are inexperienced instructors find it hard to recognize or verbalize things that have become automatic—such as anticipating the future movements of pedestrians and cyclists on the far side of the road, or feeling the car shift gears as it heads up an incline, or hearing the tires lose traction on a bit of sand. Yet such factors differentiate the expert from the novice.

This may explain why, despite powerful motivation, quicker reactions, and better vision, teenagers have three times the rate of fatal car accidents that adults do (Insurance Institute, 2012). Sometimes teenage drivers deliberately take risks (speeding, running a red light, drinking, and so on), but more often they simply misjudge and misperceive conditions that a more experienced driver would automatically notice.

The same gap between knowledge and instruction occurs when a computer expert tries to teach a novice what to do, as I know myself when my daughters try to help me with the finer points of Excel. They are unable to verbalize what they know, although they can do it very well with the computer. It is much easier to click the mouse or do the keystroke oneself than to teach what has become automatic.

A study of expert chess players (aged 17 to 81) found minor age-related declines, but expertise was much more important than age. This was particularly apparent

Same Situation, Far Apart: Don't Be Afraid The police officer in Toronto collecting slugs and the violinist in Jakarta collecting donations have both spent years refining their skills. Many adults would fear being that close to a murder victim or that close to thousands of rushing commuters, but both men have learned to practice their vocation no matter where they are. They are now experts: The cop discovered that two guns were used, and the musician earns more than $5 a day (the average for street musicians in Indonesia).

for speedy recognition that the king was threatened: Older experts did that almost as quickly as younger adults (in a fraction of a second) despite steep, age-related declines on standard tests of memory and speed (Jastrzembski et al., 2006).

When something—such as an audience, a stressor, or too much conscious thought—interferes with automatic processing, the result may be clumsy performance. This is thought to be the problem when some experienced athletes "choke under pressure"—their automatic actions are hijacked (DeCaro et al., 2011).

In a final example, medical students and doctors were asked to diagnose a difficult case of cardiac failure and pulmonary embolus. They read details of the case while their eye movements were tracked (Vilppu et al., 2016). Less than half of the students reached a correct diagnosis, but all of the experienced doctors did. The latter also read more quickly and focused on different pages than the students—presumably because they could automatically process some information and knew when unusual information was presented.

Strategic

Experts have more and better strategies, especially when problems are unexpected. Indeed, strategy may be the pivotal difference between a skilled person and an unskilled person. Expert chess players have general strategies for winning and far better specific strategies for the particular responses after a move that is their specialty (Bilalić et al., 2009).

Similarly, a strategy used by expert team leaders in both the military and civilian arenas is ongoing communication, especially during slow times. Therefore, when stress builds, no team member misinterprets the previously rehearsed plans, commands, and requirements. You have witnessed the same phenomenon in expert professors: At the beginning of the semester they institute routines and policies, strategies that avoid problems later in the term.

Of course, strategies themselves need to be updated as situations change—and no chess game, or battle, or class is exactly like another. The monthly fire drill required by some schools, the standard lecture given by some professors, and the pat safety instructions read by airline attendants before takeoff become less effective over time. I recently heard a flight attendant precede his standard talk with, "For those of you who have not ridden in an automobile since 1960, this is how you buckle a seat belt." In that preflight monologue I actually listened.

The superior strategies of the expert permit selective optimization with compensation. That is evident in studies of airplane pilots, a group for whom age-related declines in skill could lead to thousands of fatalities.

In one study, trained pilots were given directions by air traffic controllers in a flight simulation (Morrow et al., 2003). Experienced pilots took more accurate and complete notes and used their own shorthand to illustrate and emphasize what they heard. For instance, they had more graphic symbols (such as arrows) than did pilots who were trained to understand air traffic instructions but who had little flight experience. Thus, even though nonexperts were trained and had the tools (note paper, pencil), they did not use them in the way the experts did.

In actual flights, too, older pilots take more notes than younger ones do because they have mastered this strategy, perhaps to compensate for slower working memory. Another series of studies of pilots who were tested repeatedly over three years confirmed that expertise fostered better strategies, as expected (Taylor et al., 2007, 2011). But, unexpected was the conclusion that experience was particularly beneficial for those whose age and genes produced slower thinking.

Coping with Illness That hand belongs to a person with diabetes, who is getting a glucose check at a health fair in Los Angeles. This is better than avoidant coping but is not yet expert coping. The best strategy would be checking one's own levels at home and going to a specialist.

● **Observation Quiz** What expertise and skills does this nurse need? (see answer, page 608) ↑

In those longitudinal studies, some deficits in memory and reaction time began to appear as the pilots aged. But expertise meant that their judgment regarding piloting a plane was still good, and it was far better than that of pilots with less experience (Taylor et al., 2007, 2011). People show age-related losses in many studies, but experts of all ages often maintain their proficiency at their chosen occupation for years after other abilities decline. That's selective optimization.

Flexible

Finally, perhaps because they are intuitive, automatic, and strategic, experts are also flexible. The expert artist, musician, or scientist is creative and curious, deliberately experimenting and enjoying the challenge when unexpected things occur (Csikszentmihalyi, 2013). Remember Pavlov (Chapter 1). He already had won the Nobel Prize when he noticed his dogs' unexpected reaction to being fed. His expertise made him notice, then investigate, and eventually develop insights that opened a new perspective in psychology.

Consider the expert surgeon who takes the most complex cases and prefers unusual patients to typical ones because operating on the unusual ones might reveal sudden, challenging complications. Compared with the novice, the expert surgeon is not only more likely to notice telltale signs (an unexpected lesion, an oddly shaped organ, a rise or drop in a vital sign) that may signal a problem but is also more flexible and willing to deviate from standard textbook procedures if those procedures seem ineffective (Patel et al., 1999).

In the same way, experts in all walks of life adapt to individual cases and exceptions—much as an expert chef will adjust ingredients, temperature, technique, and timing as a dish develops, tasting to see whether a little more spice is needed, seldom following a recipe exactly. Standards are high: Some chefs throw food in the garbage rather than serve a dish that many people would happily eat. Expert chess players, auto mechanics, and violinists are similarly aware of nuances that might escape the novice.

In the field of education, best practices for the educator now emphasize flexibility and strategy, as each group of students has distinct and often erroneous assumptions. It is not helpful to simply teach the right answers; flexibility requires matching the instruction to the individuals (Ford & Yore, 2012).

A review of expertise finds that flexibility includes understanding which particular skills are necessary to become an expert in each profession. For example, repeated practice is needed in typing, sports, and games; collaboration skills are needed for leadership; and task management strategies are needed for aviation (Morrow et al., 2009).

Expertise, Age, and Experience

The relationship between expertise and age is not straightforward.

People who become experts need months—or even years—of practice (depending on the task) to develop that expertise (Ericsson et al., 2006). Some researchers think practice must be extensive, several hours a day for at least 10 years (Charness et al., 1996; Ericsson, 1996), but that is true in only some areas. Circumstances, training, genes, ability, practice, and age all affect expertise, which means that experts in one specific field are often quite inexpert in other areas.

Other studies also show that people become more expert, and their brains adapt while they practice whatever skills are needed in their chosen field (Park & Reuter-Lorenz, 2009). This occurs not only for motor skills—playing the violin, dancing, driving—but also for reasoning skills (Zatorre et al., 2012). The human brain is plastic lifelong; new learning is always possible, and practice is crucial.

Examples from Various Professions

An interesting example comes from perfumers: They need an acute sense of smell as they seek to develop new scents. Although the sense of smell typically declines with age, this is not so for perfumers. Experts outdid younger nonexperts: They had significantly developed those parts of the brain that were attuned to smell (Delon-Martin et al., 2013).

Practice may counteract other effects of aging (Krampe & Charness, 2006). As you read earlier in this chapter, the young have an advantage when speed is needed, but they are less adept at vocabulary and communication. This illustrates a general conclusion from research on cognitive plasticity: Experienced adults often use selective optimization with compensation, becoming expert. In many workplaces, the best employees may be the older, more experienced ones—if they want to do their best.

A study comparing decision-making skills found that, in some ways, age interfered with thinking. Older adults were sometimes too quick to be influenced by framing factors. For example, they might prefer beef that was 80 percent lean to beef that was 20 percent fat. However, for most aspects of decision making, they were better than younger adults because of their experience. For instance, they were better at knowing how likely they were to be correct in various guesses they made, avoiding both too little confidence and overconfidence (de Bruin et al., 2012).

Complicated work requires more cognitive practice and expertise than routine work; as a result, such work may have intellectual benefits for the workers themselves. In the Seattle Longitudinal Study, the cognitive demands of the occupations of more than 500 workers were measured, including the complexities involved in social interactions as well as understanding objects and data. In all three occupational challenges, older workers maintained their intellectual prowess (Schaie, 2005/2013).

One final example of the relationship between age and job effectiveness comes from an occupation familiar to all of us: driving a taxi. In major cities, taxi drivers must find the best route (factoring in traffic, construction, time of day, and many other details) while knowing where new passengers are likely to be found and how to relate to customers, some of whom might want to talk, others not.

Research in England—where taxi drivers "have to learn the layout of 25,000 streets in London and the locations of thousands of places of interest, and pass stringent examinations" (Woollett et al., 2009, p. 1407)—found not only that the drivers became more expert with time but also that their brains adjusted to the need for particular knowledge. Some regions of their brains (areas dedicated to spatial representation) were more extensive and active than those of an average person (Woollett et al., 2009). On ordinary IQ tests, the taxi drivers' scores were average, but in navigating London, their expertise was apparent.

Family Skills

This discussion of expertise has focused so far on occupations—surgeons, pilots, taxi drivers—that once had far more male than female workers. In recent years, two important shifts have occurred that add to this topic.

First, more women are working in occupations traditionally reserved for men. Remember from Chapter 4 that Virginia Apgar, when she earned her M.D. in 1933, was told she could not be a surgeon because only men were surgeons. Fortunately for the world, she became an anesthesiologist and her scale has saved millions of newborns. Today that assumption has changed; almost half the new M.D.s in the United States are women. Many of them have become surgeons (see Figure 21.3). More generally, most college women expect to have careers, husbands, and children, and many do so (Hoffnung & Williams, 2013).

The second major shift is that women's work has gained new respect. In earlier generations, women sometimes said they were "just a housewife" even though they not only cared for the house but also the biological, cognitive, and psychosocial needs of several children. Recently, however, the importance of work at home is increasingly recognized, and men as well as women do it.

We now know that not all women are good mothers or housekeepers and that some men are expert in domestic and emotional work that was once women's exclusive domain. Couples who switch traditional roles are no longer rare. Most experts now believe that for children, especially when mothers work full time, it works well when fathers have major responsibility for child rearing (Dunn et al., 2013).

It is no longer assumed that a "maternal instinct" is innate to every mother; many mothers experience postpartum depression, financial stress, or bursts of anger and do not provide responsive child care. Certainly in some families, fathers and grandparents provide better care for children than biological mothers do. As with other adult tasks, motivation and experience are crucial for caregiving.

The skill, flexibility, and strategies needed to raise a family are a manifestation of expertise. As noted in previous chapters, in their late teens and early 20s, both sexes are at their most fertile. But conception is only a start: In general, older parents are more patient, with lower rates of child abuse as well as more successful offspring.

Of course, the mere passage of time does not make a person learn to be a better parent, but age correlates with better parenting. A review of the research by an expert on the science of parenting concludes that, in general, as people gain in maturity and experience, "the more appropriate and optimal their parenting cognitions and practices are likely to be" (Bornstein, 2015, p. 91).

This is especially true if the parents have learned from experience and can listen well, as mature parents more often do. Raising a child teaches adults how to

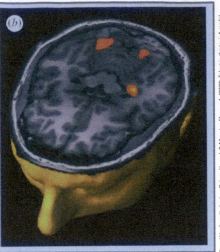

Red Means Go! The red shows the activated brain areas in London taxi drivers as they navigated the busy London streets. Not only were these areas more active than the same areas in the average person's brain, but they also had more dendrites. The longer a cabby had been driving, the more brain growth was evident.

Especially for Prospective Parents
In terms of the intellectual challenge, what type of intelligence is most needed for effective parenting? (see response, page 610)

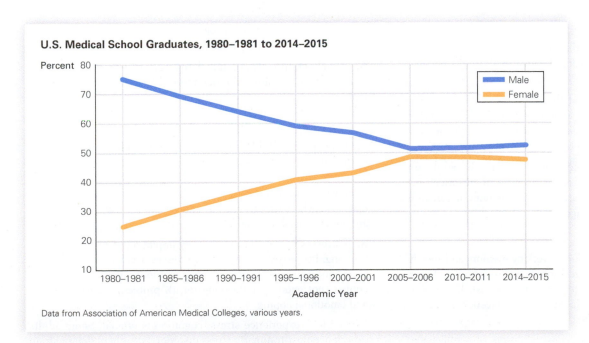

FIGURE 21.3

Expect a Woman Next time you hear "The doctor will see you now," the physician is as likely to be a woman as a man—unless the doctor is over age 40.

● ● **Response for Prospective Parents**
(from page 609): Because parenthood
demands flexibility and patience, Sternberg's
practical intelligence is probably most
needed. Anything that involves finding a
single correct answer, such as analytic
intelligence or number ability, would not be
much help.

become the intuitive, strategic, and flexible expert parent. For this, the children themselves get some credit. As my first two daughters said to the next two, "You should be grateful to me. I broke them [my husband and me] in."

Developmentalists have not yet identified all of the components necessary to become expert in child rearing, but at least we know that such expertise exists. Children raised by teenage parents are more likely to become high school dropouts and substance abusers. More experienced and mature parents are more likely to nip problems in the bud and recognize that some behaviors (that hairstyle, that music, that tattoo) are not worth fighting about. As with all aspects of adult cognition, variation is apparent, and age does not guarantee intelligence or ignorance. But experience, wisely understood, may help. Some parents are far more skilled than others.

WHAT HAVE YOU LEARNED?

1. How might a person compensate for fading memory skills?

2. What selective optimization can you see in your parents?

3. In what domain are you an expert that most people are not?

4. How does automatic processing contribute to expertise?

5. Explain how intuition might help or diminish ability.

6. In what occupations would age be an asset, and why?

7. In what occupations would age be a liability, and why?

8. What do parents learn from experience?

SUMMARY

Does Intelligence Change with Age?

1. It was traditionally assumed that intelligence was one general entity. From that assumption sprung the idea that intelligence in a measurable quantity, which Spearman called "g."

2. Cross-sectional research found that IQ scores decreased over the years of adulthood. However, longitudinal research found that the IQ of each adult tends to increase, particularly in vocabulary and general knowledge, until age 60 or so.

3. Younger adults traditionally score higher than older adults on IQ tests, not because of their age but because of historical improvements in health and education. Cross-sequential research finds both gains and losses with age.

Components of Intelligence: Many and Varied

4. Fluid intelligence—which includes working memory and speedy thought—decreases and crystallized intelligence—which is based on accumulated knowledge—increases as people age. Because of rising crystalized intelligence and falling fluid intelligence, IQ scores may be quite stable over adulthood.

5. Sternberg proposed three fundamental forms of intelligence: analytic, creative, and practical. Most research finds that, although analytic and creative abilities decline with age, practical intelligence

may improve. A fourth factor, wisdom, helps people judge which intelligence to use and how to do so.

6. Overall, cultural values and changing demands cause adults to develop some cognitive abilities more than others. Psychometric tests may not reflect these variations.

Selective Gains and Losses

7. As people grow older, they choose to focus on certain aspects of their lives, optimizing development in those areas and compensating for declines in others, as necessary. As applied to cognition, selective optimization with compensation means that people specialize in whatever intellectual skills they choose. Abilities that are not exercised may fade.

8. If stresses become stressors, they impair a person's health and thinking. People experience many stresses over the years of adulthood, and they use various coping methods, including avoidant coping (not good over the long term), problem-focused coping, and emotional coping.

9. As adults experience stress, cognition is crucial. Some adults experience post-traumatic stress disorder, but others demonstrate post-traumatic growth. The difference is less in the event than in coping with the event.

Expert Cognition

10. In addition to being more experienced, experts are better thinkers than novices for four reasons. They are more intuitive; their cognitive processes are automatic (often seeming to require little conscious thought); they use more and better strategies to perform whatever task is required; they are more flexible.

11. Expertise in adulthood is particularly apparent in the workplace, as evidenced by doctors, airplane pilots, and taxi drivers.

Experienced workers often outperform younger workers because they specialize, compensating for any losses.

12. Raising children and responding well to the emotional complexities and unanticipated challenges of family life are now recognized and valued as expert work. Expeience and maturation increase the likelihood of family expertise.

KEY TERMS

general intelligence (*g*) (p. 584)
Seattle Longitudinal Study
  (p. 586)
fluid intelligence (p. 589)
crystallized intelligence (p. 590)

analytic intelligence (p. 591)
creative intelligence (p. 592)
practical intelligence (p. 592)
cognitive artifacts (p. 595)

selective optimization with
  compensation (p. 596)
stressor (p. 597)
avoidant coping (p. 599)

problem-focused coping (p. 599)
emotion-focused coping (p. 599)
religious coping (p. 600)
expert (p. 603)

APPLICATIONS

1. The importance of context and culture is illustrated by the things that people think are basic knowledge. With a partner from the class, write four questions that you think are hard but fair as measures of general intelligence. Then give your test to your partner, and answer the four questions that your partner has prepared for you. What did you learn from the results?

2. Skill at video games is sometimes thought to reflect intelligence. Interview three or four people who play such games.

What abilities do they think video games require? What do you think these games reflect in terms of experience, age, and motivation?

3. Some people mistakenly assume that almost any high school graduate can become a teacher, since most adults know the basic reading and math skills that elementary children need to learn. Describe aspects of expertise that experienced teachers need to master, with examples from your own experience.

Adulthood:
Psychosocial Development

What Will You Know?

1. Does personality change from childhood to adulthood?
2. Why doesn't everyone get married these days?
3. Is being a parent work or joy?

"**Y**our backpack is open."

I hear that several times a day from strangers at street corners, on subways, in stores. I say, "Thank you. I know," and continue whatever I am doing.

The backpack is large, with three deep pockets. It is easier for me to zip it up halfway, leaving the top open so that I can see which books and papers are in which section. Nothing visible has any value to anyone but me, and nothing ever falls out when the backpack is strapped to my back, half-open.

But one time, as I was waiting for the train, next to me sat a young boy and next to him a friendly father who said, "Your backpack is open."

"Thank you, I know."

He was still troubled.

"Do you want me to zip it for you?"

I smiled and shook my head.

"I know you must be tired and busy," he said. "My son could zip it for you."

He seemed upset. I gave up.

"OK. Thank you."

His son zipped it up; the man was happy.

The merits of open backpacks can be argued either way, but this incident begins this chapter because it reveals three characteristics of adult development, each soon described.

First, we describe adult personality: That man and I have quite different attitudes about things being open or closed. (I keep kitchen cabinets, closet doors, and jackets open, too.) Because of basic personality differences, misunderstandings are common. He assumed, incorrectly, that he knew why my backpack was open. More consequentially, personality misunderstandings are one reason for divorce.

Then this chapter discusses the human need to interact with other people. In this case, it was stranger to stranger; usually it is between friends or family members.

The final topic of this chapter is caregiving. Adults want to take care of each other, yet they often find it hard to accept care from others. I did not want that man's help, but he really wanted to take care of me and have his son zip my backpack. I recognized his need, so I let him.

Personality Development in Adulthood

Chapter 7 explains that every infant is born with a unique temperament, and Chapter 10 describes parenting styles, two of the ingredients that contribute to adult personality. But, there is much more. Adult personality arises from many influences.

Continuity is evident: Few adults develop characteristics that are antithetical to their childhood temperament. But adults can change, not only in actions and attitudes but also in personality, usually for the better. Like a tree adding another ring of growth each year, adults continue to develop, which affects every aspect of their personality.

Theories and descriptions about how that happens vary, as you will now see.

Erikson's Theory

As you remember, Erikson originally described eight stages of development. His first stages (already explained) each begin in a particular chronological period.

His adult stages are less age-based (see Table 22.1). You have already read that identity, once thought to be achieved in adolescence, takes many years to achieve. In fact, echoes of the search for identity are apparent in late adulthood (Erikson, 1993a). The three adult stages—*intimacy versus isolation, generativity versus stagnation*, and *integrity versus despair*—do not always appear in chronological sequence, but overlap.

Erikson recognized the sociocultural aspect of human psychosocial development. This is one of the key differences between his theory and that of his mentor, Freud. The ecological approach, now accepted by almost every developmentalist, builds on the recognition of the many social influences on each person. No longer

TABLE 22.1	Erikson's Stages of Adulthood

Unlike Freud or other early theorists who thought adults simply worked through the legacy of their childhood, four of Erikson's eight psychosocial stages occur after puberty. His most famous book, *Childhood and Society* (1993a), devoted only two pages to each adult stage, but elaborations in later works have led to a much richer depiction (Hoare, 2002).

Identity Versus Role Confusion

Although Erikson originally situated the identity crisis during adolescence, he realized that identity concerns could be lifelong. Identity combines values and traditions from childhood with the current social context. Since contexts keep evolving, many adults reassess all four types of identity (sexual/gender, vocational/work, religious/spiritual, and political/ethnic).

Intimacy Versus Isolation

Adults seek intimacy—a close, reciprocal connection with another human being. Intimacy is mutual, not self-absorbed, which means that adults need to devote time and energy to one another. This process begins in emerging adulthood and continues lifelong. Isolation is especially likely when divorce or death disrupts established intimate relationships.

Generativity Versus Stagnation

Adults need to care for the next generation, either by raising their own children or by mentoring, teaching, and helping others. Erikson's first description of this stage focused on parenthood, but later he included other ways to achieve generativity. Adults extend the legacy of their culture and their generation with ongoing care, creativity, and sacrifice.

Integrity Versus Despair

When Erikson himself reached his 70s, he decided that integrity, with the goal of combating prejudice and helping all humanity, was too important to be left to the elderly. He also thought that each person's entire life could be directed toward connecting a personal journey with the historical and cultural purpose of human society, the ultimate achievement of integrity.

does any developmentalist focus on individuals of a particular age without noting the impact of family, friends, and culture.

Every adult seeks to connect with other people, experiencing the crisis Erikson called **intimacy versus isolation,** already explained in Chapter 19. The social nature of humans is particularly salient in stage six, because intimacy cannot be achieved alone. People need other people to avoid isolation.

According to Erikson, after intimacy comes **generativity versus stagnation,** when adults seek to be productive in a caring way. Erikson wrote that a mature adult "needs to be needed" (1993a, p. 266). Without generativity, adults experience "a pervading sense of stagnation and personal impoverishment" (Erikson, 1993a, p. 267).

Generativity traditionally was expressed as adults cared for the younger generation, as parents do. Observing adult devotion to children (not only from parents but also from grandparents, teachers, nurses, coaches, and many others) makes it clear how compelling is the adult need to be generative.

Generativity occurs in ways other than child rearing. Meaningful employment, important creative production, and caregiving, wherever it occurs, are ways to avoid stagnation.

Again, generativity is a very social stage. Children affect their parents by their personalities, needs, and sheer existence. As Erikson said, "The fashionable insistence on dramatizing the dependence of children on adults often blinds us to the dependence of the older generation on the younger one" (1993a, p. 266).

The final adult stage, *integrity versus despair,* is described in Chapter 25, as is Erikson's concept of a ninth stage, even later.

Maslow's Theory of Personality

Some scientists are convinced that there is something hopeful, unifying, and noble in humans, and that, if all goes well, each individual will become quite wonderful, each in his or her own way. This is the central idea of **humanism,** a theory of personality developed by Abraham Maslow (1908–1970) and many others.

Maslow witnessed the Great Depression, the rise of the Nazis, the power of fascism, World War II, the atom bomb, and then the eventual decline and defeat of all those horrors. He concluded that traditional psychological theories underrated human potential by focusing on the evil of humanity, not the potential for good. He wrote *Toward a Psychology of Being* (1962/1998), challenging psychoanalytic and behaviorist theories of personality.

Maslow believed that all people—no matter what their culture, gender, or background—have the same basic needs, eventually striving for appreciation of themselves and of everyone else. He arranged these needs in a hierarchy, often illustrated as a pyramid (see Figure 22.1):

1. Physiological: needing food, water, warmth, and air
2. Safety: feeling protected from injury and death
3. Love and belonging: having friends, family, and a community (often religious)

intimacy versus isolation The sixth of Erikson's stages of development. Every adult seeks close relationships with other people in order to live a happy and healthy life.

generativity versus stagnation The seventh of Erikson's eight stages of development. Adults seek to be productive in a caring way, often as parents. Generativity also occurs through art, caregiving, and employment.

humanism A theory that stresses the potential of all humans, who have the same basic needs regardless of culture, gender, or background.

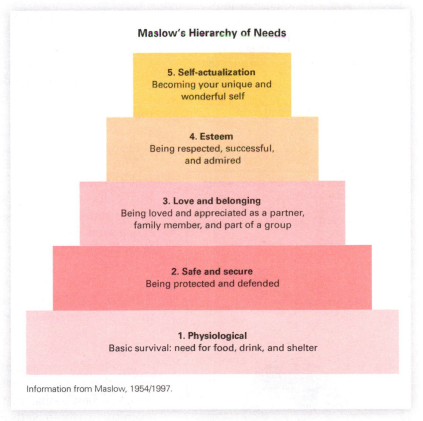

Maslow's Hierarchy of Needs

5. Self-actualization
Becoming your unique and wonderful self

4. Esteem
Being respected, successful, and admired

3. Love and belonging
Being loved and appreciated as a partner, family member, and part of a group

2. Safe and secure
Being protected and defended

1. Physiological
Basic survival: need for food, drink, and shelter

Information from Maslow, 1954/1997.

FIGURE 22.1

Moving Up, Not Looking Back Maslow's hierarchy is like a ladder: Once a person stands firmly on a higher rung, the lower rungs are no longer needed. Thus, someone who has arrived at step 4 might devalue safety (step 2) and be willing to risk personal safety to gain respect.

4. Esteem: being respected by the wider community as well as by oneself
5. Self-actualization: becoming truly oneself, fulfilling one's unique potential while appreciating all of life

After Fame Why did Oprah *(left)* quit her popular television program to pursue other projects, or Mark Ruffalo *(right)* donate his time to stop fracking? Perhaps Maslow is right. Self-actualization is the highest level in his famous hierarchy, when respect and esteem allow people to move past selfish concerns to care for the rest of humanity and nature. This applies to less famous adults as well.

This pyramid caught on almost immediately; it was one of the most "contagious ideas in behavioral science" because it seemed insightful about human psychology (Kenrick et al., 2010, p. 292). This theory is not a developmental theory in the traditional sense, in that Maslow did not believe that the five levels were connected to a particular stage or age. However, his hierarchy is sequential: Lower needs must be met before higher needs can be.

Thus, every person needs to have basic physiological needs satisfied, and to feel safe, before being able to seek love, respect, and finally self-actualization. At that highest level, when all four earlier needs have been met, people can be fully themselves—creative, spiritual, curious, appreciative of nature, able to respect everyone else.

Humanists emphasize what all people have in common, not their national, ethnic, or cultural differences. Maslow contended that everyone, universally, has the same needs, which can lead to the unique self-fulfillment of each person.

A starving man, for instance, may not be concerned for his own safety when he seeks food (level 1 precedes level 2), or an unloved woman might not care about self-respect because she needs love (level 3 precedes level 4). Maslow proposed that people who seem mean-spirited, or selfish, or nationalistic feel insecure. Destructive and inhumane actions may be the consequence of unmet lower needs. When those needs are met, self-actualization becomes possible.

This theory is relevant at every age. Babies seek food and comfort, children seek approval, emerging adults seek love, older adults seek respect, and all people have an inner drive to self-actualize. Early experiences can impede human growth: People may become thieves or even killers, unable to reach their potential, to self-actualize, if they were unsafe or unloved as children. Ideally people get past those lower levels, and the need for each person to become their unique, best self is one reason adult personality is so diverse.

Humanism is prominent among medical professionals because they recognize that illness and pain are not always physical (the first two levels) but can also be social (the next two) (Majercsik, 2005; Zalenski & Raspa, 2006). Even the very sick need love and belonging (never alone) and esteem (the dying need respect). The goal is total wellness (self-actualization), not mere absence of disease.

Echoes of humanism are also evident in education and sports: The basic idea here is that people are motivated to master knowledge or a skill that reaches their "personal best"—that is, to reach the peak of their own potential—more than when they strive to be the best in their class or star of their team (Ravizza, 2007).

In business, too, self-actualization may be the reason people strive for success (Fernando & Chowdhury, 2015). Crude competition—which produces winners and losers—is antithetical to the ethics of humanism, that everyone is wonderful in their own way.

Is this theory accurate? Not everyone thinks so. However, in a massive survey in China, elders who were high in social participation, sharing in common life, were most self-actualized (Chen & Gao, 2013).

If only I could accept that I can't accept being someone who finds it hard to accept acceptance from those who accept me for the person that I can't accept I really am.

FRY.

Maybe Next Year Self-acceptance is a gradual process over the years of adulthood, aided by the appreciation of friends and family. At some point in adulthood, people shift from striving to fulfill their potential to accepting their limitations.

Trait Theories

Many contemporary psychologists contend that adult personalities are too varied to be described by any grand theory, such as the ones proposed by Maslow and Erikson. Instead they contend that each person has hundreds of traits, each comprising one pixel of the distinct picture of personality.

The Big Five

One prominent theory is that all of the traits can be clustered on five dimensions, with each person relatively high or low on each of them. They have been called the **Big Five.** (To remember the Big Five, the acronym OCEAN is useful.)

- *Openness:* imaginative, curious, artistic, creative, open to new experiences
- *Conscientiousness:* organized, deliberate, conforming, self-disciplined
- *Extroversion:* outgoing, assertive, active
- *Agreeableness:* kind, helpful, easygoing, generous
- *Neuroticism:* anxious, moody, self-punishing, critical

Each personality is somewhere on a continuum on each of these five. The low end might be described, in the same order as above, with these five adjectives: *closed, careless, introverted, hard to please,* and *placid.*

According to trait theory, adults choose their contexts, selecting vocations, hobbies, health habits, mates, and neighborhoods in part because of their status on these Big Five. International research confirms that human personality traits (there are hundreds of them) can be grouped on these five dimensions (Carlo et al., 2014; Ching et al., 2014).

Among the actions and attitudes linked to the Big Five are education (conscientious people are more likely to complete college), cheating on exams (low on agreeableness), marriage (more often extroverts), divorce (more likely for neurotics), IQ (higher in openness), verbal fluency (again, openness and extroversion), smoking cigarettes (low in conscientiousness), and even political views (conservatives are less open) (Duckworth et al., 2007; Gerber et al., 2011; Silvia & Sanders, 2010; Giluk & Postlethwaite, 2015; Zvolensky et al., 2015).

Everyone agrees that personality is influenced by many factors beyond temperament. The paragraph above notes tendencies, not always realities.

Age Changes

Many researchers find that the strength of every trait is affected by maturation. However, when people of the same age are compared longitudinally, their traits are still evident compared to others their age. For example, extroversion tends to decrease slightly overall with age, but 20-year-old extroverts will still be extroverts at age 80, more outgoing than most other people their age, although not necessarily more than most 20-year-olds.

The general age trend is positive. During adulthood people become less neurotic and more conscientious (Clark, 2009; Lehman et al., 2013). In addition, people become more aligned with the norms of their culture and more stable in their traits. Personality change, when it occurs, is more likely early or late in life, not in the middle (Specht et al., 2011). That may be one reason that self-esteem rises from early adulthood until about age 50, as people develop whatever personality is most appreciated within their community (Orth et al., 2012).

Big Five The five basic clusters of personality traits that remain quite stable throughout adulthood: openness, conscientiousness, extroversion, agreeableness, and neuroticism.

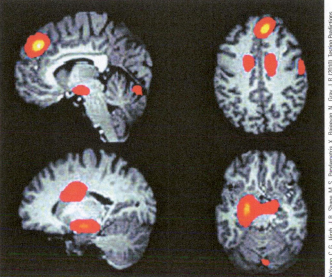

Active Brains, Active Personality The hypothesis that individual personality traits originate in the brain was tested by scientists who sought to find correlations between brain activity (shown in red) and personality traits. People who rated themselves high in four of the Big Five (conscientiousness, extroversion, agreeableness, neuroticism—but not openness) also had more activity in brain regions that are known to relate to those traits. Here are two side views *(left)* and a top and bottom view *(right)* of brains of people high in neuroticism. Their brain regions known to be especially sensitive to stress, depression, threat, and punishment (yellow bullseyes) were more active than the same brain regions in people low in neuroticism (DeYoung et al., 2010).

Especially for Immigrants and Children of Immigrants Poverty and persecution are the main reasons some people leave their home for another country, but personality is also influential. Which of the Big Five personality traits do you think is most characteristic of immigrants? (see response, page 618)

Same Situation, Far Apart: Scientists at Work Most scientists are open-minded and conscientious (two of the Big Five personality traits), as both of these women are. Culture and social context are crucial, however. If the woman on the left were in Tanzania, would she be a doctor surrounded by patients in the open air, as the Tanzanian woman on the right is? Or is she so accustomed to her North American laboratory, protected by gloves and a screen, that she could not adjust? The answer depends on personality, not knowledge.

> **THINK CRITICALLY:** Would your personality fit better in another culture?

Response for Immigrants and Children of Immigrants (from page 617): Extroversion and neuroticism, according to one study (Silventoinen et al., 2008). Because these traits decrease over adulthood, fewer older adults migrate.

One indication of this is that adults become more accepting of themselves and their community. People under the age of 30 "actively try to change their environment," moving away from home and finding new friends, changing their nurture. Later in life, context shapes traits, because once adults have chosen their vocation, family, and neighborhoods, they "change the self to fit the environment" (Kandler, 2012, p. 294).

Cultural Influences

That "change to fit the environment" is evident in how adults react to cultural mandates to have many, or few, children. Traits didn't much affect childbearing for men and women born in 1920 because the culture strongly valued fertility: Almost all adults, no matter what their personality, hoped to marry and have several children. Most did. (My maternal grandparents had 16 babies; my paternal grandparents had 5.)

By 1960, however, culture was more ambivalent about childbearing. For those born in that year, personality mattered. Women high in openness and conscientiousness had fewer children than average, sometimes choosing to have one or none (Jokela, 2012). (Some of my cousins had no children.) As in this example, cultural context matters, interacting with personality.

Culture shapes personality. As one team wrote, "personality may acculturate" (Güngör et al., 2013, p. 713). A study of well-being and self-esteem in 28 nations found that people are happiest if their personality traits match their social context. For example, extroversion is relatively highly valued in Canada and less so in Japan; Canadians and Japanese have a stronger sense of well-being if their personal ratings on extroversion are consistent with their culture's norms (Fulmer et al., 2010).

Common Themes

Every well-known theorist or scholar of adult personality echoes the same themes. Freud enunciated them first: He said that adults need *lieben und arbeiten* (to love and to work). As you just read, Maslow considered Love and Belonging, and then Success and Esteem, among the basic human needs. Trait theories recognize extroversion and conscientiousness, which are related to the same two.

Other theorists call these two needs *affiliation/achievement,* or *emotional/instrumental,* or *communion/agency.* Every theory recognizes both; every adult seeks to love and to work, each in a way that fits his or her personality. To organize our discussion, we will use Erikson's terms, *intimacy* and *generativity,* as a scaffold.

Intimacy: Connecting with Others

Humans are not meant to be loners. Decades of research finds that physical health and psychological well-being flourish best if both family members and friends are part of an adult's life (Li & Zhang, 2015).

Romantic Partners

We begin our discussion of intimacy with romance. Adults tend to be happiest and healthiest if they have a long-term partner, connected to them with bonds of affection and care all their lives.

Marriage

Traditionally, that romantic bond was codified via marriage. You already read that most emerging adults postpone marriage. That trend continues in adulthood: Although many say they would like a long and happy marriage, more and more adults never marry (see Figure 22.2).

Similar trends are found worldwide, even in nations where traditional marriage was recently prized. For example, in Japan in 1950, almost every adult was married, often before age 20. Now their average age of marriage is about 30, and an estimated 20 percent will never marry (Raymo, 2013).

Marriage continues to seem desirable even though many avoid it. Although one might think that a bad marriage would discourage people about the institution, many people who divorce try again. In the United States, 40 percent of new marriages have at least one partner who has been married before (Livingston, 2014).

What do these trends mean for societies and individuals? Societies benefit when most adults marry and stay married. Older adults are often cared for by spouses, and children are more likely to thrive if both parents are legally and emotionally dedicated to them, forming a constructive parental alliance.

Individuals may benefit, too: A satisfying marriage improves health, wealth, and happiness. However, not all marriages are satisfying, and divorce is always difficult (Fincham & Beach, 2010; R. Miller et al., 2013). The only sure way to avoid divorce is to never marry.

It was once thought that men were happier in marriage and women less happy (Bernard, 1982). Suggested reasons were that women had higher expectations for marriage and, thus, greater disillusionment, or that women did far more housework, child care, and emotional work. However, that is changing by cohort and varies by income, education, and culture (Stavrova et al., 2012).

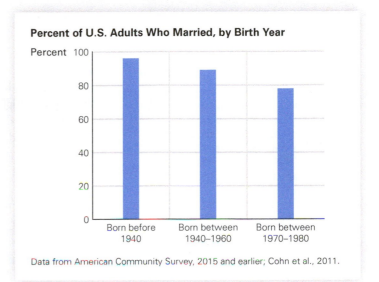

Percent of U.S. Adults Who Married, by Birth Year

Data from American Community Survey, 2015 and earlier; Cohn et al., 2011.

FIGURE 22.2

And the Future? It is not known how many single people born after 1980 will eventually marry, but projections are that fewer and fewer will. It is known that among people ages 25 to 34 in 2010, only 44 percent were married.

THINK CRITICALLY: Is marriage a failed institution?

Share My Life Marriage often requires one partner to support the other's aspirations. That is evident in the French couple *(right)*, as Nicole embraces her husband, Alain Maignan, who just completed a six-month solo sail around the world. For 20 years, he spent most of his money and time building his 10-meter boat. Less is known about the couple on the left, but here they enjoy kissing on the beach in Florida, evidence of the thrill of physical touch that they first experienced decades ago.

A recent meta-analysis in the United States found no marked gender differences in marital happiness (J. B. Jackson et al., 2014). Early in a marriage, wives tended to be slightly more satisfied with the relationship than husbands, but this shifted by about the 15-year mark, with husbands slightly more satisfied. That study found one cultural exception to overall gender neutrality: In Chinese American and Japanese American marriages, wives were more often dissatisfied than husbands (J. B. Jackson et al., 2014).

Nonmarital Romantic Relationships

As explained in Chapter 19, romantic partnerships do not always mean marriage. Cohabitation is no longer the exclusive purview of young adults; cohabitation rates are increasing for adults of all ages. Many adults prefer cohabitation to marriage.

A sizable number of adults have found a third way (neither marriage nor cohabitation) to meet their intimacy needs with a steady romantic partner. They are *living apart together* (**LAT**) They have separate residences, but especially when the partners are over age 30, they function as a couple for decades, sexually faithful, vacationing together, and so on (Duncan & Phillips, 2010).

LAT (living apart together) When a couple is committed to each other emotionally and sexually for years, yet each partner has his or her own home.

Financial patterns are a complication for LAT couples. Most married couples pool their money; many cohabiting couples do not (Hamplová et al., 2014). LAT couples struggle with this aspect of their relationship, with the women particularly wanting to pay their own way (Lyssens-Danneboom & Mortelmans, 2014).

Every couple's decision to marry, cohabit, or LAT is influenced by their families and cultures. Children are particularly influential. Cohabiters who have had children together are more likely to marry than those without, especially when the children start school. Likewise, married couples sometimes stay together for the children, and sometimes one parent leaves a violent mate to protect the children. As for LAT couples, many older parents maintain separate households because they do not want to upset their grown children (de Jong Gierveld & Merz, 2013).

LaunchPad
macmillan learning

Video: Marriage in Adulthood
http://qrs.ly/t24sqml

Partnerships Over the Years

Love is complex, as described in Chapter 19, with passion, intimacy, and commitment varying by culture, and *consummate love* only sometimes attained. A wealth of research over the years of adulthood finds that, for most adults, mutual commitment is the most crucial of the three.

A long-term committed partnership correlates with health and happiness throughout life (R. Miller et al., 2013). The reasons for this correlation are both emotional and practical. People have a deep psychological need for someone who listens, understands, and shares heartfelt goals, and people also benefit from a companion who monitors diet, exercise, and medical attention.

The passage of time makes a difference. In general, the honeymoon period tends to be happy, but frustration with a partnership increases as conflicts—even those not directly between the couple—arise (see At About This Time). Partnerships (including heterosexual married couples, committed cohabiters, same-sex couples, and LAT couples) tend to be less happy when the first child is born and again when children reach puberty (Umberson et al., 2010). Divorce risk rises and then falls.

Remember, however, that averages obscure many differences of age, ethnicity, personality, and circumstances. In the United States, Asian Americans are least likely to divorce and African Americans are most likely to do so. These ethnic differences are partly cultural and partly economic, making any broad effort to promote marriage for everyone doomed to disappoint politicians, social workers, and individuals (Johnson, 2012).

Education and religion matter too: College-educated couples are more likely to marry and less likely to divorce no matter what their ethnic background. Some unhappy couples stay married for religious reasons, and the result may be a long-lasting, conflict-filled relationship. Husbands and wives in happy marriages tend to agree that their marriage is a good one, but in unhappy marriages often one spouse is much less content than the other (Brown et al., 2012).

Contrary to outdated impressions, the **empty nest**—when parents are alone again after the children have left—is usually a time for improved relationships. Simply having time for each other, without crying babies, demanding children, or rebellious teenagers, improves intimacy. Partners can focus on their mates, doing together whatever they both enjoy. Remember *linked lives*. Partners share the emotions and accomplishments of their mate (Carr et al., 2014).

Gay and Lesbian Partners

As you remember from Chapter 19, almost everything just described applies to gay and lesbian partners as well as to heterosexual ones (Biblarz & Savci, 2010; Cherlin, 2013; Herek, 2006). A review of 15 years of same-sex marriages in Denmark, Sweden, and Norway finds that neither the greatest fears nor grandest hopes for such unions were realized (Biblarz & Stacey, 2010).

Some same-sex couples are faithful and supportive of each other; their emotional well-being thrives on their intimacy and commitment, which increases over the decades into old age. Others are conflicted: Problems of finances, communication, and domestic abuse resemble those in heterosexual marriages.

As the U.S. Supreme Court confirmed in 2015, love between partners is the crucial bond. Research on marital conflict finds that communication is essential for a happy partnership, just as it is with other-sex couples (Ogolsky & Gray, 2016). When married same-sex couples divorce, they fight about money and children, just as heterosexual couples do.

Frank Baron/Camera Press/Guardian/Redux

One Love, Two Homes Their friends and family know that Jonathan and Diana are a couple, happy together day and night, year after year. But one detail distinguishes them from most couples: Each owns a house. They commute 10 miles and are living apart together—LAT.

empty nest The time in the lives of parents when their children have left the family home. This is often a happy time for everyone.

AT ABOUT THIS TIME

Marital Happiness Over the Years

Interval After Wedding	Characterization
First 6 months	Honeymoon period—happiest of all
6 months to 5 years	Happiness dips; divorce is more common now than later in marriage
5 to 10 years	Happiness holds steady
10 to 20 years	Happiness dips as children reach puberty
20 to 30 years	Happiness rises when children leave the nest
30 to 50 years	Happiness is high and steady, barring serious health problems

Not Always These are trends, often masked by more pressing events. For example, some couples stay together because of the children, so unlike most couples, for them the empty-nest stage becomes a time of conflict or divorce.

A Dream Come True When Melissa Adams and Meagan Martin first committed to each other, they thought they could never marry, at least in their South Carolina home. On July 11th, 2015, they celebrated their union, complete with flower girl, bridesmaids, Reverend Sidden, and all the legal documents.

● **Especially for Young Couples** Suppose you are one-half of a turbulent relationship in which moments of intimacy alternate with episodes of abuse. Should you break up? (see response, page 624)

The similarity of same- and other-sex relationships surprised researchers who studied alcohol abuse in romantic couples. The scientists expected that the stress of minority sexual orientation would increase alcohol use disorder. That was *not* what the data revealed. Instead, the crucial variable was whether the couple was married or not. For both same-sex and other-sex couples, cohabiters drank to excess much more than married people did (Reczek et al., 2014).

Another finding relates to all partnerships: family connections. In a study of married gay couples in Iowa, one man decided to marry because of his mother: "I had a partner that I lived with . . . And I think she, as much as she accepted him, it wasn't anything permanent in her eyes" (Ocobock, 2013, p. 196). In this study, most family members were supportive, but some were not—again eliciting deep emotional reactions.

In heterosexual marriages as well, in-laws usually welcome the new spouse, but when they do not, the partnership may be troubled. Family influences are hard to ignore.

Divorce and Remarriage

Throughout this text, developmental events that seem isolated, personal, and transitory are shown to be interconnected and socially constructed, with enduring consequences. Relationships never improve or end in a vacuum; they are influenced by the macrosystem and exosystem. For example, a study of many nations found that the happiness as well as the likelihood of separation of married and cohabiting couples were powerfully influenced by national norms (Wiik et al., 2012).

Divorce occurs because at least one partner believes that he or she would be happier without the spouse, a conclusion reached fairly often in the United States. Divorce is a process that begins long before the official decree. Typically, happiness dips in the months before a divorce and then increases after official separation (Luhmann et al., 2012). Over the years, however, reduced income, lost friendships, and weaker relationships with offspring are common (Kalmijn, 2010; Mustonen et al., 2011).

Family problems arise from divorce not only with children (usually custodial parents become stricter and noncustodial parents become distant) but also with other relatives. The divorced adult's parents are often financially supportive but not emotionally supportive. Relationships with their in-laws may have been good but are severed when the couple splits. No wonder divorce increases loneliness (van Tilburg et al., 2015).

Sometimes divorced adults confide in their children. That may help the adults but not the children. Even if adults avoid that trap, children need extra stability and understanding just when the parents are consumed by their own emotions (H. S. Kim, 2011).

Many divorced people seek another partner (remember, their marriage rate is higher than for never-married people the same age). Initially, remarriage restores

"But you knew I was addicted to bad men when you married me."

Surprised? Many brides and grooms hope to rescue and reform their partners, but they should know better. Changing another person's habits, values, or addictions is very difficult.

intimacy, health, and financial security. For fathers, bonds with stepchildren or with a new baby may replace strained relationships with their children (Noël-Miller, 2013a).

Divorce is never easy, but the negative consequences just explained are not inevitable. If divorce ends an abusive, destructive relationship (as it does about one-third of the time), it usually benefits at least one spouse and the children (Amato, 2010).

Some divorces lead to stronger and warmer mother–child and/or father–child relationships after the marital fights are over. That helps children cope, not only immediately but also for years to come (Vélez et al., 2011).

Friends and Acquaintances

Each person is part of a **social convoy.** The term *convoy* originally referred to a group of travelers in hostile territory, such as the pioneers in ox-drawn wagons headed for California or soldiers marching across unfamiliar terrain. Individuals were strengthened by the convoy, sharing difficult conditions and defending one another.

As people move through life, their social convoy functions as those earlier convoys did, a group of people who provide "a protective layer of social relations to guide, socialize, and encourage individuals as they move through life" (Antonucci et al., 2001, p. 572).

Sometimes a friend needs care and cannot reciprocate at the time, but it is understood that later the roles may be reversed. Friends provide practical help and useful advice when serious problems—death of a family member, personal illness, job loss—arise, and companionship, information, and laughter in daily life.

Friends are a crucial part of the social convoy; they are chosen for the traits that make them reliable fellow travelers. Mutual loyalty and aid characterize friendship: An unbalanced friendship (one giving and the other taking) often ends because both parties are uncomfortable.

Friendships tend to improve over the decades of adulthood. As adults grow older, they tend to have fewer friends, but they keep their close friends and nurture those relationships (English & Carstensen, 2014).

Although most friendships last for decades, conflicting health habits may end a relationship (O'Malley & Christakis, 2011). For instance, a chain smoker and a friend who quit smoking are likely to part ways. On the other hand, shared health problems can bind a friendship together. For example, overweight people become friends with other overweight people, and together their food preferences and eating habits reinforce each other as both continue to gain weight (Powell et al., 2015).

If an adult has no close and positive friends, health suffers (Couzin, 2009; Fuller-Iglesias et al., 2013). This seems as true in poor nations as in rich ones: Universally, humans are healthier with social support and sicker when socially isolated (Kumar et al., 2012).

Family Bonds

Family links span generations and endure over time, even more than friendship networks or romantic partnerships. Childhood history influences people decades

Luke Thompson

Fellow Travelers Here that phrase is not a metaphor for life's journey, but a literal description of a good friend, Tom, carrying 30-year-old Kevan Chandler, from Fort Wayne, Indiana, as they view the Paris Opera House. Kevan was born with spinal muscular atrophy because both his parents are carriers of the recessive gene. He cannot walk, but three of his friends agreed to take him on a three-week backpacking adventure through Europe. The trip was funded by hundreds of people who read about Kevan's plans online.

social convoy Collectively, the family members, friends, acquaintances, and even strangers who move through the years of life with a person.

Dinner Every Night Not only does the Shilts family eat together at 6 P.M. every night, but all six adults and five children also sleep under the same roof. The elderly couple is on the ground floor, and each adult daughter, with husband and children, has a wing on the second floor.

THINK CRITICALLY: Does the rising divorce rate indicate stronger or weaker family links?

Response for Young Couples (from page 622): There is no simple answer, but you should bear in mind that, while abuse usually decreases with age, breakups become more difficult with every year, especially if children are involved.

after they have left their childhood home. Parental death does not stop parental influence.

For example, many studies have found that parental SES is a strong predictor of SES in adulthood. It is difficult to overcome the influence of poverty. However, detailed studies found that low income alone is not as influential as family values during childhood: Going to museums, reading books, and other practices more common with higher parental education linger into adulthood, influencing adult habits and values and, thus, SES (Erola et al., 2016).

This does not always mean that adults follow their parents' example: Sometimes the opposite occurs. One of my students complained about her life as one of 16 children; she had only one child, and she said that was enough. As she explained this to the class, it seemed apparent that her choice was in reaction to her childhood. However, other echoes of her parents' attitudes were evident.

The power of family experiences was documented in data from the twins in Denmark. They married less often than single-born Danes, but if they wed, they were less likely to divorce. According to the researchers, twins may have their intimacy needs met by each other and therefore they are less likely to seek a spouse, but if they have one, they know how to maintain a close relationship (Petersen et al., 2011).

Parents and Their Adult Children

A crucial part of family life for many adults is raising children. That is discussed soon as part of generativity. Here we focus on family bonds that meet adult intimacy needs, providing companionship, support, and affection for parents and their grown children.

Do not confuse intimacy with residence. If income allows, most adults seek to establish their own households. A study of 7,578 adults in seven nations found that physical separation did not weaken family ties. Indeed, intergenerational relationships seem to be strengthened, not weakened, when adult children lived apart from their parents (Treas & Gubernskaya, 2012), because "the intergenerational support network is both durable and flexible" (Bucx et al., 2012, p. 101). If a divorced son or daughter has custody of children, the grandparents (usually middle-aged adults) often provide child care and other help (Westphal et al., 2015).

Framed by Birth In the twenty-first century, it is unusual for fathers and sons to work together, as these two do in a framing shop. It is even more unusual for both to enjoy working together.

The recent economic recession led to "boomerang children," adults who live with their parents for a while. In the United States, in 1980 only 11 percent of 25- to 34-year-olds lived with their parents for at least a few months, but between 2008 and 2011, 29 percent did (K. Parker, 2012).

Rates of adult children living with parents are continuing to rise, reaching a peak not seen in the past 135 years—except in 1940, when the Great Depression meant that few young people could afford to leave home (DeSilver, 2016). Sharing a home among adults from different generations is not ideal for individual development, but the data illustrate that parents remain a resource for their children lifelong.

Fictive Kin

Most adults seek to maintain connections with family members, sometimes traveling great distances to attend weddings, funerals, and holidays. The power of this link is apparent when we note that, unlike friends, family members may be on opposite sides of political or social issues. Even radically different views do not usually keep them apart.

Sometimes, however, adults avoid their blood relatives because they find them toxic—not because they disagree on politics, but because their personal interaction is hostile. Such adults may become **fictive kin** in another family. They are introduced by a family member who says this person is "like a sister" or "my brother" and so on. Over time, the new family accepts them. They are not technically related (hence *fictive*), but they are treated like a family member (hence *kin*).

Fictive kin can be a lifeline to those adults who are rejected by their original family (perhaps because of their sexual orientation), or are isolated far from home (perhaps because they are immigrants), or are changing their family habits (such as stopping addiction) (Ebaugh & Curry, 2000; Heslin et al., 2011; E. Kim, 2009). A qualitative study of African American college students found that the influence of fictive kin, at college or at home, was pivotal in encouraging them to persist in their studies (Brooks & Allen, 2016).

The role for fictive kin reinforces a general theme: Adults benefit from kin, fictive or not.

Arch Rivals or Blood Brothers? Both. Fernando and Humberto Campana are designers, shown here at an exhibit of their work in Spain, far from their native Brazil. As with many siblings, competition and collaboration have inspired them all their lives.

fictive kin People who become accepted as part of a family in which they are not genetically or legally members.

WHAT HAVE YOU LEARNED?

1. What needs do long-term partners meet?
2. How are marriage and cohabiting rates changing?
3. Why would people choose to live apart together?
4. How do same-sex marriages compare to heterosexual marriages?
5. What are the consequences of divorce?
6. How do remarriages differ from first marriages?
7. Why do people need a social convoy?
8. What roles do friends play in a person's life?
9. What is the usual relationship between adult children and their parents?
10. Why do people have fictive kin?

Generativity: The Work of Adulthood

Adults satisfy their need to be generative in many ways, especially through parenthood, caregiving, and employment.

Parenthood

Although generativity can take many forms, its chief manifestation is "establishing and guiding the next generation" (Erikson, 1993a, p. 267). Many adults pass along their values as they respond to the hundreds of daily requests and unspoken needs of their children. The impact of parents on children has been discussed many times in the previous chapters. Now we look at the adult half of this interaction—the impact of parenting on the parents.

Most nonparents underestimate the generative demands of parenthood. Indeed, "having a child is perhaps the most stressful experience in a family's life" (McClain, 2011, p. 889).

Parenthood is particularly difficult when intimacy, not generativity, is a person's most urgent psychosocial need. As already noted, marital happiness may dip when a baby arrives, because intimacy needs must sometimes be postponed. Worse yet is having a baby as part of the search for identity (as teenagers may discover too late).

Children reorder adult perspectives. One sign of a good parent is the parent's realization that the infant's cries are communicative, not selfish, and that adults need to care for children more than vice versa (Katz et al., 2011).

Parents adjust to children in ways that fit their personality and culture. For example, a study of men and women who had been in the top 0.01 percent in math ability when they were in high school, and who had gone on to earn graduate degrees and impressive jobs decades later, found that parenthood changed both sexes. Compared to their peers who had not had children, the fathers worked harder to achieve more status and income, while the mothers became more communal, focusing on community and family (Ferriman et al., 2009).

Those brilliant adults became parents two decades ago, but patterns persist. A 16-nation study found changes—fathers do more child care and mothers earn

More Dad . . . and Mom Worldwide, fathers are spending more time playing with their children—daughters as well as sons, as these two photos show. Does that mean that mothers spend less time with their children? No—the data show that mothers are spending more time as well.

more money—but the gender division of labor remains (Kan et al., 2011). On average, mothers do child care, schedule doctor appointments, plan birthday parties, arrange play dates, choose schools and after-school activities, and so on more than fathers.

Even in nontraditional couples, old patterns persist. For example, one man became the prime caregiver for his infant and 2-year-old but wanted to earn a paycheck. He found a part-time job that allowed him to bring his children along (as a schoolbus driver). He said:

> In the last generation it's changed so much . . . it's almost like you're on ice that's breaking up. That's how I felt. Like I was on ice breaking up. You don't really know what or where the father role is. You kind of have to define it for yourself . . . I think that's what I've learned most from staying home with the kids . . . Does it emasculate me that my wife is making more money?
>
> [Geoff, quoted in Doucet, 2015, p. 235]

Another father in the same study opened a day-care business for his own children and several others. Both of these men were influenced by of gender roles, even as they resisted them.

No matter who does what, parenting is an ongoing challenge. Just when parents figure out how to care for their infants, or preschoolers, or schoolchildren, those children grow older, presenting new dilemmas.

Over the decades of family life, parents must adjust to babies who disrupt sleep, toddlers who have temper tantrums, preschoolers who want to explore, schoolchildren who need help with homework or friendship or skills, teenagers who are moody, or defiant, or depressed. One exasperated mother told her criticizing teenager, "I'm learning on the job, I've never been a mother of an adolescent before."

Not every child presents every problem, but privacy and income rarely seem adequate, and every child needs extra care and attention at some point. The more children a couple has, the more problems arise, as found in a multinational study (Margolis & Myrskylä, 2011). This is true for all parents, but special attention needs to be devoted to the roughly one-third of adults who become nonbiological parents. Each form of parenting provides abundant opportunities for generativity, although each mode has distinct vulnerabilities.

Adoptive Parents

The easiest form of nonbiological parenting may be adoption, since those adults are legally connected to their children for life. Moreover, adoptive children are much wanted, so the parents are ready to sacrifice their own needs to be generative for the child.

Current adoptions are usually "open," which means that the birth parents decided that someone else would be a better parent, but they still want some connection to the child. The child knows about this arrangement, which proves advantageous for all of the adults who seek the best for the child.

Strong parent–child attachments are often evident with adoption, especially when children are adopted as infants. Secure bonds can also develop if adoption occurs when the children are older, especially when the adopting mother was strongly attached to her own mother (Pace et al., 2011).

Sadly, some adopted children have spent their early years in an institution, never attached to anyone. Although some such children are resilient, many are afraid to love anyone (van IJzendoorn et al., 2011). That makes child rearing more difficult for the adoptive parent.

Video: Interview with Jay Belsky explores how problematic parenting practices are transmitted (or not) from one generation to the next.

DSM-5 recognizes *reactive attachment disorder*, when a young child cannot seem to form any attachments. This problem can occur with children who live with their biological parents, but it is particularly likely with children who have spent infancy in institutions.

The problems continue in elementary school, requiring teachers with skill and sensitivity (Spilt et al., 2016). Most children respond to their parents' guidance because they are attached to their parents. This is less true for children with attachment disorder, which means that adoptive parents need to be extraordinarily generative caregivers.

As you remember, adolescence—the time when teenagers seek their own identity—can stress any family. This stage is particularly problematic for adoptive families because all teenagers want to know their genetic and ethnic roots. One college student who feels well loved and cared for by her adoptive parents explains:

> In attempts to upset my parents sometimes I would (foolishly) say that I wish I was given to another family, but I never really meant it. Still when I did meet my birth family I could definitely tell we were related—I fit in with them so well. I guess I have a very similar attitude and make the same faces as my birth mother! It really makes me consider nature to be very strong in personality.

[A, personal communication]

Attitudes in the larger culture often increase tensions between adoptive parents and children. For example, the mistaken notion that the "real" parents are the biological ones is a common social construction that hinders a secure relationship. International and interethnic adoptions are especially controversial.

Adoptive parents who take on the complications of international or interethnic adoption are usually intensely dedicated to their children. They are very much "real" parents, seeking to protect their children from discrimination that they might not have noticed before it affected their child.

For example, one European American couple adopted a multiethnic baby and three years later requested a second baby. They said, "We made a commitment [to our daughter] that we would have a brown or Black baby. So we turned down a couple of situations because they were not right" (Sweeney, 2013, p. 51). These parents had noticed strangers' stares and didn't want their first child to be the only dark-skinned family member.

Many such adoptive parents seek multiethnic family friends and educate their children about their heritage and the prejudice they may encounter. Such *racial socialization* often occurs within minority families for their biological children. When adoptive parents do so, their adolescents who encounter frequent prejudice experience less stress because they are ready to counter with pride in their background (Leslie et al., 2013).

The same is true if the child experiences discrimination because of same-sex parents, or single parents, or international origins, or even adoption itself. Each situation provides special insights and strengths. Adults realize that; children may need to be told.

As emphasized in earlier chapters, the child's first months and years are a sensitive period for language, attachment, and neurological maturation. The older a child is at adoption, the more difficult parenting might be (Schwarzwald et al., 2015). However, difficult parenting is what most parents do. Parents usually are intensely devoted to their children, no matter what the child's special needs or atypical situation. Generativity is amazingly powerful.

A Happy Adoptive Family Social workers once discouraged interracial, biracial, and international adoptions. But the evidence from families such as this one finds a very positive result.

Brooke Fasani Auchincloss/Corbis/Getty Images

Stepparents

The average new stepchild is 9 years old. Typically, stepchildren have lived with both biological parents and then with a single parent, a grandparent, other relatives, and/or a paid caregiver, before becoming a stepchild.

Changes in living arrangements are always disruptive for children (Goodnight et al., 2013). The effects are cumulative; emotions erupt in adolescence if not before. Becoming a new stepparent to such a child, especially if the child is coping with a new school, loss of friends, or puberty, is challenging. Stepchildren may intensify their attachment to their birth parents, a reaction that upsets a stepparent who wants to become a parent to the child.

The new stepparent may expect the child to welcome a loving, better mother or father. However, the stepparent has learned about the other biological parent from a very biased reporter, namely their new spouse. Stepchildren may be hostile or distant (Ganong et al., 2011), getting sick, injured, or disruptive, or, if they are teenagers, pregnant, drunk, or arrested. That reaction in the children is understandable; so is the resentment that stepparents feel.

Few adults—biological parents or not—can live up to the generative ideal, day after day (Ganong et al., 2011). Some stepparents go to the other extreme, remaining aloof. Wrong again. Hopefully, the new couple feels happy with each other and their parenting roles, and that leads to a generative family (King et al., 2014).

Meeting the Challenge Twins pose special difficulties, and so does taking six children from three marriages on an outing, but these parents of this blended family seem to manage it well. It helps to have a spacious park nearby—this is Griffith Park, a large, urban park with hiking trails and a zoo in Los Angeles, California. Relationships within every family structure are more complex than outsiders imagine.

Foster Parents

An estimated 400,650 children were officially in foster care in the United States in 2011 (Child Welfare Information Gateway, 2013). Many others are unofficially in foster care, because someone other than their biological parents has taken them in.

This is the most difficult form of parenting of all, partly because foster children typically have emotional and behavioral needs that require intense involvement. Foster parents need to spend far more time and effort on each child than biological parents do, yet the social context tends to devalue their efforts (J. Smith et al., 2013).

Contrary to popular prejudice, adults become foster parents more often for psychosocial than financial reasons, part of the adult generativity impulse (Geiger et al., 2013). Official foster parents are paid, but they typically earn far less than a babysitter or than they would in a conventional job.

Most children are in foster care for less than a year, as the goal may be reunification with the birth parent. Children may be moved from one placement to another, or from foster care back to the original family, for reasons unrelated to the wishes, competence, or emotions of the foster parents. This makes it hard for the foster parents to develop a generative attachment to their children, and doubly admirable when they do.

The average child entering the foster-care system is 7 years old (Child Welfare Information Gateway, 2013). Many spent their early years with their birth families and are attached to them. Such human bonding is normally beneficial, not only for the children but also for the adults.

However, if birth parents are so neglectful or abusive that foster care is needed, the child's early insecure or disorganized attachment to their birth parents impedes relationships with the foster parent. Most foster children have experienced long-standing maltreatment and have witnessed violence; they are understandably suspicious of any adult (Dorsey et al., 2012).

Nonetheless, for adolescents who have been with a foster family for some time, about half of the children and adults develop a healthy, mutual attachment, a marked contrast to the relationship with their biological parents (Joseph et al., 2014).

For all forms of parenting, generative caring does not occur in the abstract; it involves a particular caregiver and care receiver. That means everything needs to be done to encourage attachment between the foster parent and child, including stable placement and support for foster parents.

Grandparents

As already mentioned, the empty-nest stage of a marriage, when children have finally grown up and started independent lives, is often a happy time for parents. Grown children are more often a source of pride than of stress. A new opportunity for generativity arises if grandchildren arrive. That event once occurred on average at age 40, but now, in developed nations, grandparenthood begins on average at about age 50 (Leopold & Skopek, 2015a).

Especially when the grandchildren's parents are troubled, grandparents worldwide believe that they must help raise their grandchildren (Herlofson & Hagestad, 2012). Specifics depend on policies, customs, gender, past parenting, and income of both adult generations, but for every adult, the generative impulse extends to caring for the youngest generation.

Grandparents try to be helpful, whether or not the grandchildren live with the grandparents, as about 5 percent do. In most such families, the parents are the major caregivers and grandparents need to be companions, not authorities. One grandmother said that her tongue was scarred because she had to bite it so often (Holmes & Nash, 2015).

Some U.S. households (about 1 percent) are two-generation families because the middle generation is missing. That is a *skipped-generation* family, with all parenting work done by the grandparents. Skipped-generation families require every ounce of generativity that grandparents can muster, often at the expense of their

Everybody Contributes A large four-generation family such as this one helps meet the human need for love and belonging, the middle level of Maslow's hierarchy. When social scientists trace who contributes what to whom, the results show that everyone does their part, but the flow is more down than up: Grandparents give more money and advice to younger generations than vice versa.

Jodi Cobb/National Geographic/Getty Images

own health and happiness. This family type sometimes is designated officially to provide kinship care (true for one-third of the foster children), and it may include formal adoption by the grandparents.

If a grandmother is employed, she is likely to retire early if she has major grandchild responsibility, because balancing a job, marriage, and family demands reduces her own health and well-being (Meyer, 2014). Stress may strain her marriage. One working grandmother reports:

> When my daughter divorced, they nearly lost the house to foreclosure, so I went on the loan and signed for them. But then again they nearly foreclosed, so my husband and I bought it. . . . I have to make the payment on my own house and most of the payment on my daughter's house, and that is hard. . . . I am hoping to get that money back from our daughter, to quell my husband's sense that the kids are all just taking and no one is ever giving back. He sometimes feels used and abused.
>
> *[quoted in Meyer, 2014, pp. 5–6]*

But before concluding that grandparents suffer when they are responsible for grandchildren, consider China, where millions of grandparents outside the urban areas become full-time caregivers because members of the middle generation have jobs in the cities, unable to take children with them. The working parents typically send money and visit when they can. For those grandparents, caring for their grandchildren correlates with *better* physical and psychological health than other Chinese elders (Baker & Silverstein, 2012). Thus, it is not the fact of grandparent care but the social context that makes it arduous.

This discussion of grandparents should not obscure the general fact that most grandparents enjoy their role, gain generativity from it, and are appreciated by their adult children. Some grandmothers are rhapsodic and spiritual about their experience. As one writes:

> Not until my grandson was born did I realize that babies are actually miniature angels assigned to break through our knee-jerk habits of resistance and to remind us that love is the real reason we're here.
>
> *[Golden, 2010, p. 125]*

Caregiving

Child care is the most common form of generativity for adults, but caregiving can and does occur in many other ways as well. Indeed, "life begins with care and ends with care" (Talley & Montgomery, 2013, p. 3). Some caregiving requires meeting physical needs—feeding, cleaning, and so on—but much of it involves fulfilling psychological needs. Caregiving is part of generative adulthood.

Kinkeepers

A prime example of caregiving in most multigenerational families is the **kinkeeper,** who gathers everyone for holidays, spreads the word about anyone's illness, relocation, or accomplishments, buys gifts for special occasions, and reminds family members of one another's birthdays and anniversaries (Sinardet & Mortelmans, 2009). Guided by their kinkeeper, all of the relatives become more generative.

Fifty years ago, kinkeepers were almost always women, usually the mother or grandmother of a large family. Now families are smaller and gender equity is more apparent, so some men or young women are kinkeepers. This role may seem burdensome, but caregiving provides both satisfaction and power (Mitchell, 2010).

kinkeeper Someone who becomes the gatherer and communications hub for their family.

Caregiving in Adulthood

Longer life expectancies for elders and a challenging economy means that more adults than ever are meeting the needs of their aging parents, children, and even their grandchildren. While children account for most of the financial strain, caring for adult parents may include hands-on caregiving. Problems arise if caregivers feel isolated, but generally caregiving adults are as happy as those who are not. Usually the benefits of close family relationships outweigh the stress of responsibilities.

U.S. HOUSEHOLDS IN 2012

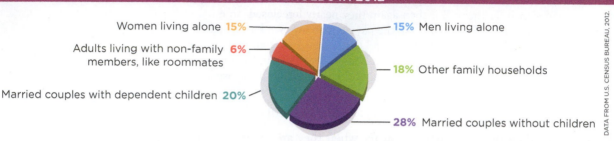

Women living alone **15%**

Adults living with non-family members, like roommates **6%**

Married couples with dependent children **20%**

15% Men living alone

18% Other family households

28% Married couples without children

DATA FROM U.S. CENSUS BUREAU, 2012.

SUPPORTING FAMILY MEMBERS

Most middle-aged adults live alone, or with someone of their generation. But of those living with another generation:

Almost half of 40- to 59-year-old adults are either raising a child under age 18 or financially supporting their grown children.

Only about 15% give financial support to both a child (of any age) and an aging parent.

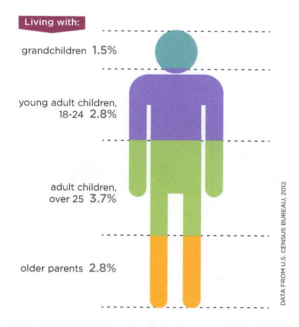

Living with:

grandchildren **1.5%**

young adult children, 18-24 **2.8%**

adult children, over 25 **3.7%**

older parents **2.8%**

DATA FROM U.S. CENSUS BUREAU, 2012.

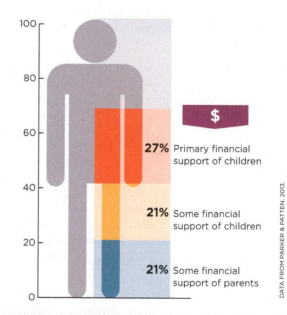

$

27% Primary financial support of children

21% Some financial support of children

21% Some financial support of parents

DATA FROM PARKER & PATTEN, 2013.

Only 16% of adults under 65 are caregivers for someone over 65. Of those 16%, less than half care for a parent. To be specific:

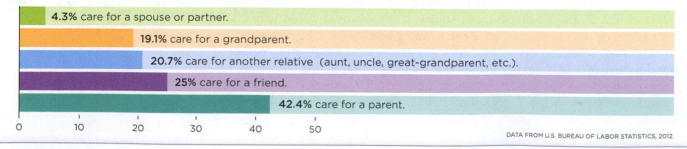

4.3% care for a spouse or partner.

19.1% care for a grandparent.

20.7% care for another relative (aunt, uncle, great-grandparent, etc.).

25% care for a friend.

42.4% care for a parent.

0   10   20   30   40   50

DATA FROM U.S. BUREAU OF LABOR STATISTICS, 2012.

Middle-aged adults have been called the **sandwich generation,** a term that evokes an image of a layer of filling pressed between two slices of bread. This analogy suggests that the middle generation is squeezed because they are expected to support their parents and their growing children. This sandwich metaphor is vivid but misleading (Gonyea, 2013; Grundy & Henretta, 2006).

Far from being squeezed, middle-aged adults who provide some financial and emotional help to their adult children are *less* likely to be depressed than those adults whose children no longer relate to them. Meanwhile, emerging adults, depicted as squeezing their parents, often take care of their parents.

The manifestation of care from emerging-adult children to their parents is not usually financial but cultural. They help their parents understand music, media, fashion, and technology—setting up their smartphones, sending digital photos, fixing computer glitches. They also are more cognizant of nutritional and medical discoveries and guidelines.

I have often experienced this in my family. For years, one of my adult daughters insisted that my Christmas gift to her should be for *me* to have a mammogram. Another daughter said that her birthday present should be to go clothes shopping with her for *myself.* She told me what to try on and advised me what to buy. All I did was pay for my own new clothes.

As for caregiving on the other side of the supposed sandwich, from middle-aged adults to their elderly parents, this is typically much less demanding than the metaphor implies. Most of the over-60 generation are capable of caring for themselves, and financial support is more likely to flow from them to their middle-aged children than vice versa. If they need daily care, a spouse, another elderly person, or a paid caregiver is more likely to provide it than a daughter or son. Middle-aged adults do their part as members of a caregiving team for older relatives, but they are not often stuck in the middle of a sandwich.

Thus, every adult of a family cares for every other one, each in their own way. The specifics depend on many factors, including childhood attachments, personality patterns, and the financial and practical resources of each generation. Mutual caregiving strengthens family bonds; wise kinkeepers share the work; everyone is generative.

Employment

Besides parenthood and caregiving, the other major avenue for generativity is employment. A well-established specialty within psychology focuses on increasing the productivity of workers and companies. That is useful for the study of development, since productivity can benefit everyone. There is extensive research regarding when and where telecommuting is beneficial, on how to organize work teams and times, and on almost every aspect of job conditions—lighting, wall colors, coffee breaks, and more.

However, here we consider the more personal details of human development, not productivity. So, we will now look at how employment affects people as they grow older.

Generativity and Work

As is evident from many terms that describe healthy adult development—*generativity, success and esteem, instrumental,* and *achievement*—adults have many psychosocial needs that work can fill.

Work meets these needs by allowing people to do the following:

- Develop and use their personal skills.
- Express their creative energy.

sandwich generation The generation of middle-aged people who are supposedly "squeezed" by the needs of the younger and older members of their families.

- Aid and advise coworkers, as mentor or friend.
- Support the education and health of their families.
- Contribute to the community by providing goods or services.

extrinsic rewards of work The tangible benefits, usually in salary, insurance, pension, and status, that come with employment.

intrinsic rewards of work The personal gratifications, such as pleasure in a job well done or friendships with coworkers, that accompany employment.

These facts highlight the distinction between the **extrinsic rewards of work** (the tangible benefits such as salary, health insurance, and pension) and the **intrinsic rewards of work** (the intangible gratifications of actually doing the job). Generativity is intrinsic.

The power of these rewards is affected by age. Extrinsic rewards tend to be more important when young people are first hired (Kooij et al., 2011).

Parents of young children are particularly concerned with income, hours, and health care. After a few years, in a developmental shift, the intrinsic rewards of work, especially relationships with coworkers, become more important (Inceoglu et al., 2012).

The power of intrinsic rewards explains why older employees are, on average, less often absent or late, and more committed to doing a good job, than younger workers are (Rau & Adams, 2014). Because of seniority, they also have more control over what they do, as well as when and how they do it. (Autonomy reduces strain and increases dedication.) Further, experienced workers are more likely to be mentors—people who help new workers navigate the job. Mentors benefit in many ways, gaining status and generativity.

Surprisingly, absolute income (whether a person earns $30,000 or $40,000 or even $100,000 a year, for instance) matters less for job satisfaction than how a person's income compares with others in their profession or neighborhood, or with their own salary a year or two ago. It is a human trait to react more strongly to losses than to gains, ignoring systemic losses unless they reduce one's personal fortune (Kahneman, 2011). Salary cuts have emotional, not just financial, effects.

For adults of any age, unemployment—especially if it lasts more than a few weeks—is destructive of mental and physical health. Generative needs are unmet, which increases domestic abuse, substance use disorder, depression, and many other social and mental health problems (Paul & Moser, 2009; Wanberg, 2012).

A meta-analysis of research on eight stressful events found that losing a job was worst. A bout of unemployment reduced self-esteem more than even divorce or death of a parent. The stress of unemployment lingered after finding a job (Luhmann et al., 2012).

Developmentalists are particularly concerned when the economy, or the automization of labor, results in fewer jobs for millions of adults. Current unemployment of emerging adults—people who are NEET (Not in Education, Employment, or Training)—may harm that generation lifelong, a "grave concern." One careful study of thousands of NEETs in Great Britain found that they seek work but are stymied by the job market and by their own traits (Goldman-Mellor, 2016, p. 201).

NOT AS WELL OFF AS OUR PARENTS WERE AT OUR AGE

Lowered Expectations It was once realistic, a "secular trend," for adults to expect to be better off than their parents had been, but hard times have reduced the socioeconomic status of many adults.

Unemployment is troubling at any age. Adults who are unemployed are 60 percent more likely to die than other people, especially if they are younger than 40 (Roelfs et al., 2011). They are twice as likely to be clinically depressed (Wanberg, 2012) and almost twice as likely to be addicted to drugs (Compton et al., 2014).

These statistics need to be put in context. The death rate is low during these years, but the depression and drug abuse rate is substantial. This means that unemployment is a significant drag on healthy development. A crucial buffer is social support from family and friends—more evidence of the importance of linked lives (Crowe & Butterworth, 2016).

What about those who have jobs? Most Americans are troubled about the large income gap between the rich and the poor. They wish that the salary distribution were less skewed. However, relatively few consider this a major problem (Norton & Ariely, 2011). Given that a sense of fairness is innate, many psychologists wonder why this isn't more troubling. One answer is that people believe that social mobility is possible, that they themselves will soon be able to earn more (Davidai & Gilovich, 2015).

Apparently, resentment about work arises not directly from wages and benefits but from how wages are determined and whether people believe that their income or status might improve. If workers have a role in setting wages, and they perceive that those wages are fair, they are more satisfied (Choshen-Hillel & Yaniv, 2011).

> **THINK CRITICALLY:** Is the connection between employment and developmental health cause or correlation?

The Changing Workplace

Employment is changing in many ways that affect adult development. We focus here on only three—diversity among workers, job changes, and alternate schedules. Dramatic shifts have occurred in all three. We will use U.S. statistics to illustrate these shifts, but these phenomena are occurring worldwide.

As you can see from Figure 22.3, the workforce is becoming more diverse. Fifty years ago, the U.S. civilian labor force was 74 percent male and 89 percent non-Hispanic White. In 2014, 53 percent were male and 80 percent non-Hispanic White (16 percent were Hispanic, 11 percent African American, and 6 percent Asian).

This shift is also notable within occupations. For example, in 1960, male nurses and female police officers were rare, perhaps 1 percent. Now 11 percent of registered nurses are men and 14 percent of police officers are women—still not equal, but a dramatic shift nonetheless (U.S. Bureau of Labor Statistics, 2016b). Job discrimination relating to gender and ethnicity still exists [16 percent of police officers but 18 percent of the population is Hispanic]—but it is much less prevalent than it once was.

These changes benefit millions of adults who would have been jobless in previous decades, but they also require workers and employers to be sensitive to differences that they did not previously notice (see A View from Science on p. 636). Younger adults may have an advantage: A 25-year-old employee is not surprised to have a female boss or a coworker from another ethnic group. Since a goal of human development is for everyone to fill their potential, reduced discrimination in employment is welcomed by developmentalists. The next two changes are not as welcome.

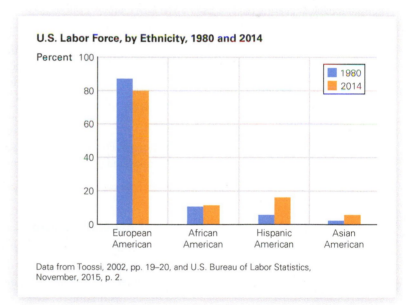

Data from Toossi, 2002, pp. 19–20, and U.S. Bureau of Labor Statistics, November, 2015, p. 2.

FIGURE 22.3

Diversity at Work The U.S. labor force is increasingly non-White, even according to Labor Department statistics (which exclude some low-wage workers). The next challenge is for women and people of all ethnic groups to be more proportionally distributed in various vocations, management positions, and workplaces.

Observation Quiz Which group has had the largest increase in labor force participation? (See answer, page 636)

Accommodating Diversity

Accommodating the various sensitivities and needs of a diverse workforce requires far more than reconsidering the cafeteria menu and the holiday schedule. Private rooms for breast-feeding, revised uniform guidelines, new office design, and changing management practices may be necessary. Exactly what is needed depends on the particular culture of the workers: Some are satisfied with conditions that others would reject.

New Zealand supervisors of European descent criticize Maori workers (descendent from Polynesians who had arrived there several hundred years before the first Europeans) for "extending the leave they were given for attending a family or tribe *hui* (gathering or meeting) without notifying them . . . If the reasons behind are not understood, such critical incidents may . . . easily lead to over-generalizations and stereotyping and finally to less employment of people who are labeled as 'unreliable'" (Podsiadlowski & Fox, 2011, p. 8).

What might those "reasons behind" be? For British New Zealanders, a funeral of a cousin might take a day. Employees from that culture resent that a Maori coworker might be gone much longer, appearing back at work a week or more later.

Yet the Maori were expected by their families to stay for several days: It would be disrespectful to leave quickly. The cultural clash regarding work schedules and family obligations led to anger and rejection.

Less obvious examples occur daily, at every workplace. Certain words, policies, jokes, or mannerisms seem innocuous to one group but hostile to others.

- Women object to racy calendars or pictures in construction offices—something male workers once accepted as routine.

- Exchanging Christmas presents, as in the office Secret Santa, may be troubling to those who are Jehovah's Witnesses or to those who are not Christian.

- Resentment may stir if a man calls a woman "honey" or if a supervisor creates a nickname for an employee with a hard-to-pronounce name.

- Comments about a celebrity of another race may be heard as insults.

Researchers have begun to explore *micro-aggressions*—small things unnoticed by one person that seem aggressive to another (Sue, 2010). Mentioning "senior moments," or being "color-blind," or the "fairer sex," or "the model minority" can be perceived as aggressive, even though the speaker believes they are benign.

The question "Where are you from?" may seem innocent, or even friendly, but it implies that someone is from elsewhere. This question may be micro-aggressive to a Hispanic American born in Puerto Rico or Texas, whose family members have been U.S. citizens for decades (Nadal et al., 2014).

Micro-aggressions can affect anyone who feels different because of their ethnicity, age, gender, sexual orientation, religion, or anything else. For example, one research group found that older workers were particularly likely to notice ageist micro-aggressions at their workplace but that some young men heard micro-aggressions about them (Chou & Choi, 2011).

To create a workplace that respects diversity, mutual effort is needed. Not only must everyone learn about sensitivities and customs, but everyone also must communicate. When an innocent comment is heard as an insult, both parties need to be more aware.

Changing Locations

Today's workers change employers more often than did workers decades ago. Hiring and firing are common. Employers constantly downsize, reorganize, relocate, outsource, or merge. Loyalty between employee and employer, once assumed, now seems quaint.

Whether they originate from the worker or the employers, changes may increase corporate profits, worker benefits, and consumer choice. However, churning employment may harm development. Losing work friendships means losing a source of social support. This problem may be worse for older adults for several reasons (Rix, 2011):

1. Seniority brings higher salaries, more respect, and greater expertise; workers who leave a job they have had for years lose these advantages.
2. Many skills required for employment were not taught decades ago, so older workers are less likely to find a new job.
3. Workers believe that age discrimination is widespread. Even if this is a misperception, stereotype threat undercuts successful job searching.
4. Especially if a new job requires relocation, long-standing intimacy and generativity are reduced.

Answer to Observation Quiz
(from page 635): Hispanic Americans. The reason is that far more Hispanic adults are of working age than was true decades ago.

If You Had to Choose Which is more important, a high salary or comfortable working conditions? Intrinsic rewards of work are scarce for these workers in Mumbai, India *(left)*, who talk to North Americans who call in confused about their computers, their bills, or their online orders, as well as for the man in eastern Colorado *(right)*. His relationships with co-workers and supervisors may not be comforting, and he may have heard that fracking increases pollution, earthquakes, and cancer (hence the protective gear). Most workers who have few psychosocial benefits at work are much younger than the average employee.

From a developmental and family perspective, this last factor is crucial. Imagine that you are a 40-year-old who has always lived in West Virginia, and your employer goes out of business. You try to find work, but no one hires you, partly because unemployment in West Virginia is among the highest in the nation. Would you move a thousand miles west to North Dakota, where the unemployment rate is half that of West Virginia (U.S. Bureau of Labor Statistics, 2016a)?

If you were unemployed and in debt, and a new job was guaranteed, you might. You would leave friends, community, and local culture, but at least you would have a paycheck.

But, would your family leave their homes, jobs, schools, churches, and friends to move with you? If not, you would be deprived of social support; but if they did, their food and housing would be expensive, their schools overcrowded, and their lives lonely (at least initially). For you and anyone who comes with you, moving means losing intimacy—harmful for psychosocial development.

Such difficulties are magnified for immigrants, who make up about 15 percent of the U.S. adult workforce and 22 percent of Canada's. Many depend on other immigrants for housing, work, religion, and social connections (García Coll & Marks, 2012). That may meet some of their intimacy and generativity needs, but their relationships with their original family and friends are strained by distance. The climate, the food, and the language are not comforting.

Developmental needs are ignored by most business owners and by many workers themselves. However, intimacy and generatively are best satisfied by a thriving social network, and each neighborhood and workplace fosters that. When that is disrupted, psychological and physical health suffers.

Changing Schedules

The standard workweek is 9 A.M. to 5 P.M., Monday through Friday—a schedule that is increasingly unusual. In the United States, about one-third of all workers have nonstandard schedules. Retail services (virtual and in-store) are increasingly available 24/7, which requires night and weekend employees. Many other parts of the economy (hospitals, police, hotels) need employees with nonstandard schedules. Employers, customers, and employees see many benefits.

Especially for Entrepreneurs Suppose you are starting a business. In what ways would middle-aged adults be helpful to you? (see response, page 638)

Insecurity More than 1 million people in the United States work as security guards, often spending long lonely nights watching video cameras, as this man does. How might his work hours, sleep schedule, and family life be different from the average office worker's?

Response for Entrepreneurs
(from page 637): As employees and as customers. Middle-aged workers are steady, with few absences and good "people skills," and they like to work. In addition, household income is likely to be higher at about age 50 than at any other time, so middle-aged adults are more likely to afford your products or services. Of course, it depends on what you are selling; some products are rarely purchased by those over age 25.

It has long been recognized that non-standard, varying schedules upset the body rhythms of adults, making them more vulnerable to physical illness as well as emotional problems. Recently, an entire issue of an academic journal was devoted to these problems (Chronobiology International, 2016).

The impact on human development, especially family life, is rarely considered when employers hire new workers. Those who are most likely to have mandatory, nonstandard schedules are parents of young children.

Weekend work, especially with mandatory overtime, is difficult for father–child relationships, because "normal rhythms of family life are impinged upon by irregular schedules" (Hook, 2012, p. 631). Mothers with nonstandard employment get less sleep and are more stressed (Kalil et al., 2014b). Couples who have less time together are more likely to divorce (Maume & Sebastian, 2012).

Another problem arises for skilled, higher income, experienced workers. They may benefit from *flextime* (some choice as to days and hours) or *telecommuting* (working via Internet, phone, and fax, often at home). They may welcome the flexibility.

However, with more skills and responsibilities also come more demands: Many such workers find that work is always in their lives, on evenings and weekends. The boundaries between work life and family life are porous, as a text message at home can interrupt family time with an unanticipated deadline, last-minute travel, or other demands.

Choices about hours, overtime, and tasks increase job satisfaction. This is true no matter how experienced the workers are, what their occupation is, or where they live (Tuttle & Garr, 2012). For instance, a nationwide study of 53,851 nurses, ages 20 to 59, found that *required* overtime was one of the few factors that reduced job satisfaction in every cohort (Klaus et al., 2012). Apparently, although employment is often satisfying, working too long and not by choice may undercut the psychological and physical benefits.

In theory, part-time work and self-employment might allow adults to balance conflicting demands. But reality does not conform to the theory. In many nations, part-time work is underpaid. Thus, workers avoid part-time employment if they can, again making a choice that inadvertently undercuts their emotional well-being and family life.

Finding the Balance

As you see, adulthood is filled with opportunities and challenges. Adults choose their mates, their locations, their lifestyles and their vocations to express their personality. Extroverts surround themselves with many social activities and introverts choose a more quiet, but no less rewarding, life.

Both men and women have many ways to meet intimacy needs, with partners of the same or other sex, marriage or cohabiting, friends and family, parents or grown children. Ideally, they find some combination that results in solid social support. Similarly, generativity can focus on raising children, caregiving of others, or satisfying work, again with more choices and flexibility than in past decades.

In some ways, then, modern life allows adults to "have it all," to combine family and work in such a way that all needs are satisfied. However, some very articulate observers suggest that "having it all" is an illusion or, at best, a mistaken ideal achievable only by the very rich and very talented (Slaughter, 2012; Sotomayor, 2014).

Compromises, trade-offs, and selective optimization with compensation may be essential to find an appropriate work–family balance. Both halves of these two sources of generativity can bring joy, but both can bring stress—and often do.

In linked lives, husbands and wives usually adjust to each other's needs, allowing them to function better as a couple than they did as singles (Abele & Volmer, 2011). A large survey found that five years after their wedding the man's salary is notably higher than it would have been if he were single, while their home was more comfortable, perhaps because the wife had worked to make it so (Kuperberg, 2012). Those benefits may reflect gender norms, but both spouses should be credited with improvements in each other's lives. In general, adults—mates, family, and friends—help each other, together balancing intimacy and generativity needs.

Because personality is enduring and variable, opinions about the impact of modern life reflect personality as well as objective research. Some people are optimists—high in extroversion and agreeableness—and they tend to believe that adulthood is better now than it used to be. Others are pessimists—high in neuroticism and low in openness—and they are likely to conclude that adults were better off before the rise of cohabitation, LAT, divorce, and economic stress. They are nostalgic for the time when most people married and stayed married, raising their children on the man's steady salary from his 9-to-5 job with one stable employer.

Data could be used to support both perspectives. For instance, in the United States, suicide is less common than it used to be (life is better), but the gap between rich and poor is increasing (life is worse). Fewer people are marrying and fewer children are born: Is that evidence for improved adult lives or the opposite? Opinions vary, partly because of the age, gender and ethnicity of the person who judges.

From a developmental perspective, personality, intimacy, and generativity are important in every adult life. Many researchers study work–family balance; their conclusions differ. Much depends on whether or not adults are able to feel in control of their lives, achieving the balance they want (Allen et al., 2012; Chan et al., 2016). As recognition of the macrosystem and exosystem makes clear, balancing work and family is depends partly on factors beyond the individual.

Every adult benefits from friends and family, caregiving responsibilities, and satisfying work. Whether finding a satisfying combination of all of this is easier or more difficult at this historical moment is debatable.

As the next trio of chapters detail, there are many possible perspectives on life in late adulthood as well. Some view the last years of life with horror, while others consider them golden. Soon you will have your own view, informed by empirical data, not prejudice.

WHAT HAVE YOU LEARNED?

1. How is generativity a distinct human need?

2. In what ways does parenthood satisfy the need to be generative?

3. Why might it be more difficult for parents to bond with nonbiological children?

4. Is it a blessing or a burden that women are more often kinkeepers and caregivers than are men?

5. Why is it a mistake to call middle-aged adults the "sandwich generation"?

6. What are some extrinsic and intrinsic rewards of employment?

7. What are the advantages of greater ethnic diversity at work places?

8. Why is changing jobs stressful?

9. How have innovations in work scheduling helped and harmed families?

SUMMARY

Personality Development in Adulthood

1. Erikson emphasized that people at every stage of life are influenced by their social context. The adulthood stages are much less age-based than the childhood stages because the need for intimacy and generativity are evident throughout adulthood.

2. Maslow and other humanists believe that people of all ethnic and national origins have the same basic needs. They first must have their physical needs met and then feel safe. Beyond that, love and respect are crucial. Finally, people can be truly themselves, becoming self-actualized.

3. Personality traits over the years of adulthood are quite stable, although many adults become closer to their culture's ideal. The Big Five personality traits—openness, conscientiousness, extroversion, agreeableness, and neuroticism—characterize personality at every age. Culture and context affect everyone.

Intimacy: Connecting with Others

4. Intimacy is a universal human need, satisfied in diverse ways, with romantic partners, friends, and family. Variations are evident, by culture and cohort.

5. Marriage is no longer the only way to establish a romantic partnership. Although societies benefit if people marry and stay married, many adults prefer cohabitation, or living apart together. Same-sex and other-sex relationships are similar in most ways.

6. Divorce sometimes may be the best end for a conflicted relationship, but divorce is difficult for both partners and their family members, not only immediately but for years before and after the decree.

7. Remarriage is common, especially for men. This solves some of the problems (particularly financial and social) of divorced adults, but the success of second marriages varies. Children add complications.

8. Friends are crucial for buffering stress and sharing secrets, for everyday companionship and guidance. This is true for both men and women, with younger adults having more friends but older adults preferring fewer, closer friends.

9. Family members have linked lives, continuing to affect one another as they all grow older. Family members are often mutually supportive, emotionally and financially, whether or not they share a household.

Generativity: The Work of Adulthood

10. Adults seek to be generative, successful, achieving, instrumental—all words used to describe a major psychosocial need that each adult meets in various ways.

11. Parenthood is a common expression of generativity. Even wanted and planned-for biological children pose challenges; foster children, stepchildren, and adoptive children bring additional stresses and joys.

12. Caregiving is more likely to flow from the older generations to the younger ones, so the "sandwich generation" metaphor is misleading. Many families have a kinkeeper, who aids generativity within the family.

13. Employment brings many rewards to adults, including intrinsic benefits such as pride and friendship. Changes in employment patterns—job switches, shift work, and the diversity of fellow workers—affect other aspects of adult development. Unemployment is particularly difficult for self-esteem.

14. Combining work schedules, caregiving requirements, and intimacy needs is not easy. Some adults benefit from new patterns within the labor market; others find that the demands of their jobs impair family well-being.

KEY TERMS

intimacy versus isolation (p. 615)
generativity versus stagnation (p. 615)

humanism (p. 615)
Big Five (p. 617)
LAT (p. 620)
empty nest (p. 621)

social convoy (p. 623)
fictive kin (p. 625)
kinkeeper (p. 631)
sandwich generation (p. 633)

extrinsic rewards of work (p. 634)
intrinsic rewards of work (p. 634)

APPLICATIONS

1. Describe a relationship that you know of in which a middle-aged person and a younger adult learned from each other.

2. Did your parents' marital and employment status affect you? How would you have fared if they had chosen other marriage or work patterns?

3. Imagine becoming a foster parent or adoptive parent yourself. What do you see as the personal benefits and costs?

4. Ask several people how their personalities have changed in the past decade. The research suggests that changes are usually minor. Is that what your interviewees say?

The Developing Person So Far:
Adulthood

BIOSOCIAL

Senescence As bodies age, internal as well as external organs show the effects of senescence. The brain slows down; skin becomes more wrinkled; the senses become less acute; lungs reduce capacity. Bodies change shape, with more fat in the middle and less strength in the muscles.

The Sexual-Reproductive System Sexual responsiveness and reproductive potential are reduced over adulthood. Women experience a dramatic drop in estrogen at menopause, which stops ovulation; men experience a more gradual decline in testosterone, which makes fatherhood less likely but not impossible.

Health Habits and Age Cigarette smoking is decreasing in North America but not in many other nations. Alcohol abuse, obesity, and inactivity are now recognized as problems, but most adults find them hard to reverse.

Measuring Health There are many ways to measure health, whether by calculating mortality, morbidity, disability, or vitality. Overall health is partly dependent on heredity, but much depends on daily habits. Education and income are critical.

COGNITIVE

What Is Intelligence? Researchers measure adult intelligence in many ways. Longitudinal research shows intelligence increasing over the years of adulthood, whereas cross-sectional research finds a decline. Cross-sequential research shows decreases in speeded tests but increases in vocabulary. Analytic intelligence is particularly valuable in universities; creative intelligence is essential in the arts. Practical intelligence, particularly social understanding, is increasingly needed through life's ups and downs.

Selective Gains and Losses Selective compensation with optimization is apparent in adulthood, as people become experts in areas of life that they choose to specialize in. In general, people are more intuitive, automatic, strategic, and flexible when dealing with problems in their area of expertise than they are in other areas. Every adult accumulates expertise in some selected area.

PSYCHOSOCIAL

Personality Development in Adulthood All the major theories of adult development note that people maintain personality traits yet show some change. For instance, people become more conscientious and less neurotic with age. The Big Five traits reflect culture and are strengthened by a person's chosen lifestyle and ecological niche.

Intimacy: Family and Friends Adults need friends and family. They usually find good friends and have rewarding relationships with their adult children and their aging parents. Marriage, cohabitation, and LAT can all be rewarding. However, breakups and divorces can be harmful for adults as well as children. Adults depend on their life partners, whether of the same sex or the other sex.

Generativity Caregiving is part of the joy as well as the obligation of adulthood. Many adults spend time and money on child rearing. Filial obligation is strong, with some adults caring for older family members. The sandwich generation concept is more myth than reality, and older generations usually provide financial and emotional support for younger generations. Employment is satisfying for many adults, although some trends, such as shift work and job change, harm optimal psychosocial development.

late adulthood

What emotions do you expect when you read about late adulthood? Sadness, fear, depression, resignation, sympathy, sorrow? Expect instead surprise and joy. You will learn that most older adults are active, alert, and self-sufficient; that dramatic loss of memory and logic ("senility") is unusual; and that many are independent and happy.

This does not mean that you should anticipate mindless contentment. Earlier personality and social connections continue; the complexities of life are evident. Joy is mixed with sorrow. Poverty, loneliness, and chronic illness are difficult. However, most older adults, most of the time, overcome such difficulties.

If you doubt this, you are not alone. Late adulthood, more than any other part of life, is a magnet for misinformation. Ageism may be worse than other -*isms*, because everyone experiences it if they live long enough, but almost no one is well prepared.

Late Adulthood:
Biosocial Development

What Will You Know?

1. How is ageism like racism?
2. Can people slow down the aging process?
3. Why would anyone want to live to 100?

I took Asa, age 1, to the playground. One mother, watching her son, warned that the sandbox would soon be crowded because the children from a nearby day-care center were coming. I asked questions, and to my delight she explained details of the center's curriculum, staffing, scheduling, and tuition as if she assumed I was Asa's mother, weighing my future options.

Soon I realized she was merely being polite, because a girl too young to be graciously ageist glanced at me and asked, "Is that your grandchild?" I nodded. "Where is the mother?" was her next question.

Later that afternoon came the final blow. As I opened the gate for a middle-aged man, he said, "Thank you, young lady." I don't think I look old, but no one would imagine I was young. That "young lady" was benevolent, but it made me realize that my pleasure at the first woman's words was a sign of my own self-deceptive prejudice.

Now we begin our study of the last phase of life, from age 65 or so until death. This chapter starts by exploring the prejudices that surround aging. We describe biosocial changes—and what can be done to mitigate them. Then we provide a perspective on diseases, an exploration of the causes of aging, and finally a celebration of centenarians.

This is not a medical textbook, but various ailments that are common in the elderly—insomnia, heart disease, diabetes, osteoporosis, arthritis, erectile dysfunction, poor vision, deafness, hypertension, pneumonia, influenza, and accidental death—are all described in context, as examples of primary or secondary aging, selective optimization, the compression of morbidity, acute or chronic illness, and so on.

Prejudice and Predictions

Prejudice about late adulthood is common among people of all ages, including young children and older adults. That is **ageism,** which "shares parallels with other prejudices, such as racism and sexism. Like any form of bias, ageism effectively reduces individuals to broad, stereotypical categories" (North, 2015, p. 30).

ageism A prejudice whereby people are categorized and judged solely on the basis of their chronological age.

Left: Josu Altzelai/age fotostock
Top: Jupiterimages/DigitalVision/Getty Images

Older and Wiser Contrary to ageist ideas, older mountain climbers are less likely to fall to their death than younger ones. Judgment is crucial; a strong safety rope like this one is a smart precaution.

THINK CRITICALLY: Why do many people contemplate aging with sorrow rather than joy?

Compared to Other *-Isms*

Every *-ism* is destructive. The harm of racism and sexism are well-known, and other *-isms*, notably ableism (the idea that those with disabilities are less worthy), are recognized as limiting human potential. But in two ways, ageism may be worse.

First, as one expert contends:

> There is no other group like the elderly about which we feel free to openly express stereotypes and even subtle hostility. . . . Most of us . . . believe that we aren't really expressing negative stereotypes or prejudice, but merely expressing true statements about older people when we utter our stereotypes.

> *[Nelson, 2011, p. 40]*

Second, those who suffer the sting of ageism may be blindsided, unprepared to counteract the prejudice they experience. This is a marked contrast to racism and sexism, for which potential victims help each other to recognize and fight the stereotype.

Parents of non-White children engage in *racial socialization,* teaching their children about heroes of their group and alerting them to prejudice that they might experience and how to combat it. Similarly, parents of girls encourage them to participate in sports leagues, to excel in science, to become leaders in politics, or business, or medicine. Of course, much more needs to be done to counter racism, sexism, and all of the other *-isms*, but at least the problem is often recognized.

That is less true for ageism. In some ways, it is unrecognized but pervasive in the media, employment, and retirement communities (Nelson, 2011). Those who are victims are unprepared, because unlike those who are African American, or female, or whatever, they were never members of this stigmatized group—until time passed and suddenly they were. Older people of every ethnic group are vulnerable to ageist stereotype threat—when reminders of possible prejudice make them anxious and less able to function (Lamont et al., 2015).

One problem with many stereotypes is that they may appear benevolent, complimentary ("young lady"), or solicitous. However, the effects are insidious, eroding the older person's feelings of competence. Ageism fosters anxiety, morbidity, and even mortality.

Believing the Stereotype

Ageism becomes a *self-fulfilling prophecy,* a prediction that comes true because people believe it. There are three harmful consequences:

- If people of any age treat older people as if they are frail and confused, that treatment might make the aged more dependent on others.
- If people believe that the norms for young adults should apply to everyone, they may try to fix the old. If they fail, they give up.
- If older people themselves think that their age makes them feeble, they stop taking care of themselves and avoid social interaction, and that itself makes them age faster.

Attitudes toward aging may be one reason that longevity varies markedly depending on where a person lives. (The estimated life span for people born in various nations was shown in Figure 20.4, page 579.) Japan has the highest life expectancy in the world—a newborn Japanese girl is expected to live well into her 80s (United Nations, 2013)—perhaps because of cultural practices such as *Respect for the Aged Day,* when everyone is supposed to heed the wisdom of the aged.

I'm Not Like Those Other Old People

My mother, in her 80s, was reluctant to enter an assisted-living apartment. She told me that she did not want to live there because too many of the people were old. Her attitude was not unusual: Many older people believe that "they" are old, but "I" am younger (Weiss & Lang, 2012).

Asked how old they feel, most 80-year-olds lop a decade or more off their age (Pew Research Center, June 29, 2009). Think of the logical lapse here. If *most* 80-year-olds feel how they imagine the average 70-year-old feels, then that feeling is, in fact, typical of 80-year-olds. Thus, 80-year-olds have a stereotype of 80-year-olds, and they believe it does not apply to them.

This same phenomenon is apparent for every aspect of functioning in late adulthood. One study asked people to estimate trajectories over the life span of six cognitive functions and four social ones (Riediger et al., 2014). People of all age groups estimated that most people would decline, usually by age 60 and clearly by age 80. That is accurate: Many declines occur.

However, on every measure, older people were most likely to estimate that their own functioning was better than the average older person (see Table 23.1). This was particularly true for memory, speed, and making new friends—the three abilities most often stereotyped as dropping markedly with age. Again, they share a cultural stereotype and then reject it when it applies to them.

In an ageist culture, for older people to feel younger than others of their chronological age is understandable, even healthy. As one commentator noted, "feeling youthful is more strongly predictive of health than any other factors including commonly noted ones like chronological age, gender, marital status and socioeconomic status" (Barrett, 2012, p. 3). Self-perception is crucial. Another study found that:

> Perceptions are a strong predictor of psychological well-being in later life . . . [and] older adults with negative self-perceptions of aging also have greater levels of disability, ill health, worse physical function and a higher risk of mortality over time.
>
> [Robertson et al., 2016, p. 71]

This study tried to zoom in on exactly what aspects of ageism were worst. The answer was that ageism undermined the sense of control. People who strongly disagreed with "as I get older, there is much I can do to maintain my independence" were most likely to have reduced memory over time (Robertson et al., 2016, p. 73).

THINK CRITICALLY: How do you compare to other people your age?

TABLE 23.1	How Do You Compare to Other People Your Age?			
	9-Year-Olds	13- to 15-Year-Olds	21- to 26-Year-Olds	70- to 76-Year-Olds
Memory	Better	Same	Worse	Better
Cognitive speed	Same	Worse	Worse	Better
Mental math	Better	Same	Worse	Better
Concentration	Same	Same	Worse	Better
New friends	Same	Worse	Worse	Better
Self-assertion	Better	Same	Same	Better

Information from Riediger et al., 2014.

Not Like the Others People in this study thought that most young adults were quite competent in these six areas and that most older people were not. That is accurate, according to laboratory research. However, when evaluating themselves, most emerging adults thought their peers were better, and most older adults thought their peers were worse.

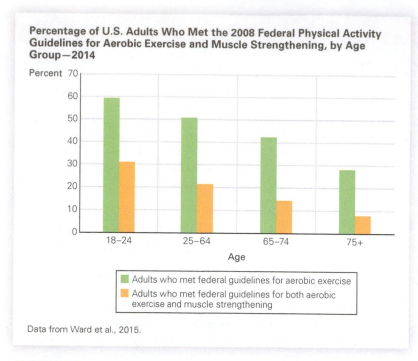

Percentage of U.S. Adults Who Met the 2008 Federal Physical Activity Guidelines for Aerobic Exercise and Muscle Strengthening, by Age Group—2014

Data from Ward et al., 2015.

FIGURE 23.1

Hearts, Lungs, and Legs As you see, most of the elderly do not meet the minimum exercise standards recommended by the Centers for Disease Control—150 minutes of aerobic exercise a week and muscle-strengthening exercises twice a week. This is especially troubling since those activities have been proven many times to safeguard the health of all the major organs, as well as to correlate with intelligence, memory, and joy.

How to Travel Exercise is not just a personal choice; it is also a cultural and cohort one. Bicycles were once considered children's toys. Now we know that every senior should be active like these men.

Observation Quiz Is this the United States? (see answer, page 650) ↑

When older people believe that they are independent and in control of their own lives, they are likely to be healthier—mentally, as well as physically—than others their age. Of course some need special care. Elders must find "a delicate balance . . . knowing when to persist and when to switch gears, . . . [and] some aspects of aging are out of one's control" (Lachman et al., 2011, p. 186). If an older person is struggling to carry a heavy bag, help might be appreciated. But do not assume; ask first, never just grab the bag.

Now we consider other specific examples of ways in which ageism can affect health.

How to Fight Insomnia

Ageism impairs the routines of daily life. It prevents depressed older people from seeking help because they resign themselves to infirmity.

One specific example is sleep. The day–night circadian rhythm diminishes with age: Many older people wake before dawn and are sleepy during the day. Older adults spend more time in bed, take longer to fall asleep, and wake frequently (about 10 times per night) (Ayalon & Ancoli-Israel, 2009). They also are more likely to nap. All of this is normal: If they choose their own sleep schedules, elders feel less tired than young adults.

However, many older people complain of sleep problems because they get up during the night, are tired in the early evening, and are wide awake at dawn. None of these is a problem, but ageism makes them so.

In one study, older adults complaining of sleep problems were mailed six booklets (one each week) (K. Morgan et al., 2012). The booklets described normal sleep patterns for people their age and gave suggestions to relieve insomnia, such as not watching TV in bed and getting up when the body woke up. Compared to similar older people who did not get the booklets, the informed elders used less sleep medication and reported better-quality sleep. Even six months after the last booklet, they were more satisfied with their sleep.

By contrast, uninformed elders in an ageist culture are distressed about sleep. Doctors might prescribe narcotics, or people might drink alcohol. These remedies can overwhelm an aging body, causing heavy sleep, confusion, nausea, depression, and unsteadiness.

Less Exercise or More?

A similar downward spiral is apparent with regard to exercise. In the United States, only 35 percent of those age 65 and over meet the recommended guidelines for aerobic exercise, a contrast to 55 percent for adults aged 18 to 64 (National Center for Health Statistics, 2016) (see Figure 23.1). Meeting the guidelines for muscle strengthening was worse; only 11 percent of the aged did so.

How are these lower rates the result of ageism? A study of the reasons older adults do not exercise found many reasons. Some still fear that exercise will harm them (people used to believe that), and for everyone social support is crucial. When older adults can exercise with others (from taking walks to joining a team), they are likely to do so (Franco et al., 2015).

However, most team sports are organized to accommodate the young; traditional dancing assumes a balanced sex ratio; many yoga, aerobics, and other classes are paced and designed for people in their 20s. If an old man tries to join a pickup basketball game, the reaction of the young players might be rejection. If an old woman dons running shorts and jogs around the park, others might snicker.

Added to the problems caused by the ageism of the culture is self-imposed ageism. Instead of pushing against stiffness, an older adult might choose comfort—reducing range of motion while impairing circulation and digestion. If balance is decreased, elders might walk less, instead of getting better shoes, a cane, or whatever.

Talk and Prejudice

Many people think they are compassionate when they infantilize the elderly, regarding them as if they were children ("so cute," "second childhood") (Albert & Freedman, 2010). Some of the elderly accept the stereotype. It is easier not to protest: At every age and for every preconceived idea, changing someone else's attitudes and assumptions is difficult.

Among the professionals most likely to harbor stereotypes are nurses, doctors, and other care workers. Their ageism is difficult to erase (Eymard & Douglas, 2012), partly because it is based on their experience in treating older patients who are sick and dependent. It is understandable—and harmful—to generalize based on one's own experience with sick and feeble elderly (Williams et al., 2009).

One noted example is **elderspeak**—the way people talk to the old (Kemper, 2015; Nelson, 2011). Like baby talk, elderspeak uses simple and short sentences, slower talk, higher pitch, louder volume, and frequent repetition. Elderspeak is especially patronizing when people call an older person "honey" or "dear," or use a nickname instead of a surname ("Billy," not "Mr. White").

Ironically, many aspects of elderspeak reduce communication (Kemper, 2015). Higher frequencies are harder for the elderly to hear, stretching out words makes comprehension worse, shouting causes anxiety, and simplified vocabulary reduces the precision of language.

Elderspeak is prevalent in hospitals, nursing homes, and lawyer's offices. Ageism makes talking down to older people seem appropriate, but professionals can learn to communicate without stereotyping (Kemper, 2015; Sprangers et al., 2015).

Destructive Protection

Some younger adults and the media discourage the elderly from leaving home. For example, whenever an older person is robbed, raped, or assaulted, sensational headlines add to fear and consequently promote ageism. In fact, street crime targets young adults, not old ones (see Figure 23.2).

The homicide rate (the most reliable indicator of violent crime, since reluctance to report is not an issue) of those over age 65 is less than one-fifth the rate for those in their 20s (FBI, 2015). To protect our relatives, perhaps we should insist that our young adults never leave the house alone—a ridiculous suggestion that makes it obvious why telling older adults to stay home is shortsighted.

Although advertisements induce younger adults to buy medical-alert devices for older relatives, it might be better to go biking with them. Lest you think that bikes are only for children, a study of five nations (Germany, Italy, Finland, Hungary, and the Netherlands) found that 15 percent of Europeans *older than* 75 ride their bicycles *every day* (Tacken & van Lamoen, 2005).

Safe Crossing Professionals least likely to use elderspeak are those like this one who interact with dozens of typical, community-dwelling elders every day.

elderspeak A condescending way of speaking to older adults that resembles baby talk, with simple and short sentences, exaggerated emphasis, repetition, and a slower rate and a higher pitch than used in normal speech.

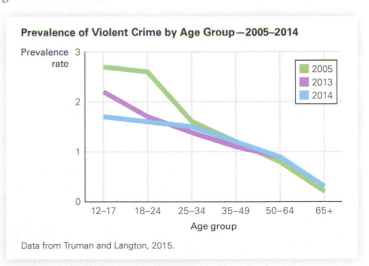

Data from Truman and Langton, 2015.

FIGURE 23.2

Victims of Crime As people grow older, they are less likely to be crime victims. These figures come from personal interviews in which respondents were asked whether they had been the victim of a violent crime—assault, sexual assault, rape, or robbery—in the past several months. This approach yields more accurate results than official crime statistics because many crimes are never reported to the police.

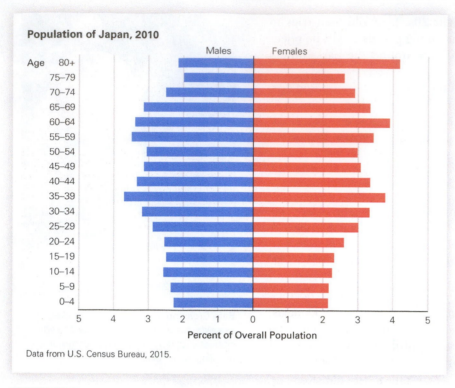

Population of Japan, 2010

Males   Females

Age   80+
75–79
70–74
65–69
60–64
55–59
50–54
45–49
40–44
35–39
30–34
25–29
20–24
15–19
10–14
5–9
0–4

5   4   3   2   1   0   1   2   3   4   5

Percent of Overall Population

Data from U.S. Census Bureau, 2015.

FIGURE 23.3

Not Yet Square But certainly not a pyramid. Changes in birth rates worldwide are already making the shape of the population square in some nations, evident in Japan for those under age 25. If trends continue, Japan will be a rectangle in 50 years!

demographic shift A shift in the proportions of the populations of various ages.

In the United States, few elders ride bikes. Protected bike paths are scarce, and many bikes are designed for speed, not stability. Laws requiring bike helmets often apply only to children—another example of ageism.

The Demographic Shift

Demography is the science that describes populations, including population by cohort, age, gender, or region. Demographers refer to "the greatest demographic upheaval in human history" (Bloom, 2011, p. 562), a **demographic shift** in the proportions of the population of various ages. In an earlier era, there were 20 times more children than older people. Indeed, a mere 50 years ago the world had 7 times more people under age 15 than over age 64. This is no longer true.

The World's Aging Population

The United Nations estimates that 8 percent of the world's population in 2015 was 65 or older, compared with only 2 percent a century earlier. This number is expected to double by the year 2050. Already 15 percent in the United States are that old, as are 16 percent in Canada, 22 percent in Italy, and 26 percent in Japan (United Nations, 2015) (see Figure 23.3).

Demographers often depict the age structure of a population as a series of stacked bars, one bar for each age group, with the bar for the youngest at the bottom and the bar for the oldest at the top. Historically, the shape was a *demographic pyramid*. Like a wedding cake, it was widest at the base, and each higher level was narrower than the one beneath it, for three reasons—none of which is currently true:

1. More babies were born than the replacement rate of one per adult, so each new generation had more children than the previous one. (**NOW FALSE**)
2. Many young children died, which made the bottom bar much wider than later ones. (**NOW FALSE**)
3. Serious illness was almost always fatal, reducing the size of each adult group. (**NOW FALSE**)

Sometimes unusual events caused a deviation from this wedding-cake pattern. For example, the Great Depression and World War II reduced the number of births. Then, postwar prosperity and the soldiers' return caused a baby boom between 1946 and 1964, just when infant survival increased. The high birth and survival rates led many demographers to predict a population explosion, with mass starvation by the year 2000 (Ehrlich, 1968).

That fear evaporated. Birth rates fell and a "green revolution" doubled the food supply. Early death has become rare; demographic stacks have become rectangles, not pyramids. Indeed, some people worry about another demographic shift: fewer babies and more elders, which will greatly affect world health and politics.

This flipped demographic pattern is not yet evident everywhere. Most nations still have more people under age 15 than over age 64. Worldwide, children outnumber elders by 3 to 1—but not 20 to 1 as they once did, or 7 to 1 as they did in

Same Situation, Far Apart: Keep Smiling
Good humor seems to be a cause of longevity, and vice versa. This is true for both sexes, including the British men on Founder's Day *(left)* and the two Indian women on an ordinary sunny day in Dwarka *(right)*.

1950. The United Nations estimates that in 2015 there were 1,915,808,000 people younger than 15 and 608,180,000 older than 64. Not until 2075 is the ratio projected to be even.

Statistics That Frighten

Unfortunately, demographic data are sometimes reported in ways designed to alarm. For instance, have you heard that people aged 80 and older are the fastest-growing age group? Or, that the number of people with Alzheimer's disease is increasing rapidly? Both true; both misleading.

In 2015 in the United States, there were four times as many people 80 and older than there were 50 years earlier (12.1 million compared with 3.1 million). That seems like a rapid increase. Furthermore, the risk of most neurocognitive disorders increases dramatically with age, which means millions more with Alzheimer's and other disorders. Stating the facts in that way triggers ageist fears of a nation burdened by hungry hordes of frail and confused elders, costing billions of dollars of health care in crowded hospitals and nursing homes.

But stop and think. The population has also grown. The percent of U.S. residents age 80 and older has doubled, not quadrupled, and in 2015 was 3.8 percent. That does not overwhelm the other 96.2 percent. Very few are in hospitals or nursing homes. (Guess the percent, the answer will appear soon.) Since Alzheimer's rates increase with age, the absolute numbers are rising—but the rate is decreasing, as Chapter 24 explains.

Another misleading set of statistics is the **dependency ratio,** which is supposed to be the proportion of the population that *depends* on care from others. This ratio is calculated by comparing the number people in the population who are dependent (considered under age 15 or over 64) with the number who are independent (considered ages 15 to 64).

Some nations have almost as many under age 15 as ages 15 to 64. Those are very poor nations: Few people reach old age, but the high birth rate makes their dependency ratio 1:1. In most nations, including the United States, life is longer and the birth rate lower, so the dependency ratio is about 2:1, that is two adults, ages 15 to 64, for every young or old person.

But, the assumption that those over age 64 are dependent is wrong. This mistake is echoed in dire predictions of what will happen when baby boomers age: Supposedly, a shrinking number of working adults will be crushed by the burden of so many old people. Social Security, Medicare, and public hospitals will be bankrupt, according to some. One article by economists argues that we do not know what

dependency ratio A calculation of the number of self-sufficient productive adults compared with the number of dependents (children and the elderly) in a given population.

will happen but that many worry that "the federal government will stagger under the weight of these elderly baby boomers" (Lee & Skinner, 1999, p.117). That specter is alarmist, ageist, and untrue.

The truth is that most elders are fiercely independent. They are more often care*givers*, not care receivers, caring not only for each other but also for children, those other "dependents." This reality was explained in an article in the leading British medical journal as "the timebomb that isn't" (Spijker & MacInnes, 2013).

Gerontologists distinguish among the *young-old*, the *old-old*, and the *oldest-old*.

- The **young-old** are the largest group of older adults. They are healthy, active, financially secure, and independent. Few people realize they are senior citizens.
- The **old-old** suffer some losses in body, mind, or social support, but they proudly care for themselves.
- Only the **oldest-old** are dependent, and they are the most noticeable.

Ages are sometimes used to demarcate these three groups, with the young-old aged 65 to 75, old-old 75 to 85, and oldest-old over 85. However, an elder of any age could be any of these. A young-old person could be 90; an oldest-old person can be 70 or 100.

Only 10 percent of those over age 64 depend on other people for basic care. Those who do need help are more likely to get it from close relatives than taxpaying strangers. On any given day in 2012, only 3 percent of U.S. residents over age 64 were currently in nursing homes or hospitals, down from 5 percent in 1990 (National Center for Health Statistics, 2015). Most older adults live independently, alone or with an aging spouse; a minority are living with adult children, and even fewer are in institutions.

Each year, some of the old are admitted to a hospital, but they do not stay long. Even among those over age 84, the annual rate of hospital admission is 21 percent. Long hospital stays are unusual—the overall average is six days (National Center for Health Statistics, 2015). Most of the elders who are admitted are treated and sent back home. Some go to a rehab facility for a few weeks, and a few go to a nursing home. Even at age 85, only about 10 percent are in long-term care institutions.

young-old Healthy, vigorous, financially secure older adults (generally, those aged 65 to 75) who are well integrated into the lives of their families and communities.

old-old Older adults (generally, those over age 75) who suffer from physical, mental, or social deficits.

oldest-old Elderly adults (generally, those over age 85) who are dependent on others for almost everything, requiring supportive services such as nursing homes and hospital stays.

John Phillips/BFI/Getty Images

Is She Old Yet? Maggie Smith began her acting career in Shakespeare's *Twelfth Night* at age 17, and has appeared every year since then in films, television, and on stage. Many people have watched her work as Professor Minerva McGonagall in eight *Harry Potter* movies and as Violet Crawley in the TV series *Downton Abbey*. She is still acting, making her a young-old.

● **Observation Quiz** How old is she? (see answer, page 654) ↑

WHAT HAVE YOU LEARNED?

1. What are the similarities among ageism, racism, and sexism?
2. What are the differences among ageism, racism, and sexism?
3. Is there any harm in being especially kind to people who are old?
4. How is elderspeak an example of ageism?
5. How does ageism interfere with treatment for insomnia?
6. Why don't the elderly exercise as much as the young?
7. How is the demographic pyramid changing?
8. Why is the dependency ratio misleading?
9. How many of those over age 65 are in nursing homes?

Selective Optimization with Compensation

Ageism distorts reality, but senescence is real. Everyone should be alert to the distortions of aging. Everyone also needs to recognize the actual effects of aging. Then, we can counteract, compensate, control, and celebrate them. Chapters 17,

20, and 21 already explained ways to decrease allostatic load by exercising daily, eating well but not too much, avoiding cigarettes and other drugs, and coping well with stress. All of these strategies may be even more important in late adulthood.

Now we highlight another strategy mentioned earlier: *selective optimization with compensation*. The elderly can compensate for the impairments of senescence and then can perform (optimize) whatever specific tasks they select. [**Life-Span Link:** Selective optimization with compensation is first described in Chapter 21.]

Selective compensation occurs on many levels—the microsystem, macrosystem, and exosystem. This means that personal choice, community practices, and technological advances are always relevant. To illustrate, we now explain three examples: sexual intercourse, driving, and the senses. Each involves all three levels, but here we emphasize one level for each.

Microsystem Compensation: Sex

Most people are sexually active throughout adulthood. Some continue to have intercourse long past age 65 (Lindau & Gavrilova, 2010) (see Figure 23.4), but generally intercourse becomes less frequent, and sometimes stops completely. Nonetheless, sexual satisfaction often increases after middle age (Heiman et al., 2011). How can that be?

Many older adults reject the idea that intercourse is the only, or best, measure of sexual activity. Instead, kissing, caressing, cuddling, sex talk, and fantasizing become more important (Chao et al., 2011). As one study explained, sex in late adulthood is "active, but with a different kind of desire" (McHugh & Interligi, 2015). A five-nation study (United States, Germany, Japan, Brazil, Spain) found that kissing and hugging, not intercourse, predicted happiness in long-lasting romances (Heiman et al., 2011). Is that optimization, compensation, or both?

The following in-depth study provides some clues.

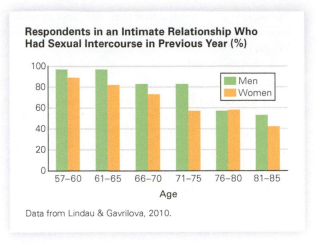

Data from Lindau & Gavrilova, 2010.

FIGURE 23.4

Your Reaction Older adults who consider their health good (most of them) were asked whether they had had sexual intercourse within the past year. If they answered yes, they were considered sexually active. What is your reaction to the data? Some young adults might be surprised that many adults, aged 60 to 80, still experience sexual intercourse. Other people might be saddened that many healthy adults over age 80 do not. However, neither reaction may be appropriate. For many elders, sexual affection is expressed in other ways than intercourse, and it continues lifelong.

Observation Quiz What are the male–female differences and how can they be explained, since all of these respondents had partners of the other sex? (see answer, page 655) ↑

(see answer, page 655)

A CASE TO STUDY

Sex Among Older Adults

Two researchers wanted to study sexual activity among the elderly, but they rejected the usual ways to study sex. They feared that laboratory measures of sexual arousal might be calibrated on young bodies and that questions about sex might be offensive or misinterpreted (Lodge & Umberson, 2012).

Accordingly, they used a method called *grounded theory*. They found 17 couples, aged 50 to 86, most married for decades, and interviewed each person privately, transcribing all 34 interviews. They read and reread the transcripts, line by line, and identified topics that came up repeatedly. They then tallied all the topics and sorted the results by age and gender.

From their intensive study, they concluded that sexual activity was more a social construction than a biological event (Lodge & Umberson, 2012). They reported that everyone said that intercourse was less frequent with age, including four couples for whom intercourse stopped completely because of the husband's health. Despite that, more of the respondents said that their sex life had improved than said it deteriorated (44 percent compared to 30 percent).

Surprisingly, the middle-aged couples, who were more likely to have intercourse, were also more likely to be in the minority who said that their sex lives had deteriorated. The older couples were likely to say that their sex lives were better than before.

The middle-aged husbands and wives had gender-specific concerns that led many to that discouraging assessment. The men were troubled by difficulty maintaining an erection, and the women were worried that they were less attractive. The solution for several middle-aged couples was for the man to take Viagra, typically at the woman's suggestion.

One woman said:

All of a sudden, we didn't have sex after I got skinny. And I couldn't figure that out . . . I look really good now and we're not having sex. It turns out that he was going through a major physical thing at that point and just had lost his sex drive. It didn't have anything to do with me, but I thought it did. I went through years thinking it was my fault. So, [I said] let's go make sure it's your fault [laughs] or let's find out what the problem is instead of me just assuming the blame.

[Irene, quoted in Lodge & Umberson, 2012, p. 435]

The authors believe that "images of masculine sexuality are premised on high, almost uncontrollable levels of penis-driven sexual desire," while the cultural ideals for women emphasize female passivity and yet "implore women to be both desirable and receptive to men's sexual desires and impulses," deeming "older women and their bodies unattractive" (p. 430).

Thus, when people in middle age first realize that aging has changed them, their reaction is distress, but their distress takes a gender-specific form. Men are distressed that their erections are slower and weaker, and women are distressed that their bodies are less youthful. Middle-aged men and women attempt to reverse aging, through drugs, hormones, lubricants, diet, hairstyles, clothes, and so on.

A few years later, this study found that couples over age 70 often realized that the young idea of good sex (which many still thought of as intercourse) was not relevant to them. Instead, they *compensated* for physical changes by *optimizing* their relationship in other ways. As one man (who still equated the word "sex" with intercourse) said:

I think the intimacy is a lot stronger even though the sex is bad. Probably more often now we do things like holding hands and wanting to be close to each other or touch each other. It's probably more important now than sex is.

[Jim, quoted in Lodge & Umberson, 2012, p. 438]

A woman said that her marriage improved because

we have more opportunities and more motivation. [Sex] was wonderful. It got thwarted, with . . . the medication he is on. And he hasn't been functional since. The doctors just said that it is going to be this way, so we have learned to accept that. But we have also learned long before that there are more ways than one to share your love.

[Helen, quoted in Lodge & Umberson, 2012, p. 437]

The authors point out that their conclusions may not be accurate for couples in the future. This cohort grew up with the social construction that men were rapacious and women had to be restrained but attractive. Both sexes were taught when they were young that sexual desire stopped before old age. It was considered deviant ("dirty old man") or ridiculous ("does she think she is a teenager?") if an older adult still felt sexy. Now the culture says that older people should be sexually active, but the aging participants in this study needed time and experience to know what that entailed.

Hot or Cold The weather is chilly and the beach is lonely, but it is evident that this senior couple is enjoying the moment. Physical attraction and intimacy continue into later adulthood, despite what younger people might think.

Older adults adjust to changes in their sexual arousal and may improve their relationship in the process (Lodge & Umberson, 2012; DeLamater, 2012). This is an example of selective optimization with compensation. A similar process occurs for individuals after divorce or the death of a partner. Since the sex drive varies from person to person, some single elders consider sex a thing of the past, some cohabit, some begin LAT (living apart together) with a new partner, and some remarry. Each older person selects whether and how to be sexual.

Neither the old myth, that no elders are sexual, nor the new myth, that all older people have strong sexual desires, is accepted by elderly people themselves. Each individual selects, optimizes, and compensates in his or her own way. Of course, with every aspect of development, individual adjustment is only part of the process. The social context makes some actions difficult, which leads to the next topic.

Answer to Observation Quiz
(from page 652): She was born in 1932. When this picture was taken, she was 83.

Macrosystem Compensation: Driving

A life-span perspective reminds us that "aging is a process, socially constructed as a problem" (Cruikshank, 2009, p. 7). The process is biological for each individual, but the problem begins in society. Selective optimization with compensation is needed in each community. One example is driving.

The Biological Process

With age, reading road signs takes longer, turning the head becomes harder, reaction time slows, and night vision worsens. The elderly compensate: Many drive slowly and reduce driving in the dark.

Relying on individuals to decide when and whether to drive is foolhardy, however. In the United States, driving is a source of pride and cars are tools of independence; the elderly are reluctant to quit. They know that some critics are ageist, and some family members are overprotective (Satariano et al., 2012). Consequently, many old people reject age-based restrictions.

Because they are cautious, elderly drivers have fewer accidents than 20-year-olds (see Visualizing Development, p. 656). They see teenagers speeding, ignoring stop signs, using cell phones, driving after drinking. They conclude that they are better drivers than these "young whippersnappers." One study found that 85 percent of older drivers rated their driving good or excellent. Their self-ratings were not affected by whether or not they had been ticketed for unsafe driving or had motor-vehicle accidents (Ross et al., 2012).

Few older drivers notice the impact of their losses. Hearing and vision are not as acute, reaction time is slower, grip strength is reduced. Another common problem is less accuracy in estimating the speed of oncoming cars. Without that, safe merging into highway traffic is difficult. Usually such losses do not cause collisions, but they might.

What the Community Can Do

Societies need to compensate for age-related reduction in driving ability, yet often they do not. For instance, many jurisdictions renew licenses by mail, even at age 80. If an older adult causes a crash, the individual is blamed, not the community.

When retesting is required, that may entail answering multiple-choice questions about road rules and reading letters on a well-lit chart while looking straight ahead. Anyone who fails should have stopped driving long ago, but proficiency does not guarantee competence. For instance, judgment and reaction time are more important than book knowledge, and peripheral vision is a stronger predictor of accidents than acuity on direct vision (Johnson & Wilkinson, 2010; Wood, 2002).

There is a solution that local jurisdictions could adopt, but few do. A national panel recommends simulated driving via a computer and video screen, with the prospective driver seated with a steering wheel, accelerator, and brakes (Staplin et al., 2012). The results of this test could allow some older adults to renew their license, some to have their licenses revoked, and many to recognize that they are less proficient than they thought.

Driving simulators are especially useful if an older adult has had a stroke or if there are signs of neurological impairment. Some are nonetheless competent

And on Icy Curves. . . Everywhere in the world, the elderly want to keep driving. Some nations require extensive training for license renewals. This is a special safety class for elderly drivers in Germany.

Axel Heimken/picture-alliance/dpa/AP Images

Answer to Observation Quiz

(from page 653): Overall, older men are about 15 percent more likely to be sexually active than older women. Why? One explanation is that, among this cohort, brides were about five years younger than grooms, so some of those older married women had partners who were no longer "sexually active." Another explanation is that, just as the high school students described in Chapter 1, men are still more likely to brag and women to demur—actual rates may be more unisex than this figure depicts.

THINK CRITICALLY: How does a driver decide whether his or her driving is impaired?

Social Comparison: Elders Behind the Wheel

Older people often change their driving habits in order to compensate for their slowing reaction time. Some states have initiated restrictions, including requiring older drivers to renew their licenses in person, to make sure they stay safe. Because most older drivers limit themselves (they avoid night, rainy, and distance driving), their crash rate is low overall, but not when measured by the rate per miles driven.

Accident Rate per Driver

Data from U.S. Census Bureau, 2012, p. 698.

Crashes per 100 Drivers

Age: <20, 20-24, 25-34, 35-44, 45-54, 55-64, 65-74, 75+

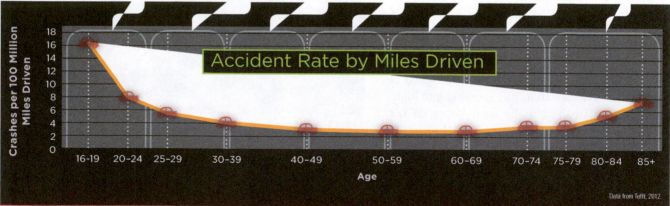

Accident Rate by Miles Driven

Crashes per 100 Million Miles Driven

Age: 16-19, 20-24, 25-29, 30-39, 40-49, 50-59, 60-69, 70-74, 75-79, 80-84, 85+

Data from Tefft, 2012.

Self-Check

Humans of all ages tend to overestimate their abilities. As a result, they may cause a kitchen fire, or fall on ice, or ignore a lump or a chest pain until it is too late.

Especially after age 65, adults who want to drive need to answer six questions:

1. **Is your vision fading?** [Ask your optometrist if any visual losses affect driving.]
2. **Do your medications affect reaction time or alertness?** [Ask both doctor and pharmacist.]
3. **Do your physical limitations affect neck-turning, foot-pushing, wheel-turning?**
4. **Do you get lost more easily now than in earlier years?**
5. **Do other drivers honk at you?** [Don't just get angry, consider the reason.]
6. **Have you had any minor accidents?** [Even a scrape or a fender bender signifies something.]

If your answers are all no, review them with someone who will be honest with you. Some of the elderly are very safe drivers whereas others can be a risk to themselves and to those around them. Before you step on the accelerator, make sure you are one of the safe ones.

drivers and some are not: Age is a poor predictor, and medical doctors are not the best judge (Vardaki et al., 2016). The individual may be even worse at self-assessment: An on-road analysis of older drivers found that some overestimated their competence and some underestimated it (Broberg & Willstrand, 2014).

Beyond retesting, sociocultural compensation can take many other forms. Larger-print signs before highway exits, mirrors that replace the need to turn the neck, illuminated side streets and driveways, non-glaring headlights and hazard flashers, and warnings of ice or fog ahead would all reduce accidents. Well-designed cars, roads, signs, lights, and guardrails, as well as appropriate laws and enforcement, would allow selective optimization. Competent elderly drivers could maintain independence.

Another social initiative is sorely needed. In one in-depth study, elderly drivers in Sweden who were aware of their problems said that free and efficient public transportation would keep them off the road (Broberg & Willstrand, 2014). This could benefit everyone, but it particularly helps the aged in many ways. In Great Britain, free bus passes were given to the elderly. That not only reduced their driving but also increased their walking and social activity (Coronini-Cronberg et al., 2012). Optimization and compensation again.

Exosystem Compensation: The Senses

Every sense becomes slower and less sharp with each passing decade. This is true for touch (particularly in fingers and toes), pain, taste (particularly for sour and bitter), smell, as well as for sight and hearing. This topic was discussed in Chapter 20 and will be revisited in Chapter 24, when we trace cognition from input to output.

All of these losses begin as an individual problem, not one related to the exosystem. Certainly, the specifics depend on each person's unique genes, past practices, and current demands. However, think about the effects of the exosystem (including historical change and cultural assumptions) on the senses. Hundreds of manufactured devices and "built" constructions can compensate for sensory loss, and their invention and availability arise from the exosystem.

(a)

(b)

(c)

(d)

Through Different Eyes These photographs depict the same scene as it would be perceived by a person with *(a)* normal vision, *(b)* cataracts, *(c)* glaucoma, or *(d)* macular degeneration. Think about how difficult it would be to find your own car if you had one of these disorders. That may help you remember to have your vision checked regularly.

© Anna Stowe/Alamy

TABLE 23.2	Common Vision Impairments Among the Elderly

- *Cataracts.* As early as age 50, about 10 percent of adults have cataracts, a thickening of the lens, causing vision to become cloudy, opaque, and distorted. By age 70, 30 percent have cataracts. They can be removed in outpatient surgery and replaced with an artificial lens.

- *Glaucoma.* About 1 percent of those in their 70s and 10 percent of those in their 90s have glaucoma, a buildup of fluid within the eye that damages the optic nerve. Early stages have no symptoms. Without treatment, glaucoma causes blindness, but the damage can be prevented. Testing is crucial, particularly for African Americans and people with diabetes, since the first signs of glaucoma may occur for them as early as age 40.

- *Macular degeneration.* About 4 percent of those in their 60s and about 12 percent of those over age 80 have a deterioration of the retina, called macular degeneration. An early warning occurs when vision is spotty (e.g., some letters missing when reading). Again, early treatment—in this case, medication—can restore some vision, but without treatment, blindness occurs about five years after macular degeneration starts.

Especially for Young Adults Should you always speak louder and slower when talking to a senior citizen? (see response, page 660)

Vision

Only 10 percent of people of either sex over age 65 see well without glasses (see Table 23.2). But many inventions, from eyeglasses (first invented in the thirteenth century) to tiny video cameras worn on the forehead that connect directly to the brain (not yet commercially available) improve sight. Changing the environment—brighter lights, halogen streetlights, newspapers with large and darker print—make a difference.

For those with severe vision losses, dogs, canes, and audio devices allow mobility and cognition. The availability of such implements depends on nationwide practices—they are free in some places, absent in others. That relates to exosystem.

Hearing

Hearing estimates vary, although everyone loses some hearing with age. Of all people in the United States over age 65, 39 percent report some trouble hearing, and 8 percent of them say that they are virtually deaf (National Center for Health Statistics, 2016). The rates among men are twice that of women. High frequencies—the voice of a small child—are lost more quickly than low frequencies—the voice of some men.

Ageism affects whether a society provides technological help. A dramatic improvement in the ability of people with severe hearing loss to enjoy concerts, plays, museums, and so on results from a "hearing loop," a small device in a room that enables people with hearing aids to hear the words or music without the distracting clatter. Installing a loop requires someone to realize that it is worth the cost. David Myers, himself now hearing-impaired, explains:

> The Americans with Disabilities Act does, however, mandate hearing assistance in public settings with 50 or more fixed seats. Such assistance typically takes the form of a checkout FM or infrared receiver with earphones. Alas, because well-meaning sound engineers fail to consider the human factor—how real people interact with technology—most such units sit unused in storage closets.
>
> To empathize, imagine yourself struggling to carve meaning out of sound as you watch a movie, attend worship, listen to a lecture, strain to hear an airport announcement, or stand at a ticket window. Which of these hearing solutions would you prefer?
>
> 1. Taking the initiative to locate, check out, wear, and return special equipment (typically a conspicuous headset that delivers generic sound)?
> 2. Pushing a button that transforms your hearing aid (or cochlear implant) into wireless loudspeakers that deliver sound customized to your own needs?
>
> Solution 1—the hearing-aid-incompatible solution—has been America's prevalent assistive-listening technology. Solution 2—the hearing-aid-compatible solution—has spread to Scandinavian countries and across the United Kingdom, where it now exists in most cathedrals and churches, in the back seats of all London taxis, and at 11,500 post offices and countless train and ticket windows.

[Myers, 2011, pp. 1–2]

universal design The creation of settings and equipment that can be used by everyone, whether or not they are able-bodied and sensory-acute.

Universal Design

Disability advocates hope more designers and engineers will think of **universal design,** which is the creation of settings and equipment that can be used by everyone, whether or not able-bodied and sensory-acute (Hussain et al., 2013; Holt, 2013). That would be a change in the exosystem. At the moment, just about everything, from houses to fashionable shoes, is designed for adults with no impairments. Many disabilities would disappear with better design.

Look around at the built environment (stores, streets, colleges, and homes); notice the print on medicine bottles; listen to the public address systems in train stations; ask why most homes have entry stairs and narrow bathrooms, why most buses and cars require a big step up to enter, why smelling remains the usual way to detect a gas leak. Then, look for signs that indicate accessibility or hearing loop availability, and find out how accurate those signs are. Too often elevators are not in service, curb cuts are not smooth, ramps are hidden, and so on.

Sensory loss need not lead to morbidity or cognitive loss, but without compensation, any disability, especially deafness and blindness, can lead to isolation, less movement, and reduced intellectual stimulation. Often illness increases and cognition declines as the senses fade. The blame for this often is aimed at individuals, but you can see now that the exosystem affects how an individual functions.

All Systems Together

As you know, in a dynamic-systems approach to development, all of the systems work together, each affecting the other. Selective optimization with compensation describes the entire disease process, because, as captured in the idea of allostatic load, many elements of body functioning interact to keep a person healthy.

Primary and Secondary Aging

To further understand this selective optimization for diseases, we need to distinguish between **primary aging,** which involves universal changes that occur with the passage of time, and **secondary aging,** which includes the consequences of particular inherited weaknesses, chosen health habits, and environmental conditions. Primary aging does not directly cause illness, but it makes compensation more difficult and thus makes almost every disease more likely.

For example, with age the heart pumps more slowly and the vascular network is less flexible, increasing the risk of stroke and heart attack. The lungs take in and expel less air with each breath, so blood oxygen is reduced and chronic obstructive pulmonary disease is more common. Digestion slows. The kidneys become less efficient, increasing problems if people become dehydrated because they drink less.

Furthermore, because of age, healing takes longer when an illness or an accident occurs. That is why young adults who contract pneumonia usually recover completely in a few weeks, but in the very old pneumonia can overwhelm a weakened body. Indeed, pneumonia often is listed as the cause of death for the oldest-old, although the underlying cause is primary and secondary aging.

The same is true for accidents of all kinds, from falls, crashes, fires, and poisons. Younger people are much more likely to recover from such insults, but 41 million people in the United States over age 65 died accidentally in 2010, making the accidental death rate for the elderly higher than for people of any other age (National Center for Health Statistics, 2015).

The data in the previous paragraph may puzzle you, since earlier chapters said that more children, adolescents, and emerging adults die of accidents than of any other cause. The answer to that puzzle is that almost no young person dies of any non-violent cause. Because heart disease, cancers, strokes, and so on are rare earlier in life but common in late adulthood, accidents are the leading cause of death from age 1 to 44 but only the eighth greatest after age 65. Older people are more cautious than younger ones, but when injury occurs, death is more likely.

Looking Good Here is Cher at age 69, still with skin that looks much younger. How a person ages depends partly on genes and partly on lifelong skin care and nutrition.

primary aging The universal and irreversible physical changes that occur to all living creatures as they grow older.

secondary aging The specific physical illnesses or conditions that become more common with aging but are caused by health habits, genes, and other influences that vary from person to person.

A developmental view of the relationship between primary and secondary aging harkens back to the lifelong toll of stress, as explained in Chapters 17 and 21. Allostatic load is measured by 10, or sometimes 16, biomarkers—including cortisol, C-reactive protein, systolic and diastolic blood pressure, waist–hip ratio, and insulin resistance. All of these indicate stress on the body, all increase with age, and all affect health.

Examples—Flu and Hypertension

Because of primary aging, medical intervention affects the old differently than the young. For this reason, drugs, surgeries, and so on that have been validated on young adults may be less effective on the elderly. Two examples are treatments for flu and hypertension.

The specific strains of flu (influenza) that circulate are slightly different each year, so the vaccine is redesigned annually to fight whatever strains are predicted. This is why North Americans need flu shots every fall for the following winter. [Timing, and sometimes the composition of the vaccine, differs in other parts of the world.]

Annual immunization is particularly recommended for those over age 65, because their other infirmities make flu sometimes fatal. Those other infirmities are primarily the result of secondary aging—caused by smoking, poor diet, inactivity, and the like—but the death rate comes partly because of primary aging, including a reduced immune system that makes the flu more devastating, even when the person is vaccinated (Mueller, 2016). In other words, the vaccine is simultaneously less powerful but more needed for the elderly.

A case in point was the 2012–2013 vaccine, which protected the elderly reasonably well against the B strains of flu but provided almost no protection against the A strain, even though it protected the young (Kelvin & Farooqui, 2013). Obviously, the vaccine needs to be calibrated for age. In addition, each nation has attitudes and policies regarding all vaccines, which leads to variable rates of vaccination. A systems approach considers not only individual choice but also various systems that can nudge, or require, people to be vaccinated (Dubov & Phung, 2015).

The importance of considering how systems interact is also apparent with hypertension. Hypertension increases with age, and it is one of the factors in allostatic load because it is part of the system of health and disease. If systolic blood pressure in a middle-aged person is above 140, the first recommendation is diet (low salt), weight loss, and exercise, all affected by the micro-, macro-, and exosystems, as explained in Chapter 20. If improving health habits does not lower blood pressure, most doctors prescribe daily medication, thus reducing the risk of strokes and heart attacks.

This is the point when system-wide senescence becomes crucial. The same blood pressure may affect the oldest-old differently than the young-old (Sabayan et al., 2012). For the frail elderly, some hypertension may be protective; drugs may *increase* the risk of death, not decrease it.

When physicians decide whether or not to prescribe pressure-lowering medication, they consider the overall body systems and the likelihood of illness (Odden et al., 2012; Nilsson, 2016). A sudden drop in blood pressure, coupled with the slowness of homeostasis in the old, may be less damaging if the drop is from high to average rather than from average to low.

Compression of Morbidity

compression of morbidity A shortening of the time a person spends ill or infirm, accomplished by postponing illness.

Probably the best example of optimization with regard to the diseases of old age is **compression of morbidity,** which is the reduction (compression) of sickness before death. Some people are in poor health for years before dying, and thus they experience a long time of morbidity. Ideally, however, a person is in good health for decades after age 65, and then, within a few days or months, experiences serious illnesses that lead to death. Years of frailty are avoided.

In this way, morbidity can be compressed even as mortality is postponed. This has certainly happened with some diseases. For instance, unlike 30 years ago, most people diagnosed today with cancer, diabetes, or a heart condition continue to be vital for decades. The World Health Organization and many experts recognize that disability is the result of person–environment interaction, so changing the environment limits disability (Phillipson, 2013). Cultures, schools, and technology can extend the time a person is young-old, forestalling the morbidity of the oldest-old (Thompson et al., 2012).

Compression of morbidity is apparent with **osteoporosis** (fragile bones). Primary aging makes bones more porous as cells that build bone (osteoblasts) are outnumbered by cells that reabsorb bone (osteoclasts) (Rachner et al., 2011). Osteoporosis is particularly common in underweight women with European ancestry, although men and people of other ethnic groups sometimes experience it.

The result of this chronic condition can be deadly, not just disabling. A fall that would have merely bruised a young person may result in a broken hip or a spine fracture, neither of which is lethal. However, both may start a cascade of medical problems with the person moving much less and thus risking heart conditions, digestive problems, and many other complications.

A fall that breaks a major bone leads to death for 10 percent of osteoporosis sufferers within a year, and it contributes to morbidity for the other 90 percent. According to the Centers for Disease Control and Prevention, a broken hip was "a leading cause of morbidity and excess mortality among older adults" (MMWR, March 31, 2000). Half of the people with broken hips never walked again; immobility caused many body systems to deteriorate.

Now let's return to compression of morbidity. Note the 2000 date above. A more recent report concludes: "In the 21st century, osteoporosis, a disease once considered an inevitable consequence of aging, is both diagnosable and treatable" (Black et al., 2012, p. 2051).

How was this compression of morbidity achieved? Early diagnosis via a bone density test (not available a few decades ago) can detect bone weakening long before the first fracture. Prevention can begin in middle age, or even earlier, with weight-bearing and muscle-strengthening exercise and a lifelong diet with sufficient calcium and vitamin D. In addition, a dozen drug treatments (including HRT) reduce bone loss.

Because a focus on chronic conditions is relatively new and treatment of osteoporosis is newer yet, scientists do not know the consequences of ingesting preventive drugs over many years. The data suggest caution (Brown et al., 2012). As you know, drugs that prevent one problem may cause another. [**Life-Span Link:** HRT (hormone replacement therapy) is discussed in Chapter 20.] Nonetheless, the 44 million people over age 50 in the United States who have weak bones need not experience the disabling breaks that those with osteoporosis once did. That is compression of morbidity.

Further, those who have weakened or broken hips can have surgery for hip replacement, which is considered one of the most common, cost-effective ways to improve the quality of later life, reducing morbidity although not necessarily mortality from other causes (Schwartsmann et al., 2015).

Osteoporosis is only one example. For almost every condition, morbidity can be compressed, although many people do not realize it. For instance, half of the elderly population has arthritis, but few know that their stiffness and immobility can be reduced (Hootman et al., 2012). The same is true for diabetes, which often goes undiagnosed until it leads to other chronic problems of the heart, kidneys, feet, eyes, and more (Caspersen et al., 2012).

Touch Your Toes? This woman can even put both feet behind her neck. Although everyone loses some flexibility with age, daily practice is crucial. Tao Porchon-Lynch has taught yoga for a half-century. At age 92, shown here, she can balance on one leg in tree pose, stretch her hamstrings in downward dog, and then relieve any remaining stress in cobra pose.

osteoporosis A disease whose symptoms are low bone mass and deterioration of bone tissue, which leads to increasingly fragile bones and greater risk of fracture.

Ralph Orlowski/Getty Images

Strike or Washout When college students, including Marcus Drendel shown here, brought Nintendo Wii bowling to a senior residence, this woman (Margaret Roeder) and hundreds of others became enthusiasts. Teams from several senior homes will compete in a championship tournament for the national title. Active sports provide exercise for mind and body at every age—unlike the mind-numbing television that some senior residences keep on day and night in their "recreation" rooms.

One crucial factor is fitness earlier in life, so the emphasis on physical fitness in adulthood means compression of morbidity in old age. That is one conclusion of a study of 18,670 people from midlife (about age 50) to old age (about age 75) (Willis et al., 2012).

Research in many nations seeks to find whether morbidity is currently compressed despite the increases in longevity. Some research finds that it is (e.g., Bardenheier et al., 2016) and others that it is not (e.g., Beltrán-Sánchez et al., 2016). Much variation is found, as might be expected from the diverse health habits of individuals. In fact, the gerontologist who first proposed compression of morbidity recognizes that there is also evidence for the opposite, expansion of morbidity. Much depends on personal habits and systemic influences (Fries, 2015).

The goal is clear: not merely to add years to life but to add life to years, via health habits, early treatment, and so on (Gremeaux et al., 2012). Data from many nations show that there is no set age when people become frail. Compression of morbidity is possible, if compensation produces selective optimization.

WHAT HAVE YOU LEARNED?

1. How is it possible for older adults to have satisfying sex lives?
2. What can be done to maintain the independence of older drivers while reducing their risk of accidents?
3. How does vision change with age?
4. How does hearing change with age?
5. How does selective optimization apply to the inevitable decreases in the senses?
6. What is the difference between primary and secondary aging?
7. How would researchers know whether compression of morbidity is occurring?
8. Why might falls be a serious health problem in old age?
9. How is compression of morbidity good for society as well as the individual?

LaunchPad
macmillan learning

Video: Portrait of Aging: Mary
http://qrs.ly/xr4sqmm

Theories of Aging

Underlying every condition and disease just mentioned is a fundamental question: Why do people age? If we could stop senescence, we could stop primary aging, reducing all diseases of the old—most cancers, most heart diseases, most strokes, and so on. Secondary aging would remain, but it would be squarely the responsibility of individuals and societies, not the inevitable result of living a long life.

Hundreds of theories and thousands of scientists have sought to understand why aging occurs. Many reasons involve policies and prejudices (Bengtson & Settersten, 2016). We focus here on theories of biological aging, which have led to the happy conclusion that "we now know that aging is modifiable" (Kennedy, 2016, p. 109). We group these theories in three clusters: wear and tear, genetic adaptation, and cellular aging.

Stop Moving? Stop Eating?

wear-and-tear theory A view of aging as a process by which the human body wears out because of the passage of time and exposure to environmental stressors.

The oldest, most general theory of aging is known as **wear-and-tear theory.** The idea is that the body wears out, part by part, after years of use. Organ reserve and repair processes are exhausted as the decades pass (Gavrilov & Gavrilova, 2006).

This theory begins by recognizing that some body parts suffer from overuse. Athletes who put repeated stress on their shoulders or knees may have chronically painful joints by middle age; workers who inhale asbestos and smoke cigarettes damage their lungs; hockey, football, and boxing athletes who suffer repeated blows to the head may destroy their brains.

In addition, sometimes the body wears out because of weather, or harmful food, or pollution, or radiation. For instance, skin cancer is caused partly by too much sun, clogged arteries are caused partly by too much animal fat, and some cancer tumors result from too much pollution and radiation.

Every older person's hands and face are wrinkled, often with discolorations known as "age spots." By contrast, the skin on the torso may be smooth and clear, even at age 80. The reason is wear and tear via daily sun, wind, and cold to the hands and face but almost never to the stomach.

However, most scientists have rejected wear and tear as a general theory of aging, because other body functions benefit from activity. Exercise improves heart and lung functioning; tai chi improves balance; weight training increases muscle mass; sexual activity stimulates the sexual-reproductive system. The slogan "use it or lose it" may apply to cognition, as well.

An astonishing finding from lower animals suggests an application of wear and tear. If an adult reduced wear and tear on digestion, metabolism, and so on by eating 1,800 calories a day instead of the usual 3,000, would that slow all aging processes? **Calorie restriction**—a drastic reduction in calories consumed—increases the life span in many organisms.

The most dramatic evidence comes from fruit flies, which can live three times as long if they eat less. Many other species benefit from calorie restriction, but not all. Some research on monkeys, mice, and other animals reports that calorie restriction extends life, but other research does not (Mattison et al., 2012).

Results may depend on small genetic differences between one species (or strain of mice) and another, or on details of the diet. Some research suggests that a high-nutrient, low-protein diet may be crucial (Bruce et al., 2010). Periodic fasting and scheduled eating may also be relevant (Fontana & Partridge, 2015).

Regarding humans, thousands of members of the Calorie Restriction Society voluntarily undereat (Roth & Polotsky, 2012). They give up some things that many people cherish, not just cake and hot dogs but also a strong sex drive and high energy. As a result, they have lower blood pressure, fewer strokes, less cancer, and almost no diabetes. But that does not convince most scientists, in part because they are a self-selective sample.

In several places (e.g., Okinawa, Denmark, and Norway), wartime occupation forced severe calorie reduction for almost everyone. People ate local vegetables and not much else, and they were often hungry. But they were less likely to die of disease (Fontana et al., 2011).

Similar results were reported from Cuba, already mentioned in Chapter 20. Because the United States led an embargo of Cuban products, that nation experienced food and gas shortages from 1991 to 1995. People ate local fruits and vegetables, walked more, and lost weight. Death, particularly due to heart disease and diabetes, was reduced (Franco et al., 2013).

In all of these examples, populations benefited when everyone ate less, particularly less meat. But in all of these nations, once more food was available, people eagerly ate more. Then disease deaths rose. Apparently, most humans choose some wear and tear in order to have the comforts they enjoy.

It's All Genetic

A second cluster of theories focuses on genes, both genes of the entire species and genes that vary from one person to another (Sutphin & Kaeberlein, 2011). About

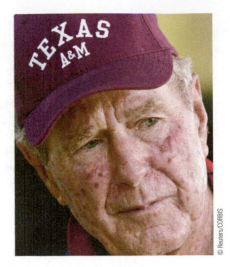

Skin Deep Those spots on former president Bush's face are signs of an anti-aging treatment, specifically nitrogen to freeze the damaged cells on his skin. For him as well as for everyone else, aging that results from wear and tear can be treated, unlike the aging that is genetic or cellular.

calorie restriction The practice of limiting dietary energy intake (while consuming sufficient quantities of vitamins, minerals, and other important nutrients) for the purpose of improving health and slowing down the aging process.

"If you give up alcohol, cigarettes, sex, red meat, cake and chocolate, and don't get too excited, you can enjoy life for a few more years yet."

THINK CRITICALLY: Do people want the comforts of daily life—driving and eating—more than longer lives?

maximum life span The oldest possible age to which members of a species can live under ideal circumstances. For humans, that age is approximately 122 years.

average life expectancy The number of years the average newborn in a particular population group is likely to live.

genetic clock A purported mechanism in the DNA of cells that regulates the aging process by triggering hormonal changes and controlling cellular reproduction and repair.

THINK CRITICALLY: For the benefit of the species as a whole, why would genes promote aging?

cellular aging The cumulative effect of stress and toxins, causing cellular damage first and eventually the death of cells.

one-third of longevity can be attributed directly to genes and the other two-thirds to epigenetic and environmental factors. Those proportions vary from person to person, as differential susceptibility would predict (Govindaraju et al., 2015).

Every species has a **maximum life span,** defined as the oldest possible age that members of that species can attain (Wolf, 2010). Genes determine the maximum: for rats, 4 years; rabbits, 13; tigers, 26; house cats, 30; brown bats, 34; brown bears, 37; chimpanzees, 55; Indian elephants, 70; finback whales, 80; humans, 122; lake sturgeon, 150; giant tortoises, 180.

Maximum life span is quite different from **average life expectancy,** which is the average life span of individuals in a particular group. In human groups, average life expectancy varies a great deal, depending on historical, cultural, and socioeconomic factors (Sierra et al., 2009).

The average human life expectancy has more than doubled in the past century and continues to rise. Worldwide, in 2015, the average is about 71 (69 for men, 73 for women). In the United States, in 2015, average life expectancy at birth is 80 (77 for men, 82 for women), eight years more than half a century ago. The U.S. average life span is projected to be six years longer by 2065 (United Nations, Department of Economic and Social Affairs, Population Division, 2015).

Average life expectancy is increasing primarily because public health measures (clean water, immunization, nutrition, newborn care) prevented many infant and child deaths. Recent medical measures have decreased midlife death from heart disease and cancer.

Eventually, however, a **genetic clock** regulates life, growth, and aging. Just as genes trigger puberty at a certain age, genes may switch on to cause gray hair, slower movement, and, eventually, death. That is true for each species.

In addition, some genes cause unusually fast or slow aging. Children born with Hutchinson-Gilford syndrome (a genetic disease also called *progeria*) stop growing at about age 5 and begin to look old, with wrinkled skin and balding heads, dying in their teens of diseases typically found in people five times their age.

Other genes seem to program a long and healthy life. People who reach age 100 usually have alleles that other people do not (Govindaraju et al., 2015).

Two alleles of the ApoE gene prove the point. ApoE2 is found in 12 percent of men in their 70s and 17 percent of men over age 85. Those numbers make it apparent that ApoE2 aids survival. However, another allele of the same gene, ApoE4, increases the rate of death by heart disease, stroke, neurocognitive disorders, and—if a person is HIV-positive—by AIDS (Kuhlmann et al., 2010).

Almost every disease is partly genetic, so disease rates vary among people with ancestors from particular parts of the world. For instance, many genes for type 2 diabetes are shared across ethnic groups, but some are more common among African Americans than other U.S. groups (Palmer et al., 2012). For genetic reasons, people with Asian ancestors develop diabetes at younger ages and lower weights than Europeans (Chan et al., 2009; Hsu et al., 2015).

Cells Quit Reproducing

The third cluster of theories examines **cellular aging,** focusing on molecules and cells. Remember, cells duplicate many times during the life span. Consequently, minor errors in copying accumulate. Early in life, the immune system repairs such errors, but eventually the immune system itself becomes less adept.

When the organism can no longer repair every cellular error, senescence occurs. This process is first apparent in the skin, an organ that replaces itself often, particularly if damage occurs (such as peeling skin with sunburn). Cellular aging also occurs inside the body, notably in cancer, as the aging immune system is increasingly unable to control abnormal cells.

Even without specific infections or stresses, healthy cells stop replicating at a certain point. This point is referred to as the **Hayflick limit,** named after the scientist who discovered it. Hayflick believes that aging is caused primarily by a natural loss of molecular fidelity—that is, by inevitable errors in transcription as each cell reproduces itself. He believes that aging is natural, built into our cells (Hayflick, 2004).

One cellular change occurs with **telomeres**—material at the ends of the chromosome that becomes shorter with each duplication. Telomeres are longer in children (except those with progeria) and shorter in older adults. Eventually, at the Hayflick limit, the telomere is gone, duplication stops, and the creature dies (Aviv, 2011).

The length of telomeres is related to both genes and stress. The more stress a person experiences, from childhood on, the shorter their telomeres are in late adulthood and the sooner they will die (J. Lin et al., 2012).

Telomere length is about the same in newborns of both sexes and all ethnic groups, but by late adulthood telomeres are longer in women than in men and longer in European Americans than in African Americans (Aviv, 2011). There are many possible causes, but cellular-aging theorists focus on the consequences: Women outlive men, and European Americans outlive African Americans, at least until age 80.

Hayflick limit The number of times a human cell is capable of dividing into two new cells. The limit for most human cells is approximately 50 divisions, an indication that the life span is limited by our genetic program.

telomeres The area of the tips of each chromosome that is reduced a tiny amount as time passes. By the end of life, the telomeres are very short.

Old Caterpillars? No, these are young chromosomes, stained to show the glowing white telomeres at the ends.

Stop the Clock?

Many scientists, as well as older people, seek to extend life. Those who restrict their calories may be extreme, but millions eat special foods (blueberries, red wine, fish oil?) or take certain drugs (sirtuins, rapamycin, resveratrol?) to extend life.

All of the theories of aging, and all of the research on genes, cells, calorie restriction, foods, drugs, antioxidants, and so on, have not yet led to any sure way to postpone death. Scientists are following numerous leads because many are convinced that something will slow aging.

For instance, a team of researchers traces about half of all adult cognitive decline to three specific diseases (Alzheimer's disease, vascular disease, and Lewy body disease—all described in Chapter 24), but much more research must be done on the underlying causes (Boyle et al., 2013). Many medical researchers believe that more funding for anti-aging research, and less for specific diseases, would reduce the cost of health care (Goldman et al., 2013).

But the opposing perspective is that anti-aging research is both foolish and unethical. Perhaps now that major causes of premature death have been prevented, further longevity is not possible. In the most advanced nations, the rate of increase in longevity has slowed down. Gerontologists are engaged in a "fiery debate" as to whether the maximum is genetically fixed (Couzin-Frankel, 2011a, p. 549).

Further, is it ethical to strive for increased longevity for wealthy 80-year-olds when many low-SES infants, children,

and young adults die? Perhaps training doctors and nurses in the poorest nations and reducing SES disparities in wealthy nations are better goals.

Many worry that by extending life, nations are adding medical costs to society. Currently, the U.S. health benefit for the aged of any income—Medicare—costs three times as much as the elderly themselves pay for the benefit. Thus, the concern is that any lengthening of life will result in less public money for schools, colleges, and health care for those under age 65.

Further, unconscious prejudice may be fueling the efforts to extend life. Compared to the average U.S. resident, older Americans are more often of European than African ancestry, native-born than immigrant, Protestant Christian than other religions, middle class than poor. The effort to extend their life, rather than, say, put research funds into gun violence, or teratogens, or early-childhood education, may be selfishly promoted by lawmakers (who know that older people vote), by senior scientists, and by the elderly themselves.

Or is it ageist and prejudiced to suggest such a thing? Opposing perspectives.

THINK CRITICALLY: Are anti-aging measures a selfish endeavor by older people who protect themselves while harming the young?

GUILLAUME SOUVANT/AFP/Getty Images

Still Together   At age 104 in 2016, the Lamolie twins are twice fortunate to be alive. The first time was at birth, when Paulette (left) weighed 3 pounds and Simone (right) 2 pounds. The second is genetic—their shared genes must include some for longevity.

The Centenarians

Most current theories of aging involve thousands of scientists in laboratories, working with fruit flies, or mice, or cells. As you just read, the scientists are finding intriguing possibilities, but also that hopeful hypothesis has not yet been proven. The search for the Fountain of Youth seems as much a fantasy as it was for Ponce de León in the sixteenth century. Given the human wish to believe that aging is not inevitable, it is useful to look at research on living human beings—those who live a very long time and those who studied them.

In the 1970s, three remote places—one in the Republic of Georgia, one in Pakistan, and one in Ecuador—were in the news because many vigorous old people lived there. Some were said to be more than 100 years old. One researcher wrote:

> Most of the aged [older than age 90] work regularly. . . . Some even continue to chop wood and haul water. Close to 40 percent of the aged men and 30 percent of the aged women report good vision; that is, that they do not need glasses for any sort of work, including reading or threading a needle. Between 40 and 50 percent have reasonably good hearing. Most have their own teeth. Their posture is unusually erect, even into advanced age. Many take walks of more than two miles a day and swim in mountain streams.
>
> *[Benet, 1974]*

More comprehensive studies (Pitskhelauri, 1982; Buettner, 2012) found that lifestyles in all three of these regions were similar in four ways:

1. *Diet.* People ate mostly fresh vegetables and herbs, with little meat or fat. They thought it better to be a little bit hungry than too full.
2. *Work.* Even the very old did farm work, household tasks, and child care.
3. *Family and community.* The elderly were well integrated into families of several generations and interacted frequently with friends and neighbors.
4. *Exercise and relaxation.* Most took a walk every morning and evening (often up and down mountains), napped midday, and socialized in the evening.

Might these factors—diet, work, social interaction, and exercise—lengthen life?

The theory that the social context promotes longevity is buttressed by evidence from bumblebees. Genetically, worker bees and queen bees are the same, but worker bees live about three months while queen bees, fed special food and treated with deference, live about five years. When a queen dies, a worker bee is chosen to become a queen, thereby living 20 times longer than that bee otherwise would have.

Maximum Life Expectancy

Surely your suspicions were raised by the preceding paragraphs. Humans have almost nothing in common with bumblebees, and the information about those long-lived people was published decades ago.

Indeed, the three regions famous for long-lived humans lack verifiable birth or marriage records. Everyone who claimed to be a centenarian was probably exaggerating, and every researcher who believed them was too eager to accept the idea that life would be long and wonderful if only the ills of modern civilization were absent (Thorson, 1995). Some people still move to those remote places in order to live longer (e.g., Volkwein-Caplan & McConatha, 2012), but most scientists consider that foolish.

Now the challenge is to increase the life span of the very old. Gerontologists are engaged in a "fiery debate" as to whether the average life span will keep rising and whether the maximum is genetically fixed (Couzin-Frankel, 2011a, p. 549). It is known that the oldest well-documented life ended at age 122, when Jeanne Calment died in southern France in 1997. No one has yet been proven to have outlived her, despite documented birth dates for a billion people who have died since then. This suggests that the maximum is set at 122, although some disagree.

Everyone agrees, however, that the last years of life can be good ones. Those who study centenarians find many quite happy (Jopp & Rott, 2006; Paúl et al., 2013). Jeanne Calment enjoyed a glass of red wine and some olive oil each day. "I will die laughing," she said.

Disease, disability, and depression may eventually set in; studies disagree about how common these problems are past age 100. Some studies find fewer physical and mental health problems after age 100 than before. For example, in Sweden, where medical care is free, centenarians were less likely to take antidepressants, but more likely to use pain medication, than those who were aged 80 or so (Wastesson et al., 2012).

In the United States, more than half of those who live past 100 show no cognitive impairment, and about one-fifth have no major diseases or disabilities (Ailshire et al., 2015). They feel happy, although they score high on standard measures of depression, which include symptoms such as fatigue that may not indicate depression for the aged (Scheetz et al., 2012).

Could centenarians be happier than octogenarians, as the Swedish data suggest? That is not known. However, it is true that more and more people live past 100, and many of them are energetic, alert, and optimistic. Social relationships in particular correlate with robust mental health (Margrett et al., 2011). Centenarians tend to be upbeat about life.

That could be considered the theme of this chapter: Attitude is crucial as senescence continues. As noted in the beginning of the chapter, ageism shortens life and makes the final years less satisfying. Don't let it. As thousands of centenarians demonstrate, a long life can be a happy one.

● **Especially for Biologists** What are some immediate practical uses for research on the causes of aging? (see response, page 668)

World's Record for Centenarians Can you sprint 100 meters in less than 30 seconds? This man, Hidekichi Miyazaki can. Maybe you need more practice. Hidekichi has been running for 103 years!

Response for Biologists
(from page 667): Although ageism and ambivalence limit the funding of research on the causes of aging, the applications include prevention of AIDS, cancer, neurocognitive disorders, and physical damage from pollution—all urgent social priorities.

WHAT HAVE YOU LEARNED?

1. Why is the wear-and-tear theory of aging no longer considered accurate?

2. Why do relatively few people follow the implications of the calorie restriction theory of aging?

3. What evidence supports the genetic theory of aging?

4. Why is the average life span so many decades lower than the maximum?

5. What damages cells as they age?

6. How can immune system failure cause aging?

7. Why would people lie about their age by adding years to it?

8. What do studies of the very old suggest about the attitudes of other people toward elders?

SUMMARY

Prejudice and Predictions

1. Stereotypes about the elderly are prevalent in the culture, evident in the assumptions and behaviors of both the young and the old. That prejudice is called ageism, and it can lead to self-fulfilling prophecies regarding health and well-being. Elderspeak is one example.

2. Demography notes the changing size of various age groups, as few babies are born and more people live long lives. What once was a pyramid is becoming a rectangle.

3. Statistics about the elderly are sometimes presented in ways to alarm younger people. Currently, about 14 percent of people in the U.S. population are elderly, with 90 percent of them self-sufficient and productive, more often caregivers than care receivers.

4. Gerontologists sometimes distinguish among the young-old, the old-old, and the oldest-old, according to each group's relative degree of dependency. Only 10 percent of those over age 65 are dependent (they are the oldest-old), and only 3 percent of the elderly are in nursing homes or hospitals.

Selective Optimization with Compensation

5. Compensation for senescence can occur at every level of the ecological system. Sexual interaction may improve with age.

6. Declines in all of the senses are more or less debilitating depending on culture and technology. Compensation is crucial, because vision losses are common and critical: Many elders have cataracts, glaucoma, or macular degeneration. Hearing also declines: Most older men are significantly hard-of-hearing.

7. Primary aging happens to everyone, reducing organ reserve in body and brain. Secondary aging depends on the individual's past health habits and genes. In many ways, age is relevant in treatment of various conditions, including flu, hypertension, and osteoporosis. Compensation is possible and brings many benefits, including compression of morbidity.

Theories of Aging

8. Hundreds of theories address the causes of aging. Wear-and-tear theory suggests that living wears out the body; it applies to some parts of the body but not to overall aging. Calorie restriction is a promising application of this theory.

9. Another theory is that genes allow humans to survive through the reproductive years but then become seriously ill and inevitably die. Some individuals have genes or alleles that lead to long life, others to shorter lives.

10. Cellular theories of aging include the idea that the processes of DNA duplication and repair are affected by aging, making repair of errors more difficult.

11. Age-related decline in the immune system may cause aging, as it contributes to elderly people's increasing vulnerability to disease.

12. Cells stop duplicating at a certain point, called the Hayflick limit. This stoppage seems to occur when the telomeres shorten and then disappear.

13. Each species seems to have a genetic timetable for decline and death. Although the average life span has clearly increased, it is disputed whether the maximum can increase.

14. The number of centenarians is increasing, and many of them are quite healthy and happy. The personalities and attitudes of the very old suggest that long-term survival may be welcomed more than feared.

KEY TERMS

ageism (p. 645)
elderspeak (p. 649)
demographic shift (p. 650)
dependency ratio (p. 651)
young-old (p. 652)
old-old (p. 652)

oldest-old (p. 652)
universal design (p. 658)
primary aging (p. 659)
secondary aging (p. 659)
compression of morbidity
    (p. 660)

osteoporosis (p. 661)
wear-and-tear theory (p. 662)
calorie restriction (p. 663)
maximum life span (p. 664)
average life expectancy (p. 664)

genetic clock (p. 664)
cellular aging (p. 664)
Hayflick limit (p. 665)
telomeres (p. 665)

APPLICATIONS

1. Write down the degree of independence of all your relatives over age 65, such as grandparents and great-grandparents, great aunts and great uncles, and so on. What percent are in nursing homes? How and why is that percent higher or lower than the national average?

2. Compensating for sensory losses is difficult because it involves learning new habits. To better understand the experience, reduce your hearing or vision for a day by wearing earplugs or dark glasses that let in only bright lights. (Use caution and common sense: Don't drive a car while wearing earplugs or cross streets while wearing dark glasses.) Report on your emotions, the responses of others, and your conclusions.

3. Ask five people of various ages whether they want to live to age 100, and record their responses. Would they be willing to eat half as much, exercise much more, experience weekly dialysis, or undergo other procedures in order to extend life? Analyze the responses.

Late Adulthood:
Cognitive Development

What Will You Know?

1. Does the brain grow or shrink in old age?
2. What kinds of memory are least apt to fade in old age? What kinds are the most apt to fade?
3. What is the difference between these four terms: Alzheimer's disease, senility, dementia, and neurocognitive disorders?
4. What gains in cognition occur in late adulthood?

I have eaten many dinners sponsored by large organizations. I am tired of them. No longer do I enjoy church suppers with lasagna and Jell-O/marshmallow salad; no longer do I appreciate chicken and chocolates at nonprofit fundraisers; no longer am I impressed with choices (red or white wine? rare or well-done beef?) at corporate events.

But recently I attended an organization's dinner that was unlike the rest. The appetizer was a cold kale and nut salad; the fish entrée was passed around family style; and the guests were mostly young, lean, and earnest. It was a celebration of 40 years of a group that works for pedestrian safety, protected bike lanes, and metered parking. Most of the hundreds of patrons arrived by foot, subway, or bike.

This chapter on cognition in late adulthood begins with this event because each generation has its own concept of how things should be. Challenging our conceptions is one of the things people of other ages do for us.

My assumptions were challenged and my ideas grew, not only by the menu but also by the conversation and the speeches. Piaget thought intelligence was the ability to expand the mind whenever disequilibrium requires new thinking, an insight that applies lifelong: New experiences require deeper, better thinking. Neurological research confirms that.

This chapter acknowledges intellectual losses of late adulthood in sensory input, memory, control processes, and output. But gains in thought, expression, and perhaps wisdom are also described. You will also learn about neurological diseases that become more frequent with age—Alzheimer's, vascular, Lewy body, frontotemporal, and more, all now called neurocognitive disorders. Understanding them will dissipate some of the fog and confusion many people have about aging cognition.

One theme is evident throughout: Cognition in late adulthood varies. Intellectual prowess after age 65 requires that people have experiences that require new concepts or skills. As you will see, this may include playing video games, or lifting weights, or storytelling, or painting, or singing, or staying on the job. For me, it meant going to dinner.

Still Thinking New dendrites can lead to new ideas. Albert Bandura was a young scholar when he developed social learning theory to explain why preschoolers attacked a doll with a hammer. Here, at age 90, he signs copies of his most recent book that explains his theory of moral disengagement, in hopes that we can develop a more compassionate, humane society.

Especially for People Who Are Proud of Their Intellect What can you do to keep your mind sharp all your life? (see response, page 674)

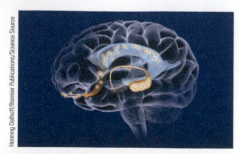

Video: Brain Development Animation: Late Adulthood shows gray matter loss in the normal aging brain.

The Aging Brain

The most feared aspect of the aging process involves the mind, not the body. Chapter 17 promised that this chapter would take an information-processing perspective, detailing steps in the intellectual process that falter in adulthood and those that do not. First, however, we need to look closely at aging in the brain.

As with many stereotypes, the notion of cognitive decline in late adulthood begins with a half-truth and then stops. In fact, "although many 70- to 80-year-old adults show evidence of age-related decline, some continue to maintain very high levels of cognitive performance" (Nyberg & Bäckman, 2011). The fear is worse than the facts.

New Brain Cells

About 10 years ago, developmentalists were thrilled to confirm something they once thought impossible: New neurons form in adulthood. As first described in Chapter 20, the brain is particularly likely to gain cells in the hippocampus, the brain structure most prominent in memory (Bergmann et al., 2015). That allows new memories to form and endure throughout life (Kempermann et al., 2016).

For decades, developmentalists have recognized another encouraging aspect of mature brains: Dendrites grow with new experiences as well as with antidepressants. Adults can shake the grip of depression and anxiety as well as add a new perspective, if needed (Mateus-Pinheiro et al., 2013).

Although neurogenesis and dendrite formation occur in many creatures, an evolutionary perspective suggests that humans have special reasons to grow brains in adulthood (Kempermann, 2016). New dendrites and neurons allow individuals to develop unique perspectives and talents as their lives unfold. This has been verified in mice, and it probably is true for humans as well—adults continue to individualize lifelong (Freund et al., 2013).

One hypothesis is that, when agriculture began (widely believed to be approximately 10,000 years ago), adults developed brains that promoted more planning, remembering, and strategizing than was previously necessary. Some skills were needed before then for the nomadic life of hunters and gatherers, but when people lived in towns, interdependence required laws, markets, and labor specialization. Adults needed to grapple with social interactions far more complex than previously. One scholar suggests:

> Moving actively in a changing world and dealing with novelty and complexity regulate adult neurogenesis. New neurons might thus provide the cognitive adaptability to conquer ecological niches rich with challenging stimuli.

> [Kempermann, 2012, p. 727]

Has this process continued since the beginning of agriculture? Probably. The Flynn effect suggests that it might, and certainly life in the twenty-first century presents new challenges to adults, requiring changed perspectives. Perhaps urbanization and globalization demand intellectual expansion. Thus, when older people cope with changing cultures, their brains continue to grow.

The positive finding that neurons are created later in life is tempered by another fact—growth of the brain in late adulthood is slow and limited (S. Lee et al., 2012), and treatment for various illnesses may kill neurons without creating new ones (Monje & Dietrich, 2012; Mashour & Avidan, 2013). New neurons develop, but they are not sufficient to restore the aging brain to its earlier state. Further, some older adults isolate themselves and criticize others. Their brains do not grow.

Atrophy Ranking

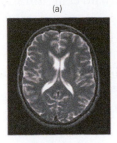
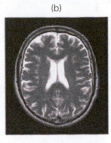
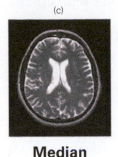
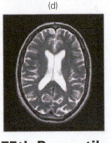
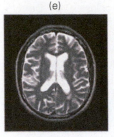

(a) (b) (c) (d) (e)

Lowest   **25th Percentile**   **Median**   **75th Percentile**   **Highest**

Not All Average A team of neuroscientists in Scotland (Farrell et al., 2009) published these images of the brains of healthy 65- to 70-year-olds. The images show normal brain loss from the lowest (5th percentile) to the highest (95th percentile). Some atrophy is inevitable (even younger brains atrophy), but few elders are merely average. On these black-and-white photos, loss is shown as white—which is not the same as the so-called "white matter" of the brain.

Senescence and the Brain

The cold fact that senescence shrinks the brain has been known for decades. Recent research has brought the good news that new brain cells and dendrites can develop, but the old news is still true—brains slow down with age.

Slower Thinking

Senescence reduces the production of neurotransmitters—including glutamate, acetylcholine, serotonin, and especially dopamine—that allow a nerve impulse to jump quickly across the synaptic gap from one neuron to another. Neural fluid decreases, myelination thins, and cerebral blood circulates more slowly. The result is an overall slowdown, evident in reaction time, movement, speech, and thought.

This severely drains the mind because speed is crucial for many aspects of cognition. In fact, some experts believe that processing speed is a basic element of the g mentioned in Chapter 21—an ability that underlies all other aspects of intelligence (Salthouse, 2004; Gow et al., 2011; Sandu et al., 2014).

Deterioration of cognition correlates with slower movement as well as with almost every kind of physical disability. For example, gait speed correlates strongly with many measures of intellect (Hausdorff & Buchman, 2013). Walks slow? Talks slow? Oh no—thinks slow!

Smaller Brains

Brain aging is evident not only in processing speed but also in size, as the total volume of the brain becomes smaller. Shrinkage is particularly notable in the hippocampus and the areas of the prefrontal cortex that are needed for planning, inhibiting unwanted responses, and coordinating thoughts (Rodrigue & Kennedy, 2011).

In every part of the brain, the volume of gray matter (crucial for processing new experiences) is reduced, in part because the cortex becomes thinner with every decade of adulthood (Zhou et al., 2013). As a consequence, many people must use their cognitive reserve to stave off serious impairment (Whalley et al., 2016). White matter generally is reduced as well, slowing the mind. However, white matter also increases in an odd way: Bright white spots appear on MRIs after age 50 or so.

These white-matter lesions are thought to result from tiny impairments in blood flow. They increase the time it takes for a thought to be processed in the brain (Rodrigue & Kennedy, 2011). Slowed transmission from one neuron to another is not the only problem. With age, transmission of impulses from entire regions of

● **Response for People Who Are Proud of Their Intellect** (from page 672): If you answered, "Use it or lose it" or "Do crossword puzzles," you need to read more carefully. No specific brain activity has proved to prevent brain slowdown. Overall health is good for the brain as well as for the body, so exercise, a balanced diet, and well-controlled blood pressure are some smart answers.

the brain, specifically from parts of the cortex and the cerebellum, is disrupted. Specifics correlate more with cognitive ability than with age (Bernard et al., 2013).

Variation in Brain Efficiency

As with every other organ, all aspects of brain senescence vary markedly from individual to individual, in part because of past health and habits. High SES correlates with less cognitive decline. There are three plausible hypotheses for this finding:

1. High-SES people began late adulthood with higher IQs, so their losses are not as noticeable.
2. Those with more education are likely to keep their minds active, and that protects the intellect.
3. Those with more income and better jobs tend to be exposed to less pollution and have lower rates of destructive drug use. They also have better medical care, nutrition and exercise. These all foster maintenance of intelligence.

The first hypothesis has substantial research support. The intellectually gifted may lose cognitive speed at the same rate as other people, but they began late adulthood as such quick thinkers that the slowdown is less apparent (Puccioni & Vallesi, 2012). But, the second hypothesis also has support: The intellectually gifted may be open to new ideas, and openness produces a more active mind (Hogan et al., 2012). This is the "use it or lose it" hypothesis, an attractive idea that has millions of older people doing crossword puzzles and Sudoku.

Finally, there is the third possibility. No one doubts that exercise, nutrition, and normal blood pressure are powerful influences on brain health, and these predict success in life (higher SES) and intelligence in old age. Some experts contend that with good health habits and favorable genes, no intellectual decrement will occur (Greenwood & Parasuraman, 2012).

Variation occurs by SES but also within each person, and some parts of the brain slow down before others. Names are forgotten faster than faces, spatial representation (Where did I put that?) faster than vocabulary (What is that called?). This variation may be strictly biological (hypothesis one) or a matter of practice (hypothesis two). No doubt it is affected by blood circulation in the brain (hypothesis three).

An Application: Multitasking

Technology often has many people multitasking (Cardoso-Leite et al., 2015). The classic example is the teenager who does homework while using several devices: listening to music, responding to text messages, watching television. Adults of all ages multitask as well. The research finds that multitasking is both more effective and less effective than many people think it is.

In some ways, human brains are designed to undertake one task at a time. Each neuron either fires or not, either on or off. Further, many intellectual tasks require sequencing in the brain. Some crucial hubs may become bottlenecks if more than one message—that is two or more tasks—are both ready to be sent at the same time. On the other hand, plasticity and automaticity mean that the brain adjusts to experience.

Multitasking becomes less common with age (Ren et al., 2013). Is that because older adults have less experience with it, or because older adults are wiser, or because older brains are less able to do several things at once?

The answer is complex, but let us begin by recognizing that, in some ways, the brain is always multitasking. We breathe, our hearts beat, thoughts occur, we feel pain or hunger, simultaneously. Neurons themselves are not multitaskers:

Each neuron turns on or off. That provides a clue about when multitasking is easy or hard. If two tasks involve substantial automaticity, and therefore avoid bottlenecks in the brain, multitasking is possible. However, if two tasks both require the same neurons, then simultaneous multitasking is impossible. Instead the brain must switch from one task to another, and that switch takes time and effort.

This is not hypothetical. In laboratories, people are asked to switch from one task to another. For example, they sit before a computer screen that has a number and a vowel, and they are asked to indicate (by pressing a button which records precisely the time between the request and the response) whether the number is odd or even or whether the letter is a vowel or a consonant. When the request is the same as the previous one—number, number, number—the reaction time is shorter than when the task is different—number, letter, letter, number. This is evidence of a *switch-cost,* that multitasking slows down thinking. It would be quicker to do 100 numbers in sequence and then 100 letters in sequence than to do all 200 intermingled.

Switch-costs are evident in many real-life situations, too—drivers react more slowly to hazards if they are in a conversation, bilingual speakers take a moment if they must switch from one language to another, and so on (Poarch & Bialystok, 2015).

However, laboratory studies also find that, with practice, switch-costs are reduced. Certain kinds of multitasking—specifically video games that require monitoring several things at once and reacting quickly—show reduced switch-costs with practice. Some studies find that this reduces switch-costs in other tasks as well. Bilingual people, who must switch often, may be better in those aspects of executive function that involved selecting some responses and inhibiting others (Poarch & Bialystok, 2015).

But caution is needed; practice at multitasking does not always help. Indeed, people who routinely use several technology devices at once are slower, not faster, at multitasking in the laboratory, especially when they think themselves excellent multitaskers (Sanbonmatsu et al., 2013).

How does this relate to late adulthood? There are two ways in which older adults may be better at multitasking than younger people.

1. Selective attention may improve. We are all bombarded with multiple senses and demands; we all need to focus on some aspects and ignore others. It is known that selective attention improves over the years of childhood; perhaps it continues to improve as people grow older.
2. Practice with multiple demands may make multitasking easier. For instance, if a cook must prepare an elaborate meal, then attention to several simmering pots and pans while washing, cutting, chopping, dicing, and so on becomes easier with practice. Some can talk to others while they cook; others find it upsetting if anyone else interrupts their multitasking to ask a question. What is possible and efficient depends on experience.

Both of those improvements in multitasking make logical sense, but they may not work in real life. In general, multitasking seems to become more difficult with age (Ren et al., 2013). The brain slows down. Split-second timing is a little slower, which means switch-costs are more noticeable. If an older person is asked to multitask at unfamiliar tasks, they will be notably slower. If stressed, they may say "Don't rush me" or "One thing at a time."

No Distraction An employment agency called "65plus" specializes in placing workers such as Andre van Krieken, shown here at his job at a railway project in the Netherlands. Older workers tend to focus on the task in front of them, which makes them steady employees.

Video: Old Age: Thinking and Moving at the Same Time features a research study demonstrating how older brains are quite adaptable.

More or Less Efficient

Lifelong, brains adjust to whatever demands are put on them. Plasticity continues, albeit more slowly. Older adults can multitask—if they have time to develop the specific skills. The key seems to be that some aspects of the task need to become automatic and other aspects need to be allocated to different parts of the brain. This eliminates the bottleneck and allows some neurons to fire on or off automatically while other neurons in other parts focus on the more complex parts of the task.

Cognitive control—allocating intellectual focus to the tasks that most need it—is necessary.

Neuroimaging—literally inside the brain—reveals how this works. As one study found, "neural signatures obtained by using EEG during game play [of participants in a multitasking study] . . . reflects the engagement of the prefrontal cortex and long range neural networks involved in cognitive control" (Anguera & Gazzaley, 2015, p. 163).

This may explain a curious finding from PET and fMRI scans: Compared with younger adults, older adults use more parts of their brains, including both hemispheres, to solve problems. This may be a sign of decline, but it may also be compensation (Sugiura, 2016). Using only one brain region may no longer be sufficient if that part has shrunk, so the older brain automatically activates more parts.

In any case, older adults are as intellectually sharp as they always were on many tasks. One control strategy is to be more mindful of the task at hand, using one's entire mind to be aware of what is demanded (Bercovitz & Pagnini, 2016). However, in performing novel multitasking that requires more cognitive resources, older adults are less proficient, perhaps because they already are using their brains to the maximum (Cappell et al., 2010).

Brain shrinkage interferes with multitasking even more than with other cognitive challenges. Switch-costs, especially for novel tasks, are evident for everyone, but young children and old adults are particularly impaired (Krampe et al., 2011) (see Figure 24.1). Recognizing this fact, many elders are selective; they may deliberately focus on one task at a time, sequencing tasks that younger people seem to do simultaneously.

Suppose that a child asks Grandpa a question about dinosaurs while he is reading the newspaper, or that a child asks Grandma which bus to take while she is getting dressed. A wise man like Grandpa puts down the newspaper and then answers, and Grandma will first dress and then think about transportation (avoiding mismatched shoes).

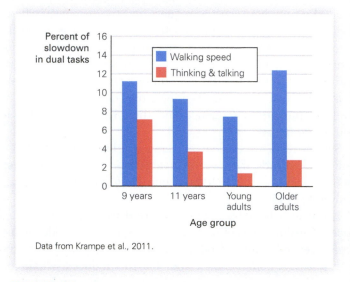

Data from Krampe et al., 2011.

FIGURE 24.1

One Task at a Time Doing two things at once impairs performance. In this study, researchers compared the speed of a sensorimotor task (walking) and a cognitive task (naming objects within a category—for example, naming as many colors, spices, insects, crimes, four-legged animals as possible within a minute or two). The participants did each task separately first, and then they did both at once. Performing them both at once resulted in performance losses for everyone. Note, however, that the eldest seemed to safeguard verbal fluency (only a 3-percent slowdown) at the expense of significantly slower walking.

Observation Quiz In the figure above, how much were the 9-year-olds affected by doing both tasks at once? (see answer, page 678) ↑

WHAT HAVE YOU LEARNED?

1. What is encouraging and discouraging about the formation of new neurons in adulthood?

2. What new challenges does historical change present to adults?

3. Why is multitasking particularly difficult in late adulthood?

● Information Processing After Age 65

Given the complexity, variation, and diversity of late-life cognition, specific details are needed to combat general stereotypes. For this purpose, the information-processing approach is useful to examine input (sensing), memory (storage), control processes (programming), and output.

Input

The first step in information processing is input. Sensation precedes perception, which precedes comprehension. As you read in Chapters 20 and 23, no sense is as sharp at age 65 as at age 15. Glasses and hearing aids mitigate severe sensory losses, but more subtle deficits impair cognition as well. In order to be perceived, information must cross the sensory threshold—the divide between what is sensed and what is not. [**Life-Span Link:** Sensory memory is explained in Chapter 12.]

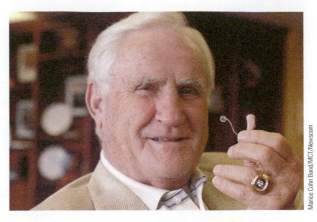

No Quitter When hearing fades, many older people avoid social interaction. Not so for Don Shula, former head coach of the Miami Dolphins, who led his team to two Super Bowl victories. He kept his players fighting, often surging ahead from behind. Here he proudly displays his hearing aid.

Sensory losses may not be noticed because the brain automatically fills in missed sights and sounds. People of all ages believe that they understand the facial expressions of their conversation partner. However, older adults are less adept at knowing where someone is looking or what their facial expression means (Hughes & Devine, 2015; Pardini & Nichelli, 2009).

Similarly, one study of point-light walkers (in the dark, the person sees only the lights on the joints, not the body of the person) found that people of all ages can interpret emotions by seeing only body movements. However, older adults were less adept—particularly at judging anger and sadness (Spencer et al., 2016).

Acute hearing is another way to detect emotional nuances. Older adults are less able to decipher the emotional content in speech, even when they hear the words correctly (Dupuis & Pichora-Fuller, 2010). Particularly for them, understanding of speech is impaired when vision is impaired (Tye-Murray et al., 2011), probably because watching lips and facial expressions aids understanding. Thus, small sensory losses—not noticed by the person or family but inevitable with age—impair cognition.

I know a father—not elderly but already with fading eyesight—who was scolding his 6-year-old daughter. Without his glasses, he could not see that her lip had started to quiver. He was surprised when she cried; he did not realize how harsh his words seemed to her.

The cognition of almost 2,000 intellectually typical older adults, average age 77, was repeatedly tested 5, 8, 10, and 11 years after the initial intake (Lin et al., 2013). At the 5-year retesting, an audiologist assessed their hearing. Between the start of the study and 11 years later, the average cognitive scores of the adults with hearing loss (who were often unaware of it) were down 7 percent, while those with normal hearing lost 5 percent.

That 2-percent difference seems small, but statistically it was highly significant (.004). Furthermore, greater hearing losses correlated with greater cognitive declines (Lin et al., 2013). Many other researchers likewise find that small input losses have a notable effect on output.

Memory

After input, the second step is processing whatever input has come from the senses. Stereotype threat impedes this processing. [**Life-Span Link:** Stereotype threat was discussed in Chapter 18.] If older people suspect memory loss,

● **Answer to Observation Quiz**
(from page 676): Nine-year-olds were the only group to slow down significantly in both tasks. Impairment was about 11 percent in walking and 7 percent in naming within a category.

● **Especially for Students** If you want to remember something that you learn in class for the rest of your life, what should you do? (see response, page 680)

anxiety itself impairs their memory (Ossher et al., 2013). Worse than that, simply knowing that they are taking a memory test makes them feel years older (Hughes et al., 2013). As you learned in Chapter 23, feeling old itself impairs health.

The more psychologists study memory, the more they realize that memory is not one function but many, each with a specific pattern of loss. Some losses of the elderly are quite normal and others pathological (Markowitsch & Staniloiu, 2012). The inability to recall a word or a name is a normal loss of one aspect of memory, and it does not indicate that memory, overall, is fading.

Losses and Gains

Generally, explicit memory (recall of learned material) shows more loss than implicit memory (recognition and habits). This means that names are harder to remember than actions. Grandpa can still swim, ride a bike, and drive a car, even if he cannot name both U.S. senators from his state.

One particular memory deficit in the elderly is *source amnesia*—forgetting the origin of a fact, idea, or snippet of conversation. Source amnesia is particularly problematic in the twenty-first century, as electronic and print information bombard the mind.

In practical terms, source amnesia means that elders might believe a rumor or political advertisement because they forget the source. Compensation requires deliberate attention to the reason behind a message before accepting a con artist's promises or the politics of a TV ad. However, elders are less likely than younger adults to analyze, or even notice, information surrounding the material they remember (Boywitt et al., 2012).

A hot political debate in the United States is about "dark money," whereby financial contributions to political candidates can be anonymous (Dawood, 2015). If dark money is banned, that will help younger voters make informed judgments, but older voters, with fragile source memory, may be less affected.

Another crucial type of memory is called *prospective memory*—remembering to do something in the future (to take a pill, to meet someone for lunch, to buy milk). Prospective memory also fades notably with age (Kliegel et al., 2008). This loss becomes dangerous if, for instance, a person cooking dinner forgets to turn off the stove, or if a driver is in the far lane of the thruway when the exit appears.

The crucial aspect of prospective memory seems to be the ability to shift the mind quickly from one task to another: Older adults get immersed in one thought and have trouble changing gears (Schnitzspahn et al., 2013). For that reason, many elders follow routine sequences (brush teeth, take medicine, get the paper) and set an alarm to remind them to leave for a doctor's appointment. That is compensation.

Working memory (remembering information for a moment before evaluating, calculating, and inferring its significance) also declines with age. Speed is critical: Some older individuals take longer to perceive and process sensations, which reduces working memory because some items fade before they can be considered (Stawski et al., 2013).

For example, a common test of working memory is to have someone repeat backward a string of digits just heard. However, if the digits are said quickly, a slow-thinking person may be unable to process each number. Speed of processing would explain why one form of memory continues to build with age—recognition memory for words. When an older person hears a word they have learned, they usually know what it means because quickness is not required.

Elders can also learn new words and phrases: For example, *Internet, smartphone, e-mail,* and *fax* were not words when today's elders were young adults, but most elders know what they mean. Speed is irrelevant for recognition memory, such as knowing that chartreuse is a color, not an animal.

Being able to recall a word on command is more difficult. An elder might know chartreuse when someone else says it, but he or she might have trouble describing something that color to someone else.

Some research finds that when older people have adequate time, working memory does not fade. Speed is crucial when comparing working memory between one older adult and another, but paying attention becomes the critical factor when a person is tested repeatedly over several days (Stawski et al., 2013).

Thus, adequate time and careful attention are both crucial. This explains interesting results from a study of reading ability. In that research, older people reread phrases more often than younger people did, but when both groups had ample time to pay attention, comprehension was not impaired by age (Stine-Morrow et al., 2010).

Control Processes

The next step in information processing involves **control processes** (discussed in Chapter 12). Many scholars believe that the underlying impairment of cognition in late adulthood is in this step, as information from all parts of the brain is analyzed by the prefrontal cortex. Control processes include selective attention, strategic judgment, and then appropriate action—the so-called executive function of the brain.

Instead of using analysis, the elderly tend to rely on prior knowledge, general principles, familiarity, and rules of thumb as they make decisions (Peters et al., 2011). Actions are based on past experiences and current emotions.

For example, casinos have noticed that elderly gamblers gravitate to slot machines rather than to games where analysis is helpful. The reason, according to a study of brain scans of young and old slot players, is that the activated parts of older brains are less often the regions in which analysis occurs (McCarrey et al., 2012). When gamblers are able to analyze the odds, as younger players do, they spend less time with slots.

One particular control process is development of strategies for retrieval. Some developmentalists believe that impaired retrieval is an underlying cause of intellectual lapses in old age because elders have many thoughts and memories that they cannot access. Since deep thinking requires recognizing and comparing the similarities and differences in various experiences, if a person cannot retrieve memories of the past, new thinking is more shallow than it might otherwise be.

Inadequate control processes may explain why many older adults have extensive vocabularies (measured by written tests) but limited fluency (when they write or talk), are much better at recognition than recall, and often experience tip-of-the-tongue forgetfulness.

Many gerontologists think elders would benefit by learning better control strategies. Unfortunately, even though "a high sense of control is associated with being happy, healthy, and wise," many older adults resist suggested strategies. They believe that declines are "inevitable or irreversible" and that no strategy can help (Lachman et al., 2009, p. 144). Efforts to improve their use of control strategies succeed, but only when the strategy is explicitly taught (Murray et al., 2015; Brom & Kliegel, 2014; McDaniel & Bugg, 2012).

control processes The part of the information-processing system that regulates the analysis and flow of information. Memory and retrieval strategies, selective attention, and rules or strategies for problem solving are all useful control processes.

Cool Thoughts and Hot Hands

As you remember from the discussion of dual processing in Chapter 15, experiential, emotional thinking is not always faulty, but sometimes analytic thinking is needed to control impulsive, thoughtless reactions.

This was apparent in a study of belief in the "hot hand," which is the idea that athletes are more likely to score if they scored in the immediately previous attempts. One study found that most people (91 percent) believe that players can be "on a roll" or that teams can have "a winning streak" (Gilovich et al., 1985).

Most people are wrong about this; the hot hand is an illusion. Of course, the best players are more likely to score than the worst ones, but statistical analysis from basketball, golf, and other sports finds that one successful shot does not affect the chance that a particular player will make the next one.

People want to believe in streaks, so they forget when streaks do not occur. This misperception has become a classic example of the human tendency to ignore data that conflict with assumptions (Kahneman, 2011).

Do people become more or less likely to follow their preconceptions rather than using logic to consider new information as they age? In one study, 455 people aged 22 to 90 were told that, overall, about half of the time basketball shots miss. That was supposed to remind them to think analytically, not emotionally. Then they were asked two questions:

1. Does a basketball player have a better chance of making a shot after having just made the last two or three shots than after missing the last two or three shots?

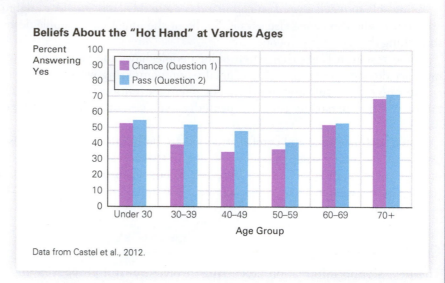

Beliefs About the "Hot Hand" at Various Ages

Data from Castel et al., 2012.

FIGURE 24.2

Hard to Chill This shows the percent of adults who answered yes to the two questions, which meant that they were not thinking analytically. As you see, the oldest participants were most likely to stick to their "hot-hand" prejudice. However, also notice that about one-fourth of those over 70 answered correctly and almost half of the younger adults did not. In this and every other study, age is only one of many factors that influence cognition.

2. Is it important to pass the ball to someone who has just made several shots in a row?

The correct answer to both questions is no, but in this study, elders were particularly likely to say yes, sticking to their hot-hand belief (Castel et al., 2012) (see Figure 24.2).

Response for Students
(from page 678): Learn it very well now, and you will probably remember it in 50 years, with a little review.

Output

The final step in information processing is output. In daily life, output is usually verbal. If the timbre and speed of a person's speech sounds old, ageism might cause listeners to dismiss the content without realizing that the substance may be profound. Then, if elders realize that what they say is ignored, they talk less. Output is diminished.

Scientists usually measure output through use of standardized tests of mental ability. As already noted, if older adults think their memory is being tested, that alone impairs them (Hughes et al., 2013). Even without stereotype threat, output on cognitive tests may not reflect ability, as you will now see.

Cognitive Tests

In the Seattle Longitudinal Study (described in Chapter 21), the measured output of all five primary mental abilities—verbal meaning, spatial orientation, inductive reasoning, number ability, and word fluency—declined, beginning at about age 60. This decline was particularly notable in spatial perception and processing speed (Schaie, 2005/2013).

Similar results are found in many tests of cognition: Thus, the usual path of cognition in late adulthood as measured by psychological tests is gradual decline, at least in output (Salthouse, 2010). However, such tests are normed and validated based on the output of younger adults. To avoid cultural bias, many questions are quite abstract and timed, since speed of thinking correlates with intelligence for younger adults.

This is reflected in how we talk about intelligence. Speed words are common: A smart person is said to be a "quick" thinker, the opposite of someone who is "slow."

Since abstract thinking and processing speed are the aspects of cognition that fade most with age, such tests may be culturally fair but age-unfair. Is there a better way to measure output in late adulthood?

Ecological Validity

Perhaps ability should be measured in everyday tasks and circumstances, not as laboratory tests assess it. To do measurements in everyday settings is to seek **ecological validity,** which may be particularly important when measuring cognition in the elderly (Marsiske & Margrett, 2006).

For example, because of changes in their circadian rhythm, older adults are at their best in the early morning, when adolescents are half asleep. If a study were to compare 85-year-olds and 15-year-olds, both tested at 7 A.M., the teenagers would be at a disadvantage. The opposite would be true if the test were at 7 P.M.

Similarly, if intellectual ability were to be assessed via a timed test, then faster thinkers (usually young) would score higher than slower thinkers (usually old), although the slower ones might know the answers if they had a few more seconds to think. Context matters, too: Who feels stressed if the tests occur on a college campus?

Indeed, age differences in prospective memory are readily apparent in laboratory tests but disappear in some naturalistic settings, a phenomenon called the "prospective memory-paradox" (Schnitzspahn et al., 2011). Motivation seems crucial; elders are less likely to forget whatever they believe is important—phoning a child on his or her birthday, for instance.

Similarly, as already noted, older adults are not as accurate as younger adults when tested on the ability to read emotions by looking at someone's face or listening to someone's voice. However, since seeing and hearing are less acute with age, those senses may not be the best way to measure empathy in older adults. Accordingly, a team decided to measure empathy when visual contact was impossible.

Their study included a hundred couples who had been together for years, and each of the participants was repeatedly asked to indicate their own emotions (how happy, enthusiastic, balanced, content, angry, downcast, disappointed, nervous they were) and to guess the emotions of their partner at that moment. Technology helped with this: The participants were beeped at various times and indicated their answers on a smartphone they kept with them. Sometimes they happened to be with their partner, sometimes not.

ecological validity The idea that cognition should be measured in settings that are as realistic as possible and that the abilities measured should be those needed in real life.

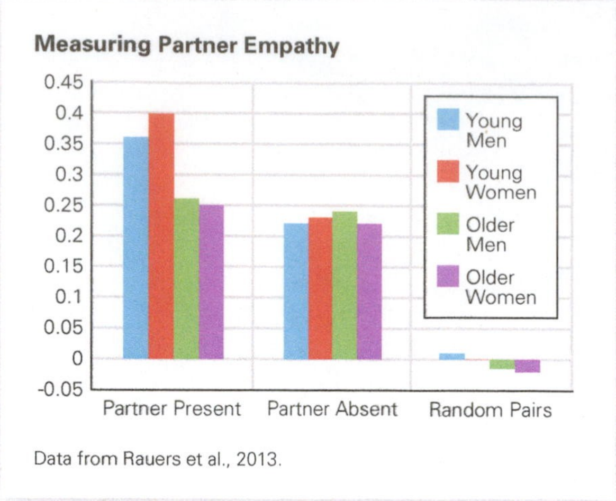

Measuring Partner Empathy

Data from Rauers et al., 2013.

FIGURE 24.3

Always on My Mind When they were together, younger partners were more accurate than older ones at knowing their partner's emotions, but older partners were as good as younger ones when they were apart. This study used "smartphone experience sampling," buzzing both partners simultaneously to ask how they and their partner felt. Interestingly, differences were found with age but not length of relationship—5, 10, 20, or 30 years of togetherness did not necessarily increase empathy when apart, but men who were in their 70s were better at absent mood assessment than men in their 20s.

When the partner was present, accuracy was higher for the younger couples, presumably because they could see and hear their mate. But when the partner was absent, the older participants were as good as the younger ones (see Figure 24.3). The key question is whether

you could predict a social partner's feelings when that person is absent: Your judgment would probably be better than chance, and although many abilities deteriorate with aging, this particular ability may remain reliable throughout your life.

[Rauers et al., 2013, p. 2215]

The fundamental ecological issue for developmentalists is what should be assessed—pure, abstract thinking or practical, contextual thought; depersonalized abilities or everyday actions? Traditional tests of cognition emphasize fluid abilities, but problem solving and emotional sensitivity may be more crucial. Those practical abilities are not measured by traditional cognitive tests, and they may improve with age.

Awareness of the need for ecological validity has helped scientists restructure research on memory. Restructured studies find fewer deficits than originally thought. However, any test may overestimate or underestimate ability. For instance, what is an accurate test of long-term memory? Many older people recount, in vivid detail, events that occurred decades ago. That is impressive . . . if the memories are accurate.

Unfortunately, "there is no objective way to evaluate the degree of ecological validity . . . because ecological validity is a subjective concept" (Salthouse, 2010, p. 77). It is impossible to be totally objective in assessing memory; memory and tests of memory always have a subjective component.

OPPOSING PERSPECTIVES

How to Measure Output

Finding the best way to measure cognition is particularly important if a decision is to be made as to whether an older person is able to live independently. An increasing number of the elderly live alone. Is this safe? Might they forget to turn off the stove, or ignore symptoms of a heart attack, or fall prey to a stranger who wants them to invest their money in a harebrained scheme?

Protection and independence are both valid goals, but they may clash.

Tests have been developed to measure practical problem solving (Law et al., 2012). Some involve short-term memory with no delay between facts and conclusions. In one such test, for instance, a person reads relevant facts; then the paper is removed and the person is asked to solve a problem based on those facts. Other tests pose practical problems, such as what to do if your refrigerator is warm or if a favorite sweater has a hole in it.

Scores on practical tests show less discrepancy between the old and the young than scores on abstract memory tests. Per-

haps only when an older person living alone fails practical tests is it time for intervention.

Unfortunately, even tests that attempt to be ecologically valid may be inaccurate (Law et al., 2012). Perhaps the best way to test cognitive ability is to be quite direct, asking questions about missed appointments, lost keys, and so on of a person or of someone who knows them well. Yet even direct questions may not be answered accurately, in part because many of the elderly do not want to admit memory loss.

Are family members accurate? Many family members and professionals, themselves growing older, do not want to admit to their own memory loss—or they may exaggerate it in someone else. Objective measurement might help.

Which measure is best? A study that compared self-assessment, spousal assessment, and tests of intellectual ability found poor correlation among them (Volz-Sidiropoulou & Gauggel, 2012). People did not accurately assess their own memories or those of their partner—with whom they had lived for an average of 30 years.

In that study, the self-assessment questions were ecologically valid, asking practical questions such as how often the person loses things around the house (Volz-Sidiropoulou & Gauggel, 2012). The formal tests of memory were also valid and well established. For instance, the examiner read a list of 15 words and asked the older person to repeat them.

Inaccurate self-assessment is characteristic of people with serious mental illness, as the study authors explain. Those who reported few memory difficulties tended to score poorly on the formal tests. This was thought to be an example of "self-serving bias"—the human tendency to think we are better than we are. That could be dangerous if people are allowed to live alone until they themselves realize they should not.

But, read the final paragraph of this feature before accepting this conclusion.

By contrast, some people in this study reported many memory problems: They typically did better on the formal tests than their self-assessment. The study authors thought this might have been their "way to protect their self-concept by claiming self-handicapping" (Volz-Sidiropoulou & Gauggel, 2012, p. 446). Thus, the perspective of researchers was that the elderly are poor at assessing their own cognition.

But wait. Can you see that the researchers might have been wrong? Is the gap between self-assessment and laboratory results evidence of self-serving bias or self-concept protection, as the researchers thought whenever the scores on self-assessment were higher or lower than the test? Or are the tests biased, not the people who took them?

We know that stereotypes are insidious, that global assessments are oversimplified, that emotions affect output. We know that individuals vary and that some but not all kinds of memory show notable age-related loss.

The final ecological question is, "What is memory for?" Older adults usually think they remember well enough. Fear of memory loss is more typical at age 60 than at age 80. Unless they develop a brain condition such as Alzheimer's disease (soon described), elders are correct: They remember how to live their daily lives. Is that enough?

WHAT HAVE YOU LEARNED?

1. How does sensory loss affect cognition?

2. Which kinds of things are harder to remember with age?

3. Why do some elderly people resist learning strategies for memory retrieval?

4. How might output be affected by the aging process?

5. What needs to be considered in ecologically valid measurement of adult intelligence?

6. What would be an ecologically valid test of cognition in late adulthood?

Neurocognitive Disorders

Most older people are less sharp than they were, but they still think and remember quite well. Others experience serious decline. They have a **neurocognitive disorder (NCD).**

neurocognitive disorder (NCD) Any of a number of brain diseases that affects a person's ability to remember, analyze, plan, or interact with other people.

The Ageism of Words

The rate of neurocognitive disorders increases with every decade after age 60. But ageism distorts and exaggerates that fact. To understand and prevent NCDs, we need to begin by using words carefully.

Senile simply means "old." If the word *senility* is used to mean "severe mental impairment," that would imply that old age always brings intellectual failure—an

ageist myth. *Dementia* (used in DSM-IV) was a more precise term than *senility* for irreversible, pathological loss of brain functioning, but *dementia* has the same root as *demon,* and thus it has inaccurate connotations.

The DSM-5 now describes neurocognitive disorders, as either *major* (previously called *dementia*) or *mild* (previously called *mild cognitive impairment*).

Memory problems occur in every cognitive disorder, although some people with NCDs have other notable symptoms, such as in judgment (they do foolish things) and moods (they are suddenly full of rage or sadness). The line between normal age-related changes, mild disorder, and major disorder is not clear, and symptoms vary depending on the specifics of brain loss as well as context. Even when the disorder is major, the individual's personality affects the symptoms.

The former word—*dementia*—and the inaccurate word—*senility*—are both still prevalent, and once a word is used it tends to obscure variations. Moreover, as two gerontologists explain, the emphasis on a medical diagnosis tends

> to ignore the subjectivity and quality of life of those who are suffering dementia, and to stigmatize, devalue, disempower, banish, objectify, and invalidate them on account of their neuropathological condition.
>
> *[George & Whitehouse, 2010, p. 351]*

In Japanese, the traditional word for neurocognitive disorder was *chihou,* translated as "foolish" or "stupid." As more Japanese reached old age, a new word, *ninchihou,* which means "cognitive syndrome," was chosen (George & Whitehouse, 2010). That is far better, for, as you remember with Down syndrome, a syndrome is a cluster of characteristics, with each person somewhat different.

Many scientists seek biological indicators (called biomarkers, as in the blood or cerebrospinal fluid) or brain indicators (as on brain scans) that predict major memory loss. However, although abnormal scores on many tests (biological, neurological, or psychological) indicate possible problems, an examination of 24 such measures found that no single test, or combination of tests, is 100 percent accurate (Ewers et al., 2012).

Two new and promising tests, a PET scan or a blood assay that reveals amyloid plaques which indicate Alzheimer's disease, are not reimbursed by Medicaid because the link between presence of amyloid and effective treatment is "insufficient." More research is needed (Centers for Medicare and Medicaid Services, 2014; Hagan et al., 2016).

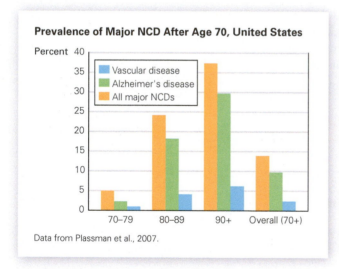

Data from Plassman et al., 2007.

FIGURE 24.4

Not Everyone Gets It Most elderly people never experience major NCD. Among people in their 70s, only 1 person in 20 does, and most of those who reach 90 or 100 do not suffer significant cognitive decline. Presented another way, the prevalence data sound more dire: Almost 4 million people in the United States have major NCD.

major neurocognitive disorder (major NCD) Irreversible loss of intellectual functioning caused by organic brain damage or disease. Formerly called *dementia,* major NCD becomes more common with age, but it is abnormal and pathological even in the very old.

Prevalence of NCDs

How many people suffer from neurocognitive disorders in their older years? To answer this question, researchers selected a representative sample of people over age 69 from every part of the United States. Each was interviewed and tested. Then the researchers interviewed someone who knew the elder well (usually an immediate relative). This information was combined with medical records and clinical judgment.

The conclusion was that 14 percent of the elders had some form of neurocognitive disorder (Plassman et al., 2007) (see Figure 24.4). Extrapolated to the overall population, this means that about 4 million U.S. residents have a serious neurocognitive disorder. Another study, this one of people already diagnosed with **major neurocognitive disorder (major NCD),** found much lower rates, about 8 percent of the aged population (Koller & Bynum, 2014). The discrepancy may either be that many people are not diagnosed or that the rate has decreased.

An estimated 47 million people (again, estimates vary from 35 million to 60 million) are affected worldwide, 60 percent of them in low-income nations (World Health Organization, 2015). The poorest nations have the lowest rates because fewer people reach old age; but as longevity increases, rates of major NCD rise as well. This has already occurred in China, where 9 million people had a serious NCD in 2010, compared to only 4 million in 1990 (K. Chan et al., 2013).

Eventually, better education and public health will reduce the rate (if not the number) of cognitive impairments everywhere. In England and Wales, the rate of major NCD for people over age 65 was 8.3 percent in 1991 but only 6.5 percent in 2011 (Matthews et al., 2013). Sweden had a similar decline (Qiu et al., 2013). In China, rates are much higher in rural areas than in cities, perhaps because rural Chinese have less education or worse health (Jia et al., 2014).

The Many Neurocognitive Disorders

As more is learned, it has become apparent that there are many types of brain disease, with each beginning in a distinct part of the brain and having particular symptoms. Once it was thought that if a person seemed to have a good memory, he or she could not be suffering from a neurocognitive disorder. That mistaken idea prevented diagnosis and treatment. Accordingly, we describe some of the many disorders now.

Alzheimer's Disease

In the past century, millions of people in every large nation have been diagnosed with **Alzheimer's disease (AD)** (now formally referred to as *major NCD due to Alzheimer's disease*). Severe and worsening memory loss is the main symptom, but the diagnosis is not definitive until an autopsy finds extensive plaques and tangles in the cerebral cortex (see Table 24.1).

Plaques are clumps of a protein called beta-amyloid in tissues surrounding the neurons; **tangles** are twisted masses of threads made of a protein called tau

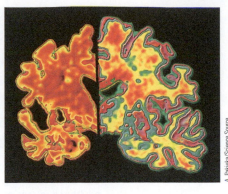

The Alzheimer's Brain This computer graphic shows a vertical slice through a brain ravaged by Alzheimer's disease *(left)* compared with a similar slice of a normal brain *(right)*. The diseased brain is shrunken because neurons have degenerated. The red indicates plaques and tangles.

A. Pakieka/Science Source

Alzheimer's disease (AD) The most common cause of major NCD, characterized by gradual deterioration of memory and personality and marked by the formation of plaques of beta-amyloid protein and tangles of tau in the brain.

plaques Clumps of a protein called beta-amyloid, found in brain tissues surrounding the neurons.

tangles Twisted masses of threads made of a protein called tau within the neurons of the brain.

TABLE 24.1	**Stages of Alzheimer's Disease**

Stage 1. People in the first stage forget recent events or new information, particularly names and places. For example, they might forget the name of a famous film star or how to get home from a familiar place. This first stage is similar to mild cognitive impairment—even experts cannot always tell the difference. In retrospect, it seems clear that President Ronald Reagan had early AD while in office, but no doctor diagnosed it.

Stage 2. Generalized confusion develops, with deficits in concentration and short-term memory. Speech becomes aimless and repetitive, vocabulary is limited, words get mixed up. Personality traits are not curbed by rational thought. For example, suspicious people may decide that others have stolen the things that they themselves have mislaid.

Stage 3. Memory loss becomes dangerous. Although people at stage 3 can care for themselves, they might leave a lit stove or hot iron on or might forget whether they took essential medicine and thus take it twice—or not at all.

Stage 4. At this stage, full-time care is needed. People cannot communicate well. They might not recognize their closest loved ones.

Stage 5. Finally, people with AD become unresponsive. Identity and personality have disappeared. When former president Ronald Reagan was at this stage, a longtime friend who visited him was asked, "Did he recognize you?" The friend answered, "Worse than that—I didn't recognize him." Death comes 10 to 15 years after the first signs appear.

LaunchPad
macmillan learning

In **Video Activity: Alzheimer's Disease,** experts and family members discuss the progression of the disease.

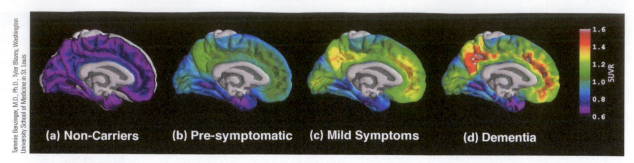

Hopeful Brains Even the brain without symptoms *(a)* might eventually develop Alzheimer's disease, but people with a certain dominant gene definitely will. They have no symptoms in early adulthood *(b)*, some symptoms in middle adulthood *(c)*, and stage-five Alzheimer's disease *(d)* before old age. Research finds early brain markers (such as those shown here) that predict the disease. This is not always accurate, but it may soon lead to early treatment that halts AD, not only in those genetically vulnerable but in everyone.

Especially for Genetic Counselors
Would you perform a test for ApoE4 if someone asked for it? (see response, page 688)

vascular disease Formerly called *vascular* or *multi-infarct dementia,* vascular disease is characterized by sporadic, and progressive, loss of intellectual functioning caused by repeated infarcts, or temporary obstructions of blood vessels, which prevent sufficient blood from reaching the brain.

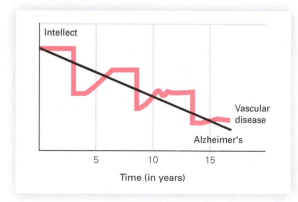

FIGURE 24.5

The Progression of Alzheimer's Disease and Vascular Disease Cognitive decline is apparent in both Alzheimer's disease (AD) and vascular disease (VaD). However, the pattern of decline for each disease is different. Victims of AD show steady, gradual decline, while those who suffer from VaD get suddenly much worse, improve somewhat, and then experience another serious loss.

within the neurons. A normal brain contains some beta-amyloid and some tau, but in brains with AD these plaques and tangles proliferate, especially in the hippocampus, a brain structure that is crucial for memory. Forgetfulness is the dominant symptom, from momentary lapses to—after years of progressive disease—forgetting the names and faces of one's own children.

An autopsy that finds massive plaques and tangles proves that a person had Alzheimer's disease. However, between 20 and 30 percent of cognitively typical elders have, at autopsy, extensive plaques in their brains (Jack et al., 2009). One explanation is that cognitive reserve enables some people to bypass the disconnections caused by plaques. Education does seem to prevent, or modify, AD (Langa, 2015).

Alzheimer's disease is partly genetic. If it develops in middle age, the affected person either has trisomy-21 (Down syndrome) or has inherited one of three genes: amyloid precursor protein (APP), presenilin 1, or presenilin 2. For these people, the disease progresses quickly, reaching the last phase within three to five years.

Most cases begin much later, at age 75 or so. Many genes have some impact, including SORL1 and ApoE4 (allele 4 of the ApoE gene). People who inherit one copy of ApoE4 (as about one-fifth of all U.S. residents do) have about a 50/50 chance of developing AD. Those who inherit two copies almost always develop the disorder if they live long enough, but they may not live long enough, because ApoE4 also predicts a stroke.

Vascular Disease

The second most common cause of neurocognitive disorder is a stroke (a temporary obstruction of a blood vessel in the brain) or a series of strokes, called transient ischemic attacks (TIAs, or ministrokes). The interruption in blood flow reduces oxygen, destroying part of the brain. Symptoms (blurred vision, weak or paralyzed limbs, slurred speech, and mental confusion) suddenly appear.

In a TIA, symptoms may vanish quickly, unnoticed. However, unless recognized and prevented, another TIA is likely, eventually causing **vascular disease,** commonly referred to as *vascular* or *multi-infarct dementia* (see Figure 24.5).

Vascular disease also correlates with the ApoE4 allele (Cramer & Procaccio, 2012). For some of the elderly, it is caused by surgery that requires general anesthesia. They suffer a ministroke, which, added to reduced cognitive reserve, damages their brains (Y. Stern, 2013).

Frontotemporal NCDs

Several types of neurocognitive disorders affect the frontal lobes and thus are called **frontotemporal NCDs,** or *frontotemporal lobar degeneration.* (Pick disease is the most common form.) These disorders cause perhaps 15 percent of all cases of NCDs in the United States. Frontotemporal NCDs tend to occur before age 70, unlike Alzheimer's or vascular disease (Seelaar et al., 2011).

In frontotemporal NCDs, parts of the brain that regulate emotions and social behavior (especially the amygdala and prefrontal cortex) deteriorate. Emotional and personality changes are the main symptoms (Seelaar et al., 2011). A loving mother with a frontotemporal NCD might reject her children, or a formerly astute businessman might invest in a foolish scheme.

Frontal lobe problems may be worse than more obvious types of neurocognitive disorders, in that compassion, self-awareness, and judgment fade in a person who otherwise seems normal. One wife, Ruth French, was furious because her husband

> threw away tax documents, got a ticket for trying to pass an ambulance and bought stock in companies that were obviously in trouble. Once a good cook, he burned every pot in the house. He became withdrawn and silent, and no longer spoke to his wife over dinner. That same failure to communicate got him fired from his job.
>
> [D. Grady, 2012, p. A1]

Finally, he was diagnosed with a frontotemporal NCD. Ruth asked him to forgive her fury. It is not clear that he understood either her anger or her apology.

Although there are many forms and causes of frontotemporal NCDs—including a dozen or so alleles—they usually progress rapidly, leading to death in about five years.

Other Disorders

Many other brain diseases begin with impaired motor control (shaking when picking up a coffee cup, falling when trying to walk), not with impaired thinking. The most common of these is **Parkinson's disease,** the cause of about 3 percent of all cases of NCDs.

Parkinson's disease starts with rigidity or tremor of the muscles as dopamine-producing neurons degenerate, affecting movement long before cognition. Middle-aged adults with Parkinson's disease usually have sufficient cognitive reserve to avoid major intellectual loss, although about one-third have mild cognitive decline (S. Gao et al., 2014).

Older people with Parkinson's develop cognitive problems sooner (Pfeiffer & Bodis-Wollner, 2012). If people with Parkinson's live 10 years or more, almost always major neurocognitive impairment occurs (Pahwa & Lyons, 2013).

Another 3 percent of people with NCD in the United States suffer from **Lewy body disease:** excessive deposits of a particular kind of protein in their brains. Lewy bodies are also present in Parkinson's disease, but in Lewy body disease they are more numerous and dispersed throughout the brain, interfering with communication between neurons. The main symptom is loss of inhibition: A person might gamble or become hypersexual.

Comorbidity is common with all of these disorders. For instance, most people with Alzheimer's disease also show signs of vascular impairment (Doraiswamy,

To Have and to Hold Ruth wanted to divorce Michael until she realized that he suffered from a frontotemporal NCD. Now she provides body warmth and comfort in his nursing home bed.

frontotemporal NCDs Deterioration of the amygdala and frontal lobes that may be the cause of 15 percent of all major neurocognitive disorders. (Also called *frontotemporal lobar degeneration.*)

Parkinson's disease A chronic, progressive disease that is characterized by muscle tremor and rigidity and sometimes major neurocognitive disorder; caused by reduced dopamine production in the brain.

Lewy body disease A form of major neurocognitive disorder characterized by an increase in Lewy body cells in the brain. Symptoms include visual hallucinations, momentary loss of attention, falling, and fainting.

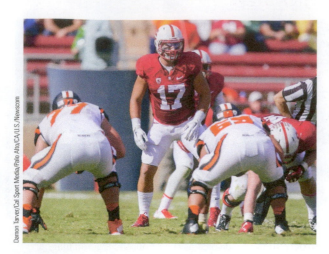

Score Please Most observers celebrate first downs, field goals, and touchdowns, but neurologists notice tackles—and shudder.

⬤◑ **Response for Genetic Counselors**
(from page 686): A general guideline for genetic counselors is to provide clients with whatever information they seek, but because of both the uncertainty of diagnosis and the devastation of Alzheimer's disease, the ApoE4 test is not available at present. This may change (as was the case with the test for HIV) if early methods of prevention and treatment become more effective.

2012). Parkinson's, Alzheimer's, and Lewy body diseases can occur together: People who have all three experience more rapid and severe cognitive loss (Compta et al., 2011).

Some other types of NCDs begin in middle age or even earlier, caused by Huntington's disease, multiple sclerosis, a severe head injury, or the last stages of syphilis, AIDS, or bovine spongiform encephalopathy (BSE, or mad cow disease). Repeated blows to the head, even without concussions, can cause *chronic traumatic encephalopathy (CTE),* which first causes memory loss and emotional changes (Voosen, 2013).

Although the rate of systemic neurocognitive disorder increases dramatically with every decade after age 60, brain disease can occur at any age, as revealed by the autopsies of a number of young professional athletes. For them, prevention includes better helmets and fewer body blows. Already, tackling is avoided in football practice.

These changes in athletic practices have come too late for thousands of adults, including Derek Boogaard, a National Hockey League enforcer who died of a drug overdose in 2011 at age 28. His autopsied brain showed traumatic brain injury, now called CTE.

For Boogaard, chronic traumatic encephalopathy may have been a cause of drug addiction and would have become major NCD if he lived longer. The brain disorder probably already occurred, undiagnosed. Another hockey player said of him, "His demeanor, his personality, it just left him . . . He didn't have a personality anymore" (John Scott, quoted in Branch, 2011, p. B13). Obviously, *senility* is not a synonym for *neurocognitive disorder.*

Preventing Impairment

Severe brain damage cannot be reversed, although the rate of decline and some of the symptoms can be treated. However, education, exercise, and good health not only ameliorate mild losses, they may prevent worse ones. That may be happening: "A growing number of studies, at least nine over the past 10 years, have shown a declining risk for dementia incidence or prevalence in high-income countries, including the US, England, The Netherlands, Sweden, and Denmark" (Langa, 2015, p. 34).

Because brain plasticity is lifelong, exercise that improves blood circulation not only prevents cognitive loss but also builds capacity and repairs damage. The benefits of exercise have been repeatedly cited in this text. Now we simply reiterate that physical exercise—even more than good nutrition and mental exercise—prevents, postpones, and slows cognitive loss of all kinds (Erickson et al., 2012; Gregory et al., 2012; Lövdén et al., 2013).

Medication to prevent strokes also protects against neurocognitive disorders. In a Finnish study, half of a large group of older Finns were given drugs to reduce lipids in their system (primarily cholesterol). Years later, fewer of them had developed NCDs than did a comparable group who were not given the drug (Solomon et al., 2010).

Avoiding specific pathogens is critical. For example, beef can be tested to ensure that it does not have BSE, condoms can protect against HIV/AIDS, and syphilis can be cured with antibiotics.

For most neurocognitive disorders, however, despite the efforts of thousands of scientists and millions of older people, no foolproof prevention or cure has been

Selective Optimization When they were younger, they sprinted; when they were middle-aged, they jogged. Now they hike with walking sticks. Exercise is beneficial at any age, but the specifics differ.

⬤◑ **Observation Quiz** What three things do you see that promote cognitive health? (see answer, page 690) ⬆

Global Prevalence of Major Neurocognitive Disorders

Major neurocognitive disorder (better known as dementia) refers to several diseases, with Alzheimer's disease the most common. Estimates of the prevalence and number of people with major NCD vary depending on how studies are conducted, but numbers are increasing in most parts of the world, as more people live to their 80s and 90s. Rates are quite low in some places, such as sub-Saharan Africa, but that might be because most people die before they are very old. In developed nations, by contrast, a person could have major NCD and live a decade or longer.

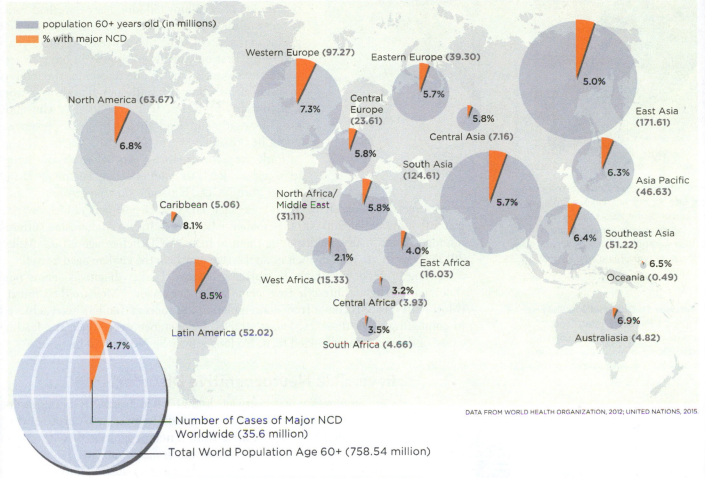

- population 60+ years old (in millions)
- % with major NCD

North America (63.67) — 6.8%
Western Europe (97.27) — 7.3%
Eastern Europe (39.30) — 5.7%
Central Europe (23.61) — 5.8%
Central Asia (7.16) — 5.8%
East Asia (171.61) — 5.0%
Asia Pacific (46.63) — 6.3%
Caribbean (5.06) — 8.1%
North Africa/Middle East (31.11) — 5.8%
South Asia (124.61) — 5.7%
Southeast Asia (51.22) — 6.4%
West Africa (15.33) — 2.1%
East Africa (16.03) — 4.0%
Oceania (0.49) — 6.5%
Latin America (52.02) — 8.5%
Central Africa (3.93) — 3.2%
South Africa (4.66) — 3.5%
Australiasia (4.82) — 6.9%

Worldwide — 4.7%
Number of Cases of Major NCD Worldwide (35.6 million)
Total World Population Age 60+ (758.54 million)

DATA FROM WORLD HEALTH ORGANIZATION, 2012; UNITED NATIONS, 2015.

HOW WILL THE NUMBERS CHANGE IN DECADES TO COME?

It is impossible to project future rates of neurocognitive disorders, since many scientists and doctors are trying to understand causes and cures, and many older people are trying to reduce their risk. However, one risk—old age—will increase. As more people reach age 80 and above, more people will experience major NCD of one kind or another.

HEALTH-CARE COSTS ASSOCIATED WITH MAJOR NCD

Alzheimer's disease and other major NCDs are among the costliest chronic diseases to society: Individuals with a major NCD have more hospital and skilled nursing facility stays and home health care visits than other older people. However, the human cost may be greater than these estimates: Many family members spend substantial time caring for people with dementia, but often that time is not calculated until the NCD is severe.

THE HEALTH-CARE PROVIDERS

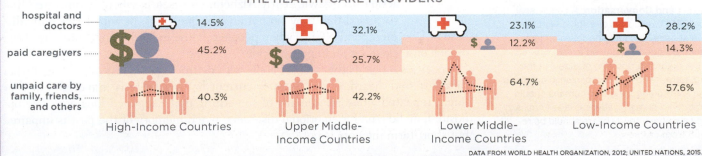

	High-Income Countries	Upper Middle-Income Countries	Lower Middle-Income Countries	Low-Income Countries
hospital and doctors	14.5%	32.1%	23.1%	28.2%
paid caregivers	45.2%	25.7%	12.2%	14.3%
unpaid care by family, friends, and others	40.3%	42.2%	64.7%	57.6%

DATA FROM WORLD HEALTH ORGANIZATION, 2012; UNITED NATIONS, 2015.

Same Situation, Far Apart: Strong Legs, Long Life As this woman in a Brooklyn, New York, senior center (*left*) and this man on a Greek beach (*right*) seem to realize, exercise that strengthens the legs is particularly beneficial for body, mind, and spirit in late adulthood.

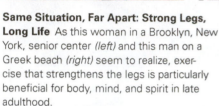

Answer to Observation Quiz
(from page 688): Social interaction, appreciation of nature, and, of course, exercise. Doing leg lifts alone at home is good, too, but this is much better.

Comfort and Conversation A cuddly seal robot, PARO, responds to petting with 12 tactile senses, encouraging touch and eye contact. Designed and used in Japan, which has the highest proportion of elders in the world, here PARO is a companion in a nursing home. Critics complain that humans should interact with humans; advocates ask critics if they also think teddy bears should be removed from children.

found. Avoiding toxins (lead, aluminum, copper, and pesticides) or adding supplements (hormones, aspirin, coffee, insulin, antioxidants, red wine, blueberries, and statins) have been tried as preventatives but have not proven effective in controlled, scientific research.

Thousands of scientists have sought to halt the production of beta-amyloid, and they have had some success in mice but not yet in humans. One current goal is to diagnose Alzheimer's disease 10 or 15 years before the first outward signs appear in order to prevent brain damage. That is one reason for the interest in mild NCDs: They often (though not always) progress to major problems. If it were known why some mild losses do not lead to major ones, prevention might be possible.

Early, accurate diagnosis, years before obvious symptoms appear, leads to more effective treatment. Drugs do not cure NCDs, but some slow progression. Sometimes surgery or stem cell therapy is beneficial. The U.S. Department of Defense estimates that more than 200,000 U.S. soldiers who were in Iraq or Afghanistan suffered traumatic brain injury, predisposing them to major NCD before age 60 (G. Miller, 2012). Measures to remedy their brain damage may help the civilian aged as well.

Among professionals, hope is replacing despair. Earlier diagnosis seems possible; many drug and lifestyle treatments are under review. "Measured optimism" (Moye, 2015, p. 331) comes from contemplating the success that has been achieved in combating other diseases. Heart attacks, for instance, were once the leading cause of death for middle-aged men. No longer. Maybe NCDs will be next.

Reversible Neurocognitive Disorder?

Care improves when everyone knows what disease is undermining intellectual capacity. Accurate diagnosis is even more crucial when memory problems do not arise from a neurocognitive disorder. Brain diseases destroy parts of the brain, but some people are thought to be permanently "losing their minds" when a reversible condition is really at fault.

Depression

The most common reversible condition that is mistaken for major NCD is depression. Normally, older people tend to be quite happy; frequent sadness or anxiety is not normal. Ongoing, untreated depression increases the risk of major NCD (Y. Gao et al., 2013).

Ironically, people with untreated anxiety or depression may exaggerate minor memory losses or refuse to talk. Quite the opposite reaction occurs with early Alzheimer's disease, when victims are often surprised that they cannot answer questions, or with Lewy body disease or frontotemporal NCDs, when people talk too much without thinking. Talk, or lack of it, provides an important clue.

Specifics provide other clues. People with neurocognitive loss might forget what they just said, heard, or did because current brain activity is impaired, but they might repeatedly describe details of something that happened long ago. The opposite may be true for emotional disorders, when memory of the past is impaired but short-term memory is not.

Malnutrition

Malnutrition and dehydration can also cause symptoms that may seem like brain disease. The aging digestive system is less efficient but needs more nutrients and fewer calories. This requires new habits, less fast food, and more grocery money (which many do not have).

Some elderly people deliberately drink less liquid because they want to avoid frequent urination, yet adequate water in the body is needed for cell health. Since homeostasis slows with age, older people are less likely to recognize and remedy their hunger and thirst, and thus they may inadvertently impair their cognition.

Beyond the need to drink water and eat vegetables, several specific vitamins may stave off cognitive impairment. Among the suggested foods to add are those containing antioxidants (vitamins C, A, E) and vitamin B-12. Homocysteine (from animal fat) may need to be avoided, since high levels correlate with major NCD (Perez et al., 2012; Whalley et al., 2014). Psychoactive drugs, especially alcohol, can cause confusion and hallucinations at much lower doses than in the young.

Obviously, any food that increases the risk of heart disease and stroke also increases the risk of vascular disease. In addition, some prescribed drugs destroy certain nutrients, although specifics require more research (Jyrkkä et al., 2012).

Indeed, well-controlled longitudinal research on the relationship between particular aspects of nutrition and NCD has not been done (Coley et al., 2015). It is known, however, that people who already suffer from NCD tend to forget to eat or tend to choose unhealthy foods, hastening their mental deterioration. It is also known that alcohol abuse interferes with nutrition, directly (reducing eating and hydration) and indirectly (blocking vitamin absorption).

Polypharmacy

At home as well as in the hospital, most elderly people take numerous drugs—not only prescribed medications but also over-the-counter preparations and herbal remedies—a situation known as **polypharmacy.** Excessive reliance on drugs can occur on doctor's orders as well as via patient ignorance.

The rate of polypharmacy is increasing in the United States. For instance, in 1988 the number of people over age 65 who took five drugs or more was 13 percent; by 2010 that number had tripled to 39 percent (Charlesworth et al., 2015).

Unfortunately, recommended doses of many drugs are determined primarily by clinical trials with younger adults, for whom homeostasis usually eliminates excess medication (Herrera et al., 2010). When homeostasis slows down, excess lingers. In addition, most trials to test the safety of a new drug exclude people who have more than one disease. That means drugs are not tested on the people who will use them most.

The average elderly person in the United States sees a physician eight times a year (National Center for Health Statistics, 2014). Typically, each doctor follows "clinical practice guidelines," which are recommendations for one specific condition. A "prescribing cascade" (when many interacting drugs are prescribed) may occur.

In one disturbing case, a doctor prescribed medication to raise his patient's blood pressure, and another doctor, noting the raised blood pressure, prescribed a drug to lower it (McLendon & Shelton, 2011–2012). Usually, doctors ask patients what medications they are taking and why, which could prevent such an error. However, people who are sick and confused may not give accurate responses.

A related problem is that people of every age forget when to take which drugs (before, during, or after meals? after dinner or at bedtime?) (Bosworth & Ayotte, 2009). Short-term memory loss makes this worse, and poverty cuts down on pill purchases.

polypharmacy Refers to a situation in which elderly people are prescribed several medications. The various side effects and interactions of those medications can result in dementia-like symptoms.

And That's Not All This 82-year-old man is shown with eight of his pill bottles. That polypharmacy alone causes side effects and drug interactions. Added to that are what he eats and drinks, including substances that might interfere with his medication.

● **Observation Quiz** What indicates that he is likely taking the right pills at the right time? (See answer, page 692) ↑

● **Answer to Observation Quiz**
(from page 691): Notice the pill containers on the left, with labels for date and time of day.

THINK CRITICALLY: Who should decide what drugs a person should take—doctor, family, or the person him- or herself?

Even when medications are taken as prescribed and the right dose reaches the bloodstream, drug interactions can cause confusion and memory loss. Cognitive side effects can occur with almost any drug, but especially with drugs intended to reduce anxiety and depression.

Following recommendations from the radio, friends, and television ads, many of the elderly try supplements, compounds, and herbal preparations that contain mind-altering toxins. And finally, since some of the elderly believe that only illegal drugs are harmful to the mind, alcohol and pill addiction are harder to recognize in the elderly.

The solution seems simple: Discontinue drugs. However, that may increase both disease and cognitive decline. One expert warns of polypharmacy but adds that "underuse of medications in older adults can have comparable adverse effects on quality of life" (Miller, 2011–2012, p. 21).

For instance, untreated diabetes and hypertension cause cognitive loss. Lack of drug treatment for those conditions may be one reason why low-income elders experience more illness, more cognitive impairment, and earlier death than do high-income elders: They may not be able to afford good medical care or life-saving drugs.

Obviously, money complicates the issue: Prescription drugs are expensive, which increases profits for drug companies, but they can also reduce surgery and hospitalization, thus saving money. As one observer notes, the discussion about spending for prescription drugs is highly polarized, emotionally loaded, with little useful debate. A war is waged over the cost of prescriptions for older people, and it is a "gloves-off, stab-you-in-the-guts, struggle to the death" (Sloan, 2011–2012, p. 56).

WHAT HAVE YOU LEARNED?

1. How does changing terminology reflect changing attitudes?

2. What changes in the prevalence of neurocognitive disorders have occurred in recent years?

3. What indicates that Alzheimer's disease is partly genetic?

4. How does the progression of Alzheimer's differ from that of vascular disease?

5. In what ways are frontotemporal NCDs worse than Alzheimer's disease?

6. Why is Lewy body disease sometimes mistaken for Parkinson's disease?

7. In addition to disease, what other conditions affect major NCD?

8. How successful are scientists at preventing major NCD?

9. What is the relationship between depression, anxiety, and neurocognitive disorders?

10. Why is polypharmacy particularly common among the elderly?

New Cognitive Development

You have learned that most older adults maintain adequate intellectual power. Some losses—in rapid reactions, for instance—are quite manageable, and most elders never experience a serious neurocognitive disorder. Beyond that, the life-span perspective holds that gains as well as losses occur during every period. [**Life-Span Link:** The multidirectional characteristic of development is discussed in Chapter 1.] Are there cognitive gains in late adulthood? Yes, according to many developmentalists. New depth, enhanced creativity, and even wisdom are possible.

Erikson and Maslow

Both Erik Erikson and Abraham Maslow were particularly interested in the elderly, interviewing older people to understand their views. Erikson's final book, *Vital Involvement in Old Age* (Erikson et al., 1986/1994), written when he was in his 90s, was based on responses from other 90-year-olds—the cohort who had been studied since they were babies in Berkeley, California.

Erikson found that in old age many people gained interest in the arts, in children, and in human experience as a whole. He observed that elders are "social witnesses," aware of the interdependence of the generations as well as of all human experience. His eighth stage, *integrity versus despair,* marks the time when life comes together in a "re-synthesis of all the resilience and strengths already developed" (Erikson et al., 1986/1994, p. 40).

Maslow maintained that older adults are more likely than younger people to reach what he originally thought was the highest stage of development, **self-actualization.** In his later years, Maslow suggested a stage even higher than self-actualization, called *self-transcendence* (Maslow, 1971/1993). Remember that Maslow rejected an age-based sequence of life, refusing to confine self-actualization to the old. However, Maslow also believed that life experience helps people move forward, so more of the old reach the final stage (D'Souza & Gurin, 2016).

The stage of self-actualization is characterized by aesthetic, creative, philosophical, and spiritual understanding (Maslow, 1954/1997). A self-actualized person might have a deeper spirituality than ever; might be especially appreciative of nature; or might find life more amusing, laughing often at himself or herself.

This seems characteristic of many of the elderly. Studies of centenarians find that they often have a deep spiritual grounding and a surprising sense of humor—surprising, that is, if one assumes that people with limited sight, poor hearing, and frequent pain have nothing to laugh about.

Life Gets Better This couple has reached the time in their lives when having a beer in an outdoor cafe while checking the Internet is not only possible, but also joyous. Not every older man is happy in late adulthood, but increasing self-actualization and laughter is common.

self-actualization The final stage in Maslow's hierarchy of needs, characterized by aesthetic, creative, philosophical, and spiritual understanding.

Learning Late in Life

Many people have tried to improve the intellectual abilities of older adults by teaching or training them in various tasks (Lustig et al., 2009; Stine-Morrow & Basak, 2011). Success has been reported in specific abilities. In one part of the Seattle Longitudinal Study, 60-year-olds who had lost some spatial understanding had five sessions of personalized training and practice. As a result, they returned to the skill level of 14 years earlier (Schaie, 2005/2013).

Another group of researchers (Basak et al., 2008) targeted control processes. Volunteers with an average age of 69 and no signs of any neurocognitive disorder were divided into an experimental group and a control group. Everyone took a battery of cognitive tests to measure executive function. None of them was a video game player.

The experimental group was taught to play a video game that was preset to begin at the easiest level. After each round, they were told their score, and another round began—more challenging in pace and memory if the earlier one was too easy. The participants seemed to enjoy trying to raise their scores. After 20 hours of game playing over several weeks, the cognitive tests were given again. Compared with the control group, the experimental group improved in mental activities that were not exactly the ones required by the video game.

Similar results have been found in many nations in which elders have been taught a specific skill. As a result, almost all researchers have accepted the conclusion that people younger than 80 can advance in cognition if the educational process is carefully targeted to their motivation and ability.

For instance, in one study in southern Europe, people who were cognitively typical but were living in senior residences were taught memory strategies and attended motivational discussions to help them understand why and how memory was important for daily functioning. Their memory improved compared to a control group, and the improvements were still evident six months later (Vranić et al., 2013).

What about the oldest-old? Learning is more difficult for them, but it is still possible. The older people are, the harder it is for them to master new skills and then apply what they know (Stine-Morrow & Basak, 2011). Older adults sometimes learn cognitive strategies and skills and maintain that learning if the strategies and skills are frequently used, but they may quickly forget new learning if it is not applied (Park & Bischof, 2013). They revert back to familiar, and often inferior, cognitive patterns.

Let's return to the question of cognitive gains in late adulthood. In many nations, education programs have been created for the old, called Universities for the Third Age in Europe and Australia, and Road Scholar (formerly Exploritas) in the United States. Classes for seniors must take into account the range of needs and motivations: Some want intellectually challenging courses, and others want practical skills (Villar & Celdrán, 2012). All of the research finds that, when motivated, older adults can learn.

Aesthetic Sense and Creativity

Robert Butler was a geriatrician responsible for popularizing the study of aging in the United States. He coined the word "ageism" and wrote a book titled *Why Survive: Being Old in America,* first published in 1975. Partly because his grandparents were crucial in his life, Butler understood that society needs to recognize the potential of the elderly.

Butler explained that "old age can be a time of emotional sensory awareness and enjoyment" (Butler et al., 1998, p. 65). For example, some of the elderly take up gardening, bird-watching, sculpting, painting, or making music, even if they have never done so before.

Elderly Artists

A well-known example of late creative development is Anna Moses, who was a farm wife in rural New York. For most of her life, she expressed her artistic impulses by stitching quilts and embroidering in winter, when farm work was slow. At age 75, arthritis made needlework impossible, so she took to "dabbling in oil."

Four years later, three of her paintings, displayed in a local drugstore, caught the eye of a New York City art dealer who happened to be driving through town. He bought them, drove to her house, and bought 15 more.

The following year, at age 80, "Grandma Moses" had a one-woman show, receiving international recognition for her unique "primitive" style. She continued to paint, and her work "developed and changed considerably over the course of her twenty-year career" (Cardinal, 2001). Anna Moses died at age 101.

Other well-known artists continue to work in late adulthood, sometimes producing their best work. Michelangelo painted the awe-inspiring frescoes in the Sistine Chapel at age 75; Verdi composed the opera *Falstaff* when he was 80; Frank Lloyd Wright completed the design of New York City's Guggenheim Museum when he was 91.

In a study of extraordinarily creative people, very few felt that their ability, their goals, or the quality of their work had been much impaired by age. The leader of

Pierre Bessard/REA/Redux

© Rodrigo Torres/Glowimages/Corbis

Exercise and the Mind Creative activity may improve the intellect, especially when it involves social activity. Both the woman in a French ceramics class *(top)*, subsidized by the government for residents of Grenoble over age 60, and the man playing the tuba in a band in Cuba *(bottom)* are gaining much more than the obvious finger or lung exercise.

that study observed, "in their seventies, eighties, and nineties, they may lack the fiery ambition of earlier years, but they are just as focused, efficient, and committed as before . . . perhaps more so" (Csikszentmihalyi, 2013, p. 207).

But an older artist does not need to be extraordinarily talented. Some of the elderly learn to play an instrument, and many enjoy singing. In China, people gather spontaneously in public parks to sing together. The groups are intergenerational—but a disproportionate number are elderly (Wei, 2013).

Music and singing are often used to reduce anxiety in those who suffer from neurocognitive impairment, because the ability to appreciate music is preserved in the brain when other functions fail (Sacks, 2008; Ueda et al., 2013). Many experts believe that creative activities—poetry and pottery, jewelry making and quilting, music and sculpture—can benefit all of the elderly (Flood & Phillips, 2007; Malchiodi, 2012). Artistic expression may aid social skills, resilience, and even brain health (McFadden & Basting, 2010).

The Life Review

In the **life review,** elders provide an account of their personal journey by writing or telling their story. They want others to know their history, not only their personal experiences but also those of their family, cohort, or ethnic group. According to Robert Butler:

> We have been taught that this nostalgia represents living in the past and a preoccupation with self and that it is generally boring, meaningless, and time-consuming. Yet as a natural healing process it represents one of the underlying human capacities on which all psychotherapy depends. The life review should be recognized as a necessary and healthy process in daily life as well as a useful tool in the mental health care of older people.
>
> *[Butler et al., 1998, p. 91]*

life review An examination of one's own role in the history of human life, engaged in by many elderly people.

Hundreds of developmentalists, picking up on Butler's suggestions, have guided elderly people in self-review. Sometimes the elderly write down their thoughts, and sometimes they simply tell their story, responding to questions from the listener.

The result of the life review is almost always quite positive, especially for the person who tells the story. For instance, of 202 elderly people in the Netherlands, half were randomly assigned to a life review process. For them, depression and anxiety were markedly reduced compared to the control group (Korte et al., 2012).

Wisdom

It is possible that "older adults . . . understand who they are in a newly emerging stage of life, and discovering the wisdom that they have to offer" (Bateson, 2011, p. 9). A massive international survey of 26 nations from every corner of the world found that most people everywhere agree that wisdom is a characteristic of the elderly (Löckenhoff et al., 2009).

Contrary to these wishes and opinions, most objective research finds that wisdom does not necessarily increase with age. Starting at age 25 or so, some adults of every age are wise, but most, even at age 80, are not (Staudinger & Glück, 2011).

An underlying quandary is that a universal definition of wisdom is elusive: Each culture and each cohort has its own concept, with fools sometimes seeming wise (as happens in Shakespearean drama) and those who are supposed to be wise

Wise or Foolish? Your opinion depends primarily on how you evaluate motorcycle transportation—as a more enjoyable and less expensive way to navigate the road, or dangerous and uncomfortable. Your evaluation could indicate wisdom—possible at any age but hard for anyone to define.

In **Video: Portrait of Aging: Bill, Age 99,** one man shares his secret to longevity.

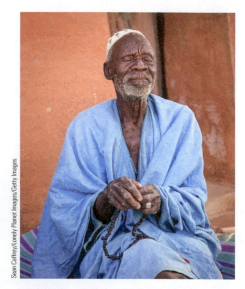

Long Past Warring Many of the oldest men in Mali, like this imam, are revered. Unfortunately, Mali has experienced violent civil wars and two national coups in recent years, perhaps because 75 percent of the male population are under age 30 and less than 2 percent are over age 70.

sometimes acting foolishly (provide your own examples). Older and younger adults differ in how they make decisions; one interpretation of these differences is that the older adults are wiser, but not every younger adult would agree (Worthy et al., 2011).

One summary describes wisdom as an "expert knowledge system dealing with the conduct and understanding of life" (Baltes & Smith, 2008, p. 58). Several factors just mentioned, including self-reflective honesty (as in integrity), perspective on past living (the life review), and the ability to put aside one's personal needs (as in self-actualization), are considered part of wisdom.

If this is true, the elderly may have an advantage in developing wisdom, particularly if they have (1) dedicated their lives to the "understanding of life," (2) learned from their experiences, and (3) become more mature and integrated (Ardelt, 2011, p. 283). That may be why popes and U.S. Supreme Court justices are usually quite old.

As two psychologists explain:

> Wisdom is one domain in which some older individuals excel. . . . [They have] a combination of psychosocial characteristics and life history factors, including openness to experience, generativity, cognitive style, contact with excellent mentors, and some exposure to structured and critical life experiences.
>
> *[Baltes & Smith, 2008, p. 60]*

These researchers posed life dilemmas to adults of various ages and asked others (who had no clue as to how old the participants were) to judge whether the responses were wise. They found that wisdom is rare at any age, but, unlike physical strength and cognitive quickness, wisdom does not fade with maturity. Thus, some people of every age were judged as wise.

Similarly, the author of a detailed longitudinal study of 814 people concludes that wisdom is not reserved for the old, but humor, perspective, and altruism increase over the decades, gradually making people wiser. He then wrote:

> To be wise about wisdom we need to accept that wisdom does—and wisdom does not—increase with age. . . . Winston Churchill, that master of wise simplicity and simple wisdom, reminds us, "We are all happier in many ways when we are old than when we are young. The young sow wild oats. The old grow sage."
>
> *[Vaillant, 2002, p. 256]*

WHAT HAVE YOU LEARNED?

1. What do Erikson and Maslow say about cognitive development in late adulthood?

2. What happens with creative ability as people grow older?

3. What is the special role of music in old age?

4. Why are scientists hesitant to say that wisdom comes from age?

SUMMARY

The Aging Brain

1. The human brain continues to add new cells and grow new dendrites as people age, but it also becomes smaller and slower. The effects of senescence are apparent not only in motor skills (such as speed of walking) but also in cognitive skills (such as how quickly an older adult remembers a name).

2. Remarkable plasticity is also apparent, with wide variation from person to person in the rate and specifics of brain slowdown. In general, older adults use more of their brains, not less, to do various tasks, and they prefer doing one task at a time, not multitasking.

Information Processing After Age 65

3. The senses become less acute with age, making it difficult for older people to register stimuli. Memory is slower, but there are many types of memory, each with a distinct trajectory. Source memory and prospective memory are less accurate, but memory for semantics, emotions, and automatic skills may be strong.

4. Control processes are less effective with age, as retrieval strategies become less efficient. Anxiety may prevent older people from using the strategies they need.

5. In daily life, most of the elderly are not seriously handicapped by cognitive difficulties. The need for ecologically valid, real-life measures of cognition is increasingly apparent to developmental scientists.

Neurocognitive Disorders

6. Neurocognitive disorders (NCDs) are characterized by cognitive loss of varying degrees. The many NCDs differ, as do individuals and families who suffer from them, but early diagnosis seems helpful.

7. Major NCD (formerly called dementia) is first characterized by minor cognitive lapses. Then more serious impairments appear, and finally major losses are evident.

8. The most common cause of cognitive loss among the elderly in the United States is Alzheimer's disease, an incurable ailment that worsens over time, as plaques and tangles increase.

9. Vascular disease (also called multi-infarct dementia) results from a series of ministrokes (transient ischemic attacks, or TIAs) that occur when impairment of blood circulation destroys portions of brain tissue.

10. Other NCDs, including frontotemporal NCDs and Lewy body disease, also become more common with age. Parkinson's disease reduces muscle control, and it can also cause neurocognitive problems, particularly in the elderly. Many other diseases also affect the brain.

11. Serious injury to the head, as sometimes occurs in tackle football and ice hockey, also causes NCDs. Societies can do much to prevent this.

12. An NCD may be mistakenly diagnosed when the individual is actually suffering from a reversible problem. Malnutrition, depression, drug addiction, and polypharmacy are among the reasons that an older person might seem to be cognitively impaired. These symptoms can disappear if the problem is recognized and treated.

New Cognitive Development

13. Older adults can and often do continue to learn as they age. Training and practice can increase cognitive skills and control processes in the aged. Surprising to some is the fact that one effective kind of training involves video games.

14. Many people become more interested and adept in creative endeavors, as well as more philosophical, as they grow older. The life review is a personal reflection that many older people undertake, remembering earlier experiences, putting their entire lives into perspective, and achieving integrity or self-actualization.

15. Wisdom does not necessarily increase as a result of age, but some elderly people are unusually wise or insightful. Learning from experience can occur at any age, but the old have an advantage in that they have had many experiences.

KEY TERMS

control processes (p. 679)
ecological validity (p. 681)
neurocognitive disorder (NCD) (p. 683)

major neurocognitive disorder (major NCD) (p. 684)
Alzheimer's disease (AD) (p. 685)
plaques (p. 685)

tangles (p. 685)
vascular disease (p. 686)
frontotemporal NCDs (p. 687)
Parkinson's disease (p. 687)

Lewy body disease (p. 687)
polypharmacy (p. 691)
self-actualization (p. 693)
life review (p. 695)

APPLICATIONS

1. At all ages, memory is selective. People forget much more than they remember. Choose someone—a sibling, a former classmate, or a current friend—who went through some public event that you did. Sit down together, write separate lists of all details each of you remembers about the event, and then compare your accounts. What insight does this exercise give you into the kinds of things adults remember and forget?

2. Many factors affect intellectual sharpness. Think of an occasion when you felt inept and an occasion when you felt smart.

How did the contexts of the two experiences differ? How might those differences affect the performance of elderly and young adults who go to a university laboratory for testing?

3. Visit someone in a hospital. Note all of the elements in the environment—such as noise, lights, schedules, and personnel—that might cause an elderly patient to feel confused.

Late Adulthood:
Psychosocial Development

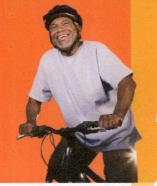

What Will You Know?

1. Do older people become sadder or more hopeful?
2. Do the elderly hope to move to a distant, warm place?
3. What do adult children owe their elderly parents?
4. Is home care better than nursing-home care?

Almost every week I walk through a park with my friend Doris, a widow in her 80s, to a meeting we both attend. Many people of all backgrounds greet her by name, including men who play chess on a park table and a woman who owns a nearby hotel.

Doris feeds squirrels and pets dogs. She is an icon for street performers, including Colin, who plays his piano (on wheels) outside on sunny days. The police once ticketed him for not having a permit. Doris organized a protest. She got Community Board 2 (she is the oldest member, reappointed by the Borough President every two years since 1964) to pass a resolution about free speech. The city withdrew Colin's ticket and the Parks Department revised their policy.

Often we stop at the mailbox for her to mail a timely greeting card: I have become one of hundreds on her list. Colorful envelopes arrive in my box—green for St. Patrick's Day, orange for Halloween, gray for Thanksgiving, red for July 4th, and multicolored for my birthday. She sent 426 Christmas cards; she orders stamps from a post office catalog.

I am unlike Doris in many ways. I never send cards, feed squirrels, or protect pianists (although Doris did get me to help Colin). We belong to opposing political parties. She has no children; I have four.

How did we become friends? Several years ago, Doris had knee surgery and needed volunteers to wheel her to her many meetings, appointments, and social engagements. Dozens of people offered their services. I did, too. Soon she could walk alone with her walker, but I have come to enjoy her anecdotes, her memories, her attitudes. I watch for cars when we cross the street, but I get more from Doris than I give. And I don't mean Thanksgiving cards.

Doris illustrates the theme of this chapter: the variability and complexity of development in later life. As you will read, some of the elderly are frail, lonely, and vulnerable because of private circumstances and public failures. For most, however, psychosocial development includes working and socializing, concern for others as well as self-care. Doris does all of this admirably. I hope to be like her someday.

Left: Milind Ketkar/Dinodia Photo/age fotostock
Top: Jupiterimages/DigitalVision/Getty Images

Not a Puppet One park regular is a puppeteer, Ricky Syers, who entertains hundreds of tourists with an array of puppets. He recently made one of Doris, one more bit of evidence that the real Doris is beloved by many—and not controlled by anyone.

self theories Theories of late adulthood that emphasize the core self, or the search to maintain one's integrity and identity.

Always Himself Leading nonviolent protest is a sign of lifelong integrity for John Lewis. In his early 20s, he was beaten and arrested dozens of times as he sought civil rights for African Americans. At age 23, he spoke at the 1963 March on Washington, when Martin Luther King, Jr. proclaimed his dream. In this photo, at age 73, he is at the unveiling of a stamp commemorating that march fifty years earlier. Lewis was elected to represent Georgia in the U.S. Congress in 1986 and has been reelected 15 times. At age 76, he led a sit-in on the Congressional floor, asking the leadership to allow discussion and a vote on a bill to require background checks for gun ownership. He did not succeed. . . yet.

integrity versus despair The final stage of Erik Erikson's developmental sequence, in which older adults seek to integrate their unique experiences with their vision of community.

Theories of Late Adulthood

Some elderly people run marathons and lead nations; others no longer walk or talk. Social scientists theorize about this diversity.

Self Theories

Certain theories of late adulthood can be called **self theories;** they focus on individuals, especially the self-concept and challenges to identity. Self-awareness of oneself begins, as you remember, before age 2, and it builds throughout childhood and adolescence. In those early decades, self-image is greatly affected by physical appearance and by other people's perceptions (Harter, 2012).

Appearance and external opinions become less crucial with age. Chronological age is almost irrelevant. Instead, a person's concept of how old they feel correlates with their satisfaction with themselves and with life (Mirucka et al., 2016).

The Self and Aging

Perhaps people become more truly themselves with age. That is what Anna Quindlen found:

> It's odd when I think of the arc of my life from child to young woman to aging adult. First I was who I was, then I didn't know who I was, then I invented someone and became her, then I began to like what I'd invented, and finally I was what I was again. It turned out I wasn't alone in that particular progression.

> [Quindlen, 2012, p. ix]

Older adults maintain their self-concept despite senescence, which alters appearance and social status in ways that might undercut self-esteem. In late adulthood, the "creation and maintenance of identity" is "a key aspect of healthy living" (Allen, 2011, p. 10). Even the oldest-old and those who suffer from neurocognitive disorders preserve their sense of self, although memory, ability, and health fade (Klein, 2012).

Self theory is one explanation for an interesting phenomenon: Older people rely more on their personal experiences than on objective statistics, or, in dual-processing terms, more on intuition than on analysis, on gut feelings more than logic. Although elders weigh emotions stronger than logic, that is not always a problem. Elders generally are happier with their decision making than younger adults are (Mikels et al., 2015).

Self theory also adds insight to elders deciding whether or not to retire. If a person relies on their work to achieve a sense of self-worth, that makes quitting work difficult. This was one conclusion from a study of physicians in their 60s who were deciding when to stop their medical practice. Many wondered who they would be and what they would do when their expert opinion was no longer needed (Onyura et al., 2015).

Integrity

The most comprehensive self theory came from Erik Erikson. His eighth and final stage of development, **integrity versus despair,** requires adults to integrate their unique experiences with their community (Erikson et al., 1986/1994). The word *integrity* is often used to mean honesty, but it also means a feeling of being whole, not scattered, comfortable with oneself. The virtue of old age, according to Erikson, is wisdom, which implies wholeness (Kroger, 2015).

As an example of integrity, many older people are proud of their personal history. They glorify their past, even boasting about bad experiences such as skipping school, taking drugs, escaping arrest, or being physically abused.

Cherished memories of the past are far better than despair because "time is now short, too short for the attempt to start another life" (Erikson, 1993a, p. 269). For every stage, the tension between the two opposing aspects (here integrity versus despair) propels growth.

In this final stage,

> life brings many, quite realistic reasons for experiencing despair: aspects of a past we fervently wish had been different; aspects of the present that cause unremitting pain; aspects of a future that are uncertain and frightening. And, of course, there remains inescapable death, that one aspect of the future which is both wholly certain and wholly unknowable. Thus, some despair must be acknowledged and integrated as a component of old age.
>
> *[Erikson et al., 1986/1994, p. 72]*

Integration of death and the self is a crucial accomplishment. The life review (explained in Chapter 14) and the acceptance of death (explained in the Epilogue) are crucial aspects of the integrity envisioned by Erikson (Zimmerman, 2012).

As Erikson wrote, the older person:

> knows that an individual life is the accidental coincidence of but one life cycle with but one segment of history and that for him all human integrity stands or falls with the one style of integrity of which he partakes. . . . In such a final consolation, death loses its sting.
>
> *[Erikson, 1986/1994, p. 140]*

As self theory contends, identity achievement echoes lifelong, with integrity attained for those who achieve identity, and despair (Erikson's opposite course) likely for those who never achieved identity. The critical need in late adulthood is "retaining a sense of identity despite decline" (Kroger, 2015, p. 77).

Holding On to the Self

Most older people consider their personalities and attitudes quite stable over their life span, even as they acknowledge physical changes of their bodies and gaps in their minds (Klein, 2012). One 103-year-old woman, wrinkled, shrunken, and severely crippled by arthritis, displayed a photo of herself as a beautiful young woman. She said, "My core has stayed the same. Everything else has changed" (quoted in Troll & Skaff, 1997, p. 166).

Many older people refuse to move from drafty and dangerous dwellings into smaller, safer apartments because leaving familiar places means abandoning personal history. That is irrational, but it is explained by self theory. Likewise, an older person may avoid surgery or refuse medicine because they fear anything that might distort their thinking or emotions: Their priority may be self-protection, even if it shortens life (Miller, 2011–2012).

The insistence on protecting the self may explain **compulsive hoarding,** saving reams of old papers, books, mementos . . . anything that might someday be useful. The fifth edition of the DSM recognizes hoarding as a psychological disorder (American Psychiatric Association, 2013, pp. 247–251), but earlier DSM editions did not. Why not?

What Is She Thinking? At her 117th birthday, Misao Okawa was the oldest living person in the world. She died a few weeks later—but not before making a statement indicating the positivity effect. She said that the secret to a long life was to eat delicious things.

compulsive hoarding The urge to accumulate and hold on to familiar objects and possessions, sometimes to the point of their becoming health and/or safety hazards. This impulse tends to increase with age.

Trash or Treasure? Tryphona Flood, threatened with eviction, admitted that she's a hoarder and got help from Megan Tolen, shown here discussing what in this four-room apartment can be discarded. Flood sits on the only spot of her bed that is not covered with stuff. This photo was taken midway through a three-year effort to clean out the apartment—the clutter was worse a year earlier.

THINK CRITICALLY: Is hoarding a universal disorder or a cohort problem?

---

socioemotional selectivity theory The theory that older people prioritize regulation of their own emotions and seek familiar social contacts who reinforce generativity, pride, and joy.

positivity effect The tendency for elderly people to perceive, prefer, and remember positive images and experiences more than negative ones.

Many elderly hoarders grew up in the Great Depression and World War II, when saving scraps and reusing products meant survival and patriotism. That habit is contrary to the current ethos: Expiration dates are now stamped on food and drugs; electronics, from computers to televisions, are quickly obsolete. A prime motive for elderly hoarders is avoiding waste. Hoarding brings them emotional satisfaction (Frost et al., 2015), which a younger person might get from replacing something old.

My friend Doris (opening anecdote) hoards old newspaper articles, records, and other things that are precious to her. She lives alone, with her possessions and two cats. She likes it that way.

Socioemotional Selectivity Theory

Another self theory is **socioemotional selectivity theory** (Carstensen, 1993). The crucial idea regarding late adulthood is that people consider what to value in their lives depending on how much of their life is ahead of them.

Consequently, when people believe that their future time is limited, they think about the meaning of their life. They then become more appreciative of family and friends, thus furthering their happiness (Hicks et al., 2012).

Socioemotional selectivity is central to self theories. In late adulthood, there is a "shift in social goals and changes in social relationships and contexts" (Nielsen, 2015, p. xvii), which challenges individuals to set personal goals, assess their abilities, and figure out how to accomplish their goals despite aging, maintaining identity.

Closely connected to socioemotional selectivity is the **positivity effect** (Hicks et al., 2012). A meta-analysis of more than 115 comparisons between younger and older adults found that the elderly perceive, prefer, and remember positive images and experiences more than negative ones (Reed et al., 2014). Unpleasant experiences are ignored, forgotten, or reinterpreted.

For that reason, stressful events (economic loss, serious illness, death of friends or relatives) become less central to identity with age. Because elders think of themselves more positively, they protect their emotional health (Boals et al., 2012), becoming more optimistic about themselves and happier because of it. A strong sense of *self-efficacy* (the idea that a person has the power to control and change a situation) is likely to correlate with a happier and longer life (Gerstorf et al., 2014).

The positivity effect may explain why, in every nation and religion, older people tend to be more patriotic and devout than younger ones. They see their national history and religious beliefs in positive terms, and they are proud to be themselves—Canadian, Czech, Chinese, or whatever. Of course, this same trait can keep them mired in their earlier prejudices—racism, or sexism, or homophobia, for instance.

Anna Quindlen was quoted on page 700 as being glad that she "was what I was again." Does this mean that she, and most older people, do not see current world problems? Consider my daughter, my mother, and me.

Too Sweet or Too Sad?

When I was young, I liked movies that were gritty, dramatic, violent. My mother questioned my choices; I told her that I hated sugar-coating. She liked romantic comedies that made her laugh; I told her that was frivolous.

Now my youngest daughter wants me to read dystopian novels. *The Hunger Games* is an example. I tell her that the world has enough poverty and conflict; I don't need to read about imaginary killing. Have I become my mother?

Many researchers have found that a positive worldview increases with age. The positivity effect correlates with believing that life is meaningful. Elders who are happy, not frustrated or depressed, agree strongly that their life has a purpose (e.g., "I have a system of values that guides my daily activities" and "I am at peace with my past") (Hicks et al., 2012). Meaningfulness and positivity correlate with a long and healthy life.

The elderly are quicker to let go of disappointments. They think positively about going forward. As a result, many studies have found "an increase in emotional well-being from middle age onward, whereas the experience of anger declines" (Brassen et al., 2012, p. 614).

Researchers have measured reactions to disappointment, not only in attitudes and actions but also in brain activity and heart rate. One study compared three groups: young adults, healthy older adults, and older adults with late-life depression.

In reaction to disappointment, the healthy older adults recovered quickly, but the other two groups took longer: The brains, bodies, and behavior of the depressed elders and the younger adults were similar. The conclusion: "emotionally healthy aging is associated with a reduced responsiveness to regretful events" (Brassen et al., 2012, p. 614) (see Figure 25.1).

A pair of researchers wondered whether the positivity effect in social interaction occurred because older adults simply avoided unpleasant people (Luong & Charles, 2014). Accordingly, they assigned younger and older adults to work on a task with a disagreeable partner.

In fact, that partner was an actor, trained to be equally nasty with everyone. For example, the actor never smiled, and said "I really don't see where you're coming from." True to expectations, compared to the younger participants, the older adults more often reported that they liked the partner and enjoyed the task. They did not try to change their partner or feel resentful (see Figure 25.2).

Perhaps anger and frustration are useful emotions and the positivity effect is too rosy. Too much acceptance may be wrong in a world that needs changing. It also may be annoying to younger people. My daughter recently apologized for criticizing me. I replied, honestly, that I had forgotten her critique. Do I ignore criticism? Am I stuck in my ways?

However, with the disagreeable partner, the elders' blood pressure rose less and it came down more quickly than it did for the younger adults. The pulse of the older participants hardly changed at all (Luong & Charles, 2014). Having a positive outlook not only makes a person happier, it also makes them healthier.

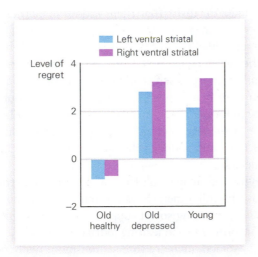

FIGURE 25.1

Let Bygones Be Bygones Areas of the brain (the ventral striatal) are activated when a person feels regret. In this experiment, brain activation correlated with past loss and then unwise choices, with participants repeating behavior that had just failed. Older adults were usually wiser, evident in brain activation as well as actions. However, elders who had been diagnosed as depressed seemed to dwell on past losses. The positivity effect had passed them by.

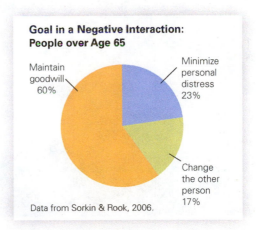

FIGURE 25.2

Keep the Peace When someone does something mean or unpleasant, what is your goal in your interaction with that person? If your goal is to maintain goodwill, as is true for most older adults, you are likely to be quicker to forgive and forget. This was much less true for younger adults in this study.

THINK CRITICALLY: Does the positivity effect avoid reality, or was my mother right?

Twice Fortunate Ageism takes many forms. Some cultures are youth-oriented, devaluing the old, while others are the opposite. These twin sisters are lucky to be alive: They were born in rural China in 1905, a period when most female twins died. When this photo was taken, they were age 103, and fortunate again, venerated because they have lived so long.

stratification theories Theories that emphasize that social forces, particularly those related to a person's social stratum or social category, limit individual choices and affect a person's ability to function in late adulthood because past stratification continues to limit life in various ways.

Stratification Theories

A second set of theories, called **stratification theories,** emphasize social forces that position each person in a social stratum or level. That positioning creates disadvantages for some and advantages for others (Wickrama et al., 2013a).

Stratification begins in the womb, as "individuals are born into a society that is already stratified—that is differentiated—along key dimensions, including sex, race, and SES" (Lynch & Brown, 2011, p. 107). Indeed, stratification affects the prenatal environment, so some newborns already suffer from being born to a disadvantaged mother.

Every form of stereotyping makes it more difficult for people to break free from social institutions that assign them to a particular path. The results are cumulative, over the entire life span (Brandt et al., 2012).

As you have also read, at each step some individuals break away from the usual path, but stratification theory contends that overcoming the liabilities of the past is increasingly difficult as life unfolds. By age 60, people who have experienced poverty and prejudice all their lives almost never are able to break free from their past and become healthy and wealthy in old age.

Stratification theory suggests that to improve the final years of life for everyone, intervention needs to begin before birth. Each stereotype adds to stratification and thus adds to the risk of problems, perhaps putting those who are female, non-white, and poor in *triple jeopardy*. However, as explained at the end of this section, not everyone agrees with that conclusion (Rosenfield, 2012).

Gender Stratification

First, consider gender. Irrational, gender-based fear may limit female independence, even in old age. For example, adult children are more likely to insist that their widowed mothers live with them than their widowed fathers. In fact, however, men living alone are more likely than women to have a sudden health crisis or to be the victim of a violent crime (5 percent versus 2 percent).

In another example of gender stratification, young women typically marry men a few years older and then outlive them. Especially in former years, many married women relied on their husbands to manage money. Thus, past gender stratification produced many old widows who were lonely, poor, and dependent for decades.

Longevity itself may result from lifelong gender stratification, in this case harming men. Boys are taught to be stoic, repressing emotions, spurning social support, and avoiding medical attention. According to the leading journal of public health in the

Twice-Abandoned Widows Traditionally in India, widows walked into the funeral pyre that cremated their husband's body, a suicide called sati. If a widow hesitated, the husband's relatives would sometimes push. Currently, sati is outlawed, but many Indian widows experience a social death: They are forbidden to meet men and remarry, except sometimes to the dead man's brother. Hundreds go to the sacred city of Vrindavan, where they are paid a pittance to chant prayers all day, as this woman does.

United States, "Compared to women, men are three times more likely not to have had contact with a health care provider for five years," which means that they do not seek the many measures of preventive care that have allowed older people to have longer, healthier lives (Elder & Griffith, 2016, p. 1157). Thus, gender stratification may harm both sexes, making men die too soon and women lonely for too long.

When gender stratification is added to ethnic and income stratification, the results are tragic. One source considers the disparity in health between African American men and other people "a public health imperative" (Bond & Herman, 2016, p. 1167).

Ethnic Stratification

Past ethnic discrimination results in poverty for many minority families, itself a result of stratification in the quality of education, the health of neighborhoods, the salary of jobs. As you remember, SES and race often coexist because of neighborhood segregation, and the result is lifelong stratification, which affects the mind as well as the body (Rosso et al., 2016).

Consider one detailed example, home ownership, a source of financial security for many seniors. Fifty years ago, stratification prevented many African Americans from buying homes, except in inner cities or isolated rural areas. Laws have reduced housing discrimination, but recent suburban homeowners were particularly likely to lose homes in the foreclosure crisis that began in 2007 and continued for years. Who had bought homes since 1990? Many African Americans. Why? Past stratification. Result: African Americans suffered a disproportionate number of foreclosures. Is this a new example of an old story: stratification causing poverty (Saegert et al., 2011)?

A particular form of ethnic stratification affects immigrant elders. Most immigrants to North America come from non-Western cultures, where younger generations are expected to care for the elderly. However, U.S. dwellings are designed for nuclear families. Further, retirement pensions and Social Security are designated for employees who worked for decades "on the books" within established companies for many years.

Thus, U.S. practices leave many older immigrants poor, lonely, and dependent on their children, who live in homes and apartments designed for nuclear families. Both likely options are onerous: unwelcome closeness in crowded, multigenerational homes, or distressing distance between elders and their descendants.

A review of studies of this dilemma among Chinese immigrants found that elderly parents and their grown children endorsed the idea of filial piety but found it difficult to practice (Lin et al., 2015). Of course, when elderly parents are in the home country and their adult children have emigrated, as often happens because of political as well as personal decisions, both generations suffer.

Always a Mother In this photo, in Nepal, a volunteer gives food to an elderly woman in an Aama Ghar, a home for elderly mothers. Is such an institution an example of self theory (identity as mother endures decades after children are independent) or stratification theory (older people segregated from ordinary life)?

Income Stratification

Finally, poverty may magnify stratification of gender, ethnicity, and immigration. Many of the poorest elderly never held jobs that paid into Social Security. Thus, past ethnic and gender discrimination affected employment, making poverty likely in old age. In adulthood, when money is scarce, that itself undercuts the ability to plan for the future (Haushofer & Fehr, 2014).

This affects low-SES people of both sexes and all races. Less education, worse health, and spotty work history (more unemployment, fewer benefits, no pensions), as a result of past SES, impair future well-being. In the recent economic crisis, many nations reduced the social safety net of medical care, low-income housing, and so on, which particularly harms the poor elderly (Phillipson, 2013).

Age Stratification

Age stratification itself affects life in many ways, including income and health. For example, workers gradually gain seniority and then age causes retirement, reducing income, social support, and status. Further, many aspects of public life,

disengagement theory The view that aging makes a person's social sphere increasingly narrow, resulting in role relinquishment, withdrawal, and passivity.

activity theory The view that elderly people want and need to remain active in a variety of social spheres—with relatives, friends, and community groups—and become withdrawn only unwillingly, as a result of ageism.

A Soldier for Democracy Poll workers like Carolyn Borcherding in Ohio are often patriotic senior citizens who work on election days, checking lists and guiding voters. Democracy in the United States depends on hundreds of thousands of such people. It is not an easy job, as both competence and friendliness are needed. In 2016, New York City had four election days, which meant 66 hours of training and work for thousands of retirees.

Especially for Social Scientists The various social science disciplines tend to favor different theories of aging. Can you tell which theories would be more acceptable to psychologists and which to sociologists? (see response, page 709)

from the design of sidewalks to the scheduling of town meetings, are designed for younger adults.

The most controversial version of age stratification is **disengagement theory** (Cumming & Henry, 1961), which holds that as people age, traditional roles become unavailable and the social circle shrinks. According to this theory, disengagement is mutual. Thus, younger adults disengage from the old, who themselves disengage, withdrawing from life's action. Elders want this disengagement.

This theory provoked a storm of protest. An opposing theory, **activity theory,** holds that the elderly seek to remain active with relatives, friends, and community groups. Activity theorists contended that if the elderly disengage, they do so unwillingly (Kelly, 1993; Rosow, 1985).

Extensive research supports activity theory. Being active correlates with happiness, intelligence, and health. This is true at younger ages as well, but the correlation between activity and well-being is particularly strong at older ages (Potočnik & Sonnentag, 2013; Bielak et al., 2012). Prioritizing social and political activities in late adulthood predicts a greater sense of well-being, postponing decline (Gerstorf et al., 2016).

Disengagement is more likely among those low in SES, which suggests that it is another harmful outcome of past economic stratification (Clarke et al., 2011). Literally being active—bustling around the house, climbing stairs, walking to work—lengthens life and increases satisfaction (Festini et al., 2016).

Critique of Stratification Theories

Both disengagement and activity theories need to be applied with caution, however. The positivity effect may mean that older people disengage from emotional events that cause anger, regret, and sadness but still actively enjoy other experiences. Current theories and research emphasize the variations in the lives of the aged, with neither disengagement nor activity theory always accurate (Johnson & Mutchler, 2014).

Indeed, people of all groups develop habits and attitudes by old age that protect them from the worst effects of stratification (Rosenfield, 2012). Evidence is spotty, and low SES and ill health are harmful at every age, but gender, ethnicity, and SES may be less damaging for the very old than they are earlier in life.

Contrary to gender stratification, differences between the sexes seem less prominent with age. Women have several advantages, including closer relationships with friends and families. Compared to younger men, older men may be advantaged as well.

The greatest gender disparities in mortality occur in the first 25 years of life, when the gender gap in life expectancy is 5 years. By age 75, that gap is less than 2 years. This means that an 80-year-old man is almost as likely to live 10 more years as an 80-year-old woman (National Center for Health Statistics, 2016). Both sexes benefit from each other, with older married couples typically sharing housework, financial decisions, and other aspects of life that were more stratified when they were younger.

Similarly, cautionary data come from comparing the aged of various ethnic groups. A study of those people who lived to 110 or longer finds that, among those living in the United States, a disproportionate number were/are non-White (Young et al., 2015). Stratification seems irrelevant after age 100.

Ethnic differences in survival after age 80 no longer favor European Americans, a phenomenon called the *race crossover* (Yao & Robert, 2011). Among centenarians, African Americans live seven months longer, on average, than European Americans. Older Asian Americans have a several-year advantage, and older Hispanic Americans may also live longer—although for them the data are less clear.

One explanation for the race crossover in longevity is called *selective survival*—the idea that only extremely healthy non-European Americans reach old age. But, other sources suggest that something about the family, social context, or culture favor older people who are non-White (Roth et al., 2016). Or, perhaps past stratification teaches coping strategies, such as humor and social bonds, that are protective by late adulthood.

One scholar suggests that older African American women in the United States have the best mental health of all the race, age, and gender groups. He does not think "stratification systems such as gender, race and class" are as debilitating in late adulthood as earlier. Instead "multiple minority statuses affect mental health in paradoxical ways . . . that refute triple jeopardy approaches" (Rosenfield, 2012, p. 1791).

> **THINK CRITICALLY:** Could years of being at the top of the social hierarchy become a liability in old age?

WHAT HAVE YOU LEARNED?

1. How does Erikson's use of the word *integrity* differ from its usual meaning?
2. How does hoarding relate to self theory?
3. What are the advantages of the positivity effect?
4. Which type of stratification is most burdensome: economic, ethnic, or gender?
5. How can disengagement be mutual?
6. Why do some scholars think stratification is less problematic in old age than earlier?

Activities in Late Adulthood

As you read, most of the research finds that active elders live longer and more happily than inactive ones. Many elders themselves bear this out. They complain that they do not have enough time each day. What keeps them so busy?

Working

Work—paid or unpaid—provides social support and status.

Paid Work

Employment history affects current health and happiness of older adults (Wahrendorf et al., 2013). Those who lost their jobs because of structural changes (a factory closing, a corporate division eliminated) are, decades later, less likely to be in good health (Schröder, 2013). Income matters as well: Those who have sufficient savings and an adequate pension are much more likely to enjoy old age.

Same Situation, Far Apart: Satisfying Work In Nice, France *(left)*, two paleontologists examine a skull bone, and in Arizona *(right)*, a woman said to be more than 100 years old prepares wool for weaving. Note their facial expressions: Elders are often happier when they continue working.

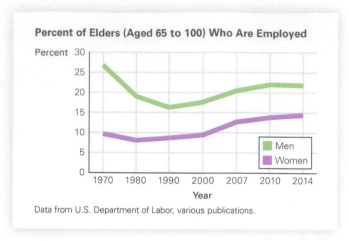

Percent of Elders (Aged 65 to 100) Who Are Employed

Data from U.S. Department of Labor, various publications.

FIGURE 25.3

Along with Everyone Else Although younger adults might imagine that older people stop work as soon as they can, this is clearly not true for everyone.

The Best New Hire Clayton Fackler, age 72, is shown here at his new job, a cashier at a Wal-Mart in Bowling Green, Ohio. He is among thousands of elderly people hired by that corporation, in part because retired seniors are reliable workers. They are also more willing than younger adults to work for minimum wage at part-time hours—a boon to employers but not for young adults.

Nonunionized low-wage workers (who need the income) and professionals (who welcome the status) are likely to stay employed in their 60s (Komp et al., 2010). Especially for low-wage workers, worries about retirement income are increasing: 41 percent of U.S. workers aged 45 to 65 fear that post-retirement income will be inadequate (Morin & Fry, 2012).

The employment rate for older workers has risen since 2005 (see Figure 25.3). The main reason is that many workers keep their jobs in order to keep their paychecks. Some private pensions have been eliminated, and many governments are reducing national pensions.

For example, in 2010, the French raised the pension age from 60 to 62, a move reversed in 2012 for those who have worked at least 40 years. In the United States, full Social Security benefits began at age 65 for those born before 1938, but now those born after 1959 must be age 67 to receive their full benefits. This reflects reality. Many workers in their mid-60s are quite capable.

Retirement

People retire for "push" reasons—they are pushed out of work, perhaps because of their poor health or fading skills. Or they may have "pull" reasons—there are things they want to do and they have adequate income to do it (De Preter et al., 2013). Not surprisingly, pull reasons correlate with better mental and physical health after retirement. Push reasons do not.

Family concerns are also influential. Remember generativity? Adults try to balance family and work needs, and therefore parenthood and grandparenthood affect retirement age. Fathers tend to work a little longer than other men; mothers tend to retire a little earlier (Hank & Korbmacher, 2013). Being a caregiving grandmother is also a reason for earlier retirement (Hochman & Lewin-Epstein, 2013).

When retirement is precipitated by poor health or fading competence, it correlates with illness, but the idea that retirement precipitates illness is more myth than fact. If quitting work leads to disengagement, it results in mental decline, otherwise not (Mazzonna & Peracchi, 2012; Rohwedder & Willis, 2010).

However, illness is far from inevitable. When retirees voluntarily leave their jobs and then engage in activities and intellectual challenges, as many do, they become healthier and happier than they were before (Coe & Zamarro, 2011).

Volunteer Work

Volunteering offers some of the benefits of paid employment (generativity, social connections). Longitudinal as well as cross-sectional research finds a strong link between health and volunteering (Cutler et al., 2011; Kahana et al., 2013).

As self theory would predict, volunteer work attracts older people who always were strongly committed to their community and had more social contacts (Pilkington et al., 2012). Beyond that, volunteering protects health, even for the very old. A meta-analysis found that volunteering cut the death rate in half, and even when various confounds (such as marital status and health before volunteering) were taken into account, simply being a volunteer correlated with a longer and healthier life (Okun et al., 2013). Half of all volunteers do so because someone asked them. Knowing someone else who volunteers (especially a husband or wife) is also an incentive (See Figure 25.4).

Researchers in Germany hypothesized that the elderly needed encouragement and suggestions for volunteering (Warner et al., 2014). Accordingly, they provided a two-hour session that explained the benefits of volunteering, the importance of planning and initiative, and how to find an activity that suited one's values and preferences. All of this was partly to undermine passive ageism. They also distributed a list of nearby volunteer opportunities.

The attendees had expressed interest, before the session, in "active retirement," but one-third of them had done no volunteering at all. Six weeks later, the people who attended the sessions volunteered almost twice as often as they had done before. Some began volunteering only after the session, and others increased the time they spent already as volunteers (Warner et al., 2014).

Home Sweet Home

One of the favorite activities of many retirees is caring for their homes and taking care of their own needs. Typically, both men and women do more housework and meal preparation (less fast food, more fresh ingredients) after retirement (Luengo-Prado & Sevilla, 2012). They go to fewer restaurants, stores, and parties because they like to stay put. Both sexes do yard work, redecorate, build shelves, hang pictures, rearrange furniture.

Gardening is particularly popular: More than half of the elderly in the United States do it (see Figure 25.5). Tending flowers, herbs, and vegetables is productive because it involves both exercise and social interaction (Schupp & Sharp, 2012).

In keeping up with household tasks and maintaining their property, almost all older people—about 90 percent, even when they are frail—prefer to **age in place** rather than move. The exception is immigrants, who sometimes move back to their original nation.

Generally, however, most of those who move do not go far. They may find a smaller apartment with an elevator and less upkeep, but they rarely uproot themselves to another city or state unless they already know people there. That is wise: Elders fare best when surrounded by long-term friends and acquaintances. Gerontologists believe that "interrupting social connections . . . might be harmful, especially for women and the frailest" (Berkman et al., 2011, p. 347).

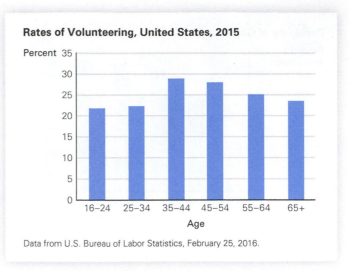

Rates of Volunteering, United States, 2015

Data from U.S. Bureau of Labor Statistics, February 25, 2016.

FIGURE 25.4
Official Volunteers As you can see, older adults volunteer less often than do middle-aged adults, according to official statistics. However, this counts people who volunteer for organizations—schools, churches, social service groups, and so on. Not counted is help given to friends, family members, neighbors, and even strangers. If that were counted, would elders have higher rates than everyone else?

THINK CRITICALLY: Can you think of another definition of *volunteering* that would increase the rate for elderly adults?

Response for Social Scientists
(from page 706): In general, psychologists favor self theories, and sociologists favor stratification theories. Of course, each discipline respects the other, but each believes that its perspective is more honest and accurate.

age in place To remain in the same home and community in later life, adjusting but not leaving when health fades.

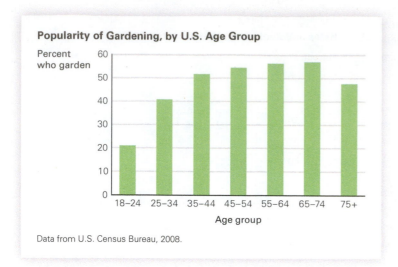

Popularity of Gardening, by U.S. Age Group

Data from U.S. Census Bureau, 2008.

FIGURE 25.5

Dirty Fingernails Almost three times as many 60-year-olds as 20-year-olds are gardeners. What is it about dirt, growth, and time that makes gardening an increasingly popular hobby as people age?

naturally occurring retirement community (NORC) A neighborhood or apartment complex whose population is mostly retired people who moved to the location as younger adults and never left.

Many of the older adults in **Video: Active and Healthy Aging: The Importance of Community** frequent senior centers for continual social contact, and some benefit from volunteering.

The preference for aging in place is evident in state statistics. Of the 50 states, Florida has the largest percentage of people over age 65, many of whom moved there not only for the climate but also because friends had already moved there. The next three states highest in proportion of population over age 65 are Maine, West Virginia, and Pennsylvania, all places where older people have aged in place.

Fortunately, aging in place has become easier. One project sent a team (a nurse, occupational therapist, and handyman) to vulnerable aged adults with good results: Most became better able to take care of themselves at home, avoiding institutions (Szanton et al., 2015). Elders themselves use selective optimization with compensation as they envision staying in their homes despite age-related problems.

About 4,000 consultants are now certified by the National Association of Homebuilders to advise about universal design, which includes making a home livable for people who find it hard to reach the top shelves, to climb stairs, to respond to the doorbell. Non-design aspects of housing also allow aging in place, such as bright lights without dangling cords, carpets affixed to the floor, and seats and grab bars in the shower.

Assistance to allow a person to age in place is particularly needed in rural areas, where isolation may become dangerous. A better setting is a neighborhood or an apartment complex that has become a **naturally occurring retirement community (NORC).**

A NORC develops when young adults move into a new suburb or large apartment building and then stay for decades. People in NORCs may live alone, after children left and partners died. They enjoy home repair, housework, and gardening, partly because their lifelong neighbors notice the new curtains, the polished door, the blooming rose bush. They share meals, gossip and entertainment.

If low-income elders are in a NORC within a high-crime neighborhood, they and their neighbors sometimes form a protective social network. NORCs can be granted public money to replace after-school karate with senior centers, or piano teachers with visiting nurses, if that is what the community needs (Greenfield et al., 2012; Vladeck & Altman, 2015).

In many other ways, public and private institutions and people can support aging in place (A. Smith, 2009). That is true for Doris, my friend who introduced this chapter. Dozens of people in the community care for her. Recently in the park, two strangers started to talk with her. Half a dozen homeless men stopped what they were doing to watch. Nothing untoward happened, but one of the men approached and said, "OK Doris, I will walk you home." Doris appreciated his protection.

Religious Involvement

Older adults attend fewer religious services than do the middle-aged, but faith and praying increase. Religious involvement correlates with physical and emotional health for several reasons:

- Religious prohibitions encourage good habits (e.g., less drug use).
- Faith communities promote caring relationships.
- Beliefs give meaning for life and death, thus reducing stress.

[Atchley, 2009; Lim & Putnam, 2010; Noronha, 2015]

Life After 65: Living Independently

Most people who reach age 65 not only survive a decade or more, but also live independently.

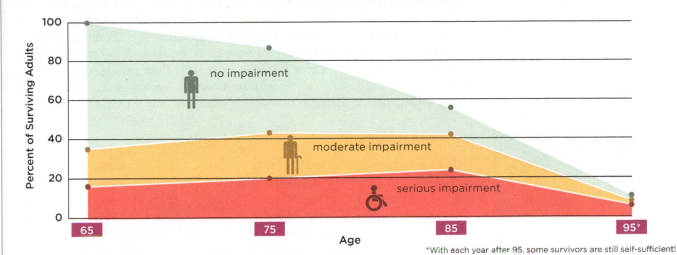

Percent of Surviving Adults

no impairment

moderate impairment

serious impairment

Age

65   75   85   95*

*With each year after 95, some survivors are still self-sufficient!

AGE 65

Of 100 people, in the next decade:

Most will care for all their basic needs. But, 35 will become unable to take care of at least one instrumental activity of daily living (IADL) like household chores, shopping, or taking care of finances, or one activity of daily living (ADL) like bathing, dressing, eating, or getting in and out of bed. And 16 are so impaired that they need extensive help, either at home or in a nursing home. 87 will survive another decade.

AGE 75

Of the 87 people who survived, in the next decade:

About half will not need help caring for their basic needs. But 43 will become unable to take care of at least one IADL or ADL. And half of these 43 become so impaired that they require extensive care. 56 will survive another decade.

AGE 85

Of the 56 people who survived, in the next decade:

Most need help. 42 will be unable to take care of at least one IADL or ADL. And 24 of them become so impaired that they require extensive care. Only 11 will survive another decade.

AGE 95

Of the 11 people who survived, in the next decade:

Those who reach 95 live for about four more years, on average. Almost three-quarters will need some help caring for their basic needs and about half require extensive care.

DATA FROM NATIONAL VITAL STATISTICS REPORTS, MAY 8, 2013.

With Whom?

Only about 10 percent of those over age 65 move in with an adult child, and less than 4% live in a nursing home or hospital.

LIVING ARRANGEMENTS OF PERSONS 65+, 2010

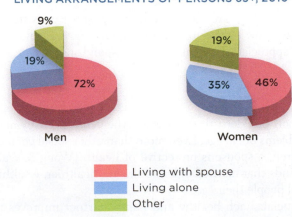

Men

Women

- Living with spouse
- Living alone
- Other

Where?

Not necessarily in a warm state.

PERSONS 65+ AS A PERCENTAGE OF TOTAL POPULATION, 2010

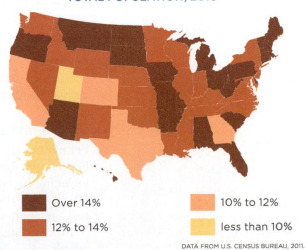

- Over 14%
- 12% to 14%
- 10% to 12%
- less than 10%

DATA FROM U.S. CENSUS BUREAU, 2011.

● Especially for Religious Leaders
Why might the elderly have strong faith but poor church attendance? (see response, page 714)

Religious identity and institutions are especially important for older members of minority groups, who often identify more strongly with their religious heritage than with their national or ethnic background. A nearby house of worship, with familiar words, music, and rituals, is one reason that American elders prefer to age in place.

Faith may explain an oddity in mortality statistics, specifically in suicide data (Chatters et al., 2011). In the United States, suicide after age 65 among elderly European American men occurs 50 times more often than among African American women. One explanation is that African American women's religious faith is often very strong, making them less depressed about their daily lives (Colbert et al., 2009).

Political Activity

It is easy to assume that elders are not political activists. Few turn out for rallies, and only about 2 percent are active in political campaigns. Indeed, only 7 percent of U.S. residents older than 65 volunteer for *any* political, civic, international, or professional group (Bureau of Labor Statistics, February 25, 2014).

By other measures, however, the elderly are very political. More than any other age group, they write letters to their representatives, identify with a political party, and vote.

In addition, they keep up with the news. For example, the Pew Research Center for the People and the Press periodically asks a cross section of U.S. residents a dozen questions about current events. The elderly almost always best the young, sometimes by a little, sometimes by a lot. For example, in April 2015 people were asked with which country did the United States recently re-establish diplomatic relations. Of those over age 65, 82 percent correctly said Cuba, as did 67 percent of those aged 18 to 29. They were also notably better at recognizing Elizabeth Warren, knowing the composition of the U.S. Senate, and spotting on a map where the Keystone XL pipeline might be built (Pew Research Center, April 28, 2015).

Many government policies affect the elderly, especially those regarding housing, pensions, prescription drugs, and medical costs. However, members of this age group do not necessarily vote their own economic interests, or vote as a bloc. Instead they are divided on most national issues, including global warming, military conflicts, and public education. Political scientists believe the idea of "gray power" (that the elderly vote as a bloc) is a myth, promulgated to reduce support for programs that benefit the old (Walker, 2012).

Douglas Graham/Associated Press

Few for Many These seniors rally to keep the U.S. Congress from reducing Social Security, Medicare, and Medicaid benefits—part of a successful National Committee to Preserve Social Security (NCPSS) campaign that has been supported by politicians of both major political parties for 30 years. This organization relies mostly on letters sent to legislators and on the human tendency to resist reductions in benefits.

Friends and Relatives

Social connections are particularly important in old age (Suitor et al., 2015). For the most part, negative relationships are abandoned, and positive ones remain. Bonds formed over the years allow people to share triumphs and tragedies with others who understand and appreciate. Siblings, old friends, and spouses are ideal convoy members.

Long-Term Partnerships

For most of the current cohort of elders, their spouse is the central convoy member, a buffer against the problems of old age. Even more than other social contacts, including friends and children, a spouse is protective of health (Wong & Waite, 2015). All of the research finds that married older adults are healthier, wealthier, and happier than unmarried people their age.

Mutual interaction is crucial: Each healthy and happy partner improves the other's well-being (Ruthig et al., 2012). Of course, not every marriage is good:

A Lover's Kiss Ralph Young wakes Ruth *(left)* with a kiss each day, as he has for most of the 78 years of their marriage. Here they are both 99, sharing a room in their Indiana residence, "more in love than ever." Half a world away, in Ukraine *(right)*, more kisses occur, with 70 newly married couples and one couple celebrating their golden anniversary. Developmental data suggest that now, several years after these photos, the two old couples are more likely to be happily married than the 70 young ones.

About one in every six long-term marriages decreases health and happiness (Waldinger & Schulz, 2010). For example, when spouses are dissatisfied with their relationship, hypertension increases (Birditt et al., 2015). But, that is not the usual pattern.

A lifetime of shared experiences—living together, raising children, and dealing with financial and emotional crises—brings partners closer. Often couples develop "an exceedingly positive portrayal" (O'Rourke et al., 2010b) of their mate, seeing their partner's personality as better than their own.

Older couples have learned how to disagree, considering conflicts to be discussions, not fights. I know one example personally.

Irma and Bill are both politically active, proud parents of two adult children, devoted grandparents, and informed about current events. They seem happily married, and they cooperate admirably when caring for their grandsons.

However, they vote for opposing candidates for almost every public office. I was puzzled until Irma explained: "We sit together on the fence, seeing both perspectives, and then, when it's time to vote, Bob and I fall on opposite sides." I know who will fall on which side, but they enjoy the discussion, listening to each other with respect.

This is apparent in many older couples. Instead of one trying to dominate the other, or one withdrawing (the demand/withdraw mode mentioned in Chapter 19), most older couples try to integrate the other's thoughts with their own (Kulik et al., 2016). Studies of adult decision making about medical issues, a common need in late adulthood, find that couples typically rely on each other's judgment more than on anyone else's (Queen et al., 2015).

Outsiders might judge many long-term marriages as unequal, since one or the other spouse usually provides most of the money, or needs most of the care, or does most of the housework. Yet such disparities do not bother most older partners, who accept each other's dependencies, remembering times (perhaps decades ago) when the situation was reversed. Equality is not the goal; equity is—and that may differ from what someone else judges (Kulik, 2016). A couple together achieve selective optimization with compensation: The one who is bedbound but alert can keep track of what the mobile but confused one must do, for instance.

Relationships with Younger Generations

Since the average couple now has fewer children, the *beanpole family,* with multiple generations but with only a few members at each level, is becoming more common (Murphy, 2011) (see Figure 25.6). With the beanpole structure, close family relationships are changing, from centering on parents and their children to involving other relatives as well (Verdery, 2015).

"They grow old too fast."

Ignorant? Each generation has much to teach as well as much to learn.

Many Households, Few Members The traditional nuclear family consists of two parents and their children living together. Today, as couples have fewer children, the beanpole family is becoming more common. This kind of family has many generations, each typically living in its own household, with only a few members in each generation.

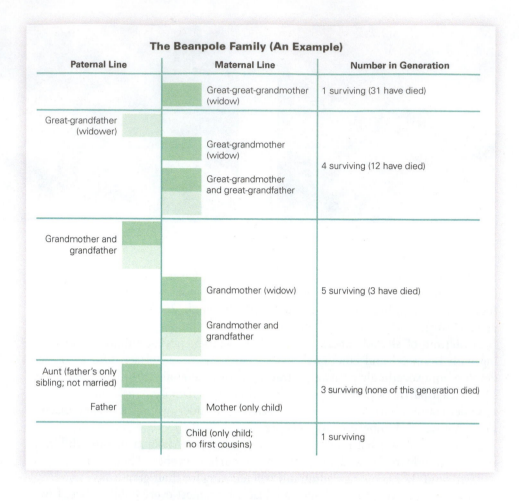

The Beanpole Family (An Example)

Paternal Line	Maternal Line	Number in Generation
	Great-great-grandmother (widow)	1 surviving (31 have died)
Great-grandfather (widower)	Great-grandmother (widow)	4 surviving (12 have died)
	Great-grandmother and great-grandfather	
Grandmother and grandfather		
	Grandmother (widow)	5 surviving (3 have died)
	Grandmother and grandfather	
Aunt (father's only sibling; not married)		3 surviving (none of this generation died)
Father	Mother (only child)	
	Child (only child; no first cousins)	1 surviving

filial responsibility The obligation of adult children to care for their aging parents.

Intergenerational Relationships

As you remember, *familism* prompts family caregiving among all relatives. One norm is **filial responsibility,** the obligation of adult children to care for their aging parents. This is a value in every nation, with some variation by culture (Saraceno, 2010).

As a value, filial responsibility is strong in Asia, but in practice, some scholars find Asians less likely to care for elderly parents than in Western cultures. For example, a survey in China found that half of adult children saw their parents only once a year or less (Kim et al., 2015).

As you also remember, older adults do not want to move in with younger generations and do so only if poverty and frailty require it. Especially in the United States, every generation values independence. That is why, after midlife and especially after the death of their own parents, members of the older generation are *less* likely to agree that children should provide substantial care for their parents and more likely to strive to be helpful to their children.

Ironically, conflict may be more frequent in emotionally close relationships than in distant ones (Silverstein et al., 2010), especially when either generation becomes dependent on the other. Aged parents want to support their children, but sometimes providing support—especially nonmaterial support (emotional support; child care, and so on)—is stressful (Bangerter et al., 2015).

In general, although interdependence and close attachment to a spouse enhances well-being, the same may not be true for relationships with grown children. As one study concludes, "it is not familial ties per se that are beneficial, but rather the quality of such ties that matters" (Holtfreter et al., 2016, p. 61).

● ● **Response for Religious Leaders** (from page 712): There are many possible answers, including the specifics of getting to church (transportation, stairs), physical comfort in church (acoustics, temperature), and content (unfamiliar hymns and language).

Some conflict is common in late-life families, as is some mutual respect. Indeed, both within families and within cultures, *ambivalence* is becoming recognized as the usual intergenerational pattern (Connidis, 2015), with mixed feelings in every generation. The degree of ambivalence varies partly by developmental age—teenagers are particularly likely to feel ambivalent about their parents (Tighe et al., 2016).

Extensive research finds many factors that affect intergenerational relationships:

- Assistance arises from both need and ability to provide.
- Frequency of contact is more dependent on geographical proximity than affection.
- Love is influenced by childhood memories.
- Sons feel stronger obligation; daughters feel stronger affection.
- National norms and policies can nudge family support, but they do not create it.

Grandparents and Great-Grandparents

Eighty-five percent of U.S. elders currently older than 65 are grandparents. (The rate was lower in previous cohorts because the birth rate fell during the 1930s, and it is expected to be lower again.) Given current longevity, the grandparent role can last for decades—35 years in the United States, according to one study (Leopold & Skopek, 2015b). Relatively few grandparents are raising young children, but most of them have elderly relatives who require some attention.

As with parents and children, specifics of the grandparent–grandchild relationship depend partly on personality and partly on the age and gender of both generations. The oldest grandparents tend to be less actively involved in day-to-day activities. Grandparents typically delight in the youngest children, provide material support for the school-age children, and offer advice and encouragement and act as a role model for the older grandchildren. Generally in the West (less so in Asia), grandparents are more involved with their daughter's children than their son's.

Same Situation, Far Apart: Happy Grandfathers No matter where they are, grandparents and grandchildren often enjoy each other partly because conflict is less likely, as grandparents are usually not as strict as parents are. Indeed, Sam Levinson quipped, "The reason grandparents and grandchildren get along so well is that they have a common enemy."

Grandparents fill one of four roles:

1. *Remote grandparents* (sometimes called *distant grandparents*) are emotionally distant from their grandchildren. They are esteemed elders who are honored, respected, and obeyed, expecting to get help when they need it.
2. *Companionate grandparents* (sometimes called *"fun-loving" grandparents*) entertain and "spoil" their grandchildren—especially in ways that the parents would not.
3. *Involved grandparents* are active in the day-to-day lives of their grandchildren. They live near them and see them daily.
4. *Surrogate parents* raise their grandchildren, usually because the parents are unable or unwilling to do so.

Currently in developed nations, most grandparents are companionate, partly because all three generations expect them to be companions, not authorities (Suitor et al., 2015). Contemporary elders usually provide babysitting and financial help but not advice or discipline (May et al., 2012).

Surrogate parents are usually in *skipped-generation* families, when the middle generation is absent. Skipped-generation families are uncommon—less than 1 percent of all grandparents in the United States are in that role at any given time (more are skipped-generation at some point in their decades of grandparenting). The health and happiness of surrogate grandparents is reduced compared to their peers from the same community who are not fully responsible for grandchildren.

LaunchPad
macmillan learning

In **Video: Grandparenting,** several individuals discuss their close, positive attachments to their grandchildren.

OPPOSING PERSPECTIVES

The Middle Generation as Gatekeeper

Every family has its own issues, and no parent or grandparent or child is perfect—especially in the eyes of other close family members. The middle generation is the one who decides how much contact the children should have with the grandparents, and that decision is not always what the grandparents wish.

Just as too much responsibility for grandchildren may impair health and happiness, the opposite—no contact at all—may be harmful as well. One Australian study focused on grandparents whose children prevented contact with the grandchildren.

One grandmother reported this conversation with her daughter:

She said: "You've never been a good mother, only when I was little". I said: "now that is ridiculous and you know that is ridiculous". She said: "you be quiet and listen to what I have to say, what I have to tell you now . . . I never want to see or hear from you the rest of your life" . . . I said: "I have fought hard. I have provided for both of your children. I've done all that I can to help you and [son-in-law]."

[Sims & Rofail, 2014]

Another grandmother in the same study said that her daughter told her

. . . you will do what I tell you, when I tell you, how I tell you or you will not be coming here again and you would never see [granddaughter] again.

[Sims & Rofail, 2014]

It is hard not to sympathize with these grandmothers, but we should acknowledge that sometimes the earlier relationship between parent and child provokes great bitterness in the middle generation. Not every grandparent is the patient, loving elder depicted by Norman Rockwell. However, these daughters need to be reminded of two findings regarding human development.

- People change over time. A grandparent can become less, or more, strict, can follow parental rules (such as for eating, screen time, hygiene) that differ from the elder's customs, and so on. As with every human relationship, mutual compromise and explicit communication is essential.
- Relationships with younger generations promote emotional and physical well-being. In that Australian study, grandparents who were shut out cited heart problems, high blood pressure, and sleepless nights.

One of the realities of human development that appears in study after study is that family connections are pivotal for optimal growth, from pregnancy (when relatives help keep the expectant mother drug-free) to the end of life (when family members provide essential comfort).

That is no less true in late adulthood, as the elderly can benefit from connections to younger generations. By the same token, grandchildren benefit from grandparents who love them.

Friendship

Friendship networks typically are reduced with each decade. Emerging adults tend to average the most friends. By late adulthood, the number of people considered friends is notably smaller (Wrzus et al., 2013). This is counterbalanced by another trend: Older adults tend to report fewer problems with the friends they do have (Schlosnagle & Strough, 2016).

Although friends are an important source of support at every age, they may be particularly crucial in late adulthood (Blieszner, 2014; Heinze et al., 2015). For example, if a romantic relationship ends in divorce or death, the chance of finding another partner (i.e., remarriage, cohabitation, or LAT) are less than 50 percent, with older women particularly unlikely to re-partner (Schimmele & Wu, 2016). But especially if death ended the relationship, many older widows do not seek another spouse. Instead of trying to replace the family member, they rely on close friends to satisfy the need for companionship (Wrzus et al., 2013).

An interesting difference is found between older and younger adults. Older adults are more likely to put effort into maintaining friendship (Lang et al., 2013). Perhaps because they realize how important friends are, or because they have learned from experience, they are likely to phone, write, e-mail, arrange excursions, remember special occasions, and so on. This has a practical application: Grown children who urge their distant parents to move closer to them may be making a mistake if they do not appreciate the long-standing social networks that surround most older people.

WHAT HAVE YOU LEARNED?

1. Why would a person keep working after age 65?

2. How does retirement affect the health of people who have worked all their lives?

3. Who is more likely to volunteer and why?

4. What are the benefits and liabilities for elders who want to age in place?

5. How does religion affect the well-being of the aged?

6. How does the political activity of older and younger adults differ?

7. What is the usual relationship between older adults who have been partners for decades?

8. Who benefits most from relationships between older adults and their grown children?

9. Which type of grandparenting seems to benefit both generations the most?

10. How does friendship differ depending on the adult's age?

The Frail Elderly

Now that we have dispelled stereotypes by describing active, happy young-old adults, we turn to the **frail elderly**—the oldest-old who are infirm, inactive, seriously disabled, or cognitively impaired. Frailty is not defined by any single disease, no matter how serious, but by an overall loss of energy and strength. It is systemic, often accompanied by weight loss and exhaustion. It can occur at any age.

Frailty at the end of life is called *terminal decline,* characterized by a loss of intellectual sharpness and happiness. Weight loss is one of the signs: At most ages, overweight is far more problematic than underweight, but when older adults lose weight, that may signify a problem.

Activities of Daily Life

One way to measure frailty, according to insurance standards and medical professionals, is by assessing a person's ability to perform the tasks of self-care. Gerontologists often assess five physical **activities of daily life (ADLs)**: eating, bathing, toileting, dressing, and moving from a bed to a chair. Sometimes personal hygiene, such as brushing teeth, and mobility, such as walking a certain number of feet, are included as ADLs.

Equally important are **instrumental activities of daily life (IADLs)**, which require intellectual competence and forethought. Indeed, difficulty with IADLs often precedes problems with ADLs since planning and problem solving help frail elders maintain self-care.

The ADLs are fairly standard: People everywhere who cannot do them need help. However, ADLs are dynamic: Most people who have difficulty with one or more of them are able to recover (Ciol et al., 2014). Recovery is especially likely if someone teaches them how to, for instance, put on shoes without bending down, or get out of bed without risking a fall. Physical therapists may be crucial.

IADLs vary from culture to culture. In developed nations, IADLs may include understanding the labels on medicine bottles, making sure the daily diet is nutritious, preparing income tax forms, using modern appliances, and making and

Same Situation, Far Apart: Partners Whether at the Vietnam Veterans Memorial in Washington, D.C. *(top)* or in the Philippines *(bottom)*, elderly people support each other in joy and sorrow. These women are dancing together, and these men are tracing the name of one of their buddies who died 40 years earlier.

frail elderly People who are physically infirm, very ill, or cognitively disabled, and consequently tired and lethargic.

activities of daily life (ADLs) Typically identified as five tasks of self-care that are important to independent living: eating, bathing, toileting, dressing, and transferring from a bed to a chair. The inability to perform any of these tasks is a sign of frailty.

instrumental activities of daily life (IADLs) Actions (for example, paying bills and car maintenance) that are important to independent living and that require some intellectual competence and forethought. The ability to perform these tasks may be even more critical to self-sufficiency than ADL ability.

TABLE 25.1	Instrumental Activities of Daily Life
Domain	**Exemplar Task**
Managing medical care	Keeping current on checkups, including teeth and eyes
	Assessing supplements as good, worthless, or harmful
Food preparation	Evaluating nutritional information on food labels
	Preparing and storing food to eliminate spoilage
Transportation	Comparing costs of car, taxi, bus, and train
	Determining quick and safe walking routes
Communication	Knowing when, whether, and how to use landline, cell, texting, mail, e-mail
	Programming speed dial for friends, emergencies
Maintaining household	Following instructions for operating an appliance
	Keeping safety devices (fire extinguishers, CO_2 alarms) active
Managing one's finances	Budgeting future expenses (housing, utilities, etc.)
	Completing timely income tax returns
	Avoiding costly scams, unread magazines

keeping doctor appointments (see Table 25.1). Professionals vary in their lists of IADLS (Chan et al., 2012).

IADLs are best maintained if the person established habits and competencies for such tasks decades earlier. This may explain the results of a study of Mexican-origin elders in the United States. Those who were born in Mexico were more likely to have trouble with IADLs than those of Mexican ancestry who were born in the United States (Garcia et al., 2015).

Whose Responsibility?

There are marked cultural differences in care for the frail elderly. Many African and Asian cultures hold sons responsible for the care of their parents. In those cultures, some men and their wives take elders into their homes, providing meals, medical care, and conversation.

However, as already mentioned, this is increasingly difficult in modern times, not only in the United States but also in other nations. The governments of China and India have mandated that children care for their parents, a mandate that itself suggests that many parents need care that they are not getting.

The problem is that demographics have changed, with more elders and fewer children than in former times. Some people still romanticize elder care, believing that frail older adults should live with their children, who should care for them. That assumption worked when the demographic pyramid meant that each surviving elder had many descendants, but it does not work for beanpole families, who may have a dozen elders.

Fortunately, as already mentioned, most older people are quite capable of caring for themselves. When an older relative needs help with ADLs, the helper is usually a husband or wife, with the assistance of siblings and adult children.

Preventing Frailty

Prevention of frailty begins with the fact that disability is dynamic, part of the many systems that support each person. Individuals, families, and the larger community must all do their part. Consider walking and cognitive loss.

Mobility

Muscles weaken with age, a condition called *sarcopenia*. The rate of muscle loss usually increases in late-late adulthood: Muscle mass at age 90 is only half of what it was at age 30 (McLean & Kiel, 2015). Sarcopenia is characteristic of elders before frailty sets in, which means that preventing muscle loss might prevent or postpone frailty (Nishiguchi et al., 2015).

Social support is crucial. For example, an elderly person who wants to age in place may live in a home with a kitchen and bathroom down steep stairs, far from the bedroom. A caregiver might bring meals, put a portable toilet in the room, and buy a remote control for a bedroom TV. Medicare may pay for a wheelchair, the local news station may highlight violent crime, the municipality may not build sidewalks and may not have good streetlights. The result: A frail person becomes more frail.

Instead, the person could exercise daily, walking with family members on pathways built to be safe and pleasant. A physical therapist—paid by the individual,

WANG ZHAO/AFP/Getty Images

Better or Worse? It depends. The advantage of having a motorized wheelchair is that a person can stay engaged in life, even, as shown here, on the streets of Beijing. The disadvantage is that riding may replace walking—but that is up to the person. This man might be on his way to strength training at the gym, and if he gets there safely and regularly, his electric wheelchair can add years to his life.

the family, or the government—could individualize the exercise regimen and select appropriate equipment (a walker? a cane? special shoes?). The house could be redesigned, or the elder could move to a place where walking is safe and encouraged—not a place where everyone is in wheelchairs.

In general, the research is clear that both attitude change and exercise carefully tailored to the individual is beneficial. However, translating that research into action—the steps of habit change outlined in Chapter 20—is a problem; impaired ADLs are a result. IADLs may follow.

Mental Capacity

Thus, all three—the elder, the family, and the community—could prevent or at least postpone frailty by improving mobility. As explained, however, problems with IADLs may be worse than problems with ADLs. Here again, the family and the community may be crucial.

Consider this example.

> A 70-year-old Hispanic man came to his family doctor following a visit to his family in Colombia, where he had appeared to be disoriented (he said he believed he was in the United States, and he did not recognize places that were known to be familiar to him) and he was very agitated, especially at night. An interview with the patient and a family member revealed a history that had progressed over the past six years, at least, of gradual worsening cognitive deficit, which that family had interpreted as part of normal aging. Recently his symptoms had included difficulty operating simple appliances, misplacement of items, and difficulty finding words, with the latter attributed to his having learned English in his late 20s. . . . [His] family had been very protective and increasingly had compensated for his cognitive problems.
>
> . . . He had a lapse of more than five years without proper control of his medical problems [hypertension and diabetes] because of difficulty gaining access to medical care. . . .
>
> Based on the medical history, a cognitive exam . . . and a magnetic resonance imaging of the brain . . . the diagnosis of moderate Alzheimer's disease was made. Treatment with ChEI [cholinesterase inhibitors] was started. . . . His family noted that his apathy improved and that he was feeling more connected with the environment.
>
> [Griffith & Lopez, 2009, p. 39]

Both the community (those five years without treatment for hypertension and diabetes) and the family (making excuses, protecting him) contributed to major neurocognitive disorder that could have been delayed, if not prevented altogether.

Often with IADLs, the elderly person him- or herself needs to understand and prevent problems. In this case, the elderly man did not take care of his health. This is a common problem, particularly for immigrant men, as explained in the section on stratification.

One strength of many immigrant communities is family support, but familism can be harmful. The trip to Colombia was ill-advised because disorientation worsens in an unfamiliar place. The man's family helped him arrange the trip, unaware of how leaving a familiar place might affect someone with a neurocognitive disorder.

The responsibility for the man's condition is shared not only by him and his protective family but also by the medical community. Nationwide, immigrants need physicians who are fluent in their language and culture. Although many immigrants speak English well, using a second language to describe intimate medical details to a doctor from another background is difficult, as is understanding exactly what medication and treatment is needed.

DeAgostini/G. SIOEN/Getty Images

Never Frail This man is playing the recorder at an Easter celebration in Arachova, a mountain town in Greece.

● **Observation Quiz** Impossible to be sure, but from what you see and know, there are seven clues that he will never be frail. How many can you name? (see answer, page 720) ↑

Answer to Observation Quiz (from page 719) He has an activity he enjoys (recorder playing), he walks regularly (that walking stick), he breathes non-polluted air (mountain town), he is religious (it is Easter, so he is probably Greek Orthodox), his community values him (he was chosen to play), he is male (men are more likely to die quickly), and he has a healthy diet (the Mediterranean diet—with lots of fish, vegetables, and olive oil, the healthiest diet we know). Of course, we cannot be certain of any of these, but chances are this man has many more healthy years.

Sweet But Sad Family support is evident here, as an older sister (Lillian, age 75) escorts her younger sister (Julia, age 71) to the doctor. Unseen is how family support wrecked their lives: The sisters lost their life savings and their childhood home because their nephew was addicted to crack.

Caring for the Frail Elderly

Prevention is best, but it is not always sufficient. Some problems, such as major NCD, can be postponed or slowed but not eliminated. Caregivers themselves are usually elderly, and they often have poor health, limited strength, and failing immune systems (Lovell & Wetherell, 2011). Thus, an aging parent who cares for the other parent is especially likely to need help.

If people have trouble with an ADL, everyone is aware of the problem. However, IADLs are worse, because elders might insist that they can submit taxes perfectly well and become angry if the IRS fines them, insist they can prepare meals but lose weight because of poor nutrition, insist they can drive but get lost, and so on.

The designated caregiver of a frail elderly person is chosen less for practical reasons (e.g., the relative with the most patience, time, and skill) than for cultural ones. Currently in the United States, the usual caregiver is the spouse (the wife twice as often as the husband) who often has no prior experience caring for a frail elder.

If no spouse is available, grown children may assume that another sibling has fewer responsibilities and thus should be the caregiver. As you might imagine, resentment is common, particularly in daughters with more education (Lin et al., 2012). They often have significant work and family responsibilities, and they bristle if their brothers assume that they must be caregivers of their parents.

Not only do family assumptions vary but nations, cultures, and ethnic groups vary as well. In northern European nations, most elder care is provided through a social safety net of senior day-care centers, senior homes, and skilled nurses; in African cultures, families are fully responsible for the aged.

Even in ideal circumstances, family members disagree about appropriate nutrition, medical help, and dependence. A family member may insist that an elderly person never enter a nursing home, but another member may say that a nursing home is the best option. Family conflict erupts, making the situation worse.

Public agencies rarely intervene unless a crisis arises. This troubles developmentalists, who study "change over time." From a life-span perspective, caregiver exhaustion and elder abuse are predictable and preventable. A study of elderly people with serious heart disease found that the burden on family caregivers depended more on their attitude and on social support than on the impairment of the patient. This suggests that professionals need to help caregivers access support *before* the need is obvious (Grigorovich et al., 2016).

The ideal is *integrated care,* in which a caregiving team comprised of some professionals and some family members cooperate to provide individualized care, whether at a long-term care facility or at someone's home (Lopez-Hartmann et al., 2012). Just as a physical therapist knows specific exercises and movements to improve mobility, a case manager can evaluate an impaired elder and develop a comprehensive plan. Some tasks are best done by a family member, some by the frail person themselves, some by a medical professional.

Integrated care does not ease the burden of caregiving, but it helps. In one study, a year after a professional helped plan and coordinate care, family caregivers improved in their overall attitude and quality of life. Although the total time spent on caregiving was not reduced by integrated care, the tasks performed changed, with more time on household tasks (e.g., meal preparation and cleanup) and less on direct care (Janse et al., 2014).

The idea that a frail person is cared for either exclusively by family or exclusively in a nursing home is not only wrong but it is destructive of everyone's health and well-being. Instead, if home care is chosen, family members need professional help, and if nursing-home care is best, family members need to visit and continue to provide emotional support. Isolation—either at home or in a nursing home—makes poor care more likely.

Elder Abuse

When caregiving results in resentment and social isolation, the risk of depression, sickness, and abuse (of either the frail person or the caregiver) escalates (G. Smith et al., 2011; Johannesen & LoGiudice, 2013). Abuse is likely if:

- the *caregiver* suffers from emotional problems or substance abuse.
- the *care receiver* is frail, confused, and demanding.
- the *care location* is isolated, where visitors are few.

Ironically, although relatives are less prepared to cope with difficult patients than professionals are, they often provide round-the-clock care with little outside help or supervision. Some caregivers overmedicate, lock doors, and use physical restraints, all of which may be abusive. That may lead to inadequate feeding, medical neglect, or rough treatment. Obvious abuse is less likely in nursing homes and hospitals, not only because laws forbid it but also because workers are not alone, nor expected to work 24/7.

Extensive public and personal safety nets are needed. Most social workers and medical professionals are suspicious if an elder is unexpectedly quiet, or losing weight, or injured. They are currently "mandated reporters," which means that they must alert the authorities if they believe abuse is occurring. Not all elder abuse is physical. It may instead be financial, yet few bankers, lawyers, and investment advisers know how to recognize abuse or are obligated to notify anyone if they become suspicious (Jackson & Hafemeister, 2011).

A major problem is awareness. If someone notices that a caregiver cashes the Social Security check, disrespects the elder, or ignores the elder's demands, is that abuse? Because of problems in the macrosystem, political and legal definitions and remedies are unclear (Lichtenberg, 2016). Accurate incidence data and intervention are complicated by definitions: If an elder feels abused but a caregiver disagrees, who is right?

Sometimes caregivers become victims, attacked by a confused elderly person. As with other forms of abuse, the dependency of the victim makes prosecution difficult, especially when secrecy, suspicion, and family pride keep outsiders away. Social isolation makes abuse possible; fear of professionals makes it worse.

LaunchPad
macmillan learning

Video: Nursing Homes
http://qrs.ly/xs4sqmt

Long-Term Care

The trend in the United States and elsewhere is away from nursing homes and toward aging in place. Currently, residents of nursing homes tend to be very old—at least age 85—and experiencing significant cognitive decline. They also are disproportionately women (because men are usually married, and they predecease their wives) with few descendants who could provide care.

A few nursing homes—e.g., Green House, or Eden, or Wellspring—provide individualized, humane care, allowing residents to decide what to eat, where to walk, how to decorate their rooms, and so on. The philosophy that residents are individuals, capable even when some ADLs are impossible, may cause a culture change in more conventional nursing homes (Grabowski et al., 2014).

In North America, good nursing-home care is available for those who can afford it and know what to look for. Some nonprofit homes are subsidized by religious organizations, and these may be good. In some European nations, the federal government subsidizes care for anyone (rich or poor) who needs it—although quality varies.

Same Situation, Far Apart: Diversity Continues No matter where they live, elders thrive with individualized care and social interaction, as is apparent here. Lenore Walker *(top)* celebrates her 100th birthday in a Florida nursing home with her younger sister nearby, and an elderly chess player in a senior residence in Kosovo *(bottom)* contemplates protecting his king. Both photos show, in details such as the women's earrings and the men's head coverings, that these elders maintain their individuality.

Especially for Those Uncertain About Future Careers Would you like to work in a nursing home? (see response, page 723)

Good care allows independence, individual choice, and privacy. As with day care for young children, continuity of care is crucial: An institution with a high rate of staff turnover is to be avoided. At every age, establishing relationships with other people is crucial: If the residents feel that their caregivers are the same, year after year, that improves well-being.

The training and the workload of the staff, especially of the aides who provide frequent, personal care, are crucial: Such simple tasks as helping a frail person out of bed can be done clumsily, painfully, or skillfully. Currently, however, most front-line workers have little training, low pay, and many patients— and almost half leave each year (Golant, 2011).

Many nursing homes now have dedicated areas and accommodation for people with Alzheimer's or other NCDs. Among the special characteristics are "memory boxes," in addition to names on the doors of the rooms. A memory box is open to view and displays photographs and other mementos so that the person knows which room is his or hers.

Many people with major NCD do not understand why they need care and often resist it. Nursing homes sometimes treat such resistance with psychoactive drugs (Kleijer et al., 2014), but other tactics can reduce anxiety (Konno et al., 2014). Among such measures are special music, friendly dogs, and favorite foods— all of which can be appreciated by someone whose memory is so impaired that reading and conversing are impossible.

Quality care is much more labor-intensive and expensive than most people realize. Variations are dramatic, primarily because of the cost of personnel. According to John Hancock Life & Health Insurance Company, in 2015 the cost of a year of a private room at a nursing home is $200,750 in Alaska and $56,575 in Louisiana. (Most people think that Medicare, Medicaid, or long-term insurance covers the entire cost—a costly misconception.)

As noted, the trend over the past 20 years has been toward a lower proportion of those over age 60 residing in nursing homes. Those few are usually more than 80 years old, frail and confused, with several medical problems (Moore et al., 2012). Most elders, most of the time, live at home.

Alternative Care

Everyone is on a continuum somewhere between needing no help at all and needing extensive, 24-hour care. Once that is understood, a range of options can be envisioned. Remember the study cited in Chapter 24 that found that major NCD is less common in England than it used to be? That study also found that the percentage of people with neurocognitive disorders in nursing homes has risen, from 56 percent in 1991 to 65 percent in 2011, primarily because of a rise in the number of oldest-old women in such places (Matthews et al., 2013).

This means that more elderly who need some care are now in the community. Aging in place, assisted living, and other options are less costly and more individualized than institutions. The number of assisted-living facilities has increased as nursing homes have decreased. Typically, assisted-living residences provide private apartments for each person and allow pets and furnishings as in a traditional home.

The "assisted" aspects vary, often one daily communal meal, special transportation and activities, household cleaning, and medical assistance, such as

Many Possibilities This couple in Wyoming *(left)* sold their house in Georgia and now live in this RV, and this Cuban woman *(right)* continues to live in her familiar home. Ideally, all of the elderly have a range of choices—and when that is true, almost no one needs nursing-home care.

supervision of pill-taking and blood pressure or diabetes monitoring, with a nurse, doctor, and ambulance if needed. In the United States, many of these forms of assistance are additional expenses.

Assisted-living facilities range from group homes for three or four elderly people to large apartment or townhouse developments for hundreds. Variation is also evident in the health, ability, and attitudes of the residents (Park et al., 2015).

Almost every state, province, or nation has its own standards for assisted-living facilities, but many such places are unlicensed. Some regions of the world (e.g., northern Europe) have many options, while others (e.g., sub-Saharan Africa) have almost none. The variations mean that family members and elders themselves need to evaluate and choose exactly what social and medical support are needed and provided.

Another form of elder care is sometimes called *village care*. Although not really a village, it is so named because of the African proverb, "It takes a whole village to raise a child." In village care, elderly people who live near each other pool their resources, staying in their homes but also getting special assistance when they need it. Such communities require that the elderly contribute financially and that they be relatively competent, so village care is not suited for everyone. However, for some it is ideal (Scharlach et al., 2012).

Overall, as with many other aspects of aging, the emphasis in living arrangements is on selective optimization with compensation. Elders need settings that allow them to be safe, social, and respected, as independent as possible. Indeed, that is true for all of human development. Each person, at each age, has individual needs and abilities. Ideally, the context supports and encourages the best in all of us.

Response for Those Uncertain About Future Careers (from page 722): Why not? The demand for good workers will obviously increase as the population ages, and the working conditions are likely to improve. An important problem is that the quality of nursing homes varies, so you need to make sure you work in one whose policies incorporate the view that the elderly can be quite capable, social, and independent.

WHAT HAVE YOU LEARNED?

1. What factors make an older person frail?

2. What is the difference between ADLs and IADLs?

3. Why might IADLs be more important than ADLs in deciding whether a person needs care?

4. What can be done to increase mobility in the aged?

5. How is cognitive decline related to prevention of frailty?

6. What three factors increase the likelihood of elder abuse?

7. What factors distinguish a good nursing home from a bad one?

8. What are the advantages and disadvantages of assisted living for the elderly?

SUMMARY

Theories of Late Adulthood

1. Self theories hold that adults make personal choices in ways that allow them to become fully themselves. One such theory arises from Erikson's last stage, integrity versus despair, in which individuals seek integrity that connects them to the human community.

2. The positivity effect and socioemotional selectivity are part of the elder's drive to maintain a sense of self.

3. Compulsive hoarding can be understood as an effort to hold onto the self, keeping objects from the past that others might consider worthless.

4. Stratification theories maintain that social forces—such as ageism, racism, and sexism—limit personal choices throughout the life span, keeping people on a particular level or stratum of society. Many believe that the most powerful stratification arises from SES.

5. Age stratification can be blamed for the disengagement of older adults. Activity theory counters disengagement theory, stressing that older people need to be active.

6. There is some evidence that stratification early in life affects later life, but there is also evidence that earlier stratification is less powerful after age 80 or so.

Activities in Late Adulthood

7. At every age, employment can provide social and personal satisfaction as well as needed income. Retirement may be welcomed by the elderly if they remain active in other ways.

8. Some elderly people perform volunteer work and are active politically—writing letters, voting, staying informed. These activities enhance health and well-being and benefit the larger society.

9. Common among retirees is an increase in religious faith (but not church attendance). Elders hope to age in place. Many of the elderly engage in home improvement or redecoration, preferring to stay in their own homes and attend their local house of worship.

10. A lifelong romantic partner is often the most important member of a person's social convoy. Older adults in long-standing marriages tend to be satisfied with their relationships and to safeguard each other's health.

11. Older adults tend to have fewer friends than younger adults, but friendship may be even more important in late adulthood than earlier.

12. Relationships with adult children and grandchildren are usually mutually supportive, although conflicts arise as well. Financially, elders more often support the younger generations than vice versa.

13. Most of the elderly prefer to maintain their independence, rather than living with younger family members. Grandparents enjoy grandchildren, but not taking over the parenting role.

The Frail Elderly

14. Most elderly people are self-sufficient, but some eventually become frail. They need help with their activities of daily life, either with physical tasks (such as eating and bathing) or with instrumental ones (such as preparing meals, doing taxes, and consulting doctors).

15. Care of the frail elderly is usually undertaken by other older adults, particularly spouses. Elder abuse may occur when the stress of care is great and social support is lacking.

16. Nursing homes, assisted living, and professional home care are of varying quality and availability. Each of these arrangements sometimes provide necessary and beneficial care. Good care for the frail elderly involves a combination of professional and family support, recognizing diversity in needs and personality.

KEY TERMS

self theories (p. 700)	positivity effect (p. 702)	naturally occurring retirement community (NORC) (p. 710)	activities of daily life (ADLs) (p. 717)
integrity versus despair (p. 700)	stratification theories (p. 704)	filial responsibility (p. 714)	instrumental activities of daily life (IADLs) (p. 717)
compulsive hoarding (p. 701)	disengagement theory (p. 706)	frail elderly (p. 717)	
socioemotional selectivity theory (p. 702)	activity theory (p. 706)		
	age in place (p. 709)		

APPLICATIONS

1. Political attitudes vary by family and by generation. Interview several generations within the same family about issues of national and local importance. How do you explain the similarities and differences between the generations? What is more influential: experience, SES, heritage, or age?

2. People of different ages, cultures, and experiences vary in their values regarding family caregiving, including the need for safety, privacy, independence, and professional help. Find four people whose backgrounds (age, ethnicity, SES) differ. Ask their opinions, and analyze the results.

3. Visit a nursing home or assisted-living residence in your community. Record details about the physical setting, the social interactions of the residents, and the activities of the staff. Would you like to work or live in this place? Why or why not?

The Developing Person So Far:
Late Adulthood

BIOSOCIAL

Ageism Prejudice based on age is common and harmful in late adulthood. Many younger adults, and even older people themselves, underestimate the health and vitality of the old. The best strategy for coping with aging seems to be selective optimization with compensation. Physiological functions change over time, but such changes can be taken in stride if individuals and communities adjust.

Disease and Aging Virtually every disease and disability becomes more common in late adulthood. Impairment of the senses occurs to almost everyone and can result in serious losses. Every condition is affected by genes and by health habits decades earlier, and most can be mitigated by early detection and treatment. The optimal goal is compression of morbidity.

Longevity Wear and tear, genes, and cellular damage all seem relevant to some aspect of aging but none has led to proven measures that halt aging. The maximum life span for every species is determined by genes. Calorie restriction succeeds in prolonging life in some species; application to humans is unproven. People who live more than 100 years have good genes and health habits and seem unusually active, happy, and supported by their community.

COGNITIVE

Brains and Thinking Some brain areas shrink with age, some kinds of memory fade, and thinking processes slow down, but new learning can produce new neurons and dendrites, and verbal memory is often unimpaired until very late in life. Sensory losses reduce input; remediating problems with vision and hearing may improve cognition. Ecologically valid cognitive assessments show that most elders are able to use their minds to remain vital and independent.

Neurocognitive Disorders Neurocognitive disorders become more common with age as cognitive reserves shrink. Alzheimer's disease is the most common one in the United States. It is rare until age 70, but the rate increases every decade after that. Another common NCD is caused by a series of strokes, each destroying part of the brain. There are many other causes, each with distinct symptoms. Some reversible problems, such as depression and polypharmacy, also cause cognitive problems.

New Cognitive Development In later adulthood, many people develop their creativity via the arts or the life review. Some elders also become wise, but wisdom is not guaranteed in the old or completely absent in the young.

PSYCHOSOCIAL

Theories, Activities, and Family Self and stratification theories note that it is not easy to maintain vitality and joy in late adulthood, but most elders remain active, caring about political and religious concerns. Some move to a smaller residence or assisted-living quarters, but most prefer to age in place. Relationships with mates, children, and grandchildren continue to be important for well-being.

The Frail Elderly A minority of elders are termed "frail": weak and failing, unable to maintain the activities of daily life or the instrumental activities. Frailty is partly the result of aging bodies and minds and partly the result of lack of self-care and the misguided care of other people and of neglectful communities.

Epilogue:
Death and Dying

What Will You Know?

1. How can death be a source of hope, not despair?
2. What is the difference between a good death and a bad one?
3. How does mourning help with grief?

My brother told me three years ago that he had fatal prostate cancer; it had already metastasized. I was angry—I thought we would both live to 100 because we ate better and exercised more than our parents, who died in their 90s. Dying was not in my plan. He accepted, not fought, death. He kept teaching and writing; I wanted him to seek the best medical care. He was angry, too—at me, for telling my daughters. He said I should tell no one, because people might discount his work.

We were both typical and irrational. Emotions at death include anger, wishful thinking, selfish concerns, legacy hopes. Irrational emotions are one reason for hospice, for bereavement customs, for arguments about when and how death occurs.

I did not want Glen to value his work more than his life. He said his only worry was about David, my nephew described in Chapter 1. I see now that we thought and valued what humans have always thought and valued.

I am now doing what this chapter prescribes, working to extend his legacy, with the help of many of his students and colleagues. I know deeply and personally what follows in this Epilogue: There is *hope* in death, *choices* in dying, and *affirmation* in mourning.

Death and Hope

A multicultural life-span perspective reveals that reactions to death are filtered through cultural prisms, as well as by the age of both the dying and the bereaved.

One emotion is constant, however: hope. It appears in many ways: hope for life after death, hope that the world is better because someone lived, hope that death occurred for a reason, hope that survivors rededicate themselves.

Cultures, Epochs, and Death

Few people have witnessed someone die. This was not always the case (see Table EP.1). If someone reached age 50 in 1900 in the United States and had had 20 high school classmates, at least 6 of those fellow students would have already died. The survivors would have visited and reassured friends who were dying at home, promising to see them in heaven. Almost everyone believed in life after death.

Now few die before old age, and if a young person dies, it usually is too quick for goodbye. Ironically, death is more feared as dying becomes less familiar (Carr, 2012).

Left: © Friedrich Stark/Alamy Stock Photo

TABLE EP.1	How Death Has Changed in the Past 100 Years

Death occurs later. A century ago, the average life span worldwide was less than 40 years (47 in the rapidly industrializing United States). Half of the world's babies died before age 5. Now newborns are expected to live to age 71 (79 in the United States); in many nations, centenarians are the fastest-growing age group.

Dying takes longer. In the early 1900s, death was usually fast and unstoppable; once the brain, the heart, or any other vital organ failed, the rest of the body quickly followed. Now death can often be postponed through medical technology: Hearts can beat for years after the brain stops functioning, respirators can replace lungs, and dialysis does the work of failing kidneys.

Death often occurs in hospitals. For most of our ancestors, death occurred at home, with family nearby. Now most deaths occur in hospitals or other institutions, with the dying surrounded by medical personnel and machines.

The causes of death have changed. People of all ages once usually died of infectious diseases (tuberculosis, typhoid, smallpox), or, for many women and most infants, in childbirth. Now disease deaths before age 50 are rare, and in developed nations most newborns (99 percent) and their mothers (99.99 percent) live.

And after death . . . People once knew about life after death. Some believed in heaven and hell; others, in reincarnation; others, in the spirit world. Prayers were repeated—some on behalf of the souls of the deceased, some for remembrance, some to the dead asking for protection. Believers were certain that their prayers were heard. People now are aware of cultural and religious diversity; many raise doubts that never occurred to their ancestors.

HIP/Art Resource, NY

Conversation Who is talking here? Unless you are an Egyptologist, you would not guess that this depicts a dead man conversing with the gods of the Underworld. Note that the deceased is relatively young and does not seem afraid—both typical for people in ancient Egypt.

Ancient Times

Paleontologists believe that 100,000 years ago Neanderthals buried their dead with tools, bowls, or jewelry, signifying belief in an afterlife (Hayden, 2012). The date is controversial: Burial could have begun 200,000 years ago or more recently—but it is certain that long ago death was an occasion for hope, mourning, and remembrance. Two ancient Western civilizations with written records—Egypt and Greece—had elaborate death rituals.

The ancient Egyptians built magnificent pyramids, refined mummification, and scripted instructions (the *Book of the Dead*) to aid the soul (*ka*), personality (*ba*), and shadow (*akh*) in reuniting after death, so the dead could bless and protect the living (Taylor, 2010).

The fate of dead Egyptians depended partly on their actions while alive, partly on the circumstances of death, and partly on proper burial. Death was a "call to action," a reason to live morally and to honor the past (Assmann, 2005, p. 19). If the dead were not appropriately respected, the living would suffer.

Another set of beliefs comes from the Greeks. Again, continuity between life and death was evident, with hope for this world and the next. The fate of a dead person depended on past deeds. A few would have a blissful afterlife, a few were condemned to torture in Hades, and most would enter a shadow world until they were reincarnated.

Three themes are apparent in all the known ancient societies, not only in Greece and Egypt but also in the Mayan, Chinese, Indian, and African cultures.

- Actions during life affected destiny after death.
- An afterlife was assumed.
- Mourners said particular prayers and made specific offerings, to prevent the spirit of the dead from haunting and hurting them.

Contemporary Religions

Now consider contemporary religions. Each faith seems distinct in its practices surrounding death. One review states, "Rituals in the world's religions, especially those for the major tragic and significant events of bereavement and death, have a bewildering diversity" (Idler, 2006, p. 285).

Some details illustrate this diversity. According to one expert, in Hinduism the casket is always open, in Islam, never (Gilbert, 2013). In many Muslim and Hindu cultures, the dead person is bathed by the next of kin; among some Native Americans (e.g., the Navajo), no family member touches the dead person. Specific rituals vary as much by region as by religion. In North America, Christians of all sects often follow local traditions. Similarly, each of the 500 Native American tribes has its own heritage (Cacciatore, 2009).

According to many branches of Hinduism, a person should die on the floor, surrounded by family, who neither eat nor wash until the funeral pyre is extinguished. By contrast, among some (but not all) Christians, the very sick should go to the hospital; if they die, then mourners gather to eat and drink, sometimes with music and dancing.

Diversity is also evident in Buddhism. The First Noble Truth of Buddhism is that life is suffering. Some rituals help believers accept death and detach from grieving in order to decrease the suffering that living without the deceased person entails. Other rituals help people connect to the dead as part of the continuity between life and death (Cuevas & Stone, 2011). Thus, some Buddhists leave the dying alone; others hover nearby.

Hospitals are supposed to prevent death, not allow it. In Thailand, where most people are Buddhist, when it becomes apparent that a hospitalized patient will soon die, an ambulance takes that person back home, where death occurs naturally. Then the person and the family can benefit from a better understanding of life, suffering, and death (Stonington, 2012).

A study of Buddhist death rituals in contemporary Cambodia finds that death customs sustain communities and families. Family members travel back to the original home, despite the economic reality that many individuals work and live far away (Davis, 2016). Often, funerals and cremation or burial become the time when distant relatives reconnect, and the dying specify that they want their bodies or ashes to be near their childhood home.

Religious practices change with historical conditions. One example comes from Korea. Koreans traditionally opposed autopsies because the body is a sacred gift. However, Koreans value science education. This created a dilemma, because medical schools need bodies to autopsy in order to teach. The solution was to start a new custom: a special religious service honoring the dead who have given their body for medical education (J-T. Park et al., 2011). The result: a dramatic increase in the number of bodies donated for research.

Autopsies create problems in the United States as well. Autopsies may be legally required and yet considered religious sacrilege. For instance, for the Hmong in Southeast Asia, any mutilation of the dead body has "horrifying meanings" and "dire consequences for . . . the spiritual well-being of surviving family and community" (Rosenblatt, 2013, p. 125).

In Minnesota, however, where many Hmong now live, autopsies may be performed immediately if the coroner has "any question about the cause of death," especially if the body will be cremated (as most Buddhists are). Minnesota law explicitly says that the next of kin do not need to be told about, much less give

Dance for the Dead This woman dances on Dia de los Muertos, wearing a traditional skull headdress. People in many Latin American communities remember death and celebrate life on November 1 (All Saints Day) and November 2 (All Souls Day) each year.

Observation Quiz Is this in Mexico? (see answer, page 730) ↑

permission for, autopsy. No autopsy is needed if a licensed physician, hospice, or hospital affirms the cause of death—but that excludes many Hmong deaths.

Ideas about death are expressed differently in various cultures. Many people believe that the spirits of ancestors visit the living. Spirits are particularly likely to appear during the Hungry Ghost Festival (in many East Asian nations), on the Day of the Dead (in many Latin American nations), or on All Souls Day (in many European nations).

People who are from none of those traditions sometimes believe that their dead family member came to them in a dream. No religion explicitly teaches that the dead become angels who protect the living, but many Westerners believe that (Walter, 2016).

Consequently, do not get distracted by death customs or beliefs that may seem odd to you, such as mummies, hungry ghosts, reincarnation, or hell. Instead, notice that death has always inspired strong emotions, often benevolent ones. It is the *denial* of death that leads to despair (Wong & Tomer, 2011). In all faiths and cultures, death is considered a passage, not an endpoint, a reason for families and strangers to come together.

Understanding Death Throughout the Life Span

Thoughts about death—as about everything else—are influenced by each person's cognitive maturation and past experiences. Here are some of the specifics.

Death in Childhood

Some adults think children are oblivious to death; others believe children should participate in funerals and other rituals, just as adults do (Talwar et al., 2011). You know from your study of childhood cognition that neither view is completely correct.

Very young children have some understanding of death, but their perspective differs from that of older people. They may not understand that the dead cannot come back to life. For that reason, a child might not immediately be sad when someone dies. Later, moments of profound sorrow might occur when reality sinks in, or simply when the child realizes that a dead parent will never again tuck them into bed at night.

Children are affected by the attitudes of others. If a child encounters death, adults should listen with full attention, neither ignoring the child's concerns nor expecting adultlike reactions (Doering, 2010). Because the limbic system matures more rapidly than the prefrontal cortex, children may seem happy one day and morbidly depressed the next.

Young children who themselves are fatally ill typically fear that death means being abandoned (Wolchik et al., 2008). Consequently, parents should stay with a dying child, holding, reading, singing, and sleeping. A frequent and caring presence is more important than logic. By school age, many children seek independence. Parents and professionals can be too solicitous; older children do not want to be babied. Often they want facts and a role in "management of illness and treatment decisions" (Varga & Paletti, 2013, p. 27).

Because the loss of a particular companion is a young child's concern, it is not helpful to say that Grandma is sleeping, that God wanted his sister in heaven, that Grandpa went on a trip, that a dog can be replaced with a puppy. The child may ask to wake up Grandma, complain to God, or phone Grandpa. The puppy might be rejected.

If a child concludes that adults are afraid to say that death has occurred, or why, the child might develop the theory that death is so horrible that adults cannot talk

Sorrow All Around When a five-day-old baby died in Santa Rosa, Guatemala, the entire neighborhood mourned. Symbols and a procession help with grief: The coffin is white to indicate that the infant was without sin and will therefore be in heaven.

Johan Ordonez/AFP/Getty Images

about it—a terrifying conclusion (Doering, 2010). Even worse is the idea that adults lie to children. Egocentric preschoolers might fear that they, personally, caused death, or that they might die soon.

Remember that cognition changes with development. As children grow older, especially if they have personal experience with death, their concepts become closer to adult ones (Bonoti et al., 2013). Concrete operational thinkers seek facts, about dying, death, and where the person goes. They want to do something: bring flowers, repeat a prayer, write a letter.

Children see no contradiction between the reality of biological death and the belief in spiritual afterlife. That may bewilder adults (Talwar et al., 2011). One complication is that children want to talk with a dying relative and be present at the death. However, many dying people prefer to shield children from their last days and hours (Lee et al., 2013).

Death in Adolescence and Emerging Adulthood

As you learned in Chapter 9, adolescents may be self-absorbed, philosophical, analytic, angry, or depressed—or all five at different moments. Counselors emphasize that adults must listen to teenagers. Self-expression is part of the search for identity; death of a loved one does not stop that search. Some adolescents use the Internet to write to the dead person or to vent their grief—an effective way to express their personal identity concerns (DeGroot, 2012).

"Live fast, die young, and leave a good-looking corpse" is advice often attributed to actor James Dean, who died in a car crash at age 24. At what stage would a person be most likely to agree? Emerging adulthood, of course. Worldwide, older teenagers and emerging adults control their anxiety about death by taking risks (de Bruin et al., 2007; Luxmoore, 2012).

Terror management theory is the idea that people protect themselves against death anxiety by denying and daring death—either by building up their self-esteem or—particularly in emerging adulthood—by risking death. Emerging adults are least likely to wear seat belts, for instance (Boal et al., 2016). When they survive, they say that death cannot get them (Landau & Sullivan, 2015).

This developmental tendency can be lethal (see Figure EP.1). As already noted, cluster suicides, foolish dares, fatal gang fights, and drug-impaired driving are common during adolescence and emerging adulthood, as is an overestimate of the odds of premature death. Three attitudes typical of older adolescents are correlated: ageism, terror management, and risk taking (Popham et al., 2011a).

When adolescents and emerging adults think about death, they sometimes become more patriotic and religious but less tolerant of other worldviews and less generous to people of other nations (Ellis & Wahab, 2013; Jonas et al., 2013). Apparently, as people try to manage terror, they try to convince themselves that loyal, conscientious members of their own group (including themselves) are especially worthy of living (Pyszczynski et al., 2015).

Death in Adulthood

When adults become responsible for work and family, attitudes shift. Death is not romanticized. Many adults quit addictive drugs, start wearing seat belts, and

Causes of Death for 15- to 24-Year-Olds, United States

Early twentieth century

Diseases 85%

Accidents 12%

Suicide 2%
Homicide 1%

Early twenty-first century

Diseases 28%

Suicide 16%

Accidents 41%

Homicide 15%

Data from U.S. Census Bureau, 1907; National Center for Health Statistics, 2012.

FIGURE EP.1

Typhoid Versus Driving into a Tree In 1905, most young adults in the United States who died were victims of diseases, usually infectious ones like tuberculosis and typhoid. In 2012, four times more died violently (accidents, homicide, suicide) than died of all the diseases combined.

terror management theory The idea that people adopt cultural values and moral principles in order to cope with their fear of death. This system of beliefs protects individuals from anxiety about their mortality and bolsters their self-esteem.

"For My Kids" Randy Pausch was a brilliant, innovative scientist at Carnegie Mellon University. When he was diagnosed with terminal pancreatic cancer, he gave a talk titled "The Last Lecture: Really Achieving Your Childhood Dreams" that became famous worldwide. He devoted the final 10 months of his life to his family—his wife, Jai, and their children, Chloë, Dylan, and Logan.

adopt other life-protective behaviors when they become parents. One of my students eagerly anticipated her first skydive, paying in advance. However, on the day before the scheduled dive, she learned that she was pregnant. She forfeited the money and bought prenatal vitamins.

To defend against the fear of death, adults do not readily accept the death of others. For instance, when the inspired poet Dylan Thomas was about age 30, he wrote to his dying father: "Do not go gentle into that good night/Rage, rage against the dying of the light" (Thomas, 2003, p. 239). Nor do adults accept their own fatal illness. A woman diagnosed at age 42 with a rare and almost always fatal cancer (a sarcoma) wrote:

> I hate stories about people dying of cancer, no matter how graceful, noble, or beautiful. . . . I refuse to accept I am dying; I prefer denial, anger, even desperation.

> *[Robson, 2010, pp. 19, 27]*

When adults hear about another's death, they want to know the deceased's age. Death in the prime of life, especially when caused by the person's own actions, is particularly disturbing. Michael Jackson, Robin Williams, and Prince were mourned by millions, in part because they were not yet old (50, 63, and 57 respectively). Older entertainers who die of natural causes after age 70 are less mourned.

Reactions to one's own mortality differ depending on developmental stage as well (see Figure EP.2). In adulthood, from ages 25 to 65, terminally ill people worry about leaving something undone or abandoning family members, especially children.

One dying middle-aged adult was Randy Pausch, a 47-year-old professor and father of three. Ten months before he died of cancer, he delivered a famous last lecture, detailing his childhood dreams and saluting those who would continue his work. After advising his students to follow their own dreams, he concluded, "This talk is not for you, it's for my kids" (Pausch, 2007). Not surprisingly, that message was embraced by his wife, also in mid-adulthood, who wrote her own book, titled *Dream New Dreams,* which deals with overcoming death by focusing on life (J. Pausch, 2012).

Adult attitudes about death are often irrational. Logically, adults should work to change social factors that increase the risk of mortality—such as air pollution, junk foods, and legal drugs, which contribute to millions of deaths in the United States annually. Instead, people react to rare events, such as anthrax and avalanches. People particularly fear deaths that seem random, out of their control.

For example, traveling by plane is feared more than by car. In fact, flying is safer: In 2015, only 569 people in the entire world died in airplane crashes, compared to 38,300 killed by motor vehicles in the United States alone.

Ironically, in the weeks after September 11, 2001, when a terrorist attack included the deliberate crash of four planes, many North Americans drove long distances instead of flying. In the next few months, 2,300 more U.S. residents died in motor-vehicle crashes than usual (Blalock et al., 2009). Not logical, but very human.

FIGURE EP.2

A Toothache Worse Than Death? A cohort of young adults (average age 21) and old adults (average age 74) were divided into three groups. One group wrote about their death (giving them overt thoughts about dying), another did a puzzle with some words about death (giving them unconscious thoughts about death), and the third wrote about dental pain (they were the control group). Then they all judged how harshly people should be punished for various moral transgressions. Those who wrote about dental pain are represented by the zero point on this graph. Compared with them, those older adults who thought about death were less punitive, but younger adults were more so.

🔵 **Observation Quiz** Which seems more powerful, conscious or unconscious thoughts about death? (see answer, page 734) ➜

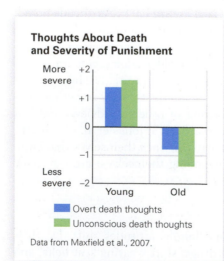

Thoughts About Death and Severity of Punishment

More severe +2

+1

0

−1

Less severe −2

Young   Old

🟦 Overt death thoughts
🟩 Unconscious death thoughts

Data from Maxfield et al., 2007.

Death in Late Adulthood

In late adulthood, attitudes shift again. Anxiety decreases; hope rises (De Raedt et al., 2013). Life-threatening illnesses reduce life satisfaction more among the middle-aged than the elderly, who often seem reconciled to death.

Indeed, many developmentalists believe that mental health among older adults includes acceptance of mortality, which increases concern for others. Some elders engage in *legacy work,* trying to leave something meaningful for later generations (Lattanzi-Licht, 2013).

As evidence of this attitude change, older people seek to reconnect with estranged family members and tie up loose ends that most young adults leave hanging (Kastenbaum, 2012). Some younger adults are troubled if their parents or grandparents allocate heirlooms, discuss end-of-life wishes, or buy a burial plot, but such actions are developmentally appropriate.

Acceptance of death does not mean that the elderly give up on living; rather, their priorities shift. In an intriguing series of studies (Carstensen, 2011), people were presented with the following scenario:

> Imagine that in carrying out the activities of everyday life, you find that you have half an hour of free time, with no pressing commitments. You have decided that you'd like to spend this time with another person. Assuming that the following three persons are available to you, with whom would you want to spend that time?
> - A member of your immediate family
> - The author of a book you have just read
> - An acquaintance with whom you seem to have much in common
>
> *[adapted from Carstensen, 2011, p. 113]*

Older adults more than younger ones choose the family member, although younger adults who have life-threatening diseases also choose family (see Figure EP.3). The researchers explain that family becomes more important when death seems near. Close family members and friends are particularly crucial when an elder is chronically ill, and a spouse dies, both of which make mortality especially salient (Karantzas & Gillath, 2017).

Near-Death Experiences

Even coming close to death may be an occasion for hope. This is most obvious in what is called a *near-death experience,* in which a person almost dies. Survivors sometimes report having left the body and moving toward a bright light while feeling peace and joy. The following classic report is typical:

> I was in a coma for approximately a week. . . . I felt as though I were lifted right up, just as though I didn't have a physical body at all. A brilliant white light appeared. . . . The most wonderful feelings came over me—feelings of peace, tranquility, a vanishing of all worries.
>
> *[quoted in Moody, 1975, p. 56]*

Near-death experiences often include religious elements (angels seen, celestial music heard). Survivors may become more spiritual, less materialistic, more compassionate. To some, near-death experiences prove that "Heaven is for real" (Burpo & Vincent, 2011). Many Americans have Christian symbolism (e.g., *heaven*). In every culture, those who report near-death experience provide similar accounts. Those who have had near-death experiences often reach a worldview, with (1) limitations of social status, (2) insignificance of material possessions, and (3) less self-centeredness (Greyson, 2015).

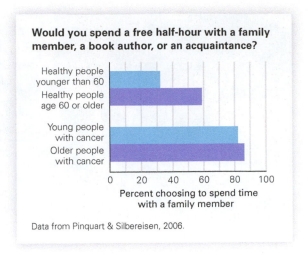

Would you spend a free half-hour with a family member, a book author, or an acquaintance?

Percent choosing to spend time with a family member

Data from Pinquart & Silbereisen, 2006.

FIGURE EP.3

Turning to Family as Death Approaches Both young and old people diagnosed with cancer (one-fourth of whom died within five years) more often preferred to spend a free half-hour with a family member rather than with an interesting person whom they did not know well.

THINK CRITICALLY: Might thoughts occur when a person is almost dead that are not limited by the neuronal connections in the brain?

Contrast or Commonality Solemn faces and red eyes are evident in the brother, widow, children, and father of Beau Biden, Vice President Joe Biden's son *(left)*—a contrast to the rousing songs at Michael Jackson's funeral *(right)*. In both cases, however, survivors memorialized the dead. Vice President Biden, for instance, began a national campaign to fight brain cancer.

Most scientists are skeptical, but many are intrigued. As one review concludes, the research:

> has been hampered by the spontaneous and unpredictable occurrence of NDEs, and has provided only indirect evidence supporting the psychological, neuro-physiological, and transcendent interpretations.

[*Greyson, 2015, p. 787*]

Answer to Observation Quiz

(from page 732): Unconscious. Young adults became more punitive; older adults became more forgiving.

WHAT HAVE YOU LEARNED?

1. Why are people less familiar with death today than they were 100 years ago? What impact might this have?

2. According to the ancient Egyptians and Greeks, what determined a person's fate after death?

3. What is one example of contrasting rituals about death?

4. What should parents remember when talking with children about death?

5. How does terror management theory explain young people's risk taking?

6. How does parenthood affect people's thoughts about their own death?

7. How do attitudes about death shift in late adulthood?

8. In what ways do people change after a near-death experience?

Choices in Dying

Do you recoil at the heading, "Choices in Dying"? If so, you may be living in the wrong century. Every twenty-first-century death involves choices, beginning with risks taken or avoided, habits sustained, and specific measures to postpone or hasten death.

It might seem that war deaths, or bystander gun deaths, or accidents of many kinds are not chosen. But always, decisions by the society, the family, or the individual make life or death more likely. For instance, 15,000 fewer motor-vehicle deaths occurred in the United States in recent years than in 1980, when such deaths reached the highest level ever. The reduction resulted from thousands of choices, by legislators, police, car designers, and drivers.

A Good Death

People everywhere hope for a good death (Vogel, 2011), one that is:

- At the end of a long life
- Peaceful
- Quick
- In familiar surroundings
- With family and friends present
- Without pain, confusion, or discomfort

Many would add that *control over circumstances* and *acceptance of the outcome* are also characteristics of a good death, but on this cultures and individuals differ. Some dying individuals willingly cede control to doctors or caregivers, and others fight every sign that death is near. Some cultures praise the dying for acceptance, others for fighting.

Modern Medicine

In some ways, modern medicine makes a good death more likely. The first item on the list has become the norm: Death usually occurs at the end of a long life.

Younger people still get sick, but surgery, drugs, radiation, and rehabilitation typically mean that, in developed countries, they go to the hospital and then return home. If young people die, death is typically quick (before medical intervention could save them), and that makes it a good death for them (if not for their loved ones).

In other ways, however, contemporary medical advances have made a bad death more likely, especially the last items on this list. When a cure is impossible, physical and emotional comfort deteriorate (Kastenbaum, 2012). Instead of acceptance, people submit to surgery and drugs that prolong pain and confusion. Hospitals sometimes exclude visitors from intensive-care units, and patients may become delirious or unconscious, unable to die in peace.

The underlying problem may be medical care itself, which is so focused on lifesaving that dying invites "the dangers of well-intentioned over 'medicalization'" (Ashby, 2009, p. 94). Dying involves emotions, values, and a community—not just a heart that might stop beating. As my religious adviser told my brother who wanted to keep it quiet that he was dying, "Cancer is a family disease." Fortunately, three factors that make a good death more likely have increased: honest conversation, the hospice, and palliative care.

Honest Conversation

In about 1960, researcher Elisabeth Kübler-Ross (1969, 1975) asked the administrator of a large Chicago hospital for permission to speak with dying patients. He told her that no one in the hospital was dying! Eventually, she found a few terminally ill patients who, to everyone's surprise, wanted very much to talk.

From ongoing interviews, Kübler-Ross identified emotions experienced by dying people and by their loved ones. She divided these emotions into five sequential stages.

1. Denial ("I am not really dying.")
2. Anger ("I blame my doctors, or my family, or God for my death.")
3. Bargaining ("I will be good from now on if I can live.")
4. Depression ("I don't care about anything; nothing matters anymore.")
5. Acceptance ("I accept my death as part of life.")

Too Late for Her When Brittany Maynard was diagnosed with progressive brain cancer that would render her unable to function before killing her, she moved from her native California to establish residence in Oregon, so she could die with dignity. A year later, the California Senate Health Committee debated a similar law, with Brittany's photo on a desk. They approved the law, 5–2.

LaunchPad
macmillan learning

Video: End of Life: Interview with Laura Rothenberg
http://qrs.ly/na4sqmv

● **Especially for Relatives of a Person Who Is Dying** Why would a healthy person want the attention of hospice caregivers? (see response, page 739)

Another set of stages of dying is based on Abraham Maslow's hierarchy of needs (Zalenski & Raspa, 2006).

1. Physiological needs (freedom from pain)
2. Safety (no abandonment)
3. Love and acceptance (from close family and friends)
4. Respect (from caregivers)
5. Self-actualization (appreciating one's unique past and present)

Maslow later suggested a possible sixth stage, *self-transcendence* (Koltko-Rivera, 2006), which emphasizes the acceptance of death and the hope for others to continue what the dying person values for them. Maslow's later stages incorporate religious faith. By contrast, few professional care providers discuss self-actualization or self-transcendence (Bergamo & White, 2016).

Other researchers have *not* found these sequential stages. Remember the woman dying of a sarcoma, cited earlier? She said that she would never accept death and that Kübler-Ross should have included desperation as a stage. Kübler-Ross herself later said that her stages have been misunderstood, as "our grief is as individual as our lives. . . . Not everyone goes through all of them or goes in a prescribed order" (Kübler-Ross & Kessler, 2014, p. 7).

Nevertheless, both lists remind caregivers that each dying person has strong emotions and needs that may be unlike that same person's emotions and needs a few days or weeks earlier. Furthermore, those emotions may differ from those of the caregivers, who themselves may have different emotions from each other.

It is vital that everyone—doctors, nurses, family, friends, and the patient—knows that a person is dying; then, appropriate care is more likely (Lundquist et al., 2011). Unfortunately, even if a patient is dying, most doctors never ask about end-of-life care. The result is not longer life but more pain, more procedures, and higher hospital bills. One study found that patients who had spoken with their doctors about terminal care had a final bill 36 percent lower than those who had not (Zhang et al., 2009).

Financial concerns aside, many caregivers never ask a dying person what is important to them. The daughter of a famous psychologist, Jack Block, knew she should ask her father before surgery what mattered to him. His answer shocked her: "If I'm able to eat chocolate ice cream and watch football on TV, then I'm willing to stay alive. I'm willing to go through a lot of pain if I have a shot at that."

That conversation was critical. It allowed her to decide what surgery he wanted, with what risks. He lived for ten more years, needing help with his ADLs, which would have been intolerable to some people. But he could think and write; he wrote two books. When he could no longer eat, he said no to a stomach tube, refused liquid nourishment, and died five days later (Gawande, 2014, pp. 183–184).

Most dying people want to talk honestly with loved ones, and with medical and religious professionals. However, it is a mistake to assume that applies to everyone. In many Asian families, telling people they are dying is thought to destroy hope (Corr & Corr, 2013a).

Remember human variability. Some people do *not* want the whole truth; some do *not* want many visitors. Some want every possible drug, surgery, and so on; others refuse anything that will cloud their thinking. Many African Americans reject prognosis. In one study, 65 percent of those with terminal cancer overestimated their survival by five years or more (Trevino et al., 2016). This is very human.

Better Ways to Die

Several practices have become more prevalent since the contrast between a good death and the usual hospital death has become clear. The hospice and the palliative care specialty are examples.

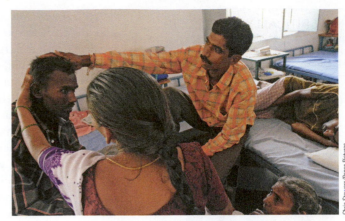

Same Situation, Far Apart: As It Should Be Dying individuals and their families benefit from physical touch and suffer from medical practices (gowns, tubes, isolation) that restrict movement and prevent contact. A good death is likely for these two terminal patients—a husband with his wife in their renovated hotel/hospital room in North Carolina *(left)*, and a man with his family in a Catholic hospice in Andhra Pradesh, India *(right)*.

Hospice

In 1950s London, Cecily Saunders opened the first modern **hospice,** where terminally ill people could spend their last days in comfort (Saunders, 1978). Thousands of other hospices have opened in many nations, and hundreds of thousands of hospice caregivers now bring medication and care to dying people where they live. In the United States, more than half of all hospice deaths occur at home (NHPCO, 2015).

Hospice professionals relieve discomfort, avoiding measures that merely delay death; their aim is to make dying easier. Comfort can include measures that some hospitals forbid: acupuncture, special foods, flexible schedules, visitors when the patient wants them (which could be 2 A.M.), massage, aromatherapy, and so on (Doka, 2013).

There are two principles for hospice care:

- Each patient's autonomy and decisions are respected. For example, pain medication is readily available, not on a schedule or minimal dosage. Most hospice patients use less medication than a doctor might prescribe, but they decide when and how much they want.
- Family members and friends are counseled before the death, taught to provide care, and guided in mourning. Their needs are as important as those of the patient. Death is thought to happen to a family, not just to an individual.

In 2014 in the United States, 46 percent of deaths occurred with hospice care, one-third of them within a week after hospice care began (NHPCO, 2015). Hospice caregivers wish they had more time to assess and meet the particular medical and emotional needs of the dying person and their loved ones. Dying and mourning are lengthy processes. It is not true that hospice care hastens death; more often death occurs later than it otherwise would (Gawande, 2014).

Unfortunately, hospice does not reach many dying people (see Table EP.2), even in wealthy nations and much less in developing ones (Kiernan, 2010). Hospice care is more common in England than in mainland Europe, more common in the western part of the United States than the Midwest, and rare in poor nations.

There are ethnic differences as well. In the United States, only 7 percent of hospice patients are Latino and only 8 percent are African American (NHPCO, 2015). Compared to European Americans,

hospice An institution or program in which terminally ill patients receive palliative care to reduce suffering; family and friends of the dying are helped as well.

TABLE EP.2	Barriers to Entering Hospice Care

- Hospice patients must be terminally ill, with death anticipated within six months, but predictions are difficult. For example, in one study of noncancer patients, physician predictions were 90 percent accurate for those who died within a week but only 13 percent accurate when death was predicted in three to six weeks (usually the patients died sooner) (Brandt et al., 2006).

- Patients and caregivers must accept death. Traditionally, entering a hospice meant the end of curative treatment (chemotherapy, dialysis, and so on). This is no longer true. Now treatment can continue. Many hospice patients survive for months, and some are discharged alive (Salpeter et al., 2012).

- Hospice care is costly. Skilled workers—doctors, nurses, psychologists, social workers, clergy, music therapists, and so on—provide individualized care day and night. Some hospices have waiting lists.

- Availability varies. Hospice care is more common in England than in mainland Europe and is a luxury in poor nations. In the United States, western states have more hospices than midwestern states do. Even in one region (northern California) and among clients of one insurance company (Kaiser), the likelihood that people with terminal cancer enter hospice care depends on exactly where they live (Keating et al., 2006).

THINK CRITICALLY: What are the possible reasons that fewer people in hospice are from non- European backgrounds?

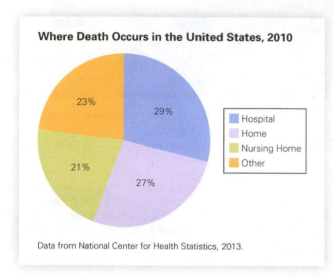

Where Death Occurs in the United States, 2010

- Hospital 29%
- Home 27%
- Nursing Home 21%
- Other 23%

Data from National Center for Health Statistics, 2013.

FIGURE EP.4

Not with Family Almost everyone prefers to die at home, yet most people die in an institution, surrounded by medical personnel and high-tech equipment, not by the soft voices and gentle touch of loved ones. The "other" category is even worse, as it includes most lethal accidents or homicides. But don't be too saddened by this chart—improvement is possible. Twenty years ago the proportion of home deaths was notably lower, and some deaths in each institution are hospice deaths.

palliative care Medical treatment designed primarily to provide physical and emotional comfort to the dying patient and guidance to his or her loved ones.

double effect When an action (such as administering opiates) has both a positive effect (relieving a terminally ill person's pain) and a negative effect (hastening death by suppressing respiration).

THINK CRITICALLY: At what point, if ever, should intervention stop to allow death?

African Americans are more often admitted to hospice from a hospital than a home and are likely to die relatively quickly (one week, on average), whereas the average hospice death occurs two weeks after admission.. The reason is thought to be cultural, not economic, since Medicare now pays most hospice expenses.

Nationally, about 15 percent of hospice patients are discharged alive. Sometimes their health has improved. However, the hospices with the highest "live discharge" rates tend to be recently founded, private, profit-making institutions: Their hospice admissions and discharges may occur for financial, not medical, reasons (Teno et al., 2014). (Originally, hospices were all nonprofit, sponsored by charitable organizations, or publicly funded.)

Home hospice care requires family or friends taught by hospice workers to provide care. Although this has led to an increase of "good deaths" at home, most deaths still occur in hospitals, and many others occur in nursing homes (see Figure EP.4).

Palliative Care

In 2006, the American Medical Association approved a new specialty, **palliative care,** which focuses on relieving pain and suffering in hospitals, homes, or hospice. Palliative doctors discuss options. Some interventions (especially surgery) may be refused if people understand the risks and benefits (Mynatt & Mowery, 2013). Palliative doctors also prescribe powerful drugs and procedures that make patients comfortable.

Morphine and other opiates have a **double effect:** They relieve pain (a positive effect), but they also slow down respiration (a negative effect). Painkillers that reduce both pain and breathing are allowed by law, ethics, and medical practice.

In England, for instance, although it is illegal to cause death, even of a terminally ill patient who repeatedly asks to die, it is legal to prescribe drugs that have a double effect. One-third of all English deaths include such drugs. This itself raises the issue of whether some narcotics are used to hasten death more than to relieve pain (Billings, 2011).

Heavy sedation is another method sometimes used to alleviate pain. Concerns have been raised that this may merely delay death rather than prolong meaningful life, since the patient becomes unconscious, unable to think or feel (Raus et al., 2011). Most people prefer to die at home, conscious, able to talk with close friends and family—even if this choice means a shorter life (Gawande, 2014).

Ethical Issues

As you see, the success of medicine has created new dilemmas. Death is no longer the natural outcome of age and disease; when and how death occurs involves human choices.

Deciding When Death Occurs

No longer does death necessarily occur when a vital organ stops. Breathing continues with respirators; stopped hearts are restarted; stomach tubes provide calories; drugs fight pneumonia.

Almost every life-threatening condition results in treatments started, stopped, or avoided, with death postponed, prevented, or welcomed. This has fostered impassioned arguments about ethics, both between nations (evidenced by radically different laws) and within them.

Religious advisers, doctors, and lawyers disagree with colleagues within their respective professions. Family members disagree with one another. Members of every group disagree with members of their own group and the other groups (Ball, 2012; Nelson-Becker et al., 2015; White et al., 2016).

One physician, a specialist in palliative care, advised his colleagues:

> The highway of aggressive medical treatment runs fast, is heavily travelled, but can lack landmarks and the signage necessary to know when it is time to make for the exit ramp . . . These signs are there and it is your responsibility to communicate them to patients and families.
>
> [Fins, 2006, p. 73]

Good advice, hard to follow.

Physicians sometimes recommend a specific treatment that might postpone death but diminish life; they sometimes tell patients a dizzying range of options and facts. Ideally they do what is most difficult—explaining realistic choices, including doing nothing, *after* learning what is important to the patient (Arnold et al., 2015).

Evidence of Death

Historically, death was determined by listening to a person's chest: No heartbeat meant death. To make sure, a feather was put to the person's nose to indicate respiration—a person who had no heartbeat and did not exhale was pronounced dead. Very rarely, but widely publicized when it happened, death was declared but the person was still alive.

Modern medicine has changed that: Hearts and lungs need not function on their own. Many life-support measures and medical interventions circumvent the diseases and organ failures that once caused death. Checking breathing with feathers is a curiosity that, thankfully, is never used today.

But how do we know when death has happened? In the late 1970s, a group of Harvard physicians concluded that death occurred when brain waves ceased, a definition now used worldwide (Wijdicks et al., 2010).

There is no international agreement as to exactly what constitutes brain death (Wahlster et al., 2015). A recent review in France notes that caution is particularly needed with newborns, as their brains have not developed mature brain waves (Szurhaj et al., 2015) (see Table EP.3). On the other hand, waiting too long to declare death makes organ donation impossible.

Euthanasia

Euthanasia (sometimes called *mercy killing*) is common for pets but rare for people. Many people see a major distinction between active and passive euthanasia, although the final result is the same. In **passive euthanasia,** a person near death is allowed to die. They may have a **DNR (do not resuscitate) order,** instructing medical staff not to restore breathing or restart the heart if breathing or pulsating stops. Passive euthanasia is legal everywhere.

Active euthanasia is deliberately doing something to cause death, such as turning off a respirator or giving a lethal drug. Some physicians condone active euthanasia when three conditions occur: (1) suffering cannot be relieved, (2) incurable illness, and (3) a patient wants to die. Active euthanasia is legal in the Netherlands, Canada, Colombia, Belgium, Luxembourg, and Switzerland, and illegal (but rarely prosecuted) elsewhere.

TABLE EP.3	Dead or Not? Yes, No, and Maybe

Brain death: Prolonged cessation of all brain activity with complete absence of voluntary movements; no spontaneous breathing; no response to pain, noise, and other stimuli. Brain waves have ceased; the electroencephalogram is flat; *the person is dead.*

Locked-in syndrome: The person cannot move, except for the eyes, but normal brain waves are still apparent; *the person is not dead.*

Coma: A state of deep unconsciousness from which the person cannot be aroused. Some people awaken spontaneously from a coma; others enter a vegetative state; *the person is not yet dead.*

Vegetative state: A state of deep unconsciousness in which all cognitive functions are absent, although eyes may open, sounds may be emitted, and breathing may continue; *the person is not yet dead.* The vegetative state can be *transient, persistent,* or *permanent.* No one has ever recovered after two years; most who recover (about 15 percent) improve within three weeks (Preston & Kelly, 2006). After sufficient time has elapsed, the person may, effectively, be dead, although exactly how many days that requires has not yet been determined (Wijdicks et al., 2010).

Response for Relatives of a Person Who Is Dying (from page 736): Death affects the entire family, including children and grandchildren. I learned this myself when my mother was dying. A hospice nurse not only gave my mother pain medication (which made it easier for me to be with her) but also counseled me. At the nurse's suggestion, I asked for forgiveness. My mother indicated that there was nothing to forgive. We both felt a peace that would have eluded us without hospice care.

passive euthanasia When a seriously ill person is allowed to die naturally, without active attempts to prolong life.

DNR (do not resuscitate) order A written order from a physician (sometimes initiated by a patient's advance directive or by a health care proxy's request) that no attempt should be made to revive a patient if he or she suffers cardiac or respiratory arrest.

active euthanasia When someone does something that hastens another person's death, with the intention of ending that person's suffering.

FIGURE EP.5

Mercy or Sin? Most Austrians of every age think euthanasia is sometimes merciful. But almost one-third disagree, and some of those think God agrees with them. If those opposite opinions are held by children of a dying parent, who should prevail?

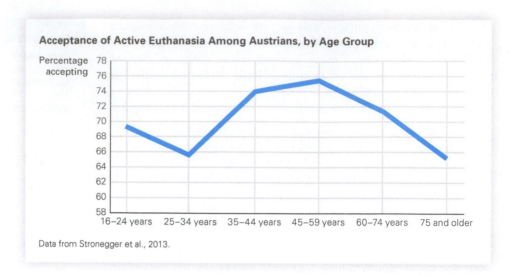

Acceptance of Active Euthanasia Among Austrians, by Age Group

Percentage accepting

Data from Stronegger et al., 2013.

physician-assisted suicide A form of active euthanasia in which a doctor provides the means for someone to end his or her own life, usually by prescribing lethal drugs.

Liberté or Death? In many nations, most people approve death with dignity but most legislators do not. This woman's sign says that 94 percent of her fellow citizens approve legalizing euthanasia.

Attitudes may be changing. For example, over the past decade in Austria, doctors in training have increasingly valued patients' autonomy, which has led to more acceptance of active euthanasia (Stronegger et al., 2013) (see Figure EP.5). In every nation surveyed, some physicians would never perform active euthanasia and others have done so.

The Doctor's Role

Between passive and active euthanasia is another option: A doctor may provide the means for patients to end their own lives, typically by prescribing lethal medication. This is called **physician-assisted suicide.**

Physician-assisted suicide is controversial. Even the name is in dispute: The laws in Oregon assert that such deaths should be called "death with dignity," not suicide. No matter what the name, acceptance varies markedly by culture. Reasons have less to do with people's personal experience than with religion, education, and local values (Verbakel & Jaspers, 2010).

Professional background also makes a difference. In the United States, although most physicians do not support euthanasia of any kind, in part because their goal is to "do no harm," doctors are more likely to support physician-assisted suicide than non-physician euthanasia. The opposite is true for the general public (Emanuel et al., 2016).

Pain: Physical and Psychological

The Netherlands has permitted active euthanasia and physician-assisted suicide since 1980 and extended the law in 2002. The patient must be aware, the request must be clearly expressed, and the goal must be to halt "unbearable suffering" (Buiting et al., 2009). Consequently, Dutch physicians first try to make the suffering bearable via better medication.

However, a qualitative analysis found that "fatigue, pain, decline, negative feelings, loss of self, fear of future suffering, dependency, loss of autonomy, being worn out, being a burden, loneliness, loss of all that makes life worth living, hopelessness, pointlessness and being tired of living were constituent elements of unbearable suffering" (Dees et al., 2011, p. 727). Medication cannot alleviate all those states of mind.

An American physician fears that doctors in the Netherlands pay too little attention to the psychological state of patients, or the ways that dying could be made easier (Gawande, 2014). Between 2011 and 2014, Dutch physicians caused 66 deaths because the person suffered severe, chronic, mental illness. This worries many American psychiatrists (Kim et al., 2016).

Meanwhile, in the United States, the states of Washington, Vermont, and California have joined Oregon in allowing physician-assisted "death with dignity" (but not other forms of active euthanasia). The Oregon law requires the following:

- The dying person must be an Oregon resident and over age 17.
- The dying person must request the lethal drugs twice orally and once in writing.
- Fifteen days must elapse between the first request and the prescription.
- Two physicians must confirm that the person is terminally ill, has less than six months to live, and is competent (i.e., not mentally impaired or depressed).

The law also requires record-keeping and annual reporting. Very few Oregon deaths (less than half of one percent in 2015) occur via physician-provided drugs. Less than half of one percent obtain the drugs, and some of those die naturally, never using the drugs.

As Table EP.4 shows, most requests were primarily for psychological, not biological, reasons—they were more concerned about their autonomy than their pain. In 2015, some 218 Oregonians obtained lethal prescriptions, and 125 legally used drugs to die. Of the remaining 93, about half died naturally, some died but it is not known if they used the drug, and some were alive in January 2016 and could use the drug in the future (generally about 10 percent use their prescriptions the year after obtaining them) (Oregon Public Health Division, 2016).

TABLE EP.4	Oregon Residents' Reasons for Requesting Physician Assistance in Dying, 2015
Percent of Patients Giving Reason (most had several reasons)	
Less able to enjoy life	96
Loss of autonomy	92
Loss of dignity	75
Burden on others	48
Loss of control over body	36
Pain	29
Financial implications of treatment	2

Data from Oregon Public Health Division, 2016, p. 6.

THINK CRITICALLY: Why would someone take all the steps to obtain a lethal prescription and then not use it?

OPPOSING PERSPECTIVES

The "Right to Die"?

Many people fear that legalizing euthanasia or physician-assisted suicide creates a **slippery slope,** that hastening death for the dying who request it will cause a slide toward killing people who are *not* ready to die—especially those who are disabled, old, poor, or of minority ethnicity. The data refute that concern.

In Oregon and the Netherlands, people from non-White groups are *less* likely to use fatal prescriptions. In fact, in Oregon, almost all of those who have done so since 1998 were European American (97 percent), had health insurance, and were well educated (72 percent had some college). There is no evidence of ageism: Most had lived a long life (average age is 71) (see Figure EP.6). Almost all (94 percent) died at home, with close friends or family nearby.

All of these statistics refute both the slippery-slope and the social-abuse arguments. People who die with physician assistance are not likely to slide anywhere they do not wish to go, nor are they likely to be pushed to die.

Nonetheless, even those who believe that people should decide their own medical care are not convinced that they themselves will choose death if given the choice. African Americans are particularly mistrustful of hospices, euthanasia, and physician-assisted suicide (Wicher & Meeker, 2012).

slippery slope The argument that a given action will start a chain of events that will culminate in an undesirable outcome.

The 1980 Netherlands law was revised in 2002 to allow euthanasia not only when a person is terminally ill but also when a person is chronically ill and in pain. The number of Dutch people who choose euthanasia is increasing, about 1 in 30 deaths in 2012. Is this a slippery slope? Some people think so, especially those who believe that God alone decides the moment of death and that anyone who interferes is defying God.

Arguing against that perspective, a cancer specialist writes:

To be forced to continue living a life that one deems intolerable when there are doctors who are willing either to end one's life or to assist one in ending one's own life, is an unspeakable violation of an individual's freedom to live—and to die—as he or she sees fit. Those who would deny patients a legal right to euthanasia or assisted suicide typically appeal to two arguments: a "slippery slope" argument, and an argument about the dangers of abuse. Both are scare tactics, the rhetorical force of which exceeds their logical strength.

[Benatar, 2011, p. 206]

Not everyone agrees with that cancer specialist. Might the decision to die be evidence of depression? If so, no physician should prescribe lethal drugs (Finlay & George, 2011). Declining ability to enjoy life was cited by 96 percent of Oregonians who requested physician-assisted suicide in 2015 (see Table EP.4). Is that a sign of sanity or depression?

Acceptance of death signifies mental health in the aged but not necessarily in the young: Should death with dignity be allowed only after age 54? That would have excluded 10 percent of Oregonians who have used the act thus far. Is the idea that only the old be allowed to choose death an ageist idea, perhaps assuming that the young don't understand what they are choosing or that the old are the ones for whom life is over?

The number of people who die by taking advantage of Oregon's law has increased steadily, from 16 in 1998 (the first year) to 125 in 2015. Some might see that as evidence of a slippery slope. Others consider it proof that the practice is useful though rare (Oregon Public Health Division, 2016).

People with disabling, painful, and terminal conditions who die after choosing futile measures to prolong life are eulogized as "fighters" who "never gave up." That indicates social approval of such choices. This same attitude about life and death is held by most voters and lawmakers around the world. The majority oppose laws that allow physician-assisted suicide.

However, that majority is not evident everywhere.

- In November 2008, in the state of Washington, just north of Oregon, 58 percent of voters approved a death with dignity law.

FIGURE EP.6

Death with Dignity The data on who chooses death with dignity in Oregon do not suggest that people of low SES are unfairly pushed to die. In fact, it is quite the opposite—people who choose physician-assisted suicide tend to be among the older, better-educated, more affluent citizens.

- In 2009, Luxembourg joined the Netherlands and Belgium in allowing active euthanasia.
- In 2011, the Montana senate refused to forbid physician-assisted suicide.
- In 2012, a legal scholar contended that the U.S. Constitution's defense of liberty includes the freedom to decide how to die (Ball, 2012).
- In 2013, Vermont joined Oregon.
- In 2014, New Mexico courts allowed such deaths, but legislators overturned this decision in 2015.

All of that might seem like a growing trend, but proposals to legalize physician-assisted suicide have been defeated in several other U.S. states and in other nations. Most jurisdictions recognize the dilemma: They do not prosecute doctors who help people die as long as it is done privately and quietly. Opposing perspectives, and opposite choices, are evident.

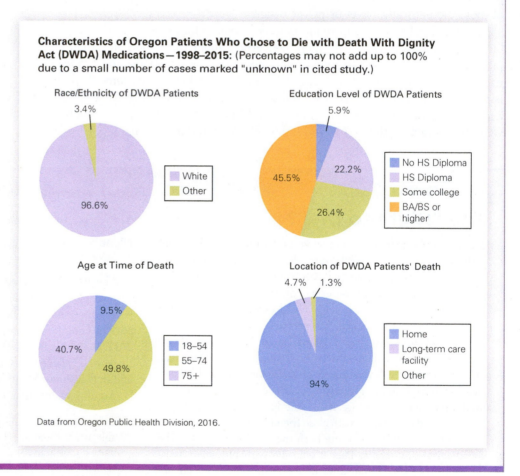

Characteristics of Oregon Patients Who Chose to Die with Death With Dignity Act (DWDA) Medications—1998–2015: (Percentages may not add up to 100% due to a small number of cases marked "unknown" in cited study.)

Race/Ethnicity of DWDA Patients
3.4%
96.6%
- White
- Other

Education Level of DWDA Patients
5.9%
22.2%
45.5%
26.4%
- No HS Diploma
- HS Diploma
- Some college
- BA/BS or higher

Age at Time of Death
9.5%
40.7%
49.8%
- 18–54
- 55–74
- 75+

Location of DWDA Patients' Death
4.7%   1.3%
94%
- Home
- Long-term care facility
- Other

Data from Oregon Public Health Division, 2016.

Advance Directives

Advance directives can describe everything regarding end-of-life care. This may include where the person wants to die and what should happen to their body after death. Typically the focus is on medical measures.

Among the explicit statements in medical directives are: whether artificial feeding, breathing, or heart stimulation should be used; whether antibiotics that might merely prolong life or pain medication that causes coma or hallucinations are desired; whether religious music or clergy are welcome; and so on.

The legality of such directives varies by jurisdiction. Sometimes a lawyer must verify the advance directive; sometimes a written request, signed and witnessed, is adequate.

Many people want personal choice about death; thus they approve of advance directives in theory but are uncertain about specifics. For example, few know that restarting the heart may extend life for decades in a healthy young adult but is likely to cause major brain damage, or merely prolong dying, in a frail elder.

Even *talking* about choices is controversial. Originally, the draft of U.S. Affordable Care Act allowed payment to doctors for describing treatment options (e.g., Kettl, 2010). Opponents called those "death panels," an accusation that almost torpedoed the entire package. As a result, that measure was scrapped: Physicians cannot bill for time spent explaining palliative care, options for treatment, or dying.

Wills and Proxies

Advance directives often include a living will and/or a health care proxy. Hospitals and hospices strongly recommend both of these. Nonetheless, most people resist: A study of cancer patients in a leading hospital found that only 16 percent had living wills and only 48 percent had designated a proxy (Halpern et al., 2011).

A **living will** indicates what medical intervention a person wants if they become unable to express their preferences. (If the person is conscious, hospital personnel ask about each specific procedure, requiring consent. Patients who are conscious can then override what they wrote in their living will.)

The reason a person might want to override their own earlier wishes is that living wills include phrases such as "incurable," "reasonable chance of recovery," and "extraordinary measures," and it is difficult to know what those phrases mean until a specific issue arises. Even then, medical judgments vary. Doctors and family members disagree about what is "extraordinary" or "reasonable."

A **health care proxy** is a person who makes medical decisions for someone who is unable to do so. That can guide medical treatment, but proxies find it difficult to allow a loved one to die. A larger problem is that few people—experts included—understand the risks, benefits, and alternatives to every medical procedure. It is hard to decide for oneself, much less for a patient or family member, exactly when the risks outweigh the benefits.

Medical professionals advocate advance directives, but

> Working within the reality of mortality, coming to death is then an inevitable part of life, an event to be lived rather than a problem to be solved. Ideally, we would live the end of our life from the same values that have given meaning to the story of our life up to that time. But in a medical crisis, there is little time, language, or ritual to guide patients and families in conceptualizing or expressing their values and goals.

> [*Farber & Farber, 2014, p. 109*]

Honest conversation is needed long before a crisis occurs (Rogne & McCune, 2014).

advance directives Any description of what a person wants to happen as they die and after they die. This can include medical measures, visitors, funeral arrangements, cremation, and so on.

Especially for People Without Advance Directives Why do very few young adults have advance directives? (see response, page 745)

living will A document that indicates what medical intervention an individual prefers if he or she is not conscious when a decision is to be expressed. For example, some do not want mechanical breathing.

health care proxy A person chosen to make medical decisions if a patient is unable to do so, as when in a coma.

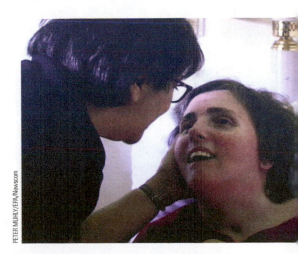

Is She Thinking? This photo of Terri Schiavo with her mother was released by those who believed Terri could recover. Other photos (not released) and other signs told the opposite story. Although autopsy showed that Terri's brain had shrunk markedly, remember that hope is part of being human. That helps explain why some people were passionately opposed to removal of Terri's stomach tube.

WHAT HAVE YOU LEARNED?

1. What is a good death?
2. According to Kübler-Ross, what are the five stages of emotions associated with dying?
3. Why doesn't everyone agree with Kübler-Ross's stages?
4. What determines whether a dying person will receive hospice care?
5. What are the guiding principles of hospice care, and why is each one important?
6. Why is the double effect legal everywhere, even though it speeds death?
7. What differences of opinion are there with respect to the definition of death?
8. What is the difference between passive and active euthanasia?
9. What are the four conditions of physician-assisted "death with dignity" in Oregon?
10. Why would a person who has a living will also need a health care proxy?

Affirmation of Life

Grief and mourning are part of living. Human relationships are life-sustaining, but every adult loses someone they love. That can lead to depression, or to life lived more deeply.

Grief

grief The deep sorrow that people feel at the death of another. Grief is personal and unpredictable.

Grief is the powerful sorrow that an individual feels at a profound loss, especially when a loved one dies. Grief is deep and personal, an anguish that can overtake daily life. Sheryl Sandberg said after her husband died, "I was swallowed up in the deep fog of grief—what I think of as the void—an emptiness that fills your heart, your lungs, constricts your ability to think or even to breathe" (Sandberg, 2016).

Normal Grief

Grief is a normal human emotion, even when it leads to unusual actions and thoughts. Grief is manifest in uncontrollable crying, sleeplessness, and irrational and delusional thoughts. When her husband died, Joan Didion kept his shoes in the closet, thinking he would need them if he came back. She wrote:

> Grief has no distance. Grief comes in waves, paroxysms, sudden apprehensions that weaken the knees and blind the eyes and obliterate the dailiness of life. . . . I see now that my insistence on spending that first night alone was more complicated than it seemed, a primitive instinct . . . There was a level on which I believed that what had happened remained reversible. That is why I needed to be alone. . . . I needed to be alone so that he could come back. This was the beginning of my year of magical thinking.

> [Didion, 2005, pp. 27, 32, 33]

Video: Bereavement: Grief in Early and Late Adulthood presents the views of a young-adult daughter and middle-aged mother on the death of the mother's brother, to whom they were both close.

When a loved one dies, loneliness, denial, anger, and sorrow come in rapid waves, overtaking normal human needs—to sleep, to eat, to think. Grief usually hits hardest in the first week after death and then lingers—with much of its impact dependent on the details of mourning, soon to be discussed.

But first, let us recognize that grief is not always normal. Some people react to death in ways that are pathological, with cognitive as well as emotional problems (Saavedra Pérez et al., 2015).

Complicated Grief

complicated grief A type of grief that impedes a person's future life, usually because the person clings to sorrow or is buffeted by contradictory emotions.

About 10 percent of all mourners experience **complicated grief,** a type of grief that impedes the person's future life (Neimeyer & Jordan, 2013; Galatzer-Levy & Bonanno, 2016).

One type of complication is called **absent grief,** when a bereaved person does not seem to grieve. This is a common first reaction, but if it continues, absent grief can trigger physical or psychological symptoms—for instance, trouble breathing or walking, sudden panic attacks, or depression. If such symptoms appear for no reason, the underlying cause might be grief that was never expressed.

One function of funerals and bereavement customs is to help everyone express their sorrow, thus avoiding absent grief. The laws of some nations—China, Chile, and Spain, for example—mandate paid bereavement leave, but this is not true in the United States (Meagher, 2013).

People who live and work where no one knows their personal lives have no one to help them grieve. Instead they may keep their sorrow private, the opposite of what mourners need.

Modern life also increases the incidence of **disenfranchised grief,** which is "not merely unnoticed, forgotten, or hidden; it is socially disallowed and unsupported" (Corr & Corr, 2013b, p. 135). For instance, many laws rule that only a current spouse or close blood relative may decide on funeral arrangements, disposal of the body, and other matters. This made sense when all adults were close to their relatives, but it may result in "gagged grief and beleaguered bereavement" when, for instance, a longtime but unmarried partner is excluded (Green & Grant, 2008, p. 275).

Parents who lose a fetus or newborn may be disenfranchised by those who say, "You never knew that baby; you can have another." Or, when a beloved dog or cat dies, outsiders may dismiss as foolish any grief at their death (Williams & Green, 2016).

Another complication is **incomplete grief.** Normally grief is a process, intense at first, diminished over time, eventually reaching closure. Customs such as viewing the dead, or throwing dirt on the grave, or scattering ashes move the process of grief forward, allowing expression and then recovery. However, many circumstances can interfere with this process.

Traumatic death is always unexpected, and that causes denial, anger, and depression to undercut the emotions of grief (Kauffman, 2013). Murders and suicides often trigger police investigations and reporters; inquiries are made when mourners need to grieve instead of answering questions.

An autopsy may prevent closure if the griever believes that the body will rise or that the soul does not immediately leave the body. Inability to recover a body, as with soldiers who are missing in action or with victims of a major flood or fire, may prevent grief from being expressed and thereby hinder completion.

After natural or human-caused disasters, including hurricanes and wars, incomplete grief is common because procuring the basics of life—food, shelter, and so on—takes precedence over emotional needs. One result of incomplete grief is that people die of causes not directly attributable to the disaster, becoming victims of the indifference of others and of their own diminished self-care. This emotional loss is also apparent when a spouse dies, with the likelihood of death increased about 40 percent—especially for widowers (who may have a harder time expressing grief) and for those who have no chronic conditions themselves (Boyle et al., 2011).

Mourning

Grief splinters people into jumbled pieces, making them vulnerable. Mourning reassembles them, making them whole again and able to rejoin the larger community. To be more specific, **mourning** is the public and ritualistic expression of bereavement, the ceremonies and behaviors that a religion or culture prescribes to honor the dead.

Empty Boots The body of a young army corporal killed near Baghdad has been sent home to his family in Mississippi for a funeral and burial, but his fellow soldiers in Iraq also need to express their grief. The custom is to hold an informal memorial service, placing the dead soldier's boots, helmet, and gun in the middle of a circle of mourners, who weep, pray, and reminisce.

absent grief When mourners do not grieve, either because other people do not allow expressions of grief or because the mourners do not allow themselves to feel sadness.

disenfranchised grief A situation in which certain people, although they are bereaved, are prevented from mourning publicly by cultural customs or social restrictions.

incomplete grief When circumstances, such as a police investigation or an autopsy, interfere with the process of grieving.

Response for People Without Advance Directives (from page 743): Young adults tend to avoid thinking realistically about their own deaths. This attitude is emotional, not rational. The actual task of preparing the documents is easy (the forms can be downloaded; no lawyer is needed). Young adults have no trouble doing other future-oriented things, such as getting a tetanus shot or enrolling in a pension plan.

mourning The ceremonies and behaviors that a religion or culture prescribes for people to express their grief after a death.

Failure of Revenge Terrorists killed 11 staff members of *Charlie Hebdo*, a satirical weekly magazine, in Paris to protest publication of disrespectful cartoons, but their act of revenge had an opposite effect. Thousands of bouquets and mourners came to the site, some with a new slogan, "Je suis Charlie." Five million copies of the publication were distributed. Public mourning, shown here, reaffirmed the value of an uncensored press. Sadly, a few people expressed revenge after the attack, killing more innocent people.

How Mourning Helps

Mourning is needed because, as you just read, the grief-stricken are vulnerable not only to irrational thoughts but also to self-destructive acts. Some eat too little or drink too much; some forget caution as they drive or even as they walk across the street.

Physical and mental health dips in the recently bereaved, and the rate of suicide increases. The death of a child is particularly hard on the parents, who sometimes distance themselves from each other or from other relatives. Shared mourning rituals are one way in which families help each other.

A large study in Sweden of children who had experienced the death of a brother or sister found that in early and middle adulthood they were more likely to die than other Swedes. That was true even if their siblings had not killed themselves, but if they had, survivors were three times as likely to commit suicide as other Swedish adults of the same age and background (Rostila et al., 2013).

Some people, and some deaths, are especially likely to benefit from the customs of mourning, and yet particularly likely not to have those rituals. For example, self-blame and anger at the deceased are especially common after suicide, making mourning complicated and private.

Customs are designed to help people move from grief toward reaffirmation (Harlow, 2005; Corr & Corr, 2013b). For this reason, eulogies emphasize the dead person's good qualities; people who did not personally know the deceased person attend wakes, funerals, or memorial services to help comfort the survivors.

If the dead person was a public figure, mourners may include thousands, even millions. They express their sorrow to one another, stare at photos and listen to music that remind them of the dead person, weep as they watch funerals on television. Mourners often pledge to affirm the best of the deceased, forgetting any criticisms they might have had in the past.

Thus, mourning allows public expression to channel and contain private grief. Examples include the Jewish custom of sitting shiva at home for a week, or the three days of active sorrow among some Muslim groups, or the 10 days of ceremonies beginning at the next full moon following a Hindu death.

Memories often return to the immediate relatives and friends on the anniversary of a death, so cultures include annual rituals such as visiting a grave or lighting a candle in memory. Many people who have distanced themselves from the religious rituals of their community find solace in returning to them when a person dies (Rosenblatt, 2013).

Mourners do whatever they believe will help the deceased. Certain prayers may be repeated to ensure a good afterlife. Some religions contend that the spirits of the dead remain on Earth and affect those still living; mourners who believe this typically provide food and other comforts to the dead so that their spirits will be benevolent. Some religions hold that the dead live on only in memory: They may preserve mementos, or name a baby after a dead person, or visit a gravesite on a particular day.

The Western practice of building a memorial, dedicating a plaque, or naming a location for a dead person is antithetical to some Eastern cultures. Indeed, some Asians believe that the spirit should be allowed to leave in peace, and thus all possessions, signs, and other evidence of the dead are removed after proper prayers.

Survivor? Two days after the typhoon Haiyan struck the Philippines, this woman mourns her husband, one of more than 6,000 dead. She herself is at risk, as she is one of more than 3 million who lost their homes. That makes her much more likely to sicken and die in the coming year than in the past one.

Same Situation, Far Apart: Gateway to Heaven or Final Rest? Many differences are obvious between a Roman Catholic burial in Mbongolwane, South Africa (left), and a Hindu cremation procession in Bali, Indonesia (right). The South Africans believe the soul goes to heaven; the Indonesians believe the body returns to the elements. In both places, however, friends and neighbors gather to honor the dead and comfort their relatives.

> **THINK CRITICALLY:** Do you think current wars are fueled by the impulse to assign blame?

Placing Blame and Seeking Meaning

A common impulse after death is for the survivors to assess blame—for medical measures not taken, for laws not enforced, for unhealthy habits not changed. The bereaved sometimes blame the dead person, sometimes themselves, and sometimes others. In November 2011, Michael Jackson's personal doctor, Conrad Murray, was found guilty and jailed for prescribing the drugs that led to the singer's death. Many fans and family members cheered at the verdict; Murray was one of the few who blamed Jackson, not himself.

For public tragedies, nations accuse one another. Blame is not rational or proportional. For instance, outrage at the assassination of Archduke Francis Ferdinand of Austria by a Serbian terrorist in 1914 provoked a conflict between Austria and Serbia—soon joined by a dozen other nations—that led to the four years and 16 million deaths of World War I. More recently, in many nations, *Islamophobia* blames millions of peace-loving Muslims for deaths caused by a small number of Muslim terrorists.

As you remember, denial and anger appear first on Kübler-Ross's list of reactions to dying and death; ideally, people move on to acceptance. Finding meaning may be crucial to the reaffirmation that follows grief.

In some cases, this search starts with preserving memories: Displaying photographs and personal effects and telling anecdotes about the dead person are central to memorial services. With major disasters, survivors often seek a goal to honor the memory of the dead. Many people believe that Israel would not have been created without the Holocaust or that marriage and love between same-sex couples would not have been recognized by the U.S. Supreme Court without HIV/AIDS.

Mourners may be helped by strangers who have experienced a similar loss. This explains groups of parents of murdered children, of mothers whose teenagers were killed by drunk drivers, of widows of firefighters who died at the World Trade Center on September 11, 2001, of relatives of passengers who died in the same plane crash, and many more.

Mourners sometimes want strangers to know about a death. Pages of paid obituaries are found in every major newspaper, and spontaneous memorials (graffiti, murals, stuffed animals, flowers) appear in public spaces, such as at a spot on a roadside where a fatal crash occurred. This practice was once discouraged, but no

The Human Touch Benetha Coleman fights Ebola in this treatment center by taking temperatures, washing bodies, and drawing blood, but she also comforts those with symptoms. Why would anyone risk working here? Benetha has recovered from Ebola, and, like many survivors of a disaster, she wants to help others who suffer.

Mommy's Memorial Praying beside the ghost bike at the spot where an 18-wheeler killed cyclist Kathryn Rickson may help these two grieve and then recover. Grief is less likely to destroy survivors when markers or rituals are observed.

longer. Authorities realize that public commemoration aids grief and mourning, building community: Public markers of bouquets and so on are dismantled only when flowers fade and time has passed (Dickinson & Hoffmann, 2010).

Organizations that combat a particular problem (such as breast cancer or handguns) find their most dedicated donors, marchers, and advocates among people who have lost a loved one to that specific danger. When someone dies, survivors often designate a charity that is connected to the deceased. Then mourners contribute, and the death has led to some good.

Another way in which people find meaning in death is to gather in vigils, rallies, or protests. As already cited, such actions can take a destructive turn, but sometimes symbols are used to attain a good result:

- When an atom bomb was dropped in Hiroshima, Japan, the aftermath led millions of children worldwide to make origami cranes. (No atom bombs since then.)
- When a cyclist was killed by a car, protesters erected "ghost bikes" and ritualistically raised their bicycles, leading to thousands of miles of bike lanes and city-wide bike sharing in New York City.
- When a racist man killed nine members of a prayer group in Charleston, South Carolina, the legislature voted to remove the Confederate flag from the State Capitol.

These are specific manifestations, but the general rule was expressed by Sandberg: "When life sucks you under, you can kick against the bottom, break the surface, and breathe again. I learned that in the face of the void—or in the face of any challenge—you can choose joy and meaning" (Sandberg, 2016).

Diversity of Reactions

As you see, how someone deals with bereavement depends on the customs and attitudes of their community. Past experiences linger. Children who lost their parents might be more distraught decades later when someone else dies. Attachment history matters (Stroebe et al., 2010). Older adults who were securely attached as children may be more likely to experience **normal grief**; those whose attachment was insecure-avoidant may have absent grief; and those who were insecure-resistant may become stuck, unable to find meaning in death and thus unable to reaffirm their own lives.

Reaffirmation does not mean forgetting; *continuing bonds* are evident years after death (Stroebe et al., 2012). Such bonds may help or hinder reaffirmation, depending on the past relationship between the individuals and on the circumstances of the death.

Although in Western nations hallucinations (seeing ghosts, hearing voices) are a sign of complicated grief, ongoing memories and thoughts of the dead person as a role model are "linked to greater personal growth" (Field & Filanosky, 2010, p. 24). Often survivors write letters or talk to the deceased person, or consider events—a sunrise, a butterfly, a rainstorm—as messages of comfort.

Bereavement theory once held that mourners should grieve and then move on. It was thought that if this progression did not take place, pathological grief could result, with the person either not grieving enough (absent grief) or grieving too long (incomplete grief). Current research finds a much wider variety of reactions (Rubin et al., 2012), with continuing bonds a normal occurrence.

normal grief The usual response to a loss. Initial sadness and then recovery are normal.

In **Video: Bereavement and Grief: Late Adulthood,** people discuss their experiences with the loss of beloved family members and friends—and all agree that these losses have been very difficult experiences.

Resilience After a Death

Earlier studies overestimated the frequency of pathological grief. For obvious reasons, scientists usually began research on mourning with mourners—that is, with people who had recently experienced the death of a loved one. With mourners, it was impossible to backtrack and study personality before the death.

Furthermore, psychologists often treated people who had difficulty dealing with a death. Some patients experienced absent grief; others felt disenfranchised grief; some were overcome by unremitting sadness many months after the loss; still others could not find meaning in a violent, sudden, unexpected death. All of these people were likely to consult therapists, who helped them while publishing descriptions of the problems and solutions.

We now know that personality has a major effect on grief and mourning (Boyraz et al., 2012). Pathological mourners are *not* typical. Almost everyone experiences several deaths over a lifetime—of parents and grandparents, of a spouse or a friend. Most feel sadness at first but then resume their customary activities, functioning as well a few months later as they did before.

The variety of reactions to death was evident in a longitudinal study that began by assessing thousands of married older adults in greater Detroit. Over several years, 319 became widows or widowers. Most were reinterviewed at six and 18 months after the death of their spouse, and about one-third were seen again four years later (Boerner et al., 2004, 2005).

General trends were evident. Almost all of the widows and widowers idealized their past marriages, remembering them more positively after the death than they experienced them at the first interview, years before the death. This idealization is a normal phenomenon that other research finds connected to psychological health, not pathology (O'Rourke et al., 2010b). After the death, many thought of their spouse several times each day. With time, such thoughts became less frequent, as expected with mourning.

This longitudinal study found notable variations. Four types of responses were evident (Galatzer-Levy & Bonanno, 2012).

1. Sixty-six percent were resilient. They were sad at first, but six months later they were about as happy and productive as they had been before the death.
2. Fifteen percent were depressed at every assessment, before as well as years after the death. If this research had begun only after the death, it might seem that the loss caused depression. However, the pre-loss assessment suggests that some of these people were chronically depressed, not stuck in grief.
3. Ten percent were *less* depressed after the death than before, often because they had been caregivers for their seriously ill partners.
4. Nine percent were slow to recover, functioning poorly at 18 months. By four years after the death, however, they functioned almost as well as they had before.

The slow recovery of this fourth group suggests that some of them experienced complicated grief. Note, however, that they were far from the majority of the participants.

Many studies show that grief and then recovery is the usual pattern, with only about 10 percent needing professional help to deal with a death. A person's health, finances, and personality all contribute to postmortem reactions.

Crucial are the person's beliefs before the death (Mancini et al., 2011). If someone tends to have a positive perspective, believing that justice will prevail and that life has meaning, then the death of a close family member may deepen, not weaken, those beliefs. Depression is less likely if a person has already accepted the reality of death.

Practical Applications

The research suggests that many people experience powerful, complicated, and unexpected emotions when death occurs. To help the griever, a friend should listen and sympathize, never implying that the person is either too grief-stricken or not grief-stricken enough.

A bereaved person *might or might not* want to visit the grave, light a candle, cherish a memento, pray, or sob. Whatever the action, he or she may want to be alone or may want company. Those who have been taught to bear grief stoically may be doubly distressed if a friend advises them to cry but they cannot. Conversely, those whose cultures expect loud wailing may resent it if they are urged to hush.

Even absent grief—in which the bereaved person does none of these things— might be appropriate. So might the opposite reaction, when people want to talk again and again about their loss, gathering sympathy, ascribing blame, and finding meaning.

As you see, assumptions might be inaccurate; people are much more varied than simple explanations of grief might suggest. One researcher cited an example of a 13-year-old girl who refused to leave home after her 17-year-old brother was shot dead going to school. The therapist was supposed to get her in school again.

It would have been easy to assume that the girl was afraid of dying on the street and to arrange for a friend to accompany her on her way to school. But careful listening revealed the real reason she stayed home: She worried that her depressed mother might kill herself if she were left alone (Crenshaw, 2013). To help the daughter, the mother had to be helped.

No matter what fears arise, what rituals are followed, or what grief entails, the result of mourning may be to give the living a deeper appreciation of themselves and others. In fact, a theme frequently sounded by those who work with the dying and the bereaved is that death leads to a greater appreciation of life, especially of the value of intimate, caring relationships.

George Vaillant is a psychiatrist who studied a group of men from the time they were Harvard students through old age. He writes this about funerals: "With tears of remembrance running down our cheeks. . . . Remembered love lives triumphantly today" (Vaillant, 2008, p. 133).

It is fitting to end this Epilogue, and this book, with a reminder of the creative work of living. As first described in Chapter 1, the study of human development is a science, with topics to be researched, understood, and explained. But the process of living is an art as well as a science, with strands of love and sorrow woven into each person's unique tapestry. Death, when it leads to hope; dying, when it is accepted; and grief, when it fosters affirmation—all add meaning to birth, growth, development, and love.

WHAT HAVE YOU LEARNED?

1. What is grief, and what are some of its signs?

2. List three types of complicated grief. Why is each type considered "complicated"?

3. What are the differences among grief, mourning, and bereavement?

4. How can a grieving person find meaning in death?

5. How might reactions such as talking to the deceased make it both easier and more difficult to adjust to the death of a loved one?

6. If a person still feels a loss six months after a death, is that pathological?

7. What should friends and relatives remember when helping someone who is grieving?

SUMMARY

Death and Hope

1. Death and dying have always led to strong emotions. However, death is not what it once was. For example, fewer people have personally witnessed the dying process.

2. In ancient times, death was considered a connection between the living, the dead, and the spirit world. People respected the dead and tried to live their lives so that their own death and afterlife would be good.

3. Every religion includes rituals and beliefs about death. These vary a great deal, but all bring hope to the living and strengthen the community.

4. Death has various meanings, depending partly on the age of the person involved. For example, young children are concerned about being separated from those they see every day; older children want to know specifics of death.

5. Terror management theory finds that some emerging adults cope with death anxiety by defiantly doing whatever is risky. Adults tend to worry about leaving something undone or abandoning family members; older adults are more accepting of death.

Choices in Dying

6. Everyone wants a good death. A death that is painless and that comes at the end of a long life is more likely than it was a century ago. However, other aspects of a good death—quick, at home, surrounded by loved ones—are less likely than they were.

7. The emotions of people who are dying change over time. Some may move from denial to acceptance, although stages of dying are much more variable than originally proposed. Honest conversation helps many, but not all, dying persons.

8. Hospice caregivers meet the biological and psychological needs of terminally ill people and their families. This can occur at home or at a specific place. Palliative care relieves pain and other uncomfortable aspects of dying.

9. Drugs that reduce pain as well as hasten dying, producing a double effect, are acceptable to many. However, euthanasia and physician-assisted suicide are controversial. A few nations and some U.S. states condone these; most do not.

10. Since 1980, death has been defined as occurring when brain waves stop; however, many measures now prolong life when no conscious thinking occurs. The need for a more precise, updated definition is apparent, but it is not agreed what the new definition should be.

11. Advance directives, such as a living will and a health care proxy, are recommended for everyone. However, no one can predict all possible interventions that may occur. Family members as well as professionals often disagree about specifics.

Affirmation of Life

12. Grief is overwhelming sorrow. It may be irrational and complicated, absent or disenfranchised.

13. Mourning rituals channel human grief, helping people move to affirm life. Most people are able to do this, although emotions of revenge may be harmful.

14. Feelings of continuing bonds with the deceased are no longer thought to be pathological. Most people who are still depressed years after a death are people who were depressed before the death. Everyone needs comfort and understanding after death, particularly after violent death.

KEY TERMS

terror management theory (p. 731)
hospice (p. 737)
palliative care (p. 738)
double effect (p. 738)
passive euthanasia (p. 739)

DNR (do not resuscitate) order (p. 739)
active euthanasia (p. 739)
physician-assisted suicide (p. 740)
slippery slope (p. 741)

advance directives (p. 743)
living will (p. 743)
health care proxy (p. 743)
grief (p. 744)
complicated grief (p. 744)

absent grief (p. 745)
disenfranchised grief (p. 745)
incomplete grief (p. 745)
mourning (p. 745)
normal grief (p. 748)

APPLICATIONS

1. Death is sometimes said to be hidden, even taboo. Ask 10 people whether they have ever been with someone who was dying. Note not only the yes and no answers but also the details and reactions. For instance, how many of the deaths occurred in hospitals?

2. Find quotes about death in *Bartlett's Familiar Quotations* or a similar collection. Do you see any historical or cultural patterns of acceptance, denial, or fear?

3. Every aspect of dying is controversial in modern society. Do an Internet search for a key term such as *euthanasia* or *grief*. Analyze the information and the underlying assumptions.

4. People of varying ages have different attitudes toward death. Ask people of different ages (ideally, at least one person younger than 20, one adult between 20 and 60, and one older person) what thoughts they have about their own death. What differences do you find?

Appendix: More About Research Methods

This appendix explains how to learn about any topic. It is crucial that you distinguish valid conclusions from wishful thinking. Such learning begins with your personal experience.

Make It Personal

Think about your life, observe your behavior, and watch the people around you. Pay careful attention to details of expression, emotion, and behavior. The more you see, the more fascinated, curious, and reflective you will become. Ask questions and listen carefully and respectfully to what other people say regarding development.

Whenever you ask specific questions as part of an assignment, **remember that observing ethical standards (see Chapter 1) comes first.** *Before* you interview anyone, inform the person of your purpose and assure him or her of confidentiality. Promise not to identify the person in your report (use a pseudonym) and do not repeat any personal details that emerge in the interview to anyone (friends or strangers). Your instructor will provide further ethical guidance. If you might publish what you've learned, get in touch with your college's Institutional Review Board (IRB).

Read the Research

No matter how deeply you think about your own experiences, and no matter how intently you listen to others whose background is unlike yours, you also need to read scholarly published work in order to fully understand any topic that interests you. Be skeptical about magazine or newspaper reports; some are bound to be simplified, exaggerated, or biased.

Professional Journals and Books

Part of the process of science is that conclusions are not considered solid until they are corroborated in many studies, which means that you should consult several sources on any topic. **Five journals in human development** are:

- *Developmental Psychology* (published by the American Psychological Association)
- *Child Development* (Society for Research in Child Development)
- *Developmental Review* (Elsevier)
- *Human Development* (Karger)
- *Developmental Science* (Wiley)

These journals differ in the types of articles and studies they publish, but all are well respected and peer-reviewed, which means that other scholars review each article submitted and recommend that it be accepted, rejected, or revised. Every article includes references to other recent work.

Also look at journals that specialize in longer reviews from the perspective of a researcher.

- *Child Development Perspectives* (from Society for Research in Child Development)
- *Perspectives on Psychological Science* (This is published by the Association for Psychological Science. APS publishes several excellent journals, none specifically on development but every issue has at least one article that is directly relevant.)

Beyond these six are literally thousands of other professional journals, each with a particular perspective or topic, including many in sociology, family studies, economics, and so on. To judge them, look for journals that are peer-reviewed. Also consider the following details: the background of the author (research funded by corporations tends to favor their products); the nature of the publisher (professional organizations, as in the first two journals above, protect their reputations); how long the journal has been published (the volume number tells you that). Some interesting work does not meet these criteria, but these are guides to quality.

Many **books** cover some aspect of development. Single-author books are likely to present only one viewpoint. That view may be insightful, but it is limited. You might consult a *handbook,* which is a book that includes many authors and many topics. One good handbook in development, now in its seventh edition (a sign that past scholars have found it useful) is:

- *Handbook of Child Psychology and Developmental Science* (7th ed.), edited by Richard M. Lerner, 2015, Hoboken, NJ: Wiley.
- Another set of handbooks—*Handbook of the Biology of Aging, Handbook of the Psychology of Aging,* and *Handbook of Aging and the Social Sciences*—is now in its eighth edition, published by Academic Press in 2016.

Dozens of other good handbooks are available, many of which focus on a particular age, perspective, or topic.

The Internet

The **Internet** is a mixed blessing, useful to every novice and experienced researcher but dangerous as well. Every library worldwide and most homes in North America, Western Europe, and East Asia have computers that provide access to journals and other information. If you're doing research in a library, ask for help from the librarians; many of them can guide you in the most effective ways to conduct online searches. In addition, other students, friends, and even strangers can be helpful.

Virtually everything is on the Internet, not only massive national and international statistics but also accounts of very personal experiences. Photos, charts, quizzes, ongoing experiments, newspapers from around the world, videos, and much more are available at a click. Every journal has a Web site, with tables of contents, abstracts, and sometimes full texts. (An abstract gives the key findings; for the full text, you may need to consult the library's copy of the print version.)

Unfortunately, you can spend many frustrating hours sifting through information that is useless, trash, or tangential. *Directories* (which list general topics or areas and then move you step by step in the direction you choose) and *search engines* (which give you all the sites that use a particular word or words) can help you select appropriate information. Each directory or search engine provides somewhat different lists; none provides only the most comprehensive and accurate sites.

Sometimes organizations figure out ways to make their links appear first, even though they are biased. With experience and help, you will find the best sites for you, but you will also encounter some junk no matter how experienced you are.

Anybody can put anything online, regardless of its truth or fairness, so you need a very critical eye. Make sure you have several divergent sources for every "fact" you find; consider who provided the information and why. Every controversial issue has sites that forcefully advocate opposite viewpoints, sometimes with biased statistics and narrow perspectives.

Here are five Internet sites that are quite reliable:

- *embryo.soad.umich.edu* The Multidimensional Human Embryo. Presents MRI images of a human embryo at various stages of development, accompanied by brief explanations.
- *childdevelopmentinfo.com* Child Development Institute. A useful site, with links and articles on child development and information on common childhood psychological disorders.
- *eric.ed.gov* Education Resources Information Center (ERIC). Provides links to many education-related sites and includes brief descriptions of each.
- *www.nia.nih.gov* National Institute on Aging. Includes information about current research on aging.
- *www.cdc.gov/nchs/hus.htm* The National Center for Health Statistics issues an annual report on health trends, called *Health, United States*.

Every source—you, your interviewees, journals, books, and the Internet—is helpful. Do not depend on any particular one. Avoid plagiarism and prejudice by citing every source and noting objectivity, validity, and credibility. Your own analysis, opinions, words, and conclusions are crucial, backed up by science, as explained in Chapter 1.

Additional Terms and Concepts

As emphasized throughout the text, the study of development is a science. Social scientists spend years in graduate school, studying methods and statistics. Chapter 1 touches on some of these matters (observation and experiments; correlation and statistical significance; independent and dependent variables; experimental and control groups; cross-sectional, longitudinal, and cross-sequential research), but there is much more. A few additional aspects of research are presented here to help you evaluate research wherever you find it.

Who Participates?

The entire group of people about whom a scientist wants to learn is called a **population.** Generally, a research population is quite large—not usually the world's entire population of more than 7 billion, but perhaps all the 4 million babies born in the United States last year, or all the 31 million Japanese currently over age 65.

The particular individuals who are studied in a specific research project are called the **participants.** They are used as a **sample** of the larger group. Ideally, the participants are a **representative sample,** that is, a sample that reflects the entire population. Every peer-reviewed, published study reports details on the sample.

Selection of the sample is crucial. People who volunteer, or people who have telephones, or people who have some particular condition are not a *random sample;* in a random sample, everyone in a particular population is equally likely to be

population The entire group of individuals who are of particular concern in a scientific study, such as all the children of the world or all newborns who weigh less than 3 pounds.

participants The people who are studied in a research project. Participants is the term now used in psychology; other disciplines still call these people "subjects."

sample A group of individuals drawn from a specified population. A sample might be the low-birthweight babies born in four particular hospitals that are representative of all hospitals.

representative sample A group of research participants who reflect the relevant characteristics of the larger population whose attributes are under study.

selected. To avoid *selection bias,* some studies are *prospective,* beginning with an entire cluster of people (for instance, every baby born on a particular day) and then tracing the development of some particular characteristic.

For example, prospective studies find the antecedents of heart disease, or child abuse, or high school dropout rates—all of which are much harder to find if the study is *retrospective,* beginning with those who had heart attacks, experienced abuse, or left school. Thus, although retrospective research finds that most high school dropouts say they disliked school, prospective research finds that some who like school still decide to drop out and then later say they hated school, while others dislike school but stay to graduate. Prospective research discovers how many students are in these last two categories; retrospective research on people who have already dropped out does not.

Research Design

Every researcher begins not only by formulating a hypothesis but also by learning what other scientists have discovered about the topic in question and what methods might be useful and ethical in designing research. Often they include measures to guard against inadvertently finding only the results they expect. For example, the people who actually gather the data may not know the purpose of the research. Scientists say that these data gatherers are **blind** to the hypothesized outcome. Participants are sometimes "blind" as well, because otherwise they might, for instance, respond the way they think they should.

Another crucial aspect of research design is to define exactly what is to be studied. Researchers establish an **operational definition** of whatever phenomenon they will be examining, defining each variable by describing specific, observable behavior. This is essential in quantitative research, but it is also useful in qualitative research. For example, if a researcher wants to know when babies begin to walk, does walking include steps taken while holding on? Is one unsteady step enough? Some parents say yes, but the usual operational definition of *walking* is "takes at least three steps without holding on." This operational definition allows comparisons worldwide, making it possible to discover, for example, that well-fed African babies tend to walk earlier than well-fed European babies.

Operational definitions are difficult to formulate, but they are essential when personality traits are studied. How should *aggression* or *sharing* or *shyness* be defined? Lack of an operational definition leads to contradictory results. For instance, critics report that infant day care makes children more aggressive, but advocates report that it makes them less passive. In this case, both may be seeing the same behavior but defining it differently. For any scientist, operational definitions are crucial, and studies usually include descriptions of how they measured attitudes or behavior.

Reporting Results

You already know that results should be reported in sufficient detail so that another scientist can analyze the conclusions and replicate the research. Various methods, populations, and research designs may produce divergent conclusions. For that reason, handbooks, some journals, and some articles are called *reviews:* They summarize past research. Often, when studies are similar in operational definitions and methods, the review is a **meta-analysis,** which combines the findings of many studies to present an overall conclusion.

Table 1.4 (p. 22) describes some statistical measures. One of them is *statistical significance,* which indicates whether or not a particular result could have occurred by chance.

blind The condition of data gatherers (and sometimes participants, as well) who are deliberately kept ignorant of the purpose of the research so that they cannot unintentionally bias the results.

operational definition A description of the specific, observable behavior that will constitute the variable that is to be studied, so that any reader will know whether that behavior occurred or not. Operational definitions may be arbitrary (e.g., an IQ score at or above 130 is operationally defined as "gifted"), but they must be precise.

meta-analysis A technique of combining results of many studies to come to an overall conclusion. Meta-analysis is powerful, in that small samples can be added together to lead to significant conclusions, although variations from study to study sometimes make combining them impossible.

A crucial statistic is **effect size,** a way of measuring how much impact one variable has on another. Effect size ranges from 0 (no effect) to 1 (total transformation, never found in actual studies). Effect size may be particularly important when the sample size is large, because a large sample often leads to highly "significant" results (results that are unlikely to have occurred by chance) that have only a tiny effect on the variable of interest.

Hundreds of statistical measures are used by developmentalists. Often the same data can be presented in many ways: Some scientists examine statistical analysis intently before they accept conclusions as valid. A specific example involved methods to improve students' writing ability between grades 4 and 12. A meta-analysis found that many methods of writing instruction have a significant impact, but effect size is much larger for some methods (teaching strategies and summarizing) than for others (prewriting exercises and studying models). For teachers, this statistic is crucial, for they want to know what has a big effect, not merely what is better than chance (significant).

Numerous articles published in the past decade are meta-analyses that combine similar studies to search for general trends. Often effect sizes are also reported, which is especially helpful for meta-analyses since standard calculations almost always find some significance if the number of participants is in the thousands.

An added problem is the "file drawer" problem—that studies without significant results tend to be filed away rather than published. Thus, an accurate effect size may be much smaller than the published meta-analysis finds, or may be nonexistent. For this reason, replication is an important step.

Overall, then, designing and conducting valid research is complex yet crucial. Remember that with your own opinions: As this appendix advises, it is good to "make it personal," but do not stop there.

effect size A way of indicating statistically how much of an impact the independent variable in an experiment had on the dependent variable.

Glossary

23rd pair The chromosome pair that, in humans, determines sex. The other 22 pairs are autosomes, inherited equally by males and females.

A

absent grief When mourners do not grieve, either because other people do not allow expressions of grief or because the mourners do not allow themselves to feel sadness.

acceleration Educating gifted children alongside other children of the same mental, not chronological, age.

accommodation The restructuring of old ideas to include new experiences.

achievement test A measure of mastery or proficiency in reading, mathematics, writing, science, or some other subject.

active euthanasia When someone does something that hastens another person's death, with the intention of ending that person's suffering.

activities of daily life (ADLs) Typically identified as five tasks of self-care that are important to independent living: eating, bathing, toileting, dressing, and transferring from a bed to a chair. The inability to perform any of these tasks is a sign of frailty.

activity theory The view that elderly people want and need to remain active in a variety of social spheres—with relatives, friends, and community groups—and become withdrawn only unwillingly, as a result of ageism.

adolescence-limited offender A person whose criminal activity stops by age 21.

adolescent egocentrism A characteristic of adolescent thinking that leads young people (ages 10 to 13) to focus on themselves to the exclusion of others.

adrenal glands Two glands, located above the kidneys, that respond to the pituitary, producing hormones.

advance directives Any description of what a person wants to happen as they die and after they die. This can include medical measures, visitors, funeral arrangements, cremation, and so on.

affordance An opportunity for perception and interaction that is offered by a person, place, or object in the environment.

age in place To remain in the same home and community in later life, adjusting but not leaving when health fades.

age of viability The age (about 22 weeks after conception) at which a fetus might survive outside the mother's uterus if specialized medical care is available.

ageism A prejudice whereby people are categorized and judged solely on the basis of their chronological age.

aggressive-rejected A type of childhood rejection, when other children do not want to be friends with a child because of his or her antagonistic, confrontational behavior.

allele A variation that makes a gene different in some way from other genes for the same characteristics. Many genes never vary; others have several possible alleles.

allocare Literally, "other-care"; the care of children by people other than the biological parents.

allostasis A dynamic body adjustment, related to homeostasis, that affects overall physiology over time. The main difference is that homeostasis requires an immediate response, whereas allostasis requires longer term adjustment.

allostatic load The stresses of basic body systems that burden overall functioning, eventually causing hypertension, obesity, and diabetes.

amygdala A tiny brain structure that registers emotions, particularly fear and anxiety.

analytic intelligence A form of intelligence that involves such mental processes as abstract planning, strategy selection, focused attention, and information processing, as well as verbal and logical skills.

analytic thought Thought that results from analysis, such as a systematic ranking of pros and cons, risks and consequences, possibilities and facts. Analytic thought depends on logic and rationality.

andropause A term coined to signify a drop in testosterone levels in older men, which normally results in reduced sexual desire, erections, and muscle mass. (Also called *male menopause*.)

animism The belief that natural objects and phenomena are alive, moving around, and having sensations and abilities that are human-like.

anorexia nervosa An eating disorder characterized by self-starvation. Affected individuals voluntarily undereat and often overexercise, depriving their vital organs of nutrition. Anorexia can be fatal.

anoxia A lack of oxygen that, if prolonged, can cause brain damage or death.

antisocial behavior Actions that are deliberately hurtful or destructive to another person.

antithesis A proposition or statement of belief that opposes the thesis; the second stage of the process of dialectical thinking.

Apgar scale A quick assessment of a newborn's health, from 0-10. Below 5 is an emergency—a neonatal pediatrician is summoned immediately. Most babies are at 7, 8, or 9—almost never a perfect 10.

apprenticeship in thinking Vygotsky's term for how cognition is stimulated and developed in people by more skilled members of society.

aptitude The potential to master a specific skill or to learn a certain body of knowledge.

assimilation The reinterpretation of new experiences to fit into old ideas.

asthma A chronic disease of the respiratory system in which inflammation narrows the airways from the nose and mouth to the lungs, causing difficulty in breathing. Signs and symptoms include wheezing, shortness of breath, chest tightness, and coughing.

attachment According to Ainsworth, "an affectional tie" that an infant forms with a caregiver—a tie that binds them together in space and endures over time.

attention-deficit/hyperactivity disorder (ADHD) A condition characterized by a persistent pattern of inattention and/or by hyperactive or impulsive behaviors; ADHD interferes with a person's functioning or development.

authoritarian parenting An approach to child rearing that is characterized by high behavioral standards, strict punishment for misconduct, and little communication from child to parent.

authoritative parenting An approach to child rearing in which the parents set limits but listen to the child and are flexible.

autism spectrum disorder (ASD) A developmental disorder marked by difficulty with social communication and interaction—including difficulty seeing things from another person's point of view—and restricted, repetitive patterns of behavior, interests, or activities.

automatization A process in which repetition of a sequence of thoughts and actions makes the sequence routine so that it no longer requires conscious thought.

autonomy versus shame and doubt Erikson's second crisis of psychosocial development. Toddlers either succeed or fail in gaining a sense of self-rule over their actions and their bodies.

average life expectancy The number of years the average newborn in a particular population group is likely to live.

avoidant coping A method of responding to a stressor by ignoring, forgetting, or hiding it.

axon A fiber that extends from a neuron and transmits electrochemical impulses from that neuron to the dendrites of other neurons.

B

babbling An infant's repetition of certain syllables, such as *ba-ba-ba*, that begins when babies are between 6 and 9 months old.

bed-sharing When two or more people sleep in the same bed.

behavioral teratogens Agents and conditions that can harm the prenatal brain, impairing the future child's intellectual and emotional functioning.

behaviorism A grand theory of human development that studies observable behavior. Behaviorism is also called *learning theory* because it describes the laws and processes by which behavior is learned.

Big Five The five basic clusters of personality traits that remain quite stable throughout adulthood: openness, conscientiousness, extroversion, agreeableness, and neuroticism.

bilingual schooling A strategy in which school subjects are taught in both the learner's original language and the second (majority) language.

binocular vision The ability to focus the two eyes in a coordinated manner in order to see one image.

blind The condition of data gatherers (and sometimes participants, as well) who are deliberately kept ignorant of the purpose of the research so that they cannot unintentionally bias the results.

body image A person's idea of how his or her body looks.

body mass index (BMI) The ratio of a person's weight in kilograms divided by his or her height in meters squared.

Brazelton Neonatal Behavioral Assessment Scale (NBAS) A test that is often administered to newborns which measures responsiveness and records 46 behaviors, including 20 reflexes.

bulimia nervosa An eating disorder characterized by binge eating and subsequent purging, usually by induced vomiting and/or use of laxatives.

bully-victim Someone who attacks others and who is attacked as well. (Also called *provocative victims* because they do things that elicit bullying.)

bullying aggression Unprovoked, repeated physical or verbal attacks, especially on victims who are unlikely to defend themselves.

bullying Repeated, systematic efforts to inflict harm on other people through physical, verbal, or social attack on a weaker person.

C

calorie restriction The practice of limiting dietary energy intake (while consuming sufficient quantities of vitamins, minerals, and other important nutrients) for the purpose of improving health and slowing down the aging process.

carrier A person whose genotype includes a gene that is not expressed in the phenotype. The carried gene occurs in half of the carrier's gametes and thus is passed on to half of the carrier's children. If such a gene is inherited from both parents, the characteristic appears in the phenotype.

cellular aging The cumulative effect of stress and toxins, causing cellular damage first and eventually the death of cells.

centration A characteristic of preoperational thought in which a young child focuses (centers) on one idea, excluding all others.

cerebral palsy A disorder that results from damage to the brain's motor centers. People with cerebral palsy have difficulty with muscle control, so their speech and/or body movements are impaired.

cesarean section (c-section) A surgical birth in which incisions through the mother's abdomen and uterus allow the fetus to be removed quickly, instead of being delivered through the vagina. (Also called simply *section*.)

charter school A public school with its own set of standards that is funded and licensed by the state or local district in which it is located.

child abuse Deliberate action that is harmful to a child's physical, emotional, or sexual well-being.

child culture The idea that each group of children has games, sayings, clothing styles, and superstitions that are not common among adults, just as every culture has distinct values, behaviors, and beliefs.

child maltreatment Intentional harm to or avoidable endangerment of anyone under 18 years of age.

child neglect Failure to meet a child's basic physical, educational, or emotional needs.

child sexual abuse Any erotic activity that arouses an adult and excites, shames, or confuses a child, whether or not the victim protests and whether or not genital contact is involved.

child-directed speech The high-pitched, simplified, and repetitive way adults speak to infants and children. (Also called *baby talk* or *motherese*.)

childhood obesity In a child, having a BMI above the 95th percentile, according to the U.S. Centers for Disease Control's 1980 standards for children of a given age.

childhood overweight In a child, having a BMI above the 85th percentile, according to the U.S. Centers for Disease Control's 1980 standards for children of a given age.

choice overload Having so many possibilities that a thoughtful choice becomes difficult. This is particularly apparent when social networking and other technology make many potential romantic partners available.

chromosome One of the 46 molecules of DNA (in 23 pairs) that virtually every cell of the human body contains and that, together, contain all the genes. Other species have more or fewer chromosomes.

circadian rhythm A day–night cycle of biological activity that occurs approximately every 24 hours.

classical conditioning The learning process in which a meaningful stimulus (such as the smell of food to a hungry animal) is connected with a neutral stimulus (such as the sound of a tone) that had no special meaning before conditioning. (Also called *respondent conditioning*.)

classification The logical principle that things can be organized into groups (or categories or classes) according to some characteristic that they have in common.

cluster suicides Several suicides committed by members of a group within a brief period.

co-sleeping A custom in which parents and their children (usually infants) sleep together in the same room.

cognitive artifacts Intellectual tools passed down from generation to generation that may assist in learning within societies.

cognitive equilibrium In cognitive theory, a state of mental balance in which people are not confused because they can use their existing thought processes to understand current experiences and ideas.

cognitive theory A grand theory of human development that focuses on changes in how people think over time. According to this theory, our thoughts shape our attitudes, beliefs, and behaviors.

cohabitation An arrangement in which a couple lives together in a committed romantic relationship but are not formally married.

cohort People born within the same historical period who therefore move through life together, experiencing the same events, new technologies, and cultural shifts at the same ages. For example, the effect of the Internet varies depending on what cohort a person belongs to.

comorbid Refers to the presence of two or more unrelated disease conditions at the same time in the same person.

complicated grief A type of grief that impedes a person's future life, usually because the person clings to sorrow or is buffeted by contradictory emotions.

compression of morbidity A shortening of the time a person spends ill or infirm, accomplished by postponing illness.

compulsive hoarding The urge to accumulate and hold on to familiar objects and possessions, sometimes to the point of their becoming health and/or safety hazards. This impulse tends to increase with age.

concrete operational thought Piaget's term for the ability to reason logically about direct experiences and perceptions.

conservation The principle that the amount of a substance remains the same (i.e., is conserved) even when its appearance changes.

control processes Mechanisms (including selective attention, metacognition, and emotional regulation) that combine memory, processing speed, and knowledge to regulate the analysis and flow of information within the information-processing system. (Also called *executive processes*.)

conventional moral reasoning Kohlberg's second level of moral reasoning, emphasizing social rules.

copy number variations Genes with various repeats or deletions of base pairs.

corporal punishment Punishment that physically hurts the body, such as slapping, spanking, etc.

corpus callosum A long, thick band of nerve fibers that connects the left and right hemispheres of the brain and allows communication between them.

correlation A number between +1.0 and −1.0 that indicates the degree of relationship between two variables, expressed in terms of the likelihood that one variable will (or will not) occur when the other variable does (or does not). A correlation indicates only that two variables are somehow related, not that one variable causes the other to occur.

cortex The outer layers of the brain in humans and other mammals. Most thinking, feeling, and sensing involves the cortex.

cortisol The primary stress hormone; fluctuations in the body's cortisol level affect human emotions.

couvade Symptoms of pregnancy and birth experienced by fathers.

creative intelligence A form of intelligence that involves the capacity to be intellectually flexible and innovative.

critical period A crucial time when a particular type of developmental growth (in body or behavior) must happen for normal development to occur, or when harm (such as a toxic substance or destructive event) can occur.

cross-sectional research A research design that compares groups of people who differ in age but are similar in other important characteristics.

cross-sequential research A hybrid research design in which researchers first study several groups of people of different ages (a cross-sectional approach) and then follow those groups over the years (a longitudinal approach). (Also called *cohort-sequential research* or *time-sequential research*.)

crystallized intelligence Those types of intellectual ability that reflect accumulated learning. Vocabulary and general information are examples. Crystallized intelligence increases with age, while fluid intelligence declines.

culture A system of shared beliefs, norms, behaviors, and expectations that persist over time and prescribe social behavior and assumptions.

cyberbullying Bullying that occurs when one person spreads insults or rumors about another by means of social media posts, e-mails, text messages, or cell phone videos.

D

deductive reasoning Reasoning from a general statement, premise, or principle, through logical steps, to figure out (deduce) specifics. (Also called *top-down reasoning*.)

Defining Issues Test (DIT) A series of questions developed by James Rest and designed to assess respondents' level of moral development by having them rank possible solutions to moral dilemmas.

demand/withdraw interaction A situation in a romantic relationship wherein one partner wants to address an issue and the other refuses, resulting in opposite reactions—one insistent on talk while the other cuts short the conversation.

demographic shift A shift in the proportions of the populations of various ages.

dendrite A fiber that extends from a neuron and receives electrochemical impulses transmitted from other neurons via their axons.

deoxyribonucleic acid (DNA) The chemical composition of the molecules that contain the genes, which are the chemical instructions for cells to manufacture various proteins.

dependency ratio A calculation of the number of self-sufficient productive adults compared with the number of dependents (children and the elderly) in a given population.

dependent variable In an experiment, the variable that may change as a result of whatever new condition or situation the experimenter adds. In other words, the dependent variable *depends* on the independent variable.

developmental psychopathology The field that uses insights into typical development to understand and remediate developmental disorders.

developmental theory A group of ideas, assumptions, and generalizations that interpret and illuminate the thousands of observations that have been made about human growth. A developmental theory provides a framework for explaining the patterns and problems of development.

deviancy training Destructive peer support in which one person shows another how to rebel against authority or social norms.

dialectical thought The most advanced cognitive process, characterized by the ability to consider a thesis and its antithesis simultaneously and thus to arrive at a synthesis. Dialectical thought makes possible an ongoing awareness of pros and cons, advantages and disadvantages, possibilities and limitations.

diathesis–stress model The view that psychological disorders, such as schizophrenia, are produced by the interaction of a genetic vulnerability (the diathesis) and stressful environmental factors and life events.

difference-equals-deficit error The mistaken belief that a deviation from some norm is necessarily inferior to behavior or characteristics that meet the standard.

differential susceptibility The idea that people vary in how sensitive they are to particular experiences. Often such differences are genetic, which makes some people affected "for better or for worse" by life events. (Also called *differential sensitivity*.)

disability Difficulty in performing normal activities of daily life because of some physical, mental, or emotional condition.

disability-adjusted life years (DALYs) A measure of the reduced quality of life caused by disability.

disenfranchised grief A situation in which certain people, although they are bereaved, are prevented from mourning publicly by cultural customs or social restrictions.

disengagement theory The view that aging makes a person's social sphere increasingly narrow, resulting in role relinquishment, withdrawal, and passivity.

disorganized attachment A type of attachment that is marked by an infant's inconsistent reactions to the caregiver's departure and return.

distal parenting Caregiving practices that involve remaining distant from the baby, providing toys, food, and face-to-face communication with minimal holding and touching.

dizygotic (DZ) twins Twins who are formed when two separate ova are fertilized by two separate sperm at roughly the same time. (Also called *fraternal twins*.)

DNR (do not resuscitate) order A written order from a physician (sometimes initiated by a patient's advance directive or by a health care proxy's request) that no attempt should be made to revive a patient if he or she suffers cardiac or respiratory arrest.

dominant–recessive pattern The interaction of a heterozygous pair of alleles in such a way that the phenotype reflects one allele (the dominant gene) more than the other (the recessive gene).

double effect When an action (such as administering opiates) has both a positive effect (relieving a terminally ill person's pain) and a negative effect (hastening death by suppressing respiration).

doula A woman who helps with the birth process. Traditionally in Latin America, a doula was the only professional who attended childbirth. Now doulas are likely to arrive at the woman's home during early labor and later work alongside a hospital's staff.

Down syndrome A condition in which a person has 47 chromosomes instead of the usual 46, with 3 rather than 2 chromosomes at the 21st site. People with Down syndrome typically have distinctive characteristics, including unusual facial features, heart abnormalities, and language difficulties. (Also called *trisomy-21*.)

drug addiction A condition of drug dependence in which the absence of the given drug in the individual's system produces a drive—physiological, psychological, or both—to ingest more of the drug.

dual processing The notion that two networks exist within the human brain, one for emotional processing of stimuli and one for analytical reasoning.

dynamic-systems approach A view of human development as an ongoing, ever-changing interaction between the physical, cognitive, and psychosocial influences. The crucial understanding is that development is never static but is always affected by, and affects, many systems of development.

dyscalculia Unusual difficulty with math, probably originating from a distinct part of the brain.

dyslexia Unusual difficulty with reading; thought to be the result of some neurological underdevelopment.

E

eclectic perspective The approach taken by most developmentalists, in which they apply aspects of each of the various theories of development rather than adhering exclusively to one theory.

ecological-systems approach A perspective on human development that considers all of the influences from the various contexts of development. (Later renamed *bioecological theory*.)

effect size A way of indicating statistically how much of an impact the independent variable in an experiment had on the dependent variable.

effortful control The ability to regulate one's emotions and actions through effort, not simply through natural inclination.

egocentrism Piaget's term for children's tendency to think about the world entirely from their own personal perspective.

elderspeak A condescending way of speaking to older adults that resembles baby talk, with simple and short sentences, exaggerated emphasis, repetition, and a slower rate and a higher pitch than used in normal speech.

embryo The name for a developing human organism from about the third week through the eighth week after conception.

embryonic period The stage of prenatal development from approximately the third week through the eighth week after conception, during which the basic forms of all body structures, including internal organs, develop.

emerging adulthood The period of life between the ages of 18 and 25. Emerging adulthood is now widely thought of as a distinct developmental stage.

emotion-focused coping A strategy to deal with stress by changing feelings about the stressor rather than changing the stressor itself.

emotional regulation The ability to control when and how emotions are expressed.

empathy The ability to understand the emotions and concerns of another person, especially when they differ from one's own.

empirical evidence Evidence that is based on observation, experience, or experiment; not theoretical.

empty nest The time in the lives of parents when their children have left the family home. This is often a happy time for everyone.

English Language Learners (ELLs) Children in the United States whose proficiency in English is low—usually below a cutoff score on an oral or written test. Many children who speak a non-English language at home are also capable in English; they are *not* ELLs.

entity theory of intelligence An approach to understanding intelligence that sees ability as innate, a fixed quantity present at birth; those who hold this view do not believe that effort enhances achievement.

epigenetics The study of how environmental factors affect genes and genetic expression—enhancing, halting, shaping, or altering the expression of genes.

epigenetics The study of how environmental factors affect genes and genetic expression—enhancing, halting, shaping, or altering the expression of genes.

equifinality A basic principle of developmental psychopathology which holds that one symptom can have many causes.

ESL (English as a Second Language) A U.S. approach to teaching English that gathers all of the non-English speakers together and provides intense instruction in English. Students' first languages are never used; the goal is to prepare them for regular classes in English.

estradiol A sex hormone, considered the chief estrogen. Females produce much more estradiol than males do.

ethnic group People whose ancestors were born in the same region and who often share a language, culture, and religion.

executive function The cognitive ability to organize and prioritize the many thoughts that arise from the various parts of the brain, allowing the person to anticipate, strategize, and plan behavior.

experience-dependent Brain functions that depend on particular, variable experiences and therefore may or may not develop in a particular infant.

experience-expectant Brain functions that require certain basic common experiences (which an infant can be expected to have) in order to develop normally.

experiment A research method in which the researcher tries to determine the cause-and-effect relationship between two variables by manipulating one (called the *independent variable*) and then observing and recording the ensuing changes in the other (called the *dependent variable*).

expert Someone with specialized skills and knowledge developed around a particular activity or area of specific interest.

extended family A family of relatives in addition to the nuclear family, usually three or more generations living in one household.

extremely low birthweight (ELBW) A body weight at birth of less than 1,000 grams (2 pounds, 3 ounces).

extrinsic motivation A drive, or reason to pursue a goal, that arises from the need to have one's achievements rewarded from outside, perhaps by receiving material possessions or another person's esteem.

extrinsic rewards of work The tangible benefits, usually in salary, insurance, pension, and status, that come with employment.

F

false positive The result of a laboratory test that reports something as true when in fact it is not true. This can occur for pregnancy tests, when a woman might not be pregnant even though the test says she is, or during pregnancy, when a problem is reported that actually does not exist.

familism The belief that family members should support one another, sacrificing individual freedom and success, if necessary, in order to preserve family unity and protect the family from outside forces.

family function The way a family works to meet the needs of its members. Children need families to provide basic material necessities, to encourage learning, to help them develop self-respect, to nurture friendships, and to foster harmony and stability.

family structure The legal and genetic relationships among relatives living in the same home. Possible structures include nuclear family, extended family, stepfamily, single-parent family, and many others.

fast-mapping The speedy and sometimes imprecise way in which children learn new words by tentatively placing them in mental categories according to their perceived meaning.

fetal alcohol syndrome (FAS) A cluster of birth defects, including abnormal facial characteristics, slow physical growth, and reduced intellectual ability, that may occur in the fetus of a woman who drinks alcohol while pregnant.

fetal period The stage of prenatal development from the ninth week after conception until birth, during which the fetus gains about 7 pounds (more than 3,000 grams) and organs become more mature, gradually able to function on their own.

fetus The name for a developing human organism from the start of the ninth week after conception until birth.

fictive kin People who become accepted as part of a family in which they are not genetically or legally members.

filial responsibility The obligation of adult children to care for their aging parents.

fine motor skills Physical abilities involving small body movements, especially of the hands and fingers, such as drawing and picking up a coin. (The word *fine* here means "small.")

fluid intelligence Those types of basic intelligence that make learning of all sorts quick and thorough. Abilities such as short-term memory, abstract thought, and speed of thinking are all usually considered part of fluid intelligence.

Flynn effect The rise in average IQ scores that has occurred over the decades in many nations.

focus on appearance A characteristic of preoperational thought in which a young child ignores all attributes that are not apparent.

foreclosure Erikson's term for premature identity formation, which occurs when an adolescent adopts his or her parents' or society's roles and values wholesale, without questioning or analysis.

formal operational thought In Piaget's theory, the fourth and final stage of cognitive development, characterized by more systematic logical thinking and by the ability to understand and systematically manipulate abstract concepts.

foster care A legal, publicly supported system in which a maltreated child is removed from the parents' custody and entrusted to another adult or family, who is reimbursed for expenses incurred in meeting the child's needs.

fragile X syndrome A genetic disorder in which part of the X chromosome seems to be attached to the rest of it by a very thin string of molecules. The cause is a single gene that has more than 200 repetitions of one triplet.

frail elderly People over age 65, and often over age 85, who are physically infirm, very ill, or cognitively disabled.

G

gender differences Differences in the roles and behaviors of males and females that are prescribed by the culture.

gender identity A person's acceptance of the roles and behaviors that society associates with the biological categories of male and female.

gender schema A cognitive concept or general belief based on one's experiences—in this case, a child's understanding of sex differences.

gene A small section of a chromosome; the basic unit for the transmission of heredity. A gene consists of a string of chemicals that provide instructions for the cell to manufacture certain proteins.

general intelligence (g) The idea of g assumes that intelligence is one basic trait, underlying all cognitive abilities. According to this concept, people have varying levels of this general ability.

generational forgetting The idea that each new generation forgets what the previous generation learned. As used here, the term refers to knowledge about the harm drugs can do.

generativity versus stagnation The seventh of Erikson's eight stages of development. Adults seek to be productive in a caring way, often as parents. Generativity also occurs through art, caregiving, and employment.

genetic clock A purported mechanism in the DNA of cells that regulates the aging process by triggering hormonal changes and controlling cellular reproduction and repair.

genetic counseling Consultation and testing by trained experts that enables individuals to learn about their genetic heritage, including harmful conditions that they might pass along to any children they may conceive.

genome The full set of genes that are the instructions to make an individual member of a certain species.

genotype An organism's entire genetic inheritance, or genetic potential.

germinal period The first two weeks of prenatal development after conception, characterized by rapid cell division and the beginning of cell differentiation.

gonads The paired sex glands (ovaries in females, testicles in males). The gonads produce hormones and mature gametes.

grammar All of the methods—word order, verb forms, and so on—that languages use to communicate meaning, apart from the words themselves.

grief The deep sorrow that people feel at the death of another. Grief is personal and unpredictable.

gross motor skills Physical abilities involving large body movements, such as walking and jumping. (The word *gross* here means "big.")

growth spurt The relatively sudden and rapid physical growth that occurs during puberty. Each body part increases in size on a schedule: Weight usually precedes height, and growth of the limbs precedes growth of the torso.

guided participation The process by which people learn from others who guide their experiences and explorations.

H

habituation The process of becoming accustomed to an object or event through repeated exposure to it, and thus becoming less interested in it.

Hayflick limit The number of times a human cell is capable of dividing into two new cells. The limit for most human cells is approximately 50 divisions, an indication that the life span is limited by our genetic program.

Head Start A federally funded early-childhood intervention program for low-income children of preschool age.

head-sparing A biological mechanism that protects the brain when malnutrition disrupts body growth. The brain is the last part of the body to be damaged by malnutrition.

health care proxy A person chosen to make medical decisions if a patient is unable to do so, as when in a coma.

helicopter parents The label used for parents who hover (like a helicopter) over their emerging-adult children. The term is pejorative, but parental involvement is sometimes helpful.

heritability A statistic that indicates what percentage of the variation in a particular trait within a particular population, in a particular context and era, can be traced to genes.

heterogamy Defined by developmentalists as marriage between individuals who tend to be dissimilar with respect to such variables as attitudes, interests, goals, socioeconomic status, religion, ethnic background, and local origin.

heterozygous Referring to two genes of one pair that differ in some way. Typically one allele has only a few base pairs that differ from the other member of the pair.

hidden curriculum The unofficial, unstated, or implicit patterns within a school that influence what children learn. For instance, teacher background, organization of the play space, and tracking are all part of the hidden curriculum—not formally prescribed, but instructive to the children.

high-stakes test An evaluation that is critical in determining success or failure. If a single test determines whether a student will graduate or be promoted, it is a high-stakes test.

hippocampus A brain structure that is a central processor of memory, especially memory for locations.

holophrase A single word that is used to express a complete, meaningful thought.

home schooling Education in which children are taught at home, usually by their parents.

homeostasis The adjustment of all of the body's systems to keep physiological functions in a state of equilibrium. As the body ages, it takes longer for these homeostatic adjustments to occur.

homogamy Defined by developmentalists as marriage between individuals who tend to be similar with respect to such variables as attitudes, interests, goals, socioeconomic status, religion, ethnic background, and local origin.

homozygous Referring to two genes of one pair that are exactly the same in every letter of their code. Most gene pairs are homozygous.

hookup A sexual encounter between two people who are not in a romantic relationship. Neither intimacy nor commitment is expected.

hormone replacement therapy (HRT) Taking hormones (in pills, patches, or injections) to compensate for hormone reduction. HRT is most common in women at menopause or after removal of the ovaries, but it is also used by men as their testosterone decreases. HRT has some medical uses but also carries health risks.

hospice An institution or program in which terminally ill patients receive palliative care to reduce suffering; family and friends of the dying are helped as well.

HPA (hypothalamus–pituitary–adrenal) axis A sequence of hormone production originating in the hypothalamus and moving to the pituitary and then to the adrenal glands.

HPG (hypothalamus–pituitary–gonad) axis A sequence of hormone production originating in the hypothalamus and moving to the pituitary and then to the gonads.

Human Genome Project An international effort to map the complete human genetic code. This effort was essentially completed in 2001, though analysis is ongoing.

humanism A theory that stresses the potential of all humans for good and the belief that all people have the same basic needs, regardless of culture, gender, or background.

humanism A theory that stresses the potential of all humans, who have the same basic needs regardless of culture, gender, or background.

hypothalamus A brain area that responds to the amygdala and the hippocampus to produce hormones that activate other parts of the brain and body.

hypothesis A specific prediction that can be tested.

hypothetical thought Reasoning that includes propositions and possibilities that may not reflect reality.

I

identification An attempt to defend one's self-concept by taking on the behaviors and attitudes of someone else.

identity achievement Erikson's term for the attainment of identity, or the point at which a person understands who he or she is as a unique individual, in accord with past experiences and future plans.

identity versus role confusion Erikson's term for the fifth stage of development, in which the person tries to figure out "Who am I?" but is confused as to which of many possible roles to adopt.

imaginary audience The other people who, in an adolescent's egocentric belief, are watching and taking note of his or her appearance, ideas, and behavior. This belief makes many teenagers very self-conscious.

imaginary friends Make-believe friends who exist only in a child's imagination; increasingly common from ages 3 through 7. They combat loneliness and aid emotional regulation.

immersion A strategy in which instruction in all school subjects occurs in the second (usually the majority) language that a child is learning.

immigrant paradox The surprising, paradoxical fact that low-SES immigrant women tend to have fewer birth complications than native-born peers with higher incomes.

immunization A process that stimulates the body's immune system by causing production of antibodies to defend against attack by a particular contagious disease. Creation of antibodies may be accomplished either naturally (by having the disease), by injection, by drops that are swallowed, or by a nasal spray.

implantation The process, beginning about 10 days after conception, in which the developing organism burrows into the uterus, where it can be nourished and protected as it continues to develop.

impulse control The ability to postpone or deny the immediate response to an idea or behavior.

in vitro fertilization (IVF) Fertilization that takes place outside a woman's body (as in a glass laboratory dish). The procedure involves mixing sperm with ova that have been surgically removed from the woman's ovary. If a zygote is produced, it is inserted into a woman's uterus, where it may implant and develop into a baby.

incomplete grief When circumstances, such as a police investigation or an autopsy, interfere with the process of grieving.

incremental theory of intelligence An approach to understanding intelligence which holds that intelligence can be directly increased by effort; those who subscribe to this view believe they can master whatever they seek to learn if they pay attention, participate in class, study, complete their homework, and so on.

independent variable In an experiment, the variable that is introduced to see what effect it has on the dependent variable. (Also called *experimental variable*.)

individual education plan (IEP) A document that specifies educational goals and plans for a child with special needs.

induction A disciplinary technique in which the parent tries to get the child to understand why a certain behavior was wrong. Listening, not lecturing, is crucial.

inductive reasoning Reasoning from one or more specific experiences or facts to reach (induce) a general conclusion. (Also called *bottom-up reasoning*.)

industry versus inferiority The fourth of Erikson's eight psychosocial crises, during which children attempt to master many skills, developing a sense of themselves as either industrious or inferior, competent or incompetent.

infertility The inability to conceive a child after trying for at least a year.

information-processing theory A perspective that compares human thinking processes, by analogy, to computer analysis of data, including sensory input, connections, stored memories, and output.

initiative versus guilt Erikson's third psychosocial crisis, in which children undertake new skills and activities and feel guilty when they do not succeed at them.

injury control/harm reduction Practices that are aimed at anticipating, controlling, and preventing dangerous activities; these practices reflect the beliefs that accidents are not random and that injuries can be made less harmful if proper controls are in place.

insecure-avoidant attachment A pattern of attachment in which an infant avoids connection with the caregiver, as when the infant seems not to care about the caregiver's presence, departure, or return.

insecure-resistant/ambivalent attachment A pattern of attachment in which an infant's anxiety and uncertainty are evident, as when the infant becomes very upset at separation from the caregiver and both resists and seeks contact on reunion.

instrumental activities of daily life (IADLs) Actions (for example, paying bills and car maintenance) that are important to independent living and that require some intellectual competence and forethought. The ability to perform these tasks may be even more critical to self-sufficiency than ADL ability.

instrumental aggression Behavior that hurts someone else because the aggressor wants to get or keep a possession or a privilege.

integrity versus despair The final stage of Erik Erikson's developmental sequence, in which older adults seek to integrate their unique experiences with their vision of community.

intelligence The ability to learn and understand various aspects of life, traditionally focused on reading and math, and more recently on the arts, movement, and social interactions.

intimacy versus isolation The sixth of Erikson's eight stages of development. Adults seek someone with whom to share their lives in an enduring and self-sacrificing commitment. Without such commitment, they risk profound aloneness and isolation.

intimacy versus isolation The sixth of Erikson's stages of development. Every adult seeks close relationships with other people in order to live a happy and healthy life.

intimate terrorism A violent and demeaning form of abuse in a romantic relationship, in which the victim (usually female) is frightened to fight back, seek help, or withdraw. In this case, the victim is in danger of physical as well as psychological harm.

intrinsic motivation A drive, or reason to pursue a goal, that comes from inside a person, such as the desire to feel smart or competent.

intrinsic rewards of work The personal gratifications, such as pleasure in a job well done or friendships with coworkers, that accompany employment.

intuitive thought Thought that arises from an emotion or a hunch, beyond rational explanation, and is influenced by past experiences and cultural assumptions.

invincibility fable An adolescent's egocentric conviction that he or she cannot be overcome or even harmed by anything that might defeat a normal mortal, such as unprotected sex, drug abuse, or high-speed driving.

irreversibility A characteristic of preoperational thought in which a young child thinks that nothing can be undone. A thing cannot be restored to the way it was before a change occurred.

K

kangaroo care A form of newborn care in which mothers (and sometimes fathers) rest their babies on their naked chests, like kangaroo mothers that carry their immature newborns in a pouch on their abdomen.

kinkeeper Someone who becomes the gatherer and communications hub for their family.

kinship care A form of foster care in which a relative of a maltreated child, usually a grandparent, becomes the approved caregiver.

knowledge base A body of knowledge in a particular area that makes it easier to master new information in that area.

L

language acquisition device (LAD) Chomsky's term for a hypothesized mental structure that enables humans to learn language, including the basic aspects of grammar, vocabulary, and intonation.

LAT (living apart together) When a couple is committed to each other emotionally and sexually for years, yet each partner has his or her own home.

lateralization Literally, sidedness, referring to the specialization in certain functions by each side of the brain, with one side dominant for each activity. The left side of the brain controls the right side of the body, and vice versa.

least restrictive environment (LRE) A legal requirement that children with special needs be assigned to the most general educational context in which they can be expected to learn.

leptin A hormone that affects appetite and is believed to affect the onset of puberty. Leptin levels increase during childhood and peak at around age 12.

life-course-persistent offender A person whose criminal activity typically begins in early adolescence and continues throughout life; a career criminal.

life-span perspective An approach to the study of human development that takes into account all phases of life, not just childhood or adulthood.

"little scientist" The stage-five toddler (age 12 to 18 months) who experiments without anticipating the results, using trial and error in active and creative exploration.

limbic system The parts of the brain that interact to produce emotions, including the amygdala, the hypothalamus, and the hippocampus. Many other parts of the brain also are involved with emotions.

linked lives Lives in which the success, health, and well-being of each family member are connected to those of other members. This includes those of another generation, as in the relationship between parents, grandparents, and children.

living will A document that indicates what medical intervention an individual prefers if he or she is not conscious when a decision is to be expressed. For example, some do not want mechanical breathing.

long-term memory The component of the information-processing system in which virtually limitless amounts of information can be stored indefinitely.

longitudinal research A research design in which the same individuals are followed over time, as their development is repeatedly assessed.

low birthweight (LBW) A body weight at birth of less than 2,500 grams (5½ pounds).

M

major depression Feelings of hopelessness, lethargy, and worthlessness that last two weeks or more.

massification The idea that establishing institutions of higher learning and encouraging college enrollment can benefit everyone (the masses).

massive open online course (MOOC) A course that is offered solely online for college credit. Typically, tuition is very low, and thousands of students enroll.

maximum life span The oldest possible age to which members of a species can live under ideal circumstances. For humans, that age is approximately 122 years.

mean length of utterance (MLU) The average number of words in a typical sentence (called utterance because children may not talk in complete sentences). MLU is often used to measure language development.

menarche A girl's first menstrual period, signaling that she has begun ovulation. Pregnancy is biologically possible, but ovulation and menstruation are often irregular for years after menarche.

menopause The time in middle age, usually around age 50, when a woman's menstrual periods cease and the production of estrogen, progesterone, and testosterone drops. Strictly speaking, menopause is dated one year after a woman's last menstrual period, although many months before and after that date are menopausal.

meta-analysis A technique of combining results of many studies to come to an overall conclusion. Meta-analysis is powerful, in that small samples can be added together to lead to significant conclusions, although variations from study to study sometimes make combining them impossible.

microbiome All of the microbes (bacteria, viruses, and so on) with all of their genes in a community; here, the millions of microbes of the human body.

middle childhood The period between early childhood and early adolescence, approximately from ages 6 to 11.

middle school A school for children in the grades between elementary school and high school. Middle school usually begins with grade 6 and ends with grade 8.

modeling The central process of social learning, by which a person observes the actions of others and then copies them.

monozygotic (MZ) twins Twins who originate from one zygote that splits apart very early in development. (Also called *identical twins*.) Other monozygotic multiple births (such as triplets and quadruplets) can occur as well.

Montessori schools Schools that offer early-childhood education based on the philosophy of Maria Montessori, which emphasizes careful work and tasks that each young child can do.

morality of care In Gilligan's view, moral principles that reflect the tendency of females to be reluctant to judge right and wrong in absolute terms because they are socialized to be nurturing, compassionate, and nonjudgmental.

morality of justice In Gilligan's view, moral principles that reflect the tendency of males to emphasize justice over compassion, judging right and wrong in absolute terms.

moratorium An adolescent's choice of a socially acceptable way to postpone making identity-achievement decisions. Going to college is a common example.

morbidity Disease. As a measure of health, morbidity usually refers to the rate of diseases in a given population—physical and emotional, acute (sudden) and chronic (ongoing).

mortality Death. As a measure of health, mortality usually refers to the number of deaths each year per hundred thousand members of a given population.

motor skill The learned abilities to move some part of the body, in actions ranging from a large leap to a flicker of the eyelid. (The word *motor* here refers to movement of muscles.)

mourning The ceremonies and behaviors that a religion or culture prescribes for people to express their grief after a death.

multifactorial Referring to a trait that is affected by many factors, both genetic and environmental, that enhance, halt, shape, or alter the expression of genes, resulting in a phenotype that may differ markedly from the genotype.

multifinality A basic principle of developmental psychopathology which holds that one cause can have many (multiple) final manifestations.

multiple intelligences The idea that human intelligence is composed of a varied set of abilities rather than a single, all-encompassing one.

myelin The coating on axons that speeds transmission of signals from one neuron to another.

myelination The process by which axons become coated with myelin, a fatty substance that speeds the transmission of nerve impulses from neuron to neuron.

N

naming explosion A sudden increase in an infant's vocabulary, especially in the number of nouns, that begins at about 18 months of age.

National Assessment of Educational Progress (NAEP) An ongoing and nationally representative measure of U.S. children's achievement in reading, mathematics, and other subjects over time; nicknamed "the Nation's Report Card."

naturally occurring retirement community (NORC) A neighborhood or apartment complex whose population is mostly retired people who moved to the location as younger adults and never left.

nature In development, nature refers to the traits, capacities, and limitations that each individual inherits genetically from his or her parents at the moment of conception.

NEET (Not in Education, Employment, or Training) Refers to older adolescents and young adults who are not in any future-oriented program and are not employed. This is a new term, because the economic recession that began in about 2007 led to a sizable number of NEET people, with many social problems.

neglectful/uninvolved parenting An approach to child rearing in which the parents are indifferent toward their children and unaware of what is going on in their children's lives.

neurodiversity The idea that people with special needs have diverse brain structures, with each person having neurological strengths and weaknesses that should be appreciated, in much the same way diverse cultures and ethnicities are welcomed.

neuron One of billions of nerve cells in the central nervous system, especially in the brain.

neurotransmitter A brain chemical that carries information from the axon of a sending neuron to the dendrites of a receiving neuron.

norm An average, or typical, standard of behavior or accomplishment, such as the norm for age of walking or the norm for greeting a stranger.

normal grief The usual response to a loss. Initial sadness and then recovery are normal.

nuclear family A family that consists of a father, a mother, and their biological children under age 18.

nurture In development, nurture includes all of the environmental influences that affect the individual after conception. This includes everything from the mother's nutrition while pregnant to the cultural influences in the nation.

O

object permanence The realization that objects (including people) still exist when they can no longer be seen, touched, or heard.

objective thought Thinking that is not influenced by the thinker's personal qualities but instead involves facts and numbers that are universally considered true and valid.

Oedipus complex The unconscious desire of young boys to replace their father and win their mother's romantic love.

old-old Older adults (generally, those over age 75) who suffer from physical, mental, or social deficits.

oldest-old Elderly adults (generally, those over age 85) who are dependent on others for almost everything, requiring supportive services such as nursing homes and hospital stays.

operant conditioning The learning process by which a particular action is followed by something desired (which makes the person or animal more likely to repeat the action) or by something unwanted (which makes the action less likely to be repeated). (Also called *instrumental conditioning.*)

operational definition A description of the specific, observable behavior that will constitute the variable that is to be studied, so that any reader will know whether that behavior occurred or not. Operational definitions may be arbitrary (e.g., an IQ score at or above 130 is operationally defined as "gifted"), but they must be precise.

organ reserve The capacity of organs to allow the body to cope with stress, via extra, unused functioning ability.

osteoporosis A disease whose symptoms are low bone mass and deterioration of bone tissue, which leads to increasingly fragile bones and greater risk of fracture.

overimitation When a person imitates an action that is not a relevant part of the behavior to be learned. Overimitation is common among 2- to 6-year-olds when they imitate adult actions that are irrelevant and inefficient.

overregularization The application of rules of grammar even when exceptions occur, making the language seem more "regular" than it actually is.

P

palliative care Medical treatment designed primarily to provide physical and emotional comfort to the dying patient and guidance to his or her loved ones.

parasuicide Any potentially lethal action against the self that does not result in death. (Also called *attempted suicide* or *failed suicide.*)

parent–infant bond The strong, loving connection that forms as parents hold, examine, and feed their newborn.

parental alliance Cooperation between a mother and a father based on their mutual commitment to their children. In a parental alliance, the parents support each other in their shared parental roles.

parental monitoring Parents' ongoing awareness of what their children are doing, where, and with whom.

parentification When a child acts more like a parent than a child. Parentification may occur if the actual parents do not act as caregivers, making a child feel responsible for the family.

participants The people who are studied in a research project. Participants is the term now used in psychology; other disciplines still call these people "subjects."

passive euthanasia When a seriously ill person is allowed to die naturally, without active attempts to prolong life.

peer pressure Encouragement to conform to one's friends or contemporaries in behavior, dress, and attitude; usually considered a negative force, as when adolescent peers encourage one another to defy adult authority.

percentile A point on a ranking scale of 0 to 100. The 50th percentile is the midpoint; half the people in the population being studied rank higher and half rank lower.

permanency planning An effort by child-welfare authorities to find a long-term living situation that will provide stability and support for a maltreated child. A goal is to avoid repeated changes of caregiver or school, which can be particularly harmful to the child.

permissive parenting An approach to child rearing that is characterized by high nurturance and communication but little discipline, guidance, or control. (Also called *indulgent parenting*.)

perseveration The tendency to persevere in, or stick to, one thought or action for a long time.

personal fable An aspect of adolescent egocentrism characterized by an adolescent's belief that his or her thoughts, feelings, and experiences are unique, more wonderful, or more awful than anyone else's.

phallic stage Freud's third stage of development, when the penis becomes the focus of concern and pleasure.

phenotype The observable characteristics of a person, including appearance, personality, intelligence, and all other traits.

physician-assisted suicide A form of active euthanasia in which a doctor provides the means for someone to end his or her own life, usually by prescribing lethal drugs.

PISA (Programme for International Student Assessment) An international test taken by 15-year-olds in 50 nations that is designed to measure problem solving and cognition in daily life.

pituitary A gland in the brain that responds to a signal from the hypothalamus by producing many hormones, including those that regulate growth and that control other glands, among them the adrenal and sex glands.

pituitary A gland in the brain that responds to a signal from the hypothalamus by producing many hormones, including those that regulate growth and sexual maturation.

plasticity genes Genes and alleles that make people more susceptible to environmental influences, for better or worse. This is part of differential sensitivity.

plasticity The idea that abilities, personality, and other human characteristics can change over time. Plasticity is particularly evident during childhood, but even older adults are not always "set in their ways."

polygamous family A family consisting of one man, several wives, and their children.

polygenic Referring to a trait that is influenced by many genes.

population The entire group of individuals who are of particular concern in a scientific study, such as all the children of the world or all newborns who weigh less than 3 pounds.

positivity effect The tendency for elderly people to perceive, prefer, and remember positive images and experiences more than negative ones.

post-traumatic stress disorder (PTSD) An anxiety disorder that develops as a delayed reaction to having experienced or witnessed a profoundly shocking or frightening event, such as rape, severe beating, war, or natural disaster. Its symptoms may include flashbacks to the event, hyperactivity and hypervigilance, displaced anger, sleeplessness, nightmares, sudden terror or anxiety, and confusion between fantasy and reality.

postconventional moral reasoning Kohlberg's third level of moral reasoning, emphasizing moral principles.

postformal thought A proposed adult stage of cognitive development, following Piaget's four stages, that goes beyond adolescent thinking by being more practical, more flexible, and more dialectical (i.e., more capable of combining contradictory elements into a comprehensive whole).

postpartum depression A new mother's feelings of inadequacy and sadness in the days and weeks after giving birth.

practical intelligence The intellectual skills used in everyday problem solving. (Sometimes called *tacit intelligence*.)

pragmatics The practical use of language that includes the ability to adjust language communication according to audience and context.

preconventional moral reasoning Kohlberg's first level of moral reasoning, emphasizing rewards and punishments.

prefrontal cortex The area of the cortex at the very front of the brain that specializes in anticipation, planning, and impulse control.

preoperational intelligence Piaget's term for cognitive development between the ages of about 2 and 6; it includes language and imagination (which involve symbolic thought), but logical, operational thinking is not yet possible at this stage.

presbycusis A significant loss of hearing associated with senescence. Presbycusis usually is not apparent until after age 60.

preterm A birth that occurs two or more weeks before the full 38 weeks of the typical pregnancy—that is, at 36 or fewer weeks after conception.

primary aging The universal and irreversible physical changes that occur to all living creatures as they grow older.

primary circular reactions The first of three types of feedback loops in sensorimotor intelligence, this one involving the infant's own body. The infant senses motion, sucking, noise, and other stimuli and tries to understand them.

primary prevention Actions that change overall background conditions to prevent some unwanted event or circumstance, such as injury, disease, or abuse.

primary sex characteristics The parts of the body that are directly involved in reproduction, including the vagina, uterus, ovaries, testicles, and penis.

private speech The internal dialogue that occurs when people talk to themselves (either silently or out loud).

problem-focused coping A strategy to deal with stress by tackling a stressful situation directly.

Progress in International Reading Literacy Study (PIRLS) Inaugurated in 2001, a planned five-year cycle of international trend studies in the reading ability of fourth-graders.

prosocial behavior Actions that are helpful and kind but are of no obvious benefit to oneself.

protein-calorie malnutrition A condition in which a person does not consume sufficient food of any kind. This deprivation can result in several illnesses, severe weight loss, and even death.

proximal parenting Caregiving practices that involve being physically close to the baby, with frequent holding and touching.

pruning When applied to brain development, the process by which unused connections in the brain atrophy and die.

psychoanalytic theory A grand theory of human development that holds that irrational, unconscious drives and motives, often originating in childhood, underlie human behavior.

psychological control A disciplinary technique that involves threatening to withdraw love and support and that relies on a child's feelings of guilt and gratitude to the parents.

puberty The time between the first onrush of hormones and full adult physical development. Puberty usually lasts three to five years. Many more years are required to achieve psychosocial maturity.

Q

qualitative research Research that considers qualities instead of quantities. Descriptions of particular conditions and participants' expressed ideas are often part of qualitative studies.

quality-adjusted life years (QALYs) A measure of how many years of high-quality life a person lives. This is distinct from DALYs, in that a person could have a disability and nonetheless have a high quality of life.

quantitative research Research that provides data that can be expressed with numbers, such as ranks or scales.

R

race A group of people who are regarded by themselves or by others as distinct from other groups on the basis of physical appearance, typically skin color. Social scientists think race is a misleading concept, as biological differences are not signified by outward appearance.

reaction time The time it takes to respond to a stimulus, either physically (with a reflexive movement such as an eyeblink) or cognitively (with a thought).

reactive aggression An impulsive retaliation for another person's intentional or accidental action, verbal or physical.

reflex An unlearned, involuntary action or movement in response to a stimulus. A reflex occurs without conscious thought.

Reggio Emilia A program of early-childhood education that originated in the town of Reggio Emilia, Italy, and that encourages each child's creativity in a carefully designed setting.

reinforcement When a behavior is followed by something desired, such as food for a hungry animal or a welcoming smile for a lonely person.

relational aggression Nonphysical acts, such as insults or social rejection, aimed at harming the social connection between the victim and other people.

religious coping The process of turning to faith as a method of coping with stress.

REM (rapid eye movement) sleep A stage of sleep characterized by flickering eyes behind closed lids, dreaming, and rapid brain waves.

reminder session A perceptual experience that helps a person recollect an idea, a thing, or an experience.

replication Repeating a study, usually using different participants, perhaps of another age, SES, or culture.

reported maltreatment Harm or endangerment about which someone has notified the authorities.

representative sample A group of research participants who reflect the relevant characteristics of the larger population whose attributes are under study.

resilience The capacity to adapt well to significant adversity and to overcome serious stress.

response to intervention (RTI) An educational strategy intended to help children who demonstrate below-average achievement in early grades, using special intervention.

role confusion A situation in which an adolescent does not seem to know or care what his or her identity is. (Sometimes called *identity* or *role diffusion*.)

rough-and-tumble play Play that mimics aggression through wrestling, chasing, or hitting, but in which there is no intent to harm.

rumination Repeatedly thinking and talking about past experiences; can contribute to depression.

S

sample A group of individuals drawn from a specified population. A sample might be the low-birthweight babies born in four particular hospitals that are representative of all hospitals.

sandwich generation The generation of middle-aged people who are supposedly "squeezed" by the needs of the younger and older members of their families.

scaffolding Temporary support that is tailored to a learner's needs and abilities and aimed at helping the learner master the next task in a given learning process.

science of human development The science that seeks to understand how and why people of all ages and circumstances change or remain the same over time.

scientific method A way to answer questions using empirical research and data-based conclusions.

scientific observation A method of testing a hypothesis by unobtrusively watching and recording participants' behavior in a systematic and objective manner—in a natural setting, in a laboratory, or in searches of archival data.

Seattle Longitudinal Study The first cross-sequential study of adult intelligence. This study began in 1956 and is repeated every seven years.

secondary aging The specific physical illnesses or conditions that become more common with aging but are caused by health habits, genes, and other influences that vary from person to person.

secondary circular reactions The second of three types of feedback loops in sensorimotor intelligence, this one involving people and objects. Infants respond to other people, to toys, and to any other object that they can touch or move.

secondary education Literally, the period after primary education (elementary or grade school) and before tertiary education (college). It usually occurs from about ages 12 to 18, although there is some variation by school and by nation.

secondary prevention Actions that avert harm in a high-risk situation, such as stopping a car before it hits a pedestrian.

secondary sex characteristics Physical traits that are not directly involved in reproduction but that indicate sexual maturity, such as a man's beard and a woman's breasts.

secular trend The long-term upward or downward direction of a certain set of statistical measurements, as opposed to a smaller, shorter cyclical variation. As an example, over the last two centuries, because of improved nutrition and medical care, children have tended to reach their adult height earlier and their adult height has increased.

secure attachment A relationship in which an infant obtains both comfort and confidence from the presence of his or her caregiver.

selective adaptation The process by which living creatures (including people) adjust to their environment. Genes that enhance survival and reproductive ability are selected, over the generations, to become more prevalent.

selective attention The ability to concentrate on some stimuli while ignoring others.

selective optimization with compensation The idea that people compensate for physical and cognitive losses, becoming more proficient in activities or topics that they choose.

self theories Theories of late adulthood that emphasize the core self, or the search to maintain one's integrity and identity.

self-awareness A person's realization that he or she is a distinct individual whose body, mind, and actions are separate from those of other people.

self-concept A person's understanding of who he or she is, in relation to self-esteem, appearance, personality, and various traits.

self-righting The inborn drive to remedy a developmental deficit; literally, to return to sitting or standing upright after being tipped over. People of all ages have self-righting impulses, for emotional as well as physical imbalance.

senescence The process of aging, whereby the body becomes less strong and efficient.

sensation The response of a sensory organ (eyes, ears, skin, tongue, nose) when it detects a stimulus.

sensitive period A time when a certain type of development is most likely, although it may still happen later with more difficulty. For example, early childhood is considered a sensitive period for language learning.

sensorimotor intelligence Piaget's term for the way infants think—by using their senses and motor skills—during the first period of cognitive development.

sensory memory The component of the information-processing system in which incoming stimulus information is stored for a split second to allow it to be processed. (Also called the *sensory register*.)

separation anxiety An infant's distress when a familiar caregiver leaves; most obvious between 9 and 14 months.

seriation The concept that things can be arranged in a logical series, such as the number sequence or the alphabet.

set point A particular body weight that an individual's homeostatic processes strive to maintain.

sex differences Biological differences between males and females, in organs, hormones, and body type.

sexting Sending sexual content, particularly photos or videos, via cell phones or social media.

sexual orientation A term that refers to whether a person is sexually and romantically attracted to others of the same sex, the opposite sex, or both sexes.

sexually transmitted infection (STI) A disease spread by sexual contact, including syphilis, gonorrhea, genital herpes, chlamydia, and HIV.

shaken baby syndrome A life-threatening injury that occurs when an infant is forcefully shaken back and forth, a motion that ruptures blood vessels in the brain and breaks neural connections.

single-parent family A family that consists of only one parent and his or her children.

situational couple violence Fighting between romantic partners that is brought on more by the situation than by the deep personality problems of the individuals. Both partners are typically victims and abusers.

slippery slope The argument that a given action will start a chain of events that will culminate in an undesirable outcome.

small for gestational age (SGA) A term for a baby whose birthweight is significantly lower than expected, given the time since conception. For example, a 5-pound (2,265-gram) newborn is considered SGA if born on time but not SGA if born two months early. (Also called *small-for-dates*.)

social comparison The tendency to assess one's abilities, achievements, social status, and other attributes by measuring them against those of other people, especially one's peers.

social construction An idea that is built on shared perceptions, not on objective reality. Many age-related terms (such as *childhood*, *adolescence*, *yuppie*, and *senior citizen*) are social constructions, connected to biological traits but strongly influenced by social assumptions.

social convoy Collectively, the family members, friends, acquaintances, and even strangers who move through the years of life with a person.

social learning theory An extension of behaviorism that emphasizes the influence that other people have over a person's behavior. Even without specific reinforcement, every individual learns many things through observation and imitation of other people. (Also called *observational learning*.)

social mediation Human interaction that expands and advances understanding, often through words that one person uses to explain something to another.

social norms approach A method of reducing risky behavior that uses emerging adults' desire to follow social norms by making them aware, through the use of surveys, of the prevalence of various behaviors within their peer group.

social referencing Seeking information about how to react to an unfamiliar or ambiguous object or event by observing someone else's expressions and reactions. That other person becomes a social reference.

social smile A smile evoked by a human face, normally first evident in infants about six weeks after birth.

sociocultural theory A newer theory which holds that development results from the dynamic interaction of each person with the surrounding social and cultural forces.

sociodramatic play Pretend play in which children act out various roles and themes in stories that they create.

socioeconomic status (SES) A person's position in society as determined by income, occupation, education, and place of residence. (Sometimes called *social class.*)

socioemotional selectivity theory The theory that older people prioritize regulation of their own emotions and seek familiar social contacts who reinforce generativity, pride, and joy.

specific learning disorder A marked deficit in a particular area of learning that is not caused by an apparent physical disability, by an intellectual disability, or by an unusually stressful home environment.

spermarche A boy's first ejaculation of sperm. Erections can occur as early as infancy, but ejaculation signals sperm production. Spermarche may occur during sleep (in a "wet dream") or via direct stimulation.

static reasoning A characteristic of pre-operational thought in which a young child thinks that nothing changes. Whatever is now has always been and always will be.

stem cells Cells from which any other specialized type of cell can form.

stereotype threat The thought in a person's mind that their appearance or behavior will be misread to confirm another person's oversimplified, prejudiced attitudes.

still-face technique An experimental practice in which an adult keeps his or her face unmoving and expressionless in face-to-face interaction with an infant.

Strange Situation A laboratory procedure for measuring attachment by evoking infants' reactions to the stress of various adults' comings and goings in an unfamiliar playroom.

stranger wariness An infant's expression of concern—a quiet stare while clinging to a familiar person, or a look of fear—when a stranger appears.

stratification theories Theories that emphasize that social forces, particularly those related to a person's social stratum or social category, limit individual choices and affect a person's ability to function in late adulthood because past stratification continues to limit life in various ways.

stressor Any situation, event, experience, or other stimulus that causes a person to feel stressed. Many circumstances that seem to be stresses become stressors for some people but not for others.

stunting The failure of children to grow to a normal height for their age due to severe and chronic malnutrition.

subjective thought Thinking that is strongly influenced by personal qualities of the individual thinker, such as past experiences, cultural assumptions, and goals for the future.

substance use disorder (SUD) The ingestion of a drug to the extent that it impairs the user's biological or psychological well-being.

substantiated maltreatment Harm or endangerment that has been reported, investigated, and verified.

sudden infant death syndrome (SIDS) A situation in which a seemingly healthy infant, usually between 2 and 6 months old, suddenly stops breathing and dies unexpectedly while asleep.

suicidal ideation Thinking about suicide, usually with some serious emotional and intellectual or cognitive overtones.

superego In psychoanalytic theory, the judgmental part of the personality that internalizes the moral standards of the parents.

survey A research method in which information is collected from a large number of people by interviews, written questionnaires, or some other means.

symbolic thought A major accomplishment of preoperational intelligence that allows a child to think symbolically, including understanding that words can refer to things not seen and that an item, such as a flag, can symbolize something else (in this case, a country).

synapse The intersection between the axon of one neuron and the dendrites of other neurons.

synchrony A coordinated, rapid, and smooth exchange of responses between a caregiver and an infant.

synthesis A new idea that integrates the thesis and its antithesis, thus representing a new and more comprehensive level of truth; the third stage of the process of dialectical thinking.

T

telomeres The area of the tips of each chromosome that is reduced a tiny amount as time passes. By the end of life, the telomeres are very short.

temperament Inborn differences between one person and another in emotions, activity, and self-regulation. It is measured by the person's typical responses to the environment.

teratogen An agent or condition, including viruses, drugs, and chemicals, that can impair prenatal development and result in birth defects or even death.

teratology The scientific study of birth abnormalities, especially on causes of biological disabilities and impairments.

terror management theory The idea that people adopt cultural values and moral principles in order to cope with their fear of death. This system of beliefs protects individuals from anxiety about their mortality and bolsters their self-esteem.

tertiary circular reactions The third of three types of feedback loops in sensorimotor intelligence, this one involving active exploration and experimentation. Infants explore a range of new activities, varying their responses as a way of learning about the world.

tertiary prevention Actions, such as immediate and effective medical treatment, that are taken after an adverse event (such as illness or injury) and that are aimed at reducing harm or preventing disability.

testosterone A sex hormone, the best known of the androgens (male hormones); secreted in far greater amounts by males than by females.

theory of mind A person's theory of what other people might be thinking. In order to have a theory of mind, children must realize that other people are not necessarily thinking the same thoughts that they themselves are. That realization seldom occurs before age 4.

theory-theory The idea that children attempt to explain everything they see and hear by constructing theories.

thesis A proposition or statement of belief; the first stage of the process of dialectical thinking.

threshold effect In prenatal development, when a teratogen is relatively harmless in small doses but becomes harmful once exposure reaches a certain level (the threshold).

time-out A disciplinary technique in which a child is separated from other people for a specified time.

transient exuberance The great but temporary increase in the number of dendrites that develop in an infant's brain during the first two years of life.

Trends in Math and Science Study (TIMSS) An international assessment of the math and science skills of fourth- and eighth-graders. Although the TIMSS is very useful, different countries' scores are not always comparable because sample selection, test administration, and content validity are hard to keep uniform.

trust versus mistrust Erikson's first crisis of psychosocial development. Infants learn basic trust if the world is a secure place where their basic needs (for food, comfort, attention, and so on) are met.

U

ultrasound An image of a fetus (or an internal organ) produced by using high-frequency sound waves. (Also called *sonogram*.)

universal design The creation of settings and equipment that can be used by everyone, whether or not they are able-bodied and sensory-acute.

V

very low birthweight (VLBW) A body weight at birth of less than 1,500 grams (3 pounds, 5 ounces).

visual cliff An experimental apparatus that gives the illusion of a sudden drop-off between one horizontal surface and another.

vitality A measure of health that refers to how healthy and energetic—physically, intellectually, and socially—an individual actually feels.

voucher Public subsidy for tuition payment at a nonpublic school. Vouchers vary a great deal from place to place, not only in amount and availability but also in restrictions as to who gets them and what schools accept them.

W

wasting The tendency for children to be severely underweight for their age as a result of malnutrition.

wear-and-tear theory A view of aging as a process by which the human body wears out because of the passage of time and exposure to environmental stressors.

withdrawn-rejected A type of childhood rejection, when other children do not want to be friends with a child because of his or her timid, withdrawn, and anxious behavior.

working memory The component of the information-processing system in which current conscious mental activity occurs. (Formerly called *short-term memory*.)

working model In cognitive theory, a set of assumptions that the individual uses to organize perceptions and experiences. For example, a person might assume that other people are trustworthy and be surprised by an incident in which this working model of human behavior is erroneous.

X

X-linked A gene carried on the X chromosome. If a male inherits an X-linked recessive trait from his mother, he expresses that trait because the Y from his father has no counteracting gene. Females are more likely to be carriers of X-linked traits but are less likely to express them.

XX A 23rd chromosome pair that consists of two X-shaped chromosomes, one each from the mother and the father. XX zygotes become females.

XY A 23rd chromosome pair that consists of an X-shaped chromosome from the mother and a Y-shaped chromosome from the father. XY zygotes become males.

Y

young-old Healthy, vigorous, financially secure older adults (generally, those aged 65 to 75) who are well integrated into the lives of their families and communities.

Z

zone of proximal development (ZPD) Vygotsky's term for the skills—cognitive as well as physical—that a person can exercise only with assistance, not yet independently.

zone of proximal development In sociocultural theory, a metaphorical area, or "zone," surrounding a learner that includes all of the skills, knowledge, and concepts that the person is close ("proximal") to acquiring but cannot yet master without help.

zygote The single cell formed from the union of two gametes, a sperm and an ovum.

References

There are dozens of standard ways to format references. I use the style recommended by the American Psychological Association, with one major change: first names (when available) rather than initials, in order to emphasize that the authors are real people, often women. This edition also includes DOI numbers, to ease checking on the Internet.

Aarnoudse-Moens, Cornelieke S. H.; Smidts, Diana P.; Oosterlaan, Jaap; Duivenvoorden, Hugo J. & Weisglas-Kuperus, Nynke. (2009). Executive function in very preterm children at early school age. *Journal of Abnormal Child Psychology*, 37(7), 981–993. doi: 10.1007/s10802-009-9327-z

Abar, Caitlin C.; Jackson, Kristina M. & Wood, Mark. (2014). Reciprocal relations between perceived parental knowledge and adolescent substance use and delinquency: The moderating role of parent–teen relationship quality. *Developmental Psychology*, 50(9), 2176–2187. doi: 10.1037 /a0037463

Abbott, Elizabeth. (2011). *A history of marriage: From same sex unions to private vows and common law, the surprising diversity of a tradition.* New York, NY: Seven Stories.

Abela, Angela & Walker, Janet (Eds.). (2014). *Contemporary issues in family studies: Global perspectives on partnerships, parenting and support in a changing world.* Malden, MA: Wiley.

Abele, Andrea E. & Volmer, Judith. (2011). Dual-career couples: Specific challenges for work-life integration. In Stephan Kaiser et al. (Eds.), *Creating balance? International perspectives on the work-life integration of professionals* (pp. 173–189). Heidelberg, Germany: Springer. doi: 10.1007/978-3-642-16199-5_10

Accardo, Pasquale. (2006). Who's training whom? *The Journal of Pediatrics*, 149(2), 151–152. doi: 10.1016/j.jpeds.2006.04.026

Adams, Caralee J. (2014). High school students' participation in advanced placement continues to grow [Web log post]. Education Week. Retrieved from http://blogs.edweek.org/edweek/college_bound/2014/02/high_school_students_participating_in_advanced_placement_continues_to_grow.html

Adamson, Lauren B. & Bakeman, Roger. (2006). Development of displaced speech in early mother-child conversations. *Child Development*, 77(1), 186–200. doi: 10.1111/j.1467-8624.2006.00864.x

Adamson, Lauren B.; Bakeman, Roger; Deckner, Deborah F. & Nelson, P. Brooke. (2014). From interactions to conversations: The development of joint engagement during early childhood. *Child Development*, 85(3), 941–955. doi: 10.1111/cdev.12189

Adolph, Karen E.; Cole, Whitney G.; Komati, Meghana; Garciaguirre, Jessie S.; Badaly, Daryaneh; Lingeman, Jesse M., . . . Sotsky, Rachel B. (2012). How do you learn to walk? Thousands of steps and dozens of falls per day. *Psychological Science*, 23(11), 1387–1394. doi: 10.1177/0956797612446346

Adolph, Karen E. & Kretch, Kari S. (2012). Infants on the edge: Beyond the visual cliff. In Alan M. Slater & Paul C. Quinn (Eds.), *Developmental psychology: Revisiting the classic studies.* Thousand Oaks, CA: Sage.

Adolph, Karen E. & Robinson, Scott. (2013). The road to walking: What learning to walk tells us about development. In Philip D. Zelazo (Ed.), *The Oxford handbook of developmental psychology* (Vol. 1, pp. 402–447). New York, NY: Oxford University Press. doi: 10.1093 /oxfordhb /9780199958450.013.0015

Adolph, Karen E.; Vereijken, Beatrix & Shrout, Patrick E. (2003). What changes in infant walking and why. *Child Development*, 74(2), 475–497. doi: 10.1111/1467-8624.7402011

Ahima, Rexford S. & Lazar, Mitchell A. (2013). The health risk of obesity—Better metrics imperative. *Science*, 341(6148), 856–858. doi: 10.1126 /science.1241244

Ahmed, Parvez & Jaakkola, Jouni J. K. (2007). Maternal occupation and adverse pregnancy outcomes: A Finnish population-based study. *Occupational Medicine*, 57(6), 417–423. doi: 10.1093/occmed/kqm038

Ailshire, Jennifer A.; Beltrán-Sánchez, Hiram & Crimmins, Eileen M. (2015). Becoming centenarians: Disease and functioning trajectories of older U.S. adults as they survive to 100. *The Journal of Gerontology Series A*, 70(2), 193–201. doi: 10.1093/gerona/glu124

Ainsworth, Mary D. Salter. (1967). *Infancy in Uganda: Infant care and the growth of love.* Baltimore, MD: Johns Hopkins Press.

Ainsworth, Mary D. Salter. (1973). The development of infant-mother attachment. In Bettye M. Caldwell & Henry N. Ricciuti (Eds.), *Child development and social policy* (pp. 1–94). Chicago, IL: University of Chicago Press.

Aizer, Anna & Currie, Janet. (2014). The intergenerational transmission of inequality: Maternal disadvantage and health at birth. *Science*, 344(6186), 856–861. doi: 10.1126 /science.1251872

Akhtar, Nameera & Jaswal, Vikram K. (2013). Deficit or difference? Interpreting diverse developmental paths: An introduction to the special section. *Developmental Psychology*, 49(1), 1–3. doi: 10.1037/a0029851

Aksglaede, Lise; Link, Katarina; Giwercman, Aleksander; Jørgensen, Niels; Skakkebæk, Niels E. & Juul, Anders. (2013). 47, XXY Klinefelter syndrome: Clinical characteristics and age-specific recommendations for medical management. *American Journal of Medical Genetics Part C: Seminars in Medical Genetics*, 163(1), 55–63. doi: 10.1002/ajmg.c.31349

Al Otaiba, Stephanie; Wanzek, Jeanne & Yovanoff, Paul. (2015). Response to intervention. *European Scientific Journal*, 1, 260–264.

Al-Hashim, Aqeela H.; Blaser, Susan; Raybaud, Charles & MacGregor, Daune. (2016). Corpus callosum abnormalities: Neuroradiological and clinical correlations. *Developmental Medicine & Child Neurology*, 58(5), 475–484. doi: 10.1111 /dmcn.12978

Al-Namlah, Abdulrahman S.; Meins, Elizabeth & Fernyhough, Charles. (2012). Self-regulatory private speech relates to children's recall and organization of autobiographical memories. *Early Childhood Research Quarterly*, 27(3), 441–446. doi: 10.1016/j.ecresq.2012.02.005

Al-Sahab, Ban; Ardern, Chris I.; Hamadeh, Mazen J. & Tamim, Hala. (2010). Age at menarche in Canada: Results from the National Longitudinal Survey of Children & Youth. *BMC Public Health*, 10(1), 736–743. doi: 10.1186/1471-2458-10-736

Al-Sayes, Fatin; Gari, Mamdooh; Qusti, Safaa; Bagatian, Nadiah & Abuzenadah, Adel. (2011). Prevalence of iron deficiency and iron deficiency anemia among females at university stage. *Journal of Medical Laboratory and Diagnosis*, 2(1), 5–11.

Al-Yagon, Michal; Cavendish, Wendy; Cornoldi, Cesare; Fawcett, Angela J.; Grünke, Matthias; Hung, Li-Yu, . . . Vio, Claudio. (2013). The proposed changes for DSM-5 for SLD and ADHD: International perspectives—Australia, Germany, Greece, India, Israel, Italy, Spain, Taiwan, United Kingdom, and United States. *Journal of Learning Disabilities*, 46(1), 58–72. doi: 10.1177/0022219412464353

Alasuutari, Pertti; Bickman, Leonard & Brannen, Julia (Eds.). (2008). *The SAGE handbook of social research methods.* Los Angeles, CA: SAGE.

Albert, Dustin; Chein, Jason & Steinberg, Laurence. (2013). The teenage brain: Peer influences on adolescent decision making. *Current Directions in Psychological Science*, 22(2), 114–120. doi: 10.1177/0963721412471347

Albert, Dustin & Steinberg, Laurence. (2011). Judgment and decision making in adolescence. *Journal of Research on Adolescence*, 21(1), 211–224. doi: 10.1111/j.1532-7795.2010.00724.x

Albert, Steven M. & Freedman, Vicki A. (2010). *Public health and aging: Maximizing function and well-being* (2nd ed.). New York, NY: Springer.

Aldwin, Carolyn M. (2007). *Stress, coping, and development: An integrative perspective* (2nd ed.). New York, NY: Guilford Press.

Aldwin, Carolyn M. (2010). Stress and coping across the lifespan. In Susan Folkman (Ed.), *The Oxford handbook of stress, health, and coping* (pp. 15–34). New York, NY: Oxford University Press.

Aldwin, Carolyn M. & Gilmer, Diane Fox. (2013). *Health, illness, and optimal aging: Biological and psychosocial perspectives* (2nd ed.). New York, NY: Springer.

Alegre, Alberto. (2011). Parenting styles and children's emotional intelligence: What do we know? *The Family Journal, 19*(1), 56–62. doi: 10.1177/1066480710387486

Alesi, Marianha; Bianco, Antonino; Padulo, Johnny; Vella, Francesco Paolo; Petrucci, Marco; Paoli, Antonio, . . . Pepi, Annamaria. (2014). Motor and cognitive development: the role of karate. *Muscle, Ligaments and Tendons Journal, 4*(2), 114–120.

Alexander, Karl L.; Entwisle, Doris R. & Olson, Linda Steffel. (2014). *The long shadow: Family background, disadvantaged urban youth, and the transition to adulthood.* New York, NY: Russell Sage Foundation.

Allen, Kathleen P. (2010). A bullying intervention system in high school: A two-year school-wide follow-up. *Studies In Educational Evaluation, 36*(3), 83–92. doi: 10.1016/j.stueduc.2011.01.002

Allen, Rebecca S.; Haley, Philip P.; Harris, Grant M.; Fowler, Stevie N. & Pruthi, Roopwinder. (2011). Resilience: Definitions, ambiguities, and applications. In Barbara Resnick et al. (Eds.), *Resilience in aging: Concepts, research, and outcomes* (pp. 1–14). New York, NY: Springer.

Allen, Tammy D.; Johnson, Ryan C.; Saboe, Kristin N.; Cho, Eunae; Dumani, Soner & Evans, Sarah. (2012). Dispositional variables and work–family conflict: A meta-analysis. *Journal of Vocational Behavior, 80*(1), 17–26. doi: 10.1016/j.jvb.2011.04.004

Allendorf, Keera. (2013). Schemas of marital change: From arranged marriages to eloping for love. *Journal of Marriage and Family, 75*(2), 453–469. doi: 10.1111/jomf.12003

Allendorf, Keera & Pandian, Roshan K. (2016). The decline of arranged marriage? Marital change and continuity in India. *Population and Development Review, 42*(3), 435–464. doi: 10.1111/j .1728-4457.2016.00149.x

Almond, Douglas. (2006). Is the 1918 influenza pandemic over? Long-term effects of in utero influenza exposure in the post-1940 U.S. population. *Journal of Political Economy, 114*(4), 672–712. doi: 10.1086/507154

Alper, Meryl. (2013). Developmentally appropriate New Media Literacies: Supporting cultural competencies and social skills in early childhood education. *Journal of Early Childhood Literacy, 13*(2), 175–196. doi: 10.1177/1468798411430101

Altbach, Philip G.; Reisberg, Liz & Rumbley, Laura E. (2010). Tracking a global academic revolution. *Change: The Magazine of Higher Learning, 42*(2), 30–39. doi: 10.1080 /00091381003590845

Alvira-Hammond, Marta; Longmore, Monica A.; Manning, Wendy D. & Giordano, Peggy C. (2014). Gainful activity and intimate partner aggression in emerging adulthood.

Emerging Adulthood, 2(2), 116–127. doi: 10.1177/2167696813512305

Alzheimer's Association. (2015). *2015 Alzheimer's disease facts and figures: Includes a special report on disclosing a diagnosis of Alzheimer's disease.* Washington, DC: Alzheimer's Association.

Amato, Michael S.; Magzamen, Sheryl; Imm, Pamela; Havlena, Jeffrey A.; Anderson, Henry A.; Kanarek, Marty S. & Moore, Colleen F. (2013). Early lead exposure (<3 years old) prospectively predicts fourth grade school suspension in Milwaukee, Wisconsin (USA). *Environmental Research, 126*, 60–65. doi: 10.1016/j .envres.2013.07.008

Amato, Paul R. (2010). Research on divorce: Continuing trends and new developments. *Journal of Marriage and Family, 72*(3), 650–666. doi: 10.1111/j.1741-3737.2010.00723.x

Ameade, Evans Paul Kwame & Garti, Helene Akpene. (2016). Age at menarche and factors that influence it: A study among female university students in Tamale, northern Ghana. *PLoS ONE, 11*(5), e0155310. doi: 10.1371/journal .pone.0155310

American College of Obstetricians and Gynecologists Committee on Obstetric Practice. (2011). Committee opinion no. 476: Planned home birth. *Obstetrics & Gynecology, 117*(2), 425–428. doi: 10.1097 /AOG.0b013e31820eee20

American Community Survey. (2014). Washington, DC: U.S. Census Bureau.

American Community Survey. (2015). Washington, DC: U.S. Census Bureau.

American Psychiatric Association. (2013). *Diagnostic and statistical manual of mental disorders: DSM-5* (5th ed.). Washington, DC: American Psychiatric Association.

American Psychological Association. (2010). Ethical principles of psychologists and code of conduct: Including 2010 amendments. http:// www.apa.org/ethics/code/index.aspx

American Psychological Association. (2012, January 11). *Stress in America™: Our health at risk.* Washington, DC: American Psychological Association.

Amodio, David M. (2014). The neuroscience of prejudice and stereotyping. *Nature Reviews Neuroscience, 15*, 670–682. doi: 10.1038/nrn3800

Anderin, Claes; Gustafsson, Ulf O.; Heijbel, Niklas & Thorell, Anders. (2015). Weight loss before bariatric surgery and postoperative complications: Data from the Scandinavian Obesity Registry (SOReg). *Annals of Surgery, 261*(5), 909–913. doi: 10.1097/SLA.0000000000000839

Anderson, Michael. (2001). 'You have to get inside the person' or making grief private: Image and metaphor in the therapeutic reconstruction of bereavement. In Jenny Hockey et al. (Eds.), *Grief, mourning, and death ritual* (pp. 135–143). Buckingham, UK: Open University Press.

Anderson, Monica. (2016, January 7). *Parents, teens and digital monitoring. Numbers, Facts and Trends Shaping the World.* Washington, DC: Pew Research Center.

Anderson, Sarah E. & Must, Aviva. (2005). Interpreting the continued decline in the average age at menarche: Results from two nationally

representative surveys of U.S. girls studied 10 years apart. *The Journal of Pediatrics, 147*(6), 753–760. doi: 10.1016/j.jpeds.2005.07.016

Andreas, Nicholas J.; Kampmann, Beate & Le-Doare, Kirsty Mehring. (2015). Human breast milk: A review on its composition and bioactivity. *Early Human Development, 91*(11), 629–635. doi: 10.1016/j.earlhumdev.2015.08.013

Anguera, Joaquin A. & Gazzaley, Adam. (2015). Video games, cognitive exercises, and the enhancement of cognitive abilities. *Current Opinion in Behavioral Sciences, 4*, 160–165. doi: 10.1016/j .cobeha.2015.06.002

Anjum, Afshan; Gait, Priyanka; Cullen, Kathryn R. & White, Tonya. (2010). Schizophrenia in adolescents and young adults. In Jon E. Grant & Marc N. Potenza (Eds.), *Young adult mental health* (pp. 362–378). New York, NY: Oxford University Press.

Ansado, Jennyfer; Collins, Louis; Fonov, Vladimir; Garon, Mathieu; Alexandrov, Lubomir; Karama, Sherif, . . . Beauchamp, Miriam H. (2015). A new template to study callosal growth shows specific growth in anterior and posterior regions of the corpus callosum in early childhood. *European Journal of Neuroscience, 42*(1), 1675–1684. doi: 10.1111 /ejn.12869

Antenucci, Antonio. (2013, November 26). Cop who bought homeless man boots promoted. *New York Post.*

Antoine, Michelle W.; Hübner, Christian A; Arezzo, Joseph C. & Hébert, Jean M. (2013). A causative link between inner ear defects and long-term striatal dysfunction. *Science, 341*(6150), 1120–1123. doi: 10.1126/science.1240405

Antonucci, Toni C.; Akiyama, Hiroko & Merline, Alicia. (2001). Dynamics of social relationships in midlife. In Margie E. Lachman (Ed.), *Handbook of midlife development* (pp. 571–598). New York, NY: Wiley.

Apgar, Virginia. (1953). A proposal for a new method of evaluation of the newborn infant. *Current Researches in Anesthesia and Analgesia, 32*, 260–267.

Apgar, Virginia. (2015). A proposal for a new method of evaluation of the newborn infant. *Anesthesia & Analgesia, 120*(5), 1056–1059. doi: 10.1213/ANE.0b013e31829bdc5c

Archambault, Isabelle; Janosz, Michel; Fallu, Jean-Sébastien & Paganim, Linda S. (2009). Student engagement and its relationship with early high school dropout. *Journal of Adolescence, 32*(3), 651–670. doi: 10.1016/j.adolescence.2008.06.007

Archer, John. (2000). Sex differences in aggression between heterosexual partners: A meta-analytic review. *Psychological Bulletin, 126*(5), 651–680. doi: 10.1037//0033-2909.126.5.651

Ardelt, Monika. (2011). Wisdom, age, and well-being. In K. Warner Schaie & Sherry L. Willis (Eds.), *Handbook of the psychology of aging* (7th ed., pp. 279–291). San Diego, CA: Academic Press. doi: 10.1016/B978-0-12-380882-0.00018-8

Arden, Rosalind; Luciano, Michelle; Deary, Ian J.; Reynolds, Chandra A.; Pedersen, Nancy L.; Plassman, Brenda L., . . . Visscher, Peter M. (2016). The association between intelligence and lifespan is mostly genetic. *International*

Journal of Epidemiology, 45(1), 178–185. doi: 10.1093/ije/dyv112

Argyrides, Marios & Kkeli, Natalie. (2015). Predictive factors of disordered eating and body image satisfaction in Cyprus. *International Journal of Eating Disorders, 48*(4), 431–435. doi: 10.1002 /eat.22310

Ariely, Dan. (2010). *Predictably Irrational: The hidden forces that shape our decisions* (Revised and Expanded ed.). New York, NY: Harper Perennial.

Arndt, Jamie; Vail III, Kenneth E.; Cox, Cathy R.; Goldenberg, Jamie L.; Piasecki, Thomas M. & Gibbons, Frederick X. (2013). The interactive effect of mortality reminders and tobacco craving on smoking topography. *Health Psychology, 32*(5), 525–532. doi: 10.1037/a0029201

Arnett, Jeffrey J. (2004). *Emerging adulthood: The winding road from the late teens through the twenties.* New York, NY: Oxford University Press.

Arnett, Jeffrey J. (2008). The neglected 95%: Why American psychology needs to become less American. *American Psychologist, 63*(7), 602–614. doi: 10.1037/0003-066X.63.7.602

Arnett, Jeffrey J. (2016). Emerging adulthood and social class: Rejoinder to Furstenberg, Silva, and du Bois-Reymond. *Emerging Adulthood, 4*(4), 244–247. doi: 10.1177/2167696815627248

Arnold, Robert M.; Back, Anthony L.; Barnato, Amber E.; Prendergast, Thomas J.; Emlet, Lillian L.; Karpov, Irina, . . . Nelson, Judith E. (2015). The Critical Care Communication project: Improving fellows' communication skills. *Journal of Critical Care, 30*(2), 250–254. doi: 10.1016/j.jcrc.2014.11.016

Aron, Arthur; Lewandowski, Gary W.; Mashek, Debra & Aron, Elaine N. (2013). The self-expansion model of motivation and cognition in close relationships. In Jeffry A. Simpson & Lorne Campbell (Eds.), *The Oxford handbook of close relationships* (pp. 90–115). New York, NY: Oxford University Press.

Aronson, Joshua; Burgess, Diana; Phelan, Sean M. & Juarez, Lindsay. (2013). Unhealthy interactions: The role of stereotype threat in health disparities. *American Journal of Public Health, 103*(1), 50–56. doi: 10.2105/AJPH.2012.300828

Arrazola, René A.; Dube, Shanta R. & King, Brian A. (2013, November 15). Tobacco product use among middle and high school students—United States, 2011 and 2012. *Morbidity and Mortality Weekly Report 62*(45), 893–897. Atlanta, GA: Centers for Disease Control and Prevention.

Arrazola, René A.; Neff, Linda J.; Kennedy, Sara M.; Holder-Hayes, Enver & Jones, Christopher D. (2014, November 14). Tobacco use among middle and high school students—United States, 2013. *Morbidity and Mortality Weekly Report 63*(45), 1021–1026. Atlanta, GA: Centers for Disease Control and Prevention.

Arrazola, René A.; Singh, Tushar; Corey, Catherine G.; Husten, Corinne G.; Neff, Linda J.; Apelberg, Benjamin J., . . . Caraballo, Ralph S. (2015, April 17). Tobacco use among middle and high school students—United States, 2011–2014. *Morbidity and Mortality Weekly Report 64*(14), 381–385. Atlanta, GA: Centers for Disease Control and Prevention.

Arterburn, David E.; Bogart, Andy; Sherwood, Nancy E.; Sidney, Stephen; Coleman, Karen J.; Haneuse, Sebastien, . . . Selby, Joe. (2013). A multisite study of long-term remission and relapse of type 2 diabetes mellitus following gastric bypass. *Obesity Surgery, 23*(1), 93–102. doi: 10.1007 /s11695-012-0802-1

Arum, Richard & Roksa, Josipa. (2011). *Academically adrift: Limited learning on college campuses.* Chicago, IL: University of Chicago Press.

Arum, Richard & Roksa, Josipa. (2014). *Aspiring adults adrift: Tentative transitions of college graduates.* Chicago, IL: University of Chicago Press.

Asbridge, Mark; Brubacher, Jeff R. & Chan, Herbert. (2013). Cell phone use and traffic crash risk: A culpability analysis. *International Journal of Epidemiology, 42*(1), 259–267. doi: 10.1093/ije /dys180

Asendorpf, Jens B.; Denissen, Jaap J. A. & van Aken, Marcel A. G. (2008). Inhibited and aggressive preschool children at 23 years of age: Personality and social transitions into adulthood. *Developmental Psychology, 44*(4), 997–1011. doi: 10.1037/0012-1649.44.4.997

Ashby, Michael. (2009). The dying human: A perspective from palliative medicine. In Allan Kellehear (Ed.), *The study of dying: From autonomy to transformation* (pp. 76–98). New York, NY: Cambridge University Press.

Ashraf, Quamrul & Galor, Oded. (2013). The 'Out of Africa' hypothesis, human genetic diversity, and comparative economic development. *American Economic Review, 103*(1), 1–46. doi: 10.1257 /aer.103.1.1

Aslin, Richard N. (2012). Language development: Revisiting Eimas et al.'s /ba/ and /pa/ study. In Alan M. Slater & Paul C. Quinn (Eds.), *Developmental psychology: Revisiting the classic studies* (pp. 191–203). Thousand Oaks, CA: Sage.

Asma, Stephen T. (2013). *Against fairness.* Chicago, IL: University of Chicago Press.

Assmann, Jan. (2005). *Death and salvation in ancient Egypt.* Ithaca, NY: Cornell University Press.

Association of American Medical Colleges. (2014). *Table 1: Medical students, selected years, 1965–2013. The state of women in academic medicine: The pipeline and pathways to leadership, 2013–2014.* Washington, DC: Association of American Medical Colleges.

Association of American Medical Colleges. (2015, November 25). *Table B-2.2: Total graduates by U.S. medical school and sex, 2010–2011 through 2014–2015. FACTS: Applicants, matriculants, enrollment, graduates, M.D.-Ph.D., and residency applicants data.* Washington, DC: Association of American Medical Colleges.

Atchley, Robert C. (2009). *Spirituality and aging.* Baltimore, MD: Johns Hopkins University Press.

Atzil, Shir; Hendler, Talma & Feldman, Ruth. (2014). The brain basis of social synchrony. *Social Cognitive & Affective Neuroscience, 9*(8), 1193–1202. doi: 10.1093/scan/nst105

Aud, Susan; Hussar, William; Planty, Michael; Snyder, Thomas; Bianco, Kevin; Fox, Mary Ann, . . . Drake, Lauren. (2010). *The condition of education 2010.* Washington, DC: National Center for Education Statistics, Institute of Education Sciences, U.S. Department of Education.

Aud, Susan; Wilkinson-Flicker, Sidney; Kristapovich, Paul; Rathbun, Amy; Wang, Xiaolei & Zhang, Jijun. (2013). *The condition of education 2013.* Washington, DC: U.S. Department of Education, National Center for Education Statistics.

Aunola, Kaisa; Tolvanen, Asko; Viljaranta, Jaana & Nurmi, Jari-Erik. (2013). Psychological control in daily parent–child interactions increases children's negative emotions. *Journal of Family Psychology, 27*(3), 453–462. doi: 10.1037/a0032891

Aven, Terje. (2011). On some recent definitions and analysis frameworks for risk, vulnerability, and resilience. *Risk Analysis, 31*(4), 515–522. doi: 10.1111/j.1539-6924.2010.01528.x

Avery, Rosemary J. & Freundlich, Madelyn. (2009). You're all grown up now: Termination of foster care support at age 18. *Journal of Adolescence, 32*(2), 247–257. doi: 10.1016 /j.adolescence.2008.03.009

Aviv, Abraham. (2011). Leukocyte telomere dynamics, human aging and life span. In Edward J. Masoro & Steven N. Austad (Eds.), *Handbook of the biology of aging* (7th ed., pp. 163–176). San Diego, CA: Academic Press. doi: 10.1016/B978-0-12-378638-8.00007-5

Ayalon, Liat & Ancoli-Israel, Sonia. (2009). Normal sleep in aging. In Teofilo L. Lee-Chiong (Ed.), *Sleep medicine essentials* (pp. 173–176). Hoboken, NJ: Wiley-Blackwell.

Ayyanathan, Kasirajan (Ed.). (2014). *Specific gene expression and epigenetics: The interplay between the genome and its environment.* Oakville, Canada: Apple Academic Press.

Azrin, Nathan H. & Foxx, Richard M. (1974). *Toilet training in less than a day.* New York, NY: Simon & Schuster.

Babchishin, Lyzon K.; Weegar, Kelly & Romano, Elisa. (2013). Early child care effects on later behavioral outcomes using a Canadian nation-wide sample. *Journal of Educational and Developmental Psychology, 3*(2), 15–29. doi: 10.5539/jedp .v3n2p15

Babineau, Vanessa; Green, Cathryn Gordon; Jolicoeur-Martineau, Alexis; Minde, Klaus; Sassi, Roberto; St-André, Martin, . . . Wazana, Ashley. (2015). Prenatal depression and 5-HTTLPR interact to predict dysregulation from 3 to 36 months–A differential susceptibility model. *Journal of Child Psychology and Psychiatry, 56*(1), 21–29. doi: 10.1111/jcpp.12246

Bagwell, Catherine L. & Schmidt, Michelle E. (2011). *Friendships in childhood & adolescence.* New York, NY: Guilford Press.

Bailey, J. Michael; Vasey, Paul L.; Diamond, Lisa M.; Breedlove, S. Marc; Vilain, Eric & Epprecht, Marc. (2016). Sexual orientation, controversy, and science. *Psychological Science in the Public Interest, 17*(2), 45–101. doi: 10.1177/1529100616637616

Baillargeon, Renée & DeVos, Julie. (1991). Object permanence in young infants: Further evidence. *Child Development, 62*(6), 1227–1246. doi: 10.1111/j.1467-8624.1991.tb01602.x

Baker, Jeffrey P. (2000). Immunization and the American way: 4 childhood vaccines. *American Journal of Public Health, 90*(2), 199–207. doi: 10.2105/AJPH.90.2.199

Baker, Lindsey A. & Silverstein, Merril. (2012). The wellbeing of grandparents caring for grandchildren in rural China and the United States. In Sara Arber & Virpi Timonen (Eds.), *Contemporary grandparenting: Changing family relationships in global contexts* (pp. 51–70). Chicago, IL: Policy Press.

Baker, Olesya & Lang, Kevin. (2013). *The effect of high school exit exams on graduation, employment, wages and incarceration.* Cambridge, MA: National Bureau of Economic Research. doi: 10.3386 /w19182

Balari, Sergio & Lorenzo, Guillermo. (2015). Should it stay or should it go? A critical reflection on the critical period for language. *Biolinguistics, 9,* 8–42.

Baldry, Anna C. & Farrington, David P. (2007). Effectiveness of programs to prevent school bullying. *Victims & Offenders, 2*(2), 183–204. doi: 10.1080/15564880701263155

Ball, Howard. (2012). *At liberty to die: The battle for death with dignity in America.* New York, NY: New York University Press.

Ball, Helen L. & Volpe, Lane E. (2013). Sudden Infant Death Syndrome (SIDS) risk reduction and infant sleep location–Moving the discussion forward. *Social Science & Medicine, 79*(1), 84–91. doi: 10.1016/j .socscimed.2012.03.025

Baltes, Paul B. (2003). On the incomplete architecture of human ontogeny: Selection, optimization and compensation as foundation of developmental theory. In Ursula M. Staudinger & Ulman Lindenberger (Eds.), *Understanding human development: Dialogues with lifespan psychology* (pp. 17–43). Boston, MA: Kluwer Academic Publishers.

Baltes, Paul B. & Baltes, Margret M. (1990). Psychological perspectives on successful aging: The model of selective optimization with compensation. In Paul B. Baltes & Margret M. Baltes (Eds.), *Successful aging: Perspectives from the behavioral sciences* (pp. 1–34). New York, NY: Cambridge University Press.

Baltes, Paul B.; Lindenberger, Ulman & Staudinger, Ursula M. (1998). Life-span theory in developmental psychology. In William Damon (Ed.), *Handbook of child psychology* (5th ed., Vol. 1, pp. 1029–1144). New York, NY: Wiley.

Baltes, Paul B.; Lindenberger, Ulman & Staudinger, Ursula M. (2006). Life span theory in developmental psychology. In William Damon & Richard M. Lerner (Eds.), *Handbook of child psychology* (6th ed., Vol. 1, pp. 569–664). Hoboken, NJ: Wiley.

Baltes, Paul B. & Smith, Jacqui. (2008). The fascination of wisdom: Its nature, ontogeny, and function. *Perspectives on Psychological Science, 3*(1), 56–64. doi: 10.1111/j.1745-6916.2008.00062.x

Baly, Michael W.; Cornell, Dewey G. & Lovegrove, Peter. (2014). A longitudinal investigation of self- and peer reports of bullying victimization across middle school. *Psychology in the Schools, 51*(3), 217–240. doi: 10.1002/pits.21747

Bandini, Julia. (2015). The medicalization of bereavement: (Ab)normal grief in the DSM-5. *Death Studies, 39*(6), 347–352. doi: 10.1080/07481187.2014.951498

Bandura, Albert. (1986). *Social foundations of thought and action: A social cognitive theory.* Englewood Cliffs, NJ: Prentice-Hall.

Bandura, Albert. (1997). The anatomy of stages of change. *American Journal of Health Promotion, 12*(1), 8–10.

Bandura, Albert. (2006). Toward a psychology of human agency. *Perspectives on Psychological Science, 1*(2), 164–180. doi: 10.1111/j.1745-6916 .2006.00011.x

Bangerter, Lauren R.; Kim, Kyungmin; Zarit, Steven H.; Birditt, Kira S. & Fingerman, Karen L. (2015). Perceptions of giving support and depressive symptoms in late life. *The Gerontologist, 55*(5), 770–779. doi: 10.1093/geront/gnt210

Banks, James R. & Andrews, Timothy. (2015). Outcomes of childhood asthma to the age of 50 years. *Pediatrics, 136*(Suppl. 3).

Banks, Jane W. (2003). Ka'nistén̲sera Teiakotíhsnie's: A native community rekindles the tradition of breastfeeding. *AWHONN Lifelines, 7*(4), 340–347. doi: 10.1177/1091592303257828

Bannon, Michael J.; Johnson, Magen M.; Michelhaugh, Sharon K.; Hartley, Zachary J.; Halter, Steven D.; David, James A., . . . Schmidt, Carl J. (2014). A molecular profile of cocaine abuse includes the differential expression of genes that regulate transcription, chromatin, and dopamine cell phenotype. *Neuropsychopharmacology, 39*(9), 2191–2199. doi: 10.1038/npp.2014.70

Barash, David P. (2016). *Out of Eden: The surprising consequences of polygamy.* New York, NY: Oxford University Press.

Barber, Brian K. (Ed.). (2002). *Intrusive parenting: How psychological control affects children and adolescents.* Washington, DC: American Psychological Association.

Barbey, Aron K.; Colom, Roberto; Paul, Erick J. & Grafman, Jordan. (2013). Architecture of fluid intelligence and working memory revealed by lesion mapping. *Brain Structure and Function, 219*(2), 485–494. doi: 10.1007/s00429-013 -0512-z

Bardenheier, Barbara H.; Lin, Ji; Zhuo, Xiaohui; Ali, Mohammed K.; Thompson, Theodore J.; Cheng, Yiling J. & Gregg, Edward W. (2016). Compression of disability between two birth cohorts of US adults with diabetes, 1992–2012: A prospective longitudinal analysis. *The Lancet Diabetes & Endocrinology, 4*(8), 686–694. doi: 10.1016/S2213-8587(16)30090-0

Barinaga, Marcia. (2003). Newborn neurons search for meaning. *Science, 299*(5603), 32–34. doi: 10.1126/science.299.5603.32

Barnett, W. Steven; Carolan, Megan E.; Squires, James H.; Brown, Kirsty Clarke & Horowitz, Michelle. (2015). *The state of preschool 2014: State preschool yearbook.* New Brunswick, NJ: National Institute for Early Education Research.

Baron-Cohen, Simon; Tager-Flusberg, Helen & Lombardo, Michael (Eds.). (2013). *Understanding other minds: Perspectives from developmental social neuroscience* (3rd ed.). New York, NY: Oxford University Press.

Barone, Joseph. (2015). *It's not your fault!: Strategies for solving toilet training and bedwetting problems.* New Brunswick, NJ: Rutgers University Press.

Barr, Rachel. (2013). Memory constraints on infant learning from picture books, television, and touchscreens. *Child Development Perspectives, 7*(4), 205–210. doi: 10.1111/cdep.12041

Barrasso-Catanzaro, Christina & Eslinger, Paul J. (2016). Neurobiological bases of executive function and social-emotional development: Typical and atypical brain changes. *Family Relations, 65*(1), 108–119. doi: 10.1111 /fare.12175

Barrett, Anne E. (2012). Feeling young—A prescription for growing older? *Aging Today, 33,* 3–4.

Barrett, Anne E. & Montepare, Joann M. (2015). "It's about time": Applying life span and life course perspectives to the study of subjective age. *Annual Review of Gerontology and Geriatrics, 35*(1), 55–77. doi: 10.1891/0198-8794.35.55

Barrett, Jon F. R.; Hannah, Mary E.; Hutton, Eileen K.; Willan, Andrew R.; Allen, Alexander C.; Armson, B. Anthony, . . . Asztalos, Elizabeth V. (2013). A randomized trial of planned cesarean or vaginal delivery for twin pregnancy. *New England Journal of Medicine, 369,* 1295–1305. doi: 10.1056/NEJMoa1214939

Barrios, Yasmin V.; Sanchez, Sixto E.; Nicolaidis, Christina; Garcia, Pedro J.; Gelaye, Bizu; Zhong, Qiuyue & Williams, Michelle A. (2015). Childhood abuse and early menarche among Peruvian women. *Journal of Adolescent Health, 56*(2), 197–202. doi: 10.1016 /j.jadohealth.2014.10.002

Barros, Romina M.; Silver, Ellen J. & Stein, Ruth E. K. (2009). School recess and group classroom behavior. *Pediatrics, 123*(2), 431–436. doi: 10.1542/peds.2007-2825

Barry, Carolyn McNamara; Padilla-Walker, Laura M. & Nelson, Larry J. (2012). The role of mothers and media on emerging adults' religious faith and practices by way of internalization of prosocial values. *Journal of Adult Development, 19*(2), 66–78. doi: 10.1007/s10804-011-9135-x

Bartels, Meike; Cacioppo, John T.; van Beijsterveldt, Toos C. E. M. & Boomsma, Dorret I. (2013). Exploring the association between well-being and psychopathology in adolescents. *Behavior Genetics, 43*(3), 177–190. doi: 10.1007/s10519-013-9589-7

Basak, Chandramallika; Boot, Walter R.; Voss, Michelle W. & Kramer, Arthur F. (2008). Can training in a real-time strategy video game attenuate cognitive decline in older adults? *Psychology and Aging, 23*(4), 765–777. doi: 10.1037/a0013494

Bass, Madeline. (2011). The tough questions: Do not attempt resuscitation discussions. In Keri Thomas & Ben Lobo (Eds.), *Advance care planning in end of life care* (pp. 113–124). New York, NY: Oxford University Press.

Basseches, Michael. (1984). *Dialectical thinking and adult development.* Norwood, NJ: Ablex.

Basseches, Michael. (1989). Dialectical thinking as an organized whole: Comments on Irwin and Kramer. In Michael L. Commons et al. (Eds.), *Adult development* (Vol. 1, pp. 161–178). New York, NY: Praeger.

Basu, Sanjay; Yoffe, Paula; Hills, Nancy & Lustig, Robert H. (2013). The relationship of sugar to population-level diabetes prevalence: An econometric analysis of repeated cross-sectional data. *PLoS ONE, 8*(2), e57873. doi: 10.1371 /journal .pone.0057873

Bateson, Mary Catherine. (2011). *Composing a further life: The age of active wisdom.* New York, NY: Vintage Books.

Bateson, Patrick. (2005). Desirable scientific conduct. *Science, 307*(5710), 645. doi: 10.1126 /science .1107915

Bateson, Patrick & Martin, Paul. (2013). *Play, playfulness, creativity and innovation.* New York, NY: Cambridge University Press.

Bauer, Patricia J.; San Souci, Priscilla & Pathman, Thanujeni. (2010). Infant memory. *Wiley Interdisciplinary Reviews: Cognitive Science, 1*(2), 267–277. doi: 10.1002/wcs.38

Baumeister, Roy F. (Ed.). (2012). *Self-esteem: The puzzle of low self-regard.* New York, NY: Springer. doi: 10.1007/978-1-4684-8956-9

Baumeister, Roy F. & Tierney, John. (2012). *Willpower: Rediscovering the greatest human strength.* New York, NY. Penguin.

Baumrind, Diana. (1967). Child care practices anteceding three patterns of preschool behavior. *Genetic Psychology Monographs, 75*(1), 43–88.

Baumrind, Diana. (1971). Current patterns of parental authority. *Developmental Psychology, 4* (1, Pt. 2), 1–103. doi: 10.1037/h0030372

Baumrind, Diana. (2005). Patterns of parental authority and adolescent autonomy. *New Directions for Child and Adolescent Development, 2005*(108), 61–69. doi: 10.1002/cd.128

Baumrind, Diana; Larzelere, Robert E. & Owens, Elizabeth B. (2010). Effects of preschool parents' power assertive patterns and practices on adolescent development. *Parenting, 10*(3), 157–201. doi: 10.1080/15295190903290790

Bax, Trent. (2014). *Youth and Internet addiction in China.* New York, NY: Routledge.

Bayley, Nancy. (1966). Learning in adulthood: The role of intelligence. In Herbert J. Klausmeier & Chester W. Harris (Eds.), *Analyses of concept learning* (pp. 117–138). New York, NY: Academic Press.

Bayley, Nancy & Oden, Melita H. (1955). The maintenance of intellectual ability in gifted adults. *The Journal of Gerontology Series B: Psychological Sciences and Social Sciences, 10*(1), 91–107. doi: 10.1093/geronj/10.1.91

Bazinger, Claudia & Kühberger, Anton. (2012). Theory use in social predictions. *New Ideas in Psychology, 30*(3), 319–321. doi: 10.1016 /j .newideapsych.2012.02.003

Beal, Susan. (1988). Sleeping position and sudden infant death syndrome. *The Medical Journal of Australia, 149*(10), 562.

Beauchaine, Theodore P.; Klein, Daniel N.; Crowell, Sheila E.; Derbidge, Christina &

Gatzke-Kopp, Lisa. (2009). Multifinality in the development of personality disorders: A Biology × Sex × Environment interaction model of antisocial and borderline traits. *Development and Psychopathology, 21*(3), 735–770. doi: 10.1017 /S0954579409000418

Beck, Melinda. (2009, May 26). How's your baby? Recalling the Apgar score's namesake. *Wall Street Journal,* p. D1.

Beck, Martha N. (1999). *Expecting Adam: A true story of birth, rebirth, and everyday magic.* New York, NY: Times Books.

Becker, Derek R.; McClelland, Megan M.; Loprinzi, Paul & Trost, Stewart G. (2014). Physical activity, self-regulation, and early academic achievement in preschool children. *Early Education and Development, 25*(1), 56–70. doi: 10.1080/10409289.2013.780505

Begos, Kevin. (2010). A wounded hero. *CR: Collaborations, Results, 5*(1), 30–35, 62–63.

Beilin, Lawrence & Huang, Rae-Chi. (2008). Childhood obesity, hypertension, the metabolic syndrome and adult cardiovascular disease. *Clinical and Experimental Pharmacology and Physiology, 35*(4), 409–411. doi: 10.1111 /j.1440-1681.2008.04887.x

Belfield, Clive R.; Nores, Milagros; Barnett, Steve & Schweinhart, Lawrence. (2006). The High/Scope Perry Preschool Program: Cost benefit analysis using data from the age-40 followup. *Journal of Human Resources, 41*(1), 162–190. doi: 10.3368 /jhr.XLI.1.162

Belin, David; Belin-Rauscent, Aude; Murray, Jennifer E. & Everitt, Barry J. (2013). Addiction: failure of control over maladaptive incentive habits. *Current Opinion in Neurobiology, 23*(4), 564–572. doi: 10.1016/j.conb.2013.01.025

Bell, Beth T. & Dittmar, Helga. (2011). Does media type matter? The role of identification in adolescent girls' media consumption and the impact of different thin-ideal media on body image. *Sex Roles, 65*(7/8), 478–490. doi: 10.1007/s11199-011-9964-x

Bell, Martha Ann & Calkins, Susan D. (2011). Attentional control and emotion regulation in early development. In Michael I. Posner (Ed.), *Cognitive neuroscience of attention* (2nd ed., pp. 322–330). New York, NY: Guilford Press.

Bellinger, David C. (2016). Lead contamination in Flint—An abject failure to protect public health. *New England Journal of Medicine, 374*(12), 1101–1103. doi: 10.1056/NEJMp1601013

Belsky, Daniel W.; Caspi, Avshalom; Houts, Renate; Cohen, Harvey J.; Corcoran, David L.; Danese, Andrea, ...; Moffitt, Terrie E. (2015). Quantification of biological aging in young adults. *Proceedings of the National Academy of Sciences of the United States of America, 112*(30), E4104–E4110. doi: 10.1073/pnas.1506264112

Belsky, Jay. (2001). Emanuel Miller lecture: Developmental risks (still) associated with early child care. *Journal of Child Psychology and Psychiatry, 42*(7), 845–859. doi: 10.1111/1469 -7610.00782

Belsky, Jay; Bakermans-Kranenburg, Marian J. & van IJzendoorn, Marinus H. (2007). For better and for worse: Differential susceptibility

to environmental influences. *Current Directions in Psychological Science, 16*(6), 300–304. doi: 10.1111/j.1467-8721.2007.00525.x

Belsky, Jay & Pluess, Michael. (2009). The nature (and nurture?) of plasticity in early human development. *Perspectives on Psychological Science, 4*(4), 345–351. doi: 10.1111 /j.1745-6924.2009.01136.x

Belsky, Jay & Rovine, Michael J. (1988). Nonmaternal care in the first year of life and the security of infant-parent attachment. *Child Development, 59*(1), 157–167. doi: 10.2307 /1130397

Belsky, Jay; Steinberg, Laurence; Houts, Renate M. & Halpern-Felsher, Bonnie L. (2010). The development of reproductive strategy in females: Early maternal harshness → earlier menarche → increased sexual risk taking. *Developmental Psychology, 46*(1), 120–128. doi: 10.1037/a0015549

Beltrán-Sánchez, Hiram; Jiménez, Marcia P. & Subramanian, S. V. (2016). Assessing morbidity compression in two cohorts from the Health and Retirement Study. *Journal of Epidemiology and Community Health, 70*(10), 1011–1016. doi: 10.1136/jech-2015-206722

Bem, Sandra L. (1981). Gender schema theory: A cognitive account of sex typing. *Psychological Review, 88*(4), 354–364. doi: 10.1037/0033 -295X.88.4.354

Ben-Zur, Hasida & Zeidner, Moshe. (2009). Threat to life and risk-taking behaviors: A review of empirical findings and explanatory models. *Personality and Social Psychology Review, 13*(2), 109–128. doi: 10.1177/1088868308330104

Benatar, David. (2011). A legal right to die: Responding to slippery slope and abuse arguments. *Current Oncology, 18*(5), 206–207. doi: 10.3747/co.v18i5.923

Bender, Heather L.; Allen, Joseph P.; Mcelhaney, Kathleen Boykin; Antonishak, Jill; Moore, Cynthia M.; Kelly, Heather O'beirne & Davis, Steven M. (2007). Use of harsh physical discipline and developmental outcomes in adolescence. *Development and Psychopathology, 19*(1), 227–242. doi: 10.1017 /S0954579407070125

Benedetto, Richard. (2004, September 17). Who's more likeable, Bush or Kerry. USA Today. http: //usatoday30.usatoday.com/news/opinion /columnist /benedetto/2004-09-17-benedetto_x.htm

Benenson, Joyce F.; Markovits, Henry; Fitzgerald, Caitlin; Geoffroy, Diana; Flemming, Julianne; Kahlenberg, Sonya M. & Wrangham, Richard W. (2009). Males' greater tolerance of same-sex peers. *Psychological Science, 20*(2), 184–190. doi: 10.1111/j.1467 -9280.2009.02269.x

Benenson, Joyce F.; Markovits, Henry; Thompson, Melissa Emery & Wrangham, Richard W. (2011). Under threat of social exclusion, females exclude more than males. *Psychological Science, 22*(4), 538–544. doi: 10.1177/0956797611402511

Benet, Sula. (1974). *Abkhasians: The long-living people of the Caucasus.* New York, NY: Holt, Rinehart & Winston.

Bengtson, Vern L. & Settersten, Richard (Eds.). (2016). *Handbook of theories of aging* (3rd ed.). New York, NY: Springer.

Benigno, Joann P.; Byrd, Dana L.; McNamara, Joseph P. H.; Berg, W. Keith & Farrar, M. Jeffrey. (2011). Talking through transitions: Microgenetic changes in preschoolers' private speech and executive functioning. *Child Language Teaching and Therapy, 27*(3), 269–285. doi: 10.1177/0265659010394385

Benn, Peter. (2016). Prenatal diagnosis of chromosomal abnormalities through chorionic villus sampling and amniocentesis. In Aubrey Milunsky & Jeff M. Milunsky (Eds.), *Genetic disorders and the fetus: Diagnosis, prevention, and treatment* (7th ed., pp. 178–266). Hoboken, NJ: Wiley-Blackwell.

Bennett, Craig M. & Baird, Abigail A. (2006). Anatomical changes in the emerging adult brain: A voxel-based morphometry study. *Human Brain Mapping, 27*(9), 766–777. doi: 10.1002/hbm.20218

Bennion, Janet & Joffe, Lisa Fishbayn (Eds.). (2016). *The polygamy question.* Boulder, CO: University Press of Colorado.

Benoit, Amelie; Lacourse, Eric & Claes, Michel. (2013). Pubertal timing and depressive symptoms in late adolescence: The moderating role of individual, peer, and parental factors. *Development and Psychopathology, 25*(2), 455–471. doi: 10.1017 /S0954579412001174

Bentley, Gillian R. & Mascie-Taylor, C. G. Nicholas. (2000). Introduction. In Gillian R. Bentley & C. G. Nicholas Mascie-Taylor (Eds.), *Infertility in the modern world: Present and future prospects* (pp. 1–13). New York, NY: Cambridge University Press.

Bercovitz, Katherine & Pagnini, Francesco. (2016). Mindfulness as an opportunity to narrow the grey digital divide. In Daniela Villani et al. (Eds.), *Integrating technology in positive psychology practice* (pp. 214–228). Hershey, PA: IGI Global. doi: 10.4018/978-1-4666-9986-1.ch009

Bergamo, David & White, Dawn. (2016). Frequency of faith and spirituality discussion in health care. *Journal of Religion and Health, 55*(2), 618–630. doi: 10.1007/s10943-015-0065-y

Bergen, Gwen; Peterson, Cora; Ederer, David; Florence, Curtis; Haileyesus, Tadesse; Kresnow, Marcie-jo & Xu, Likang. (2014). *Vital signs: Health burden and medical costs of nonfatal injuries to motor vehicle occupants—United States, 2012. Morbidity and Mortality Weekly Report 63*(40), 894–900. Atlanta, GA: Centers for Disease Control and Prevention.

Berger, Kathleen S. (1980). *The developing person* (1st ed.). New York, NY: Worth.

Bergmann, Olaf; Spalding, Kirsty L. & Frisén, Jonas. (2015). Adult neurogenesis in humans. *Cold Spring Harbor Perspectives in Biology, 7,* a018994. doi: 10.1101/cshperspect.a018994

Berkman, Lisa F.; Ertel, Karen A. & Glymour, Maria M. (2011). Aging and social intervention: Life course perspectives. In Robert H. Binstock & Linda K. George (Eds.), *Handbook of aging and the social sciences* (7th ed., pp. 337–351). San Diego, CA: Academic Press. doi: 10.1016/B978-0-12 -380880-6.00024-1

Bernard, Jessica A.; Peltier, Scott J.; Wiggins, Jillian Lee; Jaeggi, Susanne M.; Buschkuehl, Martin; Fling, Brett W., . . . Seidler, Rachael D. (2013). Disrupted cortico-cerebellar connectivity in older adults. *NeuroImage, 83,* 103–119. doi: 10.1016/j.neuroimage.2013.06.042

Bernard, Jessie S. (1982). *The future of marriage* (Revised ed.). New Haven, CT: Yale University Press.

Bernard, Kristin & Dozier, Mary. (2010). Examining infants' cortisol responses to laboratory tasks among children varying in attachment disorganization: Stress reactivity or return to baseline? *Developmental Psychology, 46*(6), 1771–1778. doi: 10.1037/a0020660

Bernard, Kristin; Lind, Teresa & Dozier, Mary. (2014). Neurobiological consequences of neglect and abuse. In Jill E. Korbin & Richard D. Krugman (Eds.), *Handbook of child maltreatment* (pp. 205–223). New York, NY: Springer. doi: 10.1007/978-94-007-7208-3_11

Bernaud, Jean-Luc. (2014). Career counseling and life meaning: A new perspective of life designing for research and applications. In Fabio A. Di & J- L. Bernaud (Eds.), *The Construction of the Identity in 21st century: A Festschrift for Jean Guichard* (pp. 29–40). New York, NY: Nova Science.

Best, Joel & Best, Eric. (2014). *The student loan mess: How good intentions created a trillion-dollar problem.* Berkeley, CA: University of California Press.

Betancourt, Theresa S.; McBain, Ryan; Newnham, Elizabeth A. & Brennan, Robert T. (2013). Trajectories of internalizing problems in war-affected Sierra Leonean youth: Examining conflict and postconflict factors. *Child Development, 84*(2), 455–470. doi: 10.1111/j.1467-8624.2012.01861.x

Beutel, Manfred E.; Klein, Eva M.; Aufenanger, Stefan; Brähler, Elmar; Dreier, Michael; Müller, Kai W., . . . Wölfling, Klaus. (2016). Procrastination, distress and life satisfaction across the age range—A German representative community study. *PLoS ONE, 11*(2), e0148054. doi: 10.1371/journal. pone.0148054

Bhatia, Tej K. & Ritchie, William C. (Eds.). (2013). *The handbook of bilingualism and multilingualism* (2nd ed.). Malden, MA: Wiley-Blackwell.

Bhatnagar, Aruni; Whitsel, Laurie P.; Ribisl, Kurt M.; Bullen, Chris; Chaloupka, Frank; Piano, Mariann R., . . . Benowitz, Neal. (2014). Electronic cigarettes: A policy statement from the American Heart Association. *Circulation, 130*(16), 1418–1436. doi: 10.1161 /CIR.0000000000000107

Bialystok, Ellen. (2010). Global-local and trail-making tasks by monolingual and bilingual children: Beyond inhibition. *Developmental Psychology, 46*(1), 93–105. doi: 10.1037/a0015466

Bianconi, Eva; Piovesan, Allison; Facchin, Federica; Beraudi, Alina; Casadei, Raffaella; Frabetti, Flavia, . . . Canaider, Silvia. (2013). An estimation of the number of cells in the human body. *Annals of Human Biology, 40*(6), 463–471. doi: 10.3109/03014460.2013.807878

Biblarz, Timothy J. & Savci, Evren. (2010). Lesbian, gay, bisexual, and transgender families. *Journal of Marriage and Family, 72*(3), 480–497. doi: 10.1111/j.1741-3737.2010.00714.x

Biblarz, Timothy J. & Stacey, Judith. (2010). How does the gender of parents matter? *Journal of Marriage and Family, 72*(1), 3–22. doi: 10.1111/j.1741-3737.2009.00678.x

Bielak, Allison A. M.; Anstey, Kaarin J.; Christensen, Helen & Windsor, Tim D. (2012). Activity engagement is related to level, but not change in cognitive ability across adulthood. *Psychology and Aging, 27*(1), 219–228. doi: 10.1037/a0024667

Bienvenu, Thierry. (2005). Rett syndrome. In Merlin G. Butler & F. John Meaney (Eds.), *Genetics of developmental disabilities* (pp. 477–519). Boca Raton, FL: Taylor & Francis.

Bilalić, Merim; McLeod, Peter & Gobet, Fernand. (2009). Specialization effect and its influence on memory and problem solving in expert chess players. *Cognitive Science, 33*(6), 1117–1143. doi: 10.1111/j.1551-6709.2009.01030.x

Billings, J. Andrew. (2011). Double effect: A useful rule that alone cannot justify hastening death. *Journal of Medical Ethics, 37*(7), 437–440. doi: 10.1136/jme.2010.041160

Bing, Hong. (2015, March 5). Has China's maverick SUSTC broken away, or been broken? *Times Higher Education.*

Birditt, Kira S.; Newton, Nicky J.; Cranford, James A. & Ryan, Lindsay H. (2015). Stress and negative relationship quality among older couples: Implications for blood pressure. *Journal of Gerontology Series B.* doi: 10.1093/geronb /gbv023

Birdsong, David. (2006). Age and second language acquisition and processing: A selective overview. *Language Learning, 56*(Suppl. 1), 9–49. doi: 10.1111/j.1467-9922.2006.00353.x

Birkeland, Marianne S.; Breivik, Kyrre & Wold, Bente. (2014). Peer acceptance protects global self-esteem from negative effects of low closeness to parents during adolescence and early adulthood. *Journal of Youth and Adolescence, 43*(1), 70–80. doi: 10.1007/s10964-013-9929-1

Birkley, Erica L. & Eckhardt, Christopher I. (2015). Anger, hostility, internalizing negative emotions, and intimate partner violence perpetration: A meta-analytic review. *Clinical Psychology Review, 37,* 40–56. doi: 10.1016/j.cpr.2015.01.002

Biro, Frank M.; Greenspan, Louise C.; Galvez, Maida P.; Pinney, Susan M.; Teitelbaum, Susan; Windham, Gayle C., . . . Wolff, Mary S. (2013). Onset of breast development in a longitudinal cohort. *Pediatrics, 132*(6), 1019–1027. doi: 10.1542 /peds.2012-3773

Biro, Frank M.; McMahon, Robert P.; Striegel-Moore, Ruth; Crawford, Patricia B.; Obarzanek, Eva; Morrison, John A., . . . Falkner, Frank. (2001). Impact of timing of pubertal maturation on growth in black and white female adolescents: The National Heart, Lung, and Blood Institute Growth and Health Study. *Journal of Pediatrics, 138*(5), 636–643. doi: 10.1067 /mpd.2001.114476

Bishop, Jacob & Verleger, Matthew A. (2013). *The flipped classroom: A survey of the research.* Paper presented at the 2013 ASEE Annual Conference.

Bjorklund, David F.; Dukes, Charles & Brown, Rhonda D. (2009). The development of memory strategies. In Mary L. Courage & Nelson Cowan (Eds.), *The development of memory in infancy and childhood* (2nd ed., pp. 145–175). New York, NY: Psychology Press.

Bjorklund, David F. & Ellis, Bruce J. (2014). Children, childhood, and development in evolutionary perspective. *Developmental Review, 34*(3), 225–264. doi: 10.1016/j.dr.2014.05.005

Bjorklund, David F. & Hawley, Patricia H. (2014). Aggression grows up: Looking through an evolutionary developmental lens to understand the causes and consequences of human aggression. In Todd K. Shackelford & Ranald D. Hansen (Eds.), *The Evolution of Violence* (pp. 159–186). New York, NY: Springer. doi: 10.1007/978-1-4614-9314-3_9

Bjorklund, David F. & Sellers, Patrick D. (2014). Memory development in evolutionary perspective. In Patricia Bauer & Robyn Fivush (Eds.), *The Wiley handbook on the development of children's memory* (Vol. 1, pp. 126–150). Malden, MA: Wiley.

Black, Dennis M.; Bauer, Douglas C.; Schwartz, Ann V.; Cummings, Steven R. & Rosen, Clifford J. (2012). Continuing bisphosphonate treatment for osteoporosis—for whom and for how long? *New England Journal of Medicine, 366,* 2051–2053. doi: 10.1056/NEJMp1202623

Blad, Evie. (2014). Some states overhauling vaccine laws. *Education Week, 33*(31), 1, 23.

Blair, Clancy. (2016). Developmental science and executive function. *Current Directions in Psychological Science, 25*(1), 3–7. doi: 10.1177/0963721415622634

Blair, Clancy & Raver, C. Cybele. (2012). Child development in the context of adversity: Experiential canalization of brain and behavior. *American Psychologist, 67*(4), 309–318. doi: 10.1037/a0027493

Blair, Clancy & Raver, C. Cybele. (2015). School readiness and self-regulation: A developmental psychobiological approach. *Annual Review of Psychology, 66,* 711–731. doi: 10.1146/annurev-psych-010814-015221

Blalock, Garrick; Kadiyali, Vrinda & Simon, Daniel H. (2009). Driving fatalities after 9/11: A hidden cost of terrorism. *Applied Economics, 41*(14), 1717–1729. doi: 10.1080/00036840601069757

Blanchard-Fields, Fredda. (2007). Everyday problem solving and emotion: An adult developmental perspective. *Current Directions in Psychological Science, 16*(1), 26–31. doi: 10.1111/j.1467-8721.2007.00469.x

Blandon, Alysia Y.; Calkins, Susan D. & Keane, Susan P. (2010). Predicting emotional and social competence during early childhood from toddler risk and maternal behavior. *Development and Psychopathology, 22*(1), 119–132. doi: 10.1017/S0954579409990307

Blas, Erik & Kurup, Anand Sivasankara (Eds.). (2010). *Equity, social determinants, and public health programmes.* Geneva, Switzerland: World Health Organization.

Bleidorn, Wiebke; Klimstra, Theo A.; Denissen, Jaap J. A.; Rentfrow, Peter J.; Potter, Jeff & Gosling, Samuel D. (2013). Personality maturation around the world: A cross-cultural examination of social-investment theory. *Psychological Science, 24*(12), 2530–2540. doi: 10.1177/0956797613498396

Bleske-Rechek, April; Somers, Erin; Micke, Cierra; Erickson, Leah; Matteson, Lindsay; Stocco, Corey, . . . Ritchie, Laura. (2012). Benefit or burden? Attraction in cross-sex friendship. *Journal of Social and Personal Relationships, 29*(5), 569–596. doi: 10.1177/0265407512443611

Bleys, Dries; Soenens, Bart; Boone, Liesbet; Claes, Stephan; Vliegen, Nicole & Luyten, Patrick. (2016). The role of intergenerational similarity and parenting in adolescent self-criticism: An actor–partner interdependence model. *Journal of Adolescence, 49,* 68–76. doi: 10.1016/j.adolescence.2016.03.003

Blieszner, Rosemary. (2014). The worth of friendship: Can friends keep us happy and healthy? *Generations, 38*(1), 24–30.

Bliss, Catherine. (2012). *Race decoded: The genomic fight for social justice.* Stanford, CA: Stanford University Press.

Bloom, Barbara & Freeman, Gulnur. (2015). *Tables of summary health statistics for U.S. Children: 2014 national health interview survey.* Atlanta, GA: U.S. Department of Health & Human Services, Centers for Disease Control and Prevention, National Center for Health Statistics.

Bloom, David E. (2011). 7 billion and counting. *Science, 333*(6042), 562–569. doi: 10.1126/science.1209290

Blurton-Jones, Nicholas G. (1976). Rough-and-tumble play among nursery school children. In Jerome S. Bruner et al. (Eds.), *Play: Its role in development and evolution* (pp. 352–363). New York, NY: Basic Books.

Boal, Winifred L.; Li, Jia & Rodriguez-Acosta, Rosa L. (2016, June 17). Seat belt use among adult workers—21 States, 2013. *Morbidity and Mortality Weekly Report 65*(23), 593–597. Atlanta, GA: Centers for Disease Control and Prevention.

Boals, Adriel; Hayslip, Bert; Knowles, Laura R. & Banks, Jonathan B. (2012). Perceiving a negative event as central to one's identity partially mediates age differences in posttraumatic stress disorder symptoms. *Journal of Aging and Health, 24*(3), 459–474. doi: 10.1177/0898264311425089

Boerner, Kathrin; Schulz, Richard & Horowitz, Amy. (2004). Positive aspects of caregiving and adaptation to bereavement. *Psychology and Aging, 19*(4), 668–675. doi: 10.1037/0882-7974.19.4.668

Boerner, Kathrin; Wortman, Camille B. & Bonanno, George A. (2005). Resilient or at risk? A 4-year study of older adults who initially showed high or low distress following conjugal loss. *The Journals of Gerontology: Series B: Psychological Sciences and Social Sciences, 60*(2), 67–73. doi: 10.1093/geronb/60.2.P67

Bögels, Susan M.; Knappe, Susanne & Clark, Lee Anna. (2013). Adult separation anxiety disorder in DSM-5. *Clinical Psychology Review, 33*(5), 663–674. doi: 10.1016/j.cpr.2013.03.006

Bogle, Kathleen A. (2008). *Hooking up: Sex, dating, and relationships on campus.* New York, NY: New York University Press.

Bohannon, John. (2015). Many psychology papers fail replication test. *Science, 349*(6251), 910–911. doi: 10.1126/science.349.6251.910

Bohlen, Tabata M.; Silveira, Marina A.; Zampieri, Thais T.; Frazão, Renata & Donato, Jose. (2016). Fatness rather than leptin sensitivity determines the timing of puberty in female mice. *Molecular and Cellular Endocrinology, 423,* 11–21. doi: 10.1016/j.mce.2015.12.022

Bollyky, Thomas J. (2012). Developing symptoms: Noncommunicable diseases go global. *Foreign Affairs, 91*(3), 134–144.

Bombard, Jennifer M.; Robbins, Cheryl L.; Dietz, Patricia M. & Valderrama, Amy L. (2013). Preconception care: The perfect opportunity for health care providers to advise lifestyle changes for hypertensive women. *American Journal of Health Promotion, 27*(3), S43–S49. doi: 10.4278/ajhp.120109-QUAN-6

Bonanno, George A. & Lilienfeld, Scott O. (2008). Let's be realistic: When grief counseling is effective and when it's not. *Professional Psychology: Research and Practice, 39*(3), 377–378. doi: 10.1037/0735-7028.39.3.377

Bonanno, Rina A. & Hymel, Shelley. (2013). Cyber bullying and internalizing difficulties: Above and beyond the impact of traditional forms of bullying. *Journal of Youth and Adolescence, 42*(5), 685–697. doi: 10.1007/s10964-013-9937-1

Bond, M. Jermane & Herman, Allen A. (2016). Lagging life expectancy for Black men: A public health imperative. *American Journal of Public Health, 106*(7), 1167–1169. doi: 10.2105/AJPH.2016.303251

Bonilla-Silva, Eduardo. (2015). The structure of racism in color-blind, "post-racial" America. *American Behavioral Scientist, 59*(11), 1358–1376. doi: 10.1177/0002764215586826

Bonoti, Fotini; Leondari, Angeliki & Mastora, Adelais. (2013). Exploring children's understanding of death: Through drawings and the death concept questionnaire. *Death Studies, 37*(1), 47–60. doi: 10.1080/07481187.2011.623216

Borke, Jörn; Lamm, Bettina; Eickhorst, Andreas & Keller, Heidi. (2007). Father-infant interaction, paternal ideas about early child care, and their consequences for the development of children's self-recognition. *Journal of Genetic Psychology, 168*(4), 365–379. doi: 10.3200/GNTP.168.4.365-380

Bornstein, Marc H. (2015). Children's parents. In Richard M. Lerner (Ed.), *Handbook of child psychology and developmental science* (7th ed., Vol. 4, pp. 55–132). New York, NY: Wiley.

Bornstein, Marc H.; Arterberry, Martha E. & Mash, Clay. (2005). Perceptual development. In Marc H. Bornstein & Michael E. Lamb (Eds.), *Developmental science: An advanced textbook* (5th ed., pp. 283–325). Mahwah, NJ: Lawrence Erlbaum Associates.

Bornstein, Marc H. & Colombo, John. (2012). Infant cognitive functioning and mental development. In Sabina Pauen (Ed.), *Early childhood development and later outcome.* New York, NY: Cambridge University Press.

Bornstein, Marc H.; Hahn, Chun-Shin & Wolke, Dieter. (2013). System and cascades in cognitive development and academic achievement. *Child Development, 84*(1), 154–162. doi: 10.1111/j.1467-8624.2012.01849.x

Bornstein, Marc H.; Mortimer, Jeylan T.; Lutfey, Karen & Bradley, Robert. (2011). Theories and processes in life-span socialization. In Karen L. Fingerman et al. (Eds.), *Handbook of life-span development* (pp. 27–56). New York, NY: Springer.

Bornstein, Marc H. & Putnick, Diane L. (2016). Mothers' and fathers' parenting practices with their daughters and sons in low- and middle-income countries. *Monographs of the Society for Research in Child Development, 81*(1), 60–77. doi: 10.1111 /mono.12226

Bornstein, Marc H.; Putnick, Diane L.; Bradley, Robert H.; Deater-Deckard, Kirby & Lansford, Jennifer E. (2016). Gender in low- and middle-income countries: Introduction. *Monographs of the Society for Research in Child Development, 81*(1), 7–23. doi: 10.1111/mono.12223

Bosworth, Hayden B. & Ayotte, Brian J. (2009). The role of cognitive and social function in an applied setting: Medication adherence as an example. In Hayden B. Bosworth & Christopher Hertzog (Eds.), *Aging and cognition: Research methodologies and empirical advances* (pp. 219–239). Washington, DC: American Psychological Association. doi: 10.1037/11882-011

Boucher, Helen C.; Peng, Kaiping; Shi, Junqi & Wang, Lei. (2009). Culture and implicit self-esteem: Chinese are "good" and "bad" at the same time. *Journal of Cross-Cultural Psychology, 40*(1), 24–45. doi: 10.1177/0022022108326195

Boundy, Ellen O.; Dastjerdi, Roya; Spiegelman, Donna; Fawzi, Wafaie W.; Missmer, Stacey A.; Lieberman, Ellice, . . . Chan, Grace J. (2016). Kangaroo mother care and neonatal outcomes: A meta-analysis. *Pediatrics, 137*(1), e20152238. doi: 10.1542/peds.2015-2238

Bourque, Francois; van der Ven, Elsje & Malla, Ashok. (2011). A meta-analysis of the risk for psychotic disorders among first- and second-generation immigrants. *Psychological Medicine, 41*(5), 897–910. doi: 10.1017 /S0033291710001406

Bouter, Lex M. (2015). Commentary: Perverse incentives or rotten apples? *Accountability in Research, 22*(3), 148–161. doi: 10.1080 /08989621.2014.950253

Bowes, Lucy; Maughan, Barbara; Caspi, Avshalom; Moffitt, Terrie E. & Arseneault, Louise. (2010). Families promote emotional and behavioural resilience to bullying: Evidence of an environmental effect. *Journal of Child Psychology and Psychiatry, 51*(7), 809–817. doi: 10.1111 /j.1469-7610 .2010.02216.x

Bowlby, John. (1983). *Attachment* (2nd ed.). New York, NY: Basic Books.

boyd, danah. (2014). *It's complicated: The social lives of networked teens.* New Haven, CT: Yale University Press.

Boyd, Wendy; Walker, Susan & Thorpe, Karen. (2013). Choosing work and care: Four Australian women negotiating return to paid work in the first year of motherhood. *Contemporary Issues in Early Childhood, 14*(2), 168–178. doi: 10.2304 /ciec.2013.14.2.168

Boyle, Chloe C.; Stanton, Annette L.; Ganz, Patricia A. & Bower, Julienne E. (2016). Posttraumatic growth in breast cancer survivors: Does age matter? *Psycho-Oncology,* (In Press). doi: 10.1002/pon.4091

Boyle, Patricia A.; Wilson, Robert S.; Yu, Lei; Barr, Alasdair M.; Honer, William G.; Schneider, Julie A. & Bennett, David A. (2013). Much of late life cognitive decline is not due to common neurodegenerative pathologies. *Annals of Neurology, 74*(3), 478–489. doi: 10.1002/ana.23964

Boyle, Paul J.; Feng, Zhiqiang & Raab, Gillian M. (2011). Does widowhood increase mortality risk?: Testing for selection effects by comparing causes of spousal death. *Epidemiology, 22*(1), 1–5. doi: 10.1097/EDE.0b013e3181fdcc0b

Boyraz, Guler; Horne, Sharon G. & Sayger, Thomas V. (2012). Finding meaning in loss: The mediating role of social support between personality and two construals of meaning. *Death Studies, 36*(6), 519–540. doi: 10.1080/07481187.2011.553331

Boywitt, C. Dennis; Kuhlmann, Beatrice G. & Meiser, Thorsten. (2012). The role of source memory in older adults' recollective experience. *Psychology and Aging, 27*(2), 484–497. doi: 10.1037/a0024729

Braams, Barbara R.; van Duijvenvoorde, Anna C. K.; Peper, Jiska S. & Crone, Eveline A. (2015). Longitudinal changes in adolescent risk-taking: A comprehensive study of neural responses to rewards, pubertal development, and risk-taking behavior. *The Journal of Neuroscience, 35*(18), 7226–7238. doi: 10.1523 /JNEUROSCI.4764-14.2015

Brabeck, Kalina M. & Sibley, Erin. (2016). Immigrant parent legal status, parent–child relationships, and child social emotional wellbeing: A middle childhood perspective. *Journal of Child and Family Studies, 25*(4), 1155–1167. doi: 10.1007 /s10826-015-0314-4

Bracken, Bruce A. & Crawford, Elizabeth. (2010). Basic concepts in early childhood educational standards: A 50-state review. *Early Childhood Education Journal, 37*(5), 421–430. doi: 10.1007 /s10643-009-0363-7

Bradley, Rachel & Slade, Pauline. (2011). A review of mental health problems in fathers following the birth of a child. *Journal of Reproductive and Infant Psychology, 29*(1), 19–42. doi: 10.1080/02646838.2010.513047

Brame, Robert; Bushway, Shawn D.; Paternoster, Ray & Turner, Michael G. (2014). Demographic patterns of cumulative arrest prevalence by ages 18 and 23. *Crime & Delinquency, 60*(3), 471–486. doi: 10.1177/0011128713514801

Branch, John. (2011, December 5). Derek Boogaard: A brain 'going bad'. *New York Times,* p. B13.

Brandone, Amanda C.; Horwitz, Suzanne R.; Aslin, Richard N. & Wellman, Henry M. (2014). Infants' goal anticipation during failed and successful reaching actions. *Developmental Science, 17*(1), 23–34. doi: 10.1111/desc.12095

Brandt, Hella E.; Ooms, Marcel E.; Ribbe, Miel W.; van der Wal, Gerrit & Deliens, Luc. (2006). Predicted survival vs. actual survival in terminally ill noncancer patients in Dutch nursing homes. *Journal of Pain and Symptom Management, 32*(6), 560–566. doi: 10.1016/j.jpainsymman .2006.06.006

Brandt, Martina & Deindl, Christian. (2013). Intergenerational transfers to adult children in Europe: Do social policies matter? *Journal of Marriage and Family, 75*(1), 235–251. doi: 10.1111/j.1741-3737.2012.01028.x

Brandt, Martina; Deindl, Christian & Hank, Karsten. (2012). Tracing the origins of successful aging: The role of childhood conditions and social inequality in explaining later life health. *Social Science & Medicine, 74*(9), 1418–1425. doi: 10.1016/j.socscimed.2012.01.004

Brassen, Stefanie; Gamer, Matthias; Peters, Jan; Gluth, Sebastian & Büchel, Christian. (2012). Don't look back in anger! Responsiveness to missed chances in successful and nonsuccessful aging. *Science, 336*(6081), 612–614. doi: 10.1126 /science.1217516

Brazelton, T. Berry & Sparrow, Joshua D. (2006). *Touchpoints, birth to 3: Your child's emotional and behavioral development* (2nd ed.). Cambridge, MA: Da Capo Press.

Breiding, Matthew J.; Smith, Sharon G.; Basile, Kathleen C.; Walters, Mikel L.; Chen, Jieru & Merrick, Melissa T. (2014). *Prevalence and characteristics of sexual violence, stalking, and intimate partner violence victimization—National intimate partner and sexual violence survey, United States, 2011. Morbidity and Mortality Weekly Report 63*(SS08), 1–18. Atlanta, GA: Centers for Disease Control and Prevention.

Breivik, Gunnar. (2010). Trends in adventure sports in a post-modern society. *Sport in Society: Cultures, Commerce, Media, Politics, 13*(2), 260–273. doi: 10.1080/17430430903522970

Bremner, J. Gavin & Wachs, Theodore D. (Eds.). (2010). *The Wiley-Blackwell handbook of infant development* (2nd ed.). Malden, MA: Wiley-Blackwell.

Brendgen, Mara; Lamarche, Véronique; Wanner, Brigitte & Vitaro, Frank. (2010). Links between friendship relations and early adolescents' trajectories of depressed mood. *Developmental Psychology, 46*(2), 491–501. doi: 10.1037/a0017413

Brennan, Arthur; Ayers, Susan; Ahmed, Hafez & Marshall-Lucette, Sylvie. (2007). A critical review of the Couvade syndrome: The pregnant male. *Journal of Reproductive and Infant Psychology, 25*(3), 173–189. doi: 10.1080/02646830701467207

Breslow, Lori; Pritchard, David E.; Deboer, Jennifer; Stump, Glenda S.; Ho, Andrew D. & Seaton, Daniel T. (2013). Studying learning in the worldwide classroom research into edX's first MOOC. *Research and Practice in Assessment, 8*(1), 13–25.

Bridgers, Sophie; Buchsbaum, Daphna; Seiver, Elizabeth; Griffiths, Thomas L. & Gopnik, Alison. (2016). Children's causal inferences from conflicting testimony and observations. *Developmental Psychology, 52*(1), 9–18. doi: 10.1037/a0039830

Bridgett, David J.; Burt, Nicole M.; Edwards, Erin S. & Deater-Deckard, Kirby. (2015). Intergenerational transmission of self-regulation: A multidisciplinary review and integrative conceptual framework. *Psychological Bulletin, 141*(3), 602–654. doi: 10.1037/a0038662

Broberg, Thomas & Willstrand, Tania Dukic. (2014). Safe mobility for elderly drivers—Considerations based on expert and self-assessment. *Accident Analysis & Prevention, 66,* 104–113. doi: 10.1016/j.aap.2014.01.014

Brody, Gene H.; Beach, Steven R. H.; Philibert, Robert A.; Chen, Yi-fu & Murry, Velma McBride. (2009). Prevention effects moderate the association of 5-HTTLPR and youth risk behavior initiation: Gene × environment hypotheses tested via a randomized prevention design. *Child Development, 80*(3), 645–661. doi: 10.1111/j.1467-8624.2009.01288.x

Brody, Gene H.; Yu, Tianyi; Chen, Yi-fu; Kogan, Steven M.; Evans, Gary W.; Windle, Michael, . . . Philibert, Robert A. (2013). Supportive family environments, genes that confer sensitivity, and allostatic load among rural African American emerging adults: A prospective analysis. *Journal of Family Psychology, 27*(1), 22–29. doi: 10.1037/a0027829

Brody, Jane E. (2012, July 24). The ideal and the real of breast-feeding. *New York Times.*

Brody, Jane E. (2013, February 26). Too many pills in pregnancy. *New York Times,* p. D5.

Brom, Sarah S. & Kliegel, Matthias. (2014). Improving everyday prospective memory performance in older adults: Comparing cognitive process and strategy training. *Psychology and Aging, 29*(3), 744–755. doi: 10.1037/a0037181

Bronfenbrenner, Urie & Morris, Pamela A. (2006). The bioecological model of human development. In William Damon & Richard M. Lerner (Eds.), *Handbook of child psychology* (6th ed., Vol. 1, pp. 793–828). Hoboken, NJ: Wiley.

Brooks, Jada E. & Allen, Katherine R. (2016). The influence of fictive kin relationships and religiosity on the Academic persistence of African American college students attending an HBCU. *Journal of Family Issues, 37*(6), 814–832. doi: 10.1177/0192513X14540160

Brooks-Gunn, Jeanne; Han, Wen-Jui & Waldfogel, Jane. (2010). First-year maternal employment and child development the first 7 years. *Monographs of the Society for Research in Child Development, 75*(2). doi: 10.1111/j.1540-5834.2010.00570.x

Brotto, Lori A. & Yule, Morag A. (2011). Physiological and subjective sexual arousal in self-identified asexual women. *Archives of Sexual Behavior, 40*(4), 699–712. doi: 10.1007/s10508-010-9671-7

Brouwer, Rachel M.; van Soelen, Inge L. C.; Swagerman, Suzanne C.; Schnack, Hugo G.; Ehli, Erik A.; Kahn, René S., . . . Boomsma, Dorret I. (2014). Genetic associations between intelligence and cortical thickness emerge at the start of puberty. *Human Brain Mapping, 35*(8), 3760–3773. doi: 10.1002/hbm.22435

Brown, B. Bradford & Bakken, Jeremy P. (2011). Parenting and peer relationships: Reinvigorating research on family–peer linkages in adolescence. *Journal of Research on Adolescence, 21*(1), 153–165. doi: 10.1111/j.1532-7795.2010.00720.x

Brown, Edna; Birditt, Kira S.; Huff, Scott C. & Edwards, Lindsay L. (2012). Marital dissolution and psychological well-being: Race and gender differences in the moderating role of marital relationship quality. *Research in Human Development, 9*(2), 145–164. doi: 10.1080/15427609.2012.681202

Brown, Steven D. & Lent, Robert W. (2016). Vocational psychology: Agency, equity, and well-being. *Annual Review of Psychology, 67,* 541–565. doi: 10.1146/annurev-psych-122414-033237

Brown, Susan L. (2010). Marriage and child well-being: Research and policy perspectives. *Journal of Marriage and Family, 72*(5), 1059–1077. doi: 10.1111/j.1741-3737.2010.00750.x

Brown, Susan L.; Manning, Wendy D. & Stykes, J. Bart. (2015). Family structure and child well-being: Integrating family complexity. *Journal of Marriage and Family, 77*(1), 177–190. doi: 10.1111/jomf.12145

Bruce, Kimberley D.; Hoxha, Sany; Carvalho, Gil B.; Yamada, Ryuichi; Wang, Horng-Dar; Karayan, Paul, . . . Ja, William W. (2010). High carbohydrate–low protein consumption maximizes Drosophila lifespan. *Experimental Gerontology, 48*(10), 1129–1135. doi: 10.1016/j.exger.2013.02.003

Brunham, Robert C.; Gottlieb, Sami L. & Paavonen, Jorma. (2015). Pelvic inflammatory disease. *New England Journal of Medicine, 372,* 2039–2048. doi: 10.1056/NEJMra1411426

Bryant, Alyssa N. & Astin, Helen S. (2008). The correlates of spiritual struggle during the college years. *Journal of Higher Education, 79*(1), 1–27. doi: 10.1353/jhe.2008.0000

Brymer, Eric & Schweitzer, Robert. (2013). Extreme sports are good for your health: A phenomenological understanding of fear and anxiety in extreme sport. *Journal of Health Psychology, 18*(4), 477–487. doi: 10.1177/1359105312446770

Bucx, Freek; Raaijmakers, Quinten & van Wel, Frits. (2010). Life course stage in young adulthood and intergenerational congruence in family attitudes. *Journal of Marriage and Family, 72*(1), 117–134. doi: 10.1111/j.1741-3737.2009.00687.x

Bucx, Freek; van Wel, Frits & Knijn, Trudie. (2012). Life course status and exchanges of support between young adults and parents. *Journal of Marriage and Family, 74*(1), 101–115. doi: 10.1111/j.1741-3737.2011.00883.x

Buettner, Dan. (2012). *The blue zones: Lessons for living longer from the people who've lived the longest.* Washington, DC: National Geographic.

Buiting, Hilde; van Delden, Johannes; Onwuteaka-Philpsen, Bregje; Rietjens, Judith; Rurup, Mette; van Tol, Donald, . . . van der Heide, Agnes. (2009). Reporting of euthanasia and physician-assisted suicide in the Netherlands: Descriptive study. *BMC Medical Ethics, 10*(18). doi: 10.1186/1472-6939-10-18

Bulpitt, Christopher J.; Beckett, Nigel; Peters, Ruth; Staessen, Jan A.; Wang, Ji-Guang; Comsa, Marius, . . . Rajkumar, Chakravarthi. (2013). Does white coat hypertension require treatment over age 80? Results of the hypertension in the very elderly trial ambulatory blood pressure side project. *Hypertension, 61*(1), 89–94. doi: 10.1161/HYPERTENSIONAHA.112.191791

Bureau of Labor Statistics. (2016, April 28). College enrollment and work activity of 2015 high school graduates [Press release]. Washington, DC: United States Department of Labor. USDL–16–0822.

Burke, Laurie A.; Neimeyer, Robert A.; Holland, Jason M.; Dennard, Sharon; Oliver, Linda & Shear, M. Katherine. (2013). Inventory of Complicated Spiritual Grief: Development and validation of a new measure. *Death Studies, 38*(4), 239–250. doi: 10.1080/07481187.2013.810098

Burke-Miller, Jane; Razzano, Lisa A.; Grey, Dennis D.; Blyler, Crystal R. & Cook, Judith A. (2012). Supported employment outcomes for transition age youth and young adults. *Psychiatric Rehabilitation Journal, 35*(3), 171–179. doi: 10.2975/35.3.2012.171.179

Burnette, Jeni L.; O'Boyle, Ernest H.; VanEpps, Eric M.; Pollack, Jeffrey M. & Finkel, Eli J. (2013). Mind-sets matter: A meta-analytic review of implicit theories and self-regulation. *Psychological Bulletin, 139*(3), 655–701. doi: 10.1037/a0029531

Burpo, Todd & Vincent, Lynn. (2011). *Heaven is for real: A little boy's astounding story of his trip to heaven and back.* Nashville, TN: Thomas Nelson.

Burri, Andrea & Spector, Timothy. (2011). Recent and lifelong sexual dysfunction in a female UK population sample: Prevalence and risk factors. *Journal of Sexual Medicine, 8*(9), 2420–2430. doi: 10.1111/j.1743-6109.2011.02341.x

Burstein, David D. (2013). *Fast future: How the millennial generation is shaping our world.* Boston, MA: Beacon Press.

Burstyn, Igor. (2014). Peering through the mist: Systematic review of what the chemistry of contaminants in electronic cigarettes tells us about health risks. *BMC Public Health, 14*(1), 18. doi: 10.1186/1471-2458-14-18

Bursztyn, Leonardo & Jensen, Robert. (2014). How does peer pressure affect educational investments? *NBER working paper series,* (Working Paper 20714).

Burt, S. Alexandra. (2009). Rethinking environmental contributions to child and adolescent psychopathology: A meta-analysis of shared environmental influences. *Psychological Bulletin, 135*(4), 608–637. doi: 10.1037/a0015702

Burt, S. Alexandra; McGue, Matt & Iacono, William G. (2009). Nonshared environmental mediation of the association between deviant peer affiliation and adolescent externalizing behaviors over time: Results from a cross-lagged monozygotic twin differences design. *Developmental Psychology, 45*(6), 1752–1760. doi: 10.1037/a0016687

Buss, David M. (2015). *Evolutionary psychology: The new science of the mind* (5th ed.). New York, NY: Routledge.

Butler, Ashley M. & Titus, Courtney. (2015). Systematic review of engagement in culturally adapted parent training for disruptive behavior. *Journal of Early Intervention, 37*(4), 300–318. doi: 10.1177/1053815115620210

Butler, Robert N.; Lewis, Myrna I. & Sunderland, Trey. (1998). *Aging and mental health: Positive psychosocial and biomedical approaches* (5th ed.). Boston, MA: Allyn & Bacon.

Buttelmann, David; Zmyj, Norbert; Daum, Moritz & Carpenter, Malinda. (2013). Selective imitation of in-group over out-group members in 14-month-old infants. *Child Development, 84*(2), 422–428. doi: 10.1111/j.1467-8624.2012.01860.x

Butterworth, Brian & Kovas, Yulia. (2013). Understanding neurocognitive developmental disorders can improve education for all. *Science, 340*(6130), 300–305. doi: 10.1126/science.1231022

Butterworth, Brian; Varma, Sashank & Laurillard, Diana. (2011). Dyscalculia: From brain to education. *Science, 332*(6033), 1049–1053. doi: 10.1126/science.1201536

Buunk, Abraham P.; Park, Justin H. & Dubbs, Shelli L. (2008). Parent-offspring conflict in mate preferences. *Review of General Psychology, 12*(1), 47–62. doi: 10.1037/1089-2680.12.1.47

Byard, Roger W. (2014). "Shaken baby syndrome" and forensic pathology: An uneasy interface. *Forensic Science, Medicine, and Pathology, 10*(2), 239–241. doi: 10.1007/s12024-013-9514-7

Byers-Heinlein, Krista; Burns, Tracey C. & Werker, Janet F. (2010). The roots of bilingualism in newborns. *Psychological Science, 21*(3), 343–348. doi: 10.1177/0956797609360758

Cabrera, Natasha. (2015). Why do fathers matter for children's development? In Susan M. McHale et al. (Eds.), *Gender and Couple Relationships* (pp. 161–168). New York, NY: Springer. doi: 10.1007/978-3-319-21635-5_9

Cacciatore, Joanne. (2009). Appropriate bereavement practice after the death of a Native American child. *Families in Society: The Journal of Contemporary Social Services, 90*(1), 46–50. doi: 10.1606/1044-3894.3844

Cacioppo, John T.; Cacioppo, Stephanie; Gonzaga, Gian C.; Ogburn, Elizabeth L. & VanderWeele, Tyler J. (2013). Marital satisfaction and break-ups differ across on-line and off-line meeting venues. *PNAS, 110*(25), 10135–10140. doi: 10.1073/pnas.1222447110

Cacioppo, Stephanie; Capitanio, John P. & Cacioppo, John T. (2014). Toward a neurology of loneliness. *Psychological Bulletin, 140*(6), 1464–1504. doi: 10.1037/a0037618

Calarco, Jessica McCrory. (2014). The inconsistent curriculum: Cultural tool kits and student interpretations of ambiguous expectations. *Social Psychology Quarterly, 77*(2), 185–209. doi: 10.1177/0190272514521438

Calder, Gillian & Beaman, Lori G. (Eds.). (2014). *Polygamy's rights and wrongs: Perspectives on harm, family, and law.* Vancouver, BC: University of British Columbia Press.

Callaghan, Bridget L. & Tottenham, Nim. (2016). The neuro-environmental loop of plasticity: A cross-species analysis of parental effects on emotion circuitry development following typical and adverse caregiving. *Neuropsychopharmacology, 41*, 163–176. doi: 10.1038/npp.2015.204

Callaghan, Tara. (2013). Symbols and symbolic thought. In Philip D. Zelazo (Ed.), *The Oxford handbook of developmental psychology* (Vol. 1). New York, NY: Oxford University Press. doi: 10.1093/oxfordhb/9780199958450.013.0034

Camchong, Jazmin; Lim, Kelvin O. & Kumra, Sanjiv. (2016). Adverse effects of cannabis on adolescent brain development: A longitudinal study. *Cerebral Cortex*, (In Press). doi: 10.1093/cercor/bhw015

Camhi, Sarah M.; Katzmarzyk, Peter T.; Broyles, Stephanie; Church, Timothy S.; Hankinson, Arlene L.; Carnethon, Mercedes R., . . . Lewis, Cora E. (2013). Association of metabolic risk with longitudinal physical activity and fitness: Coronary artery risk development in young adults (CARDIA). *Metabolic Syndrome and Related Disorders, 11*(3), 195–204. doi: 10.1089/met.2012.0120

Campbell, Frances; Conti, Gabriella; Heckman, James J.; Moon, Seong H.; Pinto, Rodrigo; Pungello, Elizabeth & Pan, Yi. (2014). Early childhood investments substantially boost adult health. *Science, 343*(6178), 1478–1485. doi: 10.1126/science.1248429

Campbell, Frances A.; Pungello, Elizabeth P.; Miller-Johnson, Shari; Burchinal, Margaret & Ramey, Craig T. (2001). The development of cognitive and academic abilities: Growth curves from an early childhood educational experiment. *Developmental Psychology, 37*(2), 231–242. doi: 10.1037/0012-1649.37.2.231

Campion, Michael C.; Ployhart, Robert E. & MacKenzie, William I. (2014). The state of research on situational judgment tests: A content analysis and directions for future research. *Human Performance, 27*(4), 283–310. doi: 10.1080/08959285.2014.929693

Cao, Liqun & Zhao, Ruohui. (2012). The impact of culture on acceptance of soft drugs across Europe. *Journal of Criminal Justice, 40*(4), 296–305. doi: 10.1016/j.jcrimjus.2012.04.002

Cappell, Katherine A.; Gmeindl, Leon & Reuter-Lorenz, Patricia A. (2010). Age differences in prefontal recruitment during verbal working memory maintenance depend on memory load. *Cortex, 46*(4), 462–473. doi: 10.1016/j.cortex.2009.11.009

Caravita, Simona C. S. & Cillessen, Antonius H. N. (2012). Agentic or communal? Associations between interpersonal goals, popularity, and bullying in middle childhood and early adolescence. *Social Development, 21*(2), 376–395. doi: 10.1111/j.1467-9507.2011.00632.x

Caravita, Simona C. S.; Di Blasio, Paola & Salmivalli, Christina. (2010). Early adolescents' participation in bullying: Is ToM involved? *The Journal of Early Adolescence, 30*(1), 138–170. doi: 10.1177/0272431609342983

Cardinal, Roger. (2001). The sense of time and place. In Jane Kallir & Roger Cardinal (Eds.), *Grandma Moses in the 21st century* (pp. 79–102). Alexandria, VA: Art Services International.

Cardoso-Leite, Pedro; Green, C. Shawn & Bavelier, Daphne. (2015). On the impact of new technologies on multitasking. *Developmental Review, 35*, 98–112. doi: 10.1016/j.dr.2014.12.001

Cardozo, Eden R.; Thomson, Alexcis P.; Karmon, Anatte E.; Dickinson, Kristy A.;

Wright, Diane L. & Sabatini, Mary E. (2015). Ovarian stimulation and in-vitro fertilization outcomes of cancer patients undergoing fertility preservation compared to age matched controls: A 17-year experience. *Journal of Assisted Reproduction and Genetics, 32*(4), 587–596. doi: 10.1007/s10815-015-0428-z

Carey, Nessa. (2012). *The epigenetics revolution: How modern biology is rewriting our understanding of genetics, disease, and inheritance.* New York, NY: Columbia University Press.

Carlo, Gustavo; Knight, George P.; Roesch, Scott C.; Opal, Deanna & Davis, Alexandra. (2014). Personality across cultures: A critical analysis of Big Five research and current directions. In Frederick T. L. Leong et al. (Eds.), *APA handbook of multicultural psychology* (Vol. 1, pp. 285–298). Washington, DC: American Psychological Association. doi: 10.1037/14189-015

Carlson, Robert G.; Nahhas, Ramzi W.; Martins, Silvia S. & Daniulaityte, Raminta. (2016). Predictors of transition to heroin use among initially non-opioid dependent illicit pharmaceutical opioid users: A natural history study. *Drug & Alcohol Dependence, 160*, 127–134. doi: 10.1016/j.drugalcdep.2015.12.026

Carlson, Scott. (2016, May 1). Should everyone go to college?: For poor kids, 'College for all' isn't the mantra it was meant to be. *The Chronicle of Higher Education.*

Carlson, Stephanie M.; Koenig, Melissa A. & Harms, Madeline B. (2013). Theory of mind. *Wiley Interdisciplinary Reviews: Cognitive Science, 4*(4), 391–402. doi: 10.1002/wcs.1232

Carmichael, Cheryl L.; Reis, Harry T. & Duberstein, Paul R. (2015). In your 20s it's quantity, in your 30s it's quality: The prognostic value of social activity across 30 years of adulthood. *Psychology and Aging, 30*(1), 95–105. doi: 10.1037/pag0000014

Carothers, Bobbi J. & Reis, Harry T. (2013). Men and women are from Earth: Examining the latent structure of gender. *Journal of Personality and Social Psychology, 104*(2), 385–407. doi: 10.1037/a0030437

Carr, Deborah. (2012). Death and dying in the contemporary United States: What are the psychological implications of anticipated death? *Social and Personality Psychology Compass, 6*(2), 184–195. doi: 10.1111/j.1751-9004.2011.00416.x

Carr, Deborah; Freedman, Vicki A.; Cornman, Jennifer C. & Schwarz, Norbert. (2014). Happy marriage, happy life? Marital quality and subjective well-being in later life. *Journal of Marriage and Family, 76*(5), 930–948. doi: 10.1111/jomf.12133

Carroll, Linda J.; Cassidy, David; Cancelliere, Carol; Côté, Pierre; Hincapié, Cesar A.; Kristman, Vicki L., . . . Hartvigsen, Jan. (2014). Systematic review of the prognosis after mild traumatic brain injury in adults: Cognitive, psychiatric, and mortality outcomes: Results of the international collaboration on mild traumatic brain injury prognosis. *Archives of Physical Medicine and Rehabilitation, 95*(3, Suppl.), S152–S173. doi: 10.1016/j.apmr.2013.08.300

Carson, Valerie; Tremblay, Mark S.; Spence, John C.; Timmons, Brian W. & Janssen, Ian. (2013). The Canadian Sedentary Behaviour Guidelines for the Early Years (zero to four years of age) and screen time among children from Kingston, Ontario. *Paediatrics & Child Health, 18*(1), 25–28.

Carstensen, Laura L. (1993). Motivation for social contact across the life span. In Janis E. Jacobs (Ed.), *Developmental perspectives on motivation: Nebraska Symposium on Motivation* (1992) (pp. 209–254). Lincoln, NE: University of Nebraska.

Carstensen, Laura L. (2011). *A long bright future: Happiness, health, and financial security in an age of increased longevity.* New York, NY: PublicAffairs.

Caruso, Federica. (2013). Embedding early childhood education and care in the socio-cultural context: The case of Italy. In Jan Georgeson & Jane Payler (Eds.), *International perspectives on early childhood education and care.* New York, NY: Open University Press.

Carwile, Jenny L.; Willett, Walter C.; Spiegelman, Donna; Hertzmark, Ellen; Rich-Edwards, Janet W.; Frazier, A. Lindsay & Michels, Karin B. (2015). Sugar-sweetened beverage consumption and age at menarche in a prospective study of US girls. *Human Reproduction, 30*(3), 675–683. doi: 10.1093/humrep/deu349

Casey, B. J. & Caudle, Kristina. (2013). The teenage brain: Self control. *Current Directions in Psychological Science, 22*(2), 82–87. doi: 10.1177/0963721413480170

Casey, B. J.; Jones, Rebecca M. & Somerville, Leah H. (2011). Braking and accelerating of the adolescent brain. *Journal of Research on Adolescence, 21*(1), 21–33. doi: 10.1111/j.1532-7795.2010.00712.x

Casey, Richard. (2008). The use of hormonal therapy in "andropause": The con side. *Canadian Urological Association Journal, 2*(1), 47–48.

Caspersen, Carl J.; Thomas, G. Darlene; Boseman, Letia A.; Beckles, Gloria L. A. & Albright, Ann L. (2012). Aging, diabetes, and the public health system in the United States. *American Journal of Public Health, 102*(8), 1482–1497. doi: 10.2105/AJPH.2011.300616

Caspi, Avshalom; Moffitt, Terrie E.; Morgan, Julia; Rutter, Michael; Taylor, Alan; Arseneault, Louise, . . . Polo-Tomas, Monica. (2004). Maternal expressed emotion predicts children's antisocial behavior problems: Using monozygotic-twin differences to identify environmental effects on behavioral development. *Developmental Psychology, 40*(2), 149–161. doi: 10.1037/0012-1649.40.2.149

Cassia, Viola Macchi; Kuefner, Dana; Picozzi, Marta & Vescovo, Elena. (2009). Early experience predicts later plasticity for face processing: Evidence for the reactivation of dormant effects. *Psychological Science, 20*(7), 853–859. doi: 10.1111/j.1467-9280.2009.02376.x

Castel, Alan D.; Rossi, Aimee Drolet & McGillivray, Shannon. (2012). Beliefs about the "hot hand" in basketball across the adult life span. *Psychology and Aging, 27*(3), 601–605. doi: 10.1037/a0026991

Catani, Claudia; Gewirtz, Abigail H.; Wieling, Elizabeth; Schauer, Elizabeth; Elbert, Thomas & Neuner, Frank. (2010). Tsunami, war, and cumulative risk in the lives of Sri Lankan schoolchildren. *Child Development, 81*(4), 1176–1191. doi: 10.1111/j.1467-8624.2010.01461.x

Cavalari, Rachel N. S. & Donovick, Peter J. (2014). Agenesis of the corpus callosum: Symptoms consistent with developmental disability in two siblings. *Neurocase: The Neural Basis of Cognition, 21*(1), 95–102. doi: 10.1080/13554794.2013.873059

Ceballo, Rosario; Maurizi, Laura K.; Suarez, Gloria A. & Aretakis, Maria T. (2014). Gift and sacrifice: Parental involvement in Latino adolescents' education. *Cultural Diversity and Ethnic Minority Psychology, 20*(1), 116–127. doi: 10.1037/a0033472

Ceci, Stephen J. (2013). Untitled response to: Rivard, Ry. (2013, November 18). Cleaning house. *Inside Higher Ed.* Retrieved from http://disq.us/p/inxceh

Cecil, Kim M.; Brubaker, Christopher J.; Adler, Caleb M.; Dietrich, Kim N.; Altaye, Mekibib; Egelhoff, John C., . . . Lanphear, Bruce P. (2008). Decreased brain volume in adults with childhood lead exposure. *PloS Medicine, 5*(5), 741–750. doi: 10.1371/journal.pmed.0050112

Center for Education Policy. (2012). *SDP strategic performance indicator: The high school effect on college-going. The SDP College-Going Diagnostic Strategic Performance Indicators.* Cambridge, MA: Harvard University, Center for Education Policy Research.

Center for Education Policy. (2013). *SDP college-going diagnostic: The school district of Philadelphia.* Cambridge, MA: Harvard University, Center for Education Policy Research.

Center, Pew Research. (2016, May 12). *Changing attitudes on gay marriage. Religion & Public Life.* Washington, DC: Pew Research Center.

Centers for Disease Control and Prevention. (2012, August). *Breastfeeding report card—United States, 2012.* Atlanta, GA: National Center for Chronic Disease Prevention and Health Promotion, Centers for Disease Control and Prevention.

Centers for Disease Control and Prevention. (2013, July). *Breastfeeding report card—United States, 2013.* Atlanta, GA: National Center for Chronic Disease Prevention and Health Promotion, Centers for Disease Control and Prevention.

Centers for Disease Control and Prevention. (2014). *Breastfeeding among U.S. children born 2001–2011, CDC National Immunization Survey.* Atlanta, GA: National Center for Chronic Disease Prevention and Health Promotion, Centers for Disease Control and Prevention.

Centers for Disease Control and Prevention. (2014). Underlying cause of death 1999–2012. Retrieved January 21, 2015, from CDC WONDER Online Database http://wonder.cdc.gov/ucd-icd10.html

Centers for Disease Control and Prevention. (2014, July). *Breastfeeding report card—United States, 2014.* Atlanta, GA: National Center for Chronic Disease Prevention and Health Promotion, Centers for Disease Control and Prevention.

Centers for Disease Control and Prevention. (2014, June 16). Teen birth rates drop, but disparities persist. http://www.cdc.gov/features/dsteen-pregnancy/

Centers for Disease Control and Prevention. (2014, October 10). *Updates on CDC's polio eradication efforts. Global Health—Polio.* Atlanta, GA: Centers for Disease Control and Prevention.

Centers for Disease Control and Prevention. (2015). Atlanta, GA: Division for Heart Disease and Stroke Prevention.

Centers for Disease Control and Prevention. (2015, January 9). *Updates on CDC's polio eradication efforts. Global Health–Polio.* Atlanta, GA: Centers for Disease Control and Prevention.

Centers for Disease Control and Prevention. (2015, May 15). *Epidemiology and prevention of vaccine-preventable diseases* (Jennifer Hamborsky et al. Eds. 13th ed.). Washington DC: Public Health Foundation.

Centers for Disease Control and Prevention. (2016). *Number of children tested and confirmed bll's ≥10 μg/dl by state, year, and bll group, children < 72 months old. CDC's National Surveillance Data (1997–2014):* U.S. Department of Health & Human Services.

Centers for Disease Control and Prevention. (2016, June 9). *Ever had sexual intercourse: High school youth risk behavior survey, 2015. Youth Risk Behavior Surveillance System: 2015 Results.* Atlanta, GA: Centers for Disease Control and Prevention.

Centers for Disease Control and Prevention, National Center for Injury Prevention and Control, Division of Analysis, Research, and Practice Integration. (2013). *Fatal Injury Reports, 1999-2013, for National, Regional, and States.* Atlanta, GA: Centers for Disease Control and Prevention.

Centers for Medicare and Medicaid Services. (2014). *Beta amyloid positron tomography in dementia and neurodegenerative disease.* Baltimore, MD: Centers for Medicare and Medicaid Services.

Centre for Community Child Health & Telethon Institute for Child Health Research. (2009). *A snapshot of early childhood development in Australia: Australian Early Development Index (AEDI) national report 2009.* Canberra, Australia: Australian Government Department of Education.

Cespedes, Elizabeth M.; McDonald, Julia; Haines, Jess; Bottino, Clement J.; Schmidt, Marie Evans & Taveras, Elsie M. (2013). Obesity-related behaviors of US- and non-US-born parents and children in low-income households. *Journal of Developmental & Behavioral Pediatrics, 34*(8), 541–548. doi: 10.1097/DBP.0b013e3182a509fb

Chafen, Jennifer J. S.; Newberry, Sydne J.; Riedl, Marc A.; Bravata, Dena M.; Maglione, Margaret; Suttorp, Marika J., . . . Shekelle, Paul G. (2010). Diagnosing and managing common food allergies. *JAMA, 303*(18), 1848–1856. doi: 10.1001/jama.2010.582

Champagne, Frances A. & Curley, James P. (2010). Maternal care as a modulating influence on infant development. In Mark S. Blumberg et al. (Eds.), *Oxford handbook of developmen-*

tal behavioral neuroscience (pp. 323–341). New York, NY: Oxford University Press. doi: 10.1093/oxfordhb/9780195314731.013.0017

Chan, Christian S. & Rhodes, Jean E. (2013). Religious coping, posttraumatic stress, psychological distress, and posttraumatic growth among female survivors four years after Hurricane Katrina. *Journal of Traumatic Stress*, 26(2), 257–265. doi: 10.1002/jts.21801

Chan, Juliana C. N.; Malik, Vasanti; Jia, Weiping; Kadowaki, Takashi; Yajnik, Chittaranjan S.; Yoon, Kun-Ho & Hu, Frank B. (2009). Diabetes in Asia: Epidemiology, risk factors, and pathophysiology. *JAMA*, 301(20), 2129–2140. doi: 10.1001/jama.2009.726

Chan, Kitty S.; Kasper, Judith D.; Brandt, Jason & Pezzin, Liliana E. (2012). Measurement equivalence in ADL and IADL difficulty across international surveys of aging: findings from the HRS, SHARE, and ELSA. *The Journals of Gerontology Series B: Psychological Sciences and Social Sciences*, 67(1), 121–132. doi: 10.1093/geronb/gbr133

Chan, Kit Yee; Wang, Wei; Wu, Jing Jing; Liu, Li; Theodoratou, Evropi; Car, Josip; . . . Rudan, Igor. (2013). Epidemiology of Alzheimer's disease and other forms of dementia in China, 1990—2010: A systematic review and analysis. *The Lancet*, 381(9882), 2016–2023. doi: 10.1016/S0140-6736 (13)60221-4

Chan, Tak Wing & Koo, Anita. (2011). Parenting style and youth outcomes in the UK. *European Sociological Review*, 27(3), 385–399. doi: 10.1093 /esr/jcq013

Chan, Xi Wen; Kalliath, Thomas; Brough, Paula; Siu, Oi-Ling; O'Driscoll, Michael P. & Timms, Carolyn. (2016). Work–family enrichment and satisfaction: The mediating role of self-efficacy and work–life balance. *The International Journal of Human Resource Management*, 27(15), 1755–1776. doi: 10.1080/09585192.2015.1075574

Chang, Alicia; Sandhofer, Catherine M. & Brown, Christia S. (2011). Gender biases in early number exposure to preschool-aged children. *Journal of Language and Social Psychology*, 30(4), 440–450. doi: 10.1177/0261927X11416207

Chang, Yevvon Yi-Chi & Chiou, Wen-Bin. (2014). Diversity beliefs and postformal thinking in late adolescence: A cognitive basis of multicultural literacy. *Asia Pacific Education Review*, 15(4), 585–592. doi: 10.1007/s12564-014-9345-6

Chao, Jian-Kang; Lin, Yen-Chin; Ma, Mi-Chia; Lai, Chin-Jen; Ku, Yan-Chiou; Kuo, Wu-Hsien & Chao, I. Chen. (2011). Relationship among sexual desire, sexual satisfaction, and quality of life in middle-aged and older adults. *Journal of Sex & Marital Therapy*, 37(5), 386–403. doi: 10.1080/0092623x.2011.607051

Charlesworth, Christina J.; Smit, Ellen; Lee, David S. H.; Alramadhan, Fatimah & Odden, Michelle C. (2015). Polypharmacy among adults aged 65 years and older in the United States: 1988–2010. *The Journals of Gerontology Series A: Biological Sciences & Medical Sciences*, 70(8), 989–995. doi: 10.1093/gerona/glv013

Charlton, Samuel G. (2009). Driving while conversing: Cell phones that distract and passengers who react. *Accident Analysis and Prevention*, 41(1), 160–173. doi: 10.1016/j.aap.2008.10.006

Charness, Michael E.; Riley, Edward P. & Sowell, Elizabeth R. (2016). Drinking during pregnancy and the developing brain: Is any amount safe? *Trends in Cognitive Sciences*, 20(2), 80–82. doi: 10.1016/j.tics.2015.09.011

Charness, Neil; Krampe, Ralf & Mayr, Ulrich. (1996). The role of practice and coaching in entrepreneurial skill domains: An international comparison of life-span chess skill acquisition. In Karl Anders Ericsson (Ed.), *The road to excellence: The acquisition of expert performance in the arts and sciences, sports, and games* (pp. 51–80). Hillsdale, NJ: Erlbaum.

Charnigo, Richard; Noar, Seth M.; Garnett, Christopher; Crosby, Richard; Palmgreen, Philip & Zimmerman, Rick S. (2013). Sensation seeking and impulsivity: Combined associations with risky sexual behavior in a large sample of young adults. *The Journal of Sex Research*, 50(5), 480–488. doi: 10.1080/00224499.2011.652264

Chartier, Karen G.; Scott, Denise M.; Wall, Tamara L.; Covault, Jonathan; Karriker-Jaffe, Katherine J.; Mills, Britain A., . . . Arroyo, Judith A. (2014). Framing ethnic variations in alcohol outcomes from biological pathways to neighborhood context. *Alcoholism: Clinical and Experimental Research*, 38(3), 611–618. doi: 10.1111/acer.12304

Chassin, Laurie; Bountress, Kaitlin; Haller, Moira & Wang, Frances. (2014). Adolescent substance use disorders. In Eric J. Mash & Russell A. Barkley (Eds.), *Child psychopathology* (3rd ed., pp. 180–124). New York, NY: Guilford Press.

Chatters, Linda M.; Taylor, Robert Joseph; Lincoln, Karen D.; Nguyen, Ann & Joe, Sean. (2011). Church-based social support and suicidality among African Americans and Black Caribbeans. *Archives of Suicide Research*, 15(4), 337–353. doi: 10.1080/13811118.2011.615703

Chaudhury, S. Raj. (2011). The lecture. In William Buskist & James E. Groccia (Eds.), *Evidence-based teaching: New directions for teaching and learning* (pp. 13–20). New York, NY: Wiley.

Chen, Edith; Cohen, Sheldon & Miller, Gregory E. (2010). How low socioeconomic status affects 2-year hormonal trajectories in children. *Psychological Science*, 21(1), 31–37. doi: 10.1177/0956797609355566

Chen, Edith & Miller, Gregory E. (2012). "Shift-and-persist" strategies: Why low socioeconomic status isn't always bad for health. *Perspectives on Psychological Science*, 7(2), 135–158. doi: 10.1177/1745691612436694

Chen, Gong & Gao, Yuan. (2013). Changes in social participation of older adults in Beijing. *Ageing International*, 38(1), 15–27. doi: 10.1007/s12126 -012-9167-y

Chen, Hong & Jackson, Todd. (2009). Predictors of changes in weight esteem among mainland Chinese adolescents: A longitudinal analysis. *Developmental Psychology*, 45(6), 1618–1629. doi: 10.1037/a0016820

Chen, Mu-Hong; Lan, Wen-Hsuan; Bai, Ya-Mei; Huang, Kai-Lin; Su, Tung-Ping; Tsai, Shih-Jen, . . . Hsu, Ju-Wei. (2016). Influence of relative age on diagnosis and treatment of Attention-deficit hyperactivity disorder in Taiwanese children. *The Journal of Pediatrics*, 172, 162–167.e161. doi: 10.1016/j.jpeds.2016.02.012

Chen, Xinyin; Cen, Guozhen; Li, Dan & He, Yunfeng. (2005). Social functioning and adjustment in Chinese children: The imprint of historical time. *Child Development*, 76(1), 182–195. doi: 10.1111/j.1467-8624.2005.00838.x

Chen, Xinyin; Rubin, Kenneth H. & Sun, Yuerong. (1992). Social reputation and peer relationships in Chinese and Canadian children: A cross-cultural study. *Child Development*, 63(6), 1336–1343. doi: 10.1111/j.1467-8624.1992.tb01698.x

Chen, Xinyin; Wang, Li & Wang, Zhengyan. (2009). Shyness-sensitivity and social, school, and psychological adjustment in rural migrant and urban children in China. *Child Development*, 80(5), 1499–1513. doi: 10.1111/j.1467-8624 .2009.01347.x

Chen, Xinyin; Yang, Fan & Wang, Li. (2013). Relations between shyness-sensitivity and internalizing problems in Chinese children: Moderating effects of academic achievement. *Journal of Abnormal Child Psychology*, 41(5), 825–836. doi: 10.1007/s10802-012-9708-6

Chen, Yijun; Corsino, Leonor; Shantavasinkul, Prapimporn Chattranukulchai; Grant, John; Portenier, Dana; Ding, Laura & Torquati, Alfonso. (2016). Gastric bypass surgery leads to long-term remission or improvement of type 2 diabetes and significant decrease of microvascular and macrovascular complications. *Annals of Surgery*, 263(6), 1138–1142. doi: 10.1097/SLA.0000000000001509

Cheng, Diana; Kettinger, Laurie; Uduhiri, Kelechi & Hurt, Lee. (2011). Alcohol consumption during pregnancy: Prevalence and provider assessment. *Obstetrics & Gynecology*, 117(2), 212–217. doi: 10.1097/AOG.0b013e3182078569

Cheng, Yvonne W.; Shaffer, Brian; Nicholson, James & Caughey, Aaron B. (2014). Second stage of labor and epidural use: A larger effect than previously suggested. *Obstetrics & Gynecology*, 123(3), 527–535. doi: 10.1097/AOG.0000000000000134

Chentsova-Dutton, Yulia E. & Vaughn, Alexandra. (2012). Let me tell you what to do: Cultural differences in advice-giving. *Journal of Cross-Cultural Psychology*, 43(5), 687–703. doi: 10.1177 /0022022111402343

Cherlin, Andrew J. (2009). *The marriage-go-round: The state of marriage and the family in America today.* New York, NY: Knopf.

Cherlin, Andrew J. (2013). Health, marriage, and same sex partnerships. *Journal of Health and Social Behavior*, 54(1), 64–66. doi: 10.1177/0022146512474430

Cheslack-Postava, Keely; Liu, Kayuet & Bearman, Peter S. (2011). Closely spaced pregnancies are associated with increased odds of autism in California sibling births. *Pediatrics*, 127(2), 246–253. doi: 10.1542/peds.2010-2371

Chikritzhs, Tanya; Stockwell, Tim; Naimi, Timothy; Andreasson, Sven; Dangardt, Frida & Liang, Wenbin. (2015). Has the leaning tower of presumed health benefits from 'moderate' alcohol use finally collapsed? *Addiction*, 110(5), 726–727. doi: 10.1111/add.12828

Child Trends. (2013). *World family map 2013: Mapping family change and child well-being outcomes.* Bethesda, MD: Child Trends.

Child Trends Data Bank. (2015, March). *Lead poisoning: Indicators on children and youth.* Bethesda, MD: Child Trends.

Child Welfare Information Gateway. (2013). *Foster care statistics, 2011.* Washington, DC: U.S. Department of Health and Human Services, Children's Bureau.

Ching, Charles M.; Church, A. Timothy; Katigbak, Marcia S.; Reyes, Jose Alberto S.; Tanaka-Matsumi, Junko; Takaoka, Shino, . . . Ortiz, Fernando A. (2014). The manifestation of traits in everyday behavior and affect: A five-culture study. *Journal of Research in Personality, 48,* 1–16. doi: 10.1016 /j.jrp.2013.10.002

Chlebowski, Rowan T.; Manson, JoAnn E.; Anderson, Garnet L.; Cauley, Jane A.; Aragaki, Aaron K.; Stefanick, Marcia L., . . . Prentice, Ross L. (2013). Estrogen plus progestin and breast cancer incidence and mortality in the Women's Health Initiative observational study. *JNCI, 105*(8), 526–535. doi: 10.1093/jnci/djt043

Choe, Daniel E.; Lane, Jonathan D.; Grabell, Adam S. & Olson, Sheryl L. (2013a). Developmental precursors of young school-age children's hostile attribution bias. *Developmental Psychology, 49*(12), 2245–2256. doi: 10.1037 /a0032293

Choe, Daniel E.; Olson, Sheryl L. & Sameroff, Arnold J. (2013b). The interplay of externalizing problems and physical and inductive discipline during childhood. *Developmental Psychology, 49*(11), 2029–2039. doi: 10.1037 /a0032054

Choi, Incheol; Dalal, Reeshad; Kim-Prieto, Chu & Park, Hyekyung. (2003). Culture and judgment of causal relevance. *Journal of Personality and Social Psychology, 84*(1), 46–59. doi: 10.1037/0022-3514 .84.1.46

Chomsky, Noam. (1968). *Language and mind.* New York, NY: Harcourt Brace & World.

Chomsky, Noam. (1980). *Rules and representations.* New York, NY: Columbia University Press.

Chong, Jessica X.; Buckingham, Kati J.; Jhangiani, Shalini N.; Boehm, Corinne; Sobreira, Nara; Smith, Joshua D., . . . Bamshad, Michael J. (2015). The genetic basis of mendelian phenotypes: Discoveries, challenges, and opportunities. *American Journal of Human Genetics, 97*(2), 199–215. doi: 10.1016 /j.ajhg.2015.06.009

Choshen-Hillel, Shoham & Yaniv, Ilan. (2011). Agency and the construction of social preference: Between inequality aversion and prosocial behavior. *Journal of Personality and Social Psychology, 101*(6), 1253–1261. doi: 10.1037 /a0024557

Chou, Rita Jing-Ann & Choi, Namkee G. (2011). Prevalence and correlates of perceived workplace discrimination among older workers in the United States of America. *Ageing and Society, 31*(6), 1051–1070. doi: 10.1017 /S0144686X10001297

Choukas-Bradley, Sophia; Giletta, Matteo; Widman, Laura; Cohen, Geoffrey L. & Prinstein, Mitchell J. (2014). Experimentally measured susceptibility to peer influence and adolescent sexual behavior trajectories: A preliminary

study. *Developmental Psychology, 50*(9), 2221–2227. doi: 10.1037/a0037300

Chow, Chong Man & Ruhl, Holly. (2014). Friendship and romantic stressors and depression in emerging adulthood: Mediating and moderating roles of attachment representations. *Journal of Adult Development, 21*(2), 106–115. doi: 10.1007 /s10804-014-9184-z

Christakis, Erika. (2016). *The importance of being little: What preschoolers really need from grown-ups.* New York, NY: Viking.

Christensen, Andrew; Eldridge, Kathleen; Catta-Preta, Adriana Bokel; Lim, Veronica R. & Santagata, Rossella. (2006). Cross-cultural consistency of the demand/withdraw interaction pattern in couples. *Journal of Marriage and Family, 68*(4), 1029–1044. doi: 10.1111/j.1741-3737 .2006.00311.x

Christian, Cindy W. & Block, Robert. (2009). Abusive head trauma in infants and children. *Pediatrics, 123*(5), 1409–1411. doi: 10.1542/peds .2009-0408

Christiansen, Dorte M.; Olff, Miranda & Elklit, Ask. (2014). Parents bereaved by infant death: Sex differences and moderation in PTSD, attachment, coping and social support. *General Hospital Psychiatry, 36*(6), 655–661. doi: 10.1016 /j .genhosppsych.2014.07.012

Chronicle of Higher Education. (2010). *Almanac of higher education 2010–2011.* Washington, DC.

Chronicle of Higher Education. (2014). *Almanac of higher education 2014–15. The Chronicle of Higher Education, 60*(45).

Chronicle of Higher Education. (2015, August 17). *The almanac of higher education 2015–16.* Washington, DC.

Chronobiology International. (2016). 22nd International Symposium on Shiftwork and Working Time: Challenges and solutions for healthy working hours (Special Issue). *Chronobiology International, 33*(6). doi: 10.1080/07420528.2016.1195632

Chuan, Toh Yong. (2015, August 24). Re-employment age will rise to 67 by 2017. *The Straits Times.*

Chudacoff, Howard P. (2011). The history of children's play in the United States. In Anthony D. Pellegrini (Ed.), *The Oxford handbook of the development of play* (pp. 101–109). New York, NY: Oxford University Press. doi: 10.1093 /oxfordhb/9780195393002.013.0009

Chuderski, Adam. (2013). When are fluid intelligence and working memory isomorphic and when are they not? *Intelligence, 41*(4), 244–262. doi: 10.1016/j.intell.2013.04.003

Cicchetti, Dante. (2013a). Annual Research Review: Resilient functioning in maltreated children–past, present, and future perspectives. *Journal of Child Psychology and Psychiatry, 54*(4), 402–422. doi: 10.1111/j.1469-7610.2012.02608.x

Cicchetti, Dante. (2013b). An overview of developmental psychopathology. In Philip D. Zelazo (Ed.), *The Oxford handbook of developmental psychology* (Vol. 2, pp. 455–480). New York, NY: Oxford University Press. doi: 10.1093 /oxfordhb/9780199958474.013.0018

Cicconi, Megan. (2014). Vygotsky meets technology: A reinvention of collaboration in the early childhood mathematics classroom. *Early Childhood Education Journal, 42*(1), 57–65. doi: 10.1007/s10643-013-0582-9

Cimpian, Andrei. (2013). Generic statements, causal attributions, and children's naive theories. In Mahzarin R. Banaji & Susan A. Gelman (Eds.), *Navigating the social world: What infants, children, and other species can teach us* (pp. 269–274). New York, NY: Oxford University Press.

Ciol, Marcia A.; Rasch, Elizabeth K.; Hoffman, Jeanne M.; Huynh, Minh & Chan, Leighton. (2014). Transitions in mobility, ADLs, and IADLs among working-age Medicare beneficiaries. *Disability and Health Journal, 7*(2), 206–215. doi: 10.1016 /j.dhjo.2013.10.007

Clark, Caron A. C.; Fang, Hua; Espy, Kimberly A.; Filipek, Pauline A.; Juranek, Jenifer; Bangert, Barbara, . . . Taylor, H. Gerry. (2013). Relation of neural structure to persistently low academic achievement: A longitudinal study of children with differing birth weights. *Neuropsychology, 27*(3), 364–377. doi: 10.1037/a0032273

Clark, Lee Anna. (2009). Stability and change in personality disorder. *Current Directions in Psychological Science, 18*(1), 27–31. doi: 10.1111/j.1467-8721.2009.01600.x

Clark, Nina A.; Demers, Paul A.; Karr, Catherine J.; Koehoorn, Mieke; Lencar, Cornel; Tamburic, Lillian & Brauer, Michael. (2010). Effect of early life exposure to air pollution on development of childhood asthma. *Environmental Health Perspectives, 118*(2), 284–290. doi: 10.1289 /ehp.0900916

Clark, Shelley; Kabiru, Caroline & Mathur, Rohini. (2010). Relationship transitions among youth in urban Kenya. *Journal of Marriage and Family, 72*(1), 73–88. doi: 10.1111/j.1741-3737.2009.00684.x

Clarke, Christina A.; Miller, Tim; Chang, Ellen T.; Chang, Daixin; Chang, Myles & Gomez, Scarlett L. (2010). Racial and social class gradients in life expectancy in contemporary California. *Social Science & Medicine, 70*(9), 1373–1380. doi: 10.1016/j.socscimed.2010.01.003

Clarke, Philippa; Marshall, Victor; House, James & Lantz, Paula. (2011). The social structuring of mental health over the adult life course: Advancing theory in the sociology of aging. *Social Forces, 89*(4), 1287–1313. doi: 10.1093/sf/89.4.1287

Clayton, P. E.; Gill, M. S.; Tillmann, V. & Westwood, M. (2014). Translational neuroendocrinology: Control of human growth. *Journal of Neuroendocrinology, 26*(6), 349–355. doi: 10.1111/jne.12156

Coe, Norma B. & Zamarro, Gema. (2011). Retirement effects on health in Europe. *Journal of Health Economics, 30*(1), 77–86. doi: 10.1016 /j.jhealeco.2010.11.002

Coghlan, Andy. (2012). DNA reveals secrets of Ötzi the ice mummy. *New Scientist, 213*(2854), 10.

Cohen, Jon. (2014). Saving lives without new drugs. *Science, 346*(6212), 911. doi: 10.1126 /science.346.6212.911

Cohen, Joachim; Van Landeghem, Paul; Carpentier, Nico & Deliens, Luc. (2013). Public acceptance of euthanasia in Europe: a survey study in 47 countries. *International Journal of Public Health*, 59(1), 143–156. doi: 10.1007/s00038-013 -0461-6

Cohen, Joel E. & Malin, Martin B. (Eds.). (2010). *International perspectives on the goals of universal basic and secondary education*. New York, NY: Routledge.

Cohen, Larry; Chávez, Vivian & Chehimi, Sana (Eds.). (2010). *Prevention is primary: Strategies for community well-being* (2nd ed.). San Francisco, CA: Jossey-Bass.

Cohen, Philip N. (2014). Recession and divorce in the United States, 2008–2011. *Population Research and Policy Review*, 33(5), 615–628. doi: 10.1007/s11113-014-9323-z

Cohn, D'Vera; Livingston, Gretchen & Wang, Wendy. (2014, April 8). *After decades of decline, a rise in stay-at-home mothers*. Washington, DC: Pew Research Center's Social & Demographic Trends project.

Cohn, D'Vera; Passel, Jeffrey S.; Wang, Wendy & Livingston, Gretchen. (2011, December 14). *Barely half of U.S. adults are married–A record low: New marriages down 5% from 2009 to 2010*. Washington, DC: Pew Research Center.

Colaco, Marc; Johnson, Kelly; Schneider, Dona & Barone, Joseph. (2013). Toilet training method is not related to dysfunctional voiding. *Clinical Pediatrics*, 52(1), 49–53. doi: 10.1177/0009922812464042

Colbert, Linda; Jefferson, Joseph; Gallo, Ralph & Davis, Ronnie. (2009). A study of religiosity and psychological well-being among African Americans: Implications for counseling and psychotherapeutic processes. *Journal of Religion and Health*, 48(3), 278–289. doi: 10.1007/s10943-008-9195-9

Cole, Pamela M.; Armstrong, Laura Marie & Pemberton, Caroline K. (2010). The role of language in the development of emotion regulation. In Susan D. Calkins & Martha Ann Bell (Eds.), *Child development at the intersection of emotion and cognition* (pp. 59–78). Washington, DC: American Psychological Association.

Coleman, Marilyn & Ganong, Lawrence H. (Eds.). (2014). *The social history of the American family: An encyclopedia*. Thousand Oaks, CA: SAGE.

Coleman-Jensen, Alisha; Rabbitt, Matthew P.; Gregory, Christian & Singh, Anita. (2015). *Household food security in the United States in 2014*. Washington, DC: U.S. Department of Agriculture, Economic Research Service.

Coleman-Jensen, Alisha; Rabbitt, Matthew P.; Gregory, Christian A. & Singh, Anita. (2016). *Household food security in the United States in 2015*. Washington, DC: United States Department of Agriculture.

Coley, Nicola; Vaurs, Charlotte & Andrieu, Sandrine. (2015). Nutrition and cognition in aging adults. *Clinics in Geriatric Medicine*, 31(3), 453–464. doi: 10.1016/j.cger.2015.04.008

Collett, DeShana & Bennett, Tamara. (2015). Putting intimate partner violence on your radar. *Journal of the American Academy of Physician Assistants*, 28(10), 24–28. doi: 10.1097/01 .JAA.0000471606.69408.ac

Collibee, Charlene & Furman, Wyndol. (2016). The relationship context for sexual activity and its associations with romantic cognitions among emerging adults. *Emerging Adulthood*, 4(2), 71–81. doi: 10.1177/2167696815604529

Collin-Vézina, Delphine; De La Sablonnière-Griffin, Mireille; Palmer, Andrea M. & Milne, Lise. (2015). A preliminary mapping of individual, relational, and social factors that impede disclosure of childhood sexual abuse. *Child Abuse & Neglect*, 43, 123–134. doi: 10.1016/j.chiabu.2015.03.010

Collins, Christine E.; Turner, Emily C.; Sawyer, Eva Kille; Reed, Jamie L.; Young, Nicole A.; Flaherty, David K. & Kaas, Jon H. (2016). Cortical cell and neuron density estimates in one chimpanzee hemisphere. *Proceedings of the National Academy of Sciences*, 113(3), 740–745. doi: 10.1073/pnas.1524208113

Collins, Rebecca L.; Martino, Steven C.; Elliott, Marc N. & Miu, Angela. (2011). Relationships between adolescent sexual outcomes and exposure to sex in media: Robustness to propensity-based analysis. *Developmental Psychology*, 47(2), 585–591. doi: 10.1037/a0022563

Colson, Eve R.; Willinger, Marian; Rybin, Denis; Heeren, Timothy; Smith, Lauren A.; Lister, George & Corwin, Michael J. (2013). Trends and factors associated with infant bed sharing, 1993–2010: The National Infant Sleep Position study. *JAMA Pediatrics*, 167(11), 1032–1037. doi: 10.1001 /jamapediatrics.2013.2560

Common Sense Media. (2013). *Zero to eight: Children's media use in America 2013*. San Francisco, CA: Common Sense Media.

Common Sense Media. (2015). *The Common Sense census: Media use by tweens and teens*. San Francisco, CA: Common Sense.

Compian, Laura J.; Gowen, L. Kris & Hayward, Chris. (2009). The interactive effects of puberty and peer victimization on weight concerns and depression symptoms among early adolescent girls. *The Journal of Early Adolescence*, 29(3), 357–375. doi: 10.1177/0272431608323656

Compta, Yaroslau; Parkkinen, Laura; O'Sullivan, Sean S.; Vandrovcova, Jana; Holton, Janice L.; Collins, Catherine, . . . Revesz, Tamas. (2011). Lewy- and Alzheimer-type pathologies in Parkinson's disease dementia: Which is more important? *Brain: A Journal of Neurology*, 134(5), 1493–1505. doi: 10.1093/brain/awr031

Compton, Wilson M.; Gfroerer, Joe; Conway, Kevin P. & Finger, Matthew S. (2014). Unemployment and substance outcomes in the United States 2002–2010. *Drug & Alcohol Dependence*, 142, 350–353. doi: 10.1016/j.drugalcdep.2014.06.012

Confer, Jaime C.; Easton, Judith A.; Fleischman, Diana S.; Goetz, Cari D.; Lewis, David M. G.; Perilloux, Carin & Buss, David M. (2010). Evolutionary psychology: Controversies, questions, prospects, and limitations. *American Psychologist*, 65(2), 110–126. doi: 10.1037/a0018413

Connidis, Ingrid Arnet. (2015). Exploring ambivalence in family ties: Progress and prospects. *Journal of Marriage and Family*, 77(1), 77–95. doi: 10.1111/jomf.12150

Coon, Carleton S. (1962). *The origin of races*. New York, NY: Knopf.

Coontz, Stephanie. (2005). *Marriage, a history: From obedience to intimacy or how love conquered marriage*. New York, NY: Viking.

Cooper, Alexia & Smith, Erica L. (2011). *Homicide trends in the United States, 1980–2008: Annual rates for 2009 and 2010*. Washington, DC: U.S. Department of Justice, Office of Justice Programs, Bureau of Justice Statistics.

Coovadia, Hoosen M. & Wittenberg, Dankwart F. (Eds.). (2004). *Paediatrics and child health: A manual for health professionals in developing countries* (5th ed.). New York, NY: Oxford University Press.

Copeland, William E.; Wolke, Dieter; Angold, Adrian & Costell, E. Jane. (2013). Adult psychiatric outcomes of bullying and being bullied by peers in childhood and adolescence. *JAMA Psychiatry*, 70(4), 419–426. doi: 10.1001/jamapsychiatry.2013.504

Copen, Casey E.; Daniels, Kimberly & Mosher, William D. (2013). *First premarital cohabitation in the United States: 2006–2010 national survey of family growth. National Health Statistics Report*. Hyattsville, MD: U.S. Department of Health and Human Services, Centers for Disease Control and Prevention, National Center for Health Statistics.

Coplan, Robert J. & Weeks, Murray. (2009). Shy and soft-spoken: Shyness, pragmatic language, and socio-emotional adjustment in early childhood. *Infant and Child Development*, 18(3), 238–254. doi: 10.1002/icd.622

Copp, Jennifer E.; Giordano, Peggy C.; Longmore, Monica A. & Manning, Wendy D. (2015). Living with parents and emerging adults' depressive symptoms. *Journal of Family Issues*, (In Press). doi: 10.1177/0192513X15617797

Corballis, Michael C. (2011). *The recursive mind: The origins of human language, thought, and civilization*. Princeton, NJ: Princeton University Press.

Corenblum, Barry. (2014). Relationships between racial–ethnic identity, self-esteem and in-group attitudes among first nation children. *Journal of Youth and Adolescence*, 43(3), 387–404. doi: 10.1007/s10964-013-0081-8

Cornaglia, Francesca; Crivellaro, Elena & McNally, Sandra. (2015). Mental health and education decisions. *Labour Economics*, 33, 1–12. doi: 10.1016/j.labeco.2015.01.005

Cornelis, Marilyn C.; Byrne, E. M.; Esko, T.; Nalls, M A.; Ganna, A.; Paynter, N., . . . Wojczynski, M. K. (2015). Genome-wide meta-analysis identifies six novel loci associated with habitual coffee consumption. *Molecular Psychiatry*, 20(5), 647–656. doi: 10.1038/mp.2014.107

Coronini-Cronberg, Sophie; Millett, Christopher; Laverty, Anthony A. & Webb, Elizabeth. (2012). The impact of a free older persons' bus pass on active travel and regular walking in England. *American Journal of Public Health*, 102(11), 2141–2148. doi: 10.2105/AJPH.2012.300946

Corr, Charles A. & Corr, Donna M. (2013a). Culture, socialization, and dying. In David K. Meagher & David E. Balk (Eds.), *Handbook of thanatology: The essential body of knowledge for the study of death, dying, and bereavement* (2nd ed., pp. 3–8). New York, NY: Routledge.

Corr, Charles A. & Corr, Donna M. (2013b). Historical and contemporary perspectives on loss, grief, and mourning. In David Meagher & David E. Balk (Eds.), *Handbook of thanatology: The essential body of knowledge for the study of death, dying, and bereavement* (2nd ed., pp. 135–148). New York, NY: Routledge.

Costa, Albert & Sebastián-Gallés, Núria. (2014). How does the bilingual experience sculpt the brain? *Nature Reviews Neuroscience, 15*(5), 336–345. doi: 10.1038/nrn3709

Côté, James E. (2009). Identity formation and self-development in adolescence. In Richard M. Lerner & Laurence Steinberg (Eds.), *Handbook of adolescent psychology* (3rd ed., Vol. 1, pp. 266–304). Hoboken, NJ: Wiley.

Côté, James E. & Levine, Charles. (2015). *Identity formation, youth, and development: A simplified approach.* New York, NY: Psychology Press.

Côté, Sylvana M.; Borge, Anne I.; Geoffroy, Marie-Claude; Rutter, Michael & Tremblay, Richard E. (2008). Nonmaternal care in infancy and emotional/behavioral difficulties at 4 years old: Moderation by family risk characteristics. *Developmental Psychology, 44*(1), 155–168. doi: 10.1037/0012-1649.44.1.155

Couzin, Jennifer. (2009). Friendship as a health factor. *Science, 323*(5913), 454–457. doi: 10.1126/science.323.5913.454

Couzin-Frankel, Jennifer. (2011a). A pitched battle over life span. *Science, 333*(6042), 549–550. doi: 10.1126/science.333.6042.549

Couzin-Frankel, Jennifer. (2011b). Aging genes: The sirtuin story unravels. *Science, 334*(6060), 1194–1198. doi: 10.1126/science.334.6060.1194

Couzin-Frankel, Jennifer. (2013a). Return of unexpected DNA results urged. *Science, 339*(6127), 1507–1508. doi: 10.1126/science.339.6127.1507

Couzin-Frankel, Jennifer. (2013b). How does fetal environment influence later health? *Science, 340*(6137), 1160–1161. doi: 10.1126/science.340.6137.1160

Couzin-Frankel, Jennifer. (2016). A cancer legacy. *Science, 351*(6272), 440–443. doi: 10.1126/science.351.6272.440

Cowan, Nelson. (2014). Working memory underpins cognitive development, learning, and education. *Educational Psychology Review, 26*(2), 197–223. doi: 10.1007/s10648-013-9246-y

Cowan, Nelson & Alloway, Tracy. (2009). Development of working memory in childhood. In Mary L. Courage & Nelson Cowan (Eds.), *The development of memory in infancy and childhood* (2nd ed., pp. 303–342). New York, NY: Psychology Press.

Coyne, Sarah M. (2016). Effects of viewing relational aggression on television on aggressive behavior in adolescents: A three-year longitudinal study. *Developmental Psychology, 52*(2), 284–295. doi: 10.1037/dev0000068

Craig, Stephanie G.; Davies, Gregory; Schibuk, Larry; Weiss, Margaret D. & Hechtman, Lily. (2015). Long-term effects of stimulant treatment for ADHD: What can we tell our patients? *Current Developmental Disorders Reports, 2*(1), 1–9. doi: 10.1007/s40474-015-0039-5

Crain, William C. (2011). *Theories of development: Concepts and applications* (6th ed.). Boston, MA: Prentice–Hall.

Cramer, Steven C. & Procaccio, Vincent. (2012). Correlation between genetic polymorphisms and stroke recovery: Analysis of the GAIN Americas and GAIN International Studies. *European Journal of Neurology, 19*(5), 718–724. doi: 10.1111/j.1468-1331.2011.03615.x

Cranwell, Brian. (2010). Care and control: What motivates people's decisions about the disposal of ashes. *Bereavement Care, 29*(2), 10–12. doi: 10.1080/02682621.2010.484929

Crenshaw, David A. (2013). The family, larger systems, and traumatic death. In David K. Meagher & David E. Balk (Eds.), *Handbook of thanatology: The essential body of knowledge for the study of death, dying, and bereavement* (2nd ed., pp. 305–309). New York, NY: Routledge.

Creswell, John W. (2009). *Research design: Qualitative, quantitative, and mixed methods approaches* (3rd ed.). Thousand Oaks, CA: Sage.

Cristia, Alejandrina; Seidl, Amanda; Junge, Caroline; Soderstrom, Melanie & Hagoort, Peter. (2014). Predicting individual variation in language from infant speech perception measures. *Child Development, 85*(4), 1330–1345. doi: 10.1111/cdev.12193

Crocetti, Elisabetta; Scrignaro, Marta; Sica, Luigia & Magrin, Maria. (2012). Correlates of identity configurations: Three studies with adolescent and emerging adult cohorts. *Journal of Youth and Adolescence, 41*(6), 732–748. doi: 10.1007/s10964-011-9702-2

Cronce, Jessica M. & Corbin, William R. (2010). College and career. In Jon E. Grant & Marc N. Potenza (Eds.), *Young adult mental health* (pp. 80–95). New York, NY: Oxford University Press.

Crone, Eveline A. & Dahl, Ronald E. (2012). Understanding adolescence as a period of social–affective engagement and goal flexibility. *Nature Reviews Neuroscience, 13*(9), 636–650. doi: 10.1038/nrn3313

Crone, Eveline A.; van Duijvenvoorde, Anna C. K. & Peper, Jiska S. (2016). Annual research review: Neural contributions to risk-taking in adolescence—developmental changes and individual differences. *Journal of Child Psychology and Psychiatry, 57*(3), 353–368. doi: 10.1111/jcpp.12502

Crosnoe, Robert; Leventhal, Tama; Wirth, Robert John; Pierce, Kim M. & Pianta, Robert C. (2010). Family socioeconomic status and consistent environmental stimulation in early childhood. *Child Development, 81*(3), 972–987. doi: 10.1111/j.1467-8624.2010.01446.x

Crosnoe, Robert; Purtell, Kelly M.; Davis-Kean, Pamela; Ansari, Arya & Benner, Aprile D. (2016). The selection of children from low-income families into preschool. *Developmental Psychology, 52*(4), 599–612. doi: 10.1037/dev0000101

Cross, Donna; Monks, Helen; Hall, Marg; Shaw, Thérèse; Pintabona, Yolanda; Erceg, Erin, . . . Lester, Leanne. (2011). Three-year results of the Friendly Schools whole-of-school intervention on children's bullying behaviour. *British Educational Research Journal, 37*(1), 105–129. doi: 10.1080/01411920903420024

Crossley, Nicolas A.; Mechelli, Andrea; Scott, Jessica; Carletti, Francesco; Fox, Peter T.; McGuire, Philip & Bullmore, Edward T. (2014). The hubs of the human connectome are generally implicated in the anatomy of brain disorders. *Brain, 137*(8), 2382–2395. doi: 10.1093/brain/awu132

Crowe, Laura & Butterworth, Peter. (2016). The role of financial hardship, mastery and social support in the association between employment status and depression: Results from an Australian longitudinal cohort study. *BMJ Open, 6*, e009834. doi: 10.1136/bmjopen-2015-009834

Crucian, Brian; Stowe, Raymond; Mehta, Satish; Uchakin, Peter; Quiriarte, Heather; Pierson, Duane & Sams, Clarence. (2013). Immune system dysregulation occurs during short duration spaceflight on board the space shuttle. *Journal of Clinical Immunology, 33*(2), 456–465. doi: 10.1007/s10875-012-9824-7

Cruikshank, Margaret. (2009). *Learning to be old: Gender, culture, and aging* (2nd ed.). Lanham, MD: Rowman & Littlefield.

Csikszentmihalyi, Mihaly. (2013). *Creativity: Flow and the psychology of discovery and invention.* New York, NY: Harper Perennial.

Cubillo, Ana; Halari, Rozmin; Smith, Anna; Taylor, Eric & Rubia, Katya. (2012). A review of fronto-striatal and fronto-cortical brain abnormalities in children and adults with Attention deficit hyperactivity disorder (ADHD) and new evidence for dysfunction in adults with ADHD during motivation and attention. *Cortex, 48*(2), 194–215. doi: 10.1016/j.cortex.2011.04.007

Cuevas, Bryan J. & Stone, Jacqueline Ilyse (Eds.). (2011). *The Buddhist dead: Practices, discourses, representations.* Honolulu, HI: University of Hawaii Press.

Cui, Ming & Donnellan, M. Brent. (2009). Trajectories of conflict over raising adolescent children and marital satisfaction. *Journal of Marriage and Family, 71*(3), 478–494. doi: 10.1111/j.1741-3737.2009.00614.x

Cuijpers, Pim; van Straten, A.; van Oppen, P. & Andersson, G. (2010). Welke psychologische behandeling, uitgevoerd door wie, is het meest effectief bij depressie? *Gedragstherapie, 43*, 79–113.

Culotta, Elizabeth. (2009). On the origin of religion. *Science, 326*(5954), 784–787. doi: 10.1126/science.326_784

Culpin, Iryna; Heron, Jon; Araya, Ricardo & Joinson, Carol. (2015). Early childhood father absence and depressive symptoms in adolescent girls from a UK cohort: The mediating role of early menarche. *Journal of Abnormal Child Psychology, 43*(5), 921–931. doi: 10.1007/s10802-014-9960-z

Cumming, Elaine & Henry, William Earl. (1961). *Growing old: The process of disengagement.* New York, NY: Basic Books.

Cumsille, Patricio; Darling, Nancy & Martínez, M. Loreto. (2010). Shading the truth: The patterning of adolescents' decisions to avoid issues, disclose, or lie to parents. *Journal of Adolescence*, 33(2), 285–296. doi: 10.1016/j.adolescence.2009.10.008

Cunningham, F. Gary; Leveno, Kenneth; Bloom, Steven; Spong, Catherine Y.; Dashe, Jodi; Hoffman, Barbara, . . . Sheffield, Jeanne S. (2014). *Williams obstetrics* (24th ed.). New York, NY: McGraw-Hill Education.

Cunradi, Carol B. (2009). Intimate partner violence among Hispanic men and women: The role of drinking, neighborhood disorder, and acculturation-related factors. *Violence and Victims*, 24(1), 83–97. doi: 10.1891/0886-6708.24.1.83

Curlin, Farr A.; Nwodim, Chinyere; Vance, Jennifer L.; Chin, Marshall H. & Lantos, John D. (2008). To die, to sleep: US physicians' religious and other objections to physician-assisted suicide, terminal sedation, and withdrawal of life support. *American Journal of Hospice and Palliative Medicine*, 25(2), 112–120. doi: 10.1177/1049909107310141

Currie, Janet & Widom, Cathy S. (2010). Long-term consequences of child abuse and neglect on adult economic well-being. *Child Maltreatment*, 15(2), 111–120. doi: 10.1177/1077559509355316

Curry, Laurel Erin; Richardson, Amanda; Xiao, Haijun & Niaura, Raymond S. (2013). Nondisclosure of smoking status to health care providers among current and former smokers in the United States. *Health Education and Behavior*, 40(3), 266–273. doi: 10.1177/1090198112454284

Cutler, Stephen J.; Hendricks, Jon & O'Neill, Greg. (2011). Civic engagement and aging. In Robert H. Binstock & Linda K. George (Eds.), *Handbook of aging and the social sciences* (7th ed., pp. 221–233). San Diego, CA: Academic Press. doi: 10.1016/B978-0-12-380880-6.00016-2

Cutuli, J. J.; Desjardins, Christopher David; Herbers, Janette E.; Long, Jeffrey D.; Heistad, David; Chan, Chi-Keung, . . . Masten, Ann S. (2013). Academic achievement trajectories of homeless and highly mobile students: Resilience in the context of chronic and acute risk. *Child Development*, 84(3), 841–857. doi: 10.1111/cdev.12013

D'Angelo, Jonathan D. & Toma, Catalina L. (2016). There are plenty of fish in the sea: The effects of choice overload and reversibility on online daters' satisfaction with selected partners. *Media Psychology*, (In Press). doi: 10.1080/15213269.2015.1121827

D'Souza, Jeevan & Gurin, Michael. (2016). The universal significance of Maslow's concept of self-actualization. *The Humanistic Psychologist*, 44(2), 210–214. doi: 10.1037/hum0000027

Dahl, Ronald E. (2004). Adolescent brain development: A period of vulnerabilities and opportunities, keynote address. *Annals of the New York Academy of Sciences*, 1021, 1–22. doi: 10.1196/annals.1308.001

Daley, Dave; Jones, Karen; Hutchings, Judy & Thompson, Margaret. (2009). Attention deficit hyperactivity disorder in pre-school children: Current findings, recommended interventions and future directions. *Child: Care, Health and Development*, 35(6), 754–766. doi: 10.1111/j.1365-2214.2009.00938.x

Dalman, Christina; Allebeck, Peter; Gunnell, David; Harrison, Glyn; Kristensson, Krister; Lewis, Glyn, . . . Karlsson, Håkan. (2008). Infections in the CNS during childhood and the risk of subsequent psychotic illness: A cohort study of more than one million Swedish subjects. *American Journal of Psychiatry*, 165(1), 59–65. doi: 10.1176/appi.ajp.2007.07050740

Damasio, Antonio R. (2012). *Self comes to mind: Constructing the conscious brain*. New York, NY: Vintage.

Damian, Lavinia E.; Stoeber, Joachim; Negru, Oana & Băban, Adriana. (2013). On the development of perfectionism in adolescence: Perceived parental expectations predict longitudinal increases in socially prescribed perfectionism. *Personality and Individual Differences*, 55(6), 688–693. doi: 10.1016/j.paid.2013.05.021

Dannefer, Dale & Patterson, Robin Shura. (2008). The missing person: Some limitations in the contemporary study of cognitive aging. In Scott M. Hofer & Duane F. Alwin (Eds.), *Handbook of cognitive aging: Interdisciplinary perspectives* (pp. 105–119). Thousand Oaks, CA: Sage. doi: 10.4135/9781412976589

Darwin, Charles. (1859). *On the origin of species by means of natural selection*. London, UK: J. Murray.

Darwin, Charles. (1971). *The descent of man and selection in relation to sex*. London: J. Murray.

Dasen, Pierre R. & Mishra, Ramesh C. (2013). Cultural differences in cognitive styles. In Bhoomika Rastogi Kar (Ed.), *Cognition and brain development: Converging evidence from various methodologies* (pp. 231–249). Washington, DC: American Psychological Association. doi: 10.1037/14043-012

Daum, Moritz M.; Ulber, Julia & Gredebäck, Gustaf. (2013). The development of pointing perception in infancy: Effects of communicative signals on covert shifts of attention. *Developmental Psychology*, 49(10), 1898–1908. doi: 10.1037/a0031111

Davidai, Shai & Gilovich, Thomas. (2015). Building a more mobile America: One income quintile at a time. *Perspectives on Psychological Science*, 10(1), 60–71. doi: 10.1177/1745691614562005

Davis, Erik W. (2016). *Deathpower: Buddhism's ritual imagination in Cambodia*. New York, NY: Columbia University Press.

Davis, Linell. (1999). *Doing culture: Cross-cultural communication in action*. Beijing, China: Foreign Language Teaching & Research Press.

Davis, R. Neal; Davis, Matthew M.; Freed, Gary L. & Clark, Sarah J. (2011). Fathers' depression related to positive and negative parenting behaviors with 1-year-old children. *Pediatrics*, 127(4), 612–618. doi: 10.1542/peds.2010-1779

Davis-Kean, Pamela E.; Jager, Justin & Collins, W. Andrew. (2009). The self in action: An emerging link between self-beliefs and behaviors in middle childhood. *Child Development Perspectives*, 3(3), 184–188. doi: 10.1111/j.1750-8606.2009.00104.x

Davison, Glen; Kehaya, Corinna & Jones, Arwel Wyn. (2014). Nutritional and physical activity interventions to improve immunity. *American Journal of Lifestyle Medicine*. doi: 10.1177/1559827614557773

Dawood, Yasmin. (2015). Campaign finance and American democracy. *Annual Review of Political Science*, 18, 329–348. doi: 10.1146/annurev-polisci-010814-104523

Dayalu, Praveen & Albin, Roger L. (2015). Huntington disease: Pathogenesis and treatment. *Neurologic Clinics*, 33(1), 101–114. doi: 10.1016/j.ncl.2014.09.003

Dayanim, Shoshana & Namy, Laura L. (2015). Infants learn baby signs from video. *Child Development*, 86(3), 800–811. doi: 10.1111/cdev.12340

Dayton, Carolyn Joy; Walsh, Tova B.; Oh, Wonjung & Volling, Brenda. (2015). Hush now baby: Mothers' and fathers' strategies for soothing their infants and associated parenting outcomes. *Journal of Pediatric Health Care*, 29(2), 145–155. doi: 10.1016/j.pedhc.2014.09.001

de Boer, Anouk; Peeters, Margot & Koning, Ina. (2016). An experimental study of risk taking behavior among adolescents: A closer look at peer and sex influences. *The Journal of Early Adolescence*, (In Press). doi: 10.1177/0272431616648453

de Bruin, Wändi Bruine; Parker, Andrew M. & Fischhoff, Baruch. (2007). Can adolescents predict significant life events? *The Journal of Adolescent Health*, 41(2), 208–210. doi: 10.1016/j.jadohealth.2007.03.014

de Bruin, Wändi Bruine; Parker, Andrew M. & Fischhoff, Baruch. (2012). Explaining adult age differences in decision-making competence. *Journal of Behavioral Decision Making*, 25(4), 352–360. doi: 10.1002/bdm.712

De Corte, Erik. (2013). Giftedness considered from the perspective of research on learning and instruction. *High Ability Studies*, 24(1), 3–19. doi: 10.1080/13598139.2013.780967

de Heering, Adelaide; de Liedekerke, Claire; Deboni, Malorie & Rossion, Bruno. (2010). The role of experience during childhood in shaping the other-race effect. *Developmental Science*, 13(1), 181–187. doi: 10.1111/j.1467-7687.2009.00876.x

de Hoog, Marieke L. A.; Kleinman, Ken P.; Gillman, Matthew W.; Vrijkotte, Tanja G. M.; van Eijsden, Manon & Taveras, Elsie M. (2014). Racial/ethnic and immigrant differences in early childhood diet quality. *Public Health Nutrition*, 17(6), 1308–1317. doi: 10.1017/S1368980013001183

de Jong Gierveld, Jenny & Merz, Eva-Maria. (2013). Parents' partnership decision making after divorce or widowhood: The role of (step)children. *Journal of Marriage and Family*, 75(5), 1098–1113. doi: 10.1111/jomf.12061

de Jonge, Ank; Mesman, Jeanette A. J. M.; Manniën, Judith; Zwart, Joost J.; van Dillen, Jeroen & van Roosmalen, Jos. (2013). Severe adverse maternal outcomes among low risk women with planned home versus hospital births in the Netherlands: Nationwide cohort study. *BMJ*, 346, f3263. doi: 10.1136/bmj.f3263

de Jonge, Huub. (2011). Purification and remembrance: Eastern and Western ways to deal with the Bali bombing. In Peter Jan Margry & Cristina Sánchez-Carretero (Eds.), *Grassroots memorials: The politics of memorializing traumatic death* (pp. 262–284). New York, NY: Berghahn Books.

de la Croix, David. (2013). *Fertility, education, growth, and sustainability*. New York, NY: Cambridge University Press.

De Lee, Joseph Bolivar. (1938). *The principles and practice of obstetrics* (7th ed.). Philadelphia, PA: W. B. Saunders Co.

De Neys, Wim & Van Gelder, Elke. (2009). Logic and belief across the lifespan: The rise and fall of belief inhibition during syllogistic reasoning. *Developmental Science, 12*(1), 123–130. doi: 10.1111/j.1467-7687.2008.00746.x

De Preter, Hanne; Van Looy, Dorien & Mortelmans, Dimitri. (2013). Individual and institutional push and pull factors as predictors of retirement timing in Europe: A multilevel analysis. *Journal of Aging Studies, 27*(4), 299–307. doi: 10.1016/j.jaging.2013.06.003

De Raedt, Rudi; Koster, Ernst H. W. & Ryckewaert, Ruben. (2013). Aging and attentional bias for death related and general threat-related information: Less avoidance in older as compared with middle-aged adults. *The Journals of Gerontology, Series B: Psychological Sciences and Social Sciences, 68*(1), 41–48. doi: 10.1093/geronb/gbs047

de Vos, Paul; Hanck, Christoph; Neisingh, Marjolein; Prak, Dennis; Groen, Henk & Faas, Marijke M. (2015). Weight gain in freshman college students and perceived health. *Preventive Medicine Reports, 2*, 229–234. doi: 10.1016/j.pmedr.2015.03.008

Dean, Angela J.; Walters, Julie & Hall, Anthony. (2010). A systematic review of interventions to enhance medication adherence in children and adolescents with chronic illness. *Archives of Disease in Childhood, 95*(9), 717–723. doi: 10.1136/adc.2009.175125

Dearing, Eric; Walsh, Mary E.; Sibley, Erin; Lee-St.John, Terry; Foley, Claire & Raczek, Anastacia E. (2016). Can community and school-based supports improve the achievement of first-generation immigrant children attending high-poverty schools? *Child Development, 87*(3), 883–897. doi: 10.1111/cdev.12507

Dearing, Eric; Wimer, Christopher; Simpkins, Sandra D.; Lund, Terese; Bouffard, Suzanne M.; Caronongan, Pia, . . . Weiss, Heather. (2009). Do neighborhood and home contexts help explain why low-income children miss opportunities to participate in activities outside of school? *Developmental Psychology, 45*(6), 1545–1562. doi: 10.1037/a0017359

Deater-Deckard, Kirby. (2013). The social environment and the development of psychopathology. In Philip D. Zelazo (Ed.), *The Oxford handbook of developmental psychology* (Vol. 2, pp. 527–548). New York, NY: Oxford University Press. doi: 10.1093/oxfordhb/9780199958474.013.0021

Deater-Deckard, Kirby & Lansford, Jennifer E. (2016). Daughters' and sons' exposure to child-rearing discipline and violence in low- and middle-income countries. *Monographs of the Society for Research in Child Development, 81*(1), 78–103. doi: 10.1111/mono.12227

DeCaro, Marci S.; Thomas, Robin D.; Albert, Neil B. & Beilock, Sian L. (2011). Choking under pressure: Multiple routes to skill failure. *Journal of Experimental Psychology, 140*(3), 390–406. doi: 10.1037/a0023466

Dees, Marianne K.; Vernooij-Dassen, Myrra. J.; Dekkers, Wim. J.; Vissers, Kris. C. & van Weel, Chris. (2011). 'Unbearable suffering': A qualitative study on the perspectives of patients who request assistance in dying. *Journal of Medical Ethics, 37*(12), 727–734. doi: 10.1136/jme.2011.045492

Degnan, Kathryn A.; Hane, Amie Ashley; Henderson, Heather A.; Moas, Olga Lydia; Reeb-Sutherland, Bethany C. & Fox, Nathan A. (2011). Longitudinal stability of temperamental exuberance and social–emotional outcomes in early childhood. *Developmental Psychology, 47*(3), 765–780. doi: 10.1037/a0021316

DeGroot, Jocelyn M. (2012). Maintaining relational continuity with the deceased on Facebook. *Omega: Journal of Death & Dying, 65*(3), 195–212. doi: 10.2190/OM.65.3.c

Dekel, Sharon; Ein-Dor, Tsachi & Solomon, Zahava. (2012). Posttraumatic growth and posttraumatic distress: A longitudinal study. *Psychological Trauma, 4*(1), 94–101. doi: 10.1037/a0021865

DeLamater, John. (2012). Sexual expression in later life: A review and synthesis. *The Journal of Sex Research, 49*(2/3), 125–141. doi: 10.1080/00224499.2011.603168

Delaunay-El Allam, Maryse; Soussignan, Robert; Patris, Bruno; Marlier, Luc & Schaal, Benoist. (2010). Long-lasting memory for an odor acquired at the mother's breast. *Developmental Science, 13*(6), 849–863. doi: 10.1111/j.1467-7687.2009.00941.x

DeLisi, Matt. (2014). Low self-control is a brain-based disorder. In Kevin M. Beaver et al. (Eds.), *The nurture versus biosocial debate in criminology: On the origins of criminal behavior and criminality* (pp. 172–183). Thousand Oaks, CA: Sage.

DeLoache, Judy S.; Chiong, Cynthia; Sherman, Kathleen; Islam, Nadia; Vanderborght, Mieke; Troseth, Georgene L., . . . O'Doherty, Katherine. (2010). Do babies learn from baby media? *Psychological Science, 21*(11), 1570–1574. doi: 10.1177/0956797610384145

Delon-Martin, Chantal; Plailly, Jane; Fonlupt, Pierre; Veyrac, Alexandra & Roye, Jean-Pierre. (2013). Perfumers' expertise induces structural reorganization in olfactory brain regions. *NeuroImage, 68*, 55–62. doi: 10.1016/j.neuroimage.2012.11.044

Deming, Michelle E.; Covan, Eleanor Krassen; Swan, Suzanne C. & Billings, Deborah L. (2013). Exploring rape myths, gendered norms, group processing, and the social context of rape among college women a qualitative analysis. *Violence Against Women, 19*(4), 465–485. doi: 10.1177/1077801213487044

Deng, Nina; Guyer, Rick & Ware, John E. (2015). Energy, fatigue, or both? A bifactor modeling approach to the conceptualization and measurement of vitality. *Quality of Life Research, 24*(1), 81–93. doi: 10.1007/s11136-014-0839-9

Denny, Dallas & Pittman, Cathy. (2007). Gender identity: From dualism to diversity. In Mitchell Tepper & Annette Fuglsang Owens (Eds.), *Sexual Health* (Vol. 1, pp. 205–229). Westport, CT: Praeger.

Deptula, Daneen P.; Henry, David B. & Schoeny, Michael E. (2010). How can parents make a difference? Longitudinal associations with adolescent sexual behavior. *Journal of Family Psychology, 24*(6), 731–739. doi: 10.1037/a0021760

Deresiewicz, William. (2014). *Excellent sheep: The miseducation of the American elite and the way to a meaningful life*. New York, NY: Free Press.

Derksen, B. J.; Duff, Melissa C.; Weldon, K.; Zhang, J.; Zambac, K. D.; Tranel, Daniel & Denburg, Natalie L. (2015). Older adults catch up to younger adults on a learning and memory task that involves collaborative social interaction. *Memory, 23*(4), 612–624. doi: 10.1080/09658211.2014.915974

Desai, Rishi J.; Hernandez-Diaz, Sonia; Bateman, Brian T. & Huybrechts, Krista F. (2014). Increase in prescription opioid use during pregnancy among medicaid-enrolled women. *Obstetrics & Gynecology, 123*(5), 997–1002. doi: 10.1097/AOG.0000000000000208

Desai, Sonalde & Andrist, Lester. (2010). Gender scripts and age at marriage in India. *Demography, 47*(3), 667–687. doi: 10.1353/dem.0.0118

DeSilver, Drew. (2016, June 8). *Increase in living with parents driven by those ages 25–34, non-college grads. Fact Tank: News in the Numbers.* Washington, DC: Pew Research Center.

Devaraj, Sridevi; Hemarajata, Peera & Versalovic, James. (2013). The human gut microbiome and body metabolism: Implications for obesity and diabetes. *Clinical Chemistry, 59*(4), 617–628. doi: 10.1373/clinchem.2012.187617

Devine, Rory T. & Hughes, Claire. (2014). Relations between false belief understanding and executive function in early childhood: A meta-analysis. *Child Development, 85*(5), 1777–1794. doi: 10.1111/cdev.12237

Devine, Rory T.; White, Naomi; Ensor, Rosie & Hughes, Claire. (2016). Theory of mind in middle childhood: Longitudinal associations with executive function and social competence. *Developmental Psychology, 52*(5), 758–771. doi: 10.1037/dev0000105

DeYoung, Colin G.; Hirsh, Jacob B.; Shane, Matthew S.; Papademetris, Xenophon; Rajeevan, Nallakkandi & Gray, Jeremy R. (2010). Testing predictions from personality neuroscience. *Psychological Science, 21*(6), 820–828. doi: 10.1177/0956797610370159

Diamond, Adele. (2012). Activities and programs that improve children's executive functions. *Current Directions in Psychological Science, 21*(5), 335–341. doi: 10.1177/0963721412453722

Diamond, Lisa M. & Fagundes, Christopher P. (2010). Psychobiological research on attachment. *Journal of Social and Personal Relationships, 27*(2), 218–225. doi: 10.1177/0265407509360906

Diamond, Milton & Sigmundson, H. Keith. (1997). Sex reassignment at birth: Long-term review and clinical implications. *Archives of Pediatric Adolescent Medicine, 151*(3), 298–304. doi: 10.1001/archpedi.1997.02170400084015

Diamond, Marian C. (1988). *Enriching heredity: The impact of the environment on the anatomy of the brain.* New York, NY: Free Press.

Dickinson, George E. & Hoffmann, Heath C. (2010). Roadside memorial policies in the United States. *Mortality: Promoting the interdisciplinary study of death and dying, 15*(2), 154–167. doi: 10.1080/13576275.2010.482775

Didion, Joan. (2005). *The year of magical thinking.* New York, NY: Knopf.

Digital Journal. (2014, August 14). 2014 Survey: How many Christians do you think watch porn? *Digital Journal.*

Dijk, Jan A. G. M. van. (2005). *The deepening divide: Inequality in the information society.* Thousand Oaks, CA: Sage.

Dijksterhuis, Ap; Bos, Maarten W.; van der Leij, Andries & van Baaren, Rick B. (2009). Predicting soccer matches after unconscious and conscious thought as a function of expertise. *Psychological Science, 20*(11), 1381–1387. doi: 10.1111/j.1467-9280.2009.02451.x

Dimler, Laura M. & Natsuaki, Misaki N. (2015). The effects of pubertal timing on externalizing behaviors in adolescence and early adulthood: A meta-analytic review. *Journal of Adolescence, 45,* 160–170. doi: 10.1016/j.adolescence.2015.07.021

Dinh, Michael M.; Bein, Kendall; Roncal, Susan; Byrne, Christopher M.; Petchell, Jeffrey & Brennan, Jeffrey. (2013). Redefining the golden hour for severe head injury in an urban setting: The effect of prehospital arrival times on patient outcomes. *Injury, 44*(5), 606–610. doi: 10.1016/j.injury.2012.01.011

Dion, Jacinthe; Blackburn, Marie-Eve; Auclair, Julie; Laberge, Luc; Veillette, Suzanne; Gaudreault, Marco, . . . Touchette, Évelyne. (2015). Development and aetiology of body dissatisfaction in adolescent boys and girls. *International Journal of Adolescence and Youth, 20*(2), 151–166. doi: 10.1080/02673843.2014.985320

DiPietro, Janet A.; Costigan, Kathleen A. & Voegtline, Kristin M. (2015). Fetal motor activity. *Monographs of the Society for Research in Child Development, 80*(3), 33–42. doi: 10.1111/mono.12176

Dirks, Doris Andrea. (2016). Transgender people at four big ten campuses: A policy discourse analysis *The Review of Higher Education, 39*(3), 371–393. doi: 10.1353/rhe.2016.0020

Diseth, Åge; Meland, Eivind & Breidablik, Hans J. (2014). Self-beliefs among students: Grade level and gender differences in self-esteem, self-efficacy and implicit theories of intelligence. *Learning and Individual Differences, 35,* 1–8. doi: 10.1016/j.lindif.2014.06.003

Dishion, Thomas J.; Poulin, François & Burraston, Bert. (2001). Peer group dynamics associated with iatrogenic effects in group interventions with high-risk young adolescents. In

Douglas W. Nangle & Cynthia A. Erdley (Eds.), *The role of friendship in psychological adjustment* (pp. 79–92). San Francisco, CA: Jossey-Bass.

Dishion, Thomas J.; Véronneau, Marie-Hélène & Myers, Michael W. (2010). Cascading peer dynamics underlying the progression from problem behavior to violence in early to late adolescence. *Development and Psychopathology, 22*(3), 603–619. doi: 10.1017/S0954579410000313

Dix, Theodore & Yan, Ni. (2014). Mothers' depressive symptoms and infant negative emotionality in the prediction of child adjustment at age 3: Testing the maternal reactivity and child vulnerability hypotheses. *Development and Psychopathology, 26*(1), 111–124. doi: 10.1017/S0954579413000898

Dobler, Robert Thomas. (2011). Ghost bikes: Memorialization and protest on city streets. In Peter Jan Margry & Cristina Sanchez-Carretero (Eds.), *Grassroots memorials: The politics of memorializing traumatic death* (pp. 169–187). New York, NY: Berghahn Books.

Dobson, Velma; Candy, T. Rowan; Hartmann, E. Eugenie; Mayer, D. Luisa; Miller, Joseph M. & Quinn, Graham E. (2009). Infant and child vision research: Present status and future directions. *Optometry & Vision Science, 86*(6), 559–560. doi: 10.1097/OPX.0b013e3181aa06d5

Dodge, Kenneth A. (2009). Mechanisms of gene-environment interaction effects in the development of conduct disorder. *Perspectives on Psychological Science, 4*(4), 408–414. doi: 10.1111/j.1745-6924.2009.01147.x

Doering, Katie. (2010). Death: The unwritten curriculum. *Encounter: Education for Meaning and Social Justice, 23*(4), 57–62.

Doka, Kenneth J. (2013). Historical and contemporary perspectives on dying. In David K. Meagher & David E. Balk (Eds.), *Handbook of thanatology: The essential body of knowledge for the study of death, dying, and bereavement* (2nd ed., pp. 17–23). New York, NY: Routledge.

Domina, Thurston; Conley, AnneMarie & Farkas, George. (2011a). The case for dreaming big. *Sociology of Education, 84*(2), 118–121. doi: 10.1177/0038040711401810

Domina, Thurston; Conley, AnneMarie & Farkas, George. (2011b). The link between educational expectations and effort in the college-for-all era. *Sociology of Education, 84*(2), 93–112. doi: 10.1177/1941406411401808

Dominelli, Paolo B. & Sheel, A. William. (2012). Experimental approaches to the study of the mechanics of breathing during exercise. *Respiratory Physiology & Neurobiology, 180*(2/3), 147–161. doi: 10.1016/j.resp.2011.10.005

Dominguez, Cynthia O. (2001). Expertise in laparoscopic surgery: Anticipation and affordances. In Eduardo Salas & Gary A. Klein (Eds.), *Linking expertise and naturalistic decision making* (pp. 287–301). Mahwah, NJ: Erlbaum.

Dominguez-Folgueras, Marta & Castro-Martin, Teresa. (2013). Cohabitation in Spain: No longer a marginal path to family formation. *Journal of Marriage and Family, 75*(2), 422–437. doi: 10.1111/jomf.12013

Dong, XinQi & Simon, Melissa A. (2011). Enhancing national policy and programs to address elder abuse. *JAMA, 305*(23), 2460–2461. doi: 10.1001/jama.2011.835

Dorais, Michel. (2009). *Don't tell: The sexual abuse of boys* (2nd ed.). Montreal, Canada: McGill-Queen's University Press.

Doraiswamy, P. Murali. (2012). Silent cerebrovascular events and Alzheimer's disease: An overlooked opportunity for prevention? *American Journal of Psychiatry, 169*(3), 251–254. doi: 10.1176/appi.ajp.2011.11121830

Dorsey, Shannon; Burns, Barbara J.; Southerland, Dannia G.; Cox, Julia Revillion; Wagner, H. Ryan & Farmer, Elizabeth M. Z. (2012). Prior trauma exposure for youth in treatment foster care. *Journal of Child and Family Studies, 21*(5), 816–824. doi: 10.1007/s10826-011-9542-4

Dotterer, Aryn M.; McHale, Susan M. & Crouter, Ann C. (2009). The development and correlates of academic interests from childhood through adolescence. *Journal of Educational Psychology, 101*(2), 509–519. doi: 10.1037/a0013987

Doucet, Andrea. (2015). Parental responsibilities: Dilemmas of measurement and gender equality. *Journal of Marriage and Family, 77*(1), 224–242. doi: 10.1111/jomf.12148

Driemeyer, Wiebke; Janssen, Erick; Wiltfang, Jens & Elmerstig, Eva. (2016). Masturbation experiences of Swedish senior high school students: Gender differences and similarities. *The Journal of Sex Research.* doi: 10.1080/00224499.2016.1167814

Dubicka, Bernadka; Carlson, Gabrielle A.; Vail, Andy & Harrington, Richard. (2008). Prepubertal mania: Diagnostic differences between US and UK clinicians. *European Child & Adolescent Psychiatry, 17*(3), 153–161. doi: 10.1007/s00787-007-0649-5

Dubois, Jessica; Poupon, Cyril; Thirion, Bertrand; Simonnet, Hina; Kulikova, Sofya; Leroy, François, . . . Dehaene-Lambertz, Ghislaine. (2015). Exploring the early organization and maturation of linguistic pathways in the human infant brain. *Cerebral Cortex,* (In Press). doi: 10.1093/cercor/bhv082

Dubov, Alex & Phung, Connie. (2015). Nudges or mandates? The ethics of mandatory flu vaccination. *Vaccine, 33*(22), 2530–2535. doi: 10.1016/j.vaccine.2015.03.048

Duckworth, Angela L. & Kern, Margaret L. (2011). A meta-analysis of the convergent validity of self-control measures. *Journal of Research in Personality, 45*(3), 259–268. doi: 10.1016/j.jrp.2011.02.004

Duckworth, Angela L.; Peterson, Christopher; Matthews, Michael D. & Kelly, Dennis R. (2007). Grit: Perseverance and passion for long-term goals. *Journal of Personality and Social Psychology, 92*(6), 1087–1101. doi: 10.1037/0022-3514.92.6.1087

Duffey, Kiyah J.; Steffen, Lyn M.; Van Horn, Linda; Jacobs, David R. & Popkin, Barry M. (2012). Dietary patterns matter: Diet beverages and cardiometabolic risks in the longitudinal Coronary

Artery Risk Development in Young Adults (CARDIA) Study. *American Journal of Clinical Nutrition*, 95(4), 909–915. doi: 10.3945 /ajcn.111.026682

Dugas, Lara R.; Fuller, Miles; Gilbert, Jack & Layden, Brian T. (2016). The obese gut microbiome across the epidemiologic transition. *Emerging Themes in Epidemiology*, 13(1). doi: 10.1186 /s12982-015-0044-5

Duggan, Maeve & Brenner, Joanna. (2013). *The demographics of social media users—2011.* Washington, DC: Pew Research Center Internet & American Life Project, Pew Research Center.

Duh, Shinchieh; Paik, Jae H.; Miller, Patricia H.; Gluck, Stephanie C.; Li, Hui & Himelfarb, Igor. (2016). Theory of mind and executive function in Chinese preschool children. *Developmental Psychology*, 52(4), 582–591. doi: 10.1037 /a0040068

Dukes, Richard L.; Stein, Judith A. & Zane, Jazmin I. (2009). Effect of relational bullying on attitudes, behavior and injury among adolescent bullies, victims and bully-victims. *The Social Science Journal*, 46(4), 671–688. doi: 10.1016/j.soscij.2009.05.006

Duman, Ronald S. & Aghajanian, George K. (2012). Synaptic dysfunction in depression: Potential therapeutic targets. *Science*, 338(6103), 68–72. doi: 10.1126/science.1222939

Dumas, A.; Simmat-Durand, L. & Lejeune, C. (2014). Pregnancy and substance use in France: A literature review. *Journal de Gynécologie Obstétrique et Biologie de la Reproduction*. doi: 10.1016/j.jgyn.2014.05.008

Duncan, Greg J. & Magnuson, Katherine. (2007). Penny wise and effect size foolish. *Child Development Perspectives*, 1(1), 46–51. doi: 10.1111 /j.1750-8606.2007.00009.x

Duncan, Greg J. & Magnuson, Katherine. (2013). Investing in preschool programs. *Journal of Economic Perspectives*, 27(2), 109–132. doi: 10.1257/jep.27.2.109

Duncan, Simon & Phillips, Miranda. (2010). People who live apart together (LATs)—How different are they? *The Sociological Review*, 58(1), 112–134. doi: 10.1111/j.1467-954X.2009.01874.x

Dunmore, Simon J. (2013). Of fat mice and men: The rise of the adipokines. *Journal of Endocrinology*, 216(1), E1–E2. doi: 10.1530/JOE-12-0513

Dunn, Marianne G.; Rochlen, Aaron B. & O'Brien, Karen M. (2013). Employee, mother, and partner: An exploratory investigation of working women with stay-at-home fathers. *Journal of Career Development*, 40(1), 3–22. doi: 10.1177/0894845311401744

Dupuis, Kate & Pichora-Fuller, M. Kathleen. (2010). Use of affective prosody by young and older adults. *Psychology and Aging*, 25(1), 16–29. doi: 10.1037/a0018777

Dutra, Lauren M. & Glantz, Stanton A. (2014). Electronic cigarettes and conventional cigarette use among US adolescents: A cross-sectional study. *JAMA Pediatrics*, 168(7), 610–617. doi: 10.1001/jamapediatrics.2013.5488

Dutton, Donald G. (2012). The case against the role of gender in intimate partner violence. *Aggression and Violent Behavior*, 17(1), 99–104. doi: 10.1016/j.avb.2011.09.002

Dutton, Edward & Lynn, Richard. (2015). A negative Flynn Effect in France, 1999 to 2008–9. *Intelligence*, 51, 67–70. doi: 10.1016/j.intell .2015.05.005

Dvornyk, Volodymyr & Waqar-ul-Haq. (2012). Genetics of age at menarche: A systematic review. *Human Reproduction Update*, 18(2), 198–210. doi: 10.1093/humupd/dmr050

Dwane, H. Dean. (2012). Self-control and perceived physical risk in an extreme sport. *Young Consumers: Insight and Ideas for Responsible Marketers*, 13(1), 62–73. doi: 10.1108 /17473611211203948

Dweck, Carol S. (2013). Social Development. In Philip D. Zelazo (Ed.), *The Oxford handbook of developmental psychology* (Vol. 2, pp. 167–190). New York, NY: Oxford University Press. doi: 10.1093 /oxfordhb/9780199958474.013.0008

Dyer, Nazly; Owen, Margaret T. & Caughy, Margaret O'Brien. (2014). Ethnic differences in profiles of mother–child interactions and relations to emerging school readiness in African American and Latin American children. *Parenting*, 14(3/4), 175–194. doi: 10.1080/15295192.2014.972756

Eagan, Kevin; Stolzenberg, Ellen Bara; Bates, Abigail K.; Aragon, Melissa C.; Suchard, Maria Ramirez & Rios-Aguilar, Cecilia. (2015). *The American freshman: National norms fall 2015.* Los Angeles: Higher Education Research Institute, UCLA.

Eagly, Alice H. & Wood, Wendy. (2013). The nature–nurture debates: 25 years of challenges in understanding the psychology of gender. *Perspectives on Psychological Science*, 8(3), 340–357. doi: 10.1177/1745691613484767

Earth Policy Institute. (2011). *Two stories of disease: Smallpox and polio.* Washington, DC: Earth Policy Institute.

Ebaugh, Helen Rose & Curry, Mary. (2000). Fictive kin as social capital in new immigrant communities. *Sociological Perspectives*, 43(2), 189–209. doi: 10.2307/1389793

Eccles, Jacquelynne S. & Roeser, Robert W. (2010). An ecological view of schools and development. In Judith L. Meece & Jacquelynne S. Eccles (Eds.), *Handbook of research on schools, schooling, and human development* (pp. 6–22). New York, NY: Routledge.

Eccles, Jacquelynne S. & Roeser, Robert W. (2011). Schools as developmental contexts during adolescence. *Journal of Research on Adolescence*, 21(1), 225–241. doi: 10.1111 /j.1532-7795.2010.00725.x

Eckholm, Erik. (2013, October 24). Case explores rights of fetus versus mother. *New York Times*, pp. A1, A16.

Edwards, Katie M.; Sylaska, Kateryna M. & Neal, Angela M. (2015). Intimate partner violence among sexual minority populations: A critical review of the literature and agenda for future research. *Psychology of Violence*, 5(2), 112–121. doi: 10.1037/a0038656

Eells, Tracy D.; Lombart, Kenneth G.; Salsman, Nicholas; Kendjelic, Edward M.; Schneiderman, Carolyn T. & Lucas, Cynthia P. (2011). Expert reasoning in psychotherapy case formulation. *Psychotherapy Research*, 21(4), 385–399. doi: 10.1080/10503307.2010.539284

Ehrenberg, Rachel. (2016). GMOs under scrutiny. *Science News*, 189(3), 22–27.

Ehrlich, Paul R. (1968). *The population bomb.* New York, NY: Ballantine Books.

Ehrlich, Sara Z. & Blum-Kulka, Shoshana. (2014). 'Now I said that Danny becomes Danny again': A multifaceted view of kindergarten children's peer argumentative discourse. In Asta Cekaite et al. (Eds.), *Children's peer talk: Learning from each other* (pp. 23–41). New York, NY: Cambridge University Press.

Eichhorst, Werner; Rodríguez-Planas, Núria; Schmidl, Ricarda & Zimmermann, Klaus F. (2012). *A roadmap to vocational education and training systems around the world.* Bonn, Germany: Institute for the Study of Labor.

Eimas, Peter D.; Siqueland, Einar R.; Jusczyk, Peter & Vigorito, James. (1971). Speech perception in infants. *Science*, 171(3968), 303–306. doi: 10.1126/science.171.3968.303

Eisenberg, Nancy; Cumberland, Amanda; Guthrie, Ivanna K.; Murphy, Bridget C. & Shepard, Stephanie A. (2005). Age changes in prosocial responding and moral reasoning in adolescence and early adulthood. *Journal of Research on Adolescence*, 15(3), 235–260. doi: 10.1111 /j.1532-7795 .2005.00095.x

Eisenberg, Nancy; Hofer, Claire; Sulik, Michael J. & Liew, Jeffrey. (2013). The development of prosocial moral reasoning and a prosocial orientation in young adulthood: Concurrent and longitudinal correlates. *Developmental Psychology*, 50(1), 58–70. doi: 10.1037/a0032990

Eisenberg, Nancy; Hofer, Claire; Sulik, Michael J. & Spinrad, Tracy L. (2014). Self-regulation, effortful control, and their socioemotional correlates. In James J. Gross (Ed.), *Handbook of emotion regulation* (2nd ed., pp. 157–172). New York, NY: Guilford Press.

Eisenberg, Nancy & Zhou, Qing. (2016). Conceptions of executive function and regulation: When and to what degree do they overlap? In James A. Griffin et al. (Eds.), *Executive function in preschool-age children: Integrating measurement, neurodevelopment, and translational research* (pp. 115–136). Washington, DC: American Psychological Association. doi: 10.1037 /14797 -006

Elder, Glen H. (1998). The life course as developmental theory. *Child Development*, 69(1), 1–12. doi: 10.1111/j.1467-8624.1998.tb06128.x

Elder, Keith & Griffith, Derek M. (2016). Men's health: Beyond masculinity. *American Journal of Public Health*, 106(7), 1157. doi: 10.2105 /AJPH.2016.303237

Elicker, James; Ruprecht, Karen M. & Anderson, Treshawn. (2014). Observing infants' and toddlers' relationships and interactions in group care. In Linda J. Harrison & Jennifer Sumsion (Eds.), *Lived spaces of infant-toddler education and care: Exploring diverse perspectives on theory, research and practice* (pp. 131–145). Dordrecht, Netherlands: Springer. doi: 10.1007/978-94-017 -8838-0_10

Elkind, David. (1967). Egocentrism in adolescence. *Child Development*, 38(4), 1025–1034.

Elkind, David. (2007). *The power of play: How spontaneous, imaginative activities lead to happier, healthier children*. Cambridge, MA: Da Capo Press.

Ellingsaeter, Anne L. (2014). Towards universal quality early childhood education and care: The Norwegian model. In Ludovica Gambaro et al. (Eds.), *An equal start?: Providing quality early education and care for disadvantaged children* (pp. 53–76). Chicago, IL: Policy Press.

Elliott, Sinikka. (2012). *Not my kid: What parents believe about the sex lives of their teenagers*. New York, NY: New York University Press.

Elliott, Vanessa J.; Rodgers, David L. & Brett, Stephen J. (2011). Systematic review of quality of life and other patient-centred outcomes after cardiac arrest survival. *Resuscitation*, 82(3), 247–256. doi: 10.1016/j.resuscitation.2010.10.030

Ellis, Bruce J. & Boyce, W. Thomas. (2008). Biological sensitivity to context. *Current Directions in Psychological Science*, 17(3), 183–187. doi: 10.1111/j.1467-8721.2008.00571.x

Ellis, Bruce J.; Shirtcliff, Elizabeth A.; Boyce, W. Thomas; Deardorff, Julianna & Essex, Marilyn J. (2011). Quality of early family relationships and the timing and tempo of puberty: Effects depend on biological sensitivity to context. *Development and Psychopathology*, 23(1), 85–99. doi: 10.1017/S0954579410000660

Ellis, Lee & Wahab, Eshah A. (2013). Religiosity and fear of death: A theory-oriented review of the empirical literature. *Review of Religious Research*, 55(1), 149–189. doi: 10.1007/s13644-012-0064-3

Ellison, Christopher G.; Musick, Marc A. & Holden, George W. (2011). Does conservative Protestantism moderate the association between corporal punishment and child outcomes? *Journal of Marriage and Family*, 73(5), 946–961. doi: 10.1111/j.1741-3737.2011.00854.x

Emanuel, Ezekiel J.; Onwuteaka-Philipsen, Bregje D.; Urwin, John W. & Cohen, Joachim. (2016). Attitudes and practices of euthanasia and physician-assisted suicide in the United States, Canada, and Europe. 3*16*(1), 79–90. doi: 10.1001/jama.2016.8499

Engelberts, Adèle C. & de Jonge, Guustaaf Adolf. (1990). Choice of sleeping position for infants: Possible association with cot death. *Archives of Disease in Childhood*, 65(4), 462–467. doi: 10.1136/adc.65.4.462

Engelhardt, H. Tristram. (2012). Why clinical bioethics so rarely gives morally normative guidance. In H. Tristram Engelhardt (Ed.), *Bioethics critically reconsidered: Having second thoughts* (pp. 151–174). New York, NY: Springer. doi: 10.1007/978-94-007-2244-6_8

English, Tammy & Carstensen, Laura L. (2014). Selective narrowing of social networks across adulthood is associated with improved emotional experience in daily life. *International Journal of Behavioral Development*, 38(2), 195–202. doi: 10.1177/0165025413515404

Enserink, Martin. (2011). Can this DNA sleuth help catch criminals? *Science*, 331(6019), 838–840. doi: 10.1126/science.331.6019.838

Epps, Chad & Holt, Lynn. (2011). The genetic basis of addiction and relevant cellular mechanisms. *International Anesthesiology Clinics*, 49(1), 3–14. doi: 10.1097/AIA.0b013e3181f2bb66

Epstein, Robert; Pandit, Mayuri & Thakar, Mansi. (2013). How love emerges in arranged marriages: Two cross-cultural studies. *Journal of Comparative Family Studies*, 44(3), 341–360.

Erdos, Caroline; Genesee, Fred; Savage, Robert & Haigh, Corinne. (2014). Predicting risk for oral and written language learning difficulties in students educated in a second language. *Applied Psycholinguistics*, 35(2), 371–398. doi: 10.1017/S0142716412000422

Erickson, Kirk I.; Miller, Destiny L.; Weinstein, Andrea M.; Akl, Stephanie L. & Banducci, Sarah. (2012). Physical activity and brain plasticity in late adulthood: A conceptual and comprehensive review. *Ageing Research*, 3(1). doi: 10.4081/ar.2012.e6

Ericsson, K. Anders. (1996). The acquisition of expert performance: An introduction to some of the issues. In Karl Anders Ericsson (Ed.), *The road to excellence: The acquisition of expert performance in the arts and sciences, sports, and games* (pp. 1–50). Hillsdale, NJ: Erlbaum.

Ericsson, K. Anders; Charness, Neil; Feltovich, Paul J. & Hoffman, Robert R. (Eds.). (2006). *The Cambridge handbook of expertise and expert performance*. New York, NY: Cambridge University Press.

Erikson, Erik H. (1968). *Identity: Youth and crisis*. New York, NY: Norton.

Erikson, Erik H. (1982). *The life cycle completed: A review*. New York, NY: Norton.

Erikson, Erik H. (1993a). *Childhood and society* (2nd ed.). New York, NY: Norton.

Erikson, Erik H. (1993b). *Gandhi's truth: On the origins of militant nonviolence*. New York, NY: Norton.

Erikson, Erik H. (1994). *Identity: Youth and crisis*. New York, NY: Norton.

Erikson, Erik H. (1998). *The life cycle completed*. New York, NY: Norton.

Erikson, Erik H.; Erikson, Joan M. & Kivnick, Helen Q. (1986). *Vital involvement in old age*. New York, NY: Norton.

Erikson, Erik H.; Erikson, Joan M. & Kivnick, Helen Q. (1994). *Vital involvement in old age*. New York, NY: Norton.

Ernst, Monique. (2016). A tribute to the adolescent brain. *Neuroscience & Biobehavioral Reviews*, 70, 334–338. doi: 10.1016/j.neubiorev.2016.06.017

Erola, Jani; Jalonen, Sanni & Lehti, Hannu. (2016). Parental education, class and income over early life course and children's achievement. *Research in Social Stratification and Mobility*, 44, 33–43. doi: 10.1016/j.rssm.2016.01.003

Errichiello, Luca; Iodice, Davide; Bruzzese, Dario; Gherghi, Marco & Senatore, Ignazio. (2016). Prognostic factors and outcome in anorexia nervosa: A follow-up study. *Eating and Weight Disorders*, 21(1), 73–82. doi: 10.1007/s40519-015-0211-2

Erskine, Holly E.; Ferrari, Alize J.; Nelson, Paul; Polanczyk, Guilherme V.; Flaxman, Abraham D.; Vos, Theo, . . . Scott, James G. (2013). Research Review: Epidemiological modelling of Attention-deficit/hyperactivity disorder and conduct disorder for the Global Burden of Disease Study 2010. *Journal of Child Psychology and Psychiatry*, 54(12), 1263–1274. doi: 10.1111/jcpp.12144

Estruch, Ramón; Ros, Emilio; Salas-Salvadó, Jordi; Covas, Maria-Isabel; Corella, Dolores; Arós, Fernando, . . . Martínez-González, Angel Miguel. (2013). Primary prevention of cardiovascular disease with a Mediterranean diet. *New England Journal of Medicine*, 368(14), 1279–1290. doi: 10.1056/NEJMoa1200303

Euling, Susan Y.; Herman-Giddens, Marcia E.; Lee, Peter A.; Selevan, Sherry G.; Juul, Anders; Sørensen, Thorkild I. A., . . . Swan, Shanna H. (2008). Examination of US puberty-timing data from 1940 to 1994 for secular trends: Panel findings. *Pediatrics*, 121(Suppl. 3), S172–S191. doi: 10.1542/peds.2007-1813D

Evans, Angela D.; Xu, Fen & Lee, Kang. (2011). When all signs point to you: Lies told in the face of evidence. *Developmental Psychology*, 47(1), 39–49. doi: 10.1037/a0020787

Evans, Gary W. & Kim, Pilyoung. (2013). Childhood poverty, chronic stress, self-regulation, and coping. *Child Development Perspectives*, 7(1), 43–48. doi: 10.1111/cdep.12013

Evans, M. D. R.; Kelley, Jonathan; Sikora, Joanna & Treiman, Donald J. (2010). Family scholarly culture and educational success: Books and schooling in 27 nations. *Research in Social Stratification and Mobility*, 28(2), 171–197. doi: 10.1016/j.rssm.2010.01.002

Ewers, Michael; Walsh, Cathal; Trojanowski, John Q.; Shaw, Leslie M.; Petersen, Ronald C.; Jack, Clifford R., . . . Hampel, Harald. (2012). Prediction of conversion from mild cognitive impairment to Alzheimer's disease dementia based upon biomarkers and neuropsychological test performance. *Neurobiology of Aging*, 33(7), 1203–1214. doi: 10.1016/j.neurobiolaging.2010.10.019

Eyer, Diane E. (1992). *Mother-infant bonding: A scientific fiction*. New Haven, CT: Yale University Press.

Eymard, Amanda Singleton & Douglas, Dianna Hutto. (2012). Ageism among health care providers and interventions to improve their attitudes toward older adults: An integrative review. *Journal of Gerontological Nursing*, 38(5), 26–35. doi: 10.3928/00989134-20120307-09

Fabiani, Monica & Gratton, Gabriele. (2009). Brain imaging probes into the cognitive and physiological effects of aging. In Wojtek Chodzko-Zajko et al. (Eds.), *Enhancing cognitive functioning and brain plasticity* (Vol. 3, pp. 1–13). Champaign, IL: Human Kinetics.

Fairhurst, Merle T.; Löken, Line & Grossmann, Tobias. (2014). Physiological and behavioral responses reveal 9-month-old infants' sensitivity to pleasant touch. *Psychological Science*, 25(5), 1124–1131. doi: 10.1177/0956797614527114

Farber, Stu & Farber, Annalu. (2014). It ain't easy: Making life and death decisions before the crisis. In Leah Rogne & Susana Lauraine McCune (Eds.), *Advance care planning: Communicating about matters of life and death* (pp. 109–122). New York, NY: Springer.

Fareed, Mohd; Anwar, Malik Azeem & Afzal, Mohammad. (2015). Prevalence and gene frequency of color vision impairments among children of six populations from North Indian region. *Genes & Diseases*, 2(2), 211–218. doi: 10.1016/j.gendis.2015.02.006

Farrell, C.; Chappell, F.; Armitage, P. A.; Keston, P.; MacLullich, A.; Shenkin, S. & Wardlaw, J. M. (2009). Development and initial testing of normal reference MR images for the brain at ages 65–70 and 75–80 years. *European Radiology*, 19(1), 177–183. doi: 10.1007/s00330-008-1119-2

Faust, Erik; Bickart, William; Renaud, Cheryl & Camp, Scott. (2015). Child pornography possessors and child contact sex offenders: A multilevel comparison of demographic characteristics and rates of recidivism. *Sex Abuse*, 27(5), 460–478. doi: 10.1177/1079063214521469

Fazzi, Elisa; Signorini, Sabrina G.; Bomba, Monica; Luparia, Antonella; Lanners, Josée & Balottin, Umberto. (2011). Reach on sound: A key to object permanence in visually impaired children. *Early Human Development*, 87(4), 289–296. doi: 10.1016/j.earlhumdev.2011.01.032

FBI. (2015). *Crime in the United States, 2014.* Clarksburg, WV: U.S. Department of Justice, Federal Bureau of Investigation, Criminal Justice Information Services Division.

Feeley, Nancy; Sherrard, Kathryn; Waitzer, Elana & Boisvert, Linda. (2013). The father at the bedside: Patterns of involvement in the NICU. *Journal of Perinatal & Neonatal Nursing*, 27(1), 72–80. doi: 10.1097/JPN.0b013e31827fb415

Feigenson, Lisa; Libertus, Melissa E. & Halberda, Justin. (2013). Links between the intuitive sense of number and formal mathematics ability. *Child Development Perspectives*, 7(2), 74–79. doi: 10.1111/cdep.12019

Feld, Barry C. (2013). *Kids, cops, and confessions: Inside the interrogation room.* New York, NY: New York University Press.

Feldman, Ruth. (2007). Parent-infant synchrony and the construction of shared timing; physiological precursors, developmental outcomes, and risk conditions. *Journal of Child Psychology and Psychiatry*, 48(3/4), 329–354. doi: 10.1111/j.1469-7610.2006.01701.x

Ferguson, Christopher J. (2013). Spanking, corporal punishment and negative long-term outcomes: A meta-analytic review of longitudinal studies. *Clinical Psychology Review*, 33(1), 196–208. doi: 10.1016/j.cpr.2012.11.002

Fergusson, David M.; Horwood, L. John & Ridder, Elizabeth M. (2005). Partner violence and mental health outcomes in a New Zealand birth cohort. *Journal of Marriage and Family*, 67(5), 1103–1119. doi: 10.1111/j.1741-3737.2005.00202.x

Fernando, Mario & Chowdhury, Rafi M. M. I. (2015). Cultivation of virtuousness and self-actualization in the workplace. In Alejo José G. Sison (Ed.), *Handbook of virtue ethics in business and management* (pp. 1–13). New York, NY: Springer. doi: 10.1007/978-94-007-6729-4_117-1

Ferrari, Marco & Quaresima, Valentina. (2012). A brief review on the history of human functional near-infrared spectroscopy (fNIRS) development and fields of application. *NeuroImage*, 63(2), 921–935. doi: 10.1016/j.neuroimage.2012.03.049

Ferriman, Kimberley; Lubinski, David & Benbow, Camilla P. (2009). Work preferences, life values, and personal views of top math/science graduate students and the profoundly gifted: Developmental changes and gender differences during emerging adulthood and parenthood. *Journal of Personality and Social Psychology*, 97(3), 517–532. doi: 10.1037/a0016030

Festini, Sara B.; McDonough, Ian M. & Park, Denise C. (2016). The busier the better: Greater busyness is associated with better cognition. *Frontiers in Aging Neuroscience*, 8(98). doi: 10.3389/fnagi.2016.00098

Fewtrell, Mary; Wilson, David C.; Booth, Ian & Lucas, Alan. (2011). Six months of exclusive breast feeding: How good is the evidence? *BMJ*, 342, c5955. doi: 10.1136/bmj.c5955

Field, Nigel P. & Filanosky, Charles. (2010). Continuing bonds, risk factors for complicated grief, and adjustment to bereavement. *Death Studies*, 34(1), 1–29. doi: 10.1080/07481180903372269

Fields, R. Douglas. (2014). Myelin—More than insulation. *Science*, 344(6181), 264–266. doi: 10.1126/science.1253851

Fikkan, Janna L. & Rothblum, Esther D. (2012). Is fat a feminist issue? Exploring the gendered nature of weight bias. *Sex Roles*, 66(9-10), 575–592. doi: 10.1007/s11199-011-0022-5

Filová, Barbora; Ostatníková, Daniela; Celec, Peter & Hodosy, Július. (2013). The effect of testosterone on the formation of brain structures. *Cells Tissues Organs*, 197(3), 169–177. doi: 10.1159/000345567

Fincham, Frank D. & Beach, Steven R. H. (2010). Of memes and marriage: Toward a positive relationship science. *Journal of Family Theory & Review*, 2(1), 4–24. doi: 10.1111/j.1756-2589.2010.00033.x

Fine, J. S.; Calello, D. P.; Marcus, S. M. & Lowry, J. A. (2012). 2011 Pediatric fatality review of the National Poison Center Database. *Clinical Toxicology*, 50(10), 872–874. doi: 10.3109/15563650.2012.752494

Fingerman, Karen L.; Berg, Cynthia; Smith, Jacqui & Antonucci, Toni C. (2011). *Handbook of lifespan development.* New York, NY: Springer.

Fingerman, Karen L.; Cheng, Yen-Pi; Birditt, Kira & Zarit, Steven. (2012a). Only as happy as the least happy child: Multiple grown children's problems and successes and middle-aged parents' well-being. *The Journals of Gerontology Series B: Psychological Sciences and Social Sciences*, 67B(2), 184–193. doi: 10.1093/geronb/gbr086

Fingerman, Karen L.; Cheng, Yen-Pi; Tighe, Lauren; Birditt, Kira S. & Zarit, Steve. (2012b). Relationships between young adults and their parents. In Alan Booth et al. (Eds.), *Early adulthood in family context* (pp. 59–85). New York, NY: Springer. doi: 10.1007/978-1-4614-1436-0_5

Fingerman, Karen L. & Furstenberg, Frank F. (2012, May 30). You can go home again. *New York Times*, p. A29.

Finkel, Deborah; Andel, Ross; Gatz, Margaret & Pedersen, Nancy L. (2009). The role of occupational complexity in trajectories of cognitive aging before and after retirement. *Psychology and Aging*, 24(3), 563–573. doi: 10.1037/a0015511

Finkelhor, David & Jones, Lisa. (2012). *Have sexual abuse and physical abuse declined since the 1990s?* Durham, NH: Crimes Against Children Research Center, University of New Hampshire.

Finlay, Ilora G. & George, R. (2011). Legal physician-assisted suicide in Oregon and the Netherlands: Evidence concerning the impact on patients in vulnerable groups—Another perspective on Oregon's data. *Journal of Medical Ethics*, 37(3), 171–174. doi: 10.1136/jme.2010.037044

Finn, Amy S.; Kraft, Matthew A.; West, Martin R.; Leonard, Julia A.; Bish, Crystal E.; Martin, Rebecca E., . . . Gabrieli, John D. E. (2014). Cognitive skills, student achievement tests, and schools. *Psychological Science*, 25(3), 736–744. doi: 10.1177/0956797613516008

Fins, Joseph. (2006). *A palliative ethic of care: Clinical wisdom at life's end.* Sudbury, MA: Jones and Bartlett.

Fiori, Katherine L. & Denckla, Christy A. (2012). Social support and mental health in middle-aged men and women: A multidimensional approach. *Journal of Aging and Health*, 24(3), 407–438. doi: 10.1177/0898264311425087

Fischer, Karin. (2016, May 1). When everyone goes to college: A lesson from South Korea. *The Chronicle of Higher Education*.

Fiset, Sylvain & Plourde, Vickie. (2013). Object permanence in domestic dogs (Canis lupus familiaris) and gray wolves (Canis lupus). *Journal of Comparative Psychology*, 127(2), 115–127. doi: 10.1037/a0030595

Fisher, Helen E. (2006). Broken hearts: The nature and risks of romantic rejection. In Ann C. Crouter & Alan Booth (Eds.), *Romance and sex in adolescence and emerging adulthood: Risks and opportunities* (pp. 3–28). Mahwah, N.J: Lawrence Erlbaum Associates.

Fisher, Helen E. (2016a). *Anatomy of love: A natural history of mating, marriage, and why we stray.* New York, NY: Norton.

Fisher, Helen E. (2016b). Broken hearts: the nature and risks of romantic rejection. In Alan Booth et al. (Eds.), *Romance and sex in adolescence and emerging adulthood* (pp. 3–28). New York, NY: Routledge.

Fitzgerald, Maria. (2015). What do we really know about newborn infant pain? *Experimental Physiology*, 100(12), 1451–1457. doi: 10.1113/EP085134

Flegal, Katherine M.; Kit, Brian K.; Orpana, Heather & Graubard, Barry I. (2013). Association of all-cause mortality with overweight and obesity using standard body mass index categories: A systematic review and meta-analysis. *JAMA*, 309(1), 71–82. doi: 10.1001/jama.2012.113905

Fletcher, Erica N.; Whitaker, Robert C.; Marino, Alexis J. & Anderson, Sarah E. (2014). Screen time at home and school among low-income children attending Head Start. *Child Indicators Research*, 7(2), 421–436. doi: 10.1007 /s12187-013-9212-8

Fletcher, Jason M. (2009). Beauty vs. brains: Early labor market outcomes of high school graduates. *Economics Letters*, 105(3), 321–325. doi: 10.1016/j.econlet.2009.09.006

Fletcher, Jason M. & Frisvold, David E. (2011). College selectivity and young adult health behaviors. *Economics of Education Review*, 30(5), 826–837. doi: 10.1016/j.econedurev.2011.04.005

Fletcher, Richard; St. George, Jennifer & Freeman, Emily. (2013). Rough and tumble play quality: Theoretical foundations for a new measure of father–child interaction. *Early Child Development and Care*, 183(6), 746–759. doi: 10.1080/03004430.2012.723439

Flood, Meredith & Phillips, Kenneth D. (2007). Creativity in older adults: A plethora of possibilities. *Issues in Mental Health Nursing*, 28(4), 389–411. doi: 10.1080/01612840701252956

Floud, Roderick; Fogel, Robert W.; Harris, Bernard & Hong, Sok Chul. (2011). *The changing body: Health, nutrition, and human development in the Western world since 1700.* New York, NY: Cambridge University Press.

Flouri, Eirini & Sarmadi, Zahra. (2016). Prosocial behavior and childhood trajectories of internalizing and externalizing problems: The role of neighborhood and school contexts. *Developmental Psychology*, 52(2), 253–258. doi: 10.1037 /dev0000076

Flynn, James R. (1999). Searching for justice: The discovery of IQ gains over time. *American Psychologist*, 54(1), 5–20. doi: 10.1037 /0003 -066X.54.1.5

Flynn, James R. (2012). *Are we getting smarter?: Rising IQ in the twenty-first century.* New York, NY: Cambridge University Press.

Fogel, Robert W. & Grotte, Nathaniel. (2011). *An overview of the changing body: Health, nutrition, and human development in the Western world since 1700. NBER working paper series.* Cambridge, MA: National Bureau of Economic Research.

Fontana, Luigi; Colman, Ricki J.; Holloszy, John O. & Weindruch, Richard. (2011). Calorie restriction in nonhuman and human primates. In J. Masoro Edward & N. Austad Steven (Eds.), *Handbook of the biology of aging* (7th ed., pp. 447–461). San Diego, CA: Academic Press. doi: 10.1016/B978 -0-12-378638-8.00021-X

Fontana, Luigi & Partridge, Linda. (2015). Promoting health and longevity through diet: From model organisms to humans. *Cell*, 161(1), 106–118. doi: 10.1016/j.cell.2015.02.020

Food and Agriculture Organization of the United Nations. (2016, February 9). *Food security indicators.* Retrieved from: http://www.fao.org/ economic /ess/ess-fs/ess-fadata/en/#.V_eas9wbqf6

Forbes, Deborah. (2012). The global influence of the Reggio Emilia Inspiration. In Robert Kelly (Ed.), *Educating for creativity: A global conversation* (pp. 161–172). Calgary, Canada: Brush Education.

Ford, Carole L. & Yore, Larry D. (2012). Toward convergence of critical thinking, metacognition, and reflection: Illustrations from natural and social sciences, teacher education, and classroom practice. In Anat Zohar & Yehudit Judy Dori (Eds.), *Metacognition in Science Education* (pp. 251–271). New York, NY: Springer. doi: 10.1007/978-94-007-2132-6_11

Forget-Dubois, Nadine; Dionne, Ginette; Lemelin, Jean-Pascal; Pérusse, Daniel; Tremblay, Richard E. & Boivin, Michel. (2009). Early child language mediates the relation between home environment and school readiness. *Child Development*, 80(3), 736–749. doi: 10.1111/j.1467-8624.2009.01294.x

Forrest, Walter. (2014). Cohabitation, relationship quality, and desistance from crime. *Journal of Marriage and Family*, 76(3), 539–556. doi: 10.1111/jomf.12105

Foster, Eugene A.; Jobling, Mark A.; Taylor, P. G.; Donnelly, Peter; de Knijff, Peter; Mieremet, Rene, . . . Tyler-Smith, C. (1998). Jefferson fathered slave's last child. *Nature*, 396(6706), 27–28. doi: 10.1038/23835

Fountain, Christine; King, Marissa D. & Bearman, Peter S. (2011). Age of diagnosis for autism: Individual and community factors across 10 birth cohorts. *Journal of Epidemiology and Community Health*, 65(6), 503–510. doi: 10.1136 /jech.2009.104588

Fowler, James W. (1981). *Stages of faith: The psychology of human development and the quest for meaning.* San Francisco, CA: Harper & Row.

Fowler, James W. (1986). Faith and the structuring of meaning. In Craig Dykstra & Sharon Parks (Eds.), *Faith development and Fowler* (pp. 15–42). Birmingham, AL: Religious Education Press.

Fox, Nathan A.; Henderson, Heather A.; Marshall, Peter J.; Nichols, Kate E. & Ghera, Melissa M. (2005). Behavioral inhibition: Linking biology and behavior within a developmental framework. *Annual Review of Psychology*, 56, 235–262. doi: 10.1146/annurev. psych.55.090902.141532

Fox, Nathan A.; Henderson, Heather A.; Rubin, Kenneth H.; Calkins, Susan D. & Schmidt, Louis A. (2001). Continuity and discontinuity of behavioral inhibition and exuberance: Psychophysiological and behavioral influences across the first four years of life. *Child Development*, 72(1), 1–21. doi: 10.1111 /1467-8624.00262

Fox, Nathan A.; Reeb-Sutherland, Bethany C. & Degnan, Kathryn A. (2013). Personality and emotional development. In Philip D. Zelazo (Ed.), *The Oxford handbook of developmental psychology* (Vol. 2, pp. 15–44). New York, NY: Oxford University Press. doi: 10.1093/oxfordhb /9780199958474.013.0002

Franck, Caroline; Budlovsky, Talia; Windle, Sarah B.; Filion, Kristian B. & Eisenberg, Mark J. (2014). Electronic cigarettes in North America: History, use, and implications for smoking cessation. *Circulation*, 129(19), 1945–1952. doi: 10.1161 /CIRCULATIONAHA.113.006416

Franco, Manuel; Bilal, Usama; Orduñez, Pedro; Benet, Mikhail; Alain, Morejón; Benjamín, Caballero, . . . Cooper, Richard S. (2013). Population-wide weight loss and regain in relation to diabetes burden and cardiovascular mortality in Cuba 1980–2010: Repeated cross sectional surveys and ecological comparison of secular trends. *BMJ*, 346(7903), f1515. doi: 10.1136/bmj. f1515

Franco, Marcia R.; Tong, Allison; Howard, Kirsten; Sherrington, Catherine; Ferreira, Paulo H.; Pinto, Rafael Z. & Ferreira, Manuela L. (2015). Older people's perspectives on participation in physical activity: A systematic review and thematic synthesis of qualitative literature. *British Journal of Sports Medicine*, 49, 1268–1276. doi: 10.1136 /bjsports-2014-094015

Frankenburg, William K.; Dodds, Josiah; Archer, Philip; Shapiro, Howard & Bresnick, Beverly. (1992). The Denver II: A major revision and restandardization of the Denver Developmental Screening Test. *Pediatrics*, 89(1), 91–97.

Franklin, Sarah. (2013). *Biological relatives: IVF, stem cells, and the future of kinship.* Durham, NC: Duke University Press.

Frazier, A. Lindsay; Camargo, Carlos A.; Malspeis, Susan; Willett, Walter C. & Young, Michael C. (2014). Prospective study of peripregnancy consumption of peanuts or tree nuts by mothers and the risk of peanut or tree nut allergy in their offspring. *JAMA Pediatrics*, 168(2), 156–162. doi: 10.1001/jamapediatrics.2013.4139

Frederick, David A.; Lever, Janet; Gillespie, Brian Joseph & Garcia, Justin R. (2016). What keeps passion alive? Sexual satisfaction is associated with sexual communication, mood setting, sexual variety, oral sex, orgasm, and sex frequency in a national U.S. study. *The Journal of Sex Research*, (In Press). doi: 10.1080/00224499.2015.1137854

Fredricks, Jennifer A. & Eccles, Jacquelynne S. (2002). Children's competence and value beliefs from childhood through adolescence: Growth trajectories in two male-sex-typed domains. *Developmental Psychology*, 38(4), 519–533. doi: 10.1037/0012-1649.38.4.519

Freeman, Joan. (2010). *Gifted lives: What happens when gifted children grow up?* New York, NY: Routledge.

Freud, Anna. (1958). Adolescence. *Psychoanalytic Study of the Child*, 13, 255–278.

Freud, Anna. (2000). Adolescence. In James B. McCarthy (Ed.), *Adolescent development and psychopathology* (pp. 29–52). Lanham, MD: University Press of America.

Freud, Sigmund. (1935). *A general introduction to psychoanalysis.* New York, NY: Liveright.

Freud, Sigmund. (1938). *The basic writings of Sigmund Freud.* New York, NY: Modern Library.

Freud, Sigmund. (1989). *Introductory lectures on psycho-analysis.* New York, NY: Liveright.

Freud, Sigmund. (1995). *The basic writings of Sigmund Freud.* New York, NY: Modern Library.

Freud, Sigmund. (2001). An outline of psychoanalysis. *The standard edition of the complete psychological works of Sigmund Freud* (Vol. 23). London, UK: Vintage.

Freund, Alexandra M. (2008). Successful aging as management of resources: The role of selection, optimization, and compensation. *Research in Human Development*, 5(2), 94–106. doi: 10.1080/15427600802034827

Freund, Alexandra M. & Blanchard-Fields, Fredda. (2014). Age-related differences in altruism across adulthood: Making personal financial gain versus contributing to the public good. *Developmental Psychology, 50*(4), 1125–1136. doi: 10.1037 /a0034491

Freund, Julia; Brandmaier, Andreas M.; Lewejohann, Lars; Kirste, Imke; Kritzler, Mareike; Krüger, Antonio, . . . Kempermann, Gerd. (2013). Emergence of individuality in genetically identical mice. *Science, 340*(6133), 756–759. doi: 10.1126 /science.1235294

Friend, Stephen H. & Schadt, Eric E. (2014). Clues from the resilient. *Science, 344*(6187), 970–972. doi: 10.1126/science.1255648

Fries, James F. (2015). On the compression of morbidity, from 1980 to 2015 and beyond. In Matt Kaeberlein & George Martin (Eds.), *Handbook of the biology of aging* (8th ed., pp. 507–524). San Diego, CA: Academic Press.

Frisina, Robert D. & Frisina, D. Robert. (2016). Hormone replacement therapy and its effects on human hearing. In Andrew H. Bass et al. (Eds.), *Hearing and Hormones* (pp. 191–209). New York, NY: Springer. doi: 10.1007/978-3-319-26597-1_8

Froiland, John M. & Davison, Mark L. (2014). Parental expectations and school relationships as contributors to adolescents' positive outcomes. *Social Psychology of Education, 17*(1), 1–17. doi: 10.1007/s11218-013-9237-3

Frost, Randy O.; Steketee, Gail; Tolin, David F.; Sinopoli, Nicole & Ruby, Dylan. (2015). Motives for acquiring and saving in hoarding disorder, OCD, and community controls. *Journal of Obsessive-Compulsive and Related Disorders, 4*, 54–59. doi: 10.1016/j.jocrd.2014.12.006

Fry, Douglas P. (2014). Environment of evolutionary adaptedness, rough-and-tumble play, and the selection of restraint in human aggression. In Darcia Narvaez et al. (Eds.), *Ancestral landscapes in human evolution: Culture, childrearing and social wellbeing* (pp. 169–188). New York, NY: Oxford University Press.

Fuligni, Allison Sidle; Howes, Carollee; Huang, Yiching; Hong, Sandra Soliday & Lara-Cinisomo, Sandraluz. (2012). Activity settings and daily routines in preschool classrooms: Diverse experiences in early learning settings for low-income children. *Early Childhood Research Quarterly, 27*(2), 198–209. doi: 10.1016/j.ecresq.2011.10.001

Fuller, Bruce & García Coll, Cynthia. (2010). Learning from Latinos: Contexts, families, and child development in motion. *Developmental Psychology, 46*(3), 559–565. doi: 10.1037 /a0019412

Fuller-Iglesias, Heather R.; Webster, Noah J. & Antonucci, Toni C. (2013). Adult family relationships in the context of friendship. *Research in Human Development, 10*(2), 184–203. doi: 10.1080/15427609.2013.786562

Fulmer, C. Ashley; Gelfand, Micheke J.; Kruglanski, Arie W.; Kim-Prieto, Chu; Diener, Ed; Pierro, Antonio & Higgins, E. Tory. (2010). On "feeling right" in cultural contexts: How person-culture match affects self-esteem and subjective well-being. *Psychological Science, 21*(11), 1563–1569. doi: 10.1177/0956797610384742

Furey, Terrence S. & Sethupathy, Praveen. (2013). Genetics driving epigenetics. *Science, 342*(6159), 705–706. doi: 10.1126 /science.1246755

Furlan, Sarah; Agnoli, Franca & Reyna, Valerie F. (2013). Children's competence or adults' incompetence: Different developmental trajectories in different tasks. *Developmental Psychology, 49*(8), 1466–1480. doi: 10.1037 /a0030509

Furstenberg, Frank F. (2010). On a new schedule: Transitions to adulthood and family change. *Future of Children, 20*(1), 67–87. doi: 10.1353 /foc.0.0038

Furukawa, Emi; Tangney, June & Higashibara, Fumiko. (2012). Cross-cultural continuities and discontinuities in shame, guilt, and pride: A study of children residing in Japan, Korea and the USA. *Self and Identity, 11*(1), 90–113. doi: 10.1080/15298868.2010.512748

Fusaro, Maria & Harris, Paul L. (2013). Dax gets the nod: Toddlers detect and use social cues to evaluate testimony. *Developmental Psychology, 49*(3), 514–522. doi: 10.1037/a0030580

Gabrieli, John D. E. (2009). Dyslexia: A new synergy between education and cognitive neuroscience. *Science, 325*(5938), 280–283. doi: 10.1126 /science.1171999

Galatzer-Levy, Isaac R. & Bonanno, George A. (2012). Beyond normality in the study of bereavement: Heterogeneity in depression outcomes following loss in older adults. *Social Science & Medicine, 74*(12), 1987–1994. doi: 10.1016 /j.socscimed .2012.02.022

Galatzer-Levy, Isaac R. & Bonanno, George A. (2016). It's not so easy to make resilience go away: Commentary on Infurna and Luthar (2016). *Perspectives on Psychological Science, 11*(2), 195–198. doi: 10.1177/1745691615621277

Galván, Adriana. (2013). The teenage brain: Sensitivity to rewards. *Current Directions in Psychological Science, 22*(2), 88–93. doi: 10.1177/0963721413480859

Galvao, Tais F.; Silva, Marcus T.; Zimmermann, Ivan R.; Souza, Kathiaja M.; Martins, Silvia S. & Pereira, Mauricio G. (2014). Pubertal timing in girls and depression: A systematic review. *Journal of Affective Disorders, 155*, 13–19. doi: 10.1016 /j.jad.2013.10.034

Gambaro, Ludovica; Stewart, Kitty & Waldfogel, Jane (Eds.). (2014). *An equal start?: Providing quality early education and care for disadvantaged children.* Chicago, IL: Policy Press.

Ganapathy, Thilagavathy. (2014). Couvade syndrome among 1st time expectant fathers. *Muller Journal of Medical Science Research, 5*(1), 43–47. doi: 10.4103/0975-9727.128944

Ganchimeg, Togoobaatar; Ota, Erika; Morisaki, Naho; Laopaiboon, Malinee; Lumbiganon, P.; Zhang, Jun, . . . Mori, Rintaro. (2014). Pregnancy and childbirth outcomes among adolescent mothers: A World Health Organization multicountry study. *BJOG, 121*(Suppl. 1), 40–48. doi: 10.1111/1471-0528.12630

Gandini, Leila; Hill, Lynn; Cadwell, Louise & Schwall, Charles (Eds.). (2005). *In the spirit of the studio: Learning from the atelier of Reggio Emilia.* New York, NY: Teachers College Press.

Ganong, Lawrence H.; Coleman, Marilyn & Jamison, Tyler. (2011). Patterns of stepchild–stepparent relationship development. *Journal of Marriage and Family, 73*(2), 396–413. doi: 10.1111/j.1741-3737.2010.00814.x

Gao, Sujuan; Unverzagt, Frederick W.; Hall, Kathleen S.; Lane, Kathleen A.; Murrell, Jill R.; Hake, Ann M., . . . Hendrie, Hugh C. (2014). Mild cognitive impairment, incidence, progression, and reversion: Findings from a community-based cohort of elderly African Americans. *The American Journal of Geriatric Psychiatry, 22*(7), 670–681. doi: 10.1016/j.jagp.2013.02.015

Gao, Wei; Lin, Weili; Grewen, Karen & Gilmore, John H. (2016). Functional connectivity of the infant human brain: Plastic and modifiable. *The Neuroscientist,* (In Press). doi: 10.1177 /1073858416635986

Gao, Yuan; Huang, Changquan; Zhao, Kexiang; Ma, Louyan; Qiu, Xuan; Zhang, Lei, . . . Xiao, Qian. (2013). Depression as a risk factor for dementia and mild cognitive impairment: A meta-analysis of longitudinal studies. *International Journal of Geriatric Psychiatry, 28*(5), 441–449. doi: 10.1002/gps.3845

García Coll, Cynthia T. & Marks, Amy K. (2012). *The immigrant paradox in children and adolescents: Is becoming American a developmental risk?* Washington, DC: American Psychological Association.

Garcia, Marc A.; Angel, Jacqueline L.; Angel, Ronald J.; Chiu, Chi-Tsun & Melvin, Jennifer. (2015). Acculturation, gender, and active life expectancy in the Mexican-origin population. *Journal of Aging and Health, 27*(7), 1247–1265. doi: 10.1177/0898264315577880

Gardner, Howard. (1983). *Frames of mind: The theory of multiple intelligences.* New York, NY: Basic Books.

Gardner, Howard. (1999). Are there additional intelligences? The case for naturalist, spiritual, and existential intelligences. In Jeffrey Kane (Ed.), *Education, information, and transformation: Essays on learning and thinking* (pp. 111–131). Upper Saddle River, NJ: Merrill.

Gardner, Howard. (2006). *Multiple intelligences: New horizons in theory and practice.* New York, NY: Basic Books.

Gardner, Howard. (2011). *Frames of mind: The theory of multiple intelligences.* New York, NY: Basic Books.

Gardner, Howard & Moran, Seana. (2006). The science of multiple intelligences theory: A response to Lynn Waterhouse. *Educational Psychologist, 41*(4), 227–232. doi: 10.1207 /s15326985ep4104_2

Gardner, Paula & Hudson, Bettie L. (1996). *Advance report of final mortality statistics, 1993. Monthly Vital Statistics Report, 44*(7, Suppl.). Hyattsville, MD: National Center for Health Statistics.

Garfin, Dana R.; Holman, E. Alison & Silver, Roxane C. (2015). Cumulative exposure to prior collective trauma and acute stress responses to the Boston Marathon bombings. *Psychological Science, 26*(6), 675–683. doi: 10.1177/0956797614561043

Gash, Don M. & Deane, Andrew S. (2015). Neuron-based heredity and human evolution. *Frontiers in Neuroscience, 9,* 209. doi: 10.3389/fnins.2015.00209

Gaskins, Audrey Jane; Mendiola, Jaime; Afeiche, Myriam; Jørgensen, Niels; Swan, Shanna H. & Chavarro, Jorge E. (2013). Physical activity and television watching in relation to semen quality in young men. *British Journal of Sports Medicine, 49*(4), 265–270. doi: 10.1136/bjsports -2012-091644

Gavin, Lorrie; MacKay, Andrea P.; Brown, Kathryn; Harrier, Sara; Ventura, Stephanie J.; Kann, Laura, . . . Ryan, George. (2009, July 17). *Sexual and reproductive health of persons aged 10–24 Years—United States, 2002–2007. Morbidity and Mortality Weekly Report* 58(SS06). Atlanta, GA: Centers for Disease Control and Prevention.

Gavrilov, Leonid A. & Gavrilova, Natalia S. (2006). Reliability theory of aging and longevity. In Edward J. Masoro & Steven N. Austad (Eds.), *Handbook of the biology of aging* (6th ed., pp. 3–42). Boston, MA: Academic Press.

Gawande, Atul. (2014). *Being mortal: Medicine and what matters in the end.* New York, NY: Metropolitan Books.

Ge, Xinting; Shi, Yonggang; Li, Junning; Zhang, Zhonghe; Lin, Xiangtao; Zhan, Jinfeng, . . . Liu, Shuwei. (2015). Development of the human fetal hippocampal formation during early second trimester. *NeuroImage, 119,* 33–43. doi: 10.1016 /j.neuroimage.2015.06.055

Geiger, Jennifer Mullins; Hayes, Megan J. & Lietz, Cynthia A. (2013). Should I stay or should I go? A mixed methods study examining the factors influencing foster parents' decisions to continue or discontinue providing foster care. *Children and Youth Services Review, 35*(9), 1356–1365. doi: 10.1016 /j.childyouth.2013.05.003

Gendron, Brian P.; Williams, Kirk R. & Guerra, Nancy G. (2011). An analysis of bullying among students within schools: Estimating the effects of individual normative beliefs, self-esteem, and school climate. *Journal of School Violence, 10*(2), 150–164. doi: 10.1080/15388220.2010.539166

Gentile, Douglas A. (2011). The multiple dimensions of video game effects. *Child Development Perspectives, 5*(2), 75–81. doi: 10.1111/j.1750-8606 .2011.00159.x

Geoffroy, Marie-Claude; Boivin, Michel; Arseneault, Louise; Turecki, Gustavo; Vitaro, Frank; Brendgen, Mara, . . . Côté, Sylvana M. (2016). Associations between peer victimization and suicidal ideation and suicide attempt during adolescence: Results from a prospective population-based birth cohort. *Journal of the American Academy of Child and Adolescent Psychiatry, 55*(2), 99–105.

George, Danny & Whitehouse, Peter. (2010). Dementia and mild cognitive impairment in social and cultural context. In Dale Dannefer & Chris Phillipson (Eds.), *The SAGE handbook of social gerontology* (pp. 343–356). Los Angeles, CA: Sage.

Georgeson, Jan & Payler, Jane (Eds.). (2013). *International perspectives on early childhood education and care.* New York, NY: Open University Press.

Gerber, Alan S.; Huber, Gregory A.; Doherty, David & Dowling, Conor M. (2011). The Big Five personality traits in the political arena. *Annual Review of Political Science, 14,* 265–287. doi: 10.1146/annurev-polisci-051010-111659

Gershoff, Elizabeth T. (2013). Spanking and child development: We know enough now to stop hitting our children. *Child Development Perspectives, 7*(3), 133–137. doi: 10.1111 /cdep.12038

Gershoff, Elizabeth T.; Lansford, Jennifer E.; Sexton, Holly R.; Davis-Kean, Pamela & Sameroff, Arnold J. (2012). Longitudinal links between spanking and children's externalizing behaviors in a national sample of White, Black, Hispanic, and Asian American families. *Child Development, 83*(3), 838–843. doi: 10.1111/j.1467-8624.2011.01732.x

Gershoff, Elizabeth T.; Purtell, Kelly M. & Holas, Igor. (2015). *Corporal punishment in U.S. public schools: Legal precedents, current practices, and future policy.* New York, NY: Springer. doi: 10.1007/978-3-319-14818-2

Gershuny, Jonathan. (2011, September 12). *Time-use surveys and the measurement of national well-being.* Centre for Time-use Research Department of Sociology, University of Oxford.

Gerstorf, Denis; Heckhausen, Jutta; Ram, Nilam; Infurna, Frank J.; Schupp, Jürgen & Wagner, Gert G. (2014). Perceived personal control buffers terminal decline in well-being. *Psychology and Aging, 29*(3), 612–625. doi: 10.1037/a0037227

Gerstorf, Denis; Hoppmann, Christiane A.; Löckenhoff, Corinna E.; Infurna, Frank J.; Schupp, Jürgen; Wagner, Gert G. & Ram, Nilam. (2016). Terminal decline in well-being: The role of social orientation. *Psychology and Aging, 31*(2), 149–165. doi: 10.1037/pag0000072

Gervais, Will M. & Norenzayan, Ara. (2012). Analytic thinking promotes religious disbelief. *Science, 336*(6080), 493–496. doi: 10.1126 /science .1215647

Gettler, Lee T. & McKenna, James J. (2010). Never sleep with baby? Or keep me close but keep me safe: Eliminating inappropriate safe infant sleep rhetoric in the United States. *Current Pediatric Reviews, 6*(1), 71–77. doi: 10.2174/157339610791317250

Gewertz, Catherine. (2014, August 19). Support slipping for Common Core, especially among teachers, poll finds [Web log post]. Education week: Curriculum matters. Retrieved from http: //blogs.edweek.org/edweek/curriculum/2014/08 /education_next_poll_shows_comm.html

Gewirtzman, Aron; Bobrick, Laura; Conner, Kelly & Tyring, Stephen K. (2011). Epidemiology of sexually transmitted infections. In Gerd Gross & Stephen K. Tyring (Eds.), *Sexually transmitted infections and sexually transmitted diseases* (pp. 13–34). New York, NY: Springer.

Ghosh, Tista; Van Dyke, Mike; Maffey, Ali; Whitley, Elizabeth; Gillim-Ross, Laura & Wolk, Larry. (2016). The public health framework of legalized marijuana in Colorado. *American Journal of Public Health, 106*(1), 21–27. doi: 10.2105 /AJPH.2015.302875

Gibbons, Ann. (2012). An evolutionary theory of dentistry. *Science, 336*(6084), 973–975. doi: 10.1126/science.336.6084.973

Gibbs, Jeremy J. & Goldbach, Jeremy. (2015). Religious conflict, sexual identity, and suicidal behaviors among LGBT young adults. *Archives of Suicide Research, 19*(4), 472–488. doi: 10.1080/13811118.2015.1004476

Giblin, Chris. (2014). Travis Pastrana makes comeback for Red Bull's inaugural straight rhythm competition. *Men's Fitness.*

Gibson, Eleanor J. (1969). *Principles of perceptual learning and development.* New York, NY: Appleton-Century-Crofts.

Gibson, Eleanor J. (1988). Exploratory behavior in the development of perceiving, acting, and the acquiring of knowledge. *Annual Review of Psychology, 39,* 1–42. doi: 10.1146/annurev .ps.39.020188.000245

Gibson, Eleanor J. (1997). An ecological psychologist's prolegomena for perceptual development: A functional approach. In Cathy Dent-Read & Patricia Zukow-Goldring (Eds.), *Evolving explanations of development: Ecological approaches to organism-environment systems* (1st ed., pp. 23–54). Washington, DC: American Psychological Association.

Gibson, Eleanor J. & Walk, Richard D. (1960). The "visual cliff". *Scientific American, 202*(4), 64–71. doi: 10.1038/scientificameri-can0460-64

Gibson, James J. (1979). *The ecological approach to visual perception.* Boston, MA: Houghton Mifflin.

Gibson-Davis, Christina & Rackin, Heather. (2014). Marriage or carriage? Trends in union context and birth type by education. *Journal of Marriage and Family, 76*(3), 506–519. doi: 10.1111/jomf.12109

Gignac, Gilles E. (2016). On the evaluation of competing theories: A reply to van der Maas and Kan. *Intelligence, 57,* 84–86. doi: 10.1016/j.intell .2016.03.006

Gilbert, Daniel T.; King, Gary; Pettigrew, Stephen & Wilson, Timothy D. (2016). Comment on "Estimating the reproducibility of psychological science". *Science, 351*(6277), 1037-b. doi: 10.1126/science.aad7243

Gilbert, Richard B. (2013). Religion, spirituality, and end-of-life decision making. In David K. Meagher & David E. Balk (Eds.), *Handbook of thanatology: The essential body of knowledge for the study of death, dying, and bereavement* (2nd ed., pp. 63–71). New York, NY: Routledge.

Giles, Amy & Rovee-Collier, Carolyn. (2011). Infant long-term memory for associations formed during mere exposure. *Infant Behavior and Development, 34*(2), 327–338. doi: 10.1016 /j.infbeh.2011.02.004

Gillen, Meghan M. & Lefkowitz, Eva S. (2012). Gender and racial/ethnic differences in body image development among college students. *Body Image, 9*(1), 126–130. doi: 10.1016 /j.bodyim.2011.09.004

Gilles, Floyd H. & Nelson, Marvin D. (2012). *The developing human brain: Growth and adversities.* London, UK: Mac Keith Press.

Gillespie, Brian Joseph; Frederick, David; Harari, Lexi & Grov, Christian. (2015). Homophily, close friendship, and life satisfaction among gay, lesbian, heterosexual, and bisexual men and women. *PLoS ONE, 10*(6), e0128900. doi: 10.1371/journal.pone.0128900

Gillespie, Michael A. (2010). Players and spectators: Sports and ethical training in the American university. In Elizabeth Kiss & J. Peter Euben (Eds.), *Debating moral education: Rethinking the role of the modern university* (pp. 293–316). Durham, NC: Duke University Press.

Gilligan, Carol. (1981). Moral development in the college years. In Arthur Chickering (Ed.), *The modern American college: Responding to the new realities of diverse students and a changing society* (pp. 139–156). San Francisco, CA: Jossey-Bass.

Gilligan, Carol. (1982). *In a different voice: Psychological theory and women's development.* Cambridge, MA: Harvard University Press.

Gilligan, Carol; Murphy, John Michael & Tappan, Mark B. (1990). Moral development beyond adolescence. In Charles Nathaniel Alexander & Ellen J. Langer (Eds.), *Higher stages of human development: Perspectives on adult growth* (pp. 208–225). New York, NY: Oxford University Press.

Gillis, John R. (2008). The islanding of children: Reshaping the mythical landscapes of childhood. In Marta Gutman & Ning de Coninck-Smith (Eds.), *Designing modern childhoods: History, space, and the material culture of children* (pp. 316–329). New Brunswick, NJ: Rutgers University Press.

Gillon, Raanan. (2015). Defending the four principles approach as a good basis for good medical practice and therefore for good medical ethics. *Journal of Medical Ethics, 41*(1), 111–116. doi: 10.1136/medethics-2014-102282

Gilovich, Thomas; Vallone, Robert & Tversky, Amos. (1985). The hot hand in basketball: On the misperception of random sequences. *Cognitive Psychology, 17*(3), 295–314. doi: 10.1016/0010-0285(85)90010-6

Giluk, Tamara L. & Postlethwaite, Bennett E. (2015). Big Five personality and academic dishonesty: A meta-analytic review. *Personality and Individual Differences, 72*(5), 59–67. doi: 10.1016/j.paid.2014.08.027

Giovino, Gary A.; Mirza, Sara A.; Samet, Jonathan M.; Gupta, Prakash C.; Jarvis, Martin J.; Bhala, Neeraj, . . . Asma, Samira. (2012). Tobacco use in 3 billion individuals from 16 countries: An analysis of nationally representative cross-sectional household surveys. *The Lancet, 380*(9842), 668–679. doi: 10.1016/S0140-6736(12)61085-X

Giuffrè, Mario; Piro, Ettore & Corsello, Giovanni. (2012). Prematurity and twinning. *Journal of Maternal-Fetal and Neonatal Medicine, 25*(3), 6–10. doi: 10.3109/14767058.2012.712350

Giumetti, Gary W. & Kowalski, Robin M. (2015). Cyberbullying matters: Examining the incremental impact of cyberbullying on outcomes over and above traditional bullying in North America. In Raúl Navarro et al. (Eds.), *Cyberbullying across the globe: Gender, family, and mental health* (pp. 117–130). New York, NY: Springer. doi: 10.1007/978-3-319-25552-1_6

Glenberg, Arthur M.; Witt, Jessica K. & Metcalfe, Janet. (2013). From the revolution to embodiment: 25 years of cognitive psychology. *Perspectives on Psychological Science, 8*(5), 573–585. doi: 10.1177/1745691613498098

Goddings, Anne-Lise & Giedd, Jay N. (2014). Structural brain development during childhood and adolescence. In Michael S. Gazzaniga & George R. Mangun (Eds.), *The cognitive neurosciences* (5th ed., pp. 15–22). Cambridge, MA: MIT Press.

Goddings, Anne-Lise; Heyes, Stephanie Burnett; Bird, Geoffrey; Viner, Russell M. & Blakemore, Sarah-Jayne. (2012). The relationship between puberty and social emotion processing. *Developmental Science, 15*(6), 801–811. doi: 10.1111/j.1467-7687.2012.01174.x

Godinet, Meripa T.; Li, Fenfang & Berg, Teresa. (2014). Early childhood maltreatment and trajectories of behavioral problems: Exploring gender and racial differences. *Child Abuse & Neglect, 38*(3), 544–556. doi: 10.1016/j.chiabu.2013.07.018

Gogtay, Nitin; Giedd, Jay N.; Lusk, Leslie; Hayashi, Kiralee M.; Greenstein, Deanna; Vaituzis, A. Catherine, . . . Ungerleider, Leslie G. (2004). Dynamic mapping of human cortical development during childhood through early adulthood. *Proceedings of the National Academy of Sciences of the United States of America, 101*(21), 8174–8179. doi: 10.1073/pnas.0402680101

Gökbayrak, N. Simay; Paiva, Andrea L.; Blissmer, Bryan J. & Prochaska, James O. (2015). Predictors of relapse among smokers: Transtheoretical effort variables, demographics, and smoking severity. *Addictive Behaviors, 42,* 176–179. doi: 10.1016/j.addbeh.2014.11.022

Golant, Stephen M. (2011). The changing residential environments of older people. In Robert H. Binstock & Linda K. George (Eds.), *Handbook of aging and the social sciences* (7th ed., pp. 207–220). San Diego, CA: Academic Press. doi: 10.1016/B978-0-12-380880-6.00015-0

Golden, Marita. (2010). Angel baby. In Barbara Graham (Ed.), *Eye of my heart: 27 writers reveal the hidden pleasures and perils of being a grandmother* (pp. 125–133). New York, NY: HarperCollins.

Golden, Neville H.; Yang, Wei; Jacobson, Marc S.; Robinson, Thomas N. & Shaw, Gary M. (2012). Expected body weight in adolescents: Comparison between weight-for-stature and BMI methods. *Pediatrics, 130*(6), e1607–e1613. doi: 10.1542/peds.2012-0897

Goldin-Meadow, Susan. (2015). From action to abstraction: Gesture as a mechanism of change. *Developmental Review, 38,* 167–184. doi: 10.1016/j.dr.2015.07.007

Goldin-Meadow, Susan & Alibali, Martha W. (2013). Gesture's role in speaking, learning, and creating language. *Annual Review of Psychology, 64,* 257–283. doi: 10.1146/annurev-psych-113011-143802

Goldman, Dana P.; Cutler, David; Rowe, John W.; Michaud, Pierre-Carl; Sullivan, Jeffrey; Peneva, Desi & Olshansky, S. Jay. (2013). Substantial health and economic returns from delayed aging may warrant a new focus for medical research. *Health Affairs, 32*(10), 1698–1705. doi: 10.1377/hlthaff.2013.0052

Goldman-Mellor, Sidra; Caspi, Avshalom; Arseneault, Louise; Ajala, Nifemi; Ambler, Antony; Danese, Andrea, . . . Moffitt, Terrie E. (2016). Committed to work but vulnerable: Self-perceptions and mental health in NEET 18-year olds from a contemporary British cohort. *Journal of Child Psychology and Psychiatry, 57*(2), 196–203. doi: 10.1111/jcpp.12459

Goldschmidt, Andrea B.; Wall, Melanie M.; Zhang, Jun; Loth, Katie A. & Neumark-Sztainer, Dianne. (2016). Overeating and binge eating in emerging adulthood: 10-year stability and risk factors. *Developmental Psychology, 52*(3), 475–483. doi: 10.1037/dev0000086

Goldstein, Joshua R. (2011). A secular trend toward earlier male sexual maturity: Evidence from shifting ages of male young adult mortality. *PLoS ONE, 6*(8), e14826. doi: 10.1371/journal.pone.0014826

Goldstein, Michael H.; Schwade, Jennifer A. & Bornstein, Marc H. (2009). The value of vocalizing: Five-month-old infants associate their own noncry vocalizations with responses from caregivers. *Child Development, 80*(3), 636–644. doi: 10.1111/j.1467-8624.2009.01287.x

Goldstein, Sam; Princiotta, Dana & Naglieri, Jack A. (Eds.). (2015). *Handbook of intelligence: Evolutionary theory, historical perspective, and current concepts.* New York, NY: Springer. doi: 10.1007/978-1-4939-1562-0

Golinkoff, Roberta M. & Hirsh-Pasek, Kathy. (2016). *Becoming brilliant: What science tells us about raising successful children.* Washington, DC: American Psychological Association.

Göncü, Artin & Gaskins, Suzanne. (2011). Comparing and extending Piaget's and Vygotsky's understandings of play: Symbolic play as individual, sociocultural, and educational interpretation. In Anthony D. Pellegrini (Ed.), *The Oxford handbook of the development of play* (pp. 48–57). New York, NY: Oxford University Press. doi: 10.1093/oxfordhb/9780195393002.013.0005

Gonyea, Judith G. (2013). Midlife, multigenerational bonds, and caregiving. In Ronda C. Talley & Rhonda J. V. Montgomery (Eds.), *Caregiving across the lifespan: Research, practice, policy* (pp. 105–130). New York, NY: Springer.

Gonzalez-Gomez, Nayeli; Hayashi, Akiko; Tsuji, Sho; Mazuka, Reiko & Nazzi, Thierry. (2014). The role of the input on the development of the LC bias: A crosslinguistic comparison. *Cognition, 132*(3), 301–311. doi: 10.1016/j.cognition.2014.04.004

Goodlad, James K.; Marcus, David K. & Fulton, Jessica J. (2013). Lead and Attention-deficit/hyperactivity disorder (ADHD) symptoms: A meta-analysis. *Clinical Psychology Review, 33*(3), 417–425. doi: 10.1016/j.cpr.2013.01.009

Goodman, Madeline J.; Sands, Anita M. & Coley, Richard J. (2015). *America's skills challenge: Millennials and the future.* Princeton, NJ: Educational Testing Service.

Goodman, Sherryl H. & Gotlib, Ian H. (Eds.). (2002). *Children of depressed parents: Mechanisms of risk and implications for treatment*. Washington, DC: American Psychological Association.

Goodnight, Jackson A.; D'Onofrio, Brian M.; Cherlin, Andrew J.; Emery, Robert E.; Van Hulle, Carol A. & Lahey, Benjamin B. (2013). Effects of multiple maternal relationship transitions on offspring antisocial behavior in childhood and adolescence: A cousin-comparison analysis. *Journal of Abnormal Child Psychology*, 41(2), 185–198. doi: 10.1007/s10802-012-9667-y

Gopnik, Alison. (2012). Scientific thinking in young children: Theoretical advances, empirical research, and policy implications. *Science*, 337(6102), 1623–1627. doi: 10.1126/science.1223416

Gordon-Hollingsworth, Arlene T.; Becker, Emily M.; Ginsburg, Golda S.; Keeton, Courtney; Compton, Scott N.; Birmaher, Boris B., . . . March, John S. (2015). Anxiety disorders in caucasian and African American children: A comparison of clinical characteristics, treatment process variables, and treatment outcomes. *Child Psychiatry & Human Development*, 46(5), 643–655. doi: 10.1007/s10578-014-0507-x

Gostin, Lawrence O. (2016). 4 Simple reforms to address mass shootings and other firearm violence. *JAMA*, 315(5), 453–454. doi: 10.1001/jama.2015.19497

Gottesman, Irving I.; Laursen, Thomas Munk; Bertelsen, Aksel & Mortensen, Preben Bo. (2010). Severe mental disorders in offspring with 2 psychiatrically ill parents. *Archives of General Psychiatry*, 67(3), 252–257. doi: 10.1001/archgenpsychiatry .2010.1

Gottman, John Mordechai; Murray, James D.; Swanson, Catherine; Tyson, Rebecca & Swanson, Kristin R. (2002). *The mathematics of marriage: Dynamic nonlinear models*. Cambridge, MA: MIT Press.

Gough, Ethan K.; Moodie, Erica E. M.; Prendergast, Andrew J.; Johnson, Sarasa M. A.; Humphrey, Jean H.; Stoltzfus, Rebecca J., . . . Manges, Amee R. (2014). The impact of antibiotics on growth in children in low and middle income countries: Systematic review and meta-analysis of randomised controlled trials. *BMJ*, 348, g2267. doi: 10.1136/bmj.g2267

Govindaraju, Diddahally; Atzmon, Gil & Barzilai, Nir. (2015). Genetics, lifestyle and longevity: Lessons from centenarians. *Applied & Translational Genomics*, 4(Suppl. 1), 23–32. doi: 10.1016 /j.atg.2015.01.001

Gow, Alan J.; Johnson, Wendy; Pattie, Alison; Brett, Caroline E.; Roberts, Beverly; Starr, John M. & Deary, Ian J. (2011). Stability and change in intelligence from age 11 to ages 70, 79, and 87: The Lothian Birth Cohorts of 1921 and 1936. *Psychology and Aging*, 26(1), 232–240. doi: 10.1037/a0021072

Graber, Julia A.; Nichols, Tracy R. & Brooks-Gunn, Jeanne. (2010). Putting pubertal timing in developmental context: Implications for prevention. *Developmental Psychobiology*, 52(3), 254–262. doi: 10.1002/dev.20438

Grabowski, David C.; O'Malley, James; Afendulis, Christopher C.; Caudry, Daryl J.; Elliot, Amy & Zimmerman, Sheryl. (2014). Culture change and nursing home quality of care. *The Gerontologist*, 54(Suppl. 1), S35–S45. doi: 10.1093/geront /gnt143

Grady, Denise. (2012, May 5). When illness makes a spouse a stranger. *New York Times*, p. A1

Grady, Jessica S.; Ale, Chelsea M. & Morris, Tracy L. (2012). A naturalistic observation of social behaviours during preschool drop-off. *Early Child Development and Care*, 182(12), 1683–1694. doi: 10.1080/03004430.2011.649266

Grainger, Sarah A.; Henry, Julie D.; Phillips, Louise H.; Vanman, Eric J. & Allen, Roy. (2015). Age deficits in facial affect recognition: The influence of dynamic cues. *The Journal of Gerontology Series B*, (In Press). doi: 10.1093/geronb/gbv100

Grant, Jon E. & Potenza, Marc N. (Eds.). (2010). *Young adult mental health*. New York, NY: Oxford University Press.

Grant, Kristen; Goldizen, Fiona C.; Sly, Peter D.; Brune, Marie-Noel; Neira, Maria; van den Berg, Martin & Norman, Rosana E. (2013). Health consequences of exposure to e-waste: A systematic review. *The Lancet Global Health*, 1(6), e350–e361. doi: 10.1016/S2214-109X(13)70101-3

Grazioplene, Rachael G.; Ryman, Sephira G.; Gray, Jeremy R.; Rustichini, Aldo; Jung, Rex E. & DeYoung, Colin G. (2015). Subcortical intelligence: Caudate volume predicts IQ in healthy adults. *Human Brain Mapping*, 36(4), 1407–1416. doi: 10.1002/hbm.22710

Greco, Daniel. (2014). Could KK be OK? *The Journal of Philosophy*, 111(4), 169–197. doi: 10.5840/jphil2014111411

Green, James A.; Whitney, Pamela G. & Potegal, Michael. (2011). Screaming, yelling, whining, and crying: Categorical and intensity differences in vocal expressions of anger and sadness in children's tantrums. *Emotion*, 11(5), 1124–1133. doi: 10.1037/a0024173

Green, Lorraine & Grant, Victoria. (2008). "Gagged grief and beleaguered bereavements?" An analysis of multidisciplinary theory and research relating to same sex partnership bereavement. *Sexualities*, 11(3), 275–300. doi: 10.1177/1363460708089421

Green, Ronald. (2015). Designer babies. In Henk ten Have (Ed.), *Encyclopedia of global bioethics*. Living Reference Work: Springer International Publishing. doi: 10.1007/978-3-319-05544-2_138-1

Greene, Melissa L. & Way, Niobe. (2005). Self-esteem trajectories among ethnic minority adolescents: A growth curve analysis of the patterns and predictors of change. *Journal of Research on Adolescence*, 15(2), 151–178. doi: 10.1111 /j.1532 -7795.2005.00090.x

Greenfield, Emily A.; Scharlach, Andrew; Lehning, Amanda J. & Davitt, Joan K. (2012). A conceptual framework for examining the promise of the NORC program and Village models to promote aging in place. *Journal of Aging Studies*, 26(3), 273–284. doi: 10.1016/j.jaging.2012.01.003

Greenfield, Patricia M. (2009). Technology and informal education: What is taught, what is learned. *Science*, 323(5910), 69–71. doi: 10.1126 /science .1167190

Greenough, William T.; Black, James E. & Wallace, Christopher S. (1987). Experience and brain development. *Child Development*, 58(3), 539–559. doi: 10.1111/j.1467-8624.1987.tb01400.x

Greenough, William T. & Volkmar, Fred R. (1973). Pattern of dendritic branching in occipital cortex of rats reared in complex environments. *Experimental Neurology*, 40(2), 491–504. doi: 10.1016/0014 -4886(73)90090-3

Greenstone, Michael & Looney, Adam. (2012). The importance of education: An economics view. *Education Week*, 32(11), 32.

Greenwood, Pamela M. & Parasuraman, R. (2012). *Nurturing the older brain and mind*. Cambridge, MA: MIT Press.

Gregg, Norman McAlister. (1941). Congenital cataract following German measles in the mother. *Transactions of the Ophthalmological Society of Australia*, 3, 35–46.

Gregg, Norman McAlister. (1991). Congenital cataract following German measles in the mother. *Epidemiology and Infection*, 107(1), iii–xiv. doi: 10.1017/S0950268800048627

Gregory, Sara M.; Parker, Beth & Thompson, Paul D. (2012). Physical activity, cognitive function, and brain health: What is the role of exercise training in the prevention of dementia? *Brain Sciences*, 2(4), 684–708. doi: 10.3390/brainsci2040684

Gremeauxa, Vincent; Gaydaa, Mathieu; Leperse, Romuald; Sosnera, Philippe; Juneaua, Martin & Nigam, Anil. (2012). Exercise and longevity. *Maturitas*, 73(4), 312–317. doi: 10.1016/j.maturitas .2012.09.012

Greyson, Bruce. (2009). Near-death experiences and deathbed visions. In Allan Kellehear (Ed.), *The study of dying: From autonomy to transformation* (pp. 253–275). New York, NY: Cambridge University Press.

Greyson, Bruce. (2015). Western scientific approaches to near-death experiences. *Humanities*, 4(4), 775–796. doi: 10.3390/h4040775

Griffin, James; Gooding, Sarah; Semesky, Michael; Farmer, Brittany; Mannchen, Garrett & Sinnott, Jan D. (2009). Four brief studies of relations between postformal thought and non-cognitive factors: Personality, concepts of god, political opinions, and social attitudes. *Journal of Adult Development*, 16(3), 173–182. doi: 10.1007 /s10804-009-9056-0

Griffin, Martyn. (2011). Developing deliberative minds: Piaget, Vygotsky and the deliberative democratic citizen. *Journal of Public Deliberation*, 7(1).

Griffith, Patrick & Lopez, Oscar. (2009). Disparities in the diagnosis and treatment of Alzheimer's disease in African American and Hispanic patients: A call to action. *Generations*, 33(1), 37–46.

Griffiths, Thomas L. (2015). Manifesto for a new (computational) cognitive revolution. *Cognition*, 135, 21–23. doi: 10.1016/j.cognition.2014.11.026

Grigorovich, Alisa; Lee, Adrienne; Ross, Heather; Woodend, A. Kirsten; Forde, Samantha & Cameron, Jill I. (2016). A longitudinal view of factors that influence the emotional well-being of family caregivers to individuals with heart failure. *Aging & Mental Health*, (In Press). doi: 10.1080/13607863.2016.1168361

Grigsby, Timothy J. H.; Forster, Myriam; Soto, Daniel W.; Baezconde-Garbanati, Lourdes & Unger, Jennifer B. (2014). Problematic substance use among Hispanic adolescents and young adults: Implications for prevention efforts. *Substance Use & Misuse, 49*(8), 1025–1038. doi: 10.3109/10826084.2013.852585

Grobman, Kevin H. (2008). Learning & teaching developmental psychology: Attachment theory, infancy, & infant memory development. http://www.devpsy.org/questions/attachment_theory_memory.html

Groh, Ashley M.; Roisman, Glenn I.; van IJzendoorn, Marinus H.; Bakermans-Kranenburg, Marian J. & Fearon, R. Pasco. (2012). The significance of insecure and disorganized attachment for children's internalizing symptoms: A meta-analytic study. *Child Development, 83*(2), 591–610. doi: 10.1111/j.1467-8624.2011.01711.x

Gross, James J. (Ed.). (2014). *Handbook of emotion regulation* (2nd ed.). New York, NY: Guilford Press.

Grossmann, Klaus E.; Bretherton, Inge; Waters, Everett & Grossmann, Karin (Eds.). (2014). *Mary Ainsworth's enduring influence on attachment theory, research, and clinical applications.* New York, NY: Routledge.

Grossmann, Tobias. (2013). Mapping prefrontal cortex functions in human infancy. *Infancy, 18*(3), 303–324. doi: 10.1111/infa.12016

Grotevant, Harold D. & McDermott, Jennifer M. (2014). Adoption: Biological and social processes linked to adaptation. *Annual Review of Psychology, 65*, 235–265. doi: 10.1146/annurev-psych-010213-115020

Grov, Christian; Gillespie, Brian Joseph; Royce, Tracy & Lever, Janet. (2011). Perceived consequences of casual online sexual activities on heterosexual relationships: A U.S. online survey. *Archives of Sexual Behavior, 40*(2), 429–439. doi: 10.1007/s10508-010-9598-z

Gruchalla, Rebecca S. & Sampson, Hugh A. (2015). Preventing peanut allergy through early consumption—Ready for prime time? *New England Journal of Medicine, 372*(9), 875–877. doi: 10.1056/NEJMe1500186

Gründer, Gerhard; Heinze, Martin; Cordes, Joachim; Mühlbauer, Bernd; Juckel, Georg; Schulz, Constanze, . . . Timm, Jürgen. (2016). Effects of first-generation antipsychotics versus second-generation antipsychotics on quality of life in schizophrenia: a double-blind, randomised study. *The Lancet Psychiatry, 3*(8), 717–729. doi: 10.1016/S2215-0366(16)00085-7

Grundy, Emily & Henretta, John C. (2006). Between elderly parents and adult children: A new look at the intergenerational care provided by the 'sandwich generation'. *Ageing & Society, 26*(5), 707–722. doi: 10.1017/S0144686X06004934

Grünebaum, Amos; McCullough, Laurence B.; Sapra, Katherine J.; Brent, Robert L.; Levene, Malcolm I.; Arabin, Birgit & Chervenak, Frank A. (2014). Early and total neonatal mortality in relation to birth setting in the United States, 2006–2009. *American Journal of Obstetrics and Gynecology, 211*(4), 390.e391–390.e397. doi: 10.1016/j.ajog.2014.03.047

Guerra, Nancy G. & Williams, Kirk R. (2010). Implementing bullying prevention in diverse settings: Geographic, economic, and cultural influences. In Eric M. Vernberg & Bridget K. Biggs (Eds.), *Preventing and treating bullying and victimization* (pp. 319–336). New York, NY: Oxford University Press.

Guerra, Nancy G.; Williams, Kirk R. & Sadek, Shelly. (2011). Understanding bullying and victimization during childhood and adolescence: A mixed methods study. *Child Development, 82*(1), 295–310. doi: 10.1111/j.1467-8624.2010.01556.x

Guerri, Consuelo & Pascual, María. (2010). Mechanisms involved in the neurotoxic, cognitive, and neurobehavioral effects of alcohol consumption during adolescence. *Alcohol, 44*(1), 15–26. doi: 10.1016/j.alcohol.2009.10.003

Güngör, Derya; Bornstein, Marc H.; De Leersnyder, Jozefien; Cote, Linda; Ceulemans, Eva & Mesquita, Batja. (2013). Acculturation of personality: A three-culture study of Japanese, Japanese Americans, and European Americans. *Journal of Cross-Cultural Psychology, 44*(5), 701–718. doi: 10.1177/0022022112470749

Guo, Siying. (2016). A meta-analysis of the predictors of cyberbullying perpetration and victimization. *Psychology in the Schools, 53*(4), 432–453. doi: 10.1002/pits.21914

Gupta, Nidhi; Goel, Kashish; Shah, Priyali & Misra, Anoop. (2012). Childhood obesity in developing countries: Epidemiology, determinants, and prevention. *Endocrine Reviews, 33*(1), 48–70. doi: 10.1210/er.2010-0028

Gurunath, Sumana; Pandian, Z.; Anderson, Richard A. & Bhattacharya, Siladitya. (2011). Defining infertility—A systematic review of prevalence studies. *Human Reproduction Update, 17*(5), 575–588. doi: 10.1093/humupd/dmr015

Gutierrez-Galve, Leticia; Stein, Alan; Hanington, Lucy; Heron, Jon & Ramchandani, Paul. (2015). Paternal depression in the postnatal period and child development: Mediators and moderators. *Pediatrics, 135*(2), e339–e347. doi: 10.1542/peds.2014-2411

Guzman, Natalie S. de & Nishina, Adrienne. (2014). A longitudinal study of body dissatisfaction and pubertal timing in an ethnically diverse adolescent sample. *Body Image, 11*(1), 68–71. doi: 10.1016/j.bodyim.2013.11.001

Guzzo, Karen Benjamin. (2014). Trends in cohabitation outcomes: Compositional changes and engagement among never-married young adults. *Journal of Marriage and Family, 76*(4), 826–842. doi: 10.1111/jomf.12123

Hackett, Geoffrey Ian. (2016). Testosterone replacement therapy and mortality in older men. *Drug Safety, 39*(2), 117–130. doi: 10.1007/s40264-015-0348-y

Haden, Catherine A. (2010). Talking about science in museums. *Child Development Perspectives, 4*(1), 62–67. doi: 10.1111/j.1750-8606.2009.00119.x

Hagan, José E.; Wassilak, Steven G. F.; Craig, Allen S.; Tangermann, Rudolf H.; Diop, Ousmane M.; Burns, Cara C. & Quddus, Arshad. (2015, May 22). Progress toward polio eradication—Worldwide, 2014–2015. *Morbidity and Mortality Weekly Report 64*(19), 527–531. Atlanta, GA: Centers for Disease Control and Prevention.

Hagues, Rachel Joy; Bae, DaYoung & Wickrama, Kandauda K. A. S. (2016). Mediational pathways connecting secondary education and age at marriage to maternal mortality: A comparison between developing and developed countries. *Women & Health,* (In Press). doi: 10.1080/03630242.2016.1159266

Haidt, Jonathan. (2013). *The righteous mind: Why good people are divided by politics and religion.* New York, NY: Vintage Books.

Hajek, Peter; Etter, Jean-François; Benowitz, Neal; Eissenberg, Thomas & McRobbie, Hayden. (2014). Electronic cigarettes: Review of use, content, safety, effects on smokers and potential for harm and benefit. *Addiction, 109*(11), 1801–1810. doi: 10.1111/add.12659

Halim, May Ling; Ruble, Diane N.; Tamis-LeMonda, Catherine S.; Zosuls, Kristina M.; Lurye, Leah E. & Greulich, Faith K. (2014). Pink frilly dresses and the avoidance of all things "girly": Children's appearance rigidity and cognitive theories of gender development. *Developmental Psychology, 50*(4), 1091–1101. doi: 10.1037/a0034906

Hall, Jeffrey A. (2011). Sex differences in friendship expectations: A meta-analysis. *Journal of Social and Personal Relationships, 28*(6), 723–747. doi: 10.1177/0265407510386192

Hall, Lynn K. (2008). *Counseling military families: What mental health professionals need to know.* New York, NY: Taylor & Francis.

Hallers-Haalboom, Elizabeth T.; Mesman, Judi; Groeneveld, Marleen G.; Endendijk, Joyce J.; van Berkel, Sheila R.; van der Pol, Lotte D. & Bakermans-Kranenburg, Marian J. (2014). Mothers, fathers, sons and daughters: Parental sensitivity in families with two children. *Journal of Family Psychology, 28*(2), 138–147. doi: 10.1037/a0036004

Halpern, Neil A.; Pastores, Stephen M.; Chou, Joanne F.; Chawla, Sanjay & Thaler, Howard T. (2011). Advance directives in an oncologic intensive care unit: A contemporary analysis of their frequency, type, and impact. *Journal of Palliative Medicine, 14*(4), 483–489. doi: 10.1089/jpm.2010.0397

Halpern-Meekin, Sarah; Manning, Wendy D.; Giordano, Peggy C. & Longmore, Monica A. (2013). Relationship churning: Physical violence, and verbal abuse in young adult relationships. *Journal of Marriage and Family, 75*(1), 2–12. doi: 10.1111/j.1741-3737.2012.01029.x

Hamerton, John L. & Evans, Jane A. (2005). Sex chromosome anomalies. In Merlin G. Butler & F. John Meaney (Eds.), *Genetics of developmental disabilities* (pp. 585–650). Boca Raton, FL: Taylor & Francis.

Hamill, Paul J. (1991). Triage: An essay. *The Georgia Review, 45*(3), 463–469.

Hamilton, Alice. (1914). Lead poisoning in the United States. *American Journal of Public Health, 4*(6), 477–480. doi: 10.2105/AJPH.4.6.477-a

Hamilton, Brady E.; Martin, Joyce A.; Osterman, Michelle J. K.; Curtin, Sally C. & Mathews, T. J. (2015, December 23). *Births: Final data for 2014. National Vital Statistics Reports*

64(12). Hyattsville, MD: National Center for Health Statistics.

Hamilton, Rashea; Sanders, Megan & Anderman, Eric M. (2013). The multiple choices of sex education. *Phi Delta Kappan, 94*(5), 34–39.

Hamilton, William L.; Cook, John T.; Thompson, William W.; Buron, Lawrence F.; Frongillo, Edward A.; Olson, Christine M. & Wehler, Cheryl A. (1997). *Household food security in the United States in 1995: Summary report of the Food Security Measurement Project.* Washington, DC: United States Department of Agriculture.

Hamlat, Elissa J.; Shapero, Benjamin G.; Hamilton, Jessica L.; Stange, Jonathan P.; Abramson, Lyn Y. & Alloy, Lauren B. (2014a). Pubertal timing, peer victimization, and body esteem differentially predict depressive symptoms in African American and Caucasian girls. *The Journal of Early Adolescence.* doi: 10.1177/0272431614534071

Hamlat, Elissa J.; Stange, Jonathan P.; Abramson, Lyn Y. & Alloy, Lauren B. (2014b). Early pubertal timing as a vulnerability to depression symptoms: Differential effects of race and sex. *Journal of Abnormal Child Psychology, 42*(4), 527–538. doi: 10.1007/s10802-013-9798-9

Hamlin, J. Kiley. (2014). The origins of human morality: Complex socio-moral evaluations by preverbal infants. In Jean Decety & Yves Christen (Eds.), *New frontiers in social neuroscience* (pp. 165–188). New York, NY: Springer. doi: 10.1007/978-3-319 -02904-7_10

Hammond, Christopher J.; Andrew, Toby; Mak, Ying Tat & Spector, Tim D. (2004). A susceptibility locus for myopia in the normal population is linked to the PAX6 gene region on chromosome 11: A genomewide scan of dizygotic twins. *American Journal of Human Genetics, 75*(2), 294–304. doi: 10.1086/423148

Hamplová, Dana. (2009). Educational homogamy among married and unmarried couples in Europe: Does context matter? *Journal of Family Issues, 30*(1), 28–52. doi: 10.1177/0192513X08324576

Hamplová, Dana; Le Bourdais, Céline & Lapierre-Adamcyk, Évelyne. (2014). Is the cohabitation–marriage gap in money pooling universal? *Journal of Marriage and Family, 76*(5), 983–997. doi: 10.1111/jomf.12138

Han, Wen-Jui. (2012). Bilingualism and academic achievement. *Child Development, 83*(1), 300–321. doi: 10.1111/j.1467-8624.2011.01686.x

Hane, Amie Ashley; Cheah, Charissa; Rubin, Kenneth H. & Fox, Nathan A. (2008). The role of maternal behavior in the relation between shyness and social reticence in early childhood and social withdrawal in middle childhood. *Social Development, 17*(4), 795–811. doi: 10.1111/j.1467-9507.2008.00481.x

Hank, Karsten & Korbmacher, Julie M. (2013). Parenthood and retirement: Gender, cohort, and welfare regime differences. *European Societies, 15*(3), 446–461. doi: 10.1080/14616696.2012.750731

Hanks, Andrew S.; Just, David R. & Wansink, Brian. (2013). Smarter lunchrooms can address new school lunchroom guidelines and childhood obesity. *The Journal of Pediatrics, 162*(4), 867–869. doi: 10.1016/j.jpeds.2012.12.031

Hanna-Attisha, Mona; LaChance, Jenny; Sadler, Richard Casey & Schnepp, Allison Champney. (2016). Elevated blood lead levels in children associated with the Flint drinking water crisis: A spatial analysis of risk and public health response. *American Journal of Public Health, 106*(2), 283–290. doi: 10.2105/AJPH.2015.303003

Hannah, Sean T.; Avolio, Bruce J. & May, Douglas R. (2011). Moral maturation and moral conation: A capacity approach to explaining moral thought and action. *Academy Management Review, 36*(4), 663–685. doi: 10.5465/amr.2010.0128

Hanushek, Eric A. & Woessmann, Ludger. (2007). *The role of education quality in economic growth.* World Bank Policy Research Working Paper No. 4122. Washington, DC: World Bank.

Hanushek, Eric A. & Woessmann, Ludger. (2009). Do better schools lead to more growth? Cognitive skills, economic outcomes, and causation. *Journal of Economic Growth, 17*(4), 267–321. doi: 10.1007/s10887-012-9081-x

Hanushek, Eric A. & Woessmann, Ludger. (2010). *The high cost of low educational performance: The long-run economic impact of improving PISA outcomes.* Paris: OECD Publishing. doi: 10.1787/9789264077485-en

Harden, K. Paige & Tucker-Drob, Elliot M. (2011). Individual differences in the development of sensation seeking and impulsivity during adolescence: Further evidence for a dual systems model. *Developmental Psychology, 47*(3), 739–746. doi: 10.1037/a0023279

Hargreaves, Andy. (2012). Singapore: The Fourth Way in action? *Educational Research for Policy and Practice, 11*(1), 7–17. doi: 10.1007/s10671-011 -9125-6

Harkness, Sara. (2014). Is biology destiny for the whole family? Contributions of evolutionary life history and behavior genetics to family theories. *Journal of Family Theory & Review, 6*(1), 31–34. doi: 10.1111/jftr.12032

Harkness, Sara; Super, Charles M. & Mavridis, Caroline J. (2011). Parental ethnotheories about children's socioemotional development. In Xinyin Chen & Kenneth H. Rubin (Eds.), *Socioemotional development in cultural context* (pp. 73–98). New York, NY: Guilford Press.

Harlor, Allen D. Buz & Bower, Charles. (2009). Hearing assessment in infants and children: Recommendations beyond neonatal screening. *Pediatrics, 124*(4), 1252–1263. doi: 10.1542/peds .2009-1997

Harlow, Ilana. (2005). Shaping sorrow: Creative aspects of public and private mourning. In Samuel C. Heilman (Ed.), *Death, bereavement, and mourning* (pp. 33–52). New Brunswick, NJ: Transaction.

Harper, Casandra E. & Yeung, Fanny. (2013). Perceptions of institutional commitment to diversity as a predictor of college students' openness to diverse perspectives. *The Review of Higher Education, 37*(1), 25–44. doi: 10.1353/rhe.2013.0065

Harris, Judith R. (1998). *The nurture assumption: Why children turn out the way they do.* New York, NY: Free Press.

Harris, Judith R. (2002). Beyond the nurture assumption: Testing hypotheses about the child's environment. In John G. Borkowski et al. (Eds.), *Parenting and the child's world: Influences on academic, intellectual, and social-emotional development* (pp. 3–20). Mahwah, NJ: Erlbaum.

Harris, Peter R.; Brearley, Irina; Sheeran, Paschal; Barker, Margo; Klein, William M. P.; Creswell, J. David, . . . Bond, Rod. (2014). Combining self-affirmation with implementation intentions to promote fruit and vegetable consumption. *Health Psychology, 33*(7), 729–736. doi: 10.1037 /hea0000065

Harrison, Kristen; Bost, Kelly K.; McBride, Brent A.; Donovan, Sharon M.; Grigsby-Toussaint, Diana S.; Kim, Juhee, . . . Jacobsohn, Gwen Costa. (2011). Toward a developmental conceptualization of contributors to overweight and obesity in childhood: The Six-Cs model. *Child Development Perspectives, 5*(1), 50–58. doi: 10.1111/j.1750 -8606.2010.00150.x

Harrison, Linda J.; Elwick, Sheena; Vallotton, Claire D. & Kappler, Gregor. (2014). Spending time with others: A time-use diary for infant-toddler child care. In Linda J. Harrison & Jennifer Sumsion (Eds.), *Lived spaces of infant-toddler education and care: Exploring diverse perspectives on theory, research and practice* (pp. 59–74). Dordrecht, Netherlands: Springer. doi: 10.1007/978-94-017 -8838-0_5

Harrist, Amanda W.; Topham, Glade L.; Hubbs-Tait, Laura; Page, Melanie C.; Kennedy, Tay S. & Shriver, Lenka H. (2012). What developmental science can contribute to a transdisciplinary understanding of childhood obesity: An interpersonal and intrapersonal risk model. *Child Development Perspectives, 6*(4), 445–455. doi: 10.1111 /cdep.12004

Hart, Betty & Risley, Todd R. (1995). *Meaningful differences in the everyday experience of young American children.* Baltimore, MD: P.H. Brookes.

Hart, Chantelle N.; Cairns, Alyssa & Jelalian, Elissa. (2011). Sleep and obesity in children and adolescents. *Pediatric Clinics of North America, 58*(3), 715–733. doi: 10.1016 /j.pcl.2011.03.007

Harter, Susan. (2012). *The construction of the self: Developmental and sociocultural foundations* (2nd ed.). New York, NY: Guilford Press.

Hartley, Catherine A. & Somerville, Leah H. (2015). The neuroscience of adolescent decision-making. *Current Opinion in Behavioral Sciences, 5*, 108–115. doi: 10.1016/j.cobeha.2015.09.004

Hartman, Sarah & Belsky, Jay. (2015). An evolutionary perspective on family studies: Differential susceptibility to environmental influences. *Family Process,* (In Press). doi: 10.1111/famp.12161

Hartshorne, Joshua K. & Germine, Laura T. (2015). When does cognitive functioning peak? The asynchronous rise and fall of different cognitive abilities across the life span. *Psychological Science, 26*(4), 433–443. doi: 10.1177/0956797614567339

Hasson, Ramzi & Fine, Jodene Goldenring. (2012). Gender differences among children with ADHD on continuous performance tests: A meta-analytic review. *Journal of Attention Disorders*, 16(3), 190–198. doi: 10.1177/1087054711427398

Hatch, J. Amos. (2012). From theory to curriculum: Developmental theory and its relationship to curriculum and instruction in early childhood education. In Nancy File et al. (Eds.), *Curriculum in early childhood education: Re-examined, rediscovered, renewed.* New York, NY: Routledge.

Hatfield, Elaine; Bensman, Lisamarie & Rapson, Richard L. (2012). A brief history of social scientists' attempts to measure passionate love. *Journal of Social and Personal Relationships*, 29(2), 143–164. doi: 10.1177/0265407511431055

Hausdorff, Jeffrey M. & Buchman, Aron S. (2013). What links gait speed and MCI with dementia? A fresh look at the association between motor and cognitive function. *Journals of Gerontology: Series A: Biological Sciences and Medical Sciences*, 68(4), 409–411. doi: 10.1093/gerona/glt002

Haushofer, Johannes & Fehr, Ernst. (2014). On the psychology of poverty. *Science*, 344(6186), 862–867. doi: 10.1126/science.1232491

Hawkes, Kristen & Coxworth, James E. (2013). Grandmothers and the evolution of human longevity: A review of findings and future directions. *Evolutionary Anthropology*, 22(6), 294–302. doi: 10.1002/evan.21382

Hawthorne, Joanna. (2009). Promoting development of the early parent-infant relationship using the Neonatal Behavioural Assessment Scale. In Jane Barlow & P. O. Svanberg (Eds.), *Keeping the baby in mind: Infant mental health in practice* (pp. 39–51). New York, NY: Routledge.

Hayden, Brian. (2012). Neandertal social structure? *Oxford Journal of Archaeology*, 31(1), 1–26. doi: 10.1111/j.1468-0092.2011.00376.x

Hayden, Elizabeth P. & Mash, Eric J. (2014). Child psychopathology: A developmental-systems perspective. In Eric J. Mash & Russell A. Barkley (Eds.), *Child psychopathology* (3rd ed., pp. 3–72). New York, NY: Guilford Press.

Hayes, DeMarquis; Blake, Jamilia J.; Darensbourg, Alicia & Castillo, Linda G. (2015). Examining the academic achievement of Latino adolescents: The role of parent and peer beliefs and behaviors. *The Journal of Early Adolescence*, 35(2), 141–161. doi: 10.1177/0272431614530806

Hayes, Peter. (2013). International adoption, "early" puberty, and underrecorded age. *Pediatrics*, 131(6), 1029–1031. doi: 10.1542/peds.2013-0232

Hayes, Rachel A. & Slater, Alan. (2008). Three-month-olds' detection of alliteration in syllables. *Infant Behavior and Development*, 31(1), 153–156. doi: 10.1016/j.infbeh.2007.07.009

Hayflick, Leonard. (2004). "Anti-aging" is an oxymoron. *Journals of Gerontology: Series A: Biological Sciences and Medical Sciences*, 59A(6), 573–578. doi: 10.1093/gerona/59.6.B573

Haynie, Dana L.; Soller, Brian & Williams, Kristi. (2014). Anticipating early fatality: Friends', schoolmates' and individual perceptions of fatality on adolescent risk behaviors. *Journal of Youth and Adolescence*, 43(2), 175–192. doi: 10.1007/s10964-013-9968-7

Hayslip, Bert; Blumenthal, Heidemarie & Garner, Ashley. (2014). Health and grandparent–grandchild well-being: One-year longitudinal findings for custodial grandfamilies. *Journal of Aging and Health*, 26(4), 559–582. doi: 10.1177/0898264314525664

Heflick, Nathan A. & Goldenberg, Jamie L. (2012). No atheists in foxholes: Arguments for (but not against) afterlife belief buffers mortality salience effects for atheists. *British Journal of Social Psychology*, 51(2), 385–392. doi: 10.1111/j.2044-8309.2011.02058.x

Heiman, Julia R.; Long, J. Scott; Smith, Shawna N.; Fisher, William A.; Sand, Michael S. & Rosen, Raymond C. (2011). Sexual satisfaction and relationship happiness in midlife and older couples in five countries. *Archives of Sexual Behavior*, 40(4), 741–753. doi: 10.1007/s10508-010-9703-3

Hein, Sascha; Tan, Mei; Aljughaiman, Abdullah & Grigorenko, Elena L. (2014). Characteristics of the home context for the nurturing of gifted children in Saudi Arabia. *High Ability Studies*, 25(1), 23–33. doi: 10.1080/13598139.2014.906970

Heinze, Justin E.; Kruger, Daniel J.; Reischl, Thomas M.; Cupal, Suzanne & Zimmerman, Marc A. (2015). Relationships among disease, social support, and perceived health: A lifespan approach. *American Journal of Community Psychology*, 56(3/4), 268–279. doi: 10.1007/s10464-015-9758-3

Helle, Nadine; Barkmann, Claus; Bartz-Seel, Jutta; Diehl, Thilo; Ehrhardt, Stephan; Hendel, Astrid, . . . Bindt, Carola. (2016). Very low birthweight as a risk factor for postpartum depression four to six weeks postbirth in mothers and fathers: Cross-sectional results from a controlled multicentre cohort study. *Journal of Affective Disorders*, 180, 154–161. doi: 10.1016/j.jad.2015.04.001

Hellerstein, Susan C.; Feldman, Sarah & Duan, Tao. (2015). China's 50% caesarean delivery rate: Is it too high? *BJOG: An International Journal of Obstetrics & Gynaecology*, 122(2), 160–164. doi: 10.1111/1471-0528.12971

Henderson, Heather A.; Pine, Daniel S. & Fox, Nathan A. (2015). Behavioral inhibition and developmental risk: A dual-processing perspective. *Neuropsychopharmacology Reviews*, 40(1), 207–224. doi: 10.1038/npp.2014.189

Hendry, Leo B. & Kloep, Marion. (2011). Lifestyles in emerging adulthood: Who needs stages anyway? In Jeffrey Jensen Arnett et al. (Eds.), *Debating emerging adulthood: Stage or process?* (pp. 77–104). New York, NY: Oxford University Press. doi: 10.1093/acprof:oso/9780199757176.003.0005

Hennessy-Fiske, Molly. (2011, February 8). CALIFORNIA; Concern about child obesity grows, poll finds; Many Californians support restricting unhealthful food and drink in schools. *Los Angeles Times*, p. AA3.

Henrich, Joseph. (2015). Culture and social behavior. *Current Opinion in Behavioral Sciences*, 3, 84–89. doi: 10.1016/j.cobeha.2015.02.001

Henrich, Joseph; Heine, Steven J. & Norenzayan, Ara. (2010). The weirdest people in the world? *Behavioral and Brain Sciences*, 33(2/3), 61–83. doi: 10.1017/S0140525X0999152X

Henry, David B.; Deptula, Daneen P. & Schoeny, Michael E. (2012). Sexually transmitted infections and unintended pregnancy: A longitudinal analysis of risk transmission through friends and attitudes. *Social Development*, 21(1), 195–214. doi: 10.1111/j.1467-9507.2011.00626.x

Herd, Pamela; Higgins, Jenny; Sicinski, Kamil & Merkurieva, Irina. (2016). The implications of unintended pregnancies for mental health in later life. *American Journal of Public Health*, 106(3), 421–429. doi: 10.2105/AJPH.2015.302973

Herek, Gregory M. (2006). Legal recognition of same-sex relationships in the United States: A social science perspective. *American Psychologist*, 61(6), 607–621. doi: 10.1037/0003-066X.61.6.607

Herlofson, Katharina & Hagestad, Gunhild. (2012). Transformations in the role of grandparents across welfare states. In Sara Arber & Virpi Timonen (Eds.), *Contemporary grandparenting: Changing family relationships in global contexts* (pp. 27–49). Chicago, IL: Policy Press.

Herman, Khalisa N.; Paukner, Annika & Suomi, Stephen J. (2011). Gene × environment interactions and social play: Contributions from rhesus macaques. In Anthony D. Pellegrini (Ed.), *The Oxford handbook of the development of play* (pp. 58–69). New York, NY: Oxford University Press. doi: 10.1093/oxfordhb/9780195393002.013.0006

Herman-Giddens, Marcia E. (2013). The enigmatic pursuit of puberty in girls. *Pediatrics*, 132(6), 1125–1126. doi: 10.1542/peds.2013-3058

Herman-Giddens, Marcia E.; Steffes, Jennifer; Harris, Donna; Slora, Eric; Hussey, Michael; Dowshen, Steven A., . . . Reiter, Edward O. (2012). Secondary sexual characteristics in boys: Data from the pediatric research in office settings network. *Pediatrics*, 130(5), e1058–e1068. doi: 10.1542/peds.2011-3291

Herrera, Angelica P.; Snipes, Shedra A.; King, Denae W.; Torres-Vigil, Isabel; Goldberg, Daniel S. & Weinberg, Armin D. (2010). Disparate inclusion of older adults in clinical trials: Priorities and opportunities for policy and practice change. *American Journal of Public Health*, 100(S1), S105–S112. doi: 10.2105/ajph.2009.162982

Herring, Ann & Swedlund, Alan C. (Eds.). (2010). *Plagues and epidemics: Infected spaces past and present.* New York, NY: Berg.

Herrmann, Esther; Call, Josep; Hernàndez-Lloreda, María Victoria; Hare, Brian & Tomasello, Michael. (2007). Humans have evolved specialized skills of social cognition: The cultural intelligence hypothesis. *Science*, 317(5843), 1360–1366. doi: 10.1126/science.1146282

Herrmann, Julia; Schmidt, Isabelle; Kessels, Ursula & Preckel, Franzis. (2016). Big fish in big ponds: Contrast and assimilation effects on math and verbal self-concepts of students in within-school gifted tracks. *British Journal of Educational Psychology*, 86(2), 222–240. doi: 10.1111/bjep.12100

Herschensohn, Julia R. (2007). *Language development and age*. New York, NY: Cambridge University Press.

Hertzog, Christopher. (2010). Regarding methods for studying behavioral development: The contributions and influence of K. Warner Schaie. *Research in Human Development*, 7(1), 1–8. doi: 10.1080/15427600903578110

Hertzog, Christopher. (2011). Intelligence in adulthood. In Robert J. Sternberg & Scott Barry Kaufman (Eds.), *The Cambridge handbook of intelligence* (pp. 174–190). New York, NY: Cambridge University Press.

Herzog, Patricia Snell; Beadle, De Andre' T.; Harris, Daniel E.; Hood, Tiffany E. & Venugopal, Sanjana. (2016). Moral and cultural awareness in emerging adulthood: Preparing for multi-faith workplaces. *Religions*, 7(4). doi: 10.3390/rel7040040

Heslin, Kevin C.; Hamilton, Alison B.; Singzon, Trudy K.; Smith, James L.; Lois, Nancy & Anderson, Ruth. (2011). Alternative families in recovery: Fictive kin relationships among residents of sober living homes. *Qualitative Health Research*, 21(4), 477–488. doi: 10.1177/1049732310385826

Hess, Thomas M.; Hinson, Joey & Hodges, Elizabeth. (2009a). Moderators of and mechanisms underlying stereotype threat effects on older adults' memory performance. *Experimental Aging Research*, 35(2), 153–177. doi: 10.1080/03610730802716413

Hess, Thomas M.; Leclerc, Christina M.; Swaim, Elizabeth & Weatherbee, Sarah R. (2009b). Aging and everyday judgments: The impact of motivational and processing resource factors. *Psychology and Aging*, 24(3), 735–740. doi: 10.1037/a0016340

Hetherington, E. Mavis. (2006). The influence of conflict, marital problem solving and parenting on children's adjustment in nondivorced, divorced and remarried families. In Alison Clarke-Stewart & Judy Dunn (Eds.), *Families count: Effects on child and adolescent development* (pp. 203–237). New York, NY: Cambridge University Press.

Hewer, Mariko. (2014). Selling sweet nothings: Science shows food marketing's effects on children's minds—and appetites. *Observer*, 27(10).

Heyes, Cecilia. (2016). Who knows? Metacognitive social learning strategies. *Trends in Cognitive Sciences*, 20(3), 204–213. doi: 10.1016/j.tics.2015.12.007

Hicks, Joshua A.; Trent, Jason; Davis, William E. & King, Laura A. (2012). Positive affect, meaning in life, and future time perspective: An application of socioemotional selectivity theory. *Psychology and Aging*, 27(1), 181–189. doi: 10.1037/a0023965

Hicks, Meredith S.; McRee, Annie-Laurie & Eisenberg, Marla E. (2013). Teens talking with their partners about sex: The role of parent communication. *American Journal of Sexuality Education*, 8(1/2), 1–17. doi: 10.1080/15546128.2013.790219

Higgins, Matt. (2006, August 7). A series of flips creates some serious buzz. *New York Times*, p. D7.

Hill, Patrick L.; Burrow, Anthony L. & Sumner, Rachel. (2013). Addressing important questions in the field of adolescent purpose. *Child Development Perspectives*, 7(4), 232–236. doi: 10.1111/cdep.12048

Hill, Sarah E.; Prokosch, Marjorie L.; DelPriore, Danielle J.; Griskevicius, Vladas & Kramer, Andrew. (2016). Low childhood socioeconomic status promotes eating in the absence of energy need. *Psychological Science*, 27(3), 354–364. doi: 10.1177/0956797615621901

Hinnant, J. Benjamin; Nelson, Jackie A.; O'Brien, Marion; Keane, Susan P. & Calkins, Susan D. (2013). The interactive roles of parenting, emotion regulation and executive functioning in moral reasoning during middle childhood. *Cognition and Emotion*, 27(8), 1460–1468. doi: 10.1080/02699931.2013.789792

Hinshaw, Stephen P. & Arnold, L. Eugene. (2015). Attention-deficit hyperactivity disorder, multimodal treatment, and longitudinal outcome: evidence, paradox, and challenge. *Wiley Interdisciplinary Reviews: Cognitive Science*, 6(1), 39–52. doi: 10.1002/wcs.1324

Hipwell, Alison E.; Keenan, Kate; Loeber, Rolf & Battista, Deena. (2010). Early predictors of sexually intimate behaviors in an urban sample of young girls. *Developmental Psychology*, 46(2), 366–378. doi: 10.1037/a0018409

Hirvonen, Riikka; Aunola, Kaisa; Alatupa, Saija; Viljaranta, Jaana & Nurmi, Jari-Erik. (2013). The role of temperament in children's affective and behavioral responses in achievement situations. *Learning and Instruction*, 27, 21–30. doi: 10.1016/j.learninstruc.2013.02.005

Hively, Kimberly & El-Alayli, Amani. (2014). "You throw like a girl:" The effect of stereotype threat on women's athletic performance and gender stereotypes. *Psychology of Sport and Exercise*, 15(1), 48–55. doi: 10.1016/j.psychsport.2013.09.001

Ho, Emily S. (2010). Measuring hand function in the young child. *Journal of Hand Therapy*, 23(3), 323–328. doi: 10.1016/j.jht.2009.11.002

Hoare, Carol Hren. (2002). *Erikson on development in adulthood: New insights from the unpublished papers*. New York, NY: Oxford University Press.

Hochman, Oshrat & Lewin-Epstein, Noah. (2013). Determinants of early retirement preferences in Europe: The role of grandparenthood. *International Journal of Comparative Sociology*, 54(1), 29–47. doi: 10.1177/0020715213480977

Hoeve, Machteld; Dubas, Judith S.; Gerris, Jan R. M.; van der Laan, Peter H. & Smeenk, Wilma. (2011). Maternal and paternal parenting styles: Unique and combined links to adolescent and early adult delinquency. *Journal of Adolescence*, 34(5), 813–827. doi: 10.1016/j.adolescence.2011.02.004

Hofer, Claire; Eisenberg, Nancy; Spinrad, Tracy L.; Morris, Amanda S.; Gershoff, Elizabeth; Valiente, Carlos, . . . Eggum, Natalie D. (2013). Mother-adolescent conflict: Stability, change, and relations with externalizing and internalizing behavior problems. *Social Development*, 22(2), 259–279. doi: 10.1111/sode.12012

Hoff, Erika. (2013). Interpreting the early language trajectories of children from low-SES and language minority homes: Implications for closing achievement gaps. *Developmental Psychology*, 49(1), 4–14. doi: 10.1037/a0027238

Hoff, Erika; Core, Cynthia; Place, Silvia; Rumiche, Rosario; Señor, Melissa & Parra, Marisol. (2012). Dual language exposure and early bilingual development. *Journal of Child Language*, 39(1), 1–27. doi: 10.1017/S0305000910000759

Hoff, Erika; Rumiche, Rosario; Burridge, Andrea; Ribota, Krystal M. & Welsh, Stephanie N. (2014). Expressive vocabulary development in children from bilingual and monolingual homes: A longitudinal study from two to four years. *Early Childhood Research Quarterly*, 29(4), 433–444. doi: 10.1016/j.ecresq.2014.04.012

Hoffman, Jessica L.; Teale, William H. & Paciga, Kathleen A. (2014). Assessing vocabulary learning in early childhood. *Journal of Early Childhood Literacy*, 14(4), 459–481. doi: 10.1177/1468798413501184

Hoffnung, Michele & Williams, Michelle A. (2013). Balancing act: Career and family during college-educated women's 30s. *Sex Roles*, 68(5-6), 321–334. doi: 10.1007/s11199-012-0248-x

Hogan, Michael J.; Staff, Roger T.; Bunting, Brendan P.; Deary, Ian J. & Whalley, Lawrence J. (2012). Openness to experience and activity engagement facilitate the maintenance of verbal ability in older adults. *Psychology and Aging*, 27(4), 849–854. doi: 10.1037/a0029066

Höjer, Ingrid & Sjöblom, Yvonne. (2014). Voices of 65 young people leaving care in Sweden: "There is so much I need to know!". *Australian Social Work*, 67(1), 71–87. doi: 10.1080/0312407X.2013.863957

Holden, Constance. (2010). Myopia out of control. *Science*, 327(5961), 17. doi: 10.1126/science.327.5961.17-c

Holland, James D. & Klaczynski, Paul A. (2009). Intuitive risk taking during adolescence. *Prevention Researcher*, 16(2), 8–11.

Holland, John L. (1997). *Making vocational choices: A theory of vocational personalities and work environments* (3rd ed.). Odessa, FL: Psychological Assessment Resources.

Hollich, George J.; Hirsh-Pasek, Kathy; Golinkoff, Roberta M.; Brand, Rebecca J.; Brown, Ellie; Chung, He Len, . . . Rocroi, Camille. (2000). *Breaking the language barrier: An emergentist coalition model for the origins of word learning*. Malden, MA: Blackwell. doi: 10.1111/1540-5834.00090

Holmboe, K.; Nemoda, Z.; Fearon, R. M. P.; Sasvari-Szekely, M. & Johnson, M. H. (2011). Dopamine D4 receptor and serotonin transporter gene effects on the longitudinal development of infant temperament. *Genes, Brain and Behavior*, 10(5), 513–522. doi: 10.1111/j.1601-183X.2010.00669.x

Holmes, Christopher J.; Kim-Spoon, Jungmeen & Deater-Deckard, Kirby. (2016). Linking executive function and peer problems from early childhood through middle adolescence. *Journal of Abnormal Child Psychology*, 44(1), 31–42. doi: 10.1007/s10802-015-0044-5

Holmes, Tabitha R. & Nash, Alison. (2015). Rules of engagement: Grandmothers, daughters and the mothering of mothers. In Margueite Guzman Bouvard (Ed.), *Mothers of adult children* (pp. 153–164). Lanham, MA: Lexington Books.

Holt, Raymond. (2013). Design for the ages: Universal design as a rehabilitation strategy (Book Review). *Disability & Society*, 28(1), 142–144. doi: 10.1080/09687599.2012.739364

Holt-Lunstad, Julianne; Smith, Timothy B.; Baker, Mark; Harris, Tyler & Stephenson, David. (2015). Loneliness and social isolation as risk factors for mortality: A meta-analytic review. *Perspectives on Psychological Science*, 10(2), 227–237. doi: 10.1177/1745691614568352

Holtfreter, Kristy; Reisig, Michael D. & Turanovic, Jillian J. (2016). Self-rated poor health and loneliness in late adulthood: Testing the moderating role of familial ties. *Advances in Life Course Research*, 27, 61–68. doi: 10.1016/j.alcr.2015.11.006

Holzer, Jessica; Canavan, Maureen & Bradley, Elizabeth. (2014). County-level correlation between adult obesity rates and prevalence of dentists. *JADA*, 145(9), 932–939. doi: 10.14219/jada.2014.48

Hong, David S. & Reiss, Allan L. (2014). Cognitive and neurological aspects of sex chromosome aneuploidies. *The Lancet Neurology*, 13(3), 306–318. doi: 10.1016/S1474-4422(13)70302-8

Hong, Jun Sung & Garbarino, James. (2012). Risk and protective factors for homophobic bullying in schools: An application of the social–ecological framework. *Educational Psychology Review*, 24(2), 271–285. doi: 10.1007/s10648-012-9194-y

Hook, Jennifer L. (2012). Working on the weekend: Fathers' time with family in the United Kingdom. *Journal of Marriage and Family*, 74(4), 631–642. doi: 10.1111/j.1741-3737.2012.00986.x

Hooley, Jill M. (2004). Do psychiatric patients do better clinically if they live with certain kinds of families? *Current Directions in Psychological Science*, 13(5), 202–205. doi: 10.1111/j.0963-7214.2004.00308.x

Hootman, Jennifer M.; Helmick, Charles G. & Brady, Teresa J. (2012). A public health approach to addressing arthritis in older adults: The most common cause of disability. *American Journal of Public Health*, 102(3), 426–433. doi: 10.2105/AJPH.2011.300423

Hopkins, J. Roy. (2011). The enduring influence of Jean Piaget. *Observer*, 24(10).

Horn, John L. & Cattell, Raymond B. (1967). Age differences in fluid and crystallized intelligence. *Acta Psychologica*, 26, 107–129. doi: 10.1016/0001-6918(67)90011-X

Horton, Megan K.; Kahn, Linda G.; Perera, Frederica; Barr, Dana B. & Rauh, Virginia. (2012). Does the home environment and the sex of the child modify the adverse effects of prenatal exposure to chlorpyrifos on child working memory? *Neurotoxicology and Teratology*, 34(5), 534–541. doi: 10.1016/j.ntt.2012.07.004

Hostinar, Camelia E.; Johnson, Anna E. & Gunnar, Megan R. (2015). Parent support is less effective in buffering cortisol stress reactivity for adolescents compared to children.

Developmental Science, 18(2), 281–297. doi: 10.1111/desc.12195

Hougaard, Karin S. & Hansen, Åse M. (2007). Enhancement of developmental toxicity effects of chemicals by gestational stress: A review. *Neurotoxicology and Teratology*, 29(4), 425–445. doi: 10.1016/j.ntt.2007.02.003

Howard, Andrea L.; Galambos, Nancy L. & Krahn, Harvey J. (2010). Paths to success in young adulthood from mental health and life transitions in emerging adulthood. *International Journal of Behavioral Development*, 34(6), 538–546. doi: 10.1177/0165025410365803

Howard, Kimberly S. (2010). Paternal attachment, parenting beliefs and children's attachment. *Early Child Development and Care*, 180(1/2), 157–171. doi: 10.1080/03004430903415031

Howe, Tsu-Hsin; Sheu, Ching-Fan; Hsu, Yung-Wen; Wang, Tien-Ni & Wang, Lan-Wan. (2016). Predicting neurodevelopmental outcomes at preschool age for children with very low birth weight. *Research in Developmental Disabilities*, 48, 231–241. doi: 10.1016/j.ridd.2015.11.003

Howell, Diane M.; Wysocki, Karen & Steiner, Michael J. (2010). Toilet training. *Pediatrics in Review*, 31(6), 262–263. doi: 10.1542/pir.31-6-262

Hoyert, Donna L.; Kochanek, Kenneth D. & Murphy, Sherry L. (1999). *Deaths: Final data for 1997*. National Vital Statistics Reports 47(19). Hyattsville, MD: National Center for Health Statistics.

Hoyert, Donna L.; Kung, Hsiang-Ching & Smith, Betty L. (2005). *Deaths: Preliminary data for 2003*. National Vital Statistics Reports 53(15). Hyattsville, MD: National Center for Health Statistics.

Hoyert, Donna L. & Xu, Jiaquan. (2012). *Deaths: Preliminary data for 2011*. National Vital Statistics Reports 61(6). Hyattsville, MD: National Center for Health Statistics.

Hrdy, Sarah B. (2009). *Mothers and others: The evolutionary origins of mutual understanding*. Cambridge, MA: Harvard University Press.

Hsia, Yingfen & Maclennan, Karyn. (2009). Rise in psychotropic drug prescribing in children and adolescents during 1992–2001: A population-based study in the UK. *European Journal of Epidemiology*, 24(4), 211–216. doi: 10.1007/s10654-009-9321-3

Hsu, William C.; Araneta, Maria Rosario G.; Kanaya, Alka M.; Chiang, Jane L. & Fujimoto, Wilfred. (2015). BMI cut points to identify at-risk Asian Americans for type 2 diabetes screening. *Diabetes Care*, 38(1), 150–158. doi: 10.2337/dc14-2391

Huang, Chiungjung. (2010). Mean-level change in self-esteem from childhood through adulthood: Meta-analysis of longitudinal studies. *Review of General Psychology*, 14(3), 251–260. doi: 10.1037/a0020543

Huang, Yvonne J. (2013). Asthma microbiome studies and the potential for new therapeutic strategies. *Current Allergy and Asthma Reports*, 13(5), 453–461. doi: 10.1007/s11882-013-0355-y

Huang, Z. Josh & Luo, Liqun. (2015). It takes the world to understand the brain. *Science*, 350(6256), 42–44. doi: 10.1126/science.aad4120

Hubbard, Raymond & Lindsay, R. Murray. (2008). Why p values are not a useful measure of evidence in statistical significance testing. *Theory Psychology*, 18(1), 69–88. doi: 10.1177/0959354307086923

Hugdahl, Kenneth & Westerhausen, René (Eds.). (2010). *The two halves of the brain: Information processing in the cerebral hemispheres*. Cambridge, MA: MIT Press.

Hughes, Claire & Devine, Rory T. (2015). Individual differences in theory of mind: A social perspective. In Richard M. Lerner (Ed.), *Handbook of child psychology and developmental science* (7th ed., Vol. 3). New York, NY: Wiley.

Hughes, Julie M. & Bigler, Rebecca S. (2011). Predictors of African American and European American adolescents' endorsement of race-conscious social policies. *Developmental Psychology*, 47(2), 479–492. doi: 10.1037/a0021309

Hughes, Jan N. & Im, Myung H. (2016). Teacher–student relationship and peer disliking and liking across grades 1–4. *Child Development*, 87(2), 593–611. doi: 10.1111/cdev.12477

Hughes, Matthew L.; Geraci, Lisa & De Forrest, Ross L. (2013). Aging 5 years in 5 minutes: The effect of taking a memory test on older adults' subjective age. *Psychological Science*, 24(12), 2481–2488. doi: 10.1177/0956797613494853

Hughey, Matthew W. & Parks, Gregory. (2014). *The wrongs of the right: Language, race, and the Republican Party in the age of Obama*. New York, NY: New York University Press.

Huh, Susanna Y.; Rifas-Shiman, Sheryl L.; Zera, Chloe A.; Edwards, Janet W. Rich; Oken, Emily; Weiss, Scott T. & Gillman, Matthew W. (2012). Delivery by caesarean section and risk of obesity in preschool age children: A prospective cohort study. *Archives of the Diseases of Childhood*, 97(7), 610–616. doi: 10.1136/archdischild-2011-301141

Hunt, Earl B. (2011a). *Human intelligence*. New York, NY: Cambridge University Press.

Hunt, Earl B. (2011b). Where are we? Where are we going? Reflections on the current and future state of research on intelligence. In Robert J. Sternberg & Scott Barry Kaufman (Eds.), *The Cambridge handbook of intelligence*. New York, NY: Cambridge University Press.

Hunt, Earl B. (2012). What makes nations intelligent? *Perspectives on Psychological Science*, 7(3), 284–306. doi: 10.1177/1745691612442905

Hunter, Jonathan & Maunder, Robert (Eds.). (2016). *Improving patient treatment with attachment theory: A guide for primary care practitioners and specialists*. New York, NY: Springer. doi: 10.1007/978-3-319-23300-0

Hunter, Myra Sally. (2012). Long-term impacts of early and surgical menopause. *Menopause*, 19(3), 253–254. doi: 10.1097/gme.0b013e31823e9b2e

Hussain, Amjad; Case, Keith; Marshall, Russell & Summerskill, Steve J. (2013). An inclusive design method for addressing human variability and work performance issues. *International Journal of Engineering and Technology Innovation*, 3(3), 144–155.

Huston, Aletha C.; Bobbitt, Kaeley C. & Bentley, Alison. (2015). Time spent in child care: How and why does it affect social development? *Developmental Psychology*, 51(5), 621–634. doi: 10.1037/a0038951

Hutchinson, Esther A.; De Luca, Cinzia R.; Doyle, Lex W.; Roberts, Gehan & Anderson, Peter J. (2013). School-age outcomes of extremely preterm or extremely low birth weight children. *Pediatrics*, 131(4), e1053–e1061. doi: 10.1542/peds.2012-2311

Huver, Rose M. E.; Otten, Roy; de Vries, Hein & Engels, Rutger C. M. E. (2010). Personality and parenting style in parents of adolescents. *Journal of Adolescence*, 33(3), 395–402. doi: 10.1016/j.adolescence.2009.07.012

Huynh, Jimmy L. & Casaccia, Patrizia. (2013). Epigenetic mechanisms in multiple sclerosis: Implications for pathogenesis and treatment. *The Lancet Neurology*, 12(2), 195–206. doi: 10.1016/S1474-4422(12)70309-5

Hvistendahl, Mara. (2014). While emerging economies boom, equality goes bust. *Science*, 344(6186), 832–835. doi: 10.1126/science.344.6186.832

Hyde, Janet S. (2007). New directions in the study of gender similarities and differences. *Current Directions in Psychological Science*, 16(5), 259–263. doi: 10.1111/j.1467-8721.2007.00516.x

Hyde, Janet S.; Lindberg, Sara M.; Linn, Marcia C.; Ellis, Amy B. & Williams, Caroline C. (2008). Gender similarities characterize math performance. *Science*, 321(5888), 494–495. doi: 10.1126/science.1160364

Hyslop, Anne. (2014). *The case against exit exams. New American Education Policy Brief.* Washington DC: New America Education Policy Program.

Idler, Ellen. (2006). Religion and aging. In Robert H. Binstock & Linda K. George (Eds.), *Handbook of aging and the social sciences* (6th ed., pp. 277–300). Amsterdam, The Netherlands: Elsevier.

Iida, Hiroko & Rozier, R. Gary. (2013). Mother-perceived social capital and children's oral health and use of dental care in the United States. *American Journal of Public Health*, 103(3), 480–487. doi: 10.2105/AJPH.2012.300845

Ikeda, Martin J. (2012). Policy and practice considerations for response to intervention: Reflections and commentary. *Journal of Learning Disabilities*, 45(3), 274–277. doi: 10.1177/0022219412442170

ILO. (2011). Database of conditions of work and employment laws. Retrieved, from International Labour Organization http://www.ilo.org/dyn/travail/travmain.home

Imdad, Aamer; Sadiq, Kamran & Bhutta, Zulfiqar A. (2011). Evidence-based prevention of childhood malnutrition. *Current Opinion in Clinical Nutrition & Metabolic Care*, 14(3), 276–285. doi: 10.1097/MCO.0b013e328345364a

Inan, Hatice Z.; Trundle, Kathy C. & Kantor, Rebecca. (2010). Understanding natural sciences education in a Reggio Emilia-inspired preschool. *Journal of Research in Science Teaching*, 47(10), 1186–1208. doi: 10.1002/tea.20375

Inceoglu, Ilke; Segers, Jesse & Bartram, Dave. (2012). Age-related differences in work motivation. *Journal of Occupational and Organizational Psychology*, 75(2), 300–329. doi: 10.1111/j.2044-8325.2011.02035.x

Inhelder, Bärbel & Piaget, Jean. (1958). *The growth of logical thinking from childhood to adolescence: An essay on the construction of formal operational structures.* New York, NY: Basic Books.

Inhelder, Bärbel & Piaget, Jean. (1964). *The early growth of logic in the child: Classification and seriation.* New York, NY: Harper & Row.

Inhelder, Bärbel & Piaget, Jean. (2013a). *The early growth of logic in the child: Classification and seriation.* New York, NY: Routledge.

Inhelder, Bärbel & Piaget, Jean. (2013b). *The growth of logical thinking from childhood to adolescence: An essay on the construction of formal operational structures.* New York, NY: Routledge.

Insel, Thomas R. (2014). Mental disorders in childhood: Shifting the focus from behavioral symptoms to neurodevelopmental trajectories. *JAMA*, 311(17), 1727–1728. doi: 10.1001/jama.2014.1193

Insurance Institute for Highway Safety. (2012). Fatality facts: Teenagers 2010. http://www.iihs.org/iihs/topics/t/teenagers/fatalityfacts/teenagers/2010

Insurance Institute for Highway Safety. (2013a). Older drivers. http://www.iihs.org/iihs/topics/t/older-drivers/fatalityfacts/older-people

Insurance Institute for Highway Safety. (2013b). Teenages: Driving carries extra risks for them. http://www.iihs.org/iihs/topics/t/teenagers/fatalityfacts/teenagers/2013

Insurance Institute for Highway Safety. (2016, February). Fatality facts: Pedestrians 2014. http://www.iihs.org/iihs/topics/t/pedestrians-and-bicyclists/fatalityfacts/pedestrians

Inzlicht, Michael & Schmader, Toni. (2012). *Stereotype threat: Theory, process, and application.* New York, NY: Oxford University Press.

Irwin, Scott; Galvez, Roberto; Weiler, Ivan Jeanne; Beckel-Mitchener, Andrea & Greenough, William. (2002). Brain structure and the functions of FMR1 protein. In Randi Jenssen Hagerman & Paul J. Hagerman (Eds.), *Fragile X syndrome: Diagnosis, treatment, and research* (3rd ed., pp. 191–205). Baltimore, MD: Johns Hopkins University Press.

Ishii, Nozomi; Kono, Yumi; Yonemoto, Naohiro; Kusuda, Satoshi & Fujimura, Masanori. (2013). Outcomes of infants born at 22 and 23 weeks' gestation. *Pediatrics*, 132(1), 62–71. doi: 10.1542/peds.2012-2857

Ivcevic, Zorana & Brackett, Marc. (2014). Predicting school success: Comparing conscientiousness, grit, and emotion regulation ability. *Journal of Research in Personality*, 52, 29–36. doi: 10.1016/j.jrp.2014.06.005

Iyengar, Sheena S. & Lepper, Mark R. (2000). When choice is demotivating: Can one desire too much of a good thing? *Journal of Personality and Social Psychology*, 79(6), 995–1006. doi: 10.1037//0022-3514.79.6.995

Jack, Clifford R.; Lowe, Val J.; Weigand, Stephen D.; Wiste, Heather J.; Senjem, Matthew L.; Knopman, David S., . . . Petersen, Ronald C. (2009). Serial PIB and MRI in normal, mild cognitive impairment and Alzheimer's disease: Implications for sequence of pathological events in Alzheimer's disease. *Brain*, 132(5), 1355–1365. doi: 10.1093/brain/awp062

Jackson, Jeffrey B.; Miller, Richard B.; Oka, Megan & Henry, Ryan G. (2014). Gender differences in marital satisfaction: A meta-analysis. *Journal of Marriage and Family*, 76(1), 105–129. doi: 10.1111/jomf.12077

Jackson, Sandra L. & Cunningham, Solveig A. (2015). Social competence and obesity in elementary school. *American Journal of Public Health*, 105(1), 153–158. doi: 10.2105/AJPH.2014.302208

Jackson, Shelly L. & Hafemeister, Thomas L. (2011). Risk factors associated with elder abuse: The importance of differentiating by type of elder maltreatment. *Violence and Victims*, 26(6), 738–757. doi: 10.1891/0886-6708.26.6.738

Jaffe, Arthur C. (2011). Failure to thrive: Current clinical concepts. *Pediatrics in Review*, 32(3), 100–108. doi: 10.1542/pir.32-3-100

Jaffe, Eric. (2004). Mickey Mantle's greatest error: Yankee star's false belief may have cost him years. *Observer*, 17(9), 37.

Jambon, Marc & Smetana, Judith G. (2014). Moral complexity in middle childhood: Children's evaluations of necessary harm. *Developmental Psychology*, 50(1), 22–33. doi: 10.1037/a0032992

James, Jenée; Ellis, Bruce J.; Schlomer, Gabriel L. & Garber, Judy. (2012). Sex-specific pathways to early puberty, sexual debut, and sexual risk taking: Tests of an integrated evolutionary–developmental model. *Developmental Psychology*, 48(3), 687–702. doi: 10.1037/a0026427

James, Will. (2012, May 25). Report faults doctors: Long Island grand jury blames physicians, pharmacists for epidemic of abuse. *Wall Street Journal*, p. A15.

Janse, Benjamin; Huijsman, Robbert; de Kuyper, Ruben Dennis Maurice & Fabbricotti, Isabelle Natalina. (2014). The effects of an integrated care intervention for the frail elderly on informal caregivers: A quasi-experimental study. *BMC Geriatrics*, 14(1). doi: 10.1186/1471-2318-14-58

Jarcho, Johanna M.; Fox, Nathan A.; Pine, Daniel S.; Etkin, Amit; Leibenluft, Ellen; Shechner, Tomer & Ernst, Monique. (2013). The neural correlates of emotion-based cognitive control in adults with early childhood behavioral inhibition. *Biological Psychology*, 92(2), 306–314. doi: 10.1016/j.biopsycho.2012.09.008

Jastrzembski, Tiffany S.; Charness, Neil & Vasyukova, Catherine. (2006). Expertise and age effects on knowledge activation in chess. *Psychology and Aging*, 21(2), 401–405. doi: 10.1037/0882-7974.21.2.401

Jednoróg, Katarzyna; Altarelli, Irene; Monzalvo, Karla; Fluss, Joel; Dubois, Jessica; Billard, Catherine, . . . Ramus, Franck. (2012). The influence of socioeconomic status on children's brain structure. *PLoS ONE*, 7(8), e42486. doi: 10.1371/journal.pone.0042486

Jensen, Alexander C.; Whiteman, Shawn D.; Fingerman, Karen L. & Birditt, Kira S. (2013). "Life still isn't fair": Parental differential treatment of young adult siblings. *Journal of Marriage and Family*, 75(2), 438–452. doi: 10.1111/jomf.12002

Jensen, Lene Arnett & McKenzie, Jessica. (2016). The moral reasoning of U.S. Evangelical and mainline protestant children, adolescents, and adults: A cultural–developmental study. *Child Development*, 87(2), 446–464. doi: 10.1111/cdev.12465

Jessop, Donna C. & Wade, Jennifer. (2008). Fear appeals and binge drinking: A terror management theory perspective. *British Journal of Health Psychology*, 13(4), 773–788. doi: 10.1348/135910707X272790

Jha, Prabhat; Ramasundarahettige, Chinthanie; Landsman, Victoria; Rostron, Brian; Thun, Michael; Anderson, Robert N., . . . Peto, Richard. (2013). 21st-Century hazards of smoking and benefits of cessation in the United States. *New England Journal of Medicine*, 368, 341–350. doi: 10.1056/NEJMsa1211128

Ji, Cheng Ye; Chen, Tian Jiao & Working Group on Obesity in China (WGOC). (2013). Empirical changes in the prevalence of overweight and obesity among Chinese students from 1985 to 2010 and corresponding preventive strategies. *Biomedical and Environmental Sciences*, 26(1), 1–12. doi: 10.3967/0895-3988.2013.01.001

Jia, Jianping; Wang, Fen; Wei, Cuibai; Zhou, Aihong; Jia, Xiangfei; Li, Fang, . . . Dong, Xiumin. (2014). The prevalence of dementia in urban and rural areas of China. *Alzheimers and Dementia*, 10(1), 1–9. doi: 10.1016/j.jalz.2013.01.012

Jimerson, Shane R.; Burns, Matthew K. & VanDerHeyden, Amanda M. (Eds.). (2016). *Handbook of response to intervention: The science and practice of multi-tiered systems of support*. New York, NY: Springer. doi: 10.1007/978-1-4899-7568-3

Johannesen, Mark & LoGiudice, Dina. (2013). Elder abuse: A systematic review of risk factors in community-dwelling elders. *Age and Ageing*, 42(3), 292–298. doi: 10.1093/ageing/afs195

Johnson, Chris A. & Wilkinson, Mark E. (2010). Vision and driving: The United States. *Journal of Neuro-Ophthalmology*, 30(2), 170–176. doi: 10.1097/WNO.0b013e3181df30d4

Johnson, Jonni L.; McWilliams, Kelly; Goodman, Gail S.; Shelley, Alexandra E. & Piper, Brianna. (2016). Basic principles of interviewing the child eyewitness. In William T. O'Donohue & Matthew Fanetti (Eds.), *Forensic interviews regarding child sexual abuse* (pp. 179–195). New York, NY: Springer. doi: 10.1007/978-3-319-21097-1_10

Johnson, Kimberly J. & Mutchler, Jan E. (2014). The emergence of a positive gerontology: From disengagement to social involvement. *The Gerontologist*, 54(1), 93–100. doi: 10.1093/geront/gnt099

Johnson, Kimberly S.; Kuchibhatla, Maragatha & Tulsky, James A. (2011). Racial differences in location before hospice enrollment and association with hospice length of stay. *Journal*

of the American Geriatrics Society, 59(4), 732–737. doi: 10.1111/j.1532-5415.2011.03326.x

Johnson, Matthew D. (2012). Healthy marriage initiatives: On the need for empiricism in policy implementation. *American Psychologist*, 67(4), 296–308. doi: 10.1037/a0027743

Johnson, Mark H. & de Haan, Michelle. (2015). *Developmental cognitive neuroscience: An introduction* (4th ed.). Hoboken, NJ: Wiley.

Johnson, Mark H. & Fearon, R. M. Pasco. (2011). Commentary: Disengaging the infant mind: Genetic dissociation of attention and cognitive skills in infants–reflections on Leppänen et al. (2011). *Journal of Child Psychology and Psychiatry*, 52(11), 1153–1154. doi: 10.1111/j.1469-7610.2011.02433.x

Johnson, Michael P. (2011). Gender and types of intimate partner violence: A response to an anti-feminist literature review. *Aggression and Violent Behavior*, 16(4), 289–296. doi: 10.1016/j.avb.2011.04.006

Johnson, Michael P. & Ferraro, Kathleen J. (2000). Research on domestic violence in the 1990s: Making distinctions. *Journal of Marriage and Family*, 62(4), 948–963. doi: 10.1111/j.1741-3737.2000.00948.x

Johnson, Michael P.; Leone, Janel M. & Xu, Yili. (2014). Intimate terrorism and situational couple violence in general surveys: Ex-spouses required. *Violence Against Women*, 20(2), 186–207. doi: 10.1177/1077801214521324

Johnson, Susan C.; Dweck, Carol S.; Chen, Frances S.; Stern, Hilarie L.; Ok, Su-Jeong & Barth, Maria. (2010). At the intersection of social and cognitive development: Internal working models of attachment at infancy. *Cognitive Science*, 34(5), 807–825. doi: 10.1111/j.1551-6709.2010.01112.x

Johnson, Teddi D. (2011). Report calls for examination of chemical safety: National coalition notes difficulty determining exposures. *The Nation's Health*, 41(6), 9.

Johnson, Wendy; McGue, Matt & Deary, Ian J. (2014). Normative cognitive aging. In Deborah Finkel & Chandra A. Reynolds (Eds.), *Behavior genetics of cognition across the lifespan: Advances in behavior genetics* (Vol. 1, pp. 135–167). New York, NY: Springer. doi: 10.1007/978-1-4614-7447-0_5

Johnston, Lloyd D.; O'Malley, Patrick M.; Bachman, Jerald G. & Schulenberg, John E. (2011). *Monitoring the future, national survey results on drug use, 1975–2010, Volume I: Secondary school students*. Ann Arbor: Institute for Social Research, The University of Michigan.

Johnston, Lloyd D.; O'Malley, Patrick M.; Bachman, Jerald G. & Schulenberg, John E. (2012). *Monitoring the future, national survey results on drug use, 1975–2011, Volume I: Secondary school students*. Ann Arbor, MI: Institute for Social Research, The University of Michigan.

Johnston, Lloyd D.; O'Malley, Patrick M.; Bachman, Jerald G.; Schulenberg, John E. & Miech, Richard A. (2014). *Monitoring the future, national survey results on drug use, 1975–2013: Volume I, Secondary school students*. Ann Arbor, MI: Institute for Social Research, The University of Michigan.

Jokela, Markus. (2012). Birth-cohort effects in the association between personality and fertility. *Psychological Science*, 23(8), 835–841. doi: 10.1177/0956797612439067

Jonas, Eva; Sullivan, Daniel & Greenberg, Jeff. (2013). Generosity, greed, norms, and death–Differential effects of mortality salience on charitable behavior. *Journal of Economic Psychology*, 35, 47–57. doi: 10.1016/j.joep.2012.12.005

Jones, Andrea M. & Morris, Tracy L. (2012). Psychological adjustment of children in foster care: Review and implications for best practice. *Journal of Public Child Welfare*, 6(2), 129–148. doi: 10.1080/15548732.2011.617272

Jones, Daniel. (2006, February 12). You're not sick, you're just in love. *New York Times*, pp. H1, H13.

Jones, Jeffrey M. (2015, October 21). *In U.S., 58% back legal marijuana use*. Washington, DC: Gallup.

Jones, Mary C. (1965). Psychological correlates of somatic development. *Child Development*, 36(4), 899–911. doi: 10.2307/1126932

Jong, Jyh-Tsorng; Kao, Tsair; Lee, Liang-Yi; Huang, Hung-Hsuan; Lo, Po-Tsung & Wang, Hui-Chung. (2010). Can temperament be understood at birth? The relationship between neonatal pain cry and their temperament: A preliminary study. *Infant Behavior and Development*, 33(3), 266–272. doi: 10.1016/j.infbeh.2010.02.001

Jonsson, Maria; Cnattingius, Sven & Wikström, Anna-Karin. (2013). Elective induction of labor and the risk of cesarean section in low-risk parous women: A cohort study. *Acta Obstetricia et Gynecologica Scandinavica*, 92(2), 198–203. doi: 10.1111/aogs.12043

Jopp, Daniela & Rott, Christoph. (2006). Adaptation in very old age: Exploring the role of resources, beliefs, and attitudes for centenarians' happiness. *Psychology and Aging*, 21(2), 266–280. doi: 10.1037/0882-7974.21.2.266

Jordet, Geir; Hartman, Esther & Vuijk, Pieter J. (2012). Team history and choking under pressure in major soccer penalty shootouts. *British Journal of Psychology*, 103(2), 268–283. doi: 10.1111/j.2044-8295.2011.02071.x

Jorgenson, Alicia Grattan; Hsiao, Ray Chih-Jui & Yen, Cheng-Fang. (2016). Internet addiction and other behavioral addictions. *Child & Adolescent Psychiatric Clinics*, 25(3), 509–520. doi: 10.1016/j.chc.2016.03.004

Jose, Anita; Daniel O'Leary, K. & Moyer, Anne. (2010). Does premarital cohabitation predict subsequent marital stability and marital quality? A meta-analysis. *Journal of Marriage and Family*, 72(1), 105–116. doi: 10.1111/j.1741-3737.2009.00686.x

Joseph, Michelle A.; O'Connor, Thomas G.; Briskman, Jacqueline A.; Maughan, Barbara & Scott, Stephen. (2014). The formation of secure new attachments by children who were maltreated: An observational study of adolescents in foster care. *Development and Psychopathology*, 26(1), 67–80. doi: 10.1017/S0954579413000540

Judd, Fiona K.; Hickey, Martha & Bryant, Christina. (2012). Depression and midlife: Are we overpathologising the menopause? *Journal of Affective Disorders*, 136(3), 199–211. doi: 10.1016/j.jad.2010.12.010

Julian, Megan M. (2013). Age at adoption from institutional care as a window into the lasting effects of early experiences. *Clinical Child and Family Psychology Review, 16*(2), 101–145. doi: 10.1007 /s10567-013-0130-6

Jung, Rex E. & Ryman, Sephira G. (2013). Imaging creativity. In Kyung Hee Kim et al. (Eds.), *Creatively gifted students are not like other gifted students: Research, theory, and practice* (pp. 69–87). Rotterdam, The Netherlands: SensePublishers. doi: 10.1007/978-94-6209-149-8_6

Juonala, Markus; Magnussen, Costan G.; Berenson, Gerald S.; Venn, Alison; Burns, Trudy L.; Sabin, Matthew A., . . . Raitakari, Olli T. (2011). Childhood adiposity, adult adiposity, and cardiovascular risk factors. *New England Journal of Medicine, 365*(20), 1876–1885. doi: 10.1056 /NEJMoa1010112

Juujärvi, Soile. (2005). Care and justice in real-life moral reasoning. *Journal of Adult Development, 12*(4), 199–210. doi: 10.1007/s10804-005-7088-7

Juvonen, Jaana & Graham, Sandra. (2014). Bullying in schools: The power of bullies and the plight of victims. *Annual Review of Psychology, 65*, 159–185. doi: 10.1146/annurev -psych-010213-115030

Jyrkkä, Johanna; Mursu, Jaakko; Enlund, Hannes & Lönnroos, Eija. (2012). Polypharmacy and nutritional status in elderly people. *Current Opinion in Clinical Nutrition & Metabolic Care, 15*(1), 1–6. doi: 10.1097 /MCO.0b013e32834d155a

Kachel, A. Friederike; Premo, Luke S. & Hublin, Jean-Jacques. (2011). Modeling the effects of weaning age on length of female reproductive period: Implications for the evolution of human life history. *American Journal of Human Biology, 23*(4), 479–487. doi: 10.1002/ajhb.21157

Kahana, Eva; Bhatta, Tirth; Lovegreen, Loren D.; Kahana, Boaz & Midlarsky, Elizabeth. (2013). Altruism, helping, and volunteering: Pathways to well-being in late life. *Journal of Aging and Health, 25*(1), 159–187. doi: 10.1177/0898264312469665

Kahneman, Daniel. (2011). *Thinking, fast and slow*. New York, NY: Farrar, Straus and Giroux.

Kahneman, Daniel; Krueger, Alan B.; Schkade, David; Schwarz, Norbert & Stone, Arthur. (2004). Toward national well-being accounts. *The American Economic Review, 94*(2), 429–434.

Kail, Robert V. (2013). Influences of credibility of testimony and strength of statistical evidence on children's and adolescents' reasoning. *Journal of Experimental Child Psychology, 116*(3), 747–754. doi: 10.1016/j.jecp.2013.04.004

Kaiser, Jocelyn. (2014a). Gearing up for a closer look at the human placenta. *Science, 344*(6188), 1073. doi: 10.1126/science.344.6188.1073

Kaiser, Jocelyn. (2014b). Ambitious children's study meets disappointing end. *Science, 346*(6216), 1441. doi: 10.1126/science.346.6216.1441

Kalil, Ariel; Dunifon, Rachel; Crosby, Danielle & Su, Jessica Houston. (2014a). Work hours, schedules, and insufficient sleep among mothers and their young children. *Journal of Marriage and Family, 76*(5), 891–904. doi: 10.1111/jomf.12142

Kalil, Ariel; Ryan, Rebecca & Chor, Elise. (2014b). Time investments in children across family structures. *The ANNALS of the American Academy of Political and Social Science, 654*(1), 50–168. doi: 10.1177/0002716214528276

Kalliala, Marjatta. (2006). *Play culture in a changing world*. Maidenhead, UK: Open University Press.

Kallio, Eeva. (2011). Integrative thinking is the key: An evaluation of current research into the development of adult thinking. *Theory Psychology, 21*(6), 785–801. doi: 10.1177/0959354310388344

Kalmijn, Matthijs. (2010). Country differences in the effects of divorce on well-being: The role of norms, support, and selectivity. *European Sociological Review, 26*(4), 475–490. doi: 10.1093 /esr/jcp035

Kalokhe, Ameeta; del Rio, Carlos; Dunkle, Kristin; Stephenson, Rob; Metheny, Nicholas; Paranjape, Anuradha & Sahay, Seema. (2016). Domestic violence against women in India: A systematic review of a decade of quantitative studies. *Global Public Health*, (In Press). doi: 10.1080/17441692.2015.1119293

Kaltiala-Heino, Riittakerttu; Fröjd, Sari & Marttunen, Mauri. (2015). Depression, conduct disorder, smoking and alcohol use as predictors of sexual activity in middle adolescence: a longitudinal study. *Health Psychology and Behavioral Medicine, 3*(1), 25–39. doi: 10.1080/21642850.2014.996887

Kan, Man Yee; Sullivan, Oriel & Gershuny, Jonathan. (2011). Gender convergence in domestic work: Discerning the effects of interactional and institutional barriers from large-scale data. *Sociology, 45*(2), 234–251. doi: 10.1177/0038038510394014

Kandel, Denise B. (Ed.). (2002). *Stages and pathways of drug involvement: Examining the gateway hypothesis*. New York, NY: Cambridge University Press.

Kandler, Christian. (2012). Nature and nurture in personality development: The case of neuroticism and extraversion. *Current Directions in Psychological Science, 21*(5), 290–296. doi: 10.1177/0963721412452557

Kang, Hye-Kyung. (2014). Influence of culture and community perceptions on birth and perinatal care of immigrant women: Doulas' perspective. *The Journal of Perinatal Education, 23*(1), 25–32. doi: 10.1891/1058-1243.23.1.25

Kanis, John A.; McCloskey, Eugene V.; Johansson, Helena; Cooper, Cyrus; Rizzoli, Rene & Reginster, Jean-Yves. (2013). European guidance for the diagnosis and management of osteoporosis in postmenopausal women. *Osteoporosis International, 24*(1), 23–57. doi: 10.1007/s00198- 012-2074-y

Kann, Laura; McManus, Tim; Harris, William A.; Shanklin, Shari L.; Flint, Katherine H.; Hawkins, Joseph, . . . Zaza, Stephanie. (2016, June 10). *Youth risk behavior surveillance—United States, 2015. Morbidity and Mortality Weekly Report 65*(6). Atlanta, GA: U.S. Department of Health and Human Services, Centers for Disease Control and Prevention.

Kanner, Leo. (1943). Autistic disturbances of affective contact. *Nervous Child, 2*, 217–250.

Kapp, Steven K.; Gillespie-Lynch, Kristen; Sherman, Lauren E. & Hutman, Ted. (2013). Deficit, difference, or both? Autism and neurodiversity. *Developmental Psychology, 49*(1), 59–71. doi: 10.1037/a0028353

Karama, Sherif; Ad-Dab'bagh, Yasser; Haier, Richard J.; Deary, Ian J.; Lyttelton, Oliver C.; Lepage, Claude & Evans, Alan C. (2009). Positive association between cognitive ability and cortical thickness in a representative US sample of healthy 6 to 18-year-olds. *Intelligence, 37*(2), 145–155. doi: 10.1016 /j.intell.2008.09.006

Karantzas, Gery C. & Gillath, Omri. (2017). Stress and wellbeing during chronic illness and partner death in later-life: The role of social support. *Current Opinion in Psychology, 13*, 75–80. doi: 10.1016/j.copsyc.2016.05.009

Karbach, Julia & Unger, Kerstin. (2014). Executive control training from middle childhood to adolescence. *Frontiers in Psychology, 5*(390). doi: 10.3389/fpsyg.2014.00390

Karevold, Evalill; Ystrom, Eivind; Coplan, Robert J.; Sanson, Ann V. & Mathiesen, Kristin S. (2012). A prospective longitudinal study of shyness from infancy to adolescence: Stability, age-related changes, and prediction of socio-emotional functioning. *Journal of Abnormal Child Psychology, 40*(7), 1167–1177. doi: 10.1007 /s10802-012-9635-6

Karl, Katherine & Peluchette, Joy. (2016). Breaking boundaries and leaving bad impressions: Toward understanding workplace encounters with helicopter parents. *Journal of Organizational Psychology, 16*(1), 93–105.

Karmiloff-Smith, Annette. (2010). A developmental perspective on modularity. In Britt Glatzeder et al. (Eds.), *Towards a theory of thinking* (pp. 179–187). Heidelberg, Germany: Springer. doi: 10.1007/978-3-642-03129-8_12

Kärnä, Antti; Voeten, Marinus; Little, Todd D.; Poskiparta, Elisa; Kaljonen, Anne & Salmivalli, Christina. (2011). A large-scale evaluation of the KiVa antibullying program: Grades 4–6. *Child Development, 82*(1), 311–330. doi: 10.1111/j.1467-8624.2010.01557.x

Kärtner, Joscha; Borke, Jörn; Maasmeier, Kathrin; Keller, Heidi & Kleis, Astrid. (2011). Sociocultural influences on the development of self-recognition and self-regulation in Costa Rican and Mexican toddlers. *Journal of Cognitive Education and Psychology, 10*(1), 96–112. doi: 10.1891/1945-8959.10.1.96

Kärtner, Joscha; Keller, Heidi & Yovsi, Relindis D. (2010). Mother–infant interaction during the first 3 months: The emergence of culture-specific contingency patterns. *Child Development, 81*(2), 540–554. doi: 10.1111/j.1467-8624.2009.01414.x

Kassebaum, Nicholas J.; Bertozzi-Villa, Amelia; Coggeshall, Megan S.; Shackelford, Katya A.; Steiner, Caitlyn; Heuton, Kyle R., . . . Lozano, Rafael. (2014). Global, regional, and national levels and causes of maternal mortality during 1990–2013: A systematic analysis for the Global Burden of Disease Study 2013. *The Lancet, 384*(9947), 980–1004. doi: 10.1016 /S0140 -6736(14)60696-6

Kastbom, Åsa A.; Sydsjö, Gunilla; Bladh, Marie; Priebe, Gisela & Svedin, Carl-Göran. (2015). Sexual debut before the age of 14 leads to poorer psychosocial health and risky behaviour in later life. *Acta Paediatrica, 104*(1), 91–100. doi: 10.1111/apa.12803

Kastenbaum, Robert J. (2012). *Death, society, and human experience* (11th ed.). Boston, MA: Pearson.

Katz, Jennifer & Schneider, Monica E. (2013). Casual hook up sex during the first year of college: Prospective associations with attitudes about sex and love relationships. *Archives of Sexual Behavior, 42*(8), 1451–1462. doi: 10.1007/s10508-013-0078-0

Katz, Kathy S.; Jarrett, Marian H.; El-Mohandes, Ayman A. E.; Schneider, Susan; McNeely-Johnson, Doris & Kiely, Michele. (2011). Effectiveness of a combined home visiting and group intervention for low income African American mothers: The Pride in Parenting program. *Maternal and Child Health Journal, 15*(Suppl. 1), 75–84. doi: 10.1007 /s10995-011-0858-x

Kauffman, Jeffery. (2013). Culture, socialization, and traumatic death. In David K. Meagher & David E. Balk (Eds.), *Handbook of thanatology: The essential body of knowledge for the study of death, dying, and bereavement* (2nd ed.). New York, NY: Routledge.

Kaufman, James C. & Sternberg, Robert J. (Eds.). (2006). *The international handbook of creativity.* New York, NY: Cambridge University Press.

Kaufman, Kenneth R. & Kaufman, Nathaniel D. (2006). And then the dog died. *Death Studies, 30*(1), 61–76. doi: 10.1080/07481180500348811

Kavanaugh, Robert D. (2011). Origins and consequences of social pretend play. In Anthony D. Pellegrini (Ed.), *The Oxford handbook of the development of play* (pp. 296–307). New York, NY: Oxford University Press. doi: 10.1093 /oxfordhb/9780195393002.013.0022

Keating, Nancy L.; Herrinton, Lisa J.; Zaslavsky, Alan M.; Liu, Liyan & Ayanian, John Z. (2006). Variations in hospice use among cancer patients. *Journal of the National Cancer Institute, 98*(15), 1053–1059. doi: 10.1093/jnci/djj298

Keil, Frank C. (2011). Science starts early. *Science, 331*(6020), 1022–1023. doi: 10.1126 /science.1195221

Kellehear, Allan. (2008). Dying as a social relationship: A sociological review of debates on the determination of death. *Social Science & Medicine, 66*(7), 1533–1544. doi: 10.1016/j.socscimed .2007.12.023

Keller, Heidi. (2014). Introduction: Understanding relationships. In Hiltrud Otto & Heidi Keller (Eds.), *Different faces of attachment: Cultural variations on a universal human need* (pp. 3–25). New York, NY: Cambridge University Press.

Keller, Heidi; Borke, Jörn; Chaudhary, Nandita; Lamm, Bettina & Kleis, Astrid. (2010). Continuity in parenting strategies: A cross-cultural comparison. *Journal of Cross-Cultural Psychology, 41*(3), 391–409. doi: 10.1177/0022022109359690

Keller, Heidi; Yovsi, Relindis; Borke, Joern; Kärtner, Joscha; Jensen, Henning & Papaligoura, Zaira. (2004). Developmental consequences of early parenting experiences: Self-recognition and self-regulation in three

cultural communities. *Child Development, 75*(6), 1745–1760. doi: 10.1111/j.1467-8624.2004.00814.x

Keller, Peggy S.; El-Sheikh, Mona; Granger, Douglas A. & Buckhalt, Joseph A. (2012). Interactions between salivary cortisol and alpha-amylase as predictors of children's cognitive functioning and academic performance. *Physiology & Behavior, 105*(4), 987–995. doi: 10.1016 /j.physbeh.2011.11.005

Kellman, Philip J. & Arterberry, Martha E. (2006). Infant visual perception. In William Damon & Richard M. Lerner (Eds.), *Handbook of child psychology* (6th ed., Vol. 2, pp. 109–160). Hoboken, NJ: Wiley.

Kelly, Daniel; Faucher, Luc & Machery, Edouard. (2010). Getting rid of racism: Assessing three proposals in light of psychological evidence. *Journal of Social Philosophy, 41*(3), 293–322. doi: 10.1111/j.1467-9833.2010.01495.x

Kelly, John R. (1993). *Activity and aging: Staying involved in later life.* Newbury Park, CA: Sage.

Kelvin, David J. & Farooqui, Amber. (2013). Extremely low vaccine effectiveness against influenza H3N2 in the elderly during the 2012/2013 flu season. *Journal of Infection in Developing Countries, 7*(3), 299–301. doi: 10.3855/jidc.3544

Kempe, Ruth S. & Kempe, C. Henry. (1978). *Child abuse.* Cambridge, MA: Harvard University Press.

Kemper, Susan. (2015). Language production in late life. In Annette Gerstenberg & Anja Voeste (Eds.), *Language development: The lifespan perspective* (pp. 59–75). Philadelphia, PA: John Benjamins Publishing Company.

Kempermann, Gerd. (2012). New neurons for 'survival of the fittest'. *Nature Reviews Neuroscience, 13*(10), 727–736. doi: 10.1038 /nrn3319

Kempermann, Gerd. (2016). Adult neurogenesis: An evolutionary perspective. *Cold Spring Harbor Perspectives in Biology,* (In Press). doi: 10.1101 /cshperspect.a018986

Kempermann, Gerd; Song, Hongjun & Gage, Fred H. (2015). Neurogenesis in the adult hippocampus. *Cold Spring Harbor Perspectives in Biology, 7,* a018812. doi: 10.1101/cshperspect. a018812

Kena, Grace; Aud, Susan; Johnson, Frank; Wang, Xiaolei; Zhang, Jijun; Rathbun, Amy, . . . Kristapovich, Paul. (2014, May). *The condition of education 2014.* Washington, DC: U.S. Department of Education, National Center for Education Statistics.

Kena, Grace; Musu-Gillette, Lauren; Robinson, Jennifer; Wang, Xiaolei; Rathbun, Amy; Zhang, Jijun, . . . Dunlop Velez, Erin. (2015). *The condition of education 2015.* Washington, DC: Department of Education, National Center for Education Statistics.

Kendall-Taylor, Nathaniel; Lindland, Eric; O'Neil, Moira & Stanley, Kate. (2014). Beyond prevalence: An explanatory approach to reframing child maltreatment in the United Kingdom. *Child Abuse & Neglect, 38*(5), 810–821. doi: 10.1016 /j.chiabu.2014.04.019

Kendler, Howard H. (2002). Unified knowledge: Fantasy or reality? *Contemporary Psychology: APA Review of Books, 47*(5), 501–503. doi: 10.1037/001200

Kennedy, Brian K. (2016). Advances in biological theories of aging. In Vern L. Bengtson & Richard Settersten (Eds.), *Handbook of theories of aging* (3rd ed., pp. 107–112). New York, NY: Springer Publishing Group.

Kenrick, Douglas T.; Griskevicius, Vladas; Neuberg, Steven L. & Schaller, Mark. (2010). Renovating the pyramid of needs: Contemporary extensions built upon ancient foundations. *Perspectives on Psychological Science, 5*(3), 292–314. doi: 10.1177/1745691610369469

Keown, Louise J. & Palmer, Melanie. (2014). Comparisons between paternal and maternal involvement with sons: Early to middle childhood. *Early Child Development and Care, 184*(1), 99–117. doi: 10.1080/03004430.2013.773510

Kerr, Margaret; Stattin, Håkan & Burk, William J. (2010). A reinterpretation of parental monitoring in longitudinal perspective. *Journal of Research on Adolescence, 20*(1), 39–64. doi: 10.1111/j.1532 -7795.2009.00623.x

Kesselring, Thomas & Müller, Ulrich. (2011). The concept of egocentrism in the context of Piaget's theory. *New Ideas in Psychology, 29*(3), 327–345. doi: 10.1016/j.newidea-psych.2010.03.008

Kessler, Ronald C.; Aguilar-Gaxiola, Sergio; Alonso, Jordi; Chatterji, Somnath; Lee, Sing; Ormel, Johan, . . . Wang, Philip S. (2009). The global burden of mental disorders: An update from the WHO World Mental Health (WMH) Surveys. *Epidemiologia e Psichiatria Sociale, 18*(1), 23–33. doi: 10.1017/S1121189X00001421

Kessler, Ronald C.; Avenevoli, Shelli; Costello, E. Jane; Georgiades, Katholiki; Green, Jennifer G.; Gruber, Michael J., . . . Merikangas, Kathleen R. (2012). Prevalence, persistence, and sociodemographic correlates of DSM-IV disorders in the National Comorbidity Survey Replication Adolescent Supplement. *Archives of General Psychiatry, 69*(4), 372–380. doi: 10.1001/archgenpsychiatry .2011.160

Kettl, Paul. (2010). One vote for death panels. *JAMA, 303*(13), 1234–1235. doi: 10.1001 /jama.2010.376

Keupp, Stefanie; Bancken, Christin; Schillmöller, Jelka; Rakoczy, Hannes & Behne, Tanya. (2016). Rational over-imitation: Preschoolers consider material costs and copy causally irrelevant actions selectively. *Cognition, 147*(3), 85–92. doi: 10.1016 /j.cognition.2015.11.007

Khafi, Tamar Y.; Yates, Tuppett M. & Luthar, Suniya S. (2014). Ethnic differences in the developmental significance of parentification. *Family Process, 53*(2), 267–287. doi: 10.1111/famp.12072

Khan, Shereen; Gagné, Monique; Yang, Leigh & Shapk, Jennifer. (2016). Exploring the relationship between adolescents' self-concept and their offline and online social worlds. *Computers in Human Behavior, 55*(Part B), 940–945. doi: 10.1016 /j.chb.2015.09.046

Kharazmi, Akram; Armanmehr, Vajihe; Moradi, Noorallah & Bagheri, Pezhman. (2015). Systematic review and meta-analysis of the lifetime prevalence of domestic violence against women in Iran. *Asian Women*, 31(4), 77–97. doi: 10.14431 /aw.2015.12.31.4.77

Kharsati, Naphisabet & Bhola, Poornima. (2014). Patterns of non-suicidal self-injurious behaviours among college students in India. *International Journal of Social Psychiatry*. doi: 10.1177/0020764014535755

Kiernan, Stephen P. (2010). The transformation of death in America. In Nan Bauer Maglin & Donna Marie Perry (Eds.), *Final acts: Death, dying, and the choices we make* (pp. 163–182). New Brunswick, NJ: Rutgers University Press.

Kiiski, Jouko; Määttä, Kaarina & Uusiautti, Satu. (2013). "For better and for worse, or until . . . ": On divorce and guilt. *Journal of Divorce & Remarriage*, 54(7), 519–536. doi: 10.1080/10502556.2013.828980

Kiley, Dan. (1983). *The Peter Pan syndrome: Men who have never grown up.* New York, NY: Dodd Mead.

Kilgore, Paul E.; Grabenstein, John D.; Salim, Abdulbaset M. & Rybak, Michael. (2015). Treatment of Ebola virus disease. *Pharmacotherapy*, 35(1), 43–53. doi: 10.1002/phar.1545

Killen, Melanie & Smetana, Judith G. (Eds.). (2014). *Handbook of moral development* (2nd ed.). New York, NY: Psychology Press.

Killgore, William D. S.; Vo, Alexander H.; Castro, Carl A. & Hoge, Charles W. (2006). Assessing risk propensity in American soldiers: Preliminary reliability and validity of the Evaluation of Risks (EVAR) scale-English version. *Military Medicine*, 171(3), 233–239.

Kim, Dong-Sik & Kim, Hyun-Sun. (2009). Body-image dissatisfaction as a predictor of suicidal ideation among Korean boys and girls in different stages of adolescence: A two-year longitudinal study. *The Journal of Adolescent Health*, 45(1), 47–54. doi: 10.1016/j.jadohealth.2008.11.017

Kim, Esther C. (2009). "Mama's family": Fictive kinship and undocumented immigrant restaurant workers. *Ethnography*, 10(4), 497–513. doi: 10.1177/1466138109347000

Kim, Hojin I. & Johnson, Scott P. (2013). Do young infants prefer an infant-directed face or a happy face? *International Journal of Behavioral Development*, 37(2), 125–130. doi: 10.1177/0165025413475972

Kim, Hyun Sik. (2011). Consequences of parental divorce for child development. *American Sociological Review*, 76(3), 487–511. doi: 10.1177/0003122411407748

Kim, Heejung S. & Sasaki, Joni Y. (2014). Cultural neuroscience: Biology of the mind in cultural contexts. *Annual Review of Psychology*, 65, 487–514. doi: 10.1146/annurev-psych-010213-115040

Kim, Joon Sik. (2011). Excessive crying: Behavioral and emotional regulation disorder in infancy. *Korean Journal of Pediatrics*, 54(6), 229–233. doi: 10.3345/kjp.2011.54.6.229

Kim, Kyungmin; Cheng, Yen-Pi; Zarit, Steven H. & Fingerman, Karen L. (2015). Relationships between adults and parents in Asia. In Sheung-Tak Cheng et al. (Eds.), *Successful Aging* (pp. 101–122). Dordrecht, Netherlands: Springer. doi: 10.1007/978-94-017-9331-5_7

Kim, Pilyoung; Strathearn, Lane & Swain, James E. (2016). The maternal brain and its plasticity in humans. *Hormones and Behavior*, 77, 113–123. doi: 10.1016/j.yhbeh.2015.08.001

Kim, Scott Y. H.; De Vries, Raymond G. & Peteet, John R. (2016). Euthanasia and assisted suicide of patients with psychiatric disorders in the Netherlands 2011 to 2014. *JAMA Psychiatry*, 73(4), 362–368. doi: 10.1001/jamapsychiatry.2015.2887

Kim-Spoon, Jungmeen; Longo, Gregory S. & McCullough, Michael E. (2012). Parent-adolescent relationship quality as a moderator for the influences of parents' religiousness on adolescents' religiousness and adjustment. *Journal of Youth and Adolescence*, 41(12), 1576–1587. doi: 10.1007/s10964-012-9796-1

Kimmel, Michael S. (2008). *Guyland: The perilous world where boys become men.* New York, NY: HarperCollins.

King, Bruce M. (2013). The modern obesity epidemic, ancestral hunter-gatherers, and the sensory/reward control of food intake. *American Psychologist*, 68(2), 88–96. doi: 10.1037/a0030684

King, Pamela E. & Roeser, Robert W. (2009). Religion and spirituality in adolescent development. In Richard M. Lerner & Laurence Steinberg (Eds.), *Handbook of adolescent psychology* (3rd ed., Vol. 1, pp. 435–478). Hoboken, NJ: Wiley.

King, Valarie; Thorsen, Maggie L. & Amato, Paul R. (2014). Factors associated with positive relationships between stepfathers and adolescent stepchildren. *Social Science Research*, 47, 16–29. doi: 10.1016/j.ssresearch.2014.03.010

Kinney, Hannah C. & Thach, Bradley T. (2009). The sudden infant death syndrome. *New England Journal of Medicine*, 361, 795–805. doi: 10.1056/NEJMra0803836

Kirby, Douglas & Laris, B. A. (2009). Effective curriculum-based sex and STD/HIV education programs for adolescents. *Child Development Perspectives*, 3(1), 21–29. doi: 10.1111/j.1750-8606.2008.00071.x

Kirk, Elizabeth; Howlett, Neil; Pine, Karen J. & Fletcher, Ben. (2013). To sign or not to sign? The impact of encouraging infants to gesture on infant language and maternal mind-mindedness. *Child Development*, 84(2), 574–590. doi: 10.1111/j.1467-8624.2012.01874.x

Kiuru, Noona; Burk, William J.; Laursen, Brett; Salmela-Aro, Katariina & Nurmi, Jari-Erik. (2010). Pressure to drink but not to smoke: Disentangling selection and socialization in adolescent peer networks and peer groups. *Journal of Adolescence*, 33(6), 801–812. doi: 10.1016/j.adolescence.2010.07.006

Klaczynski, Paul A. (2001). Analytic and heuristic processing influences on adolescent reasoning and decision-making. *Child Development*, 72(3), 844–861. doi: 10.1111/1467-8624.00319

Klaczynski, Paul A. (2011). Age differences in understanding precedent-setting decisions and authorities' responses to violations of deontic rules. *Journal of Experimental Child Psychology*, 109(1), 1–24. doi: 10.1016/j.jecp.2010.10.010

Klaczynski, Paul A.; Daniel, David B. & Keller, Peggy S. (2009). Appearance idealization, body esteem, causal attributions, and ethnic variations in the development of obesity stereotypes. *Journal of Applied Developmental Psychology*, 30(4), 537–551. doi: 10.1016/j.appdev.2008.12.031

Klaczynski, Paul A. & Felmban, Wejdan S. (2014). Heuristics and biases during adolescence: Developmental reversals and individual differences. In Henry Markovits (Ed.), *The developmental psychology of reasoning and decision-making* (pp. 84–111). New York, NY: Psychology Press.

Klaus, Marshall H. & Kennell, John H. (1976). *Maternal-infant bonding: The impact of early separation or loss on family development.* St. Louis, MO: Mosby.

Klaus, Susan F.; Ekerdt, David J. & Gajewski, Byron. (2012). Job satisfaction in birth cohorts of nurses. *Journal of Nursing Management*, 20(4), 461–471. doi: 10.1111/j.1365-2834.2011.01283.x

Kleijer, Bart C.; van Marum, Rob J.; Frijter, Dinnus H. M.; Jansen, Paul A. F.; Ribbe, Miel W.; Egberts, Antoine C. G. & Heerdink, Eibert R. (2014). Variability between nursing homes in prevalence of antipsychotic use in patients with dementia. *International Psychogeriatrics*, 26(3), 363–371. doi: 10.1017/S1041610213002019

Klein, Denise; Mok, Kelvin; Chen, Jen-Kai & Watkins, Kate E. (2014). Age of language learning shapes brain structure: A cortical thickness study of bilingual and monolingual individuals. *Brain and Language*, 131, 20–24. doi: 10.1016/j.bandl.2013.05.014

Klein, Hilary. (1991). Couvade syndrome: Male counterpart to pregnancy. *International Journal of Psychiatry in Medicine*, 21(1), 57–69. doi: 10.2190/FLE0-92JM-C4CN-J83T

Klein, Stanley B. (2012). The two selves: The self of conscious experience and its brain. In Mark R. Leary & June Price Tangney (Eds.), *Handbook of self and identity* (pp. 617–637). New York, NY: Guilford Press.

Klein, Zoe A. & Romeo, Russell D. (2013). Changes in hypothalamic–pituitary–adrenal stress responsiveness before and after puberty in rats. *Hormones and Behavior*, 64(2), 357–363. doi: 10.1016/j.yhbeh.2013.01.012

Kliegel, Matthias; Jäger, Theodor & Phillips, Louise H. (2008). Adult age differences in event-based prospective memory: A meta-analysis on the role of focal versus nonfocal cues. *Psychology and Aging*, 23(1), 203–208. doi: 10.1037/0882-7974.23.1.203

Klimstra, Theo A.; Luyckx, Koen; Germeijs, Veerle; Meeus, Wim H. J. & Goossens, Luc. (2012). Personality traits and educational identity formation in late adolescents: Longitudinal associations and academic progress. *Journal of Youth and Adolescence*, 41(3), 346–361. doi: 10.1007/s10964-011-9734-7

Klinger, Laura G.; Dawson, Geraldine; Burner, Karen & Crisler, Megan. (2014). Autism spectrum disorder. In Eric J. Mash & Russell A. Barkley (Eds.), *Child psychopathology* (3rd ed., pp. 531–572). New York, NY: Guilford Press.

Knight, Rona. (2014). A hundred years of latency: From Freudian psychosexual theory to dynamic systems nonlinear development in middle childhood. *Journal of the American Psychoanalytic Association, 62*(2), 203–235. doi: 10.1177/0003065114531044

Knott, Craig S.; Coombs, Ngaire; Stamatakis, Emmanuel & Biddulph, Jane P. (2015). All cause mortality and the case for age specific alcohol consumption guidelines: Pooled analyses of up to 10 population based cohorts. *BMJ, 350,* h384. doi: 10.1136/bmj.h384

Koch, Linda. (2015). Shaping the gut microbiome. *Nature Reviews Genetics, 16,* 2–3. doi: 10.1038 /nrg3869

Kochanek, Kenneth D.; Xu, Jiaquan; Murphy, Sherry L.; Miniño, Arialdi M. & Kung, Hsiang-Ching. (2011). *Deaths: Preliminary data for 2009. National Vital Statistics Reports 59*(4). Hyattsville, MD: National Center for Health Statistics.

Kochanska, Grazyna; Barry, Robin A.; Jimenez, Natasha B.; Hollatz, Amanda L. & Woodard, Jarilyn. (2009). Guilt and effortful control: Two mechanisms that prevent disruptive developmental trajectories. *Journal of Personality and Social Psychology, 97*(2), 322–333. doi: 10.1037/a0015471

Kohlberg, Lawrence. (1963). The development of children's orientations toward a moral order: I. Sequence in the development of moral thought. *Vita Humana, 6*(1/2), 11–33. doi: 10.1159/000269667

Kohlberg, Lawrence; Levine, Charles & Hewer, Alexandra. (1983). *Moral stages: A current formulation and a response to critics.* New York, NY: Karger.

Kohn, Alfie. (2016). *Myth of the spoiled child: Coddled kids, helicopter parents, and other phony crises.* Boston, MA: Beacon Press.

Kolb, Bryan & Gibb, Robbin. (2015). Childhood poverty and brain development. *Human Development, 58*(4/5), 215–217. doi: 10.1159/000438766

Kolb, Bryan & Whishaw, Ian Q. (2015). *Fundamentals of human neuropsychology* (7th ed.). New York, NY: Worth Publishers.

Koller, Daniela & Bynum, Julie P. W. (2014). Dementia in the USA: State variation in prevalence. *Journal of Public Health.* doi: 10.1093 /pubmed/fdu080

Kolowich, Steve. (2013). Why some colleges are saying no to MOOC deals, at least for now. *Chronicle of Higher Education.*

Kolowich, Steve. (2016, June 5). After the gold rush: MOOCs, money, and the education of Richard McKenzie. *The Chronicle of Higher Education, 62*(38).

Koltko-Rivera, Mark E. (2006). Rediscovering the later version of Maslow's hierarchy of needs: Self-transcendence and opportunities for theory, research, and unification. *Review of General Psychology, 10*(4), 302–317. doi: 10.1037/1089 -2680.10.4.302

Komp, Kathrin; van Tilburg, Theo & van Groenou, Marjolein Broese. (2010). Paid work between age 60 and 70 years in Europe: A matter of socio-economic status? *International Journal of Ageing and Later Life, 5*(1), 45–75. doi: 10.3384 /ijal.1652 -8670.105145

Konner, Melvin. (2010). *The evolution of childhood: Relationships, emotion, mind.* Cambridge, MA: Harvard University Press.

Konno, Rie; Kang, Hee Sun & Makimoto, Kiyoko. (2014). A best-evidence review of intervention studies for minimizing resistance-to-care behaviours for older adults with dementia in nursing homes. *Journal of Advanced Nursing, 70*(10), 2167–2180. doi: 10.1111/jan.12432

Konstam, Varda. (2015). *Emerging and young adulthood: Multiple perspectives, diverse narratives.* New York, NY: Springer. doi: 10.1007/978-3-319 -11301-2

Kooij, Dorien T. A. M.; Annet, H. D. E. Lange; Jansen, Paul G. W.; Kanfer, Ruth & Dikkers, Josje S. E. (2011). Age and work-related motives: Results of a meta-analysis. *Journal of Organizational Behavior, 32*(2), 197–225. doi: 10.1002/job.665

Kopp, Claire B. (2011). Development in the early years: Socialization, motor development, and consciousness. *Annual Review of Psychology, 62,* 165–187. doi: 10.1146/annurev .psych.121208.131625

Korhonen, Tellervo; Latvala, Antti; Dick, Danielle M.; Pulkkinen, Lea; Rose, Richard J.; Kaprio, Jaakko & Huizink, Anja C. (2012). Genetic and environmental influences underlying externalizing behaviors, cigarette smoking and illicit drug use across adolescence. *Behavior Genetics, 42*(4), 614–625. doi: 10.1007/s10519- 012-9528-z

Korte, J.; Bohlmeijer, E. T.; Cappeliez, P.; Smit, F. & Westerhof, G. J. (2012). Life review therapy for older adults with moderate depressive symptomatology: A pragmatic randomized controlled trial. *Psychological Medicine, 42*(6), 1163–1173. doi: 10.1017 /S0033291711002042

Kost, Kathryn & Henshaw, Stanley. (2013). *U.S. teenage pregnancies, births and abortions, 2008: State trends by age, race and ethnicity.* New York, NY: Guttmacher Institute.

Koster-Hale, Jorie & Saxe, Rebecca. (2013). Functional neuroimaging of theory of mind. In Simon Baron-Cohen et al. (Eds.), *Understanding other minds: Perspectives from developmental social neuroscience* (3rd ed., pp. 132–163). New York, NY: Oxford University Press.

Kouider, Sid; Stahlhut, Carsten; Gelskov, Sofie V.; Barbosa, Leonardo S.; Dutat, Michel; de Gardelle, Vincent, . . . Dehaene-Lambertz, Ghislaine. (2013). A neural marker of perceptual consciousness in infants. *Science, 340*(6130), 376–380. doi: 10.1126/science.1232509

Kozhimannil, Katy B. & Kim, Helen. (2014). Maternal mental illness. *Science, 345*(6198), 755. doi: 10.1126/science.1259614

Kozhimannil, Katy B.; Law, Michael R. & Virnig, Beth A. (2013). Cesarean delivery rates vary tenfold among US hospitals; Reducing variation may address quality and cost issues. *Health Affairs, 32*(3), 527–535. doi: 10.1377 /hlthaff.2012.1030

Kozo, Justine; Sallis, James F.; Conway, Terry L.; Kerr, Jacqueline; Cain, Kelli; Saelens, Brian E., . . . Owen, Neville. (2012). Sedentary behaviors of adults in relation to neighborhood walkability and income. *Health Psychology, 31*(6), 704–713. doi: 10.1037/a0027874

Kramer, Karen L. & Russell, Andrew F. (2015). Was monogamy a key step on the hominin road? Reevaluating the monogamy hypothesis in the evolution of cooperative breeding. *Evolutionary Anthropology, 24*(2), 73–83. doi: 10.1002 /evan.21445

Krampe, Ralf Th. & Charness, Neil. (2006). Aging and expertise. In K. Anders Ericsson et al. (Eds.), *The Cambridge handbook of expertise and expert performance* (pp. 723–742). New York, NY: Cambridge University Press.

Krampe, Ralf Th.; Schaefer, Sabine; Lindenberger, Ulman & Baltes, Paul B. (2011). Lifespan changes in multi-tasking: Concurrent walking and memory search in children, young, and older adults. *Gait & Posture, 33*(3), 401–405. doi: 10.1016/j.gaitpost .2010.12.012

Kreager, Derek A.; Molloy, Lauren E.; Moody, James & Feinberg, Mark E. (2016). Friends first? The peer network origins of adolescent dating. *Journal of Research on Adolescence, 26*(2), 257–269. doi: 10.1111/jora.12189

Krebs, John R. (2009). The gourmet ape: Evolution and human food preferences. *American Journal of Clinical Nutrition, 90*(3), 707S–711S. doi: 10.3945/ajcn.2009.27462B

Kremen, William S.; Moore, Caitlin S.; Franz, Carol E.; Panizzon, Matthew S. & Lyons, Michael J. (2014). Cognition in middle adulthood. In Deborah Finkel & Chandra A. Reynolds (Eds.), *Behavior genetics of cognition across the lifespan: Advances in behavior genetics* (Vol. 1, pp. 105–134). New York, NY: Springer. doi: 10.1007/978-1-4614 -7447-0_4

Kremer, Peter; Elshaug, Christine; Leslie, Eva; Toumbourou, John W.; Patton, George C. & Williams, Joanne. (2014). Physical activity, leisure-time screen use and depression among children and young adolescents. *Journal of Science and Medicine in Sport, 17*(2), 183–187. doi: 10.1016 /j.jsams.2013.03.012

Kretch, Kari S. & Adolph, Karen E. (2013). No bridge too high: Infants decide whether to cross based on the probability of falling not the severity of the potential fall. *Developmental Science, 16*(3), 336–351. doi: 10.1111/desc.12045

Krieg, Alexander & Dickie, Jane R. (2013). Attachment and hikikomori: A psychosocial developmental model. *International Journal of Social Psychiatry, 59*(1), 61–72. doi: 10.1177/0020764011423182

Krisberg, Kim. (2014). Public health messaging: How it is said can influence behaviors: Beyond the facts. *The Nation's Health, 44*(6), 1–20.

Kroger, Jane. (2015). Identity development through adulthood: The move toward "wholeness". In Kate C. McLean & Moin Syed (Eds.), *The Oxford handbook of identity development* (pp. 65–80). New York, NY: Oxford University Press. doi: 10.1093 /oxfordhb /9780199936564.013.004

Kroger, Jane & Marcia, James E. (2011). The identity statuses: Origins, meanings, and interpretations. In Seth J. Schwartz et al. (Eds.), *Handbook of identity theory and research* (pp. 31–53). New York, NY: Springer. doi: 10.1007/978-1-4419 -7988-9_2

Krogstad, Jens M. & Fry, Richard. (2014, August 18). *Dept. of Ed. projects public schools will be 'majority-minority' this fall. Fact tank: News in the numbers.* Washington, DC: Pew Research Center.

Kroncke, Anna P.; Willard, Marcy & Huckabee, Helena. (2016). Optimal outcomes and recovery. In *Assessment of autism spectrum disorder: Critical issues in clinical, forensic and school settings* (pp. 23–33). New York, NY: Springer. doi: 10.1007/978-3-319-25504-0_3

Kübler-Ross, Elisabeth. (1969). *On death and dying.* New York, NY: Macmillan.

Kübler-Ross, Elisabeth. (1975). *Death: The final stage of growth.* Englewood Cliffs, NJ: Prentice-Hall.

Kübler-Ross, Elisabeth & Kessler, David. (2014). *On grief and grieving: Finding the meaning of grief through the five stages of loss.* New York, NY: Scribner.

Kuehn, Bridget M. (2011). Scientists find promising therapies for fragile X and Down syndromes. *JAMA, 305*(4), 344–346. doi: 10.1001/jama.2010.1960

Kuhlmann, Inga; Minihane, Anne; Huebbe, Patricia; Nebel, Almut & Rimbach, Gerald. (2010). Apolipoprotein E genotype and hepatitis C, HIV and herpes simplex disease risk: A literature review. *Lipids in Health and Disease, 9*(1), 8. doi: 10.1186/1476-511X-9-8

Kuhn, Deanna. (2013). Reasoning. In Philip D. Zelazo (Ed.), *The Oxford handbook of developmental psychology* (Vol. 1, pp. 744–764). New York, NY: Oxford University Press. doi: 10.1093/oxfordhb/9780199958450.013.0026

Kulik, Liat. (2016). Spousal role allocation and equity in older couples. In Jamila Bookwala (Ed.), *Couple relationships in the middle and later years: Their nature, complexity, and role in health and illness* (pp. 135–155). Washington, DC: American Psychological Association. doi: 10.1037/14897 -008

Kulik, Liat; Walfisch, Shulamith & Liberman, Gabriel. (2016). Spousal conflict resolution strategies and marital relations in late adulthood. *Personal Relationships, 23*(3), 456–474. doi: 10.1111/pere.12137

Kumar, Gayathri S.; Pan, Liping; Park, Sohyun; Lee-Kwan, Seung Hee; Onufrak, Stephen & M., Blanck. Heidi. (2014, August 15). *Sugar-sweetened beverage consumption among adults—18 States, 2012. Morbidity and Mortality Weekly Report 63*(32), 686–690. Atlanta, GA: Centers for Disease Control and Prevention.

Kumar, Santosh; Calvo, Rocio; Avendano, Mauricio; Sivaramakrishnan, Kavita & Berkman, Lisa F. (2012). Social support, volunteering and health around the world: Cross-national evidence from 139 countries. *Social Science & Medicine, 74*(5), 696–706. doi: 10.1016/j.socscimed .2011.11.017

Kundu, Tapas K. (Ed.). (2013). *Epigenetics: Development and disease.* New York, NY: Springer. doi: 10.1007/978-94-007-4525-4

Kuperberg, Arielle. (2012). Reassessing differences in work and income in cohabitation and marriage. *Journal of Marriage and Family, 74*(4), 688–707. doi: 10.1111/j.1741-3737.2012.00993.x

Kushnerenko, Elena; Tomalski, Przemyslaw; Ballieux, Haiko; Ribeiro, Helena; Potton, Anita; Axelsson, Emma L., . . . Moore, Derek G. (2013). Brain responses to audiovisual speech mismatch in infants are associated with individual differences in looking behaviour. *European Journal of Neuroscience, 38*(9), 3363–3369. doi: 10.1111/ejn.12317

Kutob, Randa M.; Senf, Janet H.; Crago, Marjorie & Shisslak, Catherine M. (2010). Concurrent and longitudinal predictors of self-esteem in elementary and middle school girls. *Journal of School Health, 80*(5), 240–248. doi: 10.1111/j.1746-1561 .2010.00496.x

Kuwahara, Keisuke; Kochi, Takeshi; Nanri, Akiko; Tsuruoka, Hiroko; Kurotani, Kayo; Pham, Ngoc Minh, . . . Mizoue, Tetsuya. (2014). Flushing response modifies the association of alcohol consumption with markers of glucose metabolism in Japanese men and women. *Alcoholism: Clinical and Experimental Research, 38*(4), 1042–1048. doi: 10.1111/acer.12323

Kwok, Sylvia Y. C. Lai & Shek, Daniel T. L. (2010). Hopelessness, parent-adolescent communication, and suicidal ideation among Chinese adolescents in Hong Kong. *Suicide and Life-Threatening Behavior, 40*(3), 224–233. doi: 10.1521/suli.2010 .40.3.224

Kypri, Kypros; Davie, Gabrielle; McElduff, Patrick; Connor, Jennie & Langley, John. (2014). Effects of lowering the minimum alcohol purchasing age on weekend assaults resulting in hospitalization in New Zealand. *American Journal of Public Health, 104*(8), 1396–1401. doi: 10.2105/AJPH.2014.301889

Kypri, Kypros; Voas, Robert B.; Langley, John D.; Stephenson, Shaun C. R.; Begg, Dorothy J.; Tippetts, A. Scott & Davie, Gabrielle S. (2006). Minimum purchasing age for alcohol and traffic crash injuries among 15- to 19-year-olds in New Zealand. *American Journal of Public Health, 96*(1), 126–131. doi: 10.2105/AJPH.2005.073122

Labouvie-Vief, Gisela. (2015). *Integrating emotions and cognition throughout the lifespan.* New York, NY: Springer. doi: 10.1007/978-3-319-09822-7

LaBrie, Joseph W.; Grant, Sean & Hummer, Justin F. (2011). "This would be better drunk": Alcohol expectancies become more positive while drinking in the college social environment. *Addictive Behaviors, 36*(8), 890–893. doi: 10.1016/j.addbeh .2011.03.015

Lachman, Margie E.; Neupert, Shevaun D. & Agrigoroaei, Stefan. (2011). The relevance of control beliefs for health and aging. In K. Warner Schaie & Sherry L. Willis (Eds.), *Handbook of the psychology of aging* (7th ed., pp. 175–190). San Diego, CA: Academic Press.

Lachman, Margie E.; Rosnick, Christopher B. & Röcke, Christina. (2009). The rise and fall of control beliefs and life satisfaction in adulthood: Trajectories of stability and change over ten years. In Hayden B. Bosworth & Christopher Hertzog (Eds.), *Aging and cognition: Research methodologies and empirical advances* (pp. 143–160). Washington, DC: American Psychological Association. doi: 10.1037/11882-007

LaFontana, Kathryn M. & Cillessen, Antonius H. N. (2010). Developmental changes in the priority of perceived status in childhood and adolescence. *Social Development, 19*(1), 130–147. doi: 10.1111/j.1467-9507.2008.00522.x

Lagattuta, Kristin H. (2014). Linking past, present, and future: Children's ability to connect mental states and emotions across time. *Child Development Perspectives, 8*(2), 90–95. doi: 10.1111/cdep.12065

Lai, Stephanie A.; Benjamin, Rebekah G.; Schwanenflugel, Paula J. & Kuhn, Melanie R. (2014). The longitudinal relationship between reading fluency and reading comprehension skills in second-grade children. *Reading & Writing Quarterly: Overcoming Learning Difficulties, 30*(2), 116–138. doi: 10.1080/10573569.2013.789785

Laier, Christian; Pawlikowski, Mirko & Brand, Matthias. (2014). Sexual picture processing interferes with decision-making under ambiguity. *Archives of Sexual Behavior, 43*(3), 473–482. doi: 10.1007/s10508-013-0119-8

Laird, Robert D.; Marrero, Matthew D.; Melching, Jessica A. & Kuhn, Emily S. (2013). Information management strategies in early adolescence: Developmental change in use and transactional associations with psychological adjustment. *Developmental Psychology, 49*(5), 928–937. doi: 10.1037/a0028845

Lake, Neil. (2012). Labor, interrupted: Cesareans, "cascading interventions," and finding a sense of balance. *Harvard Magazine, 115*(2), 21–26.

Lalande, Kathleen M. & Bonanno, George A. (2006). Culture and continuing bonds: A prospective comparison of bereavement in the United States and the People's Republic of China. *Death Studies, 30*(4), 303–324. doi: 10.1080/07481180500544708

Lamb, Michael E. (1982). Maternal employment and child development: A review. In Michael E. Lamb (Ed.), *Nontraditional families: Parenting and child development* (pp. 45–69). Hillsdale, NJ: Erlbaum.

Lamb, Michael E. (Ed.). (2010). *The role of the father in child development* (5th ed.). Hoboken, NJ: Wiley.

Lamont, Ruth A.; Swift, Hannah J. & Abrams, Dominic. (2015). A review and meta-analysis of age-based stereotype threat: Negative stereotypes, not facts, do the damage. *Psychology and Aging, 30*(1), 180–193. doi: 10.1037/a0038586

Landau, Mark J. & Sullivan, Daniel. (2015). Terror management motivation at the core of personality. In Mario Mikulincer et al. (Eds.), *APA handbook of personality and social psychology* (Vol. 4, pp. 209–230). Washington, DC: American Psychological Association. doi: 10.1037/14343 -010

Lander, Eric S. (2015). Brave new genome. *New England Journal of Medicine, 373*, 5–8. doi: 10.1056/NEJMp1506446

Lander, Eric S. (2016). The heroes of CRISPR. *Cell, 164*(1/2), 18–28. doi: 10.1016/j.cell.2015 .12.041

Landgren, Kajsa; Lundqvist, Anita & Hallström, Inger. (2012). Remembering the chaos–But life went on and the wound healed: A four year follow up with parents having had a baby with infantile colic. *The Open Nursing Journal*, 6, 53–61. doi: 10.2174/1874434601206010053

Lando, Amy M. & Lo, Serena C. (2014). Consumer understanding of the benefits and risks of fish consumption during pregnancy. *American Journal of Lifestyle Medicine*, 8(2), 88–92. doi: 10.1177/1559827613514704

Lane, Jonathan D. & Harris, Paul L. (2014). Confronting, representing, and believing counterintuitive concepts: Navigating the natural and the supernatural. *Perspectives on Psychological Science*, 9(2), 144–160. doi: 10.1177/1745691613518078

Lang, Frieder R.; Wagner, Jenny; Wrzus, Cornelia & Neyer, Franz J. (2013). Personal effort in social relationships across adulthood. *Psychology and Aging*, 28(2), 529–539. doi: 10.1037/a0032221

Langa, Kenneth M. (2015). Is the risk of Alzheimer's disease and dementia declining? *Alzheimer's Research & Therapy*, 7(1), 34. doi: 10.1186/s13195-015-0118-1

Langer, Robert D.; Manson, JoAnn E. & Allison, Matthew A. (2012). Have we come full circle–or moved forward? The Women's Health Initiative 10 years on. *Climacteric*, 15(3), 206–212. doi: 10.3109/13697137.2012.666916

Langeslag, Sandra J. E.; Muris, Peter & Franken, Ingmar H. A. (2013). Measuring romantic love: Psychometric properties of the infatuation and attachment scales. *The Journal of Sex Research*, 50(8), 739–747. doi: 10.1080/00224499.2012.714011

Långström, Niklas; Rahman, Qazi; Carlström, Eva & Lichtenstein, Paul. (2010). Genetic and environmental effects on same-sex sexual behavior: A population study of twins in Sweden. *Archives of Sexual Behavior*, 39(1), 75–80. doi: 10.1007/s10508-008-9386-1

Language and Reading Research Consortium. (2015). The dimensionality of language ability in young children. *Child Development*, 86(6), 1948–1965. doi: 10.1111/cdev.12450

Lannegrand-Willems, Lyda; Perchec, Cyrille & Marchal, Clotilde. (2016). Vocational identity and psychological adjustment: A study in French adolescents and emerging adults. *Journal of Adolescence*, 47, 210–219. doi: 10.1016/j.adolescence.2015 .10.005

Lara-Cinisomo, Sandraluz; Fuligni, Allison Sidle & Karoly, Lynn A. (2011). Preparing preschoolers for kindergarten. In DeAnna M. Laverick & Mary Renck Jalongo (Eds.), *Transitions to early care and education* (Vol. 4, pp. 93–105). New York, NY: Springer. doi: 10.1007/978-94-007-0573-9_9

Laraway, Kelly A.; Birch, Leann L.; Shaffer, Michele L. & Paul, Ian M. (2010). Parent perception of healthy infant and toddler growth. *Clinical Pediatrics*, 49(4), 343–349. doi: 10.1177/0009922809343717

Larose, Joanie; Boulay, Pierre; Sigal, Ronald J.; Wright, Heather E. & Kenny, Glen P. (2013). Age-related decrements in heat dissipation during physical activity occur as early as the age of 40. *PLoS ONE*, 8(12), e83148. doi: 10.1371/journal .pone.0083148

Larzelere, Robert; Cox, Ronald & Smith, Gail. (2010). Do nonphysical punishments reduce antisocial behavior more than spanking? A comparison using the strongest previous causal evidence against spanking. *BMC Pediatrics*, 10(10). doi: 10.1186/1471-2431-10-10

Larzelere, Robert E. & Cox, Ronald B. (2013). Making valid causal inferences about corrective actions by parents from longitudinal data. *Journal of Family Theory & Review*, 5(4), 282–299. doi: 10.1111/jftr.12020

Larzelere, Robert E.; Cox, Ronald B. & Swindle, Taren M. (2015). Many replications do not causal inferences make: The need for critical replications to test competing explanations of nonrandomized studies. *Perspectives on Psychological Science*, 10(3), 380–389. doi: 10.1177/1745691614567904

Lattanzi-Licht, Marcia. (2013). Religion, spirituality, and dying. In David K. Meagher & David E. Balk (Eds.), *Handbook of thanatology: The essential body of knowledge for the study of death, dying, and bereavement* (2nd ed., pp. 9–16). New York, NY: Routledge.

Lau, Carissa; Ambalavanan, Namasivayam; Chakraborty, Hrishikesh; Wingate, Martha S. & Carlo, Waldemar A. (2013). Extremely low birth weight and infant mortality rates in the United States. *Pediatrics*, 131(5), 855–860. doi: 10.1542 /peds.2012-2471

Laumann, Edward O. & Michael, Robert T. (2001). Introduction: Setting the scene. In Edward O. Laumann & Robert T. Michael (Eds.), *Sex, love, and health in America: Private choices and public policies* (pp. 1–38). Chicago, IL: University of Chicago Press.

Laurent, Heidemarie K. (2014). Clarifying the contours of emotion regulation: Insights from parent–child stress research. *Child Development Perspectives*, 8(1), 30–35. doi: 10.1111/cdep.12058

Laurino, Mercy Y.; Bennett, Robin L.; Saraiya, Devki S.; Baumeister, Lisa; Doyle, Debra L.; Leppig, Kathleen, . . . Raskind, Wendy H. (2005). Genetic evaluation and counseling of couples with recurrent miscarriage: Recommendations of the National Society of Genetic Counselors. *Journal of Genetic Counseling*, 14(3), 165–181. doi: 10.1007 /s10897-005-3241-5

Laursen, Brett & Collins, W. Andrew. (2009). Parent-child relationships during adolescence. In Richard M. Lerner & Laurence Steinberg (Eds.), *Handbook of adolescent psychology* (3rd ed., Vol. 2, pp. 3–42). Hoboken, NJ: Wiley.

Laursen, Brett & Hartl, Amy C. (2013). Understanding loneliness during adolescence: Developmental changes that increase the risk of perceived social isolation. *Journal of Adolescence*, 36(6), 1261–1268. doi: 10.1016/j.adolescence.2013 .06.003

Lauster, Nathanael T. (2008). Better homes and families: Housing markets and young couple stability in Sweden. *Journal of Marriage and Family*, 70(4), 891–903. doi: 10.1111/j.1741-3737.2008 .00534.x

Lavelli, Manuela & Fogel, Alan. (2005). Developmental changes in the relationship between the infant's attention and emotion during early face-to-face communication: The 2-month transition. *Developmental Psychology*, 41(1), 265–280. doi: 10.1037/0012-1649.41.1.265

Law, Lawla L. F.; Barnett, Fiona; Yau, Matthew K. & Gray, Marion A. (2012). Measures of everyday competence in older adults with cognitive impairment: A systematic review. *Age and Ageing*, 41(1), 9–16. doi: 10.1093/ageing /afr104

Le Grange, Daniel & Lock, James (Eds.). (2011). *Eating disorders in children and adolescents: A clinical handbook.* New York, NY: Guilford Press.

Leach, Penelope. (2011). The EYFS and the real foundations of children's early years. In Richard House (Ed.), *Too much, too soon?: Early learning and the erosion of childhood.* Stroud, UK: Hawthorn.

Leaning, Jennifer & Guha-Sapir, Debarati. (2013). Natural disasters, armed conflict, and public health. *New England Journal of Medicine*, 369(19), 1836–1842. doi: 10.1056/NEJMra1109877

Leaper, Campbell; Farkas, Timea & Brown, Christia Spears. (2012). Adolescent girls' experiences and gender-related beliefs in relation to their motivation in math/science and English. *Journal of Youth and Adolescence*, 41(3), 268–282. doi: 10.1007/s10964-011-9693-z

Leavitt, Judith W. (2009). *Make room for daddy: The journey from waiting room to birthing room.* Chapel Hill, NC: University of North Carolina Press.

LeCuyer, Elizabeth A. & Swanson, Dena Phillips. (2016). African American and European American mothers' limit setting and their 36-month-old children's responses to limits, self-concept, and social competence. *Journal of Family Issues*, 37(2), 270–296. doi: 10.1177/0192513X13515883

Lee, Christine M.; Geisner, Irene M.; Patrick, Megan E. & Neighbors, Clayton. (2010). The social norms of alcohol-related negative consequences. *Psychology of Addictive Behaviors*, 24(2), 342–348. doi: 10.1037/a0018020

Lee, Dohoon; Brooks-Gunn, Jeanne; McLanahan, Sara S.; Notterman, Daniel & Garfinkel, Irwin. (2013). The Great Recession, genetic sensitivity, and maternal harsh parenting. *Proceedings of the National Academy of Sciences*, 110(34), 13780–13784. doi: 10.1073 /pnas.1312398110

Lee, David M.; Nazroo, James; O'Connor, Daryl B.; Blake, Margaret & Pendleton, Neil. (2015). Sexual health and well-being among older men and women in England: Findings from the English longitudinal study of ageing. *Archives of Sexual Behavior*, (In Press). doi: 10.1007/s10508-014 -0465-1

Lee, Geok Ling; Woo, Ivan Mun Hong & Goh, Cynthia. (2013). Understanding the concept of a "good death" among bereaved family caregivers of cancer patients in Singapore. *Palliative and Supportive Care*, 11(1), 37–46. doi: 10.1017 /S1478951511000691

Lee, Jihyun & Porretta, David L. (2013). Enhancing the motor skills of children with autism spectrum disorders: A pool-based approach. *JOPERD: The Journal of Physical Education, Recreation & Dance*, 84(1), 41–45. doi: 10.1080/07303084.2013.746154

Lee, Moosung & Ju, Eunsu. (2016). Differential selection or differential socialization? Examining the effects of part-time work on school disengagement behaviors among South Korean adolescents. *Social Psychology of Education, 19*(2), 281–302. doi: 10.1007/s11218-016-9333-2

Lee, Moosung; Oi-yeung Lam, Beatrice; Ju, Eunsu & Dean, Jenny. (2016). Part-time employment and problem behaviors: Evidence from adolescents in South Korea. *Journal of Research on Adolescence,* (In Press). doi: 10.1111/jora.12258

Lee, Ronald & Skinner, Jonathan. (1999). Will aging baby boomers bust the federal budget? *Journal of Economic Perspectives, 13*(1), 117–140. doi: 10.1257/jep.13.1.117

Lee, RaeHyuck; Zhai, Fuhua; Brooks-Gunn, Jeanne; Han, Wen-Jui & Waldfogel, Jane. (2014). Head Start participation and school readiness: Evidence from the early childhood longitudinal study–birth cohort. *Developmental Psychology, 50*(1), 202–215. doi: 10.1037/a0032280

Lee, Soojeong & Shouse, Roger C. (2011). The impact of prestige orientation on shadow education in South Korea. *Sociology of Education, 84*(3), 212–224. doi: 10.1177/0038040711411278

Lee, Shawna J. & Altschul, Inna. (2015). Spanking of young children: Do immigrant and U.S.-born Hispanic parents differ? *Journal of Interpersonal Violence, 30*(3), 475–498. doi: 10.1177/0886260514535098

Lee, Shawna J.; Altschul, Inna & Gershoff, Elizabeth T. (2015). Wait until your father gets home? Mother's and fathers' spanking and development of child aggression. *Children and Youth Services Review, 52,* 158–166. doi: 10.1016/j.childyouth.2014.11.006

Lee, Star W.; Clemenson, Gregory D. & Gage, Fred H. (2012). New neurons in an aged brain. *Behavioural Brain Research, 227*(2), 497–507. doi: 10.1016/j.bbr.2011.10.009

Lee, Yuan-Hsuan; Ko, Chih-Hung & Chou, Chien. (2015). Re-visiting Internet addiction among Taiwanese students: A cross-sectional comparison of students' expectations, online gaming, and online social interaction. *Journal of Abnormal Child Psychology, 43*(3), 589–599. doi: 10.1007/s10802-014-9915-4

Legerstee, Maria. (2013). The developing social brain: Social connections and social bonds, social loss, and jealousy in infancy. In Maria Legerstee et al. (Eds.), *The infant mind: Origins of the social brain* (pp. 223–247). New York, NY: Guilford Press.

Legewie, Joscha & DiPrete, Thomas A. (2012). School context and the gender gap in educational achievement. *American Sociological Review, 77*(3), 463–485. doi: 10.1177/0003122412440802

Lehmann, Regula; Denissen, Jaap J. A.; Allemand, Mathias & Penke, Lars. (2013). Age and gender differences in motivational manifestations of the Big Five from age 16 to 60. *Developmental Psychology, 49*(2), 365–383. doi: 10.1037/a0028277

Lehner, Ben. (2013). Genotype to phenotype: Lessons from model organisms for human genetics. *Nature Reviews Genetics, 14*(3), 168–178. doi: 10.1038/nrg3404

Leiter, Valerie & Herman, Sarah. (2015). Guinea pig kids: Myths or modern Tuskegees? *Sociological Spectrum, 35*(1), 26–45. doi: 10.1080/02732173.2014.978429

Leman, Patrick J. & Björnberg, Marina. (2010). Conversation, development, and gender: A study of changes in children's concepts of punishment. *Child Development, 81*(3), 958–971. doi: 10.1111/j.1467-8624.2010.01445.x

Lemieux, André. (2012). Post-formal thought in gerontagogy or beyond Piage. *Journal of Behavioral and Brain Science, 2*(3), 399–406. doi: 10.4236/jbbs.2012.23046

Lemish, Daphna & Kolucki, Barbara. (2013). Media and early childhood development. In Pia Rebello Britto et al. (Eds.), *Handbook of early childhood development research and its impact on global policy.* New York, NY: Oxford University Press.

Lenhart, Amanda. (2015, April 9). *Teen, social media and technology overview 2015: Smartphone facilitate shifts in communication landscape for teens. Pew Research Center: Internet, Science & Tech.* Washington, DC: Pew Research Center.

Lenhart, Amanda; Anderson, Monica & Smith, Aaron. (2015, October 1). *Teens, technology and romantic relationships. Pew Research Center: Internet, Science & Tech.* Washington, DC: Pew Research Center.

Leonard, Hayley C. & Hill, Elisabeth L. (2014). Review: The impact of motor development on typical and atypical social cognition and language: A systematic review. *Child and Adolescent Mental Health, 19*(3), 163–170. doi: 10.1111/camh.12055

Leopold, Thomas & Skopek, Jan. (2015a). The delay of grandparenthood: A cohort comparison in East and West Germany. *Journal of Marriage and Family, 77*(2), 441–460. doi: 10.1111/jomf.12169

Leopold, Thomas & Skopek, Jan. (2015b). The demography of grandparenthood: An international profile. *Social Forces, 94*(2), 801–832. doi: 10.1093/sf/sov066

Lepousez, Gabriel; Nissant, Antoine & Lledo, Pierre-Marie. (2015). Adult neurogenesis and the future of the rejuvenating brain circuits. *Neuron, 86*(2), 387–401. doi: 10.1016/j.neuron.2015.01.002

Lerner, Richard M.; Overton, F. Willis; Freund, Alexandra M. & Lamb, Michael E. (2010). *The handbook of life-span development.* Hoboken, NJ: Wiley.

Leslie, Leigh A.; Smith, Jocelyn R.; Hrapczynski, Katie M. & Riley, Debbie. (2013). Racial socialization in transracial adoptive families: Does it help adolescents deal with discriminative stress? *Family Relations, 62*(1), 72–81. doi: 10.1111/j.1741-3729.2012.00744.x

Leslie, Mitch. (2012). Gut microbes keep rare immune cells in line. *Science, 335*(6075), 1428. doi: 10.1126/science.335.6075.1428

Lester, Patricia; Leskin, Gregory; Woodward, Kirsten; Saltzman, William; Nash, William; Mogil, Catherine, . . . Beardslee, William. (2011). Wartime deployment and military children: Applying prevention science to enhance family resilience. In Shelley MacDermid Wadsworth & David Riggs (Eds.), *Risk and resilience in U.S. military families* (pp. 149–173). New York, NY: Springer. doi: 10.1007/978-1-4419-7064-0_8

Leung, Angel Nga-Man; Wong, Stephanie Siu-fong; Wong, Iris Wai-yin & McBride-Chang, Catherine. (2010). Filial piety and psychosocial adjustment in Hong Kong Chinese early adolescents. *The Journal of Early Adolescence, 30*(5), 651–667. doi: 10.1177/0272431609341046

Leung, Sumie; Mareschal, Denis; Rowsell, Renee; Simpson, David; Laria, Leon; Grbic, Amanda & Kaufman, Jordy. (2016). Oscillatory activity in the infant brain and the representation of small numbers. *Frontiers in Systems Neuroscience, 10*(4). doi: 10.3389/fnsys.2016.00004

Leventhal, Bennett L. (2013). Complementary and alternative medicine: Not many compliments but lots of alternatives. *Journal of Child and Adolescent Psychopharmacology, 23*(1), 54–56. doi: 10.1089/cap.2013.2312

Levy, Daniel & Brink, Susan. (2005). *A change of heart: How the Framingham Heart Study helped unravel the mysteries of cardiovascular disease.* New York, NY: Knopf.

Lewallen, Lynne P. (2011). The importance of culture in childbearing. *Journal of Obstetric, Gynecologic, & Neonatal Nursing, 40*(1), 4–8. doi: 10.1111/j.1552-6909.2010.01209.x

Lewandowski, Lawrence J. & Lovett, Benjamin J. (2014). Learning disabilities. In Eric J. Mash & Russell A. Barkley (Eds.), *Child psychopathology* (3rd ed., pp. 625–669). New York, NY: Guilford Press.

Lewin, Kurt. (1945). The Research Center for Group Dynamics at Massachusetts Institute of Technology. *Sociometry, 8*(2), 126–136. doi: 10.2307/2785233

Lewis, David M. G.; Conroy-Beam, Daniel; Al-Shawaf, Laith; Raja, Annia; DeKay, Todd & Buss, David M. (2011). Friends with benefits: The evolved psychology of same- and opposite-sex friendships. *Evolutionary Psychology, 9*(4), 543–563.

Lewis, John D.; Theilmann, Rebecca J.; Townsend, Jeanne & Evans, Alan C. (2013). Network efficiency in autism spectrum disorder and its relation to brain overgrowth. *Frontiers in Human Neuroscience, 7,* 845. doi: 10.3389/fnhum.2013.00845

Lewis, Kristen & Burd-Sharps, Sarah. (2010). *The measure of America 2010–2011: Mapping risks and resilience.* New York, NY: New York University Press.

Lewis, Michael. (2010). The emergence of human emotions. In Michael Lewis et al. (Eds.), *Handbook of emotions* (3rd ed.). New York, NY: Guilford Press.

Lewis, Michael & Brooks, Jeanne. (1978). Self-knowledge and emotional development. In Michael Lewis & L. A. Rosenblum (Eds.), *Genesis of behavior* (Vol. 1, pp. 205–226). New York, NY: Plenum Press.

Lewis, Michael & Kestler, Lisa (Eds.). (2012). *Gender differences in prenatal substance exposure.* Washington, DC: American Psychological Association.

Lewis, Marc D. (2013). The development of emotional regulation: Integrating normative and individual differences through developmental neuroscience. In Philip D. Zelazo (Ed.), *The Oxford handbook of developmental psychology* (Vol. 2, pp. 81–97). New York, NY: Oxford University Press. doi: 10.1093/oxfordhb/9780199958474.013.0004

Li, Jin; Fung, Heidi; Bakeman, Roger; Rae, Katharine & Wei, Wanchun. (2014). How European American and Taiwanese mothers talk to their children about learning. *Child Development*, 85(3), 1206–1221. doi: 10.1111/cdev.12172

Li, Liman Man Wai; Masuda, Takahiko & Russell, Matthew J. (2014). The influence of cultural lay beliefs: Dialecticism and indecisiveness in European Canadians and Hong Kong Chinese. *Personality and Individual Differences*, 68, 6–12. doi: 10.1016/j.paid.2014.03.047

Li, Ting & Zhang, Yanlong. (2015). Social network types and the health of older adults: Exploring reciprocal associations. *Social Science & Medicine*, 130(2), 59–68. doi: 10.1016/j.socscimed.2015 .02.007

Li, Weilin; Farkas, George; Duncan, Greg J.; Burchinal, Margaret R. & Vandell, Deborah Lowe. (2013). Timing of high-quality child care and cognitive, language, and preacademic development. *Developmental Psychology*, 49(8), 1440–1451. doi: 10.1037/a0030613

Li, Yibing & Lerner, Richard M. (2011). Trajectories of school engagement during adolescence: Implications for grades, depression, delinquency, and substance use. *Developmental Psychology*, 47(1), 233–247. doi: 10.1037 /a0021307

Liben, Lynn S. (2016). We've come a long way, baby (but we're not there yet): Gender past, present, and future. *Child Development*, 87(1), 5–28. doi: 10.1111/cdev.12490

Libertus, Klaus & Needham, Amy. (2010). Teach to reach: The effects of active vs. passive reaching experiences on action and perception. *Vision Research*, 50(24), 2750–2757. doi: 10.1016 /j.visres.2010.09.001

Libertus, Melissa E.; Feigenson, Lisa & Halberda, Justin. (2013). Is approximate number precision a stable predictor of math ability? *Learning and Individual Differences*, 25, 126–133. doi: 10.1016/j.lindif.2013.02.001

Lichtenberg, Peter A. (2016). Financial exploitation, financial capacity, and Alzheimer's disease. *American Psychologist*, 71(4), 312–320. doi: 10.1037/a0040192

Liew, Jeffrey. (2012). Effortful control, executive functions, and education: Bringing self-regulatory and social-emotional competencies to the table. *Child Development Perspectives*, 6(2), 105–111. doi: 10.1111/j.1750-8606.2011.00196.x

Lillard, Angeline S. (2013). Playful learning and Montessori education. *American Journal of Play*, 5(2), 157–186.

Lillard, Angeline S.; Lerner, Matthew D.; Hopkins, Emily J.; Dore, Rebecca A.; Smith, Eric D. & Palmquist, Carolyn M. (2013). The impact of pretend play on children's development: A review of the evidence. *Psychological Bulletin*, 139(1), 1–34. doi: 10.1037/a0029321

Lillevoll, Kjersti R.; Kroger, Jane & Martinussen, Monica. (2013). Identity status and locus of control: A meta-analysis. *Identity: An International Journal of Theory and Research*, 13(3), 253–265. doi: 10.1080/15283488.2013.799471

Lim, Chaeyoon & Putnam, Robert D. (2010). Religion, social networks, and life satisfaction. *American Sociological Review*, 75(6), 914–933. doi: 10.1177/0003122410386686

Lim, Cher Ping; Zhao, Yong; Tondeur, Jo; Chai, Ching Sing & Tsai, Chin-Chung. (2013). Bridging the gap: Technology trends and use of technology in schools. *Educational Technology & Society*, 16(2), 59–68.

Limber, Susan P. (2011). Development, evaluation, and future directions of the Olweus Bullying Prevention Program. *Journal of School Violence*, 10(1), 71–87. doi: 10.1080/15388220.2010 .519375

Lin, Alex R. (2014). Examining students' perception of classroom openness as a predictor of civic knowledge: A cross-national analysis of 38 countries. *Applied Developmental Science*, 18(1), 17–30. doi: 10.1080/10888691.2014.864204

Lin, Frank R.; Yaffe, Kristine; Xia, Jin; Xue, Qian-Li; Harris, Tamara B.; Purchase-Helzner, Elizabeth, . . . Simonsick, Eleanor M. (2013). Hearing loss and cognitive decline in older adults. *JAMA Internal Medicine*, 173(4), 293–299. doi: 10.1001/jamainternmed.2013.1868

Lin, Jue; Epel, Elissa & Blackburn, Elizabeth. (2012). Telomeres and lifestyle factors: Roles in cellular aging. *Mutation Research/Fundamental and Molecular Mechanisms of Mutagenesis*, 730(1/2), 85–89. doi: 10.1016/j.mrfmmm.2011.08.003

Lin, Xiaoping; Bryant, Christina; Boldero, Jennifer & Dow, Briony. (2015). Older Chinese immigrants' relationships with their children: A literature review from a solidarity–conflict perspective. *The Gerontologist*, 55(6), 990–1005. doi: 10.1093 /geront/gnu004

Lindau, Stacy T. & Gavrilova, Natalia. (2010). Sex, health, and years of sexually active life gained due to good health: Evidence from two US population based cross sectional surveys of ageing. *BMJ*, 340(7746), c810. doi: 10.1136/bmj.c810

Liu, Dong & Xin, Ziqiang. (2014). Birth cohort and age changes in the self-esteem of Chinese adolescents: A cross-temporal meta-analysis, 1996–2009. *Journal of Research on Adolescence*. doi: 10.1111/jora.12134

Livas-Dlott, Alejandra; Fuller, Bruce; Stein, Gabriela L.; Bridges, Margaret; Mangual Figueroa, Ariana & Mireles, Laurie. (2010). Commands, competence, and *cariño*: Maternal socialization practices in Mexican American families. *Developmental Psychology*, 46(3), 566–578. doi: 10.1037/a0018016

Livingston, Gretchen. (2014). *Four-in-ten couples are saying 'I do,' again*. Washington, DC: Pew Research Center.

Lobstein, Tim & Dibb, Sue. (2005). Evidence of a possible link between obesogenic food advertising and child overweight. *Obesity Reviews*, 6(3), 203–208. doi: 10.1111/j.1467-789X.2005.00191.x

LoBue, Vanessa. (2013). What are we so afraid of? How early attention shapes our most common fears. *Child Development Perspectives*, 7(1), 38–42. doi: 10.1111/cdep.12012

Lock, Margaret. (2013). The lure of the epigenome. *The Lancet*, 381(9881), 1896–1897. doi: 10.1016/S0140-6736(13)61149-6

Löckenhoff, Corinna E.; De Fruyt, Filip; Terracciano, Antonio; McCrae, Robert R.; De Bolle, Marleen; Costa, Paul T., . . . Yik, Michelle. (2009). Perceptions of aging across 26 cultures and their culture-level associates. *Psychology and Aging*, 24(4), 941–954. doi: 10.1037/a0016901

Lodge, Amy C. & Umberson, Debra. (2012). All shook up: Sexuality of mid- to later life married couples. *Journal of Marriage and Family*, 74(3), 428–443. doi: 10.1111/j.1741-3737.2012.00969.x

Loeber, Rolf & Burke, Jeffrey D. (2011). Developmental pathways in juvenile externalizing and internalizing problems. *Journal of Research on Adolescence*, 21(1), 34–46. doi: 10.1111/j.1532-7795 .2010.00713.x

Loeber, Rolf; Capaldi, Deborah M. & Costello, Elizabeth. (2013). Gender and the development of aggression, disruptive behavior, and delinquency from childhood to early adulthood. In Patrick H. Tolan & Bennett L. Leventh (Eds.), *Disruptive behavior disorders* (pp. 137–160). New York, NY: Springer. doi: 10.1007/978-1-4614-7557-6_6

Longo, Lawrence D. (2013). *The rise of fetal and neonatal physiology: Basic science to clinical care*. New York, NY: Springer.

Lopez-Hartmann, Maja; Wens, Johan; Verhoeven, Veronique & Remmen, Roy. (2012). The effect of caregiver support interventions for informal caregivers of community-dwelling frail elderly: A systematic review. *International Journal of Integrated Care*, 12, 1–16.

Lortet-Tieulent, Joannie; Soerjomataram, Isabelle; Ferlay, Jacques; Rutherford, Mark; Weiderpass, Elisabete & Bray, Freddie. (2014). International trends in lung cancer incidence by histological subtype: Adenocarcinoma stabilizing in men but still increasing in women. *Lung Cancer*, 84(1), 13–22. doi: 10.1016/j.lungcan.2014.01.009

Lövdén, Martin; Xu, Weili & Wang, Hui-Xin. (2013). Lifestyle change and the prevention of cognitive decline and dementia: What is the evidence? *Current Opinion in Psychiatry*, 26(3), 239–243. doi: 10.1097/YCO.0b013e32835f4135

Lovell, Brian & Wetherell, Mark A. (2011). The cost of caregiving: Endocrine and immune implications in elderly and non elderly caregivers. *Neuroscience & Biobehavioral Reviews*, 35(6), 1342–1352. doi: 10.1016/j.neubiorev.2011.02.007

Lowrey, Annie. (2014, March 16). Income gap, meet the longevity gap. *New York Times*, p. BU1.

Lubienski, Christopher; Puckett, Tiffany & Brewer, T. Jameson. (2013). Does homeschooling "work"? A critique of the empirical claims and agenda of advocacy organizations. *Peabody Journal of Education*, 88(3), 378–392. doi: 10.1080/0161956X.2013.798516

Luecken, Linda J.; Lin, Betty; Coburn, Shayna S.; MacKinnon, David P.; Gonzales, Nancy A. & Crnic, Keith A. (2013). Prenatal stress, partner support, and infant cortisol reactivity in low-income Mexican American families. *Psychoneuroendocrinology*, 38(12), 3092–3101. doi: 10.1016/j.psyneuen.2013.09.006

Luengo-Prado, María J. & Sevilla, Almudena. (2012). Time to cook: Expenditure at retirement in Spain. *The Economic Journal, 123*(569), 764–789. doi: 10.1111/j.1468-0297.2012.02546.x

Luhmann, Maike & Hawkley, Louise C. (2016). Age differences in loneliness from late adolescence to oldest old age. *Developmental Psychology, 52*(6), 943–959. doi: 10.1037 /dev0000117

Luhmann, Maike; Hofmann, Wilhelm; Eid, Michael & Lucas, Richard E. (2012). Subjective well-being and adaptation to life events: A meta-analysis. *Journal of Personality and Social Psychology, 102*(3), 592–615. doi: 10.1037 /a0025948

Luna, Beatriz; Paulsen, David J.; Padmanabhan, Aarthi & Geier, Charles. (2013). The teenage brain: Cognitive control and motivation. *Current Directions in Psychological Science, 22*(2), 94–100. doi: 10.1177/0963721413478416

Lundahl, Alyssa; Kidwell, Katherine M. & Nelson, Timothy D. (2014). Parental underestimates of child weight: A meta-analysis. *Pediatrics, 133*(3), e689–e703. doi: 10.1542/peds.2013-2690

Lundberg, Shelly; Pollak, Robert A. & Stearns, Jenna. (2016). Family inequality: Diverging patterns in marriage, cohabitation, and childbearing. *Journal of Economic Perspectives, 30*(2), 79–102. doi: 10.1257/jep.30.2.79

Lundquist, Gunilla; Rasmussen, Birgit H. & Axelsson, Bertil. (2011). Information of imminent death or not: Does it make a difference? *Journal of Clinical Oncology, 29*(29), 3927–3931. doi: 10.1200/JCO.2011.34.6247

Luo, Rufan; Tamis-LeMonda, Catherine S.; Kuchirko, Yana; Ng, Florrie F. & Liang, Eva. (2014). Mother–child book-sharing and children's storytelling skills in ethnically diverse, low-income families. *Infant and Child Development, 23*(4), 402–425. doi: 10.1002/icd.1841

Luong, Gloria & Charles, Susan T. (2014). Age differences in affective and cardiovascular responses to a negative social interaction: The role of goals, appraisals, and emotion regulation. *Developmental Psychology, 50*(7), 1919–1930. doi: 10.1037 /a0036621

Lupski, James R. (2013). Genome mosaicism: One human, multiple genomes. *Science, 341*(6144), 358–359. doi: 10.1126 /science.1239503

Luquis, Raffy R.; Brelsford, Gina M. & Rojas-Guyler, Liliana. (2012). Religiosity, spirituality, sexual attitudes, and sexual behaviors among college students. *Journal of Religion and Health, 51*(3), 601–614. doi: 10.1007/s10943-011-9527-z

Lustig, Cindy; Shah, Priti; Seidler, Rachael & Reuter-Lorenz, Patricia A. (2009). Aging, training, and the brain: A review and future directions. *Neuropsychology Review, 19*(4), 504–522. doi: 10.1007/s11065-009-9119-9

Luthar, Suniya S. & Barkin, Samuel H. (2012). Are affluent youth truly "at risk"? Vulnerability and resilience across three diverse samples. *Development and Psychopathology, 24*(2), 429–449. doi: 10.1017/S0954579412000089

Luthar, Suniya S.; Cicchetti, Dante & Becker, Bronwyn. (2000). The construct of resilience: A critical evaluation and guidelines for future work. *Child Development, 71*(3), 543–562. doi: 10.1111/1467-8624.00164

Lutz, Wolfgang; Muttarak, Raya & Striessnig, Erich. (2014). Universal education is key to enhanced climate adaptation. *Science, 346*(6213), 1061–1062. doi: 10.1126/science.1257975

Luxmoore, Nick. (2012). *Young people, death, and the unfairness of everything.* Philadelphia, PA: Jessica Kingsley.

Lyall, Donald M.; Inskip, Hazel M.; Mackay, Daniel; Deary, Ian J.; McIntosh, Andrew M.; Hotopf, Matthew, . . . Smith, Daniel J. (2016). Low birth weight and features of neuroticism and mood disorder in 83,545 participants of the UK Biobank cohort. *British Journal of Psychiatry Open, 2*(1), 38–44. doi: 10.1192/bjpo.bp.115.002154

Lynch, Scott M. & Brown, J. Scott. (2011). Stratification and inequality over the life course. In Robert H. Binstock & Linda K. George (Eds.), *Handbook of aging and the social sciences* (7th ed., pp. 105–117). San Diego, CA: Academic Press. doi: 10.1016/B978-0-12-380880-6.00008-3

Lynskey, Michael T.; Agrawal, Arpana; Henders, Anjali; Nelson, Elliot C.; Madden, Pamela A. F. & Martin, Nicholas G. (2012). An Australian twin study of cannabis and other illicit drug use and misuse, and other psychopathology. *Twin Research and Human Genetics, 15*(5), 631–641. doi: 10.1017/thg.2012.41

Lyons-Ruth, Karlen; Bronfman, Elisa & Parsons, Elizabeth. (1999). Maternal frightened, frightening, or atypical behavior and disorganized infant attachment patterns. *Monographs of the Society for Research in Child Development, 64*(3), 67–96. doi: 10.1111/1540-5834.00034

Lyssens-Danneboom, Vicky & Mortelmans, Dimitri. (2014). Living apart together and money: New partnerships, traditional gender roles. *Journal of Marriage and Family, 76*(5), 949–966. doi: 10.1111/jomf.12136

Ma-Kellams, Christine; Or, Flora; Baek, Ji Hyun & Kawachi, Ichiro. (2016). Rethinking suicide surveillance Google search data and self-reported suicidality differentially estimate completed suicide risk. *Clinical Psychological Science, 4*(3), 480–484. doi: 10.1177/2167702615593475

Maas, Megan K.; Shearer, Cindy L.; Gillen, Meghan M. & Lefkowitz, Eva S. (2015). Sex rules: Emerging adults' perceptions of gender's impact on sexuality. *Sexuality & Culture, 19*(4), 617–636. doi: 10.1007/s12119-015-9281-6

Määttä, Kaarina & Uusiautti, Satu. (2012). Changing identities: Finnish divorcees' perceptions of a new marriage. *Journal of Divorce & Remarriage, 53*(7), 515–532. doi: 10.1080/10502556.2012.682906

Mac Dougall, K.; Beyene, Y. & Nachtigall, R.D. (2013). Age shock: Misperceptions of the impact of age on fertility before and after IVF in women who conceived after age 40. *Human Reproduction, 28*(2), 350–356. doi: 10.1093/humrep/des409

MacDorman, Marian F.; Mathews, T. J.; Mohangoo, Ashna D. & Zeitlin, Jennifer. (2014). *International comparisons of infant mortality and related factors: United States and Europe, 2010. National Vital Statistics Reports 63*(5). Hyattsville, MD: National Center for Health Statistics.

MacDorman, Marian F. & Rosenberg, Harry M. (1993). *Trends in infant mortality by cause of death and other characteristics, 1960–88. Vital and Health Statistic 20*(20). Hyattsville, MD: National Center for Health Statistics.

Macgregor, Stuart; Lind, Penelope A.; Bucholz, Kathleen K.; Hansell, Narelle K.; Madden, Pamela A. F.; Richter, Melinda M., . . . Whitfield, John B. (2009). Associations of ADH and ALDH2 gene variation with self report alcohol reactions, consumption and dependence: An integrated analysis. *Human Molecular Genetics, 18*(3), 580–593. doi: 10.1093/hmg/ddn372

Mackenzie, Karen J.; Anderton, Stephen M. & Schwarze, Jürgen. (2014). Viral respiratory tract infections and asthma in early life: Cause and effect? *Clinical & Experimental Allergy, 44*(1), 9–19. doi: 10.1111/cea.12139

MacKenzie, Michael J.; Nicklas, Eric; Brooks-Gunn, Jeanne & Waldfogel, Jane. (2011). Who spanks infants and toddlers? Evidence from the fragile families and child well-being study. *Children and Youth Services Review, 33*(8), 1364–1373. doi: 10.1016/j.childyouth.2011.04.007

Macmillan, Ross & Copher, Ronda. (2005). Families in the life course: Interdependency of roles, role configurations, and pathways. *Journal of Marriage and Family, 67*(4), 858–879. doi: 10.1111 /j.1741-3737.2005.00180.x

Macosko, Evan Z. & McCarroll, Steven A. (2013). Our fallen genomes. *Science, 342*(6158), 564–565. doi: 10.1126/science.1246942

MacWhinney, Brian. (2015). Language Development. In Richard M. Lerner (Ed.), *Handbook of child psychology and developmental science* (7th ed., Vol. 2, pp. 296–338). New York, NY: Wiley.

Madden, Mary; Lenhart, Amanda; Duggan, Maeve; Cortesi, Sandra & Gasser, Urs. (2013). *Teens and technology 2013.* Washington, DC: Pew Research Center, Pew Internet & American Life Project.

Madewell, Amy N. & Ponce-Garcia, Elisabeth. (2016). Assessing resilience in emerging adulthood: The resilience scale (RS), connor–davidson resilience scale (CD-RISC), and scale of protective factors (SPF). *Personality and Individual Differences, 97*(2), 249–255. doi: 10.1016/j.paid .2016.03.036

Magill, Molly; Gaume, Jacques; Apodaca, Timothy R.; Walthers, Justin; Mastroleo, Nadine R.; Borsari, Brian & Longabaugh, Richard. (2014). The technical hypothesis of motivational interviewing: A meta-analysis of MI's key causal model. *Journal of Consulting and Clinical Psychology, 82*(6), 973–983. doi: 10.1037 /a0036833

Mahalik, James R.; Lombardi, Caitlin McPherran; Sims, Jacqueline; Coley, Rebekah Levine & Lynch, Alicia Doyle. (2015). Gender, male-typicality, and social norms predicting adolescent alcohol intoxication and marijuana use. *Social Science & Medicine, 143*, 71–80. doi: 10.1016/j.socscimed.2015.08.013

Mahmoudzadeh, Mahdi; Dehaene-Lambertz, Ghislaine; Fournier, Marc; Kongolo, Guy; Goudjil, Sabrina; Dubois, Jessica, . . . Wallois, Fabrice. (2013). Syllabic discrimination in premature human infants prior to complete formation of cortical layers. *Proceedings of the National Academy of Sciences, 110*(12), 4846–4851. doi: 10.1073 /pnas.1212220110

Majdandžić, Mirjana; Möller, Eline L.; de Vente, Wieke; Bögels, Susan M. & van den Boom, Dymphna C. (2013). Fathers' challenging parenting behavior prevents social anxiety development in their 4-year-old children: A longitudinal observational study. *Journal of Abnormal Child Psychology, 42*(2), 301–310. doi: 10.1007/s10802-013-9774-4

Majercsik, Eszter. (2005). Hierachy of needs of geriatric patients. *Gerontology, 51*(3), 170–173. doi: 10.1159/000083989

Malchiodi, Cathy A. (2012). Creativity and aging: An art therapy perspective. In Cathy A. Malchiodi (Ed.), *Handbook of art therapy* (2nd ed., pp. 275–287). New York, NY: Guilford Press.

Malina, Robert M.; Bouchard, Claude & Bar-Or, Oded. (2004). *Growth, maturation, and physical activity* (2nd ed.). Champaign, IL: Human Kinetics.

Malloy, Michael H. (2009). Impact of cesarean section on intermediate and late preterm births: United States, 2000-2003. *Birth, 36*(1), 26–33. doi: 10.1111/j.1523-536X.2008.00292.x

Mancini, Anthony D.; Prati, Gabriele & Bonanno, George A. (2011). Do shattered worldviews lead to complicated grief? Prospective and longitudinal analyses. *Journal of Social and Clinical Psychology, 30*(2), 184–215. doi: 10.1521 /jscp.2011.30.2.184

Mandler, Jean M. & DeLoache, Judy. (2012). The beginnings of conceptual development. In Sabina M. Pauen (Ed.), *Early childhood development and later outcome.* New York, NY: Cambridge University Press.

Mangan, Katherine. (2016, April 15). This former college president spent 2 years in prison: Here's what he learned. *The Chronicle of Higher Education.*

Mangels, Jennifer A.; Good, Catherine; Whiteman, Ronald C.; Maniscalco, Brian & Dweck, Carol S. (2012). Emotion blocks the path to learning under stereotype threat. *Social Cognitive Affective Neuroscience, 7*(2), 230–241. doi: 10.1093/scan /nsq100

Mann, Joshua R.; McDermott, Suzanne; Bao, Haikun & Bersabe, Adrian. (2009). Maternal genitourinary infection and risk of cerebral palsy. *Developmental Medicine & Child Neurology, 51*(4), 282–288. doi: 10.1111/j.1469-8749.2008.03226.x

Manning, Wendy D. (2015). Cohabitation and child wellbeing. *Marriage and Child Wellbeing Revisited, 25*(2), 51–66.

Manning, Wendy D.; Brown, Susan L. & Payne, Krista K. (2014). Two decades of stability and change in age at first union formation. *Journal of Marriage and Family, 76*(2), 247–260. doi: 10.1111/jomf.12090

Månsson, Johanna & Stjernqvist, Karin. (2014). Children born extremely preterm show significant lower cognitive, language and motor function levels compared with children born at term, as measured by the Bayley-III at 2.5 years.

Acta Paediatrica, 103(5), 504–511. doi: 10.1111 /apa.12585

Manzi, Claudia; Ferrari, Laura; Rosnati, Rosa & Benet-Martinez, Veronica. (2014). Bicultural identity integration of transracial adolescent adoptees: Antecedents and outcomes. *Journal of Cross-Cultural Psychology, 45*(6), 888–904. doi: 10.1177/0022022114530495

Mao, Xianyun; Bigham, Abigail W.; Mei, Rui; Gutierrez, Gerardo; Weiss, Ken M.; Brutsaert, Tom D., . . . Parra, Esteban J. (2007). A genomewide admixture mapping panel for Hispanic/Latino populations. *The American Journal of Human Genetics, 80*(6), 1171–1178. doi: 10.1086/518564

Mar, Raymond A. (2011). The neural bases of social cognition and story comprehension. *Annual Review of Psychology, 62*, 103–134. doi: 10.1146 /annurev-psych-120709-145406

Marazita, John M. & Merriman, William E. (2010). Verifying one's knowledge of a name without retrieving it: A U-shaped relation to vocabulary size in early childhood. *Language Learning and Development, 7*(1), 40–54. doi: 10.1080/15475441.2010.496099

Marcia, James E. (1966). Development and validation of ego-identity status. *Journal of Personality and Social Psychology, 3*(5), 551–558. doi: 10.1037/h0023281

Marcia, James E.; Waterman, Alan S.; Matteson, David R.; Archer, Sally L. & Orlofsky, Jacob L. (1993). *Ego identity: A handbook for psychosocial research.* New York, NY: Springer-Verlag.

Marcus, Gary F. & Rabagliati, Hugh. (2009). Language acquisition, domain specificity, and descent with modification. In John Colombo et al. (Eds.), *Infant pathways to language: Methods, models, and research disorders* (pp. 267–285). New York, NY: Psychology Press.

Margolis, Rachel & Myrskylä, Mikko. (2011). A global perspective on happiness and fertility. *Population and Development Review, 37*(1), 29–56. doi: 10.1111/j.1728-4457.2011.00389.x

Margrett, Jennifer A.; Daugherty, Kate; Martin, Peter; MacDonald, Maurice; Davey, Adam; Woodard, John L., . . . Poon, Leonard W. (2011). Affect and loneliness among centenarians and the oldest old: The role of individual and social resources. *Aging & Mental Health, 15*(3), 385–396. doi: 10.1080/13607863.2010.519327

Marin, Marie-France; Lord, Catherine; Andrews, Julie; Juster, Robert-Paul; Sindi, Shireen; Arsenault-Lapierre, Geneviève, . . . Lupien, Sonia J. (2011). Chronic stress, cognitive functioning and mental health. *Neurobiology of Learning and Memory, 96*(4), 583–595. doi: 10.1016/j.nlm .2011.02.016

Markey, Charlotte N. & Markey, Patrick M. (2012). Emerging adults' responses to a media presentation of idealized female beauty: An examination of cosmetic surgery in reality television. *Psychology of Popular Media Culture, 1*(4), 209–219. doi: 10.1037/a0027869

Markowitsch, Hans J. & Staniloiu, Angelica. (2012). Amnesic disorders. *The Lancet, 380*(9851), 1429–1440. doi: 10.1016/S0140-6736 (11)61304-4

Maron, Dina Fine. (2015, June 8). Has maternal mortality really doubled in the U.S.? *Scientific American.*

Marschark, Marc & Spencer, Patricia E. (2003). What we know, what we don't know, and what we should know. In Marc Marschark & Patricia E. Spencer (Eds.), *Oxford handbook of deaf studies, language, and education* (pp. 491–494). New York, NY: Oxford University Press.

Marshall, Eliot. (2014). An experiment in zero parenting. *Science, 345*(6198), 752–754. doi: 10.1126/science.345.6198.752

Marsiske, Michael & Margrett, Jennifer A. (2006). Everyday problem solving and decision making. In James E. Birren & K. Warren Schaie (Eds.), *Handbook of the psychology of aging* (6th ed., pp. 315–342). San Diego, CA: Academic Press. doi: 10.1016/B978-012101264-9/50017-3

Martin, Carmel. (2014). *Common Core implementation best practices. New York State Office of the Governor Common Core Implementation Panel.* Washington, DC: Center for American Progress.

Martin, Carol L.; Fabes, Richard; Hanish, Laura; Leonard, Stacie & Dinella, Lisa. (2011). Experienced and expected similarity to same-gender peers: Moving toward a comprehensive model of gender segregation. *Sex Roles, 65*(5/6), 421–434. doi: 10.1007/s11199-011-0029-y

Martin, Joyce A.; Hamilton, Brady E.; Osterman, Michelle J. K.; Curtin, Sally C. & Mathews, T. J. (2015). *Births: Final data 2013. National Vital Statistics Reports 64*(1). Hyattsville, MD: National Center for Health Statistics.

Martin, Joyce A.; Hamilton, Brady E.; Sutton, Paul D.; Ventura, Stephanie J.; Mathews, T. J. & Osterman, Michelle J. K. (2010). *Births: Final data for 2008. National Vital Statistics Reports.* Hyattsville, MD: National Center for Health Statistics.

Martin, Leslie R.; Haskard-Zolnierek, Kelly B. & DiMatteo, M. Robin. (2010). *Health behavior change and treatment adherence: Evidence-based guidelines for improving healthcare.* New York, NY: Oxford University Press.

Martin-Uzzi, Michele & Duval-Tsioles, Denise. (2013). The experience of remarried couples in blended families. *Journal of Divorce & Remarriage, 54*(1), 43–57. doi: 10.1080/10502556.2012.743828

Martinez, Gladys; Daniels, Kimberly & Chandra, Anjani. (2012, April 12). *Fertility of men and women aged 15–44 years in the United States: National Survey of Family Growth, 2006–2010. National Health Statistics Reports 51.* Washington, DC: U.S. Department Of Health And Human Services, Centers for Disease Control and Prevention National Center for Health Statistics.

Martinez, Gilbert A.; Dodd, David, A. & Samartgedes, Jo Ann. (1981). Milk feeding patterns in the United States during the first 12 months of life. *Pediatrics, 68*(6), 863–868.

Martínez-Hernáez, Angel; Carceller-Maicas, Natàlia; DiGiacomo, Susan M. & Ariste, Santiago. (2016). Social support and gender differences in coping with depression among emerging adults: A mixed-methods study. *Child and Adolescent Psychiatry and Mental Health, 10*(2). doi: 10.1186 /s13034-015-0088-x

Martinson, Melissa L. & Reichman, Nancy E. (2016). Socioeconomic inequalities in low birth weight in the United States, the United Kingdom, Canada, and Australia. *American Journal of Public Health, 106*(4), 748–754. doi: 10.2105/AJPH .2015.303007

Martorell, Reynaldo; Melgar, Paul; Maluccio, John A.; Stein, Aryeh D. & Rivera, Juan A. (2010). The nutrition intervention improved adult human capital and economic productivity. *The Journal of Nutrition, 140*(2), 411–414. doi: 10.3945/jn.109.114504

Martorell, Reynaldo & Young, Melissa F. (2012). Patterns of stunting and wasting: Potential explanatory factors. *Advances in Nutrition, 3*(2), 227–233. doi: 10.3945/an.111.001107

Marvasti, Amir B. & McKinney, Karyn D. (2011). Does diversity mean assimilation? *Critical Sociology, 37*(5), 631–650. doi: 10.1177 /0896920510380071

Mascarelli, Amanda. (2013). Growing up with pesticides. *Science, 341*(6147), 740–741. doi: 10.1126/science.341.6147.740

Mascarenhas, Maya N.; Flaxman, Seth R.; Boerma, Ties; Vanderpoel, Sheryl & Stevens, Gretchen A. (2012). National, regional, and global trends in infertility prevalence since 1990: A systematic analysis of 277 health surveys. *PloS Medicine, 9*(12), e1001356. doi: 10.1371/journal. pmed.1001356

Mashour, George A. & Avidan, Michael (Eds.). (2013). *Neurologic outcomes of surgery and anesthesia.* New York, NY: Oxford University Press.

Maski, Kiran P. & Kothare, Sanjeev V. (2013). Sleep deprivation and neurobehavioral functioning in children. *International Journal of Psychophysiology, 89*(2), 259–264. doi: 10.1016 /j.ijpsycho.2013.06.019

Maskileyson, Dina. (2014). Healthcare system and the wealth–health gradient: A comparative study of older populations in six countries. *Social Science & Medicine, 119,* 18–26. doi: 10.1016 /j.socscimed.2014.08.013

Maslow, Abraham H. (1954). *Motivation and personality* (1st ed.). New York, NY: Harper & Row.

Maslow, Abraham H. (1962). *Toward a psychology of being* (1st ed.). Princeton, NJ: D. Van Nostrand.

Maslow, Abraham H. (1971). *The farther reaches of human nature.* New York, NY: Viking Press.

Maslow, Abraham H. (1993). *The farther reaches of human nature.* New York, NY: Penguin.

Maslow, Abraham H. (1997). *Motivation and personality* (3rd ed.). New York, NY: Pearson.

Maslow, Abraham H. (1998). *Toward a psychology of being* (3rd ed.). New York, NY: Wiley.

Maslowsky, Julie; Schulenberg, John E. & Zucker, Robert A. (2014). Influence of conduct problems and depressive symptomatology on adolescent substance use: Developmentally proximal versus distal effects. *Developmental Psychology, 50*(4), 1179–1189. doi: 10.1037/a0035085

Mâsse, Louise C.; Perna, Frank; Agurs-Collins, Tanya & Chriqui, Jamie F. (2013). Change in school nutrition-related laws from 2003 to 2008: Evidence from the School Nutrition-Environment State Policy Classification System. *American Journal of Public Health, 103*(9), 1597–1603. doi: 10.2105/AJPH.2012.300896

Masten, Ann S. (2014). *Ordinary magic: Resilience in development.* New York, NY: Guilford Press.

Masten, Ann S. & Wright, Margaret O'Dougherty. (2010). Resilience over the lifespan: Developmental perspectives on resistance, recovery, and transformation. In John W. Reich et al. (Eds.), *Handbook of adult resilience* (pp. 213–237). New York, NY: Guilford Press.

Mateus-Pinheiro, António; Patrício, Patrícia; Bessa, João M.; Sousa, Nuno & Pinto, Luísa. (2013). Cell genesis and dendritic plasticity: A neuroplastic pas de deux in the onset and remission from depression. *Molecular Psychiatry, 18*(7), 748–750. doi: 10.1038/mp.2013.56

Mathews, T. J.; Menacker, Fay & MacDorman, Marian F. (2003). *Infant mortality statistics from the 2001 period linked birth/infant death data set. National Vital Statistics Reports 52*(2). Hyattsville, MD: National Center for Health Statistics.

Mathison, David J. & Agrawal, Dewesh. (2010). An update on the epidemiology of pediatric fractures. *Pediatric Emergency Care, 26*(8), 594–603. doi: 10.1097 /PEC.0b013e3181eb838d

Matsumoto, David; Hwang, Hyi Sung & Yamada, Hiroshi. (2012). Cultural differences in the relative contributions of face and context to judgments of emotion. *Journal of Cross-Cultural Psychology, 43*(2), 198–218. doi: 10.1177 /0022022110387426

Matsumoto, Yasuyo; Yamabe, Shingo; Sugishima, Toru & Geronazzo, Dan. (2011). Perception of oral contraceptives among women of reproductive age in Japan: A comparison with the USA and France. *Journal of Obstetrics and Gynaecology Research, 37*(7), 887–892. doi: 10.1111/j.1447-0756.2010 .01461.x

Matthews, Fiona E.; Arthur, Antony; Barnes, Linda E.; Bond, John; Jagger, Carol; Robinson, Louise & Brayne, Carol. (2013). A two-decade comparison of prevalence of dementia in individuals aged 65 years and older from three geographical areas of England: Results of the Cognitive Function and Ageing Study I and II. *The Lancet, 382*(9902), 1405–1412. doi: 10.1016/ S0140-6736 (13)61570-6

Mattison, Julie A.; Roth, George S.; Beasley, T. Mark; Tilmont, Edward M.; Handy, April M.; Herbert, Richard L., . . . de Cabo, Rafael. (2012). Impact of caloric restriction on health and survival in rhesus monkeys from the NIA study. *Nature, 489*(7415), 318–321. doi: 10.1038/nature11432

Maume, David J. & Sebastian, Rachel A. (2012). Gender, nonstandard work schedules, and marital quality. *Journal of Family and Economic Issues, 33*(4), 477–490. doi: 10.1007/s10834-012-9308-1

Maxfield, Molly; John, Samantha & Pyszczynski, Tom. (2014). A terror management perspective on the role of death-related anxiety in psychological dysfunction. *The Humanistic Psychologist, 42*(1), 35–53. doi: 10.1080/08873267.2012.732155

Maxfield, Molly; Pyszczynski, Tom; Kluck, Benjamin; Cox, Cathy R.; Greenberg, Jeff; Solomon, Sheldon & Weise, David. (2007). Age-related differences in responses to thoughts of one's own death: Mortality salience and judgments of moral transgressions. *Psychology and Aging, 22*(2), 341–353. doi: 10.1037/0882-7974.22.2.341

Maxwell, Lesli A. (2012). Achievement gaps tied to income found widening. *Education Week, 31*(23), 1, 22–23.

May, Lillian; Byers-Heinlein, Krista; Gervain, Judit & Werker, Janet F. (2011). Language and the newborn brain: Does prenatal language experience shape the neonate neural response to speech? *Frontiers in Psychology, 2,* 222. doi: 10.3389/fpsyg .2011.00222

May, Vanessa; Mason, Jennifer & Clarke, Lynda. (2012). Being there, yet not interfering: The paradoxes of grandparenting. In Sara Arber & Virpi Timonen (Eds.), *Contemporary grandparenting: Changing family relationships in global contexts* (pp. 139–158). Chicago, IL: Policy Press.

Mazzonnaa, Fabrizio & Peracchi, Franco. (2012). Ageing, cognitive abilities and retirement. *European Economic Review, 56*(4), 691–710. doi: 10.1016/j.euroecorev.2012.03.004

McAdams, Dan P. (2013). The psychological self as actor, agent, and author. *Perspectives on Psychological Science, 8*(3), 272–295. doi: 10.1177/1745691612464657

McAdams, Dan P. & Olson, Bradley D. (2010). Personality development: Continuity and change over the life course. *Annual Review of Psychology, 61,* 517–542. doi: 10.1146/annurev .psych.093008.100507

McAlister, Anna R. & Peterson, Candida C. (2013). Siblings, theory of mind, and executive functioning in children aged 3–6 years: New longitudinal evidence. *Child Development, 84*(4), 1442–1458. doi: 10.1111/cdev.12043

McCabe, Janice. (2011). Doing multiculturalism: An interactionist analysis of the practices of a multicultural sorority. *Journal of Contemporary Ethnography, 40*(5), 521–549. doi: 10.1177/0891241611403588

McCall, Robert B. (2013). The consequences of early institutionalization: Can institutions be improved?—Should they? *Child and Adolescent Mental Health, 18*(4), 193–201. doi: 10.1111 /camh .12025

McCarrey, Anna C.; Henry, Julie D.; von Hippel, William; Weidemann, Gabrielle; Sachdev, Perminder S.; Wohl, Michael J. A. & Williams, Mark. (2012). Age differences in neural activity during slot machine gambling: An fMRI study. *PLoS ONE, 7*(11), e49787. doi: 10.1371 /journal.pone.0049787

McCarter, Roger J. M. (2006). Differential aging among skeletal muscles. In Edward J. Masoro & Steven N. Austad (Eds.), *Handbook of the biology of aging* (6th ed., pp. 470–497). Boston, MA: Academic Press.

McCarthy, Neil & Eberhart, Johann K. (2014). Gene–ethanol interactions underlying fetal alcohol spectrum disorders. *Cellular and Molecular Life Sciences, 71*(14), 2699–2706. doi: 10.1007 /s00018-014-1578-3

McCartney, Kathleen; Burchinal, Margaret; Clarke-Stewart, Alison; Bub, Kristen L.; Owen, Margaret T. & Belsky, Jay. (2010). Testing a series of causal propositions relating time in child care to children's externalizing behavior. *Developmental Psychology*, 46(1), 1–17. doi: 10.1037/a0017886

McClain, Lauren Rinelli. (2011). Better parents, more stable partners: Union transitions among cohabiting parents. *Journal of Marriage and Family*, 73(5), 889–901. doi: 10.1111/j.1741-3737.2011 .00859.x

McClain, Natalie M. & Garrity, Stacy E. (2011). Sex trafficking and the exploitation of adolescents. *Journal of Obstetric, Gynecologic, & Neonatal Nursing*, 40(2), 243–252. doi: 10.1111 /j.1552-6909 .2011.01221.x

McCormick, Cheryl M.; Mathews, Iva Z.; Thomas, Catherine & Waters, Patti. (2010). Investigations of HPA function and the enduring consequences of stressors in adolescence in animal models. *Brain and Cognition*, 72(1), 73–85. doi: 10.1016 /j.bandc.2009.06.003

McCowan, Lesley M. E.; Dekker, Gustaaf A.; Chan, Eliza; Stewart, Alistair; Chappell, Lucy C.; Hunter, Misty, . . . North, Robyn A. (2009). Spontaneous preterm birth and small for gestational age infants in women who stop smoking early in pregnancy: Prospective cohort study. *BMJ*, 338, b1081. doi: 10.1136/bmj.b1081

McCright, Aaron M. & Dunlap, Riley E. (2011). The politicization of climate change and polarization in the American public's views of global warming, 2001–2010. *Sociological Quarterly*, 52(2), 155–194. doi: 10.1111 /j.1533-8525.2011.01198.x

McDaniel, Mark A. & Bugg, Julie M. (2012). Memory training interventions: What has been forgotten? *Journal of Applied Research in Memory and Cognition*, 1(1), 45–50. doi: 10.1016 /j.jarmac .2011.11.002

McEwen, Bruce S. & Gianaros, Peter J. (2011). Stress- and allostasis-induced brain plasticity. *Annual Review of Medicine*, 62, 431–445. doi: 10.1146/annurev-med-052209-100430

McEwen, Bruce S. & Karatsoreos, Ilia N. (2015). Sleep deprivation and circadian disruption: Stress, allostasis, and allostatic load. *Sleep Medicine Clinics*, 10(1), 1–10. doi: 10.1016/j.jsmc .2014.11.007

McFadden, Susan H. & Basting, Anne D. (2010). Healthy aging persons and their brains: Promoting resilience through creative engagement. *Clinics in Geriatric Medicine*, 26(1), 149–161. doi: 10.1016/j.cger.2009.11.004

McFarlane, Alexander C. & Van Hooff, Miranda. (2009). Impact of childhood exposure to a natural disaster on adult mental health: 20-year longitudinal follow-up study. *The British Journal of Psychiatry*, 195(2), 142–148. doi: 10.1192/bjp.bp .108.054270

McGee, Robin E. & Thompson, Nancy J. (2015, March 19). *Unemployment and depression among emerging adults in 12 states, Behavioral Risk Factor Surveillance System, 2010. Preventing Chronic Disease 12.* Atlanta, GA: Centers for Disease Control and Prevention, National Center for Chronic Disease Prevention and Health Promotion. doi: 10.5888/pcd12.140451

McGill, Natalie. (2015). States taking action to regulate e-cigarettes: FDA working to gain authority as science on products grows. *The Nation's Health*, 45(4), 1–12.

McGill, Rebecca K.; Hughes, Diane; Alicea, Stacey & Way, Niobe. (2012). Academic adjustment across middle school: The role of public regard and parenting. *Developmental Psychology*, 48(4), 1003–1018. doi: 10.1037/a0026006

McGrath, John J. & Murray, Robin M. (2011). Environmental risk factors for schizophrenia. In Daniel R. Weinberger & Paul J. Harrison (Eds.), *Schizophrenia* (3rd ed., pp. 226–244). Hoboken, NJ: Wiley. doi: 10.1002/9781444327298.ch11

McGrath, John J.; Saha, Sukanta; Al-Hamzawi, Ali O.; Alonso, Jordi; Andrade, Laura; Borges, Guilherme, . . . Kessler, Ronald C. (2016). Age of onset and lifetime projected risk of psychotic experiences: Cross-national data from the world mental health survey. *Schizophrenia Bulletin*, 42(4), 933–941. doi: 10.1093/schbul/sbw011

McGue, Matt; Irons, Dan & Iacono, William G. (2014). The adolescent origins of substance use disorders: A behavioral genetic perspective. In Scott F. Stoltenberg (Ed.), *Genes and the motivation to use substances* (pp. 31–50). New York, NY: Springer. doi: 10.1007/978-1-4939-0653-6_3

McHugh, Maureen C. & Interligi, Camille. (2015). Sexuality and older women: Desirability and desire. In Varda Muhlbauer et al. (Eds.), *Women and aging: An international, intersectional power perspective* (pp. 89–116). New York, NY: Springer. doi: 10.1007/978-3-319-09306-2_6

McKinney, Lyle & Burridge, Andrea Backscheider. (2015). Helping or hindering? The effects of loans on community college student persistence. *Research in Higher Education*, 56(4), 299–324. doi: 10.1007/s11162-014-9349-4

McLaren, Lindsay; Patterson, Steven; Thawer, Salima; Faris, Peter; McNeil, Deborah; Potestio, Melissa & Shwart, Luke. (2016). Measuring the short-term impact of fluoridation cessation on dental caries in grade 2 children using tooth surface indices. *Community Dentistry and Oral Epidemiology*, 44(3), 274–282. doi: 10.1111/cdoe.12215

McLaren, Rachel M. & Sillars, Alan. (2014). Hurtful episodes in parent–adolescent relationships: How accounts and attributions contribute to the difficulty of talking about hurt. *Communication Monographs*, 81(3), 359–385. doi: 10.1080/03637751.2014.933244

McLean, Robert R. & Kiel, Douglas P. (2015). Developing consensus criteria for sarcopenia: An update. *Journal of Bone and Mineral Research*, 30(4), 588–592. doi: 10.1002/jbmr.2492

McLendon, Amber N. & Shelton, Penny S. (2011–2012). New symptoms in older adults: Disease or drug? *Generations*, 35(4), 25–30.

McLeod, Bryce D.; Wood, Jeffrey J. & Weisz, John R. (2007). Examining the association between parenting and childhood anxiety: A meta-analysis. *Clinical Psychology Review*, 27(2), 155–172. doi: 10.1016/j.cpr.2006.09.002

McManus, I. Chris; Moore, James; Freegard, Matthew & Rawles, Richard. (2010). Science in the making: Right Hand, Left Hand. III: Estimating historical rates of left-handedness. *Laterality: Asymmetries of Body, Brain and Cognition*, 15(1/2), 186–208. doi: 10.1080/13576500802565313

McMillin, Stephen Edward; Hall, Lacey; Bultas, Margaret W.; Grafeman, Sarah E.; Wilmott, Jennifer; Maxim, Rolanda & Zand, Debra H. (2015). Knowledge of child development as a predictor of mother-child play interactions. *Clinical Pediatrics*, 54(11), 1117–1119. doi: 10.1177/0009922815581763

McNeil, Michele & Blad, Evie. (2014). U.S. comes up short on education equity, federal data indicate. *Education Week*, 33(26), 8.

McShane, Kelly E. & Hastings, Paul D. (2009). The New Friends Vignettes: Measuring parental psychological control that confers risk for anxious adjustment in preschoolers. *International Journal of Behavioral Development*, 33(6), 481–495. doi: 10.1177/0165025409103874

Meadows, Sara. (2006). *The child as thinker: The development and acquisition of cognition in childhood* (2nd ed.). New York, NY: Routledge.

Meagher, David K. (2013). Ethical and legal issues and loss, grief, and mourning. In David K. Meagher & David E. Balk (Eds.), *Handbook of thanatology: The essential body of knowledge for the study of death, dying, and bereavement* (2nd ed.). New York, NY: Routledge.

Meczekalski, Blazej; Podfigurna-Stopa, Agnieszka & Katulski, Krzysztof. (2013). Long-term consequences of anorexia nervosa. *Maturitas*, 75(3), 215–220. doi: 10.1016/j.maturitas.2013.04.014

Meece, Judith L. & Eccles, Jacquelynne S. (Eds.). (2010). *Handbook of research on schools, schooling, and human development*. New York, NY: Routledge.

Meeus, Wim. (2011). The study of adolescent identity formation 2000–2010: A review of longitudinal research. *Journal of Research on Adolescence*, 21(1), 75–94. doi: 10.1111/j.1532-7795.2010 .00716.x

Mehta, Clare M. & Strough, JoNell. (2009). Sex segregation in friendships and normative contexts across the life span. *Developmental Review*, 29(3), 201–220. doi: 10.1016/j.dr.2009.06.001

Meier, Ann; Hull, Kathleen E. & Ortyl, Timothy A. (2009). Young adult relationship values at the intersection of gender and sexuality. *Journal of Marriage and Family*, 71(3), 510–525. doi: 10.1111/j.1741-3737.2009.00616.x

Meisenberg, Gerhard & Woodley, Michael A. (2013). Are cognitive differences between countries diminishing? Evidence from TIMSS and PISA. *Intelligence*, 41(6), 808–816. doi: 10.1016 /j.intell.2013.03.009

Meltzoff, Andrew N. & Gopnik, Alison. (2013). Learning about the mind from evidence: Children's development of intuitive theories of perception and personality. In Simon Baron-Cohen et al. (Eds.), *Understanding other minds: Perspectives from developmental social neuroscience* (3rd ed., pp. 19–34). New York, NY: Oxford University Press. doi: 10.1093/acprof: oso/9780199692972.001.0001

Menary, Kyle; Collins, Paul F.; Porter, James N.; Muetzel, Ryan; Olson, Elizabeth A.; Kumar, Vipin, . . . Luciana, Monica. (2013). Associations between cortical thickness and general intelligence in children, adolescents and young adults. *Intelligence, 41*(5), 597–606. doi: 10.1016/j.intell.2013.07.010

Mendle, Jane; Harden, K. Paige; Brooks-Gunn, Jeanne & Graber, Julia A. (2010). Development's tortoise and hare: Pubertal timing, pubertal tempo, and depressive symptoms in boys and girls. *Developmental Psychology, 46*(5), 1341–1353. doi: 10.1037/a0020205

Mendle, Jane; Harden, K. Paige; Brooks-Gunn, Jeanne & Graber, Julia A. (2012). Peer relationships and depressive symptomatology in boys at puberty. *Developmental Psychology, 48*(2), 429–435. doi: 10.1037/a0026425

Mennis, Jeremy & Mason, Michael J. (2012). Social and geographic contexts of adolescent substance use: The moderating effects of age and gender. *Social Networks, 34*(1), 150–157. doi: 10.1016/j.socnet.2010.10.003

Mercer, Neil & Howe, Christine. (2012). Explaining the dialogic processes of teaching and learning: The value and potential of sociocultural theory. *Learning, Culture and Social Interaction, 1*(1), 12–21. doi: 10.1016/j.lcsi.2012.03.001

Merikangas, Kathleen R.; He, Jian-ping; Rapoport, Judith; Vitiello, Benedetto & Olfson, Mark. (2013). Medication use in US youth with mental disorders. *JAMA Pediatrics, 167*(2), 141–148. doi: 10.1001/jamapediatrics.2013.431

Merikangas, Kathleen R. & McClair, Vetisha L. (2012). Epidemiology of substance use disorders. *Human Genetics, 131*(6), 779–789. doi: 10.1007/s00439-012-1168-0

Merriam, Sharan B. (2009). *Qualitative research: A guide to design and implementation.* San Francisco, CA: Jossey-Bass.

Merrill, Anne F. & Afifi, Tamara D. (2012). Examining the bidirectional nature of topic avoidance and relationship dissatisfaction: The moderating role of communication skills. *Communication Monographs, 79*(4), 499–521. doi: 10.1080/03637751.2012.723809

Mersky, Joshua P.; Topitzes, James & Reynolds, Arthur J. (2013). Impacts of adverse childhood experiences on health, mental health, and substance use in early adulthood: A cohort study of an urban, minority sample in the U.S. *Child Abuse & Neglect, 37*(11), 917–925. doi: 10.1016/j.chiabu.2013.07.011

Merz, Emily C. & McCall, Robert B. (2011). Parent ratings of executive functioning in children adopted from psychosocially depriving institutions. *Journal of Child Psychology and Psychiatry, 52*(5), 537–546. doi: 10.1111/j.1469-7610.2010.02335.x

Messinger, Daniel M.; Ruvolo, Paul; Ekas, Naomi V. & Fogel, Alan. (2010). Applying machine learning to infant interaction: The development is in the details. *Neural Networks, 23*(8/9), 1004–1016. doi: 10.1016/j.neunet.2010.08.008

Metcalfe, Lindsay A.; Harvey, Elizabeth A. & Laws, Holly B. (2013). The longitudinal relation between academic/cognitive skills and externalizing behavior problems in preschool children. *Journal of Educational Psychology, 105*(3), 881–894. doi: 10.1037/a0032624

Meyer, Madonna Harrington. (2014). *Grandmothers at work: Juggling families and jobs.* New York, NY: New York University Press.

Michl, Louisa C.; McLaughlin, Katie A.; Shepherd, Kathrine & Nolen-Hoeksema, Susan. (2013). Rumination as a mechanism linking stressful life events to symptoms of depression and anxiety: Longitudinal evidence in early adolescents and adults. *Journal of Abnormal Psychology, 122*(2), 339–352. doi: 10.1037/a0031994

Miech, Richard A.; Johnston, Lloyd D.; O'Malley, Patrick M.; Bachman, Jerald G. & Schulenberg, John E. (2015). *Monitoring the future, national survey results on drug use, 1975–2014: Volume I, Secondary school students.* Ann Arbor, Michigan: Institute for Social Research, The University of Michigan.

Miech, Richard A.; Johnston, Lloyd D.; O'Malley, Patrick M.; Bachman, Jerald G. & Schulenberg, John E. (2016). *Monitoring the future, national survey results on drug use, 1975–2015: Volume I secondary school students.* Ann Arbor, Michigan: Institute for Social Research, The University of Michigan.

Mikels, Joseph A.; Shuster, Michael M. & Thai, Sydney T. (2015). Aging, emotion, and decision making. In Thomas M. Hess et al. (Eds.), *Aging and decision making: Empirical and applied perspectives* (pp. 170–189). San Diego, CA: Academic Press.

Miklowitz, David J. & Cicchetti, Dante (Eds.). (2010). *Understanding bipolar disorder: A developmental psychopathology perspective.* New York, NY: Guilford Press.

Miles, Lynden K. (2009). Who is approachable? *Journal of Experimental Social Psychology, 45*(1), 262–266. doi: 10.1016/j.jesp.2008.08.010

Milkman, Katherine L.; Chugh, Dolly & Bazerman, Max H. (2009). How can decision making be improved? *Perspectives on Psychological Science, 4*(4), 379–383. doi: 10.1111/j.1745-6924.2009.01142.x

Miller, Cindy F.; Martin, Carol Lynn; Fabes, Richard A. & Hanish, Laura D. (2013). Bringing the cognitive and the social together: How gender detectives and gender enforcers shape children's gender development. In Mahzarin R. Banaji & Susan A. Gelman (Eds.), *Navigating the social world: What infants, children, and other species can teach us* (pp. 306–313). New York, NY: Oxford University Press.

Miller, Greg. (2012). Engineering a new line of attack on a signature war injury. *Science, 335*(6064), 33–35. doi: 10.1126/science.335.6064.33

Miller, Gregory E. & Chen, Edith. (2010). Harsh family climate in early life: Presages the emergence of a proinflammatory phenotype in adolescence. *Psychological Science, 21*(6), 848–856. doi: 10.1177/0956797610370161

Miller, Gregory E.; Murphy, Michael L. M.; Cashman, Rosemary; Ma, Roy; Ma, Jeffrey; Arevalo, Jesusa M. G., . . . Cole, Steve W. (2014). Greater inflammatory activity and blunted glucocorticoid signaling in monocytes of chronically stressed caregivers. *Brain, Behavior, and Immunity, 41*, 191–199. doi: 10.1016/j.bbi.2014.05.016

Miller, Melissa K.; Dowd, M. Denise; Harrison, Christopher J.; Mollen, Cynthia J.; Selvarangan, Rangaraj & Humiston, Sharon. (2015). Prevalence of 3 sexually transmitted infections in a pediatric emergency department. *Pediatric Emergency Care, 31*(2), 107–112. doi: 10.1097/PEC.0000000000000284

Miller, Portia; Votruba-Drzal, Elizabeth; Coley, Rebekah Levine & Koury, Amanda S. (2014). Immigrant families' use of early childcare: Predictors of care type. *Early Childhood Research Quarterly, 29*(4), 484–498. doi: 10.1016/j.ecresq.2014.05.011

Miller, Patricia H. (2011). *Theories of developmental psychology* (5th ed.). New York, NY: Worth Publishers.

Miller, Patricia Y. & Simon, William. (1980). The development of sexuality in adolescence. In Joseph Adelson (Ed.), *Handbook of adolescent psychology* (pp. 383–407). New York, NY: Wiley.

Miller, Richard B.; Hollist, Cody S.; Olsen, Joseph & Law, David. (2013). Marital quality and health over 20 years: A growth curve analysis. *Journal of Marriage and Family, 75*(3), 667–680. doi: 10.1111/jomf.12025

Miller, Susan W. (2011–2012). Medications and elders: Quality of care or quality of life? *Generations, 35*(4), 19–24.

Mills-Koonce, W. Roger; Garrett-Peters, Patricia; Barnett, Melissa; Granger, Douglas A.; Blair, Clancy & Cox, Martha J. (2011). Father contributions to cortisol responses in infancy and toddlerhood. *Developmental Psychology, 47*(2), 388–395. doi: 10.1037/a0021066

Milunsky, Aubrey & Milunsky, Jeff M. (2016). *Genetic disorders and the fetus: Diagnosis, prevention, and treatment* (7th ed.). Hoboken, NJ: Wiley-Blackwell.

Minagawa-Kawai, Yasuyo; van der Lely, Heather; Ramus, Franck; Sato, Yutaka; Mazuka, Reiko & Dupoux, Emmanuel. (2011). Optical brain imaging reveals general auditory and language-specific processing in early infant development. *Cerebral Cortex, 21*(2), 254–261. doi: 10.1093/cercor/bhq082

Mindell, Jodi A.; Sadeh, Avi; Wiegand, Benjamin; How, Ti Hwei & Goh, Daniel Y. T. (2010). Cross-cultural differences in infant and toddler sleep. *Sleep Medicine, 11*(3), 274–280. doi: 10.1016/j.sleep.2009.04.012

Ming, Guo-li & Song, Hongjun. (2011). Adult neurogenesis in the mammalian brain: Significant answers and significant questions. *Neuron, 70*(4), 687–702. doi: 10.1016/j.neuron.2011.05.001

Miniño, Arialdi M.; Heron, Melonie P.; Murphy, Sherry L. & Kochanek, Kenneth D. (2007). *Deaths: Final data for 2004. National Vital Statistics Reports 55*(19). Hyattsville, MD: National Center for Health Statistics.

Mirucka, Beata; Bielecka, Urszula & Kisielewska, Monika. (2016). Positive orientation, self-esteem, and satisfaction with life in the context of subjective age in older adults. *Personality and Individual Differences, 99*, 206–210. doi: 10.1016/j.paid.2016.05.010

Mischel, Walter. (2014). *The marshmallow test: Mastering self-control.* New York, NY: Little, Brown and Company.

Mischel, Walter; Ebbesen, Ebbe B. & Raskoff Zeiss, Antonette. (1972). Cognitive and attentional mechanisms in delay of gratification. *Journal of Personality and Social Psychology, 21*(2), 204–218. doi: 10.1037/h0032198

Mishra, Ramesh C.; Singh, Sunita & Dasen, Pierre R. (2009). Geocentric dead reckoning in Sanskrit- and Hindi-medium school children. *Culture & Psychology, 15*(3), 386–408. doi: 10.1177/1354067x09343330

Misra, Dawn P.; Caldwell, Cleopatra; Young, Alford A. & Abelson, Sara. (2010). Do fathers matter? Paternal contributions to birth outcomes and racial disparities. *American Journal of Obstetrics and Gynecology, 202*(2), 99–100. doi: 10.1016 /j.ajog.2009.11.031

Missana, Manuela; Rajhans, Purva; Atkinson, Anthony P. & Grossmann, Tobias. (2014). Discrimination of fearful and happy body postures in 8-month-old infants: An event-related potential study. *Frontiers in Human Neuroscience, 8,* 531. doi: 10.3389/fnhum.2014.00531

Mitchell, Barbara A. (2010). Happiness in midlife parental roles: A contextual mixed methods analysis. *Family Relations, 59*(3), 326–339. doi: 10.1111/j.1741-3729.2010.00605.x

Mitchell, Edwin A. (2009). SIDS: Past, present and future. *Acta Paediatrica, 98*(11), 1712–1719. doi: 10.1111/j.1651-2227.2009.01503.x

Mitchell, Kimberly J.; Jones, Lisa M.; Finkelhor, David & Wolak, Janis. (2013). Understanding the decline in unwanted online sexual solicitations for U.S. youth 2000–2010: Findings from three Youth Internet Safety Surveys. *Child Abuse & Neglect, 37*(12), 1225–1236. doi: 10.1016/j.chiabu .2013.07.002

Mitchell, Philip B.; Meiser, Bettina; Wilde, Alex; Fullerton, Janice; Donald, Jennifer; Wilhelm, Kay & Schofield, Peter R. (2010). Predictive and diagnostic genetic testing in psychiatry. *Psychiatric Clinics of North America, 33*(1), 225–243. doi: 10.1016/j.psc.2009.10.001

Miyata, Susanne; MacWhinney, Brian; Otomo, Kiyoshi; Sirai, Hidetosi; Oshima-Takane, Yuriko; Hirakawa, Makiko, . . . Itoh, Keiko. (2013). Developmental sentence scoring for Japanese. *First Language, 33*(2), 200–216. doi: 10.1177/0142723713479436

Mize, Krystal D.; Pineda, Melannie; Blau, Alexis K.; Marsh, Kathryn & Jones, Nancy A. (2014). Infant physiological and behavioral responses to a jealousy provoking condition. *Infancy, 19*(3), 338–348. doi: 10.1111/infa.12046

MMWR. (1992). *Youth risk behavior surveillance—United States, 1991. Morbidity and Mortality Weekly Report Surveillance Summaries.* Atlanta, GA: U.S. Department of Health and Human Services, Centers for Disease Control and Prevention.

MMWR. (1995, March 24). *Youth risk behavior surveillance—United States, 1993. Morbidity and Mortality Weekly Report Surveillance Summaries* 44(SS-1). Atlanta, GA: U.S. Department of Health and Human Services, Centers for Disease Control and Prevention.

MMWR. (1996, September 27). *Youth risk behavior surveillance—United States, 1995. Morbidity and Mortality Weekly Report Surveillance Summaries* 45(SS-4). Atlanta, GA: U.S. Department of Health and Human Services, Centers for Disease Control and Prevention.

MMWR. (1998, August 14). *Youth risk behavior surveillance—United States, 1997. Morbidity and Mortality Weekly Report Surveillance Summaries* 47(SS-3). Atlanta, GA: U.S. Department of Health and Human Services, Centers for Disease Control and Prevention.

MMWR. (2000, June 9). *Youth risk behavior surveillance—United States, 1999. Morbidity and Mortality Weekly Report Surveillance Summaries* 49(SS05). Atlanta, GA: U.S. Department of Health and Human Services, Centers for Disease Control and Prevention.

MMWR. (2000, March 31). *Reducing falls and resulting hip fractures among older women. Morbidity and Mortality Weekly Report* 49(RR02), 1–12. Atlanta, GA: U.S. Department of Health and Human Services, Centers for Disease Control and Prevention.

MMWR. (2002, June 28). *Youth risk behavior surveillance—United States, 2001. Morbidity and Mortality Weekly Report Surveillance Summaries* 51(SS04). Atlanta, GA: U.S. Department of Health and Human Services, Centers for Disease Control and Prevention.

MMWR. (2004, May 21). *Youth risk behavior surveillance—United States, 2003. Morbidity and Mortality Weekly Report Surveillance Summaries* 53(SS-2). Atlanta, GA: U.S. Department of Health and Human Services, Centers for Disease Control and Prevention.

MMWR. (2006, June 9). *Youth risk behavior surveillance—United States, 2005. Morbidity and Mortality Weekly Report Surveillance Summaries* 55(SS-5). Atlanta, GA: U.S. Department of Health and Human Services, Centers for Disease Control and Prevention.

MMWR. (2008, January 18). *School-associated student homicides—United States, 1992–2006. Morbidity and Mortality Weekly Report* 57(2), 33–36. Atlanta, GA: U.S. Department of Health and Human Services, Centers for Disease Control and Prevention.

MMWR. (2008, June 6). *Youth risk behavior surveillance—United States, 2007. Morbidity and Mortality Weekly Report Surveillance Summaries* 57(SS04). Atlanta, GA: U.S. Department of Health and Human Services, Centers for Disease Control and Prevention.

MMWR. (2010, June 4). *Youth risk behavior surveillance—United States, 2009. Morbidity and Mortality Weekly Report Surveillance Summaries* 59(SS05). Atlanta, GA: U.S. Department of Health and Human Services, Centers for Disease Control and Prevention.

MMWR. (2012, July 20). *Alcohol Use and Binge Drinking Among Women of Childbearing Age—United States, 2006–2010. Morbidity and Mortality Weekly Report* 61(28), 534–538. Atlanta, GA: U.S. Department of Health and Human Services, Centers for Disease Control and Prevention.

MMWR. (2012, June 8). *Youth risk behavior surveillance—United States, 2011. Morbidity and Mortality Weekly Report* 61(4). Atlanta, GA: U.S. Department of Health and Human Services, Centers for Disease Control and Prevention.

MMWR. (2013). *Progress toward eradication of polio—Worldwide, January 2011–March 2013. Morbidity and Mortality Weekly Report* 62(17), 335–338. Atlanta, GA: Centers for Disease Control and Prevention.

MMWR. (2013, April 5). *Blood lead levels in children aged 1–5 Years—United States, 1999–2010. Morbidity and Mortality Weekly Report* 62(13), 245–248. Atlanta, GA: U.S. Department of Health and Human Services, Centers for Disease Control and Prevention.

MMWR. (2013, August 9). *Vital signs: Obesity among low-income, preschool-aged children—United States, 2008–2011. Morbidity and Mortality Weekly Report* 62(31), 629–634. Atlanta, GA: U.S. Department of Health and Human Services, Centers for Disease Control and Prevention.

MMWR. (2013, January 18). *Obesity prevalence among low-income, preschool-aged children—New York City and Los Angeles County, 2003–2011. Morbidity and Mortality Weekly Report* 62(2), 17–22. Atlanta, GA: U.S. Department of Health and Human Services, Centers for Disease Control and Prevention.

MMWR. (2013, June 21). *U.S. selected practice recommendations for contraceptive use, 2013: Adapted from the World Health Organization Selected Practice Recommendations for Contraceptive Use, 2nd Edition. Morbidity and Mortality Weekly Report: Recommendations and Reports* 62(5). Atlanta, GA: Centers for Disease Control and Prevention.

MMWR. (2014, July 25). *Human papillomavirus vaccination coverage among adolescents, 2007–2013, and postlicensure vaccine safety monitoring, 2006–2014—United States. Morbidity and Mortality Weekly Report* 63(29). Atlanta, GA: U.S. Department of Health and Human Services, Centers for Disease Control and Prevention.

MMWR. (2014, June 13). *Youth risk behavior surveillance—United States, 2013. Morbidity and Mortality Weekly Report* 63(4). Atlanta, GA: U.S. Department of Health and Human Services, Centers for Disease Control and Prevention.

MMWR. (2014, March 7). *Impact of requiring influenza vaccination for children in licensed child care or preschool programs—Connecticut, 2012–13 influenza season. Morbidity and Mortality Weekly Report* 63(9), 181–185. Atlanta, GA: U.S. Department of Health and Human Services, Centers for Disease Control and Prevention.

MMWR. (2014, March 28). *Prevalence of autism spectrum disorder among children aged 8 years—Autism and Developmental Disabilities Monitoring Network, 11 sites, United States, 2010. Morbidity and Mortality Weekly Report* 63(2). Atlanta, GA: U.S. Department of Health and Human Services, Centers for Disease Control and Prevention.

MMWR. (2014, May 2). *QuickStats: Percentage of children aged 6–17 years prescribed medication during the preceding 6 months for emotional or behavioral difficulties, by census region—National Health Interview Survey, United States, 2011–2012.*

Morbidity and Mortality Weekly Report 63(17), 389–389. Atlanta, GA: Centers for Disease Control and Prevention.

MMWR. (2014, May 16). *Racial/ethnic disparities in fatal unintentional drowning among persons aged ≤29 years—United States, 1999–2010. Morbidity and Mortality Weekly Report 63*(19), 421–426. Atlanta, GA: U.S. Department of Health and Human Services, Centers for Disease Control and Prevention.

MMWR. (2014, September 5). *Prevalence of smokefree home rules—United States, 1992–1993 and 2010–2011. Morbidity and Mortality Weekly Report 63*(35), 765–769. Atlanta, GA: Department of Health and Human Services, Centers for Disease Control and Prevention.

MMWR. (2015, November 6). *Gestational weight gain—United States, 2012 and 2013. Morbidity and Mortality Weekly Report 64*(43), 1215–1220. Atlanta, GA: Centers for Disease Control and Prevention.

MMWR. (2015, September 25). *Alcohol use and binge drinking among women of childbearing age—United States, 2011–2013. Morbidity and Mortality Weekly Report 64*(37), 1042–1046. Atlanta, GA: Centers for Disease Control and Prevention.

MMWR. (2016, January 8). *Notifiable diseases and mortality tables. Morbidity and Mortality Weekly Report 64*(52). Atlanta, GA: Centers for Disease Control and Prevention.

MMWR. (2016, June 10). *Youth risk behavior surveillance—United States, 2015. Morbidity and Mortality Weekly Report 65*(6). Atlanta, GA: U.S. Department of Health and Human Services, Centers for Disease Control and Prevention.

Moffitt, Terrie E. (2003). Life-course-persistent and adolescence-limited antisocial behavior: A 10-year research review and a research agenda. In Benjamin B. Lahey et al. (Eds.), *Causes of conduct disorder and juvenile delinquency* (pp. 49–75). New York, NY: Guilford Press.

Moffitt, Terrie E.; Arseneault, Louise; Belsky, Daniel; Dickson, Nigel; Hancox, Robert J.; Harrington, HonaLee, . . . Casp, Avshalom. (2011). A gradient of childhood self-control predicts health, wealth, and public safety. *Proceedings of the National Academy of Sciences of the United States of America, 108*(7), 2693–2698. doi: 10.1073/pnas.1010076108

Moffitt, Terrie E.; Caspi, Avshalom; Rutter, Michael & Silva, Phil A. (2001). *Sex differences in antisocial behaviour: Conduct disorder, delinquency, and violence in the Dunedin Longitudinal Study.* New York, NY: Cambridge University Press.

Mojtabai, Ramin; Stuart, Elizabeth A.; Hwang, Irving; Eaton, William W.; Sampson, Nancy & Kessler, Ronald C. (2015). Long-term effects of mental disorders on educational attainment in the National Comorbidity Survey ten-year follow-up. *Social Psychiatry and Psychiatric Epidemiology, 50*(10), 1577–1591. doi: 10.1007/s00127-015 -1083-5

Mokrova, Irina L.; O'Brien, Marion; Calkins, Susan D.; Leerkes, Esther M. & Marcovitch, Stuart. (2013). The role of persistence at preschool age in academic skills at kindergarten. *European Journal of Psychology of Education, 28*(4), 1495–1503. doi: 10.1007/s10212-013-0177-2

Moldavsky, Maria & Sayal, Kapil. (2013). Knowledge and attitudes about Attention-deficit/hyperactivity disorder (ADHD) and its treatment: The views of children, adolescents, parents, teachers and healthcare professionals. *Current Psychiatry Reports, 15*, 377. doi: 10.1007/s11920-013 -0377-0

Moles, Laura; Manzano, Susana; Fernández, Leonides; Montilla, Antonia; Corzo, Nieves; Ares, Susana, . . . Espinosa-Martos, Irene. (2015). Bacteriological, biochemical, and immunological properties of colostrum and mature milk from mothers of extremely preterm infants. *Journal of Pediatric Gastroenterology & Nutrition, 60*(1), 120–126. doi: 10.1097/MPG.0000000000000560

Molina, Brooke S. G.; Hinshaw, Stephen P.; Swanson, James W.; Arnold, L. Eugene; Vitiello, Benedetto; Jensen, Peter S., . . . Houck, Patricia R. (2009). The MTA at 8 years: Prospective follow-up of children treated for combined-type ADHD in a multisite study. *Journal of the American Academy of Child and Adolescent Psychiatry, 48*(5), 484–500. doi: 10.1097/CHI.0b013e31819c23d0

Møller, Signe J. & Tenenbaum, Harriet R. (2011). Danish majority children's reasoning about exclusion based on gender and ethnicity. *Child Development, 82*(2), 520–532. doi: 10.1111/j.1467-8624.2010.01568.x

Monahan, Kathryn C.; Steinberg, Laurence & Cauffman, Elizabeth. (2009). Affiliation with antisocial peers, susceptibility to peer influence, and antisocial behavior during the transition to adulthood. *Developmental Psychology, 45*(6), 1520–1530. doi: 10.1037/a0017417

Monahan, Kathryn C.; Steinberg, Laurence; Cauffman, Elizabeth & Mulvey, Edward P. (2013). Psychosocial (im)maturity from adolescence to early adulthood: Distinguishing between adolescence-limited and persisting antisocial behavior. *Development and Psychopathology, 25*(4), 1093–1105. doi: 10.1017/S0954579413000394

Monastersky, Richard. (2007). Who's minding the teenage brain? *Chronicle of Higher Education, 53*(19), A14–A18.

Money, John & Ehrhardt, Anke A. (1972). *Man & woman, boy & girl: The differentiation and dimorphism of gender identity from conception to maturity.* Baltimore, MD: Johns Hopkins University Press.

Monje, Michelle & Dietrich, Jörg. (2012). Cognitive side effects of cancer therapy demonstrate a functional role for adult neurogenesis. *Behavioural Brain Research, 227*(2), 376–379. doi: 10.1016/j.bbr.2011.05.012

Monks, Claire P. & Coyne, Iain (Eds.). (2011). *Bullying in different contexts.* New York, NY: Cambridge University Press.

Montgomery, Heather. (2015). Understanding child prostitution in Thailand in the 1990s. *Child Development Perspectives, 9*(3), 154–157. doi: 10.1111/cdep.12122

Monthly Vital Statistics Report. (1980). *Final mortality statistics, 1978: Advance report. Monthly Vital Statistics Report, 29*(6, Suppl. 2). Hyattsville, MD: National Center for Health Statistics.

Montirosso, Rosario; Casini, Erica; Provenzi, Livio; Putnam, Samuel P.; Morandi, Francesco; Fedeli, Claudia & Borgatti, Renato. (2015). A categorical approach to infants' individual differences during the Still-Face paradigm. *Infant Behavior and Development, 38*, 67–76. doi: 10.1016/j.infbeh .2014.12.015

Monto, Martin A. & Carey, Anna G. (2014). A new standard of sexual behavior? Are claims associated with the "hookup culture" supported by general social survey data? *The Journal of Sex Research, 51*(6), 605–615. doi: 10.1080/00224499.2014.906031

Moody, Myles. (2016). From under-diagnoses to over-representation: Black children, ADHD, and the school-to-prison pipeline. *Journal of African American Studies, 20*(2), 152–163. doi: 10.1007/s12111-016-9325-5

Moody, Raymond A. (1975). *Life after life: The investigation of a phenomenon—Survival of bodily death.* Atlanta, GA: Mockingbird Books.

Moore, Karenza & Measham, Fiona. (2008). "It's the most fun you can have for twenty quid": Motivations, consequences and meanings of British ketamine use. *Addiction Research & Theory, 16*(3), 231–244. doi: 10.1080/16066350801983681

Moore, Kelly L.; Boscardin, W. John; Steinman, Michael A. & Schwartz, Janice B. (2012). Age and sex variation in prevalence of chronic medical conditions in older residents of U.S. nursing homes. *Journal of the American Geriatrics Society, 60*(4), 756–764. doi: 10.1111/j.1532-5415.2012.03909.x

Moore, Keith L.; Persaud, T. V. N. & Torchia, Mark G. (2015). *The developing human: Clinically oriented embryology* (10th ed.). Philadelphia, PA: Saunders.

Morales, Michelle; Tangermann, Rudolf H. & Wassilak, Steven G. F. (2016). *Progress toward polio eradication—Worldwide, 2015–2016. Morbidity and Mortality Weekly Report 65*(18), 470–473. Atlanta, GA: Centers for Disease Control and Prevention.

Moran, Lyndsey R.; Lengua, Liliana J. & Zalewski, Maureen. (2013). The interaction between negative emotionality and effortful control in early social-emotional development. *Social Development, 22*(2), 340–362. doi: 10.1111/sode.12025

Moran, Lauren V.; Masters, Grace A.; Pingali, Samira; Cohen, Bruce M.; Liebson, Elizabeth; Rajarethinam, R. P. & Ongur, Dost. (2015). Prescription stimulant use is associated with earlier onset of psychosis. *Journal of Psychiatric Research, 71*, 41–47. doi: 10.1016/j.jpsychires.2015.09.012

Morawska, Alina & Sanders, Matthew. (2011). Parental use of time out revisited: A useful or harmful parenting strategy? *Journal of Child and Family Studies, 20*(1), 1–8. doi: 10.1007/s10826 -010-9371-x

Morcos, Roy N. & Kizy, Thomas. (2012). Gynecomastia: When is treatment indicated? *Journal of Family Practice, 61*(12), 719–725.

Moreno, Megan A. & Whitehill, Jennifer M. (2016). #Wasted: The intersection of substance use behaviors and social media in adolescents and young adults. *Current Opinion in Psychology, 9*, 72–76. doi: 10.1016/j.copsyc.2015.10.022

Moreno, Sylvain; Lee, Yunjo; Janus, Monika & Bialystok, Ellen. (2015). Short-term second language and music training induces lasting functional brain changes in early childhood. *Child Development, 86*(2), 394–406. doi: 10.1111/cdev.12297

Morgan, Ali Zaremba; Keiley, Margaret K.; Ryan, Aubrey E.; Radomski, Juliana Groves; Gropper, Sareen S.; Connell, Lenda Jo, . . . Ulrich, Pamela V. (2012). Eating regulation styles, appearance schemas, and body satisfaction predict changes in body fat for emerging adults. *Journal of Youth and Adolescence, 41*(9), 1127–1141. doi: 10.1007 /s10964-012-9757-8

Morgan, Ian G.; Ohno-Matsui, Kyoko & Saw, Seang-Mei. (2012). Myopia. *The Lancet, 379*(9827), 1739–1748. doi: 10.1016/S0140-6736 (12)60272-4

Morgan, Kevin; Gregory, Pamela; Tomeny, Maureen; David, Beverley M. & Gascoigne, Claire. (2012). Self-help treatment for insomnia symptoms associated with chronic conditions in older adults: A randomized controlled trial. *Journal of the American Geriatrics Society, 60*(10), 1803–1810. doi: 10.1111/j.1532-5415.2012.04175.x

Morgan, Paul L.; Staff, Jeremy; Hillemeier, Marianne M.; Farkas, George & Maczuga, Steven. (2013). Racial and ethnic disparities in ADHD diagnosis from kindergarten to eighth grade. *Pediatrics, 132*(1), 85–93. doi: 10.1542 /peds.2012 -2390

Morin, Rich & Fry, Richard. (2012, October 22). More Americans worry about financing retirement: Adults in their late 30s most concerned. *Pew Research, Social and Demographic Trends.*

Morning, Ann. (2008). Ethnic classification in global perspective: A cross-national survey of the 2000 census round. *Population Research and Policy Review, 27*(2), 239–272. doi: 10.1007/s11113-007 -9062-5

Morón, Cecilio & Viteri, Fernando E. (2009). Update on common indicators of nutritional status: Food access, food consumption, and biochemical measures of iron and anemia. *Nutrition Reviews, 67*(Suppl. 1), S31–S35. doi: 10.1111/j.1753-4887 .2009.00156.x

Morones, Alyssa. (2013). Paddling persists in U.S. schools. *Education Week, 33*(9), 1, 10–11.

Morris, Amanda S.; Silk, Jennifer S.; Steinberg, Laurence; Myers, Sonya S. & Robinson, Lara R. (2007). The role of the family context in the development of emotion regulation. *Social Development, 16*(2), 361–388. doi: 10.1111/j.1467-9507.2007.00389.x

Morris, Danielle H.; Jones, Michael E.; Schoemaker, Minouk J.; Ashworth, Alan & Swerdlow, Anthony J. (2011). Familial concordance for age at natural menopause: Results from the Breakthrough Generations Study. *Menopause, 18*(9), 956–961. doi: 10.1097 /gme.0b013e31820ed6d2

Morris, Vivian G. & Morris, Curtis L. (2013). A call for African American male teachers: The supermen expected to solve the problems of low-performing schools. In Chance W. Lewis & Ivory A. Toldson (Eds.), *Black male teachers: Diversifying the United States' teacher workforce* (pp. 151–165). Bingley, UK: Emerald Group.

Morrissey, Taryn. (2009). Multiple child-care arrangements and young children's behavioral outcomes. *Child Development, 80*(1), 59–76. doi: 10.1111/j.1467-8624.2008.01246.x

Morrow, Daniel G.; Miller, Lisa M. Soederberg; Ridolfo, Heather E.; Magnor, Clifford; Fischer, Ute M.; Kokayeff, Nina K. & Stine-Morrow, Elizabeth A. L. (2009). Expertise and age differences in pilot decision making. *Aging, Neuropsychology, and Cognition, 16*(1), 33–55. doi: 10.1080/13825580802195641

Morrow, Daniel G.; Ridolfo, Heather E.; Menard, William E.; Sanborn, Adam; Stine-Morrow, Elizabeth A. L.; Magnor, Cliff, . . . Bryant, David. (2003). Environmental support promotes expertise-based mitigation of age differences on pilot communication tasks. *Psychology and Aging, 18*(2), 268–284. doi: 10.1037/0882-7974.18.2.268

Mortimer, Jeylan T. (2010). The benefits and risks of adolescent employment. *Prevention Researcher, 17*(2), 8–11.

Mortimer, Jeylan T. (2013). Work and its positive and negative effects on youth's psychosocial development. In Carol W. Runyan et al. (Eds.), *Health and safety of young workers: Proceedings of a U.S. and Canadian series of symposia* (pp. 66–79). Washington, DC: U.S. Department of Health and Human Services, Centers for Disease Control and Prevention, National Institute for Occupational Safety and Health.

Mosher, Catherine E. & Danoff-Burg, Sharon. (2007). Death anxiety and cancer-related stigma: A terror management analysis. *Death Studies, 31*(10), 885–907. doi: 10.1080/07481180701603360

Mosher, William D.; Jones, Jo & Abma, Joyce C. (2012). *Intended and unintended births in the United States: 1982–2010. National Health Statistics Reports 55*, 1–27. Hyattsville, MD: U.S. Department of Health and Human Services, Centers for Disease Control and Prevention, National Center for Health Statistics.

Moshman, David. (2011). *Adolescent rationality and development: Cognition, morality, and identity* (3rd ed.). New York, NY: Psychology Press.

Moss, Howard B.; Chen, Chiung M. & Yi, Hsiao-ye. (2014). Early adolescent patterns of alcohol, cigarettes, and marijuana polysubstance use and young adult substance use outcomes in a nationally representative sample. *Drug & Alcohol Dependence, 136*(Suppl. 1), 51–62. doi: 10.1016 /j.drugalcdep.2013.12.011

Motel, Seth. (2014). *6 facts about marijuana.* Washington, DC: Pew Research Center.

Moulson, Margaret C.; Westerlund, Alissa; Fox, Nathan A.; Zeanah, Charles H. & Nelson, Charles A. (2009). The effects of early experience on face recognition: An event-related potential study of institutionalized children in Romania. *Child Development, 80*(4), 1039–1056. doi: 10.1111 /j.1467-8624.2009.01315.x

Moultrie, Fiona; Goksan, Sezgi; Poorun, Ravi & Slater, Rebeccah. (2016). Pain in neonates and infants. In Anna A. Battaglia (Ed.), *An intro-duction to pain and its relation to nervous system disorders* (pp. 283–293). New York, NY: Wiley.

Mowry, James B.; Spyker, Daniel A.; Brooks, Daniel E.; Mcmillan, Naya & Schauben, Jay L. (2015). 2014 Annual report of the American Association of Poison Control Centers' National Poison Data System (NPDS): 32nd Annual report. *Clinical Toxicology, 53*(10), 962–1146. doi: 10.3109/15563650.2015.1102927

Moye, Jennifer. (2015). Evidence-based treatment of neurocognitive disorders: Measured optimism about select outcomes. *The American Journal of Geriatric Psychiatry, 23*(4), 331–334. doi: 10.1016/j.jagp.2015.01.002

Mrug, Sylvie; Elliott, Marc N.; Davies, Susan; Tortolero, Susan R.; Cuccaro, Paula & Schuster, Mark A. (2014). Early puberty, negative peer influence, and problem behaviors in adolescent girls. *Pediatrics, 133*(1), 7–14. doi: 10.1542/peds.2013 -0628

Mueller, Kristen L. (2016). Flu immunity shows its age. *Science, 352*(6284), 424–425. doi: 10.1126 /science.352.6284.424-f

Muennig, Peter. (2015). Can universal pre-kindergarten programs improve population health and longevity? Mechanisms, evidence, and policy implications. *Social Science & Medicine, 127*, 116–123. doi: 10.1016/j.socscimed.2014.08.033

Mullally, Sinéad L. & Maguire, Eleanor A. (2014). Learning to remember: The early ontogeny of episodic memory. *Developmental Cognitive Neuroscience, 9*(13), 12–29. doi: 10.1016 /j.dcn.2013.12.006

Mulligan, Aisling; Anney, Richard; Butler, L.; O'Regan, M.; Richardson, T.; Tulewicz, E. M., . . . Gill, Michael. (2013). Home environment: Association with hyperactivity/impulsivity in children with ADHD and their non-ADHD siblings. *Child: Care, Health & Development, 39*(2), 202–212. doi: 10.1111/j.1365-2214.2011.01345.x

Mullis, Ina V. S.; Martin, Michael O.; Foy, Pierre & Arora, A. (2012a). *TIMSS 2011 International Results in Mathematics.* Chestnut Hill, MA: TIMSS & PIRLS International Study Center, Boston College.

Mullis, Ina V. S.; Martin, Michael O.; Foy, Pierre & Drucker, Kathleen T. (2012b). *PIRLS 2011 international results in reading.* Chestnut Hill, MA: TIMSS & PIRLS International Study Center, Boston College.

Mullis, Ina V. S.; Martin, Michael O.; Kennedy, Ann M. & Foy, Pierre. (2007). International student achievement in reading. In, *IEA's progress in international reading literacy study in primary school in 40 countries* (pp. 35–64). Chestnut Hill, MA: TIMSS & PIRLS International Study Center, Boston College.

Muñoz, Carmen & Singleton, David. (2011). A critical review of age-related research on L2 ultimate attainment. *Language Teaching, 44*(1), 1–35. doi: 10.1017/S0261444810000327

Munson, Michelle R.; Lee, Bethany R.; Miller, David; Cole, Andrea & Nedelcu, Cristina. (2013). Emerging adulthood among former system youth: The ideal versus the real. *Children and Youth Services Review, 35*(6), 923–929. doi: 10.1016 /j.childyouth.2013.03.003

Muris, Peter & Meesters, Cor. (2014). Small or big in the eyes of the other: On the developmental psychopathology of self-conscious emotions as shame, guilt, and pride. *Clinical Child and Family Psychology Review*, 17(1), 19–40. doi: 10.1007/s10567-013-0137-z

Murphy, Michael. (2011). Long-term effects of the demographic transition on family and kinship networks in Britain. *Population and Development Review*, 37(Suppl. 1), 55–80. doi: 10.1111/j.1728-4457.2011.00378.x

Murphy, Sherry L.; Xu, Jiaquan & Kochanek, Kenneth D. (2012). *Deaths: Preliminary data for 2010. National Vital Statistics Reports* 60(4). Hyattsville, MD: National Center for Health Statistics.

Murray, Brendan D.; Anderson, Michael C. & Kensinger, Elizabeth A. (2015). Older adults can suppress unwanted memories when given an appropriate strategy. *Psychology and Aging*, 30(1), 9–25. doi: 10.1037/a0038611

Murray, C. J.; Barber, R. M.; Foreman, K. J.; Abbasoglu Ozgoren, A.; Abd-Allah, F.; Abera, S. F., . . . Vos, T. (2015). Global, regional, and national disability-adjusted life years (DALYs) for 306 diseases and injuries and healthy life expectancy (HALE) for 188 countries, 1990-2013: Quantifying the epidemiological transition. *The Lancet*, 386(10009), 2145–2191. doi: 10.1016/S0140-6736(15)61340-X

Murray, Christopher J. L.; Vos, Theo; Lozano, Rafael; Naghavi, Mohsen; Flaxman, Abraham D.; Michaud, Catherine, . . . Lopez, Alan D. (2012). Disability-adjusted life years (DALYs) for 291 diseases and injuries in 21 regions, 1990—2010: A systematic analysis for the Global Burden of Disease Study 2010. *The Lancet*, 380(9859), 2197–2223. doi: 10.1016/S0140-6736(12)61689-4

Murray, Thomas H. (2014). Stirring the simmering "designer baby" pot. *Science*, 343(6176), 1208–1210. doi: 10.1126/science.1248080

Mustanski, Brian; Birkett, Michelle; Greene, George J.; Hatzenbuehler, Mark L. & Newcomb, Michael E. (2014). Envisioning an America without sexual orientation inequities in adolescent health. *American Journal of Public Health*, 104(2), 218–225. doi: 10.2105/AJPH.2013.301625

Mustonen, Ulla; Huurre, Taina; Kiviruusu, Olli; Haukkala, Ari & Aro, Hillevi. (2011). Long-term impact of parental divorce on intimate relationship quality in adulthood and the mediating role of psychosocial resources. *Journal of Family Psychology*, 25(4), 615–619. doi: 10.1037/a0023996

Myatt, Julia P. & Thorpe, Susannah K. S. (2011). Postural strategies employed by orangutans (Pongo abelii) during feeding in the terminal branch niche. *American Journal of Physical Anthropology*, 146(1), 73–82. doi: 10.1002/ajpa.21548

Myers, David G. (2002). *Intuition: Its powers and perils.* New Haven, CT: Yale University Press.

Myers, David G. (2011). Harnessing the human factor in hearing assistance. *Observer*, 24(8).

Mynatt, Blair Sumner & Mowery, Robyn L. (2013). The family, larger systems, and end-of-life decision making. In David K. Meagher & David E. Balk (Eds.), *Handbook of thanatology: The essential body of knowledge for the study of death, dying, and bereavement* (2nd ed., pp. 91–99). New York, NY: Routledge.

Nadal, Kevin L.; Mazzula, Silvia L.; Rivera, David P. & Fujii-Doe, Whitney. (2014). Microaggressions and Latina/o Americans: An analysis of nativity, gender, and ethnicity. *Journal of Latina/o Psychology*, 2(2), 67–78. doi: 10.1037/lat0000013

Næss, Kari-Anne B. (2016). Development of phonological awareness in Down syndrome: A meta-analysis and empirical study. *Developmental Psychology*, 52(2), 177–190. doi: 10.1037/a0039840

NAEYC. (2014). *NAEYC Early Childhood Program Standards and Accreditation Criteria & Guidance for Assessment.* Washington, DC: National Association for the Education of Young Children.

Nanji, Ayaz. (2005, February 8). World's smallest baby goes home. *CBS News.*

Narayan, Chandan R.; Werker, Janet F. & Beddor, Patrice Speeter. (2010). The interaction between acoustic salience and language experience in developmental speech perception: Evidence from nasal place discrimination. *Developmental Science*, 13(3), 407–420. doi: 10.1111/j.1467-7687.2009.00898.x

National Center for Education Statistics. (2009). *The condition of education 2009.* Washington, DC: Institute of Education Sciences, U.S. Department of Education.

National Center for Education Statistics. (2013a). *The Nation's report card: A first look: 2013 mathematics and reading.* Washington, DC: Institute of Education Sciences, U.S. Department of Education.

National Center for Education Statistics. (2013b). *Table 204.30: Children 3 to 21 years old served under Individuals with Disabilities Education Act (IDEA), Part B, by type of disability: Selected years, 1976–77 through 2011–12. Digest of Education Statistics.* Washington, DC: Institute of Education Sciences, U.S. Department of Education.

National Center for Education Statistics. (2013c). *Annual diploma counts and the Averaged Freshmen Graduation Rate (AFGR) in the United States by race/ethnicity: School years 2007–08 through 2011–12. Common Core Data.* Washington, DC: U.S. Department of Education, Institute of Education Sciences, National Center for Education Statistics.

National Center for Education Statistics. (2014, July). *Table 219.70: Percentage of high school dropouts among persons 16 through 24 years old (status dropout rate), by sex and race/ethnicity: Selected years, 1960 through 2013.* Washington, DC: U.S. Department of Education, Institute of Education Sciences, National Center for Education Statistics, The World of Statistics.

National Center for Health Statistics. (2011). *Health, United States, 2010: With special feature on death and dying.* Hyattsville, MD: U.S. Department of Health and Human Services, Centers for Disease Control and Prevention.

National Center for Health Statistics. (2012). *Health, United States, 2011: With special feature on socioeconomic status and health.* Hyattsville, MD: U.S. Department of Health and Human Services, Centers for Disease Control and Prevention.

National Center for Health Statistics. (2013). *Health, United States, 2012: With special feature on emergency care.* Hyattsville, MD: U.S. Department of Health and Human Services, Centers for Disease Control and Prevention.

National Center for Health Statistics. (2014). *Health, United States, 2013: With special feature on prescription drugs.* Hyattsville, MD: U.S. Department of Health and Human Services, Centers for Disease Control and Prevention.

National Center for Health Statistics. (2015). *Health, United States, 2014: With a special feature on adults aged 55–64.* Hyattsville, MD: U.S. Department of Health and Human Services, Centers for Disease Control and Prevention.

National Center for Health Statistics. (2016). *Health, United States, 2015: With a special feature on racial and ethnic health disparities.* Hyattsville, MD: U.S. Department of Health and Human Services, Centers for Disease Control and Prevention.

National Governors Association Center for Best Practices (NGA Center) and the Council of Chief State School Officers (CCSSO). (2010, October 25). *Common Core state standards initiative.* Washington, DC: National Governors Association.

National Highway Traffic Safety Administration. (2014, December 19). *U.S. Department of Transportation announces decline in traffic fatalities in 2013.* Washington, DC: U.S. Department of Transportation.

National Institute on Alcohol Abuse and Alcoholism. (2015, December). *College drinking.* Washington, DC: U.S. Department of Health and Human Services.

National Vital Statistics Reports. (2013, May 8). *Deaths: Final data for 2010. National Vital Statistics Reports* 61(4). Hyattsville, MD: National Center for Health Statistics.

National Vital Statistics Reports. (Forthcoming). *Deaths: Final data for 2012. National Vital Statistics Reports* 63(9). Hyattsville, MD: National Center for Health Statistics.

Naughton, Michelle J.; Yi-Frazier, Joyce P.; Morgan, Timothy M.; Seid, Michael; Lawrence, Jean M.; Klingensmith, Georgeanna J., . . . Loots, Beth. (2014). Longitudinal associations between sex, diabetes self-care, and health-related quality of life among youth with type 1 or type 2 diabetes mellitus. *The Journal of Pediatrics*, 164(6), 1376–1383.e1371. doi: 10.1016/j.jpeds.2014.01.027

Neary, Karen R. & Friedman, Ori. (2014). Young children give priority to ownership when judging who should use an object. *Child Development*, 85(1), 326–337. doi: 10.1111/cdev.12120

Neary, Marianne T. & Breckenridge, Ross A. (2013). Hypoxia at the heart of sudden infant death syndrome? *Pediatric Research*, 74(4), 375–379. doi: 10.1038/pr.2013.122

Needleman, Herbert L. & Gatsonis, Constantine A. (1990). Low-level lead exposure and the IQ of children: A meta-analysis of modern studies. *JAMA*, 263(5), 673–678. doi: 10.1001/jama.1990.03440050067035

Needleman, Herbert L.; Schell, Alan; Bellinger, David; Leviton, Alan & Allred, Elizabeth N. (1990). The long-term effects of exposure to low doses of lead in childhood. *New England Journal of Medicine, 322*(2), 83–88. doi: 10.1056 /NEJM199001113220203

Neggers, Yasmin & Crowe, Kristi. (2013). Low birth weight outcomes: Why better in Cuba than Alabama? *Journal of the American Board of Family Medicine, 26*(2), 187–195. doi: 10.3122 / jabfm.2013.02.120227

Nehme, Eileen K.; Oluyomi, Abiodun O.; Calise, Tamara Vehige & Kohl, Harold W. (2016). Environmental correlates of recreational walking in the neighborhood. *American Journal of Health Promotion, 30*(3), 139–148. doi: 10.4278 / ajhp.130531-QUAN-281

Neigh, Gretchen N.; Gillespie, Charles F. & Nemeroff, Charles B. (2009). The neurobiological toll of child abuse and neglect. *Trauma, Violence, & Abuse, 10*(4), 389–410. doi: 10.1177/1524838009339758

Neimeyer, Robert A. & Holland, Jason M. (2015). Bereavement in later life: Theory, assessment, and intervention. In Peter A. Lichtenberg et al. (Eds.), *APA handbook of clinical geropsychology* (Vol. 2). Washington, DC: American Psychological Association. doi: 10.1037/14459-025

Neimeyer, Robert A. & Jordan, John R. (2013). Historical and contemporary perspectives on assessment and intervention. In David K. Meagher & David E. Balk (Eds.), *Handbook of thanatology: The essential body of knowledge for the study of death, dying, and bereavement* (2nd ed., pp. 219–237). New York, NY: Routledge.

Nelson, Charles A.; Fox, Nathan A. & Zeanah, Charles H. (2014). *Romania's abandoned children: Deprivation, brain development, and the struggle for recovery.* Cambridge, MA: Harvard University Press.

Nelson, Charles A.; Zeanah, Charles H.; Fox, Nathan A.; Marshall, Peter J.; Smyke, Anna T. & Guthrie, Donald. (2007). Cognitive recovery in socially deprived young children: The Bucharest Early Intervention Project. *Science, 318*(5858), 1937–1940. doi: 10.1126/science.1143921

Nelson, Eric E.; Jarcho, Johanna M. & Guyer, Amanda E. (2016). Social re-orientation and brain development: An expanded and updated view. *Developmental Cognitive Neuroscience, 17*, 118–127. doi: 10.1016/j.dcn.2015.12.008

Nelson, Geoffrey & Caplan, Rachel. (2014). The prevention of child physical abuse and neglect: An update. *Journal of Applied Research on Children: Informing Policy for Children at Risk, 5*(1).

Nelson, Katherine. (2015). A bio-social-cultural approach to early cognitive development: Entering the community of minds. In Robert A. Scott & Stephen M. Kosslyn (Eds.), *Emerging trends in the social and behavioral sciences: An interdisciplinary, searchable, and linkable resource.* New York, NY: Wiley. doi: 10.1002/9781118900772.etrds0001

Nelson, Larry J. & Padilla-Walker, Laura M. (2013). Flourishing and floundering in emerging adult college students. *Emerging Adulthood, 1*(1), 67–78. doi: 10.1177/2167696812470938

Nelson, Todd D. (2011). Ageism: The strange case of prejudice against the older you. In Richard L. Wiener & Steven L. Willborn (Eds.), *Disability and aging discrimination: Perspectives in law and psychology* (pp. 37–47). New York, NY: Springer. doi: 10.1007/978-1-4419-6293-5_2

Nelson-Becker, Holly; Ai, Amy L.; Hopp, Faith P.; McCormick, Thomas R.; Schlueter, Judith O. & Camp, Jessica K. (2015). Spirituality and religion in end-of-life care ethics: The challenge of interfaith and cross-generational matters. *British Journal of Social Work, 45*(1), 104–119. doi: 10.1093/bjsw/bct110

Neuman, Susan B.; Kaefer, Tanya; Pinkham, Ashley & Strouse, Gabrielle. (2014). Can babies learn to read? A randomized trial of baby media. *Journal of Educational Psychology, 106*(3), 815–830. doi: 10.1037/a0035937

Nevanen, Saila; Juvonen, Antti & Ruismäki, Heikki. (2014). Does arts education develop school readiness? Teachers' and artists' points of view on an art education project. *Arts Education Policy Review, 115*(3), 72–81. doi: 10.1080/10632913.2014.913970

Nevin, Rick. (2007). Understanding international crime trends: The legacy of preschool lead exposure. *Environmental Research, 104*(3), 315–336. doi: 10.1016/j.envres.2007.02.008

Newnham, Carol A.; Milgrom, Jeannette & Skouteris, Helen. (2009). Effectiveness of a modified mother-infant transaction program on outcomes for preterm infants from 3 to 24 months of age. *Infant Behavior and Development, 32*(1), 17–26. doi: 10.1016/j.infbeh.2008.09.004

Ng, Florrie Fei-Yin; Pomerantz, Eva M. & Deng, Ciping. (2014). Why are Chinese mothers more controlling than American mothers? "My child is my report card". *Child Development, 85*(1), 355–369. doi: 10.1111/cdev.12102

Ng, Marie; Fleming, Tom; Robinson, Margaret; Thomson, Blake; Graetz, Nicholas; Margono, Christopher, . . . Gakidou, Emmanuela. (2014). Global, regional, and national prevalence of overweight and obesity in children and adults during 1980—2013: A systematic analysis for the Global Burden of Disease Study 2013. *The Lancet, 384*(9945), 766–781. doi: 10.1016/S0140 -6736(14)60460-8

Ngui, Emmanuel; Cortright, Alicia & Blair, Kathleen. (2009). An investigation of paternity status and other factors associated with racial and ethnic disparities in birth outcomes in Milwaukee, Wisconsin. *Maternal and Child Health Journal, 13*(4), 467–478. doi: 10.1007/ s10995-008-0383-8

Nguyen, Angela-MinhTu D. & Benet-Martínez, Verónica. (2013). Biculturalism and adjustment: A meta-analysis. *Journal of Cross-Cultural Psychology, 44*(1), 122–159. doi: 10.1177/0022022111435097

NHPCO. (2014). *NHPCO's facts and figures: Hospice care in America.* Alexandria, VA: National Hospice and Palliative Care Organization.

NHPCO. (2015). *NHPCO's facts and figures: Hospice care in America.* Alexandria, VA: National Hospice and Palliative Care Organization.

Niakan, Kathy K.; Han, Jinnuo; Pedersen, Roger A.; Simon, Carlos & Reijo Pera, Renee A. (2012). Human pre-implantation embryo development. *Development, 139*, 829–841. doi: 10.1242/dev .060426

Nic Gabhainn, Saoirse; Baban, Adriana; Boyce, William & Godeau, Emmanuelle. (2009). How well protected are sexually active 15-year olds? Cross-national patterns in condom and contraceptive pill use 2002-2006. *International Journal of Public Health, 54*(Suppl. 2), 209–215. doi: 10.1007/s00038-009-5412-x

Niclasen, Janni; Andersen, Anne-Marie N.; Strandberg-Larsen, Katrine & Teasdale, Thomas W. (2014). Is alcohol binge drinking in early and late pregnancy associated with behavioural and emotional development at age 7 years? *European Child & Adolescent Psychiatry, 23*(12), 1175–1180. doi: 10.1007/s00787-013-0511-x

Niedzwiedz, Claire; Haw, Camilla; Hawton, Keith & Platt, Stephen. (2014). The definition and epidemiology of clusters of suicidal behavior: A systematic review. *Suicide and Life-Threatening Behavior, 44*(5), 569–581. doi: 10.1111/sltb.12091

Nielsen, Lisbeth. (2015). Foreword: Decision making and aging: Emerging findings and research needs. In Thomas M. Hess et al. (Eds.), *Aging, emotion, and decision making* (pp. xv–xxiii). San Diego, CA: Academic Press.

Nielsen, Mark & Tomaselli, Keyan. (2010). Overimitation in Kalahari Bushman children and the origins of human cultural cognition. *Psychological Science, 21*(5), 729–736. doi: 10.1177/0956797610368808

Nielsen, Mark; Tomaselli, Keyan; Mushin, Ilana & Whiten, Andrew. (2014). Exploring tool innovation: A comparison of Western and Bushman children. *Journal of Experimental Child Psychology, 126*, 384–394. doi: 10.1016 /j.jecp.2014.05.008

Nieto, Sonia. (2000). *Affirming diversity: The sociopolitical context of multicultural education* (3rd ed.). New York, NY: Longman.

Nigg, Joel T. & Barkley, Russell A. (2014). Attention-deficit/hyperactivity disorder. In Eric J. Mash & Russell A. Barkley (Eds.), *Child psychopathology* (3rd ed., pp. 75–144). New York, NY: Guilford Press.

Nikitin, Dmitriy; Timberlake, David S. & Williams, Rebecca S. (2016). Is the e-liquid industry regulating itself? A look at e-liquid Internet vendors in the United States. *Nicotine & Tobacco Research, 18*(10), 1967–1972. doi: 10.1093/ntr/ntw091

Nilsson, Kristine Kahr & de López, Kristine Jensen. (2016). Theory of mind in children with specific language impairment: A systematic review and meta-analysis. *Child Development, 87*(1), 143–153. doi: 10.1111/cdev.12462

Nilsson, Peter M. (2016). Blood pressure strategies and goals in elderly patients with hypertension. *Experimental Gerontology*, (In Press, Corrected Proof). doi: 10.1016/j.exger.2016.04.018

Nilwik, Rachel; Snijders, Tim; Leenders, Marika; Groen, Bart B. L.; van Kranenburg, Janneau; Verdijk, Lex B. & van Loon, Luc J. C. (2013). The decline in skeletal muscle mass with aging is mainly attributed to a reduction in type II muscle fiber size. *Experimental Gerontology*, 48(5), 492–498. doi: 10.1016/j.exger.2013.02.012

Nisbett, Richard E.; Aronson, Joshua; Blair, Clancy; Dickens, William; Flynn, James; Halpern, Diane F. & Turkheimer, Eric. (2012). Intelligence: New findings and theoretical developments. *American Psychologist*, 67(2), 130–159. doi: 10.1037/a0026699

Nisbett, Richard E.; Peng, Kaiping; Choi, Incheol & Norenzayan, Ara. (2001). Culture and systems of thought: Holistic versus analytic cognition. *Psychological Review*, 108(2), 291–310. doi: 10.1037//0033-295X.108.2.291

Nishiguchi, Shu; Yamada, Minoru; Fukutani, Naoto; Adachi, Daiki; Tashiro, Yuto; Hotta, Takayuki, . . . Aoyama, Tomoki. (2015). Differential association of frailty with cognitive decline and sarcopenia in community-dwelling older adults. *JAMDA*, 16(2), 120–124. doi: 10.1016/j.jamda.2014.07.010

Noël-Miller, Claire M. (2013a). Repartnering following divorce: Implications for older fathers' relations with their adult children. *Journal of Marriage and Family*, 75(3), 697–712. doi: 10.1111/jomf.12034

Noël-Miller, Claire M. (2013b). Former stepparents' contact with their stepchildren after midlife. *The Journals of Gerontology Series B: Psychological Sciences and Social Sciences*, 68(3), 409–419. doi: 10.1093/geronb/gbt021

Norcross, John C.; Krebs, Paul M. & Prochaska, James O. (2011). Stages of change. *Journal of Clinical Psychology*, 67(2), 143–154. doi: 10.1002/jclp.20758

Nordgren, Loran F.; Harreveld, Frenk van & Pligt, Joop van der. (2009). The restraint bias: How the illusion of self-restraint promotes impulsive behavior. *Psychological Science*, 20(12), 1523–1528. doi: 10.1111/j.1467-9280.2009.02468.x

Noronha, Konrad J. (2015). Impact of religion and spirituality on older adulthood. *Journal of Religion, Spirituality & Aging*, 27(1), 16–33. doi: 10.1080/15528030.2014.963907

Norris, Pippa. (2001). *Digital divide: Civic engagement, information poverty, and the Internet worldwide.* New York, NY: Cambridge University Press.

North, Michael S. (2015). Ageism stakes its claim in the social sciences. *Generations*, 39(3), 29–33.

Norton, Michael I. & Ariely, Dan. (2011). Building a better America: One wealth quintile at a time. *Perspectives on Psychological Science*, 6(1), 9–12. doi: 10.1177/1745691610393524

Nouri, Ahmad; Etemadi, Ozra; Jazayeri, Rezvanossadat & Fatehizade, Maryam. (2016). Analysis of psychological spouse abuse against men in Iranian couples: A qualitative study. *Review of European Studies*, 8(3). doi: 10.5539/res.v8n3p1

Nucci, Larry P. & Turiel, Elliot. (2009). Capturing the complexity of moral development and education. *Mind, Brain, and Education*, 3(3), 151–159. doi: 10.1111/j.1751-228X.2009.01065.x

Nwosisi, Christopher; Ferreira, Alexa; Rosenberg, Warren & Walsh, Kelly. (2016). A study of the flipped classroom and its effectiveness in flipping thirty percent of the course content. *International Journal of Information and Education Technology*, 6(5), 348–351. doi: 10.7763/IJIET.2016.V6.712

Nyberg, Lars & Bäckman, Lars. (2011). Memory changes and the aging brain: A multimodal imaging approach. In K. Warner Schaie & Sherry L. Willis (Eds.), *Handbook of the psychology of aging* (7th ed., pp. 121–131). San Diego, CA: Academic Press. doi: 10.1016/B978-0-12-380882-0.00008-5

O'Brien, Beth A.; Wolf, Maryanne & Lovett, Maureen W. (2012). A taxometric investigation of developmental dyslexia subtypes. *Dyslexia*, 18(1), 16–39. doi: 10.1002/dys.1431

O'Conner, Rosemarie; Abedi, Jamal & Tung, Stephanie. (2012). *A descriptive analysis of enrollment and achievement among English language learner students in Pennsylvania.* Washington, DC: U.S. Department of Education, Institute of Education Sciences, National Center for Education Evaluation and Regional Assistance, Regional Educational Laboratory Mid-Atlantic.

O'Leary, Colleen M.; Nassar, Natasha; Zubrick, Stephen R.; Kurinczuk, Jennifer J.; Stanley, Fiona & Bower, Carol. (2010). Evidence of a complex association between dose, pattern and timing of prenatal alcohol exposure and child behaviour problems. *Addiction*, 105(1), 74–86. doi: 10.1111/j.1360-0443.2009.02756.x

O'Malley, A. James & Christakis, Nicholas A. (2011). Longitudinal analysis of large social networks: Estimating the effect of health traits on changes in friendship ties. *Statistics in Medicine*, 30(9), 950–964. doi: 10.1002/sim.4190

O'Meara, J. Donald. (1989). Cross-sex friendship: Four basic challenges of an ignored relationship. *Sex Roles*, 21(7), 525–543. doi: 10.1007/BF00289102

O'Rourke, Norm; Cappeliez, Philippe & Claxton, Amy. (2010a). Functions of reminiscence and the psychological well-being of young-old and older adults over time. *Aging & Mental Health*, 15(2), 272–281. doi: 10.1080/13607861003713281

O'Rourke, Norm; Neufeld, Eva; Claxton, Amy & Smith, JuliAnna Z. (2010b). Knowing me-knowing you: Reported personality and trait discrepancies as predictors of marital idealization between long-wed spouses. *Psychology and Aging*, 25(2), 412–421. doi: 10.1037/a0017873

Oakes, J. Michael. (2009). The effect of media on children: A methodological assessment from a social epidemiologist. *American Behavioral Scientist*, 52(8), 1136–1151. doi: 10.1177/0002764209331538

Obradović, Jelena. (2012). How can the study of physiological reactivity contribute to our understanding of adversity and resilience processes in development? *Development and Psychopathology*, 24(2), 371–387. doi: 10.1017/S0954579412000053

Obradović, Jelena; Long, Jeffrey D.; Cutuli, J. J.; Chan, Chi-Keung; Hinz, Elizabeth; Heistad, David & Masten, Ann S. (2009). Academic achievement of homeless and highly mobile children in an urban school district: Longitudinal evidence on risk, growth, and resilience. *Development and Psychopathology*, 21(2), 493–518. doi: 10.1017/S0954579409000273

Ocobock, Abigail. (2013). The power and limits of marriage: Married gay men's family relationships. *Journal of Marriage and Family*, 75(1), 191–205. doi: 10.1111/j.1741-3737.2012.01032.x

Odden, Michelle C.; Peralta, Carmen A.; Haan, Mary N. & Covinsky, Kenneth E. (2012). Rethinking the association of high blood pressure with mortality in elderly adults: The impact of frailty. *Archives of Internal Medicine*, 172(15), 1162–1168. doi: 10.1001/archinternmed.2012.2555

Odlaug, Brian L.; Mahmud, Waqar; Goddard, Andrew & Grant, Jon E. (2010). Anxiety disorders. In Jon E. Grant & Marc N. Potenza (Eds.), *Young adult mental health* (pp. 231–254). New York, NY: Oxford University Press.

OECD. (2010). *PISA 2009 results: Learning to learn: Student engagement, strategies and practices* (Vol. 3): PISA, OECD Publishing. doi: 10.1787/9789264083943-en

OECD. (2011). *Education at a glance 2011: OECD indicators.* Paris, France: Organisation for Economic Cooperation and Development. doi: 10.1787/eag-2011-en

OECD. (2013). *Education at a glance 2013: OECD indicators.* Paris, France: Organisation for Economic Cooperation and Development. doi: 10.1787/19991487

OECD. (2014). *Education at a glance 2014: OECD Indicators.* Paris, France: Organisation for Economic Cooperation and Development. doi: 10.1787/eag-2014-en

OECD. (2015). Life expectancy at birth. In *Health at a glance 2015: OECD indicators* (pp. 46–47). Paris, France: Organisation for Economic Cooperation and Development. doi: 10.1787/health_glance-2015-en

Ogden, Cynthia L.; Carroll, Margaret D.; Kit, Brian K. & Flegal, Katherine M. (2014). Prevalence of childhood and adult obesity in the United States, 2011–2012. *JAMA*, 311(8), 806–814. doi: 10.1001/jama.2014.732

Ogden, Cynthia L.; Gorber, Sarah C.; Dommarco, Juan A. Rivera; Carroll, Margaret; Shields, Margot & Flegal, Katherine. (2011). The epidemiology of childhood obesity in Canada, Mexico and the United States. In Luis A. Moreno et al. (Eds.), *Epidemiology of obesity in children and adolescents* (Vol. 2, pp. 69–93). New York, NY: Springer. doi: 10.1007/978-1-4419-6039-9_5

Ogolsky, Brian G. & Gray, Christine R. (2016). Conflict, negative emotion, and reports of partners' relationship maintenance in same-sex couples. *Journal of Family Psychology*, 30(2), 171–180. doi: 10.1037/fam0000148

Okun, Morris A.; Yeung, Ellen WanHeung & Brown, Stephanie. (2013). Volunteering by older adults and risk of mortality: A meta-analysis. *Psychology and Aging*, 28(2), 564–577. doi: 10.1037/a0031519

Olfson, Mark; Crystal, Stephen; Huang, Cecilia & Gerhard, Tobias. (2010). Trends in antipsychotic drug use by very young, privately insured children. *Journal of the American Academy of Child and Adolescent Psychiatry, 49*(1), 13–23. doi: 10.1016/j.jaac.2009.09.003

Oliver, Taylor L.; Meana, Marta & Snyder, Joel S. (2016). Sex differences in concordance rates between auditory event-related potentials and subjective sexual arousal. *Psychophysiology, 53*(8), 1272–1281. doi: 10.1111/psyp.12661

Olsen, James P.; Parra, Gilbert R. & Bennett, Shira A. (2010). Predicting violence in romantic relationships during adolescence and emerging adulthood: A critical review of the mechanisms by which familial and peer influences operate. *Clinical Psychology Review, 30*(4), 411–422. doi: 10.1016/j.cpr.2010.02.002

Olson, Kristina R. & Dweck, Carol S. (2009). Social cognitive development: A new look. *Child Development Perspectives, 3*(1), 60–65. doi: 10.1111/j.1750-8606.2008.00078.x

Olson, Sheryl L.; Lopez-Duran, Nestor; Lunkenheimer, Erika S.; Chang, Hyein & Sameroff, Arnold J. (2011). Individual differences in the development of early peer aggression: Integrating contributions of self-regulation, theory of mind, and parenting. *Development and Psychopathology, 23*(1), 253–266. doi: 10.1017/S0954579410000775

Olweus, Dan. (1999). Sweden. In Peter K. Smith et al. (Eds.), *The nature of school bullying: A cross-national perspective* (pp. 7–27). New York, NY: Routledge.

Onyura, Betty; Bohnen, John; Wasylenki, Don; Jarvis, Anna; Giblon, Barney; Hyland, Robert, . . . Leslie, Karen. (2015). Reimagining the self at late-career transitions: How identity threat influences academic physicians' retirement considerations. *Academic Medicine, 90*(6), 794–801. doi: 10.1097/ACM.0000000000000718

Open Science Collaboration. (2015). Estimating the reproducibility of psychological science. *Science, 349*(6251), 943. doi: 10.1126/science.aac4716

Oregon Public Health Division. (2013). *Oregon's Death with Dignity Act–2012.* Portland, OR: Oregon Health Authority, Public Health Division.

Oregon Public Health Division. (2016). *Oregon's Death with Dignity Act: 2015 Data summary.* Portland, OR: Oregon Health Authority, Public Health Division.

Orth, Ulrich; Robins, Richard W. & Widaman, Keith F. (2012). Life-span development of self-esteem and its effects on important life outcomes. *Journal of Personality and Social Psychology, 102*(6), 1271–1288. doi: 10.1037/a0025558

Osgood, D. Wayne; Ragan, Daniel T.; Wallace, Lacey; Gest, Scott D.; Feinberg, Mark E. & Moody, James. (2013). Peers and the emergence of alcohol use: Influence and selection processes in adolescent friendship networks. *Journal of Research on Adolescence, 23*(3), 500–512. doi: 10.1111/jora.12059

Osher, David; Bear, George G.; Sprague, Jeffrey R. & Doyle, Walter. (2010). How can we improve school discipline? *Educational Researcher, 39*(1), 48–58. doi: 10.3102/0013189X09357618

Osilla, Karen Chan; Miles, Jeremy N. V.; Hunter, Sarah B. & Amico, Elizabeth J. D. (2015). The longitudinal relationship between employment and substance use among at-risk adolescents. *Journal of Child & Adolescent Behavior Genetics, 3*(3). doi: 10.4172/2375-4494.1000202

Ossher, Lynn; Flegal, Kristin E. & Lustig, Cindy. (2013). Everyday memory errors in older adults. *Aging, Neuropsychology, and Cognition, 20*(2), 220–242. doi: 10.1080/13825585.2012.690365

Ostfeld, Barbara M.; Esposito, Linda; Perl, Harold & Hegyi, Thomas. (2010). Concurrent risks in sudden infant death syndrome. *Pediatrics, 125*(3), 447–453. doi: 10.1542/peds.2009-0038

Ostrov, Jamie M.; Kamper, Kimberly E.; Hart, Emily J.; Godleski, Stephanie A. & Blakely-McClure, Sarah J. (2014). A gender-balanced approach to the study of peer victimization and aggression subtypes in early childhood. *Development and Psychopathology, 26*(3), 575–587. doi: 10.1017/S0954579414000248

Over, Harriet & Gattis, Merideth. (2010). Verbal imitation is based on intention understanding. *Cognitive Development, 25*(1), 46–55. doi: 10.1016/j.cogdev.2009.06.004

Owen, Jesse; Fincham, Frank D. & Moore, Jon. (2011). Short-term prospective study of hooking up among college students. *Archives of Sexual Behavior, 40*(2), 331–341. doi: 10.1007/s10508-010-9697-x

Owsley, Cynthia. (2011). Aging and vision. *Vision Research, 51*(13), 1610–1622. doi: 10.1016/j.visres.2010.10.020

Oza-Frank, Reena & Narayan, K. M. Venkat. (2010). Overweight and diabetes prevalence among U.S. immigrants. *American Journal of Public Health, 100*(4), 661–668. doi: 10.2105/ajph.2008.149492

Pace, Cecilia Serena; Zavattini, Giulio Cesare & D'Alessio, Maria. (2011). Continuity and discontinuity of attachment patterns: A short-term longitudinal pilot study using a sample of late-adopted children and their adoptive mothers. *Attachment & Human Development, 14*(1), 45–61. doi: 10.1080/14616734.2012.636658

Padilla-Walker, Laura; Nelson, Larry; Madsen, Stephanie & Barry, Carolyn. (2008). The role of perceived parental knowledge on emerging adults' risk behaviors. *Journal of Youth and Adolescence, 37*(7), 847–859. doi: 10.1007/s10964-007-9268-1

Padilla-Walker, Laura M.; Nelson, Larry J. & Carroll, Jason S. (2012). Affording emerging adulthood: Parental financial assistance of their college-aged children. *Journal of Adult Development, 19*(1), 50–58. doi: 10.1007/s10804-011-9134-y

Pahlke, Erin & Hyde, Janet Shibley. (2016). The debate over single-sex schooling. *Child Development Perspectives, 10*(2), 81–86. doi: 10.1111/cdep.12167

Pahlke, Erin; Hyde, Janet Shibley & Allison, Carlie M. (2014). The effects of single-sex compared with coeducational schooling on students' performance and attitudes: A meta-analysis. *Psychological Bulletin, 140*(4), 1042–1072. doi: 10.1037/a0035740

Pahwa, Rajesh & Lyons, Kelly E. (Eds.). (2013). *Handbook of Parkinson's disease* (5th ed.). Boca Raton, FL: CRC Press.

Paik, Anthony. (2011). Adolescent sexuality and the risk of marital dissolution. *Journal of Marriage and Family, 73*(2), 472–485. doi: 10.1111/j.1741-3737.2010.00819.x

Palacios, Natalia & Kibler, Amanda. (2016). Oral English language proficiency and reading mastery: The role of home language and school supports. *The Journal of Educational Research, 109*(2), 122–136. doi: 10.1080/00220671.2014.927341

Palagi, Elisabetta. (2011). Playing at every age: Modalities and potential functions in non-human primates. In Anthony D. Pellegrini (Ed.), *The Oxford handbook of the development of play* (pp. 70–82). New York, NY: Oxford University Press. doi: 10.1093/oxfordhb/9780195393002.013.0007

Palatini, Paolo. (2015). Coffee consumption and risk of type 2 diabetes. *Diabetologia, 58*(1), 199–200. doi: 10.1007/s00125-014-3425-3

Palmer, Nicholette D.; McDonough, Caitrin W.; Hicks, Pamela J.; Roh, Bong H.; Wing, Maria R.; An, S. Sandy, . . . Bowden, Donald W. (2012). A genome-wide association search for type 2 diabetes genes in African Americans. *PLoS ONE, 7*(1), e29202. doi: 10.1371/journal.pone.0029202

Panksepp, Jaak & Watt, Douglas. (2011). What is basic about basic emotions? Lasting lessons from affective neuroscience. *Emotion Review, 3*(4), 387–396. doi: 10.1177/1754073911410741

Papandreou, Maria. (2014). Communicating and thinking through drawing activity in early childhood. *Journal of Research in Childhood Education, 28*(1), 85–100. doi: 10.1080/02568543.2013.851131

Pardini, Matteo & Nichelli, Paolo F. (2009). Age-related decline in mentalizing skills across adult life span. *Experimental Aging Research, 35*(1), 98–106. doi: 10.1080/03610730802545259

Park, Denise C. & Bischof, Gérard N. (2013). The aging mind: Neuroplasticity in response to cognitive training. *Dialogues in Clinical Neuroscience, 15*(1), 109–119.

Park, Denise C. & Reuter-Lorenz, Patricia. (2009). The adaptive brain: Aging and neurocognitive scaffolding. *Annual Review of Psychology, 60*, 173–196. doi: 10.1146/annurev.psych.59.103006.093656

Park, D. J. & Congdon, Nathan G. (2004). Evidence for an "epidemic" of myopia. *Annals Academy of Medicine Singapore, 33*(1), 21–26.

Park, Hyun; Bothe, Denise; Holsinger, Eva; Kirchner, H. Lester; Olness, Karen & Mandalakas, Anna. (2011). The impact of nutritional status and longitudinal recovery of motor and cognitive milestones in internationally adopted children. *International Journal of Environmental Research and Public Health, 8*(1), 105–116. doi: 10.3390/ijerph8010105

Park, Jong-Tae; Jang, Yoonsun; Park, Min Sun; Pae, Calvin; Park, Jinyi; Hu, Kyung-Seok, . . . Kim, Hee-Jin. (2011). The trend of body donation for education based on Korean social and religious culture. *Anatomical Sciences Education, 4*(1), 33–38. doi: 10.1002/ase.198

Park, Ji-Yeun; Seo, Dong-Chul & Lin, Hsien-Chang. (2016). E-cigarette use and intention to initiate or quit smoking among US youths. *American Journal of Public Health, 106*(4), 672–678. doi: 10.2105/AJPH.2015.302994

Park, Nan Sook; Jang, Yuri; Lee, Beom S.; Chiriboga, David A. & Molinari, Victor. (2015). Correlates of attitudes toward personal aging in older assisted living residents. *Journal of Gerontological Social Work, 58*(3), 232–252. doi: 10.1080/01634372.2014.978926

Parke, Ross D. (2013). Gender differences and similarities in parental behavior. In Bradford Wilcox & Kathleen K. Kline (Eds.), *Gender and parenthood: Biological and social scientific perspectives* (pp. 120–163). New York, NY: Columbia University Press.

Parke, Ross D. & Buriel, Raymond. (2006). Socialization in the family: Ethnic and ecological perspectives. In William Damon & Richard M. Lerner (Eds.), *Handbook of child psychology* (6th ed., Vol. 3, pp. 429–504). Hoboken, NJ: Wiley.

Parker, Andrew. (2012). *Ethical problems and genetics practice.* New York, NY: Cambridge University Press.

Parker, Kim. (2012). *The boomerang generation: Feeling OK about living with Mom and Dad. Pew social and demographic trends.* Washington, DC: Pew Research Center.

Parker, Kim; Horowitz, Juliana Menasce & Rohal, Molly. (2015, November 4). *Raising kids and running a household: How working parents share the load. Social & Demographic Trends.* Washington, DC: Pew Research Center.

Parker, Kim & Patten, Eileen. (2013, January 30). *The sandwich generation: Rising financial burdens for middle-aged Americans. Social & Demographic Trends.* Washington, DC: Pew Research Center.

Parker, Philip D.; Jerrim, John & Anders, Jake. (2016). What effect did the global financial crisis have upon youth wellbeing? Evidence from four Australian cohorts. *Developmental Psychology, 52*(4), 640–651. doi: 10.1037/dev0000092

Parker, Stephen. (2010). Research in Fowler's faith development theory: A review article. *Review of Religious Research, 51*(3), 233–252.

Parker, Stacey L.; Jimmieson, Nerina L.; Walsh, Alexandra J. & Loakes, Jennifer L. (2015). Trait resilience fosters adaptive coping when control opportunities are high: Implications for the motivating potential of active work. *Journal of Business and Psychology, 30*(3), 583–604. doi: 10.1007 /s10869-014-9383-4

Parks, Sharyn E.; Johnson, Linda L.; McDaniel, Dawn D. & Gladden, Matthew. (2014, January 17). *Surveillance for violent deaths—National Violent Death Reporting System, 16 states, 2010. Morbidity and Mortality Weekly Report 63*(SS01), 1–33. Atlanta, GA: U.S. Department of Health and Human Services, Centers for Disease Control and Prevention, Morbidity and Mortality Weekly Report.

Partanen, Anu. (2011, December 29). What Americans keep ignoring about Finland's school success. *The Atlantic.*

Parten, Mildred B. (1932). Social participation among pre-school children. *The Journal of Abnormal and Social Psychology, 27*(3), 243–269. doi: 10.1037/h0074524

Pascarella, Ernest T.; Martin, Georgianna L.; Hanson, Jana M.; Trolian, Teniell L.; Gillig, Benjamin & Blaich, Charles. (2014). Effects of diversity experiences on critical thinking skills over 4 years of college. *Journal of College Student Development, 55*(1), 86–92. doi: 10.1353 /csd.2014.0009

Pascarella, Ernest T. & Terenzini, Patrick T. (1991). *How college affects students: Findings and insights from twenty years of research.* San Francisco, CA: Jossey-Bass.

Patel, Vimla L.; Arocha, José F. & Kaufman, David R. (1999). Expertise and tacit knowledge in medicine. In Robert J. Sternberg & Joseph A. Horvath (Eds.), *Tacit knowledge in professional practice: Researcher and practitioner perspectives* (pp. 75–99). Mahwah, NJ: Erlbaum.

Pathela, Preeti & Schillinger, Julia A. (2010). Sexual behaviors and sexual violence: Adolescents with opposite-, same-, or both-sex partners. *Pediatrics, 126*(5), 879–886. doi: 10.1542/peds .2010-0396

Patil, Rakesh N.; Nagaonkar, Shashikant N.; Shah, Nilesh B. & Bhat, Tushar S. (2013). A cross-sectional study of common psychiatric morbidity in children aged 5 to 14 years in an urban slum. *Journal of Family Medicine and Primary Care, 2*(2), 164–168. doi: 10.4103/2249-4863.117413

Paúl, Constança; Teixeira, Laetitia & Ribeiro, Oscar. (2013). What about happiness in later life? In Constantinos Phellas (Ed.), *Aging in European societies: Healthy aging in Europe* (pp. 83–96). New York, NY: Springer. doi: 10.1007/978-1-4419 -8345-9_6

Paul, Karsten I. & Moser, Klaus. (2009). Unemployment impairs mental health: Meta-analyses. *Journal of Vocational Behavior, 74*(3), 264–282. doi: 10.1016/j.jvb.2009.01.001

Pausch, Jai. (2012). *Dream new dreams: Reimagining my life after loss.* New York, NY: Crown Archetype.

Pausch, Randy (Producer). (2007). Randy Pausch last lecture: Really achieving your childhood dreams. [Video] Retrieved from http://www .youtube.com/watch?v=ji5_MqicxSo

Pausch, Randy & Zaslow, Jeffrey. (2008). *The last lecture.* New York, NY: Hyperion.

Pawlik, Amy J. & Kress, John P. (2013). Issues affecting the delivery of physical therapy services for individuals with critical illness. *Physical Therapy, 93*(2), 256–265. doi: 10.2522/ptj.20110445

Peffley, Mark & Hurwitz, Jon. (2010). *Justice in America: The separate realities of blacks and whites.* New York, NY: Cambridge University Press.

Pelham, William E. & Fabiano, Gregory A. (2008). Evidence-based psychosocial treatments for Attention-deficit/hyperactivity disorder. *Journal of Clinical Child & Adolescent Psychology, 37*(1), 184–214. doi: 10.1080/15374410701818681

Pellegrini, Anthony D. (2011). Introduction. In Anthony D. Pellegrini (Ed.), *The Oxford handbook of the development of play* (pp. 3–6). New York, NY: Oxford University Press. doi: 10.1093 /oxfordhb /9780195393002.013.0001

Pellegrini, Anthony D. (2013). Play. In Philip D. Zelazo (Ed.), *The Oxford handbook of developmental psychology* (Vol. 2, pp. 276–299). New York, NY: Oxford University Press. doi: 10.1093 /oxfordhb/9780199958474.013.0012

Pellegrini, Anthony D.; Roseth, Cary J.; Van Ryzin, Mark J. & Solberg, David W. (2011). Popularity as a form of social dominance: An evolutionary perspective. In Antonius H. N. Cillessen et al. (Eds.), *Popularity in the peer system* (pp. 123–139). New York, NY: Guilford Press.

Pellis, Sergio M. & Pellis, Vivien C. (2011). Rough-and-tumble play: Training and using the social brain. In Anthony D. Pellegrini (Ed.), *The Oxford handbook of the development of play* (pp. 245–259). New York, NY: Oxford University Press. doi: 10.1093 /oxfordhb/9780195393002.013.0019

Peng, Duan & Robins, Philip K. (2010). Who should care for our kids? The effects of infant child care on early child development. *Journal of Children and Poverty, 16*(1), 1–45. doi: 10.1080/10796120903575085

Pennington, Charlotte R.; Heim, Derek; Levy, Andrew R. & Larkin, Derek T. (2016). Twenty years of stereotype threat research: A review of psychological mediators. *PLoS ONE, 11*(1), e0146487. doi: 10.1371/journal. pone.0146487

Pennisi, Elizabeth. (2016). The right gut microbes help infants grow. *Science, 351*(6275), 802. doi: 10.1126/science.351.6275.802

Peper, Jiska S. & Dahl, Ronald E. (2013). The teenage brain: Surging hormones—brain-behavior interactions during puberty. *Current Directions in Psychological Science, 22*(2), 134–139. doi: 10.1177/0963721412473755

Pereira, Vera; Faísca, Luís & de Sá-Saraiva, Rodrigo. (2012). Immortality of the soul as an intuitive idea: Towards a psychological explanation of the origins of afterlife beliefs. *Journal of Cognition and Culture, 12*(1/2), 101–127. doi: 10.1163/156853712X633956

Perels, Franziska; Merget-Kullmann, Miriam; Wende, Milena; Schmitz, Bernhard & Buchbinder, Carla. (2009). Improving self-regulated learning of preschool children: Evaluation of training for kindergarten teachers. *British Journal of Educational Psychology, 79*(2), 311–327. doi: 10.1348/000709908X322875

Perez, L.; Helm, L.; Sherzai, A. Dean; Jaceldo-Siegl, K. & Sherzai, A. (2012). Nutrition and vascular dementia. *The Journal of Nutrition, Health & Aging, 16*(4), 319–324. doi: 10.1007/s12603-012 -0042-z

Pérez-Fuentes, Gabriela; Olfson, Mark; Villegas, Laura; Morcillo, Carmen; Wang, Shuai & Blanco, Carlos. (2013). Prevalence and correlates of child sexual abuse: A national study. *Comprehensive Psychiatry, 54*(1), 16–27. doi: 10.1016/j.comppsych .2012.05.010

Perner, Josef. (2000). Communication and representation: Why mentalistic reasoning is a lifelong endeavour. In Peter Mitchell & Kevin John Riggs (Eds.), *Children's reasoning and the mind* (pp. 367–401). Hove, UK: Psychology Press.

Perone, Sammy; Molitor, Stephen J.; Buss, Aaron T.; Spencer, John P. & Samuelson, Larissa K. (2015). Enhancing the executive functions of 3-year-olds in the dimensional change card sort task. *Child Development*, 86(3), 812–827. doi: 10.1111/cdev.12330

Perren, Sonja; Ettekal, Idean & Ladd, Gary. (2013). The impact of peer victimization on later maladjustment: Mediating and moderating effects of hostile and self-blaming attributions. *Journal of Child Psychology and Psychiatry*, 54(1), 46–55. doi: 10.1111/j.1469-7610.2012.02618.x

Perry, William G. (1981). Cognitive and ethical growth: The making of meaning. In Arthur Chickering (Ed.), *The modern American college: Responding to the new realities of diverse students and a changing society* (pp. 76–116). San Francisco, CA: Jossey-Bass.

Perry, William G. (1998). *Forms of intellectual and ethical development in the college years: A scheme.* San Francisco, CA: Jossey-Bass.

Peters, Ellen; Dieckmann, Nathan F. & Weller, Joshua. (2011). Age differences in complex decision making. In K. Warner Schaie & Sherry L. Willis (Eds.), *Handbook of the psychology of aging* (7th ed., pp. 133–151). San Diego, CA: Academic Press. doi: 10.1016/B978-0-12-380882-0.00009-7

Peters, Stacey L.; Lind, Jennifer N.; Humphrey, Jasmine R.; Friedman, Jan M.; Honein, Margaret A.; Tassinari, Melissa S., . . . Broussard, Cheryl S. (2013). Safe lists for medications in pregnancy: Inadequate evidence base and inconsistent guidance from Web-based information, 2011. *Pharmacoepidemiology and Drug Safety*, 22(3), 324–328. doi: 10.1002/pds.3410

Petersen, Inge; Martinussen, Torben; McGue, Matthew; Bingley, Paul & Christensen, Kaare. (2011). Lower marriage and divorce rates among twins than among singletons in Danish birth cohorts 1940–1964. *Twin Research and Human Genetics*, 14(2), 150–157. doi: 10.1375/twin.14.2.150

Petersen, Jennifer L. & Hyde, Janet Shibley. (2011). Gender differences in sexual attitudes and behaviors: A review of meta-analytic results and large datasets. *The Journal of Sex Research*, 48(2/3), 149–165. doi: 10.1080/00224499.2011.551851

Petrenko, Christie L. M.; Friend, Angela; Garrido, Edward F.; Taussig, Heather N. & Culhane, Sara E. (2012). Does subtype matter? Assessing the effects of maltreatment on functioning in preadolescent youth in out-of-home care. *Child Abuse & Neglect*, 36(9), 633–644. doi: 10.1016/j.chiabu.2012.07.001

Pew Research Center. (2008, June 1). *U.S. Religious Landscape Survey: Religious beliefs and practices. Religion & Public Life.* Washington, DC: Pew Research Center.

Pew Research Center. (2009, June 11). *Depression, anxiety, stress or mental health issues.* Washington, DC: Pew Research Center.

Pew Research Center. (2009, June 29). *Growing old in America: Expectations vs. reality.* Washington, DC: Pew Research Center.

Pew Research Center. (2014, April 2). *America's new drug policy landscape: Two-thirds favor treatment, not jail, for use of heroin, cocaine. U.S. Politics & Policy.* Washington, DC: Pew Research Center.

Pew Research Center. (2014, April 16). *Global views on morality: Compare values across 40 countries. Global Attitudes & Trends.* Washington, DC: Pew Research Center.

Pew Research Center. (2015, April 7). *A deep dive into party affiliation: Sharp differences by race, gender, generation, education. U.S. Politics & Policy.* Washington, DC: Pew Research Center.

Pew Research Center. (2015, April 28). *What the public knows—In pictures, words, maps and graphs: Pew Research Center news IQ quiz. U.S. Politics & Policy.* Washington, DC: Pew Research Center.

Pew Research Center. (2015, May 12). *America's changing religious landscape: Christians decline sharply as share of population; unaffiliated and other faiths continue to grow. Religion & Public Life.* Washington, DC: Pew Research Center.

Pew Research Center. (2015, November 3). *U.S. public becoming less religious: Modest drop in overall rates of belief and practice, but religiously affiliated Americans are as observant as before. Religion & Public Life.* Washington, DC: Pew Research Center.

Peyser, James A. (2011). Unlocking the secrets of high-performing charters. *Education Next*, 11(4), 36–43.

Pfaus, James G.; Scepkowski, Lisa A.; Marson, Lesley & Georgiadis, Janniko R. (2014). Biology of the sexual response. In Deborah L. Tolman et al. (Eds.), *APA handbook of sexuality and psychology* (Vol. 1, pp. 145–203). Washington, DC: American Psychological Association. doi: 10.1037/14193-007

Pfeiffer, Ronald E. & Bodis-Wollner, Ivan (Eds.). (2012). *Parkinson's disease and nonmotor dysfunction.* New York, NY: Springer.

Phillips, Deborah A.; Fox, Nathan A. & Gunnar, Megan R. (2011). Same place, different experiences: Bringing individual differences to research in child care. *Child Development Perspectives*, 5(1), 44–49. doi: 10.1111/j.1750-8606.2010.00155.x

Phillips, Tommy M.; Wilmoth, Joe D.; Wall, Sterling K.; Peterson, Donna J.; Buckley, Rhonda & Phillips, Laura E. (2013). Recollected parental care and fear of intimacy in emerging adults. *The Family Journal*, 21(3), 335–341. doi: 10.1177/1066480713476848

Phillipson, Chris. (2013). *Ageing.* Malden, MA: Polity Press.

Piaget, Jean. (1932). *The moral judgment of the child.* London, UK: K. Paul, Trench, Trubner & Co.

Piaget, Jean. (1950). *The psychology of intelligence.* London, UK: Routledge & Paul.

Piaget, Jean. (1952). *The origins of intelligence in children.* Oxford, UK: International Universities Press.

Piaget, Jean. (1954). *The construction of reality in the child.* New York, NY: Basic Books.

Piaget, Jean. (2001). *The psychology of intelligence.* New York, NY: Routledge.

Piaget, Jean. (2011). *The origins of intelligence in children.* New York, NY: Routledge.

Piaget, Jean. (2013a). *The construction of reality in the child.* New York, NY: Routledge.

Piaget, Jean. (2013b). *The moral judgment of the child.* New York, NY: Routledge.

Piaget, Jean & Inhelder, Bärbel. (1972). *The psychology of the child.* New York, NY: Basic Books.

Piaget, Jean; Voelin-Liambey, Daphne & Berthoud-Papandropoulou, Ioanna. (2001). Problems of class inclusion and logical implication. In Robert L. Campell (Ed.), *Studies in reflecting abstraction* (pp. 105–137). Hove, UK: Psychology Press.

Pickles, Andrew; Hill, Jonathan; Breen, Gerome; Quinn, John; Abbott, Kate; Jones, Helen & Sharp, Helen. (2013). Evidence for interplay between genes and parenting on infant temperament in the first year of life: Monoamine oxidase A polymorphism moderates effects of maternal sensitivity on infant anger proneness. *Journal of Child Psychology and Psychiatry*, 54(12), 1308–1317. doi: 10.1111/jcpp.12081

Piekny, Jeanette & Maehler, Claudia. (2013). Scientific reasoning in early and middle childhood: The development of domain-general evidence evaluation, experimentation, and hypothesis generation skills. *British Journal of Developmental Psychology*, 31(2), 153–179. doi: 10.1111/j.2044-835X.2012.02082.x

Piérard, Gérald E.; Hermanns-Lê, Trinh; Piérard, Sébastien & Piérard-Franchimont, Claudine. (2015). Effects of hormone replacement therapy on skin viscoelasticity during climacteric aging. In Miranda A. Farage et al. (Eds.), *Skin, mucosa and menopause: Management of clinical issues* (pp. 97–103). New York, NY: Springer. doi: 10.1007/978-3-662-44080-3_8

Pietrantonio, Anna Marie; Wright, Elise; Gibson, Kathleen N.; Alldred, Tracy; Jacobson, Dustin & Niec, Anne. (2013). Mandatory reporting of child abuse and neglect: Crafting a positive process for health professionals and caregivers. *Child Abuse & Neglect*, 37(2/3), 102–109. doi: 10.1016/j.chiabu.2012.12.007

Pilarz, Alejandra Ros & Hill, Heather D. (2014). Unstable and multiple child care arrangements and young children's behavior. *Early Childhood Research Quarterly*, 29(4), 471–483. doi: 10.1016/j.ecresq.2014.05.007

Pilkington, Pamela D.; Windsor, Tim D. & Crisp, Dimity A. (2012). Volunteering and subjective well-being in midlife and older adults: The role of supportive social networks. *The Journals of Gerontology Series B: Psychological Sciences and Social Sciences*, 67B(2), 249–260. doi: 10.1093/geronb/gbr154

Pinderhughes, Ellen E. & Rosnati, Rosa. (2015). Introduction to special issue: Adoptees' ethnic identity within family and social contexts. *New Directions for Child and Adolescent Development*, 150, 1–3. doi: 10.1002/cad.20116

Pinker, Steven. (1999). *Words and rules: The ingredients of language.* New York, NY: Basic Books.

Pinker, Steven. (2003). *The blank slate: The modern denial of human nature.* New York, NY: Penguin.

Pinker, Steven. (2011). *The better angels of our nature: Why violence has declined.* New York, NY: Viking.

Pinquart, Martin & Silbereisen, Rainer K. (2006). Socioemotional selectivity in cancer patients. *Psychology and Aging, 21*(2), 419–423. doi: 10.1037/0882-7974.21.2.419

PISA. (2009). *Learning mathematics for life: A perspective from PISA.* Paris, France: OECD. doi: 10.1787/9789264075009-en

PISA. (2014a). *Pisa 2012 results: What students know and can do, student performance in mathematics, reading and science.* Paris, France: OECD.

PISA. (2014b). *PISA 2012 results in focus: What 15-year-olds know and what they can do with what they know.* Paris, France: OECD.

Pitskhelauri, G. Z. (1982). *The longliving of Soviet Georgia.* New York, NY: Human Sciences Press.

Pittenger, Samantha L.; Huit, Terrence Z. & Hansen, David J. (2016). Applying ecological systems theory to sexual revictimization of youth: A review with implications for research and practice. *Aggression and Violent Behavior, 26,* 35–45. doi: 10.1016/j.avb.2015.11.005

Piumatti, Giovanni & Rabaglietti, Emanuela. (2015). Different types of emerging adult university students: The role of achievement strategies and personality for adulthood self-perception and life and education satisfaction. *International Journal of Psychology and Psychological Therapy, 15*(2), 241–257.

Pizot, Cécile; Boniol, Mathieu; Mullie, Patrick; Koechlin, Alice; Boniol, Magali; Boyle, Peter & Autier, Philippe. (2016). Physical activity, hormone replacement therapy and breast cancer risk: A meta-analysis of prospective studies. *European Journal of Cancer, 52,* 138–154. doi: 10.1016 /j.ejca.2015.10.063

Plassman, Brenda L.; Langa, Kenneth M.; Fisher, Gwenith G.; Heeringa, Steven G.; Weir, David R.; Ofstedal, Mary Beth, . . . Wallace, Robert B. (2007). Prevalence of dementia in the United States: The aging, demographics, and memory study. *Neuroepidemiology, 29*(1/2), 125–132. doi: 10.1159/000109998

Plomin, Robert & Deary, Ian J. (2015). Genetics and intelligence differences: Five special findings. *Molecular Psychiatry, 20,* 98–108. doi: 10.1038/mp .2014.105

Plomin, Robert; DeFries, John C.; Knopik, Valerie S. & Neiderhiser, Jenae M. (2013). *Behavioral genetics.* New York, NY: Worth Publishers.

Plows, Alexandra. (2011). *Debating human genetics: Contemporary issues in public policy and ethics.* New York, NY: Routledge.

Pluess, Michael. (2015). Individual differences in environmental sensitivity. *Child Development Perspectives, 9*(3), 138–143. doi: 10.1111 /cdep .12120

Poarch, Gregory J. & Bialystok, Ellen. (2015). Bilingualism as a model for multitasking. *Developmental Review, 35,* 113–124. doi: 10.1016 /j.dr.2014.12.003

Podsiadlowski, Astrid & Fox, Stephen. (2011). Collectivist value orientations among four ethnic groups: Collectivism in the New Zealand context. *New Zealand Journal of Psychology, 40*(1), 5–18.

Pogrebin, Abigail. (2010). *One and the same: My life as an identical twin and what I've learned about everyone's struggle to be singular.* New York, NY: Anchor.

Pons, Ferran & Lewkowicz, David J. (2014). Infant perception of audio-visual speech synchrony in familiar and unfamiliar fluent speech. *Acta Psychologica, 149,* 142–147. doi: 10.1016 /j.actpsy.2013.12.013

Popham, Lauren E.; Kennison, Shelia M. & Bradley, Kristopher I. (2011a). Ageism, sensation-seeking, and risk-taking behavior in young adults. *Current Psychology, 30*(2), 184–193. doi: 10.1007 /s12144-011-9107-0

Popham, Lauren E.; Kennison, Shelia M. & Bradley, Kristopher I. (2011b). Ageism and risk-taking in young adults: Evidence for a link between death anxiety and ageism. *Death Studies, 35*(8), 751–763. doi: 10.1080/07481187.2011.573176

Potočnik, Kristina & Sonnentag, Sabine. (2013). A longitudinal study of well-being in older workers and retirees: The role of engaging in different types of activities. *Journal of Occupational and Organizational Psychology, 86*(4), 497–521. doi: 10.1111/joop.12003

Pottinger, Audrey M. & Palmer, Tiffany. (2013). Whither IVF assisted birth or spontaneous conception? Parenting anxiety, styles and child development in Jamaican families. *Journal of Reproductive and Infant Psychology, 31*(2), 148–159. doi: 10.1080/02646838.2012.762085

Powell, Cynthia M. (2013). Sex chromosomes, sex chromosome disorders, and disorders of sex development. In Steven L. Gersen & Martha B. Keagle (Eds.), *The principles of clinical cytogenetics* (pp. 175–211). New York, NY: Springer. doi: 10.1007/978-1-4419-1688-4_10

Powell, Kendall. (2006). Neurodevelopment: How does the teenage brain work? *Nature, 442*(7105), 865–867. doi: 10.1038/442865a

Powell, Katie; Wilcox, John; Clonan, Angie; Bissell, Paul; Preston, Louise; Peacock, Marian & Holdsworth, Michelle. (2015). The role of social networks in the development of overweight and obesity among adults: A scoping review. *BMC Pubilc Health, 15*(996). doi: 10.1186/ s12889-015-2314-0

Powell, Shaun; Langlands, Stephanie & Dodd, Chris. (2011). Feeding children's desires? Child and parental perceptions of food promotion to the "under 8s". *Young Consumers: Insight and Ideas for Responsible Marketers, 12*(2), 96–109. doi: 10.1108/17473611111141560

Power, E.; Clarke, M.; Kelleher, I.; Coughlan, H.; Lynch, F.; Connor, D., . . . Cannon, M. (2015). The association between economic inactivity and mental health among young people: a longitudinal study of young adults who are not in employment, education or training. *Irish Journal of Psychological Medicine, 32*(1), 155–160. doi: 10.1017/ipm.2014.85

Powers, Alisa & Casey, B. J. (2015). The adolescent brain and the emergence and peak of psychopathology. *Journal of Infant, Child, and Adolescent Psychotherapy, 14*(1), 3–15. doi: 10.1080/15289168.2015.1004889

Pozzoli, Tiziana & Gini, Gianluca. (2013). Why do bystanders of bullying help or not? A multidimensional model. *The Journal of Early Adolescence, 33*(3), 315–340. doi: 10.1177 /0272431612440172

Prenderville, Jack A.; Kennedy, Paul J.; Dinan, Timothy G. & Cryan, John F. (2015). Adding fuel to the fire: The impact of stress on the ageing brain. *Trends in Neurosciences, 38*(1), 13–25. doi: 10.1016/j.tins.2014.11.001

Preston, Tom & Kelly, Michael. (2006). A medical ethics assessment of the case of Terri Schiavo. *Death Studies, 30*(2), 121–133. doi: 10.1080/07481180500455608

Price, Joseph; Patterson, Rich; Regnerus, Mark & Walley, Jacob. (2016). How much more XXX is Generation X consuming? Evidence of changing attitudes and behaviors related to pornography since 1973. *The Journal of Sex Research, 53*(1), 12–20. doi: 10.1080/00224499.2014.1003773

Price, Margaret S. (2010). *Divorce and the special needs child: A guide for parents.* Philadelphia, PA: Jessica Kingsley Publishers.

Priess, Heather A.; Lindberg, Sara M. & Hyde, Janet Shibley. (2009). Adolescent gender-role identity and mental health: Gender intensification revisited. *Child Development, 80*(5), 1531–1544. doi: 10.1111/j.1467-8624.2009.01349.x

Proctor, Laura J. & Dubowitz, Howard. (2014). Child neglect: Challenges and controversies. In Jill E. Korbin & Richard D. Krugman (Eds.), *Handbook of child maltreatment* (pp. 27–61). New York, NY: Springer. doi: 10.1007/978-94-007-7208-3_2

Propper, Cathi B. & Holochwost, Steven J. (2013). The influence of proximal risk on the early development of the autonomic nervous system. *Developmental Review, 33*(3), 151–167. doi: 10.1016/j.dr.2013.05.001

Prothero, Arianna. (2016, April 20). Charters help alums stick with college. *Education Week, 35*(28), 1, 13.

Provasnik, Stephen; Kastberg, David; Ferraro, David; Lemanski, Nita; Roey, Stephen & Jenkins, Frank. (2012). *Highlights from TIMSS 2011: Mathematics and science achievement of U.S. fourth- and eighth-grade students in an international context.* Washington, DC: National Center for Education Statistics, Institute of Education Sciences, U.S. Department of Education.

Pryor, Frederic L. (2014). A note on the determinants of recent pupil achievement. *Scientific Research, 5,* 1265–1268. doi: 10.4236/ce.2014 .514143

Pryor, John H.; Eagan, Kevin; Palucki Blake, Laura; Hurtado, Sylvia; Berdan, Jennifer & Case, Matthew H. (2012). *The American freshman: National norms Fall 2012.* Los Angeles, CA: Higher Education Research Institute, UCLA.

Public Law 104–208—Sept. 30, 1996, (1996).

Puccioni, Olga & Vallesi, Antonino. (2012). Conflict resolution and adaptation in normal aging: The role of verbal intelligence and cognitive reserve. *Psychology and Aging, 27*(4), 1018–1026. doi: 10.1037/a0029106

Pucher, Philip H.; Macdonnell, Michael & Arulkumaran, Sabaratnam. (2013). Global lessons on transforming strategy into action to save mothers' lives. *International Journal of Gynecology & Obstetrics*, 123(2), 167–172. doi: 10.1016/j.ijgo.2013.05.009

Puhl, Rebecca M. & Heuer, Chelsea A. (2010). Obesity stigma: Important considerations for public health. *American Journal of Public Health*, 100(6), 1019–1028. doi: 10.2105/AJPH.2009.159491

Puts, David. (2016). Human sexual selection. *Current Opinion in Psychology*, 7, 28–32. doi: 10.1016/j.copsyc.2015.07.011

Pyszczynski, Tom; Solomon, Sheldon & Greenberg, Jeff. (2015). Thirty years of terror management theory: From genesis to revelation. *Advances in Experimental Social Psychology*, 52, 1–70. doi: 10.1016/bs.aesp.2015.03.001

Qaseem, Amir; Barry, Michael J.; Denberg, Thomas D.; Owens, Douglas K. & Shekelle, Paul. (2013). Screening for prostate cancer: A guidance statement from the clinical guidelines committee of the American College of Physicians. *Annals of Internal Medicine*, 158(10), 761–769. doi: 10.7326/0003-4819-158-10-201305210-00633

Qin, Desiree B. & Chang, Tzu-Fen. (2013). Asian fathers. In Natasha J. Cabrera & Catherine S. Tamis-LeMonda (Eds.), *Handbook of father involvement: Multidisciplinary perspectives* (2nd ed., pp. 261–281). New York, NY: Routledge.

Qin, Jiabi; Sheng, Xiaoqi; Wang, Hua; Liang, Desheng; Tan, Hongzhuan & Xia, Jiahui. (2015). Assisted reproductive technology and risk of congenital malformations: A meta-analysis based on cohort studies. *Archives of Gynecology and Obstetrics*, 292(4), 777–798. doi: 10.1007/s00404-015-3707-0

Qin, Lili; Pomerantz, Eva M. & Wang, Qian. (2009). Are gains in decision-making autonomy during early adolescence beneficial for emotional functioning? The case of the United States and China. *Child Development*, 80(6), 1705–1721. doi: 10.1111/j.1467-8624.2009.01363.x

Qiu, Chengxuan; von Strauss, Eva; Bäckman, Lars; Winblad, Bengt & Fratiglioni, Laura. (2013). Twenty-year changes in dementia occurrence suggest decreasing incidence in central Stockholm, Sweden. *Neurology*, 80(20), 1888–1894. doi: 10.1212/WNL.0b013e318292a2f9

Queen, Tara L.; Berg, Cynthia A. & Lowrance, William. (2015). A framework for decision making in couples across adulthood. In Thomas M. Hess et al. (Eds.), *Aging and decision making: Empirical and applied perspectives* (pp. 372–392). San Diego, CA: Academic Press.

Quindlen, Anna. (2012). *Lots of candles, plenty of cake*. New York, NY: Random House.

Rabkin, Nick & Hedberg, Eric C. (2011). *Arts education in America: What the declines mean for arts participation*. Washington, DC: National Endowment for the Arts.

Rachner, Tilman D.; Khosla, Sundeep & Hofbauer, Lorenz C. (2011). Osteoporosis: Now and the future. *The Lancet*, 377(9773), 1276–1287. doi: 10.1016/S0140-6736(10)62349-5

Raeburn, Paul. (2014). *Do fathers matter?: What science is telling us about the parent we've overlooked*. New York, NY: Farrar, Straus and Giroux.

Rahilly, Elizabeth P. (2015). The gender binary meets the gender-variant child: Parents' negotiations with childhood gender variance. *Gender & Society*, 29(3), 338–361. doi: 10.1177/0891243214563069

Rajaratnam, Julie Knoll; Marcus, Jake R.; Flaxman, Abraham D.; Wang, Haidong; Levin-Rector, Alison; Dwyer, Laura, . . . Murray, Christopher J. L. (2010). Neonatal, postneonatal, childhood, and under-5 mortality for 187 countries, 1970–2010: A systematic analysis of progress towards Millennium Development Goal 4. *The Lancet*, 375(9730), 1988–2008. doi: 10.1016/S0140-6736 (10)60703-9

Ramo, Danielle E.; Young-Wolff, Kelly C. & Prochaska, Judith J. (2015). Prevalence and correlates of electronic-cigarette use in young adults: Findings from three studies over five years. *Addictive Behaviors*, 41, 142–147. doi: 10.1016/j.addbeh.2014.10.019

Ramscar, Michael & Dye, Melody. (2011). Learning language from the input: Why innate constraints can't explain noun compounding. *Cognitive Psychology*, 62(1), 1–40. doi: 10.1016/j.cogpsych.2010.10.001

Ranciaro, Alessia; Campbell, Michael C.; Hirbo, Jibril B.; Ko, Wen-Ya; Froment, Alain; Anagnostou, Paolo, . . . Tishkoff, Sarah A. (2014). Genetic origins of lactase persistence and the spread of pastoralism in Africa. *The American Journal of Human Genetics*, 94(4), 496–510. doi: 10.1016/j.ajhg.2014.02.009

Rand, David G. & Nowak, Martin A. (2016). Cooperation among humans. In Dirk Messner & Silke Weinlich (Eds.), *Global cooperation and the human factor in international relations* (pp. 113–138). New York, NY: Routledge.

Raspberry, Kelly A. & Skinner, Debra. (2011). Negotiating desires and options: How mothers who carry the fragile X gene experience reproductive decisions. *Social Science & Medicine*, 72(6), 992–998. doi: 10.1016/j.socscimed.2011.01.010

Rau, Barbara L. & Adams, Gary A. (2014). Recruiting older workers: Realities and needs of the future workforce. In Daniel M. Cable et al. (Eds.), *The Oxford handbook of recruitment* (pp. 88–109). New York, NY: Oxford University Press. doi: 10.1093/oxfordhb/9780199756094.013.0007

Rauers, Antje; Blanke, Elisabeth & Riediger, Michaela. (2013). Everyday empathic accuracy in younger and older couples: Do you need to see your partner to know his or her feelings? *Psychological Science*, 24(11), 2210–2217. doi: 10.1177/0956797613490747

Raus, Kasper; Sterckx, Sigrid & Mortier, Freddy. (2011). Is continuous sedation at the end of life an ethically preferable alternative to physician-assisted suicide? *The American Journal of Bioethics*, 11(6), 32–40. doi: 10.1080/15265161.2011.577510

Ravallion, Martin. (2014). Income inequality in the developing world. *Science*, 344(6186), 851–855. doi: 10.1126/science.1251875

Ravizza, Kenneth. (2007). Peak experiences in sport. In Daniel Smith & Michael Bar-Eli (Eds.), *Essential readings in sport and exercise psychology* (pp. 122–125). Champaign, IL: Human Kinetics.

Ray, Brian D. (2013). Homeschooling rising into the twenty-first century: Editor's introduction. *Peabody Journal of Education*, 88(3), 261–264. doi: 10.1080/0161956X.2013.796822

Raymo, James M. (2013). Cohabitation in Japan. *Family Focus, National Council on Family Relations*, (FF57), F9–F11.

Raz, Naftali & Lindenberger, Ulman. (2013). Life-span plasticity of the brain and cognition: From questions to evidence and back. *Neuroscience & Biobehavioral Reviews*, 37(9), 2195–2200. doi: 10.1016/j.neubiorev.2013.10.003

Reardon, Sean F. (2013). The widening income achievement gap. *Educational Leadership*, 70(8), 10–16.

Reavey, Daphne; Haney, Barbara M.; Atchison, Linda; Anderson, Betsi; Sandritter, Tracy & Pallotto, Eugenia K. (2014). Improving pain assessment in the NICU: A quality improvement project. *Advances in Neonatal Care*, 14(3), 144–153. doi: 10.1097/ANC.0000000000000034

Reche, Marta; Valbuena, Teresa; Fiandor, Ana; Padial, Antonia; Quirce, Santiago & Pascual, Cristina. (2011). Induction of tolerance in children with food allergy. *Current Nutrition & Food Science*, 7(1), 33–39. doi: 10.2174/157340111794941085

Reczek, Corinne; Liu, Hui & Spiker, Russell. (2014). A population-based study of alcohol use in same-sex and different-sex unions. *Journal of Marriage and Family*, 76(3), 557–572. doi: 10.1111/jomf.12113

Reddy, Marpadga A. & Natarajan, Rama. (2013). Role of epigenetic mechanisms in the vascular complications of diabetes. In Tapas K. Kundu (Ed.), *Epigenetics: Development and disease* (pp. 435–454). New York, NY: Springer. doi: 10.1007/978-94-007-4525-4_19

Reed, Andrew E.; Chan, Larry & Mikels, Joseph A. (2014). Meta-analysis of the age-related positivity effect: Age differences in preferences for positive over negative information. *Psychology and Aging*, 29(1), 1–15. doi: 10.1037/a0035194

Reed, Rebecca G. & Raison, Charles L. (2016). Stress and the immune system. In Charlotte Esser (Ed.), *Environmental influences on the immune system* (pp. 97–126). New York, NY: Springer. doi: 10.1007/978-3-7091-1890-0_5

Regnerus, Mark & Uecker, Jeremy. (2011). *Premarital sex in America: How young Americans meet, mate, and think about marrying*. New York, NY: Oxford University Press. doi: 10.1093/acprof:oso/9780199743285.001.0001

Reich, Justin. (2015). Rebooting MOOC research. *Science*, 347(6217), 34–35. doi: 10.1126/science.1261627

Reich, John W.; Zautra, Alex J. & Hall, John Stuart (Eds.). (2010). *Handbook of adult resilience*. New York, NY: Guilford Press.

Reijntjes, Albert; Vermande, Marjolijn; Thomaes, Sander; Goossens, Frits; Olthof, Tjeert; Aleva, Liesbeth & Van der Meulen,

Matty. (2015). Narcissism, bullying, and social dominance in youth: A longitudinal analysis. *Journal of Abnormal Child Psychology*, 44(1), 63–74. doi: 10.1007/s10802 -015-9974-1

Reisner, Sari L.; Katz-Wise, Sabra L.; Gordon, Allegra R.; Corliss, Heather L. & Austin, S. Bryn. (2016). Social epidemiology of depression and anxiety by gender identity. *Journal of Adolescent Health*, 59(2), 203–208. doi: 10.1016/j.jadohealth .2016.04.006

Remington, Gary & Seeman, Mary V. (2015). Schizophrenia and the influence of male gender. *Clinical Pharmacology & Therapeutics*, 98(6), 578–581. doi: 10.1002/cpt.201

Ren, Jie; Wu, Yan D.; Chan, John S. Y. & Yan, Jin H. (2013). Cognitive aging affects motor performance and learning. *Geriatrics & Gerontology International*, 13(1), 19–27. doi: 10.1111/j.1447-0594.2012 .00914.x

Rendell, Luke; Fogarty, Laurel; Hoppitt, William J. E.; Morgan, Thomas J. H.; Webster, Mike M. & Laland, Kevin N. (2011). Cognitive culture: Theoretical and empirical insights into social learning strategies. *Trends in Cognitive Sciences*, 15(2), 68–76. doi: 10.1016/j.tics.2010.12.002

Rest, James. (1993). Research on moral judgment in college students. In Andrew Garrod (Ed.), *Approaches to moral development: New research and emerging themes* (pp. 201–211). New York, NY: Teachers College Press.

Rest, James; Narvaez, Darcia; Bebeau, Muriel J. & Thoma, Stephen J. (1999). *Postconventional moral thinking: A neo-Kohlbergian approach.* New York, NY: Psychology Press.

Reuter-Lorenz, Patricia A. & Sylvester, Ching-Yune C. (2005). The cognitive neuroscience of working memory and aging. In Roberto Cabeza et al. (Eds.), *Cognitive neuroscience of aging: Linking cognitive and cerebral aging* (pp. 186–217). New York, NY: Oxford University Press.

Reutskaja, Elena & Hogarth, Robin M. (2009). Satisfaction in choice as a function of the number of alternatives: When "goods satiate". *Psychology and Marketing*, 26(3), 197–203. doi: 10.1002 /mar.20268

Reynolds, Arthur J. (2000). *Success in early intervention: The Chicago Child-Parent Centers.* Lincoln, NE: University of Nebraska Press.

Reynolds, Arthur J. & Ou, Suh-Ruu. (2011). Paths of effects from preschool to adult well-being: A confirmatory analysis of the Child-Parent Center Program. *Child Development*, 82(2), 555–582. doi: 10.1111/j.1467-8624.2010.01562.x

Rhoades, Kimberly A.; Leve, Leslie D.; Eddy, J. Mark & Chamberlain, Patricia. (2015). Predicting the transition from juvenile delinquency to adult criminality: Gender-specific influences in two high-risk samples. *Criminal Behaviour and Mental Health*, (In Press). doi: 10.1002/cbm.1957

Rhodes, Marjorie. (2013). The conceptual structure of social categories: The social allegiance hypothesis. In Mahzarin R. Banaji & Susan A. Gelman (Eds.), *Navigating the social world: What infants, children, and other species can teach us* (pp. 258–262). New York, NY: Oxford University Press.

Rich, Motoko. (2013, April 11). Texas considers backtracking on testing. *New York Times*, p. 12.

Richards, Jennifer S.; Hartman, Catharina A.; Franke, Barbara; Hoekstra, Pieter J.; Heslenfeld, Dirk J.; Oosterlaan, Jaap, . . . Buitelaar, Jan K. (2014). Differential susceptibility to maternal expressed emotion in children with ADHD and their siblings? Investigating plasticity genes, prosocial and antisocial behaviour. *European Child & Adolescent Psychiatry*, 24(2), 209–217. doi: 10.1007/s00787-014-0567-2

Richert, Rebekah A.; Robb, Michael B. & Smith, Erin I. (2011). Media as social partners: The social nature of young children's learning from screen media. *Child Development*, 82(1), 82–95. doi: 10.1111/j.1467-8624.2010.01542.x

Ridgers, Nicola D.; Salmon, Jo; Parrish, Anne-Maree; Stanley, Rebecca M. & Okely, Anthony D. (2012). Physical activity during school recess: A systematic review. *American Journal of Preventive Medicine*, 43(3), 320–328. doi: 10.1016/j.amepre .2012.05.019

Ridpath, Alison; Driver, Cynthia R.; Nolan, Michelle L.; Karpati, Adam; Kass, Daniel; Paone, Denise, . . . Kunins, Hillary V. (2014, December 19). *Illnesses and deaths among persons attending an electronic dance-music festival—New York City, 2013. orbidity and Mortality Weekly Report* 63(50), 1195–1198. Atlanta, GA: Centers for Disease Control and Prevention.

Riediger, Michaela; Voelkle, Manuel C.; Schaefer, Sabine & Lindenberger, Ulman. (2014). Charting the life course: Age differences and validity of beliefs about lifespan development. *Psychology and Aging*, 29(3), 503–520. doi: 10.1037/a0036228

Riegel, Klaus F. (1975). Toward a dialectical theory of development. *Human Development*, 18(1-2), 50–64. doi: 10.1159/000271475

Riglin, Lucy; Frederickson, Norah; Shelton, Katherine H. & Rice, Frances. (2013). A longitudinal study of psychological functioning and academic attainment at the transition to secondary school. *Journal of Adolescence*, 36(3), 507–517. doi: 10.1016/j.adolescence.2013.03.002

Rindermann, Heiner; Becker, David & Coyle, Thomas R. (2016). Survey of expert opinion on intelligence: Causes of international differences in cognitive ability tests. *Frontiers in Psychology*, 7(399). doi: 10.3389/fpsyg.2016.00399

Riordan, Jan & Wambach, Karen (Eds.). (2009). *Breastfeeding and human lactation* (4th ed.). Sudbury, MA: Jones and Bartlett Publishers.

Rioux, Charlie; Castellanos-Ryan, Natalie; Parent, Sophie & Séguin, Jean R. (2016). The interaction between temperament and the family environment in adolescent substance use and externalizing behaviors: Support for diathesis–stress or differential susceptibility? *Developmental Review*, 40(10), 117–150. doi: 10.1016/j. dr.2016.03.003

Rivard, Ry. (2013, November 18). Cleaning house. *Inside Higher Ed.*

Rivas-Drake, Deborah & Mooney, Margarita. (2009). Neither colorblind nor oppositional: Perceived minority status and trajectories of academic adjustment among Latinos in elite higher education. *Developmental Psychology*, 45(3), 642–651. doi: 10.1037/a0014135

Rivera, Juan Ángel; de Cossío, Teresita González; Pedraza, Lilia S.; Aburto, Tania C.; Sánchez, Tania G. & Martorell, Reynaldo. (2014). Childhood and adolescent overweight and obesity in Latin America: A systematic review. *The Lancet Diabetes & Endocrinology*, 2(4), 321–332. doi: 10.1016 / S2213-8587(13)70173-6

Rix, Sara E. (2011). Employment and aging. In Robert H. Binstock & Linda K. George (Eds.), *Handbook of aging and the social sciences* (7th ed., pp. 193–206). San Diego, CA: Academic Press. doi: 10.1016/B978-0-12-380880-6.00014-9

Robbins, Cynthia L.; Schick, Vanessa; Reece, Michael; Herbenick, Debra; Sanders, Stephanie A.; Dodge, Brian & Fortenberry, Dennis. (2011). Prevalence, frequency, and associations of masturbation with part. *JAMA Pediatrics*, 165(12), 1087–1093. doi: 10.1001/ archpediatrics.2011.142

Robelen, Erik W. (2011). More students enrolling in Mandarin Chinese. *Education Week*, 30(27), 5.

Robert, L. & Labat-Robert, J. (2015). Longevity and aging: Role of genes and of the extracellular matrix. *Biogerontology*, 16(1), 125–129. doi: 10.1007/s10522-014-9544-x

Roberts, Brent W. & Davis, Jordan P. (2016). Young adulthood is the crucible of personality development. *Emerging Adulthood*, 4(5), 318–326. doi: 10.1177/2167696816653052

Roberts, Richard D. & Lipnevich, Anastasiya A. (2012). From general intelligence to multiple intelligences: Meanings, models, and measures. In Karen R. Harris et al. (Eds.), *APA educational psychology handbook* (Vol. 2, pp. 33–57). Washington, DC: American Psychological Association. doi: 10.1037/13274-002

Roberts, Soraya. (2010, January 1). Travis Pastrana breaks world record for longest rally car jump on New Year's Eve. *New York Daily News.*

Robertson, Deirdre A.; King-Kallimanis, Bellinda L. & Kenny, Rose Anne. (2016). Negative perceptions of aging predict longitudinal decline in cognitive function. *Psychology and Aging*, 31(1), 71–81. doi: 10.1037/pag0000061

Robins, Richard W.; Trzesniewski, Kali H. & Donnellan, M. Brent. (2012). A brief primer on self-esteem. *Prevention Researcher*, 19(2), 3–7.

Robinson, Ken. (2015). Afterword. In Pasi Sahlberg, *Finnish lessons 2.0: What can the world learn from educational change in Finland?* (pp. 205–206). New York, NY.

Robinson, Leah E.; Wadsworth, Danielle D.; Webster, E. Kipling & Bassett, David R. (2014). School reform: The role of physical education policy in physical activity of elementary school children in Alabama's Black Belt region. *American Journal of Health Promotion*, 38(Suppl. 3), S72–S76. doi: 10.4278/ajhp.130430-ARB-207

Robson, Ruthann. (2010). Notes on my dying. In Nan Bauer Maglin & Donna Marie Perry (Eds.), *Final acts: Death, dying, and the choices we make* (pp. 19–28). New Brunswick, NJ: Rutgers University Press.

Roca, María; Parr, Alice; Thompson, Russell; Woolgar, Alexandra; Torralva, Teresa; Antoun, Nagui, . . . Duncan, John. (2010). Executive function and fluid intelligence after frontal lobe lesions. *Brain, 133*(1), 234–247. doi: 10.1093/brain/awp269

Rochat, Philippe. (2013). Self-conceptualizing in development. In Philip D. Zelazo (Ed.), *The Oxford handbook of developmental psychology* (Vol. 2, pp. 378–397). New York, NY: Oxford University Press. doi: 10.1093/oxfordhb/9780199958474.013.0015

Rodrigue, Karen M. & Kennedy, Kristen M. (2011). The cognitive consequences of structural changes to the aging brain. In K. Warner Schaie & Sherry L. Willis (Eds.), *Handbook of the psychology of aging* (7th ed., pp. 73–91). San Diego, CA: Academic Press. doi: 10.1016/B978-0-12-380882-0.00005-X

Roebers, Claudia M.; Schmid, Corinne & Roderer, Thomas. (2009). Metacognitive monitoring and control processes involved in primary school children's test performance. *British Journal of Educational Psychology, 79*(4), 749–767. doi: 10.1348/978185409X429842

Roelfs, David J.; Shor, Eran; Davidson, Karina W. & Schwartz, Joseph E. (2011). Losing life and livelihood: A systematic review and meta-analysis of unemployment and all-cause mortality. *Social Science Medicine, 72*(6), 840–854. doi: 10.1016 /j.socscimed.2011.01.005

Roenneberg, Till; Allebrandt, Karla; Merrow, Martha & Vetter, Céline. (2012). Social jetlag and obesity. *Current Biology, 22*(10), 939–943. doi: 10.1016/j.cub.2012.03.038

Rogne, Leah & McCune, Susana Lauraine (Eds.). (2014). *Advance care planning: Communicating about matters of life and death.* New York, NY: Springer.

Rogoff, Barbara. (2003). *The cultural nature of human development.* New York, NY: Oxford University Press.

Rogoff, Barbara. (2016). Culture and participation: A paradigm shift. *Current Opinion in Psychology, 8*, 182–189. doi: 10.1016/j.copsyc.2015.12.002

Rohwedder, Susann & Willis, Robert J. (2010). Mental retirement. *Journal of Economic Perspectives, 24*(1), 119–138. doi: 10.1257/jep.24.1.119

Romagnolo, Donato F. & Selmin, Ornella I. (Eds.). (2016). *Mediterranean diet: Dietary guidelines and impact on health and disease.* New York, NY: Springer. doi: 10.1007/978-3-319-27969-5

Romeo, Russell D. (2013). The teenage brain: The stress response and the adolescent brain. *Current Directions in Psychological Science, 22*(2), 140–145. doi: 10.1177/0963721413475445

Romito, Patrizia & Beltramini, Lucia. (2011). Watching pornography: Gender differences, violence and victimization. An exploratory study in Italy. *Violence Against Women, 17*(10), 1313–1326. doi: 10.1177/1077801211424555

Rook, Graham A. W.; Lowry, Christopher A. & Raison, Charles L. (2014). Hygiene and other early childhood influences on the subsequent function of the immune system. *Brain Research*(Corrected Proof). doi: 10.1016 /j.brainres.2014.04.004

Roopnarine, Jaipaul; Patte, Michael; Johnson, James & Kuschner, David (Eds.). (2015). *International perspectives on children's play.* New York, NY: McGraw Hill.

Roopnarine, Jaipaul L. & Hossain, Ziarat. (2013). African American and African Caribbean fathers. In Natasha J. Cabrera & Catherine S. Tamis-LeMonda (Eds.), *Handbook of father involvement: Multidisciplinary perspectives* (2nd ed., pp. 223–243). New York, NY: Routledge.

Rose, Amanda J.; Schwartz-Mette, Rebecca A.; Glick, Gary C.; Smith, Rhiannon L. & Luebbe, Aaron M. (2014). An observational study of co-rumination in adolescent friendships. *Developmental Psychology, 50*(9), 2199–2209. doi: 10.1037 /a0037465

Rose, Nikolas. (2016). Reading the human brain: How the mind became legible. *Body & Society, 22*(2), 140–177. doi: 10.1177/1357034X15623363

Rose, Steven. (2008). Drugging unruly children is a method of social control. *Nature, 451*(7178), 521. doi: 10.1038/451521a

Roseberry, Sarah; Hirsh-Pasek, Kathy; Parish-Morris, Julia & Golinkoff, Roberta M. (2009). Live action: Can young children learn verbs from video? *Child Development, 80*(5), 1360–1375. doi: 10.1111/j.1467-8624.2009.01338.x

Rosenbaum, James E. (2011). The complexities of college for all. *Sociology of Education, 84*(2), 113–117. doi: 10.1177/0038040711401809

Rosenblatt, Paul C. (2013). Culture, socialization, and loss, grief, and mourning. In David K. Meagher & David E. Balk (Eds.), *Handbook of thanatology: The essential body of knowledge for the study of death, dying, and bereavement* (2nd ed., pp. 121–126). New York, NY: Routledge.

Rosenfeld, Michael J. & Thomas, Reuben J. (2012). Searching for a mate: The rise of the Internet as a social intermediary. *American Sociological Review, 77*(4), 523–547. doi: 10.1177/0003122412448050

Rosenfield, Sarah. (2012). Triple jeopardy? Mental health at the intersection of gender, race, and class. *Social Science & Medicine, 74*(11), 1791–1801. doi: 10.1016/j.socscimed.2011.11.010

Rosiek, Jerry & Kinslow, Kathy. (2016). *Resegregation as curriculum: The meaning of the new racial segregation in U.S. public schools.* New York, NY: Routledge.

Rosin, Hanna. (2014, March 19). The overprotected kid. *The Atlantic.*

Rosow, Irving. (1985). Status and role change through the life cycle. In Robert H. Binstock & Ethel Shanas (Eds.), *Handbook of aging and the social sciences* (2nd ed., pp. 62–93). New York, NY: Van Nostrand Reinhold.

Ross, Heidi & Wang, Yimin. (2013). Reforms to the college entrance examination in China: Key issues, developments, and dilemmas. *Chinese Education & Society, 46*(1), 3–9. doi: 10.2753 /CED1061-1932460100

Ross, Josephine; Anderson, James R. & Campbell, Robin N. (2011). *I remember me: Mnemonic self-reference effects in preschool children.* Boston, MA: Wiley-Blackwell.

Ross, Josephine; Yilmaz, Mandy; Dale, Rachel; Cassidy, Rose; Yildirim, Iraz & Zeedyk, M. Suzanne. (2016). Cultural differences in self-recognition: the early development of autonomous and related selves? *Developmental Science,* (In Press). doi: 10.1111/desc.12387

Ross, Lesley A.; Dodson, Joan E.; Edwards, Jerri D.; Ackerman, Michelle L. & Ball, Karlene. (2012). Self-rated driving and driving safety in older adults. *Accident Analysis & Prevention, 48*, 523–527. doi: 10.1016/j.aap.2012.02.015

Ross, Patrick A.; Newth, Christopher J. L.; Leung, Dennis; Wetzel, Randall C. & Khemani, Robinder G. (2016). Obesity and mortality risk in critically ill children. *Pediatrics, 137*(3), e20152035. doi: 10.1542/peds.2015-2035

Ross, Robert; Hudson, Robert; Stotz, Paula J. & Lam, Miu. (2015). Effects of exercise amount and intensity on abdominal obesity and glucose tolerance in obese adults: A randomized trial. *Annals of Internal Medicine, 162*(5), 325–334. doi: 10.7326/M14-1189

Rosselli, Mónica; Ardila, Alfredo; Lalwani, Laxmi N. & Vélez-Uribe, Idaly. (2016). The effect of language proficiency on executive functions in balanced and unbalanced Spanish–English bilinguals. *Bilingualism: Language and Cognition, 19*(3), 489–503. doi: 10.1017/S1366728915000309

Rossignol, Michel; Chaillet, Nils; Boughrassa, Faiza & Moutquin, Jean-Marie. (2014). Interrelations between four antepartum obstetric interventions and cesarean delivery in women at low risk: A systematic review and modeling of the cascade of interventions. *Birth, 41*(1), 70–78. doi: 10.1111/birt.12088

Rosso, Andrea L.; Flatt, Jason D.; Carlson, Michelle C.; Lovas, Gina S.; Rosano, Caterina; Brown, Arleen F., . . . Gianaros, Peter J. (2016). Neighborhood socioeconomic status and cognitive function in late life. *American Journal of Epidemiology, 183*(12), 1088–1097. doi: 10.1093/aje/kwv337

Rostila, Mikael; Saarela, Jan & Kawachi, Ichiro. (2013). Suicide following the death of a sibling: A nationwide follow-up study from Sweden. *BMJ Open, 3*(4), e002618. doi: 10.1136/bmjopen-2013-002618

Rotatori, Anthony; Bakken, Jeffrey P.; Burkhardt, Sandra A.; Obiakor, Festus E. & Sharma, Umesh. (2014). *Special education international perspectives: Practices across the globe.* Bingley, UK: Emerald.

Roth, David L.; Skarupski, Kimberly A.; Crew, Deidra C.; Howard, Virginia J. & Locher, Julie L. (2016). Distinct age and self-rated health crossover mortality effects for African Americans: Evidence from a national cohort study. *Social Science & Medicine, 156*, 12–20. doi: 10.1016 /j.socscimed.2016.03.019

Roth, Lauren W. & Polotsky, Alex J. (2012). Can we live longer by eating less? A review of caloric restriction and longevity. *Maturitas, 71*(4), 315–319. doi: 10.1016/j.maturitas.2011.12.017

Rothrauff, Tanja C.; Cooney, Teresa M. & An, Jeong Shin. (2009). Remembered parenting styles and adjustment in middle and late adulthood. *The Journals of Gerontology Series B: Psychological Sciences and Social Sciences, 64B*(1), 137–146. doi: 10.1093/geronb/gbn008

Rothstein, Mark A. (2015). The moral challenge of Ebola. *American Journal of Public Health, 105*(1), 6–8. doi: 10.2105/AJPH.2014.302413

Rouchka, Eric C. & Cha, I. Elizabeth. (2009). Current trends in pseudogene detection and characterization. *Current Bioinformatics, 4*(2), 112–119. doi: 10.2174/157489309788184792

Rovee-Collier, Carolyn. (1987). Learning and memory in infancy. In Joy Doniger Osofsky (Ed.), *Handbook of infant development* (2nd ed., pp. 98–148). New York, NY: Wiley.

Rovee-Collier, Carolyn. (1990). The "memory system" of prelinguistic infants. *Annals of the New York Academy of Sciences, 608,* 517–542. doi: 10.1111/j.1749-6632.1990.tb48908.x

Rovee-Collier, Carolyn & Cuevas, Kimberly. (2009). The development of infant memory. In Mary L. Courage & Nelson Cowan (Eds.), *The development of memory in infancy and childhood* (2nd ed., pp. 11–41). New York, NY: Psychology Press.

Rovee-Collier, Carolyn & Hayne, Harlene. (1987). Reactivation of infant memory: Implications for cognitive development. In Hayne W. Reese (Ed.), *Advances in child development and behavior* (Vol. 20, pp. 185–238). London, UK: Academic Press.

Rovner, Alisha J.; Nansel, Tonja R.; Wang, Jing & Iannotti, Ronald J. (2011). Food sold in school vending machines is associated with overall student dietary intake. *Journal of Adolescent Health, 48*(1), 13–19. doi: 10.1016/j.jadohealth.2010.08.021

Rowe, Meredith L.; Denmark, Nicole; Harden, Brenda Jones & Stapleton, Laura M. (2016). The role of parent education and parenting knowledge in children's language and literacy skills among White, Black, and Latino families. *Infant and Child Development, 25*(2), 198–220. doi: 10.1002/icd.1924

Rubertsson, C.; Hellström, J.; Cross, M. & Sydsjö, G. (2014). Anxiety in early pregnancy: Prevalence and contributing factors. *Archives of Women's Mental Health, 17*(3), 221–228. doi: 10.1007/s00737-013-0409-0

Rubin, Kenneth H.; Bowker, Julie C.; McDonald, Kristina L. & Menzer, Melissa. (2013). Peer relationships in childhood. In Philip D. Zelazo (Ed.), *The Oxford handbook of developmental psychology* (Vol. 2, pp. 242–275). New York, NY: Oxford University Press. doi: 10.1093/oxfordhb/9780199958474.013.0011

Rubin, Simon Shimshon; Malkinson, Ruth & Witztum, Eliezer. (2012). *Working with the bereaved: Multiple lenses on loss and mourning.* New York, NY: Routledge.

Rudd, R. A.; Aleshire, N.; Zibbell, J. E. & Gladden, R. Matthew. (2016). Increases in drug and opioid overdose deaths—United States, 2000–2014. *American Journal of Transplantation*(16), 4. doi: 10.1111/ajt.13776

Rudolph, Karen D. (2014). Puberty as a developmental context of risk for psychopathology.

In Michael Lewis & Karen D. Rudolph (Eds.), *Handbook of developmental psychopathology* (pp. 331–354). New York, NY: Springer. doi: 10.1007/978-1-4614-9608-3_17

Ruetschlin, Catherine & Draut, Tamara. (2013). *Stuck: Young America's persistent jobs crisis.* New York, NY: Demos.

Rulfs, Monika. (2011). Marking death: Grief, protest and politics after a fatal traffic accident. In Peter Jan Margry & Cristina Sanchez-Carretero (Eds.), *Grassroots memorials: The politics of memorializing traumatic death* (pp. 145–168). New York, NY: Berghahn Books.

Runions, Kevin C. & Shaw, Thérèse. (2013). Teacher–child relationship, child withdrawal and aggression in the development of peer victimization. *Journal of Applied Developmental Psychology, 34*(6), 319–327. doi: 10.1016/j.appdev.2013.09.002

Russell, Charlotte K.; Robinson, Lyn & Ball, Helen L. (2013). Infant sleep development: Location, feeding and expectations in the postnatal period. *The Open Sleep Journal, 6*(Suppl. 1: M9), 68–76. doi: 10.2174/1874620901306010068

Russell, Stephen T.; Everett, Bethany G.; Rosario, Margaret & Birkett, Michelle. (2014). Indicators of victimization and sexual orientation among adolescents: Analyses from youth risk behavior surveys. *American Journal of Public Health, 104*(2), 255–261. doi: 10.2105/AJPH.2013.301493

Russo, Theresa J. & Fallon, Moira A. (2014). Coping with stress: Supporting the needs of military families and their children. *Early Childhood Education Journal, 43*(5), 407–416. doi: 10.1007/s10643-014-0665-2

Ruthig, Joelle C.; Trisko, Jenna & Stewart, Tara L. (2012). The impact of spouse's health and well-being on own well-being: A dyadic study of older married couples. *Journal of Social and Clinical Psychology, 31*(5), 508–529. doi: 10.1521/jscp.2012.31.5.508

Rutter, Michael; Sonuga-Barke, Edmund J.; Beckett, Celia; Castle, Jennifer; Kreppner, Jana; Kumsta, Robert, . . . Gunnar, Megan R. (2010). Deprivation-specific psychological patterns: Effects of institutional deprivation. *Monographs of the Society for Research in Child Development, 75*(1). doi: 10.1111/j.1540-5834.2010.00547.x

Ryan, Alan S. (1997). The resurgence of breastfeeding in the United States. *Pediatrics, 99*(4), E12.

Ryan, Alan S.; Rush, David; Krieger, Fritz W. & Lewandowski, Gregory E. (1991). Recent declines in breast-feeding in the United States, 1984 through 1989. *Pediatrics, 88*(4), 719–727.

Ryan, Alan S.; Zhou, Wenjun & Acosta, Andrew. (2002). Breastfeeding continues to increase into the new millennium. *Pediatrics, 110*(6), 1103–1109. doi: 10.1542/peds.110.6.1103

Ryan, Erin L. (2012). "They are kind of like magic": Why U.S. mothers use baby videos with 12- to 24-month-olds. *Journalism and Mass Communication, 2*(7), 771–785.

Saavedra Pérez, Heidi C.; Ikram, Mohammad Afran; Direk, Nese; Prigerson, Holly G.; Freak-Poli, Rosanne; Verhaaren, Benjamin F.

J., . . . **Tiemeier, Henning.** (2015). Cognition, structural brain changes and complicated grief. A population-based study. *Psychological Medicine, 45*(7), 1389–1399. doi: 10.1017/S0033291714002499

Sabayan, Behnam; Oleksik, Anna M.; Maier, Andrea B.; van Buchem, Mark A.; Poortvliet, Rosalinde K. E.; de Ruijter, Wouter, . . . Westendorp, Rudi G. J. (2012). High blood pressure and resilience to physical and cognitive decline in the oldest old: the Leiden 85-plus study. *Journal of the American Geriatrics Society, 60*(11), 2014–2019. doi: 10.1111/j.1532-5415.2012.04203.x

Sabol, T. J.; Soliday Hong, S. L.; Pianta, R. C. & Burchinal, M. R. (2013). Can rating Pre-K programs predict children's learning? *Science, 341*(6148), 845–846. doi: 10.1126/science.1233517

Sacks, Oliver. (2008). *Musicophilia: Tales of music and the brain.* New York, NY: Vintage Books.

Sacks, Oliver W. (1995). *An anthropologist on Mars: Seven paradoxical tales.* New York, NY: Knopf.

Sadeh, Avi; Mindell, Jodi A.; Luedtke, Kathryn & Wiegand, Benjamin. (2009). Sleep and sleep ecology in the first 3 years: A web-based study. *Journal of Sleep Research, 18*(1), 60–73. doi: 10.1111/j.1365-2869.2008.00699.x

Sadler, Troy D.; Romine, William L.; Stuart, Parker E. & Merle-Johnson, Dominike. (2013). Game-based curricula in biology classes: Differential effects among varying academic levels. *Journal of Research in Science Teaching, 50*(4), 479–499. doi: 10.1002/tea.21085

Saegert, Susan; Fields, Desiree & Libman, Kimberly. (2011). Mortgage foreclosure and health disparities: Serial displacement as asset extraction in African American populations. *Journal of Urban Health, 88*(3), 390–402. doi: 10.1007/s11524-011-9584-3

Saewyc, Elizabeth M. (2011). Research on adolescent sexual orientation: Development, health disparities, stigma, and resilience. *Journal of Research on Adolescence, 21*(1), 256–272. doi: 10.1111/j.1532-7795.2010.00727.x

Sahlberg, Pasi. (2011). *Finnish lessons: What can the world learn from educational change in Finland?* New York, NY: Teachers College Press.

Sahlberg, Pasi. (2015). *Finnish lessons 2.0: What can the world learn from educational change in Finland?* (2nd. ed.). New York, NY: Teachers College.

Sahoo, Krushnapriya; Sahoo, Bishnupriya; Choudhury, Ashok Kumar; Sofi, Nighat Yasin; Kumar, Raman & Bhadoria, Ajeet Singh. (2015). Childhood obesity: Causes and consequences. *Journal of Family Medicine and Primary Care, 4*(2), 187–192. doi: 10.4103/2249-4863.154628

Salmivalli, Christina. (2010). Bullying and the peer group: A review. *Aggression and Violent Behavior, 15*(2), 112–120. doi: 10.1016/j.avb.2009.08.007

Salpeter, Shelley R.; Luo, Esther J.; Malter, Dawn S. & Stuart, Brad. (2012). Systematic review of noncancer presentations with a median survival of 6 months or less. *The American Journal of Medicine, 125*(5), 512.e511–512.e516. doi: 10.1016/j.amjmed.2011.07.028

Salter, Nicholas P. & Highhouse, Scott. (2009). Assessing managers' common sense using situational judgment tests. *Management Decision, 47*(3), 392–398. doi: 10.1108/00251740910946660

Salthouse, Timothy A. (2004). What and when of cognitive aging. *Current Directions in Psychological Science, 13*(4), 140–144. doi: 10.1111/j.0963-7214 .2004.00293.x

Salthouse, Timothy A. (2010). *Major issues in cognitive aging.* New York, NY: Oxford University Press.

Samaras, Nikolass; Frangos, Emilia; Forster, Alexandre; Lang, P. O. & Samaras, Dimitrios. (2012). Andropause: A review of the definition and treatment. *European Geriatric Medicine, 3*(6), 368–373. doi: 10.1016/j.eurger.2012.08.007

Samek, Diana R.; Goodman, Rebecca J.; Erath, Stephen A.; McGue, Matt & Iacono, William G. (2016). Antisocial peer affiliation and externalizing disorders in the transition from adolescence to young adulthood: Selection versus socialization effects. *Developmental Psychology, 52*(5), 813–823. doi: 10.1037/dev0000109

SAMHSA. (2009). *Results from the 2008 National Survey on Drug Use and Health: National findings* Rockville, MD: U.S. Department of Health and Human Services, Office of Applied Studies.

SAMHSA. (2014). *Results from the 2013 National Survey on Drug Use and Health: Summary of national findings. NSDUH Series.* Rockville, MD: U.S. Department of Health And Human Services, Substance Abuse and Mental Health, Services Administration Center for Behavioral Health Statistics and Quality.

Samuels, Christina A. (2013). Study reveals gaps in graduation rates: Diplomas at risk. *Education Week, 32*(32), 5.

Samuels, Christina A. & Klein, Alyson. (2013). States faulted on preschool spending levels. *Education Week, 32*(30), 21, 24.

Sanbonmatsu, David M.; Strayer, David L.; Medeiros-Ward, Nathan & Watson, Jason M. (2013). Who multi-tasks and why? Multi-tasking ability, perceived multi-tasking ability, impulsivity, and sensation seeking. *PLoS ONE, 8*(1), e54402. doi: 10.1371/journal.pone.0054402

Sanchez, Gabriel R. & Vargas, Edward D. (2016). Taking a closer look at group identity: The link between theory and measurement of group consciousness and linked fate. *Political Research Quarterly, 69*(1), 160–174. doi: 10.1177/1065912915624571

Sandberg, Sheryl & UC Berkeley (Producer). (2016). Sheryl Sandberg Gives UC Berkeley Commencement Keynote Speech. Retrieved from https://www.youtube.com/watch?v=iqm-XEqpayc

Sander, Libby. (2013). Campus counseling centers see rising numbers of severe problems. *Chronicle of Higher Education, 59*(33), A18.

Sandu, Anca-Larisa; Staff, Roger T.; McNeil, Chris J.; Mustafa, Nazahah; Ahearn, Trevor; Whalley, Lawrence J. & Murray, Alison D. (2014). Structural brain complexity and cognitive decline in late life— A longitudinal study in the Aberdeen 1936 Birth Cohort. *NeuroImage, 100,* 558–563. doi: 10.1016/j.neuroimage.2014.06.054

Santelli, John S. & Melnikas, Andrea J. (2010). Teen fertility in transition: Recent and historic trends in the United States. *Annual Review of Public Health, 31,* 371–383. doi: 10.1146/annurev .publhealth.29.020907.090830

Sanz Cruces, José Manuel; Hawrylak, María Fernández & Delegido, Ana Benito. (2015). Interpersonal variability of the experience of falling in love. *International Journal of Psychology and Psychological Therapy, 15*(1), 87–100.

Saraceno, Chiara. (2010). Social inequalities in facing old-age dependency: A bi-generational perspective. *Journal of European Social Policy, 20*(1), 32–44. doi: 10.1177/0958928709352540

Saraiva, Linda; Rodrigues, Luís P.; Cordovil, Rita & Barreiros, João. (2013). Influence of age, sex and somatic variables on the motor performance of pre-school children. *Annals of Human Biology, 40*(5), 444–450. doi: 10.3109/03014460.2013.802012

Şaşmaz, Tayyar; Öner, Seva; Kurt, A. Öner; Yapıcı, Gülçin; Yazıcı, Aylin Ertekin; Buğdaycı, Resul & Şiş, Mustafa. (2014). Prevalence and risk factors of Internet addiction in high school students. *European Journal of Public Health, 24*(1), 15–20. doi: 10.1093/eurpub/ckt051

Satariano, William A.; Guralnik, Jack M.; Jackson, Richard J.; Marottoli, Richard A.; Phelan, Elizabeth A. & Prohaska, Thomas R. (2012). Mobility and aging: New directions for public health action. *American Journal of Public Health, 102*(8), 1508–1515. doi: 10.2105 /AJPH.2011.300631

Satterwhite, Catherine Lindsey; Torrone, Elizabeth; Meites, Elissa; Dunne, Eileen F.; Mahajan, Reena; Ocfemia, M. Cheryl Bañez, . . . Weinstock, Hillard. (2013). Sexually transmitted infections among US women and men: Prevalence and incidence estimates, 2008. *Sexually Transmitted Diseases, 40*(3), 187–193. doi: 10.1097/OLQ.0b013e318286bb53

Saudino, Kimberly J. & Micalizzi, Lauren. (2015). Emerging trends in behavioral genetic studies of child temperament. *Child Development Perspectives, 9*(3), 144–148. doi: 10.1111 /cdep .12123

Sauer, Mark V.; Wang, Jeff G.; Douglas, Nataki C.; Nakhuda, Gary S.; Vardhana, Pratibashri; Jovanovic, Vuk & Guarnaccia, Michael M. (2009). Providing fertility care to men seropositive for human immunodeficiency virus: Reviewing 10 years of experience and 420 consecutive cycles of in vitro fertilization and intracytoplasmic sperm injection. *Fertility and Sterility, 91*(6), 2455–2460. doi: 10.1016 /j.fertnstert.2008.04.013

Saunders, Cicely M. (1978). *The management of terminal disease.* London, UK: Arnold.

Savioja, Hanna; Helminen, Mika; Fröjd, Sari; Marttunen, Mauri & Kaltiala-Heino, Riittakerttu. (2015). Sexual experience and self-reported depression across the adolescent years. *Health Psychology and Behavioral Medicine, 3*(1), 337–347. doi: 10.1080/21642850.2015.1101696

Saw, Seang-Mei; Cheng, Angela; Fong, Allan; Gazzard, Gus; Tan, Donald T. H. &

Morgan, Ian. (2007). School grades and myopia. *Ophthalmic and Physiological Optics, 27*(2), 126–129. doi: 10.1111/j.1475-1313.2006.00455.x

Saxton, Matthew. (2010). *Child language: Acquisition and development.* Thousand Oaks, CA: Sage.

Sayette, Michael A.; Reichle, Erik D. & Schooler, Jonathan W. (2009). Lost in the sauce: The effects of alcohol on mind wandering. *Psychological Science, 20*(6), 747–752. doi: 10.1111/j.1467-9280 .2009.02351.x

Scarr, Sandra. (1985). Constructing psychology: Making facts and fables for our times. *American Psychologist, 40*(5), 499–512. doi: 10.1037/0003 -066x.40.5.499

Schafer, Markus H.; Morton, Patricia M. & Ferraro, Kenneth F. (2014). Child maltreatment and adult health in a national sample: Heterogeneous relational contexts, divergent effects? *Child Abuse & Neglect, 38*(3), 395–406. doi: 10.1016/j.chiabu.2013.08.003

Schaie, K. Warner. (1958). Rigidity-flexibility and intelligence: A cross-sectional study of the adult life span from 20 to 70 years. *Psychological Monographs, 72*(9), 1–26. doi: 10.1037/h0093788

Schaie, K. Warner. (2005). *Developmental influences on adult intelligence: The Seattle Longitudinal Study.* New York, NY: Oxford University Press.

Schaie, K. Warner. (2013). *Developmental influences on adult intelligence: The Seattle Longitudinal Study* (2nd ed.). New York, NY: Oxford University Press.

Schaller, Jessamyn. (2013). For richer, if not for poorer? Marriage and divorce over the business cycle. *Journal of Population Economics, 26*(3), 1007–1033. doi: 10.1007/s00148-012-0413-0

Schanler, Richard. J. (2011). Outcomes of human milk-fed premature infants. *Seminars in Perinatology, 35*(1), 29–33. doi: 10.1053/j.semperi .2010.10.005

Schardein, James L. (1976). *Drugs as teratogens.* Cleveland, OH: CRC Press.

Scharlach, Andrew; Graham, Carrie & Lehning, Amanda. (2012). The "Village" model: A consumer-driven approach for aging in place. *The Gerontologist, 52*(3), 418–427. doi: 10.1093/ geront /gnr083

Scheetz, Laura T.; Martin, Peter & Poon, Leonard W. (2012). Do centenarians have higher levels of depression? Findings from the Georgia centenarian study. *Journal of the American Geriatrics Society, 60*(2), 238–242. doi: 10.1111 /j.1532-5415.2011 .03828.x

Scheibehenne, Benjamin; Greifeneder, Rainer & Todd, Peter M. (2010). Can there ever be too many options? A meta-analytic review of choice overload. *Journal of Consumer Research, 37*(3), 409–425. doi: 10.1086/651235

Schermerhorn, Alice C.; D'Onofrio, Brian M.; Turkheimer, Eric; Ganiban, Jody M.; Spotts, Erica L.; Lichtenstein, Paul, . . . Neiderhiser, Jenae M. (2011). A genetically informed study of associations between family functioning and child psychosocial adjustment. *Developmental Psychology, 47*(3), 707–725. doi: 10.1037/a0021362

Schifrin, Barry S. & Cohen, Wayne R. (2013). The effect of malpractice claims on the use of caesarean section. *Best Practice & Research Clinical Obstetrics & Gynaecology, 27*(2), 269–283. doi: 10.1016/j.bpobgyn.2012.10.004

Schiller, Ruth A. (1998). The relationship of developmental tasks to life satisfaction, moral reasoning, and occupational attainment at age 28. *Journal of Adult Development, 5*(4), 239–254. doi: 10.1023/A:1021406426385

Schimmele, Christoph. M. & Wu, Zheng. (2016). Repartnering after union dissolution in later life. *Journal of Marriage & Family, 78*(4), 1013–1031. doi: 10.1111/jomf.12315

Schlosnagle, Leo & Strough, JoNell. (2016). Understanding adult age differences in the frequency of problems with friends. *International Journal of Ageing & Human Development,* (In Press). doi: 10.1177/0091415016657558

Schmader, Toni. (2010). Stereotype threat deconstructed. *Current Directions in Psychological Science, 19*(1), 14–18. doi: 10.1177/0963721409359292

Schnitzspahn, Katharina M.; Ihle, Andreas; Henry, Julie D.; Rendell, Peter G. & Kliegel, Matthias. (2011). The age-prospective memory-paradox: An exploration of possible mechanisms. *International Psychogeriatrics, 23*(4), 583–592. doi: 10.1017/S1041610210001651

Schnitzspahn, Katharina M.; Stahl, Christoph; Zeintl, Melanie; Kaller, Christoph P. & Kliegel, Matthias. (2013). The role of shifting, updating, and inhibition in prospective memory performance in young and older adults. *Developmental Psychology, 49*(8), 1544–1553. doi: 10.1037/a0030579

Schoebi, Dominik; Karney, Benjamin R. & Bradbury, Thomas N. (2012). Stability and change in the first 10 years of marriage: Does commitment confer benefits beyond the effects of satisfaction? *Journal of Personality and Social Psychology, 102*(4), 729–742. doi: 10.1037/a0026290

Schoen, Robert & Cheng, Yen-Hsin Alice. (2006). Partner choice and the differential retreat from marriage. *Journal of Marriage and Family, 68*(1), 1–10. doi: 10.1111/j.1741-3737.2006.00229.x

Schoenfeld, Elizabeth A.; Bredow, Carrie A. & Huston, Ted L. (2012). Do men and women show love differently in marriage? *Personality and Social Psychology Bulletin, 38*(11), 1396–1409. doi: 10.1177/0146167212450739

Schön, Daniele; Boyer, Maud; Moreno, Sylvain; Besson, Mireille; Peretz, Isabelle & Kolinsky, Régine. (2008). Songs as an aid for language acquisition. *Cognition, 106*(2), 975–983. doi: 10.1016/j.cognition.2007.03.005

Schoon, Ingrid. (2006). *Risk and resilience: Adaptations in changing times.* New York, NY: Cambridge University Press.

Schore, Allan & McIntosh, Jennifer. (2011). Family law and the neuroscience of attachment, Part I. *Family Court Review, 49*(3), 501–512. doi: 10.1111/j.1744-1617.2011.01387.x

Schröder, Mathis. (2013). Jobless now, sick later? Investigating the long-term consequences of involuntary job loss on health. *Advances in Life Course Research, 18*(1), 5–15. doi: 10.1016/j.alcr.2012.08.001

Schroeder, Steven A. (2013). New evidence that cigarette smoking remains the most important health hazard. *New England Journal of Medicine, 368*(4), 389–390. doi: 10.1056/NEJMe1213751

Schulenberg, John; O'Malley, Patrick M.; Bachman, Jerald G. & Johnston, Lloyd D. (2005). Early adult transitions and their relation to well-being and substance use. In Richard A. Settersten et al. (Eds.), *On the frontier of adulthood: Theory, research, and public policy* (pp. 417–453). Chicago, IL: University of Chicago Press.

Schulenberg, John; Patrick, Megan E.; Maslowsky, Julie & Maggs, Jennifer L. (2014). The epidemiology and etiology of adolescent substance use in developmental perspective. In Michael Lewis & Karen D. Rudolph (Eds.), *Handbook of Developmental Psychopathology* (pp. 601–620). New York, NY: Springer. doi: 10.1007/978-1-4614-9608-3_30

Schupp, Justin & Sharp, Jeff. (2012). Exploring the social bases of home gardening. *Agriculture and Human Values, 29*(1), 93–105. doi: 10.1007/s10460-011-9321-2

Schwartsmann, Carlos Roberto; Spinelli, Leandro de Freitas; Boschin, Leonardo Carbonera; Yépez, Anthony Kerbes; Crestani, Marcus Vinicius & Silva, Marcelo Faria. (2015). Correlation between patient age at total hip replacement surgery and life expectancy. *Acta Ortopedica Brasileira, 23*(6), 323–325.

Schwarz, Alan. (2013, December 15). The selling of Attention deficit disorder. *New York Times,* p. A1.

Schwarz, Alan & Cohen, Sarah. (2013, March 31). A.D.H.D. seen in 11% of U.S. children as diagnoses rise. *New York Times.*

Schwarzwald, Heidi; Collins, Elizabeth Montgomery; Gillespie, Susan & Spinks-Franklin, Adiaha I. A. (2015). *International adoption and clinical practice.* New York, NY: Springer. doi: 10.1007/978-3-319-13491-8

Schweinhart, Lawrence J.; Montie, Jeanne; Xiang, Zongping; Barnett, W. Steven; Belfield, Clive R. & Nores, Milagros. (2005). *Lifetime effects: The High/Scope Perry Preschool Study through age 40.* Ypsilanti, MI: High/Scope Press.

Schweinhart, Lawrence J. & Weikart, David P. (1997). *Lasting differences: The High/Scope Preschool curriculum comparison study through age 23.* Ypsilanti, MI: High/Scope Educational Research Foundation.

Schwingel, Andiara; Linares, Deborah E.; Gálvez, Patricia; Adamson, Brynn; Aguayo, Liliana; Bobitt, Julie, . . . Marquez, David X. (2015). Developing a culturally sensitive lifestyle behavior change program for older Latinas. *Qualitative Health Research, 25*(12), 1733–1746. doi: 10.1177/1049732314568323

Schytt, Erica & Waldenström, Ulla. (2010). Epidural analgesia for labor pain: Whose choice? *Acta Obstetricia et Gynecologica Scandinavica, 89*(2), 238–242. doi: 10.3109/00016340903280974

Scott, Diane L.; Lee, Chang-Bae; Harrell, Susan W. & Smith-West, Mary B. (2013). Permanency for children in foster care: Issues and barriers for adoption. *Child & Youth Services, 34*(3), 290–307. doi: 10.1080/0145935X.2013.826045

Scott, Lisa S. & Monesson, Alexandra. (2010). Experience-dependent neural specialization during infancy. *Neuropsychologia, 48*(6), 1857–1861. doi: 10.1016/j.neuropsychologia.2010.02.008

Scott, Mindy E.; Schelar, Erin; Manlove, Jennifer & Cui, Carol. (2009). *Young adult attitudes about relationships and marriage: Times may have changed, but expectations remain high.* Washington, DC: Child Trends.

Sears, William & Sears, Martha. (2001). *The attachment parenting book: A commonsense guide to understanding and nurturing your baby.* Boston, MA: Little Brown.

Sedlak, Andrea J. & Ellis, Raquel T. (2014). Trends in child abuse reporting. In Jill E. Korbin & Richard D. Krugman (Eds.), *Handbook of child maltreatment* (pp. 3–26). New York, NY: Springer. doi: 10.1007/978-94-007-7208-3_1

Seedat, Soraya; Scott, Kate Margaret; Angermeyer, Matthias C.; Berglund, Patricia; Bromet, Evelyn J.; Brugha, Traolach S., . . . Kessler, Ronald C. (2009). Cross-national associations between gender and mental disorders in the world health organization world mental health surveys. *Archives of General Psychiatry, 66*(7), 785–795. doi: 10.1001/archgenpsychiatry.2009.36

Seelaar, Harro; Rohrer, Jonathan D.; Pijnenburg, Yolande A. L.; Fox, Nick C. & van Swieten, John C. (2011). Clinical, genetic and pathological heterogeneity of frontotemporal dementia: A review. *Journal of Neurology, Neurosurgery, & Psychiatry, 82*(5), 476–486. doi: 10.1136/jnnp.2010.212225

Séguin, Jean R. & Tremblay, Richard E. (2013). Aggression and antisocial behavior: A developmental perspective. In Philip D. Zelazo (Ed.), *The Oxford handbook of developmental psychology* (Vol. 2, pp. 507–526). New York, NY: Oxford University Press. doi: 10.1093/oxfordhb/9780199958474.013.0020

Seligman, Hilary K. & Schillinger, Dean. (2010). Hunger and socioeconomic disparities in chronic disease. *New England Journal of Medicine, 363*(1), 6–9. doi: 10.1056/NEJMp1000072

Şendil, Çağla Öneren & Erden, Feyza Tantekin. (2014). Peer preference: A way of evaluating social competence and behavioural well-being in early childhood. *Early Child Development and Care, 184*(2), 230–246. doi: 10.1080/03004430.2013.778254

Senior, Jennifer. (2014). *All joy and no fun: The paradox of modern parenthood.* New York, NY: Ecco.

Sepkowitz, Kent A. (2013). Energy drinks and caffeine-related adverse effects. *JAMA, 309*(3), 243–244. doi: 10.1001/jama.2012.173526

Seppa, Nathan. (2013a). Urban eyes: Too much time spent indoors may be behind a surge in near-sightedness. *Science News, 183*(3), 22–25. doi: 10.1002/scin.5591830323

Seppa, Nathan. (2013b). Home births more risky than hospital deliveries: Records suggest babies born at home are more prone to unresponsiveness after five minutes. *Science News, 184*(8), 14. doi: 10.1002/scin.5591840813

Servick, Kelly. (2015). Mind the phone. *Science, 350*(6266), 1306–1309. doi: 10.1126/science.350 .6266.1306

Settersten, Richard A. (2015). Relationships in time and the life course: The significance of linked lives. *Research in Human Development, 12*(3/4), 217–223. doi: 10.1080/15427609.2015.1071944

Severson, Kim & Blinder, Alan. (2014, January 7). Test scandal in Atlanta brings more guilty pleas. *New York Times,* p. A9.

Seyfarth, Robert M. & Cheney, Dorothy L. (2012). The evolutionary origins of friendship. *Annual Review of Psychology, 63,* 153–177. doi: 10.1146 /annurev-psych-120710-100337

Shah, Nirvi. (2011). Policy fight brews over discipline. *Education Week, 31*(7), 1, 12.

Shah, Prakesh; Balkhair, Taiba; Ohlsson, Arne; Beyene, Joseph; Scott, Fran & Frick, Corine. (2011). Intention to become pregnant and low birth weight and preterm birth: A systematic review. *Maternal and Child Health Journal, 15*(2), 205–216. doi: 10.1007/s10995-009-0546-2

Shai, Iris & Stampfer, Meir J. (2008). Weight-loss diets: Can you keep it off? *American Journal of Clinical Nutrition, 88*(5), 1185–1186.

Shanahan, Timothy & Lonigan, Christopher J. (2010). The National Early Literacy Panel: A summary of the process and the report. *Educational Researcher, 39*(4), 279–285. doi: 10.3102/0013189x10369172

Shattuck, Rachel M. & Kreider, Rose M. (2013). *Social and economic characteristics of currently unmarried women with a recent birth: 2011. American Community Survey Reports.* Washington, DC: U.S. Department of Commerce.

Sheeran, Paschal; Harris, Peter R. & Epton, Tracy. (2014). Does heightening risk appraisals change people's intentions and behavior? A meta-analysis of experimental studies. *Psychological Bulletin, 140*(2), 511–543. doi: 10.1037/a0033065

Shek, Daniel T. L. & Yu, Lu. (2016). Adolescent internet addiction in Hong Kong: Prevalence, change, and correlates. *Journal of Pediatric & Adolescent Gynecology, 29*(1 Suppl.), S22–S30. doi: 10.1016/j.jpag.2015.10.005

Shenzhen Daily. (2014, April 8). The pros and cons of SUSTC's development. *Shenzhen Daily.*

Sherin, Jonathan E. & Bartzokis, George. (2011). Human brain myelination trajectories across the life span: Implications for CNS function and dysfunction. In Edward J. Masoro & Steven N. Austad (Eds.), *Handbook of the biology of aging* (7th ed., pp. 333–346). San Diego, CA: Academic Press. doi: 10.1016/B978-0-12-378638-8.00015-4

Shi, Bing & Xie, Hongling. (2012). Popular and nonpopular subtypes of physically aggressive preadolescents: Continuity of aggression and peer mechanisms during the transition to middle school. *Merrill-Palmer Quarterly, 58*(4), 530–553. doi: 10.1353/mpq.2012.0025

Shi, Rushen. (2014). Functional morphemes and early language acquisition. *Child Development Perspectives, 8*(1), 6–11. doi: 10.1111/cdep.12052

Shirtcliff, Elizabeth A.; Dahl, Ronald E. & Pollak, Seth D. (2009). Pubertal development: Correspondence between hormonal and physical development. *Child Development, 80*(2), 327–337. doi: 10.1111/j.1467-8624.2009.01263.x

Shirtcliff, Elizabeth A.; Phan, Jenny M.; Lubach, Gabriele R.; Crispen, Heather R. & Coe, Christopher L. (2013). Stability of parental care across siblings from undisturbed and challenged pregnancies: Intrinsic maternal dispositions of female rhesus monkeys. *Developmental Psychology, 49*(11), 2005–2016. doi: 10.1037 /a0032050

Shoda, Tonya M.; McConnell, Allen R. & Rydell, Robert J. (2014). Having explicit-implicit evaluation discrepancies triggers race-based motivated reasoning. *Social Cognition, 32*(2), 190–202. doi: 10.1521/soco.2014.32.2.190

Shulman, Shmuel & Connolly, Jennifer. (2013). The challenge of romantic relationships in emerging adulthood: Reconceptualization of the field. *Emerging Adulthood, 1*(1), 27–39. doi: 10.1177/2167696812467330

Shutts, Kristin; Kinzler, Katherine D. & DeJesus, Jasmine M. (2013). Understanding infants' and children's social learning about foods: Previous research and new prospects. *Developmental Psychology, 49*(3), 419–425. doi: 10.1037/a0027551

Shwalb, David W.; Shwalb, Barbara J. & Lamb, Michael E. (Eds.). (2013). *Fathers in cultural context.* New York, NY: Psychology Press.

Siegal, Michael & Surian, Luca (Eds.). (2012). *Access to language and cognitive development.* New York, NY: Oxford University Press.

Siegler, Robert S. (2009). Improving the numerical understanding of children from low-income families. *Child Development Perspectives, 3*(2), 118–124. doi: 10.1111/j.1750-8606.2009.00090.x

Siegler, Robert S. (2016). Continuity and change in the field of cognitive development and in the perspectives of one cognitive developmentalist. *Child Development Perspectives, 10*(2), 128–133. doi: 10.1111/cdep.12173

Siegler, Robert S. & Chen, Zhe. (2008). Differentiation and integration: Guiding principles for analyzing cognitive change. *Developmental Science, 11*(4), 433–448. doi: 10.1111/j.1467-7687 .2008.00689.x

Siegler, Robert S. & Mu, Yan. (2008). Chinese children excel on novel mathematics problems even before elementary school. *Psychological Science, 19*(8), 759–763. doi: 10.1111/j.1467-9280.2008 .02153.x

Sierra, Felipe; Hadley, Evan; Suzman, Richard & Hodes, Richard. (2009). Prospects for life span extension. *Annual Review of Medicine, 60,* 457–469. doi: 10.1146/annurev. med.60.061607.220533

Sigurdson, J. F.; Wallander, J. & Sund, A. M. (2014). Is involvement in school bullying associated with general health and psychosocial adjustment outcomes in adulthood? *Child Abuse &*

Neglect, 38(10), 1607–1617. doi: 10.1016/j.chiabu .2014.06.001

Silberman, Steve. (2015). *Neurotribes: The legacy of autism and the future of neurodiversity.* New York, NY: Avery.

Silk, Jessica & Romero, Diana. (2014). The role of parents and families in teen pregnancy prevention: An analysis of programs and policies. *Journal of Family Issues, 35*(10), 1339–1362. doi: 10.1177/0192513X13481330

Sillars, Alan; Smith, Traci & Koerner, Ascan. (2010). Misattributions contributing to empathic (in)accuracy during parent-adolescent conflict discussions. *Journal of Social and Personal Relationships, 27*(6), 727–747. doi: 10.1177/0265407510373261

Silventoinen, Karri; Hammar, Niklas; Hedlund, Ebba; Koskenvuo, Markku; Ronnemaa, Tapani & Kaprio, Jaakko. (2008). Selective international migration by social position, health behaviour and personality. *European Journal of Public Health, 18*(2), 150–155. doi: 10.1093/eurpub/ckm052

Silverman, Arielle M. & Cohen, Geoffrey L. (2014). Stereotypes as stumbling-blocks: How coping with stereotype threat affects life outcomes for people with physical disabilities. *Personality and Social Psychology Bulletin, 40*(10), 1330–1340. doi: 10.1177/0146167214542800

Silverstein, Merril; Gans, Daphna; Lowenstein, Ariela; Giarrusso, Roseann & Bengtson, Vern L. (2010). Older parent–child relationships in six developed nations: Comparisons at the intersection of affection and conflict. *Journal of Marriage and Family, 72*(4), 1006–1021. doi: 10.1111/j.1741 -3737.2010.00745.x

Silvia, Paul J. & Sanders, Camilla E. (2010). Why are smart people curious? Fluid intelligence, openness to experience, and interest. *Learning and Individual Differences, 20*(3), 242–245. doi: 10.1016/j.lindif.2010.01.006

Simmons, Joseph P.; Nelson, Leif D. & Simonsohn, Uri. (2011). False-positive psychology: Undisclosed flexibility in data collection and analysis allows presenting anything as significant. *Psychological Science, 22*(11), 1359–1366. doi: 10.1177/0956797611417632

Simons, Ronald L.; Simons, Leslie Gordon; Lei, Man-Kit; Beach, Steven R. H.; Brody, Gene H.; Gibbons, Frederick X. & Philibert, Robert A. (2013). Genetic moderation of the impact of parenting on hostility toward romantic partners. *Journal of Marriage and Family, 75*(2), 325–341. doi: 10.1111/jomf.12010

Simons-Morton, Bruce; Haynie, Denise; Liu, Danping; Chaurasia, Ashok; Li, Kaigang & Hingson, Ralph. (2016). The effect of residence, school status, work status, and social influence on the prevalence of alcohol use among emerging adults. *Journal of Studies on Alcohol and Drugs, 77*(1), 121–132. doi: 10.15288/jsad.2016.77.121

Simpson, Jeffry A. & Kenrick, Douglas. (2013). *Evolutionary social psychology.* Hoboken, NJ: Taylor & Francis.

Simpson, Jeffry A. & Rholes, W. Steven (Eds.). (2015). *Attachment theory and research: New directions and emerging themes.* New York, NY: Guilford.

Sims, Margaret & Rofail, Maged. (2014). Grandparents with little or no contact with grandchildren-impact on grandparents. *Journal of Aging Science, 2*(1), 117–124. doi: 10.4172/2329-8847 .1000117

Sinardet, Dave & Mortelmans, Dimitri. (2009). The feminine side to Santa Claus. Women's work of kinship in contemporary gift-giving relations. *The Social Science Journal, 46*(1), 124–142. doi: 10.1016/j.soscij.2008.12.006

Sinclair, Samantha & Carlsson, Rickard. (2013). What will I be when I grow up? The impact of gender identity threat on adolescents' occupational preferences. *Journal of Adolescence, 36*(3), 465–474. doi: 10.1016/j.adolescence.2013.02.001

Singer, Irving. (2009). *The nature of love: Courtly and romantic* (Vol. 2). Cambridge, MA: MIT Press.

Singh, Amika; Uijtdewilligen, Léonie; Twisk, Jos W. R.; van Mechelen, Willem & Chinapaw, Mai J. M. (2012). Physical activity and performance at school: A systematic review of the literature including a methodological quality assessment. *Archives of Pediatrics & Adolescent Medicine, 166*(1), 49–55. doi: 10.1001/archpediatrics.2011.716

Singh, Leher. (2008). Influences of high and low variability on infant word recognition. *Cognition, 106*(2), 833–870. doi: 10.1016/j.cognition .2007.05.002

Singh, Tushar; Arrazola, René A.; Corey, Catherine G.; Husten, Corinne G.; Neff, Linda J.; Homa, David M. & King, Brian A. (2016, April 15). *Tobacco use among middle and high school students—United States, 2011–2015. Morbidity and Mortality Weekly Report 65*(14), 361–367. Atlanta, GA: Centers for Disease Control and Prevention.

Sinnott, Jan D. (2008). Cognitive and representational development in adults. In Kelly B. Cartwright (Ed.), *Literacy processes: Cognitive flexibility in learning and teaching* (pp. 42–68). New York, NY: Guilford.

Sinnott, Jan D. (2009). Cognitive development as the dance of adaptive transformation: Neo-Piagetian perspectives on adult cognitive development. In M. Cecil Smith & Nancy DeFrates-Densch (Eds.), *Handbook of research on adult learning and development* (pp. 103–134). New York, NY: Routledge.

Sinnott, Jan D. (2014). *Adult development: Cognitive aspects of thriving close relationships.* New York, NY: Oxford University Press.

Sisk, Cheryl L. (2016). Hormone-dependent adolescent organization of socio-sexual behaviors in mammals. *Current Opinion in Neurobiology, 38*, 63–68. doi: 10.1016/j.conb.2016.02.004

Sisson, Susan B.; Krampe, Megan; Anundson, Katherine & Castle, Sherri. (2016). Obesity prevention and obesogenic behavior interventions in child care: A systematic review. *Preventive Medicine, 87*, 57–69. doi: 10.1016 /j.ypmed.2016.02.016

Sjöström, Lars; Peltonen, Markku; Jacobson, Peter; Ahlin, Sofie; Andersson-Assarsson, Johanna; Anveden, Åsa, . . . Carlsson, Lena M. S. (2014). Association of bariatric surgery with long-term remission of type 2 diabetes and with microvascular and macrovascular complica-

tions. *JAMA, 311*(22), 2297–2304. doi: 10.1001 /jama.2014.5988

Skinner, B. F. (1953). *Science and human behavior.* New York, NY: Macmillan.

Skinner, B. F. (1957). *Verbal behavior.* New York, NY: Appleton-Century-Crofts.

Skinner, Ellen A. & Zimmer-Gembeck, Melanie J. (2010). Perceived control and the development of coping. In Susan Folkman (Ed.), *The Oxford handbook of stress, health, and coping* (pp. 35–61). New York, NY: Oxford University Press.

Skoog, Therése & Stattin, Håkan. (2014). Why and under what contextual conditions do early-maturing girls develop problem behaviors? *Child Development Perspectives, 8*(3), 158–162. doi: 10.1111/cdep.12076

Skorikov, Vladimir B. & Vondracek, Fred W. (2011). Occupational identity. In Seth J. Schwartz et al. (Eds.), *Handbook of identity theory and research* (pp. 693–714). New York, NY: Springer. doi: 10.1007/978-1-4419-7988-9_29

Slaughter, Anne-Marie. (2012). Why women still can't have it all. *The Atlantic, 310*(1), 84–102.

Slavich, George M. & Cole, Steven W. (2013). The emerging field of human social genomics. *Clinical Psychological Science, 1*(3), 331–348. doi: 10.1177/2167702613478594

Slining, Meghan; Adair, Linda S.; Goldman, Barbara D.; Borja, Judith B. & Bentley, Margaret. (2010). Infant overweight is associated with delayed motor development. *The Journal of Pediatrics, 157*(1), 20–25.e21. doi: 10.1016 /j.jpeds.2009.12.054

Sloan, John. (2011-2012). Medicating elders in the evidence-free zone. *Generations, 35*(4), 56–61.

Sloan, Ken. (2009). The role of personality in a manager's learning effectiveness. *European Journal of Social Sciences, 12*(1), 31–42.

Sloan, Mark. (2009). *Birth day: A pediatrician explores the science, the history, and the wonder of childbirth.* New York, NY: Ballantine Books.

Small, Meredith F. (1998). *Our babies, ourselves: How biology and culture shape the way we parent.* New York, NY: Anchor Books.

Smetana, Judith G.; Ahmad, Ikhlas & Wray-Lake, Laura. (2016). Beliefs about parental authority legitimacy among refugee youth in Jordan: Between- and within-person variations. *Developmental Psychology, 52*(3), 484–495. doi: 10.1037/dev0000084

Smith, Aaron & Anderson, Monica. (2016, February 29). *5 facts about online dating.* Washington, DC: Pew Research Center.

Smith, Aaron & Duggan, Maeve. (2013, October 21). *Online dating & relationships: Methods. Internet, Science & Tech.* Washington, DC: Pew Research Center.

Smith, Allison E. (2009). *Ageing in urban neighbourhoods: Place attachment and social exclusion.* Bristol, UK: Policy.

Smith, Christian & Snell, Patricia. (2009). *Souls in transition: The religious and spiritual lives of emerging adults.* New York, NY: Oxford University Press.

Smith, Caitlin J. & Ryckman, Kelli K. (2015). Epigenetic and developmental influences on the risk of obesity, diabetes, and metabolic syndrome. *Diabetes, Metabolic Syndrome and Obesity, 8*, 295–302. doi: 10.2147/DMSO.S61296

Smith, G. Rush; Williamson, Gail M.; Miller, L. Stephen & Schulz, Richard. (2011). Depression and quality of informal care: A longitudinal investigation of caregiving stressors. *Psychology and Aging, 26*(3), 584–591. doi: 10.1037/a0022263

Smith, Jacqueline; Boone, Anniglo; Gourdine, Ruby & Brown, Annie W. (2013). Fictions and facts about parents and parenting older first-time entrants to foster care. *Journal of Human Behavior in the Social Environment, 23*(2), 211–219. doi: 10.1080/10911359.2013.747400

Smith, Linda B. (2005). Cognition as a dynamic system: Principles from embodiment. *Developmental Review, 25*(3/4), 278–298. doi: 10.1016/j.dr.2005.11.001

Smith, Michelle I.; Yatsunenko, Tanya; Manary, Mark J.; Trehan, Indi; Mkakosya, Rajhab; Cheng, Jiye, . . . Gordon, Jeffrey I. (2013). Gut microbiomes of Malawian twin pairs discordant for kwashiorkor. *Science, 339*(6119), 548–554. doi: 10.1126/science.1229000

Smith, Peter K. (2010). *Children and play: Understanding children's worlds.* Malden, MA: Wiley-Blackwell.

Smith, Shaunna. (2015). Epic fails: Reconceptualizing failure as a catalyst for developing creative persistence within teaching and learning experiences. *Journal of Technology and Teacher Education, 23*(3), 329–355.

Smith, Shaunna & Henriksen, Danah. (2016). Fail again, fail better: Embracing failure as a paradigm for creative learning in the arts. *Art Education, 69*(2), 6–11.

Smithells, R. W.; Sheppard, S.; Schorah, C. J.; Seller, M. J.; Nevin, N. C.; Harris, R., . . . Fielding, D. W. (2011). Apparent prevention of neural tube defects by periconceptional vitamin supplementation. *International Journal of Epidemiology, 40*(5), 1146–1154. doi: 10.1093/ije/dyr143

Smolak, Linda & Levine, Michael P. (Eds.). (2015). *The Wiley handbook of eating disorders.* Malden, MA: John Wiley & Sons.

Snider, Terra Ziporyn. (2012). Later school start times are a public-health issue. *Education Week, 31*(31), 25, 27.

Snipes, Daniel J.; Green, Brooke A.; Javier, Sarah J.; Perrin, Paul B. & Benotsch, Eric G. (2014). The use of alcohol mixed with energy drinks and experiences of sexual victimization among male and female college students. *Addictive Behaviors, 39*(1), 259–264. doi: 10.1016/j.addbeh.2013.10.005

Snow, Catherine E.; Porche, Michelle V.; Tabors, Patton O. & Harris, Stephanie R. (2007). *Is literacy enough? Pathways to academic success for adolescents.* Baltimore, MD: Brookes Publishing Company.

Snow, J. B. (2015). *Narcissist and the Peter Pan syndrome: Emotionally unavailable and emotionally immature men.* Amazon Digital Services LLC: J.B. Snow Publishing.

Snyder, Thomas D. & Dillow, Sally A. (2013). *Digest of education statistics, 2012.* Washington, DC: National Center for Education Statistics, Institute of Education Sciences, U.S. Department of Education.

Snyder, Thomas D. & Dillow, Sally A. (2015, May). *Digest of education statistics 2013.* Washington, DC: National Center for Education Statistics, Institute of Education Sciences, U.S. Department of Education.

Soderstrom, Melanie; Ko, Eon-Suk & Nevzorova, Uliana. (2011). It's a question? Infants attend differently to yes/no questions and declaratives. *Infant Behavior and Development, 34*(1), 107–110. doi: 10.1016/j.infbeh.2010.10.003

Soley, Gaye & Hannon, Erin E. (2010). Infants prefer the musical meter of their own culture: A cross-cultural comparison. *Developmental Psychology, 46*(1), 286–292. doi: 10.1037/a0017555

Solheim, Elisabet; Wichstrøm, Lars; Belsky, Jay & Berg-Nielsen, Turid Suzanne. (2013). Do time in child care and peer group exposure predict poor socioemotional adjustment in Norway? *Child Development, 84*(5), 1701–1715. doi: 10.1111/cdev.12071

Solomon, Andrew. (2012). *Far from the tree: Parents, children and the search for identity.* New York, NY: Scribner.

Solomon, Alina; Sippola, Risto; Soininen, Hilkka; Wolozin, Benjamin; Tuomilehto, Jaakko; Laatikainen, Tiina & Kivipelto, Miia. (2010). Lipid-lowering treatment is related to decreased risk of dementia: A population-based study (FINRISK). *Neuro-Degenerative Diseases, 7*(1/3), 180–182. doi: 10.1159/000295659

Somerville, Leah H. (2013). The teenage brain: Sensitivity to social evaluation. *Current Directions in Psychological Science, 22*(2), 121–127. doi: 10.1177/0963721413476512

Soons, Judith P. M. & Kalmijn, Matthijs. (2009). Is marriage more than cohabitation? Well-being differences in 30 European countries. *Journal of Marriage and Family, 71*(5), 1141–1157. doi: 10.1111/j.1741-3737.2009.00660.x

Sophian, Catherine. (2013). Vicissitudes of children's mathematical knowledge: Implications of developmental research for early childhood mathematics education. *Early Education and Development, 24*(4), 436–442. doi: 10.1080/10409289.2013.773255

Søreide, Kjetil. (2012). The epidemiology of injury in bungee jumping, BASE jumping, and skydiving. *Epidemiology of Injury in Adventure and Extreme Sports, 58,* 112–129. doi: 10.1159/000338720

Sorkin, Dara H. & Rook, Karen S. (2006). Dealing with negative social exchanges in later life: Coping responses, goals, and effectiveness. *Psychology and Aging, 21*(4), 715–725. doi: 10.1037/0882-7974.21.4.715

Soska, Kasey C.; Adolph, Karen E. & Johnson, Scott P. (2010). Systems in development: Motor skill acquisition facilitates three-dimensional object completion. *Developmental Psychology, 46*(1), 129–138. doi: 10.1037/a0014618

Sotomayor, Sonia. (2014). *My beloved world.* New York, NY: Vintage Books.

Sousa, David A. (2014). *How the brain learns to read* (2nd ed.). Thousand Oaks, CA: SAGE.

Sowell, Elizabeth R.; Thompson, Paul M. & Toga, Arthur W. (2007). Mapping adolescent brain maturation using structural magnetic resonance imaging. In Daniel Romer & Elaine F. Walker (Eds.), *Adolescent psychopathology and the developing brain: Integrating brain and prevention science* (pp. 55–84). New York, NY: Oxford University Press.

Spape, Jessica; Timmers, Amanda D.; Yoon, Samuel; Ponseti, Jorge & Chivers, Meredith L. (2014). Gender-specific genital and subjective sexual arousal to prepotent sexual features in heterosexual women and men. *Biological Psychology, 102,* 1–9. doi: 10.1016/j.biopsycho.2014.07.008

Sparks, Sarah D. (2012). Form + function = Finnish schools. *Education Week, 31*(36), 9.

Spear, Linda. (2013). The teenage brain: Adolescents and alcohol. *Current Directions in Psychological Science, 22*(2), 152–157. doi: 10.1177/0963721412472192

Spearman, Charles E. (1927). *The abilities of man, their nature and measurement.* New York, NY: Macmillan.

Specht, Jule; Egloff, Boris & Schmukle, Stefan C. (2011). Stability and change of personality across the life course: The impact of age and major life events on mean-level and rank-order stability of the Big Five. *Journal of Personality and Social Psychology, 101*(4), 862–882. doi: 10.1037/a0024950

Spelke, Elizabeth S. (1993). Object perception. In Alvin I. Goldman (Ed.), *Readings in philosophy and cognitive science* (pp. 447–460). Cambridge, MA: MIT Press.

Spencer, Justine M. Y.; Sekuler, Allison B.; Bennett, Patrick J.; Giese, Martin A. & Pilz, Karin S. (2016). Effects of aging on identifying emotions conveyed by point-light walkers. *Psychology and Aging, 31*(1), 126–138. doi: 10.1037/a0040009

Spencer, Steven J.; Logel, Christine & Davies, Paul G. (2016). Stereotype threat. *Annual Review of Psychology, 67,* 415–437. doi: 10.1146/annurev-psych-073115-103235

Sperling, Gene B. & Winthrop, Rebecca. (2016). *What works in girls' education: Evidence for the world's best investment.* Washington, DC: Brookings Institution Press.

Sperry, Debbie M. & Widom, Cathy S. (2013). Child abuse and neglect, social support, and psychopathology in adulthood: A prospective investigation. *Child Abuse & Neglect, 37*(6), 415–425. doi: 10.1016/j.chiabu.2013.02.006

Spijker, Jeroen & MacInnes, John. (2013). Population ageing: The timebomb that isn't? *BMJ, 347,* f6598. doi: 10.1136/bmj.f6598

Spilt, Jantine L.; Vervoort, Eleonora; Koenen, Anne-Katrien; Bosmans, Guy & Verschueren, Karine. (2016). The socio-behavioral development of children with symptoms of attachment disorder: An observational study of teacher sensitivity in special education. *Research in Developmental Disabilities, 56,* 71–82. doi: 10.1016/j.ridd.2016.05.014

Sprangers, Suzan; Dijkstra, Katinka & Romijn-Luijten, Anna. (2015). Communication skills training in a nursing home: Effects of a brief intervention on residents and nursing aides. *Clinical Interventions in Aging, 10,* 311–319. doi: 10.2147/CIA.S73053

Sprietsma, Maresa. (2010). Effect of relative age in the first grade of primary school on long-term scholastic results: International comparative evidence using PISA 2003. *Education Economics, 18*(1), 1–32. doi: 10.1080/09645290802201961

Ssozi, John & Amlani, Shirin. (2015). The effectiveness of health expenditure on the proximate and ultimate goals of healthcare in sub-Saharan Africa. *World Development, 76,* 165–179. doi: 10.1016/j.worlddev.2015.07.010

Staff, Jeremy & Schulenberg, John. (2010). Millennials and the world of work: Experiences in paid work during adolescence. *Journal of Business and Psychology, 25*(2), 247–255. doi: 10.1007/s10869-010-9167-4

Standifer, Rhetta L.; Raes, Anneloes M. L.; Peus, Claudia; Passos, Ana Margarida; Santos, Catarina Marques & Weisweiler, Silke. (2015). Time in teams: cognitions, conflict and team satisfaction. *Journal of Managerial Psychology, 30*(6), 692–708. doi: 10.1108/JMP-09-2012-0278

Standing, E. M. (1998). *Maria Montessori: Her life and work.* New York, NY: Plume.

Staplin, Loren; Lococo, Kathy H.; Martell, Carol & Stutts, Jane. (2012). *Taxonomy of older driver behaviors and crash risk.* Washington, DC: Office of Behavioral Safety Research National Highway Traffic Safety Administration U.S. Department of Transportation.

Starr, Christine R. & Zurbriggen, Eileen L. (2016). Sandra Bem's gender schema theory after 34 years: A review of its reach and impact. *Sex Roles,* (In Press). doi: 10.1007/s11199-016-0591-4

Staudinger, Ursula M. & Glück, Judith. (2011). Psychological wisdom research: Commonalities and differences in a growing field. *Annual Review of Psychology, 62,* 215–241. doi: 10.1146/annurev.psych.121208.131659

Stavrova, Olga; Fetchenhauer, Detlef & Schlösser, Thomas. (2012). Cohabitation, gender, and happiness: A cross-cultural study in thirty countries. *Journal of Cross-Cultural Psychology, 43*(7), 1063–1081. doi: 10.1177/0022022111419030

Stawski, Robert S.; Almeida, David M.; Lachman, Margie E.; Tun, Patricia A. & Rosnick, Christopher B. (2010). Fluid cognitive ability is associated with greater exposure and smaller reactions to daily stressors. *Psychology and Aging, 25*(2), 330–342. doi: 10.1037/a0018246

Stawski, Robert S.; Sliwinski, Martin J. & Hofer, Scott M. (2013). Between-person and within-person associations among processing speed, attention switching, and working memory in younger and older adults.

Experimental Aging Research, 39(2), 194–214. doi: 10.1080/0361073X.2013.761556

Steel, Piers. (2011). *The procrastination equation: How to stop putting things off and start getting stuff done.* New York, NY: Harper.

Steel, Piers & Ferrari, Joseph. (2013). Sex, education and procrastination: An epidemiological study of procrastinators' characteristics from a global sample. *European Journal of Personality*, 27(1), 51–58. doi: 10.1002/per.1851

Steele, Claude M. (1997). A threat in the air: How stereotypes shape intellectual identity and performance. *American Psychologist*, 52(6), 613–629. doi: 10.1037//0003-066X.52.6.613

Steinberg, Laurence. (2004). Risk taking in adolescence: What changes, and why? *Annals of the New York Academy of Sciences*, 1021, 51–58. doi: 10.1196/annals.1308.005

Steinberg, Laurence. (2009). Should the science of adolescent brain development inform public policy? *American Psychologist*, 64(8), 739–750. doi: 10.1037/0003-066x.64.8.739

Steinberg, Laurence. (2014). *Age of opportunity: Lessons from the new science of adolescence.* Boston, MA: Houghton Mifflin Harcourt.

Steinberg, Laurence. (2015). The neural underpinnings of adolescent risk-taking: the roles of reward-seeking, impulse control, and peers. In Gabriele Oettingen & Peter M. Gollwitzer (Eds.), *Self-regulation in adolescence* (pp. 173–192). New York, NY: Cambridge University Press.

Steinberg, Laurence & Monahan, Kathryn C. (2011). Adolescents' exposure to sexy media does not hasten the initiation of sexual intercourse. *Developmental Psychology*, 47(2), 562–576. doi: 10.1037/a0020613

Stenseng, Frode; Belsky, Jay; Skalicka, Vera & Wichstrøm, Lars. (2015). Social exclusion predicts impaired self-regulation: A 2-year longitudinal panel study including the transition from preschool to school. *Journal of Personality*, 83(2), 212–220. doi: 10.1111/jopy.12096

Stenseng, Frode; Belsky, Jay; Skalicka, Vera & Wichstrøm, Lars. (2016). Peer rejection and Attention deficit hyperactivity disorder symptoms: Reciprocal relations through ages 4, 6, and 8. *Child Development*, 87(2), 365–373. doi: 10.1111/cdev.12471

Stephens, Rick & Richey, Mike. (2013). A business view on U.S. education. *Science*, 340(6130), 313–314. doi: 10.1126/science.1230728

Sterling, Kymberle L. & Mermelstein, Robin. (2011). Examining hookah smoking among a cohort of adolescent ever smokers. *Nicotine & Tobacco Research*, 13(12), 1202–1209. doi: 10.1093/ntr/ntr146

Sterling, Peter. (2012). Allostasis: A model of predictive regulation. *Physiology & Behavior*, 106(1), 5–15. doi: 10.1016/j.physbeh.2011.06.004

Stern, Gavin. (2015). For kids with special learning needs, roadblocks remain. *Science*, 349(6255), 1465–1466. doi: 10.1126/science.349.6255.1465

Stern, Mark; Clonan, Sheila; Jaffee, Laura & Lee, Anna. (2015). The normative limits of choice: Charter schools, disability studies, and questions of inclusion. *Educational Policy*, 29(3), 448–477. doi: 10.1177/0895904813510779

Stern, Peter. (2013). Connection, connection, connection.... *Science*, 342(6158), 577. doi: 10.1126/science.342.6158.577

Stern, Yaakov (Ed.). (2013). *Cognitive reserve: Theory and applications.* New York, NY: Psychology Press.

Sternberg, Robert J. (1988). Triangulating love. In Robert J. Sternberg & Michael L. Barnes (Eds.), *The psychology of love* (pp. 119–138). New Haven, CT: Yale University Press.

Sternberg, Robert J. (2003). *Wisdom, intelligence, and creativity synthesized.* New York, NY: Cambridge University Press.

Sternberg, Robert J. (2008). Schools should nurture wisdom. In Barbara Z. Presseisen (Ed.), *Teaching for intelligence* (2nd ed., pp. 61–88). Thousand Oaks, CA: Corwin Press.

Sternberg, Robert J. (2011). The theory of successful intelligence. In Robert J. Sternberg & Scott Barry Kaufman (Eds.), *The Cambridge handbook of intelligence* (pp. 504–526). New York, NY: Cambridge University Press.

Sternberg, Robert J. (2012). Why I became an administrator . . . and why you might become one too: Applying the science of psychology to the life of a university. *Observer*, 25(2), 21–22.

Sternberg, Robert J. (2015). Multiple intelligences in the new age of thinking. In Sam Goldstein et al. (Eds.), *Handbook of intelligence* (pp. 229–241). New York, NY: Springer. doi: 10.1007/978-1-4939-1562-0_16

Stevens, Gillian. (2015). Trajectories of English acquisition among foreign-born Spanish-language children in the United States. *International Migration Review*, 49(4), 981–1000. doi: 10.1111/imre.12119

Stevenson, Richard J.; Oaten, Megan J.; Case, Trevor I.; Repacholi, Betty M. & Wagland, Paul. (2010). Children's response to adult disgust elicitors: Development and acquisition. *Developmental Psychology*, 46(1), 165–177. doi: 10.1037/a0016692

Stewart, Destin N. & Szymanski, Dawn M. (2012). Young adult women's reports of their male romantic partner's pornography use as a correlate of their self-esteem, relationship quality, and sexual satisfaction. *Sex Roles*, 67(5), 257–271. doi: 10.1007/s11199-012-0164-0

Stieb, David M.; Chen, Li; Eshoul, Maysoon & Judek, Stan. (2012). Ambient air pollution, birth weight and preterm birth: A systematic review and meta-analysis. *Environmental Research*, 117, 100–111. doi: 10.1016/j.envres.2012.05.007

Stierand, Marc & Dörfler, Viktor. (2015). The role of intuition in the creative process of expert chefs. *The Journal of Creative Behavior*, (In Press). doi: 10.1002/jocb.100

Stigler, James W. & Hiebert, James. (2009). *The teaching gap: Best ideas from the world's teachers for improving education in the classroom.* New York, NY: Free Press.

Stiles, Joan & Jernigan, Terry. (2010). The basics of brain development. *Neuropsychology Review*, 20(4), 327–348. doi: 10.1007/s11065-010-9148-4

Stine, Gerald J. (2013). *AIDS update 2014* (23rd ed.). New York, NY: McGraw Hill.

Stine-Morrow, Elizabeth A. L. & Basak, Chandramallika. (2011). Cognitive interventions. In K. Warner Schaie & Sherry L. Willis (Eds.), *Handbook of the psychology of aging* (7th ed., pp. 153–171). San Diego, CA: Academic Press. doi: 10.1016/B978-0-12-380882-0.00010-3

Stine-Morrow, Elizabeth A. L.; Noh, Soo Rim & Shake, Matthew C. (2010). Age differences in the effects of conceptual integration training on resource allocation in sentence processing. *Quarterly Journal of Experimental Psychology*, 63(7), 1430–1455. doi: 10.1080/17470210903330983

Stipek, Deborah. (2013). Mathematics in early childhood education: Revolution or evolution? *Early Education & Development*, 24(4), 431–435. doi: 10.1080/10409289.2013.777285

Stolk, Lisette; Perry, John R. B.; Chasman, Daniel I.; He, Chunyan; Mangino, Massimo; Sulem, Patrick, . . . Lunetta, Kathryn L. (2012). Meta-analyses identify 13 loci associated with age at menopause and highlight DNA repair and immune pathways. *Nature Genetics*, 44, 260–268. doi: 10.1038/ng.1051

Stolt, Suvi; Matomäki, Jaakko; Lind, Annika; Lapinleimu, Helena; Haataja, Leena & Lehtonen, Liisa. (2014). The prevalence and predictive value of weak language skills in children with very low birth weight–A longitudinal study. *Acta Paediatrica*, 103(6), 651–658. doi: 10.1111/apa.12607

Stoltenborgh, Marije; van IJzendoorn, Marinus H.; Euser, Eveline M. & Bakermans-Kranenburg, Marian J. (2011). A global perspective on child sexual abuse: Meta-analysis of prevalence around the world. *Child Maltreatment*, 16(2), 79–101. doi: 10.1177/1077559511403920

Stone, Richard. (2011). Daring experiment in higher education opens its doors. *Science*, 332(6026), 161. doi: 10.1126/science.332.6026.161

Stonington, Scott D. (2012). On ethical locations: The good death in Thailand, where ethics sit in places. *Social Science & Medicine*, 75(5), 836–844. doi: 10.1016/j.socscimed.2012.03.045

Strait, Dana L.; Parbery-Clark, Alexandra; O'Connell, Samantha & Kraus, Nina. (2013). Biological impact of preschool music classes on processing speech in noise. *Developmental Cognitive Neuroscience*, 6, 51–60. doi: 10.1016/j.dcn.2013.06.003

Strasburger, Victor C.; Wilson, Barbara J. & Jordan, Amy B. (2009). *Children, adolescents, and the media* (2nd ed.). Los Angeles, CA: Sage.

Straus, Murray A. & Paschall, Mallie J. (2009). Corporal punishment by mothers and development of children's cognitive ability: A longitudinal study of two nationally representative age cohorts. *Journal of Aggression, Maltreatment & Trauma*, 18(5), 459–483. doi: 10.1080/10926770903035168

Stremmel, Andrew J. (2012). A situated framework: The Reggio experience. In Nancy File et al. (Eds.), *Curriculum in early childhood education: Re-examined, rediscovered, renewed* (pp. 133–145). New York, NY: Routledge.

Stroebe, Margaret S.; Schut, Henk & Boerner, Kathrin. (2010). Continuing bonds in adaptation to bereavement: Toward theoretical integration. *Clinical Psychology Review, 30*(2), 259–268. doi: 10.1016/j.cpr.2009.11.007

Stroebe, Wolfgang; Postmes, Tom & Spears, Russell. (2012). Scientific misconduct and the myth of self-correction in science. *Perspectives on Psychological Science, 7*(6), 670–688. doi: 10.1177/1745691612460687

Stroebe, Wolfgang & Strack, Fritz. (2014). The alleged crisis and the illusion of exact replication. *Perspectives on Psychological Science, 9*(1), 59–71. doi: 10.1177/1745691613514450

Stronegger, Willibald J.; Burkert, Nathalie T.; Grossschädl, Franziska & Freidl, Wolfgang. (2013). Factors associated with the rejection of active euthanasia: A survey among the general public in Austria. *BMC Medical Ethics, 14*, 26. doi: 10.1186/1472-6939-14-26

Stupica, Brandi; Sherman, Laura J. & Cassidy, Jude. (2011). Newborn irritability moderates the association between infant attachment security and toddler exploration and sociability. *Child Development, 82*(5), 1381–1389. doi: 10.1111/j.1467-8624.2011.01638.x

Su, Ya-Hui. (2011). The constitution of agency in developing lifelong learning ability: The 'being' mode. *Higher Education, 62*(4), 399–412. doi: 10.1007/s10734-010-9395-6

Suchy, Frederick J.; Brannon, Patsy M.; Carpenter, Thomas O.; Fernandez, Jose R.; Gilsanz, Vicente; Gould, Jeffrey B., . . . Wolf, Marshall A. (2010). National Institutes of Health Consensus Development Conference: Lactose intolerance and health. *Annals of Internal Medicine, 152*(12), 792–796. doi: 10.7326/0003-4819-152-12-201006150 -00248

Sue, Derald Wing (Ed.). (2010). *Microaggressions and marginality: Manifestation, dynamics, and impact.* Hoboken, NJ: Wiley.

Sugiura, Motoaki. (2016). Functional neuroimaging of normal aging: Declining brain, adapting brain. *Ageing Research Reviews, 30*, 61–72. doi: 10.1016/j.arr.2016.02.006

Suitor, J. Jill; Gilligan, Megan & Pillemer, Karl. (2015). Stability, change, and complexity in later-life families. In Linda K. George & Kenneth F. Ferraro (Eds.), *Handbook of aging and the social sciences* (8th ed., pp. 206–226). San Diego, CA: Academic Press.

Suleiman, Ahna B. & Brindis, Claire D. (2014). Adolescent school-based sex education: Using developmental neuroscience to guide new directions for policy and practice. *Sexuality Research and Social Policy, 11*(2), 137–152. doi: 10.1007 /s13178-014-0147-8

Sulek, Julia P. (2013, April 30). Audrie Pott suicide: Parents share grief, quest for justice in exclusive interview. *San Jose Mercury News.*

Sullivan, Jas M. & Ghara, Alexandra. (2015). Racial identity and intergroup attitudes: A multiracial youth analysis. *Social Science Quarterly, 96*(1), 261–272. doi: 10.1111/ssqu.12089

Sullivan, Sheila. (1999). *Falling in love: A history of torment and enchantment.* London, UK: Macmillan.

Sullivan, Shannon. (2014). *Good white people: The problem with middle-class white anti-racism.* Albany, NY: State University of New York Press.

Sun, L.; Guo, X.; J., Zhang; Liu, H.; S., Xu; Xu, Y. & Tao, F. (2016). Gender specific associations between early puberty and behavioral and emotional characteristics in children. *Zhonghua Liu Xing Bing Xue Za Zhi, 37*(1), 35–39. doi: 10.3760/cma .j.issn.0254-6450.2016.01.007

Sun, Min & Rugolotto, Simone. (2004). Assisted infant toilet training in a Western family setting. *Journal of Developmental & Behavioral Pediatrics, 25*(2), 99–101. doi: 10.1097/00004703-200404000 -00004

Sunita, T. H. & Desai, Rathnamala M. (2013). Knowledge, attitude and practice of contraception among women attending a tertiary care hospital in India. *International Journal of Reproduction, Contraception, Obstetrics and Gynecology, 2*(2), 172–176. doi: 10.5455/2320-1770.ijrcog20130612

Suomi, Steven J. (2002). Parents, peers, and the process of socialization in primates. In John G. Borkowski et al. (Eds.), *Parenting and the child's world: Influences on academic, intellectual, and social-emotional development* (pp. 265–279). Mahwah, NJ: Erlbaum.

Susman, Elizabeth J.; Houts, Renate M.; Steinberg, Laurence; Belsky, Jay; Cauffman, Elizabeth; DeHart, Ganie, . . . Halpern-Felsher, Bonnie L. (2010). Longitudinal development of secondary sexual characteristics in girls and boys between ages 9-1/2 and 15-1/2 years. *Archives of Pediatrics & Adolescent Medicine, 164*(2), 166–173. doi: 10.1001/archpediatrics.2009.261

Sutphin, George L. & Kaeberlein, Matt. (2011). Comparative genetics of aging. In Edward J. Masoro & Steven N. Austad (Eds.), *Handbook of the biology of aging* (7th ed., pp. 215–242). San Diego, CA: Academic Press. doi: 10.1016/B978-0 -12-378638-8.00010-5

Sutton-Smith, Brian. (2011). The antipathies of play. In Anthony D. Pellegrini (Ed.), *The Oxford handbook of the development of play* (pp. 110–115). New York, NY: Oxford University Press. doi: 10.1093/oxfordhb/9780195393002.013.0010

Suurland, Jill; van der Heijden, Kristiaan B.; Huijbregts, Stephan C. J.; Smaling, Hanneke J. A.; de Sonneville, Leo M. J.; Van Goozen, Stephanie H. M. & Swaab, Hanna. (2016). Parental perceptions of aggressive behavior in preschoolers: Inhibitory control moderates the association with negative emotionality. *Child Development, 87*(1), 256–269. doi: 10.1111 /cdev.12455

Swaab, D. F. & Hofman, M. A. (1984). Sexual differentiation of the human brain: A historical perspective. *Progress in Brain Research, 61*, 361–374.

Swan, Gary E. & Lessov-Schlaggar, Christina N. (2009). The effects of tobacco smoke on cognition and the brain. In Shari R. Waldstein & Merrill F. Elias (Eds.), *Neuropsychology of cardiovascular disease* (2nd ed.). New York, NY: Psychology Press.

Swan, Suzanne C.; Gambone, Laura J.; Caldwell, Jennifer E.; Sullivan, Tami P. & Snow, David L. (2008). A review of research on women's use of violence with male intimate partners. *Violence and Victims, 23*(3), 301–314. doi: 10.1891/0886 -6708.23.3.301

Swanson, Christopher B. (2014). Graduation rate breaks 80 percent. *Education Week, 33*(33, Suppl. 1), 24–26.

Swanson, H. Lee. (2013). Meta-analysis of research on children with learning disabilities. In H. Lee Swanson et al. (Eds.), *Handbook of learning disabilities* (2nd ed., pp. 627–642). New York, NY: Guilford Press.

Sweeney, Kathryn A. (2013). Race-conscious adoption choices, multiraciality and color-blind racial ideology. *Family Relations, 62*(1), 42–57. doi: 10.1111/j.1741-3729.2012.00757.x

Synovitz, Linda & Chopak-Foss, Joanne. (2013). Precocious puberty: Pathology, related risks, and support strategies. *Open Journal of Preventive Medicine, 3*(9), 504–509. doi: 10.4236 /ojpm.2013.39068

Szanton, Sarah L.; Wolff, Jennifer L.; Leff, Bruce; Roberts, Laken; Thorpe, Roland J.; Tanner, Elizabeth K., . . . Gitlin, Laura N. (2015). Preliminary data from Community Aging in Place, advancing better living for elders, a patient-directed, team-based intervention to improve physical function and decrease nursing home utilization: The first 100 individuals to complete a Centers for Medicare and Medicaid Services innovation project. *Journal of the American Geriatrics Society, 63*(2), 371–374. doi: 10.1111/jgs.13245

Szurhaj, William; Lamblin, Marie-Dominique; Kaminska, Anna & Sédiri, Haouaria. (2015). EEG guidelines in the diagnosis of brain death. *Clinical Neurophysiology, 45*(1), 97–104. doi: 10.1016 /j.neucli.2014.11.005

Taber, Daniel R.; Stevens, June; Evenson, Kelly R.; Ward, Dianne S.; Poole, Charles; Maciejewski, Matthew L., . . . Brownson, Ross C. (2011). State policies targeting junk food in schools: Racial/ethnic differences in the effect of policy change on soda consumption. *American Journal of Public Health, 101*(9), 1769–1775. doi: 10.2105 /ajph.2011.300221

Taber-Thomas, Bradley & Perez-Edgar, Koraly. (2015). Emerging adulthood brain development. In Jeffrey Jensen Arnett (Ed.), *The Oxford handbook of emerging adulthood* (pp. 126–141). New York, NY: Oxford University Press.

Tacken, Mart & van Lamoen, Ellemieke. (2005). Transport behaviour and realised journeys and trips. In Heidrun Mollenkopf et al. (Eds.), *Enhancing mobility in later life: Personal coping, environmental resources and technical support: The out-of-home mobility of older adults in urban and rural regions of five European countries* (pp. 105–139). Amsterdam, The Netherlands: IOS Press.

Tackett, Jennifer L.; Herzhoff, Kathrin; Harden, K. Paige; Page-Gould, Elizabeth & Josephs, Robert A. (2014). Personality × hormone interactions in adolescent externalizing psychopathology. *Personality Disorders: Theory, Research, and Treatment, 5*(3), 235–246. doi: 10.1037/per0000075

Taga, Keiko A.; Markey, Charlotte N. & Friedman, Howard S. (2006). A longitudinal investigation of associations between boys' pubertal timing and adult behavioral health and well-being. *Journal of Youth and Adolescence*, 35(3), 380–390. doi: 10.1007/s10964-006-9039-4

Taillieu, Tamara L.; Afifi, Tracie O.; Mota, Natalie; Keyes, Katherine M. & Sareen, Jitender. (2014). Age, sex, and racial differences in harsh physical punishment: Results from a nationally representative United States sample. *Child Abuse & Neglect*, 38(12), 1885–1894. doi: 10.1016/j.chiabu .2014.10.020

Tajalli, Hassan & Garba, Houmma A. (2014). Discipline or prejudice? Overrepresentation of minority students in disciplinary alternative education programs. *Urban Review*. doi: 10.1007/s11256 -014-0274-9

Talley, Ronda C. & Montgomery, Rhonda J. V. (2013). Caregiving: A developmental lifelong perspective. In Ronda C. Talley & Rhonda J. V. Montgomery (Eds.), *Caregiving across the lifespan: Research, practice, policy* (pp. 3–10). New York, NY: Springer.

Talwar, Victoria; Harris, Paul L. & Schleifer, Michael (Eds.). (2011). *Children's understanding of death: From biological to religious conceptions.* New York, NY: Cambridge University Press.

Tamis-LeMonda, Catherine S.; Bornstein, Marc H. & Baumwell, Lisa. (2001). Maternal responsiveness and children's achievement of language milestones. *Child Development*, 72(3), 748–767. doi: 10.1111/1467-8624.00313

Tamis-LeMonda, Catherine S.; Kuchirko, Yana & Song, Lulu. (2014). Why is infant language learning facilitated by parental responsiveness? *Current Directions in Psychological Science*, 23(2), 121–126. doi: 10.1177/0963721414522813

Tamm, Leanne; Epstein, Jeffery N.; Denton, Carolyn A.; Vaughn, Aaron J.; Peugh, James & Willcutt, Erik G. (2014). Reaction time variability associated with reading skills in poor readers with ADHD. *Journal of the International Neuropsychological Society*, 20(3), 292–301. doi: 10.1017/S1355617713001495

Tan, Cheryl H.; Denny, Clark H.; Cheal, Nancy E.; Sniezek, Joseph E. & Kanny, Dafna. (2015, September 25). *Alcohol use and binge drinking among women of childbearing age—United States, 2011–2013. Morbidity and Mortality Weekly Report* 64(37), 1042–1046. Atlanta, GA: Centers for Disease Control and Prevention.

Tan, Joseph S.; Hessel, Elenda T.; Loeb, Emily L.; Schad, Megan M.; Allen, Joseph P. & Chango, Joanna M. (2016). Long-term predictions from early adolescent attachment state of mind to romantic relationship behaviors. *Journal of Research on Adolescence*, (In Press). doi: 10.1111 /jora.12256

Tan, Patricia Z.; Armstrong, Laura M. & Cole, Pamela M. (2013). Relations between temperament and anger regulation over early childhood. *Social Development*, 22(4), 755–772. doi: 10.1111/j.1467 -9507.2012.00674.x

Taneri, Petek Eylul; Jong, Jessica C. Kiefte-de; Bramer, Wichor M.; Daan, Nadine M. P.; Franco, Oscar H. & Muka, Taulant. (2016). Association of alcohol consumption with the onset of natural menopause: a systematic review and meta-analysis. *Human Reproduction Update*, 22(4), 516–528. doi: 10.1093/humupd /dmw013

Tang, Jie; Yu, Yizhen; Du, Yukai; Ma, Ying; Zhang, Dongying & Wang, Jiaji. (2014). Prevalence of Internet addiction and its association with stressful life events and psychological symptoms among adolescent Internet users. *Addictive Behaviors*, 39(3), 744–747. doi: 10.1016/j.addbeh.2013.12.010

Tanner, Jennifer L. & Arnett, Jeffrey Jensen. (2011). Presenting emerging adulthood: What makes emerging adulthood developmentally distinctive. In Jeffrey Jensen Arnett et al. (Eds.), *Debating emerging adulthood: Stage or process?* (pp. 13–30). New York, NY: Oxford University Press. doi: 10.1093/acprof: oso/9780199757176.003.0002

Tanner, Jennifer L.; Arnett, Jeffrey J. & Leis, Julie A. (2009). Emerging adulthood: Learning and development during the first stage of adulthood. In M. Cecil Smith & Nancy DeFrates-Densch (Eds.), *Handbook of research on adult learning and development* (pp. 34–67). New York, NY: Routledge.

Tanumihardjo, Sherry A.; Gannon, Bryan & Kaliwile, Chisela. (2016). Controversy regarding widespread vitamin A fortification in Africa and Asia. *Advances in Nutrition*, 7, 5A.

Tarbetsky, Ana L.; Collie, Rebecca J. & Martin, Andrew J. (2016). The role of implicit theories of intelligence and ability in predicting achievement for Indigenous (Aboriginal) Australian students. *Contemporary Educational Psychology*, (In Press). doi: 10.1016/j.cedpsych.2016.01.002

Tarullo, Amanda R.; Garvin, Melissa C. & Gunnar, Megan R. (2011). Atypical EEG power correlates with indiscriminately friendly behavior in internationally adopted children. *Developmental Psychology*, 47(2), 417–431. doi: 10.1037 / a0021363

Tarun, Kumar; Kumar, Singh Sanjeet; Manish, Kumar; Sunita & Ashok, Sharan. (2016). Study on relationship between Anemia and academic performance of adolescent girls. *International Journal of Physiology*, 4(1), 81–86. doi: 10.5958/2320 -608X.2016.00017.2

Taveras, Elsie M.; Gillman, Matthew W.; Kleinman, Ken P.; Rich-Edwards, Janet W. & Rifas-Shiman, Sheryl L. (2013). Reducing racial/ethnic disparities in childhood obesity: The role of early life risk factors. *JAMA Pediatrics*, 167(8), 731–738. doi: 10.1001/jamapediatrics.2013.85

Tay, Marc Tze-Hsin; Au Eong, Kah Guan; Ng, C. Y. & Lim, M. K. (1992). Myopia and educational attainment in 421,116 young Singaporean males. *Annals Academy of Medicine Singapore*, 21(6), 785–791.

Taylor, John H. (Ed.). (2010). *Journey through the afterlife: Ancient Egyptian Book of the Dead.* Cambridge, MA: Harvard University Press.

Taylor, Joy L.; Kennedy, Quinn; Adamson, Maheen M.; Lazzeroni, Laura C.; Noda, Art; Murphy, Greer M. & Yesavage, Jerome A. (2011). Influences of APOE ε4 and expertise on performance of older pilots. *Psychology and Aging*, 26(2), 480–487. doi: 10.1037/a0021697

Taylor, Joy L.; Kennedy, Quinn; Noda, Art & Yesavage, Jerome A. (2007). Pilot age and expertise predict flight simulator performance: A 3-year longitudinal study. *Neurology*, 68(9), 648–654. doi: 10.1212/01.wnl.0000255943.10045.c0

Taylor, Kate. (2013, August 20). Man slaps two supporters at Quinn event. *New York Times*, p. A16.

Taylor, Marjorie; Shawber, Alison B. & Mannering, Anne M. (2009). Children's imaginary companions: What is it like to have an invisible friend? In Keith D. Markman et al. (Eds.), *Handbook of imagination and mental simulation* (pp. 211–224). New York, NY: Psychology Press.

Taylor, Paul. (2014). *The next America: Boomers, millennials, and the looming generational showdown.* New York, NY: PublicAffairs.

Taylor, Robert Joseph; Chatters, Linda M.; Woodward, Amanda Toler & Brown, Edna. (2013). Racial and ethnic differences in extended family, friendship, fictive kin, and congregational informal support networks. *Family Relations*, 62(4), 609–624. doi: 10.1111/fare.12030

Taylor, Rachael W.; Murdoch, Linda; Carter, Philippa; Gerrard, David F.; Williams, Sheila M. & Taylor, Barry J. (2009). Longitudinal study of physical activity and inactivity in preschoolers: The FLAME study. *Medicine & Science in Sports & Exercise*, 41(1), 96–102. doi: 10.1249 /MSS.0b013e3181849d81

Taylor, Shelley E. (2006). Tend and befriend: Biobehavioral bases of affiliation under stress. *Current Directions in Psychological Science*, 15(6), 273–277. doi: 10.1111/j.1467-8721.2006.00451.x

Taylor, Shelley E.; Klein, Laura Cousino; Lewis, Brian P.; Gruenewald, Tara L.; Gurung, Regan A. R. & Updegraff, John A. (2000). Biobehavioral responses to stress in females: Tend-and-befriend, not fight-or-flight. *Psychological Review*, 107(3), 411–429. doi: 10.1037//0033-295X.107.3.411

Taylor, Valerie J. & Walton, Gregory M. (2011). Stereotype threat undermines academic learning. *Personality and Social Psychology Bulletin*, 37(8), 1055–1067. doi: 10.1177/0146167211406506

Taylor, Zoe E.; Eisenberg, Nancy; Spinrad, Tracy L.; Eggum, Natalie D. & Sulik, Michael J. (2013). The relations of ego-resiliency and emotion socialization to the development of empathy and prosocial behavior across early childhood. *Emotion*, 13(5), 822–831. doi: 10.1037/a0032894

Te Morenga, Lisa; Mallard, Simonette & Mann, Jim. (2013). Dietary sugars and body weight: Systematic review and meta-analyses of randomised controlled trials and cohort studies. *BMJ*, 346, e7492. doi: 10.1136/bmj.e7492

Teachman, Jay. (2010). Work-related health limitations, education, and the risk of marital disruption. *Journal of Marriage and Family*, 72(4), 919–932. doi: 10.1111/j.1741-3737.2010.00739.x

Tefft, Brian C. (2012). *Motor vehicle crashes, injuries, and deaths in relation to driver age: United States, 1995—2010*. Washington, DC: AAA Foundation for Traffic Safety.

Telzer, Eva H.; Ichien, Nicholas T. & Qu, Yang. (2015). Mothers know best: Redirecting adolescent reward sensitivity toward safe behavior during risk taking. *Social Cognitive & Affective Neuroscience*, 10(10), 1383–1391. doi: 10.1093/scan/nsv026

Temple, Jeff R.; Le, Vi Donna; van den Berg, Patricia; Ling, Yan; Paul, Jonathan A. & Temple, Brian W. (2014). Brief report: Teen sexting and psychosocial health. *Journal of Adolescence*, 37(1), 33–36. doi: 10.1016/j.adolescence.2013.10.008

Teng, Zhaojun; Liu, Yanling & Guo, Cheng. (2015). A meta-analysis of the relationship between self-esteem and aggression among Chinese students. *Aggression and Violent Behavior*, 21(6), 45–54. doi: 10.1016/j.avb.2015.01.005

Teno, Joan M.; Plotzke, Michael; Gozalo, Pedro & Mor, Vincent. (2014). A national study of live discharges from hospice. *Journal of Palliative Medicine*, 17(10), 1121–1127. doi: 10.1089/jpm.2013.0595

Teo, Alan R. (2010). A new form of social withdrawal in Japan: A review of hikikomori. *International Journal of Social Psychiatry*, 56(2), 178–185. doi: 10.1177/0020764008100629

Teo, Alan R.; Fetters, Michael D.; Stufflebam, Kyle; Tateno, Masaru; Balhara, Yatan; Choi, Tae Young, . . . Kato, Takahiro A. (2015). Identification of the hikikomori syndrome of social withdrawal: Psychosocial features and treatment preferences in four countries. *International Journal of Social Psychiatry*, 61(1), 64–72. doi: 10.1177/0020764014535758

Teoh, Yee San & Lamb, Michael E. (2013). Interviewer demeanor in forensic interviews of children. *Psychology, Crime & Law*, 19(2), 145–159. doi: 10.1080/1068316X.2011.614610

Terry, Nicole Patton; Connor, Carol McDonald; Johnson, Lakeisha; Stuckey, Adrienne & Tani, Novell. (2016). Dialect variation, dialect-shifting, and reading comprehension in second grade. *Reading and Writing*, 29(2), 267–295. doi: 10.1007/s11145-015-9593-9

Terry-McElrath, Yvonne M.; Turner, Lindsey; Sandoval, Anna; Johnston, Lloyd D. & Chaloupka, Frank J. (2014). Commercialism in US elementary and secondary school nutrition environments: Trends from 2007 to 2012. *JAMA Pediatrics*, 168(3), 234–242. doi: 10.1001/jamapediatrics.2013.4521

Tessier, Karen. (2010). Effectiveness of hands-on education for correct child restraint use by parents. *Accident Analysis & Prevention*, 42(4), 1041–1047. doi: 10.1016/j.aap.2009.12.011

Tetzlaff, Anne & Hilbert, Anja. (2014). The role of the family in childhood and adolescent binge eating. A systematic review. *Appetite*, 76(1), 208. doi: 10.1016/j.appet.2014.01.050

Thaler, Richard H. (2015). *Misbehaving: The making of behavioral economics*. New York, NY: W. W. Norton & Co.

Thaler, Richard H. & Sunstein, Cass R. (2008). *Nudge: Improving decisions about health, wealth, and happiness*. New Haven, CT: Yale University Press.

The Associated Press. (2004). David Reimer, 38, subject of the John/Joan case. *New York Times*.

The College Board. (2012). *The College Board 2012 national survey of school counselors and administrators report on survey findings: Barriers and supports to school counselor success*. New York, NY: The College Board National Office for School Counselor Advocacy (NOSCA).

Thoma, Stephen J. & Dong, Yangxue. (2014). The Defining Issues Test of moral judgment development. *Behavioral Development Bulletin*, 19(3), 55–61. doi: 10.1037/h0100590

Thomaes, Sander; Reijntjes, Albert; Orobio de Castro, Bram; Bushman, Brad J.; Poorthuis, Astrid & Telch, Michael J. (2010). I like me if you like me: On the interpersonal modulation and regulation of preadolescents' state self-esteem. *Child Development*, 81(3), 811–825. doi: 10.1111/j.1467-8624.2010.01435.x

Thomas, Alexander & Chess, Stella. (1977). *Temperament and development*. New York, NY: Brunner/Mazel.

Thomas, Bianca Lee & Viljoen, Margaretha. (2016). EEG brain wave activity at rest and during evoked attention in children with Attention-deficit/hyperactivity disorder and effects of methylphenidate. *Neuropsychobiology*, 73(1), 16–22. doi: 10.1159/000441523

Thomas, Dylan. (2003). *The poems of Dylan Thomas* (Rev. ed.). New York, NY: New Directions.

Thomas, Michael S. C.; Van Duuren, Mike; Purser, Harry R. M.; Mareschal, Denis; Ansari, Daniel & Karmiloff-Smith, Annette. (2010). The development of metaphorical language comprehension in typical development and in Williams syndrome. *Journal of Experimental Child Psychology*, 106(2/3), 99–114. doi: 10.1016/j.jecp.2009.12.007

Thompson, Charis. (2014). Reproductions through technology. *Science*, 344(6182), 361–362. doi: 10.1126/science.1252641

Thompson, Clarissa A. & Siegler, Robert S. (2010). Linear numerical-magnitude representations aid children's memory for numbers. *Psychological Science*, 21(9), 1274–1281. doi: 10.1177/0956797610378309

Thompson, Ross A. & Raikes, H. Abigail. (2003). Toward the next quarter-century: Conceptual and methodological challenges for attachment theory. *Development and Psychopathology*, 15(3), 691–718. doi: 10.1017/S0954579403000348

Thompson, William W.; Zack, Matthew M.; Krahn, Gloria L.; Andresen, Elena M. & Barile, John P. (2012). Health related quality of life among older adults with and without functional limitations. *American Journal of Public Health*, 102(3), 496–502. doi: 10.2105/AJPH.2011.300500

Thomson, Keith Stewart. (2015). *Private doubt, public dilemma: Religion and science since Jefferson and Darwin*. New Haven, CT: Yale University Press.

Thomson, Samuel; Marriott, Michael; Telford, Katherine; Law, Hou; McLaughlin, Jo & Sayal, Kapil. (2014). Adolescents with a diagnosis of anorexia nervosa: Parents' experience of recognition and deciding to seek help. *Clinical Child Psychology Psychiatry*, 19(1), 43–57. doi: 10.1177/1359104512465741

Thornberg, Robert & Jungert, Tomas. (2013). Bystander behavior in bullying situations: Basic moral sensitivity, moral disengagement and defender self-efficacy. *Journal of Adolescence*, 36(3), 475–483. doi: 10.1016/j.adolescence.2013.02.003

Thornton, Arland; Axinn, William G. & Xie, Yu. (2007). *Marriage and cohabitation*. Chicago, IL: University of Chicago Press.

Thorson, James A. (1995). *Aging in a changing society*. Belmont, CA: Wadsworth.

Thuné-Boyle, Ingela C. V.; Stygall, Jan; Keshtgar, Mohammed R. S.; Davidson, Tim I. & Newman, Stanton P. (2013). Religious/spiritual coping resources and their relationship with adjustment in patients newly diagnosed with breast cancer in the UK. *Psycho-Oncology*, 22(3), 646–658. doi: 10.1002/pon.3048

Tighe, Lauren A.; Birditt, Kira S. & Antonucci, Toni C. (2016). Intergenerational ambivalence in adolescence and early adulthood: Implications for depressive symptoms over time. *Developmental Psychology*, 52(5), 824–834. doi: 10.1037/a0040146

Tishkoff, Sarah A.; Reed, Floyd A.; Friedlaender, Françoise R.; Ehret, Christopher; Ranciaro, Alessia; Froment, Alain, . . . Williams, Scott M. (2009). The genetic structure and history of Africans and African Americans. *Science*, 324(5930), 1035–1044. doi: 10.1126/science.1172257

Tobey, Emily A.; Thal, Donna; Niparko, John K.; Eisenberg, Laurie S.; Quittner, Alexandra L. & Wang, Nae-Yuh. (2013). Influence of implantation age on school-age language performance in pediatric cochlear implant users. *International Journal of Audiology*, 52(4), 219–229. doi: 10.3109/14992027.2012.759666

Tolman, Deborah L.; Davis, Brian R. & Bowman, Christin P. (2016). "That's just how it is": A gendered analysis of masculinity and femininity ideologies in adolescent girls' and boys' heterosexual relationships. *Journal of Adolescent Research*, 31(1), 3–31. doi: 10.1177/0743558415587325

Tolman, Deborah L. & McClelland, Sara I. (2011). Normative sexuality development in adolescence: A decade in review, 2000–2009. *Journal of Research on Adolescence*, 21(1), 242–255. doi: 10.1111/j.1532-7795.2010.00726.x

Tomalski, Przemyslaw & Johnson, Mark H. (2010). The effects of early adversity on the adult and developing brain. *Current Opinion in Psychiatry*, 23(3), 233–238. doi: 10.1097/YCO.0b013e3283387a8c

Tomasello, Michael. (2006). Acquiring linguistic constructions. In William Damon & Richard M. Lerner (Eds.), *Handbook of child psychology* (6th ed., Vol. 2, pp. 255–298). Hoboken, NJ: Wiley.

Tomasello, Michael. (2016). The ontogeny of cultural learning. *Current Opinion in Psychology*, 8, 1–4. doi: 10.1016/j.copsyc.2015.09.008

Tomasello, Michael & Herrmann, Esther. (2010). Ape and human cognition. *Current Directions in Psychological Science, 19*(1), 3–8. doi: 10.1177/0963721409359300

Tonn, Jessica L. (2006). Later high school start times a reaction to research. *Education Week, 25*(28), 5, 17.

Toossi, Mitra. (2002). *A century of change: The U.S. labor force, 1950–2050. Monthly Labor Review*, 15–28. Washington, DC: U.S. Bureau of Labor Statistics, United States Department of Labor.

Torbeyns, Joke; Schneider, Michael; Xin, Ziqiang & Siegler, Robert S. (2015). Bridging the gap: Fraction understanding is central to mathematics achievement in students from three different continents. *Learning and Instruction, 37*, 5–13. doi: 10.1016/j.learninstruc.2014.03.002

Tottenham, Nim. (2012). Human amygdala development in the absence of species-expected caregiving. *Developmental Psychobiology, 54*(6), 598–611. doi: 10.1002/dev.20531

Tough, Paul. (2012). *How children succeed: Grit, curiosity, and the hidden power of character*. Boston, MA: Houghton Mifflin Harcourt.

Travers, Brittany G.; Tromp, Do P. M.; Adluru, Nagesh; Lange, Nicholas; Destiche, Dan; Ennis, Chad, . . . Alexander, Andrew L. (2015). Atypical development of white matter microstructure of the corpus callosum in males with autism: A longitudinal investigation. *Molecular Autism, 6*. doi: 10.1186/s13229-015-0001-8

Trawick-Smith, Jeffrey. (2012). Teacher–child play interactions to achieve learning outcomes: Risks and opportunities. In Robert C. Pianta (Ed.), *Handbook of early childhood education* (pp. 259–277). New York, NY: Guilford Press.

Treas, Judith & Gubernskaya, Zoya. (2012). Farewell to moms? Maternal contact for seven countries in 1986 and 2001. *Journal of Marriage and Family, 74*(2), 297–311. doi: 10.1111/j.1741-3737 .2012.00956.x

Tremblay, Angelo & Chaput, Jean-Philippe. (2012). Obesity: The allostatic load of weight loss dieting. *Physiology & Behavior, 106*(1), 16–21. doi: 10.1016/j.physbeh.2011.05.020

Trenholm, Christopher; Devaney, Barbara; Fortson, Ken; Quay, Lisa; Wheeler, Justin & Clark, Melissa. (2007). *Impacts of four Title V, Section 510 abstinence education programs final report*. Washington, DC: U.S. Department of Health and Human Services, Mathematica Policy Research, Inc.

Trevino, Kelly M.; Zhang, Baohui; Shen, Megan J. & Prigerson, Holly G. (2016). Accuracy of advanced cancer patients' life expectancy estimates: The role of race and source of life expectancy information. *Cancer, 122*(12), 1905–1912. doi: 10.1002/cncr.30001

Trickett, Penelope K.; Noll, Jennie G. & Putnam, Frank W. (2011). The impact of sexual abuse on female development: Lessons from a multigenerational, longitudinal research study. *Development and Psychopathology, 23*(2), 453–476. doi: 10.1017/S0954579411000174

Troll, Lillian E. & Skaff, Marilyn McKean. (1997). Perceived continuity of self in very old age. *Psychology and Aging, 12*(1), 162–169. doi: 10.1037/0882-7974.12.1.162

Trompeter, Susan E.; Bettencourt, Ricki & Barrett-Connor, Elizabeth. (2012). Sexual activity and satisfaction in healthy community-dwelling older women. *The American Journal of Medicine, 125*(1), 37–43.e31. doi: 10.1016/j.amjmed.2011.07.036

Tronick, Edward. (1989). Emotions and emotional communication in infants. *American Psychologist, 44*(2), 112–119. doi: 10.1037//0003-066X .44.2.112

Tronick, Edward & Weinberg, M. Katherine. (1997). Depressed mothers and infants: Failure to form dyadic states of consciousness. In Lynne Murray & Peter J. Cooper (Eds.), *Postpartum depression and child development* (pp. 54–81). New York, NY: Guilford Press.

Truman, Jennifer L. & Langton, Lynn. (2015). *Criminal victimization, 2014*. Washington, DC: U.S. Department of Justice, Office of Justice Programs, Bureau of Justice Statistics.

Truog, Robert D. (2007). Brain death: Too flawed to endure, too ingrained to abandon. *The Journal of Law, Medicine & Ethics, 35*(2), 273–281. doi: 10.1111/j.1748-720X.2007.00136.x

Tsai, Kim M.; Telzer, Eva H. & Fuligni, Andrew J. (2013). Continuity and discontinuity in perceptions of family relationships from adolescence to young adulthood. *Child Development, 84*(2), 471–484. doi: 10.1111/j.1467-8624.2012.01858.x

Tsethlikai, Monica & Rogoff, Barbara. (2013). Involvement in traditional cultural practices and American Indian children's incidental recall of a folktale. *Developmental Psychology, 49*(3), 568–578. doi: 10.1037/a0031308

Ttofi, Maria M.; Bowes, Lucy; Farrington, David P. & Lösel, Friedrich. (2014). Protective factors interrupting the continuity from school bullying to later internalizing and externalizing problems: A systematic review of prospective longitudinal studies. *Journal of School Violence, 13*(1), 5–38. doi: 10.1080/15388220.2013.857345

Tudge, Jonathan R. H.; Doucet, Fabienne; Odero, Dolphine; Sperb, Tania M.; Piccinini, Cesar A. & Lopes, Rita S. (2006). A window into different cultural worlds: Young children's everyday activities in the United States, Brazil, and Kenya. *Child Development, 77*(5), 1446–1469. doi: 10.1111/j.1467-8624.2006.00947.x

Tugade, Michele M. (2010). Positive emotions, coping, and resilience. In Susan Folkman (Ed.), *The Oxford handbook of stress, health, and coping* (pp. 186–199). New York, NY: Oxford University Press.

Tummeltshammer, Kristen S.; Wu, Rachel; Sobel, David M. & Kirkham, Natasha Z. (2014). Infants track the reliability of potential informants. *Psychological Science, 25*(9), 1730–1738. doi: 10.1177/0956797614540178

Turner, Heather A.; Finkelhor, David; Ormrod, Richard; Hamby, Sherry; Leeb, Rebecca T.; Mercy, James A. & Holt, Melissa. (2012). Family context, victimization, and child trauma symptoms: Variations in safe, stable, and nurturing relationships during early and middle childhood. *American Journal of Orthopsychiatry, 82*(2), 209–219. doi: 10.1111/j.1939-0025.2012.01147.x

Tuttle, Robert & Garr, Michael. (2012). Shift work and work to family fit: Does schedule control matter? *Journal of Family and Economic Issues, 33*(3), 261–271. doi: 10.1007/s10834-012-9283-6

Twenge, Jean M.; Gentile, Brittany; DeWall, C. Nathan; Ma, Debbie; Lacefield, Katharine & Schurtz, David R. (2010). Birth cohort increases in psychopathology among young Americans, 1938–2007: A cross-temporal meta-analysis of the MMPI. *Clinical Psychology Review, 30*(2), 145–154. doi: 10.1016/j.cpr.2009.10.005

Twenge, Jean M.; Sherman, Ryne A. & Wells, Brooke E. (2015). Changes in American adults' sexual behavior and attitudes, 1972–2012. *Archives of Sexual Behavior, 44*(8), 2273–2285. doi: 10.1007/s10508-015-0540-2

Tye-Murray, Nancy; Spehar, Brent; Myerson, Joel; Sommers, Mitchell S. & Hale, Sandra. (2011). Cross-modal enhancement of speech detection in young and older adults: Does signal content matter? *Ear and Hearing, 32*(5), 650–655. doi: 10.1097/AUD.0b013e31821a4578

U.S. Bureau of Labor Statistics. (2012, June 22). *American time use survey–2011 Results*. Washington, DC: U.S. Department of Labor.

U.S. Bureau of Labor Statistics. (2013, April 30). *Employment characteristics of families, 2012. TED: The editor's desk*. Washington, DC: U.S. Department of Labor.

U.S. Bureau of Labor Statistics. (2014, February 25). *Volunteering in the United States—2013*. Washington, DC: U.S. Department of Labor.

U.S. Bureau of Labor Statistics. (2015). *The employment situation–July 2015*. Washington, DC: U.S. Department of Labor.

U.S. Bureau of Labor Statistics. (2015, November). *Labor force characteristics by race and ethnicity, 2014. BLS Reports*. Washington, DC: U.S. Department of Labor.

U.S. Bureau of Labor Statistics. (2016, February 25). *Volunteering in the United States—2015*. Washington, DC: U.S. Department of Labor.

U.S. Bureau of Labor Statistics. (2016a). *Local area unemployment statistics: Latest numbers, unemployment rates, seasonally adjusted*. Washington, DC: U.S. Department of Labor.

U.S. Bureau of Labor Statistics. (2016b). *Labor force statistics from the current population survey: Employed persons by detailed occupation, sex, race, and Hispanic or Latino ethnicity. Household data annual averages*. Washington, DC: U.S. Department of Labor.

U.S. Census Bureau. (1907). *Statistical Abstract of the United States 1906*. Washington, DC: U.S. Department of Commerce.

U.S. Census Bureau. (2008). *Statistical abstract of the United States: 2009*. Washington, DC: U.S. Department of Commerce.

U.S. Census Bureau. (2011). *America's families and living arrangements: 2011*. U.S. Department of Commerce, Economics and Statistics Administration, U.S. Census Bureau.

U.S. Census Bureau. (2012). *American community survey reports: The foreign-born population in the United States: 2010*.

U.S. Census Bureau. (2012). *Statistical abstract of the United States: 2012*. Washington, DC: U.S. Department of Commerce.

U.S. Census Bureau. (2012). *Table 1114. Licensed drivers and number in accidents by age: 2009. Statistical Abstract of the United States, 2012*. Washington, DC: U.S. Census Bureau.

U.S. Census Bureau. (2013a). *America's families and living arrangements: 2012*. Washington, DC: U.S. Department of Commerce, Economics and Statistics Administration, U.S. Census Bureau.

U.S. Census Bureau. (2013b). *2009–2013 American Community Survey 5-year estimates: Poverty. American FactFinder*. Washington, DC: U.S. Department of Commerce, United States Census Bureau.

U.S. Census Bureau. (2014). *America's families and living arrangements: 2014*. Washington, DC: U.S. Department of Commerce, Economics and Statistics Administration, U.S. Census Bureau.

U.S. Census Bureau. (2015). Mid-year population by five year age groups and sex–custom region–Japan. Retrieved, from U.S. Census Bureau, International Data Base.

U.S. Census Bureau. (2015). *America's families and living arrangements: 2015: Households (H table series). Table H3: Households by Race and Hispanic Origin of Household Reference Person and Detailed Type*. Washington, DC: U.S. Department of Commerce, Economics and Statistics Administration, U.S. Census Bureau.

U.S. Census Bureau. (2016a). *Selected population profile in the United States: 2014 American community survey 1-year estimates. American FactFinder*. Washington, DC: U.S. Department of Commerce.

U.S. Census Bureau. (2016b). *Selected population profile in the United States: 2009 American community survey 1-year estimates. American FactFinder*. Washington, DC: U.S. Department of Commerce.

U.S. Census Bureau, Population Division. (2010, June). *Monthly resident population estimates by age, sex, race and Hispanic origin for the United States: April 1, 2000 to July 1, 2009*. Washington, DC: U.S. Census Bureau.

U.S. Department of Agriculture. (2015, September 9). *Food insecurity rates were for Hispanics and non-Hispanic Blacks than for non-Hispanic Whites and other race/ethnic groups. Food Security in the United States*. Washington, DC: U.S. Department of Agriculture.

U.S. Department of Education. (2015, April). *A matter of equity: Preschool in America*. Washington, DC: U.S. Department of Education.

U.S. Department of Health and Human Services. (1999, December 31). *Child maltreatment 1999*. Washington, DC: Administration on Children, Youth and Families, Children's Bureau.

U.S. Department of Health and Human Services. (2000, December 31). *Child maltreatment 2000*. Washington, DC: Administration on Children, Youth and Families, Children's Bureau.

U.S. Department of Health and Human Services. (2003). *Child maltreatment 2001*. Washington, DC: Administration for Children and Families, Administration on Children Youth and Families, Children's Bureau.

U.S. Department of Health and Human Services. (2005, December 31). *Child maltreatment 2005*. Washington, DC: Administration on Children, Youth and Families, Children's Bureau.

U.S. Department of Health and Human Services. (2008). *Child maltreatment 2006*. Washington, DC: Administration for Children and Families, Administration on Children Youth and Families, Children's Bureau.

U.S. Department of Health and Human Services. (2008). *2008 Physical activity guidelines for Americans*. Washington, DC: U.S. Department of Health and Human Services. ODPHP No. U0036.

U.S. Department of Health and Human Services. (2010). *Head Start impact study: Final report*. Washington, DC: Administration for Children and Families.

U.S. Department of Health and Human Services. (2010, January). *Child maltreatment 2009*. Washington, DC: Administration for Children and Families, Administration on Children, Youth and Families, Children's Bureau.

U.S. Department of Health and Human Services. (2011). *The Surgeon General's call to action to support breastfeeding*. Washington, DC: U.S. Department of Health and Human Services, Office of the Surgeon General.

U.S. Department of Health and Human Services. (2011, December 31). *Child maltreatment 2010*. Washington, DC: Administration for Children and Families, Administration on Children Youth and Families, Children's Bureau.

U.S. Department of Health and Human Services. (2015, January 15). *Child maltreatment 2013*. Washington, DC: Administration for Children and Families, Administration on Children, Youth and Families, Children's Bureau.

U.S. Department of Health and Human Services. (2016). *Physical activity guidelines for Americans*. Washington, DC: U.S. Department of Health and Human Services.

U.S. Department of Health and Human Services. (2016, January 25). *Child maltreatment 2014*. Washington, DC: Administration for Children and Families, Administration on Children, Youth and Families, Children's Bureau.

U.S. Department of Transportation. (2013a). *Traffic safety facts, pedestrians: 2011 data*. Washington, DC: National Center for Statistics and Analysis.

U.S. Department of Transportation. (2013b). *Traffic safety facts, children: 2011 data*. Washington, DC: National Center for Statistics and Analysis.

U.S. Preventive Services Task Force. (2002). Postmenopausal hormone replacement therapy for primary prevention of chronic conditions: Recommendations and rationale. *Annals of Internal Medicine, 137*(10), 834–839. doi: 10.7326/0003-4819 -137-10-200211190-00013

Uchida, Yukiko & Norasakkunkit, Vinai. (2015). The NEET and Hikikomori spectrum: Assessing the risks and consequences of becoming culturally marginalized. *Frontiers in Psychology, 6*(1117). doi: 10.3389/fpsyg.2015.01117

Uddin, Monica; Koenen, Karestan C.; de los Santos, Regina; Bakshis, Erin; Aiello, Allison E. & Galea, Sandro. (2010). Gender differences in the genetic and environmental determinants of adolescent depression. *Depression and Anxiety, 27*(7), 658–666. doi: 10.1002/da.20692

Ueda, Tomomi; Suzukamo, Yoshimi; Sato, Mai & Izumi, Shin-Ichi. (2013). Effects of music therapy on behavioral and psychological symptoms of dementia: A systematic review and meta-analysis. *Ageing Research Reviews, 12*(2), 628–641. doi: 10.1016/j.arr.2013.02.003

Umana-Taylor, Adriana J. & Guimond, Amy B. (2010). A longitudinal examination of parenting behaviors and perceived discrimination predicting Latino adolescents' ethnic identity. *Developmental Psychology, 46*(3), 636–650. doi: 10.1037 /a0019376

Umberson, Debra; Pudrovska, Tetyana & Reczek, Corinne. (2010). Parenthood, childlessness, and well-being: A life course perspective. *Journal of Marriage and Family, 72*(3), 612–629. doi: 10.1111/j.1741-3737.2010.00721.x

Underwood, Emily. (2013). Why do so many neurons commit suicide during brain development? *Science, 340*(6137), 1157–1158. doi: 10.1126 /science.340.6137.1157

UNESCO. (2011). Institute for statistics database. Retrieved from: http://www.uis.unesco.org /Pages/default.aspx

UNESCO. (2012). *Global education digest, 2012: Opportunities lost: The impact of grade repetition and early school leaving*. Montreal, Canada: United Nations Educational, Scientific and Cultural Organization Institute for Statistics.

UNESCO. (2014). *Country profiles. UNESCO Institute for Statistics Data Centre*. Montreal, Canada: UNESCO, Université de Montréal at the Montreal's École des hautes études.

UNICEF. (2012). *The state of the world's children 2012: Children in an urban world*. New York, NY: United Nations.

UNICEF. (2014, July). *Education: Secondary net attendance ration–Percentage*. UNICEF Global Databases. Retrieved from: http://data.unicef.org

UNICEF. (2014a, October). *Low birthweight: Percentage of infants weighing less than 2,500 grams at birth*. UNICEF global databases, based on DHS, MICS, other national household surveys, data from routine reporting systems, UNICEF and WHO. Retrieved from: http://data.unicef.org /nutrition/low-birthweight.html

UNICEF. (2014b, October). *Infant and young child feeding*. UNICEF Global Databases. Retrieved from: http://www.unicef.org/nutrition /index_breastfeeding.html

United Nations. (2012). *World population prospects: The 2010 revision*. New York, NY: Population Division of the United Nations Department of Economic and Social Affairs of the United Nations Secretariat, Department of Economic and Social Affairs.

United Nations. (2013). *World population prospects: The 2012 revision, Volume 1: Comprehensive tables*. New York, NY: Department of Economic and Social Affairs, Population Division.

United Nations. (2015, July). *Probabilistic population projections based on the World Population Prospects: The 2015 Revision.* New York: Population Division, DESA.

United Nations. (2016a). *Life expectancy at birth, females.* United Nations Statistics Division.

United Nations. (2016b). *Life expectancy at birth, males.* United Nations Statistics Division.

United Nations, Department of Economic and Social Affairs, Population Division. (2015). *World population prospects: The 2015 revision.* New York, NY.

United Nations Office on Drugs and Crime. (2009, February). *Global report on trafficking in persons. United Nations Global Initiative to Fight Human Trafficking.* New York, NY: United Nations.

Ursache, Alexandra; Blair, Clancy; Stifter, Cynthia & Voegtline, Kristin. (2013). Emotional reactivity and regulation in infancy interact to predict executive functioning in early childhood. *Developmental Psychology, 49*(1), 127–137. doi: 10.1037 /a0027728

Vaala, Sarah E.; Linebarger, Deborah L.; Fenstermacher, Susan K.; Tedone, Ashley; Brey, Elizabeth; Barr, Rachel, . . . Calvert, Sandra L. (2010). Content analysis of language-promoting teaching strategies used in infant-directed media. *Infant and Child Development, 19*(6), 628–648. doi: 10.1002/icd.715

Vadillo, Miguel A.; Kostopoulou, Olga & Shanks, David R. (2015). A critical review and meta-analysis of the unconscious thought effect in medical decision making. *Frontiers in Psychology, 6*(636). doi: 10.3389/fpsyg.2015.00636

Vaillant, George E. (2002). *Aging well: Surprising guideposts to a happier life from the landmark Harvard Study of Adult Development.* Boston, MA: Little Brown.

Vaillant, George E. (2008). *Spiritual evolution: A scientific defense of faith.* New York, NY: Broadway Books.

Valdez, Carmen R.; Chavez, Tom & Woulfe, Julie. (2013). Emerging adults' lived experience of formative family stress: The family's lasting influence. *Qualitative Health Research, 23*(8), 1089–1102. doi: 10.1177/1049732313494271

Valeri, Beatriz O.; Holsti, Liisa & Linhares, Maria B. M. (2015). Neonatal pain and developmental outcomes in children born preterm: A systematic review. *Clinical Journal of Pain, 31*(4), 355–362. doi: 10.1097/AJP.0000000000000114

Vallor, Shannon. (2012). Flourishing on Facebook: Virtue friendship & new social media. *Ethics and Information Technology, 14*(3), 185–199. doi: 10.1007/s10676-010-9262-2

Valsiner, Jaan. (2006). Developmental epistemology and implications for methodology. In Richard M. Lerner & William Damon (Eds.), *Handbook of child psychology* (6th ed., Vol. 1, pp. 166–209). Hoboken, NJ: Wiley.

Van Agt, H. M. E.; de Ridder-Sluiter, J. G.; Van den Brink, G. A.; de Koning, H. J. & Reep van den Bergh, C. (2015). The predictive value of early childhood factors for language outcome in pre-school children. *Journal of Child and Adolescent Behaviour, 3*(6). doi: 10.4172/2375-4494.1000266

van Batenburg-Eddes, Tamara; Butte, Dick & van de Looij-Jansen, Petra. (2012). Measuring juvenile delinquency: How do self-reports compare with official police statistics? *European Journal of Criminology, 9*(1), 23–37. doi: 10.1177/1477370811421644

van de Bongardt, Daphne; Reitz, Ellen; Sandfort, Theo & Deković, Maja. (2015). A meta-analysis of the relations between three types of peer norms and adolescent sexual behavior. *Personality and Social Psychology Review, 19*(3), 203–234. doi: 10.1177/1088868314544223

van den Akker, Alithe; Deković, Maja; Prinzie, Peter & Asscher, Jessica. (2010). Toddlers' temperament profiles: Stability and relations to negative and positive parenting. *Journal of Abnormal Child Psychology, 38*(4), 485–495. doi: 10.1007 /s10802-009-9379-0

van den Ban, Els; Souverein, Patrick; Swaab, Hanna; van Engeland, Herman; Heerdink, Rob & Egberts, Toine. (2010). Trends in incidence and characteristics of children, adolescents, and adults initiating immediate- or extended-release methylphenidate or atomoxetine in the Netherlands during 2001-2006. *Journal of Child and Adolescent Psychopharmacology, 20*(1), 55–61. doi: 10.1089 /cap.2008.0153

van Goozen, Stephanie H. M. (2015). The role of early emotion impairments in the development of persistent antisocial behavior. *Child Development Perspectives, 9*(4), 206–210. doi: 10.1111 /cdep.12134

Van Hecke, Wim; Emsell, Louise & Sunaert, Stefan (Eds.). (2016). *Diffusion tensor imaging: A practical handbook.* New York, NY: Springer. doi: 10.1007/978-1-4939-3118-7

Van Horn, Linda V.; Bausermann, Robert; Affenito, Sandra; Thompson, Douglas; Striegel-Moore, Ruth; Franko, Debra & Albertson, Ann. (2011). Ethnic differences in food sources of vitamin D in adolescent American girls: The National Heart, Lung, and Blood Institute Growth and Health Study. *Nutrition Research, 31*(8), 579–585. doi: 10.1016 /j.nutres.2011.07.003

Van Houtte, Mieke. (2015). Lower-track students' sense of academic futility: Selection or effect? *Journal of Sociology,* (In Press). doi: 10.1177/1440783315600802

van IJzendoorn, Marinus H.; Bakermans-Kranenburg, Marian J.; Pannebakker, Fieke & Out, Dorothée. (2010). In defence of situational morality: Genetic, dispositional and situational determinants of children's donating to charity. *Journal of Moral Education, 39*(1), 1–20. doi: 10.1080/03057240903528535

van IJzendoorn, Marinus H.; Palacios, Jesús; Sonuga-Barke, Edmund J. S.; Gunnar, Megan R.; Vorria, Panayiota; McCall, Robert B., . . . Juffer, Femmie. (2011). Children in institutional care: Delayed development and resilience. *Monographs of the Society for Research in Child Development, 76*(4), 8–30. doi: 10.1111/j.1540-5834.2011.00626.x

van Nunen, Karolien; Kaerts, Nore; Wyndaele, Jean-Jacques; Vermandel, Alexandra & Van Hal, Guido. (2015). Parents' views on toilet training (TT): A quantitative study to identify the beliefs and attitudes of parents concerning TT. *Journal of Child Health Care, 19*(2), 265–274. doi: 10.1177/1367493513508232

Van Puyvelde, Martine; Vanfleteren, Pol; Loots, Gerrit; Deschuyffeleer, Sara; Vinck, Bart; Jacquet, Wolfgang & Verhelst, Werner. (2010). Tonal synchrony in mother-infant interaction based on harmonic and pentatonic series. *Infant Behavior and Development, 33*(4), 387–400. doi: 10.1016 /j.infbeh.2010.04.003

van Tilburg, Theo G.; Aartsen, Marja J. & van der Pas, Suzan. (2015). Loneliness after divorce: A cohort comparison among Dutch young-old adults. *European Sociological Review, 31*(3), 243–252. doi: 10.1093/esr/jcu086

Vandenbosch, Laura & Eggermont, Steven. (2015). The role of mass media in adolescents' sexual behaviors: Exploring the explanatory value of the three-step self-objectification process. *Archives of Sexual Behavior, 44*(3), 729–742. doi: 10.1007 /s10508-014-0292-4

Vandermassen, Griet. (2005). *Who's afraid of Charles Darwin? Debating feminism and evolutionary theory.* Lanham, MD: Rowman & Littlefield.

Vandewater, Elizabeth A.; Park, Seoung Eun; Hébert, Emily T. & Cummings, Hope M. (2015). Time with friends and physical activity as mechanisms linking obesity and television viewing among youth. *International Journal of Behavioral Nutrition and Physical Activity, 12*(Suppl. 1), S6. doi: 10.1186/1479-5868-12-S1-S6

Vanhalst, Janne; Luyckx, Koen; Scholte, Ron H. J.; Engels, Rutger C. M. E. & Goossens, Luc. (2013). Low self-esteem as a risk factor for loneliness in adolescence: Perceived–but not actual–social acceptance as an underlying mechanism. *Journal of Abnormal Child Psychology, 41*(7), 1067–1081. doi: 10.1007/s10802-013-9751-y

Vardaki, Sophia; Dickerson, Anne E.; Beratis, Ion; Yannis, George & Papageorgiou, Sokratis G. (2016). Simulator measures and identification of older drivers with mild cognitive impairment. *American Journal of Occupational Therapy, 70*(2). doi: 10.5014/ajot.2016.017673

Varga, Colleen M.; Gee, Christina B. & Munro, Geoffrey. (2011). The effects of sample characteristics and experience with infidelity on romantic jealous. *Sex Roles, 65*(11/12), 854–866. doi: 10.1007/s11199-011-0048-8

Varga, Mary Alice & Paletti, Robin. (2013). Life span issues and dying. In David K. Meagher & David E. Balk (Eds.), *Handbook of thanatology: The essential body of knowledge for the study of death, dying, and bereavement* (2nd ed., pp. 25–31). New York, NY: Routledge.

Varian, Frances & Cartwright, Lara. (2013). *The situational judgement test at a glance.* Hoboken, NJ: Wiley-Blackwell.

Varner, Fatima & Mandara, Jelani. (2014). Differential parenting of African American adolescents as an explanation for gender disparities in achievement. *Journal of Research on Adolescence, 24*(4), 667–680. doi: 10.1111/jora.12063

Vedantam, Shankar. (2011, December 5). *What's behind a temper tantrum? Scientists deconstruct the screams. Hidden Brain.* Washington DC: NPR.

Veenstra, René; Lindenberg, Siegwart; Munniksma, Anke & Dijkstra, Jan Kornelis. (2010). The complex relation between bullying, victimization, acceptance, and rejection: Giving special attention to status, affection, and sex differences. *Child Development*, 81(2), 480–486. doi: 10.1111/j.1467-8624.2009.01411.x

Vélez, Clorinda E.; Wolchik, Sharlene A.; Tein, Jenn-Yun & Sandler, Irwin. (2011). Protecting children from the consequences of divorce: A longitudinal study of the effects of parenting on children's coping processes. *Child Development*, 82(1), 244–257. doi: 10.1111/j.1467-8624.2010.01553.x

Vennemann, Mechtild M.; Hense, Hans-Werner; Bajanowski, Thomas; Blair, Peter S.; Complojer, Christina; Moon, Rachel Y. & Kiechl-Kohlendorfer, Ursula. (2012). Bed sharing and the risk of sudden infant death syndrome: Can we resolve the debate? *The Journal of Pediatrics*, 160(1), 44–48. doi: 10.1016/j.jpeds.2011.06.052

Verbakel, Ellen & Jaspers, Eva. (2010). A comparative study on permissiveness toward euthanasia: Religiosity, slippery slope, autonomy, and death with dignity. *Public Opinion Quarterly*, 74(1), 109–139. doi: 10.1093/poq/nfp074

Verdery, Ashton M. (2015). Links between demographic and kinship transitions. *Population and Development Review*, 41(3), 465–484. doi: 10.1111/j.1728-4457.2015.00068.x

Verona, Sergiu. (2003). Romanian policy regarding adoptions. In Victor Littel (Ed.), *Adoption update* (pp. 5–10). New York, NY: Nova Science.

Verweij, Karin J. H.; Creemers, Hanneke E.; Korhonen, Tellervo; Latvala, Antti; Dick, Danielle M.; Rose, Richard J., . . . Kaprio, Jaakko. (2016). Role of overlapping genetic and environmental factors in the relationship between early adolescent conduct problems and substance use in young adulthood. *Addiction*, 111(6), 1036–1045. doi: 10.1111/add.13303

Vianna, Eduardo & Stetsenko, Anna. (2006). Embracing history through transforming it: Contrasting Piagetian versus Vygotskian (activity) theories of learning and development to expand constructivism within a dialectical view of history. *Theory & Psychology*, 16, 81–108. doi: 10.1177/0959354306060108

Vikan, Arne; Camino, Cleonice & Biaggio, Angela. (2005). Note on a cross-cultural test of Gilligan's ethic of care. *Journal of Moral Education*, 34(1), 107–111. doi: 10.1080/03057240500051105

Viljaranta, Jaana; Aunola, Kaisa; Mullola, Sari; Virkkala, Johanna; Hirvonen, Riikka; Pakarinen, Eija & Nurmi, Jari-Erik. (2015). Children's temperament and academic skill development during first grade: Teachers' interaction styles as mediators. *Child Development*, 86(4), 1191–1209. doi: 10.1111/cdev.12379

Villar, Feliciano & Celdrán, Montserrat. (2012). Generativity in older age: A challenge for Universities of the Third Age (U3A). *Educational Gerontology*, 38(10), 666–677. doi: 10.1080/03601277.2011.595347

Vilppu, Henna; Mikkilä-Erdmann, Mirjamaija; Södervik, Ilona & Österholm-Matikainen, Erika. (2016). Exploring eye movements of experienced and novice readers of medical texts concerning the cardiovascular system in making a diagnosis. *Anatomical Sciences Education*, (In Press). doi: 10.1002/ase.1621

Vitale, Susan; Sperduto, Robert D. & Ferris, Frederick L. (2009). Increased prevalence of myopia in the United States between 1971–1972 and 1999–2004. *Archives of Ophthalmology*, 127(12), 1632–1639. doi: 10.1001/archophthalmol.2009.303

Vladeck, Fredda & Altman, Anita. (2015). The future of the NORC-supportive service program model. *Public Policy Aging Report*, 25(1), 20–22. doi: 10.1093/ppar/pru050

Vogel, Ineke; Verschuure, Hans; van der Ploeg, Catharina P. B.; Brug, Johannes & Raat, Hein. (2010). Estimating adolescent risk for hearing loss based on data from a large school-based survey. *American Journal of Public Health*, 100(6), 1095–1100. doi: 10.2105/ajph.2009.168690

Vogel, Lauren. (2011). Dying a "good death". *Canadian Medical Association Journal*, 183(18), 2089–2090. doi: 10.1503/cmaj.109-4059

Volkovich, Ella; Ben-Zion, Hamutal; Karny, Daphna; Meiri, Gal & Tikotzky, Liat. (2015). Sleep patterns of co-sleeping and solitary sleeping infants and mothers: A longitudinal study. *Sleep Medicine*, 16(11), 1305–1312. doi: 10.1016/j.sleep.2015.08.016

Volkwein-Caplan, Karin A. E. & McConatha, Jasmin Tamahseb. (2012). *The social geography of healthy aging*. Maidenhead, U.K.: Meyer et Meyer Sport (UK) Ltd.

Volz-Sidiropoulou, Eftychia & Gauggel, Siegfried. (2012). Do subjective measures of attention and memory predict actual performance? Metacognition in older couples. *Psychology and Aging*, 27(2), 440–450. doi: 10.1037/a0025384

Voosen, Paul. (2013, July 15). A brain gone bad: Researchers clear the fog of chronic head trauma. *The Chronicle Review*, B6–B10.

Vranić, Andrea; Španić, Ana Marija; Carretti, Barbara & Borella, Erika. (2013). The efficacy of a multifactorial memory training in older adults living in residential care settings. *International Psychogeriatrics*, 25(11), 1885–1897. doi: 10.1017/S1041610213001154

Vygotsky, Lev S. (1980). *Mind in society: The development of higher psychological processes*. Cambridge, MA: Harvard University Press.

Vygotsky, Lev S. (1987). Thinking and speech. In Robert W. Rieber & Aaron S. Carton (Eds.), *The collected works of L. S. Vygotsky* (Vol. 1, pp. 39–285). New York, NY: Springer.

Vygotsky, Lev S. (1994a). The development of academic concepts in school aged children. In René van der Veer & Jaan Valsiner (Eds.), *The Vygotsky reader* (pp. 355–370). Cambridge, MA: Blackwell.

Vygotsky, Lev S. (1994b). Principles of social education for deaf and dumb children in Russia. In Rene van der Veer & Jaan Valsiner (Eds.), *The Vygotsky reader* (pp. 19–26). Cambridge, MA: Blackwell.

Vygotsky, Lev S. (2012). *Thought and language*. Cambridge, MA: MIT Press.

Wade, Tracey D.; O'Shea, Anne & Shafran, Roz. (2016). Perfectionism and eating disorders. In Fuschia M. Sirois & Danielle S. Molnar (Eds.), *Perfectionism, health, and well-being* (pp. 205–222). New York, NY: Springer. doi: 10.1007/978-3-319-18582-8_9

Wadsworth, Martha E. & Markman, Howard J. (2012). Where's the action? Understanding what works and why in relationship education. *Behavior Therapy*, 43(1), 99–112. doi: 10.1016/j.beth.2011.01.006

Wagenaar, Karin; van Weissenbruch, Mirjam M.; van Leeuwen, Flora E.; Cohen-Kettenis, Peggy T.; Delemarre-van de Waal, Henriette A.; Schats, Roel & Huisman, Jaap. (2011). Self-reported behavioral and socioemotional functioning of 11- to 18-year-old adolescents conceived by in vitro fertilization. *Fertility and Sterility*, 95(2), 611–616. doi: 10.1016/j.fertnstert.2010.04.076

Wagmiller, Robert L. (2015). The temporal dynamics of childhood economic deprivation and children's achievement. *Child Development Perspectives*, 9(3), 158–163. doi: 10.1111/cdep.12125

Wagner, Jenny; Hoppmann, Christiane; Ram, Nilam & Gerstorf, Denis. (2015). Self-esteem is relatively stable late in life: The role of resources in the health, self-regulation, and social domains. *Developmental Psychology*, 51(1), 136–149. doi: 10.1037/a0038338

Wagner, Katie; Dobkins, Karen & Barner, David. (2013). Slow mapping: Color word learning as a gradual inductive process. *Cognition*, 127(3), 307–317. doi: 10.1016/j.cognition.2013.01.010

Wagner, Paul A. (2011). Socio-sexual education: A practical study in formal thinking and teachable moments. *Sex Education: Sexuality, Society and Learning*, 11(2), 193–211. doi: 10.1080/14681811.2011.558427

Wahlster, Sarah; Wijdicks, Eelco F. M.; Patel, Pratik V.; Greer, David M.; Hemphill, J. Claude; Carone, Marco & Mateen, Farrah J. (2015). Brain death declaration: Practices and perceptions worldwide. *Neurology*, 84(18), 1870–1879. doi: 10.1212/WNL.0000000000001540

Wahrendorf, Morten; Blane, David; Bartley, Mel; Dragano, Nico & Siegrist, Johannes. (2013). Working conditions in mid-life and mental health in older ages. *Advances in Life Course Research*, 18(1), 16–25. doi: 10.1016/j.alcr.2012.10.004

Wainer, Allison L.; Hepburn, Susan & Griffith, Elizabeth McMahon. (2016). Remembering parents in parent-mediated early intervention: An approach to examining impact on parents and families. *Autism*, (In Press). doi: 10.1177/1362361315622411

Waldinger, Robert J. & Schulz, Marc S. (2010). What's love got to do with it? Social functioning, perceived health, and daily happiness in married octogenarians. *Psychology and Aging*, 25(2), 422–431. doi: 10.1037/a0019087

Walker, Alan. (2012). The new ageism. *The Political Quarterly, 83*(4), 812–819. doi: 10.1111/j.1467 -923X.2012.02360.x

Walker, Christa L. Fischer; Rudan, Igor; Liu, Li; Nair, Harish; Theodoratou, Evropi; Bhutta, Zulfiqar A., . . . Black, Robert E. (2013). Global burden of childhood pneumonia and diarrhoea. *The Lancet, 381*(9875), 1405–1416. doi: 10.1016 /S0140-6736(13)60222-6

Walker, Lawrence J. (1984). Sex differences in the development of moral reasoning: A critical review. *Child Development, 55*(3), 677–691. doi: 10.2307/1130121

Wallis, Claudia. (2014). Gut reactions: Intestinal bacteria may help determine whether we are lean or obese. *Scientific American, 310*(6), 30–33. doi: 10.1038/scientificamerican0614-30

Wallis, Christopher J. D.; Lo, Kirk; Lee, Yuna; Krakowsky, Yonah; Garbens, Alaina; Satkunasivam, Raj, . . . Nam, Robert K. (2016). Survival and cardiovascular events in men treated with testosterone replacement therapy: an intention-to-treat observational cohort study. *The Lancet Diabetes & Endocrinology, 4*(6), 498–506. doi: 10.1016 / S2213-8587(16)00112-1

Walter, Tony. (2016). The dead who become angels: Bereavement and vernacular religion. *Omega: Journal of Death & Dying, 73*(1), 3–28. doi: 10.1177/0030222815575697

Wambach, Karen & Riordan, Jan. (2014). *Breastfeeding and human lactation* (5th ed.). Burlington, MA: Jones & Bartlett Publishers.

Wanberg, Connie R. (2012). The individual experience of unemployment. *Annual Review of Psychology, 63*, 369–396. doi: 10.1146/annurev -psych-120710-100500

Wang, Chao; Xue, Haifeng; Wang, Qianqian; Hao, Yongchen; Li, Dianjiang; Gu, Dongfeng & Huang, Jianfeng. (2014). Effect of drinking on all-cause mortality in women compared with men: A meta-analysis. *Journal of Women's Health, 23*(5), 373–381. doi: 10.1089/jwh.2013.4414

Wang, Hua & Wellman, Barry. (2010). Social connectivity in America: Changes in adult friendship network size from 2002 to 2007. *American Behavioral Scientist, 53*(8), 1148–1169. doi: 10.1177/0002764209356247

Wang, Jingyun & Candy, T. Rowan. (2010). The sensitivity of the 2- to 4-month-old human infant accommodation system. *Investigative Ophthalmology and Visual Science, 51*(6), 3309–3317. doi: 10.1167/iovs.09-4667

Wang, Wendy. (2012). *The rise of intermarriage: Rates, characteristics vary by race and gender.* Washington, DC: Pew Research Center, Pew Research on Social and Demographic Trends.

Wang, Wendy & Taylor, Paul. (2011). *For millennials, parenthood trumps marriage.* Washington, DC: Pew Social & Demographic Trends.

Ward, Brian W.; Clarke, Tainya C.; Freeman, Gulnur & Schiller, Jeannine S. (2015, June). *Early release of selected estimates based on data from the 2014 National Health Interview Survey. National Health Interview Survey Early Release Program.* Washington, DC: U.S. Department of Health and Human Services, Centers for Disease Control and Prevention, National Center for Health Statistics.

Warneken, Felix. (2015). Precocious prosociality: Why do young children help? *Child Development Perspectives, 9*(1), 1–6. doi: 10.1111 /cdep.12101

Warner, Lisa M.; Wolff, Julia K.; Ziegelmann, Jochen P. & Wurm, Susanne. (2014). A randomized controlled trial to promote volunteering in older adults. *Psychology and Aging, 29*(4), 757–763. doi: 10.1037/a0036486

Wastesson, Jonas W.; Parker, Marti G.; Fastbom, Johan; Thorslund, Mats & Johnell, Kristina. (2012). Drug use in centenarians compared with nonagenarians and octogenarians in Sweden: A nationwide register-based study. *Age and Ageing, 41*(2), 218–224. doi: 10.1093/ageing /afr144

Watson, John B. (1924). *Behaviorism.* New York, NY: The People's Institute Pub. Co.

Watson, John B. (1928). *Psychological care of infant and child.* New York, NY: Norton.

Watson, John B. (1972). *Psychological care of infant and child.* New York, NY: Arno Press.

Watson, John B. (1998). *Behaviorism.* New Brunswick, NJ: Transaction.

Webb, Alexandra R.; Heller, Howard T.; Benson, Carol B. & Lahav, Amir. (2015). Mother's voice and heartbeat sounds elicit auditory plasticity in the human brain before full gestation. *Proceedings of the National Academy of Sciences, 112*(10), 3152–3157. doi: 10.1073/pnas.1414924112

Webber, Douglas A. (2015). *Are college costs worth it?: How individual ability, major choice, and debt affect optimal schooling decisions.* Bonn, Germany: Institute for the Study of Labor.

Wei, Si. (2013). A multitude of people singing together. *International Journal of Community Music, 6*(2), 183–188. doi: 10.1386/ijcm.6.2.183_1

Weinstein, Netta & DeHaan, Cody. (2014). On the mutuality of human motivation and relationships. In Netta Weinstein (Ed.), *Human motivation and interpersonal relationships: Theory, research, and applications* (pp. 3–25). New York, NY: Springer. doi: 10.1007/978-94-017-8542-6_1

Weiss, David & Lang, Frieder R. (2012). "They" are old but "I" feel younger: Age-group dissociation as a self-protective strategy in old age. *Psychology and Aging, 27*(1), 153–163. doi: 10.1037/a0024887

Weiss, Nicole H.; Tull, Matthew T.; Lavender, Jason & Gratz, Kim L. (2013). Role of emotion dysregulation in the relationship between childhood abuse and probable PTSD in a sample of substance abusers. *Child Abuse & Neglect, 37*(11), 944–954. doi: 10.1016/j.chiabu.2013.03.014

Weiss, Noel S. & Koepsell, Thomas D. (2014). *Epidemiologic methods: Studying the occurrence of illness* (2nd ed.). New York, NY: Oxford University Press.

Wellman, Henry M.; Fang, Fuxi & Peterson, Candida C. (2011). Sequential progressions in a theory-of-mind scale: Longitudinal perspectives. *Child Development, 82*(3), 780–792. doi: 10.1111/j.1467-8624.2011.01583.x

Wendelken, Carter; Baym, Carol L.; Gazzaley, Adam & Bunge, Silvia A. (2011). Neural indices of improved attentional modulation over middle childhood. *Developmental Cognitive Neuroscience, 1*(2), 175–186. doi: 10.1016 /j.dcn.2010.11.001

Wenner, Melinda. (2009). The serious need for play. *Scientific American Mind, 20*(1), 22–29. doi: 10.1038/scientificamericanmind0209-22

Werner, Nicole E. & Hill, Laura G. (2010). Individual and peer group normative beliefs about relational aggression. *Child Development, 81*(3), 826–836. doi: 10.1111/j.1467-8624.2010.01436.x

Westphal, Sarah Katharina; Poortman, Anne-Rigt & Van der Lippe, Tanja. (2015). What about the grandparents? Children's postdivorce residence arrangements and contact with grandparents. *Journal of Marriage and Family, 77*(2), 424–440. doi: 10.1111/jomf.12173

Weymouth, Bridget B.; Buehler, Cheryl; Zhou, Nan & Henson, Robert A. (2016). A meta-analysis of parent–adolescent conflict: Disagreement, hostility, and youth maladjustment. *Journal of Family Theory & Review, 8*(1), 95–112. doi: 10.1111 /jftr.12126

Whalley, Lawrence J.; Duthie, Susan J.; Collins, Andrew R.; Starr, John M.; Deary, Ian J.; Lemmon, Helen, . . . Staff, Roger T. (2014). Homocysteine, antioxidant micronutrients and late onset dementia. *European Journal of Nutrition, 53*(1), 277–285. doi: 10.1007/s00394-013-0526-6

Whalley, Lawrence J.; Staff, Roger T.; Fox, Helen C. & Murray, Alison D. (2016). Cerebral correlates of cognitive reserve. *Psychiatry Research Neuroimaging, 247*, 65–70. doi: 10.1016 /j.pscychresns.2015 .10.012

Whitbourne, Susan K.; Sneed, Joel R. & Sayer, Aline. (2009). Psychosocial development from college through midlife: A 34-year sequential study. *Developmental Psychology, 45*(5), 1328–1340. doi: 10.1037/a0016550

Whitbourne, Susan K. & Whitbourne, Stacey B. (2014). *Adult development and aging: Biopsychosocial perspectives* (5th ed.). Hoboken, NJ: Wiley.

White, Douglas B.; Ernecoff, Natalie; Buddadhumaruk, Praewpannarai; Hong, Seoyeon; Weissfeld, Lisa; Curtis, Randall, . . . Lo, Bernard. (2016). Prevalence of and factors related to discordance about prognosis between physicians and surrogate decision makers of critically ill patients. *JAMA, 315*(19), 2086–2094. doi: 10.1001 /jama.2016.5351

White, Rebecca M. B.; Deardorff, Julianna; Liu, Yu & Gonzales, Nancy A. (2013). Contextual amplification or attenuation of the impact of pubertal timing on Mexican-origin boys' mental health symptoms. *Journal of Adolescent Health, 53*(6), 692–698. doi: 10.1016/j.jadohealth.2013.07.007

Whiteside-Mansell, Leanne; Bradley, Robert H.; Casey, Patrick H.; Fussell, Jill J. & Conners-Burrow, Nicola A. (2009). Triple risk: Do difficult temperament and family conflict increase the likelihood of behavioral maladjustment in children born low birth weight and preterm? *Journal of Pediatric Psychology, 34*(4), 396–405. doi: 10.1093/jpepsy/jsn089

Whitfield, Keith E. & McClearn, Gerald. (2005). Genes, environment, and race: Quantitative genetic approaches. *American Psychologist, 60*(1), 104–114. doi: 10.1037/0003-066X.60.1.104

Whitton, Sarah W. & Kuryluk, Amanda D. (2013). Intrapersonal moderators of the association between relationship satisfaction and depressive symptoms: Findings from emerging adult. *Journal of Social and Personal Relationships, 30*(6), 750–770. doi: 10.1177/0265407512467749

Wicher, Camille P. & Meeker, Mary Ann. (2012). What influences African American end-of-life preferences? *Journal of Health Care for the Poor and Underserved, 23*(1), 28–58. doi: 10.1353/hpu .2012.0027

Wickrama, Kandauda; Mancini, Jay A.; Kwag, Kyunghwa & Kwon, Josephine. (2013a). Heterogeneity in multidimensional health trajectories of late old years and socioeconomic stratification: A latent trajectory class analysis. *Journal of Gerontology Series B, 68*(2), 290–297. doi: 10.1093/geronb/gbs111

Wickrama, Kandauda; O'Neal, Catherine Walker & Lorenz, Fred O. (2013b). Marital functioning from middle to later years: A life course–stress process framework. *Journal of Family Theory & Review, 5*(1), 15–34. doi: 10.1111/jftr.12000

Widman, Laura; Choukas-Bradley, Sophia; Helms, Sarah W.; Golin, Carol E. & Prinstein, Mitchell J. (2014). Sexual communication between early adolescents and their dating partners, parents, and best friends. *The Journal of Sex Research, 51*(7), 731–741. doi: 10.1080/00224499.2013.843148

Widom, Cathy Spatz; Czaja, Sally J. & DuMont, Kimberly A. (2015a). Intergenerational transmission of child abuse and neglect: Real or detection bias? *Science, 347*(6229), 1480–1485. doi: 10.1126/science.1259917

Widom, Cathy Spatz; Horan, Jacqueline & Brzustowicz, Linda. (2015b). Childhood maltreatment predicts allostatic load in adulthood. *Child Abuse & Neglect, 47*, 59–69. doi: 10.1016/j.chiabu.2015.01.016

Wiik, Kenneth Aarskaug; Keizer, Renske & Lappegård, Trude. (2012). Relationship quality in marital and cohabiting unions across Europe. *Journal of Marriage and Family, 74*(3), 389–398. doi: 10.1111/j.1741-3737.2012.00967.x

Wijdicks, Eelco F. M.; Varelas, Panayiotis N.; Gronseth, Gary S. & Greer, David M. (2010). Evidence-based guideline update: Determining brain death in adults; Report of the quality standards subcommittee of the American Academy of Neurology. *Neurology, 74*(23), 1911–1918. doi: 10.1212/WNL.0b013e3181e242a8

Wilcox, W. Bradford (Ed.). (2011). *The sustainable demographic dividend: What do marriage and fertility have to do with the economy?* New York, NY: Social Trends Institute.

Wilcox, William B. & Kline, Kathleen K. (2013). *Gender and parenthood: Biological and social scientific perspectives.* New York: NY: Columbia University Press.

Wiley, Andrea S. (2011). Milk intake and total dairy consumption: Associations with early menarche in NHANES 1999-2004. *PLoS ONE, 6*(2), e14685. doi: 10.1371/journal.pone.0014685

Wilhelm, William Joseph & Gunawong, Panom. (2016). Cultural dimensions and moral reasoning: A comparative study. *International Journal of Sociology and Social Policy, 36*(5/6), 335–357. doi: 10.1108/IJSSP-05-2015-0047

Wilkinson, Stephen. (2015). Prenatal screening, reproductive choice, and public health. *Bioethics, 29*(1), 26–35. doi: 10.1111/bioe.12121

Williams, Anne M.; Chantry, Caroline; Geubbels, Eveline L.; Ramaiya, Astha K.; Shemdoe, Aloisia I.; Tancredi, Daniel J. & Young, Sera L. (2016). Breastfeeding and complementary feeding practices among HIV-exposed infants in coastal Tanzania. *Journal of Human Lactation, 32*(1), 112–122. doi: 10.1177/0890334415618412

Williams, Bronwen & Green, Rebecca. (2016). Experiences of bereavement following the death of animals. *Mental Health Practice, 19*(9), 29–33. doi: 10.7748/mhp.19.9.29.s21

Williams, Joshua L.; Corbetta, Daniela & Guan, Yu. (2015). Learning to reach with "sticky" or "non-sticky" mittens: A tale of developmental trajectories. *Infant Behavior and Development, 38*, 82–96. doi: 10.1016/j.infbeh.2015.01.001

Williams, Kristine N.; Herman, Ruth; Gajewski, Byron & Wilson, Kristel. (2009). Elderspeak communication: Impact on dementia care. *American Journal of Alzheimer's Disease and Other Dementias, 24*(1), 11–20. doi: 10.1177/1533317508318472

Williams, Lela Rankin; Fox, Nathan A.; Lejuez, C. W.; Reynolds, Elizabeth K.; Henderson, Heather A.; Perez-Edgar, Koraly E., . . . Pine, Daniel S. (2010). Early temperament, propensity for risk-taking and adolescent substance-related problems: A prospective multimethod investigation. *Addictive Behaviors, 35*(2), 1148–1151. doi: 10.1016/j.addbeh.2010.07.005

Williams, Preston. (2009, March 5). Teens might need to sleep more, but schools have to work efficiently. *Washington Post*, p. LZ10.

Williams, Shirlan A. (2005). Jealousy in the cross-sex friendship. *Journal of Loss and Trauma, 10*(5), 471–485. doi: 10.1080/15325020500193937

Willis, Benjamin L.; Gao, Ang; Leonard, David; DeFina, Laura F. & Berry, Jarett D. (2012). Midlife fitness and the development of chronic conditions in later life. *JAMA Internal Medicine, 172*(17), 1333–1340. doi: 10.1001/archinternmed.2012 .3400

Willoughby, Michael T.; Mills-Koonce, W. Roger; Gottfredson, Nisha C. & Wagner, Nicholas J. (2014). Measuring callous unemotional behaviors in early childhood: Factor structure and the prediction of stable aggression in middle childhood. *Journal of Psychopathology and Behavioral Assessment, 36*(1), 30–42. doi: 10.1007/s10862-013-9379-9

Wilmshurst, Linda. (2011). *Child and adolescent psychopathology: A casebook* (2nd ed.). Thousand Oaks, CA: Sage.

Wilson, Kathryn R.; Hansen, David J. & Li, Ming. (2011). The traumatic stress response in child maltreatment and resultant neuropsychological effects. *Aggression and Violent Behavior, 16*(2), 87–97. doi: 10.1016/j.avb.2010.12.007

Wilson, Stephan M. & Ngige, Lucy W. (2006). Families in sub-Saharan Africa. In Bron B. Ingoldsby & Suzanna D. Smith (Eds.), *Families in global and multicultural perspective* (2nd ed., pp. 247–273). Thousand Oaks, CA: Sage.

Wimer, Christopher; Nam, JaeHyun; Waldfogel, Jane & Fox, Liana. (2016). Trends in child poverty using an improved measure of poverty. *Academic Pediatrics, 16*(3, Suppl.), S60–S66. doi: 10.1016 /j.acap.2016.01.007

Wittchen, Hans-Ulrich. (2012). The burden of mood disorders. *Science, 338*(6103), 15. doi: 10.1126/science.1230817

Wolchik, Sharlene A.; Ma, Yue; Tein, Jenn-Yun; Sandler, Irwin N. & Ayers, Tim S. (2008). Parentally bereaved children's grief: Self-system beliefs as mediators of the relations between grief and stressors and caregiver-child relationship quality. *Death Studies, 32*(7), 597–620. doi: 10.1080/07481180802215551

Wolenberg, Kelly M.; Yoon, John D.; Rasinski, Kenneth A. & Curlin, Farr A. (2013). Religion and United States physicians' opinions and self-predicted practices concerning artificial nutrition and hydration. *Journal of Religion and Health, 52*(4), 1051–1065. doi: 10.1007/s10943-013 -9740-z

Wolf, Norman S. (Ed.). (2010). *Comparative biology of aging.* New York, NY: Springer.

Wolfe, Christy D.; Zhang, Jing; Kim-Spoon, Jungmeen & Bell, Martha Ann. (2014). A longitudinal perspective on the association between cognition and temperamental shyness. *International Journal of Behavioral Development, 38*(3), 266–276. doi: 10.1177/0165025413516257

Wolff, Jason J.; Gerig, Guido; Lewis, John D.; Soda, Takahiro; Styner, Martin A.; Vachet, Clement, . . . Piven, Joseph. (2015). Altered corpus callosum morphology associated with autism over the first 2 years of life. *Brain, 138*(7), 2046–2058. doi: 10.1093/brain/awv118

Wolff, Mary S.; Teitelbaum, Susan L.; McGovern, Kathleen; Pinney, Susan M.; Windham, Gayle C.; Galvez, Maida, . . . Biro, Frank M. (2015). Environmental phenols and pubertal development in girls. *Environment International, 84*, 174–180. doi: 10.1016/j.envint.2015.08.008

Wong, Jaclyn S. & Waite, Linda J. (2015). Marriage, social networks, and health at older ages. *Journal of Population Ageing, 8*(1/2), 7–25. doi: 10.1007/s12062-014-9110-y

Wong, Paul T. P. & Tomer, Adrian. (2011). Beyond terror and denial: The positive psychology of death acceptance. *Death Studies, 35*(2), 99–106. doi: 10.1080/07481187.2011.535377

Wong, Sowan & Goodwin, Robin. (2009). Experiencing marital satisfaction across three cultures: A qualitative study. *Journal of Social and Personal Relationships, 26*(8), 1011–1028. doi: 10.1177/0265407509347938

Wood, Joanne M. (2002). Aging, driving and vision. *Clinical and Experimental Optometry*, 85(4), 214–220. doi: 10.1111/j.1444-0938.2002.tb03040.x

Woodward, Amanda L. & Markman, Ellen M. (1998). Early word learning. In Deanna Kuhn & Robert S. Siegler (Eds.), *Handbook of child psychology* (5th ed., Vol. 2, pp. 371–420). Hoboken, NJ: Wiley.

Woollett, Katherine; Spiers, Hugo J. & Maguire, Eleanor A. (2009). Talent in the taxi: A model system for exploring expertise. *Philosophical Transactions of the Royal Society of London*, 364(1522), 1407–1416. doi: 10.1098/rstb.2008 .0288

Woolley, Jacqueline D. & Ghossainy, Maliki E. (2013). Revisiting the fantasy–reality distinction: Children as naïve skeptics. *Child Development*, 84(5), 1496–1510. doi: 10.1111/cdev.12081

World Bank. (2013). *World DataBank*. Washington, DC: World Bank.

World Bank. (2014). *Table 2.11: World Development indicators, participation in education*. Washington, DC: World Bank.

World Bank. (2016). *World development indicators: Mortality rate, infant (per 1,000 live births)*. Retrieved from: http://data.worldbank.org/indicator /SP.DYN.IMRT.IN

World Health Organization. (2006). WHO Motor Development Study: Windows of achievement for six gross motor development milestones. *Acta Paediatrica*, 95(Suppl. 450), 86–95. doi: 10.1111/j .1651-2227.2006.tb02379.x

World Health Organization. (2011). *Global recommendations on physical activity for health: Information sheet: global recommendations on physical activity for health 5–17 years old*. Geneva, Switzerland: World Health Organization.

World Health Organization. (2012). *Dementia: A public health priority*. Geneva, Switzerland: World Health Organization.

World Health Organization. (2013). *World health statistics 2013*. Geneva, Switzerland: World Health Organization.

World Health Organization. (2014). *Infant and young child feeding data by country*. Retrieved from: http://www.who.int/nutrition/databases /infantfeeding/countries/en/

World Health Organization. (2014, May 7). *Air quality deteriorating in many of the world's cities. Media centre, News releases*. Geneva, Switzerland: World Health Organization.

World Health Organization. (2015). *First WHO ministerial conference on global action against dementia*. Geneva, Switzerland: World Health Organization.

World Health Organization. (2015). *Global status report on road safety 2015*. Geneva, Switzerland: World Health Organization.

World Health Organization. (2016). Global Health Observatory (GHO) data: Country statistics. http://www.who.int/gho/countries/en/

Worthy, Darrell A.; Gorlick, Marissa A.; Pacheco, Jennifer L.; Schnyer, David M. & Maddox, W. Todd. (2011). With age comes wisdom: Decision making in younger and older adults. *Psychological Science*, 22(11), 1375–1380. doi: 10.1177/0956797611420301

Wosje, Karen S.; Khoury, Philip R.; Claytor, Randal P.; Copeland, Kristen A.; Hornung, Richard W.; Daniels, Stephen R. & Kalkwarf, Heidi J. (2010). Dietary patterns associated with fat and bone mass in young children. *American Journal of Clinical Nutrition*, 92(2), 294–303. doi: 10.3945 /ajcn.2009.28925

Wrzus, Cornelia; Hänel, Martha; Wagner, Jenny & Neyer, Franz J. (2013). Social network changes and life events across the life span: A meta-analysis. *Psychological Bulletin*, 139(1), 53–80. doi: 10.1037/a0028601

Wu, Ming-Yih & Ho, Hong-Nerng. (2015). Cost and safety of assisted reproductive technologies for human immunodeficiency virus-1 discordant couples. *World Journal of Virology*, 4(2), 142–146. doi: 10.5501/wjv.v4.i2.142

Wu, Pai-Lu & Chiou, Wen-Bin. (2008). Postformal thinking and creativity among late adolescents: A post-Piagetian approach. *Adolescence*, 43(170), 237–251.

Wurm, Susanne; Tomasik, Martin & Tesch-Römer, Clemens. (2008). Serious health events and their impact on changes in subjective health and life satisfaction: The role of age and a positive view on ageing. *European Journal of Ageing*, 5(2), 117–127. doi: 10.1007/s10433-008-0077-5

Xiang, Jing; Korostenskaja, Milena; Molloy, Cynthia; deGrauw, Xinyao; Leiken, Kimberly; Gilman, Carley, . . . Murray, Donna S. (2016). Multi-frequency localization of aberrant brain activity in autism spectrum disorder. *Brain and Development*, 38(1), 82–90. doi: 10.1016/j.braindev .2015.04.007

Xu, Fei. (2013). The object concept in human infants: Commentary on Fields. *Human Development*, 56(3), 167–170. doi: 10.1159/000351279

Xu, Fei & Kushnir, Tamar. (2013). Infants are rational constructivist learners. *Current Directions in Psychological Science*, 22(1), 28–32. doi: 10.1177/0963721412469396

Xu, Yaoying. (2010). Children's social play sequence: Parten's classic theory revisited. *Early Child Development and Care*, 180(4), 489–498. doi: 10.1080/03004430802090430

Yadav, Priyanka; Banwari, Girish; Parmar, Chirag & Maniar, Rajesh. (2013). Internet addiction and its correlates among high school students: A preliminary study from Ahmedabad, India. *Asian Journal of Psychiatry*, 6(6), 500–505. doi: 10.1016 /j.ajp.2013.06.004

Yang, Rongwang; Zhang, Suhan; Li, Rong & Zhao, Zhengyan. (2013). Parents' attitudes toward stimulants use in China. *Journal of Developmental & Behavioral Pediatrics*, 34(3), 225. doi: 10.1097 /DBP.0b013e318287cc27

Yao, Li & Robert, Stephanie A. (2011). Examining the racial crossover in mortality between African American and white older adults: A multilevel survival analysis of race, individual socioeconomic status, and neighborhood socioeconomic context. *2011*(Article ID 132073). doi: 10.4061/2011/132073

Yerkes, Robert Mearns. (1923). Testing the human mind. *Atlantic Monthly*, 131, 358–370.

Yeung, Wei-Jun Jean & Alipio, Cheryll. (2013). Transitioning to adulthood in Asia: School, work, and family life. *The ANNALS of the American Academy of Political and Social Science*, 646(1), 6–27. doi: 10.1177/0002716212470794

Young, Elizabeth A.; Korszun, Ania; Figueiredo, Helmer F.; Banks-Solomon, Matia & Herman, James P. (2008). Sex differences in HPA axis regulation. In Jill B. Becker et al. (Eds.), *Sex differences in the brain: From genes to behavior* (pp. 95–105). New York, NY: Oxford University Press.

Young, John K. (2010). Anorexia nervosa and estrogen: Current status of the hypothesis. *Neuroscience & Biobehavioral Reviews*, 34(8), 1195–1200. doi: 10.1016/j.neubiorev.2010.01.015

Young, Larry J. & Barrett, Catherine E. (2015). Can oxytocin treat autism? *Science*, 347(6224), 825–826. doi: 10.1126/science.aaa8120

Young, Robert D.; Muir, Mark E. & Adams, John M. (2015). Validated worldwide supercentenarians, living and recently deceased. *Rejuvenation Research*, 18(1), 96–100. doi: 10.1089/rej.2015.1678

Yu, Edward & Lippert, Adam M. (2016). Neighborhood crime rate, weight-related behaviors, and obesity: A systematic review of the literature. *Sociology Compass*, 10(3), 187–207. doi: 10.1111/soc4.12356

Yu, Xiao-ming; Guo, Shuai-jun & Sun, Yu-ying. (2013). Sexual behaviours and associated risks in Chinese young people: A meta-analysis. *Sexual Health*, 10(5), 424–433. doi: 10.1071/SH12140

Yudell, Michael; Roberts, Dorothy; DeSalle, Rob & Tishkoff, Sarah. (2016). Taking race out of human genetics. *Science*, 351(6273), 564–565. doi: 10.1126/science.aac4951

Zachry, Anne H. & Kitzmann, Katherine M. (2011). Caregiver awareness of prone play recommendations. *American Journal of Occupational Therapy*, 65(1), 101–105. doi: 10.5014/ajot.2011.09100

Zagheni, Emilio; Zannella, Marina; Movsesyan, Gabriel & Wagner, Brittney. (2015). Time is economically valuable: Production, consumption and transfers of time by age and sex. In Emilio Zagheni et al. (Eds.), *A comparative analysis of European time transfers between generations and genders* (pp. 19–33). New York, NY: Springer. doi: 10.1007/978-94-017-9591-3_2

Zalenski, Robert J. & Raspa, Richard. (2006). Maslow's hierarchy of needs: A framework for achieving human potential in hospice. *Journal of Palliative Medicine*, 9(5), 1120–1127. doi: 10.1089/jpm.2006.9.1120

Zapf, Jennifer A. & Smith, Linda B. (2007). When do children generalize the plural to novel nouns? *First Language*, 27(1), 53–73. doi: 10.1177/0142723707070286

Zarate, Carlos A. (2010). Psychiatric disorders in young adults: Depression assessment and treatment. In Jon E. Grant & Marc N. Potenza (Eds.), *Young adult mental health* (pp. 206–230). New York, NY: Oxford University Press.

Zatorre, Robert J. (2013). Predispositions and plasticity in music and speech learning: Neural correlates and implications. *Science, 342*(6158), 585–589. doi: 10.1126/science.1238414

Zatorre, Robert J.; Fields, R. Douglas & Johansen-Berg, Heidi. (2012). Plasticity in gray and white: Neuroimaging changes in brain structure during learning. *Nature Neuroscience, 15,* 528–536. doi: 10.1038/nn.3045

Zehr, Mary Ann. (2010). Bilingual education, immersion found to work equally well. *Education Week, 29*(29), 6.

Zeiders, Katharine H.; Umaña-Taylor, Adriana J. & Derlan, Chelsea L. (2013). Trajectories of depressive symptoms and self-esteem in Latino youths: Examining the role of gender and perceived discrimination. *Developmental Psychology, 49*(5), 951–963. doi: 10.1037/a0028866

Zeifman, Debra M. (2013). Built to bond: Coevolution, coregulation, and plasticity in parent-infant bonds. In Cindy Hazan & Mary I. Campa (Eds.), *Human bonding: The science of affectional ties* (pp. 41–73). New York, NY: Guilford Press.

Zelazo, Philip David. (2015). Executive function: Reflection, iterative reprocessing, complexity, and the developing brain. *Developmental Review, 38,* 55–68. doi: 10.1016/j.dr.2015.07.001

Zentall, Shannon R. & Morris, Bradley J. (2010). "Good job, you're so smart": The effects of inconsistency of praise type on young children's motivation. *Journal of Experimental Child Psychology, 107*(2), 155–163. doi: 10.1016/j.jecp.2010.04.015

Zhang, Baohui; Wright, Alexi A.; Huskamp, Haiden A.; Nilsson, Matthew E.; Maciejewski, Matthew L.; Earle, Craig C., . . . Prigerson, Holly G. (2009). Health care costs in the last week of life: Associations with end-of-life conversations. *Archives of Internal Medicine, 169*(5), 480–488. doi: 10.1001/archinternmed.2008.587

Zhao, Jinxia & Wang, Meifang. (2014). Mothers' academic involvement and children's achievement: Children's theory of intelligence as a mediator. *Learning and Individual Differences, 35,* 130–136. doi: 10.1016/j.lindif.2014.06.006

Zhou, Cindy Ke; Levine, Paul H.; Cleary, Sean D.; Hoffman, Heather J.; Graubard, Barry I. & Cook, Michael B. (2016). Male pattern baldness in relation to prostate cancer–specific mortality: A prospective analysis in the NHANES I Epidemiologic Follow-Up Study. *American Journal of Epidemiology, 183*(3), 210–217. doi: 10.1093/aje/kwv190

Zhou, Dongming; Lebel, Catherine; Evans, Alan & Beaulieu, Christian. (2013). Cortical thickness asymmetry from childhood to older adulthood. *NeuroImage, 83,* 66–74. doi: 10.1016/j.neuroimage.2013.06.073

Zhu, Qi; Song, Yiying; Hu, Siyuan; Li, Xiaobai; Tian, Moqian; Zhen, Zonglei, . . . Liu, Jia. (2010). Heritability of the specific cognitive ability of face perception. *Current Biology, 20*(2), 137–142. doi: 10.1016/j.cub.2009.11.067

Zieber, Nicole; Kangas, Ashley; Hock, Alyson & Bhatt, Ramesh S. (2014). Infants' perception of emotion from body movements. *Child Development, 85*(2), 675–684. doi: 10.1111/cdev.12134

Ziegler, Matthias; Danay, Erik; Heene, Moritz; Asendorp, Jens & Bühner, Markus. (2012). Openness, fluid intelligence, and crystallized intelligence: Toward an integrative model. *Journal of Research in Personality, 46*(2), 173–183. doi: 10.1016/j.jrp.2012.01.002

Zimmer-Gembeck, Melanie J. (2016). Peer rejection, victimization, and relational self-system processes in adolescence: Toward a transactional model of stress, coping, and developing sensitivities. *Child Development Perspectives, 10*(2), 122–127. doi: 10.1111/cdep.12174

Zimmerman, Frederick J. (2014). Where's the beef? A comment on Ferguson and Donnellan (2014). *Developmental Psychology, 50*(1), 138–140. doi: 10.1037/a0035087

Zimmerman, Frederick J.; Christakis, Dimitri A. & Meltzoff, Andrew N. (2007). Associations between media viewing and language development in children under age 2 years. *The Journal of Pediatrics, 151*(4), 364–368. doi: 10.1016/j.jpeds.2007.04.071

Zimmerman, Marc A.; Stoddard, Sarah A.; Eisman, Andria B.; Caldwell, Cleopatra H.; Aiyer, Sophie M. & Miller, Alison. (2013). Adolescent resilience: Promotive factors that inform prevention. *Child Development Perspectives, 7*(4), 215–220. doi: 10.1111/cdep.12042

Zimmermann, Camilla. (2012). Acceptance of dying: A discourse analysis of palliative care literature. *Social Science & Medicine, 75*(1), 217–224. doi: 10.1016/j.socscimed.2012.02.047

Zolotor, Adam J. (2014). Corporal punishment. *Pediatric Clinics of North America, 61*(5), 971–978. doi: 10.1016/j.pcl.2014.06.003

Zubrzycki, Jaclyn. (2012). Experts fear handwriting will become a lost art. *Education Week, 31*(18), 1, 13.

Zucker, Kenneth J.; Cohen-Kettenis, Peggy T.; Drescher, Jack; Meyer-Bahlburg, Heino F. L.; Pfäfflin, Friedemann & Womack, William M. (2013). Memo outlining evidence for change for Gender Identity Disorder in the DSM-5. *Archives of Sexual Behavior, 42*(5), 901–914. doi: 10.1007/s10508-013-0139-4

Zvolensky, Michael J.; Taha, Farah; Bono, Amanda & Goodwin, Renee D. (2015). Big Five personality factors and cigarette smoking: A 10-year study among US adults. *Journal of Psychiatric Research, 63,* 91–96. doi: 10.1016/j.jpsychires.2015.02.008

Name Index

Subject Index